EARLIER BRITISH PAINTINGS

IN THE WALKER ART GALLERY AND SUDLEY HOUSE

Earlier British Paintings
in the Walker Art Gallery and Sudley House

Alex Kidson

National Museums Liverpool

LIVERPOOL
UNIVERSITY PRESS

First published 2012 by

Liverpool University Press
4 Cambridge Street
Liverpool
L69 7ZU

and

National Museums Liverpool
127 Dale Street
Liverpool
L2 2JH

British Library Cataloguing-in-Publication data
A British Library CIP record is available

ISBN 978-1-84631-816-0

Designed by Anne Odling-Smee and Ana Gomes,
O-SB Design
www.o-sb.co.uk

Printed and bound by Bell & Bain Ltd
www.bell-bain.com

Contents

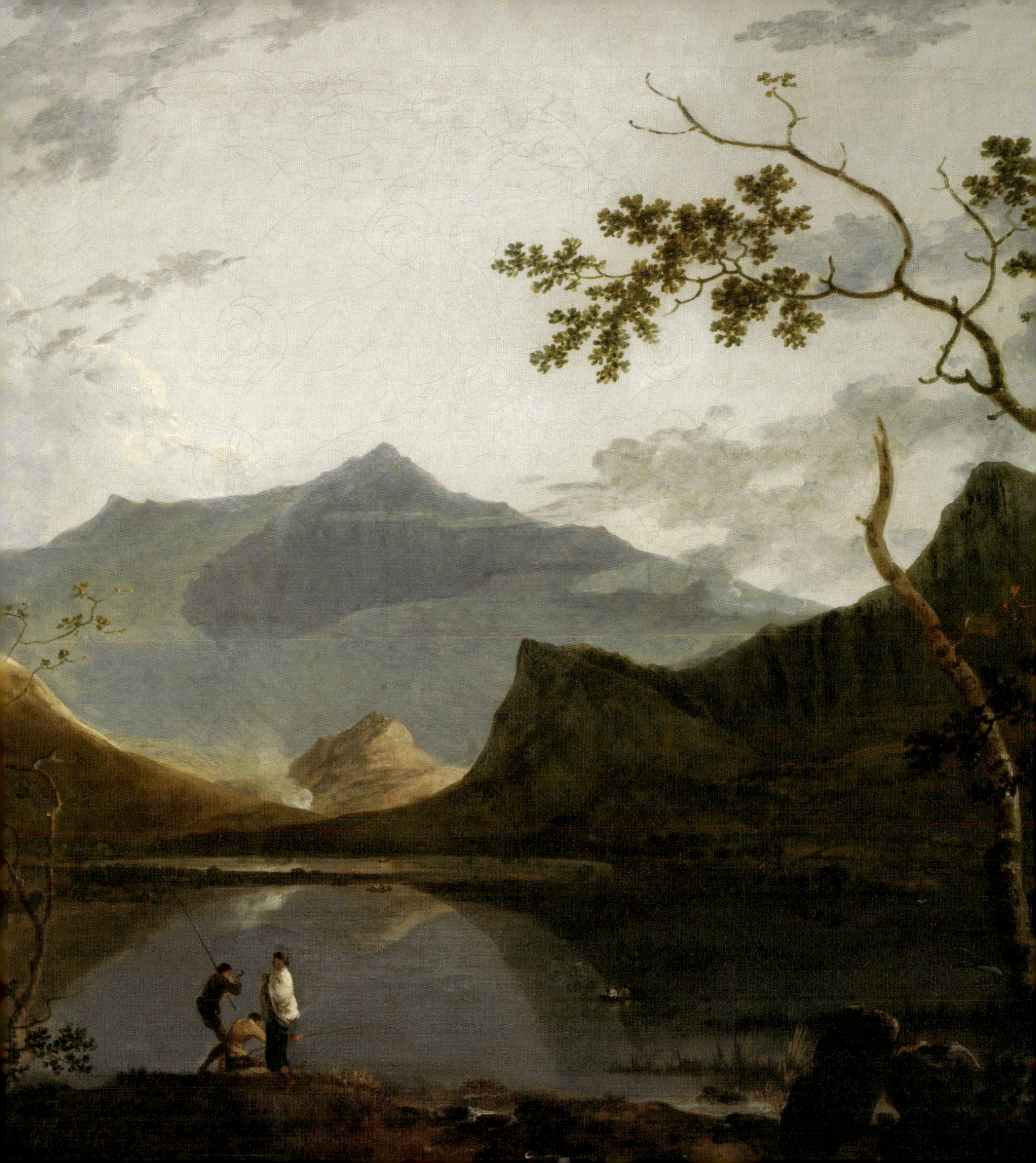

Foreword

Richard Wilson
Snowdon from Llyn Nantlle
(detail)

The early British paintings from the Walker Art Gallery and Sudley House today form one of the most significant parts of our renowned, Liverpool-based collections. Some of these works have been catalogued as part of numerous exhibitions worldwide but this is the first time that they have been addressed as a full group by period, and their strengths – and weaknesses – carefully examined. Likewise, the highpoints and shortcomings of the gallery's own collecting policy are uncovered. Almost 60 years had passed following the opening of the Walker in 1877 before the core of the holdings that are examined here started to develop. Indeed, this catalogue stands as a testament to the proactive and determined curatorship over half a century of the gallery's directors, Frank Lambert (with Col. Vere Cotton), Hugh Scrutton and Timothy Stevens. Successively, but with a shared vision spanning decades, they formed a collection that balanced both local and national agendas in collecting. An assessment of their combined achievement has long been overdue. Likewise, the catalogue celebrates key parts of the remarkable collection amassed by George Holt at Sudley House, bequeathed to the city of Liverpool in 1944 by his daughter, Emma.

Alex Kidson's longstanding relationship with the Walker and Sudley as, successively, Assistant Keeper of British Art and Curator of British Art from 1982 to 2008, his intimate knowledge of the paintings, and his eloquent prose, have made him the ideal person for this undertaking. He commenced this cataloguing project as part of his curatorial responsibilities for a much wider part of the collection, and in parallel to his work on numerous exhibitions. Some of the latter, such as his survey of George Romney in 2002, emerged directly as a result of his affinity for eighteenth-century British art. But the demands of this heavy workload meant that this cataloguing project has spanned many years, the task finally completed during a period when he was unencumbered by the daily distractions of curatorial duties.

This book is one of a series of catalogues that examines in-depth particular aspects of our collections. It complements Alex's survey of the earlier British paintings in the Lady Lever Art Gallery, published in 1999. In this new Walker volume, which incorporates Sudley House, he focuses on paintings by British artists born before 1770. The catalogue also weaves a path through the history of collecting and taste not just at the Walker but in Liverpool and further afield.

Notable amongst the many artists and themes embraced within this catalogue is a wealth of sporting pictures, amongst which the work of the local artist Charles Towne emerges, by number, one of the most significant groups within the Walker's holdings. Of some 90 paintings, 64 were bequeathed in 1979 by Colonel J. R. Danson, and this catalogue stands as a testament to his rigorous pursuit of Towne's work. His bequest also symbolises the generosity of the individuals and organisations, particularly the Art Fund, whose donations have helped to build the Walker's holdings of early British paintings.

The information contained here, whilst it represents the most erudite, scholarly inquiry, is not intended to be the definitive word on these paintings. Rather, like all such projects, it marks a significant milestone in their history and understanding. It is a research tool, setting trails for the current and future study of these paintings and, it is hoped, is a catalyst for the uncovering of new revelations in the future.

Ann Bukantas
Head of Fine Art, National Museums Liverpool

Acknowledgements

This catalogue has been a very long time in preparation, and I owe a great debt to those colleagues at the Walker, former and present, whose patience has been tried by its slow progress. Foremost among them are Timothy Stevens, Mary Bennett and Edward Morris, respectively Director, Keeper of British Art and Keeper of Foreign Art at the date I joined the gallery, each of whom had themselves carried out research on many of these paintings, and who must often in the early days have doubted their wisdom in entrusting the continuation of their work to a young Assistant Keeper of little experience. Without their faith this catalogue would never have been written. I have also received much valued support and encouragement from Julian Treuherz, Head of Art Galleries from 1989 to 2007, Reyahn King, present Director of Art Galleries, and Ann Bukantas, Head of Fine Art since 2002.

Among the many other colleagues in National Museums Liverpool who have contributed to this catalogue I should like to make special mention of the late Hugh Macandrew, who in the early 1960s at the Walker did much ground-breaking work on George Stubbs and on the Roscoe-Fuseli circle in Liverpool and whose entries on the paintings concerned are preserved in gallery files; Martin Hopkinson, who in his time at the Walker unearthed many fresh references; Dr Mark Evans, whose draft entries on many of the sixteenth- and seventeenth-century paintings (as well as a number of sporting pictures) have shaped my own; and Xanthe Brooke, who as Curator of European Art during my time at the Walker has minded the paintings in this catalogue which have traditionally been viewed in the gallery as 'continental' – in particular, I have shamelessly cannibalised her research on the portrait of Henry VIII, after Holbein. I have also benefited greatly from discussions with, and assistance from, Nicola Christie, David Crombie, John Edmondson, Jessica Feather, Jim France, Rebecca Kench, Moira Lindsay, Frank Milner, Harriet Owen-Hughes, Sandra Penketh, Jacqueline Ridge, Jane Sellars, Joseph Sharples, Katherine Stainer-Hutchins and Lucy Wood. Much of this catalogue was typed by Lynda Rea with unfailing efficiency, patience and good humour; and Jon Murden, Kay Carson, Karen Miller and Jennifer Phillip provided invaluable help in the later stages.

All catalogues of this kind are essentially collaborative in character, and represent the accumulation of information supplied over a long period, not just by fellow-curators but also by volunteers, past owners and members of the public. I have tried to make reference to these contributions wherever possible, but a brief mention in a footnote is a barely adequate form of thanks. I am especially grateful to David Mannings and Hugh Belsey for their generous assistance with Sir Joshua Reynolds and Thomas Gainsborough respectively, and to Catharine MacLeod in respect of a number of late seventeenth-century pictures. My particular thanks for their help in a variety of ways go also to Tabitha Barber, Melanie Blake, Marijke Booth, Julia Carder, Venetia Constantine, Malcolm Cormack, Paul Crossley, Jane Cunningham, Ellie Dawkins, Elizabeth Einberg, Judy Egerton, Guillaume Faroult, Peter Funnell, Shihoko Gomyo, Emmeline Hallmark, Karen Hearn, David Moore-Gwyn, Lisa Murray, Tomoko Okabe, Lucy Peltz, Joy Pepe, Martin Postle, Roger Quarm, Jacob Simon, Helen Smailes, John Sunderland, Barbara Thompson, Peter Urquhart, Norma Watt, and Nicholas White, as well as to the staffs of Liverpool City Libraries and Liverpool Record Office, the Heinz Archive at the National Portrait Gallery, the Department of Prints and Drawings at the British Museum, the Yale Center for British Art and the Paul Mellon Centre for Studies in British Art. To Brian Allen, Director of Studies at the Paul Mellon Centre and his colleagues I am most grateful for the award of a publication grant that underwrote this volume, and further most generous financial assistance was provided by Penny Treadwell. My thanks go also to this book's designers, Anne Odling-Smee and Ana Gomes, and to Helen Tookey and Anthony Cond at Liverpool University Press.

My greatest debt of all is to my wife Suzanne May, who has lived with this book for far longer than she expected and without whose loving support it could not have been completed.

Notes to the user

This catalogue covers the 311 paintings in the collection of the Walker Art Gallery and Sudley House at the end of 2009 by British artists born before 1770. The term 'British artists' has been interpreted to mean, besides native artists, ones born abroad who worked in Britain; and this catalogue includes a number of works that are discussed in the gallery's existing 'Foreign Schools' catalogues (omitted, however, is an early landscape by Philippe de Loutherbourg painted while he was still in France). It has also been decided to re-catalogue the relevant works in Mary Bennett's *Merseyside Painters, People and Places* (1978), not only because their omission would have been difficult to justify in the interests of completeness, but also because in many cases further research has yielded fresh information and sometimes new attributions, or else simply a different interpretation of the work concerned. The decision to create a cut-off date of 1770 was taken in the interest of the project's manageability. It means that around 300 British paintings in the gallery by artists born in the years 1770–1809 (at which point Edward Morris's catalogue of Victorian paintings takes over) remain uncatalogued; it is hoped that these will form the basis of a sequel volume.

The order of works is alphabetical by artist. Sections devoted to individual artists contain four types of work, placed in the following order:

(i) documented works and works where there is no reason to doubt the traditional attribution, designated by the plain name of the artist and grouped in order of date

(ii) works newly or fairly recently attributed to the artist, designated by the prefix 'attributed to'

(iii) versions of known works by the artist, whether or not autograph, designated by the prefix 'after', and

(iv) works which stand in a looser relation to the named artist, designated by the prefix 'called'. The status of these works – typically traditional but dubious attributions of continuing historic interest – is discussed in the individual entries, which are arranged in inventory order number.

Finally, at the end of the catalogue there is a section of works attributed to 'British School' where there is no convincing attribution to an artist or where it seemed more important to lose sight of a traditional attribution than to keep it in view.

The main body of each entry offers a summary of the current state of knowledge of the work concerned, but in certain respects this summary is selective. For instance, although condition reports of varying antiquity exist for many of the works, no up-to-date systematic condition check has been carried out for the purpose of this catalogue, and the entries therefore generally only discuss the work's condition (and then briefly) where it impinges upon its attribution or historical status, or else its direct visual impact. The same applies to frames. More critically, the view of each painting presented is from a present-day perspective and no systematic effort is made to record every previous reference to the work, although it is hoped that the footnotes are sufficient to enable readers to find these for themselves. A full record is given, where known, for the work's exhibition history before it entered the gallery, but loans to some minor (chiefly uncatalogued) exhibitions are omitted thereafter. In the provenance, an elipsis is used to indicate gaps in knowledge of the work's history; thus a provenance without an elipsis (as for instance with Gainsborough's *Lady Molyneux*) indicates that the ownership of the painting is known from the day it was painted. In two further cataloguing conventions, measurements have been rounded to the nearest half-centimetre, and the names of auction houses and dealers have been given in the singular form in provenances and references to individual sales, but in full elsewhere.

The term 'gallery files' has been used to refer to the object files on each work of art held in the gallery's curatorial offices, and the term 'gallery archives' to denote material held elsewhere in the gallery. The following abbreviations have been used:

BI British Institution

CIC Sandra Penketh: *Concise Illustrated Catalogue of British Paintings in the Walker Art Gallery and at Sudley* (Liverpool, 1995)

Complete Peerage G. E. Cokayne, revised by Vicary Gibbs, H. A. Doubleday, Lord Howard de Walden, Duncan Warrand, Geoffrey H. White and R. S. Lea: *The Complete Peerage of England, Scotland, Ireland, Great Britain and the United Kingdom, Extant, Extinct or Dormant,* 12 vols in 13 (London, 1910–59)

Croxteth 1746 Inventory Inventory of the goods and chattels of the 6th Viscount Molyneux taken in 1746 after his death (Lancashire Record Office, Preston, Molyneux Manuscripts, DDM 11/55)

Croxteth 1900s Inventory Ms inventory of paintings in the billiard room, card room and smoking room of Croxteth Hall dating from about 1904, found among the papers of R. D. Ratcliffe, National Museums Liverpool archives; copy in gallery archives

Croxteth 1946 Inventory Inventory of Paintings and Drawings at Croxteth Hall taken by Laurence Haward, January 1946; copy in gallery archives

FC Edward Morris and Martin Hopkinson: *Walker Art Gallery Foreign Catalogue* (Liverpool, 1977)

FD Kenneth Garlick, Angus McIntyre and Kathryn Cave, eds: *The Diary of Joseph Farington,* 16 vols (New Haven and London, 1978–84)

GrRA Algernon Graves: *The Royal Academy of Arts: A Complete Dictionary of ontributors and Their Work from Its Foundation in 1769 to 1904, 8 vols* (London, 1905–06)

GrSA Algernon Graves: *The Society of Artists of Great Britain 1760–1791 [and] The Free Society of Artists 1761–1783: A Complete Dictionary of Contributors and Their Work from the Foundation of the Societies to 1791* (London, 1907)

LA Liverpool Academy

LAOE Edward Morris and Emma Roberts: *The Liverpool Academy and Other Exhibitions of Contemporary Art in Liverpool 1774–1867: A History and Index of Artists and works Exhibited* (Liverpool, 1998)

LRI Liverpool Royal Institution

LRO Liverpool Record Office

MPPP Mary Bennett: *Merseyside Painters, People and Places* (Liverpool, 1978)

NML National Museums Liverpool

ODNB H. G. C. Matthew and B. Harrison, eds: *The Oxford Dictionary of National Biography,* 60 vols (Oxford, 2004)

RA Royal Academy

SA Society of Artists of Great Britain

Alex Kidson
October 2010

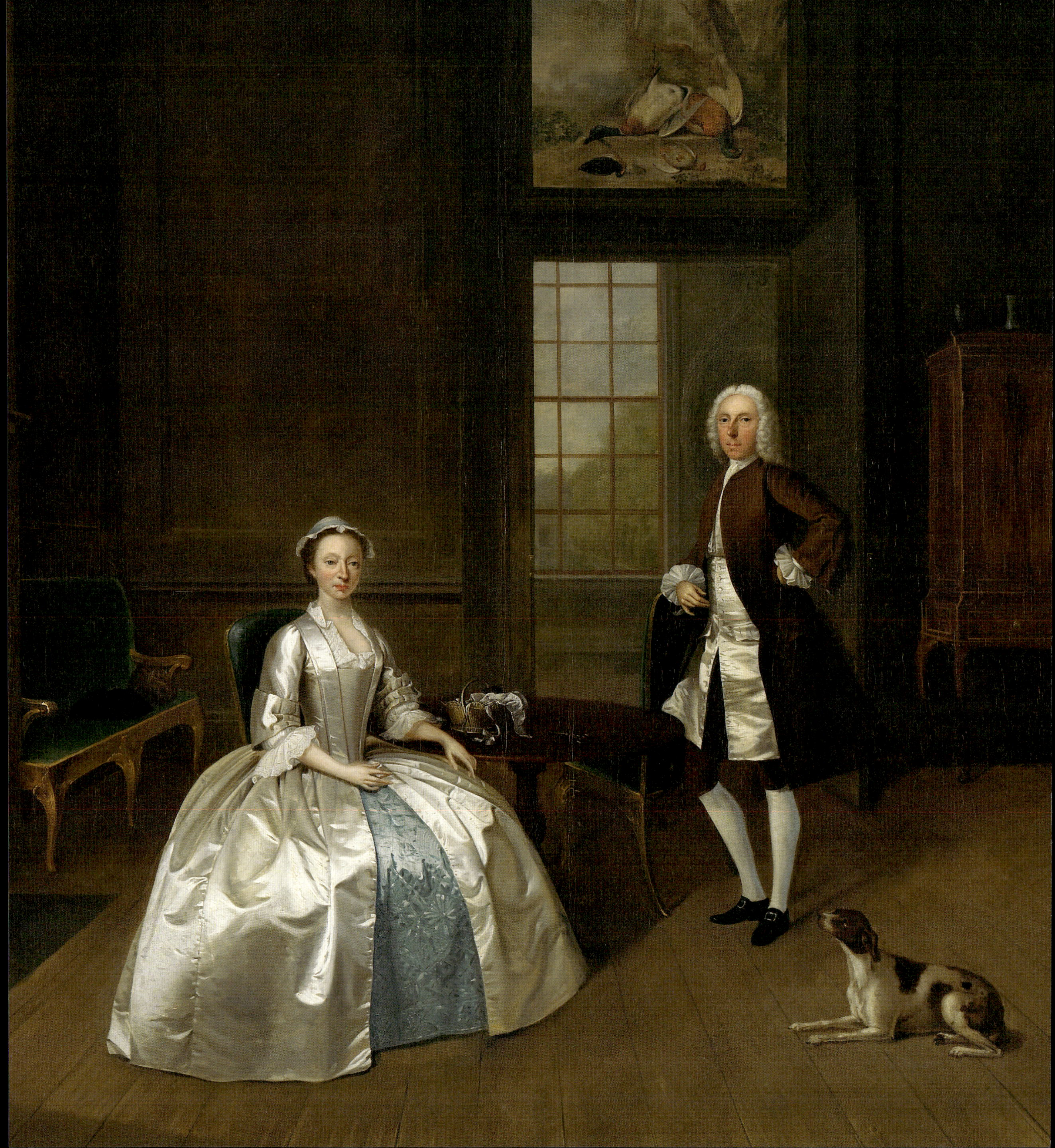

Introduction

Arthur Devis
Mr and Mrs William Atherton
(detail)

The history of the Walker Art Gallery's acquisition of early British oil paintings, as defined by the 311 works in this catalogue, falls into three clear-cut sections.[1] For the first 55 years of the gallery's existence – the heyday of the annual Liverpool Autumn Exhibitions when the acquisition of contemporary art out of the exhibitions was viewed as the institution's chief *raison d'être* – British old masters were almost wholly below the curatorial horizon. From 1933, the date of the completion of the gallery's modern extension, a sea-change occurred, and over the next 47 years three successive directors of the gallery, Frank Lambert, Hugh Scrutton and Timothy Stevens, made it one of their most urgent priorities to transform the Walker's holding of earlier British pictures into one that was representative of both national and local histories of artistic development. Between 1933 and 1980, no fewer than 261 of the 311 paintings in this catalogue entered the gallery. Since 1980, the pace has reverted to that of the early years: new priorities have governed those acquisitions that have taken place; the claims of historic British art have been critically tested against other areas of the collection in more urgent need of development, and it has become easier to view the Walker's holdings of early British paintings as now commensurate with its aspirations as a gallery of European stature. Only 16 paintings in this catalogue have entered the collection in the last 30 years.

In the third quarter of the nineteenth century, Liverpool Corporation assembled, through gift and bequest, a number of paintings, both foreign and British, envisaged as standing apart from the existing private resources of art display in Liverpool and forming the core of a new public provision of art for the city. When the Walker eventually opened in 1877, 12 of the paintings in this catalogue were already owned by the Corporation. Whilst many of them were historical curiosities, copies and in one case – a supposed

1. For a shorter summary of this and the following paragraphs, see the section 'Rococo, Classicism & Romanticism', in *The Walker* (London, 1994; 2nd edn 2003) pp. 42–4 (written by the present author); and for its place in the broader context of the gallery's development, 'The History of the Gallery and Its Collections', *ibid.*, pp. 8–13; also Edward Morris: *Public Art Collections in North-west England: A Guide* (Liverpool, 2001) pp. 84–97.

Reynolds – a painfully bad forgery, three were considerable pictures which have stood the test of time and have emerged, in their different ways, as icons of the collection. They were Benjamin West's *Death of Nelson*; Sir Martin Archer Shee's full-length portrait of the figurehead of Liverpool culture, William Roscoe; and Roscoe's own first major purchase of British art, Henry Fuseli's *Death of Oedipus*. Marking the inception of Roscoe's long championship of Fuseli in the period 1790–1810,[2] this painting was a powerful symbol of the dawn of artistic taste in Liverpool, and its donor to the Corporation, James Aikin, had gone out of his way in the 1830s to rescue it from London and return it to the city where it belonged. Yet arguably its presence in the collection from the outset was more of a hindrance than a help: it ticked so many boxes that it discouraged the gallery from embracing a more nuanced vision of past collecting in the city.

In the first 40 years of the gallery's existence only 19 pictures in this catalogue were added to the collection, and of these, only eight were bought. The gallery's first purchase of a historic British picture, in 1879, from a local dealer, was a portrait of obscure antecedents bearing an optimistic attribution to Sir Godfrey Kneller, and of sitters who had no visible connection with Liverpool. That a recent conservation treatment has serendipitously revealed this work to be one of hitherto unsuspected quality and interest cannot disguise the fact that the entire rationale of its acquisition was that the picture was on offer cheap locally; and for the next 30 years, the gallery's attitude towards spending on early British pictures (at this time funds for purchases derived solely from attendance receipts from the Autumn Exhibitions) continued to be opportunistic, based upon the availability of a bargain. In 1885 and 1893, the gallery managed in this fashion to buy its first Towne and its first Caddick respectively; while in 1888 the Corporation finally agreed to buy privately for £50 – one-seventh of the price that had originally been asked 24 years earlier – Samuel Drummond's huge *Death of Nelson* (which was presumably regarded as providing an educative comparison with West's version of the same subject, but which spent much of the next 70 years rolled up in store, an experience from which it has never recovered). In these first years only one acquisition really stood out, the gift in 1880 from local JP and progressive farmer Robert Neilson of Joseph Wright of Derby's *Annual Girandola at the Castel Sant'Angelo, Rome*: a work of spectacular visual appeal but one whose

2. H. Macandrew: 'Henry Fuseli and William Roscoe', *Liverpool Bulletin* vol. 8 (1959–60) pp. 5–52.

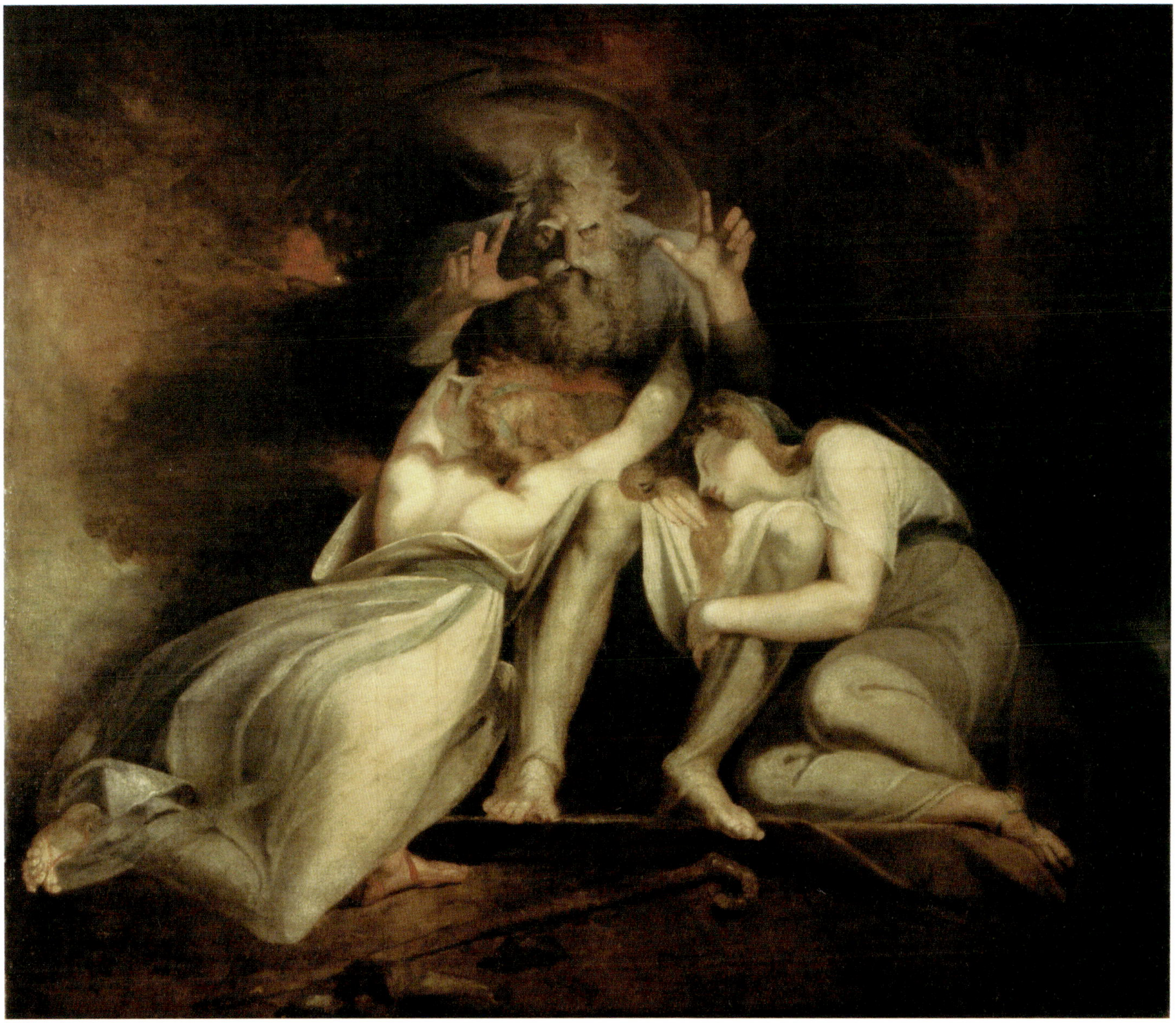

Plate 1
Henry Fuseli: *The Death of Oedipus*
WAG 1537

place in the history of local collecting had by that date been lost sight of. That this painting was in all probability owned by Thomas Moss Tate, a member of the family that were Wright's key patrons in Liverpool in his own lifetime, and continued a Wright cult in the town for decades after his death,[3] has only recently been recognised.

It was 1910 before the gallery flexed its muscles and – from the dizzying source of an auction at Christie's – made a purchase of what today might be termed a heritage picture; even if the work's price, 21 guineas, was hardly an augury of its significance. This was George Stubbs's magnificent *Horse Frightened by a Lion*. The man responsible for buying it, Edward Rimbault Dibdin, had moved from Edinburgh to Liverpool in 1877 and had moved in the city's artistic circles long before he took over as curator of the gallery in 1904. In 1918, shortly before his retirement, Dibdin published a historical survey of early art in Liverpool that was far in advance of any other piece of writing on the subject, and was evidently the fruit of years of patient accumulation of information and sifting of detail (it remains useful today).[4] It may not be coincidental that in the year that Dibdin took over the reins, the gallery received a bequest from the local collector (and Stubbs aficionado), Revd S. A. Thompson Yates, of three works whose claims to be authentic paintings by – and of – Stubbs rested stubbornly on local tradition but which could not, even then, have sustained serious visual scrutiny; and Dibdin's subsequent purchase of *A Horse Frightened by a Lion* – together with the gallery's second Caddick (bought in 1908) and what was thought to be its first Richard Wright (in 1914) clearly reflects his growing interest in and sensitisation to what might be termed local heritage issues.

Unhappily, Dibdin (who lived until 1941) retired in 1918 and his successor, Arthur Quigley, showed less independence of mind. One likely reason behind Quigley's almost complete blanking of early British pictures was the building of the Lady Lever Art Gallery in Port Sunlight, founded in 1913 and finally opened in 1922. In its holdings historic British paintings were spectacularly well represented. The 1st Viscount Leverhulme's thinking, in the later phase of his collecting when it was specifically geared to filling the gallery, had been strongly coloured by the notion of creating

3. MPPP, pp. 198–9; Elizabeth E. Barker: '*Swallowing Up All the Business*: Joseph Wright of Derby in Liverpool', in E. Barker and A. Kidson: *Joseph Wright of Derby in Liverpool*, exh. cat., Walker Art Gallery and Yale Center for British Art, New Haven (2007) pp. 74, 83.

4. E. R. Dibdin: 'Liverpool Art and Artists in the Eighteenth Century', *Walpole Society* vol. 6 (1917–18) pp. 59–93.

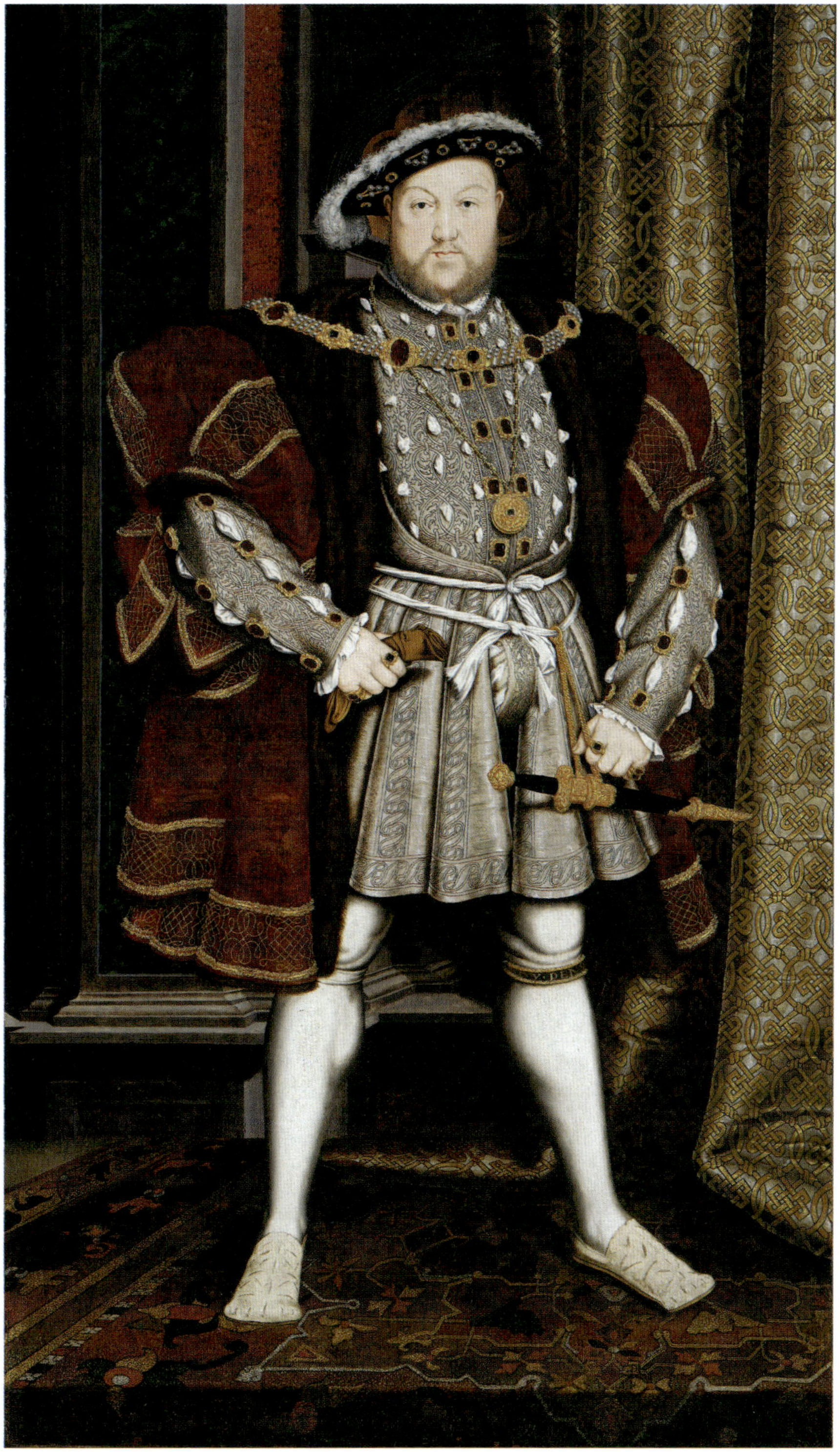

Plate 3
After Hans Holbein the Younger: *King Henry VIII*
WAG 1350

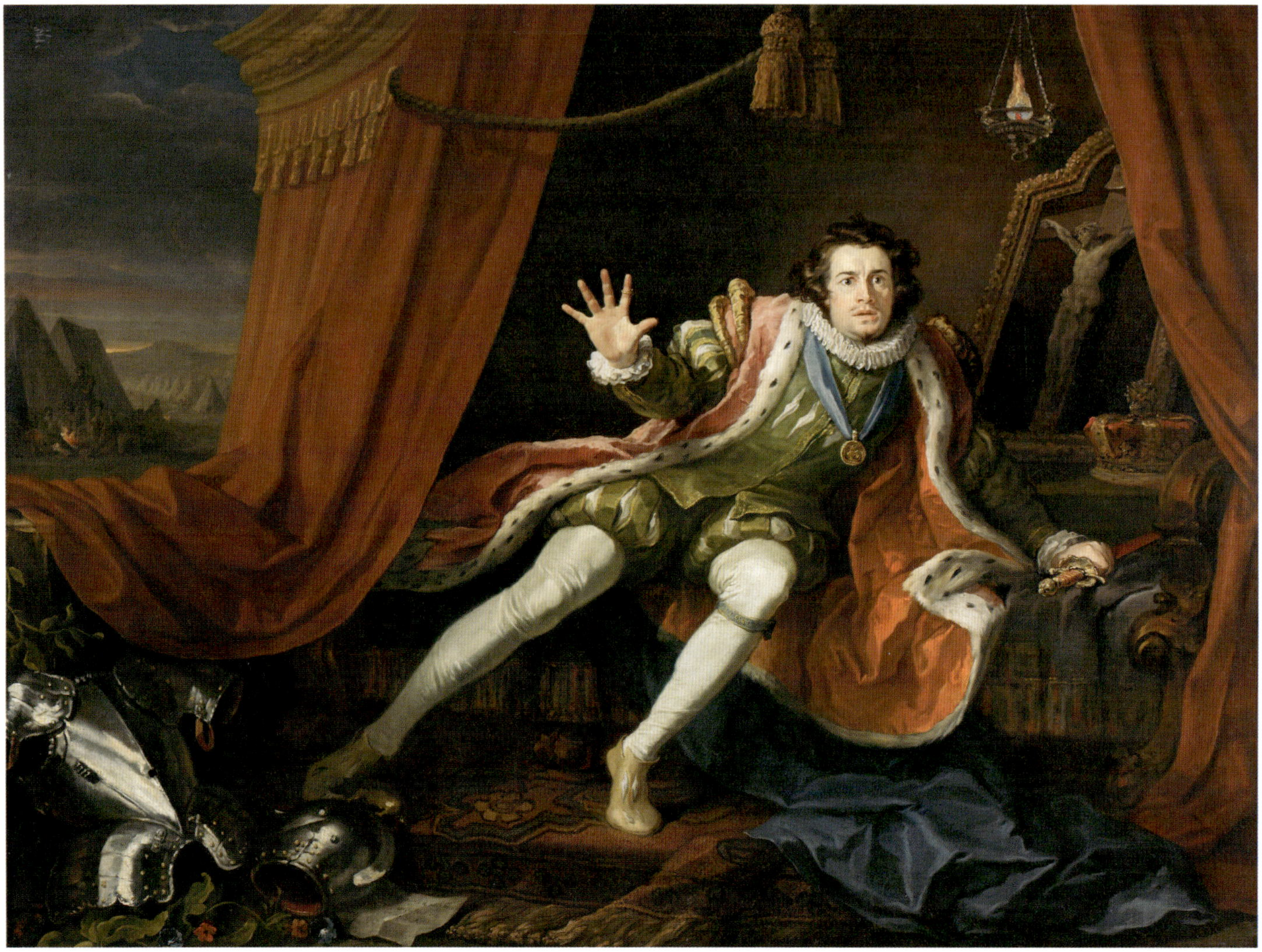

Plate 4
William Hogarth: *David Garrick as Richard III*
WAG 634

bought Hogarth's iconic *David Garrick as Richard III*. Yet as correspondence in gallery files reveals, that acquisition culminated a long search for a masterpiece by Hogarth which is best regarded as an epilogue to the Cotton and Lambert years; and after 1956 there is a perceptible fault-line that incorporated both a pause for breath and a subsequent shift in collecting priorities. When the gallery's attention to earlier British paintings resumed, a much greater interest began to be shown in the local heritage, which Cotton and Lambert had mostly ignored. The apogee of this later phase was reached with the acquisition in 1975 of Gainsborough's magnificent full-length of Isabella, Viscountess Molyneux following the winding up of the estate of Hugh, 7th and last Earl of Sefton of Croxteth Hall. His death without heirs in 1972, followed by that of his Countess eight years later, enabled the gallery, through a mixture of purchase and bequest, to represent in-depth the history of local aristocratic patronage of British painting for the first time. Fourteen paintings in this catalogue were acquired from the collections at Croxteth between 1973 and 1975, and a further 18 came by bequest from the Countess of Sefton in 1980.

*

Of the 16 paintings in this catalogue acquired by the Walker since 1980, nearly all date from the period 1720–80 and nearly all illustrate further historical aspects of local visual culture that had hitherto been unrepresented in the collection. The most remarkable of these works are five portraits by Wright of Derby from the period he spent in the city between 1768 and 1771. Taken together with the self-portrait by Winstanley formerly in the collection of the Earls of Derby at Knowsley, three Caddicks from the 1740s and 1760s, the gallery's first autograph Richard Wright, the great Wilson landscape (one of four) commissioned by Henry Blundell of Ince Blundell as early as the mid-1760s and (somewhat serendipitously) the only known portrait in oils by Peter Romney, brother of George, dating from his membership of the original Liverpool Society of Artists in 1769, their chief effect has been to emphasise the extent to which there was artistic life in Liverpool before the era of William Roscoe.[11] The side-effects of this more nuanced view of the conditions in which Roscoe's enthusiasm

11. This theme was also explored in the gallery's 2007–08 Joseph Wright of Derby exhibition (see n. 3) in which the inclusion of drawings and prints helped further to demonstrate the range of activity in the town.

for art developed have had significant implications for the gallery's hitherto hagiographical representation (fuelled by numerous bequests from many different branches of the Roscoe family) of the figure of Roscoe himself. It has permitted the gradual realisation that Roscoe, as an apologist for and collector of English art in late eighteenth- and early nineteenth-century Liverpool, was far from a lone hand.

The Walker's representation of Roscoe as the owner of British paintings (considering their minor place in his collection overall) is generous, but in its concentration upon his advocacy of Fuseli and his liking for the local John Williamson it is misleading. Roscoe also owned landscapes by[12] Gainsborough and Richard Wilson, three works by Wright, and characteristic subjects by William Hodges, Angelica Kauffman, George Morland and John Hamilton Mortimer, while among local artists he owned eight paintings by Chubbard, Stringer and William Woodworth, not only his commissions from Williamson.[13] Once these are factored in, Roscoe's taste seems less outré and more in keeping with that of his Liverpool confrères, especially his elder brother-in-law Daniel Daulby, who had begun to collect paintings several years earlier than Roscoe and was evidently an important influence on the younger man's approach.[14] Fuseli's biographer John Knowles may have noted that the artist befriended Roscoe – then 26 – on his trip to Liverpool in 1779, but it was Daulby who bought a major work by the artist first: his huge *Owen Glendower, Hotspur and Mortimer Dividing the Kingdom* (now in Birmingham Museum and Art Gallery); and this work, together with Benjamin West's extraordinary *Saul and the Witch of Endor* (Wadsworth Atheneum, Hartford) purchased directly from the artist on a visit to London in 1779[15] acted as beacons of the Sublime in Daulby's collection in very much the same way that Fuseli's *Death of Oedipus* was later to do in Roscoe's. Even Roscoe's bias towards one 'national' artist – Fuseli – and one local one – Williamson – along with his specialisation in a specific area of Old Master collecting (Italian primitives) appears modelled upon his brother-in-law's twin predilections

12. The term 'by' is used henceforward to mean 'then thought to be by', although some of the attributions of the period are likely to have been suspect.

13. See the catalogue of Roscoe's sale, Winstanley, Liverpool, 6th day, 28 September 1816, lots 133–56; also Roscoe's household inventory of 1820, pp. 2–5, 7, 9, 12 and 33 (copy in gallery archives) for 38 foreign and British paintings which as gifts or family items had been spared inclusion in his sale as a bankrupt four years earlier.

14. For a summary of Daulby's collecting of British pictures see Peter Urquhart: 'Daulby's Albums', *Transactions of the Romney Society* vol. 13 (2008) pp. 16–23.

15. In a letter of 2 June 1779 to his friend Matthew Gregson (*Gregson Papers*, LRO 920/GRE/2/18/1) Daulby described a visit to London where he and Thomas Vernon 'visited West, Romney, *Carter*, &c, Angelica has many fine pieces in this Exhibition, she with Cipriani & the late Mortimer stand in the front rank in my Opinion. I have seen some good pieces of Wests but like Mortimer better'. Previously, in the summer of 1777, Daulby had written to Sir Joshua Reynolds enquiring about the availability of one of his fancy pictures and sitting to him for his portrait (see John Ingamells and John Edgcumbe, eds: *The Letters of Sir Joshua Reynolds* [New Haven and London, 2000] pp. 69–70 [letter 64]).

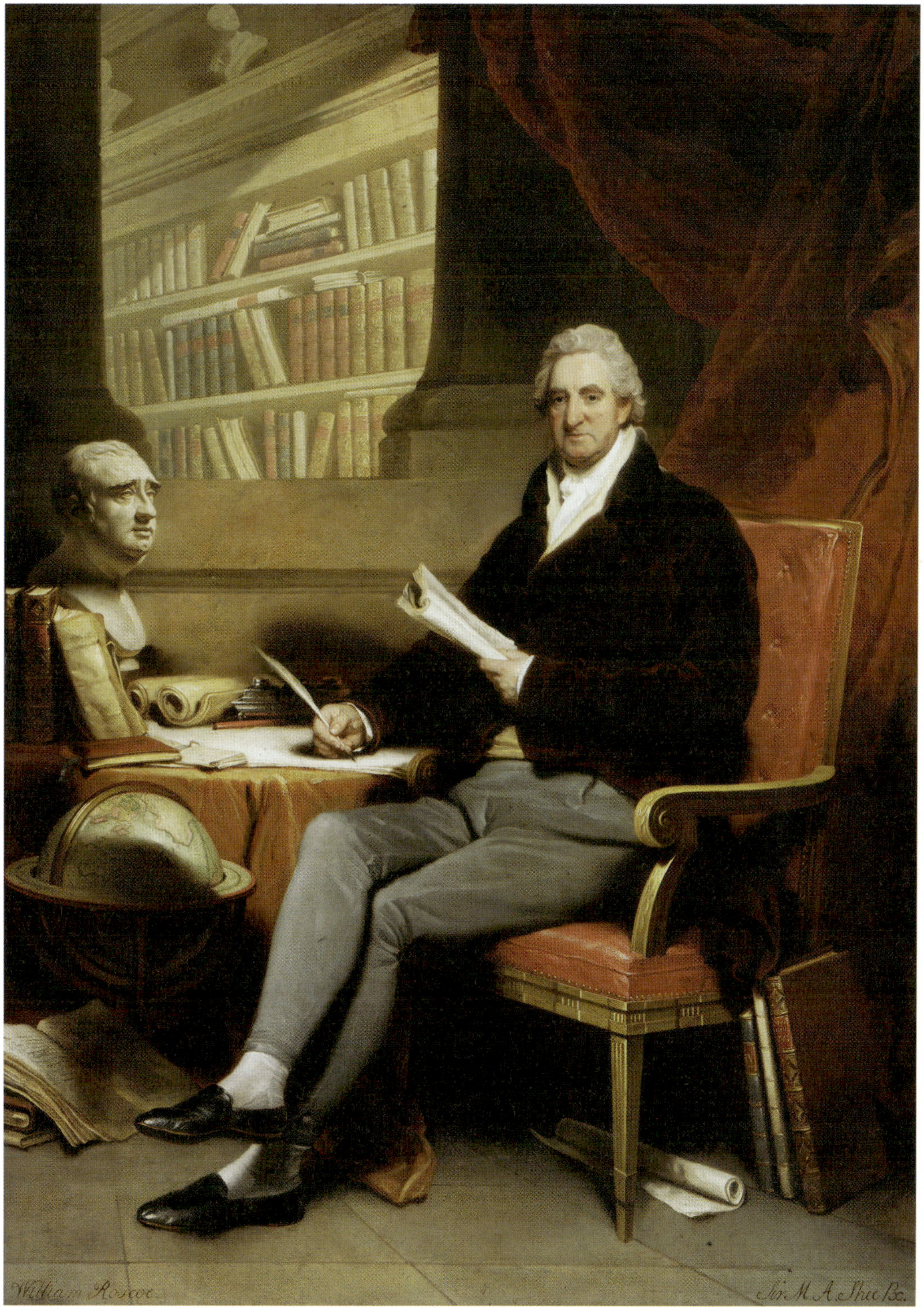

Plate 5
Martin Archer Shee: *William Roscoe*
WAG 3130

for Joseph Wright and Thomas Chubbard and his obsession with the prints of Rembrandt. However, not one of the 33 British paintings included in Daulby's posthumous sale in 1798[16] is in the Walker, and even if the net is widened to take in the 174 British paintings listed in Daulby's inventory of his collection made not long before his death,[17] the tally is still only three family portraits by William Tate and possibly (the identification is uncertain) two small landscapes by Chubbard. It would be only fitting if one day Daulby's beloved Wright, *Julia in a Cavern*, described in his sale catalogue as 'this celebrated picture… justly esteemed to be the *chef d'oeuvre* of that celebrated master' were to rejoin them in the gallery's collection.

The story of the Walker's neglect of Daulby is largely repeated with the three other leading local collectors of paintings in the late eighteenth century. Henry Blundell of Ince Blundell, whose chief interest, antique marbles, is well represented in the holdings of National Museums Liverpool, also owned nearly 200 paintings by 1803,[18] a number of which he had acquired in his youth, at a date long before Daulby was active. Although British pictures were even more of a minority in his collection than they were in Roscoe's, they included works by Reynolds, Penny, Stubbs and Wilson, as well as locals Caddick, Towne and Richard Wright. This group, fascinating as the earliest significant non-aristocratic collection of pictures in the Liverpool area, is now represented by a single work, Wilson's *Phaeton*, acquired in 1999. Edward Rogers, who with Daulby and Roscoe was on the committee of the Society for the Promotion of Painting and Design in Liverpool in the late 1780s, owned two considerable works by Stubbs; three large landscapes by Zuccarelli; five smaller works each by Fuseli and George Morland; two Monamys; two historical works by William Craig; two portraits by Cornelius Johnson; and – portentously for the artist's immediate future – two landscapes by Ibbetson. Of the 40 British paintings in his sale, conducted by Thomas Vernon after his death in 1797,[19] none is in the Walker. The same is true for the 39 British paintings in the collection of Roscoe's friend William Clarke auctioned by Winstanley in 1806.[20] Among these were Wilson's *Summit of Cader Idris* (now at Tate Britain) which Clarke

16. Daulby's sale, Thomas Vernon, Liverpool, 27 August 1798 (82 lots).
17. Daniel Daulby: (ms) *Catalogue of the Books, Prints, Pictures and Drawings of Daniel Daulby, Liverpool, 1793* LRO H 091.5 DAU (copy in gallery archives).
18. See (Henry Blundell): *An Account of the Statues, Busts, Bass-relieves, Cinerary Urns, and Other Ancient Marbles, and Paintings at Ince Collected by H. B.* (Liverpool, 1803) pp. 211–65.
19. Rogers's sale, Thomas Vernon, Liverpool, 24 July 1797 (88 lots).
20. Clarke's sale, Winstanley, Liverpool, 7–8 July 1806 (141 lots of which 75 lots comprised a total of 92 paintings).

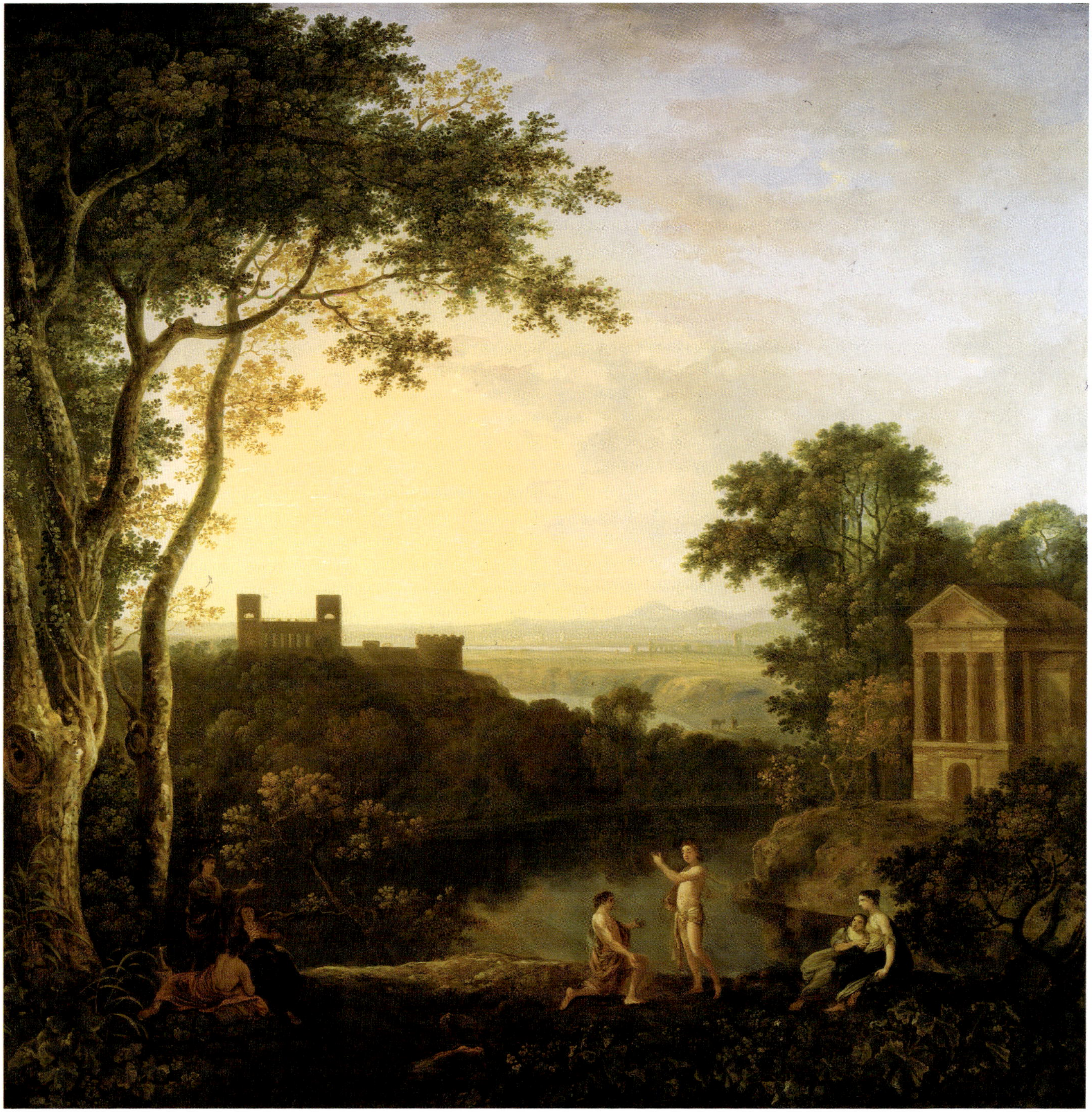

Plate 6
Richard Wilson: *Landscape with Phaeton's Petition to Apollo*
WAG 1999.58

seems to have acquired privately from Daulby, Wright's *Julia*, purchased at Daulby's sale; a Zuccarelli purchased at Rogers's; works by Gainsborough and Fuseli that (with the Wilson) passed to Roscoe; landscapes by Wyck, Marlow, Barret and Webber; marines by Scott, Serres and Swain; as well as no fewer than eight works by Caddick.

It is of course something of a tall order at over two centuries' remove to identify many of the pictures owned by this band of pioneer collectors; and the same is true of the paintings included in the historic early exhibitions in Liverpool, particularly that of 1774 mounted by the Society of Artists in Liverpool, which was the first exhibition of a provincial art society in England.[21] Of its 85 catalogued items, 27 are identifiable as oil paintings, which are by eight of the 24 exhibitors. Frustratingly, although three of these eight artists – Chubbard, John Rathbone and William Tate – are represented in the Walker, it is impossible positively to identify any contributions to the exhibition among their works in the gallery (even though there are several possible candidates).[22] When it comes to the larger and more impressive sequel exhibitions of 1784 and 1787, the situation is even less favourable. Of the 21 local exhibitors (excluding honorary exhibitors) in these, Chubbard and Tate apart, only Richard Caddick and John Pennington from the 1784 exhibition, Charles Towne and Thomas Hazlehurst from the 1787 one, and John Williamson, who showed in both, are represented in the Walker (Pennington and Hazlehurst are too youthful to appear in this catalogue). Of these seven artists' works in the Walker's collection, only two portraits of Roscoe by Williamson were 1784 or 1787 exhibits. Among the significant local artists who contributed to the 1784 and 1787 exhibitions who are not represented in the Walker at all are Peter Holland, Patrick McMorland and William Woodworth, all three of whom were collected by Daulby (Woodworth also by Roscoe); the two Stringers of Knutsford, Ottwell Worrall; and the landscape painter William Jackson. The last four of these had all been contributors to the 1774 exhibition, and both Holland and Jackson would remain resident in Liverpool at least until the late 1790s. Among their colleagues recorded in Liverpool street directories at this date, again not represented in the Walker, were the eminent marine painter and portraitist John Jenkinson (whose work is,

21. For a full list of the 1774 exhibits see Joseph Mayer: *Early Exhibitions of Art in Liverpool with Some Notes for a Memoir of George Stubbs R.A.* (Liverpool, 1876) pp. 21–31.

22. Cat. 42, *A Landscape* by Rathbone, could be WAG 734, and cat. 66, *Portrait of a Gentleman* by William Tate could be WAG 2541. Cats. 50–51, two portraits by Sharples, are possible candidates for WAG 2397–8, here catalogued as British School.

however, in the Merseyside Maritime Museum) and the portraitists John McCree and Samuel Moore.

If one looks forward into the era of the second Liverpool Academy (1810–14 and 1822 onwards), a similar pattern emerges with younger artists who do not belong in the present catalogue. Alongside names that are familiar from long exposure in the gallery there are exhibitors who were evidently stalwarts of the Academy and yet whose work is now completely forgotten. By that period, a perceptible emerging taste for early British pictures in Liverpool is to be detected among a wider circle of wealthy picture-lovers following Daulby's and Roscoe's lead.[23] A snapshot of this taste is provided by the exhibition *The Paintings; the works of the Old Masters of Various Schools, and of Deceased British Artists* held by the Liverpool Royal Institution in 1823, whose catalogue lists (together with 109 foreign works; a proportion in keeping with Roscoe's picture collection) 26 British works lent by such men as John Moss, John Gladstone and William Gregson. Of these 26 paintings, 16 were by three artists: Wilson (with six), Morland and Wright of Derby (five each) – with Reynolds and Gainsborough lagging far behind (three between them), Hogarth nowhere at all, history paintings likewise, and just a trace of exoticism supplied by two pictures by Philippe-Jacques de Loutherbourg and one by Nathan T. Fielding, who had lived in Liverpool for a few years before 1810.[24] None of these paintings – and none of their owners – is present in this catalogue; and yet small as the group is, it has a perceptible and distinctive flavour. In its avoidance of the mainstream metropolitan tradition, in the bias shown for three artists who were all perceived in their own day as in some sense outsiders, in its flirtation with quirkiness, it already epitomises a strain of Liverpudlian cultural pride that has persisted ever since. The various strands of this emerging tradition in the eighteenth and early nineteenth centuries set William Roscoe's achievement in context; and if this tradition is one that the gallery wishes to record, it still has some collecting to do.

23. A convenient list of the names and residences of many of this generation of collectors is given in Henry Smithers: *Liverpool, Its Commerce, Statistics and Institutions, with a History of the Cotton Trade* (Liverpool, 1825) p. 340.

24. Of him the catalogue noted that he 'painted many curious heads of old men and women, in which he imitated nature most exactly. His style was the reason for his gaining the name of the English *Denner.* He painted some landscapes in a highly finished style… The woman who was the original of this picture was an inhabitant of Liverpool, and was painted when she had reached her hundredth year' (*The Paintings, the Works of the Old Masters of Various Schools, and of Deceased British Artists,* exh. cat., Liverpool Royal Institution [1823] p. 30). Two landscapes in oils by Fielding are in the collection of the Victoria Museum and Gallery, University of Liverpool.

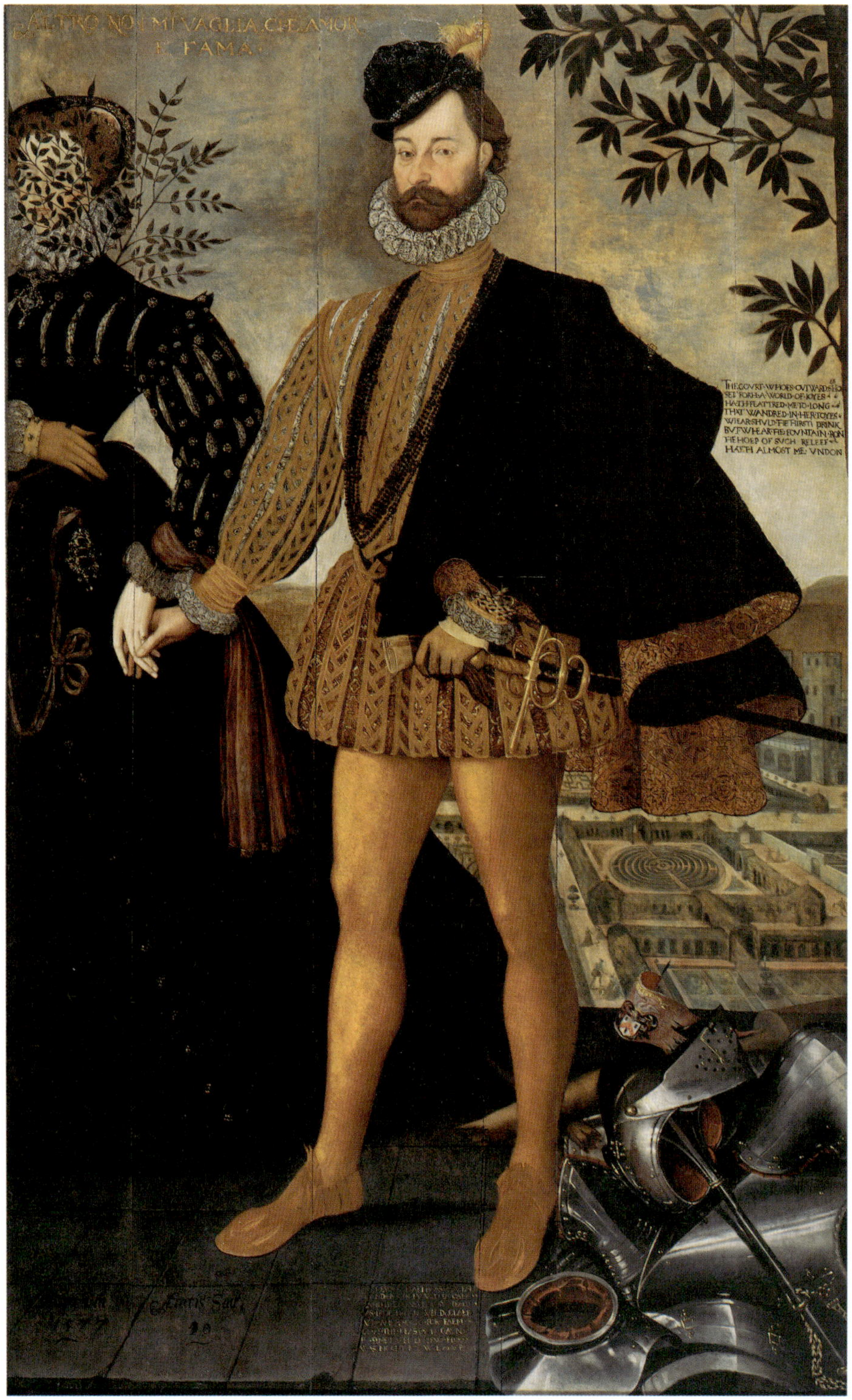

Plate 7
British School: *George Delves and a Female Companion*
WAG 3089

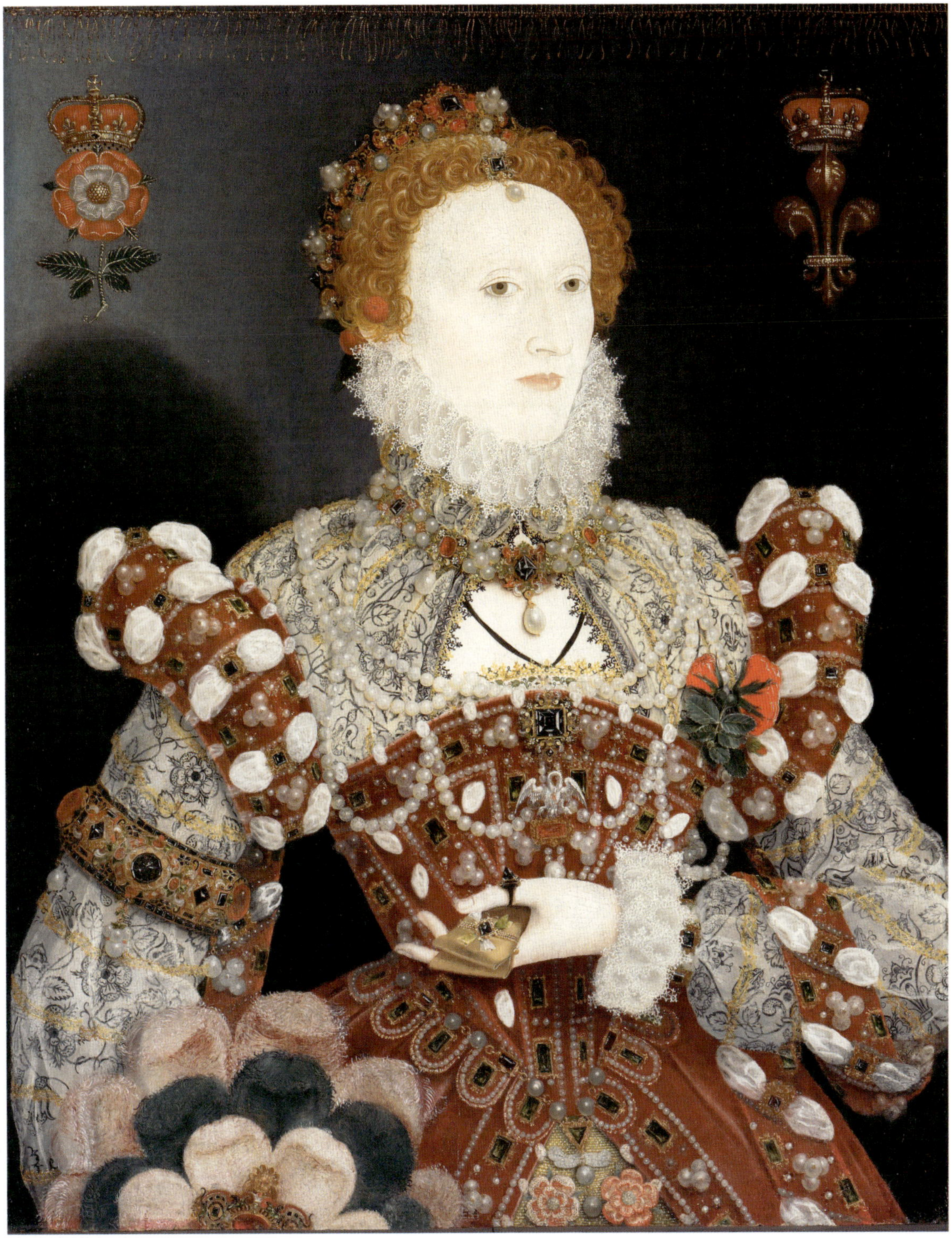

Plate 8
called Nicholas Hilliard: *Queen Elizabeth I: the Pelican Portrait*
WAG 2994

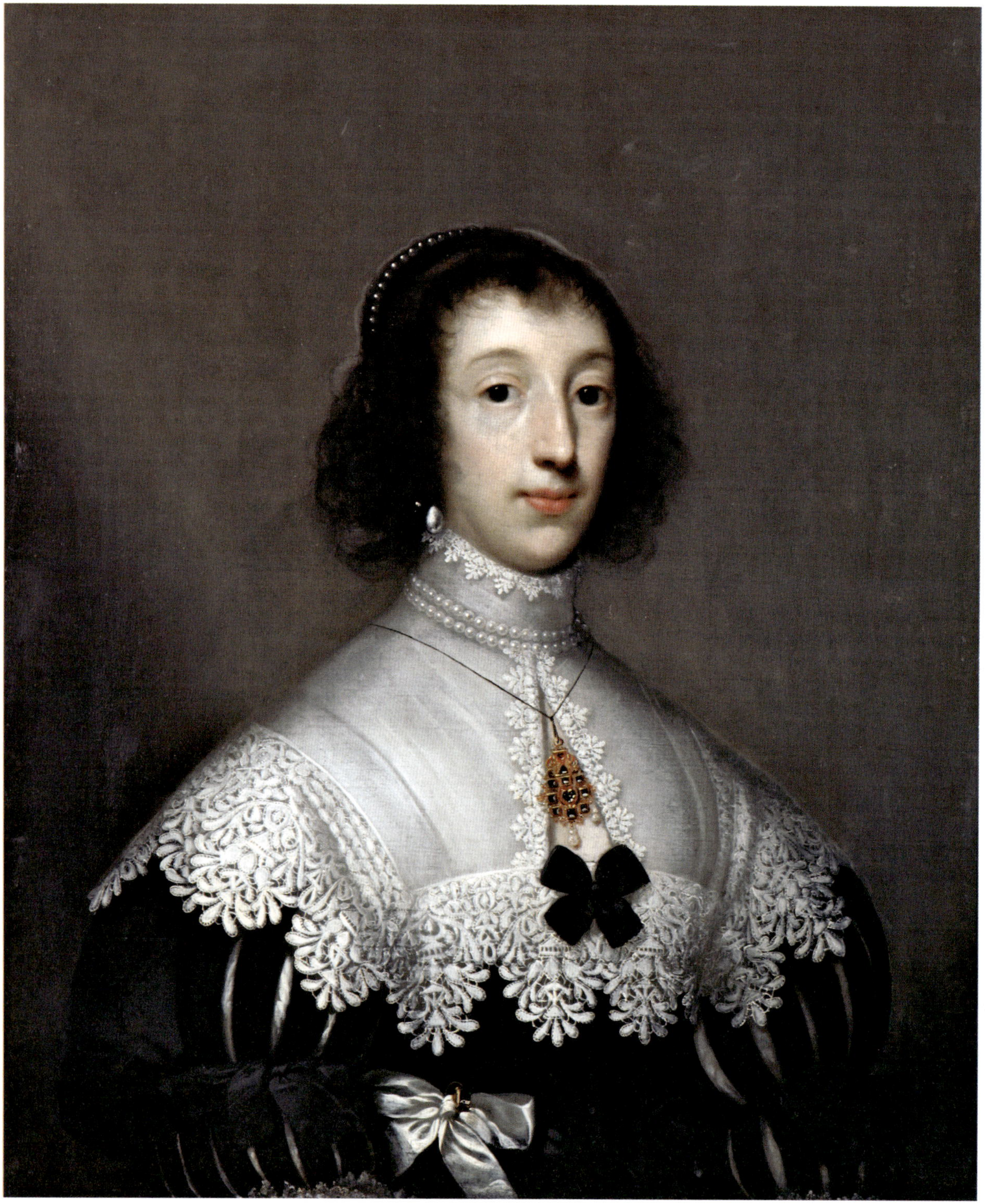

Plate 9
Cornelius Johnson: *Portrait of a Lady*
WAG 2995

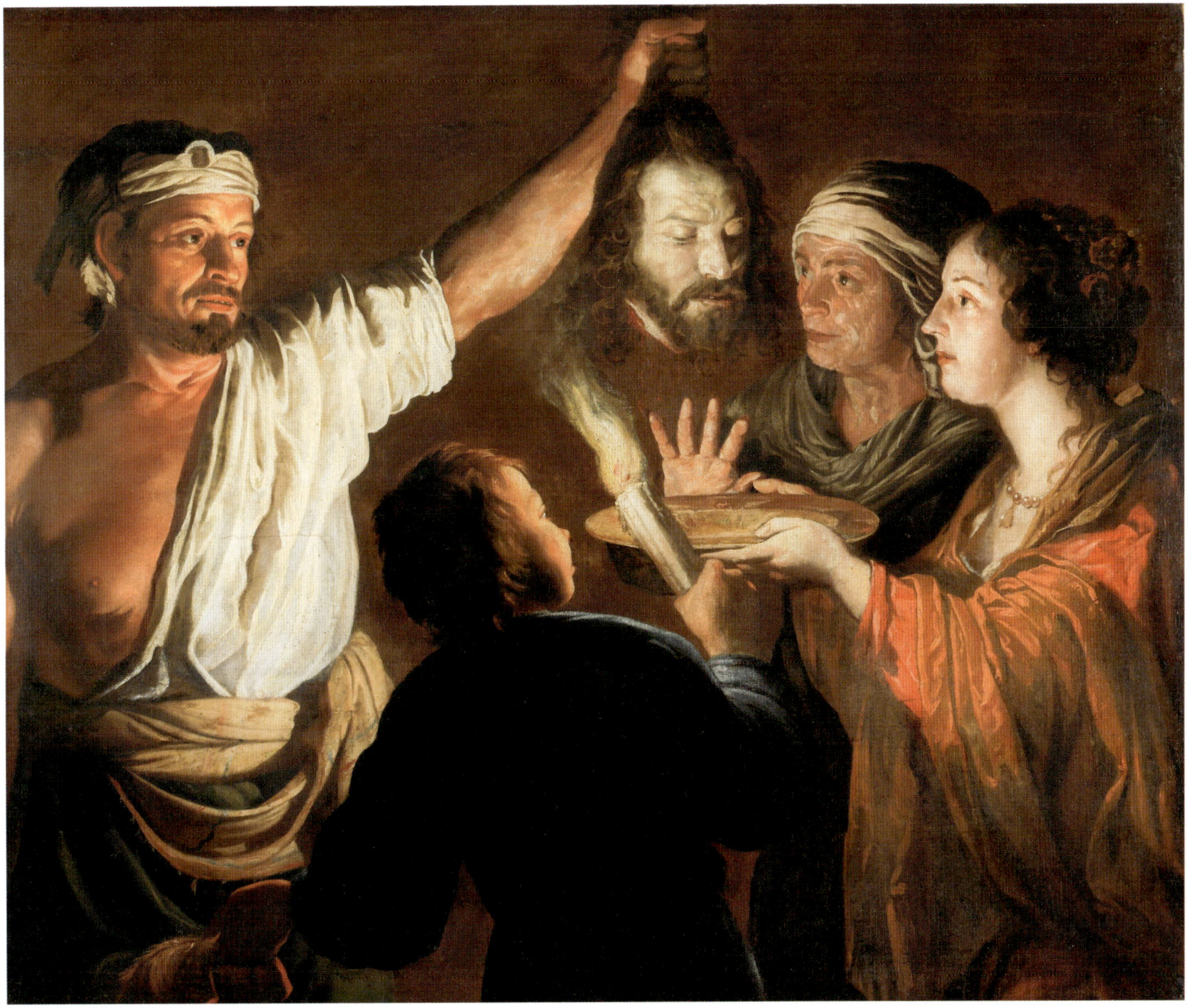

Plate 10
William Dobson: *The Executioner with the Head of John the Baptist*
WAG 2993

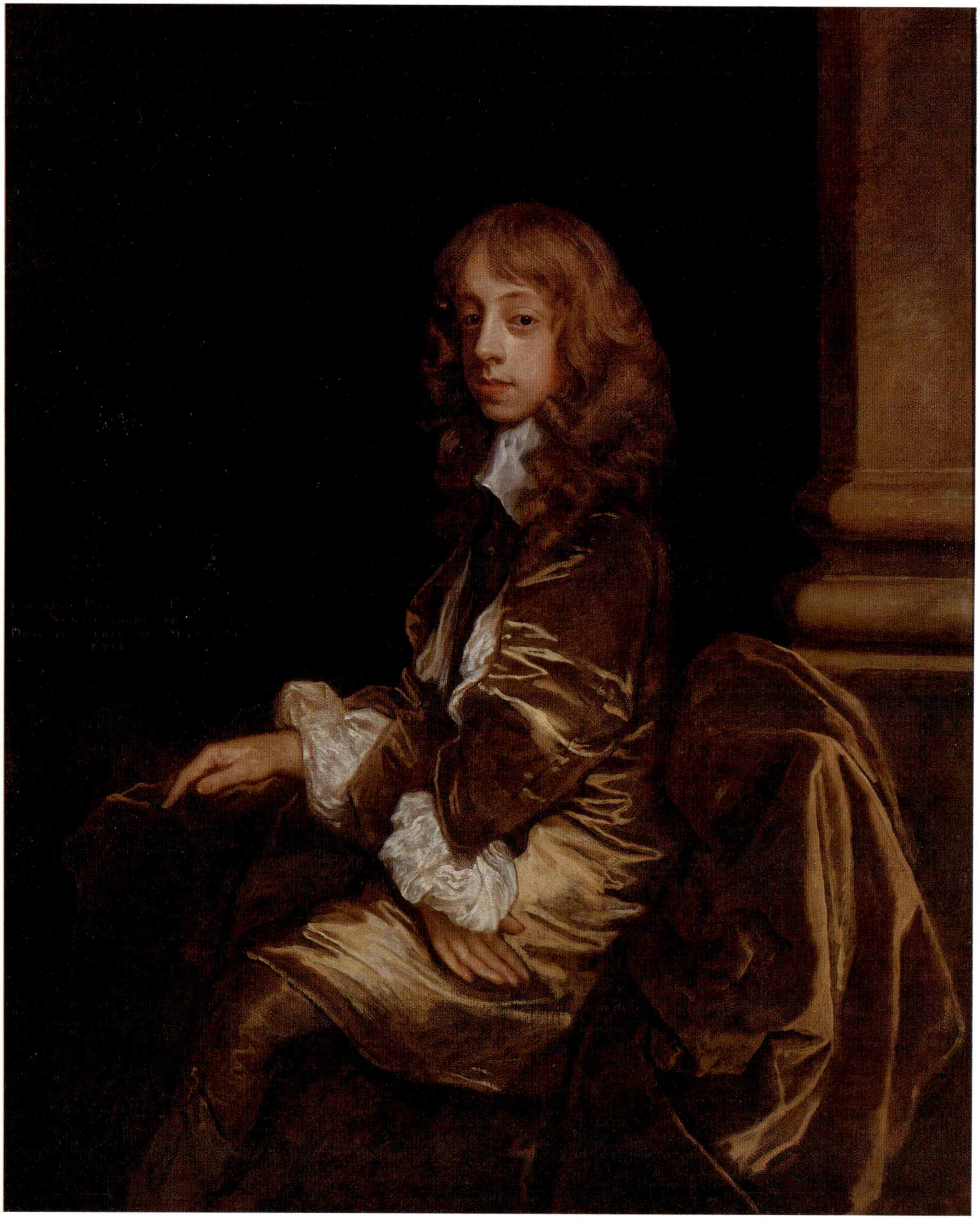

Plate 11
Peter Lely: *Josceline Percy, Lord Percy*
WAG 2945

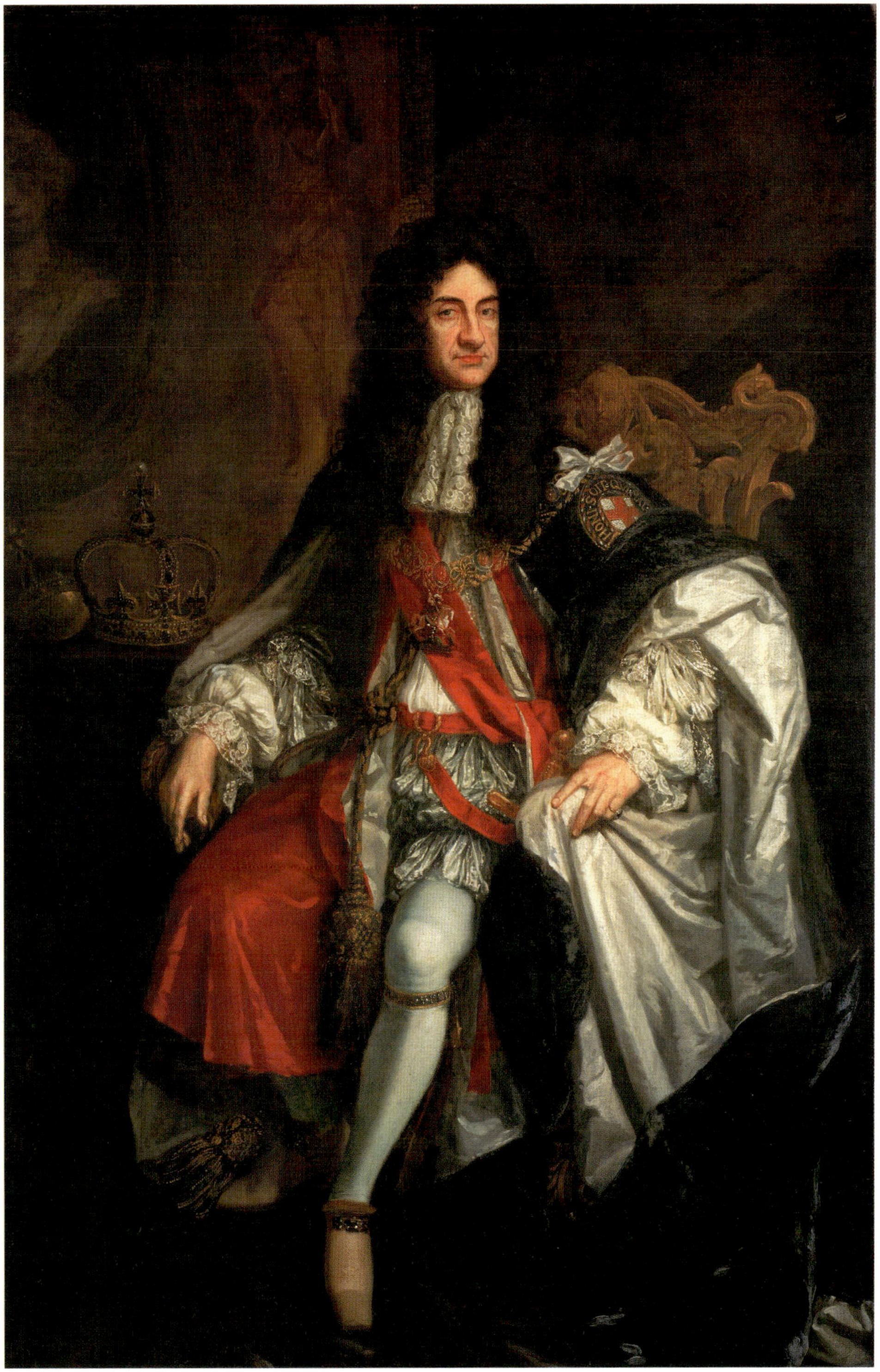

Plate 12
Godfrey Kneller: *King Charles II*
WAG 3023

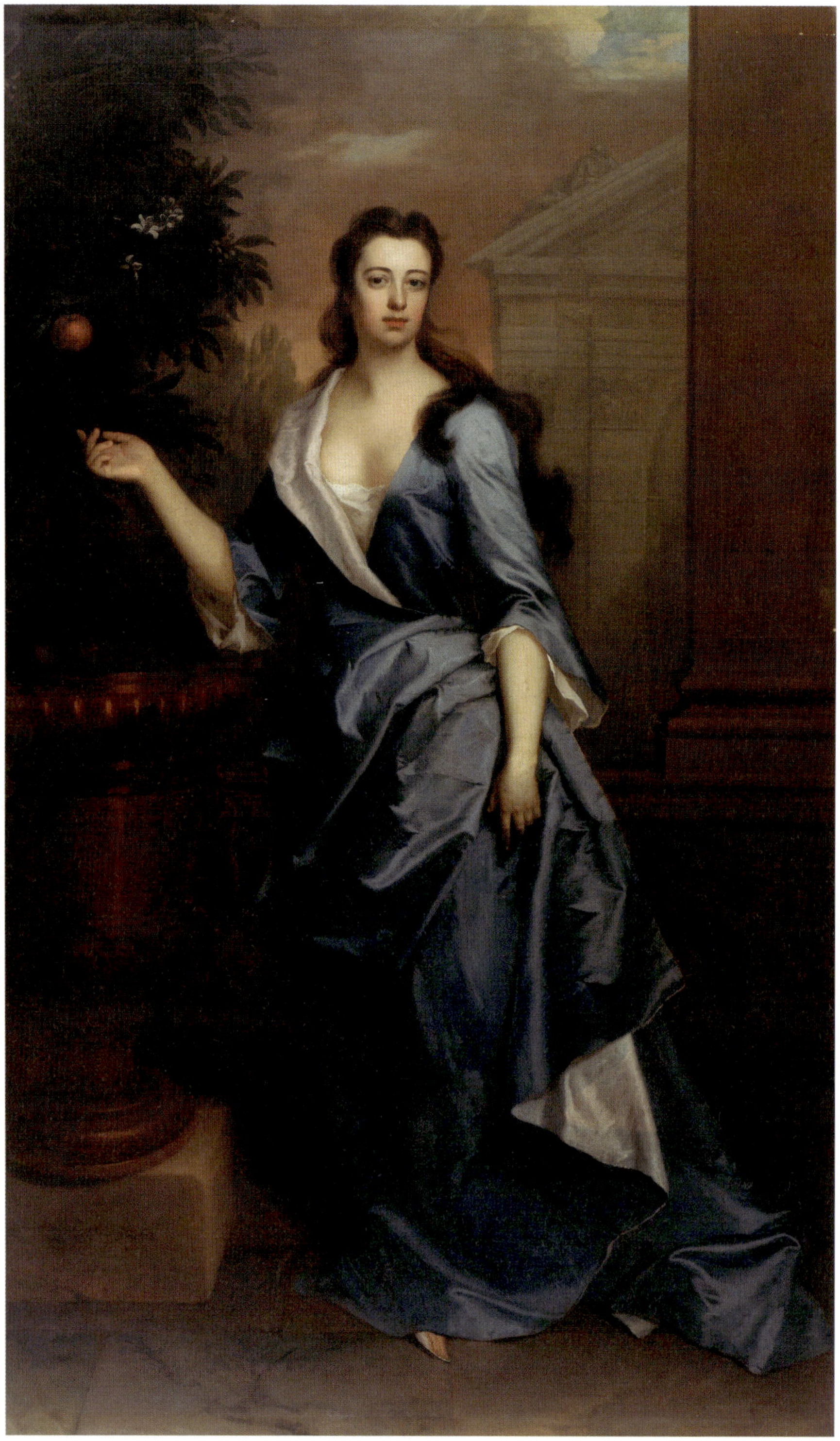

Plate 13
Michael Dahl: *Henrietta Maria, Baroness Ashburnham*
WAG 2359

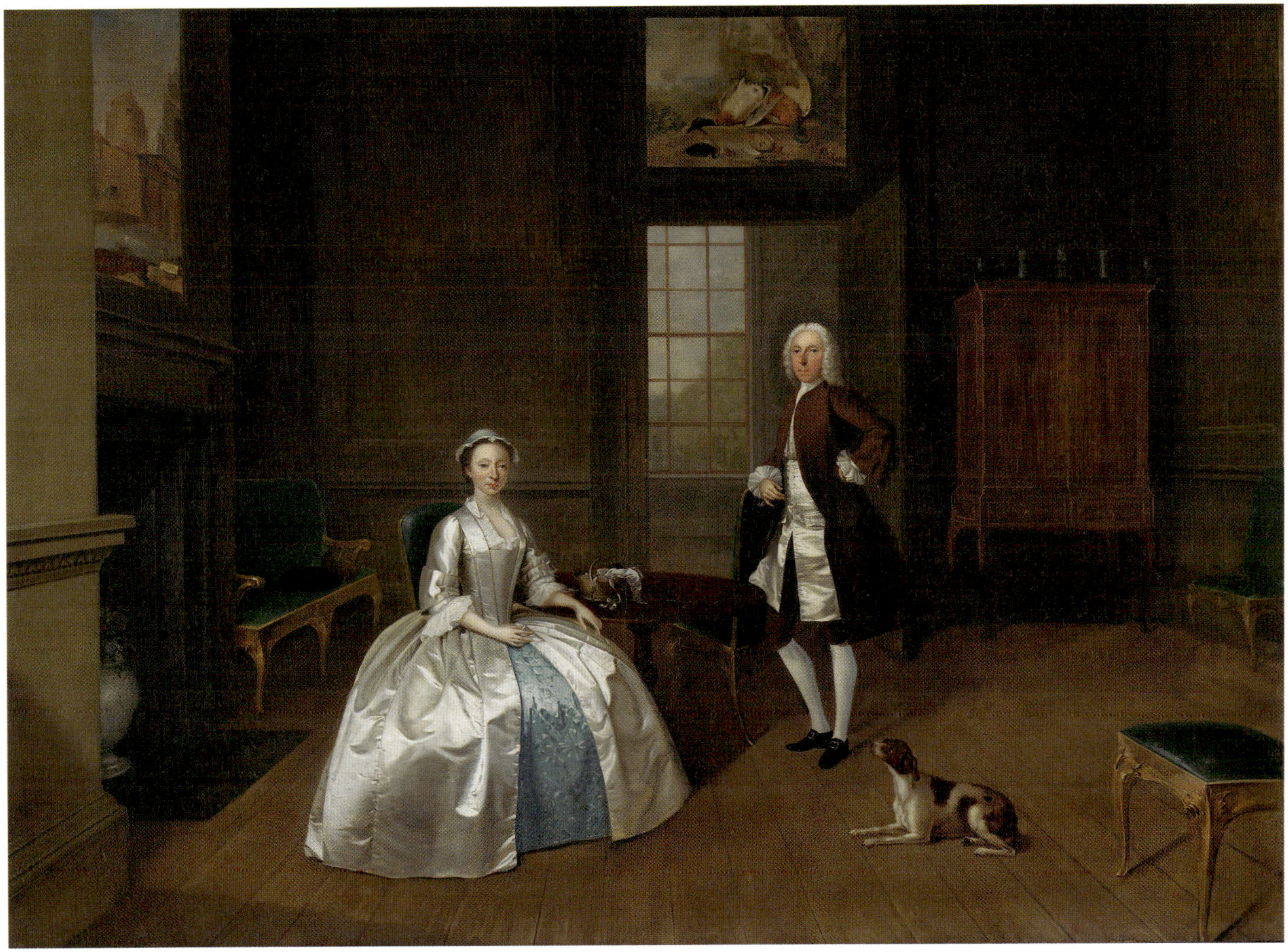

Plate 14
Arthur Devis: *Mr and Mrs William Atherton*
WAG 1353

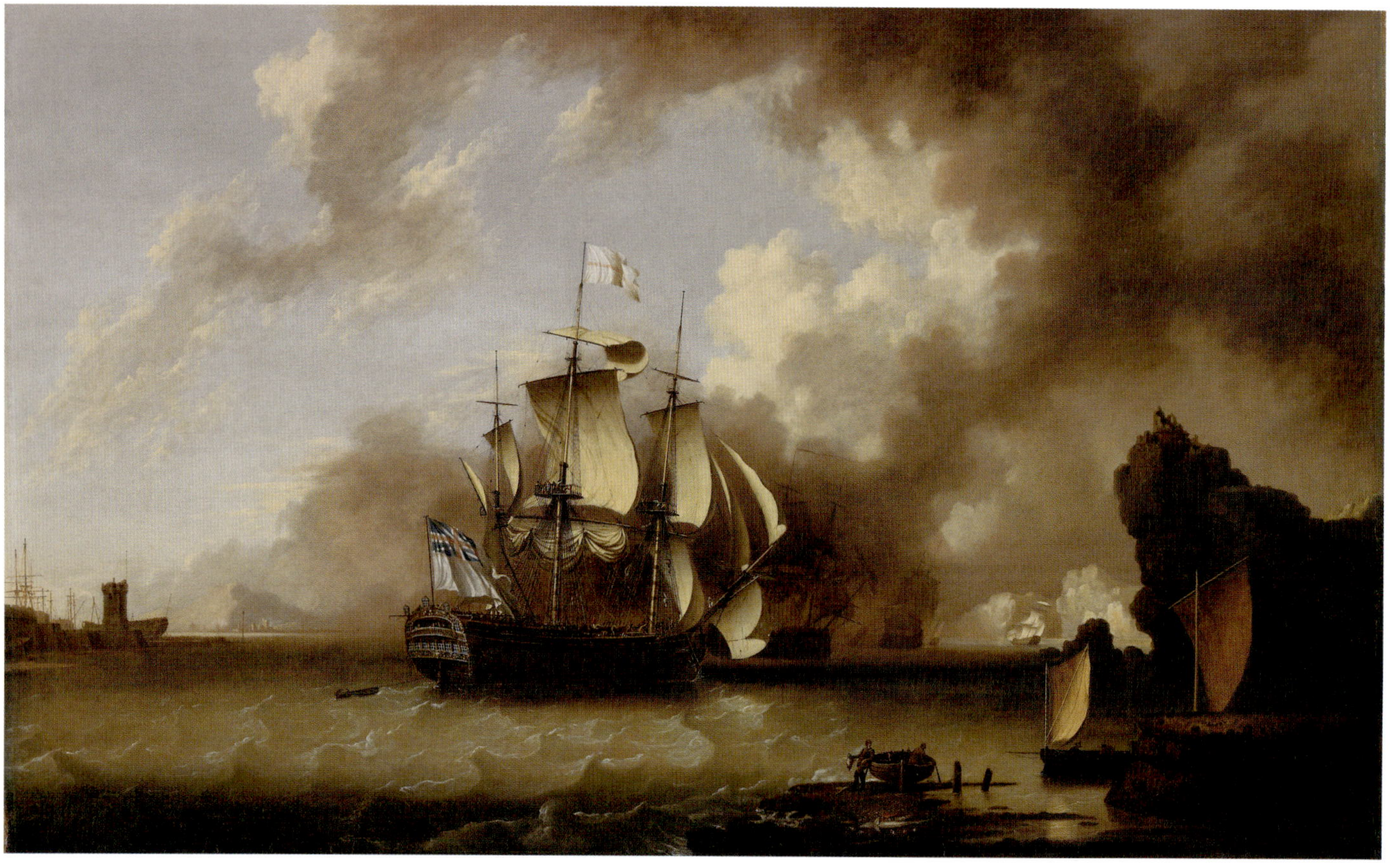

Plate 15
Richard Wright: *Man of War in a Harbour*
WAG 2006.21

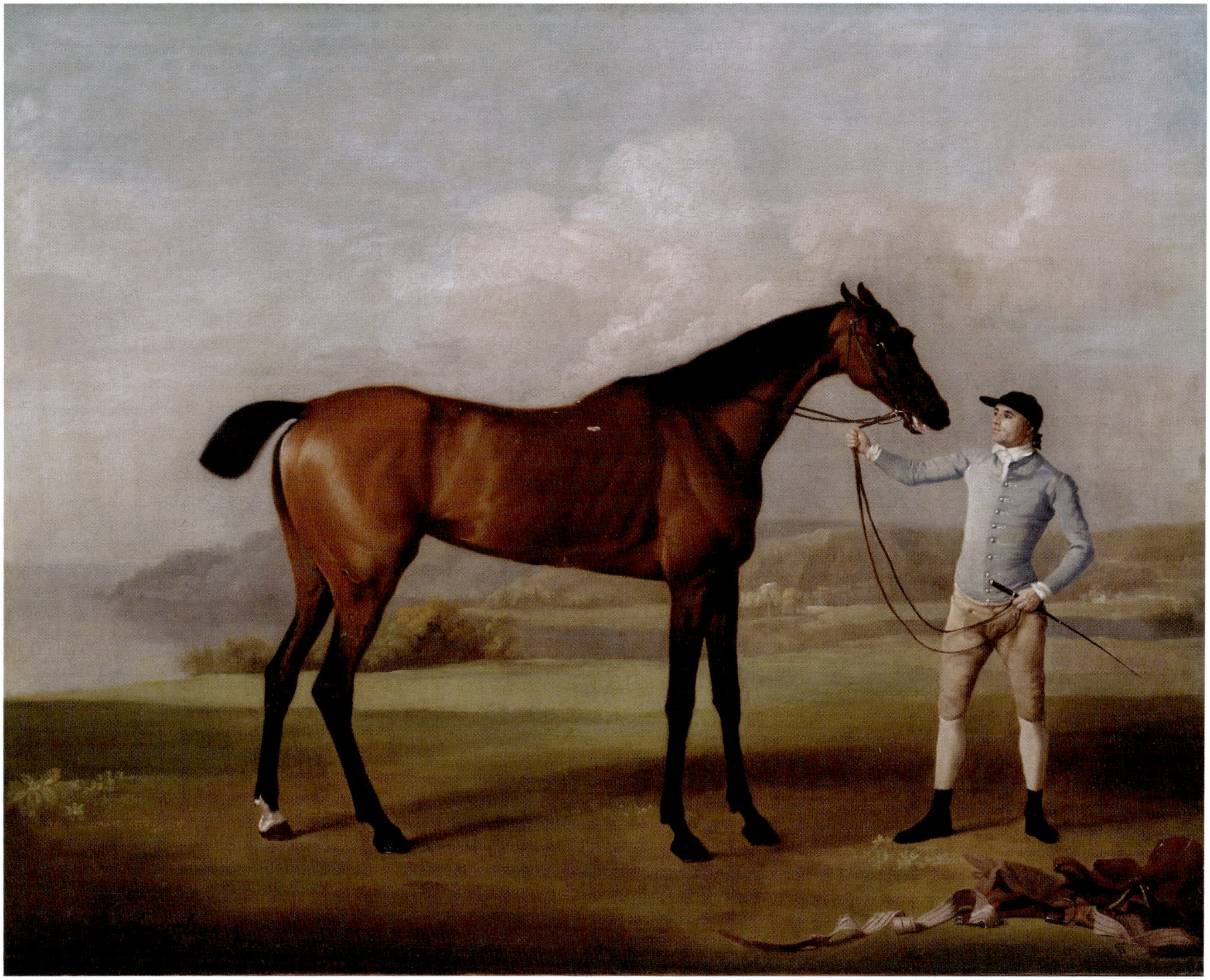

Plate 16
George Stubbs: *Molly Long-legs with her Jockey*
WAG 2389

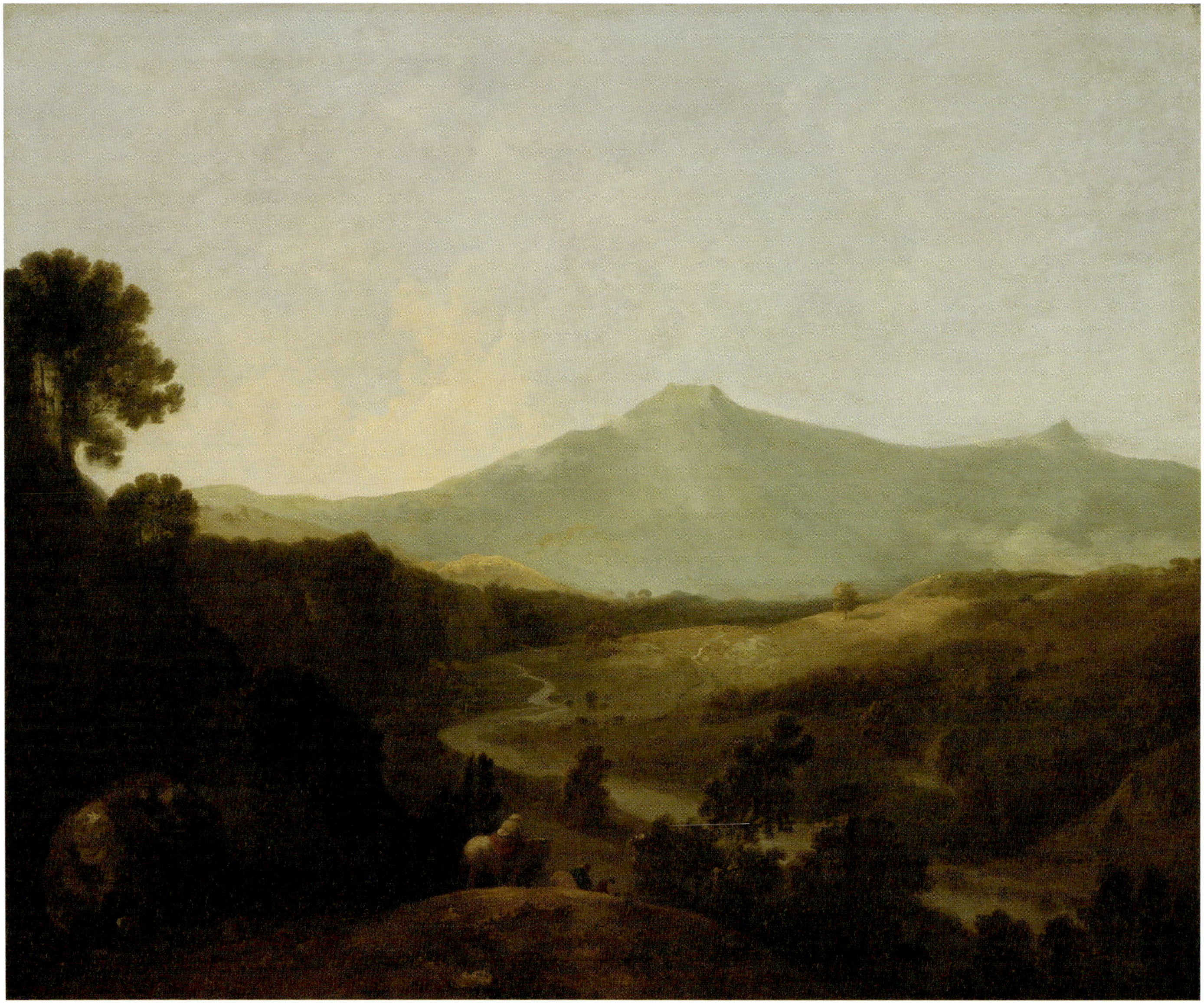

Plate 17
Richard Wilson: *The Valley of the Mawddach and Cader Idris Mountain*
WAG 2428

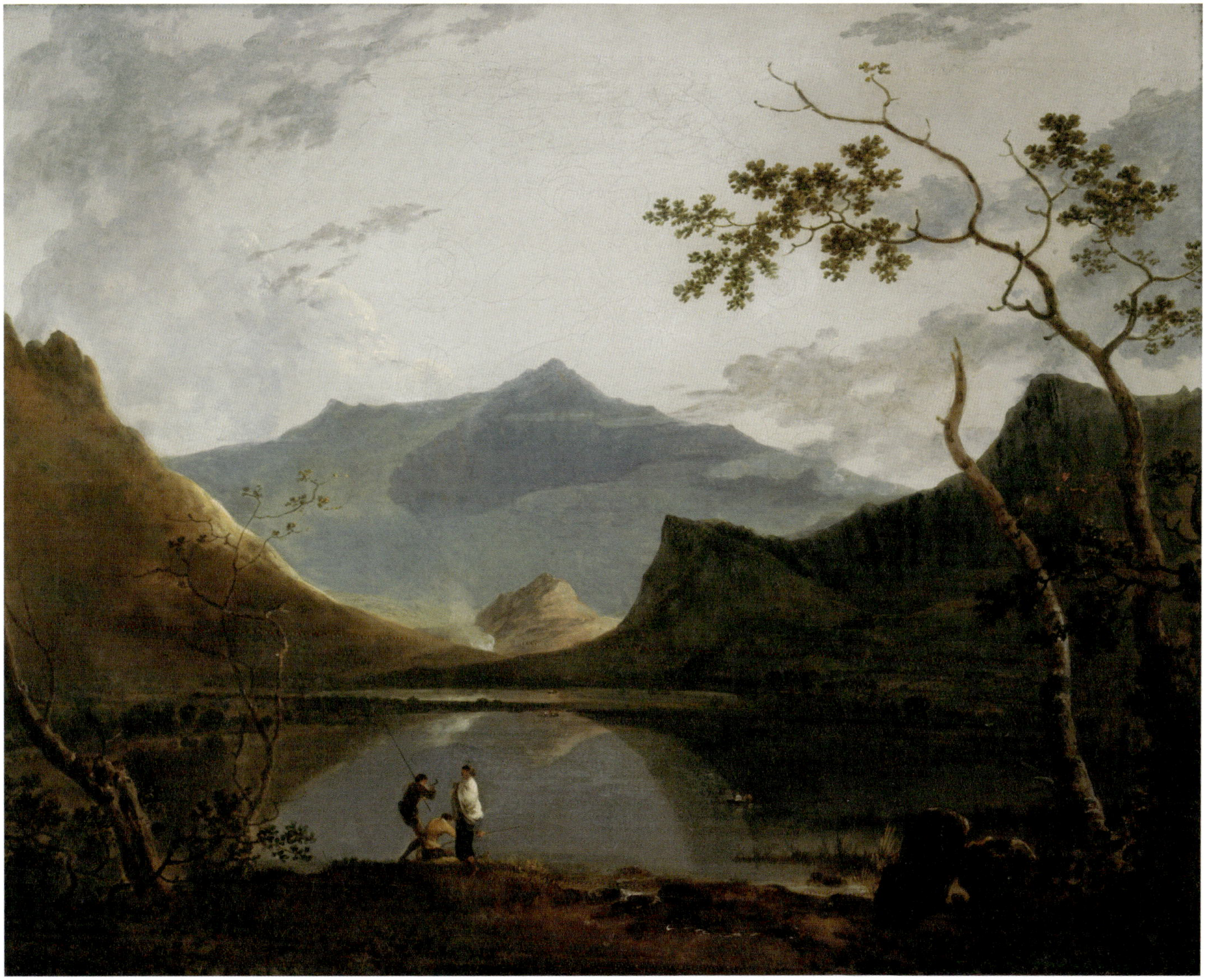

Plate 18
Richard Wilson: *Snowdon from Llyn Nantlle*
WAG 2429

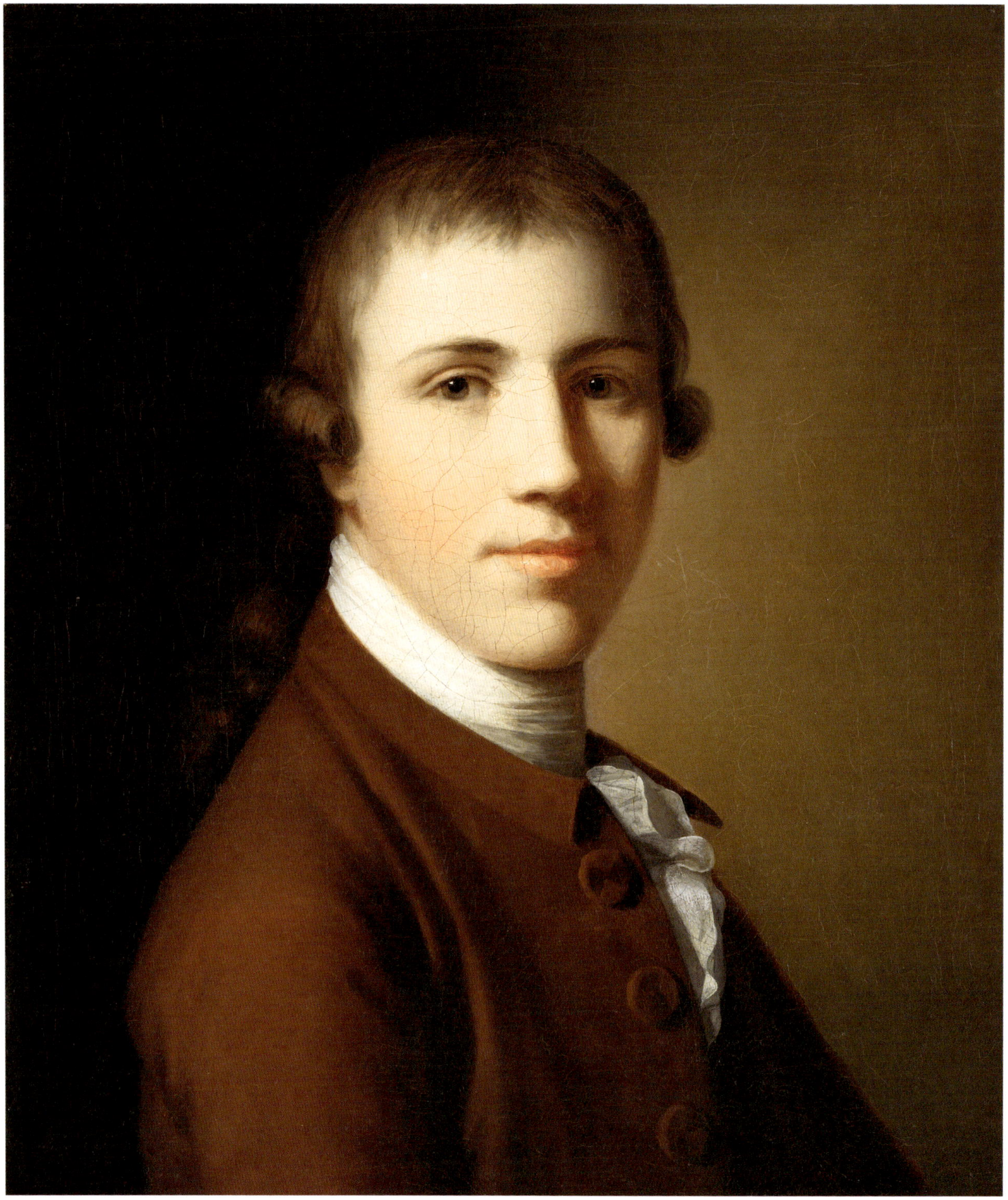

Plate 19
Richard Caddick: *Portrait of a Young Man*
WAG 3109

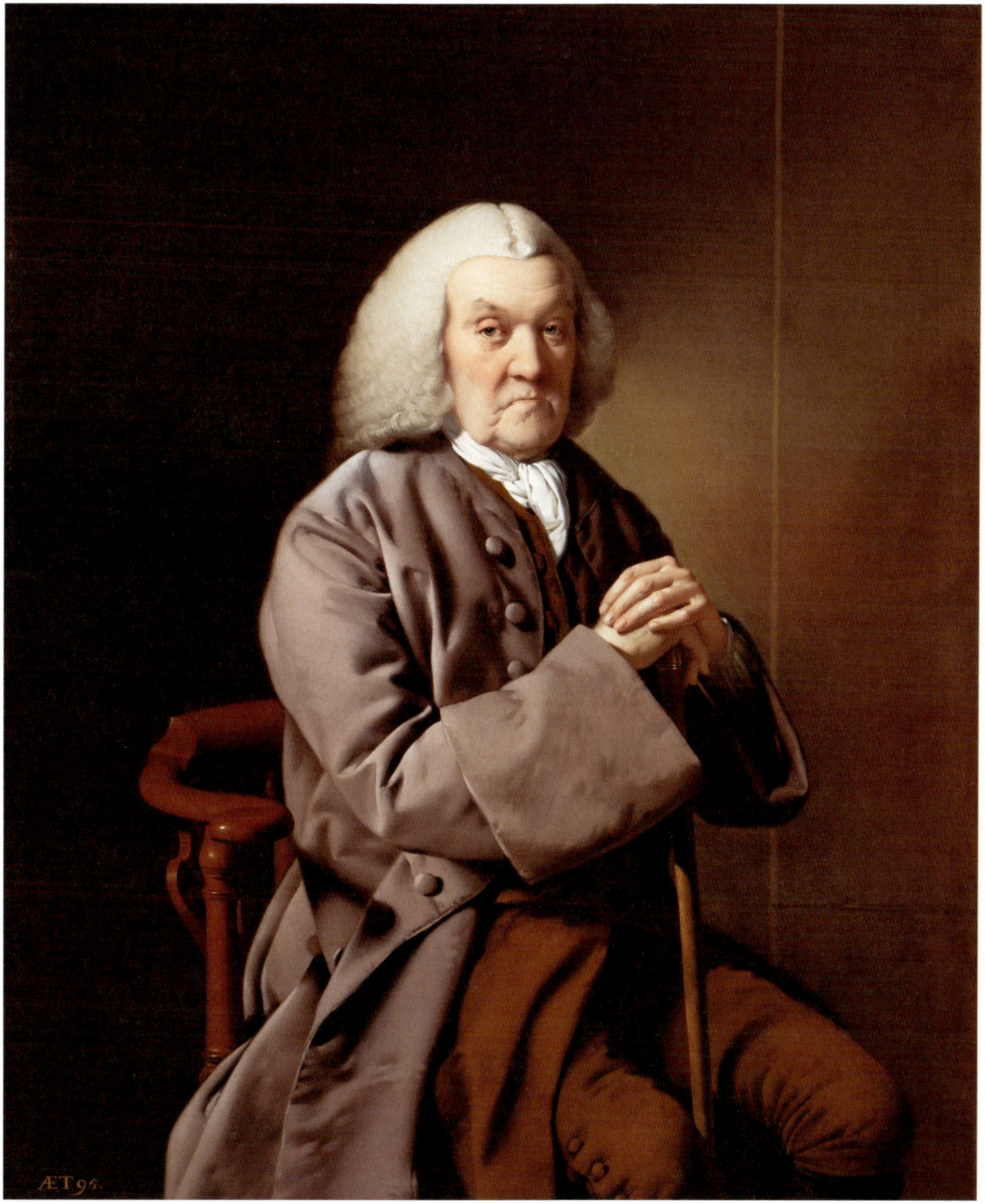

Plate 20
Joseph Wright (of Derby): *Richard Gildart*
WAG 10637

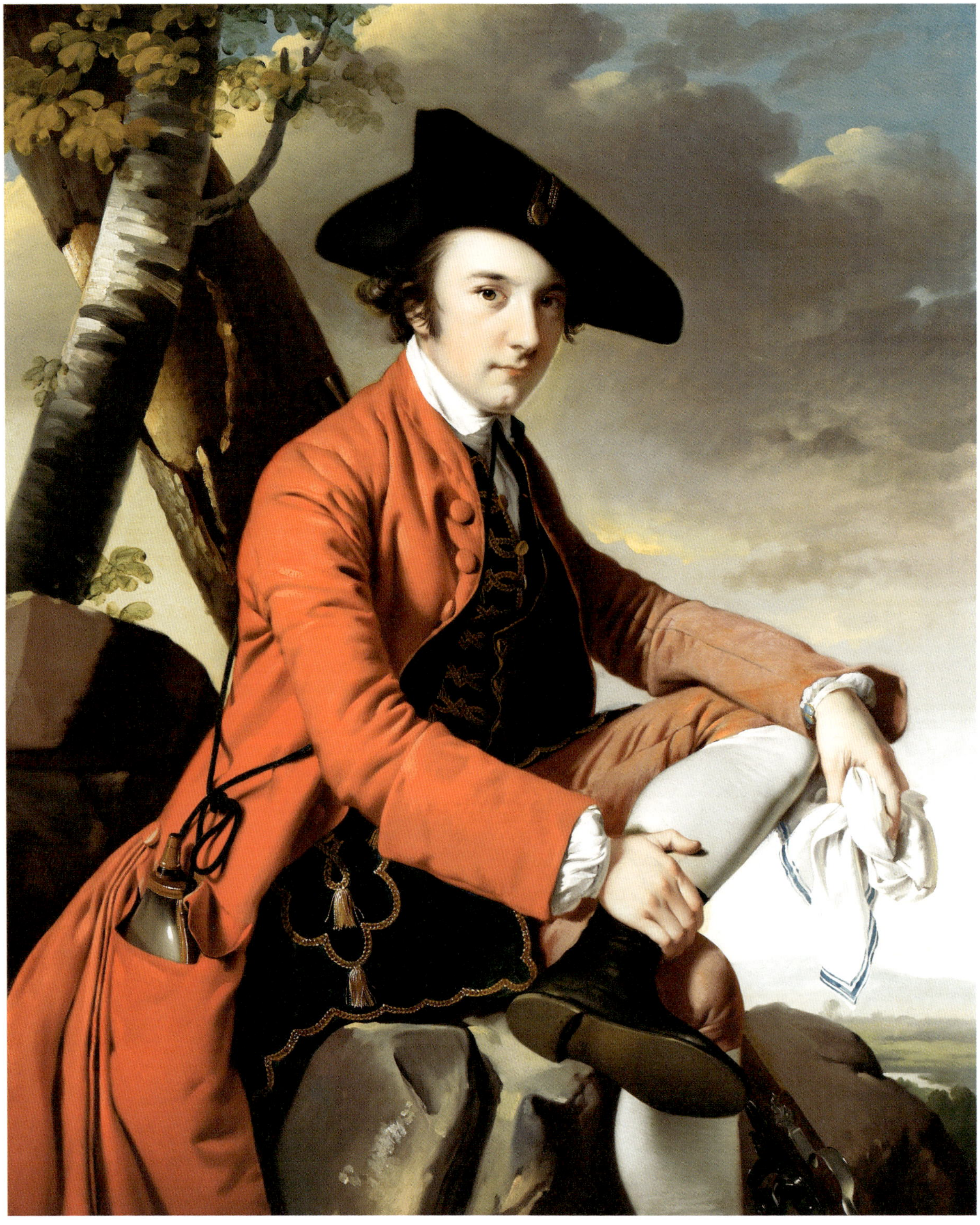

Plate 21
Joseph Wright (of Derby): *Fleetwood Hesketh*
WAG 10846

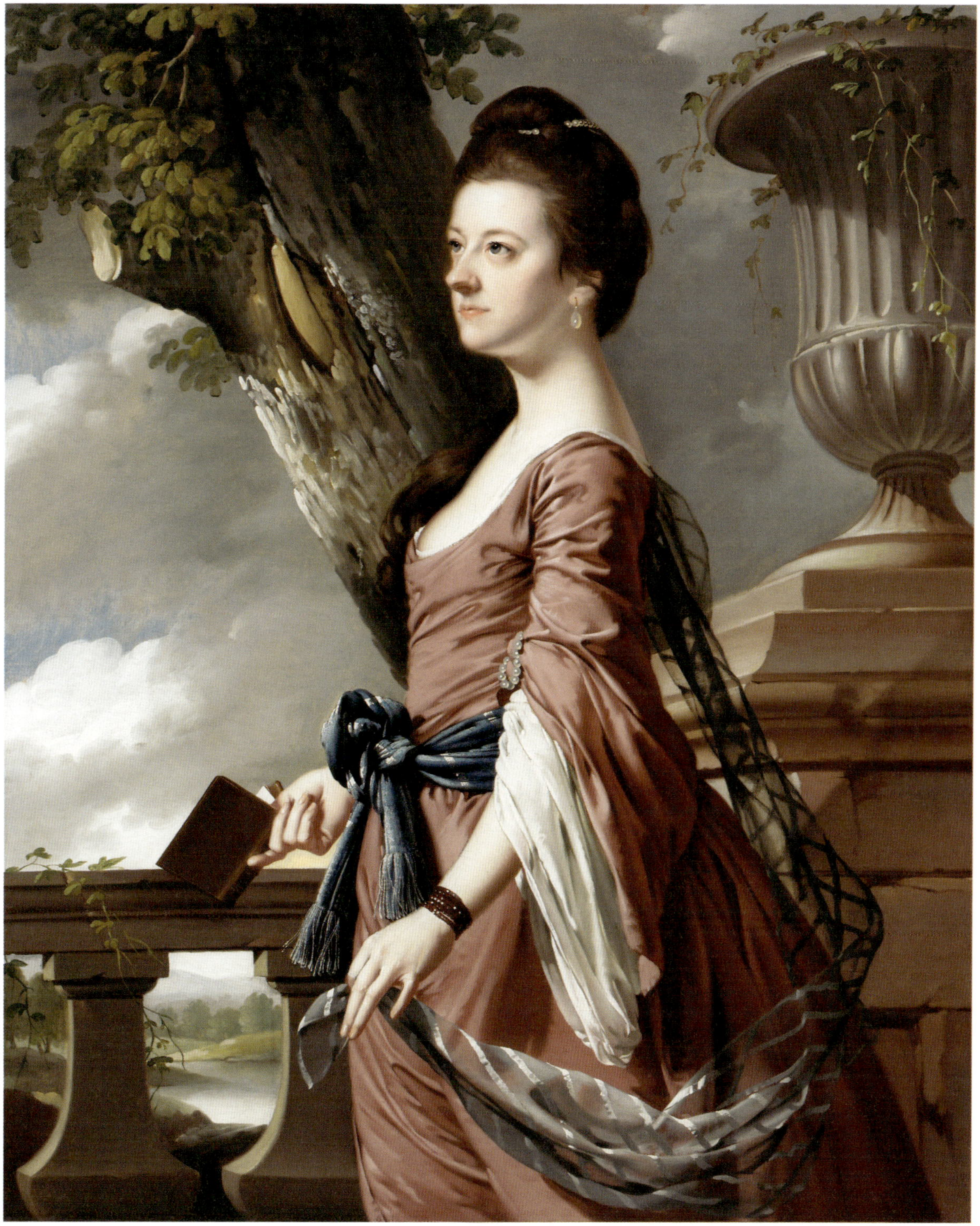

Plate 22
Joseph Wright (of Derby): *Mrs Frances Hesketh*
WAG 10847

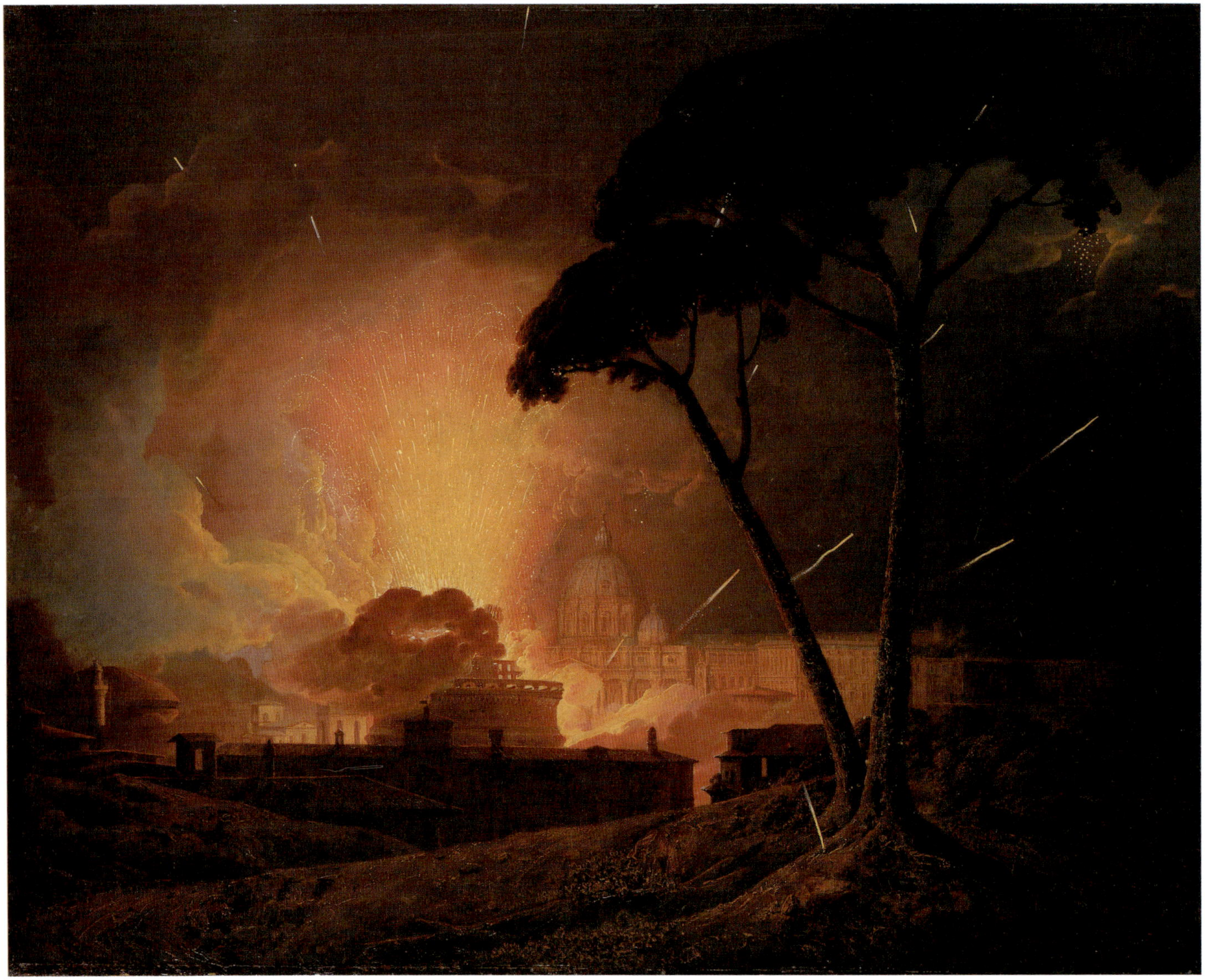

Plate 23
Joseph Wright (of Derby): *The Annual Girandola at the Castel Sant'Angelo, Rome*
WAG 1428

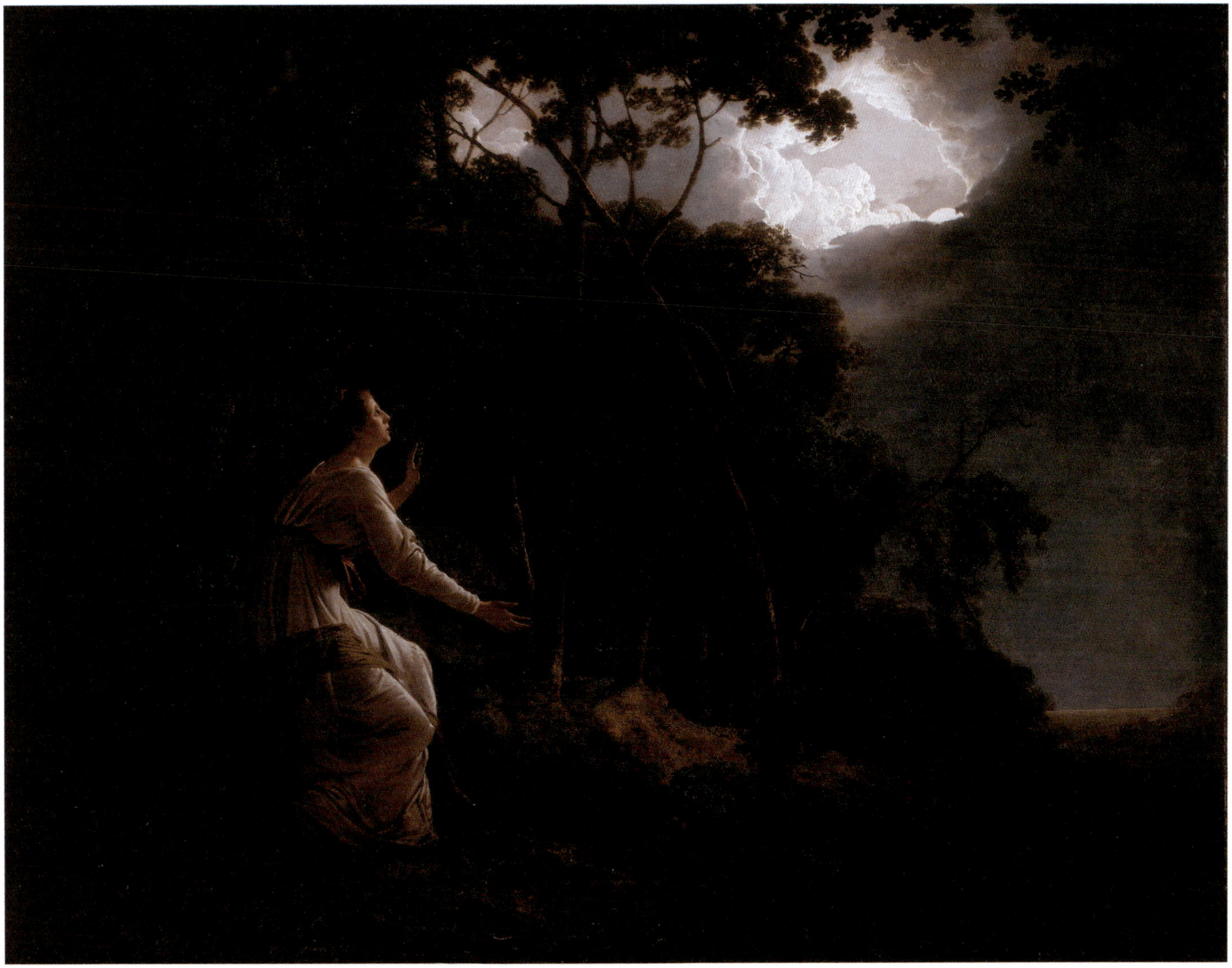

Plate 24
Joseph Wright (of Derby): *The Lady in Milton's 'Comus'*
WAG 2500

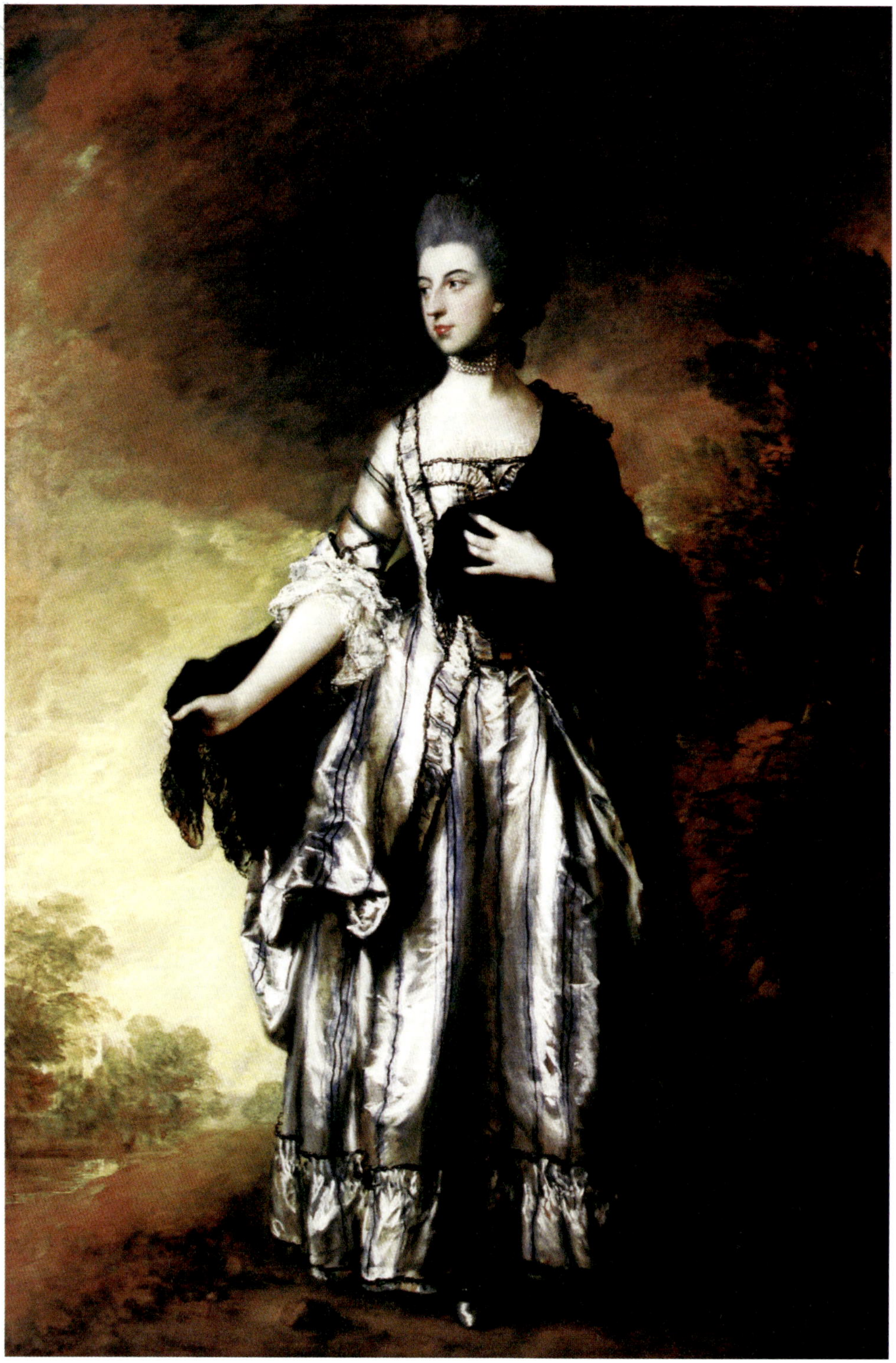

Plate 25
Thomas Gainsborough: *Isabella, Viscountess Molyneux*
WAG 8780

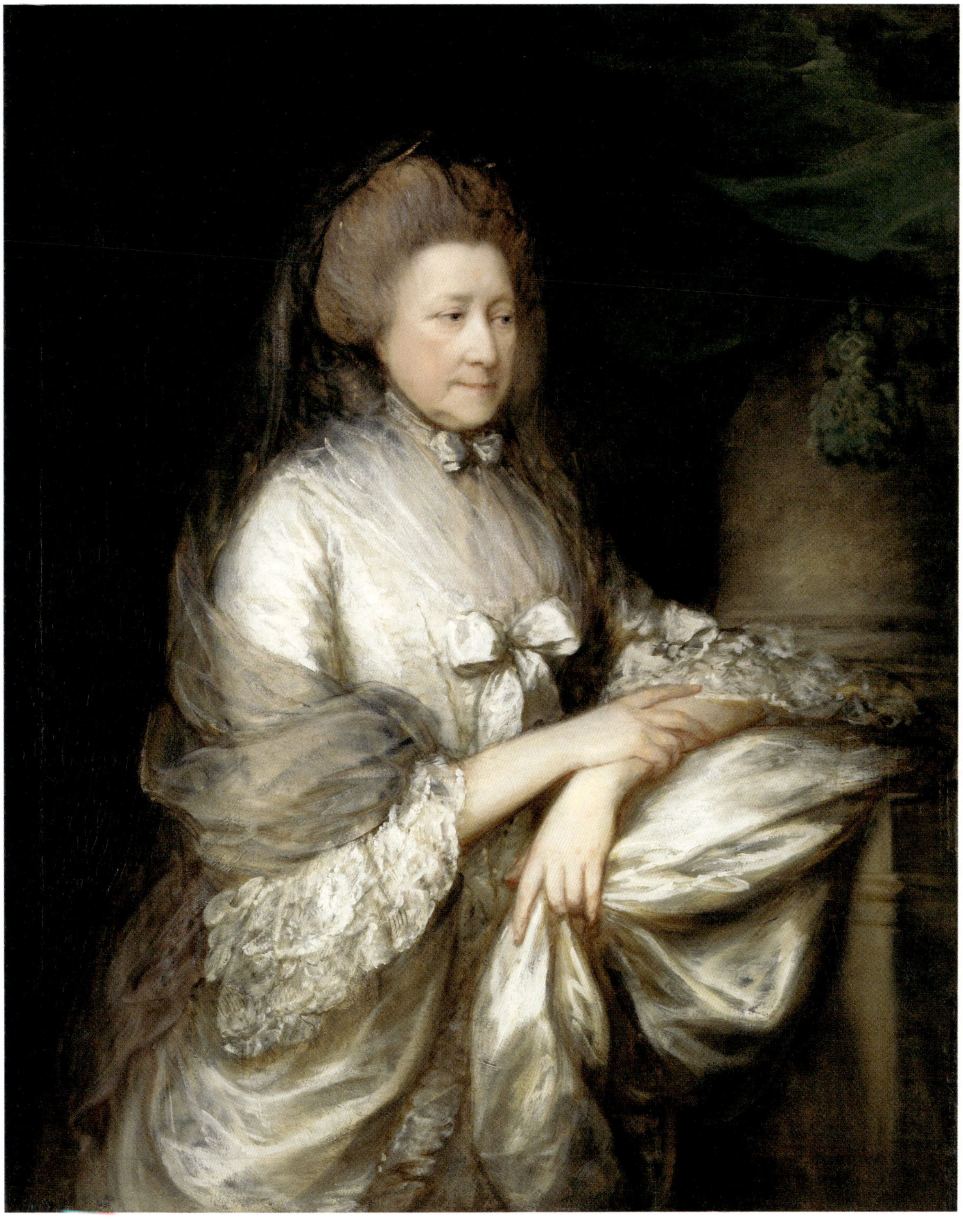

Plate 26
Thomas Gainsborough: *Elizabeth, Viscountess Folkestone*
WAG 229

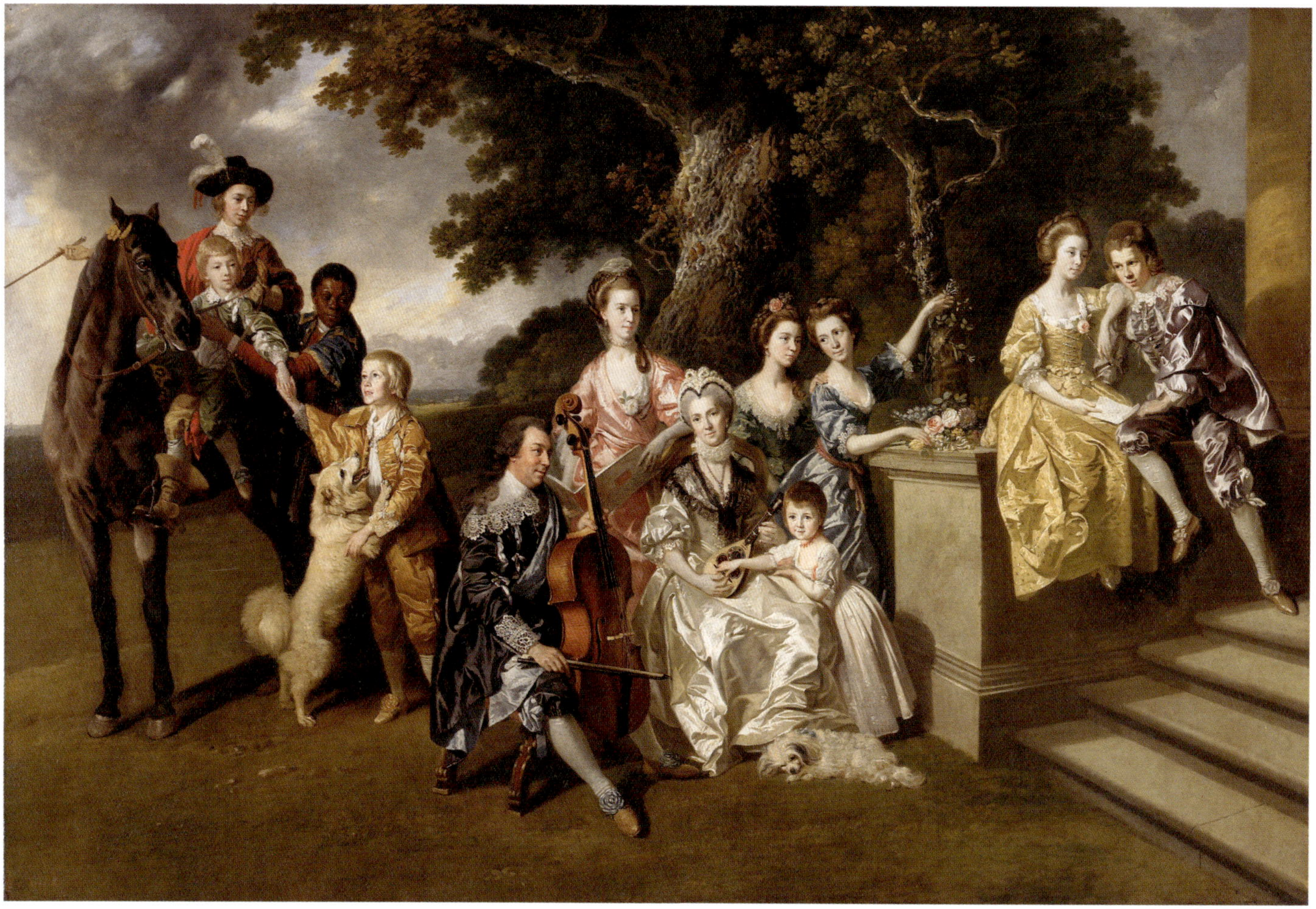

Plate 27
Johan Zoffany: *The Family of Sir William Young*
WAG 2395

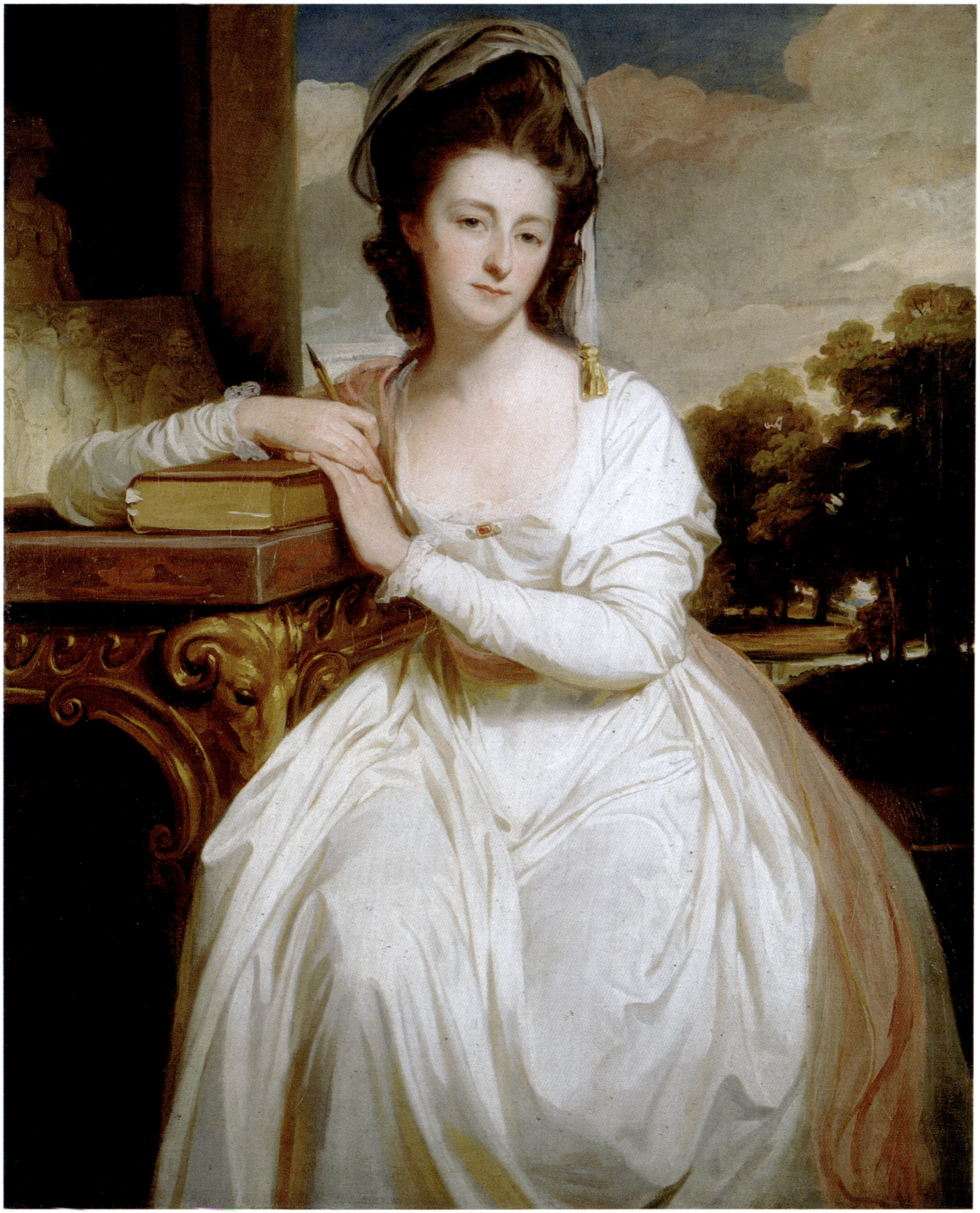

Plate 28
George Romney: *Charlotte Bettesworth, Mrs John Sargent*
WAG 294

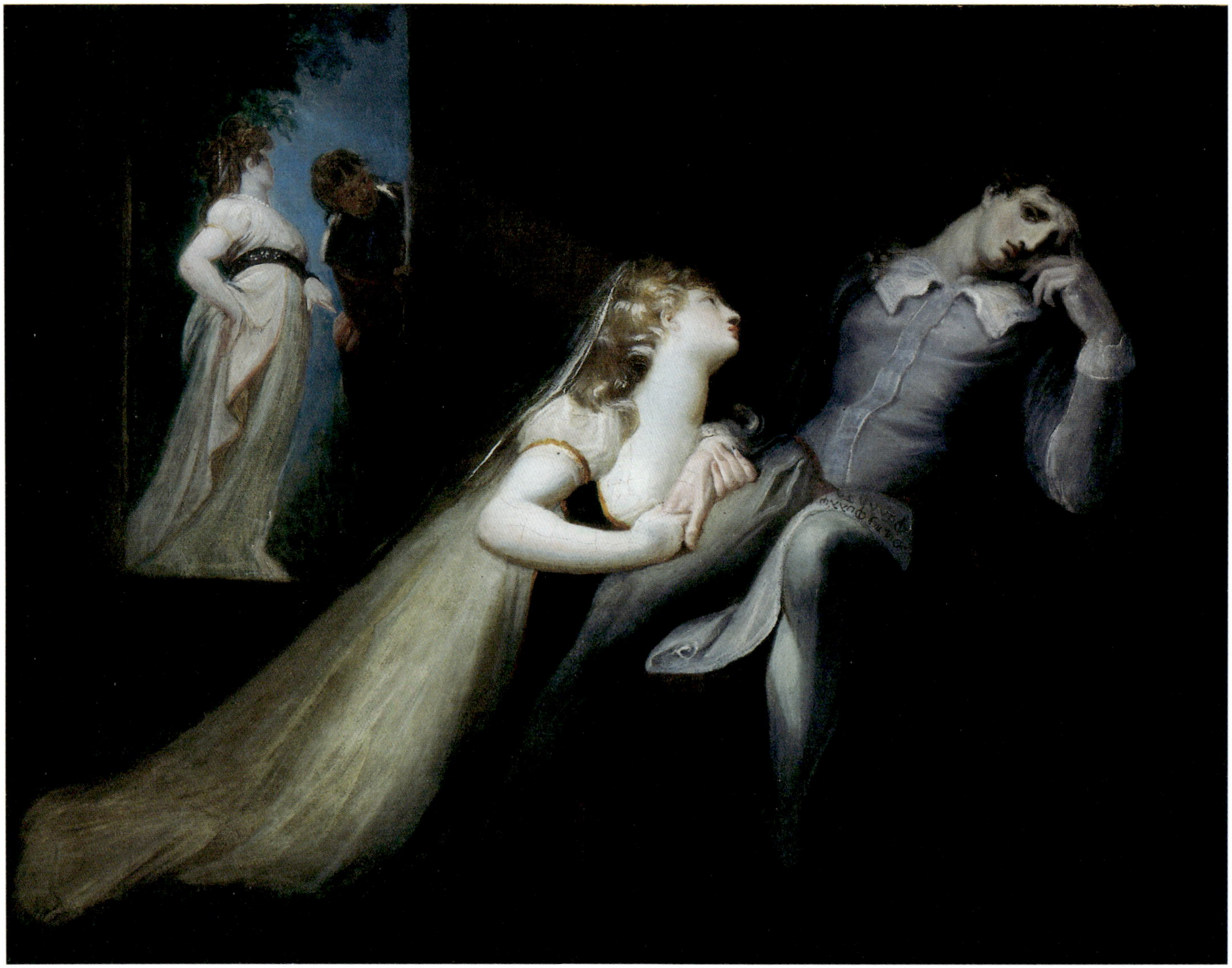

Plate 29
Henry Fuseli: *The Return of Milton's Wife*
WAG 1539

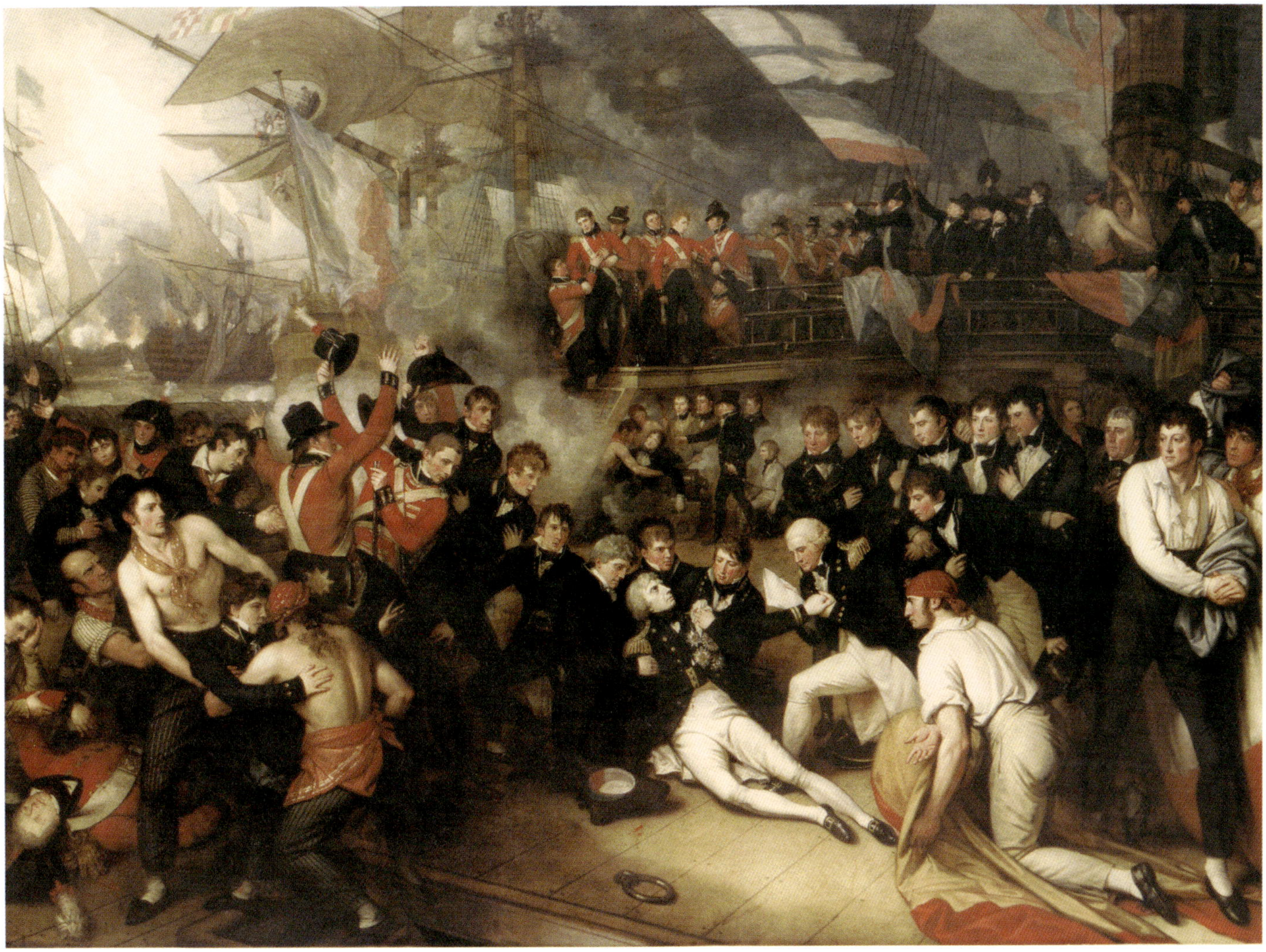

Plate 30
Benjamin West: *The Death of Nelson*
WAG 3132

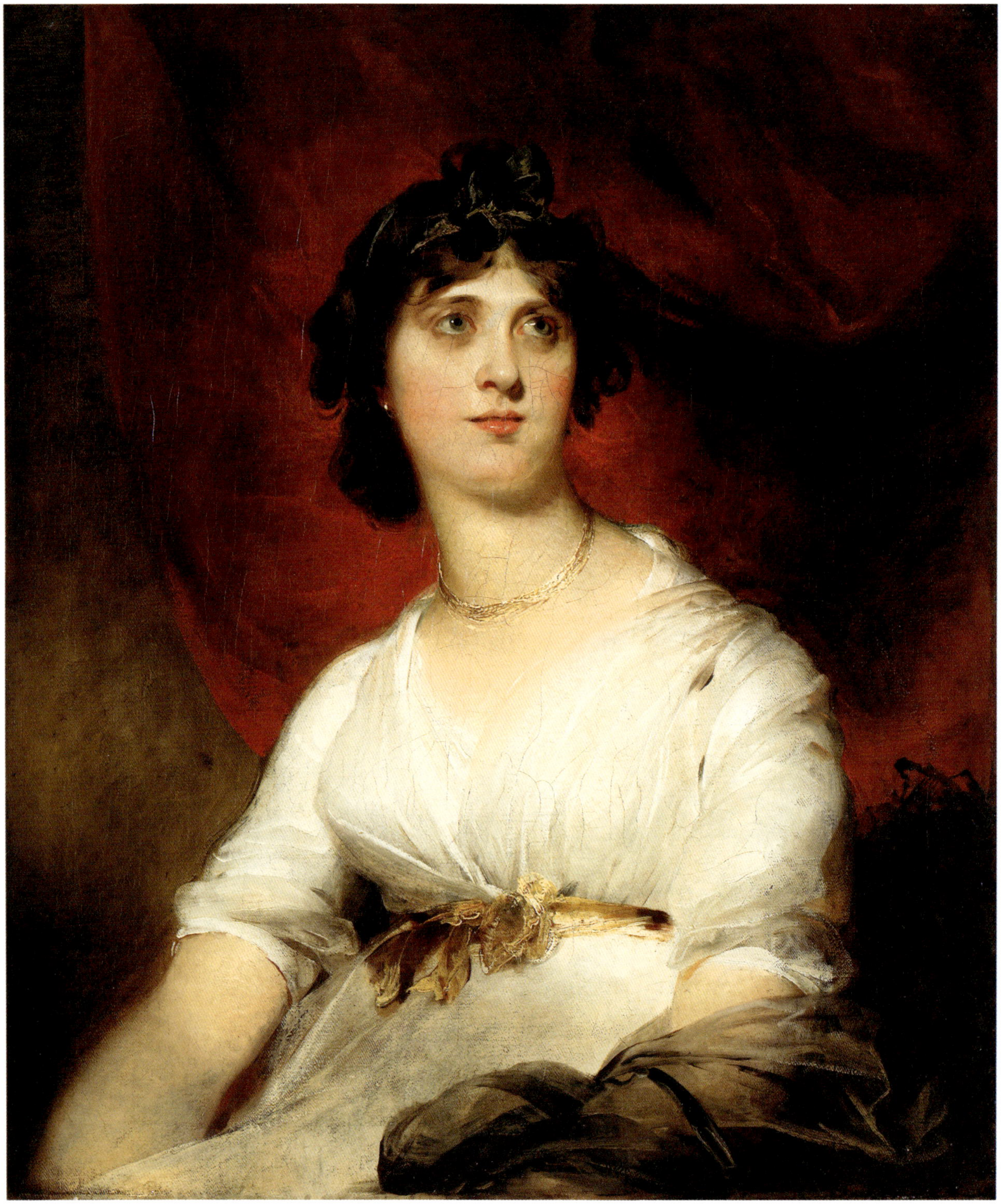

Plate 31
Thomas Lawrence: *Mrs Cecilia Lock*
WAG 252

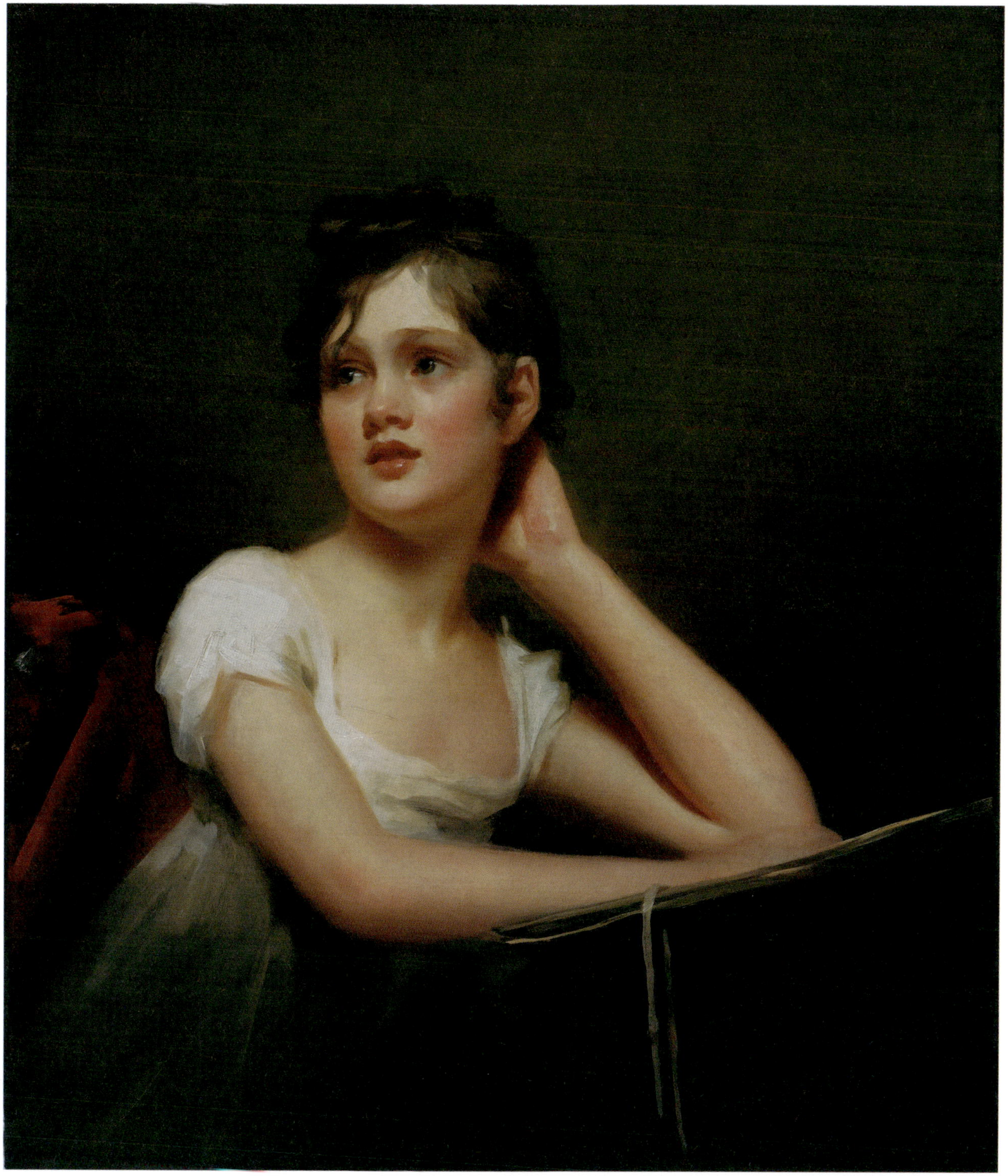

Plate 32
Henry Raeburn: *Girl Sketching*
WAG 289

Catalogue

attributed to

John White Abbott

1763–1851

Landscape with a Pedlar's Cart

WAG 118
oil on canvas, 91.5 × 159 cm
date: about 1787–94

When it entered the Walker's collection in 1948, WAG 118 was attributed to Thomas Gainsborough,[1] but it was quickly recognised to be the work of an imitator[2] before later being re-attributed to Abbott.[3] The attribution was made from comparisons with a handful of other paintings (of disparate character, themselves being attributed to Abbott for the first time) and from a consideration of stylistic features of these works against Abbott's prints of the 1790s.[4] Abbott, an amateur 'gentleman' artist, began exhibiting at the Royal Academy in 1793, showing one or two landscapes each year until 1805. The scale of WAG 118 suggests it may well have been one of them, but their titles are too unspecific to permit identification. A number included figures and cattle, and one of them, shown in 1794, was described by one critic as in 'the first [i.e. Suffolk period] manner of the late lamented GAINSBOROUGH'.[5] From the description which followed, this work cannot have been WAG 118 but it was clearly in a very similar vein. Arguably, the crowded and elaborate composition of WAG 118 carries a suggestion of immaturity, so that it perhaps dates from a little earlier than 1794. The costumes, especially that of the young man asleep on the bank in the lower centre, reinforce this notion.[6]

Although the work has the appearance of being an invented landscape, it is possible that the castle on the hilltop is a depiction of a real place, perhaps in Devon, Abbott's native county.

PROVENANCE

...F. J. Nettlefold by 1933; presented by him 1948.

Notes

1. W. Armstrong: *Thomas Gainsborough and His Place in English Art* (London, 1898) p. 83, where the work is assigned to the period 1748–54; followed by C. R. Grundy: *Catalogue of Pictures and Drawings, Nettlefold Collection* 4 vols (London, 1935) vol. 2, p. 104; Grundy's minimal entry, however, clearly manifests his dissatisfaction with the attribution.
2. Ellis Waterhouse described WAG 118 as 'absolutely impossible as a Gainsborough'; *letter*, 20 November 1954, gallery files.
3. John Hayes: *The Landscape Paintings of Thomas Gainsborough* 2 vols (London, 1982) vol.1, pp. 254–5.
4. Hayes, *op. cit.*, p. 295, n. 71, compares the splayed legs of a donkey etched by Abbott in 1793 (British Museum, 1880-3-13-16) with the treatment of the horse in the painting *Horseman on a Country Road*; the treatment of the horse's legs in WAG 118 is very similar.
5. Unidentified newspaper, quoted by Hayes, *op. cit.*, p. 252.
6. Waterhouse, *loc. cit.*, called WAG 118 'a fancy painting of the 1780s in the style of Gainsborough of the 1750s' and described the woman in the cart as '[belonging] to the age of, say, the later Wheatleys'.

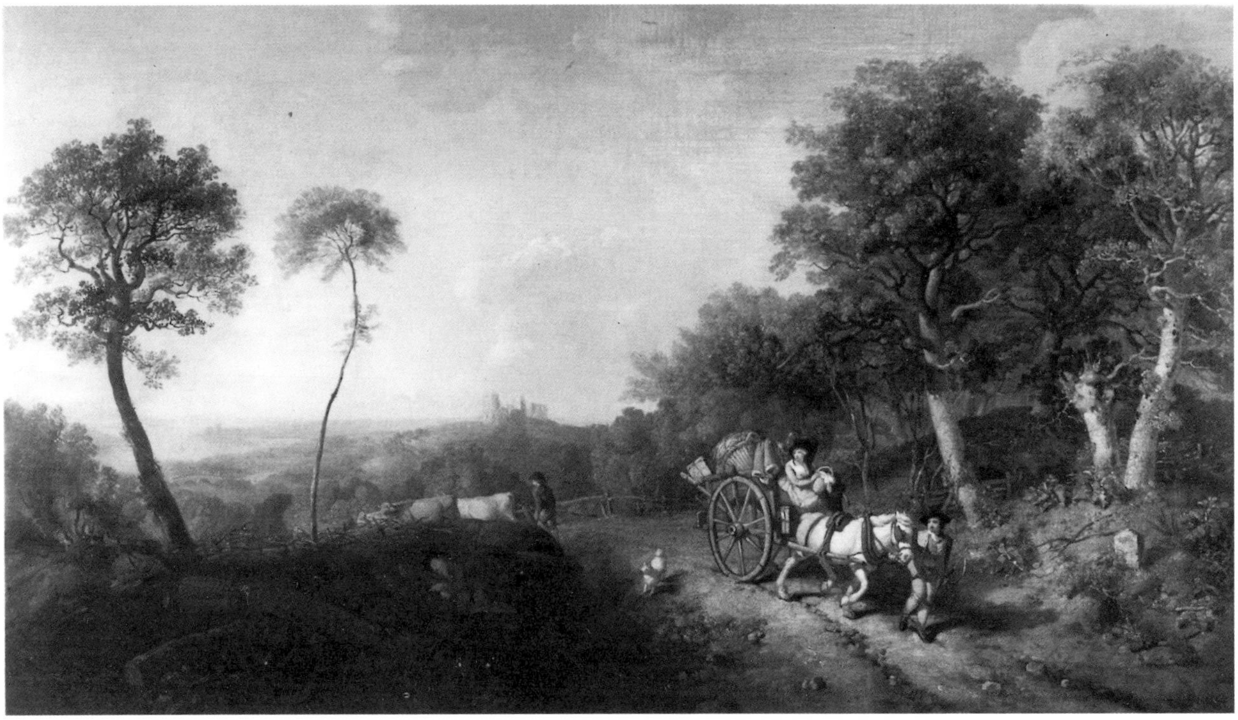

WAG 118

Joseph Allen

1769–1839

A Sculptor with a Bust of Henry Blundell[1]

WAG 8532
oil on canvas, 122 × 100.5 cm
date: 1807–08

The sitter has been identified as George Bullock (d. 1818), successively modeller in rice paste, sculptor and furniture designer, one of the leading artistic entrepreneurs of the Regency period. He may have been born in Birmingham, and he was certainly there as a youth, for his mother, a noted wax modeller, was based there between 1794 and 1798. Bullock himself had moved to Liverpool at least by 1804 and probably earlier: Bullock's elder brother William, whose activities as a silversmith and jeweller, 'statue figure manufacturer' and museum owner to some extent replicated and overlapped with George's, was in the town by 1801. George himself modelled a wax portrait of Henry Blundell of Ince Blundell in that year and by 1803 he was familiar to William Roscoe. The bust of Blundell which appears in the background of WAG 8532 was executed in marble no later than the spring of 1804, for it must have been the work exhibited in that year at the Royal Academy; Bullock later showed it at the first exhibition of the re-founded Liverpool Academy in 1810 (appropriately, despite its being an old work, since Blundell had become patron of the institution and Bullock its president). In Liverpool Bullock was initially partner of the looking-glass manufacturer William Stoakes and from 1806 with the architect Joseph Gandy, with whom he was involved in the remodelling of Storrs Hall (see WAG 3059, pp. 4–5). He resigned as President of the Liverpool Academy and held major sales

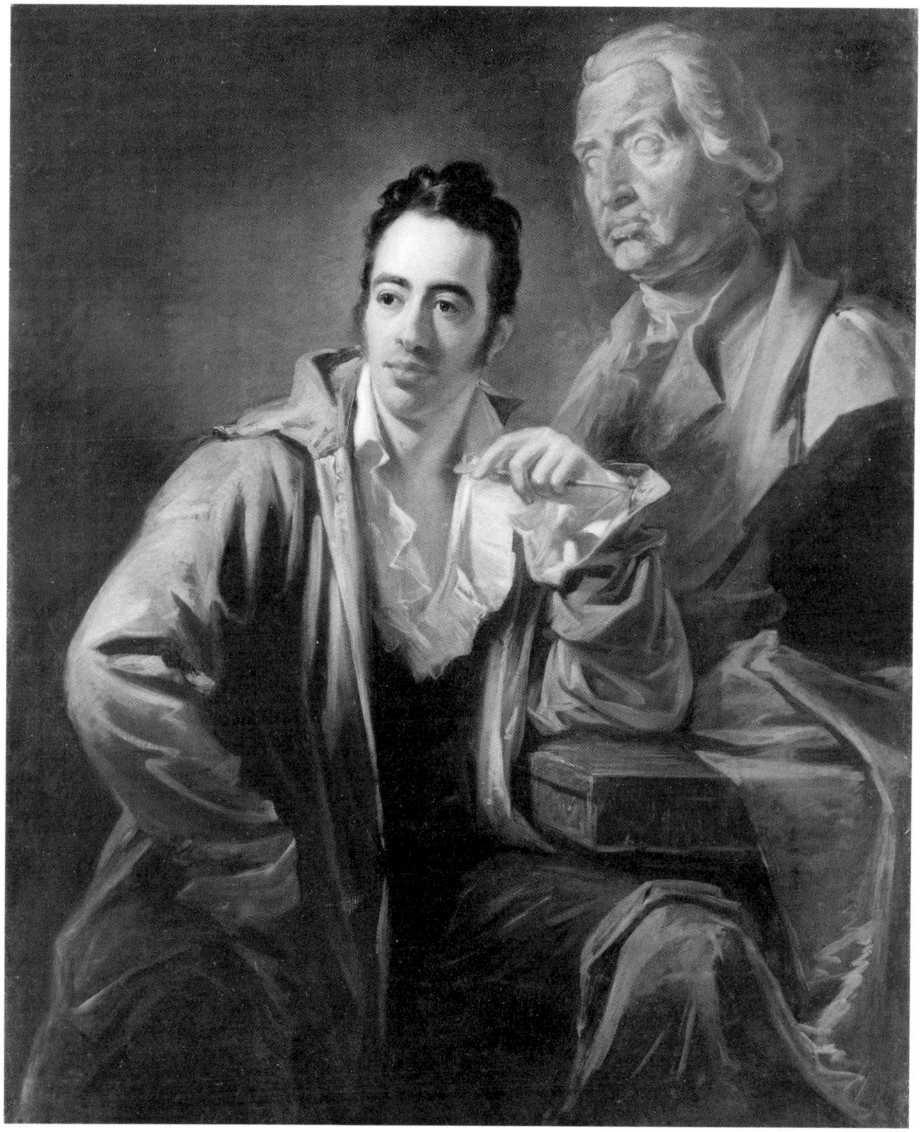

WAG 8532

of his stock in 1812, but retained some presence in Liverpool until 1814.[2] In his final years in London, Bullock devoted himself increasingly to the design and production of furniture and built up an impressive list of friends and clients, who included the Duke of Atholl and Sir Walter Scott.[3]

Allen must have completed WAG 8532 in 1807 or the early months of 1808; he is not known to have been in Liverpool before the earlier year and the work was shown at the Royal Academy (under the title above) in the latter one. He showed his portrait of Peter Whitfield Brancker (WAG 9055, p. 4) at the same exhibition and he also painted Col. Bolton (WAG 3059) at this period. The figure in WAG 8532 is unusually strongly lit and spiritedly painted by the side of Allen's normally more sober portraiture and it has been observed that this is probably a conscious reflection of Bullock's extrovert and dynamic personality.[4] It has also been noted that the instrument Bullock holds is a modelling tool rather than a chisel, suggesting that he is shown with his original model for the bust of Blundell rather than the marble. This is confirmed by the presence in WAG 8532 of the frilled tail of the cravat as depicted in the known plaster model, which was replaced by a plain shirt front in the marble.[5] In having Allen portray him working on a sculpture that by that date was several years old, Bullock was perhaps consciously expressing his sense of debt to Blundell, whose agent he had probably been as early as 1804.[6]

PROVENANCE

...John Lane; Sotheby 1 July 1925 (1); ...[?] Giovanni Castano, Boston, Mass., 1948;[7] ...Burgess Stanley, Medfield, Mass., by 1971; from whom bt. by the gallery in 1973.

EXHIBITIONS

RA 1808 (29); *George Bullock, Cabinet Maker* Blairman & Sons, London 1988 (57).

NOTES

1. In *CIC*, p. 4, titled *George Bullock with a Bust of Henry Blundell.* The present title is that used when the work was first exhibited.
2. *MPPP*, pp. 19–20 and especially Lucy Wood: 'George Bullock in Birmingham and Liverpool', in Lucy Wood and Martin Levy, eds: *George Bullock, Cabinet Maker*, exh. cat., Blairman & Sons, London and Sudley Art Gallery, Liverpool (1988) pp. 40–7. Bullock's birthdate is uncertain; at his death he was stated to be 35, but conflicting circumstantial evidence exists that he may have been born around 1778; Wood, *op. cit.*, p. 40.
3. For Bullock's London career see especially Clive Wainwright: 'George Bullock and his Circle', in Wood and Levy, *op. cit.*, pp. 13–39.
4. *MPPP*, *loc. cit.*
5. *MPPP*, p. 19; for a plaster version of the bust made from the original model, sold by Bullock in December 1807 to Stephen Tempest, see Wood and Levy, *op. cit.*, pp. 131–2 (cat. 60); for the marble itself see Wood and Levy, *op. cit.*, pp. 130–1 (cat. 59); the catalogue entries were written by Timothy Stevens.
6. Wood and Levy, *loc. cit.* (cat. 59).
7. In 1948 he sent a photograph of WAG 8532 to the National Portrait Gallery in the belief that the bust was a portrait of George Washington; Lucy Wood, reporting information from Giles Elwood, *email*, May 2004, gallery files.

Peter Whitfield Brancker

WAG 9055
oil on canvas, 126 × 100 cm
date: 1807–08

The sitter (1750–1836) was a Liverpool merchant trading with the West Indies. He was elected to the town's Common Council in 1793 and Bailiff in 1795. He was active in the Council's support of the slave trade and in 1798 was presented with a piece of plate in recognition of his efforts. He was Mayor in 1801. In 1804 he was Major Commandant of the Artillery in the Liverpool volunteer force raised to defend the town against French invasion. He married a Miss Aspinall and was thus presumably related to John Bridge Aspinall (see WAG 7041, p. 19 and WAG 7026, p. 328). He was described as a man 'of strong individuality and resource'[1] – a description reflected in Allen's treatment. The small golden object that Brancker holds in his right hand is presumably a snuff-box.

Although WAG 9055 was shown at the Royal Academy in London in 1808 – evidence that Allen regarded the portrait as felicitous – the artist had almost certainly established strong links in Liverpool by this date and painted WAG 9055 in the town. The original frame is very close in design to that of WAG 3059 (below) which suggests that both were made in Liverpool.

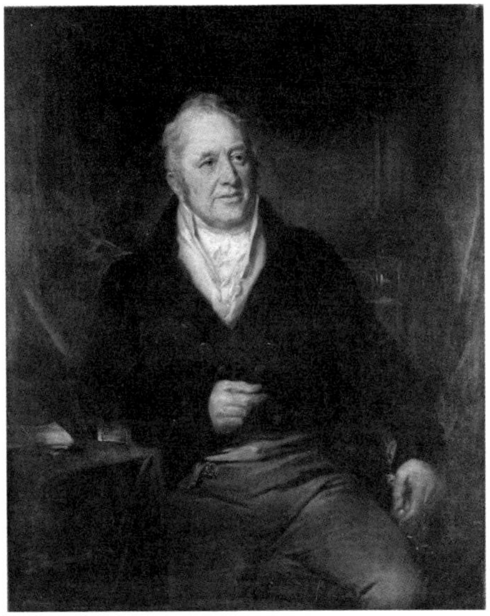

WAG 9055

PROVENANCE

By descent in the family of the sitter's son John Brancker to Mrs Cubitt, Fritton House, Great Yarmouth; presented by her trustees in 1975.

EXHIBITION

RA 1808 (43).

REFERENCE

1. *MPPP*, p. 20; and for Brancker's links with the slave trade see Gomer Williams: *History of the Liverpool Privateers and Letters of Marque, with an Account of the Liverpool Slave Trade* (London, 1897) pp. 613–4 and 683. The attribution of WAG 9055 to Allen and the identification of the sitter are confirmed by a fragment of an old label from the reverse preserved in gallery files.

Colonel John Bolton

WAG 3059
oil on canvas, 127.5 × 102 cm
date: about 1807–10

John Bolton was born in Ulverston, Lancashire, 22 March 1756, and was apprenticed to Messrs Rawson and Chorley, Liverpool merchants, in whose service he spent some years in the West Indies, about 1773–90. On his return to Liverpool he set up as a merchant on his own and met with great success. He was involved in the slave trade and was later a president of the West India Association. In 1797 he married Elizabeth Littledale of Whitehaven (1768–1848), a connection of the Fletchers of Allerton Hall, Liverpool; the couple had no children and after their death WAG 3059 passed into Fletcher family ownership. From around the time of his marriage Bolton took a leading part in the local defence movement of the French Revolutionary War; in 1797

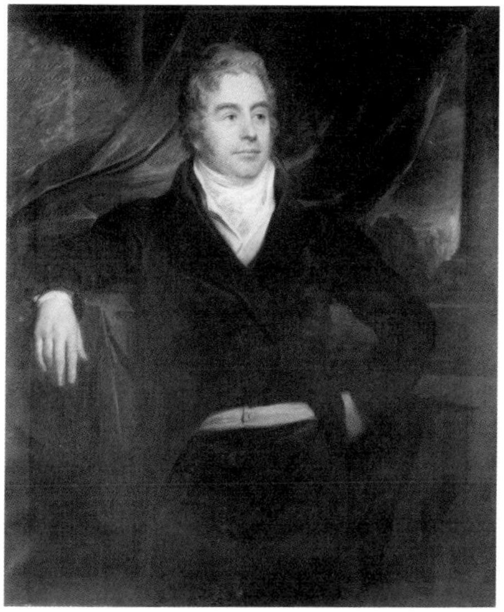

WAG 3059

he contributed £500 to the government scheme to defend Britain against French invasion and in 1803 he raised and equipped 800 men – 'Bolton's Invincibles' – for the First Battalion of Liverpool Volunteers (see WAG 9547, pp. 223–4); this was disbanded in 1806. In 1804 he was elected to the Common Council of Liverpool but declined to take his seat; from 1807, however, his involvement in local politics grew as he became a supporter of George Canning and the Tories (see WAG 3078, pp. 106–7) and his house in Duke Street was one of the headquarters of Liverpool's Canningite party. In 1808 he purchased Storrs Hall, Windermere, which he employed the architect Joseph Gandy (1771–1843) to remodel for him, and he became a leading figure of society in the Lake District. He died in Liverpool 24 February 1837 and was buried in Bowness-on-Windermere.[1]

The attribution of this painting to Allen[2] is based on the fact that a companion picture ascribed to Allen was sold with it in 1922 (when WAG 3059 itself was attributed to Opie), the circumstance that Allen is known to have been working in Liverpool in about 1807–10[3] (he was one of the founding members of the Liverpool Academy in 1810) and on stylistic criteria (it strongly resembles WAG 9055, above). With his square head and square-cut grey hair Bolton is immediately recognisable as the same man as in a portrait drawing by Henry Edridge dated 1805 (Sotheby 20 November 1986 [62, part]) and he appears several years older in WAG 3059. It is possible that WAG 3059 was painted in the Lake District since Allen is also thought to have worked there around 1810,[4] but the fact that it is in a very similar frame to WAG 9055 argues that it was carried out in Liverpool.

PROVENANCE

Passed from Mrs Bolton to her relations the Fletchers of Allerton Hall; by descent to T. Alfred Fletcher; Christie 23 June 1922 (150);[5] bt. Carpenter (5 gns.); …acquired by the gallery in unknown circumstances before 1955.

NOTES

1. *MPPP*, pp. 20–1, citing G. W. Mathews, 'John Bolton, a Liverpool Merchant 1756–1837', *Transactions of the Historic Society of Lancashire and Cheshire [for the year 1941]* vol. 93 (1942), pp. 98–115, and other sources. For a less salubrious view of Bolton see David Thomason: 'New Light on John Bolton of Storrs', *Quarto: Abbot Hall Quarterly Bulletin* vol. 24 no. 1 (April 1986) pp. 4–9.
2. The attribution was first published in *MPPP*.
3. Allen exhibited at the Royal Academy from the address 18 Ludgate Hill London in 1808 and 1809, but the fact that among his exhibits in 1808 were the portraits of George Bullock (WAG 8532) and Peter Whitfield Brancker (WAG 9055) is proof that he had already established important contacts in Liverpool by that date; from 1810 to 1815 Allen was absent from exhibitions in London but he showed at the Liverpool Academy in 1810, 1811 and 1812 from 'Manchester, or Mr Bullock's, Bold Street, Liverpool' (*LAOE*, p. 42). WAG 3059 is a candidate for the *Portrait of a Gentleman* that was his sole exhibit at the LA in 1811 (cat. 72).
4. Allen's portrait of George Strickland at Sizergh Castle is dateable from the sitter's age to around 1810–15.
5. Christie's stencil 469 *DN* is on the reverse.

Thomas, Eleanor and Anne Lance

WAG 7391
oil on canvas, 142 × 175.5 cm

Mrs Thomas Lance

WAG 7392
oil on canvas, 127 × 101.5 cm

Thomas Lance

WAG 7393
oil on canvas, 127 × 101.5 cm

date: 1808–10

Thomas Lance (1769–1829), insurance broker and merchant of Liverpool, is recorded as living at 5 Great George Street in 1805 and 1807 and at Wavertree outside Liverpool by 1810. His wife Eleanor (d. 1843) was the fifth daughter of Robert Maddock of Flookersbrook, Cheshire.[1] The three children in the portrait are Eleanor (1793–1876), who married Commander John Philipps Philipps, R. N., Thomas (1794–1879) and Anne (1796–1864), who married as his second wife H. R. Hughes of Bache Hall outside Chester.[2]

The portraits were traditionally attributed in family records to 'Sir William Allen',[3] and were sold under this name in 1970, but by that date they had already been re-ascribed to Joseph Allen,[4] who worked in Liverpool between 1807 and 1810. From the ages of the children, the three portraits – presumably commissioned together – may be dated to 1808–10, and this is also supported by the fact that the family inventory described Mr Lance as 'of Wavertree'.[5]

The portraits of Mr and Mrs Lance are relatively conventional, but the conception of WAG 7391 is much more interesting. The sitters are shown being interrupted in their preparations for a family recital by the arrival of a fourth person out of picture. The effect, with its

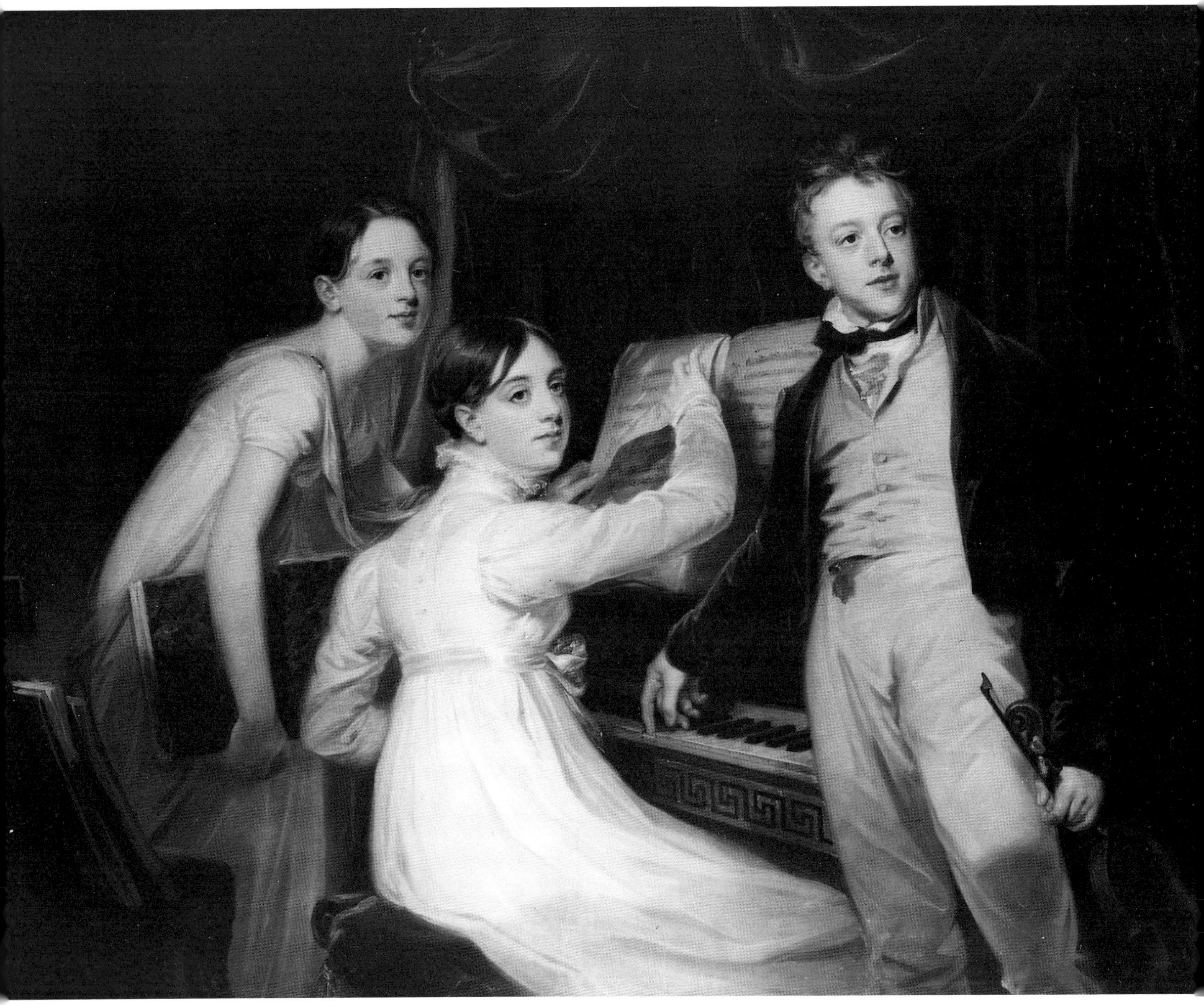

WAG 7391

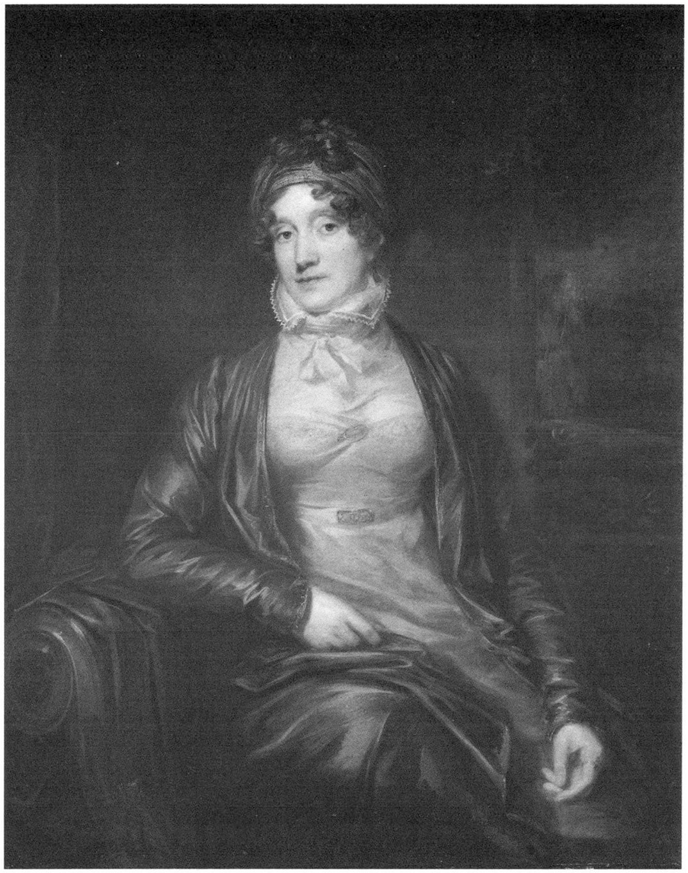

WAG 7392

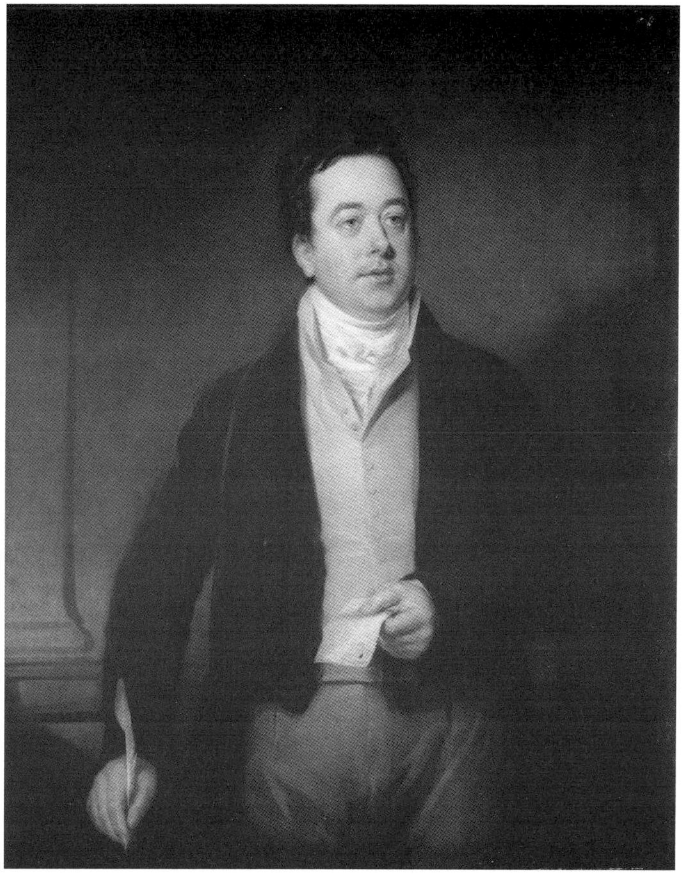

WAG 7393

natural poses and expressions and arrested movements, is informal and highly captivating. It is tempting to wonder if this was how Allen encountered the children on his first visit to the family home. If Anne was expected to hold her stooping pose throughout the sittings, it represents a *tour de force* of patience. This may explain why she inherited the picture, rather than her elder siblings.

PROVENANCE

By descent to Anne Hughes, née Lance, the youngest girl in the picture; her son H. R. Hughes of Kinmel Park, Abergele; by descent at Kinmel to David Fetherstonhaugh; Spencer premises sale at Kinmel 14–15 October 1970 (651 [WAG 7393], 652 [WAG 7392] and 653 [WAG 7931]); bt. by the gallery.

NOTES

1. *MPPP*, p. 21. Mrs Lance's birthdate is there given as 1755, following information from David Fetherstonhaugh, *letters*, 29 October 1970 and 16 March 1971, gallery files. He established from a family inventory made by his grandfather, H. R. Hughes, that she was baptised on 8 December that year; however, this would mean not only that she was 14 years older than her husband but that she had the three children in WAG 7391 between the ages of 38 and 41. This is not impossible, but subsequent efforts to trace her baptism in December 1755 in Chester parish records have been unsuccessful. However, according to David Fetherstonhaugh, *loc. cit.*, Mrs Lance was aged 88 when she died on 29 August 1843; this would mean that her baptism would have taken place in December 1754, not 1755.
2. David Fetherstonhaugh, *letter*, 29 October 1970, gallery files.
3. The attribution (i.e. to the Scottish-born portraitist Sir William Allan [1782–1850]) is impossible since Allan was in Russia between 1805 and 1814.
4. John Steegmann: *A Survey of Portraits in Welsh Houses* 2 vols (Cardiff, 1957–62) vol. 1, pp. 107–8.
5. David Fetherstonhaugh, *loc. cit.*

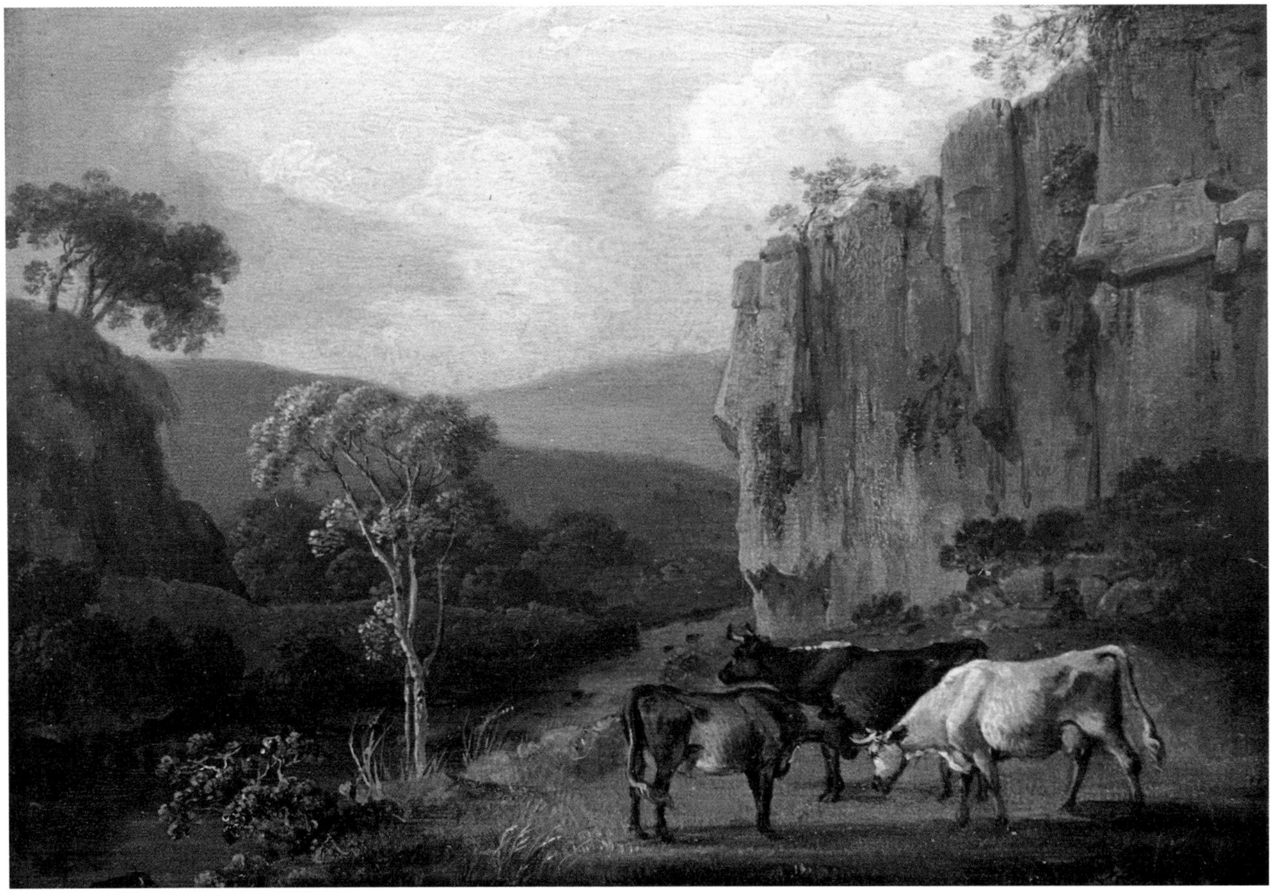

WAG 9557

attributed to

William Anderson

1757–1837

Three Cattle Grazing by a Stream under a Cliff Face

WAG 9557
oil on panel, 16.5 × 23 cm
date: unknown, perhaps 1815–35

The painting was exhibited at the Walker Art Gallery in 1977 and entered the collection in 1979 as by Charles Towne (pp. 187-235), but the attribution to him is unacceptable.[1] It presumably derives from the inscription *TOWNE* on the lower edge of the frame (the design of which is unlike the majority of the frames on Towne's paintings). The overall composition and the landscape details are uncharacteristic of Towne's work and the cows are painted with an eye to their underlying form which is at odds with his normal pre-occupation with surface and outline.

From the stencil on the reverse,[2] WAG 9557 is identifiable as one of a pair of works by Anderson auctioned at Christie's in 1891. Anderson is chiefly known as a marine painter, but did also occasionally paint landscapes, and comparison with two other such works by him, one signed and dated 1818,[3] the other, the same size as WAG 9557, dated 1836,[4] supports the conclusion that this is his work.

PROVENANCE

...F. Haines & Sons; Christie 24 March 1891 (69, part); bt. in (£2 15s.); ...Col. J. R. Danson; his bequest 1979.

EXHIBITION

Danson Collection of Paintings by Charles Towne Walker Art Gallery 1977 (12).

NOTES

1. WAG 9557 was first published as 'manner of Towne' in *CIC*, p. 282.
2. The stencil is *929d*, which was applied to lots 64–74 of Christie's sale of 24 March 1891. Lot 69, the only lot to comprise landscapes, was Anderson's *Ragnold Park* and *On the Tees*, a pair.
3. *Rustics and Cattle by a Country Church, a River beyond*, on panel, sold Sotheby 6 July 1983 (252, part); the treatment of the cows is closely comparable to that of WAG 9557.
4. Repr. Col. M. H. Grant: *A Chronological History of the Old English Landscape Painters in Oil from the XVIth Century to the XIXth Century, etc.*, 8 vols (revised edn, Leigh-on-Sea, 1957–61) vol. 4, pl. 328.

George Barret

about 1732–84

The Powerscourt Waterfall

WAG 1758
oil on canvas, 103.5 × 127.5 cm
date: probably about 1764

The 120-metre high waterfall is situated in the Powerscourt demesne near Enniskerry, Co. Wicklow, about 20 miles south of Dublin. It was already a well-known beauty spot when Barret began to make his first paintings of the scenery on the Powerscourt estate about 1760;[1] these were probably commissions from the 2nd Viscount Powerscourt, a noted patron of the arts who also took a considerable interest in the landscaping and laying out of the estate.[2] A key figure behind their commissioning, however, must have been Edmund Burke. He was acquainted with Lord Powerscourt at Trinity College Dublin at the period in which he was writing his *Philosophical Enquiry into the Origin of Our Ideas of the Sublime and the Beautiful* (1756) and he is said to have introduced Lord Powerscourt to Barret.[3] The waterfall, and the Dargle Valley, also in the demesne, may have represented for Burke the epitome of the landscape Sublime. On its arrival at the Liverpool Royal Institution in 1843 WAG 1758 was said to have been owned by Burke,[4] and Burke took considerable interest in

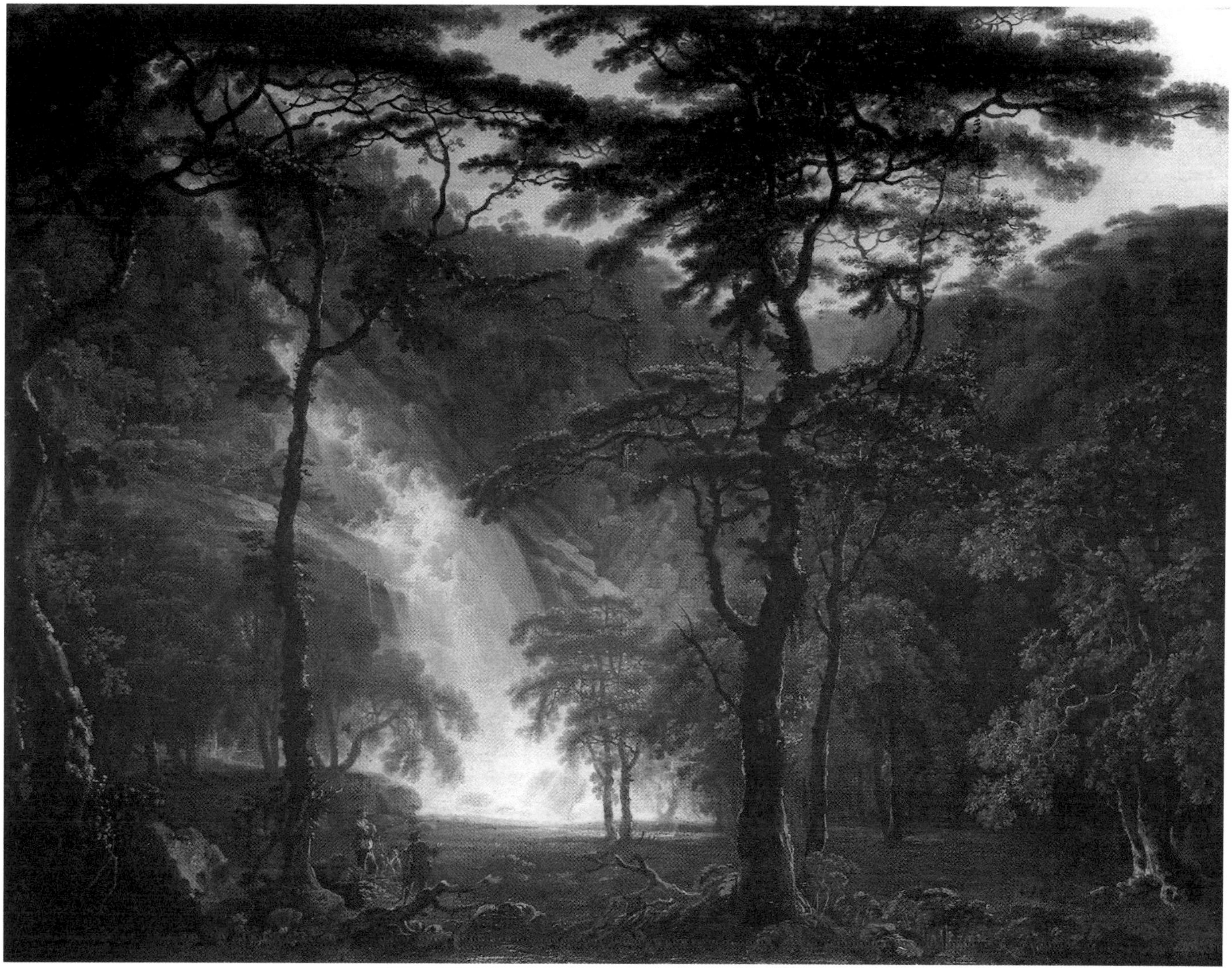

WAG 1758

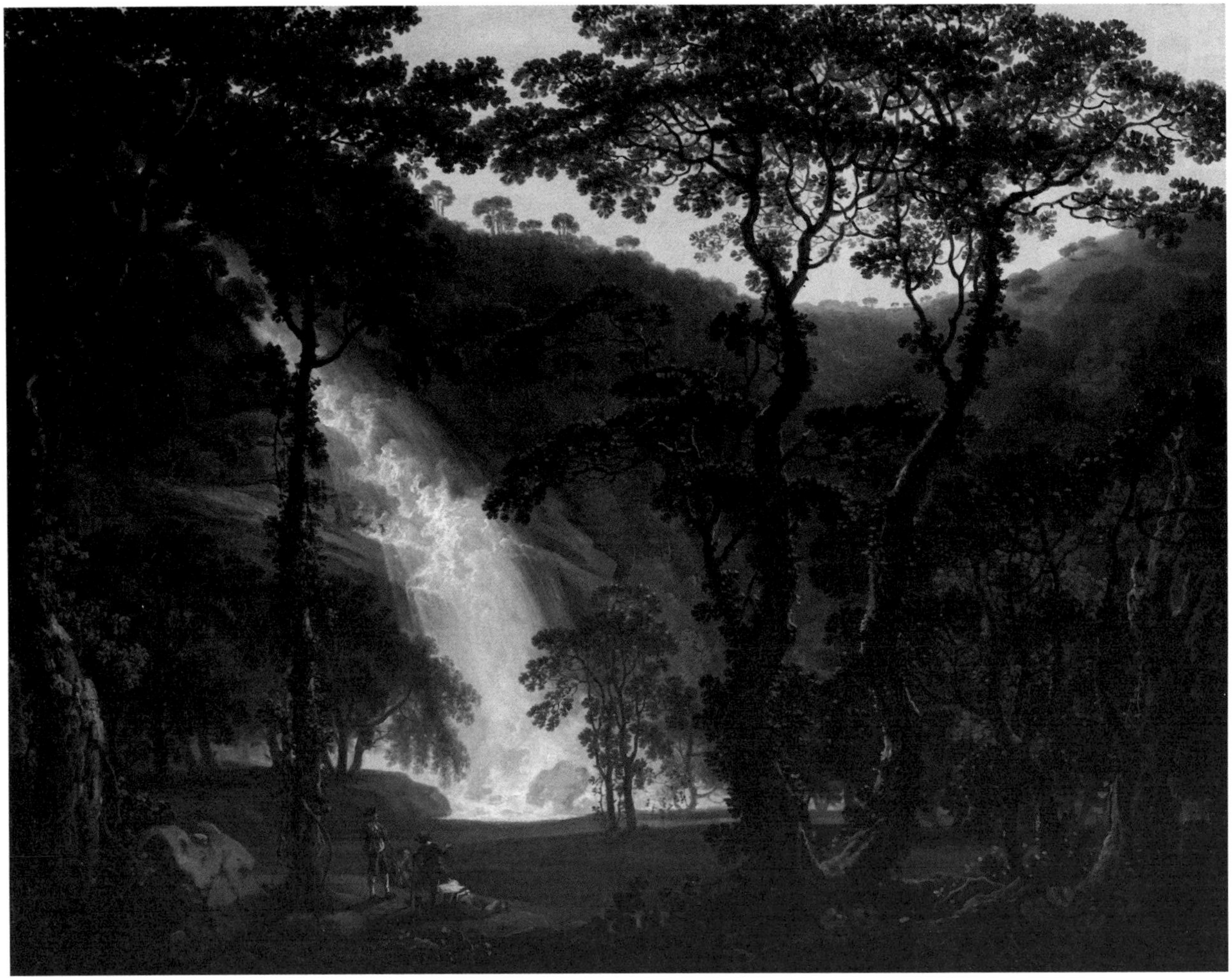

Fig.1 *Powerscourt Waterfall* by George Barret, oil on canvas.
National Gallery of Ireland, Dublin. © National Gallery of Ireland

Barret's career not only in Ireland but also in England after his move there in 1763.[5]

Other versions of WAG 1758 are known. A very similar canvas, the same size, and differing only in the slightly more elaborate disposition of the foreground curtain of trees, the presence of a fourth figure in the foreground, and a more brilliant and theatrical handling of the light (arguing that it is the prime version) is in the National Gallery of Ireland, Dublin (fig. 1).[6] Another work, with deer in place of the figures, was formerly in the collection of Col. M. H. Grant. A different treatment of the view, showing the waterfall from the higher ground of the deer park, is in the Ulster Museum, Belfast (fig. 2);[7] a version of this remained at Powerscourt until sold in the premises sale there in 1984.[8] It is tempting to argue, both from the local provenance of the two latter canvases and also from their more artless vision of the landscape, that they embody Barret's first vision of Powerscourt, and that one or other of them is identifiable as the *Waterfall in Powerscourt Park* that Barret was proposing to have engraved in February 1762. WAG 1758 and the National Gallery of Ireland painting, on the other hand, with their less literal and more sophisticated conception – a fusion of the Burkean Sublime and Beautiful[9] – and their greater technical maturity, perhaps represent Barret's return to the subject after his move to England. One or other of the two is likely to be the work exhibited at the Society of Artists in 1764.

PROVENANCE

...[? Edmund Burke]; ...Liverpool Royal Institution by 1843;[10] transferred to the gallery 1893 and presented 1948.

EXHIBITIONS

[? SA 1764 (3)];[11] [? New Institution Gallery, Liverpool 1838–39 (95 or 96)].[12]

NOTES

1. Barret advertised in *Faulkner's Journal* on 27 February 1762 a proposal to have engraved by John Dixon four Powerscourt landscapes, namely *Powerscourt House and the Adjacent Country, A View in the Dargle Called Castle Rock, A View in the Dargle Called the Dahool* and *The Waterfall in Powerscourt Park*. Although the engravings are not known to have been executed, it seems likely that the subjects were already in existence as paintings. The first has tentatively been identified as the *View of Powerscourt* now in the Yale Center for British Art, New Haven (B.1981-25-35), which is stylistically quite different from WAG 1758 and if by Barret (it was formerly attributed to Thomas Roberts) must be a very early work (see J. H. Plumb: *The Pursuit of Happiness*, exh. cat., Yale Center for British Art, New Haven [1977], p. 35 [cat. 26], where it is dated 1755–60). It is not known whether the Yale painting was commissioned by Viscount Powerscourt.

2. The Knight of Glin: *Powerscourt*, in Christie's premises sale catalogue, 24–25 September 1984.

3. *Ibid.*; and see also Brian Fitzgerald, ed.: *The Life and Letters of Emily Duchess of Leinster*, 3 vols (Dublin, 1949–1957) vol. 1, *passim*.

4. 'A Waterfall Called the Dargle. Painted for the late Edmund Burke'; *Liverpool Royal Institution 1843 Catalogue*, p. 32, cat. 117.

5. W. G. Strickland: *A Dictionary of Irish Artists* 2 vols (reprint, Shannon, 1969) vol. 1, pp. 29, 31; and see, for example, the letters from Edmund Burke to James Barry of mid-February 1767, 26 April 1767 and 24 August 1767 in Tim McLoughlin, ed: *The Correspondence of James Barry* (http://www.texte.ie/barry/).

6. NGI 174; see N. Figgis and B. Rooney: *Irish Paintings in the National Gallery of Ireland vol. 1* (Dublin, 2001) pp. 43–6.

7. Ulster Museum No. 2418 (175-1964), 73 × 70 cm; see Eileen Black: *Irish Oil Paintings 1572–c. 1830* (Belfast, 1991) pp. 12–3.

8. Christie at Powerscourt, 24–25 September 1984 (16).

9. Figgis and Rooney, *op. cit.*, p. 44, citing John Hutchinson: *James Arthur O'Connor* exh. cat., National Gallery of Ireland, Dublin (1985) p. 83.

10. Lot 56 in the Burke sale, Christie 5 June 1812, was *A View in the Dargle*. It was preceded in the sale by its supposed pendant, lot 55, a *View of Windermere*. This (and perhaps the following lot also) was bought *Winsta* (£6 5s.). The latter seems likely to have been Thomas Winstanley (1749–1823), the Liverpool dealer and auctioneer who would later be one of the key figures in the creation of the Liverpool Royal Institution. In March 1821 what sounds as though it is the *Windermere* was sold, the property of 'a refined connoisseur' by the auctioneer G Stanley [sic] of 21 Old Bond Street (15–16 March 1821, lot 55: *a Mountainous Scene, with Figures on a Lake Firing at Deer*; formerly owned by Edmund Burke). In June 1832 the same G. Stanley, now at Maddox Street, Hanover Square, sold, the property of 'A Gentleman of Taste', *Waterfall in the Woods at Powerscourt: Painted for Edmund Burke* (26 June 1832, lot 90). It is tempting to think these were old items of Winstanley stock, that G. Stanley could have been a relation of Winstanley, and that if the latter work was bought in in 1832, it was subsequently set aside for donation to the LRI; however, this is speculation. According to Getty Provenance files Stanley was active as an auctioneer in London between 1815 and 1841, having previously worked for Peter Coxe. I am grateful to Eleanor O'Donovan, University of Limerick, for this information.

11. *View of the Waterfall at Powerscourt in Ireland*. Fintan Cullen: *Visual Politics: The Representation of Ireland 1750–1930* (Cork, 1997) p. 15, has suggested that this work and its pendant, cat. 4, *View on the Dargle, Both on the Estate of the Rt. Hon. Lord Viscount Powerscourt*, are the earliest images of Ireland to have been exhibited in London.

12. It seems possible that nos 95 and 96 in this exhibition, both titled *View in Ireland, Co. Wicklow*, were identical with the views described in n. 10. No owner is given, and all the works in the exhibition were for sale.

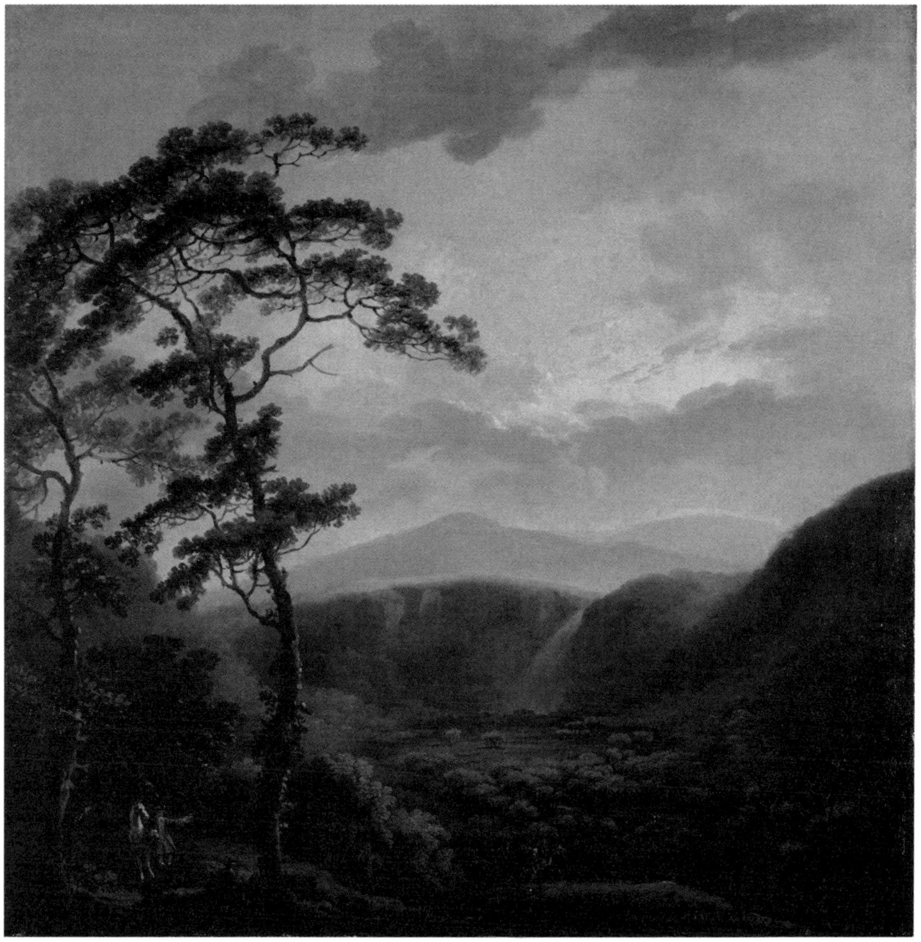

Fig.2 *The Waterfall at Powerscourt* by George Barret, oil on canvas. Photograph reproduced courtesy the Trustees of National Museums Northern Ireland.

Thomas Beach

1738–1806

The Honourable Mrs Craven

WAG 8632
oil on canvas, 75 × 64 cm
signed and dated: *T. Beach pt./1776* (bottom left)
date: 1776

An old label on the reverse of WAG 8632 reads *The Hon.ble Mrs Craven / Grandmother and Godmother / to Maria M. Countess of Sefton*. The sitter is Mary Hickes, who was the daughter of Revd Baptist Hickes of Stretton-on-the-Foss, Glos. She married Revd John Craven, Rector of Felton, Shropshire; their son William (b.1738) succeeded his uncle as 6th Baron Craven in 1769,[1] and the latter's daughter Maria married the 2nd Earl of Sefton, in whose family the painting descended (see WAG 10502, p. 13). Presumably it was one of the 'three portraits by Beechy [sic] of members of the Craven family' seen at Croxteth Hall by Edward Twycross in the 1840s.[2]

The Hon. Mrs Craven, who had been a widow for 24 years at the date the portrait was undertaken, presumably sat for it in conjunction with the large *Craven Family* portrait which Beach worked on in 1776–77 (see fig. 4, p. 14). Comparison of the features and dress here with those of the elderly lady at the right in the family group confirms that they are the same person. Beach made several individual studies for the figures in the family picture and it is tempting to suggest this is Beach's first trial for the figure of Hon. Mrs Craven. Later he decided to portray her holding her granddaughter Arabella, a grouping for which he also made a study (fig. 3).[3] He made numerous other portraits of members of the Craven family at the same period.[4]

PROVENANCE

By descent to the sitter's granddaughter Maria, Countess of Sefton; thence with the Earls of Sefton; bt. in 1974 from the executors of Hugh, 7th Earl of Sefton.[5]

NOTES

1. *Complete Peerage* vol. 3, p. 504.
2. Edward Twycross: *The Mansions of England and Wales Illustrated in a Series of Views of the Principal Seats, with Historical and Topographical Descriptions. The County Palatine of Lancaster* 5 vols (London, 1847) vol. 3, p. 10. See, however, n. 4.
3. Exhibited in *The British Face*, Colnaghi, London

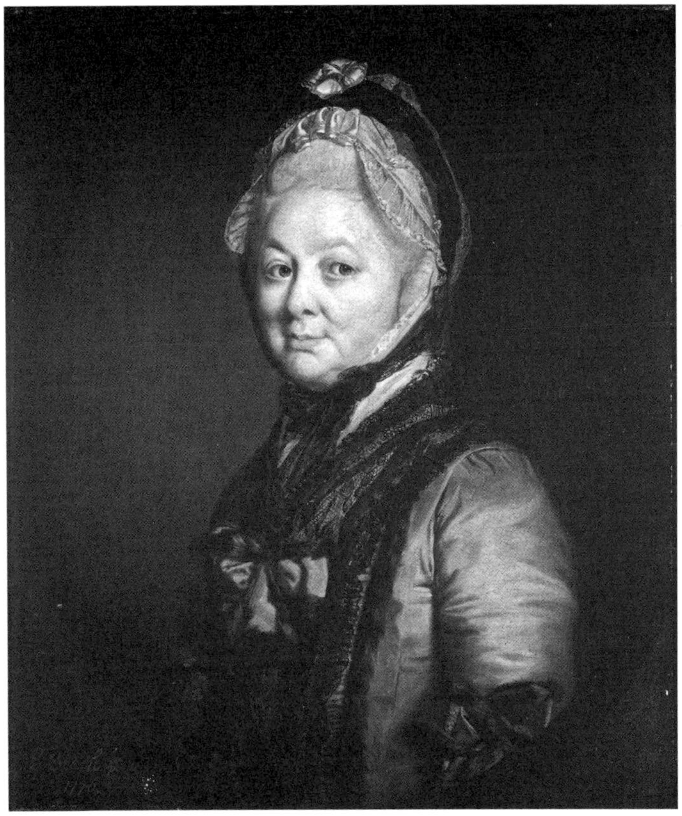

WAG 8632

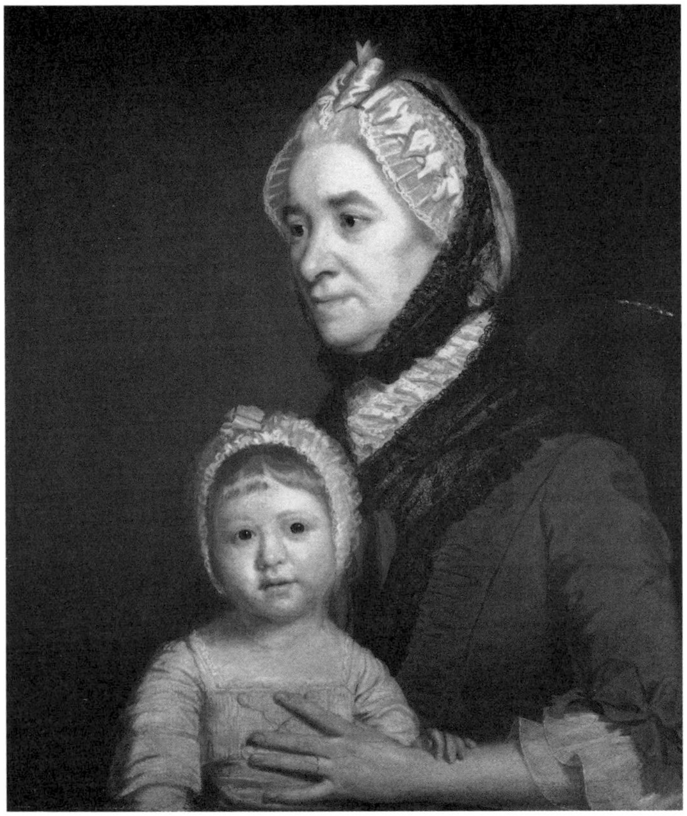

Fig. 3 *Hon. Arabella Craven and Her Nurse* by Thomas Beach, oil on canvas. Exh. Colnaghi & Co. 1986; photo Prudence Cuming Associates.

1986 (41) as *The Hon. Arabella Craven and Her Nurse.*
4. These include whole-lengths of Lady and Lord Craven (exh. SA 1776, cats. 3 and 4); Sotheby 27 November 1968 (3–4); the portrait of Lady Craven is now in the Getty Museum, Los Angeles; *William, 7th Baron and 1st Earl Craven as a Boy*; Sotheby 27 November 1968 (1) (three further portraits by Beach in this sale, not of family members, are nevertheless likely to have been commissioned by the Cravens); the small versions of Lord Craven and his son (if not copies) in the Croxteth Hall sale, Christie on the premises 17–19 September 1973, lots 1007, 1013, 1039 (it is unclear whether these may account for the pictures mentioned by Twycross; see n. 2); also a portrait of an elderly gentleman dated 1778 identified as 'Mr John Craven' (Phillips 11 December 1984 [51]). For the family group and Beach's other studies for figures in that work see WAG 10502 (below).
5. The work was not included in the catalogue of the Croxteth Hall sale, Christie 17–19 September 1973 (see n. 4).

Maria Craven, Later Countess of Sefton, as a Young Girl

WAG 10502
oil on canvas, 75.5 × 63 cm
signed and dated: *T. Beach pt./1776* (bottom right)
date: 1776

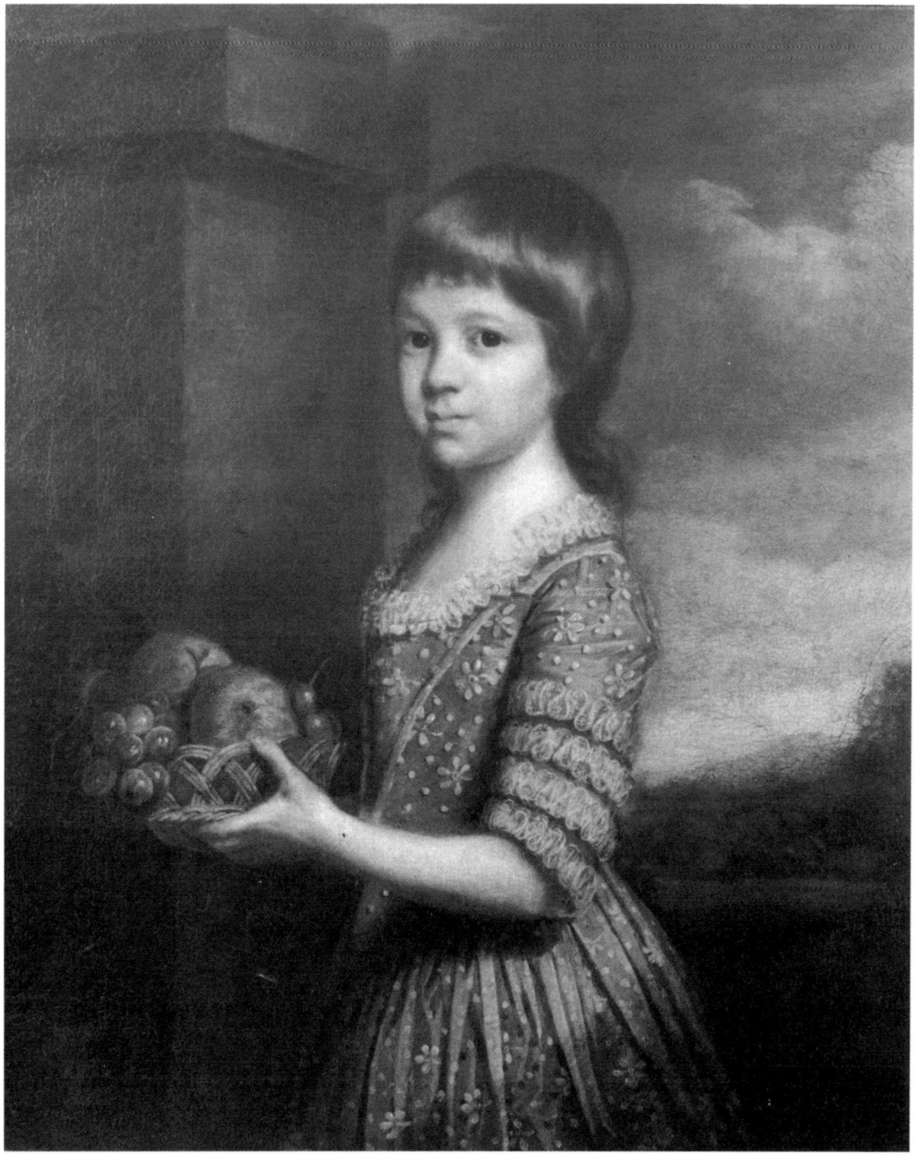

WAG 10502

The sitter was the second child (and second daughter) of William, 6th Baron Craven and his wife Elizabeth, daughter of Augustus, 4th Earl of Berkeley. She was born in 1769. On 1 January 1792 she married William Philip, Viscount Molyneux of Croxteth Hall near Liverpool, who succeeded his father as 2nd Earl of Sefton in 1795.[1] She and her husband became familiar figures in Whig society during the Regency period (being mentioned frequently in *The Creevey Papers*).[2] She died 9 March 1851.

The portrait is a study for one of the figures in Beach's large group, *The Craven Family* dating from 1777 (fig. 4).[3] That work depicts the six eldest children of the 6th Baron, together with their paternal grandmother (see WAG 8632, above) and a second adult female who is probably a nurse.[4] Beach probably made individual studies similar to WAG 10502 for all the family members portrayed in the large group, although only some of these are traced.[5] Small changes in the placement of Maria's hand and in the arrangement of the fruit are visible.

PROVENANCE
By descent in the Craven family; Phillips 11 December 1984 (53); bt. Agnew for the gallery.

NOTES
1. *Complete Peerage* vol. 11, p. 593.
2. Sir Herbert Maxwell, ed.: *The Creevey Papers* 2 vols (London, 1903) *passim*. Thomas Creevey was probably Lord Sefton's half-brother.
3. Sotheby 27 November 1968 (2); subsequently with Agnew's; sold again Christie 12 April 1991 (12) and with Christopher Gibbs 1994.
4. The figures are identified in anon: *Catalogue of*

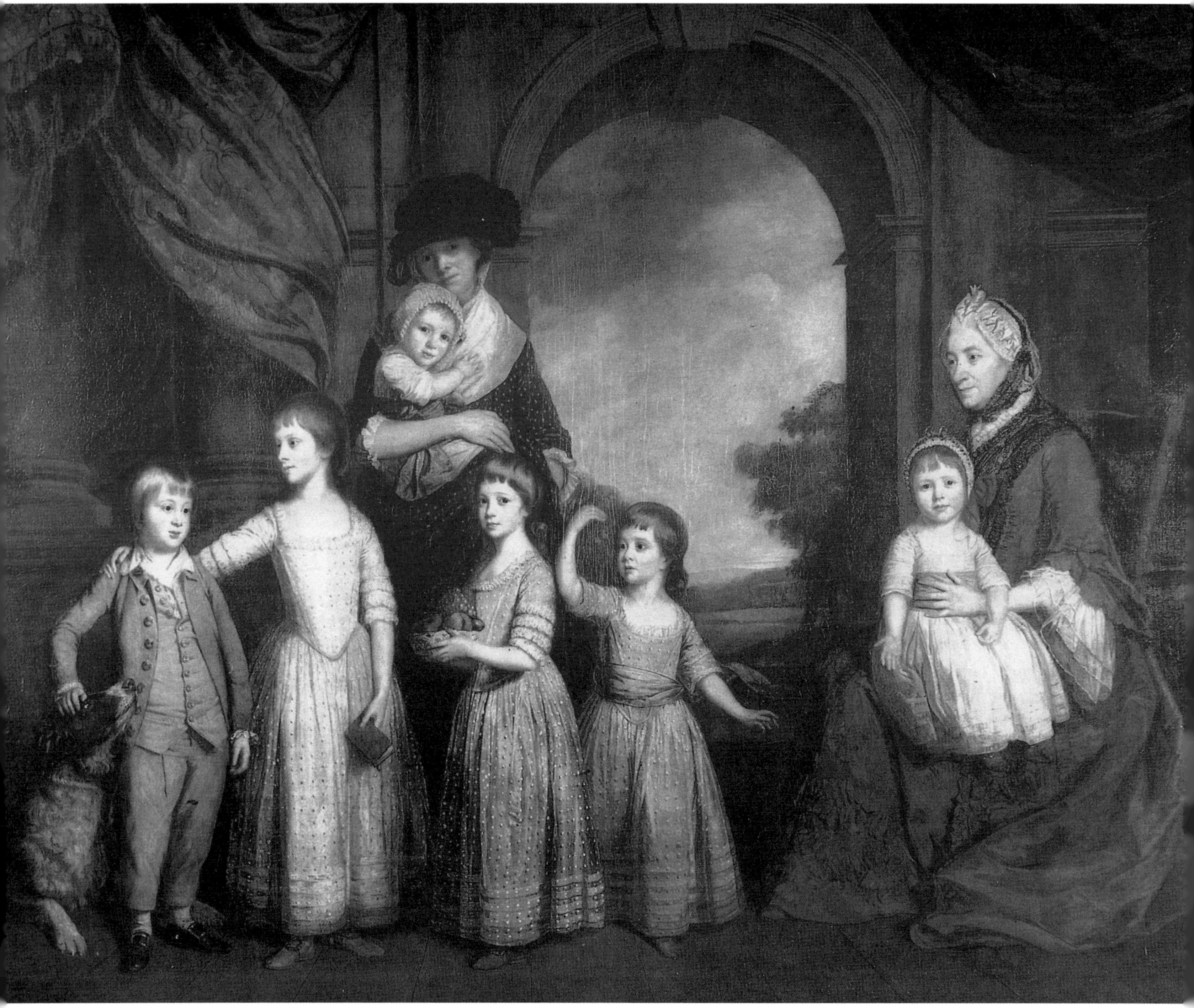

Fig. 4 *The Craven Family* by Thomas Beach, oil on canvas.
Photo courtesy Christopher Gibbs.

the Pictures at Combe Abbey, Warwickshire, the Seat of William Earl of Craven (privately printed, 1866) p. 11 (cat. 124) as 'Mrs Medoby, Lady Sefton, Lord Craven, Miss Craven, Mr B. Craven, Mr St. John'. It has sometimes been incorrectly assumed (for example Sotheby's sale catalogue of 27 November 1968, lot 2) that the first and last of these names refer to the two adult figures in the picture rather than the two eldest daughters. 'Mrs Medoby' must be an old misreading of 'Mrs Madocks', the married name of the eldest daughter, Elizabeth (*Burke's Peerage*, 105th edn [1978] p. 623) and 'Mr St. John' is an error for Mrs St John, as Arabella became by her marriage to Gen. Hon. Frederick St John in 1793.
5. Lot 50 in Phillips's sale, 11 December 1984 (see Provenance) was of Hon. Mrs Craven holding Arabella (see fig. 3, p. 12); lot 52 was a study for the figure of Elizabeth and lot 54 (misidentified as of Maria) was a study for the figure of the third daughter Georgiana, who remained unmarried and thus known as Miss Craven. The remaining children were William, the future 7th Baron and 1st Lord Craven (b. 1770) and Berkeley (b. December 1776), who must be the child in arms and depicted at the age of only a few months. A third son, Keppel Richard, was born in 1779 (*Burke's Peerage, loc. cit.*).

William Beechey

1753–1839

Portrait of a Lady

WAG 2501
oil on canvas, 77 × 64 cm
date: about 1800–1805

Although the attribution of WAG 2501 to Beechey has been questioned,[1] it seems acceptable. A routine work, the portrait nevertheless shows some felicitous touches around the face, and the gloved hand and umbrella are neatly painted. It does not have the appearance of a copy. From the costume it has been dated to the first half of the 1800s.[2]

The portrait entered the Walker's collection with the title *Mrs Greaves*, but no information exists about her and the identification is uncertain.[3]

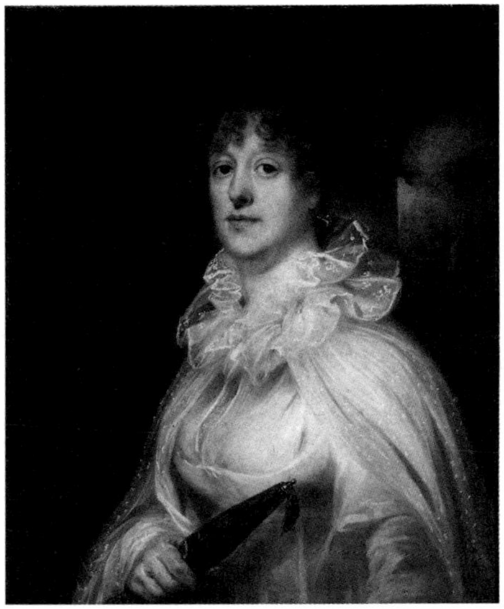

WAG 2501

PROVENANCE
...George Audley;[4] his bequest 1932.

NOTES
1. WAG 2501 was called 'manner of Beechey' in *CIC*, p. 16.
2. Anne Buck, *letter*, 12 September 1968, gallery files. The years 1792–1807 are those for which Beechey's ms account books (RA Library, London) are missing.
3. The Heinz archive at the National Portrait Gallery contains no portraits of a Mrs Greaves dating from the 1800s. George Romney's half-length portrait of Mrs George Bustard Greaves painted in 1786 (sold at Christie's 28 April 1922 [41]; photograph in the Ellis Waterhouse files, Paul Mellon Centre for Studies in British Art, London) shows a younger woman, but she does not at all resemble the lady portrayed in WAG 2501. A note in gallery files, of unknown authority, claims that Mrs Greaves's maiden name was Bulwer-Lytton, but this seems doubtful; this name was taken by royal licence by the writer Edward Bulwer only in 1843.
4. The painting does not appear in the 1923 catalogue of George Audley's collection of paintings, implying that he purchased it after that date.

called
Charles Brooking

1723–1759

Men of War in Harbour

WAG 1994.116
oil on canvas, 93 × 132 cm
date: unknown; perhaps about 1745–55

Held to be an autograph work by Brooking when it entered the gallery, WAG 1994.116 is of copy quality and is probably based on an unidentified work or works by Peter Monamy or else Willem van de Velde (of whom it is less typical). It is known that Brooking trained himself by making copies of such works and given the presence of the inscription *C. Brooking* in the lower left corner, WAG 1994.116 may genuinely be by him. Nevertheless, the quality of the handling is too low to accept this scenario uncritically.[1]

PROVENANCE
...George Palmer Holt before 1978;[2] his bequest 1990.

Notes
1. I am grateful to Ellie Hughes for discussing WAG 1994.116 with me, *verbally*, February 2008.
2. WAG 1994.116 was lent by Holt to the Walker Art Gallery in that year.

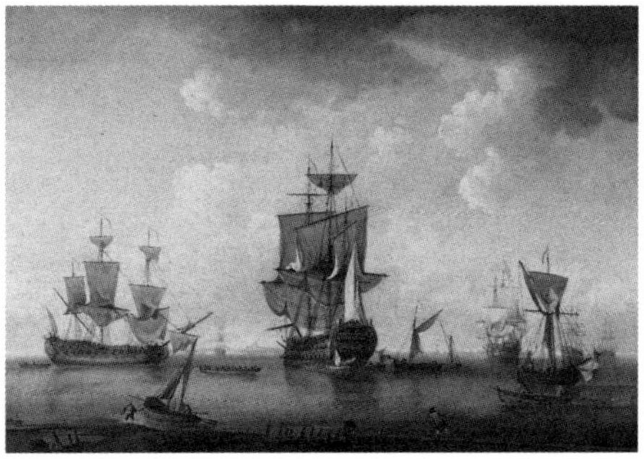

WAG 1994.116

Men of War Firing

WAG 1994.117
oil on canvas, 67 × 83.5 cm
date: unknown; perhaps about 1745–55

As with WAG 1994.116 (above), the work is inscribed in the lower left corner *C. Brooking pt*, but is of copy quality. It is based on a subject associated with Peter Monamy,[1] in which naval ships, the largest flying a plain red flag at its mainmast, are practising gunnery. This work is not a pendant to WAG 1994.116 but it appears to be by the same hand. Although it is known that Brooking trained himself by making such copies it is impossible to state with confidence that this painting is an autograph work by him.[2]

PROVENANCE
...George Palmer Holt before 1978;[3] his bequest 1990.

NOTES
1. Two very similar versions of the subject were sold as by Monamy in the same sale at Christie, 15 February 1988: lot 75, *The Morning Gun*, 45 × 65 cm; and lot 78, *Men-o'-war firing salutes and other shipping in a calm*, 46.5 × 58.5 cm; the former, which has an extra longboat at the left, a small sailing boat standing to the warship, and an additional ship in the right centre on the horizon, is the version followed by the artist of WAG 1994.117.
2. I am grateful to Ellie Hughes for discussing WAG 1994.117 with me, *verbally*, February 2008.
3. WAG 1994.117 was lent by Holt to the Walker Art Gallery in that year.

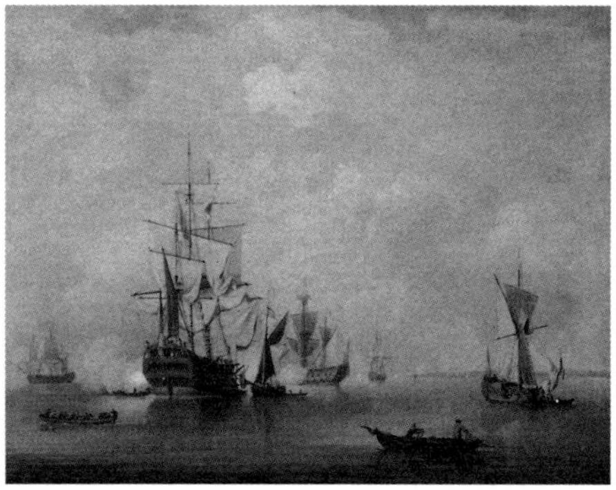

WAG 1994.117

Mather Brown

1761–1831

Lord Loughborough

WAG 2578
oil on canvas, 105.5 × 72.5 cm
date: about 1785–88

The sitter is Alexander Wedderburn (1733–1805) in his robes as Lord Chief Justice of Common Pleas, the position to which he was promoted on 14 June 1780, the same day that he was elevated to the peerage as Baron Loughborough of Leicester. Appointed Lord Chancellor in 1793, a position he retained until 1801, and then created 1st Earl of Rosslyn, Lord Loughborough was one of the most formidable figures in British law during the last 30 years of the eighteenth century. Scottish by birth, he owed his first advancement to his friendship with King George III's favourite, Lord Bute. He soon acquired a reputation for his political opportunism, twice changing sides in the House of Commons between 1769 and 1771 in a naked display of his desire for advancement. Recognised by his contemporaries as ambitious and a skilled operator, Lord Loughborough also enjoyed a reputation for strict moral probity[1] (it was he who hounded William Beckford out of England after the latter's affair with his second wife's kinsman, William Courtenay).

This oil sketch is for a whole-length portrait that appears never to have been completed (certainly, none is known). A half-length portrait to which, despite major differences, it is clearly related (Scottish National Portrait Gallery, Edinburgh; fig. 5) was published as an engraved mezzotint on 27 May 1791, so was presumably completed in 1789–90.[2] Although it is not out of the question that the full-length commission resulted from the completion of the half-length, appearances suggest that the reverse was the case, and that Brown's original idea for the portrait had to be modified and scaled down. Arguably, Lord Loughborough appears slightly more youthful in WAG 2578 than in the half-length; while perhaps more pertinently, Brown's only known preliminary drawing for the portrait, executed in black and white chalk on blue paper (National Gallery of Scotland, Edinburgh; fig. 6)[3] anticipates the design of WAG 2578 rather than the half-length (although, again, there are significant differences between them). In WAG 2578 the splay-legged pose of the figure seen in the drawing, which is reminiscent of Sir Joshua Reynolds's full-length portrait of King George III of 1779 (RA), has become less prominent, while Lord Loughborough's head has been turned a little further round to the side. The whole composition is squeezed into a narrower format. But the elements of the setting are similar, which argues that there was only a short interval between drawing and oil sketch. WAG 2578 is uncharacteristic of Brown's work and entered the Walker's collection as by Reynolds.[4]

Two further portraits of Lord Loughborough by Brown are known. One, a head and shoulders oval portrait (private collection, Massachusetts, USA in 1982; fig. 7) appears to have derived from different sittings although, from the fact that an engraving of it was published in April 1792, it must date from approximately the same period as WAG 2578.[5] The second, a variant of WAG 2578 and the Scottish National Portrait Gallery half-length, but with Lord Loughborough now as Lord Chancellor, was included in Brown's small historical composition of the mid-1790s, *George III Receiving the Turkish Ambassador.*

PROVENANCE
...Mrs D. H. Townes-Luttrell (née Dorothy Hope Wedderburn, only surviving daughter of Sir

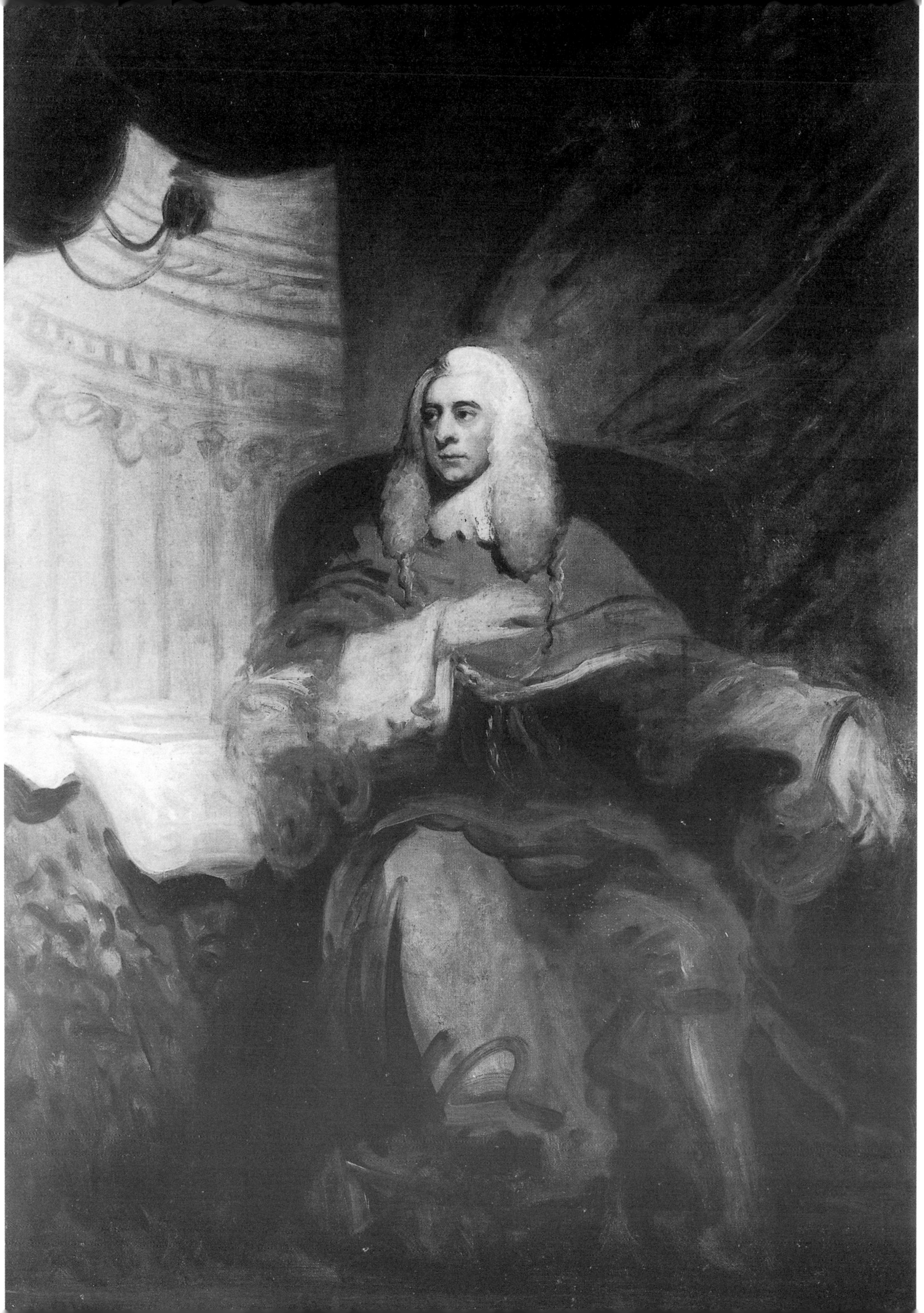

WAG 2578

William Wedderburn, 4th Bt.);[6] Burton Knowles, 1–2 March 1934 (367); bt. Spink; David Minlore; L. V. Riches;[7] from whom bt. 1942.

EXHIBITIONS

Some Acquisitions of the Walker Art Gallery Liverpool 1935–1945 National Gallery, London 1945 (7); *Art in the Georgian Home* York City Art Gallery and tour 1949 (5).

NOTES

1. *Complete Peerage* vol. 11, pp. 172–5; Alexander Murdoch: 'Wedderburn, Alexander, first earl of Rosslyn', *ODNB* vol. 57, pp. 908–10.
2. Dorinda Evans: *Mather Brown, Early American Artist in England* (1982) p. 223, cat. 151.
3. *Ibid.*, p. 267, cat. 366.
4. The attribution to Reynolds was discarded shortly after the 1949 exhibition (when John Summerson, in the catalogue, pointed out that WAG 2578 was unrelated to Reynolds's portrait of Lord Loughborough in Lincoln's Inn). The work was called 'British School' for some years before being identified as by Brown in the late 1950s (gallery files).
5. Evans, *op. cit.*, p. 223, cat.152.
6. Presumably, but not certainly, by descent; the patron would not have typically acquired a preparatory sketch from the artist. The work did not appear in Brown's posthumous sale, Foster, 14 July 1831.
7. According to Riches, he purchased WAG 2578 directly from Mrs Townes-Luttrell 'through an intermediary' (*letter*, undated, gallery files). The provenance given is as stated in Evans, *op. cit.*, p. 223.

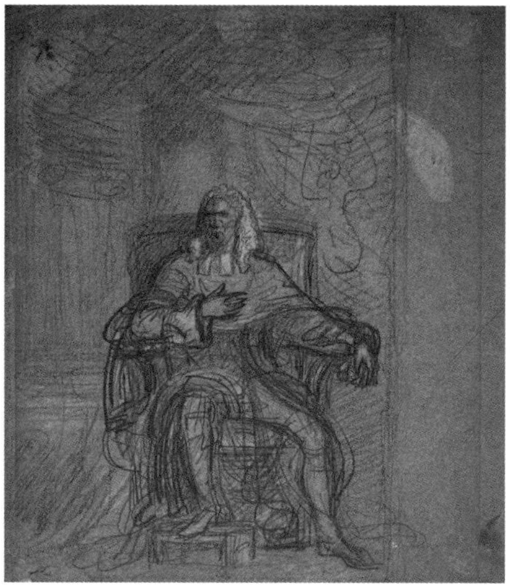

Fig. 6 *Study for the Painting of Alexander Wedderburn, 1st Earl of Rosslyn* by Mather Brown, black and white chalk on blue paper. © National Galleries of Scotland.

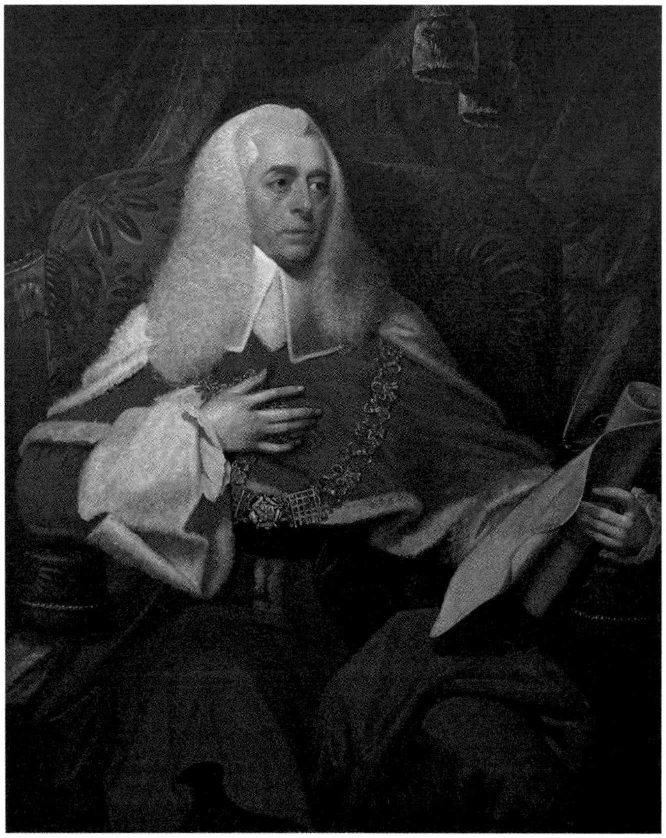

Fig. 5 *Lord Loughborough* by Mather Brown, oil on canvas. © National Galleries of Scotland.

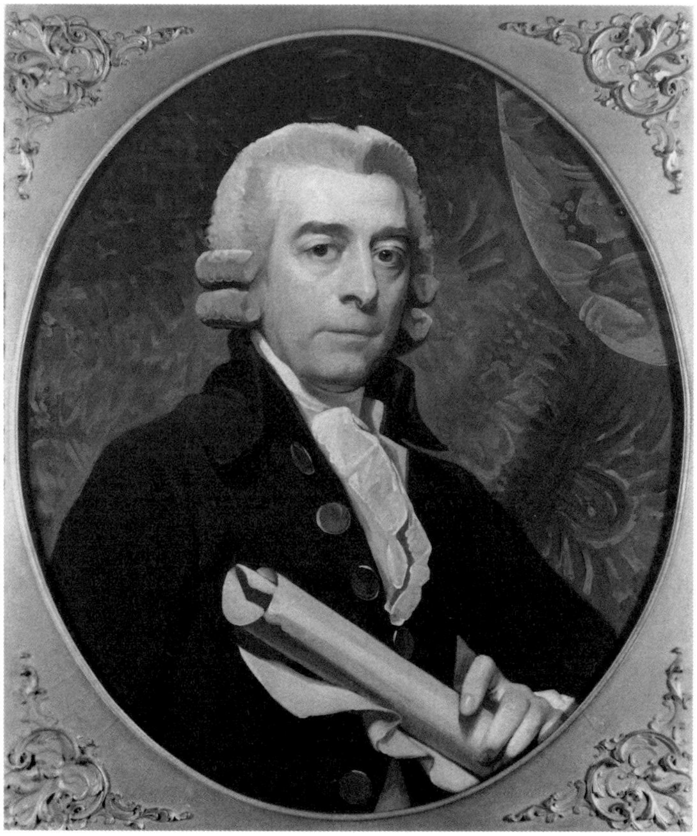

Fig. 7 *Alexander Wedderburn, 1st Earl of Rosslyn* by Mather Brown, oil on canvas. Photo courtesy Schweitzer Gallery, New York.

John Bridge Aspinall

WAG 7041
oil on canvas, 76 × 64 cm
signed: *Mather Brown/pinxt* (lower right)
date: 1808–10

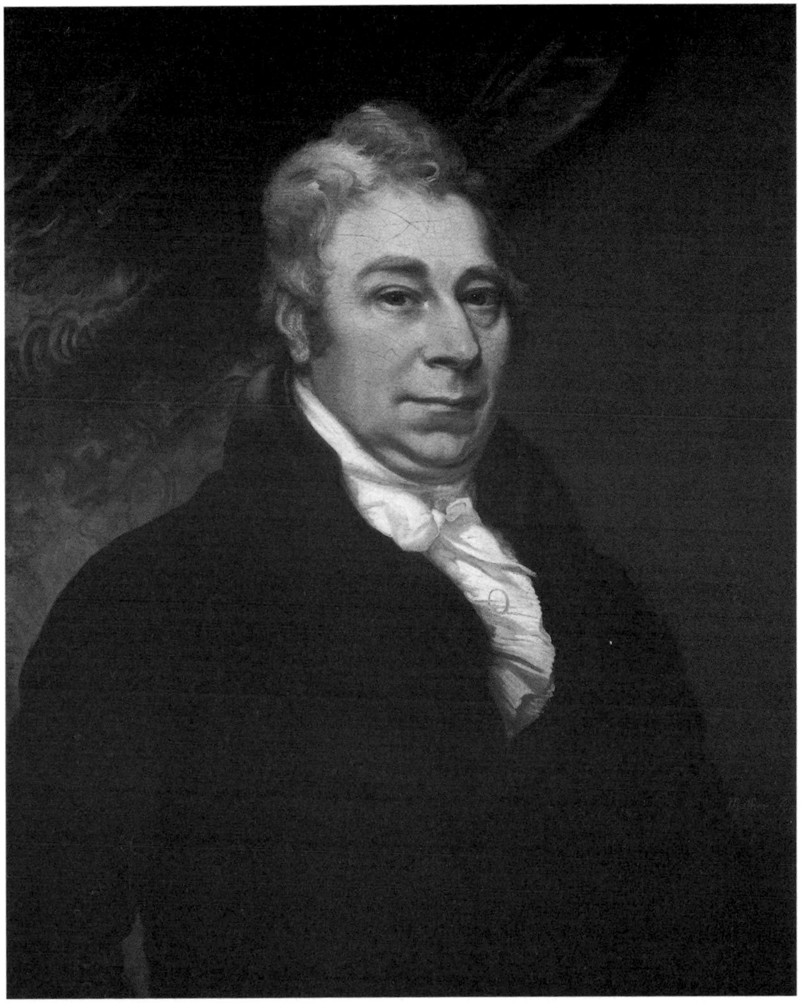

WAG 7041

Aspinall (1758/59–1830) was a Liverpool merchant who by 1787 was in trade with the West Indies, initially from premises on the south side of the Old Dock and then, by 1790, from addresses in Duke Street. He is probably identifiable as the John Aspinall who with James Aspinall concurrently had a plumbers and glaziers business in Park Lane, Liverpool, since another James Aspinall, presumably their father, is recorded as a plumber and glazier on his own in 1766 and until 1781 at the original Old Dock address. John Bridge Aspinall was prominent in local politics as a Tory, was a supporter of General Isaac Gascoyne, MP for Liverpool 1796–1831, and was successively Bailiff of Liverpool (1801) and Mayor (1803). He seems to have retired from the plumbing and glazing business shortly before this portrait was painted, and he disappears from Liverpool street directories after 1816. He owned a house in the country, Clehongar Hall, and also had property in Bath, where he died. His descendants remained prominent in Liverpool public life in the nineteenth century.[1]

WAG 7041 was one of three works shown by Brown at the inaugural exhibition in 1810 of the Liverpool Academy (the successor to the Society for Promoting Painting and Design in Liverpool which had flourished briefly in the 1780s). Although Brown's address was given in the exhibition catalogue as Cavendish Square, London, he had in fact left London by 1808 and had been in Bath before working his way northwards to Liverpool, where he had arrived by June 1810 as the Academy was in the process of being organised.[2] The portrait is a stock, no frills, head-and-shoulders treatment and it cannot have taken long to produce, but given the short interval between Brown's arrival in Liverpool and the opening of the exhibition at the beginning of August, it is tempting to conjecture that Brown had painted it in Bath, or at least had made initial contact with Aspinall there.

PROVENANCE

By descent to Capt. O. Addison Williamson; by whom presented to Liverpool Corporation 1949; transferred in 1967 from the City Estates Committee.

EXHIBITIONS

LA 1810 (52); *The Taste of Yesterday* Walker Art Gallery 1970 (6); *American Artists in Europe* Walker Art Gallery 1976 (22).

NOTES

1. MPPP, p. 55; *Gore's Liverpool Directory*, 1766–1816, *passim*; a notice of his retirement from business in Park Lane is in the *Liverpool Courier*, 3 August 1808, p. 1, although in street directories he continues to be described as 'merchant' until 1814 (in 1816 he is 'Esq.'). His memorial tablet in Bath Abbey carries the following inscription (kindly communicated by Gillian Hylson-Smith and Amina Wright): *Sacred to the memory of / John Bridge Aspinall, Esquire / of this city / and of Liverpool / and / Clehongar Hall, County of Chester / died the 3rd of May 1830 / Aged 71 years / He was an active magistrate / Beneficent to his fellow creatures / Kind to his family / And Just to all.* For two portraits of Aspinall as Mayor see WAG 2587 (p. 311) and WAG 7026 (p. 328).
2. Dorinda Evans: *Mather Brown, Early American Artist in England* (Middletown, 1982) pp. 151–2, 155.

Richard Caddick

1748–1831

Miss Elizabeth Wood, Later Mrs Proudlove

WAG 10381
oil on canvas, 29.5 × 25 cm
date: 1768–69

A memorandum formerly on the reverse of WAG 10381 (fig. 8) written by the sitter's brother reads,

This is an excellent likeness of my Sister Elizabeth painted by Mr Richard Caddick of Liverpool about the year 1768 or 9. She was born Feby 2nd 1742, married to John Proudlove of Sandbach May 25th 1771 and died March 6th 1788. The children of the above John and Elizabeth Proudlove were born as under. James, born June 5th 1772 Died May 16th aged 20 1793. Richard, born Jany 27th 1775 died Octr 1st 1775. John, born August 14th 1776, Died Decr 19th 1829. aged 52. – Enoch, born May 21st 1778 – died May 1819 aged 44. – Henry, born March 4th 1780. Elizabeth, born Feby 15th 1782. Aaron, born May 18th – Mary, born Feby 15th – 1788 – died May 25th 1788. – I believe the above to be correct Enoch Wood Burslem April 6. 1838.

It has been suggested that the portrait in fact post-dates the sitter's marriage, perhaps partly on the basis that the work was traditionally titled *Mrs Proudlove* and perhaps from the costume and the general conception of the work;[1] however, the prominent cup and saucer are surely wares made by the Wood family firm, appropriate to a depiction of the daughter of Aaron Wood (see WAG 10379, p. xxx). The sitter was the artist's cousin and WAG 10381 may well have been painted on a trip to Liverpool.[2] The disproportion between the head and hand and the torso suggest a relatively immature artist, and the date proposed in the memorandum above seems likely to be correct.

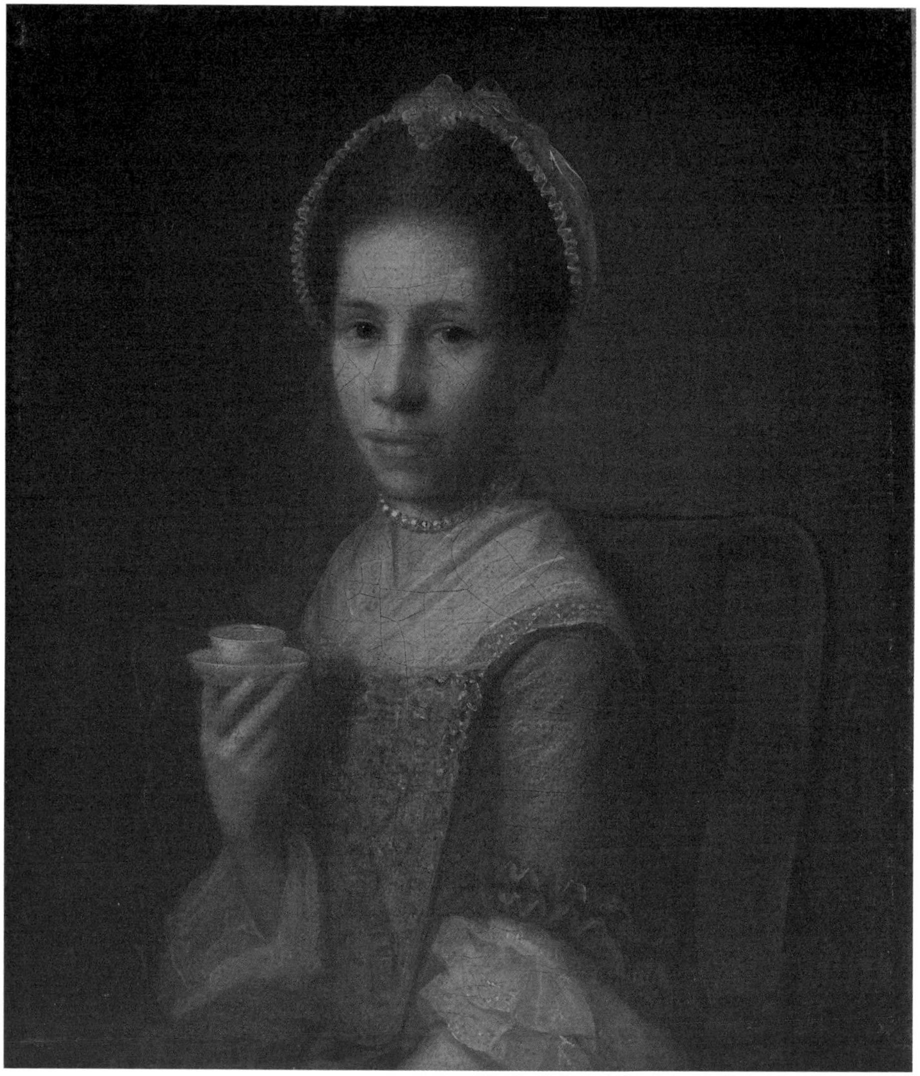

WAG 10381

PROVENANCE
By descent to Mrs C. Wood, Gollanfield, Inverness; from whom bt. by private treaty 1983.

EXHIBITION
Joseph Wright of Derby in Liverpool Walker Art Gallery and Yale Center for British Art, New Haven 2007–08 (6).

NOTES
1. Mary Bennett, *note*, gallery files; Frank Falkner: *The Wood Family of Burslem* (London, 1912) pp. 35–6 and caption to plate XXVIII, illustration 104, titles the work thus, and it was referred to as *Mrs Proudlove* in private lists of Wood family portraits at Gollanfield (gallery files).
2. Enoch Wood, Elizabeth's younger brother, spent three months with the Caddicks in Liverpool about 1770 (see cat. 10380, p. 26).

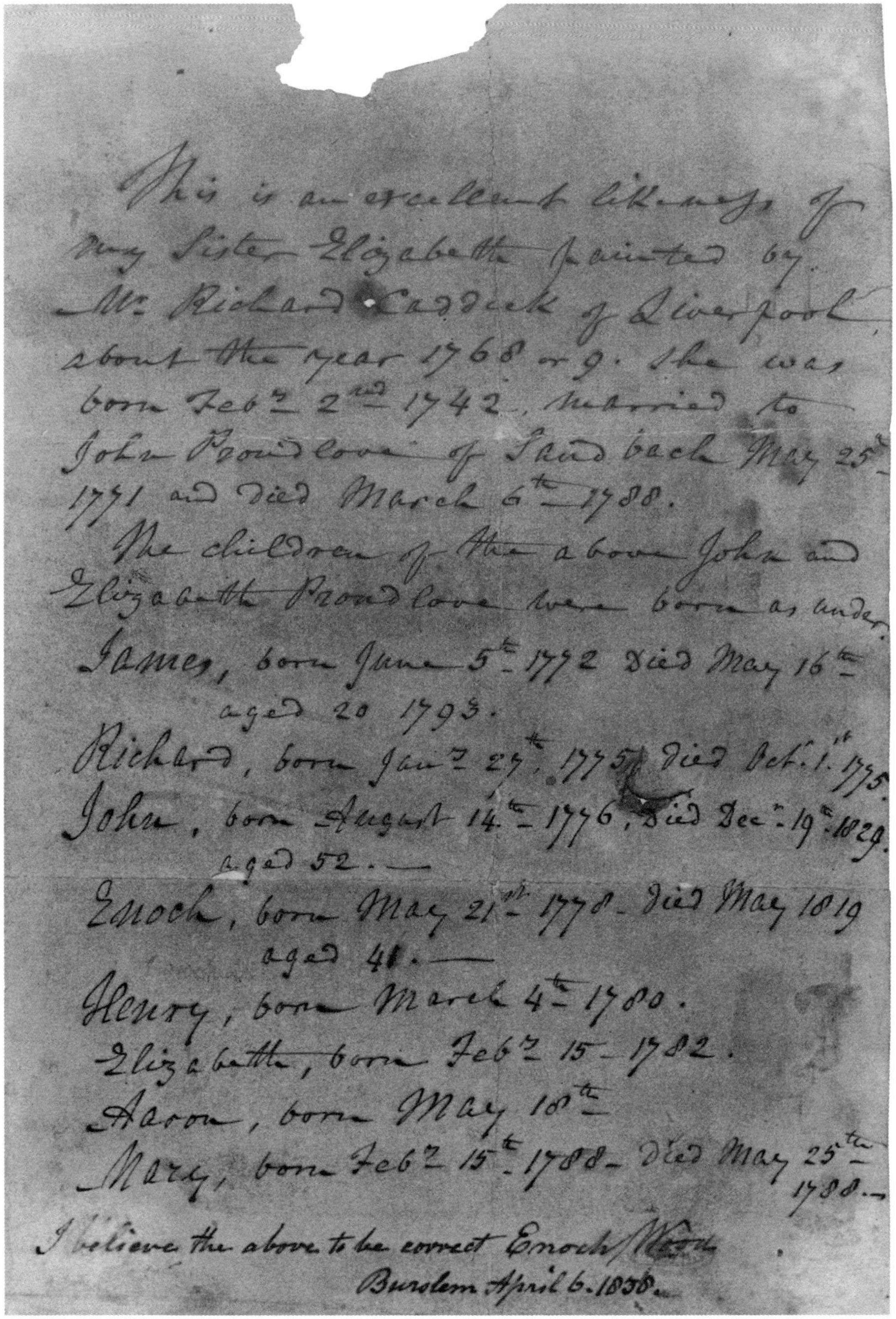
This is an excellent likeness of
my Sister Elizabeth painted by
Mr Richard Caddick of Liverpool
about the year 1768 or 9. She was
born Feby 2nd 1742, married to
John Proudlove of Sandbach May 25
1771 and died March 6th 1788.
The children of the above John and
Elizabeth Proudlove were born as under
James, born June 5th 1772 died May 16th
aged 20 1793.
Richard, born Jany 27th 1775 died Oct. 1st 1775
John, born August 14th 1776, died Decr 19th 1829
aged 52.—
Enoch, born May 21st 1778 died May 1819
aged 41.—
Henry, born March 4th 1780.
Elizabeth, born Feby 15 1782.
Aaron, born May 18th
Mary, born Feby 15th 1788 died May 25th 1788.—
I believe the above to be correct Enoch Wood
Burslem April 6. 1838.

Fig. 8 *Memorandum* by Enoch Wood formerly on the reverse of WAG 10381. Walker Art Gallery.

Portrait of a Young Man

WAG 3109
oil on canvas, 50 × 42 cm
date: about 1770–75

When acquired by the gallery in 1893, WAG 3109 was said to be a portrait of William Roscoe.[1] This young man, however, bears no resemblance to Roscoe in other likenesses (compare the later portraits by Shee, pp. 162–4, and Williamson, pp. 250–2). The sitter seems much more likely to be a member of the artist's own family, for a copy of WAG 3109 (fig. 9) descended until 1983 in the collection of the Wood family of Burslem, who were related to the Caddicks by marriage (see above and pp. 25–6). It is tempting to think that the sitter is Richard Caddick himself. At least two further portraits of Richard are recorded: one also formerly in the Wood family collection, stated on a frame label to be by his younger brother William and to date from 1780,[2] and a head depicting him as an older man, formerly owned by Miss Sudlow of Liverpool.[3] Making allowance for age difference, the likenesses in these works seem comparable to the present portrait. Furthermore, there is a distinct resemblance to the man second from the left in the portrait traditionally titled *The Caddick Family* (WAG 3108, pp. 22–3). Although the figures in the latter work are uncertain, the similarity offers further circumstantial evidence for the identification.

The label on the frame of the copy referred to above gives the artist of that work as William Caddick, Richard's father.[4] However, the handling of paint in WAG 3109 is unlike that in any work currently known to be by William, and an attribution to Richard seems preferable. If this is a self-portrait, his age suggests a dating in the early 1770s. It

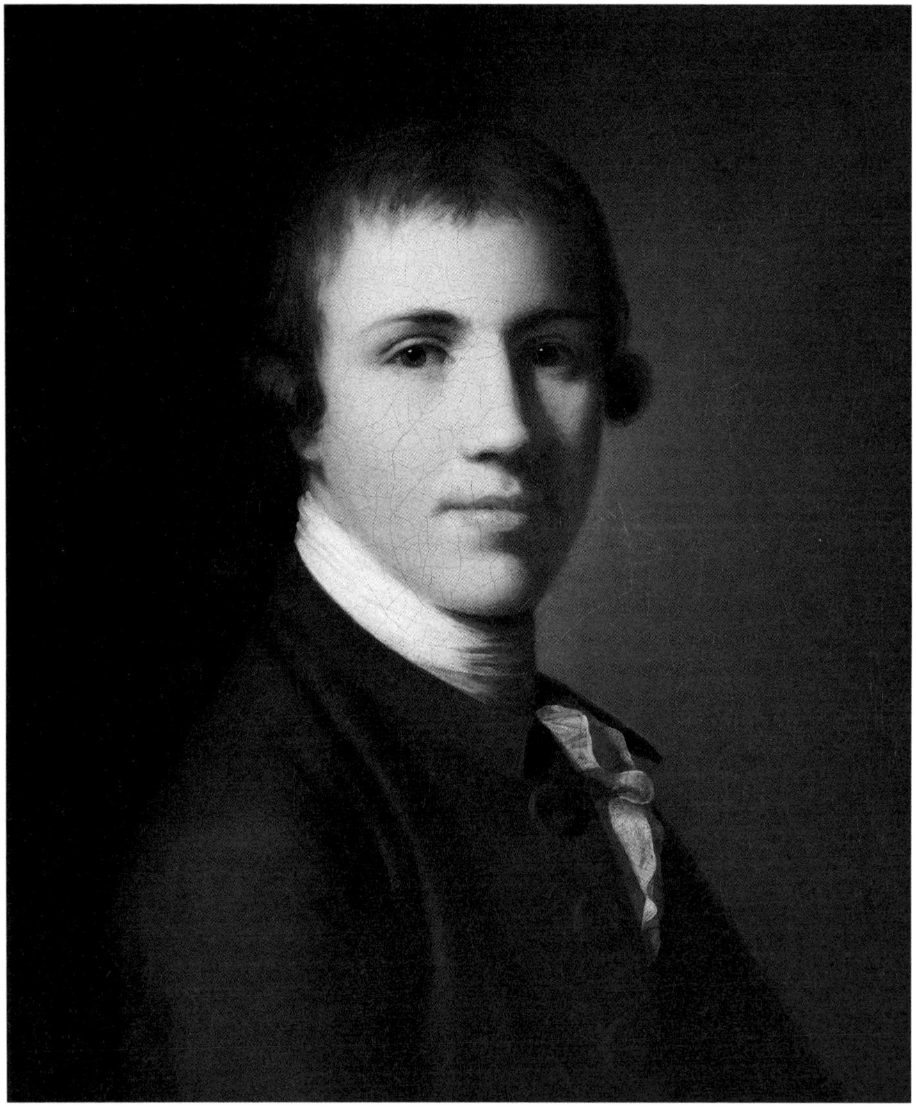

WAG 3109

does not seem fanciful to detect in WAG 3109 exposure to the Liverpool portraits of Joseph Wright of Derby: the strong lighting, the pose close to the picture plane, and the keen attention to details of costume all take their cue from the older artist's recent work in the town.[5]

PROVENANCE

...[? Joseph Mayer; Branch and Leete Liverpool 16 December 1887 (232)];[6] ...John Hargreaves, Rock Ferry; from whom bt. 1893.

EXHIBITIONS

The Liverpool School of Painters Harrogate 1924 (49); *Roscoe Centenary* Liverpool City Library 1931 (1); *British Art Exhibition* Manchester City Art Gallery 1934 (13); *Joseph Wright of Derby in Liverpool* Walker Art Gallery and Yale Center for British Art, New Haven 2007–08 (7).

NOTES

1. *Forty-first Annual Report of the Committee of the Free Public Library, Museum, and Walker Art Gallery of the City of Liverpool, for the Year Ending 31 December 1893* (1894) p. 28; see also the caption to the reproduction in *Connoisseur*, vol. 36 (1913) p. 152, and E. R. Dibdin: 'Liverpool Art and Artists in the

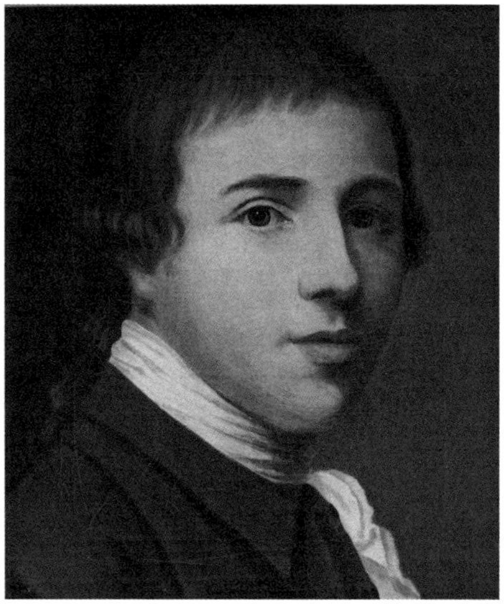

Fig. 9 *Self Portrait* after Richard Caddick, oil on canvas. Private collection; photo courtesy the owner.

Eighteenth Century', *Walpole Society* vol. 6 (1917–18), pl. XXIX (a). *MPPP*, p. 66, raises the possibility that WAG 3110 (p. 27) is in fact a portrait of William Roscoe and the name got swapped to WAG 3109 in error, conjecturally when the two pictures were in the collection of Joseph Mayer.
2. Frank Falkner: *The Wood Family of Burslem* (London, 1912) p. 35, repr. pl. XXVIII, illustration no.103.
3. *Ibid.*, p. 34, repr. pl. XXVII, illustration no.100.
4. It is possible that this attribution refers to the authorship of the copy only, but this seems unlikely.
5. As is suggested in E. Barker and A. Kidson, *Joseph Wright of Derby in Liverpool* exh. cat., Walker Art Gallery and Yale Center for British Art, New Haven (2007) p. 128.
6. Attributed to Richard Caddick in the sale catalogue.

The Caddick Family

WAG 3108
oil on canvas, 74 × 100 cm
date: about 1788–89

The title of WAG 3108 is traditional but creates difficulties. When purchased by the gallery, the work was believed to represent the family of Richard Caddick (seated) and his wife Martha.[1] But they had only one child, a daughter also named Martha; and she was born in 1797, whereas the painting has been dated from the costumes to the later 1780s.[2] Subsequently, it has been recognised that it is more likely that the seated man is William Caddick, Richard's father, who would have been in his late sixties at this date.[3] He is shown holding an album of coloured prints, an appropriate activity for the father of an artistic family. His wife Eliza was five years his junior, but although the woman at the right looks somewhat younger than 63–64,[4] there does seem to be some resemblance between her and the young woman in WAG 10380 (p. 26), and it would be natural for Richard to flatter his mother in the context of a formal family group. More problematic are the identities of the three men at the left. Conjecturally, they are William and Eliza's three sons,[5] Richard himself (b .1748), William (b. 1756) and John (b. 1762); but this hypothesis requires the likeness of William to be posthumous as he died in 1784. Possibly the left-hand figure, with the face in shadow and turned away from the viewer, and significantly, resting against a plinth supporting an urn, is intended for him. Nothing is known of John, but on the assumption that he reached maturity, he could be the figure standing in the centre. Richard himself has been thought to be this figure,[6] but he seems more likely to be the man second from the left conversing with his (putative) fellow-portraitist William: an identification that receives some corroboration from other likenesses and presumed likenesses of him, including WAG 3109 (above) and a head that descended to Miss Sudlow with the present work.[7]

The difficulty of being certain that the sitters are the Caddicks has led to the alternative suggestion, from the prominence of the vases, that these are members of the Wood family of Burslem.[8] However, Aaron Wood, the *paterfamilias* of the branch of the Woods closest to the Caddicks, died in 1785, and it is not possible to configure the sitters in WAG 3108 with the ages of remaining Wood family members. It might equally be proposed that this is simply a conversation piece of a cultivated Liverpool family that for some reason was never collected and remained on Richard's hands.

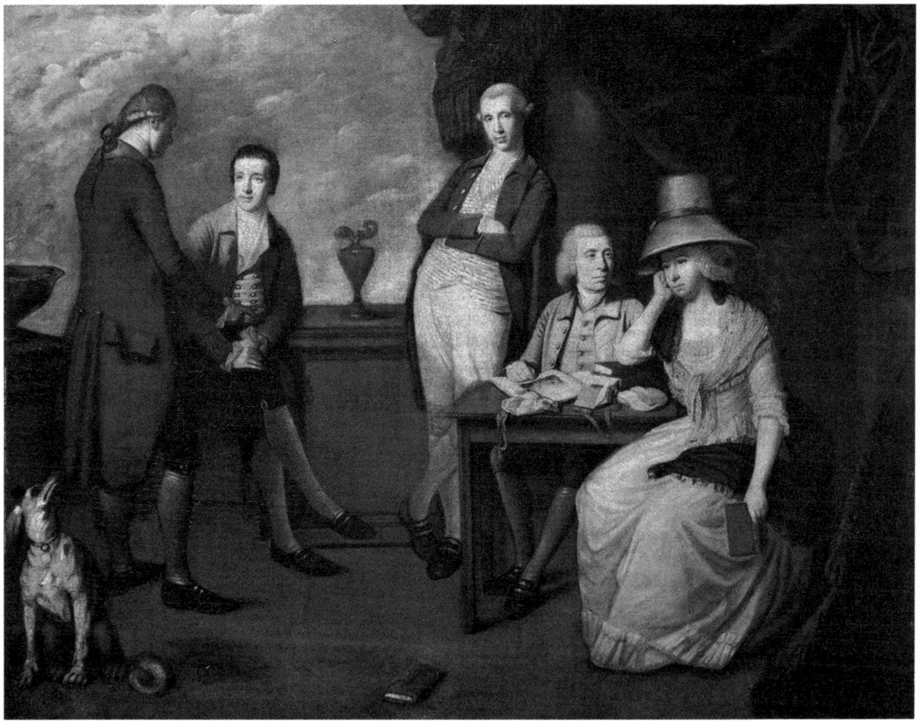

WAG 3108

PROVENANCE

By descent to Miss Alice Sudlow, Liverpool;[9] from whom bt. 1908.

EXHIBITIONS

The Liverpool School of Painters Harrogate 1924 (23); *The Taste of Yesterday* Walker Art Gallery 1970 (14).

NOTES

1. This identification, which was repeated by Frank Falkner: *The Wood Family of Burslem* (London, 1912) p. 34 and by E. Rimbault Dibdin: 'Liverpool Art and Artists in the Eighteenth Century', *Walpole Society* vol. 6 (1917–18) p. 71, derived from Peter Entwistle: [volume of ms notes on] *Liverpool Artists and Engravers*, LRO 942/ENT/33, p. 82. Entwistle's notes appear to have been based on conversations with Alice Sudlow herself; see *MPPP*, pp. 64, 66.
2. Anne Buck, *letter*, 24 November 1956, gallery files. She cites a note from the *New Ladies' Magazine*, 1788, concerning this style of hat: 'the round is made very narrow and falls down like the roof of a house'.
3. *MPPP*, p. 66.
4. *Ibid.* states categorically that this figure 'is too young for William's wife Eliza' but could be the wife or sister of one of the younger men; but this seems at odds with the whole conception of the portrait.
5. They had one further son William (1753–55); *MPPP*, p. 63.
6. *MPPP*, p. 66.
7. Repr. Dibdin, *op. cit.*, pl. XXV(a).
8. *MPPP*, *loc. cit.*
9. Her father was the nephew of Thomas Smith, an engraver listed in Liverpool street directories 1834–35, who married Martha Caddick, Richard Caddick's daughter – apparently after the latter's death in 1831, since at his death she is recorded as a spinster; *MPPP*, p. 64.

attributed to

Richard Caddick

1748–1831

Joseph Brooks

WAG 1135
oil on canvas, 223.5 × 152.5 cm
date: 1774

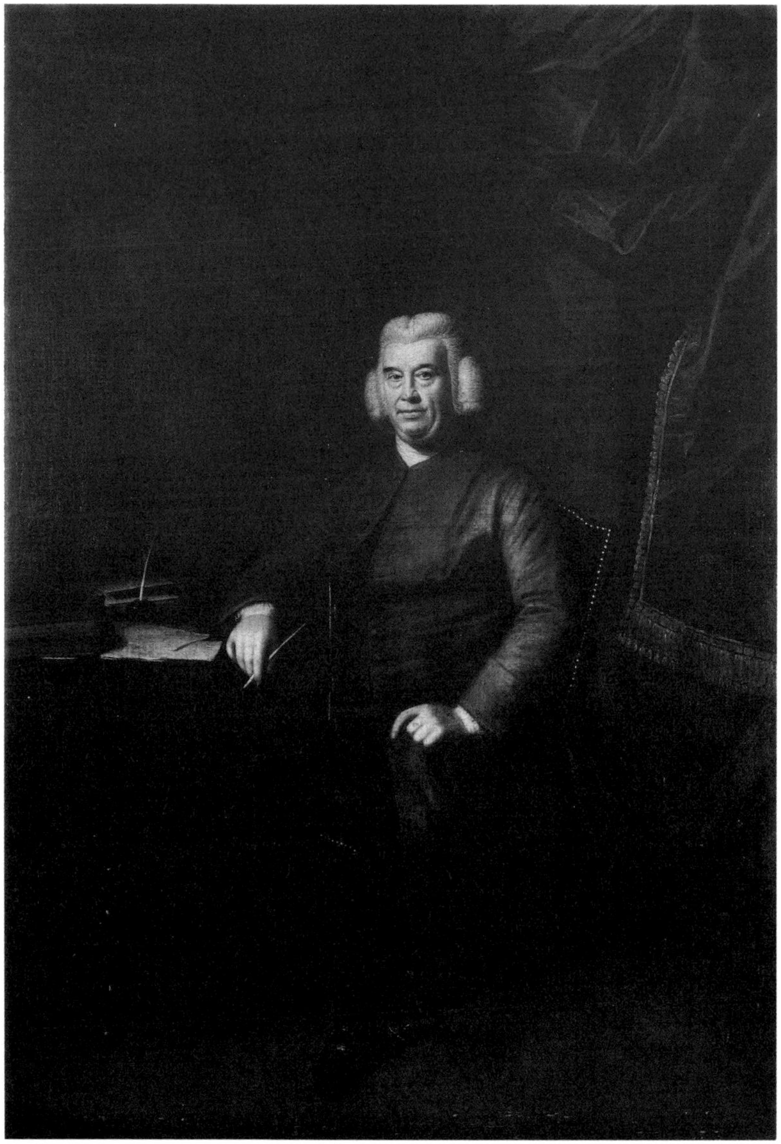

WAG 1135

This is the largest painting, and only full-length, known by any of the Caddicks. It was commissioned in April 1774 by the Parish of Liverpool, whose treasurer Brooks was. The Vestry minutes of the 5th of that month record that 'the thanks of this Vestry are returned to Mr Joseph Brooks…for his diligent, active and just discharge of his said office, and in order to preserve a grateful remembrance of his services, it is ordered that his Picture at full length be executed by one of the most masterly hands in this Kingdom and that the same be for ever hereafter hung up in the Committee Room of the Parish Poor House'.[1] According to a note in the papers of the Liverpool antiquarians John Holt and Matthew Gregson, 'the execution of this work, at the request and recommendation of Mr Brooks, was given to his Townsman Mr Caddick, a work which does the artist much credit – the Sum paid for the Piece was 40 guineas'.[2] The note, probably drawn up in the late eighteenth century, goes on to mention that Caddick in his youth was a comrade of George Stubbs, which confirms that William Caddick, and not one of his sons, was the artist to whom the commission was given.[3] Willliam Caddick was a neighbour and tenant of Brooks in Old Hall Street in Liverpool,[4] and was then Liverpool's best-known portrait painter.

But it is not so certain that William Caddick actually executed the work. He may have been responsible for Brooks's face,[5] but in general the brushy, soft-edged handling of paint in WAG 1135 seems closer to the manner of Richard Caddick than the harder, more literal style of the works known to be by his father. It seems eminently plausible that William would have regarded the commission as an opportunity for his 25 year-old son, working within the family business, to cut his teeth on a major work, and the quotation of the pose of Hogarth's *Captain Coram* (1740, Foundling Hospital, London) also seems much more likely to be the contrivance of an ambitious younger artist. In 1825, when Richard Caddick was still living in Liverpool, Henry Smithers described WAG 1135 as by Richard,[6] and Richard's name also appeared on the first tablet fixed to the frame.[7]

Joseph Brooks (1706/07–88) was a leading merchant of Liverpool, trading in timber and rope. He was also a limeburner and, with his brother Jonathan, the chief builder in the town. He was extensively involved in the construction of the Exchange (Town Hall) in the years before 1754 and with the rebuilding of St Nicholas's Parish Church in the Gothic style, 1774–75. He was a philanthropist and much concerned with poor relief.[8] WAG 1135 appears to portray him doing the parish accounts, even if no text is legible on the sheets of paper or the spines of the volumes depicted in the picture.

PROVENANCE

Commissioned by the Parish of Liverpool 1774; transferred from the Parish Offices to the gallery 1928.

EXHIBITIONS

Historical Exhibition of Liverpool Art Walker Art Gallery 1908 (12); *Liverpool Academy 150th Anniversary Exhibition* Walker Art Gallery 1960 (7).

NOTES

1. Henry Peet, *Liverpool Vestry Books 1681–1834* 2 vols (Liverpool, 1912–15) vol. 1, p. 237.
2. *Holt-Gregson Papers*, LRO 942/HOL/1, p. 27.
3. *MPPP*, p. 65.
4. *MPPP*, *loc. cit.*
5. WAG 1135 was described by Henry Smithers: *Liverpool, Its Commerce, Statistics and Institutions* (Liverpool, 1825) pp. 400ff., as an excellent likeness; William Caddick's chief reputation as a portraitist was for his ability to capture a good likeness; see also WAG 10379 and WAG 10380; also Alex Kidson: 'The Liverpool Art Scene 1745–1770', in E. Barker and A. Kidson: *Joseph Wright of Derby in Liverpool*, exh. cat., Walker Art Gallery and Yale Center for British Art, New Haven (2007), pp. 38–9, n. 53.
6. Smithers, *loc. cit.*
7. *MPPP*, *loc. cit.*
8. See *MPPP*, *loc. cit.*, for further biographical information on Brooks; and citing Sir J. A. Picton: *Memorials of Liverpool* 2 vols (London, 1873) vol. 2, pp. 66, 151–2; see also H. M. Colvin: *A Biographical Dictionary of British Architects* (3rd edn, New Haven and London, 1995) p. 164; this gives Brooks's birth date as 1707, *MPPP* as 1706.

William Caddick

1719/20–94

Aaron Wood

WAG 10379
oil on canvas,[1] 33.5 × 27 cm
date: 1747

A manuscript note[2] on the reverse of WAG 10379 written by the sitter's son reads,

Memorandum / This is a striking likeness of Aaron Wood / Modeller – Son of Ralph and Elizabeth, born in the year 1717 April / 17th – and died May 12th 1785 – Aged 68 – This likeness / was taken by Wm Caddick Liverpool in the year 1747 in / the 30th year of his [A.W's] age. – / He was Modeler to all the Potters in Staffordshire at / the later End of the time when white ware or White Stone ware was made. Enoch Wood / Nb I have heard my father say, his father was never known to / sw[e]ar, Chew / or smoke Tobacco, take Snuff, or whistle or Sing in his life / & was considered the most pleasing lively & merriest man in the Country… (fig. 10)

The latter part of this note refers to Aaron Wood's father Ralph (1686–1763), who was a miller of Cheddleton, Staffordshire.[3] He married Elizabeth Hammond and had nine children, four sons and five daughters, of whom Aaron was the second son. With his elder brother Ralph (1715–72) and Moses (b. 1719) it was Aaron who started the Wood family's well-known pottery business, which was carried on by Enoch (1759–1840), the

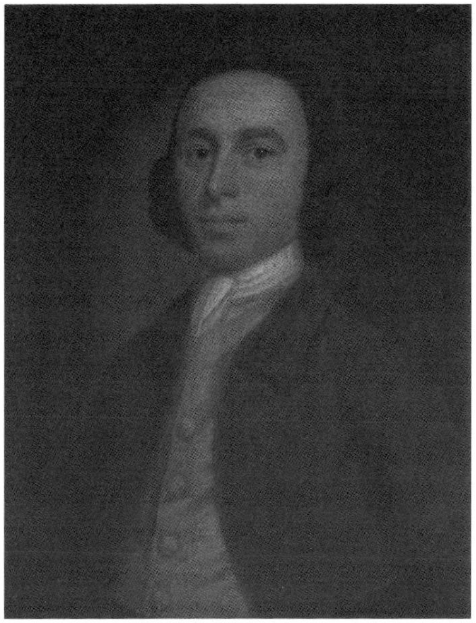

WAG 10379

Fig. 10 *Memorandum* by Enoch Wood formerly on the reverse of WAG 10379. Walker Art Gallery.

writer of the memorandum.[4]

Aaron's youth 'was spent in assiduous attention to his craft of Designing, Modelling and Block-Cutting, in this he was destined to excel and to leave eventually a reputation which time has enlarged far beyond the Pottery districts where his life was wholly spent'.[5] He was apprenticed to Thomas Wedgwood until 1743, and then worked for the potter John Mitchell until he set up independently in 1750. He married Mary Meir about 1739 and with her had eight children, of whom the eldest was a daughter, Sarah, born 1740, and the youngest was Enoch. His eldest son, William, was apprenticed to Josiah Wedgwood for four years in 1762 and at the end of that term stayed on at Wedgwood's Etruria works as a modeller.[6]

This is one of a group of portraits of members of the Wood family painted by William Caddick in the mid-1740s. The first seems to have been the portrait of Aaron's father Ralph (in the same collection as WAG 10379 until 1983), which according to Enoch Wood was painted in 1744.[7] The portrait of Eliza, Aaron's sister (and the artist's wife; see WAG 10380, below) may have been executed around the same time as WAG 10379, but the two works differ in conception and treatment and do not appear to be pendants.

PROVENANCE

By descent to Mrs C. Wood, Gollanfield, Inverness; from whom bt. by private treaty 1983.

NOTES

1. The canvas has been relined and fixed to a new stretcher bearing a Charles Roberson stamp.
2. The note is in ink on laid paper which has been mounted on card, and the card has been sealed to the reverse of the canvas on all four sides. The bottom of the note is damaged and the last sentences are illegible and lost.
3. It is misquoted by Frank Falkner: *The Wood Family of Burslem* (London, 1912), pp. 31–2, to make it appear that Enoch is describing his father, Aaron Wood himself.
4. See *ibid.* (in which WAG 10379 is reproduced as pl. XXIV, illustration 89) *passim*; also C. Hussey: 'Henley Hall, Shropshire – II', *Country Life* (23 August 1946) pp. 348–51; *MPPP*, p. 63.
5. Falkner, *op. cit.*, p. 21.
6. Falkner, *op. cit.*, pp. 21–30.
7. Repr. Falkner, *op. cit.*, pl. II, illustration 8.

Mrs William Caddick, neé Elizabeth Wood

WAG 10380
oil on canvas, 29 × 22 cm
date: about 1747

A manuscript note fixed to the reverse of WAG 10380,[1] written by the sitter's nephew, reads,

This is an excellent likeness of My Fathers sister Elizabeth who was married to Mr William Caddick of Liverpool an eminent Portrait Painter. This is a sample of his Painting soon after his marriage to her. When I was Eleven years old my Father sent me by ⁎ Morrises Waggon to his house in Liverpool for 3 month only to be instructed by him & his Sons Richard & William in the art of drawing, Perspective, Anatomy &c &c … After my return he sent me to School to the Revd Richard Benteley & my Brother in law Aaron Wedgwood, who were then parteners in that school, neither of them paid much attention to it, & is [sic] was soon discontinued Enoch Wood ⁎ Morrises Waggon Hind wheel came off (a Cotter Pin was wanting) & I was crush'd under the Hollow of that great broad wheel, which rolld off the Paved road to the soft dirty side, where I had leapd from the hind part while it was falling & crushed me so as to appear lifeless, the hind part of [sic] Body of the loaded wagon lay upon upon [sic] the wheel while I was under it untill neighbouring farmers brot rails & levers to raise the the [sic] wheel, while I crept out alive to the astonished men who assisted to releve me, I fortunately was not seriously wounded. E. Wood. (fig. 11)

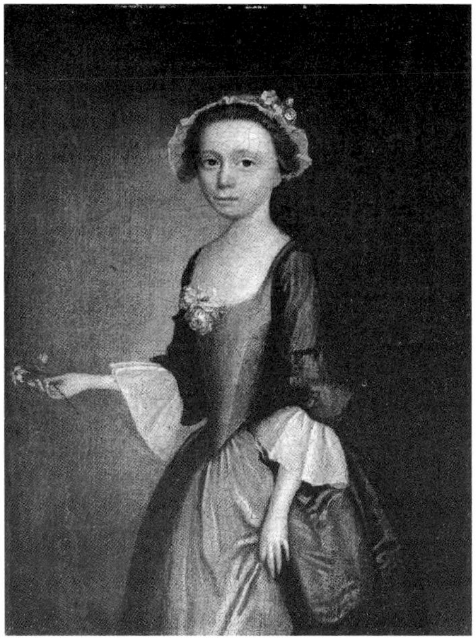

WAG 10380

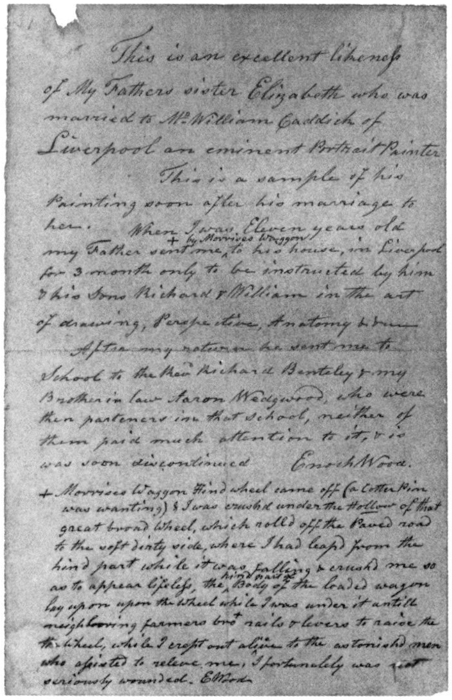

Fig. 11 *Memorandum* by Enoch Wood formerly on the reverse of WAG 10380. Walker Art Gallery.

Elizabeth Wood (1724–1795) was the daughter of Ralph Wood of Cheddleton, Staffordshire, and his wife Elizabeth, and the sister of Ralph and Aaron Wood who founded the Wood pottery firm in Burslem.[2] The date of her marriage to William Caddick has not emerged, but it was probably some time in 1747.[3] Their eldest child, Richard (see pp. 21-2) was born on 7 June 1748, and they had five more children: William, born 8 October 1753, who died an infant; a second William, born 16 June 1756, who became a portrait painter and died in 1784;[4] Ann, born 3 April 1758, who died an infant; John, born 9 February 1762; and finally a second Ann, born 2 October 1764. Eliza died on 10 September 1795 and was buried in St Nicholas's Parish Church Liverpool three days later.

The style of WAG 10380 appears slightly less mature than that of WAG 10379 (above) and the two works are not obviously pendants. Although Enoch Wood says that the portrait was painted after her marriage, the Wood family provenance suggests that it was done for her father, so it may just pre-date it.

PROVENANCE

By descent to Mrs C. Wood, Gollanfield, Inverness; from whom bt. by private treaty 1983.

NOTES

1. The note was mounted on card which was tacked to the stretcher; it is now preserved in gallery files.
2. See Frank Falkner: *The Wood Family of Burslem* (London, 1912) *passim*; *MPPP*, p. 63.
3. The diary of Caddick's visit to London with William Clarke in the summer of 1746, and heir subsequent stay in Cheshire (*Roscoe Papers*, LRO 920/ROS/612) does not mention Eliza.
4. It was probably he rather than his father who exhibited a portrait of a lady in the character of Circe at the RA in 1780 (cat.81); see *GrRA* vol. 1 p. 373.

attributed to

William Caddick

1719–94

Portrait of a Young Man, Perhaps George Stubbs

WAG 3110
oil on canvas, 39 × 31.5 cm
date: unknown, perhaps about 1744–48

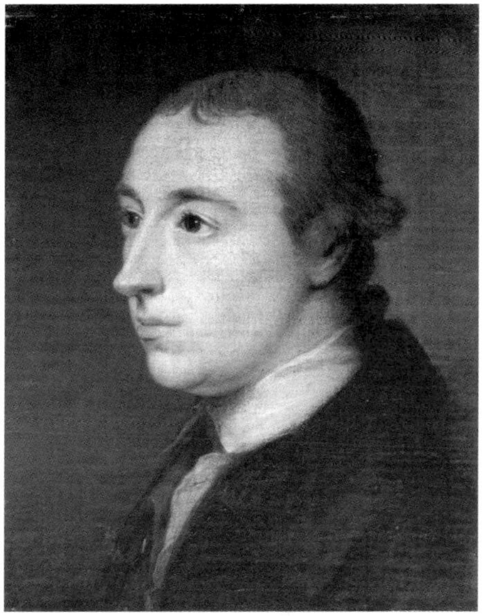

WAG 3110

When it was acquired by the gallery, WAG 3110 was identified as a portrait of George Stubbs by Richard Caddick.[1] If the identification of the sitter is correct, the attribution is impossible: Stubbs was already 24 at the date of Richard Caddick's birth. Richard's father William, however, is supposed to have studied alongside Stubbs in the early 1740s,[2] and the notion that that this is an early work by William Caddick is well worth weighing. The handling of the sitter's features, and of his mouth in particular, is close to that in *Aaron Wood* (WAG 10379, pp. 25-6) and although the paint is more thickly applied than in that work, it lacks the softer touch found in works attributed to Richard. The supposition that WAG 3110 is an immature work is strengthened by the weak handling of the eyes, which are poorly integrated with the rest of the face. The dress, with the ribbon at the back of the sitter's hair, also supports a dating in the mid-1740s rather than two decades or more later. The identification of the sitter as Stubbs turns on comparison with other known authentic likenesses of him, all of which show him much later in life. Both the broad receding forehead and the rounded, jowly chin show strong similarities, even if the nose is much longer and sharper than in any accredited portrait of Stubbs.[3]

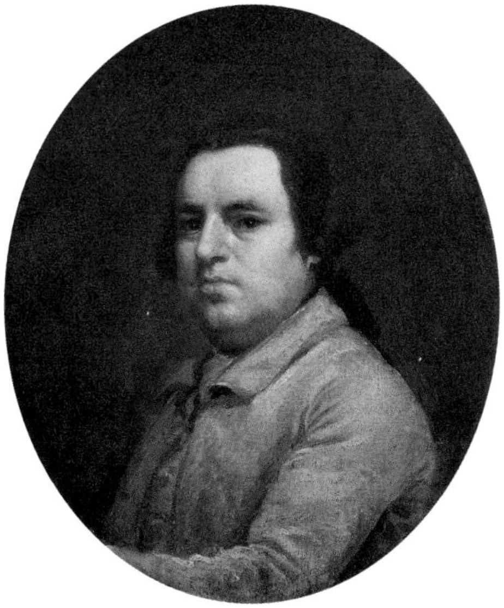

Fig. 12 *Self Portrait*, c.1756–60 by George Stubbs, oil on copper. Yale Center for British Art, Paul Mellon Fund.

Assessment of WAG 3110 is complicated by the painting's indifferent condition, which may be owing to an insensitive later relining. The remains of the original portrait, measuring 35 × 28 cm, have been lined to a larger canvas and the edges crudely matched in. There are extensive discoloured retouchings on the face and areas of matt overpaint above the varnish to the right of the head below the ear and along the left-hand edge of the face.

PROVENANCE
...[? Joseph Mayer; Branch and Leete Liverpool 16 December 1887 (234); ...Studley Martin; ...Branch and Leete Liverpool 29 January 1889 (430)]; ...Revd S. A. Thompson Yates; his bequest 1904.

EXHIBITION
British Art Exhibition Manchester City Art Gallery 1934 (20).

NOTES
1. *Annual Report of the Committee of the Public Libraries, Museums and Art Gallery of the City of Liverpool...1904* (Liverpool, 1905) p. 81; and see also E. R. Dibdin: 'Liverpool Art and Artists in the Eighteenth Century', *Walpole Society* vol. 6 (1917–18) p. 71.
2. *Holt-Gregson Papers*, LRO 942/HOL/1, p. 27.
3. Stubbs's earliest known self-portrait, presumed to have been painted about 1756–60, was sold at Christie 8 June 2006 (35) (fig. 12). Sir Walter Gilbey: *Life of George Stubbs R. A.* (London, 1898) p. 227, identified a work in Joseph Mayer's collection, perhaps WAG 3110, as a portrait of Stubbs by Thomas Chubbard. In the sale of Studley Martin, who is known to have acquired from Mayer's collection, lot 430, again perhaps identifiable as WAG 3110, was described as *Portrait of George Stubbs* by 'R. Puddick'.

Thomas Chubbard

1737/38–1809

Bridge over Rapids by a Mill[1]

WAG 8623
oil on card fixed on canvas, 22 × 27 cm

Landscape with Bridge and Cottages

WAG 8624
oil on card fixed on canvas, 21.5 × 27 cm
signed and dated: *Thos. Chubbard/delt. 1775* (on reverse)
date: 1775

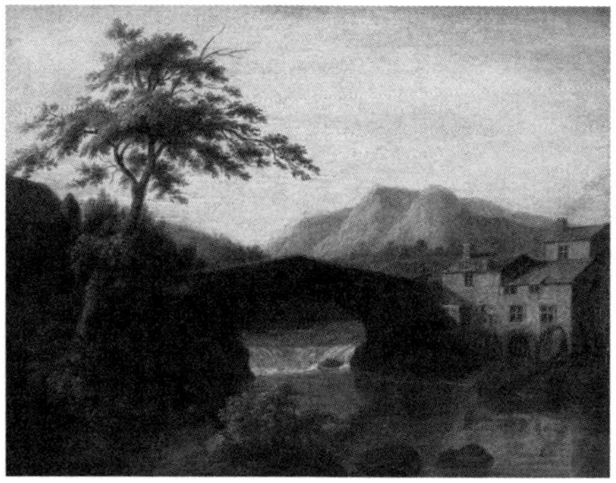

WAG 8623

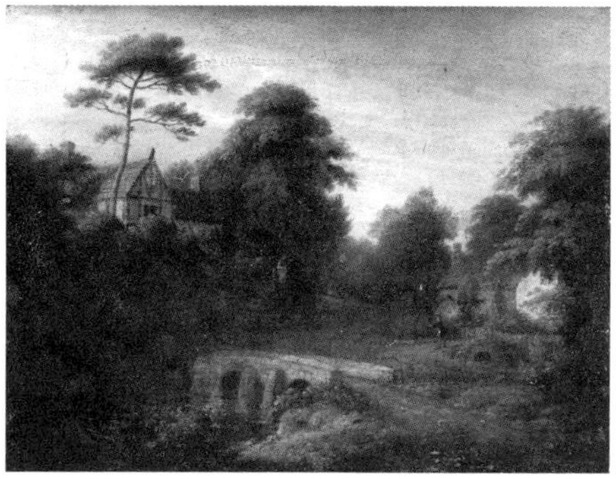

WAG 8624

This pair of small landscapes painted on card are the only oils by Chubbard currently known. They were perhaps intended as an illustration of the contrast between the landscape Sublime and Picturesque, and are possibly to be identified as the *Water Mill, Morning* and *Cottage Scene, Evening* listed by Daniel Daulby in manuscript catalogues of his paintings in the 1790s.[2] Daulby (see WAG 2541, pp. 182–3) was a friend and major patron of Chubbard, owning over a dozen of his paintings (including the fascinatingly titled *Garrick in the Character of King Lear with Shakespeare as Kent and Ben Jonson as Edgar*) and collaborating with him in the mid-1790s, when he had retired to Rydal, on an album of views in the Lake District based on his own and others' designs.[3] The view in WAG 8623 may be a recollection of Rydal Bridge with Nab Scar behind.

WAG 8623 was cleaned in 2007.

PROVENANCE
[? Bt. from the artist by Daniel Daulby]; ... Godolphin Gallery, Dublin; from whom bt. 1974.

EXHIBITION
[WAG 8623 only] *Joseph Wright of Derby in Liverpool* Walker Art Gallery and Yale Center for British Art, New Haven 2007–08 (76).

NOTES
1. In MPPP, p. 70, titled *Bridge over Rapids by a Mill with Mountainous Landscape*, in CIC, p. 56 *Bridge over Rapids by a Mill* and in the 2007–08 exhibition catalogue *Mountainous Landscape with a Bridge and a Mill*.
2. Nos 86 and 87 in Daniel Daulby: (ms) *Catalogue of the Books, Prints, Pictures & Drawings of Daniel Daulby, Liverpool, 1793* LRO H 091.5 DAU, p. 49.
3. The album was almost certainly bequeathed by Daulby to his brother-in-law William Roscoe, and descended in Roscoe's family. It was acquired by the Wordsworth Trust in 2000, and was shown in the 2007–08 exhibition (cat. 82). See Peter Urquhart: 'Daulby's Albums', *Transactions of the Romney Society* vol. 13 (2008) pp. 16–23.

Francis Cotes

1726–70

Mary, Lady Cunliffe

WAG 1514
oil on canvas, 126.5 × 101.5 cm

Sir Robert Cunliffe

WAG 1515
oil on canvas, 127.5 × 101.5 cm
signed and dated: *F Cotes pixt/1768* (initials in monogram, top left)
date: 1768

Robert Cunliffe (1719–78) was the second son of Liverpool merchant and MP Foster Cunliffe and his wife Margaret née Carter, and the younger brother of Ellis Cunliffe, MP for Liverpool from 1755 to 1767, who was created a baronet in 1759. On Ellis's death Robert succeeded him in the baronetcy (according to the terms of a special remainder) and also inherited his estate, Saighton Tower,

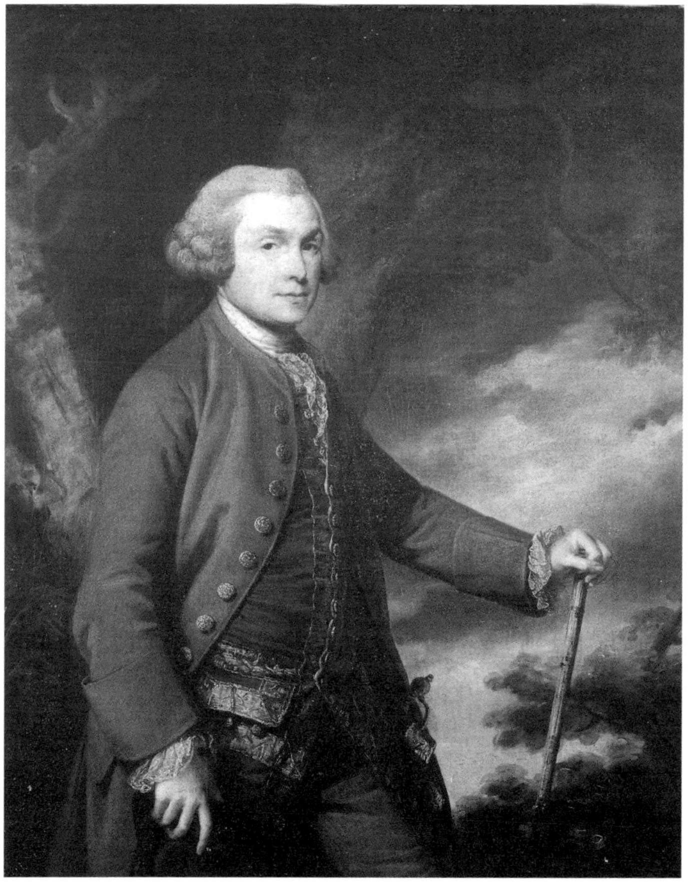

WAG 1515

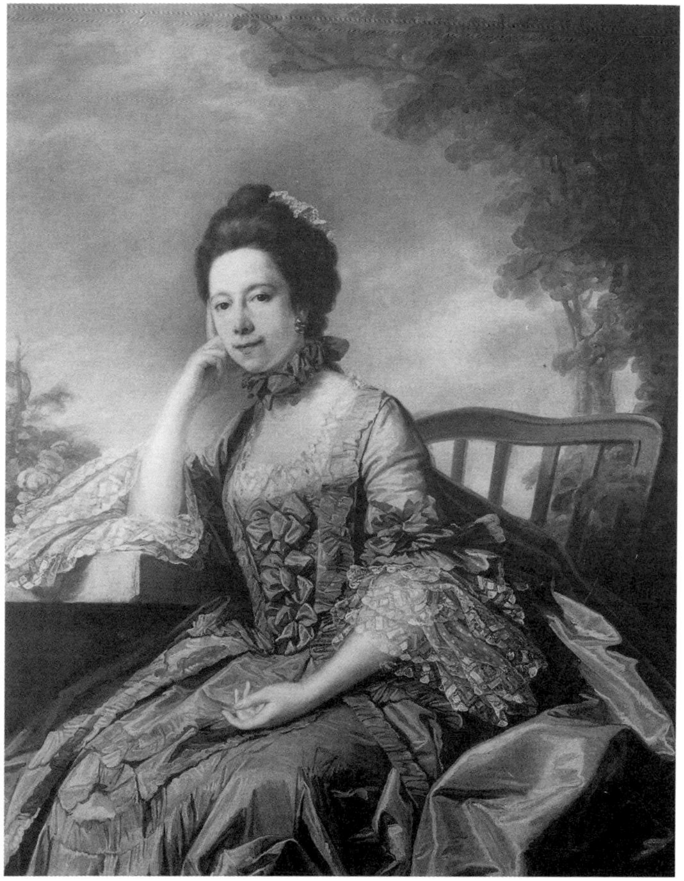

WAG 1514

three miles south-east of Chester. Robert did not pursue the career of an MP, as did his father and brother; but like them he is recorded among the company of Liverpool merchants trading with Africa in 1750, and he became an Alderman of the town.[1] His wife Mary (1721–91), whom he married in 1752, was the daughter of Ichabod Wright, a Nottingham banker. The couple had three daughters and a son, Foster, who succeeded his father as 3rd Baronet in 1778 and who purchased Acton Hall, where WAG 1515 and WAG 1514 hung until they left the family in 1950.

Notwithstanding the inscription on WAG 1514 at the upper right, *Mary, wife of / Sir Robt. Cunliffe 1765*, Cotes's portraits must have been undertaken together, as pendants, rather than three years apart.[2] They were almost certainly commissioned to mark Sir Robert's succession to the baronetcy in October 1767, and their choice to sit to Cotes was very probably determined by the fact that Mary Cunliffe, Sir Robert's niece, had sat as a young girl to the artist in 1766.[3] Lady Cunliffe wears a shot pink and grey silk sack gown with green silk ruching and bows, a dress calculated to facilitate a characteristic display of Cotes's beautiful handling of fabric. The pose of her arms, set against the gently curved back of her garden chair, imparts a fine rhythm to the figure. Sir Robert is dressed in a reddish-brown suit and a greenish waistcoat with gold braiding. The pose of the outstretched arm holding a cane that descends at an angle towards the body is a favourite Cotes device.

The condition of WAG 1515 is poor. The work, having been separated from its companion in 1950, was damaged in a fire shortly afterwards and remains in a smoke-blackened and blistered state which conservators have deemed it prudent not to disturb (for its appearance in 1950 see fig. 13). Deciding to reunite it with its pendant at little expense, the Walker Art Gallery purchased it through a firm of fire-loss adjusters in 1953.

PROVENANCE

By family descent; [WAG 1515] Christie 1 February 1950 (108); bt. Agnew; from whom bt. by Mr Cunliffe Fraser; from whom bt. by the gallery 1953 [WAG 1514] Christie 1 February 1950 (109); bt. by the gallery.

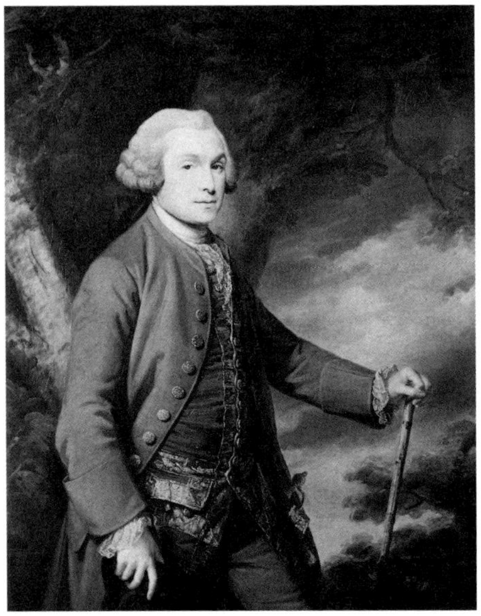

Fig. 13 WAG 1515 before being damaged by fire in 1950. Photo courtesy Sotheby's.

EXHIBITION

[WAG 1514 only] *Selected Acquisitions of the Walker Art Gallery Liverpool 1945–1955* Agnew's, London 1955 (26).[4]

NOTES

1. *MPPP*, p. 75.
2. Edward Mead Johnson: *Francis Cotes* (Oxford, 1976) pp. 77–8 (cat. 176) accepts the date of 1765 at face value. However, he had previously pointed out (*letter*, 11 October 1970, gallery files) that 'the costume and the style of the painting seem to indicate a later date' and 'this is the only instance in Cotes's *oeuvre* that I can recall in which the date is inscribed on the painting instead of appearing with the signature (as in the portrait of Sir Robert)'. Johnson's inference that the inscription was a later addition was explicitly suggested by *MPPP, loc. cit.* It seems likely that the inscriber misread the last digit on the date of the pendant; her husband could not have been referred to as 'Sir Robert' before succeeding to his title in October 1767.
3. Johnson, *op. cit.*, p. 81 (cat. 196).
4. Both portraits were loaned to the Walker Art Gallery, with other paintings from the Cunliffe family collection, between 1918 and 1928 (register of loans, gallery archives).

called

John Crome

1768–1821

A Wooded Landscape with a Grassy Knoll

WAG 2947
oil on panel,[1] 29.5 × 38 cm
date: unknown, perhaps 1825–50

When presented to the gallery in 1951, WAG 2947 was believed to be an authentic work by Crome; but the attribution has since been contested and most recent authorities have concluded that the work is not by him.[2] Nor is it related to any known Crome composition, and the amorphous, somewhat showy paint handling of the bank, the gentle and summary tonal treatment of the distant foliage, and the overall silvery tonality of the painting are all untypical of his work; however the motif of a dead tree with silhouetted branches standing on a knoll is characteristic of his landscapes, and especially familiar from his etchings.[3] Even if none of these contains these precise forms, they appear to have been a general inspiration to the artist of WAG 2947, who may be described as one of Crome's many unidentified imitators.[4]

PROVENANCE

...R. J. Marnham; ...Leggatt;[5] from whom bt. in 1951 by Owen Owen Ltd., Liverpool, for presentation to the gallery.

EXHIBITION

Selected Acquisitions of the Walker Art Gallery Liverpool 1945–1955 Agnew's, London 1955 (10).

NOTES

1. The panel has two long horizontal cracks running through the centre and has been thinned, cradled and supported by battens along the vertical edges.
2. Derek Clifford at first believed the work to be authentic, from sight of a photograph, July 1967, and dated it to 1807 (curatorial note, gallery files). However, in his and Timothy Clifford's *John Crome* (London, 1968) p. 251, the work was described as 'not by Crome, or possibly, or in part, by Crome'. WAG 2947 was accepted as a Crome by Francis Hawcroft, *verbally* (note in gallery files), but was rejected by Norman Goldberg and omitted from his *John Crome the Elder* 2 vols (Oxford, 1978). It was

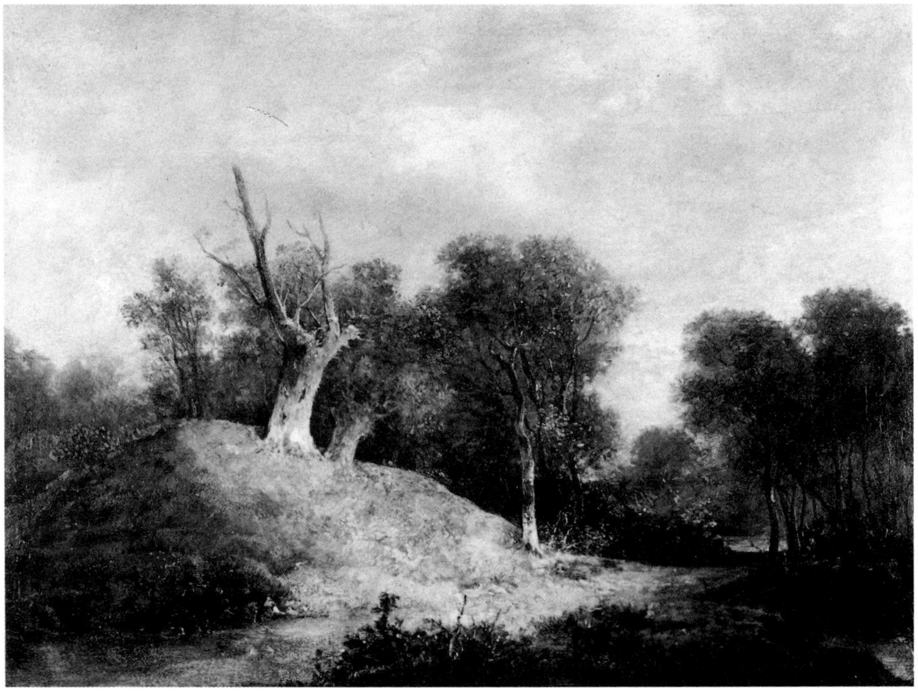

WAG 2947

also rejected, from a photograph, by Norma Watt, Castle Museum, Norwich, *verbally*, 20 April 1998.
3. See, for example, the small tree just right of centre in the 1812 etching *At Hackford* (Goldberg, *op. cit.*, vol. 1, cat. 225, p. 281) and the tree stump on a knoll at the left of *A Composition* (Goldberg, *op. cit.*, vol. 1, cat. 228, p. 282).
4. A suggested re-attribution to George Vincent was also rejected by Norma Watt, *loc. cit.*
5. According to Leggatt Bros, WAG 2947 was also in the collection of a Dr Gregory although it is unclear whether before or after it was owned by Marnham; *letter*, 29 March 1962, gallery files.

Michael Dahl

1656–1743

Henrietta Maria, Baroness Ashburnham

WAG 2359
oil on canvas, 232 × 136 cm
signed and dated *M Dahl: 1717* (lower left)
date: 1717

The sitter (1686/87–1718) was the younger daughter and third child of William 9th Earl of Derby (1656–1702) and his wife Lady Elizabeth Butler. On the death of her father without a surviving son she became the owner of the manor of Everton, north of Liverpool.[1] In 1706 she married John Annesley, 4th Earl of Anglesey, with whom she had one daughter. After his death (in 1710) she remarried on 24 July 1714, as his second wife, John Ashburnham, 3rd Baron Ashburnham. Three months before this, upon the death of her elder sister Elizabeth, she had become *suo jure* Baroness Strange. Lord and Lady Ashburnham also had one daughter, Henrietta Bridget.[2] Lady Ashburnham died on 26 June 1718, the year after WAG 2359 was painted.

Lady Ashburnham is portrayed notably informally dressed, in a blue wrapping gown over a plain linen chemise. To add to the air of fetching deshabille, she is

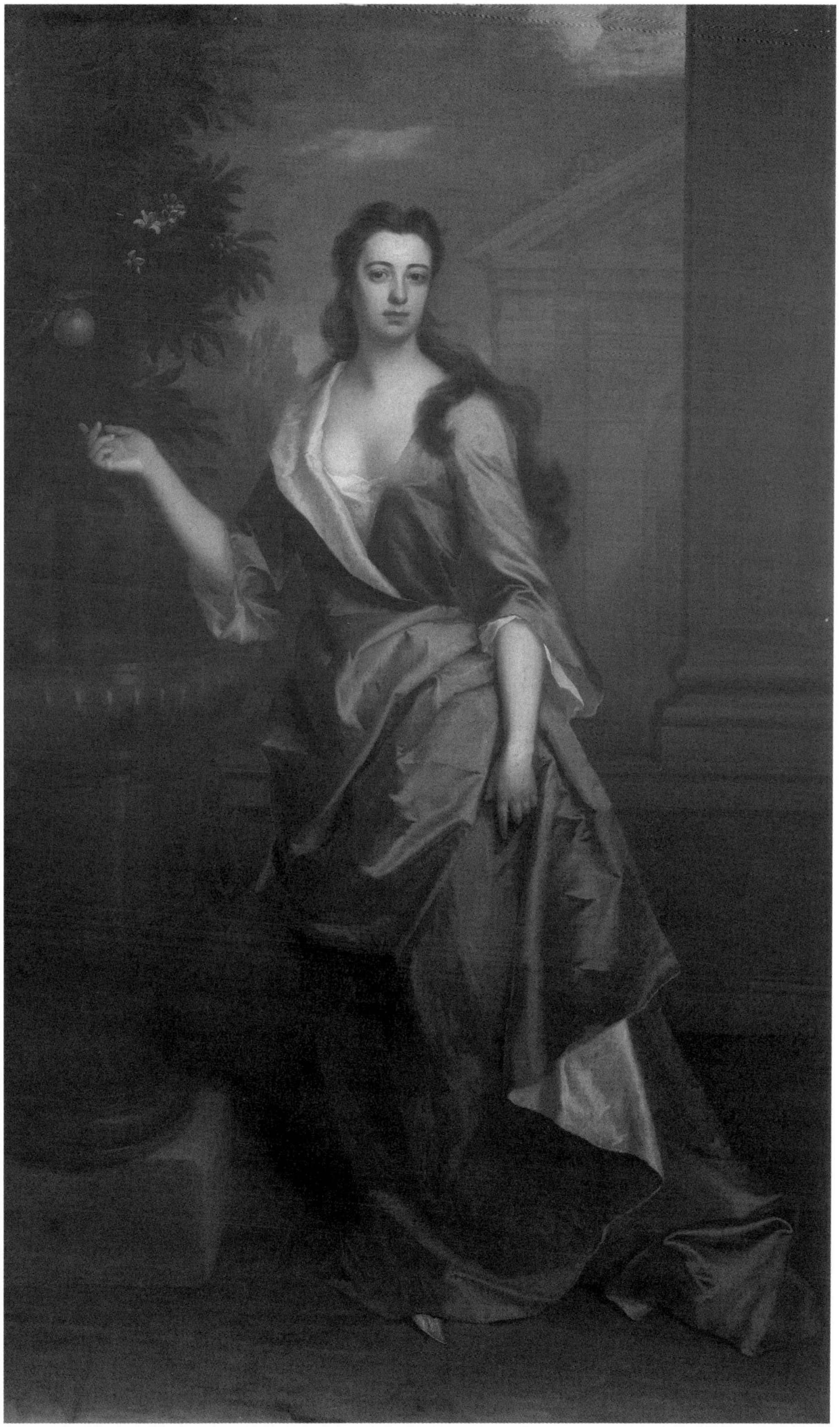

WAG 2359

keeping the gown from slipping open by pressing against it with her left elbow, while her long hair has unwound itself from her curled ringlet.[3] With her right hand she points to a small orange tree planted in a brass urn. This is probably a dual reference to her direct descent from William, Prince of Orange ('the Silent')[4] and to the fact that her husband's barony of Ashburnham had been one of the first created by William III of Orange on his succession to the throne of England in 1689.[5] As the heiress of one of the country's leading Catholic families, Lady Henrietta was unlikely to have signalled her pleasure in the Protestant succession, but her husband, although a Tory, strongly supported it,[6] and WAG 2359 was painted as a belated pendant to Dahl's portrait of the Baron.[7] Dahl also included an orange tree in a smaller portrait that he made of the Baroness.[8]

At the right-hand side a column in shadow, and behind Lady Henrietta's figure a large pedimented portico, add classical leavening to what otherwise would have been a portrait of strongly baroque character. The portico is curiously insubstantial even for a background garden ornament, but the angle of the pediment plays a crucial formal role in the construction of the design.

PROVENANCE

By descent in the family of the Earls of Ashburnham; Sotheby 15 July 1953 (108); bt. Agnew (£120); from whom bt. by Major Philip R. England; by whom presented to the gallery 1954.

EXHIBITION

Selected Acquisitions of the Walker Art Gallery Liverpool 1945–1955 Agnew's, London 1955 (22).

NOTES

1. R. Stewart-Brown: 'Maps and Plans of Liverpool and District', *Transactions of the Historic Society of Lancashire and Cheshire [for the Year 1910]* vol. 62 (1911) p. 146.
2. A full-length portrait by Hysing of 'Lady Henrietta Ashburnham with John 2nd Earl of Ashburnham' (sold Sotheby 9 July 1986 [50]) cannot therefore show the subject of WAG 2359: if of the 2nd Earl with his mother this portrait must depict Baron Ashburnham's third wife, Jemima Grey.
3. Aileen Ribeiro, *letter*, 8 November 1979, gallery files.
4. William the Silent's daughter Charlotte von Nassau-Dillenburg married Claude de la Tremoille, Duc de Thouars; their daughter Charlotte was the wife of the 7th Earl of Derby.
5. FC, p. 51. For the argument that the inclusion of an orange tree in an English portrait of this period signified allegiance to William III see John Ingamells: 'A Hanoverian Party on a Terrace by Philip Mercier', *Burlington Magazine* vol. 118 (July 1976) pp. 511–5.
6. FC, *loc. cit.*, citing Henry Horwitz, *Revolution Politicks* (Cambridge, 1968) p. 242.
7. The portrait of Baron Ashburnham was sold in the same sale as WAG 2359 (Sotheby 15 July 1953 [104]; bt. Gooden & Fox); although apparently not signed and dated it shows the sitter in Coronation robes and must have been painted directly after the coronation of George I in October 1714. It is referred to in an entry dated 25 February 1714 (i.e. 1715) in a cash book formerly at Ashburnham: 'paid Mr Dahl painter for my lord's whole length picture £44 10s –d' (quoted in the 1953 sale catalogue).
8. Sotheby 15 July 1953 (109), 108 × 76 cm.

Arthur Devis

1711–87

Mr and Mrs William Atherton

WAG 1353
oil on canvas, 91.5 × 127 cm
date: about 1742–43

William Atherton (1703–45) was a wealthy Preston woollen-draper. The third son of John and Catherine Atherton, he was active in the politics of the town from an early age, and was an ally of the artist's father Anthony Devis. He was a Burgess by 1722, served as Bailiff in 1724, the year after the elder Devis served in the same position, and was elected onto the Town Council in 1728, the year before Anthony Devis. Atherton was Mayor of Preston in 1732 and 1738, and an Alderman from 1740 until his death. He married Lucy, daughter of Richard Lonsdale of High Riley (with whom he had four sons and three daughters) in 1730. WAG 1353 was formerly assumed by family descendants to have been painted in that year on the couple's return from their honeymoon,[1] only in more recent times having been re-dated to a later period.

Although interior settings are relatively uncommon in Devis's conversation pieces, WAG 1353 has generally been held to be an at least partially accurate representation of a room on the upper storey of the Athertons' house on the east side of Preston's Market Square. The view of a country park though the window is fictive, for the area in the immediate vicinity 'comprised a network of narrow passages leading through butchers' shops and slaughter houses'.[2] However, the furnishings have been assumed to be the Athertons' actual possessions. These include a large Chinese jar in the fireplace, a fine cabinet of around 1730, perhaps by the Lancaster firm of Gillow,[3]

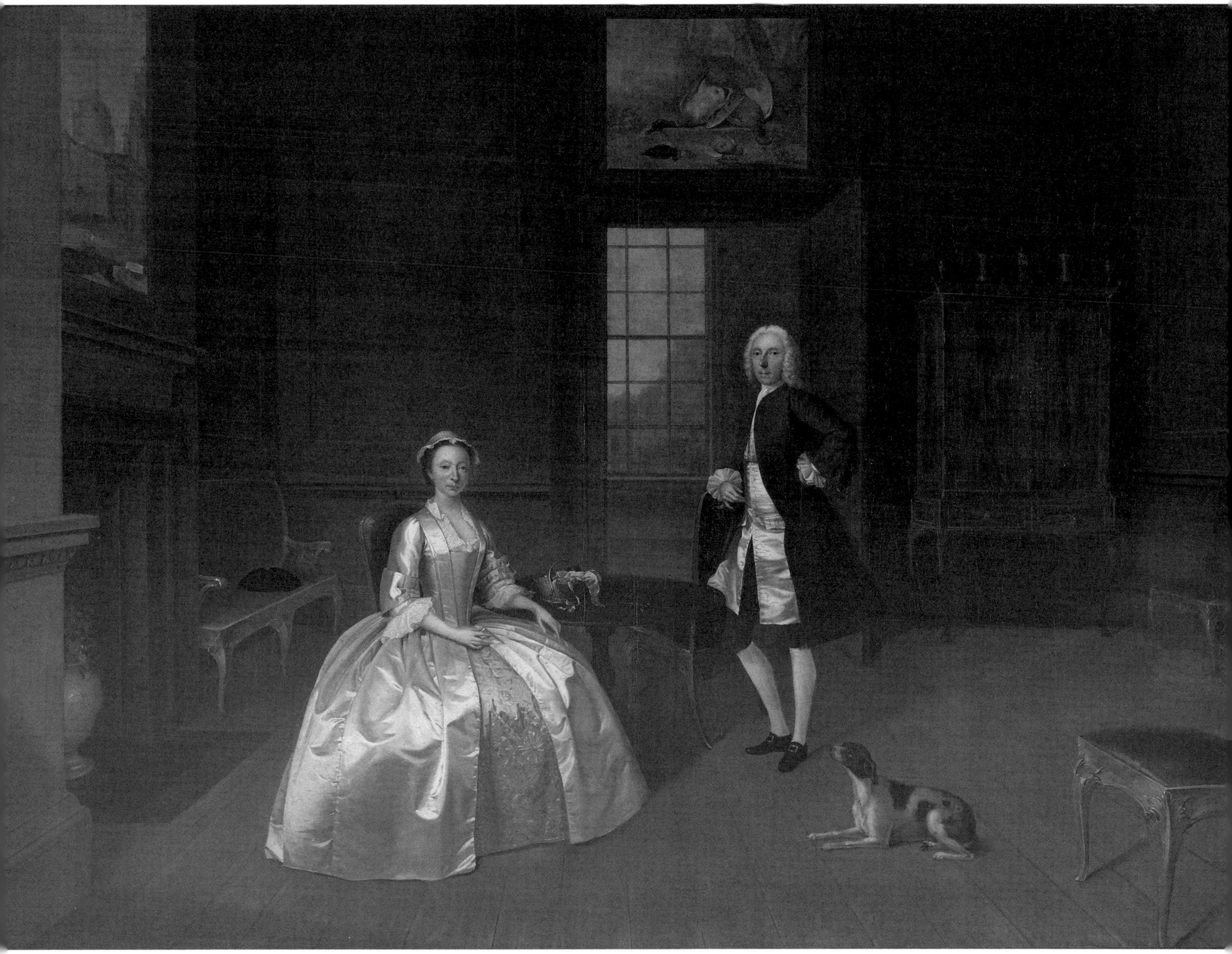

WAG 1353

a high-quality suite of chairs, stools and settee with gilt frames covered in green velvet, and two paintings (including, over the fireplace, a capriccio with a view of the Castel Sant 'Angelo in Rome that has been supposed to have been painted by Devis himself).[4] The sparseness of the furnishing of the room has been regarded as unlikely to be a true reflection of the Athertons' lifestyle and as more probably a pictorial invention on the artist's part designed to accentuate a feeling of space and grandeur around the figures.[5] Both husband and wife are noticeably formally attired, he in a long silk waistcoat and she in a satin skirt with a front opening revealing a quilted petticoat. It has been pointed out that the stiff pose of Mrs Atherton is close to illustrations in François Nivelon's *Rudiments of Genteel Behaviour* (1737) and with her needlework basket at her left hand she is the embodiment of correct comportment and accomplishment as valued by her class.[6] The painting has been recognised as one of the culminating works of the first phase of Devis's career in Lancashire, before his family moved to London, and has been dated to about 1742 to 1744.[7]

Between 2003 and 2007 WAG 1353 underwent a major conservation treatment to remove areas of blanching on the paint surface: these had been caused by lead salts within the paint reacting to environmental changes.[8]

PROVENANCE

By descent to Frances, Lady Daresbury; from whom bt. 1940.

EXHIBITIONS

Loan Exhibition of English Conversation Pieces 25 Park Lane, London 1930 (94); *Lancashire Art* Harris Museum and Art Gallery, Preston 1937 (23); *Some Acquisitions of the Walker Art Gallery Liverpool 1935–1945* National Gallery, London 1945 (4); *One Hundred Years of British Painting 1730–1830* Museu de Arte Antiga, Lisbon and Prado, Madrid 1949 (14); *British Painting 1730–1850, Hogarth to Turner* Kunsthalle, Hamburg and tour of Scandinavia 1949–50 (36); *Painting and Sculpture in England 1700–1750* Walker Art Gallery 1958 (7); *The Conversation Piece in Georgian England* Iveagh Bequest, Kenwood 1965 (11); *The Conversation Piece: Arthur Devis and his Contemporaries* Yale Center for British Art, New Haven 1980 (11); *Polite Society by Arthur Devis* Harris Museum and Art Gallery, Preston and National Portrait Gallery, London 1983–84 (14); *Home and Garden* Geffrye Museum, London 2003 (8); *British Vision: Observation and Imagination in British Art* Museum voor Schone Kunsten, Ghent 2007–08 (2).

NOTES

1. Information supplied by Lady Daresbury in 1940; note in gallery files.
2. Stephen Sartin: *Polite Society by Arthur Devis*, exh. cat., Harris Museum, Preston and National Portrait Gallery, London (1983) p. 46 (cat. 14).
3. For the cabinet's date see David Dewing *Home and Garden*, exh. cat., Geffrye Museum, London (2003) p. 30 (cat. 8); for the 'similarity' to cabinets by Gillow, see John Cornforth, 'Intimacy of the Conversation Piece', *Country Life* vol. 138 (1 July 1965) p. 13, followed by Ellen D'Oench: *The Conversation Piece: Arthur Devis and his Contemporaries*, exh. cat., Yale Center for British Art, New Haven (1980) p. 48 (cat. 11).
4. D'Oench, *loc. cit.*, pointing out that this work is more detailed than most of the *capriccii* in Devis's painted interiors.
5. Dewing, *loc. cit.*
6. Jacques Carré: 'La représentation du savoir-vivre dans la *Conversation-piece* anglaise au XVIIIe siècle', in Alain Montandon, ed.: *Convivialité et Politesse. Du gigot, des mots et autres savoir-vivre* (Clermont-Ferrand, 1993) p. 98; and see also Dewing, *loc. cit.*
7. D'Oench, *loc. cit.*, and also her *Arthur Devis*, unpublished Ph.D. thesis, Yale University (1979) pp. 60–1, dates WAG 1353 to 1743–44; Sartin, *loc. cit.*, suggests 1742–44. He points out that Atherton was appointed Steward of the Guild Marchant of Preston in 1742, though he does not explicitly connect the commissioning of Devis's portrait to this event.
8. Rebecca Kench, treatment report dated August 2007, gallery files.

William Dobson

1611–46

The Executioner with the Head of John the Baptist

WAG 2993
oil on canvas, 110.5 × 130 cm
date: about 1640–43

Described as 'the only English Caravaggesque picture known',[1] WAG 2993 is a copy of an early work by the Dutch artist Matthias Stom (or Stomer). Stom's original (private collection, UK; fig. 14) is thought to have been painted in the late 1620s. It may have been brought to England by one of his presumed teachers, Gerrit van Honthorst, when the latter arrived at the invitation of King Charles I in 1628, or if not, then in response to budding connoisseurship of Caravaggist painting in royalist circles in the 1630s created in the wake of Honthorst's brief stay.[2] That Stom's picture had passed into the collection of one of the king's courtiers, or was at least well known in royalist circles, may be inferred from the tradition that Dobson painted his copy in Oxford when he was effectively official painter in the city to the exiled king and his courtiers; and its celebrity is also suggested by the fact that Dobson particularly cherished his own copy of it and is supposed to have refused to part with it for as long as he lived. This was stated by Carlo Gambarini in his 1731 *Description of the Earl of Pembroke's Pictures*.[3] In the same year George Vertue wrote after a visit to Wilton, 'by Dobson. A decollation of St John. which Sr. P. Lelly reckoned the chief history picture that he did. – (the St. John was Prince Rupert himself. as I have heard. painted at Oxford.)'.[4] Vertue's story that the model for the head of St John was Prince Rupert is disproved by the fact that the face is identical in Stom's original, and it

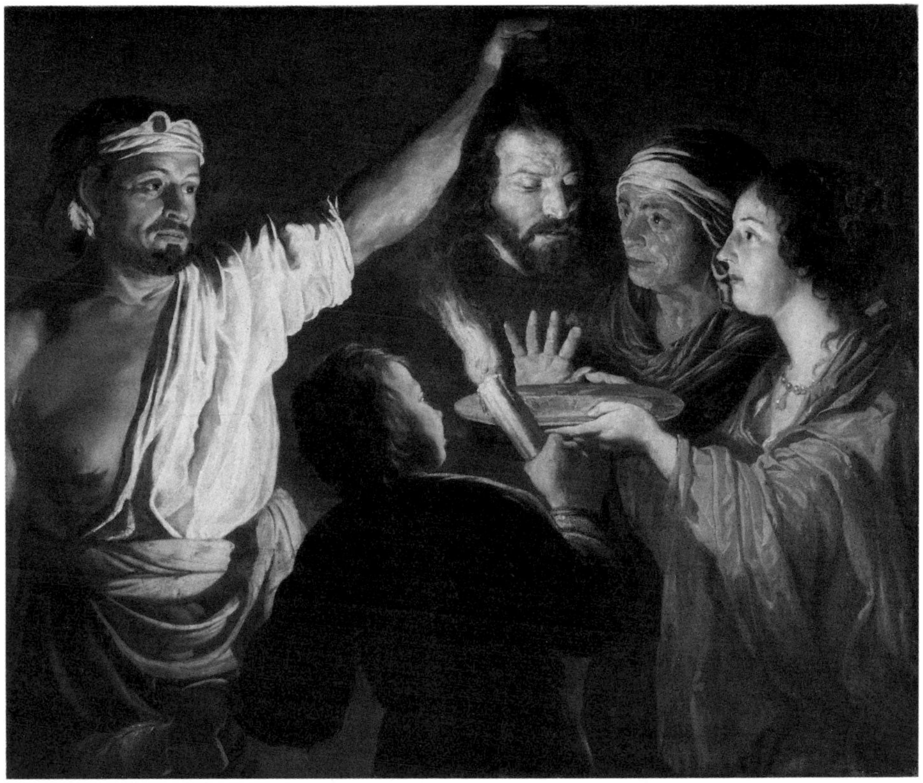

WAG 2993

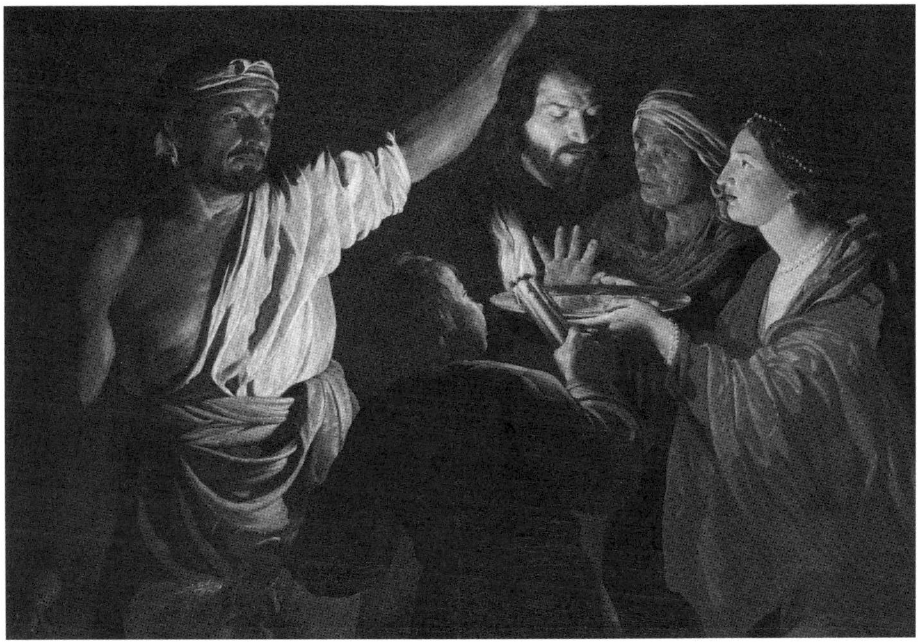

Fig. 14 *The Executioner with the Head of John the Baptist* by Matthias Stom, oil on canvas. Private collection, UK; photo R. B. Fleming & Co.

seems likely that both he and Gambarini were recycling stories purveyed by the guides at Wilton House. Recently it has been proposed, *pace* Vertue, that Dobson is less likely to have painted WAG 2993 in Oxford than in London, around 1640.[5]

Dobson's work is very close to Stom's but differs in two chief particulars. First, although it is virtually the same height it is 22 cm narrower, and lacks the right arm of the executioner present in the original; this suggests that the canvas has been trimmed at the left. Second, the face of Salome is treated more naturalistically by Dobson. The implication of this is unclear, but the resemblance between the two faces is too great to allow that Dobson was portraying a specific model and it seems most likely that he regarded Stom's waxy treatment of Salome's face as an artistic solecism.

Nevertheless, the fact that Dobson had thought fit to vary the face of Salome may have influenced the artist Isaac Fuller when he copied WAG 2993 sometime before his death in 1672. According to Vertue – reporting a conversation with Fuller's pupil C. Woodfield (d. 1724) some years before he saw Dobson's original at Wilton – the woman in Fuller's copy was Fuller's mistress, and the old woman, in his version holding a bag to put the Baptist's head in, was his mistress's mother. Vertue added, presumably from Woodfield's information, that Dobson's original was 'afterwards' in the possession of a tavern keeper in Oxford, a telling remark that suggests that it was not when Fuller copied it.[6]

In 1694 WAG 2993 was purchased from a Mrs Hall, who has been tentatively identified as the widow of Anthony Hall (d. 1691) landlord of the Mermaid Inn, Oxford from 1667, by Thomas Herbert, 8th Earl of Pembroke. The negotiation was conducted from London by the Earl's friend, the author John Aubrey, who had known Dobson in his teens at Oxford, in correspondence with Edward Lhuyd in Oxford. From the letters which passed between these two men, it appears that Mrs Hall was acting on behalf of an obscure 'Mrs Walker' (perhaps a mistake for Miss Whicker, the wife of John Moreton who leased the Mermaid Inn from 1654.) Mrs Hall valued the painting at £20, but was eventually persuaded to sell it for £14.[7] It is not clear how Lord Pembroke's interest was stimulated, but it seems very likely that Aubrey himself, who had been familiar with the collections at Wilton since a boy in the 1630s, put him up to it.[8]

The painting remained a well-known ornament of the collections at Wilton, being described (as well as by Vertue and Gambarini) by Horace Walpole, in his *Anecdotes of Painting*[9] and by Gustav Waagen in his *Treasures of Art in Great Britain*, who observed that Dobson had modelled his conception and effect on Honthorst.[10] In 1763 James Kennedy, in his *Description of the Curiosities in Wilton House*, enthused, 'The Painter is an Honour to the *English* Nation. This Picture is so finely painted, and with such strong Expressions, as to make him inferior to few of the best *Italian* Masters. King *Charles* 1st called him the *English* Tintoret…'.[11] In 1786 John Dean published a mezzotint after the painting. This adds a strip at the top of the composition so that the whole of the executioner's hand holding the head of the Baptist is visible, while truncating an equivalent amount of the composition at the bottom, cutting off the hand of the boy holding the taper.

PROVENANCE

Retained by the artist until his death; …'an Oxford tavern keeper', probably Mrs Anthony Hall; from whom bt. in 1694 for £14 through John Aubrey by Thomas, 8th Earl of Pembroke; by descent at Wilton House; Christie 22 June 1951 (34, part);[12] bt. Arcade Gallery (£73 10s.); from whom bt. by Sir Thomas Barlow; from whom bt. by the gallery through Colnaghi 1955.

EXHIBITIONS

Festival Exhibition of Art During the Civil War Worcester 1951 (15); *William Dobson 1611–1646* Tate Gallery, London 1951 (26); *William Dobson 1611–1646* National Portrait Gallery, London 1983 (4); *Matthias Stom: Isaac Blessing Jacob* Barber Institute of Fine Arts, Birmingham 1999–2000 (12).

NOTES

1. Benedict Nicolson: *The International Caravaggesque Movement: Lists of Pictures by Caravaggio and His Followers throughout Europe from 1590 to 1650* (Oxford, 1979) p. 46.
2. Richard Verdi: *Matthias Stom: Isaac Blessing Jacob*, exh. cat., Barber Institute of Fine Arts, Birmingham (1999) pp. 33–4. The identity of Dobson's prototype emerged in 1952 and was published in that year by Benedict Nicolson: 'Caravaggio and the Netherlands', *Burlington Magazine* vol. 94 (September 1952) p. 251; Oliver Millar, in the catalogue of the Dobson exhibition at the Tate Gallery the previous year, had described Dobson's work as 'clearly a copy of a (so far unidentified) Caravaggesque picture but of some independent value as an indication of Dobson's interests.'
3. Count Carlo Gambarini: *A Description of the Earl of Pembroke's Pictures* (Westminster, 1731) pp. IX, 79.
4. Lord Ilchester and H, M. Hake, eds. 'Vertue Notebooks Volume IV', *Walpole Society* vol. 24, 1935–36 (1936) p. 19. Vertue's reference to Lely's opinion is taken from Gambarini (see n. 3).
5. Malcolm Rogers: *William Dobson 1611–46* exh. cat., National Portrait Gallery, London (1983) p. 27. It is perhaps coincidental, but seems curious nevertheless, that at Oxford Dobson set up his studio in rooms in St John's College (Ian Roy and Dietrich Reinhart: 'Oxford and the Civil Wars', in N. Tyacke, ed.: *The History of the University of Oxford* [Oxford, 1997] p. 705).
6. Mrs A. Esdaile, ed.: 'Vertue Notebooks Volume I', *Walpole Society* vol. 18, 1929–1930 (1930) p. 135.
7. For a full discussion of this episode see Kate Bennett: 'John Aubrey, William and Judith Dobson and the 8th Earl of Pembroke: The Provenance of William Dobson's *Executioner with John the Baptist's Head*', *Notes and Queries* NS vol. 49, no. 3 (September 2002) pp. 352–5.
8. Aubrey had stayed in touch with Dobson's widow Judith and had bought at least one painting from her in the 1660s (Bennett, *op. cit.*, p. 353) so he would no doubt have been aware of the painting's whereabouts. But it is also tempting to wonder whether he was aware of a (now unknown) historical link between Dobson's painting and the Earl's grandfather, Philip 5th Earl of Pembroke, one of the outstanding connoisseurs of painting in Charles I's circle in the 1630s (who, however, had drifted towards the Parliamentary side by the time Charles's court was resident in Oxford in the early 1640s).
9. Horace Walpole *Anecdotes of Painting in England… with additions by the Rev. James Dallaway* ed. R. N. Wornum, 3 vols (London, 1862) vol. 2, p. 2.
10. Gustav Waagen: *Treasures of Art in Great Britain*, 3 vols (London, 1854), vol. 3, p. 154.
11. James Kennedy: *A Description of the Curiosities in Wilton House* (Salisbury, 1763) p. 69.
12. Sold, with *The Triumphal Return of David* by Antonio Tempesta, as 'G. Honthorst, after…by W. Dobson'.

Samuel Drummond

1765–1844

The Death of Nelson

WAG 3088
oil on canvas,[1] 315 × 409 cm
signed: *Drummond* (lower right)
date: 1806–07

Drummond spent his teens as an apprentice in the Baltic fleet of London, during which time he is said to have been present at three naval engagements;[2] and of all the painters who made artistic capital from the death of Admiral Nelson at the battle of Trafalgar on 21 October 1805, it was he who explored the subject's potential most fully and over the longest period of time. His initial response was no doubt conditioned by the knowledge that Benjamin West was already working on a full-scale treatment; West's painting was virtually complete by mid-March 1806 and went on public display at his house two months later where it drew thousands of visitors (see p. 241). Probably unwilling overtly to compete with the older artist, Drummond contented himself with showing a *Sketch for a Death of Lord Nelson* at the 1806 Royal Academy, biding his time until the following season, when he showed two major paintings of the subject at the British Institution. In 1812 and 1813 he exhibited what may have been the same two pictures, or may have been new ones, at the Liverpool Academy;[3] and in 1825 he showed a *Battle of Trafalgar* at the British Institution (cat.

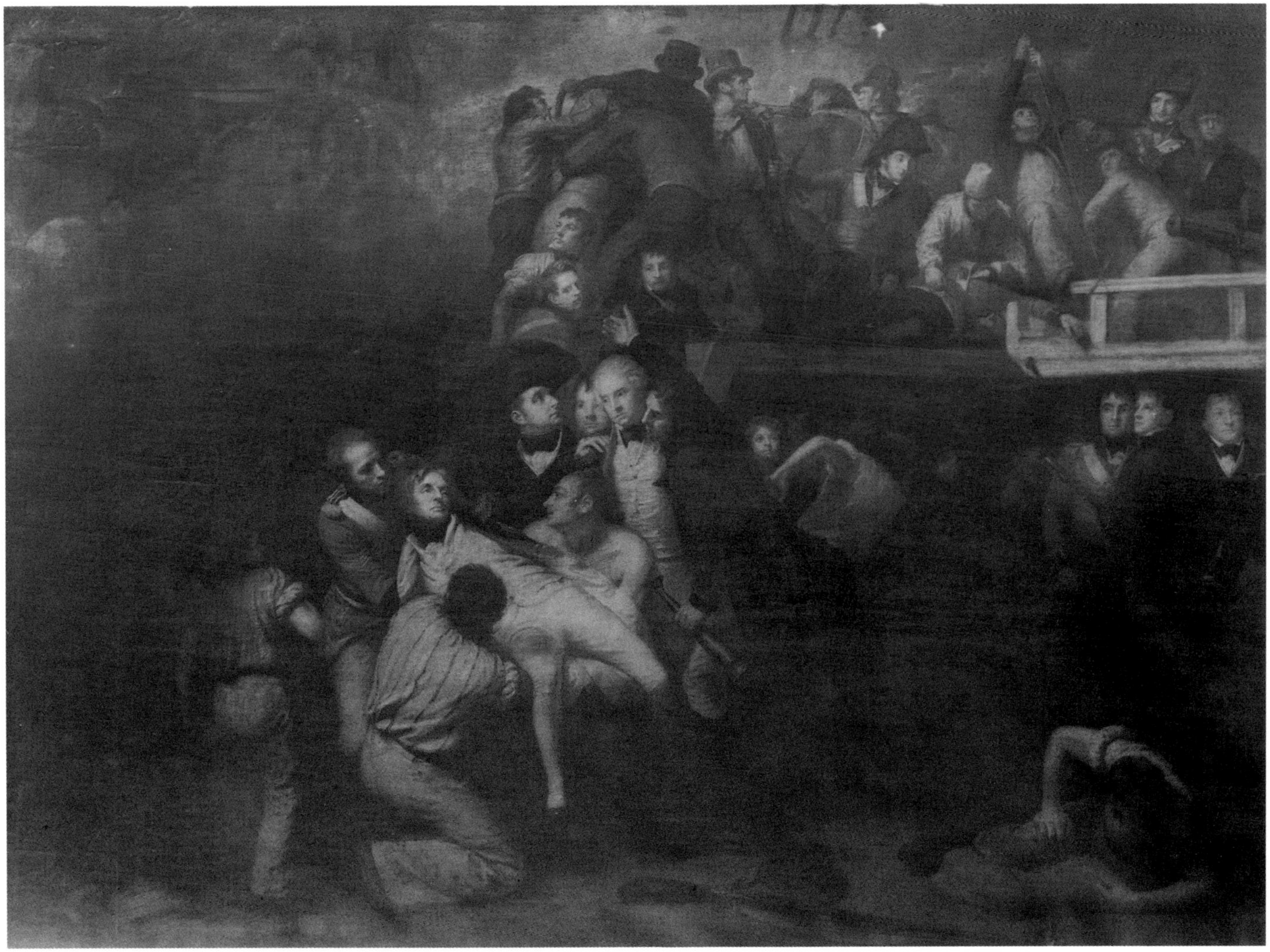

WAG 3088

262); it was probably this canvas that was shown, under the same title, at the Royal Birmingham Society of Arts in 1829 (cat. 313).

WAG 3088 is identifiable as one of the two exhibits at the British Institution in 1807: no. 126, whose measurements were given in the catalogue as 10 feet by 13 feet 6 inches. These are the approximate dimensions of WAG 3088, and in any case none of Drummond's other known treatments of the subject was on anything like this colossal scale. The other Nelson subject shown in the same exhibition (cat. 10) is also identified: it is the upright composition measuring 125 × 100 cm that was with the Sabin Galleries London in 1971, housed in its magnificent original frame bearing the legend *Trafalgar*, which accounts for the dimensions recorded in the 1807 British Institution catalogue of 68 × 58 inches.[4] Drummond's own etching of *The Death of Nelson*, which he published on 9 October 1809 (fig. 15) is based on this canvas. That Drummond chose it as the basis of his print suggests he regarded it as the more satisfactory of his two 1807 exhibits and it is thus probably slightly the later of the two.

The relationship between Drummond's other exhibited versions of the subject and the canvases known today remains conjectural. The latter are:

(a) 76 × 64 cm; Government Art Collection; purchased from Sir Bruce Ingram in 1963; this is a reduced and simplified version of the Sabin Galleries painting.

(b) 58 × 74 cm; also Government Art Collection; purchased from Sotheby, 12 January 1980 (60) (fig. 16). In

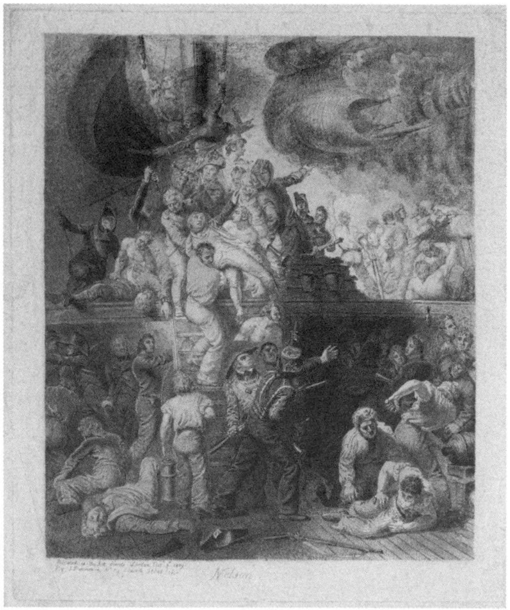

Fig. 15 *The Death of Nelson* by Samuel Drummond, etching. © National Portrait Gallery, London.

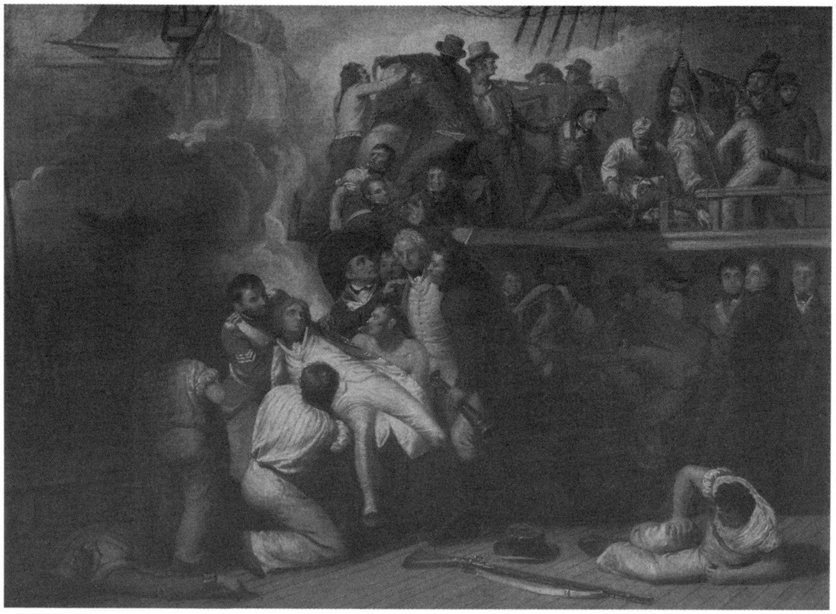

Fig. 16 *The Death of Nelson* by Samuel Drummond, oil on canvas. © Crown copyright: UK Government Art Collection.

compositional terms, this is the closest to WAG 3088 and, although fully finished, could be regarded as a preparation for it. It may therefore be a candidate for the 'sketch' exhibited at the Royal Academy in 1806 (although (d) below seems a better one). W. T. Annis's engraving of Drummond's subject (undated, but believed to have been published about 1810) follows this version.[5] A further variant of it is depicted in Drummond's *Self-portrait Painting 'The Death of Lord Nelson'* (Royal Collection).

(c) 77.5 × 98 cm; Castle Museum, Norwich; purchased from Frost & Reed Ltd, 1972; previously auctioned at Christie 24 May 1968 (36) (fig. 17). This is a landscape-format elaboration of the Sabin picture, in which Nelson is being carried below from an upper deck and where the composition most obviously strives for a religious feeling; the parallels with Rubens's celebrated *Descent from the Cross* in Antwerp Cathedral are here unmistakeable. It has been tentatively identified as the picture exhibited at the British Institution in 1825.[6]

(d) 89 × 125 cm; Ben Burgess Nelson Memorabilia Collection, Norfolk; purchased from a private collection at an auction in Ireland (fig. 18). Although this canvas contains several of the motifs present in WAG 3088 and other versions – the slumped, splay-legged figure of Nelson; the powder-monkey with the rolled sleeves, the dying sailor in the foreground (badly out of proportion here) – the below-decks conception is markedly different, and closest to historical reality. It is also very loosely handled. Accordingly, it seems to have much the best claim to be the 'sketch' shown at the RA in 1806. If this is correct, Drummond's approach from this initial take on the subject can be seen as having become gradually more idealised and pictorial, with Nelson being depicted progressively higher up the ship and in more Christ-like guise.

Three further variants of the above (together with a drawing marking the evolution of (d) into the Sabin Gallery painting) are in the National Maritime Museum, Greenwich:

(e) 58 × 71 cm (inv. 0543); a coarse but vibrant sketch on panel related to the foreground group in WAG 3088 but varying some of the figures.

(f) 71 × 83 cm (inv. 0547): a less finished and less detailed version of (c) above, although larger, which suggests it may be an abandoned second version rather than a preliminary trial.

(g) 74 × 90 cm (inv. 0551): this is a larger version of (b) above, somewhat coarser in quality. The relation between the two remains hard to determine.

Nothing is known about the gestation and early history of WAG 3088. When it was shown at the British Institution in 1807, it was titled *The Death of Nelson, with Portraits*, implying that Drummond,

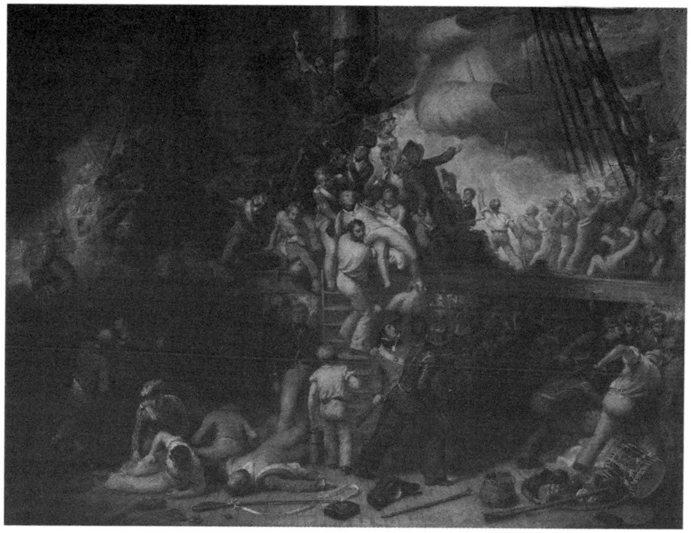

Fig. 17 *The Death of Nelson* by Samuel Drummond, oil on canvas. Castle Museum Norwich; photo courtesy Leger Galleries.

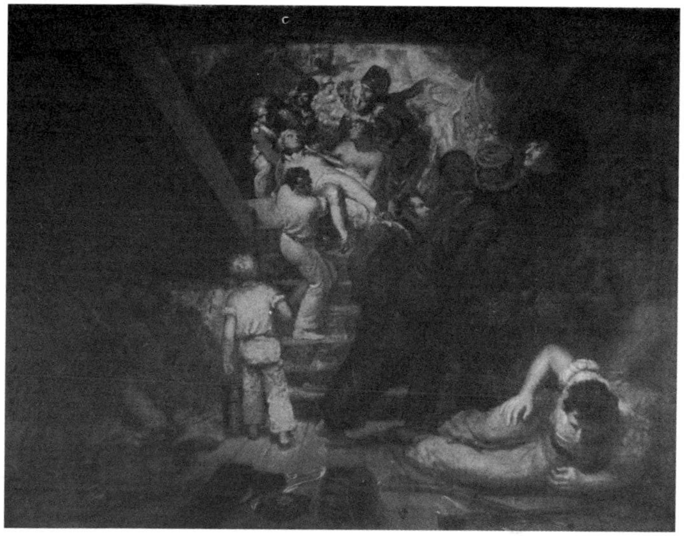

Fig. 18 *The Death of Nelson* by Samuel Drummond, oil on canvas. Ben Burgess Memorabilia Collection, Great Yarmouth; photo courtesy J. Saunders, Liverpool.

as West had before him, had sought out officers and sailors from the *Victory* to sit for the picture in the interest of historical verisimilitude. The figure in the white waistcoat in the centre looking grimly down on the dying Nelson has been identified as Captain Hardy and the man behind him as William Bligh.[7] It is evident, however, that in contrast to West's polite treatment of record, Drummond's vision was always less decorous. The figure of Nelson is calculatedly ungainly and off-centre, far from the centre of attention.

In 1839 the *Art Union* reported that 'Mr Drummond is about to dispose, by raffle, of his large painting The Death of Nelson…this work, executed when he was in his vigour, obtained, in 1826, the first premium at the British Institution, although the painter had no fewer than thirty-eight competitors'.[8] Drummond did not exhibit at the BI in 1826 and it seems unlikely that this is a reference to his *Battle of Trafalgar* shown there in 1825, whose framed dimensions were recorded in the catalogue as only 50 × 60 inches, so there seems no good reason to discount the likelihood that this is a garbled reference to WAG 3088.

PROVENANCE

…Henry W. Hoskins, Hinton St George, Somerset by 1864;[9] from whom bt. 1888.

EXHIBITION

BI 1807 (126).

NOTES

1. Re-lined; the dimensions are those of the twentieth-century lining canvas; the dimensions of the surviving original canvas are approximately 302 × 407 cm. The painting is in poor condition, with extensive vertical cracking and paint losses over the whole surface; these are the result of the painting having been rolled up and inadequately stored in one of the gallery's cellars during the period 1888–1959. In the latter year the painting was unrolled and examined, and it was subsequently re-lined, re-stretched and stabilised (conservation notes in gallery files). The work was rolled from the left-hand edge towards the right, as may be deduced from the fact that the distance between damaged areas progressively widens towards the right-hand side. In May 1873, while the painting was on deposit in the Free Public Library, the Liverpool painter William J. J. C. Bond supervised its cleaning (*Libraries, Museums and Arts Committee Extracts* [7 May 1873]).
2. G. Quilley: 'Drummond, Samuel', *ODNB* vol. 16, pp. 980–1.
3. *LAOE*, p. 203; the 1812 exhibit (cat. 209) was accompanied by the quotation, 'When victory shines on life's last ebbing sands / O who would not die with the brave' – Burns. The 1813 exhibit, no. 26 in the catalogue, was priced at £300, a sum indicative of a large picture.
4. Christie 22 January 1971 (165). Quilley, *loc. cit.*, states that the *Death of Nelson* exhibited at the BI in 1807 was well reviewed by the press but he does not differentiate between the two versions.
5. A same-size variant of this painting was formerly with Fleming Galleries, London and Portsmouth (photograph in the Witt Library, Courtauld Institute of Art); another version, recorded as 72 × 90 cm, probably not autograph, was in the Ashton collection, London, 1954. The latter may be a copy of (g) above.
6. Norfolk Museums Service website, accessed 16 March 2009.
7. Curatorial note in gallery files.
8. *Art Union* (1839) p. 105.
9. Hoskins offered WAG 3088 to Liverpool Corporation on loan, for public exhibition in June 1864; in October the same year, after it had been put on display in the Library, he offered it for sale for £350 (stating that his late uncle had given £500 for it). This offer was declined (*Libraries, Museums and Arts Committee Extracts* [1877] *passim*). The gallery eventually bought the work for £50.

Henry Fuseli

1741–1825

The Death of Oedipus

WAG 1537
oil on canvas, 150 × 166.5 cm
date: 1783–84

The subject of WAG 1537 is taken from Sophocles's play *Oedipus at Colonus*, the second of his so-called Theban trilogy. Oedipus, King of Thebes, blinded himself when he discovered that, in fulfilment of a prophecy, he had killed his father and married his mother, acts which had brought a curse on his kingdom. Banished from Thebes, but accompanied by his two daughters Antigone and Ismene, the old man is in exile at Colonus where, in the grove of the Furies, he receives the portents of his death. He bids his daughters farewell and enters the underworld. In the play, a messenger describes the moment:

It thundered from the netherworld; the maids Shivered, and crouching at their father's knees, Wept, beat their breast, and uttered a long wail...[1]

Fuseli pasted these words, written in the original Greek,[2] on his preliminary drawing for WAG 1537, a gesture calling attention to his abilities as a classical scholar. The works of Sophocles, written in the second half of the fifth century BCE, were little known in Britain before the last two decades of the eighteenth century, but then Greek drama began to enjoy a vogue. New translations of Euripides and Aeschylus were published by Revd Robert Potter in 1778 and 1781 respectively and he was working on a translation of Sophocles at the same time as Fuseli was painting WAG 1537. Thus Fuseli with this work was positioning himself on the cusp of literary fashion and emphasising his advanced tastes.

The finished painting was exhibited at the Royal Academy in 1784, two years before the appearance of a companion work illustrating an earlier episode in the same play, *Oedipus Cursing His Son Polynices* (National Gallery of Art, Washington DC; fig. 19). Despite the two-year gap between the two pictures, the assumption that they were conceived separately is premature. A finished preparatory drawing for *Oedipus Cursing Polynices*, in reverse to the painting but otherwise closely comparable, is dated *ROMA DEC 1777* (Nationalmuseum Stockholm) and other drawings for the subject are in the Roman Sketchbook of 1776–78 in the British Museum.[3] Fuseli's preliminary drawing for WAG 1537 bears a manuscript inscription (again pasted on): *Lond. Jun.* 83.[4]

The painting was not widely noticed at the exhibition. The *London Chronicle* and *Public Advertiser*, in their (shared) opening survey, observed that 'Mr Fuseli's *Oedipus* has great merit'[5] but longer mentions did not appear until the exhibition was well under way. The *Morning Post and Daily Advertiser* wrote,

We confess ourselves to be great enthusiasts in favour of this master; the subject of the picture under our consideration is truly sublime, and the artist has conceived it with the utmost vigour and enthusiasm. The tone of the colouring is to a miracle what the subject required and we look over those inadequacies in drawing that only offend our eyes, when there is so much for the mind to enjoy and dwell upon. Fuseli will draw, while those who now possess little else, will find it impossible to reach those higher excellencies that he is master of in so great a degree.[6]

The *Morning Chronicle and London Advertiser*, on the other hand, commented,

Fuseli, seldom appears otherwise to us, than as an active mind, strongly deviating into the greatest errors – his 147, *Oedipus and his daughters, is to us an attempt at the heroic degenerating into the most ridiculous bombast. – The countenance and figure of Oedipus are written and shrivelled into nothing. – As to the daughters, at least she on the right hand of the father, the appearance of her Dorsal muscles is yet more ludicrous! – Handy dandy! – which is the top of her back and which is the bottom?*[7]

Comparison of WAG 1537 with the preliminary drawing and also with William Ward's mezzotint, published 26 August 1785 (fig. 20),[8] suggests that the painting has been cut down slightly on both sides, bringing the daughters' feet much closer to the edges of the picture. The effect of this is to increase the formal rigour of the triangular design, and it was probably done by Fuseli himself soon after Ward's print appeared.[9] The artificial interlocking of the three figures and the curious positioning of the figure of Antigone in particular, with her facial expression scarcely legible, has received criticism, yet the mannerism seems central to Fuseli's artistic purpose, encouraging in the viewer a sense of the elemental and supernatural character of the scene and its distance from daily reality.[10] The positioning of Oedipus's hands not only plays a key compositional role but unlocks the recognition that being blind, the king cannot see the portents of his death; he hears them, in the form of a roll of thunder. Fuseli himself may have intended Oedipus's gesture as expressive of terror; he later supposedly said that the 'old man... was afraid of going to Hell'.[11] The other portent of his death, the flash of lightning visible in Ward's engraving, cannot now be seen in WAG 1537, which has darkened and is in worn condition.

The two Oedipus canvases were both bought by William Roscoe and they were almost certainly his first purchases of paintings from Fuseli. The artist offered them to Roscoe in October 1791

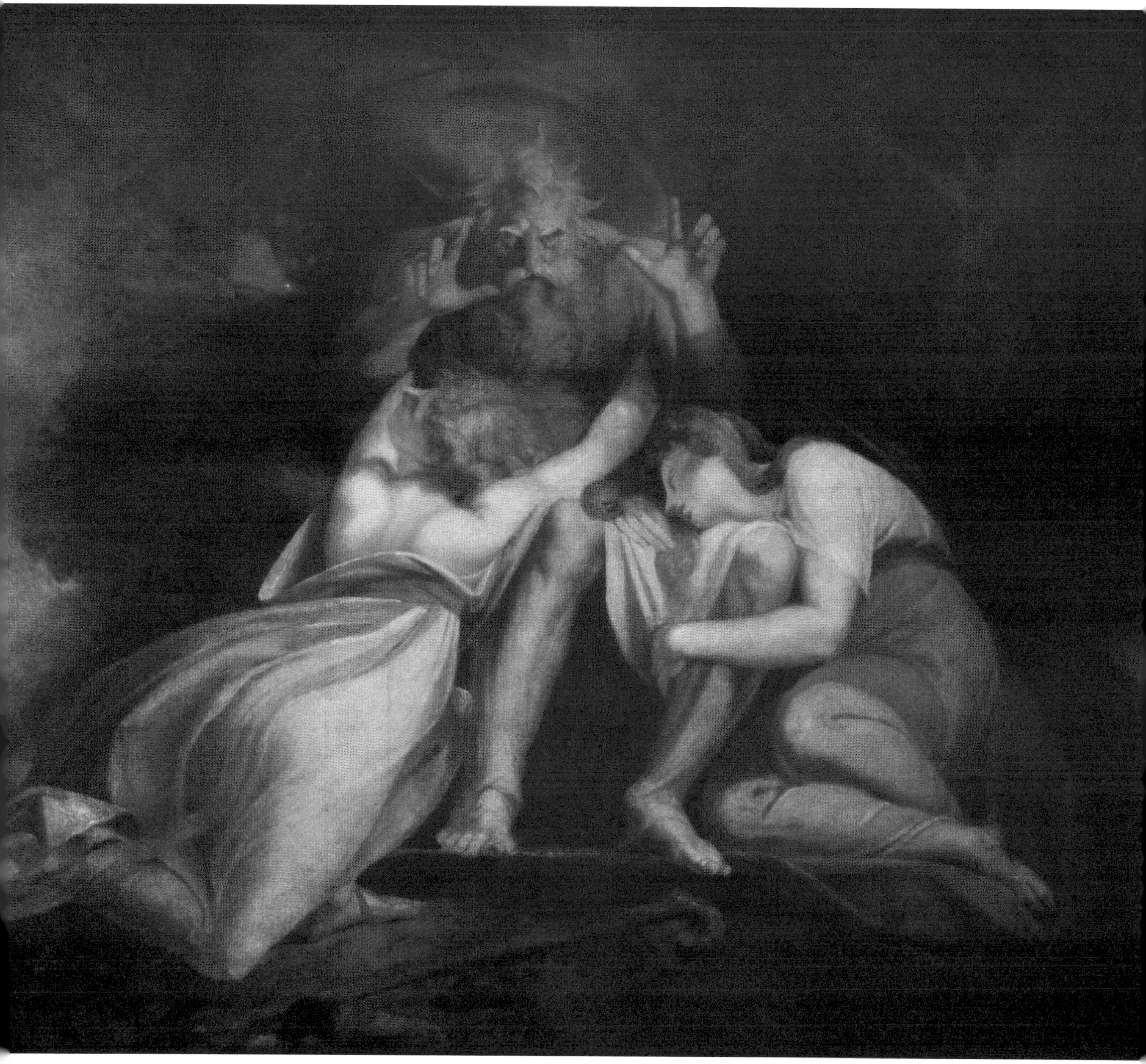

WAG 1537

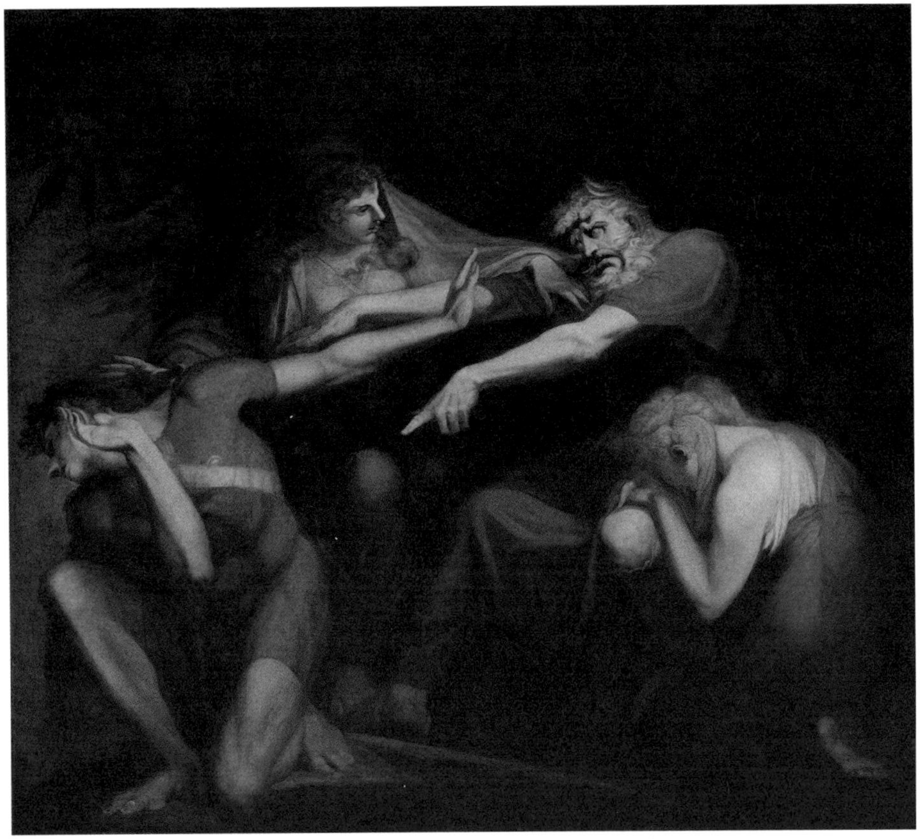

Fig. 19 *Oedipus Cursing Polynices* by Henry Fuseli, oil on canvas. National Gallery of Art, Washington D.C., Paul Mellon Collection. Image courtesy National Gallery of Art, Washington D.C.

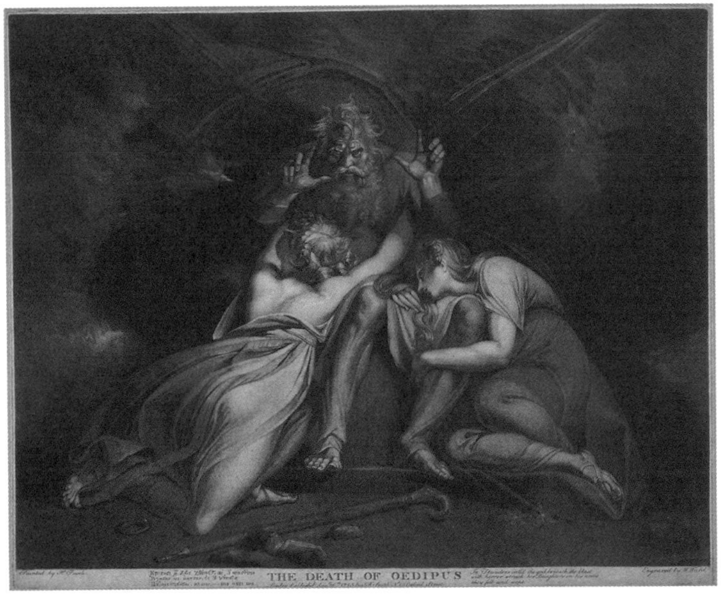

Fig. 20 *Oedipus and his Daughters* after Henry Fuseli, engraving by William Ward. Christie 18 March 2008 (530); © Christie's Images Limited (2011).

and sent them to Liverpool (separately, because Roscoe appears to have expressed some reservation about one of them, which he later retracted) in 1792.[12] Their acquisition was a milestone in Roscoe's long commitment to Fuseli's art,[13] and an early consensus about their place in the culture of Liverpool is detectible in James Aikin's 'rescuing' of WAG 1537 from London and his eventual presentation of the work to the city, while the Walker Art Gallery was being built and shortly before it opened.

PROVENANCE

Bt. from Fuseli by William Roscoe; Winstanley, Liverpool, 28 September 1816 (155); bt. Robinson (26 gns.); ...Sir Thomas Lawrence; Christie 15 May 1830 (53); bt. Peacock (20 gns.); ...E. H. Baily 1832;[14] ...James Aikin by 1842;[15] presented to Liverpool Corporation 1876; transferred to the gallery 1878.[16]

EXHIBITIONS

RA 1784 (147); Society of British Artists, Suffolk Street 1832 (21); *Second Exhibition of Objects Illustrative of the Fine Arts* [...] Liverpool Mechanics Institution 1842 (655); *International Exhibition* London 1862 (325); *Bosch, Goya et le Fantastique* Musée des Beaux-Arts, Bordeaux 1957 (59).

NOTES

1. Sophocles, *Oedipus at Colonus* lines 1606–08, translated by F. Storr; Loeb Classical Library (London and New York, 1916); Fuseli would no doubt have known that the speech had been singled out by Longinus in his treatise *On The Sublime*, as is pointed out by Edward Morris and Mark Evans: *Walker Art Gallery Liverpool Supplementary Foreign Schools Catalogue* (Liverpool, 1984) p. 7.
2. The following translation of them appeared on the letters of William Ward's engraving (see n. 5): 'In Thunders called the god beneath his blast / with horror struck his Daughters, on his knees / they fell and wept'.
3. Reproduced in C. Haenlein: 'A Fuseli Oedipus Lost and Found', *Apollo*, vol. 100 (1974) p. 34.
4. The drawing was sold at Christie 16 July 1974 (74) and was most recently recorded in a private collection in New York (David H. Weinglass: *Preliminary Renumbered and Revised Fuseli Catalogue Raisonné* 6 vols [privately printed, 1992] vol. 3, p. 349 [cat. 785]).
5. *London Chronicle* (24–27 April 1784) p. 408, repeated by the *Public Advertiser* (27 April 1784) p. 3.
6. *Morning Post and Daily Advertiser* (4 May 1784) p. 2.
7. *Morning Chronicle and London Advertiser* (15 May 1784) p. 3.
8. See David H. Weinglass: *Prints and Engraved*

Illustrations by and after Henry Fuseli (Aldershot, 1994) p. 80 (cat. 74). Weinglass corrects Gert Schiff's statement in his *Johann Heinrich Füssli. Text und Oeuvrekatalog* 2 vols (Zürich, 1973), vol. 2 p. 487 (cat. 712a) that the work was also engraved by J. R. Smith, showing that Smith merely published Ward's engraving.

9. In the catalogue of Roscoe's sale in 1816 the painting's width dimension was given as 5 ft. 6 inches, i.e. the same as it is at present. It would have been most unlike Roscoe to have had the work altered; indeed, when one of the Oedipus paintings was slightly damaged in transit to Liverpool, Roscoe referred the problem to Fuseli; see H. Macandrew: 'Henry Fuseli and William Roscoe', *Liverpool Bulletin* vol. 8 (1959–60) p. 23. Furthermore, the width measurement of *Oedipus Cursing Polynices* is also 166 cm, and if it was painted to form a pendant to WAG 1537 that argues that the latter was already at that width in about 1785–86.

10. Schiff, *op. cit.*, vol. 1, pp. 134–5 described the work as over-conceptualised, Oedipus's gesture bordering on the comic, the figure of Antigone unbelievable, and the work overall as lacking naturalness.

11. Allan Cunningham: *The Lives of the Most Eminent British Painters* rev. Mrs Charles Heaton, 3 vols (London, 1879) vol. 2, p. 256.

12. Macandrew, *op. cit.*, pp. 22–3, summarising the correspondence of Fuseli and Roscoe between the autumn of 1791 and December 1792.

13. In a letter to Fuseli dated 31 January 1812, Roscoe wrote of the artist's works in his collection: 'to me these pictures possess a value beyond even their intrinsic merits. They remind me of former days and are associated with some of the pleasantest hours of my life.' David H. Weinglass: *The Collected English Letters of Henry Fuseli* (Millwood, 1982) p. 386; quoted by Morris and Evans, *loc. cit.*

14. Lent by Baily to the 1832 exhibition.

15. Lent by Aikin to the 1842 exhibition.

16. *Libraries, Museums and Arts Committee Extracts* (22 August 1878).

The Return of Milton's Wife

WAG 1539
oil on canvas, 87.5 × 112 cm
date: 1798–99

The subject of WAG 1539 is one of the best-known episodes in the life of John Milton (1608–74), recounted by all his biographers. The poet's first wife, Mary Powell, daughter of an Oxfordshire Royalist unsympathetic to Milton's political views, deserted him in 1642[1] after less than a month of marriage, returning to her father and rebuffing all her husband's attempts to get her to come home. Not long after King Charles I's defeat at the Battle of Naseby in June 1645, however, and aware that her husband, despite his married state, was seriously courting another woman (a moral position he had meanwhile justified through the publication of several tracts on the grounds for divorce), Mary returned to him. In the words of the account probably used by Fuseli as his chief source,[2] William Hayley's recent *Life of Milton*,

While he was conversing with a relation, whom he frequently visited in St Martin's-lane, the door of an adjoining apartment was suddenly opened: he beheld his repentant wife kneeling at his feet, and imploring his forgiveness. After the natural struggles of honest pride and just resentment, he forgave and received her, 'partly from the intercession of their common friends, and partly', says his nephew, 'from his own generous nature, more inclinable to reconciliation than to perseverance and revenge'.

Fenton justly remarks, that the strong impression which this interview must have made on Milton 'contributed much to the painting of that pathetic scene in Paradise Lost in which Eve addresses herself to Adam for pardon and peace;' the verses, charming as they are, acquire new charms, when we consider them as descriptive of the poet himself and the penitent destroyer of his domestic comfort.[3]

The couple in the background are evidently meant to represent Milton's relative, whose name was Blackborough, and his wife: the figure of the woman has been recognised as a favourite Fuseli figure who appears in a number of his drawings.[4] The reconciliation must have taken place no later than October 1645, since the couple's first daughter was born in July 1646. Their marriage lasted until Mary's death in 1652, although, in the words of Doctor Johnson's rival account of Milton in his *Lives of the Poets*,[5] Milton 'probably did not much love her' and 'did not long continue the pretence of lamenting her'. Johnson's negative view of Milton as a hater of women and domestic tyrant was one of the aspects of his biography that Hayley attempted to rebut;[6] yet characteristically,[7] Fuseli himself does not choose to depict a happy and sentimental scene of marital reunion, focusing instead on the moment of suspense beforehand, in which Milton is still wrestling with doubt, unsure of whether to forgive his wife. The artist's 'very expressive and visibly *con amore*' handling of Mary Powell's face has, however, been noted.[8]

The painting is one of the last products of Fuseli's decade-long creative absorption with Milton in the 1790s, which had culminated in the opening of his Milton Gallery on 20 May 1799. The project had been conceived by Fuseli in the summer of 1790 as a rival to the Boydell Shakespeare Gallery, opened the previous year; it had been given impetus by the radical publisher John Johnson's idea in 1791 for a new edition of Milton's poems to be undertaken by William Cowper and illustrated by Fuseli, and it had been financially supported in considerable measure throughout the 1790s by William Roscoe.[9] The subject of WAG 1539 (in contrast to that of WAG 1538; see pp. 46–7) did not feature in the original Milton Gallery, as Fuseli

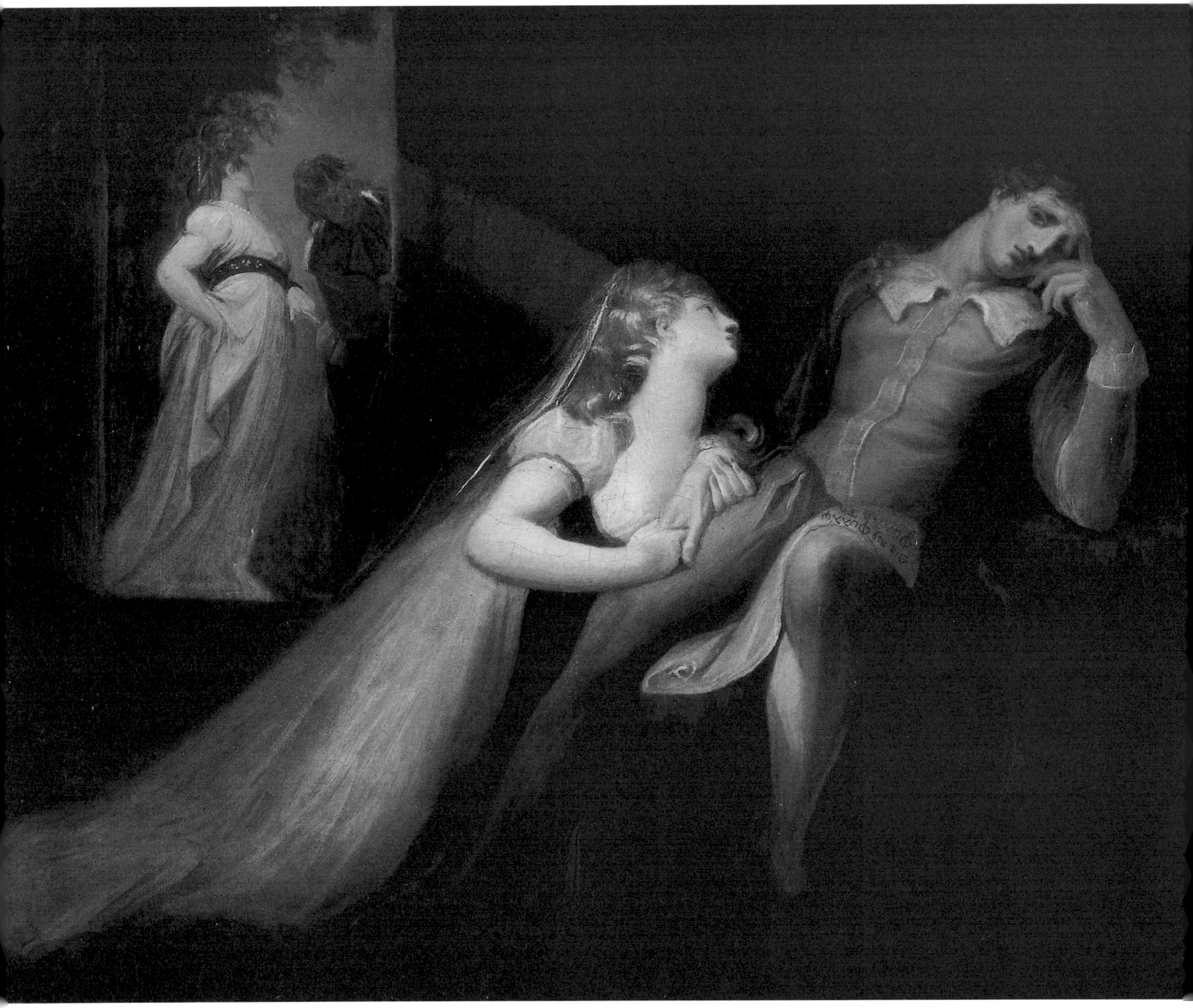

WAG 1539

first exhibited it in 1799, but it has been identified as one of the works that Fuseli added to the revamped second exhibition of the following year in a bid to give it greater popular appeal.[10] Fuseli may have been attracted to it from Hayley's observation of how it informed a celebrated passage of *Paradise Lost*. In the radical circles frequented by Fuseli and Johnson, Milton's epic poem, and the figure of its revolutionary anti-hero Satan, defined the poet's cultural significance.[11]

WAG 1539 is mentioned in a letter from Fuseli to Roscoe of 18 June 1800, where it is described as '*Milton's wife pleading & imploring his pardon*'; one of 'ten to twenty pictures at your service, from Milton, Shakspeare, Spenser, Sophocles – highly finished, portable, fit for any room, & most of them interesting & not too deep subjects'.[12] It was one of five paintings that Fuseli sent to Roscoe at the beginning of November 1800,[13] and Fuseli specified its price, 30 guineas, in a further letter of 1 December.[14] Roscoe was attempting to sell Fuseli's pictures for him in Liverpool, but he was unsuccessful with WAG 1539 and it remained on his hands. It was not included in his bankruptcy sale of 1816.

By the time WAG 1539 entered the gallery's collection in 1914 its subject matter had been lost sight of and it had been re-titled *The Blind Milton*; it continued to be known as this until 1958.[15] The work's condition, particularly the extensive cracking associated with the use of bitumen over much of the lower right-hand side, had long given cause for concern[16] when a full conservation treatment was undertaken in 1996. In the course of this, two old varnish layers, 'restorer's glazes' between the layers, and extensive retouching and overpainting underneath the second layer – which included much of Mary Powell's bare flesh and a long curl of hair lying over her chest – were removed. X-rays revealed that Fuseli had made an alteration to Mary's bodice.[17] The cleaning revealed much more clearly a Greek inscription on Milton's scroll that had formerly been described as 'indecipherable' and 'without any particular significance';[18] however, it has continued to defy efforts to decode it.

PROVENANCE

Sent by Fuseli to William Roscoe on consignment 1 November 1800; retained by Roscoe; by descent to his grandson, Sir Henry Enfield Roscoe FRS; by whom presented 1914.

EXHIBITIONS

Paintings and Drawings by Fuseli Roland, Browse and Delbanco, London 1948 (31); *Johann Heinrich Füssli Das Verlorene Paradies* Staatsgalerie, Stuttgart 1997–98 (90).

NOTES

1. Not 1643, as stated in several of the early biographies, followed by Edward Morris and Mark Evans: *Walker Art Gallery Liverpool Supplementary Foreign Schools Catalogue* (Liverpool, 1984) p. 8 and Christoph Becker: *Johann Heinrich Füssli Das Verlorene Paradies* exh. cat., Staatsgalerie Stuttgart (1997) p. 66.
2. As is suggested by the fact that in his letter to Roscoe of 4 November 1800, Fuseli refers to another Milton subject that he is sending to Liverpool under the title *Milton, a Youth, an Incident Told in Hayley's Life of Him. An Italian Female Looking at Him as He Sleeps* (*Roscoe Papers*, LRO 920/ROS/1672). Ironically, this incident is not mentioned in Hayley's *Life*.
3. Joseph A. Wittreich Jr, ed.: *The Life of Milton (Second Edition 1796) by William Hayley* (Gainesville, 1970) pp. 91–2. The St Martin's Lane referred to by Hayley was not the familiar street of that name near the church of St Martin-in-the-Fields, but a lane by St Martin's-le-Grand Church, Aldersgate Street.
4. For example, in *Hero, Ursula and Beatrice* (Kunstsammlung Basel 1914/130) and *A Seated Courtesan* (Kunsthaus Zürich 1934/1); Gert Schiff, *letter*, 20 August 1958, gallery files.
5. George Birkbeck Hill, ed.: *Samuel Johnson, Lives of the English Poets, Vol. 1, Cowley to Dryden* (Hildesheim, 1968) p. 116.
6. For a discussion of the dialectic between Hayley's and Johnson's lives of Milton see, for example, Wittreich, *op. cit.*, pp. x–xii.
7. For Fuseli's view of Northcote's inadequacy as a painter of dramatic historical scenes, see John Knowles: *The Life and Writings of Henry Fuseli* 3 vols (London, 1831), vol. 1, p. 383; cited by Hugh Macandrew, 'Henry Fuseli and William Roscoe', *Liverpool Bulletin* vol. 8 (1959–60) p. 25.
8. G. Schiff: *Johann Heinrich Füssli. Text und Oeuvrekatalog* 2 vols (Zürich, 1973), vol. 1, p. 220. WAG 1539 is no. 919 in Schiff's catalogue (vol. 2, p. 523) and is no. 1097 in David H. Weinglass: *Preliminary Renumbered and Revised Fuseli Catalogue Raisonné* 6 vols (privately printed, 1992) vol. 4, p. 524.
9. Macandrew, *op. cit.*, *passim*, especially pp. 15–26. See also G. Schiff: *Johann Heinrich Füsslis Milton-Galerie* (Zürich, 1963).
10. Becker, *loc. cit.*
11. The literature on this topic is extensive and interpretation nuanced. For broader discussions of the politics of Milton and Miltonic imagery in the late eighteenth century see, for example, Marcia Pointon: *Milton in English Art* (Manchester, 1970) and Dustin Griffin: *Regaining Paradise: Milton and the Eighteenth Century* (Cambridge, 1986).
12. Fuseli to Roscoe, *letter*, 18 June 1800, *Roscoe Papers*, LRO 920/ROS/1665.
13. Fuseli to Roscoe, *letter*, 4 November 1800, *loc. cit.* (n. 2).
14. Fuseli to Roscoe, *letter*, 4 December 1800, *Roscoe Papers*, LRO 920/ROS/1675.
15. The subject was identified by Gert Schiff, *letter*, 20 August 1958, *loc. cit.*
16. It was noted by Macandrew, *op. cit.*, p. 26.
17. Conservation report by Helen Brett dated 30 January 1997, gallery files.
18. Macandrew, *loc. cit.*

Milton When a Boy Instructed by His Mother

WAG 1538
oil on canvas, 91.5 × 72.5 cm
date: 1799–1800

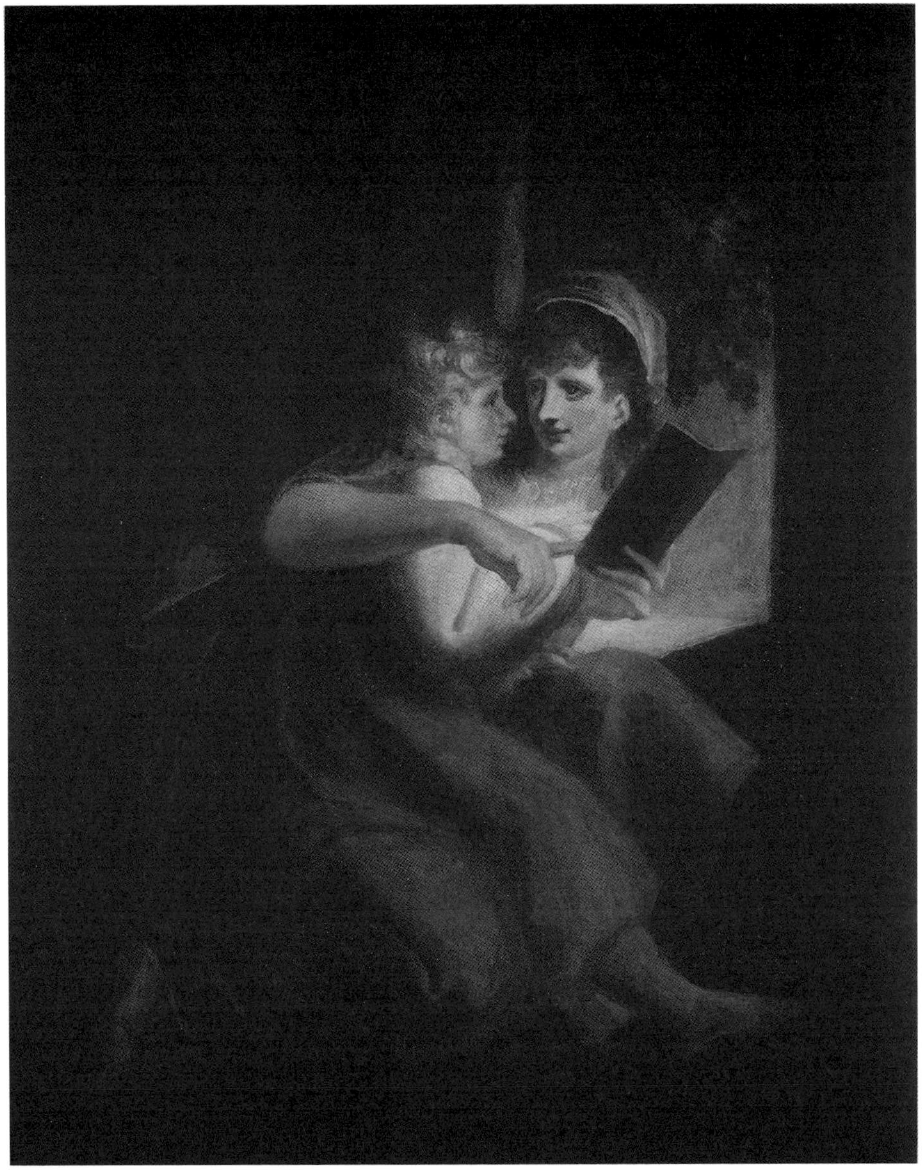

WAG 1538

As with WAG 1539, this work is a product of Fuseli's creative obsession with Milton in the 1790s (see above). An important difference, however, is that it is a replica of a subject that the artist had included in his original Milton Gallery, rather than a new one. Why Fuseli should have been concerned to depict the young poet being taught by his mother is not immediately obvious; as has been observed, 'Milton's education owed no special debt to his mother',[1] and none of his biographers make anything of the notion. It has been pointed out that the childhood of famous men was a favourite theme with artists at this period[2] (as indeed was the depiction of motherhood itself). More pertinently, Fuseli's own education had been powerfully informed by his mother,[3] and the subject may thus have been invented by him to express his personal identification with Milton. Fuseli added a further psychological layer to this idea by making a preparatory drawing for the subject (Ulster Museum, Belfast; fig. 21) in which the features of the mother are those of his wife.[4] In all, he seems to have made three paintings of the subject: the Milton Gallery picture which, significantly, he retained in his possession all his life,[5] 'a larger but much more unfinished picture...which...I sold to Mr Cuthbert at the beginning of my exhibition for 50 guineas',[6] and third (on a standard kit-cat canvas) WAG 1538, in which the figure of Milton's mother does not resemble Mrs Fuseli.[7]

This canvas is first heard of in a letter from Fuseli to William Roscoe of October 1799 when it is described as being in preparation.[8] Fuseli sent the work to Roscoe at the beginning of November 1800, in a consignment which also included WAG 1539, as well as the painting *Silence: A Mother with Her Two Children*, an illustration of Milton's *Il Penseroso* that the artist seems to have viewed as a pendant to WAG 1538.[9] In a letter to Roscoe of 4 December 1800, Fuseli priced these two works at 25 guineas. In the same letter he wrote that in three of the works despatched to Liverpool, including WAG 1538, he had

> *had an eye...to...the Suprapluteal (if you will forgive the barbarous word!) ornaments of the Athenaeum, figures or groups allusive to the particular branch of Litterature, books of Natr. History, Prints, Botany etc. placed in their library – such a picture might be over every shelf, or painted on the folding doors &*

panels of the Cases, and would not require to be executed on a much larger scale. It is true, you have not encouraged the thought, but your influence, I cannot help thinking, might bring it about.[10]

In the event, Roscoe did not pursue the idea of using Fuseli's pictures to decorate the Athenaeum (the library and reading rooms he had helped establish in Liverpool the previous year); nor did he sell WAG 1538.[11] It remained in his own possession and descended after his death (together with WAG 1539) to his youngest son Henry.

The condition of WAG 1538 is poor. The paint surface is disfigured by cracking associated with the use of bitumen and is extensively repainted.

PROVENANCE

Sent by Fuseli in November 1800 to William Roscoe; by descent to Sir Henry Enfield Roscoe, FRS; by whom presented 1914.[12]

EXHIBITION

Johann Heinrich Füssli Das Verlorene Paradies Staatsgalerie, Stuttgart 1997–98 (82).

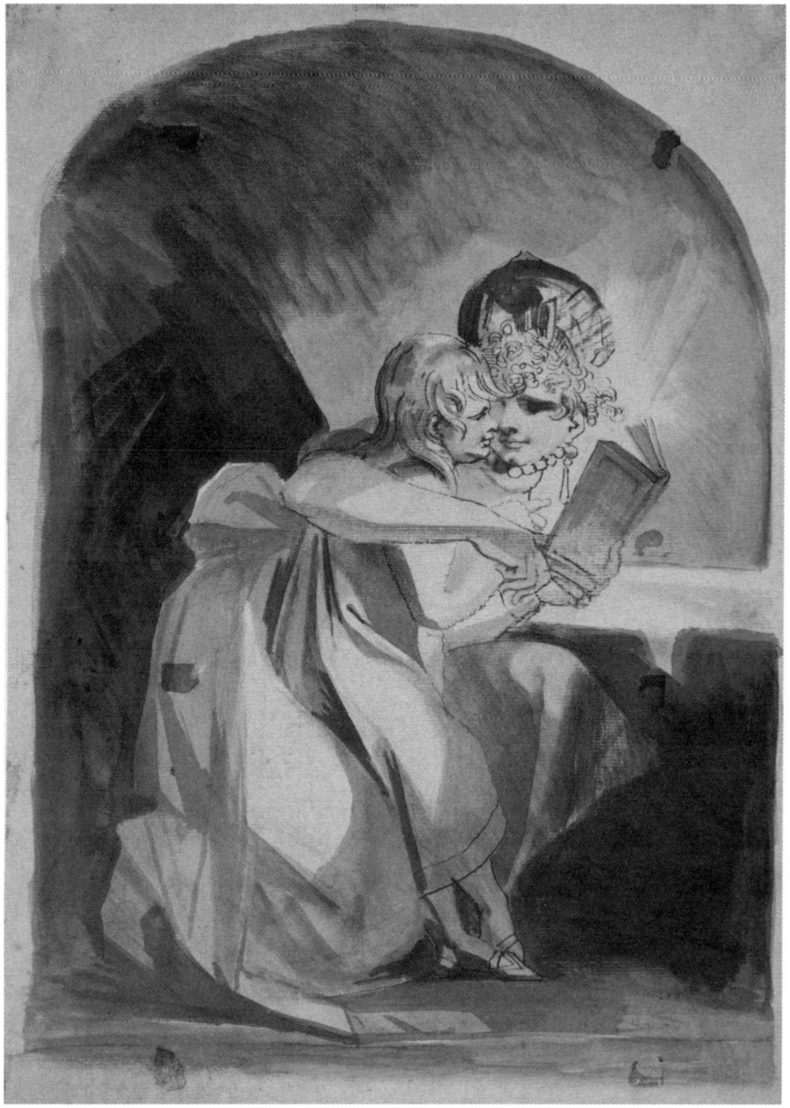

Fig. 21 *Milton when a Boy, Instructed by his Mother* (c.1796-98) by Henry Fuseli, ink and wash on paper. Photograph reproduced courtesy the Trustees of National Museums Northern Ireland.

NOTES

1. Edward Morris and Mark Evans: *Walker Art Gallery Liverpool Supplementary Foreign Schools Catalogue* (Liverpool, 1984) p. 8.
2. G. Schiff: *Johann Heinrich Füssli. Text und Oeuvrekatalog* 2 vols (Zürich, 1973) vol. 1, p. 219.
3. Morris and Evans, *loc. cit.*
4. Schiff, *loc. cit.* Schiff also proposes Fuseli's debt to a drawing by Raphael, engraved by Marcantonio Raimondi, of the Madonna teaching an unwilling Jesus to read (O. Fischel, ed.: *Raphaels Zeichnungen* 9 vols [Berlin, 1913–72] cat. 375).
5. Schiff, *op. cit.*, p. 522, correcting the view of H. Macandrew: 'Henry Fuseli and William Roscoe', *Liverpool Bulletin* vol. 8 (1959–60) p. 26, n. 160, that the work of this title in Fuseli's posthumous sale was a print; Schiff, however, may have misunderstood Macandrew's footnote.
6. Fuseli to Roscoe, *letter*, 4 November 1800, *Roscoe Papers*, LRO 920/ROS/1672; Fuseli had given Roscoe the same information, in more abbreviated form, in his letter of 14 October 1799 (see n. 8).
7. Comparison between the reproduction of WAG 1538 in Macandrew, *op. cit.*, p. 18, fig. 5, and more recent photographs, reveals the extent of retouching of the face and figure of Milton's mother after 1960. Her black wristband (noted by Macandrew, p. 26 and again by Schiff, *op. cit.*, p. 523, cat. 917, as one of the differences between WAG 1538 and the Milton Gallery canvas) has been removed. Though it is not specifically mentioned as part of the treatment, this may have been carried out during J. Coburn Witherop's restoration of the painting in 1968 (copy of his invoice, gallery files).
8. Fuseli to Roscoe, *letter*, 14 October 1799, *Roscoe Papers*, LRO 920/ROS/1663.
9. Fuseli to Roscoe, *letter*, 4 November 1800, *Roscoe Papers*, *loc. cit.* (n. 6).
10. Fuseli to Roscoe, *letter*, 4 December 1800, Roscoe Papers, LRO 920/ROS/1675.
11. David H. Weinglass: Preliminary Renumbered and Revised Fuseli Catalogue Raisonné 6 vols (privately printed, 1992) vol. 4, p. 522 (cat. 1095) claims that it was one of the six works by Fuseli that failed to sell at the sale; however, (as Macandrew, *op. cit.*, p. 25 states) the picture is not listed in the sale catalogue and WAG 1538 would seem to be one of the three unspecified works by Fuseli listed among 'articles added' in Roscoe's 1820 household inventory that as 'gifts' etc., had been spared inclusion in the sale.
12. When presented to the gallery WAG 1538 was titled *The Young Milton*, which is misleading since this is the informal title given to another Milton subject (Milton Gallery no. 39).

Thomas Gainsborough

1727–88

Sir Robert Clayton

WAG 2579
oil on canvas, 127 × 101 cm
date: 1769

The sitter (about 1740–99) was the son of Sir Kenrick Clayton, 2nd Baronet, of Marden, Surrey, and his wife Henrietta, daughter of Henry Herring, a Director of the Bank of England. He was educated at Clare College Cambridge and in 1767 married Mary, daughter of the London merchant Frederick Standert. In 1768 he was elected MP for Bletchingley, a constituency the family controlled by virtue of their large Surrey estates. He succeeded his father as 3rd Baronet in 1769. Over the following decade he got into serious financial difficulties, and contracted with his cousin John Kenrick to sell him the reversion of his Bletchingley estate after his death. In politics he was a Rockinghamite Whig, voting consistently against the ministries of Lord North and William Pitt the Younger and becoming a friend of Charles James Fox.[1]

Gainsborough's portrait is dateable to 1769 on the basis of an inscription on the lining canvas, presumably copied from one on the back of the original canvas: *Sir Robert Clayton Bart.* MP*/ of Marden. 1769./ by T. Gainsborough R.A.*[2] Presumably the work was commissioned to mark his succession to the baronetcy, and the sittings took place in Bath.

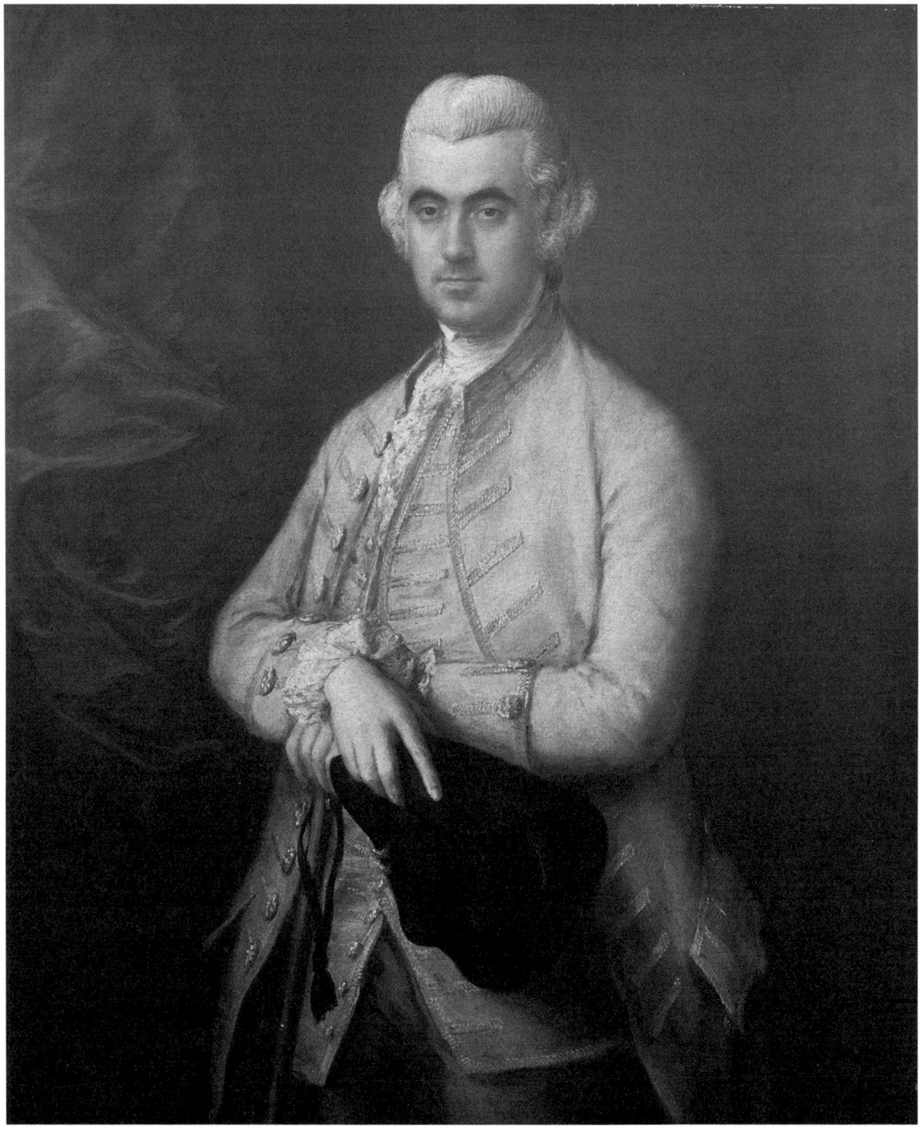

WAG 2579

PROVENANCE

By descent to Sir Harold Clayton, 10th Bt.; Christie 23 June 1950 (34); bt. Agnew (£682 10s.); Tooth; bt. by the *Liverpool Daily Post* and *Echo* December 1950 for presentation to the gallery.

EXHIBITIONS

Ninth Annual Exhibition on behalf of the Artists' General Benevolent Institution Agnew's, London 1903 (9); *Recent Acquisitions* Tooth's, London 1950 (11); *Selected Acquisitions of the Walker Art Gallery Liverpool 1945–1955* Agnew's, London 1955 (15).

NOTES

1. Sir Lewis Namier and John Brooke: *The History of Parliament: The House of Commons 1754–1790* 3 vols (London, 1964) vol. 2, pp. 218–9.
2. This date was accepted by Sir Ellis Waterhouse, *letter*, 10 May 1951, gallery files, and published in his *Gainsborough* (1958) p. 60 (cat. 152); at the date of its acquisition by the gallery WAG 2579 was generally thought to date from considerably later in Gainsborough's career (*letters* from Dudley Tooth, 19 December 1950, Mary Woodall, 2 May 1951 and C. K. Adams, 5 May 1951, gallery files).

Isabella, Viscountess Molyneux

WAG 8780
oil on canvas, 236 × 155 cm
date: 1769

Born in 1748, Lady Isabella was the second child, and second daughter, of William Stanhope, who succeeded to the title of 2nd Earl of Harrington in 1756, and his wife Lady Caroline Fitzroy. At the age of 20 she married Charles William, 8th Viscount Molyneux, of Croxteth Hall outside Liverpool, who in 1771 was advanced to the title of 1st Earl of Sefton. Their only child, William Philip, who succeeded his father as 2nd Earl of Sefton in 1795, was born in 1772. She held a position of some prominence in London society (despite the relative anonymity of her husband). In March 1774 she was chosen as the third in a series of 'Court Beauties' featured by the *London Magazine*, which wrote: 'Of this lady we need say no more than – She's so charming / Age buds at the sight of her, and swells to youth'. The accompanying circular head and shoulders engraving appears to derive loosely from Gainsborough's portrait, especially in the dress she wears.[1] A feature titled *Scale of Bon Ton* in the *Morning Post* comparing 9 attributes of 12 leading ladies of fashion and marking them out of 20, scored Lady Sefton 16 for her figure and 14 for her beauty, but only 4 for sense and 3 for wit.[2] Georgiana, Duchess of Devonshire described her in a journal written for her mother in 1777 as 'a compound of vanity, nonsence folly & good-nature – for tho' many people deny her the last qualification I am sure she possesses it only she always contrives to put her faults in the clearest light'.[3] In the early 1770s her family name, Harrington, was given to an area of urban development in south Liverpool on land owned by Lord Sefton.[4] She died in 1819.

Lady Molyneux must have sat to Gainsborough on a visit to Bath at the end of 1768 or early in 1769, just after her marriage (which took place on 27 November 1768 at the church of St Martin-in-the-Fields, London).[5] She was portrayed at the same period by Tilly Kettle and Sir Joshua Reynolds (with whom her sittings in London began on 18 February 1769).[6] Gainsborough depicts her in a pose which has been described as both Van Dyckian and Watteauesque,[7] walking towards the viewer. She wears a white silk dress decorated with light blue and black stripes, and a matching overdress. Her shawl is black with black lace edging, and her one visible shoe is white with a diamond buckle. She wears pearls around her throat and in her hair, and small hoop earrings. It is uncertain whether this was a costume actually worn by Lady Molyneux or one that Gainsborough had on hand in his studio, partly because only the head and hands in WAG 8780 look as though they are painted from the life, with the remainder appearing to have been done from a lay figure, and partly because the identical dress occurs in another portrait by Gainsborough, of Lady Bolton (São Paulo Museum of Art), which was painted at around the same date.[8] The visible pentimento around the exquisitely modelled right hand suggests that Lady Molyneux returned for a final sitting to enable Gainsborough to pull the work together; given the likely brevity of her stay in Bath, this would in turn suggest that the costume was completed very quickly, as indeed the virtuosity of the paint handling confirms. The strikingly low horizon is a feature of other Gainsborough full-lengths of this period which has been interpreted as a device anticipating the work's being hung in an elevated position, either at exhibition or in the client's home. The artist's close integration of figure and background through colour harmony and paint textures has been interpreted as a conscious effort to address the issue of the unnatural viewpoint.[9]

Gainsborough may have selected WAG 8780 as one of his four exhibits at the 1769 exhibition of the Royal Academy because the sitter was a person of fashion, and would get the work noticed, even though his title, *Portrait of a Lady. Whole Length*, preserved Lady Molyneux's anonymity. According to the later testimony of the portraitist Sir William Beechey (who was only 15 years old at the date of the exhibition), the work attracted considerable attention at the RA, but it is not clear that this was the case.[10] Horace Walpole in his copy of the catalogue wrote that the work was 'ungrateful'.[11] However, one review, placed in a number of journals including the *St James's Chronicle*, listed *Lady Molyneux* (proof that her anonymity was punctured immediately) among 'the Pictures that have this Season chiefly attracted the Attention of the Connoisseurs at the Royal Academy, in Pall-Mall'.[12] The work's subsequent reputation as the epitome of Gainsborough's art of the late 1760s – supposedly implicit in his decision to send it to the inaugural exhibition of the Royal Academy – has arguably been hard-won. Notwithstanding the publication of G. H. Every's engraving in 1887, it has chiefly depended on two clusters of appearances in exhibitions: one in the period 1928–36 and the other between 1998 and 2002 (see below). The latter followed upon the full conservation treatment which the work received in 1997.[13]

Several copies and related works exist. Although some of these have been described as preliminary studies, it is clear that they all postdate WAG 8780.[14]

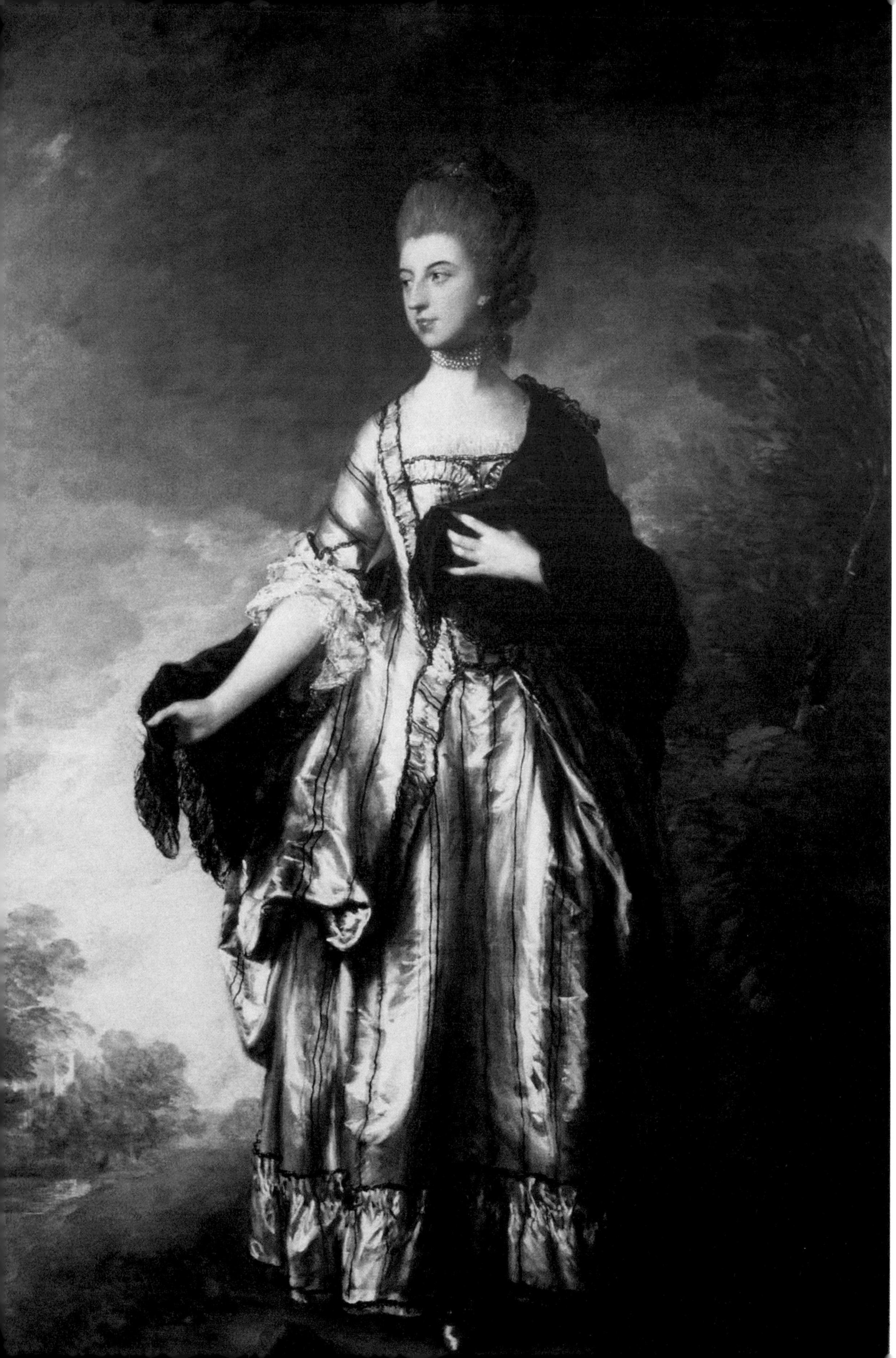

WAG 8780

PROVENANCE

By descent to Hugh, 7th Earl of Sefton (d. 1972); accepted in lieu of death duties by H. M. Government 1973 and transferred to the gallery 1975.

EXHIBITIONS

RA 1769 (35); *First Exhibition of Objects Illustrative of the Fine Arts* [...] Liverpool Mechanics Institution 1840 (1245);[15] BI 1848 (177) *Loan Exhibition of Pictures by T. Gainsborough R. A. on behalf of the National Art Collections Fund* Agnew's, London 1928 (14); *British Art* RA 1934 (345); *British Art Exhibition* Manchester City Art Gallery 1934 (54); *Twee Eeuwen Engelsche Kunst* [*Two Centuries of English Art*] Stedelijk Museum, Amsterdam 1936 (45); *Paintings and Drawings by Thomas Gainsborough 1727–1788* Victoria Art Gallery, Bath 1951 (23); *Thomas Gainsborough* Palazzo dei Diamanti, Ferrara 1998 (13); *Mehr Licht: Europa um 1770* Städel, Frankfurt 1999–2000 (33); *Gainsborough* Tate Britain, London 2002 (44).

NOTES

1. *London Magazine* (1774) p. 112 and fp.
2. See J. D. Gross, ed.: *Byron's Corbeau Blanc: The Life and Letters of Lady Melbourne* (Houston, 1997) pl. 21, for an unsourced and undated illustration. The article appears to have been a publicity stunt on behalf of Lady Sefton's younger sister, Amelia Countess of Barrymore, who scored 17 or more in every category.
3. Correspondence of the 5th Duke of Devonshire, *Chatsworth Mss*, no. 181; quoted in *MPPP*, p. 99.
4. Jane Longmore: 'The Urban Renaissance in Liverpool', in Elizabeth E. Barker and Alex Kidson: *Joseph Wright of Derby in Liverpool* exh. cat., Walker Art Gallery and Yale Center for British Art, New Haven (2007) p. 10.
5. John Hayes: *Gainsborough Paintings and Drawings* (London, 1975) p. 45; Hayes is incorrect in saying that the marriage took place at Christmas.
6. David Mannings and Martin Postle: *Sir Joshua Reynolds: A Complete Catalogue of His Paintings* 2 vols (New Haven and London, 2000) vol. 1 p. 336 (cat. 1267). James Watson's engraving after Tilly Kettle's portrait was published on 1 July 1769, implying that the canvas had been completed some months earlier (an impression of this print is in the Walker Art Gallery's collection). Three further portraits identified as of her and possibly painted around the same date are (i) a whole-length measuring 212 × 132.5 cm, sold Sotheby New York 6 October 1995 (49) with an attribution to Thomas Hickey; on grounds of likeness this seems very plausibly to depict her and at about the age she is in WAG 8780; and (ii) two pastels measuring 61 × 47 cm sold as the property of the Earl of Harrington at Sotheby 6 May 1964 (3a) and (9); in the former of these she is described as 'in uniform'.
7. For the description as Van Dyckian see especially Ellis Waterhouse: *Gainsborough* (London, 1958) p. 21: 'an eighteenth-century version of Van Dyck of hardly surpassable refinement' (quoted by Susan Sloman: *Gainsborough in Bath* [New Haven and London, 2002] p. 86); also, for example, Keith Roberts: 'A Local Lady of Merit', *Observer Magazine* (10 June 1979) p. 80, Werner Busch's catalogue entry in *Mehr Licht: Europa um 1770*, exh. cat., Städel, Frankfurt (1999) pp. 58–9 (cat. 33), where specific prototypes in Van Dyck's English portraiture are most fully adduced, and Christine Riding's catalogue entry in *Gainsborough* exh. cat.,Tate Britain, London (2002) p. 110 (cat. 44). Riding observes that WAG 8780 is 'arguably closer to seventeenth-century courtly prototypes than any portrait [Gainsborough] had hitherto executed'. For the Watteauesque character of the pose, see Selby Whittingham: '"What You Will" or Some Notes regarding the Influence of Watteau on Turner and Other British Artists (1)', *Turner Studies* vol. 5 no. 1 (1985) p. 21, n. 8. Whittingham observes that the pose is that of Watteau's *Pélerine*, engraved as a separate figure, in *L'Ile de Cythère*.
8. For the date of the portrait of Lady Bolton see Waterhouse, *op. cit.*, p. 55 (cat. 71). The foregoing observations on Lady Molyneux's costume rely on notes on the portrait made by Hugh Belsey for his forthcoming catalogue *raisonné* of Gainsborough's portraits, kindly communicated.
9. Sloman, *op. cit.*, p. 58.
10. G. W. Fulcher: *The Life of Thomas Gainsborough* (London, 1856) p. 79. W. T. Whitley: *Artists and their Friends in England 1700–1799* 2 vols (London, 1928) vol. 1 p. 258, stated that the exhibition attracted little notice in contemporary newspapers.
11. Fulcher, *loc. cit.*
12. *St James's Chronicle* (2–4 May 1769) p. 3. Similar articles appeared in the *Public Advertiser* (4 May 1769), *Lloyd's Evening Post* (1–3 May 1769), *London Chronicle* (4–6 May 1769), *Middlesex Journal* (2–4 May 1769) and *Whitehall Evening Post* (2–4 May 1769).
13. In 1952 WAG 8780 was damaged by smoke in the fire which engulfed the eighteenth-century wing of Croxteth Hall; it was in this condition when it arrived at the gallery in 1975. The work was conserved in 1997 by David Crombie of the Paintings Conservation Department of the then National Museums and Galleries on Merseyside and the frame was regilded by the Senior Framing Conservator, Roy Irlam. The treatment revealed that a 12.5 cm wide strip of canvas had been joined to the whole length of the right-hand side of the picture, in two sections, probably in the nineteenth century. This strip replaced either the original right-hand tacking edge or possibly (to save work) both tacking edges which may have been damaged or torn away from the stretcher; if this latter supposition is correct, the figure of Lady Sefton would have been moved fractionally across the composition to the left. Although the join had been well disguised the painting technique on this strip was completely different from Gainsborough's own (David Crombie, condition report dated 19 June 1997, gallery files). The earlier very brown condition of WAG 8780 may have affected Sir Ellis Waterhouse's view of the work as an instance of Gainsborough's interest in studying and painting his portraits in subdued light at the end of the 1760s (Waterhouse, *op. cit.*, p. 22); cleaning revealed that the figure, and especially the dress, is painted with very strong contrasts of light and shadow.
14. These works include (i) an oil sketch measuring about 23 × 18 cm, still at Croxteth Hall, included as lot 1021 in the catalogue of the Croxteth premises sale, Christie 17–20 June 1973 but withdrawn from the sale; this appears to be a copy dating from the nineteenth century; (ii) an oil sketch measuring 53.5 × 42.5 cm owned by the Earl of Wemyss when lent by him in 1925 to the Burlington Fine Arts Club (36) and to the exhibition in Park Lane 1936 (47); this also appears to be a work of the nineteenth century; (iii) a work measuring 44.5 × 35.5 cm owned by Archduke Salvador, New York, 1927, subsequently with Trotti, Paris and Knoedler; (iv) a poor copy measuring 74 × 62 cm in the Nationalmuseum, Stockholm (NM 2788); (v) a copy by Alice de Rothschild (d. 1922) now at Waddesdon; and (vi) an unrelated work measuring 76 × 64 cm in the possession of Ehrich Galleries, New York 1929–30; sold to American Art Association New York 18 April 1934 (147); said to depict Lady Molyneux but doubtfully of her; possibly an authentic work by Gainsborough, but if so, a later work than WAG 8780 (reproduced *Burlington Magazine* December 1929, supplement, pl. 27). All but the first of these were noted by Ellis Waterhouse: 'Preliminary Checklist of Portraits by Thomas Gainsborough', *Walpole Society* vol. 33 (1953) p. 96.
15. The critic of the *Liverpool Journal* noted that 'the drapery is rich and effective, and well arranged; the face intelligent; the air noble; the hands unobtrusively, but well, finished. A fastidious critic might find fault with the narrowness of the shoulders, the imperfect development of the bust, and the sketchy, undecided character of the neck' (*Descriptive Notices of Some of the Most Interesting Articles at the Exhibition Now Open in the Mechanics' Institution, Liverpool, Extracted, by Permission, from the LIVERPOOL JOURNAL of Saturday, June 18th, 1840* p. 15).

Elizabeth, Viscountess Folkestone

WAG 229
oil on canvas, 127 × 101.5 cm
date: about 1779–80

Lady Folkestone (1711–82) was the eldest daughter of Robert Marsham, 1st Baron Romney, and his wife Elizabeth, the daughter of Admiral Sir Cloudesley Shovell. She married in 1741, as his second wife, Sir Jacob Bouverie (1694–1761), with whom she had two sons. She outlived her husband by 21 years, dying at South Warnborough, and being buried at Britford, Wiltshire.[1] Her husband was elevated to the peerage as Viscount Folkestone in 1747.

WAG 229 has generally been thought to date from the second half of the 1770s.[2] In 1776 Gainsborough carried out a posthumous full-length of the sitter's late husband for the Society of Arts, based on an earlier portrait by Thomas Hudson.[3] It seems natural to connect that work to the present commission despite their very different characters. However, several other members of Lady Folkestone's extended family sat to Gainsborough over a wide time span: her stepson and his third wife, 1770–73;[4] her three step-grandsons in 1773–74;[5] her sister at the end of the 1770s;[6] and her nephew's wife and the latter's children in the later 1780s.[7] Of these satellite works the closest in style to WAG 229 is the portrait of Lady Harriet Marsham, Lady Folkestone's sister, and it has most recently been proposed that WAG 229 dates from about 1780, within a year or two of the date of that work.[8]

X-radiography reveals that Gainsborough made numerous alterations to WAG 229 in the course of painting the work. Lady Folkestone appears originally to have been posed seated, with a red curtain at the upper left and probably an open landscape at upper right.[9] Her face was taken in sharper profile and her arms and hands were arranged differently, with the left arm brought lower down without the jutting-elbow pose and the right hand portrayed to the knuckles, without the outstretched forefingers. A dense area of lead white is visible in x-radiographs under the area of edge of the forefinger, possibly corresponding to the former establishment of a horizon line of a landscape.[10] The changes to the composition made by Gainsborough occasionally appear as visible strokes or pentimenti beneath the paint layer. In general, the work, which is unlined,[11] has been admired as a very pure and unadulterated example of Gainsborough's painting technique.[12]

PROVENANCE

By descent to the sitter's son, Philip Bouverie-Pusey (d.1828); by descent; bt. from the Bouverie-Pusey family by Agnew; from whom bt. by George Holt January 1896 (3,000 gns.); Emma Holt Bequest 1945.

EXHIBITIONS

Exhibition of Twenty Pictures by Masters of the Early English School on behalf of the Liverpool Royal Infirmary Agnew's, Liverpool 1902 (4);[13] *Loan Collection of Portraits* Birmingham Museum and Art Gallery 1903 (22); *Loan Exhibition of Works of Early British Masters* Manchester City Art Gallery 1909 (13); *59th Liverpool Autumn Exhibition* Walker Art Gallery 1933 (4); *Some Acquisitions of the Walker Art Gallery Liverpool 1935–1945* National Gallery, London 1945 (10); *European Masters of the Eighteenth Century* RA 1954–55 (396).

NOTES

1. Lord Radnor, *letter*, 17 February 1945, gallery files.
2. E. K. Waterhouse: 'Preliminary Check List of Portraits by Thomas Gainsborough', *Walpole Society* vol. 33 (1953) p. 40, and his *Gainsborough* (London, 1958), p. 67 (cat. 262); M. Bennett and E. Morris: *Sudley* (Liverpool, 1971) p. 30. Alex Kidson: *Sudley: The Emma Holt Bequest* (Liverpool, 1992) p. 11 suggested that Lady Folkestone 'appears perhaps about sixty years old', in effect proposing a date in the early 1770s.
3. E. K. Waterhouse: *Gainsborough* p. 67 (cat. 261). Hudson's original half-length, dated 1759, was sold at Christie 27 June 1980 (155).
4. *William 1st Earl of Radnor*, 126 × 100 cm, 1770; and a second portrait of him, 74 × 61 cm, dated 1773; *Anne, Countess of Radnor*, 76 × 63 cm, dated 1773; Waterhouse, *op. cit.*, p. 86 (cats. 569–71). See also W. T. Whitley: *Thomas Gainsborough* (1915) p.105.
5. Hons. William Henry, Bartholomew, and Edward Bouverie; each 74 × 61 cm; Waterhouse, *op. cit.*, p. 55 (cats. 75–77).
6. *Hon. Harriet Marsham*, 76 × 63 cm; Barber Institute of Fine Arts, Birmingham University; Waterhouse, *op. cit.*, p. 80 (cat. 469) repr. pl. 169.
7. *Frances, Countess of Romney*, 76 × 63 cm; Waterhouse, *op. cit.*, p. 87 (cat. 585), and *The Marsham Children*, 240 × 180 cm, Berlin, Gemäldegalerie; Waterhouse, *op. cit.*, p. 80 (cat. 470).
8. Hugh Belsey, *verbally*, 17 February 2005. He compared the technique in WAG 229 to that of *Madame Lebrun*, Art Gallery of South Australia, Adelaide; for which see R. Radford: *Island to Empire: 300 Years of British Art 1550–1850* (Adelaide, 2005) pp. 150–3.
9. I am grateful to Nicola Christie, at the time Senior Paintings Conservator, National Museums Liverpool, for discussing the x-radiographs with me, 18 May 2007. There are traces of crimson paint on the left-hand tacking edge and sky-blue paint on the right-hand tacking edge of WAG 229.
10. Nicola Christie, *ibid.*
11. A wax strip-lining was carried out by J. Coburn Witherop in the mid-1960s; invoice in gallery files.
12. 'It has never been relined and has always been in the country – the main reason, in my opinion, for its extraordinary purity. The picture has never been varnished: the accumulated household dirt has merely been removed from the surface by careful washing. There is not a tittle of restoration or reparation anywhere. So far as my experience goes it is absolutely unique in condition, and as a specimen of the wonderful Art of the Master is *the most perfect masterpiece I know*.' Copy of a memorandum made by Sir William Agnew, 10 December 1895, gallery files.
13. Exhibited as *Portrait of a Lady*; lender unspecified but described in the catalogue as a well-known citizen of Liverpool.

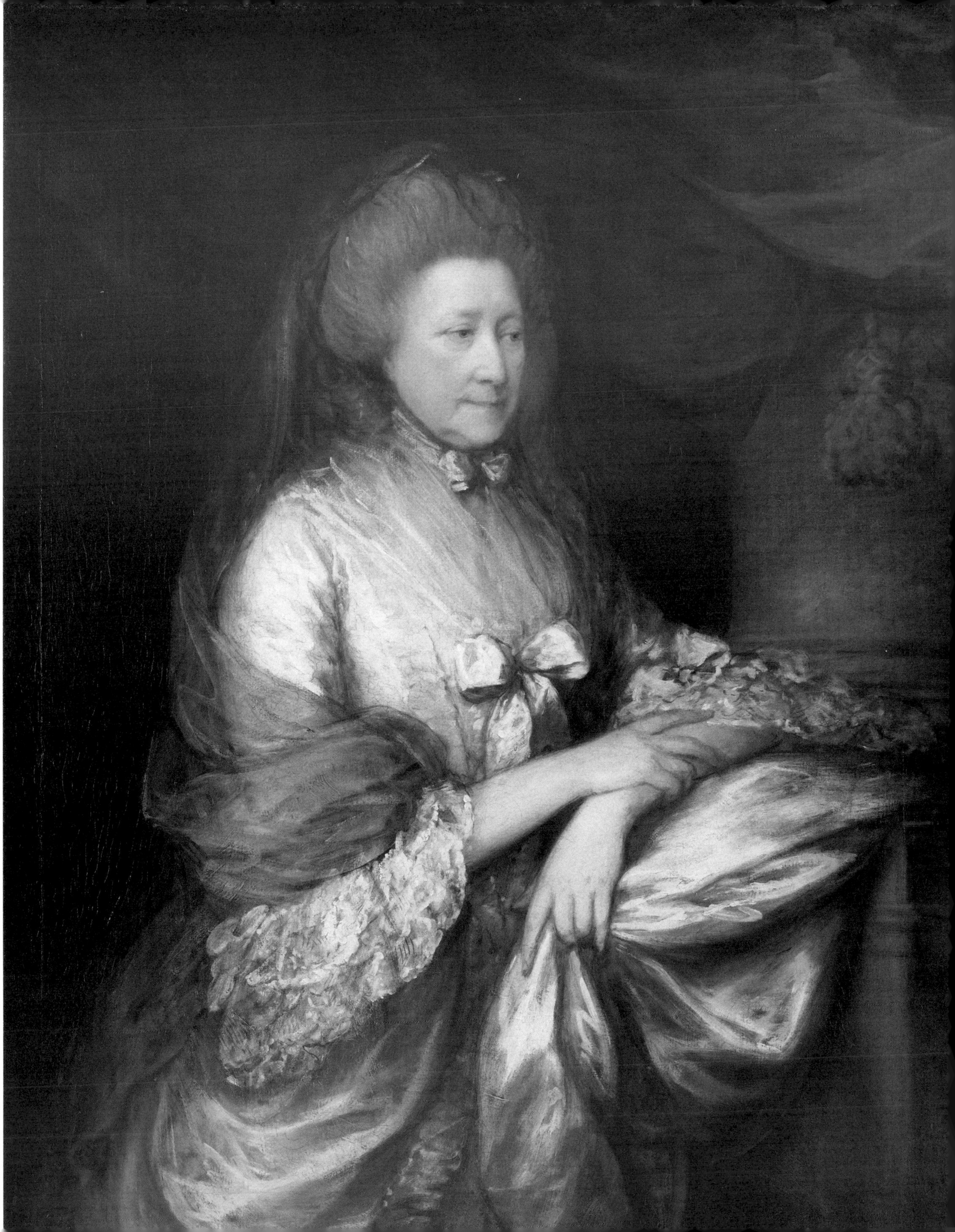

WAG 229

after

Thomas Gainsborough

1727–88

Wooded Landscape with Figures in a Country Cart and Cattle

WAG 228

oil on canvas, 97 × 136 cm

date: unknown, perhaps about 1790–1815

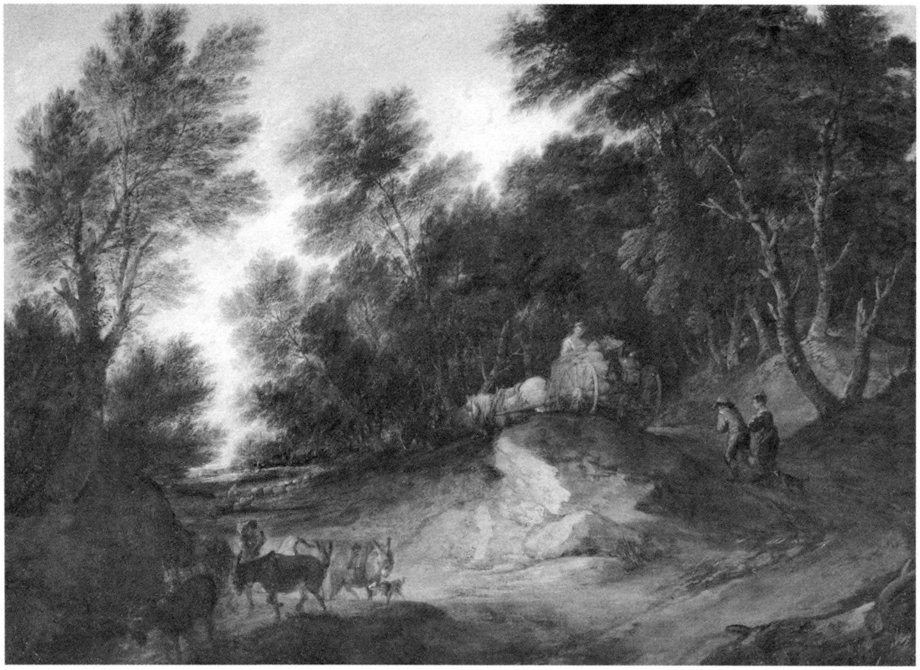

WAG 228

Purchased by George Holt as by Gainsborough, WAG 228 has subsequently been identified as a copy with variations, by a later artist, of Gainsborough's *Wooded Landscape with Figures in a Country Cart and Donkeys* (Penrhyn Castle [Douglas-Pennant Collection] The National Trust; fig. 22).[1] Gainsborough's original, substantially larger than WAG 228 at 142 × 190 cm, has been dated to 1777–78.[2] The chief difference between it and WAG 228 consists in the presence in the left foreground of a group of donkeys instead of a herd of cows. Otherwise the composition of WAG 228 follows the original closely, with only the slightly more open handling of the foliage of the trees striking a further divergent note.

Neither the date of WAG 228 nor the identity of the copyist is known. It displays considerable sensitivity to Gainsborough's idiom. The idea that it may have been painted when the Penrhyn version was on public exhibition seems to be ruled out, since that work is not known to have been shown in public prior to 1865.[3] Nevertheless, there were clearly opportunities for other artists to copy it since two further versions, closer to the size of the original, are known.[4] William Esdaile, the first recorded owner of WAG 228, bought one other Gainsborough landscape at Christie's in 1801, but is not recorded as purchasing any other work by the artist at auction in the first two decades of the nineteenth century.[5]

PROVENANCE

...William Esdaile (d.1837); his son-in-law R. Goring Thomas; Christie 16 May 1863 (125) bt. in; R. Goring Thomas;[6] Christie 12 May 1888 (25) bt. Henson; from whom bt. by Gooden; from whom bt. by George Holt July 1889; Emma Holt Bequest 1945.

EXHIBITIONS

Old Masters RA 1881 (50); Grosvenor Gallery, London 1888 (155); *Exhibition of English Landscapes in Aid of the Arists' General Benevolent Institution* Agnews, London 1926 (3); *Some Acquisitions of the Walker Art Gallery Liverpool 1935–1945* National Gallery, London 1945 (11).

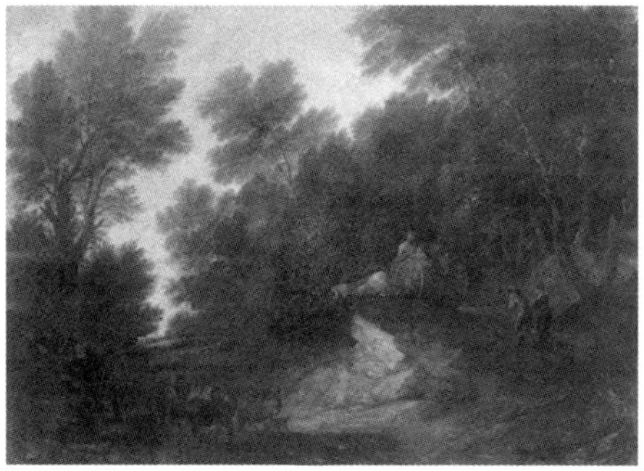

Fig. 22 *Wooded Landscape with Figures in a Country Cart and Cattle* by Thomas Gainsborough, oil on canvas. Penrhyn Castle, The Douglas-Pennant Collection (The National Trust); © National Trust Images.

NOTES

1. John Hayes: *The Landscape Paintings of Thomas Gainsborough* 2 vols (London, 1982) vol. 2, p. 468. Ellis Waterhouse: *Gainsborough* (London, 1958) pp. 116–7 (cat. 935) and pl. 193, held WAG 228 to be an authentic work by Gainsborough. The entry on the work in George Holt's ms catalogue of pictures records the presence of a signature in the bottom left-hand corner, which was also noted by Agnew's in 1920 when it was sent by Emma Holt to be cleaned (gallery files). This is no longer visible, but knowledge of its former existence probably informed Hayes's demotion of the work.
2. Hayes, *loc. cit.*; and compare also vol. 1, pp. 128, 164, 167. Hayes views it as one of Gainsborough's most rhythmic and 'Picturesque' landscapes.
3. Hayes, *loc. cit.*
4. Hayes, *loc. cit.*; however, according to Ellis Waterhouse, *letter*, 27 May 1946 (gallery files) the painting lent by E. Bolton to the British exhibition in Nice 1934 was copied from WAG 228, not the Penrhyn version.
5. Hayes, *op. cit.*, p. 561; and see B. Fredericksen, ed.: *The Index of Paintings Sold in the British Isles during the Nineteenth Century*, vols 1–4 (Oxford, 1988–96).
6. Lent by Goring Thomas to the 1881 and 1888 exhibitions.

attributed to

Sawrey Gilpin

1733–1807

Frightened Horses in a Landscape

WAG 2392
oil on panel, 22.5 × 28 cm
date: about 1800–05

This work entered the Walker's collection as *King George III's Racehorses* by George Stubbs. On the back is pasted what appears to be an extract from a sale catalogue:

394 / Landscape, with Portraits of Three Horses, 10½ × 8 / Two being Clementina and King of Trumps, the latter a piebald. The picture was presented by the painter to Mr Armstrong, Veterinary Surgeon to Geo. III, and these horses no doubt belonged to the King, for it is now found that he kept racehorses, and ran them under an assumed name.

The source of this text is unknown, but it has been assumed, by a process of elimination, to come from the sale catalogue of Edward Quaile,[1] and if so, it dates from after 1881, when Quaile lent the picture to the Liverpool Art Club's *British Artists* exhibition. The information is highly suspect: at best garbled, perhaps wholly fictitious. A veterinary surgeon named William Armstrong graduated from the London Veterinary College in July 1810, lived in Birmingham, and died in 1837; and he is known to have specialised in horses.[2] However, there is no evidence that he was ever employed by George III;[3] and if he genuinely was presented with the work by Stubbs, it must have been when he was still a youth. There is also no evidence that George III owned horses named Clementina or King of Trumps,[4] although the General Stud Book does list three separate racehorses called Clementina in the period 1789–92, none of which appear to have any connection with the story related above.

The style of WAG 2392 does not at all resemble the work of Stubbs, and for some years the painting has been attributed to Sawrey Gilpin.[5] Two works by Gilpin in UK galleries in which the depiction of the horses bears a distinct resemblance to their treatment in WAG 2392 are *A Grey Arab* (Fitzwilliam Museum, Cambridge)[6] and *Frightened Horses in a Storm* (Tullie House Museum, Carlisle).[7] Furthermore, Gilpin painted groups of three racehorses for both George III and

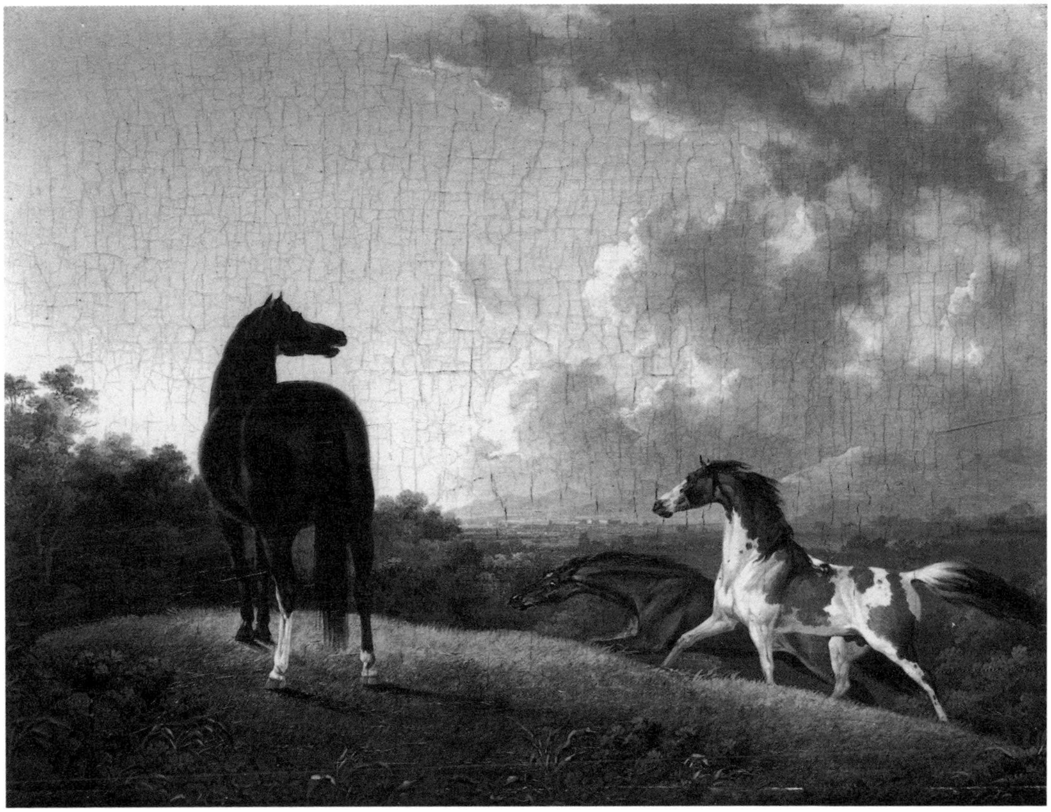

WAG 2392

the future George IV, on both occasions combining three horses of different colours. The composition of the painting done for George III (Royal Collection)[8] is unrelated to WAG 2392; the painting for the Prince of Wales has disappeared, but it is known to have measured 64 × 84 inches and depicted a roan, a brown and a white. It occupied Gilpin throughout the summer of 1804 and was probably the painting exhibited at the Royal Academy in 1805 (205).[9] WAG 2392 could turn out to be a reduced version of it,[10] if the white horse was altered to a piebald.

PROVENANCE

...John Bowman; Christie 28 January 1876 (96); bt. Scott; ...Edward Quaile by 1881; ...Revd S. A. Thompson Yates; his bequest 1904.

EXHIBITIONS

Loan Collection of Oil Paintings by British Artists born before 1801 Liverpool Art Club 1881 (224); *Animals in Art* Whitechapel Art Gallery, London 1907 (Upper Gallery, 36); *Historical Exhibition of Liverpool Art* Walker Art Gallery 1908 (531); *The Liverpool School of Painters* Harrogate 1924 (34).

NOTES

1. Draft catalogue entry by Hugh Macandrew, about 1962, gallery files. However, the sale has not been traced and its existence is conjectural.
2. J. R. Barber-Lomax, Wellcome Foundation, *letter*, 22 October 1962, gallery files.
3. R. C. Mackworth-Young, Librarian of the Royal Archives, Windsor, *letter*, 7 December 1961, gallery files.
4. Mackworth-Young, *loc. cit.*
5. The attribution was first proposed by Basil Taylor, *letter*, July 1963, gallery files, where he stated that the 'anxious mood' of the composition was typical of Gilpin. Taylor may have been thinking particularly of Gilpin's *A Grey Arab* (see n. 6). The attribution of WAG 2392 to Gilpin was first published in CIC.
6. Repr. Basil Taylor: *Stubbs* (London, 1971) fig. 7, where dated 1770–80; but see also J. W. Goodison: *Fitzwilliam Museum Cambridge Catalogue of Paintings III. The British School* (Cambridge, 1977) p. 88, who points out that the composition is related to Gilpin's *Portrait of Jupiter, the Property of Col. Thornton*, exhibited at the RA in 1792 (408), citing the reproduction of the latter in W. Shaw Sparrow: *A Book of Sporting Painters* (London, 1931) p. 41.
7. Repr. D. A. Cross: 'Sawrey Gilpin R.A., Rival of Stubbs', *The Armitt Journal*, vol. 1 (1998) p. 76; probably the *Horses in a Thunderstorm* exhibited at the RA in 1799 (131).
8. Oliver Millar: *Later Georgian Pictures in the Collection of Her Majesty the Queen* 2 vols (London, 1969) vol.1, p. 46, no. 825; vol. 2, pl. 23; and see nos 819–24 and pls 210–22 for further works by Gilpin in the Royal Collection.
9. Millar, *op. cit.*, vol.1, p. 45.
10. Goodison, *loc. cit.*, observes that 'Gilpin is known to have painted "cabinet versions" of his large pictures'.

Thomas Gooch

1750–1802

A Stallion with Its Groom

WAG 9810
oil on paper on board backed to canvas,[1]
44.5 × 55 cm
signed and dated: *T Gooch/1794*
(bottom left)
date: 1794

The work is presumably a Sefton heirloom, and may have been commissioned or purchased by William, Viscount Molyneux, the future 2nd Earl of Sefton. Both horse and groom are strongly characterised, suggesting that Gooch has portrayed individuals, rather than invented a generic scene.[2] The work is recorded at Croxteth in 1946.[3]

PROVENANCE

...Hugh, 7th Earl of Sefton by 1946; by descent to Josephine, Countess of Sefton; her bequest 1980.

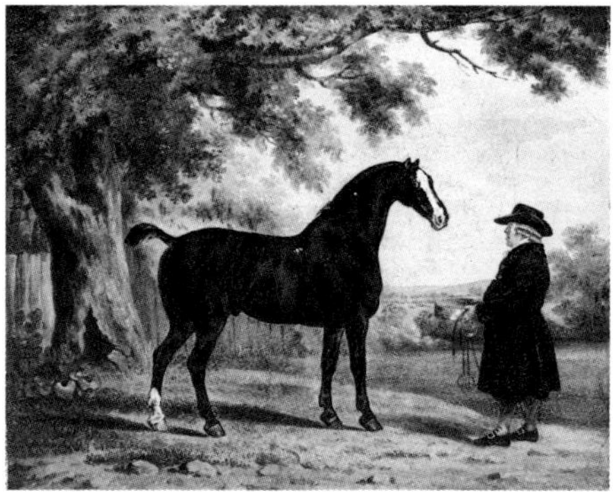

WAG 9810

NOTES

1. The painting was strip-lined with sailcloth in 1997.
2. Gooch's 13 exhibits at the Royal Academy in 1794 included six 'character' studies of different types of horse (including no. 236: *The Stallion; a Character*). No. 47 in the same exhibition was his *Curricle Horse, the Property of a Nobleman*. In 1795 his two exhibits were *Portrait of a Hunter* (101) and *Portrait of a Favourite Hackney* (311). WAG 9810 could be one of these (although this horse is perhaps rather sturdy to pull a curricle).
3. *Croxteth 1946 Inventory* no. 25.

after

Gawen Hamilton

1697–1737

The Card Party

WAG 2269
oil on canvas, 69.5 × 58.5 cm
date: unknown, perhaps about 1730–40

On its acquisition by the gallery WAG 2269 was attributed to Hogarth, and believed to represent the family of Sir James Thornhill, with Hogarth himself in the background. The basis of this belief was a letter to Charles Baring Wall pasted to the back of the work:

29 Pall Mall 17 April 1844 / Dear Sir, My Brothers account of the picture you were so good to purchase is, as nearly as I can recollect, as follows. / It was painted by Hogarth and the tradition is that it was called his propriatory [sic] piece – He having married a Daughter of Sir James Thornhill against her father's consent, on the occasion of the reconciliation presented this picture to Sir James. / Sir James Thornhill bequeathed it to his son – who in his necessities pawned it – the picture was never redeemed – and the Grandson of the Pawnbroker gave it to my brother, I think about ten or twelve years since. / I have to acknowledge the receipt of your draft for £100. – as the price of the said picture. / I have the honour to be Dear Sir your obliged Servant F. Croix.

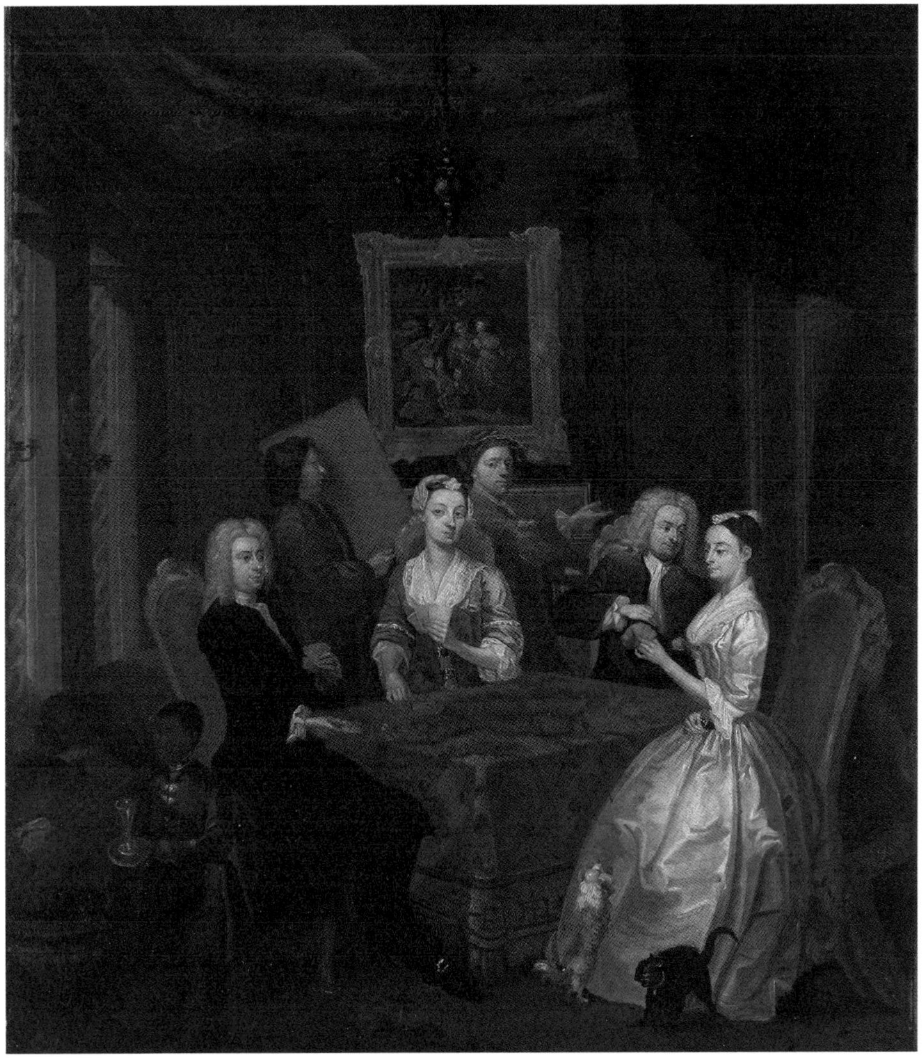

WAG 2269

Subsequently, the work was re-attributed to Gawen Hamilton, both on stylistic grounds and because of the close resemblance of the figure in the centre background to what is traditionally identified as a self-portrait on the right-hand side of Hamilton's *Club of Artists* (National Portrait Gallery, London; fig. 23).[1] Comparison with two other versions of *The Card Party*, one at Tate Britain, London (fig. 24) and one sold at Sotheby 15 November 1989 (31)[2] reveals that WAG 2269 is of inferior quality to both and must be an early copy.

The view that Sir James Thornhill and his wife are portrayed has stood the test of time; however, it has recently been argued that the figure in the cap is not Hamilton, but the artist Dietrich Ernst André (1680–1734; also known as Andreae) who worked with Thornhill between 1722 and 1724 on the decoration of the Great Hall at Greenwich, supplying large allegorical scenes in grisaille.[3] Supporting the view that the relationship between André and Thornhill is the central subject of the work is the fact that in the background hangs a painting by André's teacher, Justus van Bentum, an *Allegory of Painting and Sculpture*, a singularly apposite piece to allude to the kind of work (painting masquerading as sculpture) which André supplied for Thornhill.[4] According to George Vertue, while in England André married a 'folish extravagant woman' whom he left behind when he returned to Germany,[5] and it seems very plausible that the figure holding her cards in her left hand is Mrs André. But instead of her husband standing behind her, it seems much more natural to assume that he is the man sitting next to her[6] and that the card party is made up of two married couples, with the Thornhills, recognisable from other portraits of them,[7] sitting at the right. The setting must be their house, partly because it is to Thornhill's wife Judith (d. 1757) that the dog and cat are paying their attentions, and partly because only a very distinguished artist is likely to have had a slave (depicted in an iron collar) to serve the drinks. That leaves the artist in the background free to be Hamilton after all. It is tempting to infer, from the proximity of his figure to Mrs André's, and the fact that the two of them are looking out of the composition at the viewer, that there was some connection between them (and even that this was what lay behind André's return to Germany). It is unclear whether Hamilton's original composition is dateable to as early as 1722–24, the years when André worked for Thornhill, or whether the work is retrospective. The similarity of Hamilton's self-portrait in this work to the one in the *Club of Artists*, which dates from 1735, suggests the latter. However, it must predate 1734, the year in which Thornhill died. The degree to which the work may be connected with Hogarth's estrangement from and reconciliation with Thornhill in the years 1729–31 remains unresolved, but it may be premature to conclude that this is entirely a red herring, especially if a dating of around 1730–32 is accepted.[8]

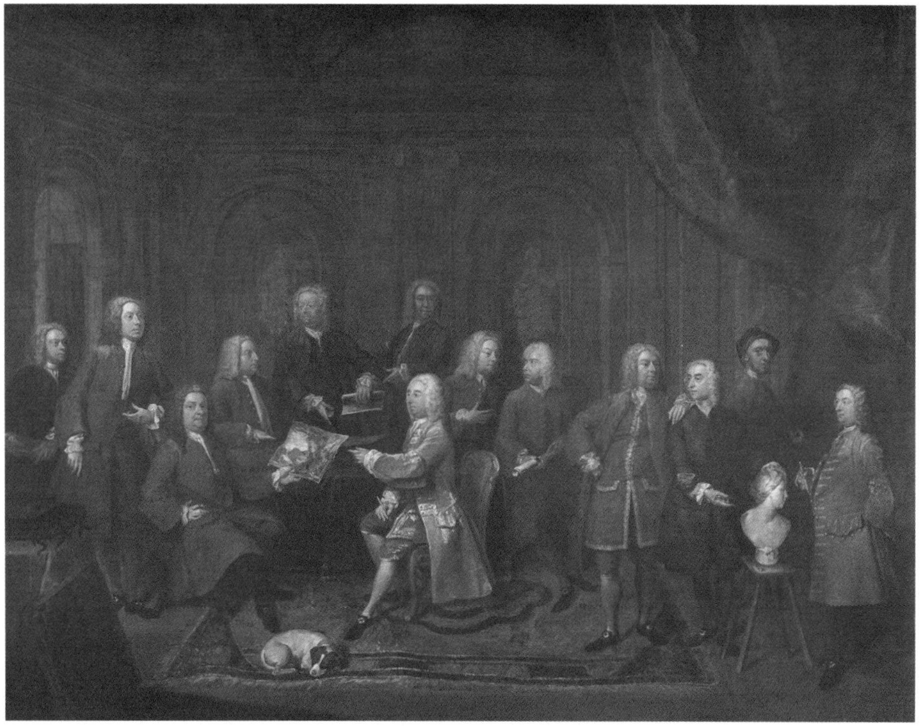

Fig. 23 *A Club of Artists* by Gawen Hamilton, oil on canvas.
© National Portrait Gallery, London.

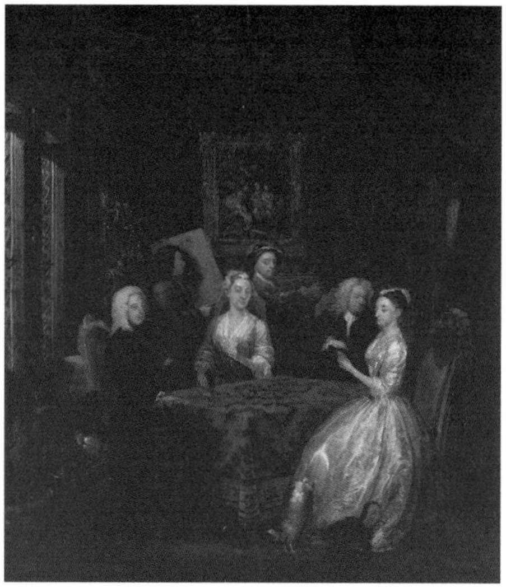

Fig. 24 *An Elegant Company Playing Cards* by Gawen Hamilton, oil on canvas. © Tate, London 2011.

PROVENANCE

...Mr Croix;[9] from whom bt. before 1844 by Charles Baring Wall; by descent to his cousin Thomas Baring (1799–1873); bequeathed to his nephew, 2nd Baron Northbrook; by descent; Christie 5 December 1941 (37); bt. Allan; ... Leggatt; from whom bt. by the gallery 1945.

EXHIBITIONS

Art in the Georgian Home York City Art Gallery and tour 1949 (10); *Selected Acquisitions of the Walker Art Gallery Liverpool 1945–1955* Agnew's, London 1955 (17); *Painting in England 1700–1750* Walker Art Gallery 1958 (10).

NOTES

1. The re-attribution was made in correspondence between Hugh Scrutton, Walker Art Gallery, and David Baxandall, National Galleries of Scotland, 1953–54, on the basis of earlier correspondence between Ralph Fastnedge and John Tillotson (see n. 2); Tillotson, who had bought his version of the painting as by Hogarth in November 1951, was aware of the resemblance to the likeness in the *Club of Artists* at least by February 1952 (*letters*, gallery files). Ralph Edwards: *Early Conversation Pieces* (London, 1954) p. 66 endorsed the view that the figure is the same in both works.

2. The Tate version emerged in a sale at Sotheby 25 June 1941 (106); bt. Sabin; and was sold again at Christie 23 November 1951 (106); bt. Spink for John Tillotson; Tillotson immediately had the slave painted out (*letter*, 20 February 1952, gallery files); this figure was re-instated during conservation at the Tate in 1986. The same conservation treatment revealed heavy overpainting and yielded the suggestion that the canvas had originally been left unfinished (Elizabeth Einberg and Judy Egerton: *Tate Gallery Catalogues: The Age of Hogarth. British Painters Born 1675–1709* (London, 1988) p. 36; entry by Elizabeth Einberg). The version sold at Sotheby in 1989 is the one mentioned in the *Gentleman's Magazine* (1794) pp. 903–4 as having been in the collection of 'the late Mr Hammond of Colchester, an ingenious coach and house painter who, it is said, worked some time under Mr Hogarth', and was then owned by Revd Charles Onley of Stisted Hall, Essex; it descended in his family until sold at Christie 16 June 1894 (56); bt. Colnaghi; in 1929 it was owned by Otto Bundy, Vienna, attributed to Hogarth under the title *A Card Table with Peg Woffington*. This, which may also be a copy of the Tate picture, lacks the spaniel present in the latter work and in WAG 2269.

3. Einberg, *op. cit.*, p. 38.

4. *Ibid.* The painting was identified by Einberg when van Bentum's monogrammed canvas appeared at Sotheby 13 February 1985 (38).

5. Einberg, *op. cit.*, p. 39.

6. Einberg's argument that the standing figure at the back is André depends on her opinion that the likeness of this man to Hamilton as he appears in the *Club of Artists* is 'arguable' (*op. cit.*, p. 36) whereas his likeness to a self-portrait by André in the Kunsthalle, Hamburg (her fig. 10, p. 37) is 'marked'. This view is difficult to accept. For one thing, André was in his early forties during his stay in England, which seems the age of the figure at the left but not the man in the background; for another, this argument leaves Einberg without a good candidate for the figure at the left. If Hamilton's picture was indeed done some time after the event depicted (see main text) this would be an explanation for why the likeness of André is a weak and generalised one.

7. Einberg, *op. cit.*, p. 39, cites Jonathan Richardson's portrait drawing of Thornhill of 1733 (British Museum) and the unattributed portrait of Lady Thornhill at Nostell Priory.

8. Ralph Edwards: 'Three Hogarth Conversations', *Apollo* vol. 98 (October 1973) p. 267, describes *A Card Party* as 'obviously close in date' to Hamilton's *Thomas Wentworth, Earl of Strafford and his Family*, signed and dated 1732. It also shows a strong compositional similarity to the five figures in the left-centre of Hogarth's *Wollaston Family* of 1730 (repr. Jenny Uglow: *Hogarth* [London, 1997] p. 164).

9. See main text above; this man was the brother of the F. Croix whose letter to Charles Baring Wall is attached to the reverse of WAG 2269. It is tempting to wonder whether the latter's account of the work's acquisition by his brother is garbled and it is in fact the version owned by John Andrews and sold after his death at Christie 3 March 1832 (i.e. 'ten

or twelve years ago') (84) as Hogarth: *The Family of James Thornhill Playing at Cards, with a Portrait of the Painter in the Background*; bt. Donovan (noted by Einberg, *op. cit.*, p. 36).

Joseph Highmore

1692–1780

King George II

WAG 3160
oil on canvas, 241.5 × 147.5 cm
signed: *Jos. Highmore pinx.* (bottom left)
date: unknown, perhaps about 1740–55

George II (1683–1760) succeeded his father George I as king of Great Britain in 1727. Brought up in Hanover, he came to England for the first time at the age of 31 in 1714, and he always spoke English with a thick German accent. His 33-year reign witnessed the fragmentation of the Whig hegemony of politics associated with the figure of Sir Robert Walpole, two major wars (the war of the Austrian Succession and the Seven Years war; George II is often remembered as the last British monarch to lead his troops in battle, at Dettingen, in 1743) and the defeat of the Jacobite uprising of 1745. George II enjoyed music and was a notable patron of George Frederick Handel, but notoriously 'hated boetry and bainting'. However, he was portrayed by a succession of artists, including (besides Highmore) Sir Godfrey Kneller, Charles Jervas, Enoch Seeman, Bartholomew Dandridge, Thomas Hudson, William Kent, and in later years John Shackleton (his principal painter-in-ordinary from 1749) and Robert Edge Pine.

Although WAG 3160 may be broadly assigned to the period 1730–55, its precise date is difficult to ascertain. According to George Vertue, writing in 1731, Highmore who

coud not obtain the Honour of the King or Queen setting to him for their pictures did by stealth draw them first on paper at Several Views, and afterwards by Memory in some parts & copying those pictures before Painted by Sr. G. Kneller – he made two pictures which he thought to be more like their Majestyes than others done before. This in time to come may explain how them two prints lately done by Faber came to be subscribed Hymore pinxit.[1]

The print of the king by John Faber published in 1731 in half-length format (fig. 25) has been assumed to derive from a lost original painted by Highmore in a bid for royal favour;[2] size apart, it exhibits considerable differences in detail from Highmore's two currently known full-lengths, and borrows much more closely, especially in the pose of the right arm, from Kneller's 1716 full-length portrait of George as Prince of Wales (Royal Collection).[3] One of the full-lengths was commissioned as long afterwards as 1755 by Charles, Marquis of Rockingham (fig. 26);[4] the history of the other – WAG 3160, perhaps the earlier of the two, judging by the king's apparent age – remains obscure. It has been conjectured that it is the whole-length of the king that remained, with a pendant of Queen Caroline, in Highmore's possession and was auctioned after his retirement in his studio sale at Langford's, 5 March 1762 (67);[5] but this scenario does not square easily with its emergence in the collection of the Earls of Falmouth. It seems more likely that the work was commissioned either by Hugh Boscawen, 1st Viscount Falmouth (about 1680–1734) who had been comptroller of the household of King George I and in the early part of George II's reign may have harboured (vain) hopes of a return to political favour; or by his eldest son, Hugh, 2nd Viscount (1707–82) who was appointed Captain of the Yeomen of the Guard to George II in 1747. However, to date no trace of WAG 3160 in Boscawen family ownership in the eighteenth or nineteenth centuries has emerged.

In WAG 3160 the king wears a blue ermine-lined robe of state used for less formal occasions, the ribbon of the Order of St George (appropriate to his name) and the Garter below his left knee. The orb and sceptre are absent and the crown of St Edmund is placed inconspicuously in shadow behind him. The image is less one of royal authority than of a monarch acting in line with Whig parliamentary principles. In commissioning his version for the Rockingham Club in York, the Marquis of Rockingham must have been aware of the political dimension of Highmore's treatment of the king.

PROVENANCE

...Evelyn, 8th Viscount Falmouth; Sotheby premises sale at Mereworth Castle, Kent 16 December 1925 (129); bt. Permain; ...Sir Ernest Royden; by whom presented to the gallery 1952.

EXHIBITION

The Taste of Yesterday Walker Art Gallery 1970 (3).

NOTES

1. Mrs A. Esdaile, Lord Ilchester and H. M. Hake, eds: 'Vertue Notebooks Volume III', *Walpole Society* vol. 22 1933–34 (1934) p. 54.
2. Alison S. Lewis: 'Joseph Highmore 1692–1780', PhD thesis, Harvard University, 1975 (Xerox University Microfilms, Ann Arbor 1979) pp. 70–3, 89–90, 368 (cat. 1) and 553 (cat. LP1).
3. Sir Oliver Millar: *Tudor, Stuart and Earlier Georgian Pictures in the Collection of Her Majesty the Queen* 2 vols (London, 1963) vol. 1, pp. 144–5; repr. vol. 2, pl. 147. An entirely separate, equestrian portrait of George II in armour measuring 75 × 62 cm was later painted by Highmore; Lewis, *op. cit.* pp. 370–1 (cat. 3). Perhaps commissioned by Charles, 2nd Duke of Richmond, Master of the Horse at George II's coronation, it was sold at Sotheby 15 July 1987 (49).
4. See John Ingamells: *Pictures in the Mansion House York* (York, 1970) pp. 3–6 and Ingamells: 'The State Room Portraits in the York Mansion House', *Connoisseur* vol. 176 (February 1971) pp. 77–83.
5. Lewis, *op. cit.* p. 553 (cat. LP2).

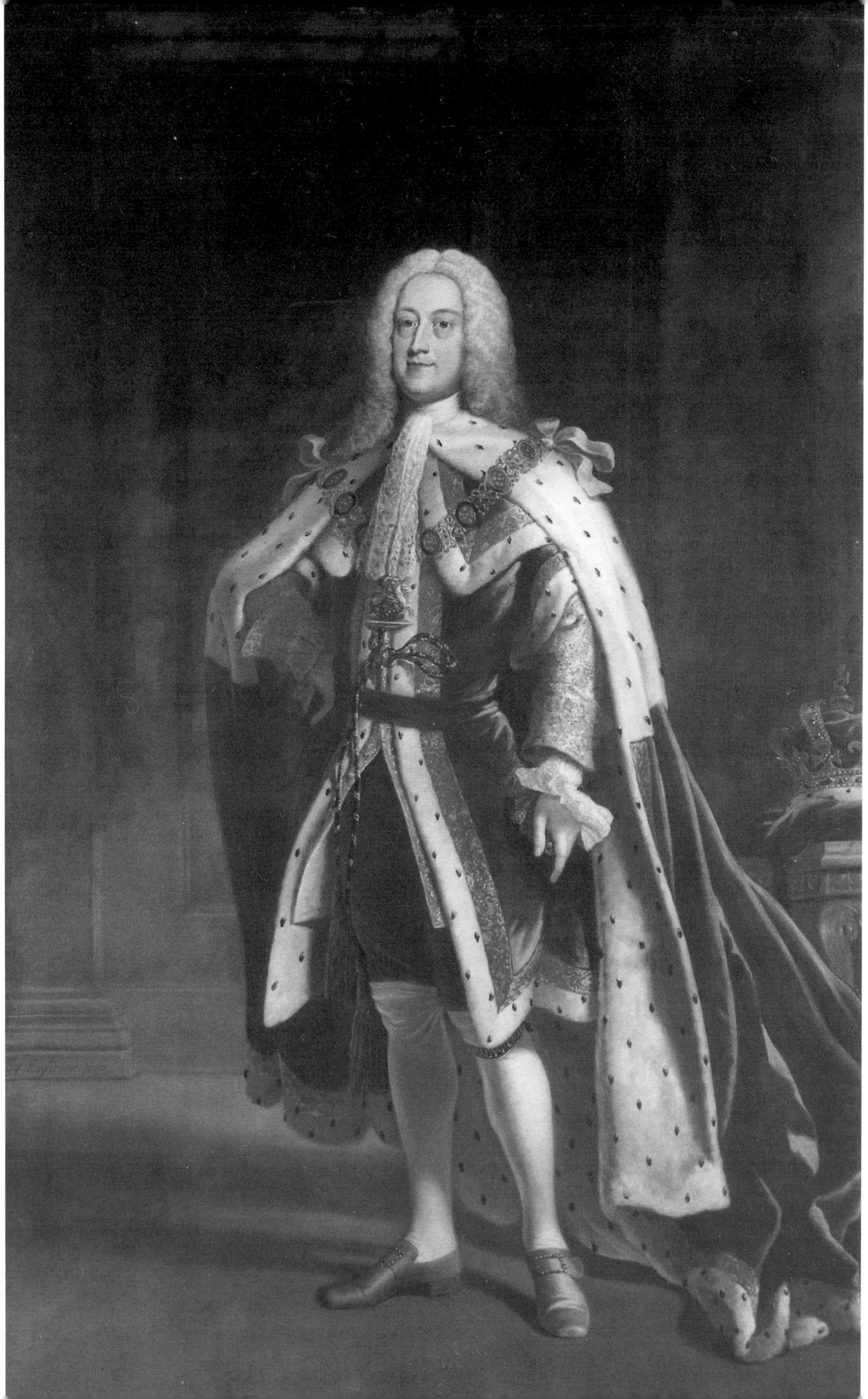

WAG 3160

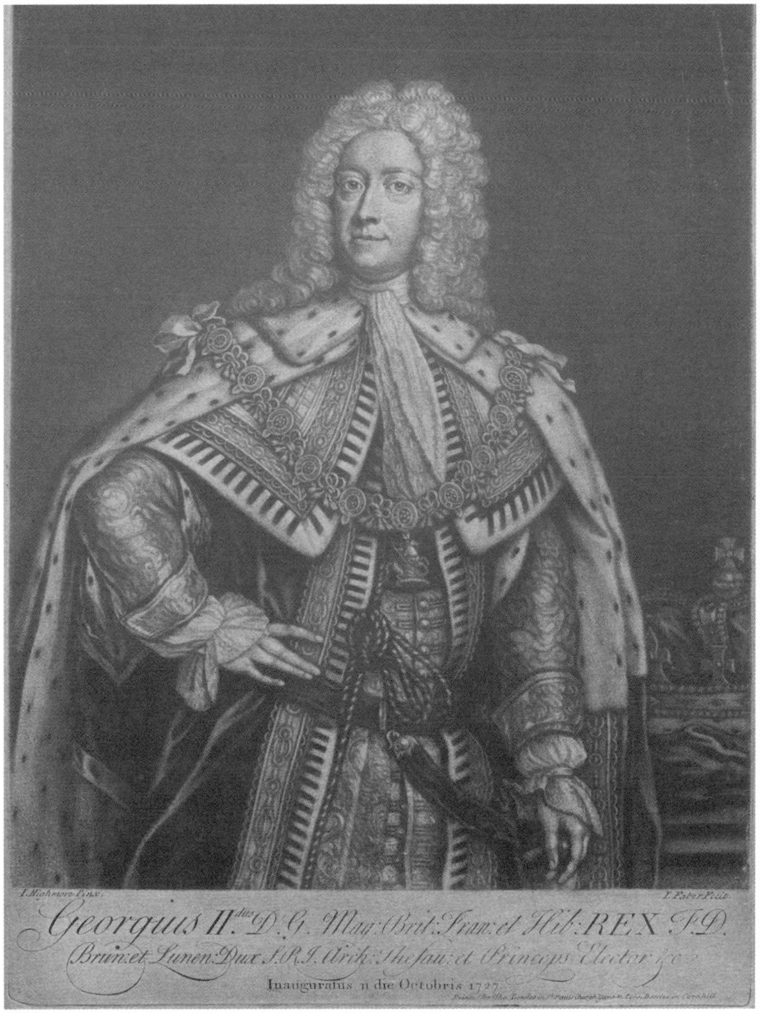

Fig. 25 *King George II* after Joseph Highmore, engraving by John Faber.
© National Portrait Gallery, London.

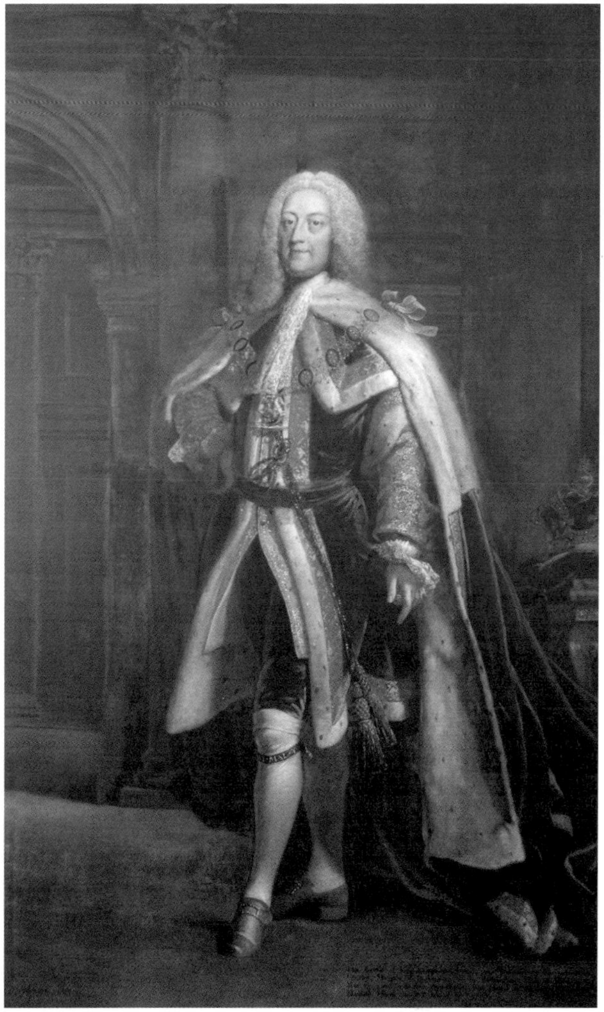

Fig. 26 *George II* by Joseph Highmore, oil on canvas.
Mansion House, York.

Anne, Duchess of Chandos

WAG 1354
oil on canvas, 126.5 × 103 cm
signed and dated: *Jos. Highmore/pinx. 1746*
(bottom left)
date: 1746

The sitter (date of birth unknown, d. 1759) was the daughter of John Wells of Marylebone and Newbury, Berks. She was a chambermaid at the Pelican Inn, Newbury and married to an ostler named Jeffries when she met Henry, 2nd Duke of Chandos (1708–71). According to the most familiar account of their union, the Duke (who had been widowed in 1738) and a companion were dining at the inn on their way up to London when

a stir in the Inn yard led to their being told that a man was going to sell his wife, and they are leading her up with a halter round her neck. They went to see. The Duke was smitten by her beauty and patient acquiescence in a process which would (as then supposed) free her from a harsh and ill-conditioned husband. He bought her, and subsequently married her (at Keith's chapel) Christmas Day 1744.[1]

According to other sources, the Duke married Anne clandestinely in 1738, but only made the marriage public in 1744, upon the death of his father and his succession to the Dukedom.[2] The marriage scandalised London society,[3] but it was a happy one. The couple had one child, Augusta Ann (1748–79).[4]

Highmore's portrait emphasises the sitter's newly acquired social rank: she wears the ermine-lined robes of a peeress and her duchess coronet is prominently placed by her right hand. Her expression perhaps conveys a touch of exultation. The robes – possibly the work of a drapery painter – are voluptuously handled, with a solidity that contrasts with the delicate treatment of the lace at her breast and cuffs. It is tempting to wonder whether the Duchess's choice of Highmore to sit to was based on the fact that in 1743–44 he had painted 12 scenes from Samuel Richardson's celebrated novel *Pamela* (1740), in which the eponymous heroine, a maidservant, finally wins the hand in marriage of the upper-class Mr B.

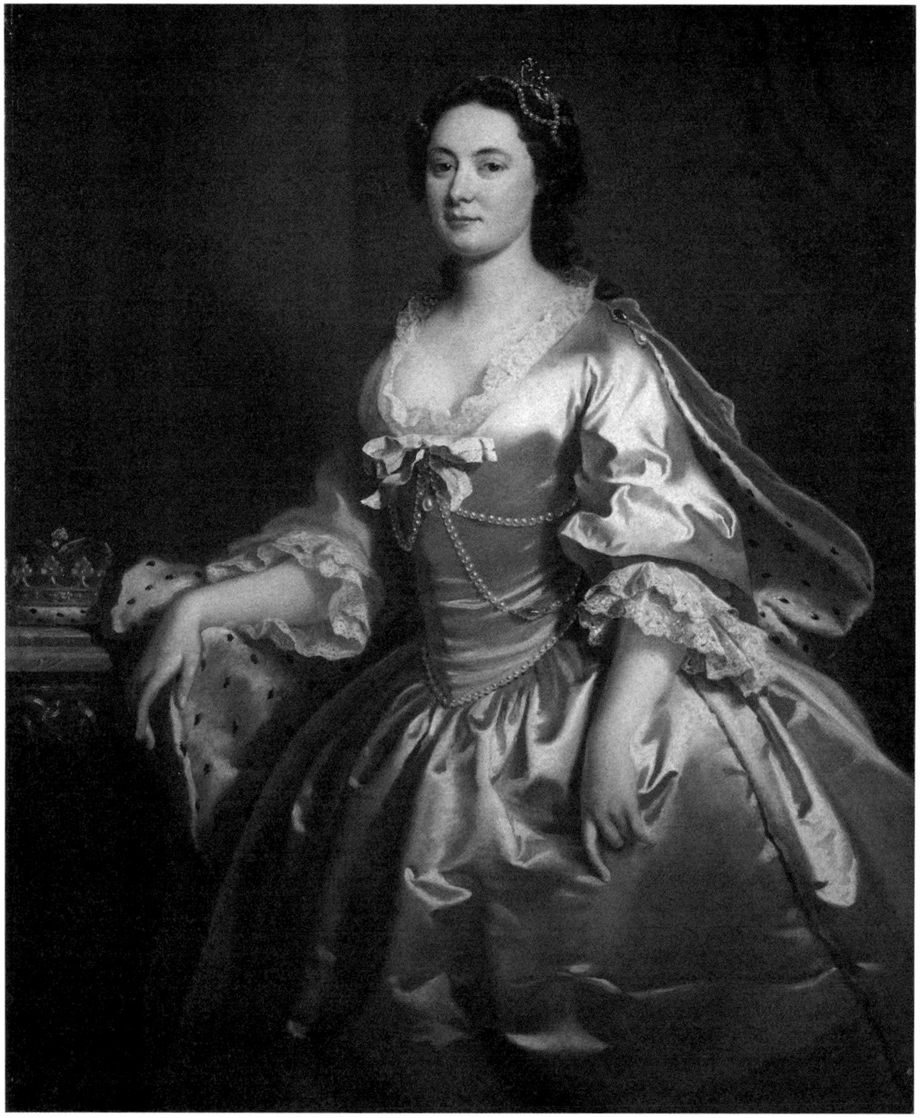

WAG 1354

PROVENANCE

Henry, 2nd Duke of Chandos; his third wife Elizabeth; presumably passed to the children of her sister, Mrs Anne Henniker; by descent at Thornham Hall, Suffolk to Charles Henry, 6th Baron Henniker; John D. Wood at Thornham Hall 27 May 1937 (1009); bt. Colnaghi; from whom bt. by the gallery 1940.

EXHIBITIONS

Burlington Magazine Exhibition Sotheby's, London 1940 (18); *Painting and Sculpture in England 1700–1750* Walker Art Gallery 1958 (16); *Paintings by Joseph Highmore* Iveagh Bequest, Kenwood 1963 (29).

NOTES

1. E. W.: 'The Duke of Chandos Buying a Wife', *Notes and Queries* (4th series) vol. 6 (August 1870) p. 179.

2. Alison S. Lewis: 'Joseph Highmore 1692–1870', PhD thesis, Harvard University, 1975 (Xerox University Microfilms, Ann Arbor 1979) p. 400 (cat. 40).
3. C. H. Collins Baker and Muriel I. Baker: *The Life and Circumstances of James Brydges, 1st Duke of Chandos* (Oxford, 1949) pp. 2, 5, 261, 263.
4. Her portrait by Highmore, also 127 × 102 cm, was commissioned about 1755; Lewis *op. cit.*, p. 402 (cat. 42).

called

Nicholas Hilliard

1547–1619

Queen Elizabeth I: The Pelican Portrait

WAG 2994
oil on panel, 78.5 × 61 cm
date: about 1573–75

Queen Elizabeth I (1533–1603) was the second daughter of King Henry VIII; the issue of his second marriage, to Anne Boleyn.[1] She succeeded to the throne after the death of her elder half-sister, Mary I, in 1558. During the course of her 45-year reign, England's position as a European power was consolidated and Protestantism was re-established as the country's official faith; however, her disinclination to marry and bear an heir engendered an element of perpetual political instability. Elizabeth had a disciplined attitude to ruling her nation which led her to adopt the role of figurehead, even martyr, for her people. This image is enshrined in WAG 2994, most notably in the bleached and unrealistic depiction of her features that presents her as distant icon, and in the pelican pendant at her breast. The pelican is a bird that draws its own blood by pecking at itself, and is a traditional emblem of Christ's self-sacrifice for humankind.

The work has traditionally been related to a miniature portrait of Elizabeth dated 1572 (National Portrait Gallery; fig. 27) which has generally been attributed to Nicholas Hilliard. It has been argued that this miniature was taken from the life and was the product of the sitting which Hilliard later referred to in his *Treatise concerning the Art of Limning.*[2] WAG 2994 is one of several portraits in large of the queen made shortly afterwards adapting the miniature's treatment of pose and costume, of which the most closely related to it (and the same size) is the so-called *Phoenix Portrait* (National Portrait Gallery, on long loan to Tate Britain; fig. 28). In this, the face (although it is spatially handled in a different way) is a mirror image of that in WAG 2994. It has recently been confirmed that both portraits were made from a cartoon intended to be used from both sides,[3] while dendrochronological analysis has shown that their two panel supports were constructed from the same two planks of wood.[4] This evidence supports the view that the two works were made virtually in conjunction with each other. Although the costume in WAG 2994 is more elaborate than that in the miniature, the similarity between them suggests that the *Pelican Portrait* postdates the miniature by no more than a year or two. Certainly, the costume in both the *Pelican* and *Phoenix* portraits has been dated to the mid-1570s,[5] as against a later portrait in the series (private collection) which appears to have been based on use of the same cartoon but whose costume has been placed at around 1583–84.[6] It has been argued, from the nature of the relationship between the miniature, the (putative) cartoon, and the large pictures, that the latter are also by Hilliard[7] yet this attribution has never been wholly accepted. Hilliard would later in his *Treatise* describe the medium of oils as 'vile in limning',[8] and his training as a goldsmith and practice as a miniaturist had to date carried no implication that he was skilled in the techniques of painting in oil. One recent suggestion is that both the *Pelican* and the *Phoenix* portraits are workshop productions involving more than one hand, but that there are sufficiently close stylistic similarities with the miniature in the handling of Elizabeth's ringlets and ruff (especially) that it is difficult to avoid the conclusion that Hilliard worked on the large portraits also.[9] A second recent suggestion, however, is that both miniature and WAG 2994 are the work of the Flemish-born female miniaturist, Lievine Teerlinc (c. 1519–76), who worked for the English court from the time of her employment by Katherine Parr in the mid-1540s.[10]

In WAG 2994 the queen wears a gold coronet decorated with jewels and pearls, one of which hangs forward and touches her forehead. Pearls are a traditional symbol of the Virgin Mary, and this pearl, together with the one at the queen's neck and the profusion of them on her costume, probably denote her conscious espousal of virginity,[11] as do the cherries worn in her hair. The dress is of deep red velvet whose high narrow rolled sleeves and bodice are slashed with drawn-out linen ornament. Underneath the dress is a lawn partlet or vest with loose sleeves decorated with the Tudor rose in black work. Around her neck is a high lace ruff of extreme delicacy and there is a carcanet at her throat. A red rose is tucked into her bodice. On her right arm is an armlet decorated with rubies and dodecahedral pointed star-cut diamonds.[12] In her left hand she holds what appears to be a pouch (rather than a glove)[13] ringed with a jewel, and concealing her right hand is a feather fan with a jewel at its centre. Infra-red photography has revealed that many changes were made during painting to details of the costume and the fan.[14] At the upper left is a crowned Tudor rose, symbol of Elizabeth's monarchy and

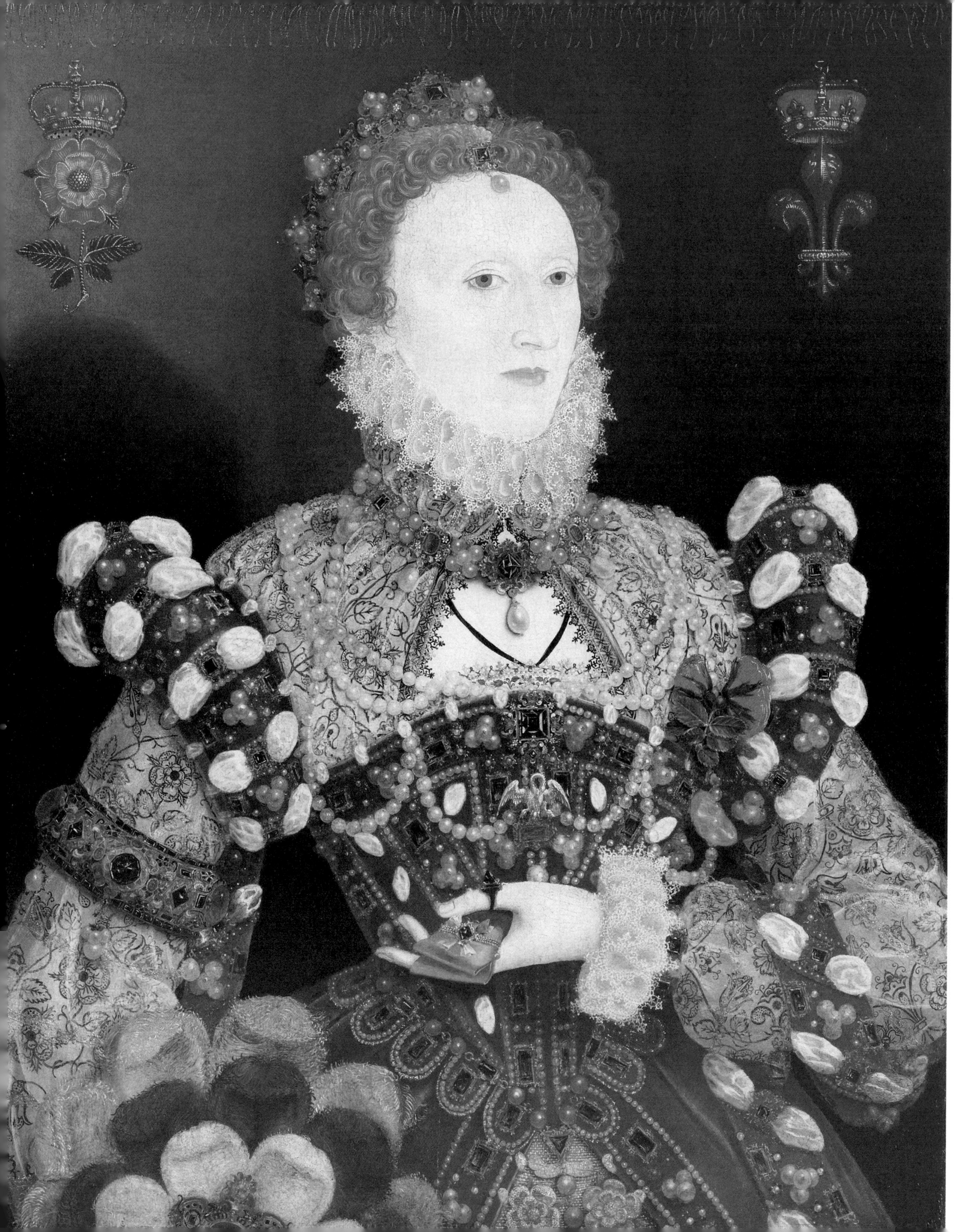

WAG 2994

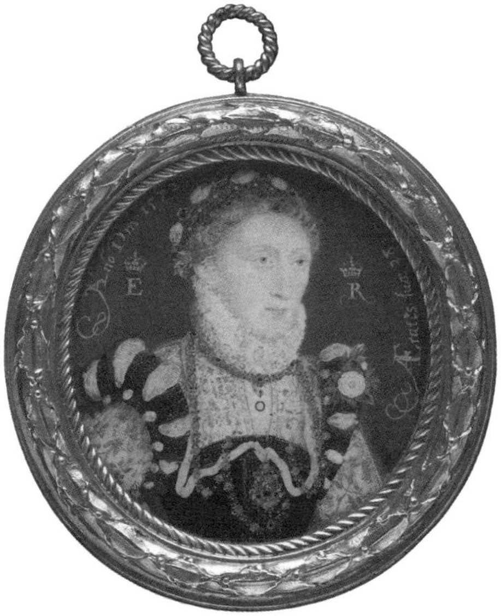

Fig. 27 *Queen Elizabeth I* by Nicholas Hilliard, watercolour on vellum.
© National Portrait Gallery, London.

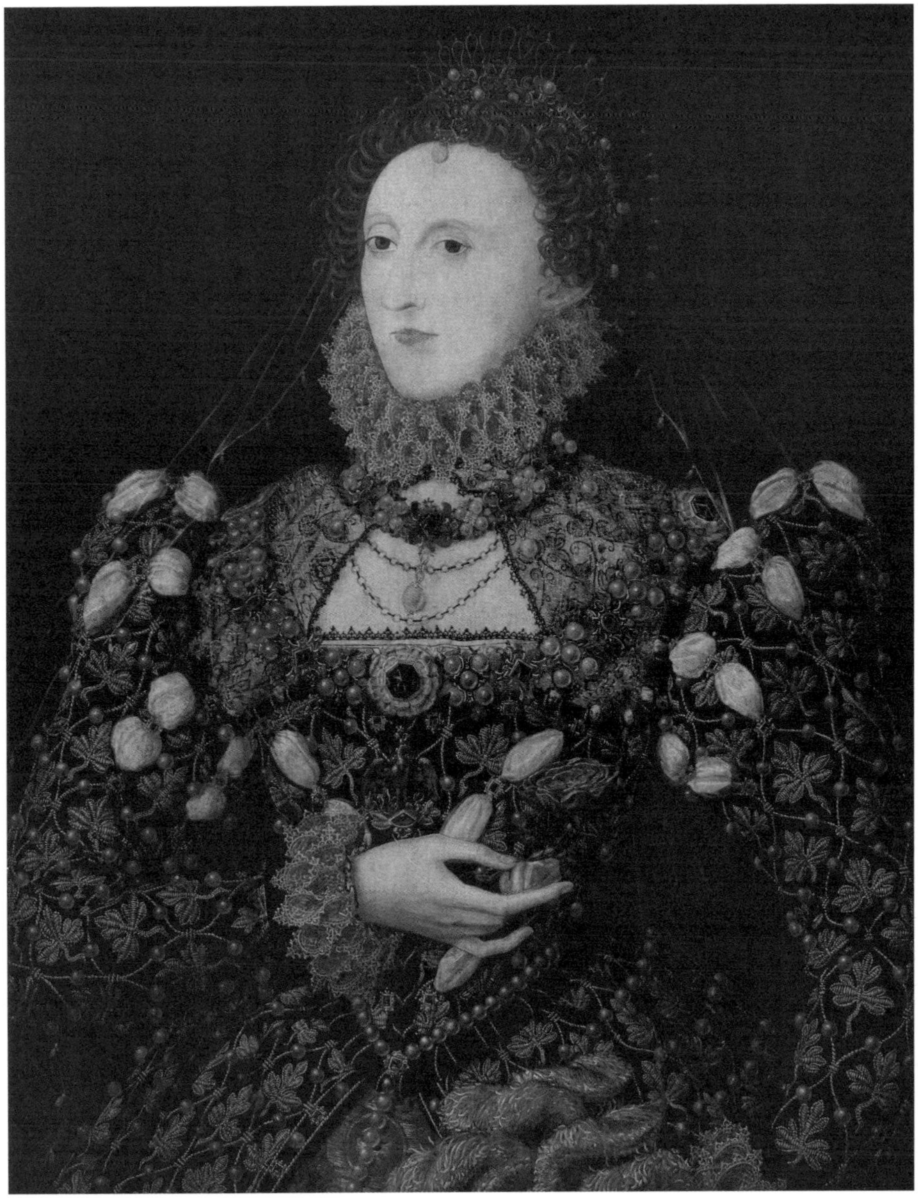

Fig. 28 *Queen Elizabeth I ('The Phoenix Portrait')* attributed to Nicholas Hilliard, oil on panel. Tate, on permanent loan from the National Portrait Gallery.
© National Portrait Gallery, London.

on her right, emblematic of her claims to the throne of France and suggestive of a possible French context for the production of the work, a crowned *fleur-de-lys*[15] (these attributes are not present in the *Phoenix Portrait*). Both flowers have further associations with the Virgin Mary.

When WAG 2994 was acquired by the gallery, the whole background was overpainted a deep brown colour. This overpaint was removed during a conservation treatment in 1962–63 to reveal the original deep indigo pigment, the shadow of the queen's head beneath the Tudor rose and the gold tasselling at the top.[16] The work, which is painted on three oak panels (of an approximate width, seen from the front from left to right, of 19.3 cm narrowing to 17.5 cm, 27 cm narrowing to 26.5 cm and 15 cm widening to 16.5 cm)[17] has suffered chronically from blistering. The largest damaged areas are in the background to the right of the queen's head, in the centre of her skirt, and on the ruff at her left wrist. There are many smaller patches of damage on the face and costume. The work was most recently stabilised in 1983–85.

The early history of WAG 2994 is unknown. According to its previous owner, it was acquired by Thomas Howard, later 1st Earl of Suffolk (1561–1626) who distinguished himself at the Armada in 1588.[18] This is not intrinsically unlikely,[19] although it is certain that the work cannot have been painted for him, for his father had been executed for treason in 1572 when he was 11 years old and the Howard family only returned to court favour in 1584. The painting is recorded at Charlton Park, the Wiltshire home of the Earls of Suffolk in 1697 (among the 'Pictures hanging at the Upper end of the Hall over the Long Table')[20] and remained there until it was sold by the Countess of Suffolk in 1930.

PROVENANCE

...Earls of Suffolk and by descent to Margaret, Countess of Suffolk; from whom bt. through Spink in 1930 by E. P. Jones, JP, Greenbank, Chester; by whom given to the gallery 1945.

EXHIBITIONS

The Reign of Queen Elizabeth Grosvenor Place, London 1933 (198); *Some Acquisitions of the Walker Art Gallery Liverpool 1935–1945* National Gallery, London 1945 (2); *Nicholas Hilliard and Isaac Oliver* Victoria and Albert Museum, London 1947 (108); *Kings and Queens of England* Walker Art Gallery 1953 (13); *Primitives to Picasso* RA 1962 (81); *The Age of Shakespeare* Whitworth Art Gallery, Manchester 1964 (1); *Elizabeth I* National Maritime Museum, Greenwich 2003 (193).

NOTES

1. This entry makes extensive use of an earlier draft entry by Mark Evans.
2. Roy Strong: *Portraits of Queen Elizabeth I* (Oxford, 1963) p. 89 (cat. M3).
3. A colloquium at the Conservation Department of the National Portrait Gallery, London, 10 September 2010, presented by Sally Marriott and Tarnya Cooper, reporting comparative scientific analysis of WAG 2994 and the *Phoenix Portrait* (hereafter *NPG Colloquium*).
4. *NPG Colloquium*, citing Ian Tyers: 'Tree-ring analysis of the National Portrait Gallery "Phoenix" and the Walker Art Gallery "Pelican" portraits of Elizabeth I by Nicholas Hilliard' unpublished report, August 2010. The planks used to construct the tri-partite supports of the two paintings derived from trees felled in the Eastern Baltic after 1557 (the plank used for both central sections) and after 1561 (the plank used for the four outer sections).
5. For the *Phoenix Portrait* see especially Roy Strong: *National Portrait Gallery: Tudor and Jacobean Portraits* 2 vols (London, 1969) vol. 1, pp. 101–2; also Karen Hearn: *Dynasties* exh. cat., Tate Gallery, London (1995) pp. 80–1 (cat. 34). For the costumes and their dating see Janet Arnold: *Queen Elizabeth's Wardrobe Unlock'd* (Leeds, 1988) pp. 22–4, 74, where it is proposed that the costume worn in WAG 2994 is from about 1574 and that worn in the *Phoenix Portrait* from about 1576.
6. Arnold, *op. cit.*, pp. 24–5.
7. The association of WAG 2994 with Hilliard was first made by C. R. Beard: 'The "Pelican Portrait" of Queen Elizabeth', *Connoisseur* vol. 92 (October 1933) pp. 263–4; Strong (1963) p. 60 (cat. P 23) attributed it '? By Nicholas Hilliard'. In his *The English Icon: Elizabethan and Jacobean Portraiture* (London, 1969) p. 159 he observed of the attribution that WAG 2994 would be difficult to connect with anyone else and in his *Gloriana: The Portraits of Queen Elizabeth I* (London, 1983) p. 79 WAG 2994 was 'long and rightly' attributed to Hilliard.
Part of the evidence in favour of the artist of WAG 2994 being Hilliard resides in a document dating from 1577 that refers to the artist responsible for Elizabeth's 'pourtraicture entiere' being then in France, as Hilliard was at that date. This, however, may have been coincidental or the artist may have been an associate or travelling companion of Hilliard's; the same document describes this artist as 'ung Francois'; see Roy Strong: *The English Renaissance Miniature* (London, 1983) p. 82.
8. N. Hilliard: *A Treatise concerning the Arte of Limning* ed. R. K. R. Thornton and T. G. S. Cain (Ashington, 1981) p. 91.
9. *NPG colloquium*.
10. Susan E. James: *The Feminine Dynamic in English Art, 1485–1603* (Farnham, 2009) pp. 322–4. According to James, a Tudor rose was the 'signature emblem' of Teerlinc.
11. Frances A. Yates: *Astraea* (London, 1975) p. 78.
12. Herbert Tillander, *letters*, 8 February and 30 March 1992 (gallery files).
13. *NPG Colloquium*. The identification as a glove was made by Janet Arnold, *op. cit.*, p. 22.
14. *NPG Colloquium*.
15. James, *op. cit.*, p. 324, relates the *fleur-de-lys* to the negotiations with the court of France over the possible marriage of Elizabeth to the Duc d'Alençon.
16. Micro-photography suggests that the background was originally a deep purple, achieved by the addition of a thin crimson-purple glaze over the indigo paint. This glaze appears to have been mostly removed with the overpaint, but traces of it survive. Other unusual pigments used in WAG 2994 revealed by micro-photography include verditer, silver and tin sulphide (mosaic gold); *NPG Colloquium*.
17. Tyers, *op. cit.*, p. 13. The figures closely match those for the boards of the *Phoenix Portrait* in reverse.
18. E. Peter Jones, *copy letter*, 6 August 1952, gallery files.
19. Oliver Millar: 'Abraham van der Doort's Catalogue of the Collections of Charles I', *Walpole Society* vol. 37 (1960) pp. 109–10, 113–5, lists numerous miniatures of Henry VIII and Edward VI given to King Charles I by 'my Lord of Suffolk'.
20. John Jacob: 'Ranger's House Blackheath: A New Gallery of English Portraits', *Apollo* vol. 101 (January 1975) p. 17. It is also described in John Britton: *The Beauties of Wiltshire* 3 vols (London, 1801–25) vol. 3, p. 63: 'A female head, between a rose and a fleur-de-lis, both crowned; on the breast a pelican; the right hand elevated and holding a cross of jewels, with a chain of pearls, and having a ring on the thumb.'

William Hogarth

1697–1764

David Garrick as Richard III

WAG 634
oil on canvas, 190.5 × 251 cm
date: 1745

One of the great masterpieces of eighteenth-century British art and an icon of theatrical portraiture, WAG 634 shows the actor David Garrick (1717–79) in his signature role. The 24 year-old aspiring actor, hitherto a virtual unknown on the fringes of the London theatrical world, became a sensation almost overnight following his playing of the role of Richard III at Goodman's Fields theatre on 19 October 1741. It was recognised that Garrick's manner of acting, with its emphasis on naturalism and the accurate depiction of particular emotion, offered a fundamental challenge to then-conventional acting styles wedded to stateliness, propriety and artifice; and also that it was justified by its obvious popular appeal with audiences.[1] Garrick's method was rooted in his own exceptional personal vivacity, physical mobility and intellectual curiosity, but behind it lay potent cultural forces.[2] It has been noted that even at the outset of his acting career Garrick was less a revolutionary than a refiner of trends already espoused by his older colleague Charles Macklin.[3]

Act V Scene 3 of Shakespeare's play is set on the eve of the Battle of Bosworth Field, in which Richard will be killed. Garrick is depicted by Hogarth at the climactic moment of the scene in the performing version of the play by Colley Cibber (1671–1757).[4] That Garrick is performing Cibber's text is confirmed by the fact that this, unlike Shakespeare's original, makes mention of the armed camp, with watchmen by a fire, that

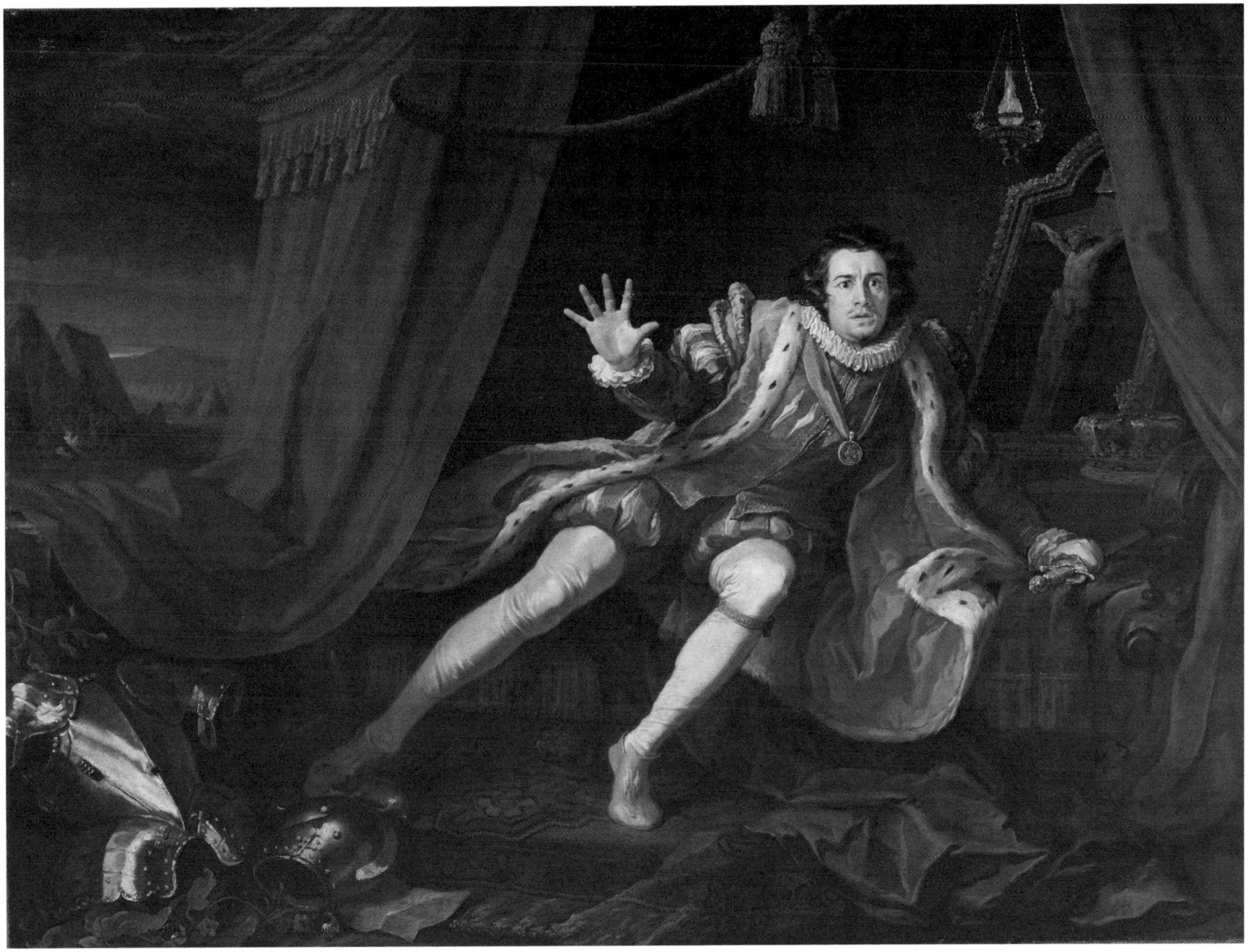

WAG 634

is visible in the background of WAG 634. Furthermore, Cibber's version of Shakespeare's fifth act fundamentally alters the staging so that only Richard III's tent appears on stage, rather than the two tents of Richard and his enemy, Henry Earl of Richmond (the future Henry Tudor) for which Shakespeare's original calls.[5] In Cibber's revision, Richard wakes from his nightmare after the disappearance of the ghost of the murdered Lancastrian King Henry VI (rather than, in Shakespeare's original, the ghost of the Duke of Buckingham). He starts up from his dream with (in Cibber's text) the words,

Give me another horse: Bind up my wounds!
Have mercy, Heaven, Ha! – soft! – 'Twas but a dream:
But then so terrible, it shakes my soul
Cold drops of sweat hang on my trembling Flesh,
My blood grows chilly, and I freeze with horror.
O Tyrant Conscience! How thou dost afflict me!

According to one of Garrick's first biographers, Garrick played this passage by calling 'Give me another horse' in a manly tone, and then advanced towards the front of the stage before crying 'Bind up my wounds', finally falling to his knees to say 'Have mercy, Heaven'; thus at the precise moment depicted by Hogarth, Garrick is calling for another horse.[6] The same account notes that Garrick's face at this point was already 'a spectacle of horror',[7] anticipating Cibber's phrase, not in Shakespeare's original text, 'I freeze with horror'. This is the prompt for Hogarth's adaptation of Garrick's expression from the depiction of *l'horreur* in Charles Le Brun's *Méthode pour apprendre à dessiner les passions* (1698).[8]

The influence of French historical painting and in particular of Le Brun's *The Tent of Darius (The Queen of Persia at the Feet of Alexander)* (Palace of Versailles, 1661) on Hogarth's conception of *Garrick as Richard III* has often been noted.[9] Although Hogarth would already have been familiar with Girard Audran's engravings after Le Brun's Alexander cycle he may have taken the opportunity to visit Versailles and see the original during his trip to Paris in the summer of 1743. The similarity in the treatment of the royal tent is particularly evident and is probably a deliberate allusion. Hogarth's engagement with the style of French history painting stands in marked contrast to his earlier theatrical and 'historical' paintings of modern moral subjects, in which the overall scale is much smaller, the figures smaller in proportion to the picture area, and the compositional principles more picaresque.[10] In *Garrick as Richard III* he espoused an enormous scale and a unified design in accordance with 'Academic' principles. The props are arranged around the central figure in a smooth and undistracting oval rather than requiring the eye to jump from place to place, as his earlier narrative technique had demanded. The most important of these props is the crumpled paper at the king's feet on which is written *Jockey of Norfolk be not so bold / Dicken thy master is bought & sold*. The note, which has been handed on to the king, is addressed to his ally the Duke of Norfolk and informs him that the king's fate in battle has been sealed by another part of his army having decided to change sides. Clockwise from this are the king's helmet and body armour, lying separately to create the sense of a decapitated body; the armed camp, with behind it a portentous blood-red streak of dawn in the sky; the waning light in the brazier; a framed crucifix, emblem of martyrdom; the deposed crown, and lastly, the sword which the stricken king has grasped as if for support. Each of these elements is intended to be read as if functioning in a historical picture to increase the sense of impending doom. Yet if the viewer's sense of being present at a theatrical performance is very differently managed from, say, Hogarth's earlier *Beggar's Opera* paintings, it is still the case that the scene is perfectly legible as a moment in a particular staging. The figure of Garrick is strongly spotlit from the front, with the rest of the scene left in half-light, and the curtained off enclave in which the action is taking place anticipates the 'stage within a stage' effect with which Garrick became associated in other Shakespearian productions.[11] There is no reason to doubt that the costume is that worn by Garrick, although it is anachronistic, being 'Jacobethan' rather than of the late fifteenth century (the armour too, which Hogarth is said to have borrowed from the Tower of London, has also been dated to the early seventeenth century).[12] Around his neck Garrick wears the medallion of the Order of the Garter, whose image of a heroic knight on horseback both contrasts with the king's mental anguish and anticipates his end for the want of a horse.[13]

Although Garrick was to become friends with many artists and encouraged them to paint him as a form of publicity, it is clear that the initiative for this work was not his but Hogarth's and that Hogarth conceived it in terms of employing Garrick's new-found celebrity for his own artistic ends. The artistic revolution that Garrick embodied offered a parallel for the similar sea-change Hogarth anticipated making with the painting, not only in his own art but in the public sphere of the visual arts generally.[14] It has been pointed out that although Garrick became friendly with Hogarth, his correspondence does not indicate that they were intimate,[15] and it is certain that he did not commission WAG 634. That he may not even have sat to Hogarth in the artist's own painting room is suggested by the fact that his face is painted on a separate piece of canvas, measuring 76 × 63.5 cm (the standard 'three-quarters' prepared canvas used by portrait painters) which has been inserted into the larger work. This canvas extends from the tip of the brazier at the top right to the bottom inner edge of Garrick's left thigh just above his stockinged kneecap at bottom left. Hogarth's highly unusual procedure carries the strong suggestion that, conscious of Garrick's frequent acting commitments outside London and knowing he could not rely on Garrick attending his studio, he was determined to capture the actor's expression of horror as an initial step, and took the likeness at Garrick's. This receives corroboration from the fact that the small canvas appears to have been folded nearly in half horizontally, as if for ease of transportation. Hogarth's procedure carries the further implication that the artist did not want Garrick to know precisely what use he would make of the head and feared the actor's interference: thus, for example, the elongated figure of the king cannot be an accurate transcription of the figure of Garrick, who was rather short, but it elegantly articulates Hogarth's evolving theory of the beauty of the serpentine line that would ultimately find expression in his *Analysis of Beauty* (1753). On this view, it seems likely that Hogarth began the work not long before Garrick left London for the provinces in the summer of 1745, and painted most of it while Garrick was away.[16] This scenario is supported by the evidence in Garrick's letters to friends during his absence of the interest he was taking in Hogarth's progress. Writing to his friend Somerset Draper on 23 October, he reported that his friend William Windham 'sends me

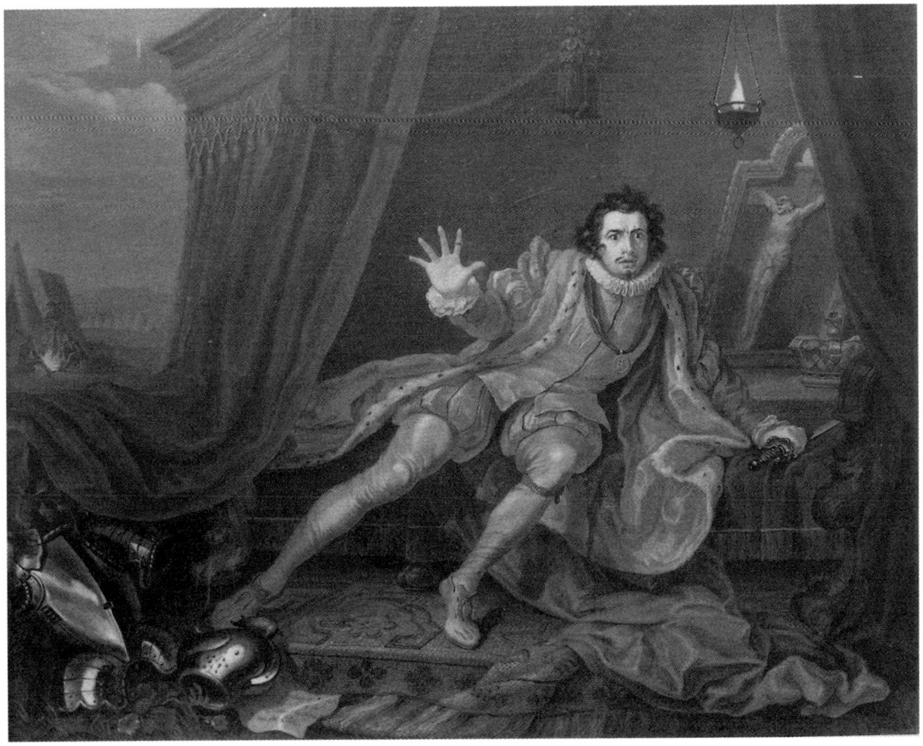

Fig. 29 *David Garrick as Richard III* after William Hogarth, by Jacobus Vrymoet, oil on canvas. Lawrence Fine Art Auctioneers, Crewkerne; photo Colin Jeffrey.

a great account of *Hogarth's* picture – have you seen it lately?';[17] and on 1 December that year he wrote again to Draper, from Dublin, asking 'Pray, does *Hogarth* go on with my picture, and does he intend a print from it?'[18] These remarks suggest that Hogarth was reportedly close to finishing the picture by late October, but that Garrick believed it was still unfinished on 1 December. There may well have been some hold-up, since the print by Charles Grignion (made with Hogarth's assistance, the artist insisting on engraving the head of Garrick himself, and according to Grignion rubbing it out several times until he finally got it right) although lettered with the publication date 20 June 1746, was issued only in mid-July.[19]

It is unknown when precisely Hogarth sold WAG 634 to 'Mr Duncombe' for £200, a price of which the artist boasted for the rest of his life, as putting him into the 'old master' league;[20] and the identity of this person has never certainly been established. The Thomas Duncombe who in the early eighteenth century built a new mansion at Duncombe Park outside Helmsley, where WAG 634 was recorded as hanging at least by 1810,[21] died in 1746; and his eldest son Thomas (whose exact birthdate is unknown) may barely have come of age by that date.[22] Whoever the buyer was, it seems probable that (although he may first have commissioned the magnificently carved frame) he almost immediately removed the painting from London: it had no close imitators in the field of theatrical painting (Francis Hayman's depiction of the identical subject, shown at the first Society of Arts exhibition in 1760, is as different as it is possible to imagine)[23] and no early copies of it are known.[24] On the other hand, Grignion's print immediately became a best-seller,[25] and it is noticeable that it and not the painting itself provided the basis for Vertue's highly favourable comments on Hogarth's achievement.[26] The print was evidently the source for the many imitations based on WAG 634 in other media, including prints, cartoons, tapestries and Staffordshire porcelain, that emerged in the late eighteenth and nineteenth centuries.[27]

PROVENANCE

Bt. from Hogarth by Mr [? Thomas] Duncombe; by descent to Charles, 3rd Earl of Feversham; bt. Agnew 1955; from whom bt. by the gallery 1956, with the assistance of the Art Fund.

EXHIBITIONS

BI 1856 (137); *Art Treasures* Manchester 1857 (Paintings by Modern Masters, 22); *3rd Special Exhibition of National Portraits* South Kensington 1868 (792); *Yorkshire Fine Art and Industrial Exhibition* Exhibition Hall, York 1879 (457);[28] Grosvenor Gallery, London 1888 (28); *British Theatrical Loan Exhibition* Dudley House, London 1933 (2151); *59th Liverpool Autumn Exhibition* Walker Art Gallery 1933 (20); *British Portraits* RA 1956 (205); *Painting and Sculpture in England 1700–1750* Walker Art Gallery 1958 (20); *Shakespeare in Art* Nottingham University Art Gallery 1961 (13); *Shakespeare in Art* Arts Council Gallery, London 1964 (11); *Shakespeare and the Theatre* Guildhall Art Gallery, London 1964 (18); *Hogarth* Tate Britain, London 2007 (105).

NOTES

1. Ronald Paulson: *Hogarth: His Life, Art and Times* 3 vols (New Brunswick, 1971) vol. 2, pp. 24–6; Jenny Uglow: *Hogarth* (London, 1997) p. 398.
2. Paulson, *ibid.*; and for contemporary theatrical performance and cultural attitudes to Shakespeare in particular see Robin Simon: *Hogarth, France and British Art* (London, 2007) pp. 93–112. Simon's discussion of WAG 634 is the most extended to date and this entry is indebted to it.
3. Paulson, *op. cit.*, p. 26.
4. Simon, *op. cit.*, pp. 103–6.
5. Simon, *op. cit.*, pp. 96, 106.
6. Simon, *op. cit.*, p. 106.
7. *Ibid.*, referring to Arthur Murphy's *Life of Hogarth* (1801) as cited by Iain Mackintosh and Geoffrey Ashton: *Thirty Different Likenesses: David Garrick in Portrait and Performance*, exh. cat., Buxton Museum and Art Gallery (1981) p. 1.
8. Simon, *op. cit.*, pp. 97–8; Martin Kemp: *The Human Animal in Western Art and Science* (Chicago and London, 2007) pp. 66–7; Kemp notes that Hogarth plays down the extremity of Le Brun's depiction of Horror to avoid distorting Garrick's

likeness and in the interest of composing 'a dramatic narrative in the grand tradition'.
9. Frederick Antal: *Hogarth and His Place in European Art* (London, 1962) p. 69 seems to have been the first to compare WAG 634 with Le Brun's *Tent of Darius*.
10. Paulson, *op. cit.*, p. 28.
11. See, for example, Benjamin Wilson's *David Garrick and Anne Bellamy in Shakespeare's 'Romeo and Juliet'* of 1753 (Yale Center for British Art, New Haven).
12. V. Cumming: *Understanding Fashion History* (London 2004) p. 116; James G. Mann: 'Sir John Smythe's Armour in Portraiture', *Connoisseur* vol. 90 (August 1932) pp. 88–97, identifying the suit as one of 'Greenwich' armour and probably that borrowed from the Tower by Colley Cibber for a performance of Shakespeare's *King Henry VIII* in 1727; Uglow, *op. cit.*, p. 400.
13. Mark Hallett and Christine Riding: *Hogarth* exh. cat., Tate Britain, London (2007) p. 204 (cat. 105).
14. Paulson, *op. cit.*, p. 28.
15. *Ibid.*
16. Paulson, *op. cit.*, pp. 27–8.
17. David M. Little and George M. Kahrl, eds: *The Letters of David Garrick* 3 vols (London, 1963) vol. 1, p. 65.
18. Little and Kahrl, *op. cit.*, vol. 1, p. 70.
19. R. Paulson: *Hogarth's Graphic Works* 2 vols (New Haven and London, 1965) vol. 1, p. 191.
20. Paulson, *Hogarth: His Life*, p. 31; Uglow, *op. cit.*, p. 401.
21. Kathleen Maclarnon: 'William Bankes and His Collection of Spanish Paintings at Kingston Lacy', *Burlington Magazine* vol. 122 (February 1990) pp. 115, n. 11 and 116. Bankes described WAG 634 on his visit to Duncombe Park as 'indifferent' and mistook the king that Garrick was playing for Richard II.
22. According to Lewis Namier and John Brooke, eds: *The History of Parliament: The House of Commons 1754–1790* 3 vols (London, 1964), vol. 2 pp. 353–4, the younger Thomas Duncombe was born about 1724. He married Lady Diana Howard in 1749 and entered Parliament in 1751. He died in 1779. That he was the purchaser of WAG 634 is strongly implied in the reference of J. Nichols: *Biographical Anecdotes of William Hogarth* (London, 1785 edn) p. 283: 'The late Mr *Duncombe*, of *Duncombe Park* in *Yorkshire* gave 200l. for the original picture, which is now in the possession of his family'. (Nichols continued: 'The expression of the countenance is happily hit off, but the figure is abundantly too large and muscular'.) The most prominent 'Mr Duncombe' in the late 1740s was this Thomas Duncombe's older cousin, Anthony Duncombe (about 1695–1763) who in 1747 was advanced to the peerage as Baron Feversham; however this man's estates were in Wiltshire, he had no direct connection with Duncombe Park and he had heirs in the shape of two daughters. It is also unlikely that Nichols would have referred to him as 'the late Mr Duncombe'.
23. For Hayman's painting see Brian Allen: *Francis Hayman* (New Haven and London, 1987) pp. 116–7 (cat. 42).
24. The earliest copy recorded in gallery files is one measuring 42 × 51 cm signed and dated Jacobus Vrymoet 1785, with T. G. Lawrence Fine Art Auctioneers, Crewkerne, Somerset January 1974 (fig. 29), which was stated to have a Garrick family provenance. A nearly full-size copy in a North Yorkshire private collection appears to have been made from the original at Duncombe Park in the first two decades of the nineteenth century (*letter* from the owner, gallery files).
25. Uglow, *op. cit.*, p. 401.
26. Mrs A. Esdaile, Lord Ilchester and H. M. Hake, eds: 'Vertue Notebooks Volume III', *Walpole Society* vol. 22 1933–34 (1934) p. 130: 'the end of June came out a Print of K. Richd 3 in the Character of Garrick the present famous player or Comedian. whose performances are much admired – by all persons – His picture is painted by Hogarth – and the engraved plate by him and Grignon a young man that first learnt of Gravelot to draw and Engrave – this operation may stand as a peece of reputation being the Invention, painting & Engraving of Natives of England. this and many other products of Engravings are come to an Equal perfection in most particulars to any foreign works of Italy, france or Dutchlanders'.
27. Satirical prints based on WAG 634 include *Charles the Third, King of the Orkneys*, published by S. W. Fores 16 June 1784 and *'Ritchie's Himself Again' – (Till further Notice)* by Linley Sambourne published in *Punch*, 28 April 1888 (repr. Leonée Ormond: 'Edward Linley Sambourne: A Cartoonist in the Art World', *British Art Journal* vol. 3 no. 1 [Autumn 2001] p. 11); one known tapestry (reversing the composition of painting and print) is in the collection of the Shakespeare Memorial Theatre Stratford-upon-Avon and another was in an English private collection in 1994; differently decorated Staffordshire figures dating from the later nineteenth century are reproduced in Thomas Balston: *Staffordshire Portrait Figures of the Victorian Age* (London, 1958) pl. 45, George Bruce: 'Staffordshire Pottery', *Ideal Home* (January 1965) p. 107, Bonita LaMarche: 'Staffordshire Figurines from the Jerome Irving Smith Collection', *Bulletin of the Detroit Institute of Arts* vol. 65, no. 4 (1990) p. 48, and Lars Tharp: *Hogarth's China* (London, 1997) p. 20.
28. 'The Gallery of Ancient Masters included the splendid collection of Pictures and Statuary from Duncombe Park, which were rescued from the recent fire… This collection formed a great attraction to the Exhibition, and our thanks are due to Lord Feversham for the trust he reposed in us by thus placing under our care these valuable Works of Art, which have long been the admiration of all those who have had the privilege of seeing them in his Lordship's galleries' (*Report of the Executive Committee of the Fine Art and Industrial Exhibition Presented to a Meeting of the Donors and Contributors to the Loan Fund* [York, 1880] p. 8). Hogarth's painting and the entirety of Lord Feversham's collection remained at the Exhibition Hall throughout 1880 and into 1881 (see *Yorkshire Fine Art and Industrial Institution York: Report of the Council to be Presented to the Contributors to the Loan and Donation Fund at the Annual Meeting, to Be Held on Thursday the 24th February 1881* [York, 1881] p. 6).

Portrait of a Lady

WAG 6218
oil on canvas, 76 × 63.5 cm
signed and dated: *W Hogarth/1745* (bottom left)[1]
date: 1745

The sitter in WAG 6218 is unidentified, although it has been suggested that she is Arabella Bate (date of birth unknown, d. 1804), daughter of William Bate of Foston, Derbyshire and his wife Arabella,

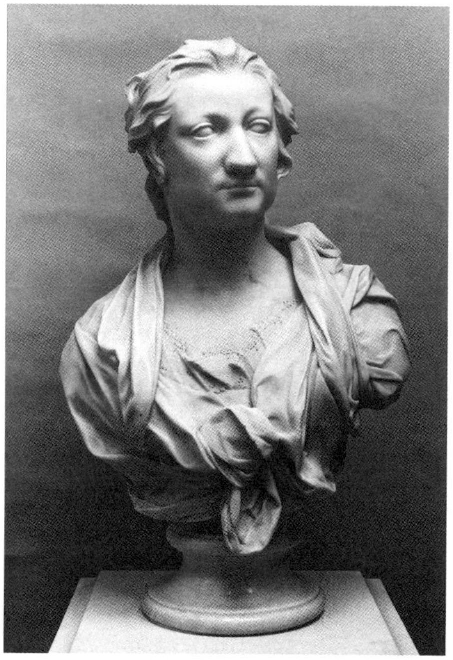

Fig. 30 *Arabella Bate* by Louis-François Roubiliac, marble. Private collection, UK. Photo Conway Library, The Courtauld Institute of Art, London.

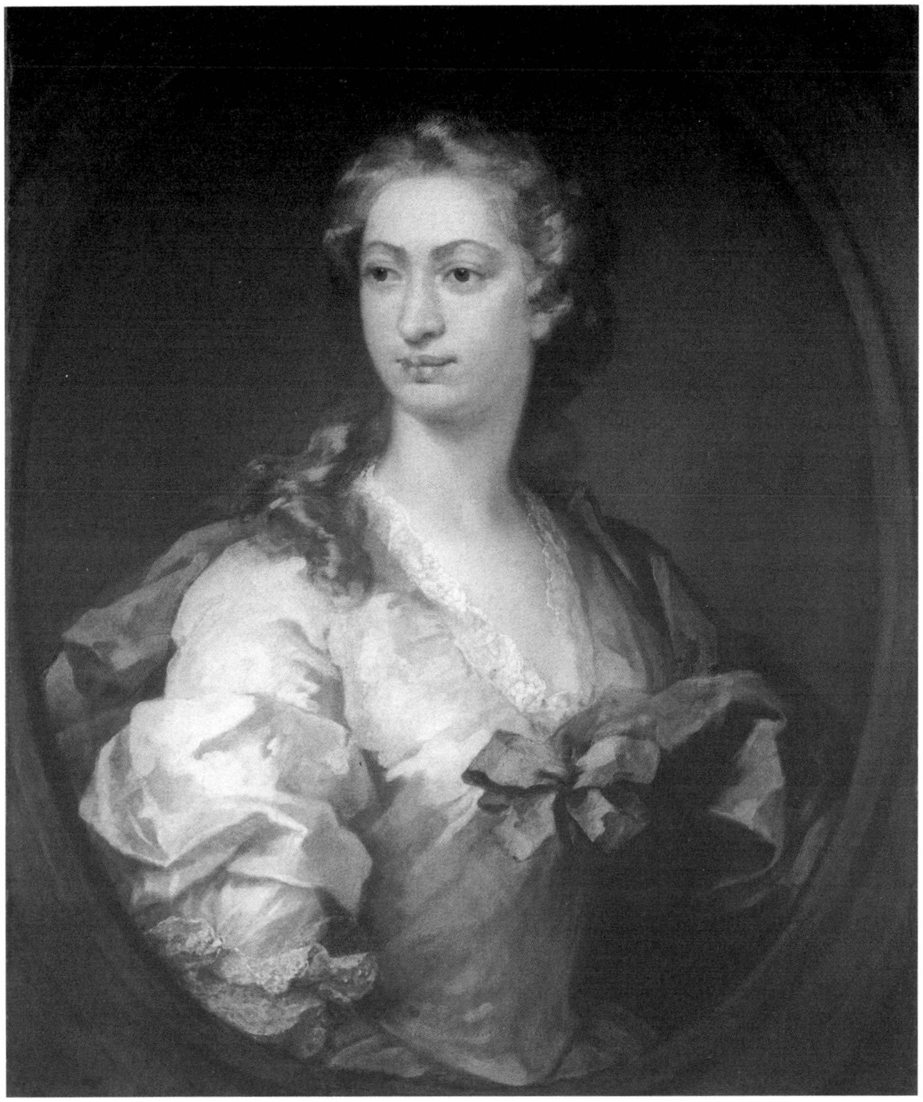

WAG 6218

née Chambers, who in 1746 married the London Huguenot merchant George René Aufrère (1715–1801). A strong resemblance has been observed between Hogarth's sitter and Arabella as she was portrayed in 1748 in a marble bust by Louis-François Roubiliac (private collection, Lincolnshire; fig. 30) and it has been proposed that, as part of a campaign in the late 1730s and 1740s to re-invigorate the tradition of the 'sculptural' bust portrait within a fictive frame, Hogarth was engaging in an artistic dialogue with Roubiliac. WAG 6218 takes its place as a mature work within this phase of Hogarth's career.[2]

The strongly 'Rococo' character of WAG 6218 has often been noted, and indeed it has been suggested that the portrait consciously exemplifies Hogarth's notions of grace and beauty as later set out in his *Analysis of Beauty* (1753), with its emphasis on a serpentine line and advocacy of the use of reflected light.[3]

PROVENANCE

...J. G. Fuller, 15 Royal Crescent, Ramsgate 1896; ...Arthur Fisk, Geneva; Sotheby 20 November 1963 (114); bt. Bernard (£1,700); Tooth; from whom bt. in 1964 by the gallery.

EXHIBITIONS

Dvě století britského malířství [*Two centuries of British Painting*] Narodnì Galerie, Prague and tour of Central Europe 1969–70 (78); *La Peinture Britannique de Gainsborough à Bacon* Galerie des Beaux-Arts, Bordeaux 1977 (24).

NOTES

1. The last digit is unclear and has been read as a 4, for example, by the painting's former owner J. G. Fuller who wrote on a label stuck to the stretcher: *This picture is / signed & dated (1744) / By W. Hogarth / in the left hand / bottom corner / J. G. Fuller / 1896.* A second label gives his name and address.
2. Robin Simon: *Hogarth, France and British Art* (London, 2007) pp. 180–1. He suggests that WAG 6218 may have been undertaken to mark Miss Bate's engagement.
3. David Mannings: 'Reynolds, Hogarth and Van Dyck', *Burlington Magazine* vol. 126 (November 1984) pp. 689–90.

called

William Hogarth

1697–1764

A Smoking Party

WAG 1733
oil on canvas, 62 × 73.5 cm
date: unknown, perhaps about 1725–50

When WAG 1733 entered the gallery it was thought to be an authentic work by Hogarth; however the attribution was doubted by the early twentieth century.[1] WAG 1733 was subsequently viewed as a later pastiche of Hogarth in the vein of such works as *A Midnight Modern Conversation* (1730–31; Yale Center for British Art, New Haven) or *Lord George Graham in His Cabin* (1745; National Maritime Museum, Greenwich) and held to date from the late eighteenth or early nineteenth centuries.[2] More recently it

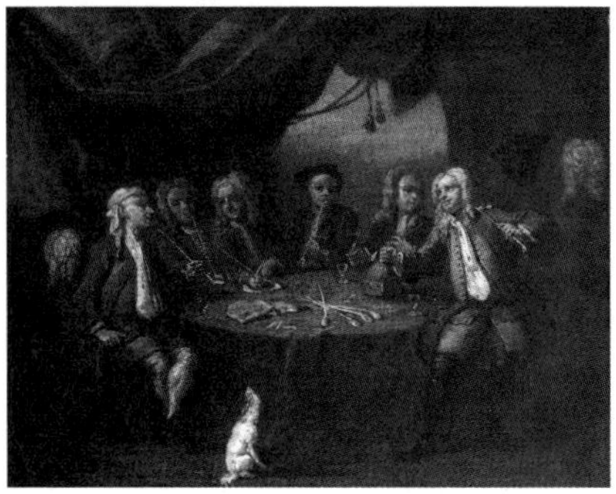

WAG 1733

has been suggested that the work is by a contemporary rival or even precursor.[3] The coarse and sketchy handling of paint is quite unlike Hogarth's, although the faces are distinctively characterised. It is possible that the figure in the centre of the composition looking directly at the viewer is the artist. There is a vague indication in the background of silhouetted buildings and towers that suggests that the setting is London.

PROVENANCE

...John Bate;[4] his bequest 1885.

NOTES

1. On an accession card predating 1917 (gallery files) the work is 'atttributed to Hogarth'.
2. Present inventory card dating from the 1960s (gallery files). The painting is on a standard size 'three-quarters' canvas of 63 × 75 cm favoured by British artists throughout this period.
3. Elizabeth Einberg, *letter*, 14 October 2009 (gallery files) observed that the work 'looks quite early, of the 1720s'; Robin Simon, *verbally*, described it as '1720s, one of several unknown hands that got dumped into the Hogarth basket in the nineteenth century' (reported by Elizabeth Einberg, *email*, 22 October 2009).
4. Bate's bequest also included four works by the nineteenth-century Liverpool artists William Davis and James Campbell (the three by Campbell of distinctly Hogarthian character) that appear likely to have been acquired in the 1860s and 1870s; see *MPPP*, pp. 68–9, 87. A label on the reverse of Sanderson Carver & Gilder Mount Pleasant Liverpool dates from the same period.

after

Hans Holbein the Younger

1497/98–1543

King Henry VIII

WAG 1350
oil on oak panel, 239 × 134.5 cm
date: about 1540–47

One of a group of full-length portraits of Henry VIII derived from the figure of the king in Holbein's mural for Whitehall Palace, which depicted the king with his father Henry VII, his mother Elizabeth of York, and his third wife, Jane Seymour.[1] Holbein executed the mural on the south wall of the king's privy chamber in the palace shortly after the king's marriage to Jane on 30 May 1536 (although he probably completed it only after the queen's death in October 1537).[2] The appearance of the mural, which was destroyed by fire in 1698, is known from a copy dated 1667 by Remigius van Leemput (Royal Collection; fig. 31). Holbein's surviving cartoon for the left-hand portion of the Whitehall mural (National Portrait Gallery, London; fig. 32), in which the figure of the king is slightly turned rather than head-on to the viewer, must have provided the basis for later copyists to work from; the outline of the figure, despite the change of angle, is almost identical to that in WAG 1530.[3] Although the cartoon is pricked, it shows no sign of charcoal dust in the holes, implying that it was used to make a second cartoon and the latter was used for copying purposes.[4]

Although WAG 1530 is first documented in the possession of the Seymour family in 1850,[5] there is evidence that they had owned it for generations before that date.[6] It is thought to have been painted for Edward Seymour (about 1500–52), Viscount Beauchamp, from 1536 Earl of Hertford and from 1547 Duke of Somerset, elder brother of Queen Jane and uncle to Henry VIII's heir, Edward VI. Seymour, who mostly owed his political career to his sister's rise to favour, became the most powerful figure at court in the later part of Henry VIII's reign and after the king's death in 1547 appointed himself Lord Protector during his nephew's minority before falling victim to a power struggle and being executed for treason in 1552. Although WAG 1530 has not been traced in inventories of his possessions, it is known that he owned a portrait of Jane Seymour and that in 1542 he paid 'Hance who made Quene Jane's picture' ten shillings; almost certainly a reference to Holbein.[7]

Of a sequence of six discrete full-length portraits of Henry that were made in the decades following the completion of Holbein's mural,[8] WAG 1350 is thought to be the second. It is probably slightly later in date than the version at Petworth House, whose provenance also implies that it was made for Edward Seymour, and appears to be by a different artist whose brief was to eliminate perceived defects in the earlier picture.[9] Chiefly, he created a work of more handsome proportions (the Petworth picture is somewhat narrower in proportion to its height than WAG 1530) and invented a much more discreet treatment of the recess decorated by a scallop shell behind Henry's head which is so visually distracting in the Petworth picture, introducing a long curtain which more effectively sets off the king's figure. The identity of the artist of WAG 1350 is unknown, but from the similarity of the treatment of Henry's black patterned silver doublet and his medallion, with its repeated letter H, to their equivalents in Holbein's earlier autograph head of the king (on which Holbein had based the head in his cartoon; Museo Thyssen-Bornemisza, Madrid) he has been identified as a close associate of Holbein's

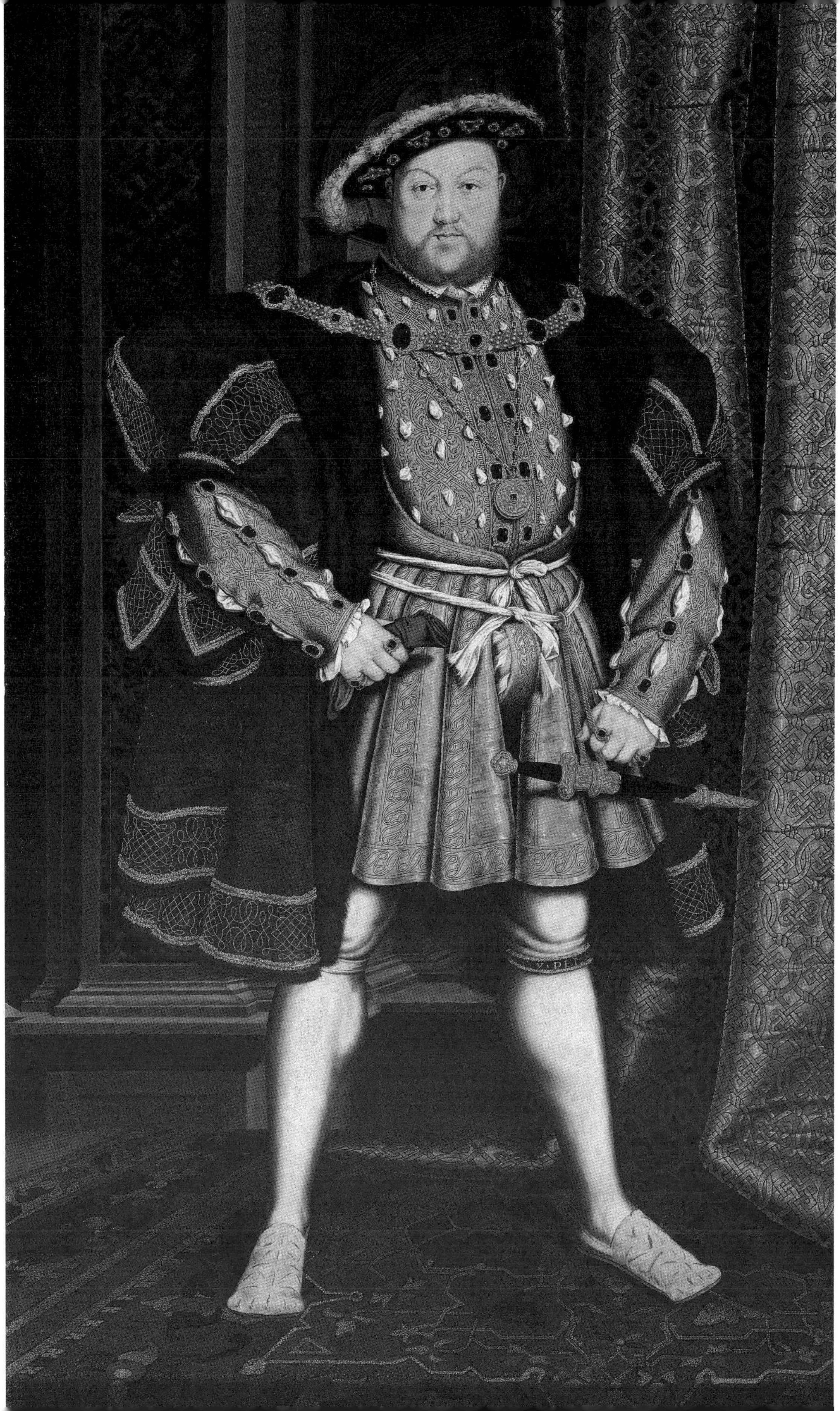

WAG 1350

in his workshop.[10] The full-length portrait of Henry VIII at Trinity College Cambridge is signed *HE* (presumably Hans Eworth) and dated 1567, and comparison between the distinctive underdrawing on this work with that on the version at Chatsworth indicates that the latter is also by this artist, whilst confirming that WAG 1350, which in the past has been ascribed to Eworth too, is not by him. [11] Dendrochronological analysis of the panels of these four paintings provides striking circumstantial evidence in support of the chronology Petworth–Walker–Trinity–Chatsworth and for an extended gap of years between the first two and the last two.[12] The latest of the six joined boards on which WAG 1350 is painted[13] has a *terminus post quem* tree-ring date of 1522 and the equivalent for the Trinity picture is 1546 for a work inscribed by the artist 1567; the same relation (although this is a highly speculative inference) would suggest a date for the painting of WAG 1350 of about 1543. Two further versions of the portrait on canvas, at Parham Park and at Belvoir Castle, postdate the Trinity and Chatsworth pictures, and the Belvoir canvas has been thought to date from as late as the early seventeenth century.[14]

In each of the six pictures Henry's figure is fractionally different in its internal measurements[15] (which suggests that the second cartoon was freshly re-traced for each work), and the costume, jewellery and accoutrements, carpet and background are systematically altered from one picture to the next in a way which suggests that a principle of variation was consciously adhered to.[16] Technical variation in the manner of execution is also clear-cut.[17] Nevertheless, all the works replicate exactly Henry's bullish square-on pose in the Whitehall Palace mural, which Holbein had belatedly adjusted from his cartoon[18] and which was a key component of the overpowering effect the mural is said to have had on visitors to the privy chamber.[19] Overlooking the Whitehall mural's specifically dynastic frame of reference, Holbein's actual depiction of the king strikingly dispensed with the traditional and distancing effect of royal robes, crowns and regalia and instead focused upon Henry's larger-than-life personality and the immediacy of his monumental and positively priapic[20] physicality; in the full-lengths the viewer is conscious of his authority as a person without being given any direct visual evidence that he is a monarch. Holbein's approach may well have been determined by Henry's intensifying conflict with the Roman Catholic Church. In November 1534, by the Act of Supremacy the king had established himself rather than the Pope as the head of the Church in England, a supreme assertion of his own willpower and personal desire over and above any reflection of political actuality. The lines inscribed on the stone plinth in the centre of Holbein's original mural have been termed 'brutally partisan and anti-Papal in tone'[21] and given that Edward Seymour was at the head of the pro-Protestant faction at court, it seems likely that WAG 1350 and its companions functioned explicitly as icons of political support for Henry's religious reforms and later, of the Protestant cause in general.

PROVENANCE

[? Commissioned by, or painted for, Edward Seymour, from 1547 1st Duke of Somerset]; by descent to Henry Danby Seymour 1850; by descent to his brother Alfred Seymour; his daughter Miss Jane Seymour (1873–1943); Christie 19 January 1945 (48); bt. by the gallery.

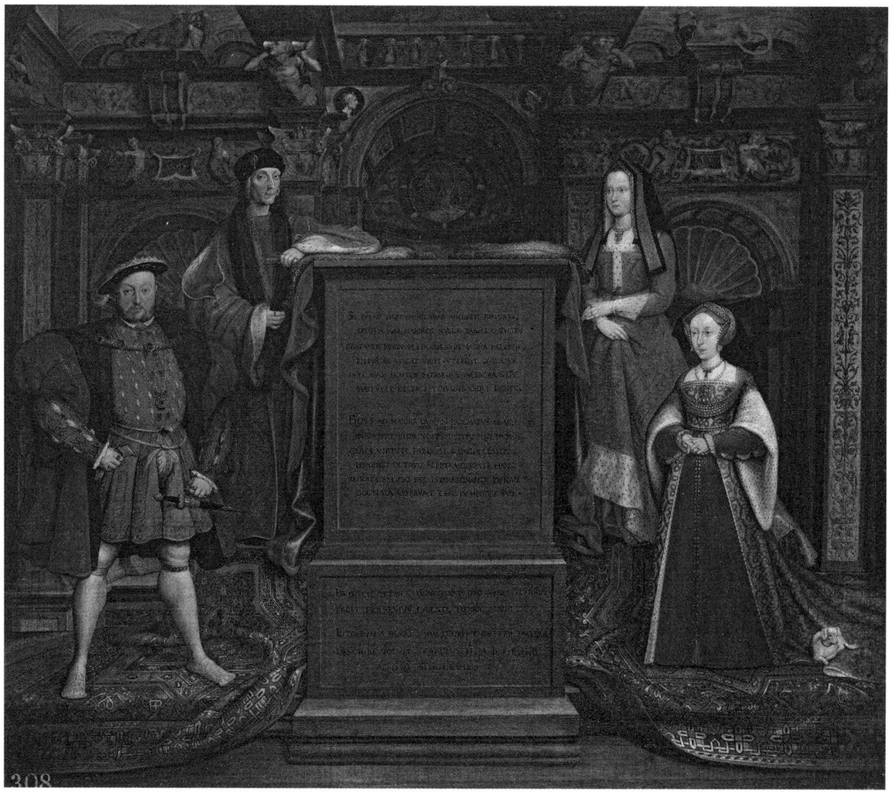

Fig. 31 *Allegory of the Tudor Succession* after Hans Holbein, by Remigius van Leemput, oil on canvas. The Royal Collection © 2010 Her Majesty Queen Elizabeth II.

EXHIBITIONS

1st Special Exhibition of National Portraits South Kensington 1866 (144); *Some Acquisitions of the Walker Art Gallery Liverpool 1935–1945* National Gallery London, 1945 (1); *Works by Holbein and Other Masters of the 16th and 17th centuries* RA 1950–51 (206); *Kings and Queens of England* Walker Art Gallery 1953 (3); *L'Europe Humaniste* Palais des Beaux-Arts, Brussels 1954–55 (41); *Henry VIII Revealed: Holbein's Portrait and Its Legacy* Walker Art Gallery 2003 (no cat. no.); *Gothic: Art for England 1400–1547* Victoria & Albert Museum, London 2004 (351); *Holbein in England* Tate Britain, London 2006 (131).

NOTES

1. This entry is very largely based on Xanthe Brooke and David Crombie: *Henry VIII Revealed: Holbein's Portrait and Its Legacy* exh. cat., Walker Art Gallery (2003) (hereafter *B&C*). This is in effect a 118-page catalogue entry and explores the physical and contextual aspects of the painting in consummate detail; further bibliographical references may be found there.
2. *B&C*, p. 17.
3. See the diagram in *B&C*, Appendix A, p. 113.
4. Susan Foister: *Holbein in England*, exh. cat., Tate Britain, London (2006) p. 95 (cat. 104).
5. Gustav Waagen: *Treasures of Art in Great Britain* 3 vols (London, 1854) vol. 2, p. 241. Waagen's account is of a visit to Henry Seymour Danby's London house made four years previously, when the work was hanging on the staircase. Waagen observed that 'there are a number of pictures of this class in England attributed to Holbein; but this is one of the few that may be considered genuine, having probably come into the possession of the family at the time of Henry VIII's marriage with Jane Seymour. The original modelling of the head is much obscured now by dirt; the hands, however, are more distinct and very delicate. The rich dress, hangings, and carpets, are executed with singular solidity and care.'
6. In a handwritten catalogue of the Seymour family's collection of paintings at East Knoyle House, probably drawn up about 1881 by Alfred Seymour (Wiltshire Record Office 1126/16), the provenance of the subject pictures is carefully listed, but none is given for the 56 family portraits, implying that they had been in the family some time previously; WAG 1530, which is no. 1 in the catalogue, is said to have been 'always in the possession of my family and in all probability was originally painted for one member of it' (*B&C*, p. 64).
7. *B&C*, p. 45, citing Historical Manuscripts Commission no. 58: *Report on the Manuscripts of the Most Honourable the Marquss of Bath Preserved at Longleat* 5 vols (London, 1904–81) vol. 4, p. 338.
8. Other full-lengths are known whose status is unclear, for instance the version 228.5 × 137 cm in the historic collection assembled by Sir Henry Lee, courtier of Henry VIII from 1545, at Ditchley Park, sold Sotheby 24 May 1933 (53) as 'School of Holbein' and described in the catalogue as depicting Henry

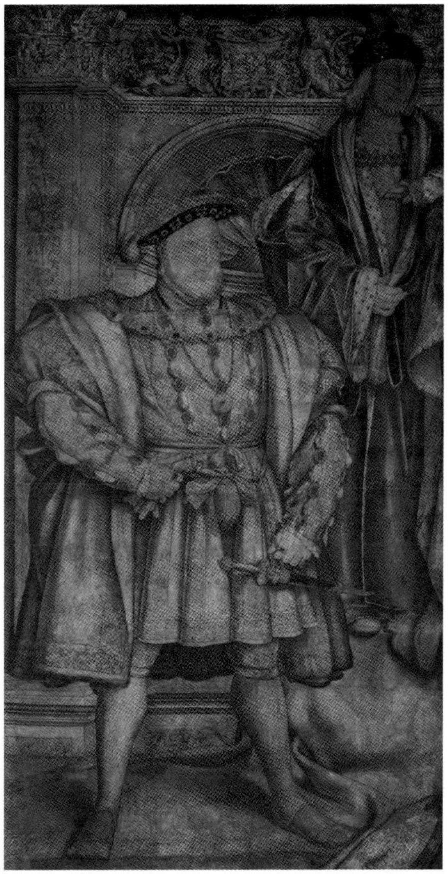

Fig. 32 *Henry VIII with Henry VII* by Hans Holbein, ink and wash on paper mounted on canvas. © National Portrait Gallery, London.

'standing legs apart, in red doublet trimmed with fur, gloves in right hand at hip, left hand holding a sheathed dagger'. Well known among other variants are those in the Royal Collection (originally to a half-length pattern, to which legs have been added) and the half-lengths in the Museo d'Arte Antica, Rome and in the Art Gallery of South Australia, Adelaide. In the former, which is inscribed with Henry's age, 49, indicating a date of 1540–41, the treatment of the face is notably close to that in WAG 1350.
9. *B&C*, p. 41.
10. Foister, *op. cit.*, p. 118 (cat. 131).
11. Roy Strong: *National Portrait Gallery: Tudor and Jacobean Portraits* 2 vols (London, 1969) vol. 1, p. 159, pl. 309; in his *Holbein and Henry VIII* (London, 1967) p. 44 n. 1, pl. 38, he had described WAG 1350 as 'after Hans Holbein'.
12. *B&C*, pp. 103–9.
13. From left to right, the six planks of imported Baltic oak on which WAG 1530 is painted measure, from top to bottom: 170–172 mm; 210–204 mm; 292–301 mm; 266 mm; 197–195 mm and 200–202 mm. It is thought that the left-hand and two right-hand planks may have come from the same tree; *B&C*, pp. 104, 114.
14. *B&C*, p. 74.
15. See the chart in *B&C*, Appendix A, p. 113.
16. In WAG 1530 Henry wears a white shirt with a frilled collar, a silver tunic with three rows of slashes in the arms, through which the shirt protrudes, a red velvet gown decorated with gold embroidery and lined with brown (lynx?) fur, a black jewel-studded hat lined with white fur at the brim, white stockings with the Order of the Garter below his left knee, displaying the letters VTY PENS (apparently an anomalous treatment of the words *Honi soiT qui mal Y PENSe*). He wears an extraordinary collar of huge rubies interspersed with rows of pearls and diamonds that has been identified as probably the collar worn by the king at a reception at Greenwich Palace in January 1540, which was described by Edward Hall as 'a coller of such Balystes [rubies] and Perle that few men ever saw the lyke'. Hanging from a chain of alternating twisting columns and initial 'H's is a gold circular pendant with a single black-foiled diamond at its centre. To cement the impression of richness and ostentation, he stands on a rare Star Ushak carpet from Anatolia in Turkey. For a discussion of the variations in the treatment of the costume, jewellery and carpet between the full-length versions and their relation to the original Whitehall mural, see *B&C*, pp. 35–41, 77–83.
17. In WAG 1530 the chalk ground layer was sealed by a mixture of lead white in oil applied across the whole surface. The underdrawing was set out directly on to this layer. This underdrawing is characterised by a fine line that is even in width but sometimes a little hesitant in execution; it is not characteristic of Holbein's own drawing technique. A grey modelling layer was applied unevenly to the areas of the curtain and carpet and the pattern of the curtain was then painted up to the drawn edge of the figure. In David Crombie's words, WAG 1350 'exhibits noticeable variations in the handling and build-up of paint across its surface. Many areas are quite thinly painted, such as the curtain, parts of the architecture, the tunic and the flesh, while others, such as the green architectural marbling and areas of the carpet, show more complex layering' (*B&C*, p. 92; and for the underdrawing p. 87). In its early years at the gallery, WAG 1530 was repeatedly treated for flaking paint, for example in 1955, 1960 and 1968 (J. Coburn Witherop, *treatment notes*, gallery files); however, this problem has stabilised in the more recent past.
18. A drawing in the Staatliche Graphische Sammlung, Munich may be a copy of a drawing by Holbein used to convert Henry's face as depicted in the cartoon to his face as painted in the Whitehall mural. It is inscribed on the reverse *Hans Swarttung*, perhaps one of Holbein's assistants. Foister, *op. cit.*, p. 118 (cat. 130), points out that this drawing's

treatment of Henry's frilled shirt collar aligns it particularly closely to WAG 1350 although she refrains from suggesting that Swarttung may have been responsible for painting WAG 1350.

19. Strong, *Holbein and Henry VIII*, p. 39 quoted Karel von Mander's description in his *Lives of the Illustrious Netherlandish and German Painters*, that the king 'was so lifelike that the spectator felt abashed, annihilated in his presence'; B&C, p. 27.

20. This term is justly employed by Richard Marks in 'Postscript', *Gothic: Art for England 1400–1547* exh. cat., Victoria & Albert Museum, London (2004) p. 456.

21. B&C, p. 31.

extinct. This portrait would thus be of Edward's widow, about whom nothing has emerged.

PROVENANCE:

... [? Ralph Abbott; Christie 3 May 1902 (67); bt. Leggatt (350 gns.)]; ...Hon. Anne Cunliffe-Lister;[2] Christie 28 November 1930 (141); bt. Agnew; presented by Hugh Agnew to mark the re-opening of the gallery 1951.

REFERENCES:

1. Miss B. Copinger Hill, *letter*, 4 July 1960, gallery files, stated that the Hill of Buxhall family pedigree contained no reference to them. An alternative, even more suspect identification is Mrs LeBlanc Smith. This name appears on the mount of a photograph in the Witt Library of what appears to be WAG 2948 in an altered state, which was supposedly with Colnaghi, passed to A. Tooth & Sons by May 1902, and to have been sold by Tooth in October 1907; however, a subtitle on the mount puzzlingly reads *Lady in White Dress*, suggesting that the wrong photograph could have been pasted to the mount in error. William McKay and William Roberts, *John Hoppner R.A.* (London, 1909) do not list the portrait under either *Lady James, Mrs. LeBlanc Smith* or *Mrs. Hill*.

2. According to Philip, Earl of Swinton, letter, 12 October 1960, gallery files, Mrs. Cunliffe-Lister would not have inherited this picture but she purchased several paintings in the period 1918-1928.

John Hoppner

1758–1810

Portrait of a Lady, Perhaps Lady James

WAG 2948

oil on canvas, 76.2 × 63.5 cm

date: about 1796–1800

The traditional attribution to Hoppner may be accepted on stylistic grounds. The sitter is in a grey dress whose style is of the later 1790s, a date also indicated by the informal hairstyle with the headband. The conception of the portrait emphasises the sitter's personality rather than her looks.

The early history of WAG 2948 is unknown and the identity of the sitter is problematic. She was identified in the 1930 sale catalogue as the wife of James Hill of Buxhall, Suffolk, but no couple of this name has been traced.[1] What could well be this work (*Portrait of a lady in grey dress with lace frill*, 30 × 25 inches) was sold with its pendant at Christie's on 3 May 1902. In the auctioneer's copy of the catalogue (Christie's archives) the lots are annotated in manuscript *Mrs James* and *Mr James son of Sir William James*. The latter (about 1721-1783), a naval captain, M.P. and Baronet, had one son, Edward William James, who died young in November 1792, when the James baronetcy became

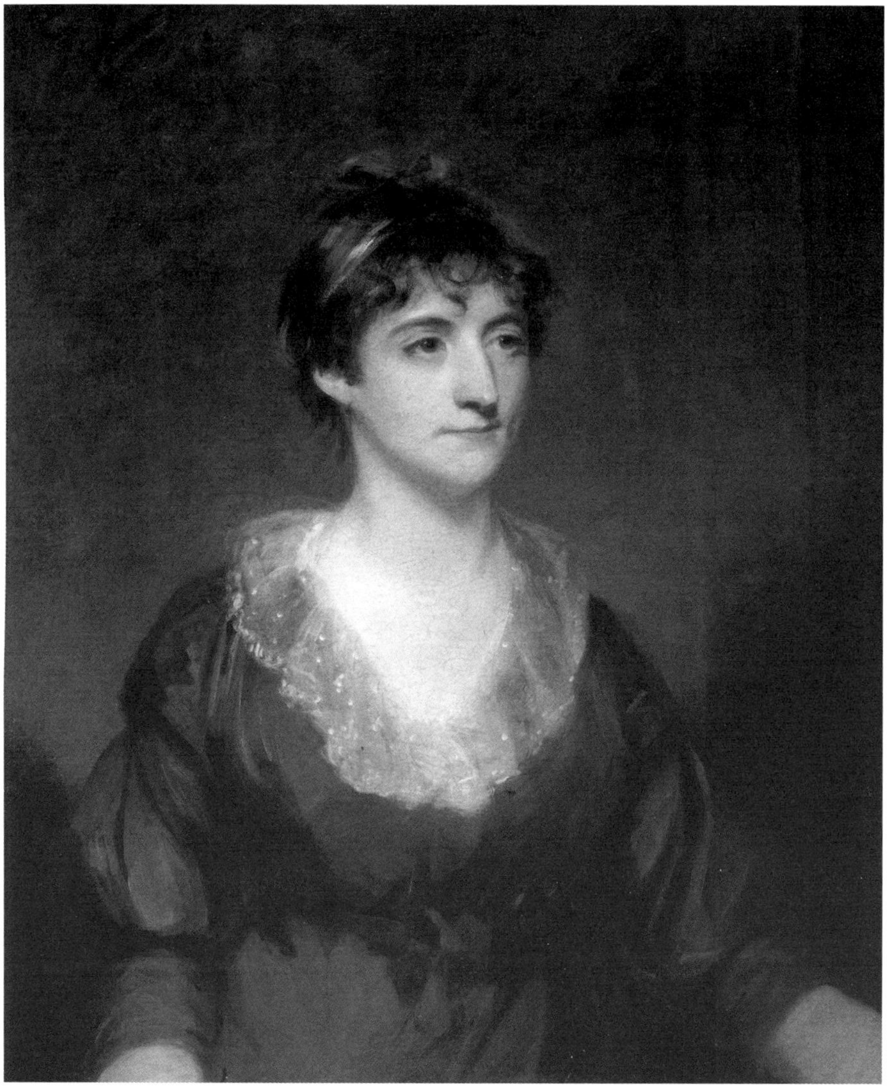

WAG 2948

The Prince of Wales (Later King George IV)

WAG 7022
oil on canvas, 228.5 × 152.5 cm
date: 1807

The Prince of Wales's visit to Liverpool on 18 September 1806 during his tour of England culminated in a Mayoral dinner held at Lillyman's Hotel in Castle Street. At this, the Prince offered to sit for his portrait to Hoppner and present the work to the Corporation; 'to correspond with the picture of the duke of Clarence now in the Possession of the Corporation' (i.e. WAG 7019, pp. 159-61).[1] Hoppner had been the Prince's official portrait painter for nearly 20 years,[2] and had painted him on many occasions; two of the resulting canvases had been exhibited at the Royal Academy in 1792 and 1796,[3] and others had involved adaptation of earlier portraits of the Prince by Reynolds.[4] The commission from Liverpool anticipated by six months the appearance at the RA of a third portrait of the Prince by Hoppner (RA 1807 [cat. 74]) and WAG 7022 has been assumed to be the exhibited canvas.[5] However, this may be incorrect. Alternative candidates, both of which were in Hoppner's possession at the time of his death, exist in the shape of 'an extra-sized Half Length...delivered to Sir Gore Ouseley to be taken to Persia',[6] and a full-length that the Prince later presented to the 2nd Marquess of Hertford. The 'extra-sized Half Length' sent to Persia is now lost, but is known to have depicted the Prince in Garter Robes, as WAG 7022 and the Hertford full-length both do also. The two full-lengths certainly are visually very closely related,[7] and it seems fair to say that the three canvases emerged more or less together, as one creative entity.

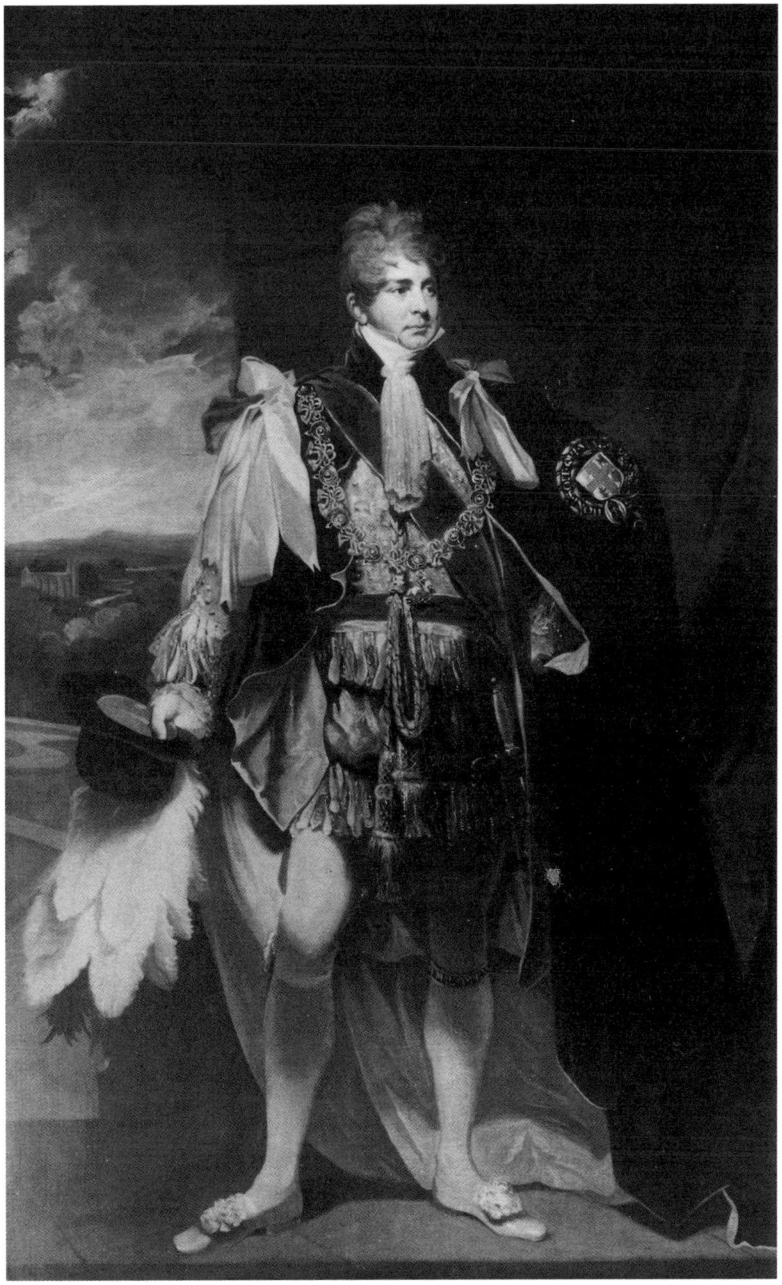

WAG 7022

Farington's diary, which refers to Lord Hertford's full-length as Hoppner's original,[8] offers some clues as to the work's gestation. The Prince apparently only began sittings to Hoppner about a fortnight before the Academy sending-in day (i.e. in April 1807) having failed to keep a number of earlier appointments. Hoppner was worried that his own health, which 'did not enable [him] to make great exertions', would prevent him from finishing the canvas destined for the Royal Academy in time, whereupon the Prince 'put his hands to Hoppner's cheeks & patting them said, "Oh! you have constitution enough to do anything"'.[9]

At the sitting, at which he was accompanied by the Duke of Clarence, the Prince of Wales found that the belt which belonged to his robes was 'too wide by 10 or 12 inches, so much had He shrunk in size'.[10] By August 1807 a copy of Hoppner's whole-length painted by Samuel Lane was already in existence, for which Hoppner had paid Lane 50 guineas. 'Hoppner asked [Lane] to paint another copy at a lower rate, which He wd. keep upon speculation but Lane declined doing it at a lower price, saying the copy had employed Him 6 weeks.'[11] It is tempting to suspect that the commission for the second copy was then passed to William Owen, whose known whole-length copy is in King's College, University of London;[12] and it is also tempting to think that it is Lane's copy that was delivered to Liverpool. WAG 7022 does have a slightly slick manner that suggests it is the work of a copyist, rather than an original. Noticeably, Hoppner abandoned his initial intention of visiting Liverpool to install the portrait, stating in a letter to Sir John Leicester that he had 'made the Corporation a very handsome present in this (for HRH talks of paying for it!) without adding the time and expense of a long journey'.[13] The sense of Hoppner's words is not clear, but presumably they anticipated his receiving the 160 guineas which the Corporation's 'Prince of Wales Visit Committee' authorised John Foster to pay him, on 12 December 1807, 'with the wish that this payment should not be communicated to the Prince of Wales and also [with the understanding] that the Committee relied on the liberality & Honor of Mr. Hoppner to refund the money in the event of the Prince hereafter causing him to be paid for the said picture'.[14] Hoppner nevertheless may have scented, if not double payment for the work, at least a way of confusing the issue by commissioning extra copies of the work, for which he would pay out less than he received.

Hoppner's composition, if not the Liverpool version of it specifically, soon became well known. Three engravings based on it were issued in quick succession by E. Scriven (published 1 January 1812 by T. Clay), William Say, 1812, and Henry Meyer (published 1 February 1815 by T. Baines). The last of these is lettered *from Hoppner's celebrated portrait*. A reduced copy by James Holmes (active 1798–1847) is at Temple Newsam, Leeds.

The frame of WAG 7022 was presumably executed in Liverpool, as it was intended to correspond to the frame on Shee's portrait of the Duke of Clarence.[15]

PROVENANCE

Painted for the Corporation of Liverpool; transferred from the City Estates Committee 1968.

EXHIBITIONS

[? RA 1807 (74)]; *Kings and Queens of England* Walker Art Gallery 1953 (37).

NOTES

1. *Minute Book of the Prince of Wales Visit Committee 1806–9* LRO 352 MIN/COU/1/2/10, p. 73.
2. The earliest designation of the artist as portrait painter to the Prince of Wales appears to be in the catalogue of the Royal Academy exhibition of 1789; John Ingamells: *The Wallace Collection Catalogue of Pictures 1, British, German, Italian, Spanish* (London, 1985) p. 109.
3. Sir Oliver Millar: *Later Georgian Pictures in the Royal Collection* 2 vols (London, 1969) vol. 1, p. 50 and Ingamells, *loc. cit.*, agree that the balance of probabilities is that the half-length in the Wallace Collection (p. 563) was the portrait exhibited at the RA in 1792 (100) and the whole-length in the Royal Collection (cat. 834) the one shown at the RA in 1796 (98). John H. Wilson: 'The Life and Work of John Hoppner', PhD thesis, University of London, 1992, p. 252, for example, believes the reverse is the case; his view is substantiated by Farington's note in his diary in January 1796 that 'Hoppner told me that He is now painting a *half length* [my emphasis] of the Prince of Wales for the Queen' (*FD*, vol. 3, p. 474 [entry for 18 January 1796]). This work, not currently accounted for, looks as though it ought to be the one shown in 1796.
4. Hoppner's portraits of the Prince that depend on Reynolds's prototypes include a whole-length at York and one formerly in the collection of Wilson Gale Braddyll at Conishead Priory (for which see M. Davies: *National Gallery Catalogues: The British School* [London, 1959] pp. 82 and 83, n. 5).
5. For example by William McKay and William Roberts: *John Hoppner R.A.* (London, 1909) pp. 94–5, followed by Richard Walker: *Regency Portraits* 2 vols (London, 1985) vol. 1, p. 209; also Wilson, *op. cit.*, p. 252.
6. Ingamells, *loc. cit.*
7. Ingamells, *loc. cit.*, observes that WAG 7022 and the Marquess of Hertford's picture are in effect only variants of the Royal Collection whole-length that had already been shown at the Royal Academy in the 1790s (see n. 3) and suggests that Sir Gore Ouseley's picture was the one exhibited in 1807.
8. *FD*, vol. 8, p. 3108 (entry of 18 August 1807).
9. *FD*, vol. 8, p. 3036 (entry of 2–4 May 1807).
10. *Ibid.*
11. *FD*, vol. 8, p. 3108 (entry of 18 August 1807).
12. Perhaps on the basis of this copy, Owen was appointed to succeed Hoppner as portrait painter to the Prince of Wales in 1810 and was commissioned for a copy of Hoppner's 1790s' (Royal Collection) whole-length; this copy is at St James's Palace; Millar, *op. cit.*, p. 55.
13. Hoppner to Sir John Leicester, *letter*, n.d., Tabley archives, University of Manchester; quoted by McKay and Roberts, *op. cit.*, p. 95.
14. *Minute Book of the Prince of Wales Visit Committee*, p. 117.
15. *Ibid.*

called

John Hoppner

1758–1810

Portrait of a Lady

WAG 633
oil on canvas, 74.5 × 61 cm
date: unknown, perhaps 1875–85

George Holt purchased WAG 633 as by Hoppner in 1887 and it was still accepted as his work by the authors of the standard Hoppner catalogue in 1914.[1] The attribution had, however, been questioned when the picture was exhibited (as by Hoppner) at Birmingham in 1900 when it was suggested that it might instead be an early Raeburn.[2] Although it is stylistically reminiscent of both artists – the colour range and relation of figure to background recall Hoppner, while the shaping of the sitter's

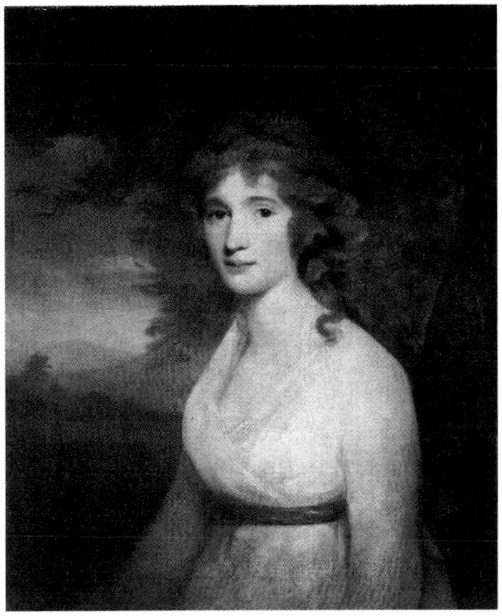

WAG 633

hair and bust have more in common with Raeburn – WAG 633 is a weak work and probably a pastiche. The scale of the figure seems misapplied to a 30 × 25 inch canvas, the drawing of the arms and bust is poor and the paint-strokes on the sash are coarsely executed. The painting purports from the costume and the hairstyle to date from the early 1790s. No identification has ever been put forward for the sitter.

PROVENANCE

...W. A. Tollemache; Christie 2 April 1887 (119); bt. Philpot; from whom bt. Agnew; bt. by George Holt June 1887;[3] Emma Holt Bequest 1945.

EXHIBITIONS

Winter Exhibition Grosvenor Gallery, London 1889 (52); *Loan Collection of Portraits* Birmingham Museum and Art Gallery 1900 (14); *Loan Exhibition of Pictures in Aid of the Funds of the Children's Infirmary* Agnew's, Liverpool 1904 (1); *International Fine Art Exhibition* Rome 1911 (British section, 42).

NOTES

1. William McKay and William Roberts: *John Hoppner R.A.* (2nd edn, London, 1914) p. 288.
2. W. Wallis and A. B. Chamberlain, eds: *Loan Collection of Portraits* [...] (exh. cat.) Birmingham Museum and Art Gallery (1900) p. 19.
3. Agnew's bill for £315 is dated 29 June 1887 (gallery archives).

called
Jacob Huysmans
1633–96

Lady Mary Molyneux

WAG 8640
oil on canvas, 128.5 × 103 cm
date: unknown, perhaps 1669–1715

This is one of the series of Molyneux family portraits of the late seventeenth and early eighteenth centuries which formed part of the historic collection at Croxteth Hall (for a general discussion of which see British School WAG 8627, pp. 329-30). There is a degree of uncertainty over the identity of the sitter but she has been assumed to be Mary, the eldest daughter of Caryll, 3rd Viscount Molyneux (1622–1700) and his wife Mary, née Barlow.[1] Her date of birth is uncertain, but given that her parents married around 1650, it may be placed in the early 1650s. She was the sister of Hon. Richard Molyneux and William, 4th Viscount Molyneux (for whom see British School WAG 8627 and 8631 [pp. 331-2] respectively) and married Sir Thomas Preston, Bt., of Furness.

The portrait was previously attributed to 'School of Kneller'[2] and then 'School of Lely'[3] before being ascribed to Huysmans.[4] The artist was much employed by Catholic families such as the Molyneux, and this portrait uses one of his recognisable stock poses. From the costume and hairstyle, it has been dated to the second half of the 1660s (implying that the sitter is still in her teens).[5] However, as with the other portraits in the group, WAG 8640 is probably a later copy, perhaps commissioned for the new wing at Croxteth completed in 1714. Its quality is not high enough for it to be an original work by Huysmans.

PROVENANCE

By descent at Croxteth Hall; bt. in 1974 from the executors of Hugh, 7th Earl of Sefton.

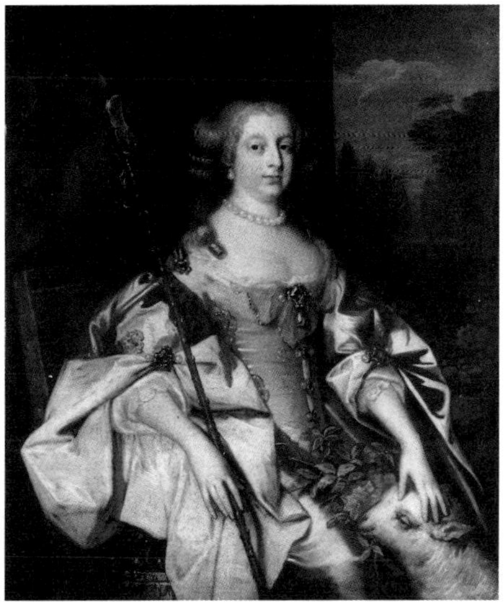

WAG 8640

NOTES

1. *MPPP*, p. 128, where an alternative candidate for the sitter was suggested in the shape of Mary (d. 1725), wife of Hon. Richard Molyneux. She was the daughter of William, 1st Marquess of Powys and later married Francis, Viscount Montagu and Sir George Maxwell. In support of this notion is the fact that WAG 8640 is the same size as the portrait of Richard (British School WAG 8627), is painted in a rather similar style, and is in a frame of very similar design. However, this identification was discounted in *MPPP* on the basis of comparison with Largillière's portrait of her at Coughton Court, which shows a more slender woman with a narrower face and higher brow. A further alternative might be Mary, née Barlow, wife of the 3rd Viscount. There is doubt over the date of her death, which is given as 1661 in *Complete Peerage*, vol. 9, p. 47, but as 1691 in other sources; if the latter is correct she is likely to have been aged around 40 in the later 1660s. Against this latter identification is the family's traditional title for WAG 8640, *Lady Mary Molyneux*, which strictly indicates the daughter of a peer; a commoner who had married into the Molyneux family would properly be termed 'Mary, Lady Molyneux'.
2. *Croxteth 1946 Inventory*, no. 2. No. 111 in the same inventory was a possible pendant, *A Young Man as a Shepherd in a Landscape*, 50 × 40 inches, by 'School of Kneller'.
3. This attribution was made by curators at the gallery, 1974.
4. Sir Oliver Millar, *letter*, 3 February 1976, gallery files; independently confirmed by Catharine MacLeod, *verbally*, 9 December 2008.
5. MacLeod, *loc. cit.*; thus correcting the proposed dating of between about 1680 and 1696 (Huysmans's death) in *CIC*, p. 147.

Julius Caesar Ibbetson

1759–1817

Mountain Landscape with Cattle on a Lakeside Path[1]

WAG 9811
oil on canvas, 51 × 66.6 cm

Mountain Landscape with Travellers on a Lakeside Path[2]

WAG 9812
oil on canvas, 51 × 66.5 cm
date: about 1788–93

The traditional attribution of WAG 9811–9812 to Ibbetson has not been questioned,[3] but they are not wholly characteristic of his – usually more topographically accurate and sharply observed – landscapes with figures, and are hard to place within his *oeuvre*. Neither their date nor the locations represented are known. Clearly they are a pair, and they are probably intended to function as opposite and contrasting views from the same spot. They have been dated to 1798,[4] perhaps on the basis that Ibbetson moved to the north-west to work in that year and on the assumption that they were acquired by the Sefton family directly from the artist. However, they do not appear in twentieth-century inventories of Croxteth Hall and there are indications that they were purchased by the last Countess of Sefton.[5] WAG 9811 seems to be a more fanciful treatment of the same landscape as that depicted by John Rathbone in WAG 2687 (pp. 129-30), which is dated 1788 and has been tentatively identified as a view in Borrowdale in the Lake District.[6] Ibbetson is said to have worked with Rathbone in early life and he is known to have been painting Lake District subjects by the late 1780s, long before his permanent move to the north-west.[7] The sensibility towards the landscape

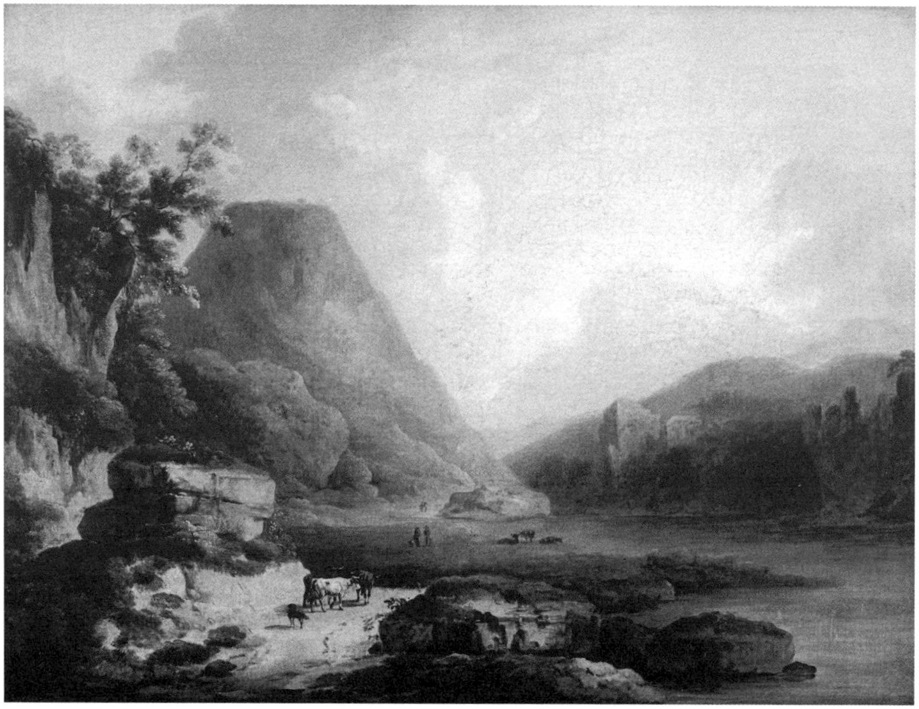

WAG 9811

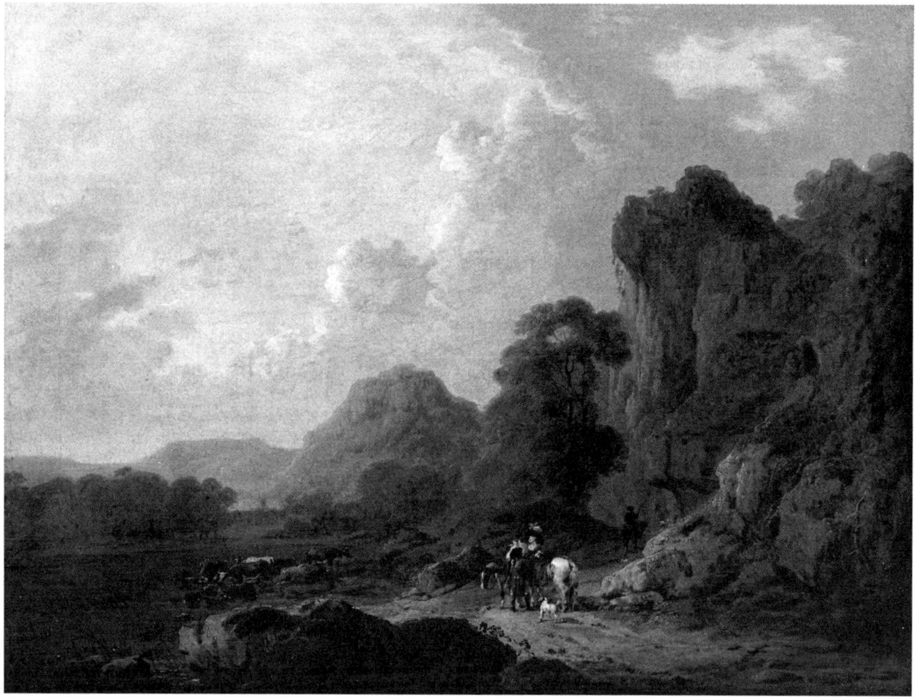

WAG 9812

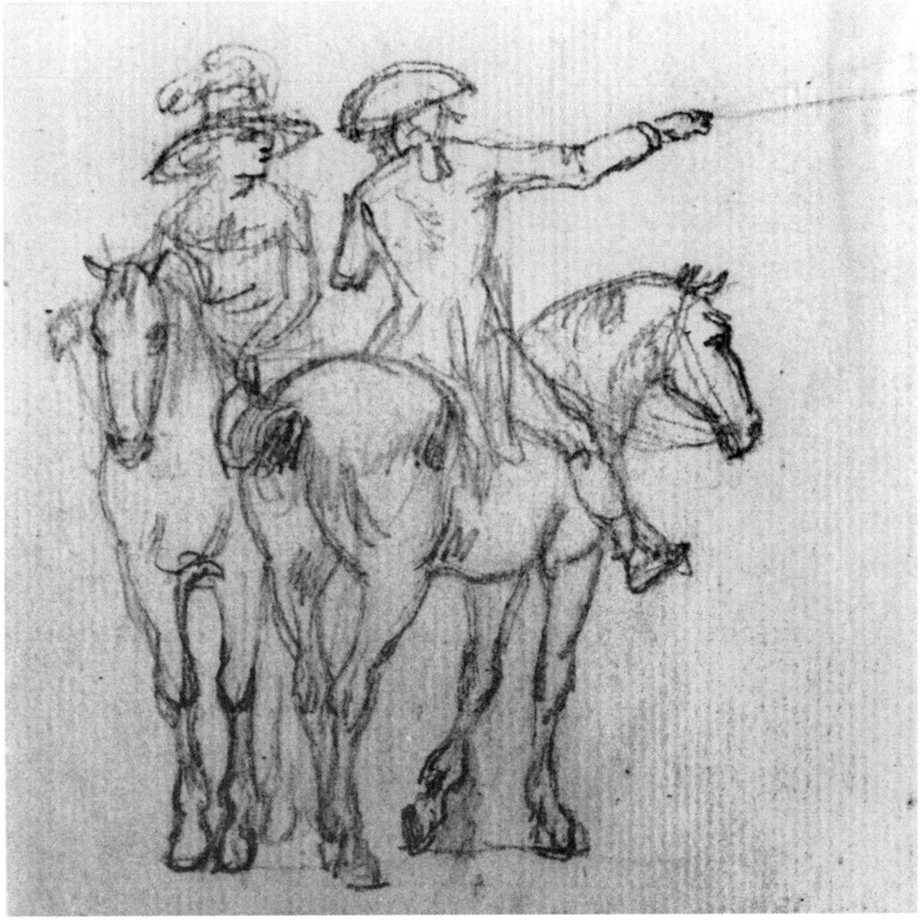

Fig. 33 *A Man and Woman on Horseback* by Julius Caesar Ibbetson, graphite, ink and wash on paper. Private collection; photo © Suzanne Higgott, courtesy of the Witt Library, The Courtauld Institute of Art, London.

displayed in WAG 9811–9812 seems redolent of theories of the Picturesque characteristic of the 1780s, in which landscape motifs were subjugated to prescribed aesthetic norms, rather than of the more Romantic attitudes prevalent both generally in British landscape painting and in Ibbetson's own work by the end of the 1790s, in which greater truth to locality, atmosphere and mood was manifest. Among comparable works by the artist, perhaps one of the closest in style is the *Gypsies with an Ass Race* of 1792 (Birmingham Museum and Art Gallery).[8] A dating of no later than the early 1790s is also suggested by the costumes of the two travellers in WAG 9812. A study of a man and woman on horseback in a collection of sketches by Ibbetson (fig. 33)[9] may, despite differences, be for this couple, given the style of their hats and the man's similarly outstretched right arm.

PROVENANCE

...Josephine, Countess of Sefton; her bequest 1980.

EXHIBITION

Julius Caesar Ibbetson 1759–1817 Abbot Hall Art Gallery, Kendal 1982 (6) [WAG 9811] and (7) [WAG 9812].

NOTES

1. Titled *Cattle on Path by a Lake* in CIC, p. 147.
2. Titled *Rocky River Landscape with Cattle* in CIC, p. 147.
3. See James Mitchell: *Julius Caesar Ibbetson (1759–1817) The Berchem of England* (London, 1999) pp. 98, 100.
4. In the 1982 exhibition catalogue, followed by Mitchell, *loc. cit.* In CIC, *loc. cit.*, WAG 9811–9812 were dated between about 1785 and about 1810.
5. There are labels on the backs of both works of the Squire Gallery, 12 Baker Street London.
6. On this basis it is tempting to locate the setting of WAG 9811–9812 somewhere close to the south-east corner of Derwentwater, looking respectively south and north, but the specific topography is unrecognisable and if this is correct, it is as though he has derived the landscape forms at second or third hand. WAG 9811–9812 are perhaps potboilers of the kind that Ibbetson made for dealers throughout much of his early career.
7. See, for example, his *Derwentwater with Skiddaw*, 92 × 125 cm, dated 1788, formerly in the collection at Sheffield Park, Sussex (photograph in Witt Library files).
8. Repr. Rotha M. Clay: *Julius Caesar Ibbetson* (London, 1948) pl. 12, between pp. 12 and 13.
9. Suzanne Gaynor: 'A Catalogue of Drawings by Julius Caesar Ibbetson in a Private Collection', MA report, Courtauld Institute of Art, 1978, cat. 113.

Lower Rydal Waterfall

WAG 1819
oil on canvas on glass,[1] 91.5 × 66.5 cm
date: 1798

An inscription on the back of the canvas, written by Ibbetson himself, reads:

Correct View of the Lower / RYDAL waterfall / in Sr Michael le Fleming's Garden / Drawn from Nature October and finished / in December 1798 by JULIUS IBBETSON / for Mr T. Vernon of Liverpool / who pays more liberally than [drawing of a Ducal crown] or [a Marquis's coronet] or [an Earl's coronet] or [a Baron's coronet] or [a Bishop's mitre].[2]

This inscription refers to the contract, initially for six months but eventually extended to three years, that the artist had earlier that year entered into, on the advice of Charles Greville, Sir George Beaumont and other London well-wishers, with the Liverpool auctioneer and picture-dealer Thomas Vernon.[3] In 1797 Vernon had auctioned two works by Ibbetson in his sale of the collection of Edward Rogers, and evidently admired the artist's work;[4] it is possible that he put out feelers to bring him to Liverpool. Vernon's eventual insolvency in 1801 was to cause Ibbetson great financial hardship.

The two falls at Rydal, situated at the point where Rydal Beck descends off Rydal Fell just before joining the River Rothay below Rydal Water, were a well-known destination for tourists of the Lake District in search of the Picturesque. In 1668–69 the owner of the Rydal estate, Sir Daniel Fleming (1633–1701) had built a small stone hut (which he referred to as 'my grott-house') from which to view the lower fall, and he added the bridge behind the fall in 1682. The view was noted as early as 1692 by Revd Thomas Machell, who described it as 'very surprising'. In his *Observations relative Chiefly to Picturesque Beauty, Made in the Year 1772, on Several Parts of England* [...], William Gilpin wrote,

tho' but a miniature, [it] is so beautiful, both in itself, and in its accompaniments, as to deserve particular notice. It is seen from a summer-house; before which its rocky cheeks, circling on each side form a little area; appearing through the window like a picture in a frame. The water falls within a few yards of the eye, which, being rather above its level, has a long perspective view of the stream, as it hurries from the higher grounds; tumbling, in various little breaks, through its rocky channel, darkened with thicket, till it arrives at the edge of the precipice, before the window; from whence it rushes into the bason [sic], which is formed by nature in the native rock. The dark colour of the stone, taking still a deeper tinge from the wood, which hangs over it, sets off to wonderful advantage the sparkling lustre of the stream; and produces an uncommon effect of light...[5]

Nineteenth-century tours of the Lake District continued to single out the experience.[6] Sir Michael le Fleming (1748–1806), referred to in Ibbetson's

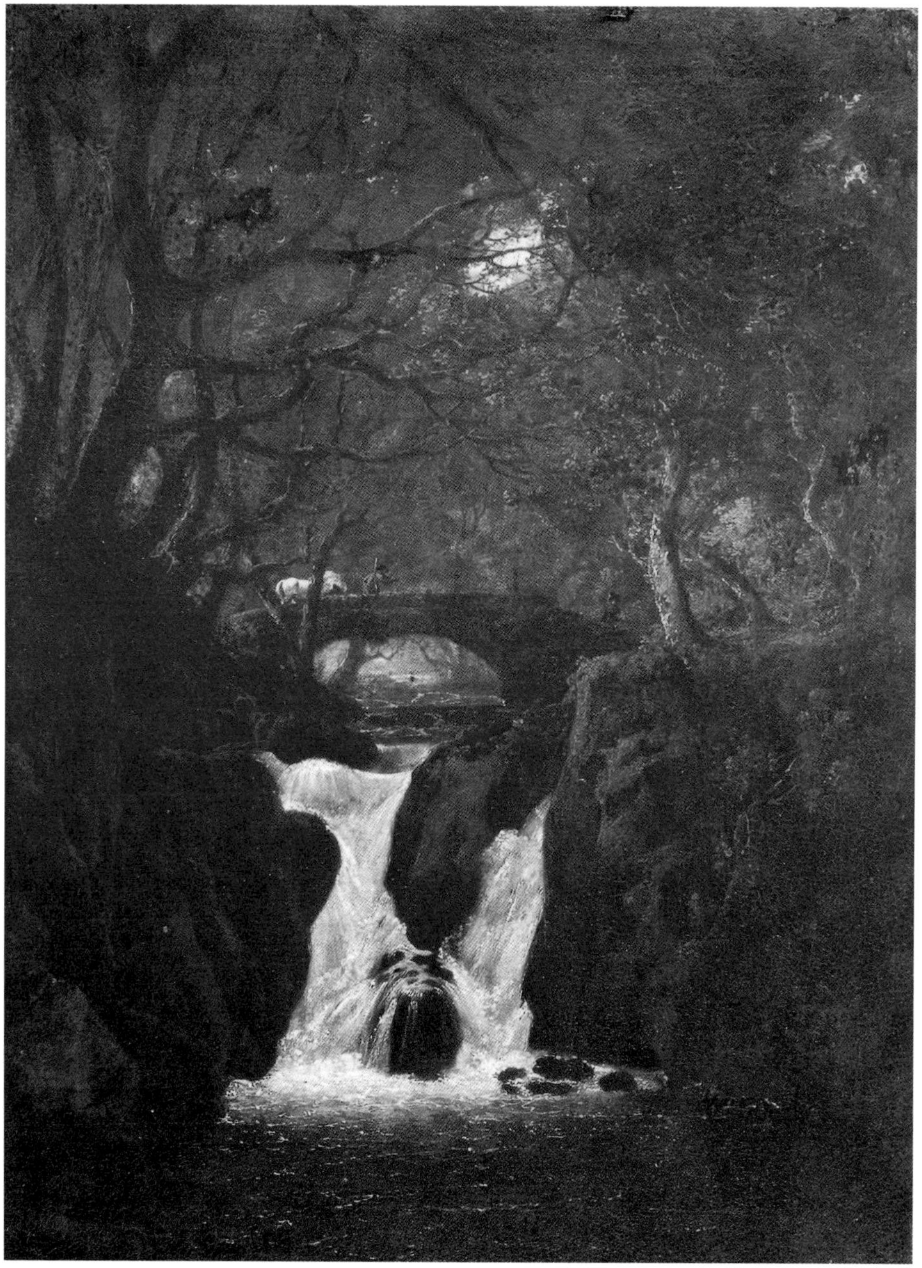

WAG 1819

inscription, was Sir Daniel's great-nephew. He was MP for Westmorland from 1774 until his death and enjoyed a reputation as a lover of literature and art; James Boswell described him as 'a very fashionable baronet in the brilliant world'.[7]

Although we have Ibbetson's word that the painting was based on a drawing taken on the spot,[8] the finished work is uncharacteristic of his usual landscape style in its rather claustrophobic conception (although he returned to the idea in his *North Esk: A Sketching Lesson* of 1800)[9] and more especially in technique (even if judgement about this should be to some extent reserved in view of the work's heavily restored condition).[10] It is tempting to think that Ibbetson was under instruction from Vernon to produce a work similar to Wright of Derby's recent painting of Rydal Falls (Derby Museum and Art Gallery; fig. 34) which, although it had been sold to the Manchester collector J. Leigh Philips at the end of 1795, had derived from one of the tours of the Lakes that Wright had made with Liverpool friends (notably Thomas Moss Tate) in 1793 and 1794.[11] Vernon may well have scented the opportunity to sell a similar view to a member of Tate's circle.

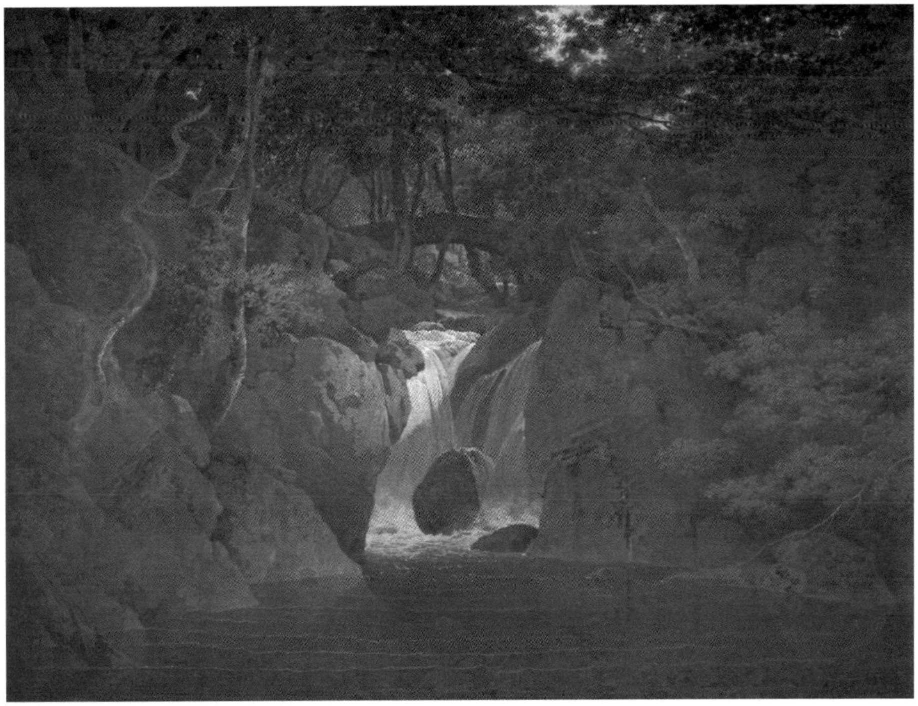

Fig. 34 *Rydal Waterfall* by Joseph Wright of Derby, oil on canvas. © 2011 Derby Museums and Art Gallery.

PROVENANCE

...[? Winstanley, Manchester, 29 February 1828 (114) (as *A Waterfall, Rydal*)];[12] ...James Mather Darbishire, Liverpool, about 1900;[13] by descent to Mrs Joyce B. Darbishire; from whom bt. 1958.

EXHIBITION

RA 1799 (257).

NOTES

1. The canvas was stuck down onto glass in the early years of the twentieth century; Joyce Darbishire, *letter*, 3 April 1958, gallery files.
2. An identical inscription is painted onto a plaque fixed to the frame. The tone of Ibbetson's wording suggests irony (a note of comparable ambiguity concerning the dealer Panton Betew, 'Un-Amateur', is written on the reverse of Ibbetson's very early landscape *The Thames at Millbank*, about 1781; private collection, Cheshire). However, given that Ibbetson was heavily dependent on Vernon for his livelihood at this date, the inscription has in the past been taken as genuinely effusive (*curatorial note*, gallery files).
3. Rotha M. Clay: *Julius Caesar Ibbetson* (London, 1948) pp. 61ff., quoting Ibbetson's own *Memoir*, in the second edition of his *Painting in Oils* (London, 1828).
4. Rogers's sale was held in the Linen Hall, Marble Street, Williamson Square, Liverpool, 24 July 1797. The text on the cover of the catalogue describes the contents as *A Capital and Extensive Collection of Valuable Pictures by Much Esteemed Masters, among Which Are Undoubted Pictures by*...IBBETSON. Ibbetson's works in the sale were lot 32, *A View near London* and lot 36 *One* (landscape).
5. Partially quoted in *MPPP*, p. 129.
6. *Ibid.*
7. James Boswell: *The Life of Doctor Johnson*; quoted in Sir Lewis Namier and John Brooke, eds: *The History of Parliament: The House of Commons 1754–1790*, 3 vols (London, 1964) vol. 2, p. 438.
8. The drawing is untraced. One candidate for it (in a private collection) is a close-up pen and ink landscape-format sketch depicting a waterfall of about the same height as the fall in WAG 1819, with similar rocky outcrops but lacking the bridge and the overhanging trees; see Suzanne Gaynor: 'A Catalogue of Drawings by Julius Caesar Ibbetson in a Private Collection', MA report, Courtauld Institute of Art, 1978, cat. 53.
9. Repr. *Julius Caesar Ibbetson*, exh. cat., Iveagh Bequest, Kenwood (1957) p. 21 (cat. 28).
10. Joyce Darbishire, *loc. cit.*, recalled that her father had had the work conserved around 1910 but described it as in poor condition when she offered it to the gallery.
11. Benedict Nicolson: *Joseph Wright of Derby, Painter of Light* 2 vols (London, 1968), vol. 1, p. 19; *MPPP*, p. 198.
12. Clay, *op. cit.*, p. 78, nn. 4 and 5, implies the existence of a second version of the work. It may be significant that adjacent lots in the same sale included a landscape by William Tate (lot 113) and an *Eruption of Vesuvius* by Wright of Derby (lot 118), suggesting that the vendor had bought Ibbetson's picture within the climate of taste for Wright's works.
13. *MPPP*, p. 129, notes that the Darbishire family appears to have had stronger connections with Manchester than Liverpool in the nineteenth century.

Hugh Mulligan

WAG 2529
oil with watercolour on panel,
20.5 × 15.5 cm
date: 1800

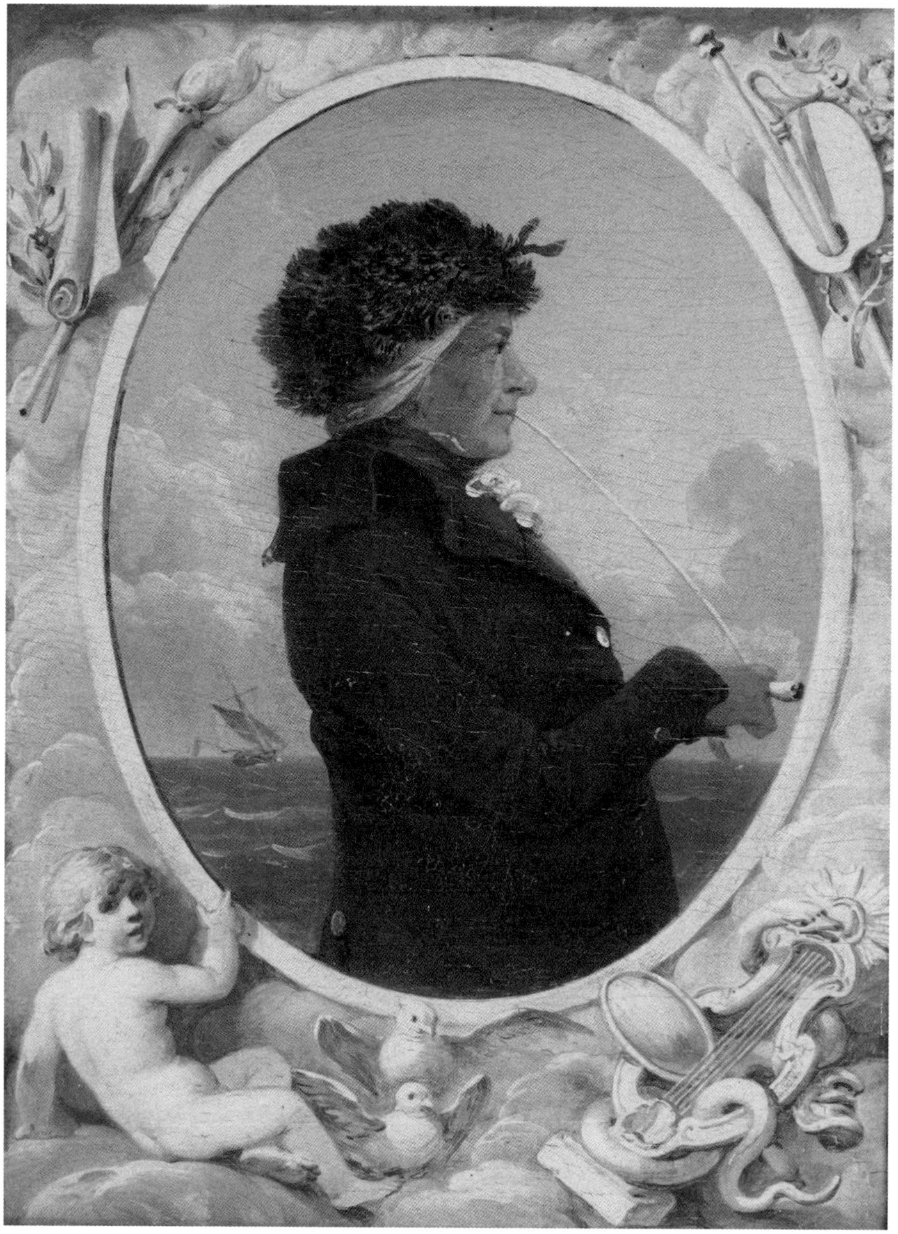

WAG 2529

Ibbetson painted this informal portrait of Hugh Mulligan, Liverpool engraver and bookseller, in 1800, on board a ship conveying the two men from Hull to Leith, where they were to join the dealer Thomas Vernon on a tour of Scotland.[1] According to the artist, writing to William Roscoe from Troutbeck on 17 September 1803 when presenting him with the picture, 'I painted him from a small black lead sketch & it is like, but the disguise of a fur cap, a nightcap & silk handkerchief, will prevent His being so easily recognized.'[2] Ibbetson's letter (whose scathing remarks about 'Vernon's Scotch campaign' reflect the subsequent souring of relations between the two men in 1801) makes it clear that WAG 2529 itself, as well as the preliminary drawing in black lead (now untraced), was made at sea. The artist told Roscoe that he had made the picture for himself, but that his wife had suggested that it might make an appropriate gift to Mrs Roscoe on their learning that Roscoe had subscribed to Ibbetson's recent publication, *Painting in Oil*. In that treatise, Ibbetson had recommended a technique of painting with a limited palette of oil colours mixed with a transparent medium of the artist's own invention (which he called 'Gumtion') over a watercolour underpainting. He had used this technique in the present picture.[3]

Mulligan (1746/47–1802) was one of Roscoe's oldest friends. Between the ages of 10 and 15, he had worked as a painter of ceramics at William Reid's China Factory on Brownlow Hill in Liverpool, which adjoined the property of Roscoe's publican and market-gardener father. According to Joseph Mayer, Mulligan gave the young Roscoe instruction (by implication in drawing and engraving)[4] and Roscoe himself later wrote that Mulligan had been 'a kind of Mentor to my youthful years, and my acquaintance with him, under different circumstances, continued till his death…'.[5] The two men were members of the Nonconformist congregation at Benn's Garden Chapel (whose registers record the baptism of four of Mulligan's daughters by his wife Sarah Granger between 1777 and 1784),[6] and both were strongly opposed to slavery, Mulligan's sentiments finding expression in his *Poems, Chiefly on Slavery and Oppression, with Notes and Illustrations* published in 1788. In Liverpool street directories Mulligan is listed during the period 1777–1800 as an engraver; in 1790 also as a potter, and in 1796 and 1800 also as a bookseller in Whitechapel.[7]

Pasted on the back of WAG 2529 is a long manuscript written by the artist after Mulligan's death in December 1802, which is in two halves.[8] The first, which is prefaced by a description of how the painting came into being, is a character study of Mulligan (headed *Hugo Mulliganus* N.O.B.A.) in the artist's characteristically forthright and effusive style:

> *...poor little Mully! the kindest hearted of all mor[tal]s the most Philanthropic, benevolent & sensible creature that ever groped his way through the world in chill penury's blind alleys...like a sensitive plant among thistles or St Fond beset by bagpipers did'st thou pass through this purgatory without any real solace but an excellent heart, thy Sarah Granger, possessing every perfection of the dulcinea adored by the inimitable knight of La Mancha, and thy beloved pipe of tobacco...sometimes indeed*
>
> *'in oblivion's grateful cup thoud'st drown*
> *the galling sneer, the supercilious frown,*
> *the strange reserve, the proud affected state*
> *of upstart knaves grown rich and fools grown*
> *great'*
>
> *but where is the wonder. It is only that it happened so very seldom that the painter of Hugo never witnessed it but once...*[9]

The second section of the document, headed *To Posterity Greeting*, is a sardonic message to readers 200 years in the future describing the perfection of life in 1803, which closely resembles a similar text written on the back of a self-portrait by Ibbetson dating from 1804.[10]

The portrait is set within a feigned oval whose corners are painted in grisaille with symbols of the arts: a torch and scroll, a palette and mahlsticks, a lyre with sun, serpent, mirror and masks, and a cherub with two doves. An ink and wash study for this border belonged in 1954 to Miss E. L. Godfrey of Dorset (19.5 × 14.5 cm; fig. 35).[11] A same-sized copy of WAG 2529 was owned in 1972 by Paul Rich, Farnham. The whole text of Ibbetson's original inscription is also pasted on the reverse of this and it is inscribed *copied by P McCreery*, who has been identified as Phoebe McCreery, daughter of the Liverpool printer who was a friend of Roscoe and of Ibbetson himself.[12]

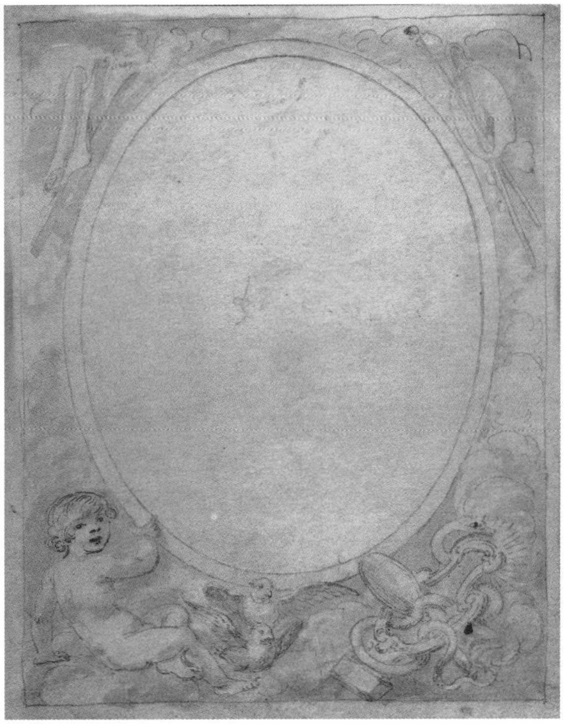

Fig. 35 *Study of a Cartouche for the Portrait of Hugh Mulligan* by Julius Caesar Ibbetson, graphite, ink and wash on paper. Private collection; photo courtesy of Mills Media.

PROVENANCE

Presented by the artist to William Roscoe; by descent to Mrs A. M. Roscoe; her bequest 1950.

EXHIBITIONS

Third Exhibition Illustrative of Objects Illustrative of the Fine Arts [...] Liverpool Mechanics Institution 1844 (no cat. no);[13] *Cleaned Pictures* Walker Art Gallery 1955 (39); *Julius Caesar Ibbetson* Iveagh Bequest, Kenwood 1957 (29).

NOTES

1. Rotha Mary Clay: *Julius Caesar Ibbetson* (London, 1948) pp. 64–5.
2. *Roscoe Papers*, LRO 920/ROS/2197. The letter is quoted in full in Ralph Fastnedge: 'A Rediscovered Portrait by J. C. Ibbetson', *Liverpool Bulletin* vol. 4 nos 1–2 (1954) pp. 49–52; and extensively in *MPPP*, pp. 129–30.
3. Fastnedge, *op. cit.*, p. 52.
4. Joseph Mayer: *Roscoe and the Influence of his Writings on the Fine Arts* (Liverpool, 1853) p. 24.
5. Henry Roscoe: *Life of William Roscoe* 2 vols (1833) vol. 1, p. 10.
6. Ms *note* by Mary Bennett, gallery files.
7. *MPPP*, p. 129.
8. Quoted in full by Fastnedge, pp. 49–50, and in *MPPP*, p. 130. Some readings of the text differ from mine.
9. The quotation is from Charles Churchill's poem *Night, an Epistle to Robert Lloyd* (1761). The reference to St Fond beset by bagpipers must refer to Barthelemy Faujas de Saint-Fond's *Travels in England, Scotland and the Hebrides*, 2 vols (London, 1799).
10. Clay, *op. cit.*, pp. XIX, 122; pl. 103.
11. Suzanne Gaynor: 'A Catalogue of Drawings by Julius Caesar Ibbetson in a Private Collection', MA report, Courtauld Institute of Art, 1978, cat. 143. Other drawings for decorative surrounds, possibly trials for the surround of WAG 2529, are in the same group of drawings.
12. *MPPP*, p. 131. The initial is not certainly *P*.
13. The artist's name is not given in the catalogue (p. 17, case 4), but the lender was Mrs W. S. Roscoe.

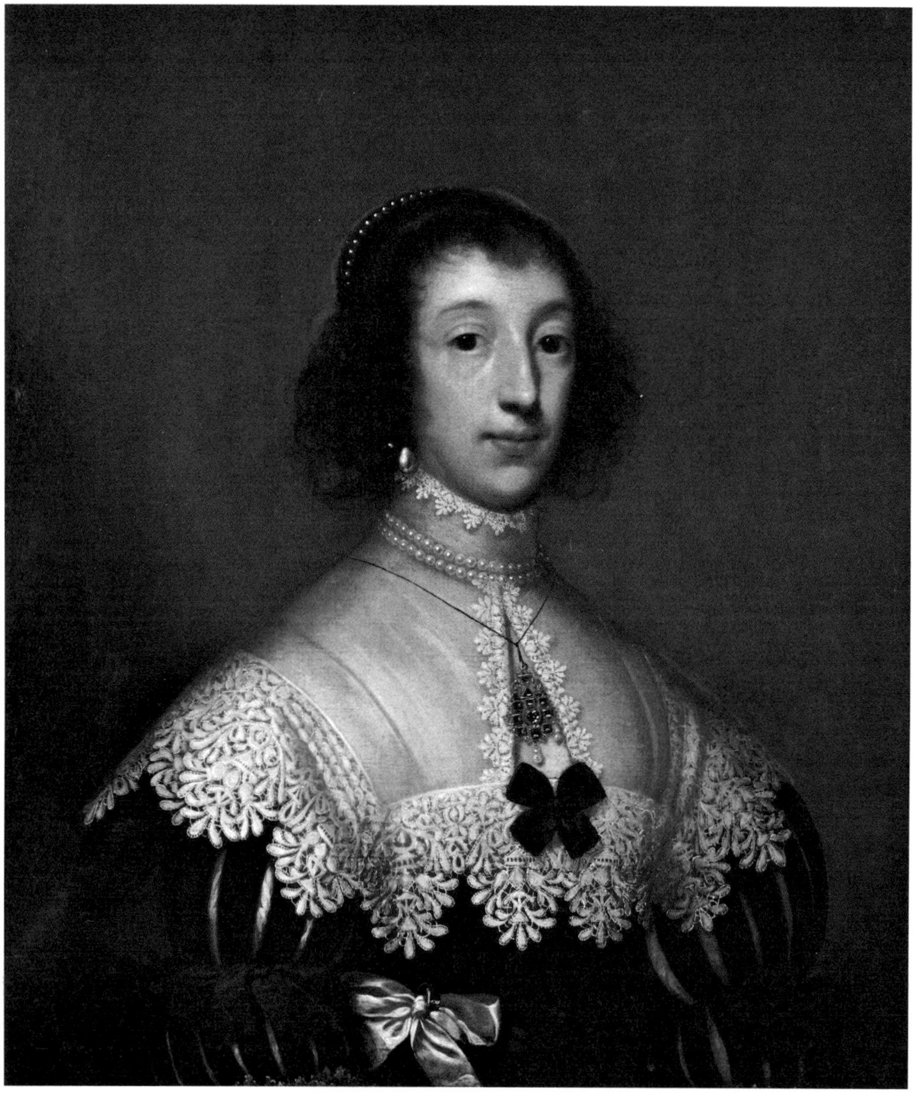

WAG 2995

Cornelius Johnson

1593–1661

Portrait of a Lady

WAG 2995
oil on canvas, 77 × 64 cm
signed and dated: *C. J. fecit/1633* (bottom left)
date: 1633

The sitter is unidentified.[1] She wears a black satin dress with slashed sleeves and a lawn collar trimmed with lace. A black pendant jewel hangs at her throat and a black ring is tied by a white bow at her waist. These may signify that she had recently been widowed. WAG 2995 is a characteristic example of Johnson's female bust portraiture of this period (compare his *Lady Morley*, dated 1633 (Killerton House, Acland Collection, The National Trust), or his *Margaret, Lady Hungerford*, also dated 1633 (sold Christie 16–17 July 1970 [133]; fig. 36). Pentimenti are visible above the head

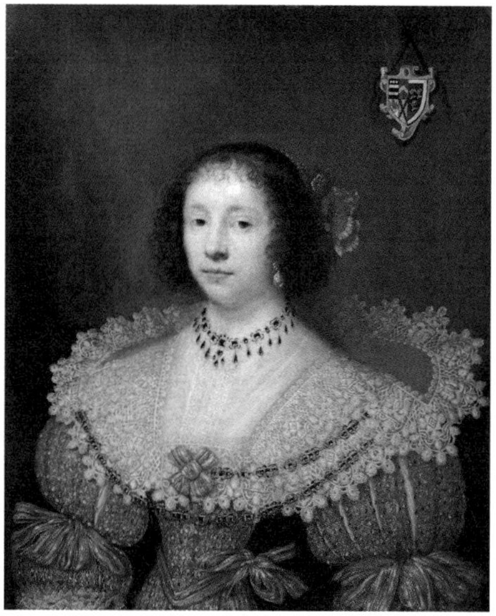

Fig. 36 *Margaret Lady Hungerford* by Cornelius Johnson, oil on canvas. Christie 16–17 July 1970 (199); © English Heritage Photo Library/The Bridgeman Art Library.

and above the lace at the right-hand shoulder. Some damage has occurred along the bottom edge, where the tacking edge has separated from the stretcher in the right-hand corner. The background has been repainted and allowed to cover the edge of the sitter's veil.[2]

PROVENANCE

...Colnaghi 1948; from whom bt. by K. R. Palmer, Banniskirk, Caithness;[3] bt. back by Colnaghi 1955;[4] from whom bt. by the gallery 1956.

NOTES

1. The portrait does not appear in A. J. Finberg: 'A Chronological List of Portraits by Cornelius Johnson, or Jonson', *Walpole Society*, vol. 10 (1921–22) pp. 1–37.
2. Condition and treatment report by J. Coburn Witherop dated February 1956, gallery files.
3. Information on the back of a photograph of WAG 2995 in the Heinz Archive, National Portrait Gallery. WAG 2995 is possibly to be identified with the *Lady in Slashed Black and White Dress with Large Lace Collar, Half Length, Turned to the Right*, 75 × 62 cm, sold in the Sir Hugo G. de Bathe sale, Sotheby 13 May 1931 (45), bt. Leggatt (£440).
4. R. Thesiger, Colnaghi & Co, *letter*, 24 January 1956, cited in a draft entry by Mark Evans, gallery files (the letter itself is missing): 'It is a picture which we sold some years ago and have just bought back'.

after

Cornelius Johnson

1593–1661

Sir Thomas Lucy and His Family

WAG 9822
oil on canvas, 75 × 132 cm
date: about 1740–44

Sir Thomas Lucy (1585–1640) of Charlecote, near Stratford-on-Avon was JP and deputy-lieutenant of Warwickshire for nearly three decades in the 1610s–30s and MP for Warwickshire 1614–28 and again 1640. He married Alice, daughter of Thomas Spencer of Claverdon in 1611 or 1612. In all they had 13 chidren, of whom the seven eldest are portrayed in WAG 9822. Their eldest son, Spencer (1614–49), enters the picture carrying a bowl of apples from the garden, which is formally laid out in newly fashionable style.[1] The next two sons, Robert (d. 1660) and Richard (1621–77), not yet breeched, play with their dog on a luxurious Indo-Persian carpet.[2] These three sons would inherit Charlecote in turn. In the centre stand the two eldest daughters, Constance, who hands her mother a dish of cherries, perhaps an allusion to her virtuousness,[3] and Margaret, holding her father's hand. The child at the right has been identified as the fourth son, George. Although the pattern of the dress is similar to those of Constance and Margaret, which might suggest that this is the third daughter, Bridget, and although the child also wears the same distinctive jewel as the older girls, it is wearing a tiny male doublet and also is holding a bow, which seems more likely to be a male attribute.[4] Bridget may thus be the seventh child, being held by its nurse at the back of the picture.

The original painting, dateable from the number of the children and their apparent ages to 1624–25, and traditionally attributed to Johnson, is believed to have perished in the Great Fire of London in 1666.[5] Previously to this, a copy of it had been made by a different artist[6] for the Great Hall at Charlecote (fig. 37), and it is from this picture that WAG 9822, one of several known versions,[7] is copied.

A letter from Caryll, 6th Viscount Molyneux to his second cousin George Lucy dated 8 January 1745,[8] in which he writes to congratulate him on his inheritance of Charlecote, refers to WAG 9822. In the course of his letter Lord Molyneux refers to two naval battle pictures at Charlecote: 'I should be very glad for to have them coppied out by ye same hand as did yt of my mother's family, wch I return you many thanks for, or by some other good hand. Ye family piece is very much admired by

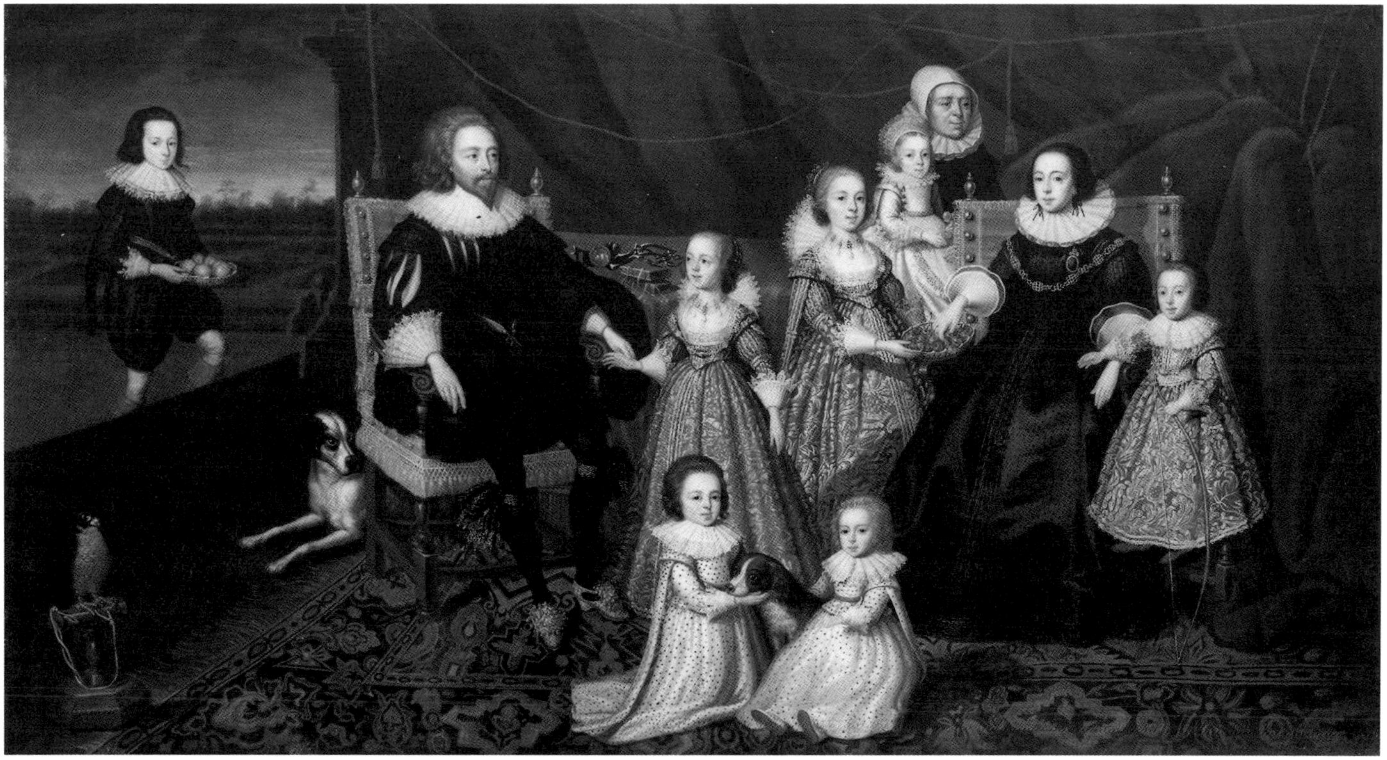

WAG 9822

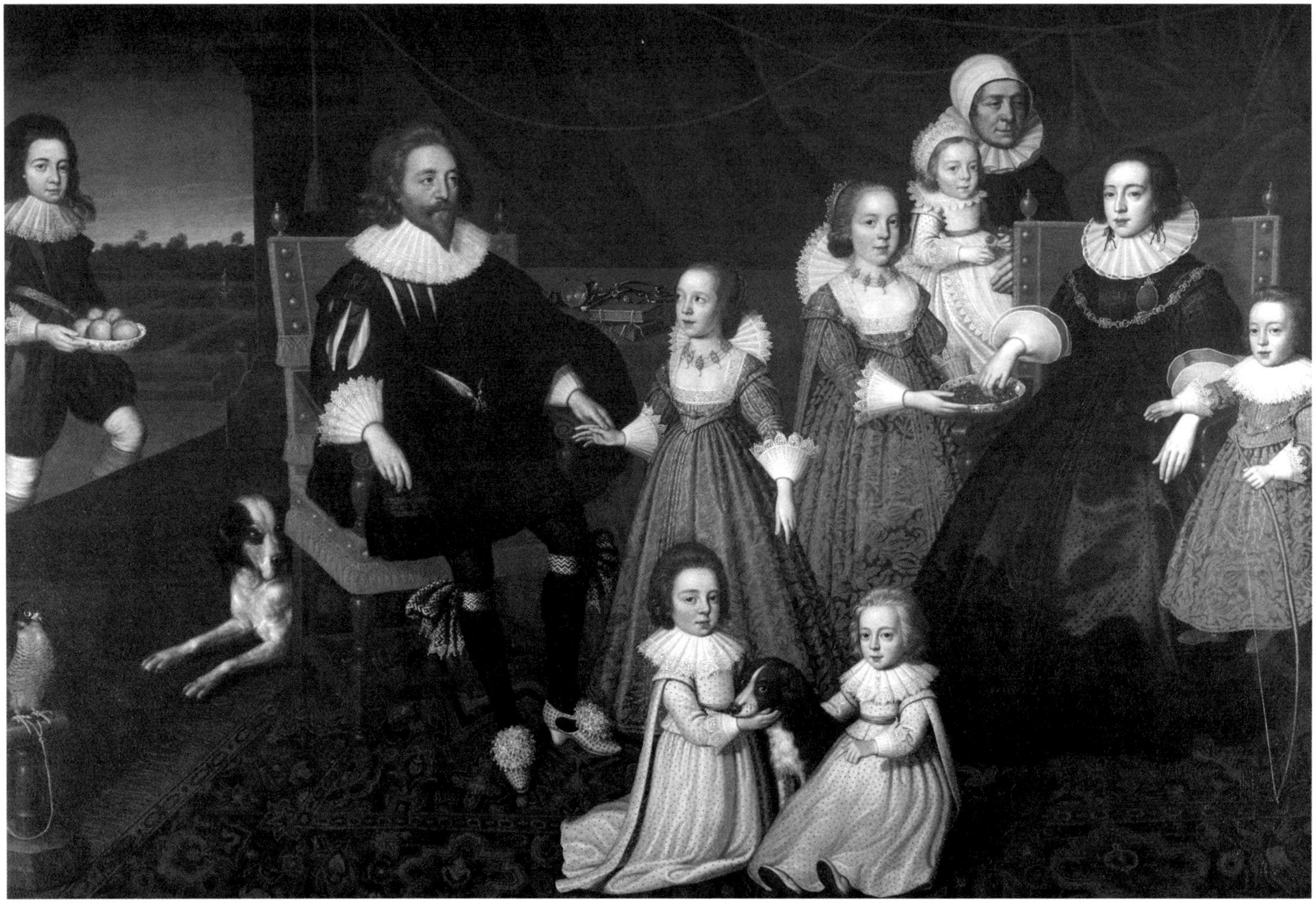

Fig. 37 *Sir Thomas Lucy and Alice Spencer, Lady Lucy, with Seven of Their Children* attributed to Cornelius Johnson, oil on canvas. Charlecote Park, The Fairfax-Lucy Collection (The National Trust); © NTPL/Derrick Witty.

every one'.[9] This suggests that WAG 9822 dates from only shortly before 1745 and it seems possible that it was an unsolicited gift to the Molyneux family from their kinsmen. Both the 6th Viscount and his elder brother Richard, 5th Viscount Molyneux (see pp. 114-5) were the sons of Bridget Lucy, who married William, 4th Viscount Molyneux in about 1675 and was the daughter of Robert Lucy, the elder of the two boys in the foreground. The painter of WAG 9822 has not been identified.

PROVENANCE

Painted for, or perhaps commissioned by, Caryll, 6th Viscount Molyneux; by descent to Josephine, Countess of Sefton; her bequest 1980.

EXHIBITION

First Exhibition of Objects Illustrative of the Fine Arts [...] Liverpool Mechanics Institution 1840 (1243).[10]

NOTES

1. For a discussion of the garden see Sir Roy Strong: *The Artist and the Garden* (New Haven and London, 2000) pp. 36–8.
2. Identified as Indo-Persian or Herat by John Mills, National Gallery, *letter*, 21 March 1984, gallery files.
3. James Hall: *Dictionary of Subjects and Symbols in Art* (rev. edn, London, 1996) p. 330. In conjunction with the apples (traditional emblems of Adam and Eve's tree of knowledge and the fall of humanity) they may suggest that the artist is appropriating traditional religious imagery for secular use.
4. For the identification of the children generally, see Alice Fairfax-Lucy: *Charlecote and the Lucys: The Chronicle of an English Family* (Oxford, 1958) p. 126; these have been supplemented by typescript notes on the Charlecote painting by Alastair Laing, kindly supplied in 1993, gallery files. Fairfax-Lucy identifies the right-hand child as Bridget, but Laing as George. That this is a boy is also proposed by Valerie Cumming, *letter*, 9 April 1984, gallery files.
5. The attribution to Johnson is given by Fairfax-Lucy, *op. cit.*, pp. 125–6; the date is given by J. Lees-Milne: 'Two Portraits at Charlecote Park by William Larkin', *Burlington Magazine* vol. 94 (December 1952) p. 324. The attribution to Johnson derives from notes made by George Vertue following a visit to Charlecote in 1737. Vertue wrote that the Charlecote picture was after a portrait by Johnson that had been destroyed in

'the Fire' – presumably a reference to the Great Fire of London (see Lord Ilchester and H. M. Hake, eds: 'Vertue Notebooks Volume IV', *Walpole Society* vol. 24 1935–36 [1936] p. 136; also Lord Ilchester et al., eds: 'Vertue Notebooks Volume VI', *Walpole Society* vol. 30 1951–52 (1955) p. 79.
6. Laing, notes, *loc. cit.*, observed that the Charlecote picture was restored and cleaned in 1990 and this not only 'made it crystal clear that it is not by Johnson'; there was 'nothing that would point to its being a copy of an original by him'. Laing questioned Vertue's view that it was a copy at all.
7. Other versions include what Vertue ('Vertue Notebooks Volume IV', *loc. cit.*) described as a sketch, measuring 42 × 50 cm, which was on loan at Charlecote in 1958 but subsequently withdrawn; also a small sketch owned by Lord Braye, Stanford Hall (Laing, notes, *loc. cit.*).
8. The letter is the first of a sequence of four dateable on internal evidence 1744–45; 1744 here is old style, in which New Year 1745 falls in March. Possibly WAG 9822 is the *Family Piece* listed in the *1746 Croxteth Inventory* p. 1, in the hall, valued at 2 guineas.
9. *Lucy Mss*, Warwickshire Record Office, LG/1396. The name of the painter is not referred to at any point in these papers.
10. Lent by the 3rd Earl of Sefton as *Portraits of the Lucy Family as Immortalized by Shakespeare* (Shakespeare having been thought to have based his Justice Shallow on an earlier Thomas Lucy). The critic of the *Liverpool Journal* observed of the work, 'a very curious specimen of a very ancient school of art', noting 'the bad perspective, the absence of *chiar' oscuro*, the inartificial grouping, and the stiffness of figures…and at the same time the very careful and elaborate finish, not merely of the faces, but of the drapery and jewellery' (*Descriptive Notices of Some of the Most Interesting Articles at the Exhibition Now Open in the Mechanics' Institution, Liverpool, Extracted, by Permission, from the* LIVERPOOL JOURNAL *of Saturday, June 18th, 1840* p. 15).

Richard Jones

1767–1840

Snipe Shooting

WAG 2328
oil on canvas, 45.5 × 61 cm
date: unknown, perhaps 1825–35

The painting has been dated to about 1830,[1] although it may be from slightly earlier or later.

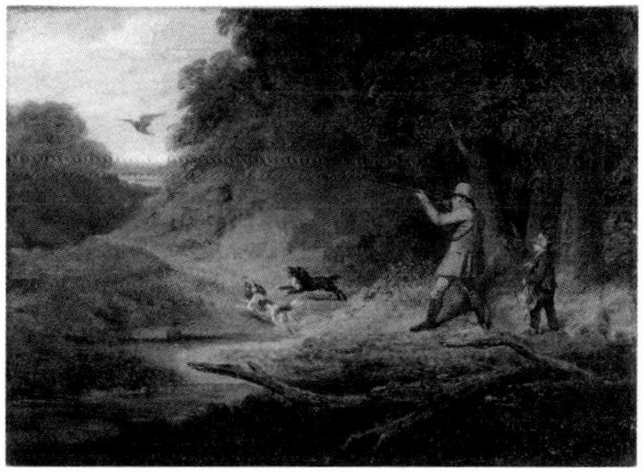

WAG 2328

PROVENANCE
…Walter Stone before 1934; Mary Stone Bequest 1944.

EXHIBITIONS
Sporting Pictures from the Walter Stone Collection Bluecoat Gallery, Liverpool 1946 (15); *A Selection of Sporting Pictures from the Walter Stone Collection* Bluecoat Gallery, Liverpool 1953 (12).

REFERENCE
1. *The Walter Stone Collection of Sporting Pictures at Whitton Hall, Westbury, Shropshire* (privately printed, 1938) p. 22, cat. 26. Stone's dates were occasionally errant. WAG 2328 is not among the works exhibited by Jones at the Royal Academy 1818–20 and the Royal Birmingham Society of Artists 1830–35. The painting is unsigned and the attribution may be Stone's.

Michael Keeling

about 1750–1820

Mrs Catherine Morey

WAG 2502
oil on canvas, 91.5 × 71 cm
signed and dated: *Micl. Keeling/pinx 1817* (bottom right)
date: 1817

Keeling seems to have been based in London in the first decade of the nineteenth century but to have moved to the provinces thereafter, perhaps in late 1809 or 1810.[1] At his death he was living in Staffordshire, and such evidence as exists suggests he was working chiefly in Lancashire and the Potteries in the preceding years.[2] However, it appears unlikely that WAG 2502 was painted in the Midlands. The sitter was baptised at Bepton, Sussex, on 11 July 1777, the daughter of John Turner and his wife Martha née Bettesworth. On 3 December 1798, at Linch, Sussex, she married as his second wife John Morey, 11 years older than herself, who, following in his father's footsteps, was a butcher at Portsea, Hants, and who in 1805 became the licensee of the Spread Eagle inn at Midhurst, Sussex.[3] After her husband's death, Mrs Morey lived first at Easebourne near Midhurst and then at Clifton, near Bristol. Her will is dated 11 January 1848 but the date and place of her death are unknown.[4] Her daughter Kate, one of numerous children, was born at North Marden on 8 November 1802 and in 1823 married Robert Weale, an inspector of Poor Laws,[5] and one of her grandsons was Alexander Stewart, Rector of Liverpool 1875–1915.[6] According to family tradition, Catherine Morey always wore a wig, in spite of having a fine head of chestnut hair.[7]

PROVENANCE
By descent from the sitter to her great-great granddaughter, Mrs N. Bicknell; by whom presented 1944.

EXHIBITION
Some Acquisitions of the Walker Art Gallery Liverpool 1935–1945 National Gallery, London 1945 (97).

NOTES
1. Keeling exhibited at the Royal Academy in 1782, 1800, 1806 and 1808–09 from London addresses but is missing thereafter. There is tenuous evidence to suggest he was the chief assistant of George Romney during the late 1780s and 1790s (see A. Kidson: *George Romney 1734–1802*, exh. cat., Walker Art Gallery, National Portrait Gallery, London and Huntington Art Collections, San Marino [2002] p. 38, n. 96).
2. Keeling's late pictures include *William Adams* (1819) who was a porcelain manufacturer in the Potteries (U. Thieme and F. Becker: *Allgemeines Lexikon der Bildenden Künstler* […] 37 vols [Leipzig, 1907–50] vol. 20 pp. 54–5) and *John Hall* (founder of the Liverpool Corn Exchange) and *Mrs John*

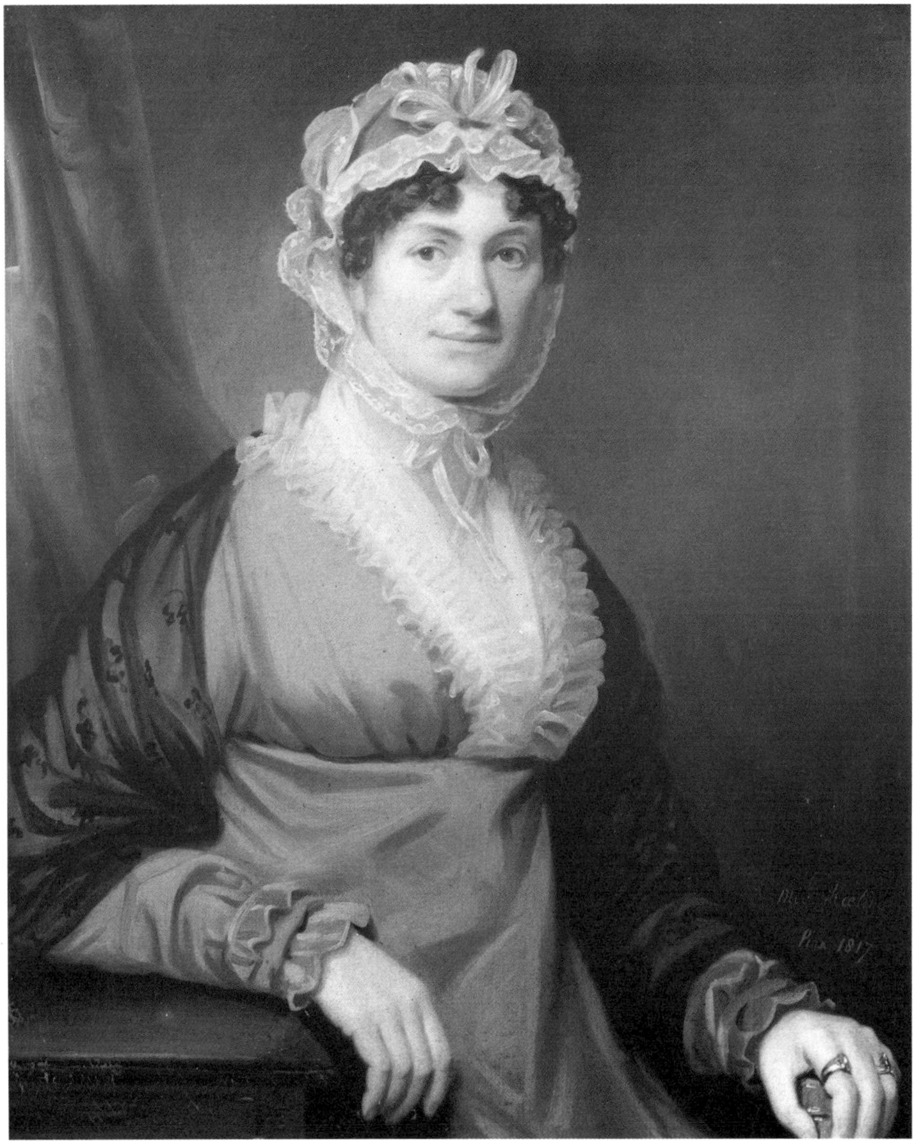

WAG 2502

Hall, who were resident in Liverpool in 1819 when Keeling painted their portraits (sold by H. P. Rigby at Christie 17 July 1908 [66]). Gore's Liverpool street directory of 1818 does not list Keeling.
3. http://www.archerfamily.org.uk/family/morey.htm; consulted 24 September 2010. It seems probable that Mrs Morey was related to Charlotte Bettesworth (see p. 148) who was also from West Sussex, and it is tempting to think that Mrs Morey patronised Keeling from knowledge of his former connection with Romney (see n. 1), to whom Charlotte had sat.
4. Helen Quartermaine, *email*, 28 September 2010, with biographical research on the Morey and Weale families.
5. *Ibid.*
6. *Some Acquisitions of the Walker Art Gallery Liverpool 1935–1945* exh. cat., National Gallery, London (1945) p. 17 (cat. 97).
7. Information from Mrs N. Bicknell, *letter*, 12 April 1944, gallery files. Mrs Bicknell was Robert and Kate Weale's great-granddaughter.

Godfrey Kneller

1646–1723

King Charles II

WAG 3023
oil on canvas, 225 × 144 cm
signed and dated: *Godfrey Kneller/ ad vivum fecit/ Ao 1685* (centre left)
date: 1685

This is Kneller's last portrait of Charles II. The term used by the artist in his signature, *ad vivum* (from the life) has two significant implications: first that, although the king died (aged 54) on 6 February in the year to which the portrait is dated, WAG 3023 was begun while he was still alive and he was able to give at least one sitting; and second that the portrait was destined for a patron for whom the knowledge that it had been taken from the life was important. Given that the facial likeness is generally based on Kneller's earlier portraits of Charles,[1] and that Kneller had already portrayed him, as here, in Garter robes,[2] the 1685 sitting or sittings must have been primarily concerned with setting the pose. Although Sir Peter Lely had invented a similar one for his 1675 portrait of Charles, this is, for a royal portrait, rather casual. Accordingly, the work has been viewed in the past as a contribution to the Van Dyckian, 'swagger' tradition in British portraiture;[4] yet the effect of the pale left leg thrust forward in direct line with the king's pale face and scarf, balanced on each side by the white sleeves of his shirt is far from sumptuous. It is tempting to think that the design, with its cruciform shape placed against a generally sombre backdrop, makes coded reference to the king's increased religiosity at the end of his life, which led him on his deathbed to convert to the Roman Catholic faith. Although the forms are not easy to distinguish, Charles's head

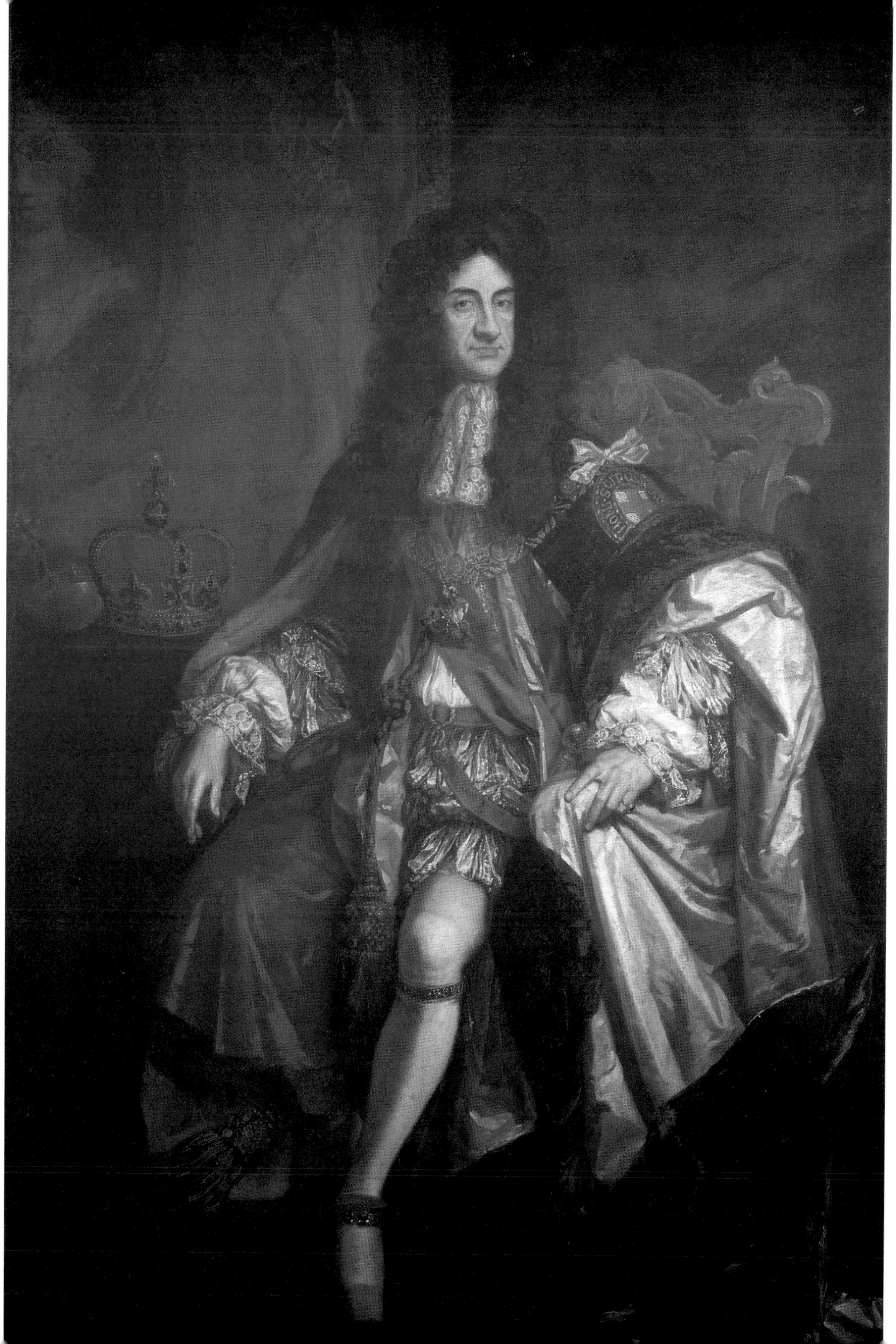

WAG 3023

seems to be placed between a shadowy figure again posed in the form of a crucifix hanging behind his right arm and a little head carved into the chair-back, in a visual pun sitting on his shoulder and whispering into his ear.[5] Also in shadow, and further away from the king as if discarded, are the trappings of monarchy in the shape of the crown and orb, and an oval portrait of a woman, no doubt intended either for Charles's Queen, Catherine of Braganza,[6] or one of the royal mistresses.

The early history of WAG 3023 is obscure. It may well be the portrait of Charles by Kneller on a list of pictures in the collection of James II at Whitehall that had never belonged to Charles himself.[7] This seems to be the same work as one seen in about 1720 at St James's House by George Vertue, who described it as signed and dated 1685; it was still at St James's House in 1758 when it was seen by Horace Walpole. This canvas is known to have been a full-length depicting Charles seated in Garter robes, so if not WAG 3023 was clearly of the same type.[8] Only one other full-length version of the picture is currently traced, in the collection at Powis Castle. A smaller replica was sold at Christie's in 1972.[9]

PROVENANCE

...Sir Cuthbert Quilter by 1901; Christie 26 June 1936 (34); bt. Leggatt (£367 10s); Lord Brocket; Sotheby 16 July 1952 (57); bt. by the gallery.

EXHIBITIONS

Monarchs of Great Britain and Ireland New Gallery, London 1901–02 (115); *Kings and Kings Queens of England* Walker Art Gallery 1953 (21); *Selected Acquisitions of the Walker Art Gallery Liverpool 1945–1955* Agnew's, London 1955 (38); *The Swagger Portrait* Tate Gallery, London 1992–23 (17).

NOTES

1. For Kneller's earlier portraits of Charles, dating back to 1678, see J. D. Stewart: *Sir Godfrey Kneller and the English Baroque Portrait* (Oxford, 1983), p. 98 (cats. 148–153); WAG 3023 is his cat. 154. Stewart describes it (p. 27) as his 'most masterly' portrait of Charles and believes it to have been completed before the King's death.
2. Stewart, *loc. cit.*, cats. 148–49 and 151–52 also show the king in Garter robes.
3. In the collection of the Dukes of Grafton, Euston Hall, Norfolk, repr. Sir Oliver Millar: *Lely* exh. cat., National Portrait Gallery, London (1978) p. 68 (cat. 52).
4. See Andrew Wilton: *The Swagger Portrait* exh. cat., Tate Gallery, London (1992) p. 96 (cat. 17); in Wilton's eyes, 'despite the relaxed pose and conversational air...this is essentially an image of state'.
5. It is unclear whether Kneller is depicting a real chair (or throne); a similar (but not identical) elaborately carved wooden chair, with winged angels holding a throne over the king's head, is shown in Thomas Hawker's full-length portrait of the king, based on Kneller's pose (but Riley's head) in the National Portrait Gallery (NPG 4691). After the monarch's death, his furniture became the perquisite of either the Lord Chamberlain or the Lord Great Chamberlain, although it has not been possible to identify this chair among the numerous thrones preserved in the Bertie family at Grimsthorpe Castle (for which see Hugh Roberts: 'Royal Thrones 1760–1840', *Furniture History* vol. 25 [1989] pp. 61–2).
6. As is stated in the 1952 Sotheby's sale catalogue.
7. Sir Oliver Millar: *The Tudor, Stuart and Early Georgian Pictures in the Collection of Her Majesty the Queen* 2 vols (London, 1963) vol. 1, p. 141.
8. *Ibid.*
9. Christie 3 March 1972 (107), measuring 120 × 76 cm. A half-length version, 127 × 101.5 cm, showing Charles in Garter robes, but varying the pose of his right arm, is at Ranger's House, Blackheath, and another version of this was with Bearne's, Torquay, July 1983.

William Clayton, Later Lord Sundon

WAG 6272
oil on canvas, 127 × 101.5 cm
signed and dated: *G.Kneller f./1719*
(lower right)
date: 1719

William Clayton (baptised 1671, d. 1752) came from a Bedfordshire family with estates at Sundon in the county. In 1688 he was appointed Clerk to the Auditor of the Receipt and held a number of political appointments before coming to the fore through his friendship with John, Duke of Marlborough, whose estate manager he was in 1713. The following year Clayton married Charlotte Dyve, a close friend of Sarah, Duchess of Marlborough, and in 1716 the Duke brought him into Parliament as MP for one of the boroughs that he controlled, New Woodstock, which he represented until 1722. He was a Lord Commissioner of the Treasury under both George I and George II, and after relinquishing his seat at New Woodstock he was MP successively for St Albans, Westminster, Plympton Erle and St Mawes. His wife, meanwhile, enjoyed considerable behind-the-scenes power as friend and lady of the bedchamber to Princess, later Queen, Caroline. William Clayton was created Baron Sundon of Armagh in the Irish Peerage in 1735.[1] He is not to be confused with Sir William Clayton, 1st Baronet, of Marden Hall Surrey, MP for Bletchingley 1715–44, nor with William Clayton, MP for Liverpool 1698–1708 and 1713–15.[2]

An earlier portrait of Clayton attributed to Kneller which, judging from the sitter's apparent age, dates from several years before WAG 6272, was paired with a companion portrait of his wife.[3] WAG 6272 itself is not recorded as having a pendant, but two other versions of it, possibly dating from after Kneller's death,

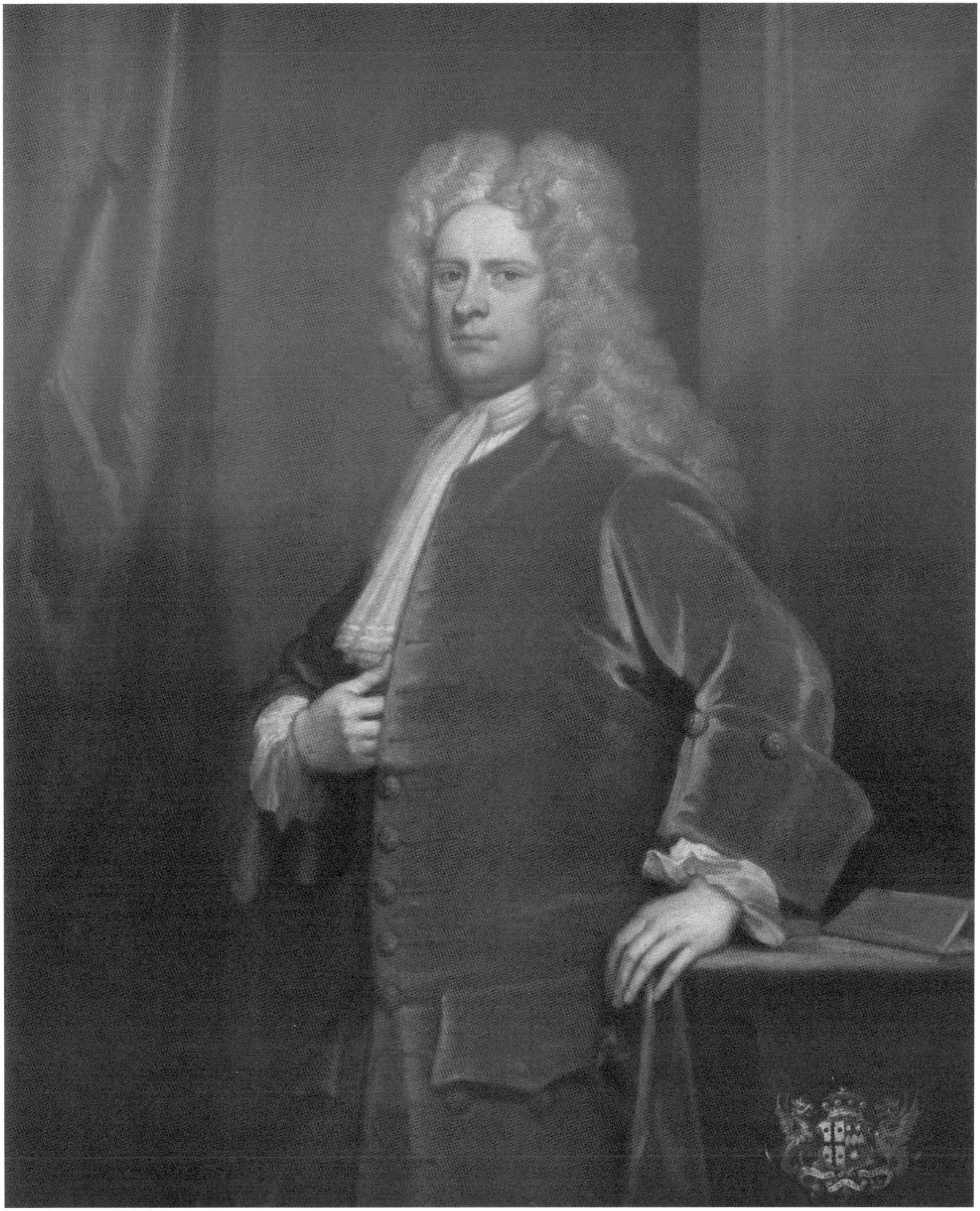

WAG 6272

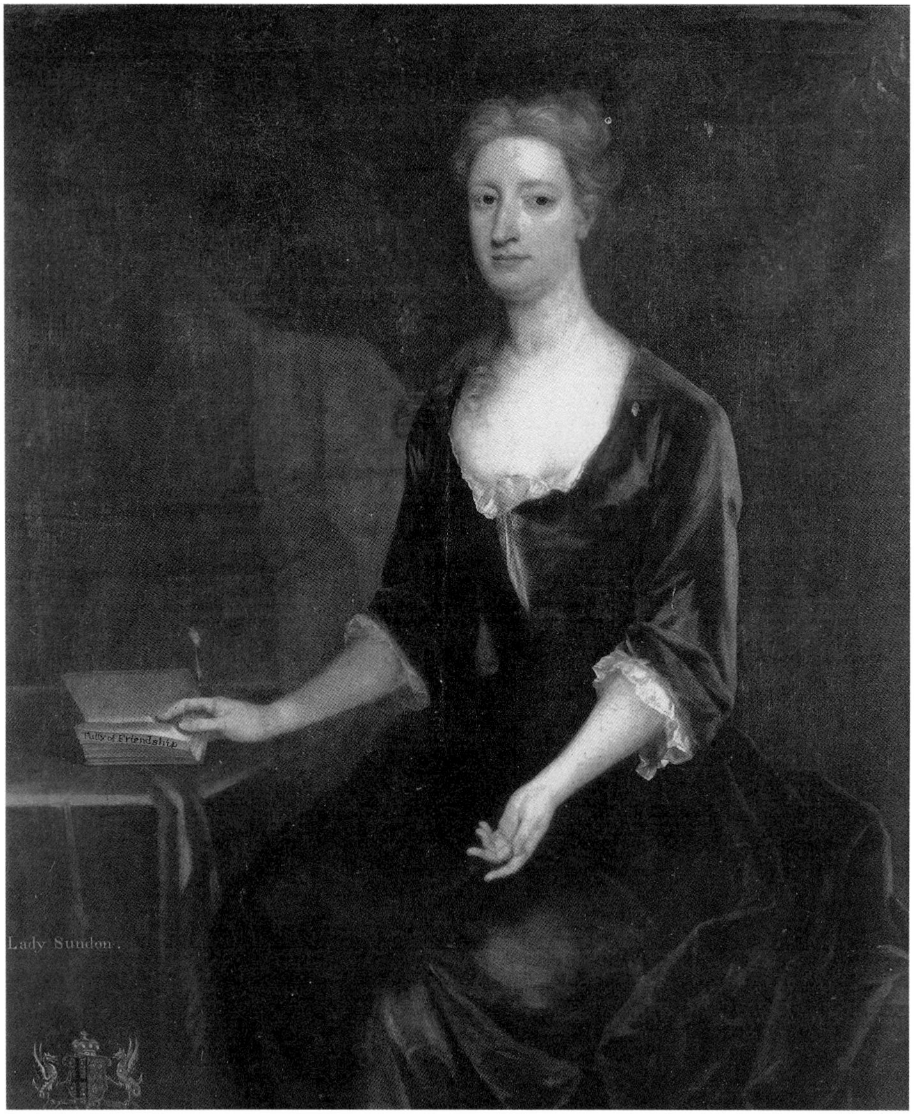

Fig. 38 *Charlotte Clayton* attributed to Godfrey Kneller, oil on canvas. Sotheby 1 February 1956 (142, part.). Photo National Portrait Gallery, London; Unknown Collection.

were also executed with pendants of Mrs Clayton.[4] In all seven of these canvases the conjoined arms of the Clayton family with its Latin motto *Probitatem quam Divitias* ('honesty rather than riches') and the Dyve family are surmounted by the coronet of a Baron, showing the arms to have been added to the painting after 1735 in each case.

It has been observed that WAG 6272 epitomises 'the canonical "hand-in-waistcoat" [portrait] in its fully Anglicized form', in which all traces of the Continental fashion present in Kneller's earlier portraits has disappeared, replaced by

> *the pure graphic equivalent of Dryden's 'good plain English'. The preference is for a more angular line and for a firmer cloth that replaces softly draped imported fabrics. Along with this marked simplicity of dress, Kneller has also adopted a less facile painting style. The sobriety of this pictorial language appears to follow in the wake of a linguistic change. It speaks in a prose style that is plain and forthright, and thus is the answer to the zealous plea for a distinctly national style that was first voiced in the 1660s.*[5]

Certainly, the stylistic contrast between WAG 6272 and Kneller's earlier portrait of Clayton is striking.

There is a small repaired damage in the upper part of the canvas above and just to the left of the sitter's head, and there is considerable degradation at the top of the canvas where the original tacking edge appears to have failed.

PROVENANCE

...Arthur G.Isaacson, Liverpool; his bequest, through his son Brian H. Isaacson, 1965.[6]

NOTES

1. *Complete Peerage*, vol. 12 pp. 490–1; Romney Sedgwick: *The History of Parliament: The House of Commons 1715–54* 2 vols (London, 1970) vol. 1, p. 558; Philip Carter: 'Clayton, [née Dyve] Charlotte, Lady Sundon', ODNB vol. 11, pp. 978–9.
2. It is clear from correspondence in gallery files at the time of acquisition that the portrait was originally bequeathed to Liverpool Corporation and accepted in the belief that it represented the MP for Liverpool.
3. Good quality versions of this pair, formerly in the collection of Michael Copeman, a descendant of the sitters, were sold at Christie South Kensington 10 July 2009 (61 and 62); copy-quality versions were owned in 1998 by Sir David Clayton. However, J. D. Stewart: *Sir Godfrey Kneller and the English Baroque Portrait* (Oxford, 1983), does not include any versions of this type in his catalogue of Kneller's portraits.
4. Stewart, *op. cit.*, p. 133 (cat. 732) lists only WAG 6272 as by Kneller. The other versions are: (i) A pair that has remained together. These were sold at Sotheby 2 November 1955 (95 and 96) and again at Sotheby 1 February 1956 (142 [a pair]), and from photographs they seem to be the canvases sold at Sotheby New York 15 October 1987 (155 [a pair]), the portrait of William Clayton as by Jervas after Kneller, but the portrait of Charlotte Clayton (fig. 38) as simply by Jervas. (ii) A pair that has been split up. Of this pair, the portrait of William Clayton has a long Latin inscription showing it to have been presented by Clayton to Dr John Freind in 1728 in thanks for Freind's intervention during a dangerous illness, and if painted in that year postdates Kneller's death. This was sold by Lady A. G. Clayton at Sotheby 23 June 1950 (40), and bought by the

Courtauld Institute of Art, who later sold it to the Government Art Collection. The companion portrait of Charlotte Clayton was owned in 1958 by C. G. Traherne of Coedarhydyglyn (Mary Beal, Government Art Collection, *letter*, 2 April 1980, gallery files). Carter, *op. cit.*, refers to a double portrait of husband and wife, known from a stipple engraving by E. Harding 'after Kneller', which was published in J. Adolphus: *The British Cabinet* (1799).
5. Arline Meyer: 'Re-dressing Classical Statuary: The Eighteenth-century "Hand-in-waistcoat" Portrait', *Art Bulletin* vol. 77 no. 1 (March 1995) p. 59.
6. Arthur Isaacson, who died in 1949, bequeathed the portrait to his son with the stipulation that if he wished to dispose of it, it must first be offered to Liverpool Corporation. Brian Isaacson offered the portrait to the Corporation following the death of his mother in 1965.

after
Godfrey Kneller
1646–1723

Alexander Pope

WAG 8654
oil on canvas, 74 × 61 cm
date: about 1725–35

The poet Alexander Pope (1688–1744) was painted three times by Kneller, in 1716, 1721 and 1722.[1] WAG 8654 is a version of the 1721 portrait. It is of good quality, and although it is perhaps more likely to have been painted by one of Kneller's pupils, it is not out of the question that it is an autograph work. It has also been attributed to Jonathan Richardson the Elder.[2]

The iconography of the portrait is distinctive and must have been established by Pope himself, presumably as a more elaborate variation on the profile portrait that Richardson had painted of him, crowned with laurel, in 1718. The profile pose in imitation of an antique medallion probably refers to Pope's dialogue with Addison on the subject, carried out in Addison's *Dialogues on Medals* and Pope's poetical response in the epistle *To Mr Addison, Occasioned by His Dialogues on Medals*, a work which was first published in 1720 although it had perhaps been written earlier.[3] The pose probably also alluded to the poet's namesake, Alexander the Great, especially to a well-known ancient coin in which Alexander, in profile to the right, wears the horns of Ammon in the belief that he was the son of Jupiter Ammon.[4] The wreath of ivy on the poet's head has been linked to Pope's own appropriation of ivy as an attribute of the critic in his *Essay on Criticism*, where it had previously been regarded as the attribute of poets alone.[5] The *ourobouros*, the snake coiled around the edge of the painting and consuming its own tail, is an ancient symbol of eternity.[6]

The prime version of WAG 8654, so identified because it is the only one that Kneller signed and dated, is in the collection of Lord Home of the Hirsel.[7] Numerous other versions are known.[8]

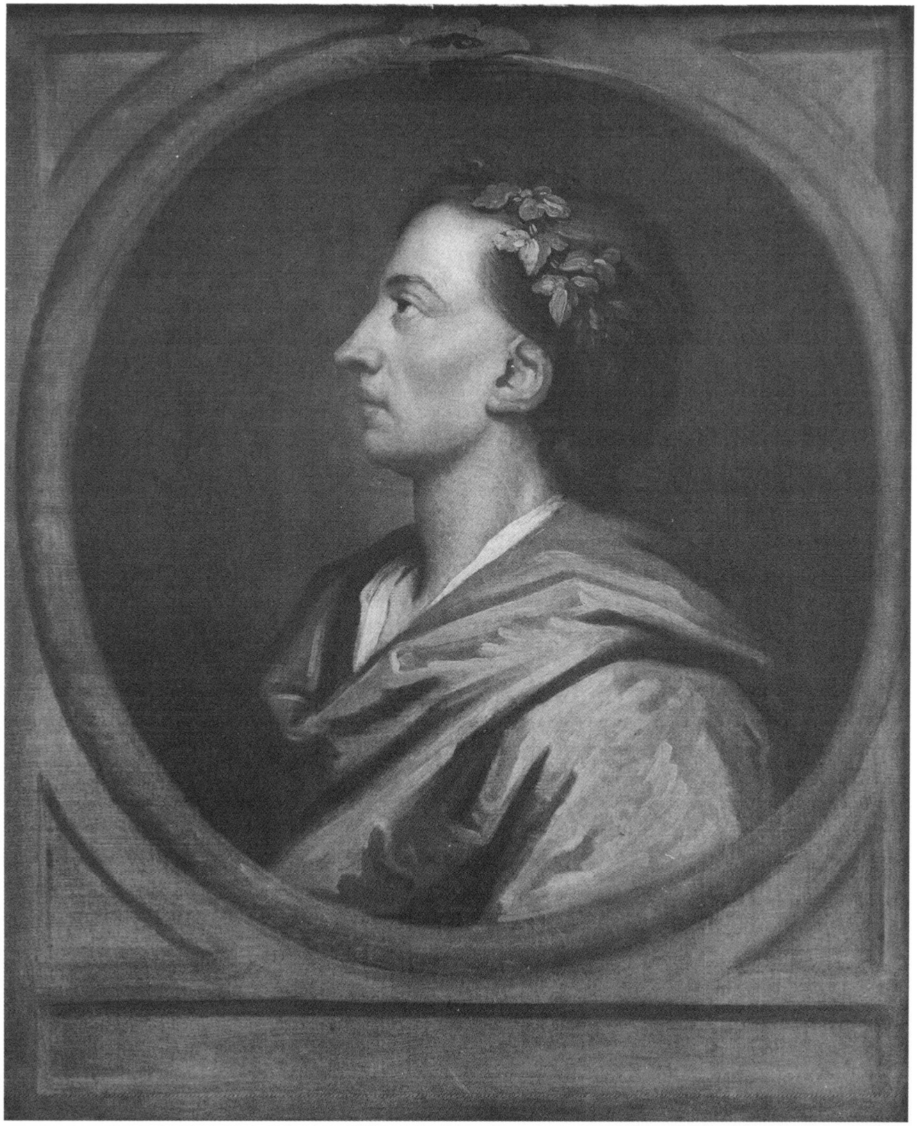

WAG 8654

Interest attaches to WAG 8654 from the possibility that it was a gift from Pope to his great friend and fellow-Catholic John Caryll (1667–1736). Pope and Caryll are known to have corresponded about the possibility of an exchange of friendship portraits as early as June 1711 and a few months prior to this, in January 1711, Caryll in a letter to Pope had banteringly compared him to Alexander the Great.[9] Clearly, if this was a friendship portrait for Caryll, it was a belated one, yet it must leave open the possibility that WAG 8654 was painted by Kneller himself. The evidence that it was given to Caryll is circumstantial, depending on the work's likely provenance. Caryll's grandson and heir, John Baptist Caryll (1713–88) married Dorothy, daughter of the 5th Viscount Molyneux. She died in 1760 and Caryll, without heirs, had disposed of his property and emigrated abroad, to join the Jacobite court of Charles Stuart, the Young Pretender, by the end of the 1760s.[10]

PROVENANCE

[? John Caryll; by descent to his grandson John Baptist Caryll; passed to his in-laws, the Molyneux family of Croxteth Hall;]...William, 4th Earl of Sefton by 1863;[11] by descent to Hugh, 7th Earl of Sefton; Christie premises sale at Croxteth Hall 19 September 1973 (1020); bt. by the gallery.

NOTES

1. For the many portraits of Pope by Kneller and other artists see especially W. K. Wimsatt: *The Portraits of Alexander Pope* (New Haven and London, 1965) together with J. Riely and W. K. Wimsatt: 'A Supplement to *The Portraits of Alexander Pope*', in René Wellek and Alvaro Ribeiro, eds: *Evidence in Literary Scholarship: Essays in Memory of James Marshall Osborn* (Oxford, 1979) pp. 123–64. Kneller's 1721 portrait is no. 6 on Wimsatt's list.
2. John Kerslake: *National Portrait Gallery: Early Georgian Portraits* 2 vols (London, 1977), vol. 1, p. 219.
3. Wimsatt, *op. cit.*, p. 50.
4. J. D. Stewart: *Sir Godfrey Kneller*, exh. cat., National Portrait Gallery London (1971), pp. 9, 65 (cat. 82); also Riely and Wimsatt, *op. cit.*, pp. 128–9.
5. Wimsatt, *op. cit.*, p. 51.
6. *Ibid.*
7. J. D. Stewart: *Sir Godfrey Kneller and the English Baroque Portrait* (Oxford, 1983) p. 124 (cat. 578); Wimsatt, *op. cit.*, p. 52 (cat. 6.2); also FC, p. 99.
8. Wimsatt, *op. cit.*, pp. 52–9, lists eight oils (of which WAG is cat. 6.4) one autograph chalk drawing on oiled paper (his 6.1; Stewart, 1983, p. 177 [drawings cat. 90]), which is in the British Museum (1888-7-19-65) and is probably the basis for Kneller's oil portrait, three watercolours (including one signed by A. B. Lens) and Faber's mezzotint published in 1738. Two further versions were listed by Riely and Wimsatt, *ibid.* Three oil versions which have emerged since the publication of the latter (which may be the same as some of the versions listed in Wimsatt and Riely and Wimsatt) include one sold Christie 26 October 1990 (200); one with Historical Portraits London, September 1991, and one with Roy Davids, Oxfordshire, July 1995.
9. Riely and Wimsatt, *op. cit.*, pp. 128–9.
10. It is most likely that Caryll presented the work to his late wife's cousin, the young 8th Viscount Molyneux (later 1st Earl of Sefton), but it is also possible that Caryll and his wife gifted the work to the former's namesake (and apparently, fourth cousin once removed) Caryll, 6th Viscount Molyneux (1683–1745) who had almost certainly been named for Caryll's great-grandfather John Caryll, 1st Baron Caryll of Durford, one of the leading Catholic politicians of the 1670s and 1680s. The two families, who were related following Mary Caryll's marriage to Richard, 1st Viscount Molyneux, had almost certainly been close since the 1610s. The portrait is not present in the *Croxteth 1746 Inventory* but it would appear that this excluded paintings which had the status of family heirlooms, including family portraits.
11. The annotation *Ld. Sefton's Novr 27 1863* appears on a very early photograph of WAG 8654 preserved in the Heinz Archive, National Portrait Gallery.

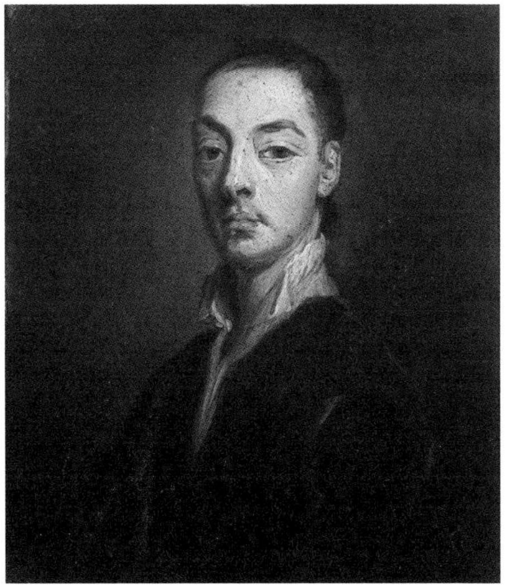

WAG 2537

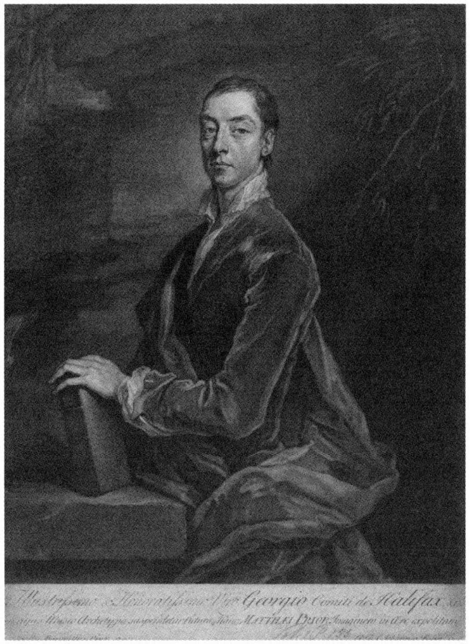

Fig. 39 *Matthew Prior* after Godfrey Kneller, engraving by John Faber. Yale Center for British Art, Paul Mellon Collection.

Matthew Prior

WAG 2537
oil on copper, 18.5 × 16 cm
date: unknown, perhaps 1730–60

Kneller's original half-length portrait of the diplomat and poet Matthew Prior (1664–1721) was painted in 1700 and is now in Trinity College, Cambridge.[1] John Faber's engraving of it (fig. 39) was published in 1728, and may have been the source for WAG 2537, which is a reduced, bust-length version of indifferent quality. The copyist has simplified the costume and the background and has altered Prior's features so that he appears more boyish. Other versions of Kneller's original are known.[2]

PROVENANCE

...[? William Roscoe];[3] ...by descent to Mrs M. Roscoe; her bequest 1950.

NOTES

1. See J. D. Stewart: *Sir Godfrey Kneller and the English Baroque Portrait* (Oxford, 1983) p. 124 (cat.

590); also J. D. Stewart: *Sir Godfrey Kneller*, exh. cat., National Portrait Gallery, London (1971) p. 63 (cat. 80). The portrait was undertaken in that short time-frame when Prior was associating with leading Whigs and was a member of the Kit-Cat Club.
2. They include a version formerly in the Bingham Mildmay collection, sold Christie 20 November 1992 (17) and again Sotheby 8 November 1995 (39); also one in the Victoria & Albert Museum, London, Dyce Bequest no. 64.
3. The portrait was not included in Roscoe's bankruptcy sale and is not mentioned in Roscoe's household inventory of 1820 (unless it is to be identified as *Port[rait] of Shenstone* [p. 4] or as the *Portrait* or *Head of a man* among the added items on p. 33).

Marcellus Laroon

1679–1772

Owen MacSwiney

WAG 5600
oil on canvas, 60.5 × 47.5 cm
date: about 1735–36

The work was unattributed, and its sitter unidentified, when it entered the gallery, apparently in the 1950s. It was ascribed to Laroon on the basis of comparison with the head, eighth from the left, in Laroon's *A Nobleman's Levée* (private collection; fig. 40).[1] The identification of the sitter had its source in George Vertue's note of 1740:[2] 'Captain Laron [i.e. Laroon] did some portraits from the life well painted in a bold free manner. with good Spirit. his own picture Mr Swiney. and others as big as life'.[3] Comparison with other likenesses of MacSwiney (who was also known as Swiny) confirms that WAG 5600 is a portrait of him: John Faber's engraving, published in 1752, of J. B. Vanloo's portrait painted in 1738 and Peter Van Bleeck's portrait of 1737 (known from a copy in the National Portrait Gallery, London; fig. 41, and from Van Bleeck's own mezzotint of 1749) both show a slightly older man, and WAG 5600 was therefore presumably executed about 1735–36, soon after MacSwiney's return to London from a long period abroad. It seems very likely to be the portrait from life 'well painted in a bold free manner' described by Vertue.

Owen MacSwiney, born near Enniscorthy, Ireland in 1676, came to London in 1703. He wrote a successful play, *The Quacks, or Love's The Physician* (a version of Molière's *L'Amour Médécin*) in 1705, and further pieces in the period 1706–09 when he was successfully managing the Queen's Theatre in the Haymarket. He was transferred to Drury Lane Theatre in 1710 and may have met Laroon, at that time more a soldier and an actor-singer than a painter, there. Both men became members of Kneller's Academy in Great Queen Anne

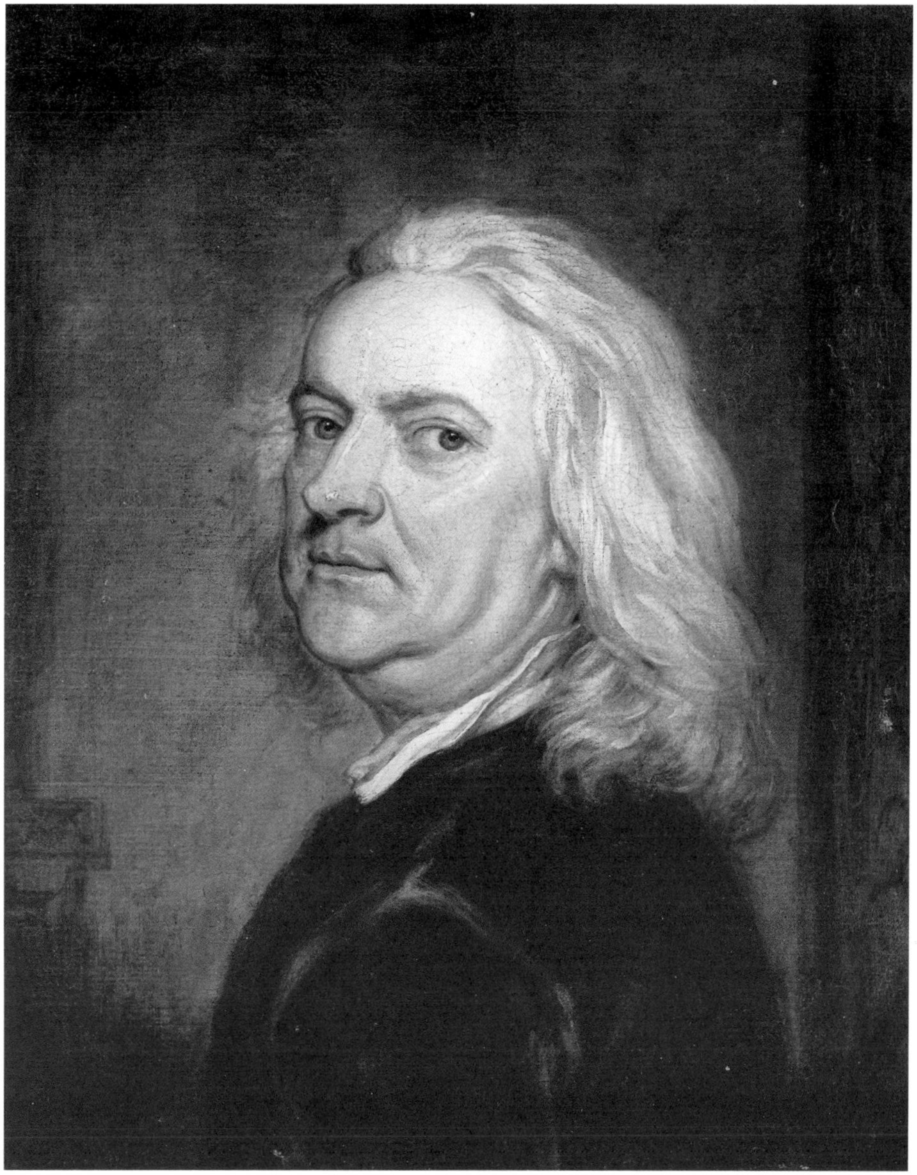

WAG 5600

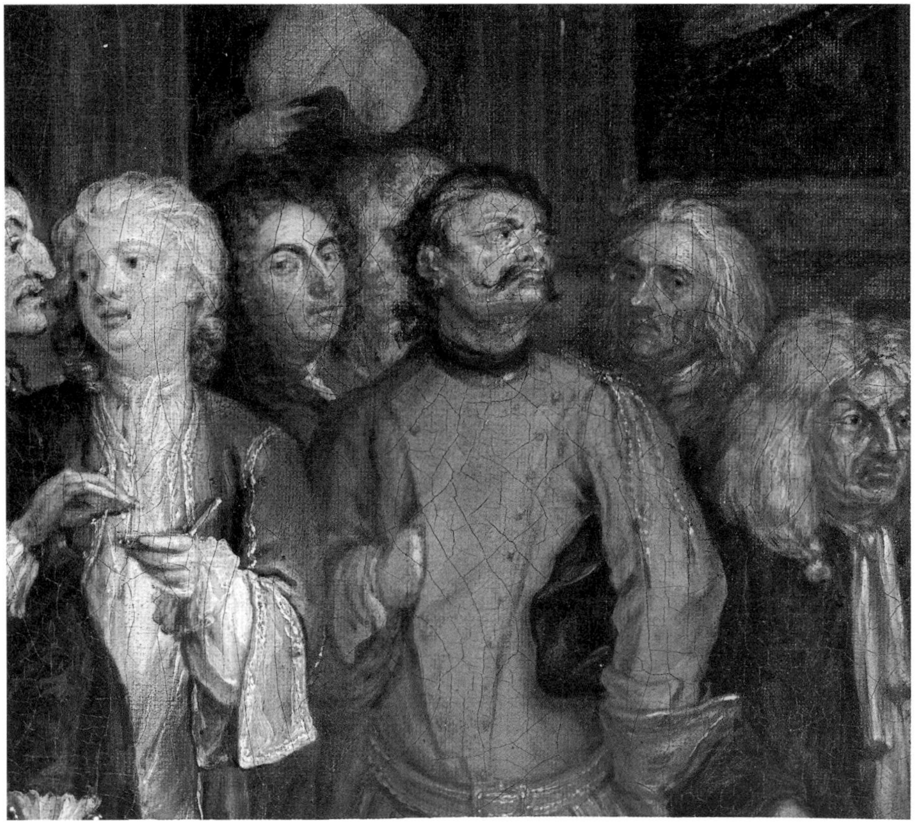

Fig. 40 Detail from *A Nobleman's Levée* by Marcellus Laroon, oil on canvas. Private collection/The Bridgeman Art Library.

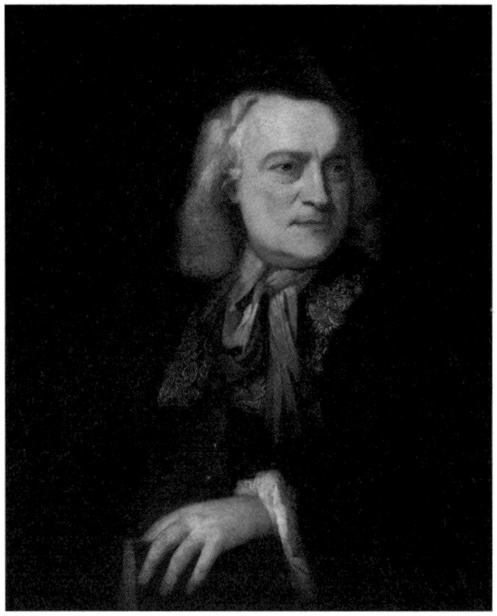

Fig. 41 *Owen MacSwiney* after Peter van Bleeck, oil on canvas. © National Portrait Gallery, London.

Street in 1711, MacSwiney by this time encountering difficulties as a theatre manager and developing a second career as an art dealer. When the Queen's Theatre, to which he had returned in 1711, went bankrupt two years later, MacSwiney fled abroad, eventually settling for many years in Venice. He returned to England in the early 1730s in order to complete his project of commissioning designs for mausolea commemorating the 'heroic or monumental actions of the renowned great Noblemen and others in England'. This appeared in 1741 as *Tombeaux des Princes, des Grand Capitaines et autres homme illustres de la Grand Bretagne*. MacSwiney died on 2 October 1754, leaving his fortune to the actress Peg Woffington.[4]

Whether WAG 5600 was a conscious study for the figure in *A Nobleman's Leveé* is unclear. From the slight physiognomic variations between the two heads, it seems unlikely. A similar ambiguous relationship exists between the fifth head from the left in the group picture and a presumed self-portrait by Laroon.[5] In *A Nobleman's Leveé* the two figures are depicted standing beside each other, an indication that they know each other well.

PROVENANCE

... Found in the gallery; transferred to the permanent collection 1960.[6]

NOTES

1. The comparison was first made by Mary Bennett in 1967, on the appearance of *A Nobleman's Leveé* at the Tate Gallery's *Laroon* exhibition. The attribution was confirmed by Robert Raines, *letter*, 3 October 1967, gallery files.
2. The identification was made by Mark Evans, whose research on WAG 5600 in the early 1980s, preserved in gallery files, forms the basis of the present entry.
3. Lord Ilchester and H. M. Hake, eds: 'Vertue Notebooks Volume III', *Walpole Society* vol. 22 1933–34 (1934) p. 82.
4. I. Bignamini: 'George Vertue, Art Historian and Art Institutions in London 1689–1768', *Walpole Society*, vol. 54 (1988) pp. 75, 80–1, 116. See also Elizabeth Gibson: 'Swiny [McSwiny, Swiney, MacSwiny, MacSwinny] Owen', *ODNB* vol. 53, pp. 518–20; and R. Raines: *Marcellus Laroon* (London, 1967) pp. 43, 49, 53.
5. Raines, *op. cit.*, pp. 113–4, identifies this as a portrait owned by Paul Mellon (now in the Yale Center for British Art, New Haven, B.1981.25.407); this work has, however, subsequently been re-attributed to the elder Marcellus Laroon and dated to about 1700 (see M. Cormack: *A Concise Catalogue of Paintings in the Yale Center of British Art* [New Haven, 1985] p. 142). Raines's dating for *A Nobleman's Leveé* of about 1730 (*op. cit.*, p. 114), suggested just before WAG 5600 came to his attention, must be several years too early.
6. Believed to have been deposited by a member of the Rathbone family around 1954 (note in gallery files).

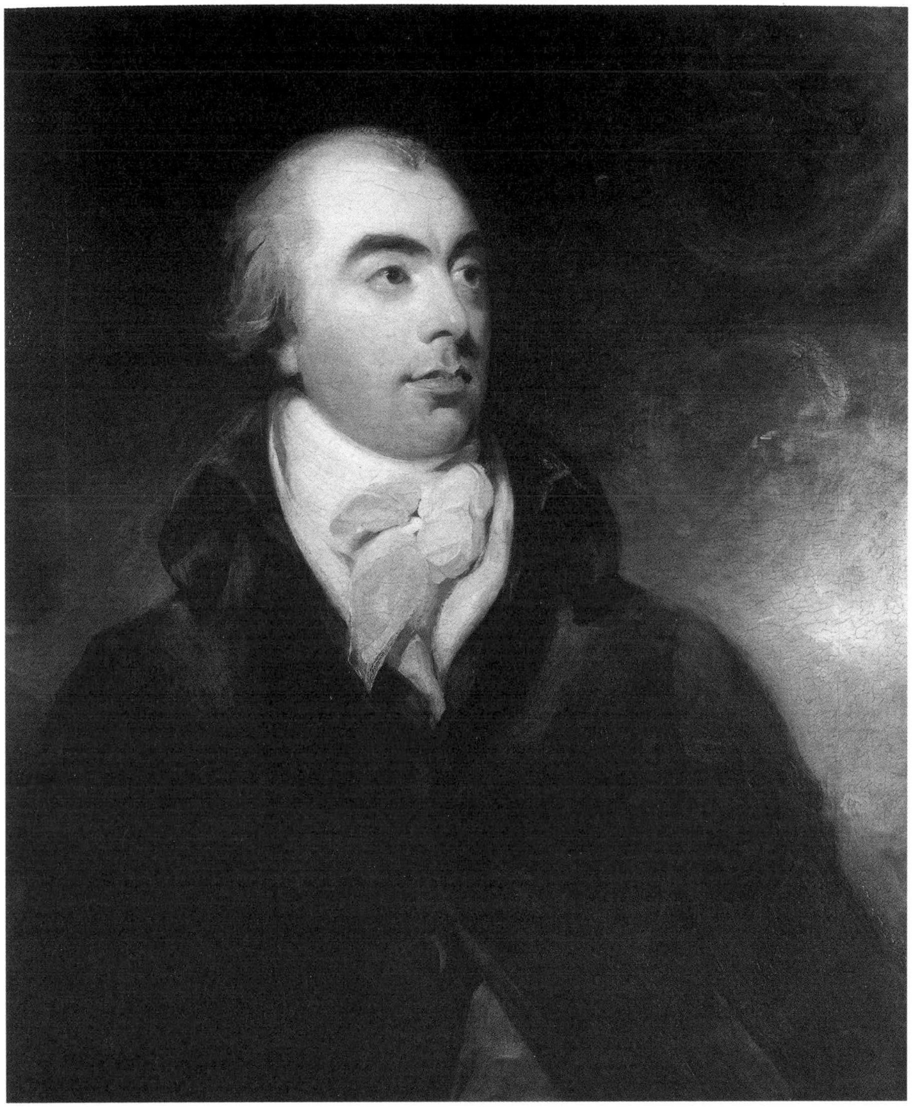

WAG 2580

Thomas Lawrence

1769–1830

John Bradburne

WAG 2580
oil on canvas, 76 × 63.5 cm
date: about 1795–1800

Little is known about John Bradburne. In the latter part of his life he lived at 'Woodlands', Windlesham, near Ascot in Surrey (the house is now Windlesham Manor) and Windlesham Parish registers record his burial on 15 June 1809. His age at death is stated as 52.[1] He is listed as a freeholder of Windlesham, and also among land tax assessments, in the years 1799–1808, suggesting that he came to live in the district about 1798.[2] From the twelfth to the seventeenth centuries the family lived at Bradbourne, near Ashbourne, Derbyshire, but they had moved away by the eighteenth century.[3]

It has been suggested that WAG 2580 was painted between 1795 and 1800.[4] Lawrence painted a companion portrait of Bradburne's wife at about the same time.[5]

PROVENANCE

By descent to J. E. Bradburne; Christie 19 July 1929 (75); bt. Tooth (720 gns.); ...Agnew; from whom bt. 1949.

EXHIBITIONS

Coronation Exhibition of British Pictures Agnew's, London 1937 (40); *Selected Acquisitions of the Walker Art Gallery Liverpool 1945–1955* Agnew's, London 1955 (6); *De Gainsborough à Bacon* Galerie des Beaux-Arts, Bordeaux 1977 (31).

NOTES

1. Revd J. J. Cresswell, Rector of Windlesham, *letter*, 2 August 1961, gallery files.
2. M. Gollancz, Surrey County Archivist, *letter*, 24 July 1961, gallery files.
3. Information from F. J. H. Lisemore, Vicar of Ashbourne, *letter*, 15 August 1961, gallery files.
4. K. Garlick: *Sir Thomas Lawrence* (Oxford, 1989) pp. 156–7 (cat. 124).
5. Garlick, *op. cit.*, p.157. This portrait, currently untraced, was sold at Christie 5 July 1907 (101); bt. Agnew, and was subsequently with Duveen.

Mrs Cecilia Lock

WAG 252
oil on canvas, 76.5 × 63.5 cm
date: 1796–97

The identity of the sitter in WAG 252 has been obscured. The portrait was sold at Christie's in 1885 and purchased shortly afterwards by George Holt under the title *Mrs Beauclerk*, that is, Emily Charlotte Ogilvie (1778–1832) who married Charles George Beauclerk of South Lodge, Horsham, Sussex, in April 1799. However, circumstantial evidence indicates that the sitter is Mrs Beauclerk's elder sister Cecilia (1775–1824) who married Charles Lock, second son of William Lock of Norbury in 1795.[1] The two girls were the daughters of Emily Duchess of Leinster (for whom see WAG 1356, pp. 126–8) by her second husband, William Ogilvie.

Lawrence is known to have painted a portrait of Mrs Lock, presumed untraced, which was exhibited at the Royal Academy in 1797.[2] The sitter was identified in a review of the exhibition in the *Monthly Mirror*, which remarked about Lawrence's picture, 'the arm is defective both in form and proportion'; a comment that, as has been pointed out, could well apply to WAG 252.[3] Mrs Lock at that date would have been in her 22nd year, which seems about right for the sitter in WAG 252; and a further piece of evidence exists in the form of a miniature after WAG 252 by Henry Bone, dated 1800, which has traditionally been titled *Mrs James Locke* [sic].[4] What became of Lawrence's 1797 exhibition picture is not clear. Although the artist painted a 30 × 25 inch portrait of her husband at around the same time,[5] the two paintings are not known to have been together at any point in their history. Given that the lots accompanying WAG 252 in the 1885 sale make it clear that the vendor was linked to the Beauclerk family,[6] it is very tempting to suspect that the portrait of Mrs Lock passed into the possession of her sister and brother-in-law, and subsequently became misidentified as a portrait of her sister.

Three tenuous pieces of evidence support this view. The first is that the immediately preceding lot in the 1885 sale was another portrait by Lawrence titled *Mrs Beauclerk*, clearly from the same period as WAG 252, showing the sitter in a yellow dress in a landscape (fig. 42). Although shown in profile rather than full face, this woman does not seem to be the same person as the sitter in WAG 252 but she does look quite like her, and the notion that she is her sister, and three or four years her junior, seems very plausible.[7] Second, moving back in time, in 1832 Major Charles Beauclerk lent 'two portraits of ladies' by Lawrence to the winter exhibition of the Society of British Artists. Although not identified, these could well have been portraits of his wife and late sister-in-law, and identical with lots 88 and 89 in the 1885 sale.[8] Third, it has been pointed out that Lawrence was originally commissioned, some time before 26 February 1796, for a whole-length double portrait of the Ogilvie daughters;[9] and it has been surmised, in default of any further evidence for the existence of this work, that the commission was converted into separate portraits of the two.[10] This could imply that the two likenesses were always envisaged as 'belonging together'.

PROVENANCE

...[? Major Beauclerk, probably the brother-in-law of the sitter 1832]; ...B. N. Johnson; Christie 1 August 1885 (89); bt. Agnew; from whom bt. by George Holt, December 1886 (£315); Emma Holt Bequest 1945.

EXHIBITIONS

(?) RA 1797 (237); (?) *Winter Exhibition of the Works of Deceased and Living British Artists* Society of British Artists 1832 (28) or (193).

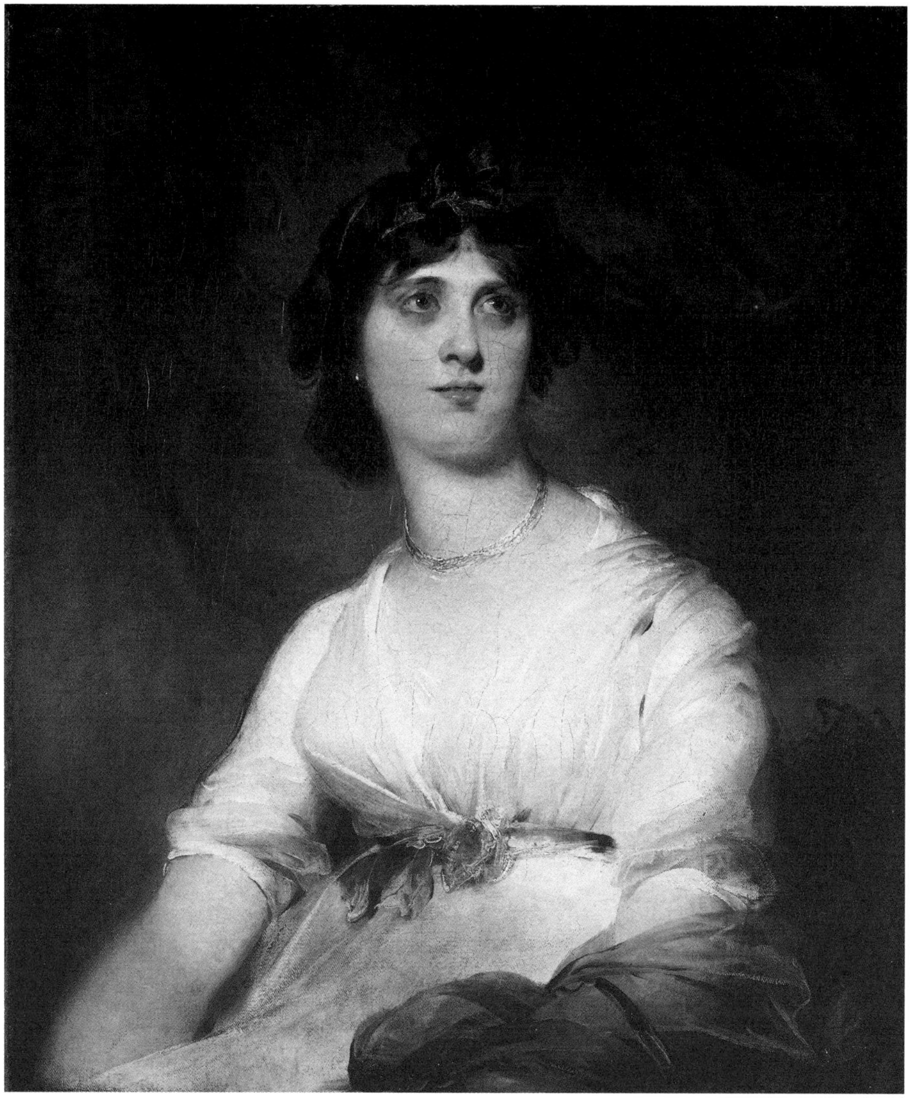

WAG 252

NOTES

1. This possibility was raised by M. Bennett and E. Morris: *Sudley* (Liverpool, 1971) pp. 43–4; at the date of this publication recent cleaning had only just confirmed that WAG 252 was an autograph work by Lawrence.

2. Joseph Farington noted in his diary that Mrs Lock was sitting to Lawrence at the beginning of February 1797; FD, vol. 3, p. 762 (entry of 2 February 1797).

3. K. Garlick, *Sir Thomas Lawrence* (Oxford, 1989) p. 227 (cat. 503).

4. Sold at Sotheby Parke-Bernet, Monaco 25–26 June 1976 (398), repr. and again Christie Geneva 26 April 1977 (103), repr.

5. Garlick, *op. cit.*, p. 226 (cat. 502); dated 'probably c.1797–98'; Garlick: 'Catalogue of Paintings, Drawings and Pastels of Sir Thomas Lawrence', *Walpole Society* vol. 39 (1964) p. 128; dated about 1795.

6. For example, lot 83 is *Topham Beauclerk Esq* by Cotes and lot 87 is *Lady Diana Spencer Wife of Topham Beauclerk Esq.* by Powell after Reynolds; lots 72–76 are works by Lady Diana Beauclerk. In the auctioneer's copy of the 1885 sale catalogue (Christie's archives) the printed title of lot 89 *Mrs Beauclerk* is crossed through and *Mrs Locke* substituted.

7. Garlick, *Sir Thomas Lawrence*, p. 247 (cat. 616). This work may be the *Portrait of a Lady* exhibited by Lawrence at the RA in 1796 (116) which is otherwise unaccounted for. What may from the likeness be another portrait of the same sitter, also (doubtfully) attributed to Lawrence and titled *Mrs Beauclerk*, was sold at Christie 21 January 1977 (54); this is certainly not of the same person as the sitter in WAG 252.

8. Sir Walter Armstrong: *Lawrence* (London, 1913) p.113. The *Two Portraits of the Same Lady, in Different Positions* included in Lawrence's studio sale Christie 18 June 1831 (64); bt. Wansey (one of which, sold as *Miss Bloxam* at Christie 13 July 1951 (26); bt. Agnew, is the identical composition to the 'profile' *Mrs Beauclerk*; fig.42), were presumably second versions, in one case already mis-identified, of lots 88 and 89 in the 1885 sale. The vendor at the 1951 sale was the great-grandson of Mr Wansey (Garlick [1964] p. 154).

9. FD, vol. 2, p. 500 (entry of 26 February 1796); cited by Garlick (1989) p. 227.

10. Garlick, *Sir Thomas Lawrence*, *loc. cit.*

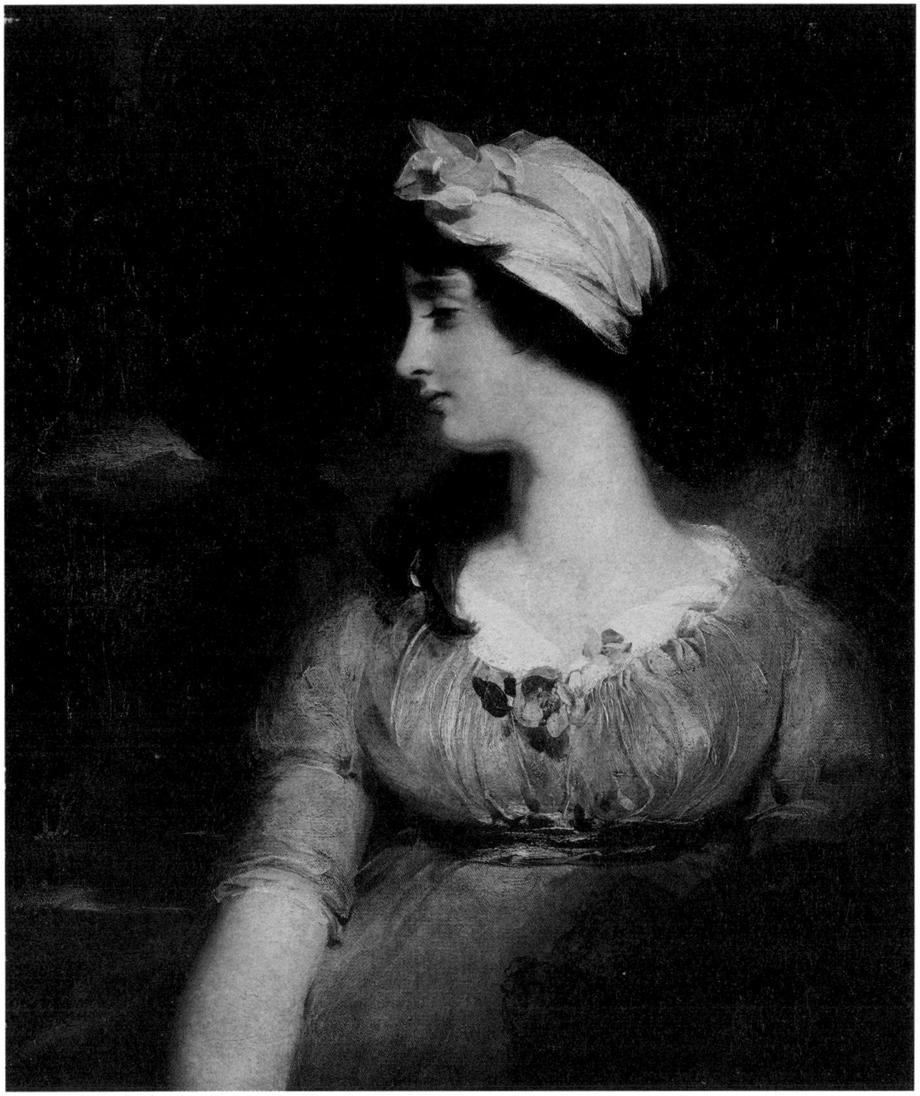

Fig. 42 *Mrs Emily Beauclerk* by Thomas Lawrence, oil on canvas. Sotheby New York, 25 April 1985 (82); photo courtesy of Sotheby's.

King George III

WAG 7021
oil on canvas, 270 × 175 cm
date: 1800–21

In 1792 George III sat to Lawrence, his new Principal Painter, for a whole-length commissioned for the city of Coventry by its Pittite MPs, Sir Sampson Gideon and John Wilmot (Herbert Art Gallery, Coventry; fig. 43).[1] The two men had recently defeated a pair of Whigs in a fiercely contested election and wished to demonstrate their loyalty to the crown in an age of revolutionary turmoil; and this portrait, the only one for which the king ever gave Lawrence sittings, became the basis for numerous replicas and variants that were ordered from the artist later in the reign.[2] WAG 7021 seems to have been the first replica to be commissioned from him: Lawrence told Joseph Farington that he was anticipating making a start on a full-length for Liverpool in July 1800,[3] and this probably pre-dated a commission from the king himself for a smaller version intended as a gift to the Prime Minister, Henry Addington.[4] Lawrence procrastinated on both commissions.

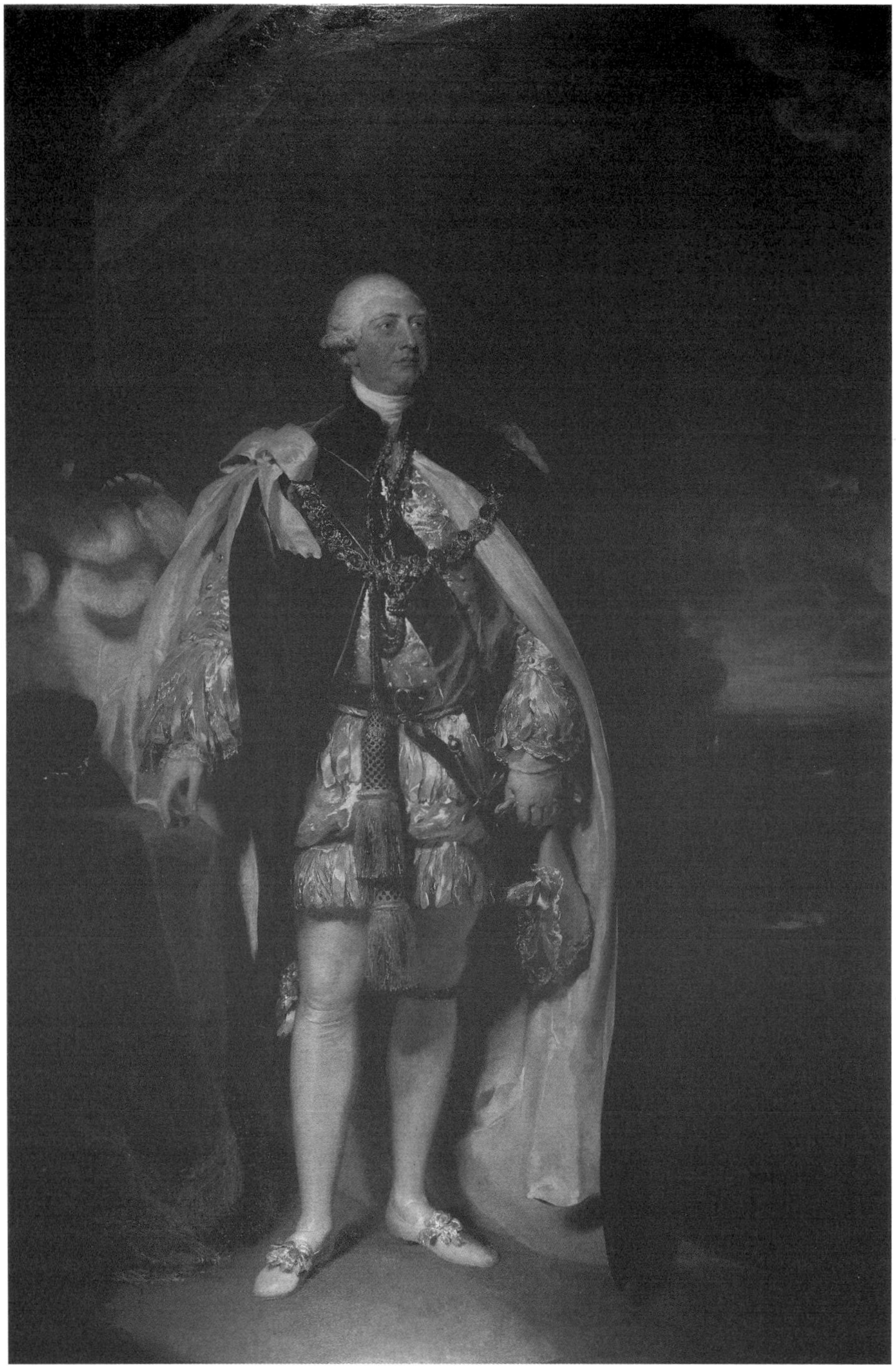

WAG 7021

The picture for Addington has been identified as the one on which Lawrence was working in March 1809.[5] In the event, the Liverpool portrait had still not been delivered in July 1821, over a year after the king's death. On 4 July that year, the Council resolved that

the Mayor be requested to communicate to Sir Thomas Lawrence the great dissatisfaction felt by this Council as not having been yet furnished with the Portrait of his late Majesty and particularly so as from the strong and repeated assurances of Sir Thomas Lawrence they have been induced to believe it would have been finished a long time since.[6]

WAG 7021 was painted in the following two months, and a letter from Lawrence stating that it had been completed was read at a council meeting on 5 September.[7]

The portrait shows the king at the age of 53, in Garter Robes, with the east end of Eton College chapel (as if being viewed from the north terrace of Windsor Castle) in the distance. WAG 7021 differs from the Coventry version in a number of ways: the figure is slightly further back from the picture plane; the face is a little fuller; the pose of the right hand is altered; less of Eton College chapel is visible; and the architectural background and the sky are both simplified. It lacks the brilliance of the original but is of good quality, and may be largely autograph.

WAG 7021 was conserved in 1993–94 after being damaged in Liverpool Town Hall. In 2002 it suffered further damage in the shape of a scratch approximately 20 cm long on the blue robes, at lower right.

PROVENANCE

Painted for the Corporation of Liverpool; transferred from the City Estates Committee 1968.

EXHIBITIONS

First Exhibition of Objects Illustrative of the Fine Arts [...] Liverpool Mechanics Institution 1840 (54);[8] *Kings and Queens of England* Walker Art Gallery 1953 (35).

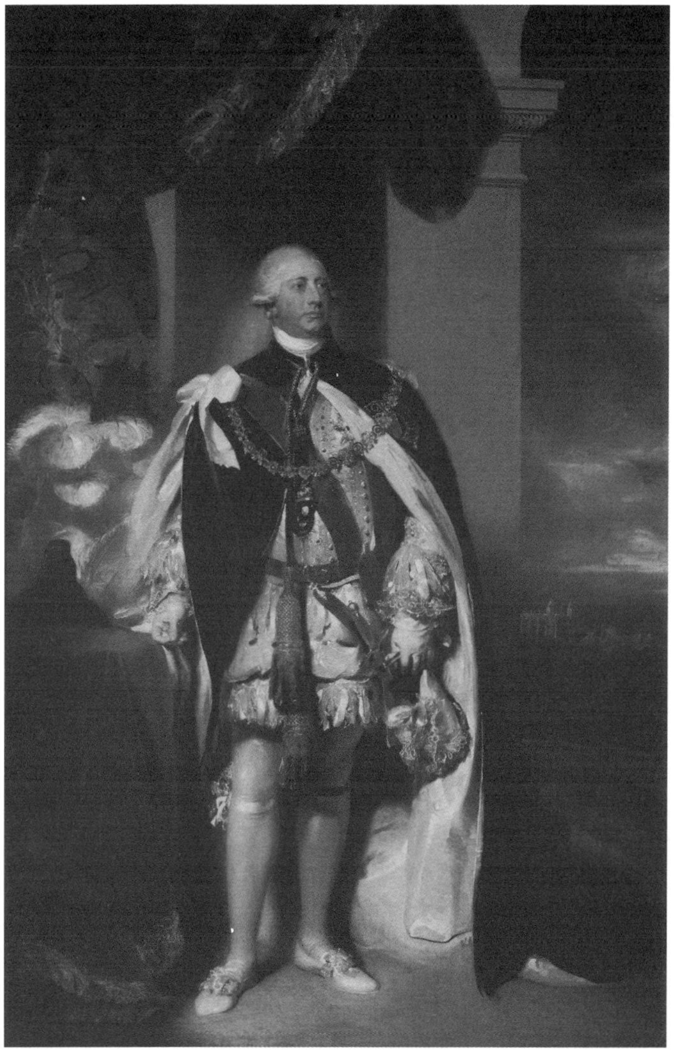

Fig. 43 *King George III* by Thomas Lawrence, oil on canvas. Herbert Art Gallery, Coventry.

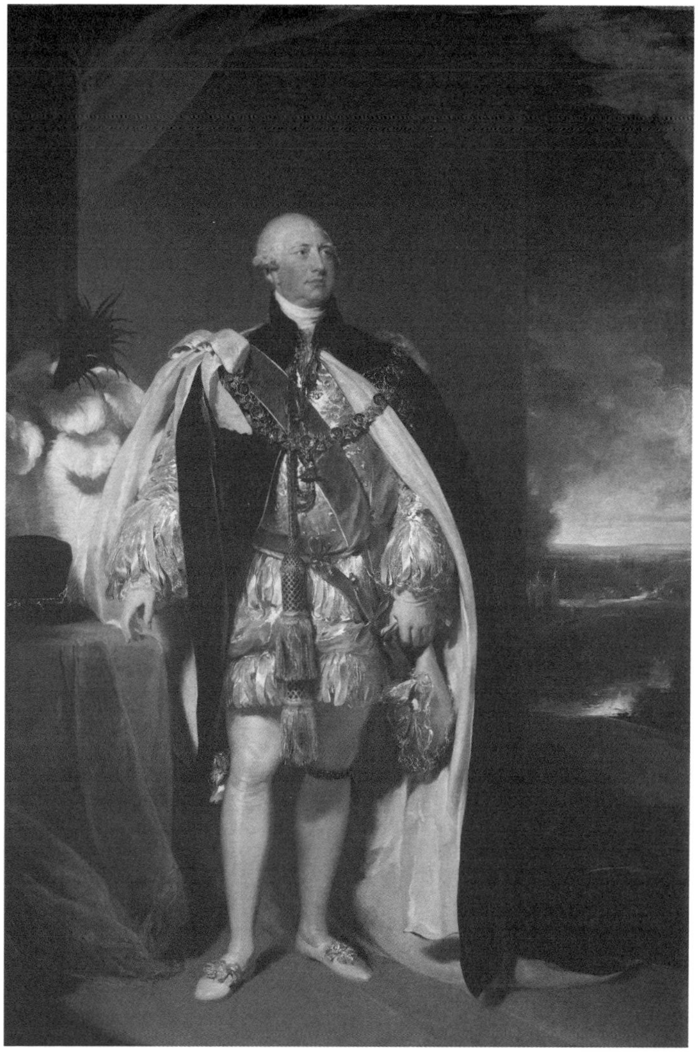

Fig. 44 *King George III* by Thomas Lawrence, oil on canvas. The Royal Collection © 2011, Her Majesty Queen Elizabeth II; photo A. C. Cooper.

NOTES

1. It was exhibited at the RA in 1792 (65); K. Garlick: *Sir Thomas Lawrence* (Oxford, 1989), p. 192, cat. 324(a).

2. Further whole-length replicas include one in the Royal Collection, painted as part of the Waterloo Chamber series between 1818 and 1823 (Sir O. Millar: *The Later Georgian Pictures in the Collection of Her Majesty the Queen* 2 vols [London, 1969] vol. 1, p. 60, cat. 871) (fig. 44); and one formerly in the collection of the Earl of Dartmouth at Patshull. A three-quarter length version measuring 67¾ × 46¼ inches, perhaps the version originally intended for Henry Addington (see n. 4) is also in the Royal Collection (Millar, *op. cit.*, pp. 60–1, no. 872). A version to the waist, perhaps cut down from a whole-length, was sold at Sotheby's, 23 March 1966 (81) and a circular version 30 inches in diameter is at Schloss Marienburg. John Woodward, in the *Kings and Queens of England* exhibition catalogue (see above) claimed that the head in the whole-length Waterloo Chamber replica was derived from later sittings.

3. FD, vol. 4, p. 1421 (entry of 17 July 1800); cited by Sir Michael Levey: *Sir Thomas Lawrence* (New Haven and London, 2005), p. 144.

4. The gestation of this portrait apparently dates from February 1802, when Addington declined to approach the King on Lawrence's behalf for fresh sittings (*FD*, vol. 5, p. 1749 [entry of 17 February 1802]; cited by Levey, *op. cit.*, p. 328). Millar, *op. cit.*, p. 61, is mistaken in his belief that Addington's intended intervention was related to the Liverpool commission.

5. Garlick, *op. cit.*, pp. 192–3, cat. 324[b].

6. *Liverpool Town Books, vol. 15, 1819–27* LRO 352 MIN/COU/1/15, p. 198.

7. *Liverpool Town Books, vol. 15, 1819–27* LRO 352 MIN/COU/1/15, p. 206.

8. Lent by Liverpool Corporation; the portrait was lent to Newsham House, Liverpool in August 1872 (*Libraries, Museums and Arts Committee Extracts*, 7 August 1872).

Thomas William Coke of Holkham

WAG 2581
oil on canvas, 92.5 × 71 cm
date: 1815–16

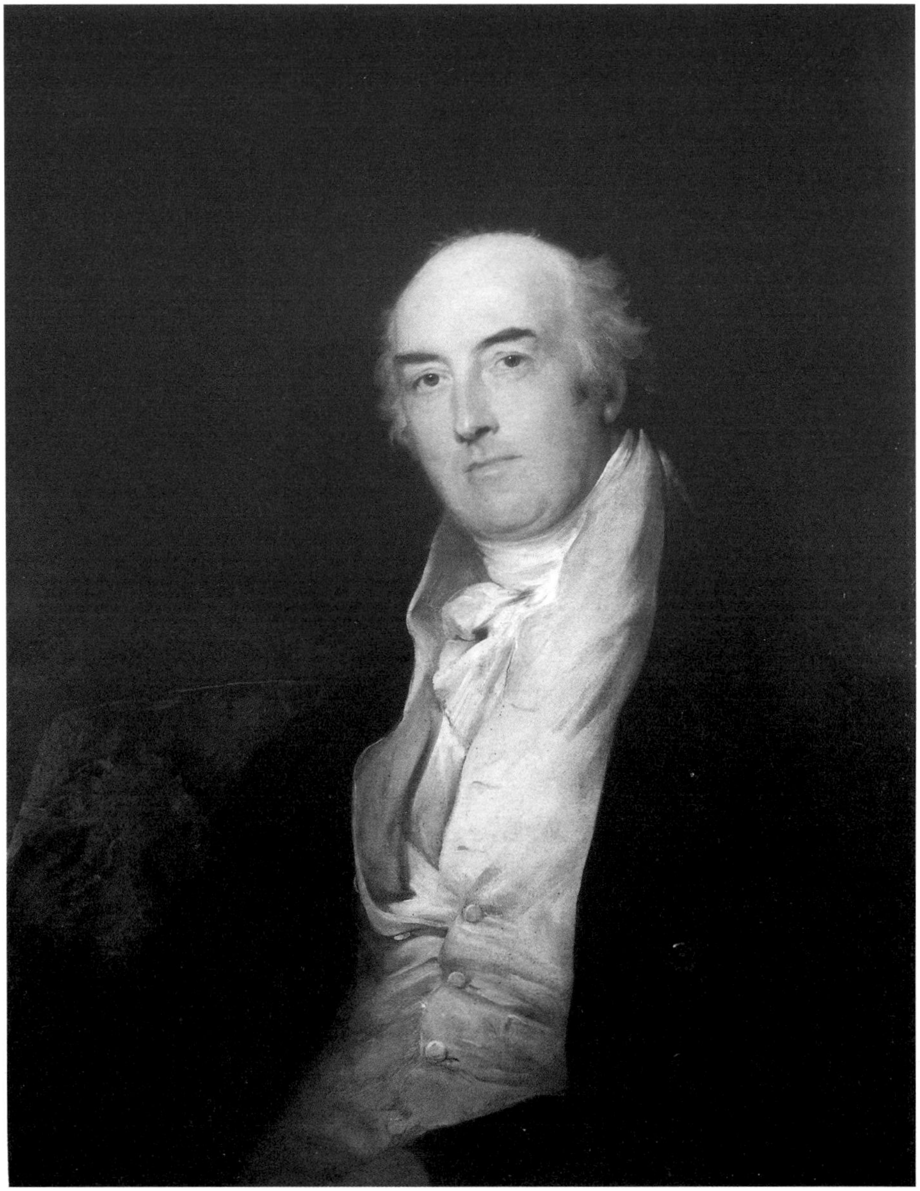

WAG 2581

Thomas William Coke (1754–1842) was the eldest son of Wenman Coke of Holkham, Norfolk and his second wife Elizabeth (née Chamberlayne-Denton). In his lifetime he was celebrated as an agriculturist who introduced new farming methods on his estates and developed efficient systems of leasing his land to tenants. It is now accepted that he took great pains to cultivate this reputation, and that many of the innovations that he claimed to have pioneered were well known when he succeeded to the Holkham estate. Coke was also MP for Norfolk for over 50 years (1776–1832, with one gap of six years between 1784 and 1790 and one of a few months in 1807); he considered himself as 'the first commoner of England' and refused a peerage six times, finally accepting the seventh offer, in 1837, when he was created Earl of Leicester. He was an ardent Whig: a follower of Charles James Fox and in his later years a supporter of Parliamentary reform.[1] Shared political beliefs were at the heart of his friendship with William Roscoe of Liverpool. They began corresponding in 1812 and Roscoe first visited Coke at Holkham in November 1814. Coke at about this time or shortly afterwards asked Roscoe to arrange and catalogue the manuscripts in his library and to supervise the repair of many of the books which were sent to Liverpool to be rebound. In the autumn of 1815 he asked Roscoe for his portrait to hang in the library, which was commissioned from Martin Archer Shee (see WAG 3130, pp. 162–4). Coke himself sat for WAG 2581 – his second portrait by Lawrence[2] – at about the same time.[3]

Although WAG 2581 does not appear to have been considered at the outset as a reciprocal gift to Roscoe, Roscoe may always have envisaged a print from Lawrence's new portrait being used as the frontispiece for his catalogue of the Holkham library (which he began in 1815, although work on it ran on into the late 1820s and it was never published).[4] A mezzotint after WAG 2581 by Charles Turner was published in 1818 and re-issued the following year with a dedication to Viscountess Anson, Coke's daughter. The print may have reinforced the general feeling in Coke's family circle that WAG 2581 was not a good likeness,[5] and this may explain why in September

1824 Roscoe wrote to Lawrence – who had kept the portrait in his own possession – requesting permission to have a new engraving done by Edward Smith of Liverpool.[6] Lawrence agreed to this but perhaps unwillingly, for the following month Roscoe was obliged to agree that apart from a few impressions set aside for Coke's private use, prints would only be sold with the catalogue itself.[7] Lawrence still had the portrait in May 1825 but he sent it to Roscoe for the new engraving the following month,[8] and it remained with him thereafter. Roscoe wrote to Coke in January 1829[9] asking whether he should return the portrait to him or to Lawrence, and this question was still unresolved in January 1831;[10] but Coke must have given it to him very soon afterwards (Roscoe died 27 June 1831). In the meanwhile Smith's engraving had been completed in 1826, at Roscoe's expense;[11] but this was as unpopular in Coke's circle as the painting itself, and Roscoe was informed that it was not to be published.[12]

PROVENANCE

Given by the sitter to William Roscoe in 1831; by descent to William Malin Roscoe; by descent to his widow, Mrs A. M. Roscoe; her bequest 1950.

EXHIBITIONS

Selected Acquisitions of the Walker Art Gallery Liverpool 1945–1955 Agnew's, London 1955 (24); *Cleaned Pictures* Walker Art Gallery 1955 (41).

NOTES

1. The standard biography of Coke is R. A. C. Parker: *Coke of Norfolk* (Oxford, 1975); and see also R. G. Thorne, ed.: *The History of Parliament: The House of Commons 1790–1820* 5 vols (London, 1986) vol. 3, pp. 477–80; and J. V. Beckett: 'Coke, Thomas William First Earl of Leicester of Holkham', *ODNB* vol. 12, pp. 475–8.
2. The earlier portrait, a whole-length begun in 1807 and completed several years later, was engraved by Charles Turner in 1814. It is in the Shire Hall, Norwich; K. Garlick: 'A Complete Catalogue of the Paintings, Drawings and Pastels of Sir Thomas Lawrence', *Walpole Society* vol. 39 (1964) p. 57; and Garlick: *Sir Thomas Lawrence* (1989) p. 222 (cat. 479a). A reduced copy is at Hinton Ampner. The engraving by W. T. Fry of 1821 which Garlick ('A Complete Catalogue', *loc. cit.*) states is after WAG 2581 is in fact derived from this earlier portrait.
3. Garlick ('A Complete Catalogue' and *Sir Thomas Lawrence, loc. cit.*) gives a date of about 1818 for WAG 2581 but a letter from Dawson Turner to Roscoe, 16 April 1817 (*Roscoe Papers*, LRO 920/ROS/4889) which describes the unfavourable response of Coke's family to the portrait indicated that it was, if not finished, then well advanced by then. What is presumably WAG 2581, rather than the 1807 full-length, is the subject of some 'Lines supposed to be address'd to Lawrence on seeing his ill-drawn portrait of Thomas William Coke Esq[r], M.P.' written by Abbot Upcher 'as I was returning from Holkham to Sheringham in my Carrigge' [sic] on internal evidence in the second half of 1816; Susan Yaxley, ed.: *Sherringhamia, The Journal of Abbot Upcher 1813–1816* (Stibbard, 1986) pp. 32–3.
4. The catalogue, much revised and extended by Frederick Madden, was completed in 1828 but was considered too expensive to publish; *MPPP*, p. 191.
5. See n. 3.
6. *Draft letter*, Roscoe to Lawrence, September 1824, LRO 920/ROS/2369.
7. *Copy letter*, Roscoe to Lawrence, 15 October 1824, LRO 920/ROS/2370.
8. *Copy letter*, Roscoe to Lawrence, 23 May 1825, LRO 920/ROS/2371; and *letter*, Roscoe to Coke, 22 June 1825, Holkham Archives, Holkham Hall, F/TWC 5, fol. 174r.
9. *Draft letter*, Roscoe to Coke, January 1829, LRO 920/ROS/990.
10. *Draft letter*, Roscoe to Fisher, Son & Co., 3 January 1831, LRO 920/ROS/1511. This company had requested 'a copy' of the portrait of Coke for their publication *The National Portrait Gallery*.
11. Smith's *receipt* for £20 on account of 'the Engraving of Mr. Coke' dated Liverpool 25 October 1826, LRO 920/ROS/4437.
12. See n. 10.

King George IV

WAG 3129
oil on canvas, 250 × 162.5 cm
date: unknown, perhaps 1822–30

This is a repetition of Lawrence's whole-length in the Royal Collection, which was painted in the second half of 1821[1] and exhibited at the Royal Academy in 1822.[2] That portrait was itself based (with a very slight modification to the likeness)[3] on Lawrence's earlier whole-length of George IV as Prince of Wales in Garter robes shown at the RA in 1818, the original of which was presented by the Prince to the Mansion House in Dublin (now in the Hugh Lane Gallery, Dublin).[4] Lawrence made many copies of the 1818 work and it effectively had the status of his official portrait of George even after he succeeded to the throne; typically, copies done after 1820 replaced the hat of the order of the Garter with the crown. The present type was much less common and is known in only a handful of versions: apart from WAG 3129 and the original in the Royal Collection (in which the coronation robes are actually painted over the top of the Garter robes, with the top of the 'Garter' collar, part of the belt, and the outline of the original robes on the floor still visible)[5] there are versions at Goodwood House[6] and (of inferior quality)[7] at the RA. The king is shown wearing the collars of the Golden Fleece, the Guelphic Order and the Bath as well as the Garter, and he rests his hand on the 'Table des Grands Capitaines' originally made for Napoleon Bonaparte in 1806

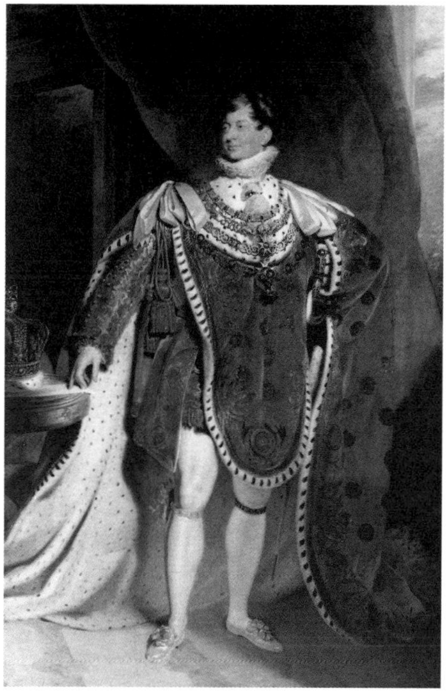

WAG 3129

which was a gift to the Prince Regent from Louis XVIII of France in 1817. The sword is still in the Royal Collection at Windsor.

The quality of WAG 3129 – although it is recognisably a studio copy – has been described as 'excellent',[8] and it has been suggested that Lawrence himself painted the head.[9] It is substantially smaller than the Royal Collection prototype,[10] and is in an unusual slim period frame with reddish-bronze undergilding. There are numerous losses and visible touches along and near the bottom edge of the canvas and there is a repaired area of damage on the shoulder to the left-hand side of the head.[11]

PROVENANCE

...Sir Ernest Royden;[12] by whom presented 1953.

NOTES

1. Unidentified newspaper report dated 20 November 1821 (National Art Library, Victoria & Albert Museum, *Press Cuttings Volumes* vol. 3, p. 819); cited by Sir Michael Levey: *Sir Thomas Lawrence* (New Haven and London, 2005) p. 333; an earlier article dated 11 August 1821 (*ibid.*) had reported, 'His Majesty, immediately after his Coronation, commissioned Sir T. Lawrence, President of the Royal Academy, to paint a new Portrait of him in his Coronation robes, and seated in St. Edward's chair, with the Crown of England upon his head, and the Sceptre in his hand, as he appeared enthroned in the Abbey. The picture, which is of great magnitude, to admit various concomitants, is already far advanced, and probably will be the most successful from the pencil of the President. It promises far to excel in magnificence and splendour, the famous Picture of the Pope, by the same Artist, belonging to His Majesty. When finished, it is the intention of his Majesty to present duplicates of it to various Corporation Halls in the United Kingdom.' See also Sir Oliver Millar: *Later Georgian Pictures in the Collection of Her Majesty the Queen* 2 vols (London, 1969) vol. 1, p. 61 (cat. 873), citing a letter written by Sir George Nayler on 8 December 1821 (Royal Archives) that refers to 'His Majesty's Portrait now painting by Sir Thomas Lawrence'.
2. K. Garlick: 'A Catalogue of the Paintings, Drawings and Pastels of Sir Thomas Lawrence', *Walpole Society* vol. 39 (1964) p. 87; and K. Garlick: *Sir Thomas Lawrence* (Oxford, 1989) p. 194 (cat. 325[e]).
3. Levey, *op. cit.*, p. 241; the newspaper report of 20 November 1821 (see n. 1) mentions that 'the King sat for the last time, at Buckingham House, on Monday last'.
4. Garlick, 'A Catalogue', p. 86; Garlick, *Sir Thomas Lawrence*, pp. 193–4 (cat. 325[d]).
5. Millar, *loc. cit.*
6. Garlick, 'A Catalogue', p. 87; Garlick, *Sir Thomas Lawrence*, p. 194.
7. John Woodward: 'Four Royal Portraits at the Walker Art Gallery', *Liverpool Bulletin* vol. 4 (1954) p. 17.
8. Woodward, *op. cit.*, p. 16.
9. John Woodward, *letter*, 2 March 1961, gallery files.
10. The Royal Collection picture measures 289.5 × 200.5 cm, and its composition extends further to the left, right and top so that the whole of the crown is visible at the left, as well as the whole of an ocular arch at top left and a small piece of curtain at top right. However, the absence of these extensions in WAG 3129 is not sufficient to account for the whole of the differential.
11. Copy *invoice* from J. Coburn Witherop dated 30 November 1971, gallery files.
12. Efforts by Hugh Macandrew to establish the earlier provenance of WAG 3129 (recorded in gallery files) succeeded only in establishing that the painting was at Hill Bark, Sir Ernest Royden's home on the Wirral, before 7 August 1952.

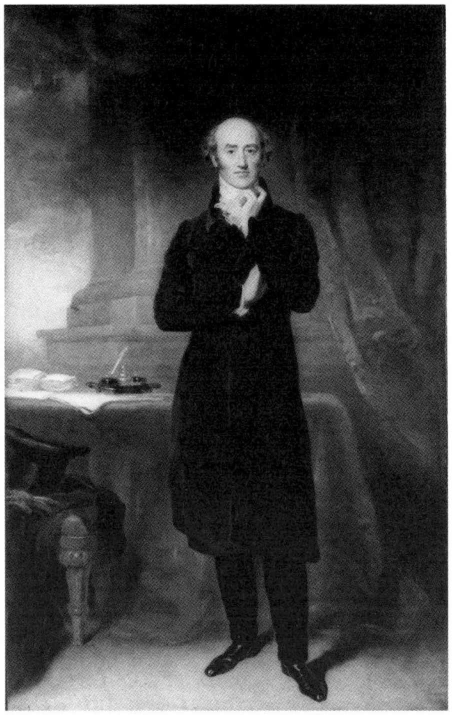

WAG 3078

called

Thomas Lawrence

1769–1830

George Canning

WAG 3078
oil on canvas, 240 × 147.3 cm
date: about 1823–35

One of Britain's leading political figures in the first three decades of the nineteenth century, Canning (1770–1827) was MP for Liverpool between 1812 and 1822. He was the son of a barrister who died when he was one year old, and was brought up by his uncle Stratford Canning, a London merchant banker with Whig connections. Canning himself, however, was a follower of Pitt; he entered Parliament in 1793, was appointed Under Secretary of State for Foreign Affairs in 1796; was twice Foreign Secretary, between 1807 and 1809 and again from 1822 until 1827; and became First Lord of the Treasury for four months before his death. Famed above all for his speeches in the House of Commons, Canning was a workaholic, individualistic and ambitious, admired and distrusted at the same time. He had received overtures from the merchant community in Liverpool to stand as MP in 1810, having impressed them by his opposition to the American intercourse bill of 1806; eventually he stood at the election of 1812, heading the poll without having to go to any expense. Following his victory, a Canning Club was formed in Liverpool, which he described as 'gratifying and glorious beyond my most sanguine dreams of popular ambition... I hardly ever thought that it would have fallen in my way to come in so close contact with so large a portion of the people, and be so received.'[1] He gave up his Liverpool seat in 1822 in favour of his political lieutenant, William Huskisson.[2]

The early history of WAG 3078 is unknown, but its presentation (documentation untraced) to Liverpool Corporation only 25 years after Canning's death strongly suggests that it originated as a commission from within the city. Given the portrait's close relationship to other portraits of Canning undertaken by Lawrence in the first half of the 1820s (discussed below), the likeliest scenario must be that it was meant to mark the ending of Canning's term as MP, in September 1822. It may have been commissioned as a presentation portrait by Canning himself, though this remains speculative. No trace of the work survives in Lawrence's papers, and the work is of uneven quality, but parts of it may be by Lawrence himself.

Canning's body and dress in WAG 3078 are identical to their appearance in a whole-length that was originally commissioned from Lawrence by George IV in 1825, of which the chief versions are now in the Royal Collection and at Harewood House. The former of these (fig. 45) was paid for by George IV sometime early in 1828 (Lawrence's receipt is dated 7 April that year) and was finished by the following year when Charles Turner's engraving of it was published, but it was still in Lawrence's studio at the time of his death;[3] the second was also in Lawrence's studio at his death and delivered to Lady Canning in April 1831.[4] Numerous smaller variants are also known.[5] However, Canning's face in WAG 3078 appears slightly younger than it does in the works begun in 1825, and also different, and unique to this canvas, is the treatment of the arms and hands. The placement of the left hand under the chin is a variation of the treatment in Lawrence's earlier kit-cat portrait of Canning, begun in or shortly after 1820 for Thomas Lord Binning (Private Collection, USA; fig. 46);[6] and it is thus tempting to conclude that the head

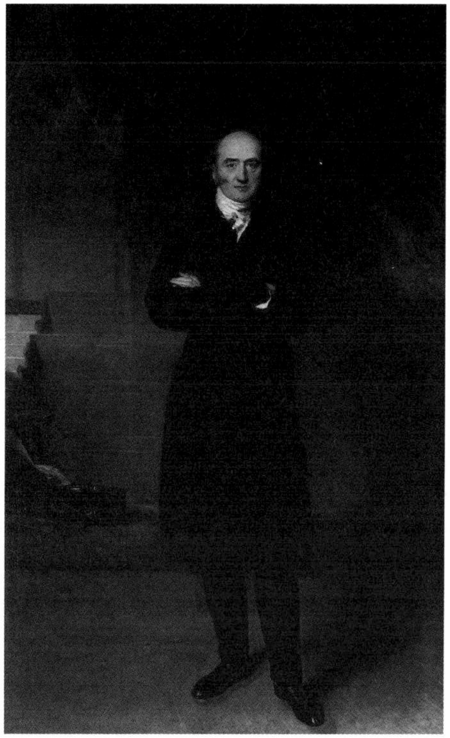

Fig. 45 *George Canning* by Thomas Lawrence, oil on canvas. The Royal Collection © 2011 Her Majesty Queen Elizabeth II.

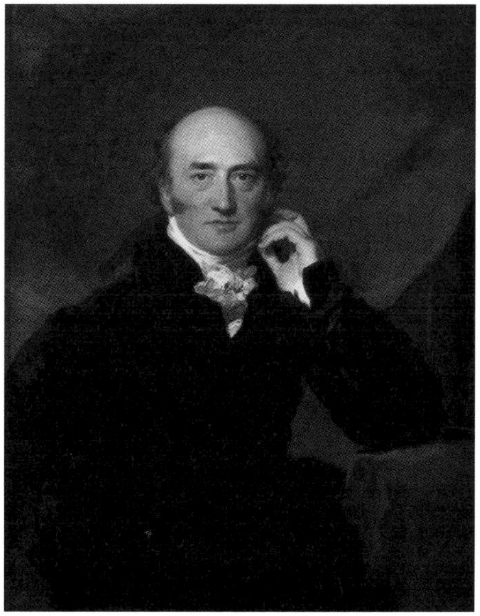

Fig. 46 *George Canning* by Thomas Lawrence, oil on canvas. Private collection, USA; photo courtesy Christie's.

and hands of WAG 3078 were painted in the wake of this portrait and before the alternative treatment with the folded arms had been developed for the 1825 whole-length commission.[7] On this view, Canning's torso in WAG 3078 was most likely added some time after 1825 but before 1831, while the 1825 full-lengths were still in Lawrence's studio. The background, which is completely unrelated to the background of any other Lawrence portrait of Canning, and of a formulaic and rather hastily painted character (the huge top hat on the chair seems far too large for Canning's head) may have been added later still. This certainly seems to be the work of a different, less accomplished hand.

PROVENANCE

...Presented to Liverpool Corporation in 1852;[8] transferred to the gallery before 1882.[9]

EXHIBITION

3rd Special Exhibition of National Portraits South Kensington 1868 (237).

NOTES

1. Quoted by Wendy Hinde: *Canning* (London, 1973) p. 262.
2. See Derek Beales: 'Canning, George', *ODNB* (2004) vol. 9, pp. 911–22; R. G. Thorne, ed.: *History of Parliament: The House of Commons, 1790–1820* 5 vols (London, 1986) vol. 3, pp. 378–404.
3. Sir Oliver Millar: *The Later Georgian Pictures in the Collection of Her Majesty the Queen* 2 vols (London, 1969) vol. 1, pp. 65–6 (cat. 887).
4. K. Garlick: 'A Catalogue of the Paintings, Drawings and Pastels of Sir Thomas Lawrence', *Walpole Society* vol. 39 (1964) p. 49.
5. Garlick, *loc. cit.*, records the following: the version measuring 132 × 104 cm in the Waterloo Chamber at Windsor Castle; in K. Garlick: *Sir Thomas Lawrence* (Oxford, 1989) p.163 (under cat. 160c), this is described as 'from a hand other than Lawrence's'; the copy by Richard Evans in the National Portrait Gallery, London (NPG 1338, 88 × 58 cm); two modern copies by M. Ayoub, one in the Foreign Office, London, one owned in 1936 by Viscount Allendale; and a 76 × 63.5 cm bust version in a private collection, Washington DC; to these may be added the small versions sold at Christie 11 March 1966 (155) and 21 July 1989 (249).
6. Exh. *Thomas Lawrence, Regency Power and Brilliance*, National Portrait Gallery, London and Yale Center for British Art, New Haven 2010–11 (48); this canvas seems the likeliest candidate for the

portrait of Canning by Lawrence exhibited at the RA in 1825 (cat. 83); R. Cooper's engraving of it was published in 1823, and Charles Turner's in 1827.
7. WAG 3078 is not directly related to Lawrence's 1826 full-length of Canning painted for Sir Robert Peel (National Portrait Gallery, London; Garlick [1989], p. 164, cat. 160d); this portrait is not known to have been copied and seems to have left Lawrence's studio in timely fashion, unlike the canvases begun in 1825.
8. See Charles Dyall: *First Decade of the Walker Art Gallery: A Report of Its Operations from 1877–1887* (Liverpool, 1888) p. 7; the painting was cleaned and re-varnished and the frame re-gilt by Samuel Alker in 1865 for £6.12s.0d. (Library, Museum and Art Gallery Committee *Minutes*, 19 October 1865).
9. Charles Dyall: *Walker Art Gallery Descriptive Catalogue of the Permanent Collection of Pictures* (Liverpool, 1882) p. 27 (cat. 103). The painting was hanging in the galleries of the Library and Museum Building in 1875 (Library, Museum and Art Committee: *Statement of the Works of Art Purchased by or Presented to the Corporation of Liverpool* [1875] no.2).

Peter Lely

1618–80

Josceline Percy, Lord Percy

WAG 2945
oil on canvas, 127 × 101.5 cm
date: 1658

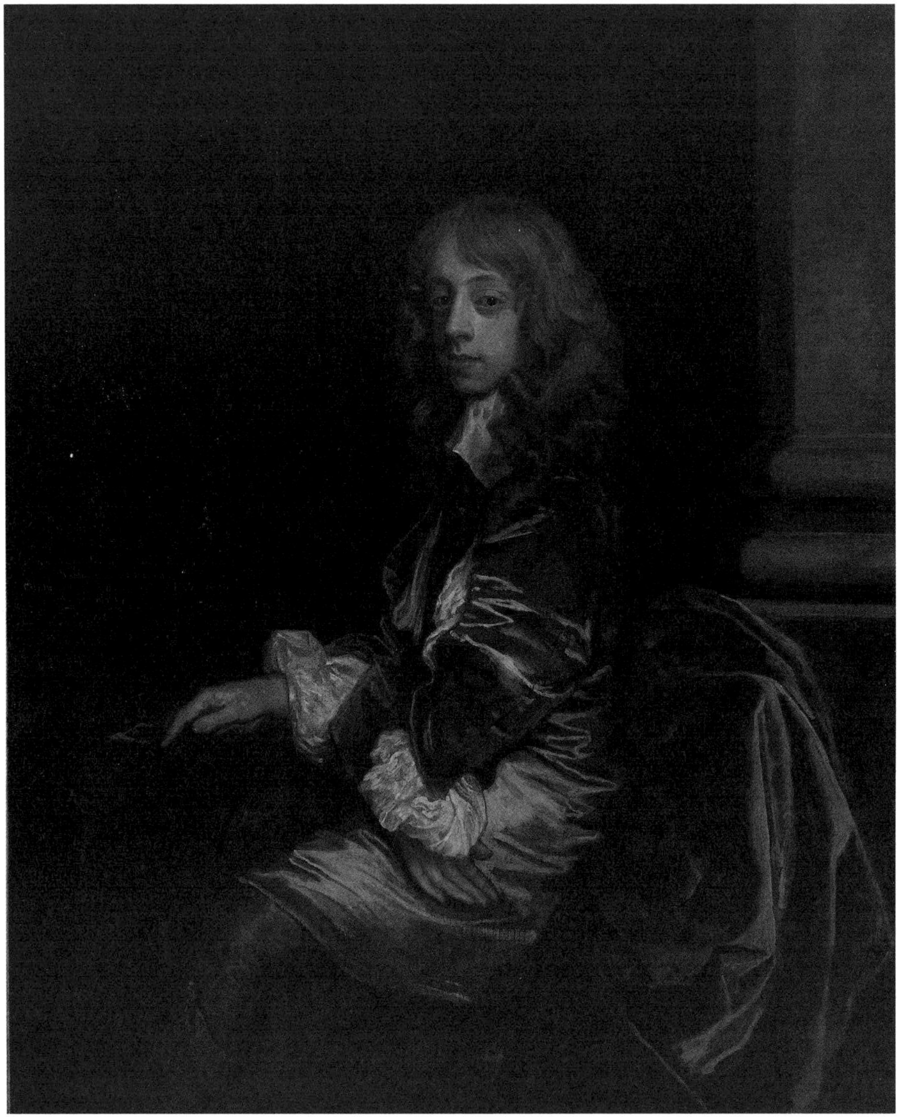
WAG 2945

The identity of the sitter is established by an inscription at centre left of the canvas: *IOSCELINE PIERCY 11TH EARL OF/NORTHUMBERLAND/DIED AT TURIN 21ST MAY 1670/AETAT* [the age has been omitted].[1] Lord Percy (1644–70) was the eldest son and heir of Algernon Percy, 10th Earl of Northumberland by his second wife, Lady Elizabeth Howard, daughter of Theophilus, 2nd Earl of Suffolk. He was made Lord Lieutenant of Northumberland jointly with his father in 1660, and was Page of Honour at the coronation of Charles II in April 1661. In December 1662 he married Lady Elizabeth Wriothesley, daughter of Thomas, 4th Earl of Southampton. Their daughter Elizabeth was born in 1666, and a son, Henry, in February 1669 (he died aged only ten months, that December). Lord Percy succeeded his father as 11th Earl of Northumberland in October 1668 and the same year was created Lord Lieutenant of Sussex (the family's main residence was at Petworth House in that county). In September 1669, with his wife and daughter, he left England for a tour of Italy, but died of a fever at Turin. With his death, in default of a direct male heir, the Earldom of Northumberland became extinct.[2]

Lord Percy's father, the 10th Earl of Northumberland, was Lely's most significant patron at the start of his career in England (commissioning from him, among other paintings, a number of portraits of Charles I and his family).[3] WAG 2945 is the third of a series of five

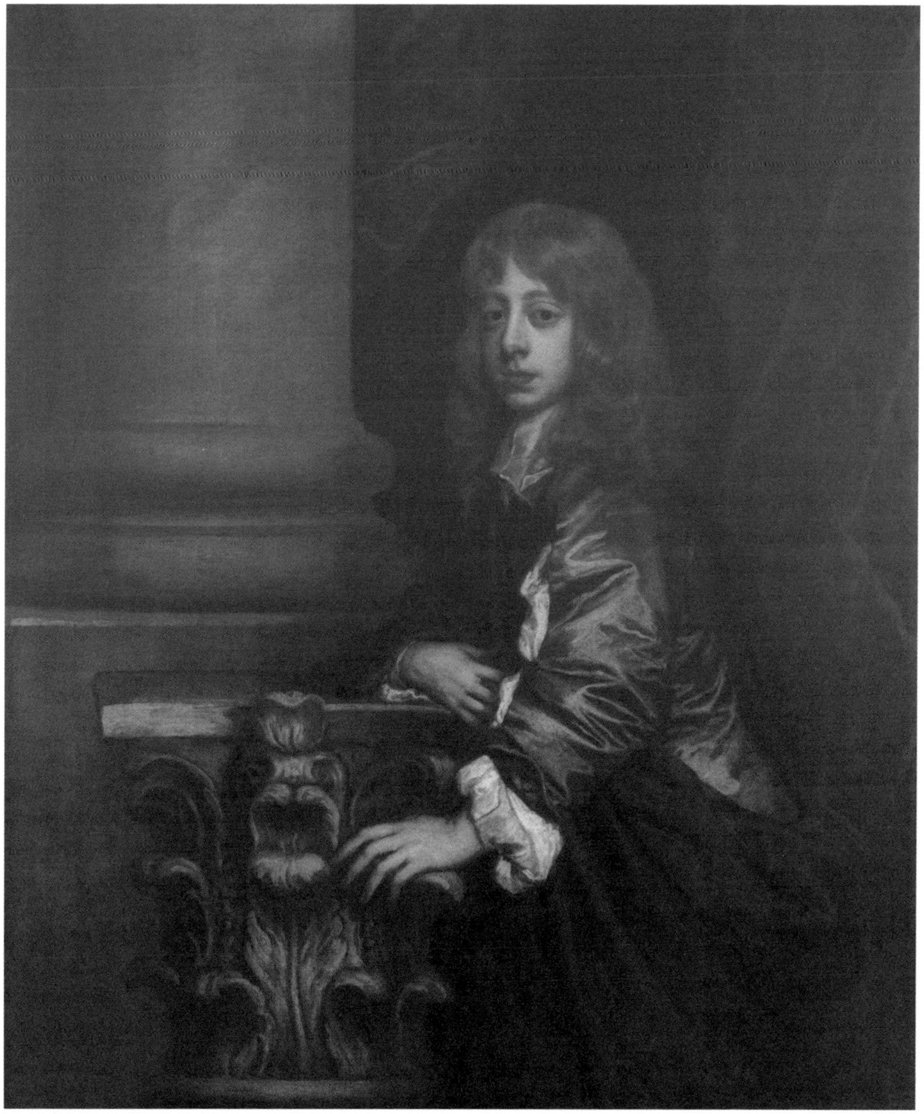

Fig. 47 *Josceline Percy, later 11th Earl of Northumberland* by Peter Lely, oil on canvas. Syon House, collection of the Duke of Northumberland; photo Photographic Survey, The Courtauld Institute of Art, London.

portraits (excluding repetitions) that Lely made of the Earl's eldest son. The first, carried out when Lord Percy was about six years old, shows him in hunting dress, as a young Adonis.[4] The second, probably painted around six years later (fig. 47), is close to WAG 2945 in basic type, but with differences to the pose of the arms and in the placement of the background column.[5] Although in this portrait Lord Percy looks distinctly more youthful than he does in WAG 2945, it seems possible that Lely based the likeness in the latter on this earlier picture in order to minimise the need for fresh sittings. The treatment of the body, with its Van Dyckian pose of the near arm and effetely folded hand, is very close to that in his portrait of the Earl of Carnarvon of the later 1650s. Lely painted two further portraits of Lord Percy in the later 1660s together with pendant portraits of his wife. These may date from after Lord Percy's succession to the Earldom of Northumberland.[6]

The date of WAG 2945 has been the subject of debate[7] but the portrait is most likely to have been painted in 1658, when Lord Percy was 14 years old. It is identifiable as the work that shows up in the artist's accounts for the year ending on 31 January 1659, where a payment of £20 is recorded for 'Drawing my Lord Percy's picture sent to Hadham'.[8] 'Hadham' must refer to Little Hadham Hall, residence of Lord Percy's step-sister Lady Elizabeth Capel (who was a favourite of their father);[9] her daughter, Lady Anne Capel married into the Howard family of Castle Howard, where the painting remained until 1944.[10] By that date, it was in indifferent condition, suffering badly from flaking, especially on the left-hand side, and having had the eyes vandalised;[11] it is also thought to have been damaged in an earlier fire in the house.[12] It was conserved by the gallery in the late 1940s.[13]

PROVENANCE

Painted for the sitter's father, Algernon, 10th Earl of Northumberland; by whom given to his daughter Lady Elizabeth Capel; by descent to her daughter, Lady Ann Capel, who in 1688 married Charles, 3rd Earl of Carlisle; by descent at Castle Howard to Hon. Geoffrey Howard; Christie 18 February 1944 (51); bt. Arcade Gallery; from whom bt. by the gallery 1945.

NOTES

1. The script of the inscription is that found on many portraits in the Carlisle collection. Sir Oliver Millar, *letter*, 6 February 2007, gallery files.

2. *Complete Peerage*, vol. 9 (1936), pp. 739–40.

3. R. B. Beckett: *Lely* (London, 1951) p. 39 (cats. 78–9) and compare Oliver Millar: *Sir Peter Lely*, exh. cat., National Portrait Gallery, London (1978), pp. 37–8 (cat. 6).

4. 163.5 × 137 cm, Petworth House; Beckett, *op. cit.*, p. 56 (cat. 390). A second version of this work was in the same 1944 Castle Howard sale as WAG 2945. Beckett's date of about 1656 seems too late for this and Oliver Millar, *letter*, 28 August 1950, gallery files, proposed a date of about 1650, pointing out its typological resemblance to Lely's portraits of Lord

Romney at Althorp and the Duke of Gloucester at Hampton Court.
5. 121 × 98 cm, Syon House; Beckett, *op. cit.*, p. 56 (cat. 391). This must be *A Picture of Sr Jocelin Percy to the Knees*, value £5, listed as no. 76 in the inventory of Petworth House taken by Symon Stone in 1671, preserved among the papers of the Duke of Northumberland, Northumberland Record Office; reprinted by Jeremy Wood: 'Van Dyck and the Earl of Northumberland: Taste and Collecting in Stuart England', in Susan J. Barnes and Arthur K. Wheelock, eds: *Van Dyck 350* (College Park, 1994) pp. 306–8.
6. One (122 × 91.5 cm) is at Chatsworth and another, with its pendant of Lady Elizabeth (both 125 × 99 cm), is at Alnwick Castle.
7. Beckett, *op. cit.*, proposed about 1659; Millar (letter of 28 August 1950) and FC, p. 105, about 1660; Mark Evans (draft entry, gallery files) on the view that Lord Percy appeared perhaps as young as 12, suggested about 1656–60.
8. Wood, *op. cit.*, p. 313. I am grateful to Sir Oliver Millar for this reference.
9. Millar, *letter*, 1 March 2007, gallery files.
10. It is recorded in Lord Hawkesbury: *Catalogue of the Portraits* [...] *at Castle Howard* (privately printed, 1904) p. 38 (cat. 545).
11. Millar, *letter*, 6 February 2007.
12. Millar, *letter*, 29 January 2007, gallery files.
13. Millar, *letter*, 22 August 1950, gallery files, observed that the portrait 'looks well now that it has been attended to'.

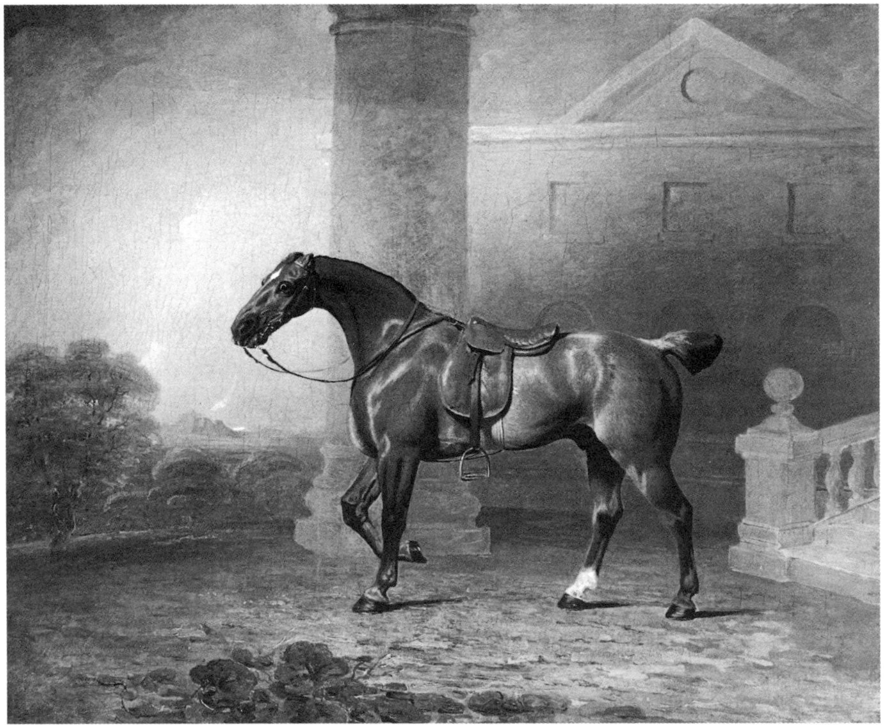

WAG 9800

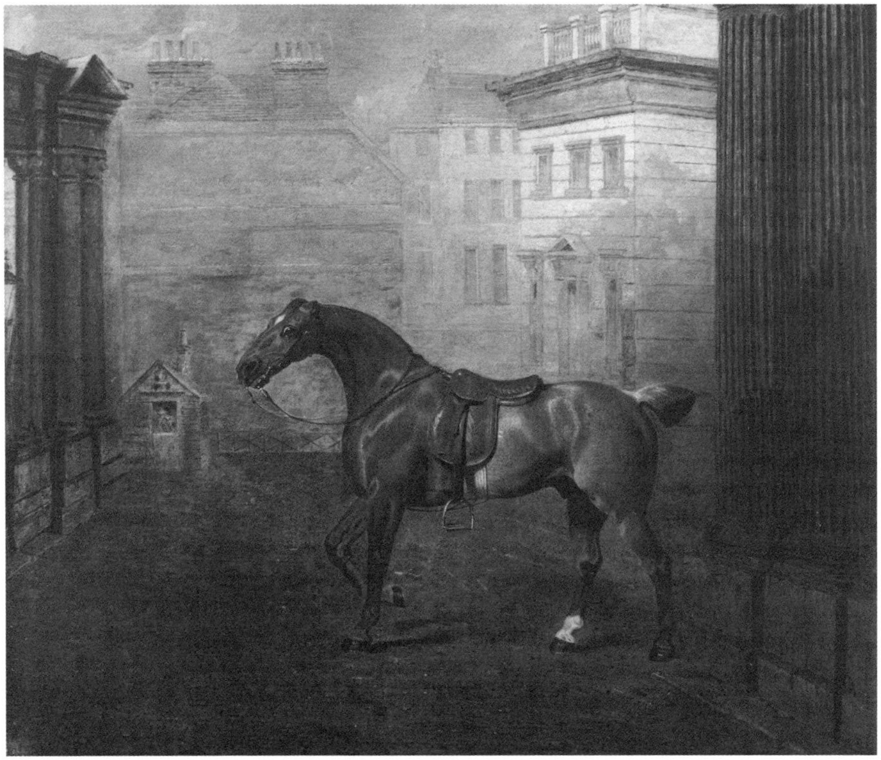

Fig. 48 *The Prince of Wales's Favourite Hack* by Benjamin Marshall, oil on canvas. The Royal Collection © 2011 Her Majesty Queen Elizabeth II.

Benjamin Marshall

1767–1835

The Prince of Wales's Favourite Roan Hack

WAG 9800
oil on canvas, 63.5 × 76.5 cm
date: about 1800

This is a reduced variant of a horse portrait carried out for George, Prince of Wales (Royal Collection; fig. 48) which has been dated to about 1794.[1] WAG 9800, however, was engraved for the November 1802 issue of *The Sporting Magazine*, and comparison with other dated works by Marshall of the period just after 1800 suggests that it dates from those years rather than earlier.[2] The text accompanying the *Sporting Magazine* engraving does not name the horse but states that it had formerly belonged to Lord Egremont[3] and then Mr Tattersall, and that the Prince of Wales rode it constantly and had once trotted it six miles in 21½ minutes. A later inscription on the back of WAG 9800[4] suggests that the name of the horse is Road Hackney, but this appears likely to be either a misreading of the words *Roan Hack* or else a corruption of Hackney Road, where the artist lived at no. 20, London Terrace. Two other horses painted by Marshall for the Prince were Mistake and Tiger, the latter described as 'a favourite' hack of the Prince; and it seems likely that he commissioned portraits of all three horses at the same time. [5] The very loosely brushed-in architectural features of the background were probably introduced to assist the task of the engraver; the building has not been identified.

PROVENANCE

...Mrs V. M. C. Heyworth; Christie 3 July 1964 (66); bt. Siller (2,200 gns.); ...Josephine, Countess of Sefton; her bequest 1980.

NOTES

1. Oliver Millar: *Later Georgian Pictures in the Collection of Her Majesty the Queen* 2 vols (London, 1969) vol. 1, p. 83 (cat. 942); followed by A. Noakes: *Ben Marshall 1768–1835* (Leigh-on-Sea, 1978) p. 30 (cat. 8). The painting measures 89 × 101.5 cm and is signed *Ben Marshall Pt. for G.P.W.* The horse is shown against the colonnade of Carlton House, and with houses in Pall Mall in the background.
2. Compare for example Marshall's *Musk, a Bay Hunter, the Property of Captain Ricketts*, 86.5 × 101 cm, signed and dated 1800, sold Sotheby 23 April 1975 (120), or *The Little Groom with His Two Chestnuts*, 107 × 127 cm signed and dated 1802, sold Sotheby 17 March 1982 (93) for the treatment of the horses, and compare also *Osterley with His Groom*, signed and dated 1804, with Spink 1937, for the treatment of the background architecture.
3. Not Lord Egmont, as stated in the 1964 sale catalogue.
4. The inscription reads in full: *Road Hackney / Favourite of his Majesty when / Prince of Wales / Ben Marshal / Pinxit.* It evidently dates from 1820–30 when George was on the throne.
5. See Sir John Hanbury Williams: 'Celebrated Horses by Celebrated Painters in the Royal Collection at Windsor Castle', *Connoisseur* vol. 111 (June 1943) pp. 109–114 for illustrations of Marshall's *Mistake* (p. 110) and *Tiger* (p. 113). Two versions of *Tiger* exist, one in the Royal Collection, the same size as the Royal Collection version of the present work (Millar, *loc. cit.* [cat. 940], where described as a light chestnut hack) and the other, which was engraved, the same size as WAG 9800. The composition of *Mistake* is unrelated to that of WAG 9800. He is described by Hanbury Williams as a dock-tailed gelding, 'his ears thrown back as if ill-tempered'. Hanbury Williams cites Thomas Lister, 4th Baron Ribblesdale: *The Queen's Hounds and Stag-hunting Recollections* (London, 1897) to the effect that the Prince of Wales's two favourite hacks were *Tiger* and *Tobacco Stopper*, both of which 'carried him to perfection'; in default of contrary evidence, it seems very possible that WAG 9800 depicts *Tobacco Stopper*.

Anti-Gallican

WAG 9801
oil on canvas, 103 × 128 cm
signed and dated: *B Marshall pt/1821* (bottom left)
date: 1821

The light bay colt Anti-Gallican (the name, popular in the period of the Napoleonic wars, and already given to another colt foaled in 1793, means 'opposed to anything French') was got in 1817 by Lord Stawell's Waxy out of Pantina.[1] He won two races at Newmarket for Lord Stawell in April 1820, at the Craven Meeting and at the First Spring Meeting,[2] but at some point after this was sold to R. Pettit, who commissioned this portrait the following year. In 1822, for Pettit, Anti-Gallican won the same two races at Newmarket that he had won in 1820, being ridden by the jockey J. Robinson. Later that same year he was sent to Russia.[3]

The work is a typical example of the stock racehorse portrait, frequently on a landscape-format 'half-length' (127 × 101 cm) canvas, that Marshall evolved towards the end of the 1810s and painted throughout the 1820s.[4] Characteristically in these works the horse is accompanied on the same plane by two or three figures, usually a groom and the trainer or stable-owner (rather than the owner of the horse

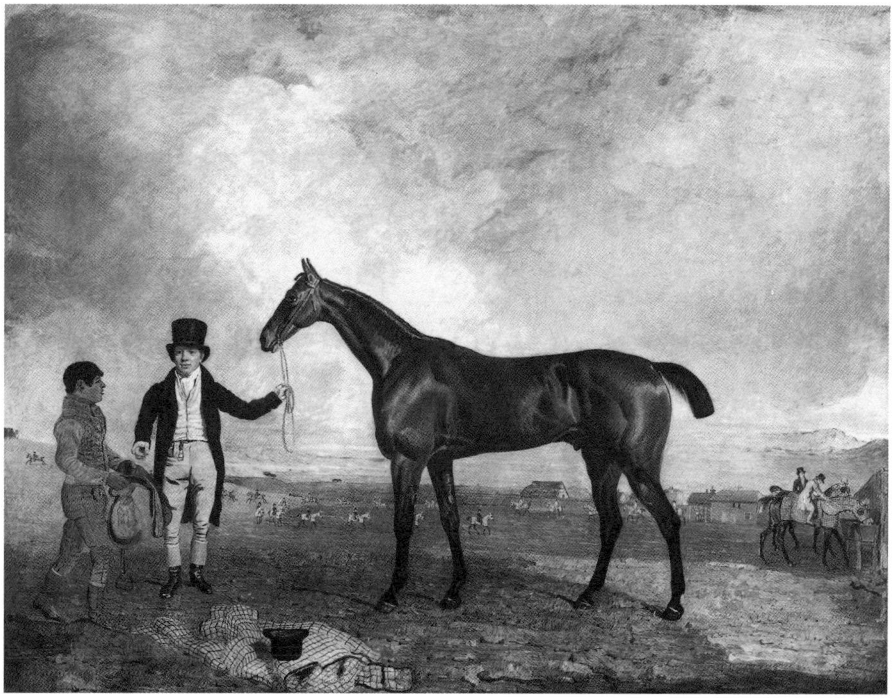

WAG 9801

itself); these figures are generally very similarly depicted, as types rather than individuals;[5] the terrain is broken and the background panoramic, usually filled with distant incident.

PROVENANCE

Painted for R. Pettit, the horse's owner; by descent;[6] bt. through Ellis & Smith[7] by Leggatt, 1934; from whom bt. in 1935 by Cedric Clifton Brown; Christie 6 November 1959 (93); bt. Leger; Ackermann 1961; from whom bt. in 1964 by Hugh, 7th Earl of Sefton; by descent to Josephine Countess of Sefton; her bequest 1980.

EXHIBITION

The Noble Horse Metropolitan Teien Art Museum, Tokyo 1998 (28).

NOTES

1. *The General Stud Book* vol. 3 (London, 1832) p. 295; and for the earlier Anti-Gallican, *The General Stud Book* vol. 1 (London, 1827) p. 385.
2. *The Racing Calendar for the Year 1820* vol. 48 (1821) pp. 7, 14.
3. *The Racing Calendar for the Year 1822* vol. 50 (1823) pp. 8, 18, 469.
4. For example *Sailor*, 99 × 124 cm, signed and dated 1819, in which very similar accoutrements lie in the foreground; *Banker*, 99 × 125 cm, signed and dated 1821, and *Mameluke*, 73 × 91.5 cm, signed and dated 1827.
5. See, for example, Marshall's *Skiff with His Groom and John Howe, the Owner of His Stables*, Christie 20 April 1990 (110); the depiction of John Howe is almost identical to the figure holding Anti-Gallican's bridle.
6. A. Noakes: *Ben Marshall 1768–1835* (Leigh-on-Sea, 1978) p. 48 (where the date of WAG 9801 is wrongly given as 1823, following the 1959 sale catalogue) states that Leggatts bought the picture from Pettit's descendants; this is also stated in a note on the back of an old photograph in the Witt Library.
7. This was stated verbally by Leggatt Bros to Mark Evans, 30 January 1984 (Mark Evans's draft entry, gallery files).

George Morland

1763–1804

Lake Scene and Cottage

WAG 274
oil on canvas, 31.5 × 38.5 cm
signed: *G. Morland pinxt.* (bottom right)
date: about 1790–95

A potboiler, but of good quality and lively character, WAG 274 may be dated on stylistic grounds to about 1790–95.[1] The man in the foreground is carrying an oar towards the boat in which he and his companion are about to go fishing; what appears to be their net is in the boat's stern. WAG 274 was cleaned and the craquelure partially infilled in 1962.[2]

PROVENANCE

...T. Mott Whitehouse; Christie 29 March 1890 (68); bt. Agnew (£61 19s.); from whom bt. by George Holt March 1891 (£84, including new frame); Emma Holt Bequest 1945.

NOTES

1. The form of the signature is also characteristic of works of this date. David Winter: 'George Morland (1763–1804)', PhD thesis, Stanford University, 1977, p. 192 (cat. P162) dates WAG 274 to 1793–95.
2. Treatment report dated 4 December 1962, gallery files.

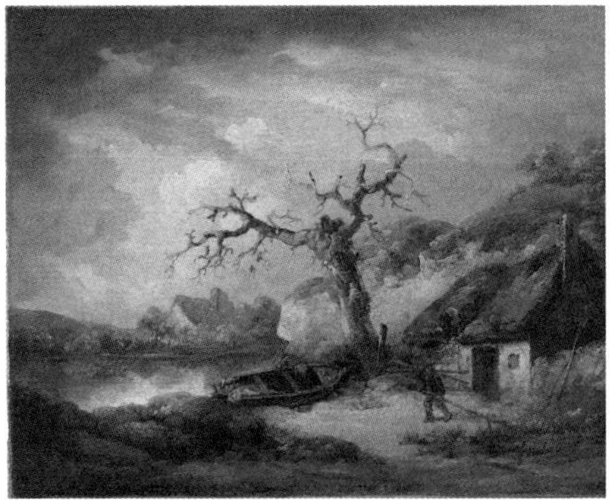

WAG 274

Gypsy Encampment

WAG 2399
oil on canvas, 87.5 × 118 cm
signed: *G. morland* (bottom right)
date: about 1790–95

The artist is said to have spent three days living in a gypsy camp,[1] and he made numerous paintings of gypsies. The subject is especially prevalent in his work from around 1789 to 1795;[2] WAG 2399 has been dated to 1793–94[3] but is perhaps, on grounds of style, a little earlier.

PROVENANCE

...William Rathbone, Liverpool by 1842;[4] by descent; presented by the Rathbone family 1945.

EXHIBITIONS

Second Exhibition of Objects Illustrative of the Fine Arts [...] Liverpool Mechanics Institution 1842 (631); *Oil Paintings by British Artists born before 1801* Liverpool Art Club 1881 (159); *Some Acquisitions of the Walker Art Gallery Liverpool 1935–1945* National Gallery, London 1945 (17); *George Morland 1763–1804* Reading Museum and Art Gallery 1975 (15).

NOTES

1. Ralph Richardson: *George Morland* (London, 1895) p. 67, citing F. W. Blagdon's *Authentic Memoirs of the Late George Morland* (London, 1806).
2. A *Gypsy Encampment* slightly smaller than WAG 2399 (84.5 × 108 cm) signed and dated 1789 was lent to the *Old Masters* exhibition at the Royal Academy in 1883 by the Earl of Normanton (G. C. Williamson: *George Morland* [London, 1907] p. 131). The *Moonlight, with Gypsies by a Fire* exhibited by Morland at the Free Society of Artists in 1782 (cat. 95), although too early in date to be WAG 2399, anticipates his interest in the subject; Morland also showed at the Society of Artists in 1790 *Landscape with Gypsies* (cat. 191), *Encampment with Gypsies, Now Engraving by J. Grozer* (cat. 201) and *Gypsies Dressing Dinner* (cat. 208) (GrSA, p. 174). William Ward's engraving *Gypsies* after Morland was published in 1792 and Grozer's *Gypsies Tent* after Morland in 1793. Williamson, *op. cit.*, fp. 52, reproduces a further *Gypsy Encampment* owned by F. Abbiss Phillips signed and dated 1795. An undated *Gypsy Camp*, 30 × 40.5 cm, is in the Brooklyn Museum.
3. David Winter: 'George Morland (1763–1804)', PhD thesis, Stanford University, 1977, p. 191 (cat. P157).
4. Lent by Rathbone to the 1842 exhibition. WAG 2399 could be the *Gypsies in a Wood* lent to the *Old Masters of Various Schools and Deceased British Artists* exhibition at the Liverpool Royal Institution 1823 (cat. 103) by Jos. Walker.

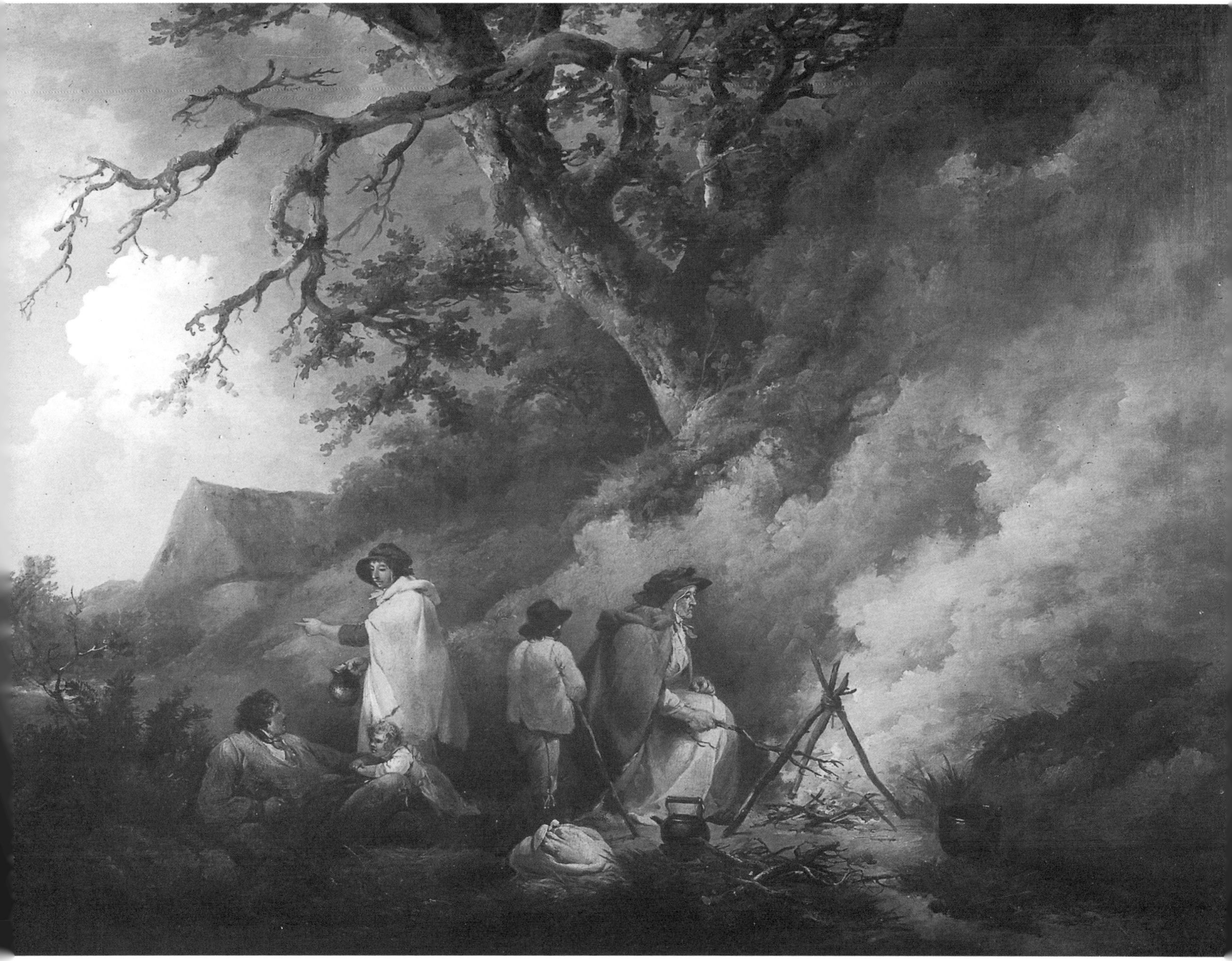

WAG 2399

after

Garret Morphy

active 1673, died 1716

Richard, Later 5th Viscount Molyneux

WAG 8629
oil on canvas, 76.5 × 62 cm

Mrs Mary, Later Lady, Molyneux

WAG 8630
oil on canvas, 76 × 63 cm
date: unknown, perhaps 1710–20

This pair of portraits is part of the group of late seventeenth- and early eighteenth-century Molyneux family portraits formerly at Croxteth Hall outside Liverpool (for a general discussion of which see British School WAG 8627, p. 329). WAG 8629 is the one portrait in the group in which the sitter is securely identified, thanks to the inscription under the coat of arms at upper right, which reads *Richard Vyc. Molyneux*. Born in 1679, he was the eldest son of William, 4th Viscount by his first wife Bridget, née Lucy (of the Lucy family of Charlecote Hall, Warwicks; see pp. 87–9). Richard's wife, the subject of WAG 8630, was Mary Brudenell (1680–1766) daughter of Francis Lord Brudenell, son of the 2nd Earl of Cardigan.[1] The coat of arms in WAG 8629 shows the arms of the Molyneux and Brudenell families conjoined. The couple, who married in February 1705, had three children: a son who died in infancy in 1706, and two daughters, Mary and Dorothy. Richard succeeded his father as 5th Viscount in 1718 and died in 1738.

Both WAG 8629 and WAG 8630, the former obviously, the latter somewhat less clearly, are copies from a pair of portraits by the Irish artist Garret Morphy (now in the National Gallery of Ireland, Dublin, figs. 49–50). Morphy's portraits have been assumed to date from the time of the couple's marriage in 1705,[2] but WAG 8629–30 may well be somewhat later. They are not only crude and weak, arguing that little supervision of the copying took place, but appear intentionally to have eliminated certain specific details of costume and hairstyle in Morphy's originals,[3] suggesting that these were felt to have become dated. Although it is not evident whether the inscribed motto in WAG 8629 is a later addition, it at least must have been painted after Richard's succession to the Viscountcy in 1718, and it seems possible that both portraits date from then or later.

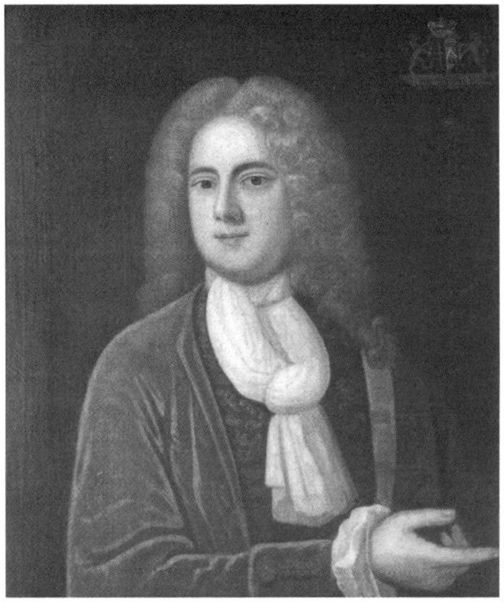

WAG 8629

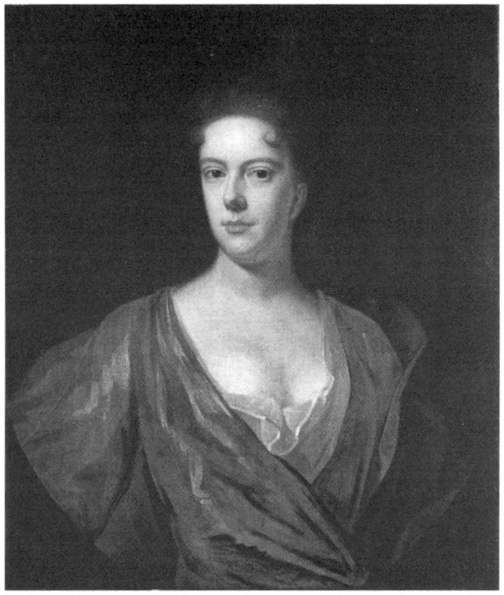

WAG 8630

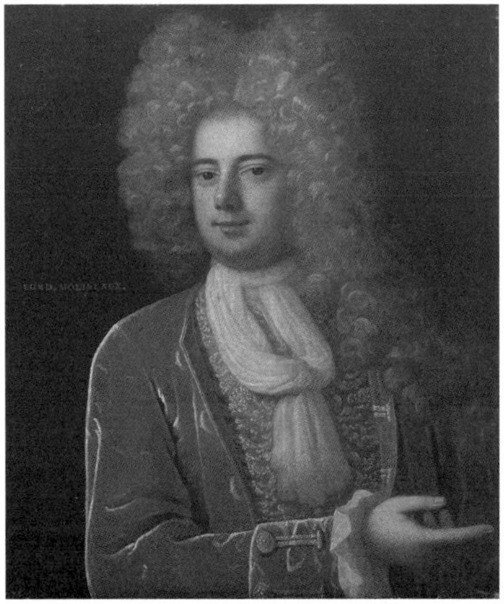

Fig. 49 *Richard, 5th Viscount Molyneux* by Garret Morphy, oil on canvas. National Gallery of Ireland, Dublin. © National Gallery of Ireland.

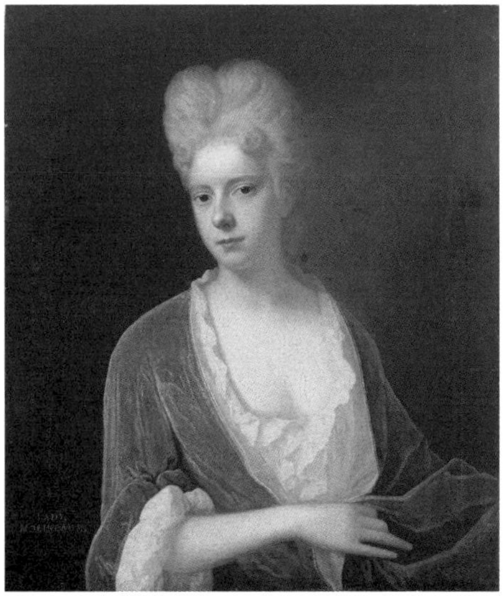

Fig. 50 *Mary, Viscountess Molyneux* by Garret Morphy, oil on canvas. National Gallery of Ireland, Dublin. © National Gallery of Ireland.

PROVENANCE

By descent at Croxteth Hall; bt. in 1974 from the executors of Hugh, 7th Earl of Sefton.

NOTES

1. WAG 8630 bears the inscription *Mrs Mary Molyneux* on its lining canvas, presumably recording an inscription on the back of the original canvas, and was similarly titled in the *1946 Croxteth Inventory*, no. 98. The suggestion made in *MPPP*, p. 49 that the sitter could be Mary, the second wife of the 4th Viscount, whom he married in 1716, or Mary the wife of Hon. Richard Molyneux (d. 1694) – for whom see WAG 8640 (p. 79, n. 1) – falls on the grounds that these ladies would from the start have been known as 'Lady Mary' or 'Mary, Lady Molyneux'.

2. Nicola Figgis and Brendan Rooney: *Irish Paintings in the National Gallery of Ireland, Vol. 1* (Dublin, 2001), pp. 368–72. It is unclear who commissioned Morphy's originals, which descended in the family of the 4th Viscount's sister Frances. She, her husband Neil O'Neill, and the 4th Viscount himself all themselves sat to Morphy (see Jane Fenlon: 'Garret Morphy and his Circle', *Irish Art Review Yearbook* [1991–92], pp. 142–4) and any one of them may have co-ordinated patronage of the artist; but equally they may all have sat at separate times. A complicating factor is that the identity of the sitters in Morphy's Molyneux portraits has been contested: the portrait now held to be of the 4th Viscount (also National Gallery of Ireland) was formerly held to be of Caryll, 3rd Viscount and the portraits of the 5th Viscount and his wife were believed to represent the 4th Viscount and his first wife. The revised identifications (which imply that the inscriptions *LORD MOLINEAUX* and *LADY MOLINEAUX* on the two latter works are later additions) were first put forward by Fenlon, *loc. cit.*, following a visit to Liverpool in 1990 and were followed by Figgis and Rooney, *loc. cit.*

3. However, the copyist has retained the 5th Viscount's Steinkirk neckcloth, which became fashionable from 1692, and his wife's 'favourites', the little curls at her temples, a French fashion from the mid-1690s (Figgis and Rooney, *loc. cit.*).

James Northcote

1746–1831

Self-portrait

WAG 2596
oil on canvas, 77 × 64.5 cm
date: 1811–12

A well-known historical and portrait painter in the last two decades of the eighteenth century and first three of the nineteenth, Northcote was born in Plymouth, the son of a watchmaker. He was the pupil and studio assistant of his fellow-Devonian, Sir Joshua Reynolds, between 1771 and 1776, and spent the years 1777–79 in Italy, where he painted the first three of a long series of self-portraits that, by the first decade of the nineteenth century, had been recognised by contemporaries as a pre-eminent strand within his work. In his later years, Northcote developed

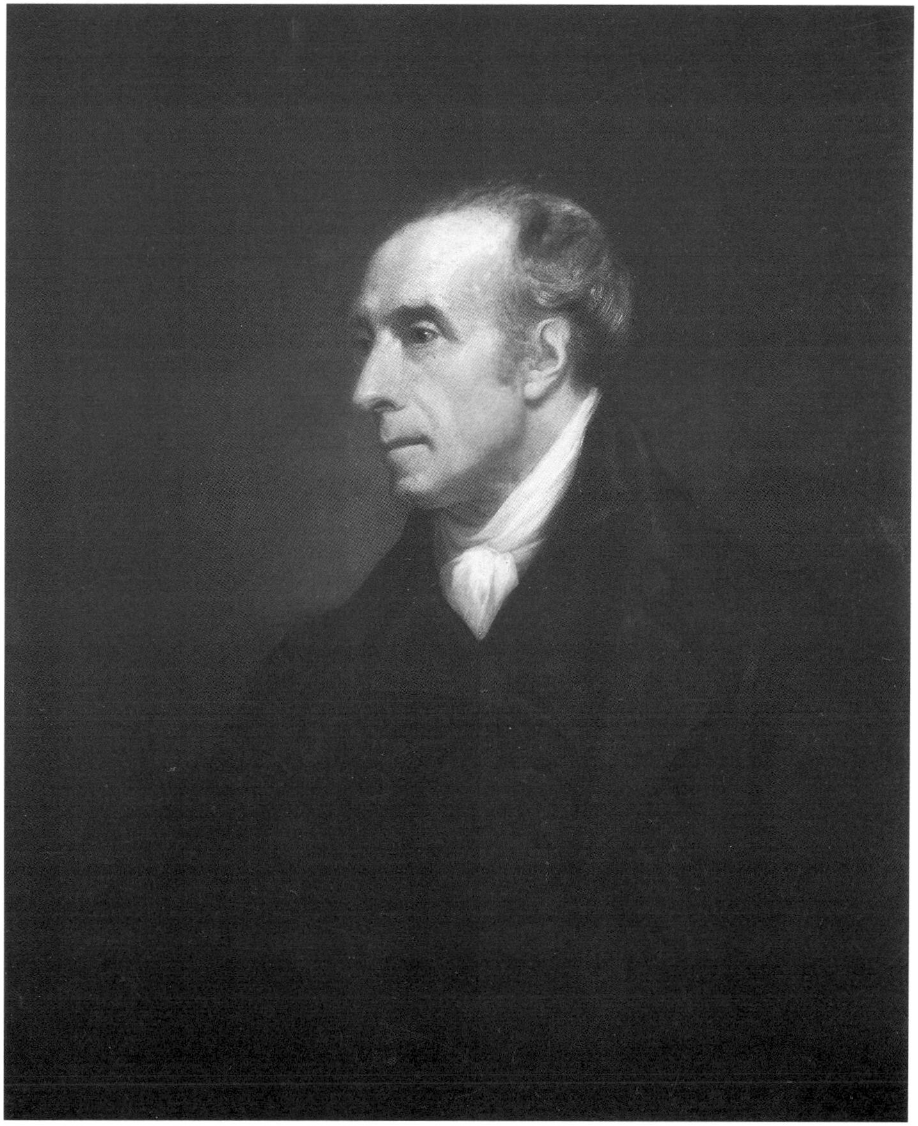

WAG 2596

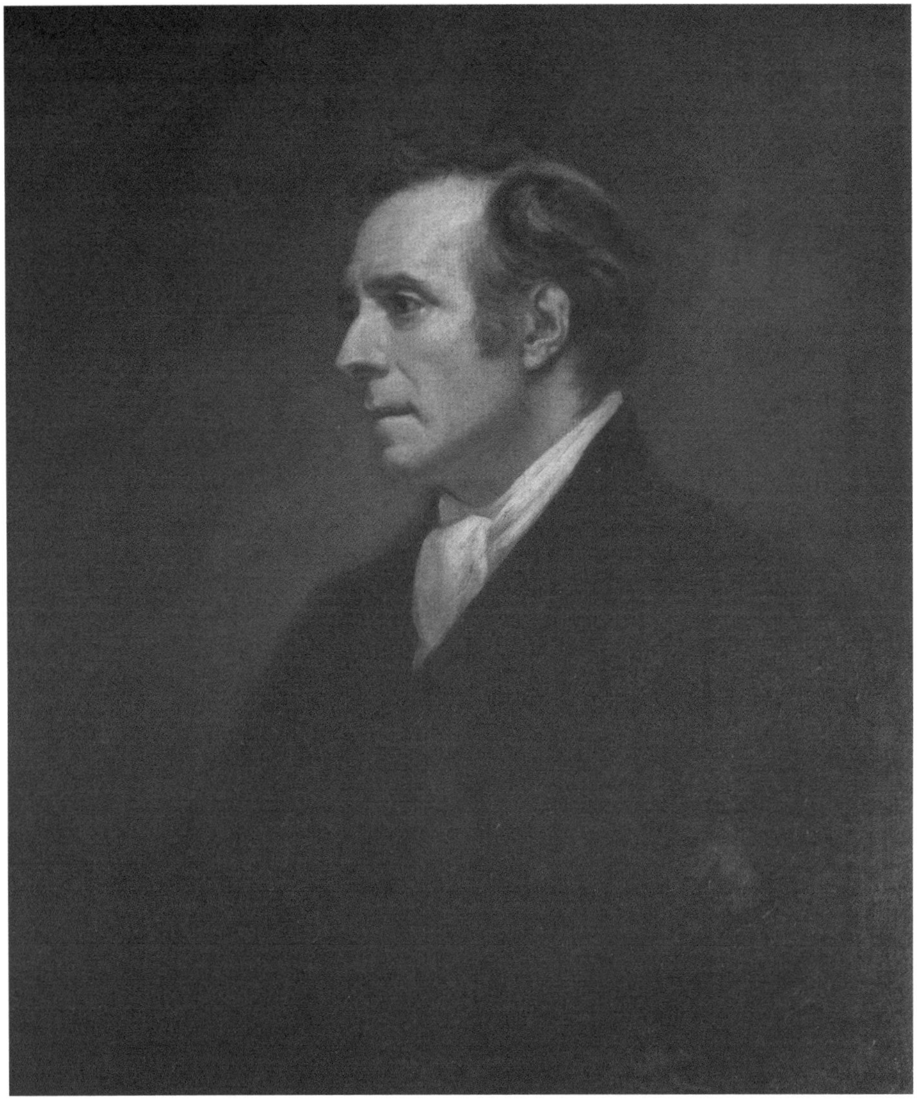

Fig. 51 *Self-portrait* by James Northcote, oil on canvas. Tabley House, University of Manchester; photo Photographic Survey, The Courtauld Institute of Art, London.

the reputation of a character and wit, whose observations and *bons mots* were cherished and preserved for posterity; and he wrote a successful biography of his master Reynolds, first published in 1813 and re-issued in an expanded two-volume version six years later.[1]

WAG 2596 must be the work recorded by Northcote in his account book under the year 1812 as no. 570: *Portrait of myself sold at Liverpool 20 guineas.*[2] Northcote that year sent a self-portrait, together with a *Study of a Philosopher's Head*, to the exhibition of the Liverpool Academy, which had been re-founded in 1810 and was attempting to attract entries from London.[3] Although the provenance is not watertight (for it is not known who bought the work in Liverpool and where) there seems no good reason to question the assumption that it is the same work as the one recorded in the ownership of the Liverpool Royal Institution at least by 1836[4] and said to have been presented to the LRI by one of its proprietors, Richard Rathbone, about 1824.[5]

The work is based closely on a self-portrait Northcote had painted in 1802 for Sir John Leicester (Tabley House, University of Manchester, fig. 51).[6] Northcote has aged himself, and slightly lengthened his nose, but the conception is otherwise identical, down to the treatment of the neck-cloth and strands of hair. Between the two works, Northcote had painted another very similar self-portrait, shown at the Royal Academy in 1808, which, according to Northcote himself, his colleagues declared to be 'the finest portrait that had ever been sent to the Royal Academy' (given by the artist to Jacquetta, wife of Sir Stafford Northcote, 7th Bt.).[7] Later self-portraits by Northcote of 1823 and 1827 repeat the same basic formula with greater variations.[8]

PROVENANCE

Sold by the artist in Liverpool; ...Richard Rathbone before 1836; by whom presented to the Liverpool Royal Institution; transferred to the Walker Art Gallery 1948.

EXHIBITIONS

LA 1812 (181); *Loan Exhibition of Works of Early British Masters* Manchester City Art Gallery 1909 (75); *Liverpool Academy 150th Anniversary Exhibition* Walker Art Gallery 1960 (21).

NOTES

1. See Martin Postle: 'Northcote, James', ODNB vol. 41, pp. 135–9; also S. Gwynn: *Memorials of an Eighteenth-century Portrait Painter* (London, 1898) and Jacob Simon: 'The Account Book of James Northcote', *Walpole Society* vol. 58 (1995–96) pp. 21–125.
2. Simon, *op. cit.*, p. 95.
3. The two exhibits of 1812 were followed in 1813 by *The Flight of the Angels Appearing to the Shepherds at the Birth of Christ* (cat. 113) and *The Interior View of Goring Church* (cat. 207); Northcote did not show again in Liverpool after this date (*LAOE*, p. 455).
4. *LRI 1836 Catalogue*, p. 30; provenance unrecorded.
5. Rathbone, who also presented three Flemish and two Dutch pictures to the Institution, is first recorded as the donor in the *LRI 1859 Catalogue*, p. 88; however, a copy of the Institution's 1819 catalogue annotated by Thomas Winstanley around 1824 gives Rathbone as the previous owner (note in gallery files). The location of this catalogue is unknown.

6. Simon, *op. cit.*, p.75 (no. 390).
7. FD, vol. 9, p. 3256 (entry of 10 April 1808). This portrait was sold at Sotheby 8 April 1992 (49).
8. The 1823 portrait was sold at Christie New York 6 October 1994 (113); the 1827 one is in the National Portrait Gallery; see Richard Walker: *National Portrait Gallery Regency Portraits* 2 vols (London, 1985) vol.1, pp. 371–2.

John Opie

1761–1807

Mrs Ann Elliott

WAG 283
oil on canvas,[1] 77 × 64.5 cm
date: about 1800

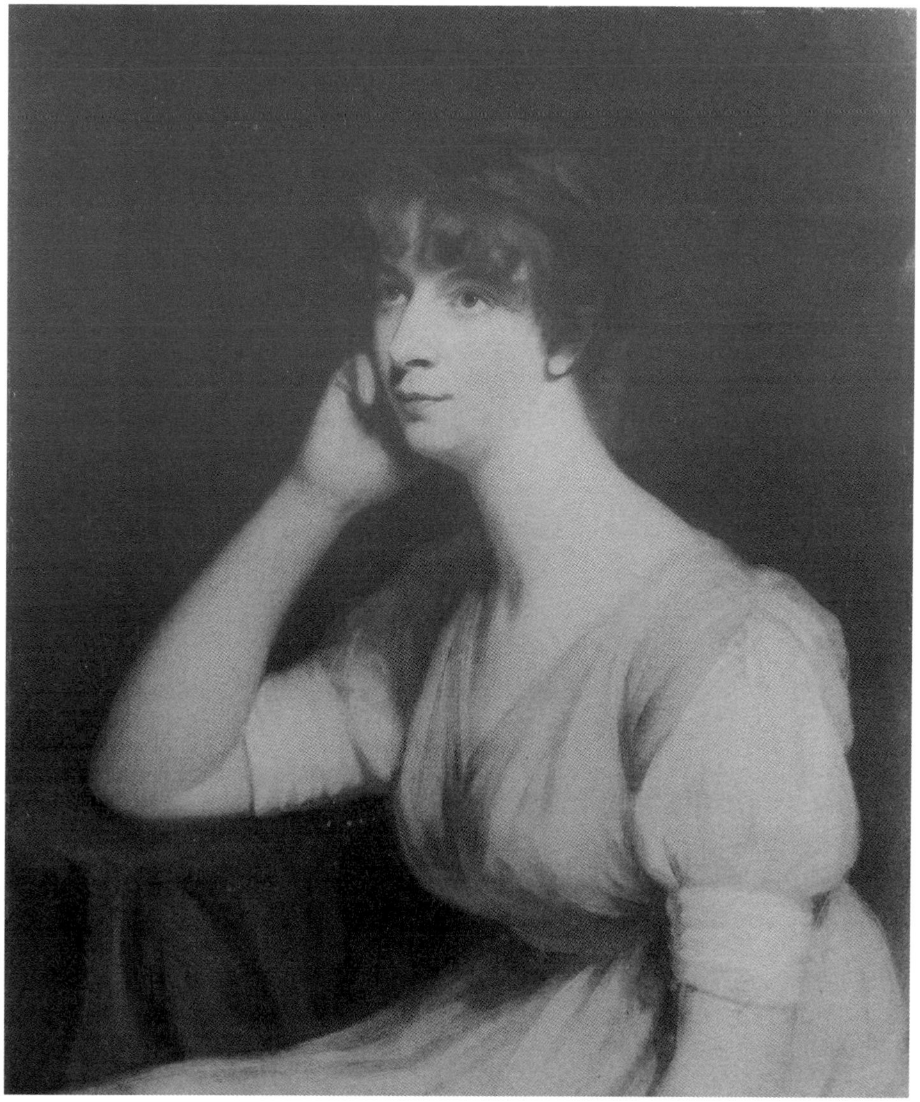

WAG 283

Ann Maria Elliott was the daughter of George Maltby, a master-weaver of Norwich, and his wife Mary; and sister of Edward Maltby (1770–1859), future Bishop of Durham.[2] Her father was Deacon of the Presbyterian Octagon Chapel in Norwich which had been frequented by the family of Opie's second wife Amelia Alderson,[3] and it seems certain that it was she who introduced Mrs Elliott to Opie, presumably not long after her marriage to him in 1798. Opie seems to have made several portraits of Mrs Elliott, and comparison between WAG 283 and a related work, in which she is shown in white rather than her present buff dress,[4] suggests that he viewed her more as a model than as a formal client: the emphasis is on her personality and intellect, rather than her looks or fashionable attire. Both works have been dated to about 1800.[5]

PROVENANCE

Said to have been bought from Opie by Revd Pretyman, Prebend of Norwich;[6] by descent to his grand-daughter Mrs Fraser-Tytler; from whom bt. by Agnew; from whom bt. by George Holt June 1889; Emma Holt Bequest 1945.

EXHIBITION

Pictures by Artists Contemporary with Those Represented in the Wrigley Collection Bury Art Gallery 1913 (29).

NOTES

1. Canvas stamp of *Jas. Poole, High Holborn*, with customs stamp 644/J75/75.
2. See E. A. Varley: 'Maltby, Edward', ODNB vol. 36, pp. 361–3. Little biographical information exists on Ann Maria Elliott. She was married to a Lt.-Col. Elliott (see Dudley Heath: 'Some Recently Discovered Miniatures by Robertson, Plimer, Cosway, Engleheart and Smart', *Connoisseur* vol. 25 [September 1909] p. 26), and is said by Ada Earland: *John Opie and His Circle* (1911) p. 275, to have died about 1853. Potential confusion exists between her and the celebrated courtesan Ann Elliott (d. 1769) who was apostrophised by Richard Cosway as 'one of the Three Graces', since Cosway made miniatures of both her and the present Ann Elliott; for the latter see Christie 20 March 1989 (132) where the 'Graces' story is erroneously applied to her.
3. See Gary Kelly: 'Opie [née Alderson] Amelia', ODNB vol. 41, p. 889.
4. Repr. Earland, *op. cit.*, fp. 273, owned in 1911 by F. M. Bland.
5. J. Rogers: *Opie and His Works* (London, 1878) p. 90 dated WAG 283 'about 1800'; followed by Earland, *op. cit.*, p. 275, who dated the other version 'about 1799'. A third portrait by Opie of Mrs Elliott was owned by the artist Charles Cope and sold by his

executors at Christie 8 June 1872 (100).
6. Pretyman was presumably related to George Pretyman, Bishop of Lincoln, who was married to Ann and Edward Maltby's cousin Elizabeth and who had helped direct Edward Maltby's education (see Varley, *op. cit.*, p. 362).

attributed to

Joseph Paul

1804–87

Landscape with Tree

WAG 216
oil on canvas,[1] 76 × 63.5 cm
date: unknown, perhaps 1825–50

The composition of WAG 216 is loosely based on John Crome's masterpiece *The Poringland Oak* (Tate Britain, London; fig. 52), and, in the detail of the cottage in the background, on his etching of 1812, *The Hall Moor Road near Hingham*.[2] It has long been recognised to be by an imitator of Crome's work, rather than by Crome himself.[3] The attribution to Paul, who is said to have been one of Crome's last pupils and who enjoyed a long career as a pasticheur of Norwich School subjects,[4] is particularly suggested by the treatment of the sunlit branch at the lower right of the tree, with its distinctive 'antlered' effect. The warm tonality, the thick, clogged handling of paint, and the sentimentalised depiction of the bathers, are all also consistent with an attribution to Paul.

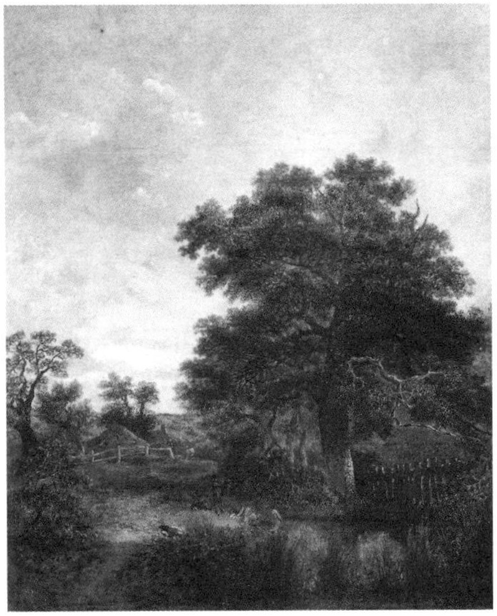

WAG 216

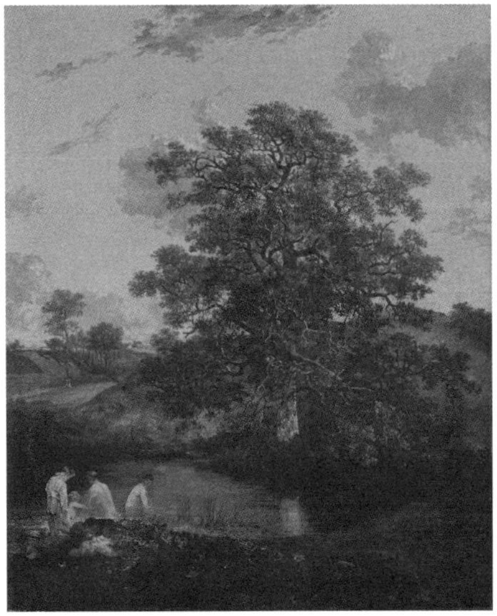

Fig. 52 *The Poringland Oak* by John Crome, oil on canvas. © Tate, London, 2011.

PROVENANCE

...Mrs Owen Roe 1889; bt. Gooden; from whom bt. 12 May 1891 by George Holt; Emma Holt Bequest 1945.

EXHIBITIONS

Old Masters RA 1889 (138); *Loan Exhibition of Works of Early British Masters* Manchester City Art Gallery 1909 (28).

NOTES

1. The canvas, which has been re-lined with a heavy glue lining, seems originally to have consisted of two pieces, joined together horizontally at a point about 53 cm from the bottom. The joint cuts across the topmost foliage of the tree, and is disguised by considerable retouching (condition and treatment report, August 1967, gallery files).
2. D. and T. Clifford: *John Crome* (London, 1968) pp. 169, 177, 232; and compare C. H. Collins Baker: *Crome* (London, 1921) p. 59: 'I know of two derivatives of the true "Poringland Oak", one, very clever, in Mr Hollingsworth's collection; the other in that of Miss Holt, at Mossley Hill.'
3. See n. 2; the similar opinion of Miklos Rajnai was conveyed by John Gage, *letter*, 11 February 1970 (gallery files).
4. On Paul see Norfolk Museums Service: *Joseph Paul (1804–1887)* (typescript; n.d.); also A. Kidson: *Earlier British Paintings in the Lady Lever Art Gallery* (Liverpool, 1999) pp.116–7.

Edward Penny

1714–91

William Farrington

WAG 6170
oil on canvas, 76 × 63 cm
date: 1744

The canvas is inscribed on the reverse *William – Farrington Esqr / of Shaw Hall / Lancashire / 1744 / Aetis 24 / Edward Pennee*. Born in 1721, William was the son of George Farrington and Margaret Bradshaw who married in 1717. The Farrington (or as they spelt it Ffarington) family was long established in the district and was closely connected to the Earls of Derby to whom numerous Farringtons had acted as Secretaries, Comptrollers of the Household, and Stewards; they had also been High Sheriffs of Lancashire, Constables of Lancaster Castle and Mayors of Preston. William himself (who was first cousin of the younger Joseph Farington, artist and famous diarist) was High Sheriff of Lancashire and knighted in 1761. He had a particular interest in art and antiquities, and travelled to Italy in 1765 where he made several purchases.[1] Soon after inheriting Shaw Hall in 1742 he altered and enlarged the house and a *Catalogue of the Pictures at Shawe Hall* drawn up by him sometime between 1761 and his death in 1782 lists numerous old masters as well as family portraits.[2] WAG 6170 cannot be positively identified on this list, which mentions only one work by Penny, a head of Mr Wright of Mobberley.[3] Although several unattributed portraits of 'Sir Wm. Ffarington' are also

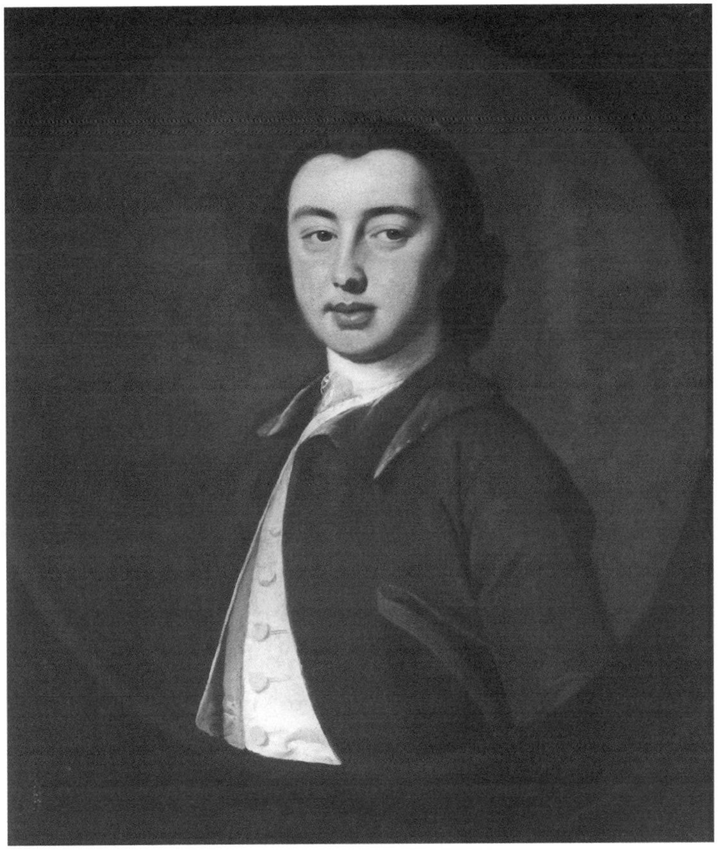

WAG 6170

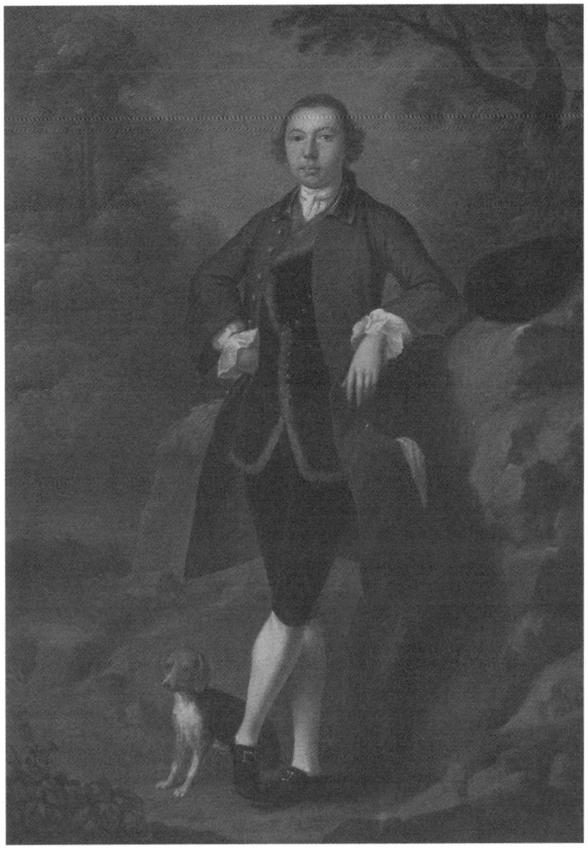

Fig. 53 *William Farington of Shawe Hall, Lancashire* by Arthur Devis, oil on canvas. Yale Center for British Art, Paul Mellon Collection.

recorded on the list, and it is conceivable that WAG 6170 is one of these,[4] a much more likely scenario (given that the portrait's known provenance begins with a man named Wallis-Wright) is that this portrait was sent to Mobberley as the other half of an exchange of friendship portraits, for both of which Penny was employed. The existence of a portrait of Farrington's mother by Penny dated 1742[5] indicates that the family had already commissioned work from the artist, who had just returned from Italy and, being originally from Cheshire, would have been considered a promising local young talent. The sitter's likeness appears closely comparable to that in two portraits of Farrington by Arthur Devis dating from the early 1740s.[6]

PROVENANCE

[? Painted for Mr Wright of Mobberley and by descent to] Major Aubrey Wallis-Wright about 1922;[7] ...[? A. W. Holliday 1930];[8] ...Christie 22 October 1943 (131); bt. Arnot (7 gns.); ...Christie 16 November 1962 (58); (bt. in);[9] 'a gentleman'; Christie 8 February 1963 (140); bt. Agnew (18 gns.) for the gallery.

NOTES

1. J. Ingamells: *A Dictionary of British and Irish Travellers in Italy 1701–1800* (New Haven and London, 1997) pp. 348–9; and see also *FD*, vol. 1, p.xiv.
2. *Farrington Papers* DDF6, Lancashire Record Office, Preston.
3. *Ibid.*, fol. 7: in the Yellow Bed Chamber, no. 2, William Farrington's cash-book (*Farrington Papers* DDF 32) p. 20, shows that this was conveyed to Shaw Hall from Warrington in October 1744.
4. The likeliest candidate would be no. 9 in the Breakfast Room.
5. This was at Rufford Hall, Lancs (about ten miles from Shaw Hall) in 1965. According to George Vertue, Penny only returned to England from his visit to Italy in 1743, but he appears to have been in Venice, the last port of call on his Grand Tour, in January 1742, so it seems likely that he was in fact back in England later that year; see Ingamells, *op. cit.*, p. 756.
6. Arthur Devis: *William Farington of Shawe Hall, Lancashire*, about 1743, Yale Center for British Art, New Haven (Paul Mellon Collection, fig. 53). This derives from Devis's *Robert Gwillym and William Farington* of the same date (Yale University Art Gallery); see Ellen D'Oench: *The Conversation Piece: Arthur Devis and His Contemporaries*, exh. cat., Yale Center for British Art, New Haven (1980) pp. 47–8 (cats. 9–10).
7. James Greig, ed.: *Farington's Diary: The Diary of Joseph Farington R. A.* 8 vols (London, 1922–28), vol. 1, p. 65, n.
8. Annotation to a photograph of WAG 6170 in the Heinz Archive, National Portrait Gallery.
9. WAG 6170 was consigned to the 1962 sale by James Bourlet, the London art handling company, as part of a large group of items owned by a client.

Henry Pickering

active 1740, died 1770/71

Mrs Thomas Johnson and Her Daughter

WAG 7015
oil on canvas, 126 × 100 cm
signed and dated: *H. Pickering Pinxt. 1759*
(on the base of the pillar)

Thomas Johnson

WAG 7016
oil on canvas, 127 × 101 cm
date: 1759

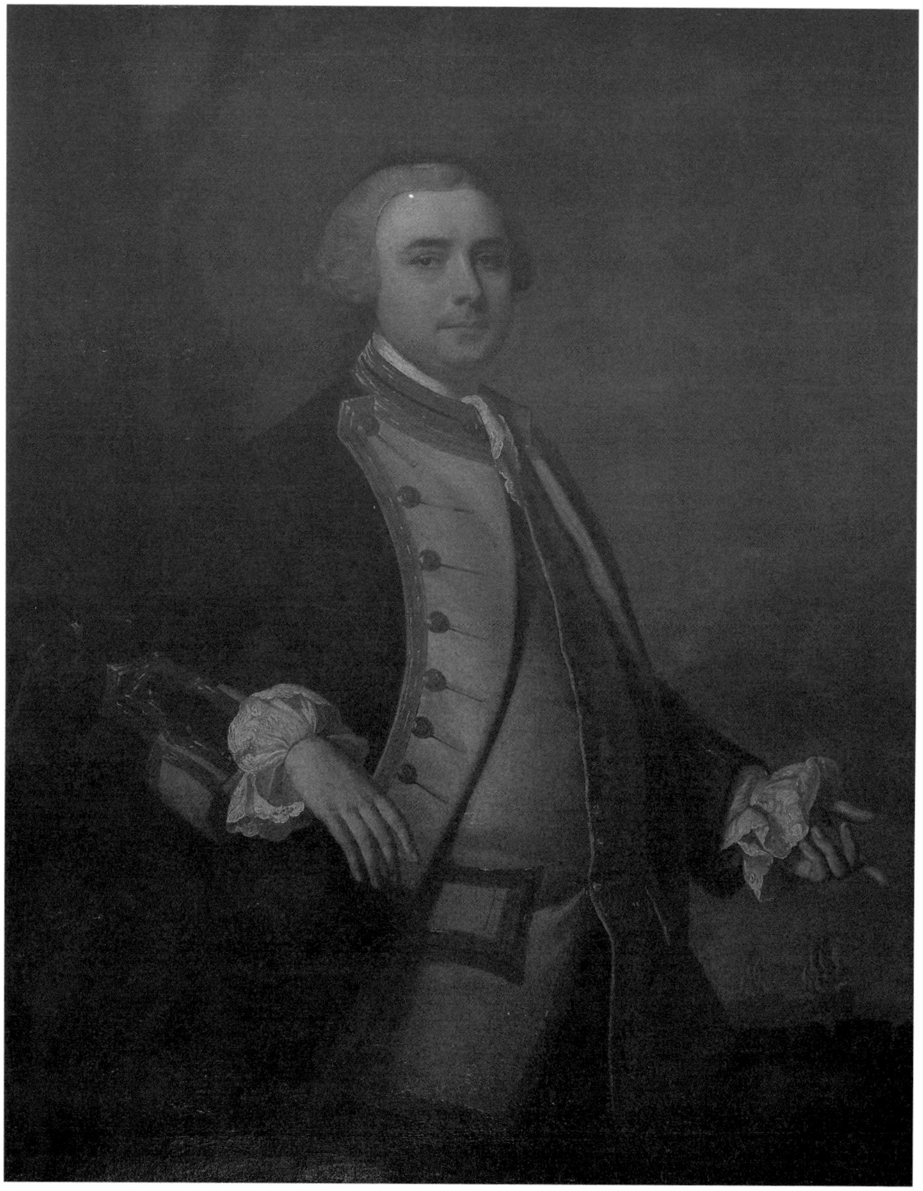

WAG 7016

A label on the reverse of WAG 7016, dating from after its purchase by Liverpool Corporation, reads, *Mr Thomas Johnson / Mayor of Liverpool 1766–7. / The Uniform is that of a Colonel of / a regiment raised by him to repel a / threatened French invasion of the town. / Portrait painted by Pickering / purchased in 1912.* In an article about the new volunteer regiments, *Williamson's Advertiser*, 14 March 1760, describes Johnson as 'Captain' rather than Colonel. The article goes on to describe the uniform worn by his 'company of the train of artillery' as 'the uniform of the navy, blue and buff, with gold lace hats'.[1] The volunteer regiments, together with batteries to defend the sea approaches to Liverpool, had been mooted in meetings between the Mayor and merchants of the town held in early November 1759.[2] Therefore, if Johnson decided to commission the pair of portraits as a consequence of his new position of importance, they were painted right at the end of that year, going by the date inscribed on WAG 7015.

Little is known about the sitters. Johnson is listed in the Liverpool street directories of 1766, 1767 and 1769 as a merchant in Lord Street; in the first year he was a Town Councillor, in the second, Mayor, and in the third, Alderman. He died on 24 February 1771.[3] His burial has not been traced and neither for certain has his marriage nor the baptism of the daughter in WAG 7015.[4] The locket held by Mrs Johnson does not provide any clue to her identity.

Pickering, a provincial painter who moved from town to town in the Midlands, may have painted WAG 7015–16 on an extended visit from Manchester, where he was chiefly based in later life.[5] He was well known for employing drapery painters to complete his portraits, and there is a distinct hint of this in WAG 7015.

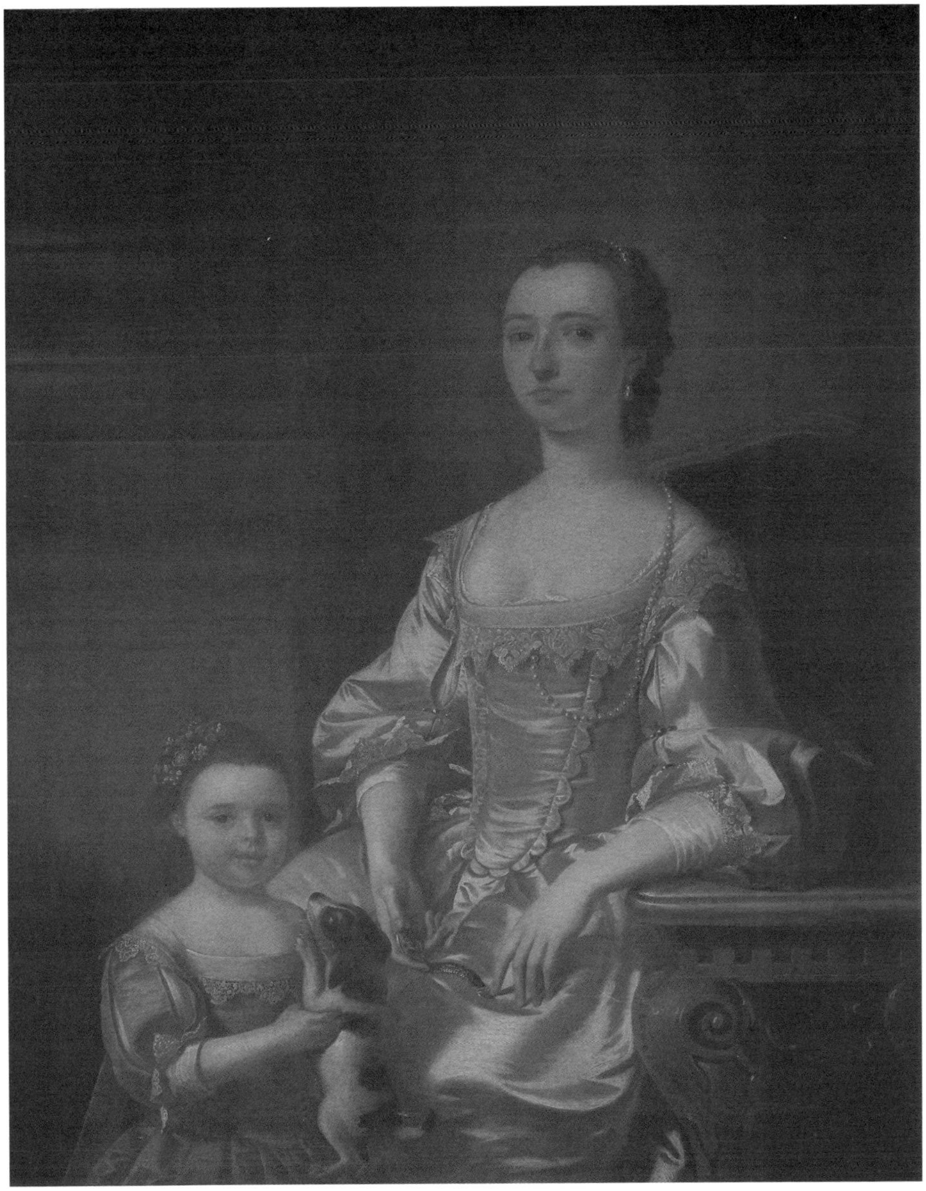

WAG 7015

PROVENANCE

…Bt. by Liverpool Corporation 1912; transferred from the City Estates Committee 1968.

NOTES

1. *Williamson's Advertiser*, 14 March 1760, quoted in Sir J. A. Picton; *Memorials of Liverpool* 2 vols (Liverpool, 1873) vol. 1, p. 220.
2. Picton, *op. cit.*, vol. 1, pp. 218–9.
3. *Liverpool General Advertiser or the Commercial Register*, 1 March 1771, p. 3: 'Sunday Last died Thomas Johnson Esq; an Alderman of this Corporation'.
4. Liverpool church registers of the 1750s list numerous Thomas Johnsons. The likeliest candidate for him appears to be Captain Thomas Johnson, described in 1755 as a mariner of Duke Street (a street of merchant houses) whose youngest daughter Ann was baptised at St George's Church on 5 July 1753. He had married Ellen Anton of West Kirby at the same church on 10 February 1746, and the couple had two elder and two younger children, born between 1750 and 1755 (the younger ones both sons). However, the identification is highly speculative; for example, it seems unlikely that his wife should have been depicted solely with their third child.
5. For other possible paintings executed by Pickering in Liverpool at this time, see Alex Kidson: 'The Liverpool Art Scene 1745–1770', in E. Barker and A. Kidson: *Joseph Wright of Derby in Liverpool*, exh. cat., Walker Art Gallery and Yale Center for British Art, New Haven (2007) p. 38, n. 28.

Henry Raeburn

1756–1823

Mrs Ann Graham

WAG 2582
oil on canvas, 78 × 63.5 cm
date: about 1795

The sitter is Ann, only daughter of Sir Henry Stirling of Ardoch. She was born about 1740 and married William Graham of Airth, near Stirling, on 6 February 1760. William Graham died in 1790 at the age of 60,[1] and Mrs Graham is portrayed by Raeburn in widow's garb. This, in conjunction with the style of the costume[2] and with Mrs Graham's apparent age, suggests that WAG 2582 dates from no later than the mid-1790s, and a date of about 1795 is supported by considerations of Raeburn's stylistic development.[3]

A copy of WAG 2582 which remained in the possession of the Stirling family was traditionally identified as of Mrs Graham's daughter Mary (1762–1820) who married John Stirling of Kippendavie in 1781. He and his youngest daughter Jean were painted as a full-length double portrait by Raeburn in about 1813 (Forbes-Leith Collection, Fyvie Castle) and it was assumed that John Stirling must have commissioned this portrait of his wife at the same time.[4] However, WAG 2582 is stylistically quite distinct from the Fyvie double portrait. It is not known when Mrs Graham died but it is likely that

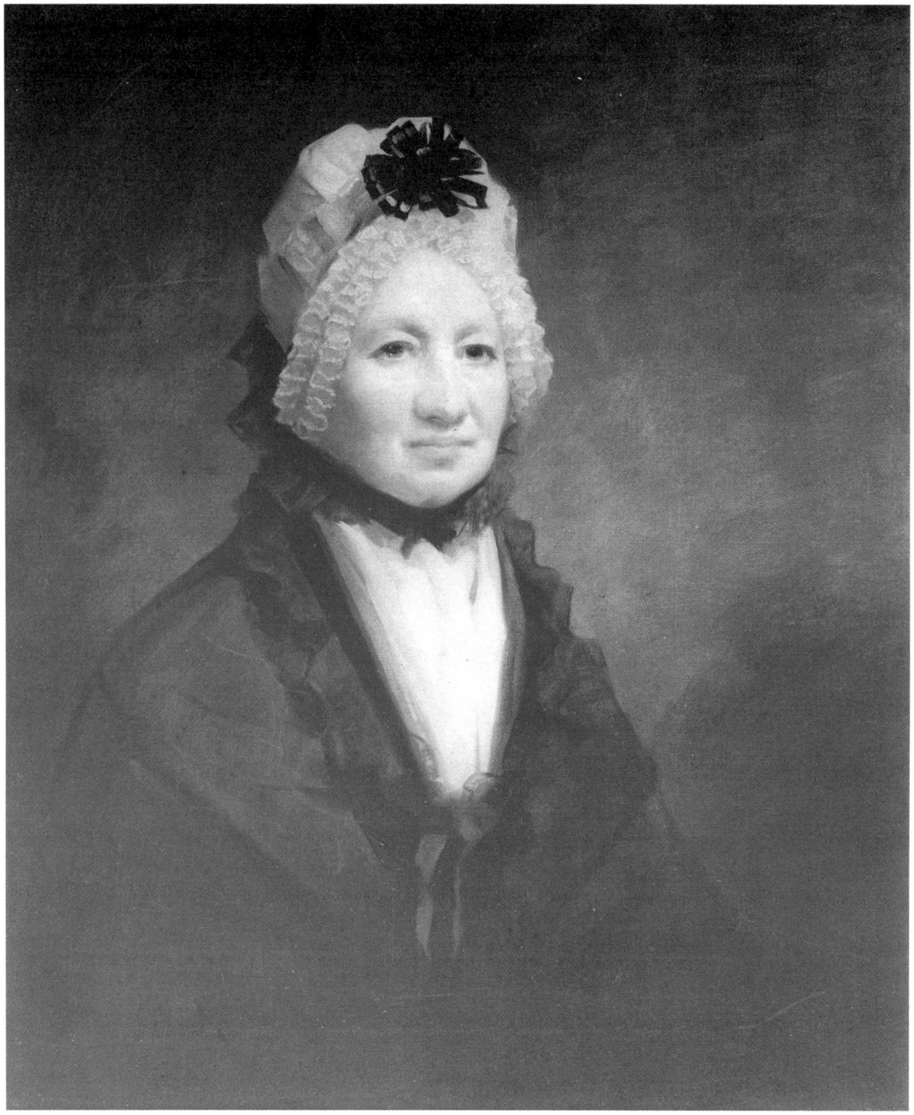

WAG 2582

WAG 2582 had by 1813 passed from her possession into that of her daughter Mary and thus acted as a spur for the Stirlings' later commission from Raeburn.

PROVENANCE

[? By descent to the sitter's second daughter, Mrs Mary Stirling and] by descent in the Stirling family to Col. J. A. Stirling, Kippenross House, Dunblane; from whom bt. in 1912 by Agnew;[5] bt. by Holbrook Gaskell; Christie 11 June 1920 (37); bt. in by Gaskell's executor, James King of Liverpool; from whom re-purchased by Agnew in or before 1933;[6] from whom bt. December 1933.

EXHIBITIONS

59th Liverpool Autumn Exhibition Walker Art Gallery 1933 (33); *Some Acquisitions of the Walker Art Gallery Liverpool 1935–1945* National Gallery, London 1945 (15); *Dve století britského malírství* [*Two Centuries of British Painting*] Narodnì Galerie, Prague and tour of Central Europe 1969–70 (108).[7]

NOTES

1. *Burke's Landed Gentry* 2 vols (2nd edn, London, 1853) vol. 2, supplement p. 141.
2. Anne Buck, *letter*, 28 March 1961, gallery files, described the shaping of the cap as fashionable for the 1790s, and 'not really characteristic of 1800–20'.
3. Duncan Thomson, *verbally*, 15 November 2007.
4. P. D. Stirling, Kippenross (younger brother of the vendor of WAG 2582) *letter*, 30 May 1945, gallery files; and re-iterated in a second letter dated 5 April 1961. Perhaps influenced by the same consideration, David Mackie: 'Raeburn: Life and Art. A Complete Catalogue of the Artist's Work', PhD thesis, University of Edinburgh, 1994, dated WAG 2582 to perhaps about 1810. WAG 2582 is mentioned in no Raeburn literature prior to Mackie's thesis. The copy referred to by Stirling was at Philipstoun House, Linlithgow, in 1961.
5. Mackie, *loc. cit.*, gives this date for the work's purchase by Agnew's; Stirling, *op. cit.*, gives about 1907–10.
6. Lent by Agnew's to the 1933 exhibition.
7. WAG 2582 was damaged in transit between the Prague and Bratislava showings of this exhibition when the canvas and stretcher became detached from the frame and the varnish surface was scratched in three places (P. Cannon-Brookes, *letter*, 18 September 1969, gallery files). The damage was repaired at the end of the exhibition by J. Coburn Witherop.

Girl Sketching

WAG 289
oil on canvas, 76 × 63.5 cm
date: about 1811–17

The identity of the sitter in WAG 289 is unknown. George Holt, in his manuscript catalogue of his pictures (gallery archives), perhaps in receipt of a verbal tradition, but possibly in recognition of the picture's exceptional informality and even intimacy, identified her as 'Miss Raeburn', that is, a member of the artist's own family, putatively a grand-daughter. It is unlikely that she is the artist's grand-daughter; Raeburn's two sons, Peter and Henry (born in 1781 and 1783 respectively) would have been too young to have had a nearly grown-up daughter at the presumptive date of this work, which has been placed in the 1810s.[1] The painting was not titled *Miss Raeburn* but only *A Young Girl Sitting, Leaning on a Portfolio* when it was exhibited in 1876 and when sold at Christie's in 1887.

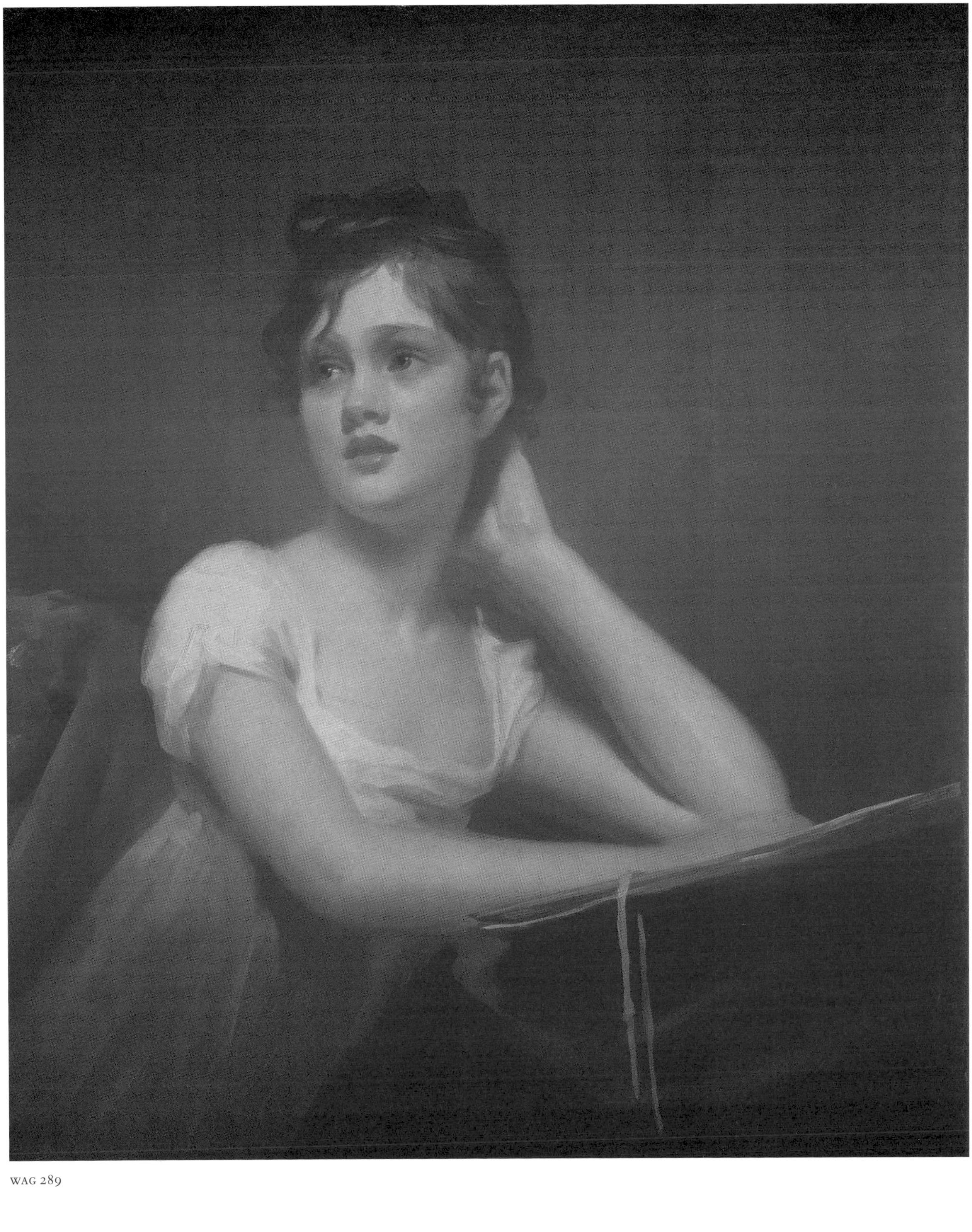

WAG 289

More likely the sitter is a relative of WAG 289's first recorded owner, James Thomson Gibson-Craig (1799–1886), in later life celebrated Edinburgh bibliophile and in his youth a member of Raeburn's circle. In the early 1810s Gibson-Craig's father, also James, commissioned from Raeburn three portraits of himself, his wife Anne and his eldest son William (acquired in 2001 by Heriot-Watt University, Edinburgh) and it may be that this is a portrait, undertaken at about the same time, of one of the elder of the seven daughters of the marriage; perhaps Anne (d. 1869) who in 1828 married John Hay Mackenzie. Another possibility is James Gibson-Craig's wife Jane, second daughter of Sir John Peter Grant of Rothiemurchus (1774–1848); she was born about 1800, married Gibson-Craig (as her second husband) in 1841 and died in 1863.

PROVENANCE

...James Thomson Gibson-Craig; Christie 23 April 1887 (24); bt. Agnew (£173 5s); bt. from Agnew in June 1887 by George Holt; by descent; Emma Holt Bequest 1945.

EXHIBITIONS

Raeburn Edinburgh 1876 (141); *International Exhibition* Glasgow 1888 (308); *International Exhibition* Glasgow 1901 (22); *Exhibition of Twenty Pictures by Masters of the Early English School on Behalf of the Liverpool Royal Infirmary* Agnew's, Liverpool 1902 (1);[2] *Loan Collection of Portraits* Birmingham Museum and Art Gallery 1903 (40); *Liverpool Autumn Exhibition* Walker Art Gallery 1907 (1158);[3] *59th Liverpool Autumn Exhibition* Walker Art Gallery 1933 (30); *Some Acquisitions of the Walker Art Gallery Liverpool 1935–1945* National Gallery, London 1945 (16); *Treasures from Sudley: A Liverpool Shipowner's Home* Haworth Art Gallery, Accrington and tour 2005–06 (no cat.).

NOTES

1. Robin Hutchison, Scottish National Portrait Gallery, *letter*, 12 February 1959, gallery files. J. L. Caw: *Portraits by Sir Henry Raeburn* (Edinburgh 1909), included WAG 289 (under the title *Girl Sketching*) as 27th of 56 portraits in an album 'arranged in approximate chronological order' (p. vii). David Mackie: 'Raeburn: Life and Art. A Complete Catalogue of the Artist's Work', PhD thesis, University of Edinburgh, 1994, dated WAG 289 to about 1820; this may have been in order to accommodate the hypothesis that the sitter was Raeburn's grand-daughter. Duncan Thomson, *letter*, 12 October 2009, gallery files, suggested 'a bit later than 1815 but not as late as 1820'.
2. *A Girl Sketching*, lender unspecified; but the exhibition catalogue stated that the work had been lent to the Glasgow exhibition in 1901 and that all the exhibits were lent by 'well known citizens of Liverpool'.
3. Without title; but lent by Mrs Holt.

Allan Ramsay

1713–84

Mrs Elizabeth Symonds

WAG 1355
oil on canvas, 127.5 × 101.5 cm
signed and dated: *A. Ramsay. 1740*
(lower left, on the pedestal)
date: 1740

The sitter (christened 25 March 1716, died April 1776) was the daughter of John Cotman of Yarmouth. She married on 17 April 1740, as his second wife, Cotton Symonds (1703–61) of Ormesby Hall, Norfolk, son of Jonathan Symonds and his wife Mary née Cotton. He carried out notable improvements to the house and gardens at Ormesby and he became High Sherriff of Norfolk in 1756. The couple remained childless, and after Elizabeth's death Ormesby and its contents passed to her husband's relation Nathaniel Symonds, with remainder to his son (Cotton Symonds's godson) James. Elizabeth was buried in Ormesby Church.[1]

Ramsay was in his 27th year and at the first peak of his career[2] when he painted WAG 1355. The work must have been painted in London, not Norfolk, and was almost certainly commissioned to mark the sitter's wedding. Mrs Symonds wears a silver-coloured sack dress with wide robings, and a separate muslin bodice with light pink bow and a plain muslin cap.[3] The urn in the background may indicate that her father was recently deceased (and the fact that she was now an heiress may well have been the *raison d'être* for her marriage); however, the fact that the portrait has traditionally been known under the title *Miss Elizabeth Cotman*, when taken with the obscurity of the work's early history, perhaps indicates that it was commissioned for her natal family, rather than for her husband.

PROVENANCE

...Bt. from an unknown source by Clement Parsons (1864–1940) some years before 1920;[4] by descent to Dr Richard Parsons, Kirkby-in-Furness;[5] from whom bt. by the gallery 1952.

EXHIBITIONS

Selected Acquisitions of the Walker Art Gallery Liverpool 1945–1955 Agnew's, London 1955 (3); *Painting and Sculpture in England* Walker Art Gallery 1958 (37); *Ramsay and Wilkie* Paisley Museum and Art Gallery 1967 (28).

NOTES

1. Biographical information on the Symonds family derived from J. H. Druery: *Historical and Topographical Notices of Great Yarmouth* (London, 1826) pp. 116, 123, 126, Charles J. Palmer, ed.: *The History of Great Yarmouth by Henry Manship* (Great Yarmouth, 1854) and Philip Morant, *The History and Antiquities of the County of Essex* 2 vols (London, 1768) vol. 2, p. 302, cited by Richard Parsons, *letter*, 21 February 1952, gallery files.
2. The total of 36 portraits painted or begun by Ramsay in 1740 was easily his highest annual figure to date and remained his highest until 1748; see A. Smart and J. Ingamells: *Allan Ramsay: A Complete Catalogue of his Paintings* (New Haven and London, 1999) p. 421.
3. Aileen Ribeiro, *letter*, 8 November 1979, gallery files.
4. Parsons, *loc. cit.*, stated that the portrait was purchased, not inherited by Clement Parsons (who was descended from the Cotton family, i.e. collateral relations of the sitter's mother-in-law), that it had been at Clement Parsons's house in Broadway, Worcestershire between 1920 and 1940 and that he had known the work previously at two of his uncle's houses in London.
5. Smart and Ingamells, *op. cit.*, p. 188, state that Parsons bought WAG 1355 in 1940 at his uncle's sale but Parsons himself, *loc. cit.*, stated only that 'it came to me on his death' and gallery files state that it was inherited.

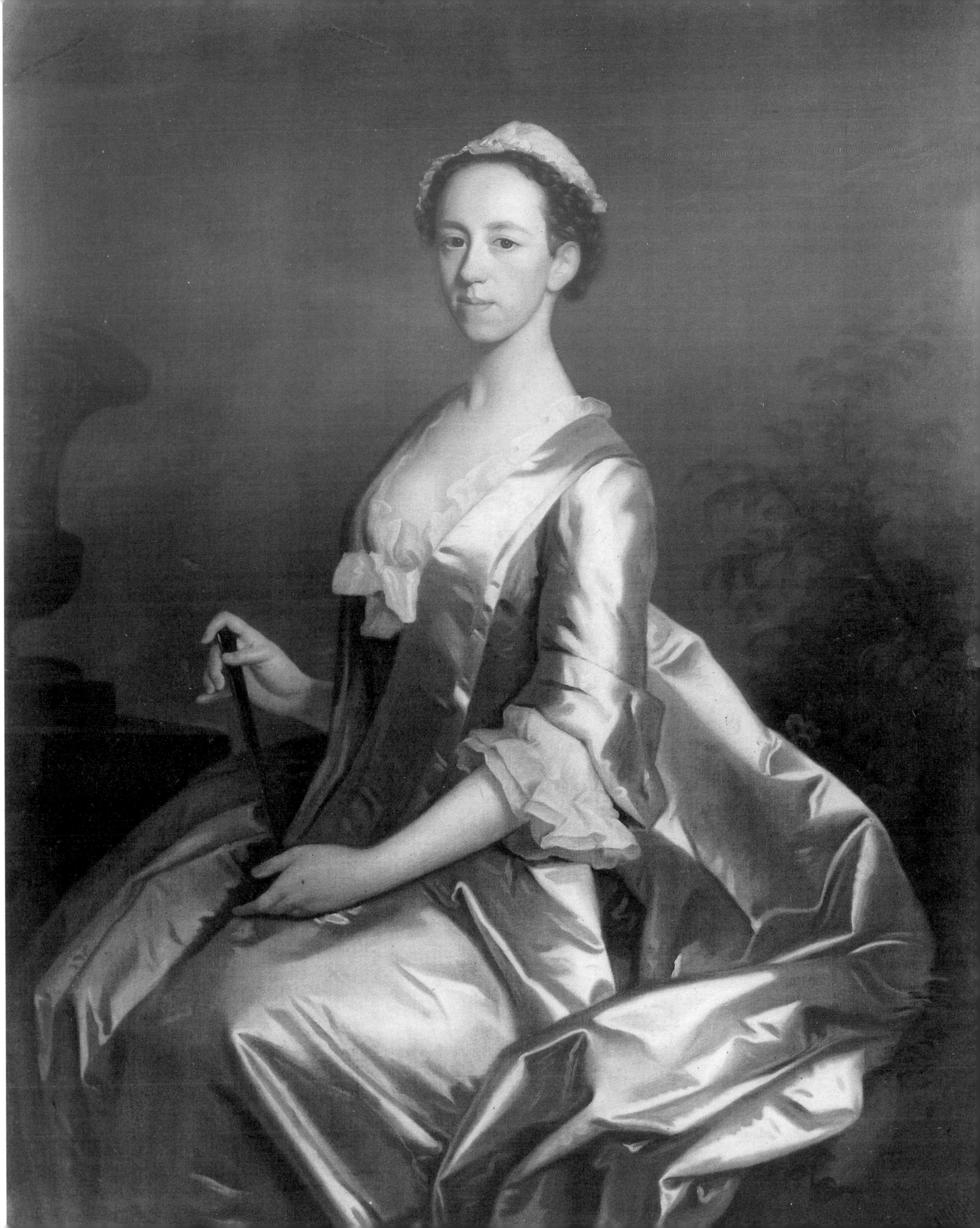

WAG 1355

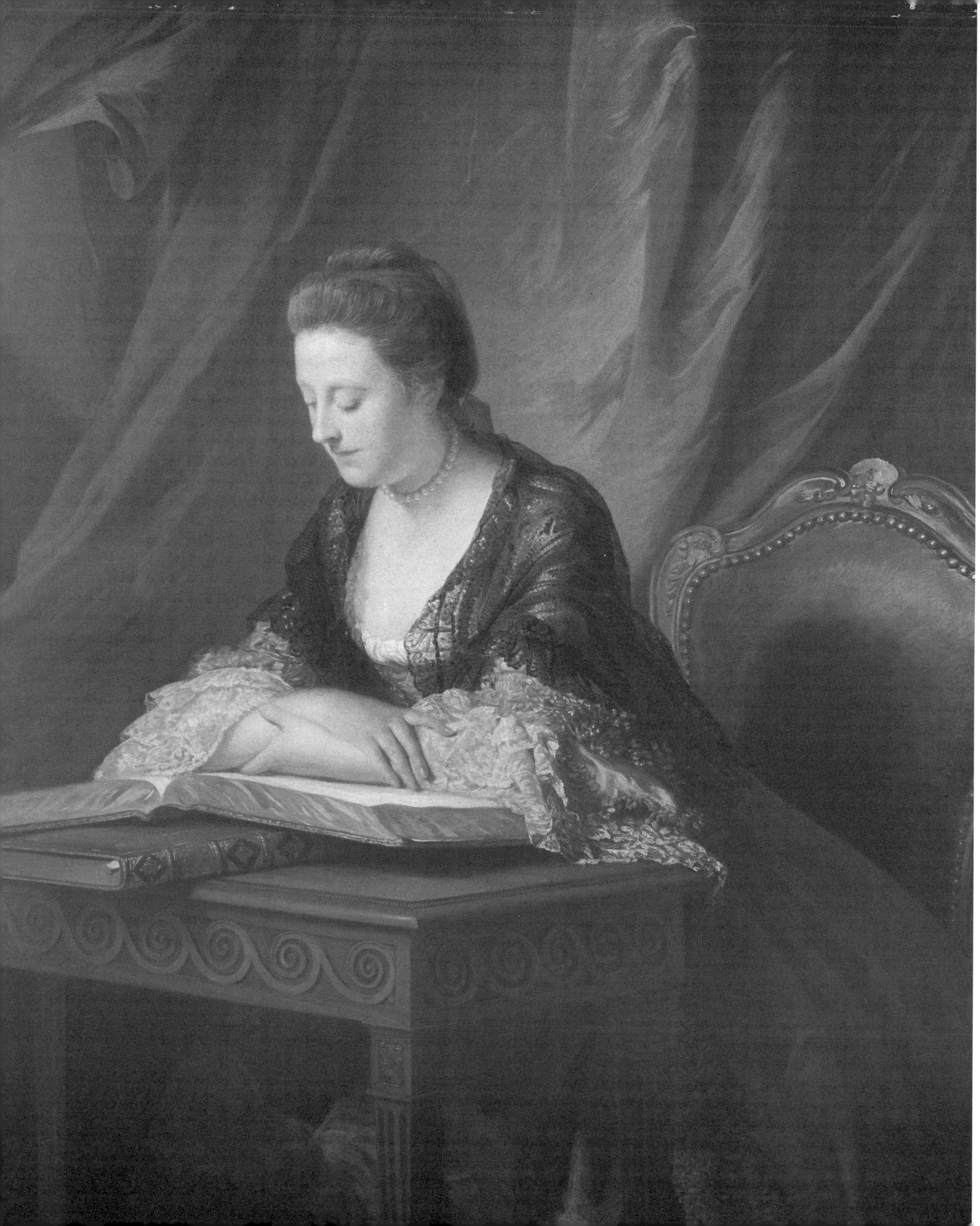

WAG 1356

Emily, Marchioness of Kildare

WAG 1356
oil on canvas, 125.5 × 102 cm
date: 1764–66

The sitter is Lady Emily Lennox (1731–1814), second surviving daughter of Charles, 2nd Duke of Richmond and his wife Lady Sarah Cadogan. In 1747, at the age of 15, she married James Fitzgerald, Earl of Kildare and Viscount Leinster; he was created Marquis of Kildare in 1761 and 1st Duke of Leinster in 1766. The couple lived chiefly in Ireland where they had 19 children (the best known of whom was the Irish radical Lord Edward Fitzgerald) and where Emily played a major role in developing the family estate at Carton, near Maynooth west of Dublin. After Lord Leinster's death in 1773, Emily married William Ogilvie, her sons' tutor, scandalising polite society. With him she had two daughters, one of whom is the subject of WAG 252 (pp. 99-101).[1]

The present canvas is identifiable as the one commissioned by Lady Emily's sister, Caroline, Baroness Holland, for her gallery of family portraits at Holland House. Another version of it is at Carton. The relative status of the two works has become obscured, partly because both versions came together in the possession of the Dukes of Leinster for a period in the nineteenth century, and partly because they were not painted synchronously with the corresponding portraits of Lady Emily's husband, for which Lord Kildare gave Ramsay sittings in 1762.[2] Lady Emily herself demurred at sitting to Ramsay in 1762, when first asked to do so by her sister, claiming that she looked too old and tired,[3] and although to this Baroness Holland responded 'you'll be handsome enough these twenty years to make the best picture in our room, if the painter does you justice',[4] something of Lady Kildare's concern about her looks remains implicit in Ramsay's selection of a half-profile and downward-looking pose for her face. In September 1763 Lady Caroline wrote to her sister again:

I beg you will, as soon as ever you come to town, settle with Ramsay to do your picture for the gallery. I shall be vastly sorry to let slip this opportunity. You'll see your name marked for one of the half-lengths in the Gallery, there are but two full-lengths in the room, so if the mark should be effaced you can't mistake, as the rest are either heads or half-lengths of a particular size, which Ramsay will go and see, tho' he knows it already...[5]

Evidently, Emily did finally sit to Ramsay at some point in the first half of 1764; on 20 September that year Lady Holland wrote to her, 'I suppose Ramsay will never let me have your picture home, for I hear he has not done anything to the original since you sat last.'[6] This observation seems to confirm both that Emily's sittings had been some time previously, and that they had been for an 'original' not destined for Holland House, that is, for the version intended for Carton. If Ramsay's strategy of placing Emily behind a table is to be construed as a means to disguise the fact that she was pregnant, this places the sittings in May or June 1764; she had given birth to Lord Edward Fitzgerald on 15 October 1763, but would have known she was pregnant again with Lord Robert Fitzgerald (b. January 1765) by May the following year.

Ramsay was completing WAG 1356 in the first half of 1766. On 25 April Lady Holland wrote to Emily – now evidently about the picture destined for herself: 'I saw your sweet face at Ramsay's t'other day: 'tis a heavenly picture indeed';[7] and on 9 June she reported that 'your sweet face is come home and put up in my gallery...I like it of all things and think it very like'.[8] The inscription on WAG 1356 on the frieze of the table, *Allen* [sic] *Ramsay. 1765*, may correctly record when most of the work on the canvas was done, but with its incorrect spelling of the artist's first name, it cannot be a signature and was probably added later (the pendant bears the same inscribed date[9] although it must be the version painted in 1762). WAG 1356 differs from the version at Carton by being smaller in size (an orthodox 'half-length' canvas of 127 × 102 cm – as intended by Lady Holland – instead of an enlarged one of 141 × 114 cm). It also features a simpler treatment of the hair, and a more sober colour scheme, with the contrast of blues and pinks in the Carton picture slightly toned down. But if it is a replica, it is nevertheless of autograph quality, and perhaps by virtue of its presence in London from 1766 to 1841 (when Lady Holland is said to have given it to the then Duke of Leinster)[10] it has acquired the greater prominence of the two; Henry Bone's miniature copy exhibited at the RA in 1821 is evidently from the colour scheme, taken from it and not the version at Carton.[11]

Ramsay made a drawing for Lady Emily's intimate crossed-hands pose (National Gallery of Scotland; fig. 54) as if the conception was unfamiliar to him; yet he had already used the motif in his 1761 portrait of Lady Susan Fox-Strangways (Lady Holland's sister-in-law), for which he had made a very similar drawing.[12] He may also have been familiar with its earlier usage by Joshua Reynolds in his portraits of Lady Caroline Keppel (1757–59) and the courtesan Kitty Fisher (1759–60).[13] Lady Emily is portrayed reading a volume of the Byzantine historian Procopius – perhaps simply an allusion to her book-learning.[14] The domestic, private character of the portrait has been viewed as establishing a consciously gendered counterpoint to the public and military depiction of her husband.[15]

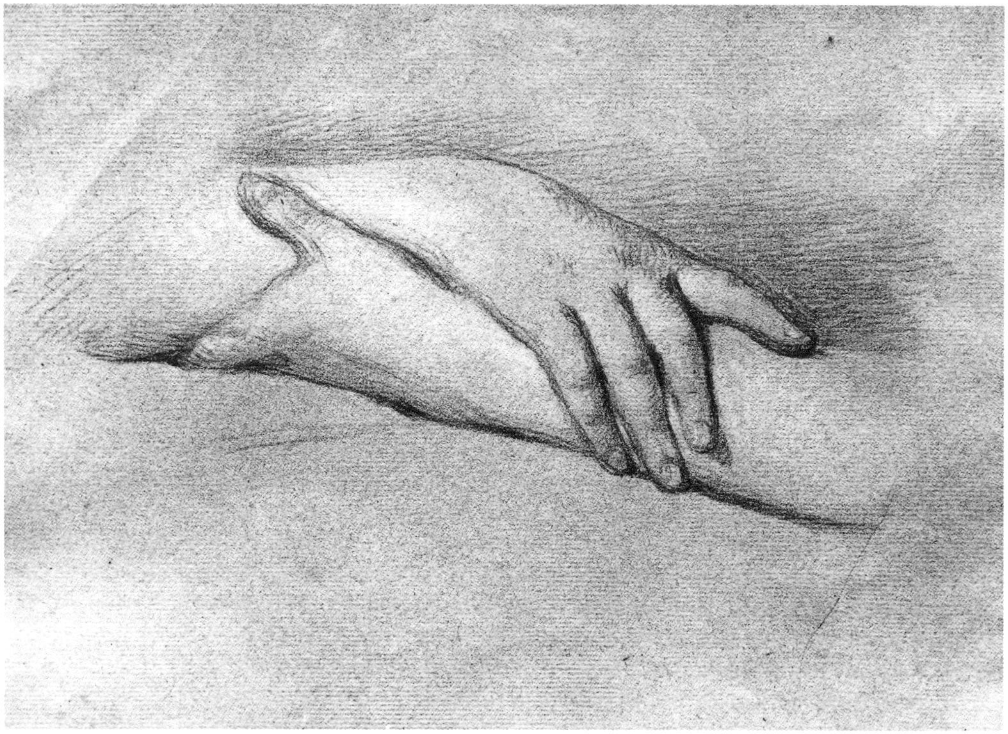

Fig. 54 *Two Female Hands Clasped. Study for the Painting of Lady Emily Lennox, Countess of Kildare* by Allan Ramsay. Black, white and red chalk on paper. ©National Galleries of Scotland.

PROVENANCE

Painted for the sitter's sister, Caroline, Baroness Holland; by descent at Holland House to Elizabeth, Lady Holland (1771–1845); by whom given in 1841 to Augustus Frederick, 3rd Duke of Leinster; by descent; [? Robinson & Fisher 1 March 1900 (102); bt. Graves (£498 15s)]; ...Mrs Gladys Bruen; Christie 13 July 1951 (14);[16] bt. in and bt. privately through Christie's by the gallery.

EXHIBITIONS

Cleaned Pictures Walker Art Gallery 1955 (38); *Selected Acquisitions of the Walker Art Gallery Liverpool 1945–1955* Agnew's, London 1955 (20); *Allan Ramsay* Iveagh Bequest, Kenwood 1958 (33); *British Painting 1700–1960* Pushkin Museum, Moscow and Hermitage, Leningrad 1960 (11); *Primitives to Picasso* RA 1962 (62); *Englische Malerei Der Grossen Zeit* Wallraf-Richartz Museum, Cologne and European tour 1966–67 (40).

NOTES

1. For an extended biographical treatment see especially Stella Tillyard: *Aristocrats* (London, 1994) *passim*; her sittings to Ramsay are mentioned at pp. 151–2.
2. A. Smart and J. Ingamells: *Allan Ramsay: A Complete Catalogue of His Paintings* (New Haven and London, 1999) cats. 317 and 317a (p. 147) suggest that WAG 1356 is Ramsay's prime version of the portrait of Lady Kildare and the Carton picture the replica, partly on the grounds that WAG 1356 shows her with an earlier, flatter hair-style and the Carton version with later, fashionably higher-piled hair. The difference seems marginal but the hair is more elaborately coiffured in the Carton picture. Of Ramsay's three autograph portraits of Lord Kildare (Smart and Ingamells, *op. cit.*, cats. 318, 318a and 318b), 318a, and not, *pace* Smart and Ingamells 318, is the first, according to Lord Kildare done expressly for Lady Holland's gallery, and the sitting for which he described in a letter to his wife of 18 May 1762 (Brian Fitzgerald, ed.: *The Correspondence of Emily, Duchess of Leinster* 3 vols [Dublin, 1949–57] vol. 1, p. 133); this leaves 318 as the portrait in his blue Master-General's coat for which Lord Kildare sat again to Ramsay, at his wife's wish, in December 1762 (Fitzgerald, *op. cit.*, vol. 1, p. 153), and 318b (at Carton) as the replica of 318a. 318b is thus the pendant to 317a, and 318a is the pendant to 317. On this view the pendants were executed in the reverse order to each other in the sequence Lord Kildare for Holland House, Lord Kildare for Carton, Lady Kildare for Carton, Lady Kildare for Holland House (WAG 1356).
3. Tillyard, *op. cit.*, p. 151.
4. Fitzgerald, *op. cit.*, vol. 1, p. 336.
5. Fitzgerald, *op. cit.*, vol. 1, p. 388.
6. Fitzgerald, *op. cit.*, vol. 1, p. 413.
7. Fitzgerald, *op. cit.*, vol. 1, p. 444.
8. Fitzgerald, *op. cit.*, vol. 1, p. 488.
9. Smart and Ingamells, *op. cit.*, p. 148 (cat. 318a). See also n. 2.
10. Lord Ilchester: *The Home of the Hollands 1605–1820* (London, 1937) p. 71.
11. Sold at Sotheby 11 July 1991 (385).
12. Smart and Ingamells, *op. cit.*, p. 354, fig. 528 (the painting) and p. 395, fig. 699 (the drawing).
13. Ramsay himself had employed similar, though less distinctive crossed-arm poses in his portraits of Emma, Lady Hudson of 1742 and Mrs Mary Barnardiston of 1745 (see Smart and Ingamells, *op. cit.*, p. 244, fig. 113 and p. 270, fig. 208).
14. Procopius is best known for his *Secret History*, an unofficial and scabrous account of the lives of the Emperor Justinian and his wife Theodora, so Lady Emily's reading material may be more entertaining than first appearances suggest.
15. Kate Retford: *The Art of Domestic Life: Family Portraiture in Eighteenth-century England* (New Haven and London, 2006) pp. 38–41.
16. The stencil *667JX* appears on the reverse. The sale catalogue states that the picture had come from the collection of the Duke of Leinster.

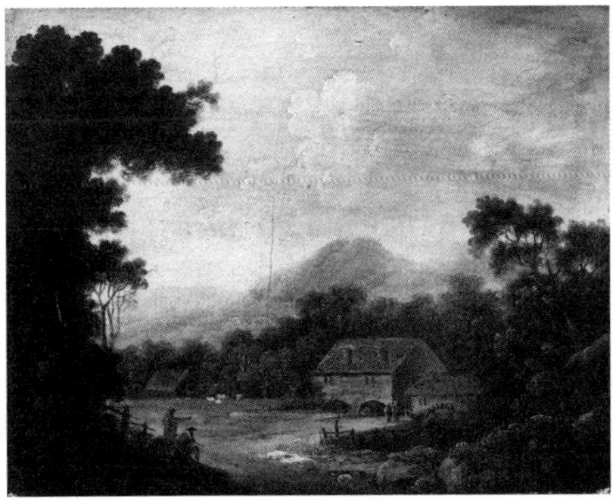

WAG 734

John Rathbone

1750–1807

Landscape with Water-mill

WAG 734
oil on panel, 28.5 × 33.5 cm
date: unknown, perhaps 1770–80

Many of the stylistic features of WAG 734 are strongly reminiscent of the landscapes of Richard Wilson (pp. 262–273): from the handling of the tall tree at the left with its dark, strongly silhouetted florets of foliage and the fluffy white clouds to the cheese-like boulders and the casually painted figures in the foreground. Especially when viewed in the context of such a visually different work as WAG 2687, dated 1788 (below), this suggests that WAG 734 is a youthful and immature painting done when Rathbone was gaining the soubriquet 'the Manchester Wilson'.[1] Conceivably, it is one of the three now untraced landscapes that Rathbone showed at the Liverpool Society of Artists exhibition of 1774 (although the only evidence for this is that the work emerged in a Liverpool collection 100 years later). The location depicted (if a real place) is unidentified.

The condition of WAG 734 is poor. There is a vertical crack about 20 cm long running up the panel from the bottom about 12 cm from the left-hand edge, and there are paint losses along all four edges, especially in the corners.

PROVENANCE

…Philip H. Rathbone;[2] by whom presented 1883.

EXHIBITION

Liverpool Academy 150th Anniversary Walker Art Gallery 1960 (1).

NOTES

1. See W. G. Constable: *Wilson* (London, 1953) pp. 147–8 and pls 157b–158a for Rathbone as an imitator of Wilson.
2. There is no known family connection between him and the artist.

Mountain Landscape with Cattle and Resting Herdsman

WAG 2687
oil on canvas, 92.5 × 130 cm
signed and dated: *J. Rathbone/1788* (bottom left)
date: 1788

The work has formerly been published under the title *View in Borrowdale*.[1] This identification of the location was made on the basis of a watercolour by John Glover (fig. 55) inscribed, apparently by the artist, *On the Derwent in Borrowdale, Cumberland*, and depicting a river valley with a rocky outcrop bearing a considerable resemblance to the one in WAG 2687.[2] However, the broader topography of Glover's view has less in common with Rathbone's, and attempts to locate in Borrowdale the precise spot depicted have not been successful. More certain is that the viewpoint is the same as the one depicted by Julius Caesar Ibbetson in WAG 9811 (p. 80) and it seems possible that the cows, horses and figure in WAG 2687 could actually be the latter's work. The two men are recorded as having collaborated on paintings and at least one dated Lake District subject by Ibbetson from 1788 is known.[3] Unusually large by Rathbone's normal standards and executed in a crisp, strongly-lit manner suggesting an effort to emulate the recent landscapes of Joseph Wright of Derby, WAG 2687 is a formal work perhaps intended for exhibition,[4] in

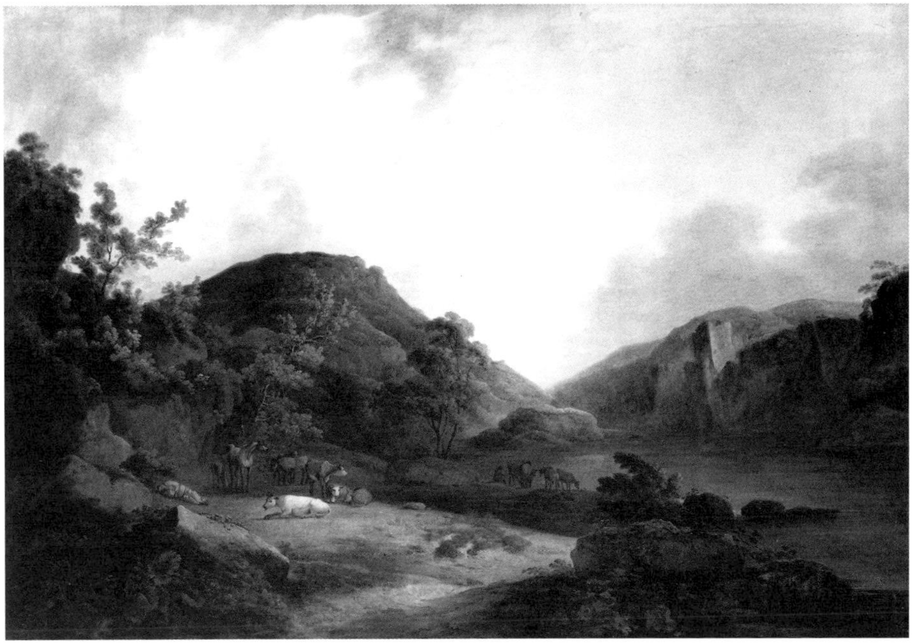

WAG 2687

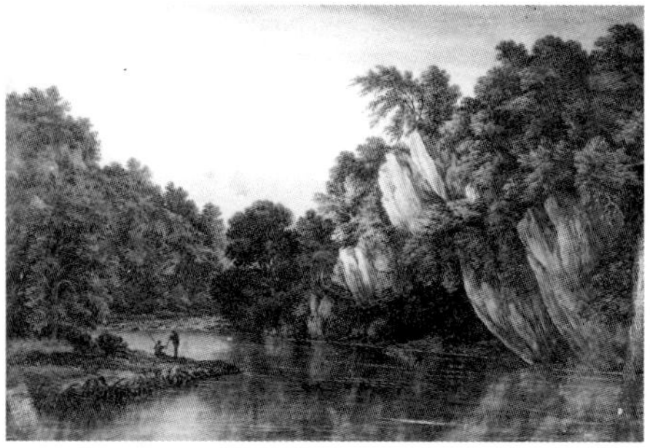

Fig. 55 *View in Borrowdale* by John Glover, watercolour on paper. Sotheby, 15 November 1990 (93); photo courtesy of Sotheby's Picture Library.

which topographical accuracy is unlikely to have weighed significantly among the artist's creative priorities.

PROVENANCE

...Mrs H. A. Bright; by whom presented 1908.

NOTES

1. *CIC*, p. 225.
2. Sold Sotheby 15 November 1990 (93, part).
3. *Derwentwater with Skiddaw*, 92 × 125 cm; see p. 81, n. 7.
4. In 1788 Rathbone exhibited at the RA *View on Derwentwater in Cumberland* (cat. 417) which could be a loose reference to Borrowdale; also *View in Dovedale, Derbyshire – Morning* (cat. 413); attempts to locate the view depicted in WAG 2687 in Dovedale have been in vain.

Joshua Reynolds

1723–92

Mrs Catherine Heywood

WAG 291
oil on canvas, 76 × 63.5 cm
date: 1755–56

The sitter (born at Woodhouse Eaves, Leicestershire on 20 July 1732; d. 1784) was daughter and co-heiress of General Chiverton Hartopp. In 1755 she married James Modyford Heywood (about 1730–98) of Maristow, Devon (the county of which her father became High Sheriff). The couple had one son (born 2 January 1756) and five daughters.[1]

Mrs Heywood had an initial appointment with Reynolds on 22 March 1755 and cancelled further appointments on the 25th and 27th. By that date her husband had already had seven sittings with Reynolds for his own portrait, which was nearly finished, and it seems probable that the two works were intended as pendants and to celebrate their marriage (although the portrait of Mr Heywood is untraced and its dimensions are unknown).[2] No further sittings from Mrs Heywood are recorded, giving rise to the assumption that her portrait was mostly carried out in 1756 – a year for which Reynolds's sitter-book does not survive. This would have been after the birth of her son, but it is tempting to think nevertheless that the prominence of the muff is one of Reynolds's sly visual jokes: an allusion to her pregnancy in 1755.

Mrs Heywood is wearing a light blue

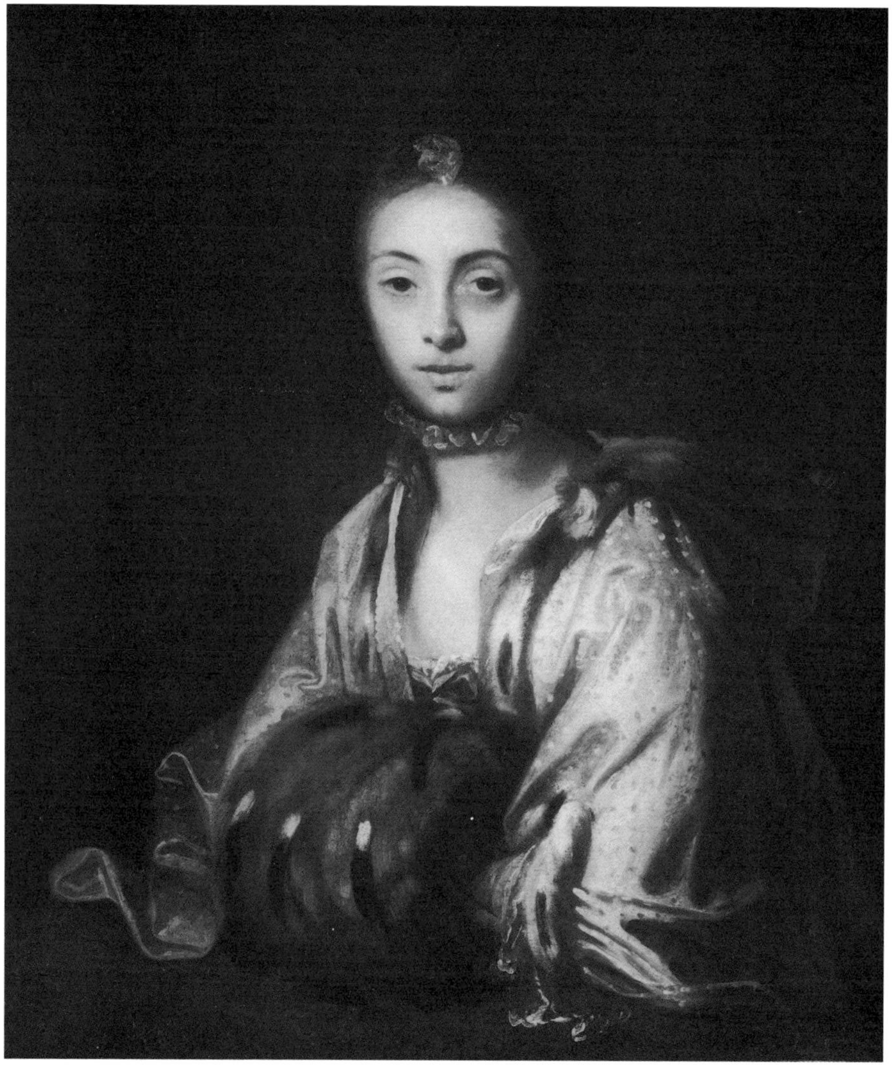

WAG 291

ruched dress and a rose-pink mantle, and is wearing a muff, a device which enables the artist to dispense with painting the hands. In 2000 WAG 291 was described as being in poor condition.[3] In fact, shortly before that date the work had received a full conservation treatment aimed at correcting the

> *crude, unnecessarily extensive and degraded [earlier] restorations…exacerbated by previous over-cleaning, heavy lining (inducing weave interference) and the faded tones of Reynolds's carmine pink which stand out stark against the misleading muddy effects of mis-matched repaints and old discoloured and patchily degraded varnish.*[4]

PROVENANCE

By descent to the sitter's daughter Sophia, Mrs John Musters of Colwick Hall, Notts; by descent to J. C. Musters 1885; bt. Agnew July 1888; bt. George Holt April 1889; Emma Holt Bequest 1945.

EXHIBITIONS

Old Masters RA 1885 (66); *Twenty Masterpieces of the English School, for the Benefit of the Artists' General Benevolent Institution* Agnew's, London 1899 (14).

NOTES

1. Sir Lewis Namier and John Brooke: *The History of Parliament: The House of Commons 1754–1790* 3 vols (London, 1964) vol. 2, p. 622; Mary Bennett and Edward Morris: *Sudley* (Liverpool, 1971) pp. 61–2; David Mannings and Martin Postle: *Sir Joshua Reynolds: A Complete Catalogue of His Paintings* 2 vols (New Haven and London, 2000) vol. 1 p. 256 (cats. 900–901). Mrs Heywood's sister Mary became Lady Howe, subject of the celebrated full-length by Gainsborough (Iveagh Bequest, Kenwood).
2. Mannings and Postle, *loc. cit.* (cat. 900).
3. Mannings and Postle, *loc. cit.* (cat. 901).
4. Katherine Stainer-Hutchins, treatment proposal dated 15 July 1997, gallery files. The treatment, funded by a Woodmansterne Art Conservation Award, was carried out by Natasha Duff.

Miss Elizabeth Ingram

WAG 6200
oil on canvas, 127 × 101.5 cm
signed and dated: *J.R 1757*
(on base of column)
date: 1757

The sitter (1733–85) was the eldest child of William Ingram of Wakefield (d. 1753)[1] and his wife Sarah, née Bradley. She was the first of her family to sit to Reynolds, her mother following in 1759[2] and one of her brothers, presumably the eldest, William (1736–70) who was making his fortune as a banker in Liverpool in 1762.[3] Elizabeth's sittings took place on 16, 18, 20, 24 and 28 May 1757, with a cancelled appointment on the 23rd. No payment is recorded but in his pocket-book of 1759 against the week of 17 December Reynolds noted that Miss Ingram's portrait was to be sent away.[4]

Miss Ingram wears a blue satin 'masquerade' gown with tasselled oversleeves, a gauzy headscarf fastened with a clasp decorated with pearls, and ropes of pearls and a jewel at her bosom.[5] The effect is to emphasise her affluence, but if the strategy of leaving the work unclaimed in Reynolds's studio for two years was in the hope of it being spotted by an eligible bachelor, the sitter (or her mother) was doomed to disappointment: Miss Ingram remained unmarried in Wakefield for the rest of her life. Although Reynolds made considerable use of drapery-painters during the 1750s, there seems no doubt that he painted Miss Ingram's dress himself, an indication that he took the commission seriously. Nevertheless, there is a hint of the formulaic in the way the clichéd Van Dyckian pose of the figure, with its out-thrust elbow, is given a rather cold, classical setting, with its heavy column in the background; perhaps Reynolds adopted this solution in order to make the best of his client's rather narrow face and long neck. As so often, Reynolds's flesh tints have faded to leave the face with a ghostly pallor.

PROVENANCE

By descent to the sitter's great-nephew, H. F. Ingram 1863; by descent to his nephew Ingram Fuller Godfrey; his great-nephew W. H. S. Godfrey; from whom bt. through Agnew by the gallery 1964, with the assistance of the Art Fund.

EXHIBITIONS

BI 1863 (108); *Exhibition of Works by Sir Joshua Reynolds P.R.A. 1723–1792* Birmingham Museum and Art Gallery 1961 (24); *La peinture britannique de Gainsborough à Bacon* Galerie des Beaux-Arts, Bordeaux 1977 (48).

NOTES

1. He was the son of William Bradley (d. 1749) Wakefield agent for the estates of the Earls of Strafford. Anne Countess of Strafford appears to have sat to Reynolds shortly before Miss Ingram (David Mannings and Martin Postle: *Sir Joshua Reynolds: A Complete Catalogue of his Paintings* 2 vols [New Haven and London, 2000] vol. 1 p. 467 [cat. 1856]) possibly accounting for the Ingrams' choice of artist.
2. She had five appointments with Reynolds between 14 and 25 May 1759; Mannings and Postle, *op. cit.*, p. 275 (cat. 987).
3. *Ibid.* His portrait appears not to have been completed. For his activities in Liverpool see John Hughes: *Liverpool Banks and Bankers 1760–1837: A History of the Circumstances Which Gave Rise to the Industry and the Men who Founded and Developed It* (Liverpool, 1906) p. 132. Ingram retired from business in 1767.
4. Mannings and Postle, *op. cit.*, p. 274 (cat. 983).
5. *Ibid.*

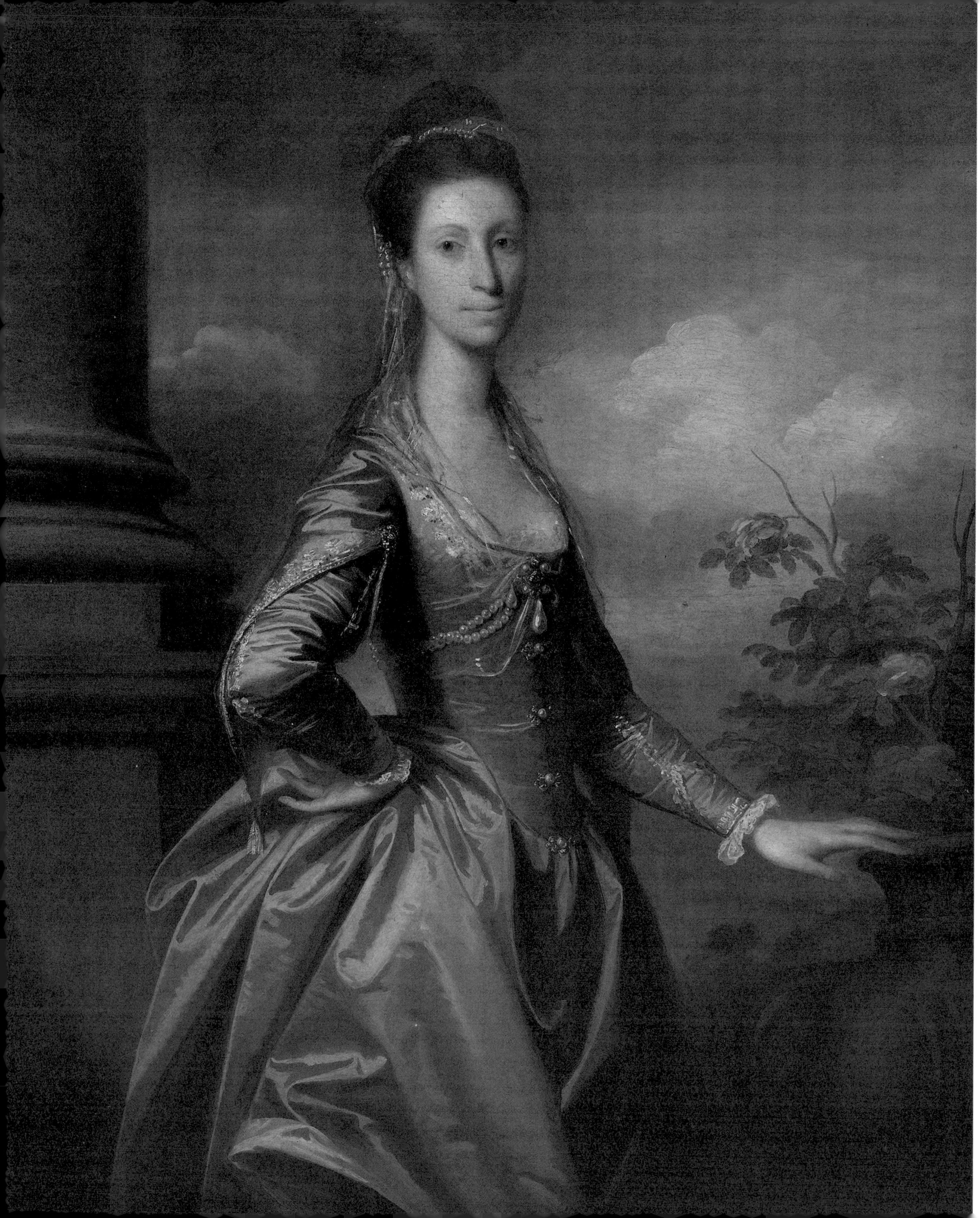

WAG 6200

Mrs Lydia Gostling

WAG 290
oil on canvas, 76.5 × 64 cm
date: 1782

The sitter (1757–1828) was the third daughter of Revd Benjamin Newcome, Rector of St Mildred, Poultry, London, and his wife Sarah, née Green. In March 1776 she married (at St George's Bloomsbury, where her eldest brother was curate) her maternal first cousin, George Gostling, a Proctor in Doctor's Commons. With him, between 1777 and 1788, she had seven children, five boys and two girls. Her early married life was spent at Gostling's London residence, 7 Godliman Street, but in December 1782 her husband's father died and the couple became the owners of his estate at Whitton Place, near Twickenham. Lydia inherited it after her husband's death in 1820 and lived there for the remaining eight years of her life.[1]

She began sitting to Reynolds in August 1782 shortly after giving birth to her fourth child;[2] appointments are recorded on 9, 13, 16, 19 and 30 August (each time at 11 o'clock) and she cancelled a further appointment on 29 October.[3] Reynolds's ledger records two payments for the work; one of 35 guineas (probably a slip of the pen for 25 as Reynolds's price for a three-quarters at this time was 50 guineas) in April 1783 and one of 25 guineas at an unspecified date between 1779 and 1785 – this was probably the initial payment and the one in April 1783 the second one, on the completion of the portrait.[4]

Reynolds exhibited WAG 290 (as *Portrait of a Lady*) at the 1783 Royal Academy. His choice is surprising in the sense that the work is a routine head and shoulders commission and its subject is a woman who was not in the public eye. Nevertheless there is an experimental feel to the portrait, especially in the rather lurid colouration of the dress: the combination of pink and sky blue is uncharacteristic of Reynolds and some of the brushstrokes on the dress have a rather superficial bravura out of keeping with his customary old-masterish approach, to the extent of raising the issue as to whether the work was later retouched.[5]

The reviewer of the Royal Academy in the *Public Advertiser* described WAG 290 as 'amongst the best Female Portraits in the Room, if not the very best',[6] whereas the reviewer of the *Morning Chronicle* decided that there was insufficient contrast between it and its neighbour – Fuseli's *Weird Sisters*.[7]

PROVENANCE

By descent to the sitter's grand-daughter, Emily Gostling;[8] her husband, Col. Charles Edward Gostling-Murray; Christie 23 June 1881 (771); bt. in; Christie 3 May 1884 (141); bt. Agnew; bt. Baron F. de Rothschild; returned by exchange to Agnew

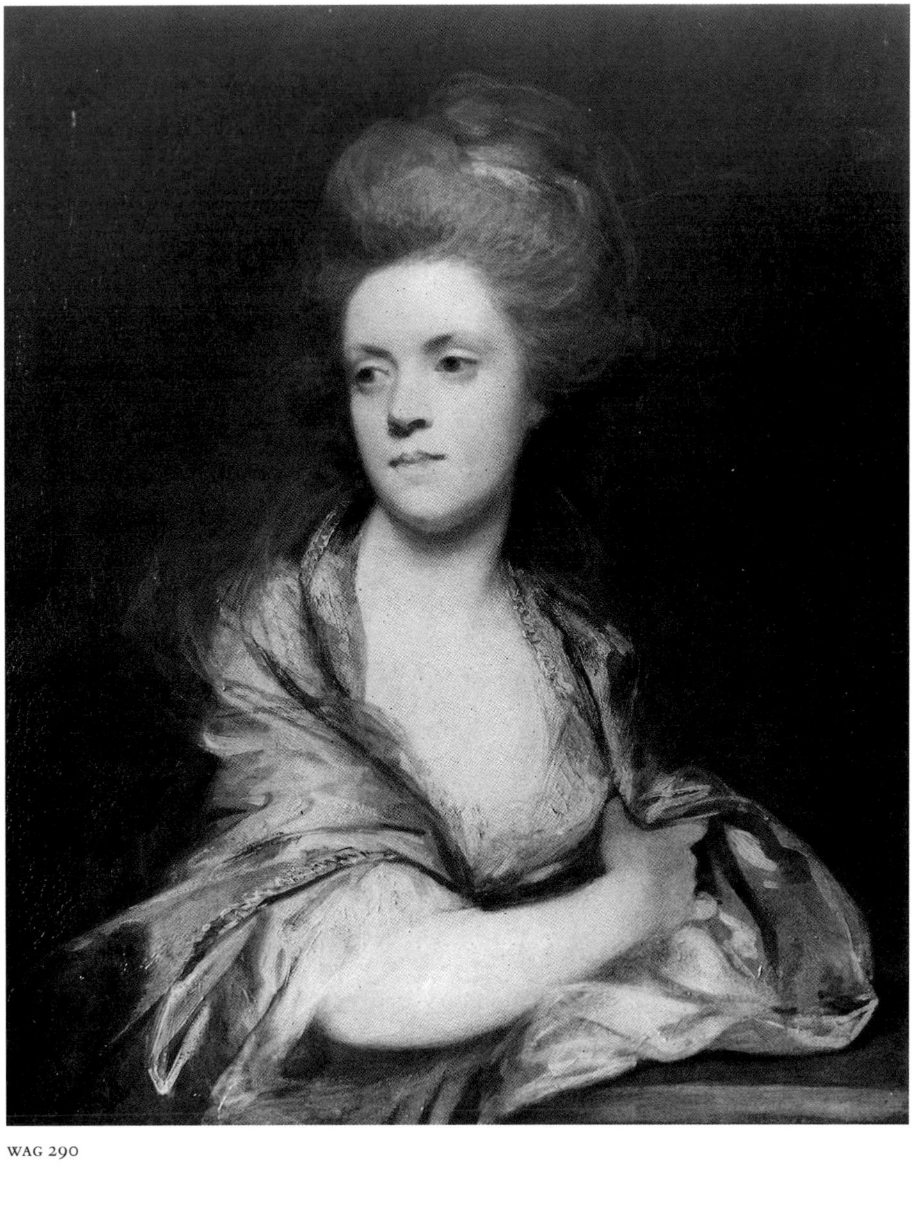

WAG 290

1886; bt. in December 1886 by George Holt; Emma Holt Bequest 1945.

EXHIBITIONS

RA 1783 (11); *Twenty Masterpieces of the English School, for the Benefit of the Artists' General Benevolent Institution* Agnew's, London 1899 (15); *Loan Collection of Portraits* Birmingham Museum and Art Gallery 1900 (8); *59th Liverpool Autumn Exhibition* Walker Art Gallery 1933 (13); *Some Acquisitions of the Walker Art Gallery Liverpool 1935–1945* National Gallery, London 1945 (8).

NOTES

1. Biographical information derived from P. Foster and D. H. Simpson: *Whitton Park and Whitton Place* (Twickenham Local History Society, Paper No. 41, 1979) pp. 20–9; also P. Foster, *letter*, 8 November 1968, gallery files.
2. The child was Augustus Gostling, baptised 7 June 1782; Foster, *letter*.
3. David Mannings and Martin Postle: *Sir Joshua Reynolds: A Complete Catalogue of His Paintings* 2 vols (New Haven and London, 2000) vol. 1 p. 222 (cat. 747). They cite a note in Reynolds's 1782 sitter-book under Sunday 18 August: 'Mrs Goslin Clapham near the Church'. The meaning of this is unclear.
4. *Ibid.*
5. David Mannings and Martin Postle, *verbally*, 20 September 1990, at Sudley, expressed the view that only the head was by Reynolds and that the dress was a late nineteenth-century confection, with possibly the lips and pupils having also been improved at that date; in 2000 Mannings wrote, 'considerably repainted, the contours sharpened up and the face prettified' (*loc. cit.*).
6. *Public Advertiser* (29 April 1783) p. 2.
7. *Morning Chronicle and London Advertiser* (9 May 1783) p. 3.
8. As was pointed out by Mary Bennett and Edward Morris: *Sudley* (Liverpool, 1971) p. 62, both Reynolds himself and the reviewer of the RA exhibition in the *Morning Chronicle* spelt the name Goslin or Gosling, and the latter spelling was given in A. Graves and W. V. Cronin: *A History of the Works of Sir Joshua Reynolds, P.R.A.* 4 vols (London 1899–1901) vol. 1, p. 374, who accordingly misidentified the sitter as Mrs Gosling, wife of the banker of that name. The reviewer in the *Public Advertiser* spelt the name correctly.

after
Joshua Reynolds
1723–92

Mrs Hartley and Child

WAG 327
oil on canvas, 91.5 × 71 cm
date: unknown, perhaps 1813–35

This is a copy, the same size as the original, of Reynolds's *A Nymph, with a Young Bacchus*, painted in 1771 and shown at the Royal Academy in 1773 (Tate Britain).[1] Although it has been suggested that WAG 327 was painted directly from the original[2] – which would imply that it was either made by a pupil in Reynolds's studio before the original was sold to Lord Carysfort in 1774–75, or else was copied at one of the exhibitions to which the original was lent in the early part of the nineteenth century[3] – visual evidence suggests that its source was the engraving published by G. Nutter in 1800 (re-issued 1801). Nutter's engraving has the curl of hair descending between the eyes of the child which is lacking in Reynolds's original and it also has the extra drape on Mrs Hartley's shoulder, while the tassel at the waist of Mrs Hartley's dress in the original is absent in WAG 327 and Nutter's print alike. The most striking difference between the two painted versions is in the face of the child, which in the original has blond hair, a higher brow and more compressed features. WAG 327 has darkened and much of the detail in the original, especially in the background, is invisible.[4]

Elizabeth Hartley (1750/51–1824), one of London's favourite actresses in the decade before the emergence of Mrs Siddons, may have been a discovery of Reynolds's.[5] She first sat to him in July 1771 before making her major acting debut in Edinburgh that winter. She subsequently performed in Bristol before making her London debut as Jane Shore – the role with which she was most closely associated – at Covent Garden in the summer of 1772. The actor John Moody, acting as a talent scout in Bristol for the Garricks, described her as having 'a good figure, with a handsome small face, and very much freckled; her hair red and her neck and shoulders well-turned' and as 'ignorant and stubborn', with 'a slovenly good-nature about her that renders her prodigiously vulgar'.[6] It has been noted that Reynolds's composition is loosely based on Michelangelo's *Doni Tondo* (Uffizi, Florence).[7] As the title under which Reynolds's original picture was first exhibited makes clear, his conception is not that of a portrait proper but of a fancy picture whose model would be recognised by its public audience.

PROVENANCE

...Angerstein family;[8] bt. Permain; ...Polak; bt. George Holt 24 August 1887; Emma Holt Bequest 1945.

NOTES

1. David Mannings and Martin Postle: *Sir Joshua Reynolds: A Complete Catalogue of His Paintings* 2 vols (New Haven and London, 2000) vol. 1 p. 245 (cat. 854). WAG 327 is one of four copies recorded.
2. David Mannings and Martin Postle, *verbally*,

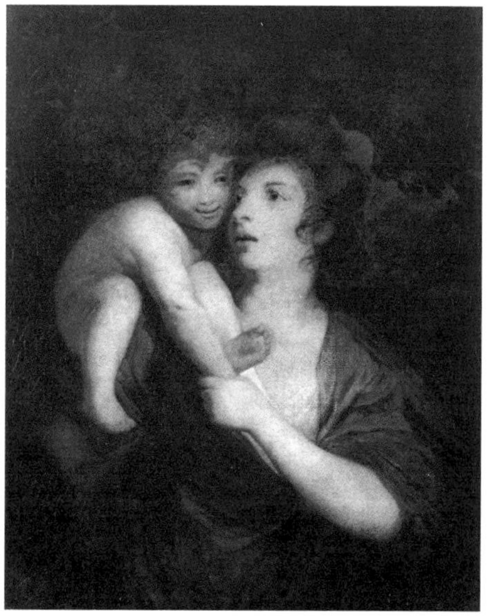

WAG 327

at Sudley, 20 September 1990.

3. Reynolds's painting, titled *Mrs Hartley and Child*, was shown at the Reynolds exhibition at the British Institution in 1813 (at which copying was permitted) and was also exhibited at the Royal Manchester Institution in 1831.

4. The painting was conserved in 1958 to treat serious mildew growth and tears along the turnover edges of the lining canvas. It was strip-lined but was not fully cleaned, and it was noted that there were numerous darkened retouchings and that the varnish layer was very heavy and discoloured (Gigi Crompton, examination and treatment report dated 20 March 1958, gallery files).

5. As noted by Martin Postle: *The Creation of Celebrity*, exh. cat., Palazzo dei Diamanti, Ferrara and Tate Britain, London (2005) p. 188 (cat. 53).

6. John Boaden, ed.: *The Private Correspondence of David Garrick* 2 vols (2nd edn, London, 1835) vol. 1, p. 476, quoted by Mannings and Postle, *loc. cit.*

7. Mannings and Postle, *loc. cit.*

8. Efforts to trace the identity of the owner have been unsuccessful; the work is not listed in the catalogue of John Julius Angerstein's collection of 1823 (Cecil Gould, *letter*, 19 September 1969, gallery files).

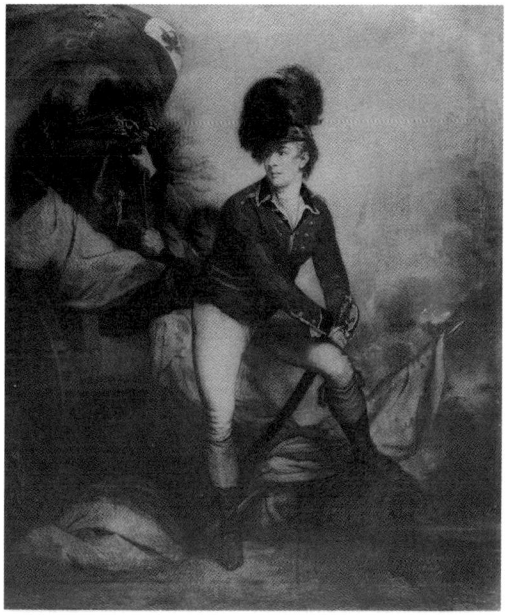

WAG 2504

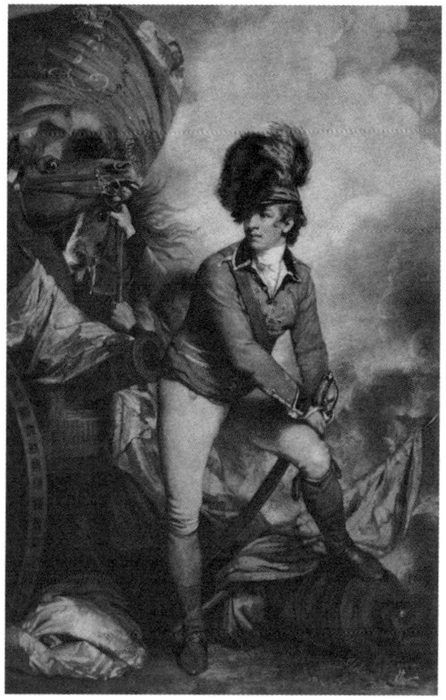

Fig. 56 *Sir Banastre Tarleton* after Sir Joshua Reynolds, engraving by J. R. Smith. © Trustees of the British Museum.

Colonel Sir Banastre Tarleton

WAG 2504
oil on canvas, 76.5 × 64 cm
date: unknown, perhaps 1800–30

This is a small copy (on a standard 'three-quarters' canvas) of Reynolds's celebrated full-length portrait of Col. Tarleton exhibited at the Royal Academy in 1782 (National Gallery, London).[1] It does not follow the proportions of the original canvas, being wider in relation to the height, and the artist has grafted extraneous passages of paint along both sides, particularly at the right, and also at the bottom. No attempt has been made to replicate in detail Reynolds's depiction of the rolling clouds of smoke behind Tarleton's figure, and the actual transcription of his facial features is also inaccurate, with the head appearing in a more front-on position and the eyes enlarged. This suggests that the artist's source was John Raphael Smith's engraving, published 11 October 1782 (fig. 56), which displays similar elements of variation from the original painting itself. WAG 2504 also has numerous differences of colouration from Reynolds's work, most noticeably in the pale banner draped over the cannon at left, and in the green of Tarleton's jacket, which lacks the blue-ish hue of the original although it is no doubt a more faithful rendition of the colour of the coats actually worn by 'Tarleton's Green Horse'.

When it was acquired by the gallery WAG 2504 was said to have been painted by Frances Reynolds (1729–1807) the sister of Sir Joshua Reynolds.[2] She is known to have copied portraits by her brother but the style of her known works does not resemble this picture and the attribution has been rejected.[3] WAG 2504 has been dated approximately to the first 30 years of the nineteenth century.[4] If the artist did make the copy from Reynolds's canvas, which seems counter-intuitive, this could have been done at the British Institution in 1823 or at the Society of British Artists, Suffolk Street in 1834. WAG 2504 is one of a number of recorded copies or variants of Reynolds's portrait made in the period 1795–1900.[5]

Banastre Tarleton (1754–1833) was the second son of the Liverpool merchant and sometime mayor John Tarleton (1719–73). His exploits as commander of the British Legion during the American War of Independence gained him celebrity status on his return to England after the surrender at Yorktown. In London he immediately sat for full-length portraits to Thomas Gainsborough as well as Reynolds, and began a liaison with the actress, Mary 'Perdita' Robinson, who had just been discarded by the Prince of Wales. He was MP for Liverpool 1790–1806, married Susan Bertie, daughter of the Duke of Ancaster in 1798, and was promoted to the rank of General in 1812.[6]

PROVENANCE

...Major J. H. Grindley by 1920;[7] bt. in 1933 from Grindley & Palmer, Liverpool.

NOTES

1. For Reynolds's portrait see especially Judy Egerton: *National Gallery Catalogues: The British School* (London, 1998) pp. 218–27 and David Mannings and Martin Postle: *Sir Joshua Reynolds: A Complete Catalogue of His Paintings* 2 vols (New Haven and London, 2000) vol. 1, pp. 439–40 (cat. 1733).
2. *Liverpool Post and Mercury* 25 January 1933, p. 5.
3. Mannings and Postle, *op. cit.*, p. 440; WAG 2504 had previously been published as 'after Reynolds' in *MPPP* and *CIC*.
4. Mannings and Postle, *verbally*, 20 September 1990; cf. Mannings and Postle, *loc. cit.*, where WAG 2504 is described as 'apparently an early 19th-century picture'.
5. Those listed by Mannings and Postle, *loc. cit.*, are: (i) by Sir William Beechey, 84 × 58.5 cm, sold at Christie 19 November 1910 (108); (ii) unattributed, 82.5 × 63.5 cm, sold at Christie 14 December 1934 (20), formerly in the collection of the Earl of Carrington; (iii) unattributed, 53.5 × 38 cms, in Tarleton family ownership until sold in 1951; (iv) by T. Stone, 91.5 × 71 cm, signed and dated 1795, Brighton Museum and Art Gallery; (v) unattributed, 49 × 32 cm; Musée Bonnat, Bayonne (probably copied from the engraving, as Tarleton is shown in a red coat). Other anonymous copies are known from their appearance in the salerooms.
6. For Tarleton see especially Egerton, *loc. cit.*; also Robert D. Bass: *The Green Dragoon. The Lives of Banastre Tarleton and Mary Robinson* (London, 1958).
7. *Liverpool Post and Mercury, loc. cit.* According to the report, the painting was owned by Grindley in Bristol, with the possible implication that he acquired it there. However, a very similar canvas (not mentioned in Mannings and Postle, *loc. cit.*) is owned by the Athenaeum in Liverpool.

called

Joshua Reynolds

1723–92

Mrs Bower of Plymouth

WAG 2505
oil on canvas, 61.5 × 51 cm
date: unknown, perhaps 1850–70

This portrait was presented to Liverpool in 1873 as an authentic work by Reynolds, but the attribution is unacceptable.[1] The loose handling of paint is completely uncharacteristic of his technique and the issue is whether WAG 2505, whose size is not that of any of the standard eighteenth-century prepared canvases, can conceivably be by one of his pupils or studio assistants, or whether, as seems much more probable, it is an out-and-out forgery. If the latter, it probably dates from only shortly before its acquisition by the Corporation. WAG 2505 purports, from the sitter's costume, to date from around 1765–70. However, in support of the notion that it is a forgery (considerations of style apart) is the curious form of the work's title, specifying the sitter's domicile; no plausible candidate for a Mrs Bower resident in Plymouth has emerged but the fact that Reynolds was born close to Plymouth was presumably intended to corroborate the attribution. Reynolds's documented portrait of Mrs Bower – the wife of the ecclesiastic Archibald Bower (1686–1766), but not from Plymouth – is unrelated to the present composition; previously unknown, it emerged at a sale at Foster's in 1871.[2]

WAG 2505 was described in the early twentieth century as in poor condition, with a tear across the sitter's brow;[3] this damage has been repaired. Nothing is known of the work's earlier history.

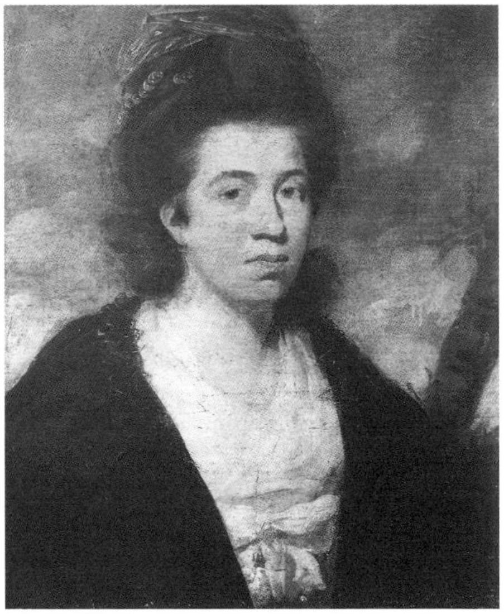

WAG 2505

PROVENANCE

...W. Sproston Caine; by whom presented to the Corporation of Liverpool 1873; transferred to the gallery before 1882.

NOTES

1. The attribution to Reynolds was retained in both Charles Dyall: *Walker Art Gallery Descriptive Catalogue of the Permanent Collection of Pictures* (Liverpool, 1882) p. 36 (cat. 140) and the gallery's 1927 catalogue, p. 152.
2. D. Mannings and M. Postle: *Sir Joshua Reynolds: A Complete Catalogue of His Paintings* 2 vols (New Haven and London, 2000) vol. 1, p.101 (cat. 229).
3. Note in gallery files.

Jonathan Richardson the Elder

1665–1745

Portrait of the Artist's Son, Jonathan

WAG 2270
oil on canvas, 76 × 63 cm
date: 1732

The younger Jonathan Richardson was born in 1694, the son of the artist and his wife Elizabeth, née Bray, who had married the previous year. Father and son remained exceptionally close, the former using the latter as his literary collaborator and agent, advisor, amanuensis and virtual *alter ego*. The son travelled to Italy in 1720 at his father's behest and his reports on the works of art he saw there formed the basis of the elder Richardson's *An Account of Some of the Statues, Bas-reliefs, Drawings, and Pictures in Italy, &c, with Remarks*, published in 1722, which for many years enjoyed a reputation as the leading guide to art in Italy written in England. The following decade the two collaborated again on *Explanatory Notes and Remarks on Milton's 'Paradise Lost'*, published in 1734. The younger Richardson made a few paintings but no work by him is now identifiable. He died in London in 1771.[1]

Especially after he began to scale down his business as a professional portraitist in the late 1720s, the elder Richardson regularly used his son as a model, both for paintings and more frequently drawings. His portrait drawings were well known to contemporaries, and at the time of the younger Richardson's posthumous sale at Langford's in 1772, Horace Walpole noted that his father seemed 'to have amused himself with writing a short poem and drawing his own, or his son's portrait every day'.[2] As Walpole's comment testifies, Richardson often drew or painted his son in conjunction with portraits of himself, and because the family likeness between the two was strong (and it may have been part of Richardson's purpose to emphasise it) it became easy for their identities to be confused. At least two drawings which are close in conception and date to WAG 2270, showing the younger Richardson in profile to the left, have been mis-identified as portraits of the father; one of these, in which Richardson seems to have employed black chalk as well as his more usual pencil, bears a particularly close resemblance to the image in WAG 2270.

It is inscribed in the artist's own hand *Richardson given to the poet Pope* and dated *26 Sep 1734*[3] and must have been based on WAG 2270, which bears the inscribed date *12 Aug 1732*.[4] WAG 2270 itself was sold in 1951 and entered the Walker's collection as a self-portrait by the elder Jonathan Richardson, and the sitter's identity was only published definitively in 1977.[5]

WAG 2270 was painted at the period of the Richardsons' Milton project, although it may have been based on an earlier drawing dated 13 February 1729 (British Museum; fig. 57). In about 1732 Richardson painted an allegorical portrait of himself and his son with the figure of Milton crowned with a laurel wreath (private collection, North Carolina; fig. 58) in which the younger Richardson, as in WAG 2270, is dressed in red and wears a red silk cap. Although the figures in that work, which measures 25 × 30 inches, are much smaller, it seems possible that WAG 2270 was done as some sort of trial for the figure of the younger Richardson there.

The later history of WAG 2270 is

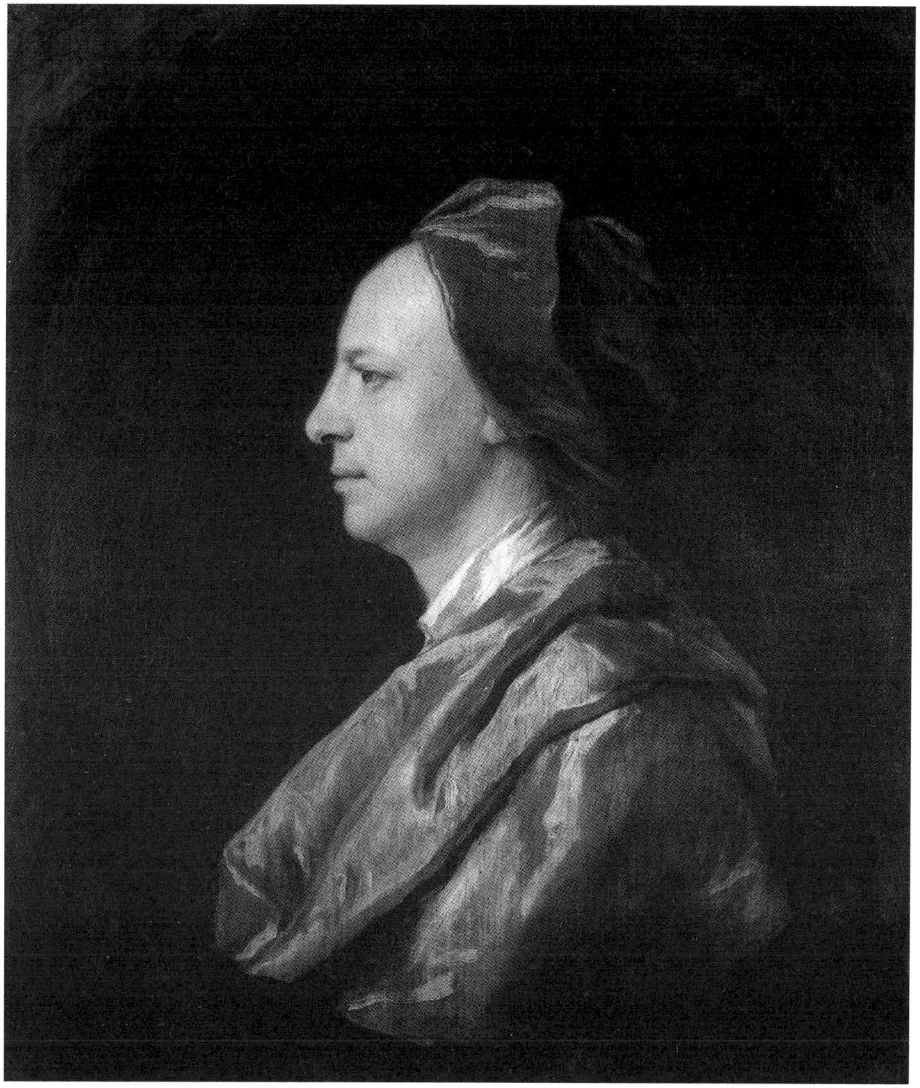

WAG 2270

obscure. It is not out of the question that it remained in the sitter's possession and was one of the portraits, mis-identified as self-portraits by his father, auctioned in his posthumous sale.[6] By 1826 sight had been lost of both artist and sitter, for in that year a lithograph by M. Gauci was published identifying the portrait as of John Gay (author of *The Beggar's Opera*) by Hogarth (fig. 59). The sitter was still identified as Gay when the work was lent by Lady Clifden to the 1867 National Portrait Exhibition, although by that time the attribution had returned to Richardson. The date at which the work was converted into a painted oval is unknown; it may be significant that Gauci's lithograph does not show it in an oval format. The grey overpainting in the corners is coarsely applied leaving the original background and even the reddish-brown ground visible in places. In the course of relining, the original canvas tacking edges were flattened out and lined to the lining canvas with the tack heads still in place.

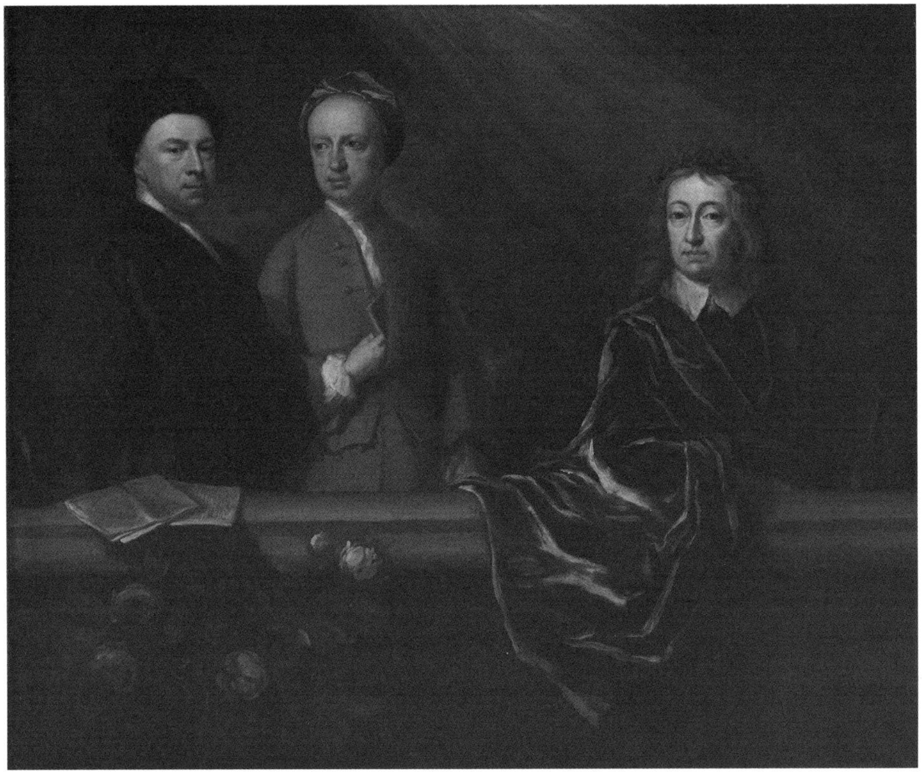

Fig. 58 *Allegorical Self-portrait with Jonathan Richardson Junior and John Milton* by Jonathan Richardson, oil on canvas. Private collection, N. Carolina.

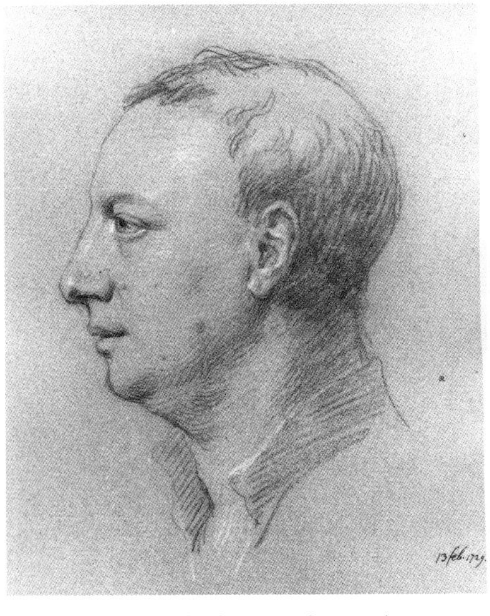

Fig. 57 *Jonathan Richardson Junior* by Jonathan Richardson, black and white chalks on paper. © Trustees of the British Museum.

PROVENANCE

...[? George, 1st Baron Dover (1797–1860); by descent to] Henry, 3rd Viscount Clifden (d.1866); Lady Clifden;[7] ...[? Lord Annesley (or Lord Annaly)];[8] ...Harold, 1st Viscount Mackintosh of Halifax; Christie 4 May 1951 (41); bt. Agnew for the gallery (£31.10s.6d.).

EXHIBITIONS

2nd Special Exhibition of National Portraits South Kensington 1867 (177); *Selected Acquisitions of the Walker Art Gallery Liverpool 1945–1955* Agnew's, London 1955 (5); *Painting and Sculpture in England 1700–1750* Walker Art Gallery 1958 (42).

NOTES

1. See Carol Gibson-Wood: *Jonathan Richardson, Art Theorist of the English Enlightenment* (New Haven and London, 2000); also her 'Richardson, Jonathan, the Elder', ODNB vol. 46, pp. 827–8.
2. Horace Walpole: *Anecdotes of Painting in England...with additions by the Rev. James Dallaway* ed. R. N. Wornum, 3 vols (London, 1862) vol. 2, p. 277; quoted by Gibson-Wood, *op. cit.*, p. 134.
3. 11¼ × 8¾ inches; untraced; sold as a self-portrait by the elder Richardson Sotheby 28 June 1920 (648) from the Wellesley collection. The other mis-identified drawing is *ECM 31* in Edward Croft-Murray's catalogue of the British Museum's Richardson drawings; Gibson-Wood, *op. cit.*, pl. 58, p. 121.
4. According to the 1951 Christie sale catalogue, the inscription has darkened and the letters forming the month are now extremely hard to read. The signature also recorded by the sale catalogue is now invisible.
5. John Kerslake: *National Portrait Gallery: Early Georgian Portraits*, 2 vols (London, 1977) vol. 1, p. 231.
6. Lot 45 in the sale was *His Own Portrait* and lot 77 was *His Own Portrait 3 qrs.*
7. Lent by Lady Clifden to the 1867 exhibition. The work does not appear in either of the Clifden sales at Robinson and Fisher in May 1895 and June 1896.
8. In the 1951 sale catalogue, the name is printed as 'Lord Annerlay', but no peer of this name is recorded and it is presumably an error for either 'Annesley' or 'Annaly'. No details concerning his ownership have emerged.

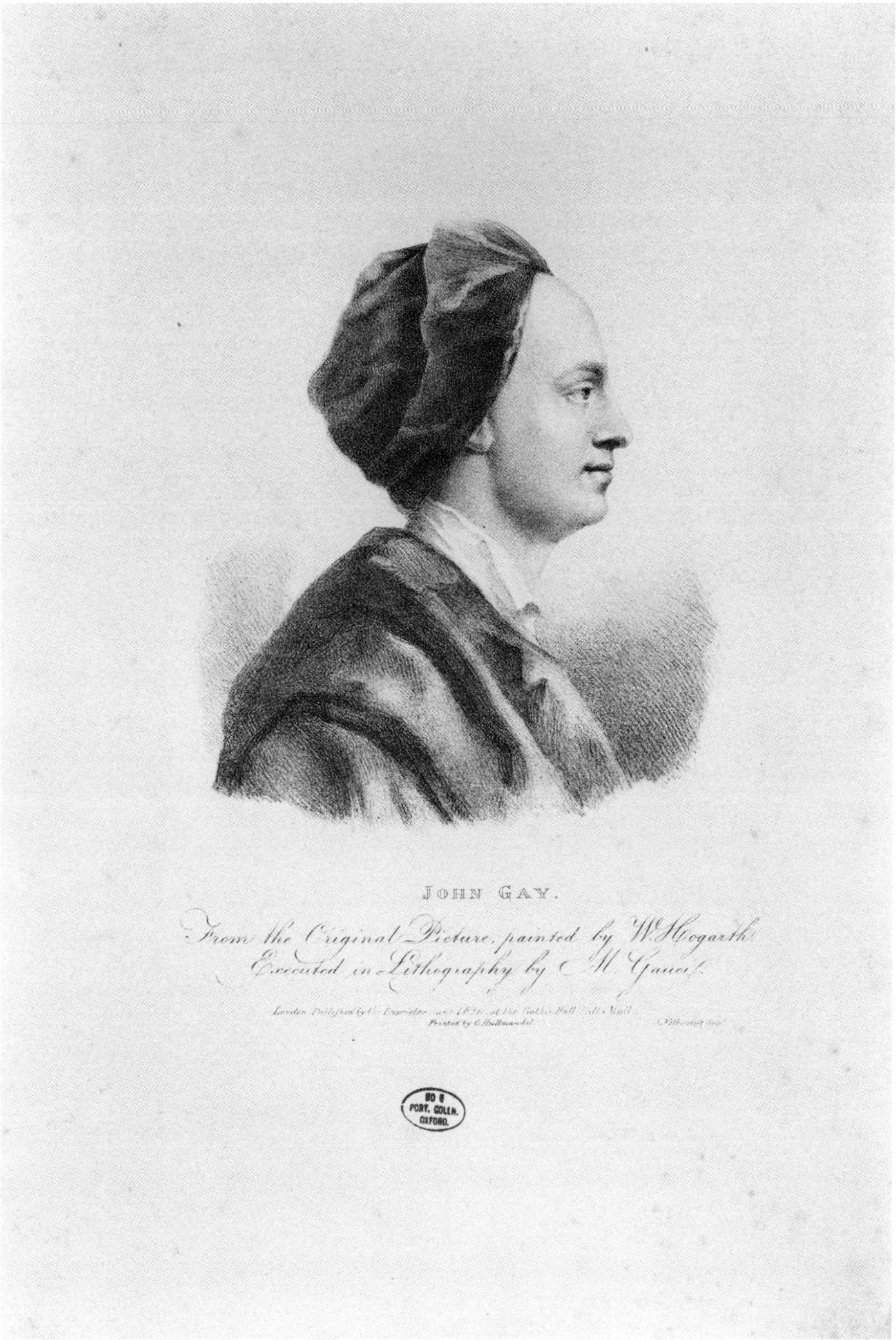

Fig. 59 *Jonathan Richardson Junior, titled John Gay* after Jonathan Richardson, lithograph by M. Gauci. Ashmolean Museum, University of Oxford.

John Francis Rigaud

1742–1810

Thomas Bentley

WAG 2548
oil on canvas, 105.5 × 85 cm
date: 1772–73

Thomas Bentley was born at Scropton, Derbyshire in 1731,[1] the son of a farmer of the same name. He was educated at Finderne Presbyterian Academy near Derby, and he remained part of Dissenting circles in adult life. After an apprenticeship to a Manchester wool and cotton merchant, he visited France and Italy in 1753, and on his return set up as a warehouseman and agent in wool and cotton in Liverpool the following year. He remained in Liverpool until 1769.

Bentley was a cultivated man, prominent in literary and philosophical circles in Liverpool. He helped found the Dissenting Academy at Warrington[2] and the Liverpool Library in the late 1750s; he wrote for *The Gentleman's Magazine* and *The Monthly Review*; from 1766 he was involved with plans for a system of canals linking Liverpool with the Potteries; he drained part of Chat Moss, and was an early and keen opponent of the slave trade. In 1762 he met and befriended Josiah Wedgwood, becoming his agent in Liverpool for the exportation of Wedgwood ware. In 1767, Wedgwood offered to make Bentley his partner. After initially hesitating, Bentley accepted. Leaving Liverpool, he spent some time with Wedgwood at Etruria, before moving to London in 1769 to head Wedgwood's London operation. His cultivation and social skills were an important factor in the development of the company, and he introduced the young Flaxman to work for Wedgwood in 1774. Twice married, Bentley died at Turnham Green, 26 November 1780.

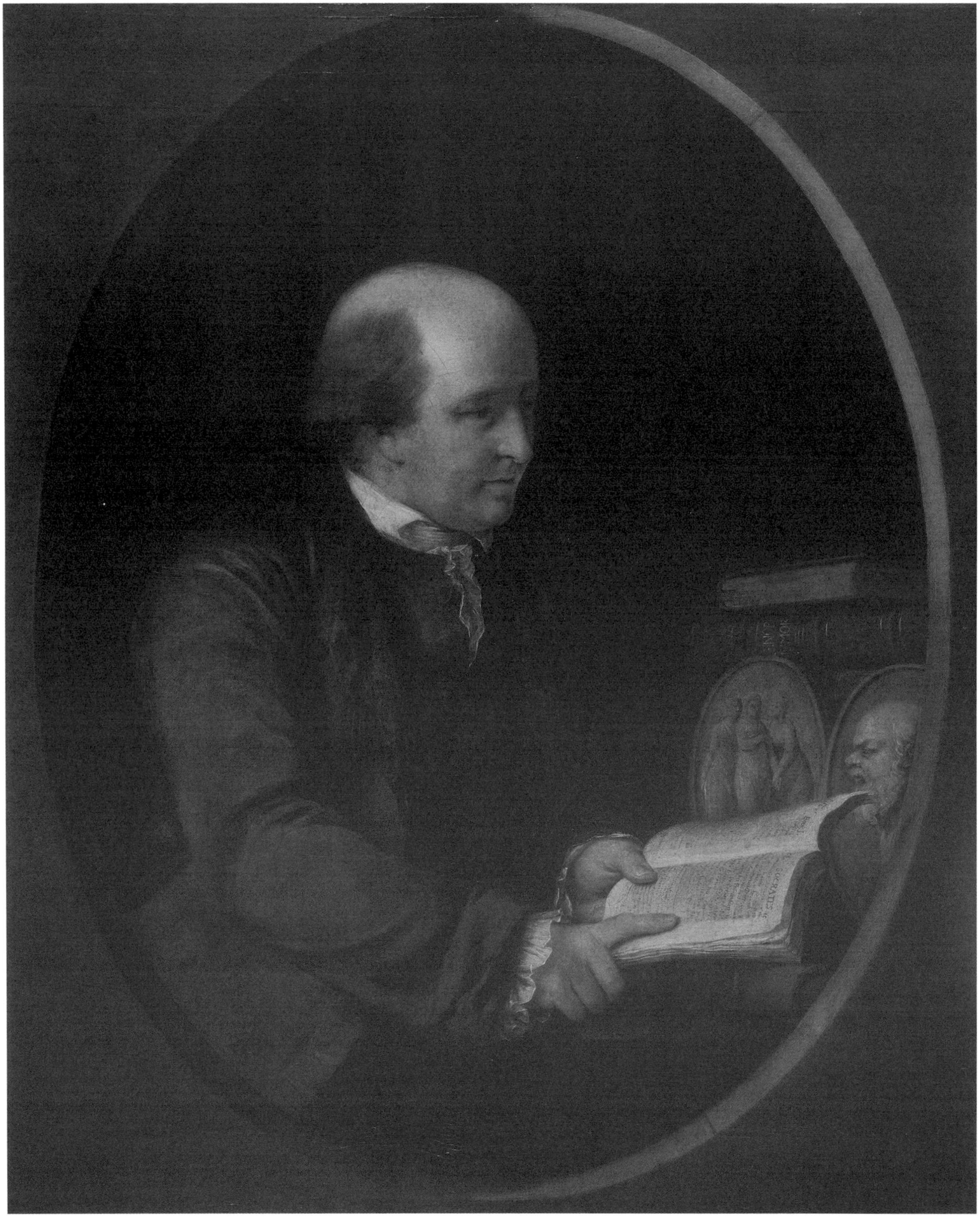

WAG 2548

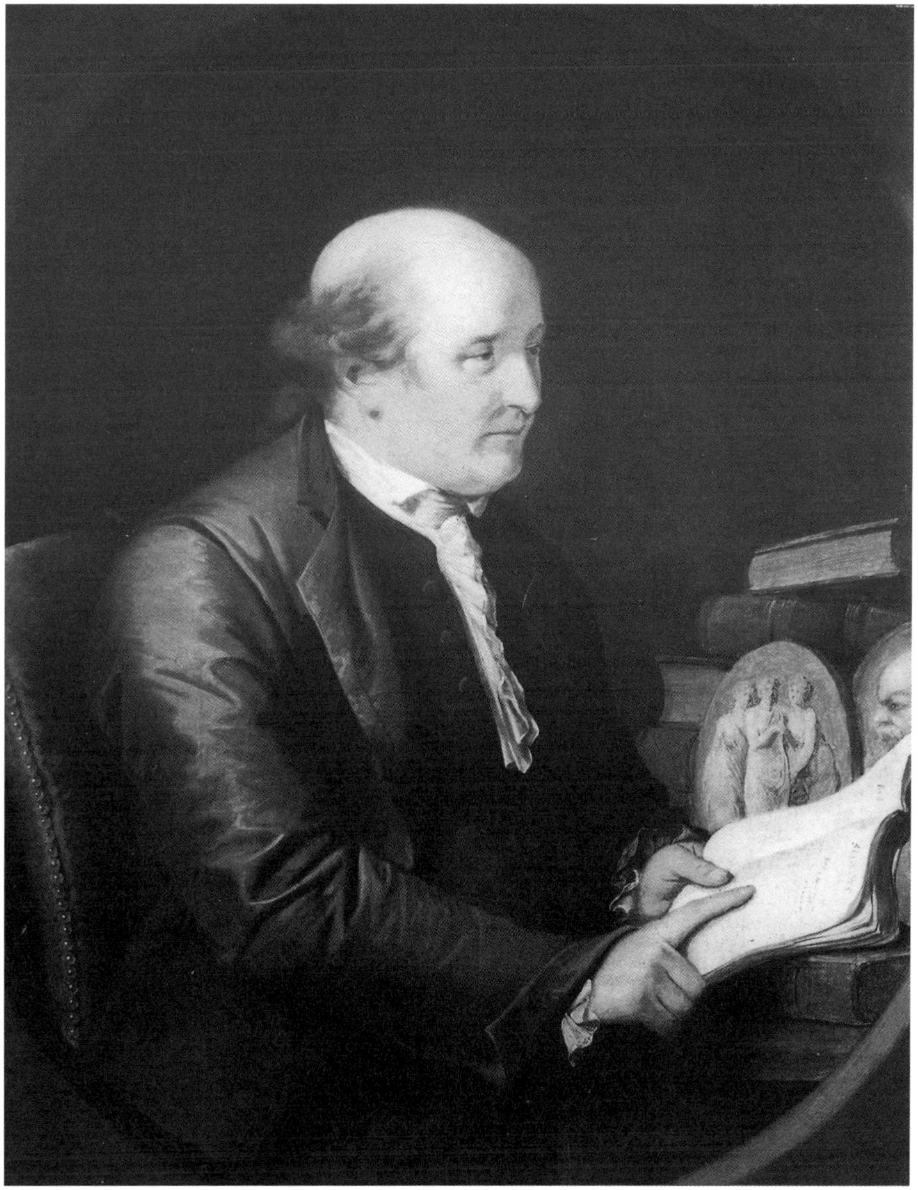

Fig. 60 *Thomas Bentley* after J. F. Rigaud, oil on canvas. Courtesy of The Wedgwood Museum.

A monument to him by Scheemakers was erected by Wedgwood in Chiswick Church, and Wedgwood also issued four medallion portraits of him, two in his lifetime, two posthumously.[3]

The present canvas must be the work exhibited by Rigaud at the Royal Academy in 1773. In the memoir of his father which he wrote in 1854, Stephen Francis Dutilh Rigaud recalled:

this year [1773] he exhibited the following six pictures... No. 5 [deleted] Portrait of a Gentleman 'Mr Bentley, <Director> of a new manufacture of porcelain in imitation of the Etruscan vases &c <generally known by the name of Wedgwood ware.> I have represented him contemplating the analogy between moral and natural beauty. He has in his hand the life of Socrates, who was the greatest Philosopher and admirer of the beauties of Nature, and at the same time an able Sculptor. The medallion of Socrates is resting on some books, which are the works and characteristics of Xenophon [sic; see below]. This picture has great strength, relief, and likeness; nevertheless, it has more the appearance of the simple representation of a Philosopher, than of a Portrait.[4]

At the RA the work was badly hung and little noticed by reviewers but the critic of the *Public Advertiser*, having noted that it was almost invisible, commented that 'the Peculiarities of it are hardly to be observed, and yet they are the Things principally worthy of Regard. They are strongly expressive of the Character and Disposition of a Gentleman who does Honour to this Country by the Judgement and Taste with which he conducts one of its most elegant Manufactures'.[5] A further version of the work (Wedgwood Museum, Barlaston; fig. 60) has been thought to be the first,[6] but it is significantly smaller in both dimensions, is a more caricatured likeness, is less detailed in the handling of the text on the open page of the *Life of Socrates*, and truncates the medallion of Socrates specifically referred to by Stephen Rigaud. On balance, therefore, WAG 2548 has the superior claim to be Rigaud's original.[7]

The book which Bentley is shown reading is John Gilbert Cooper's *Life of Socrates* (1749; fourth edition 1771), which Cooper based on passages from Xenophon's *Memorabilia* (itself one of the books in the stack on the right-hand side of the portrait) and dialogues of Plato. The volume underneath the open book is inscribed *CHARACTERISTICKS* and must be intended for the *Characteristicks of Men, Manners, Opinions, Times, [etc.]* by Anthony Cooper, 3rd Earl of Shaftesbury (Closterman's well-known engraved portrait of whom prominently features volumes of Xenophon and Plato). The passage Bentley reads is from Book I page 14 of Cooper's *Life*:

as several Authors affirm, the celebrated Graces, carv'd on the walls of the Citadel at Athens behind the statue of Minerva, were his Performances. An early indication of the Propensity of his Mind to Beauty! From this, compar'd with his Life and Doctrines, we may perceive what invariable Analogy there is between a Taste for moral and for natural comeliness.[8]

Rigaud's inclusion of a Wedgwood-like relief of the Three Graces[9] alongside the Socrates relief drives home his intended comparison between the philosopher and Bentley himself as connoisseurs of moral and natural beauty.

PROVENANCE

[? Mrs Bentley; her niece Mrs Elizabeth Caldwell; her daughter Mrs William Stanley Roscoe; by descent to] Mrs A. M. Roscoe; her bequest 1950.[10]

EXHIBITION

RA 1773 (249).

NOTES

1. *MPPP*, p. 52, states that he was born on 1 January 1730 (old style) – i.e. 1731 in the reformed calendar. The biography which follows summarises that in *MPPP*; see also James Boardman: *Bentleyana, A Memoir of Thomas Bentley* (Liverpool, 1851); Eliza Meteyard: *The Life of Josiah Wedgwood* (London, 1865); R. Bentley: *Thomas Bentley of Liverpool, Etruria and London* (Guildford, 1927); and Alison Kelly: 'Bentley, Thomas', *ODNB* vol. 5, pp. 304–5.
2. In 1757, according to *MPPP*, *loc. cit.*; in 1759 according to John Ingamells: *National Portrait Gallery: Mid-Georgian Portraits* (London, 2004) p. 54.
3. For the medallion portrait on Scheemakers's monument, see Anthony Burton: *Josiah Wedgwood: A Biography* (London, 1976) fp. 177. The four Wedgwood medallions are (i) by Joachim Smith, about 1773–74 (R. Reilly and G. Savage: *Wedgwood, The Portrait Medallions* [London, 1973] p. 60, and R. Reilly: *Wedgwood Jasper* [London, 1994] p. 14); (ii) attributed to William Hackwood, 1778, in two variants (Reilly and Savage, *op. cit.*, pp. 60–1); (iii) attributed to Hackwood, 1780 (Reilly and Savage, *op. cit.*, p. 61); (iv) a larger medallion recorded in Wedgwood's oven books in October 1782 (Reilly and Savage, *op. cit.*, p. 61). For other portraits of Bentley, which included one by William Caddick, see the discussion in *MPPP*, p. 52.
4. William L. Pressly, ed.: '*Facts and Recollections of the XVIIIth Century in a Memoir of John Francis Rigaud, Esq., R.A.*, by Stephen Francis Dutilh Rigaud, Abridged and Edited with an Introduction and Notes', *Walpole Society* vol. 50 (1984) p. 54.
5. *Public Advertiser* (28 April 1773) p. 2.
6. Ingamells, *loc. cit.*
7. Pressly, *op. cit.*, p. 144, n. 16, prefers the view that both WAG 2548 and the Wedgwood Museum portrait are copies of Rigaud's lost original, but he concedes he has based this opinion on photographs; however, the quality of WAG 2548 when viewed in the flesh seems above that of a copy. Both versions descended from Mrs Elizabeth Caldwell, niece of the second Mrs Bentley.
8. *MPPP*, *loc. cit.*, pointing out that Rigaud has transposed a left-hand page to a right-hand one for visual effect.
9. *MPPP*, *loc. cit.*, notes that known Wedgwood plaques of the Three Graces are smaller in size and of a different design to the type depicted here.
10. When it entered the gallery, WAG 2548 was attributed (as the version that later entered the Wedgwood Museum also was at the time) to Wright of Derby. It is possible that Wright was commissioned for a copy of Rigaud's portrait since his account book lists, after 1780, *a Copy of Mr Bentley Kit cat, £21* (Benedict Nicolson: *Joseph Wright of Derby, Painter of Light* 2 vols [London, 1968] vol. 1, p. 180); however, no such canvas is currently known and the identification remains conjectural. WAG 2548 was catalogued in *MPPP* (1978) as 'British School, eighteenth century' and was described as apparently 'by a provincial hand'.

John Riley

1646–91

Thomas Sprat

WAG 2996
oil on canvas,[1] 237.5 × 149 cm
date: about 1685–87

Thomas Sprat (1635–1713), Bishop of Rochester from 1684 until his death, was born at Beaminster, Dorset and was educated at Wadham College, Oxford. In his youth he was best known as a literary figure and a wit. He was a friend of Abraham Cowley, on whom he wrote his *Ode on the English Ovid* (1657) as well as a panegyric, *An Account of the Life and Writing [of Abraham Cowley]* originally in Latin, which was included in Cowley's *English Works* (1668). He became a member of the Royal Society in 1663 and under its auspices wrote *Observations on Monsieur de Sorbier's Voyage to England* (1665) and *The History of the Royal Society* (1667). He was ordained as a priest in 1661 and received a series of preferments culminating in his appointment as Dean of Westminster in 1683 (a post he was permitted to retain on being elevated to the see of Rochester the following year). Sprat was instinctively a strong Royalist, a position which stood him in good stead during the reign of Charles II but which caused him difficulties in the more turbulent reign of James II. As a member of James II's commission for ecclesiastical affairs, Sprat was perceived as a henchman of the King's pro-Catholic religious policy, and he was unable to negotiate the politics of the Glorious Revolution and the succession of William III without appearing an unprincipled opportunist. Seeing the way the wind was blowing, Sprat resigned from the King's ecclesiastical commission in August 1688, joined with fellow bishops in pressing James to accept a free Parliament, and following the king's flight, wrote prayers giving thanks for Britain's delivery from Popery. He took the oath of allegiance to William and Mary on 4 March 1689. In 1692, nevertheless, he was suspected of conspiring to restore James to the throne. Although he was found innocent, Sprat from that point on began to take a less prominent role in public affairs. He retained his reputation as a fine preacher and a master of the English language.[2]

This portrait, showing Sprat in a bishop's Convocation robes, must have been painted between November 1684, when he was consecrated Bishop of Rochester, and 1691, the year in which John Riley died. A date of about 1690 has been proposed[3] (perhaps on the basis that such an ambitious commission must have

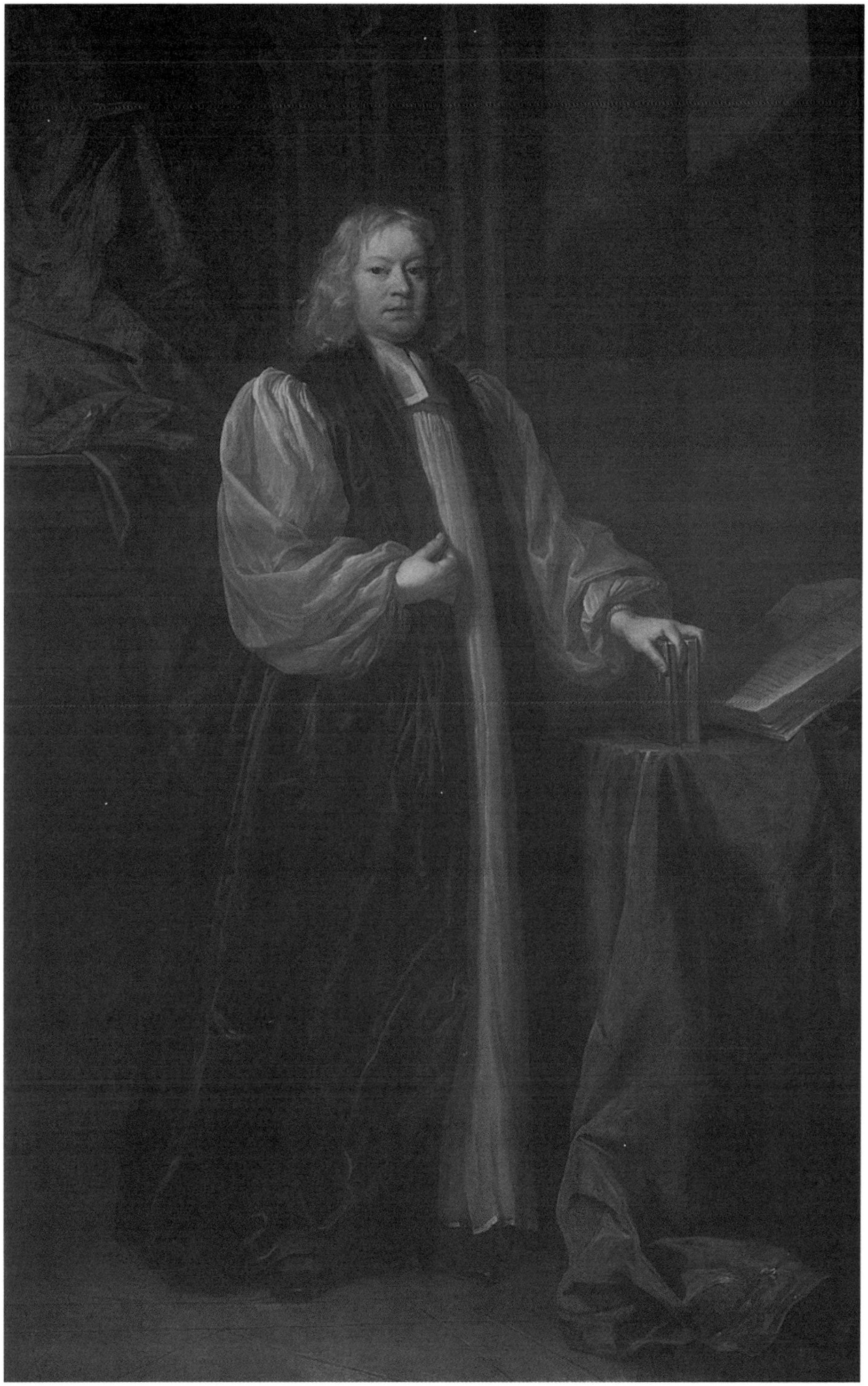

WAG 2996

been given after Riley's appointment as joint Principal Painter to William III), but there may be a case for an earlier dating. It has been suggested that WAG 2996 is a joint production between Riley (who tended to concentrate on heads) and another member of his studio, the preferred candidate being J. B. Closterman, whose 'Baroque continental manner' has been adduced in the treatment of the drapery.[4] Closterman seems to have been most closely associated with Riley in the first half of the 1680s, and a dating of about 1685 arguably works better in terms of Sprat's apparent age (he looks youthful even for 50), as well as supporting the notion that the portrait was commissioned to mark Sprat's elevation to the see of Rochester. Nevertheless, on the view that Closterman's manner would have become diffused within Riley's studio,[5] the later dating cannot be ruled out. One possible piece of evidence is the inscribed small Roman *VII* at the top of the left hand page of the large volume open on the table. This inscription could be interpreted as a coded allusion to Sprat's *Roman* (Catholic) tendencies during the Trial of the *Seven* Bishops, the famous case which fuelled popular and parliamentary opposition to James II in 1687–88.[6]

Despite its size and formality, the portrait does not seem to have had an official function, for no reduced copies are known and only one engraving, that published by David Loggan, seems to be even loosely based on it.[7] If it is to be identified as the portrait seen by George Vertue sometime after 1725 'at Earls Court near Kinsington at Mr Wrights. a gallery of pictures whole lenghts modern – about 12 or 14 / Dr Sprat Bp Rochester'[8] (and WAG 2996 is the only known full-length portrait of Sprat), then it is likely to have been retained by him as a personal possession and disposed of after his death.

PROVENANCE

…[? Mr Wright of Earl's Court about 1725]; … bt. in the early 1920s by the Tillotson family, Liverpool; presented to the gallery in 1953 by Geoffrey Tillotson.

EXHIBITIONS

Selected Acquisitions of the Walker Art Gallery Liverpool 1945–1955 Agnew's, London 1955 (35); *Cleaned Pictures* Walker Art Gallery 1955 (31).

NOTES

1. WAG 2996 was relined around 1923 shortly after it became the property of the Tillotson family, and was given a new stretcher at the same time. The condition and treatment report prepared by J. Coburn Witherop in 1954 after WAG 2996 was acquired by the gallery (gallery files) records that the original stretcher was diagonally braced in the corners. The report noted that the relining was unsatisfactory, since heavy ironing which attempted to even out the surface caused considerable damage to the paint layer, especially in the thinly painted areas of the draperies. The head had remained in good condition, but the work had been badly damaged in other areas before the 1920s relining. The report also noted the existence of pentimenti to Sprat's right hand, which has been repositioned, and at the bottom of the canvas where a step was overpainted as a level stone-paved floor. (See also Coburn Witherop's note in the 1955 exhibition catalogue, p. 56.)
2. See John Morgan: 'Sprat, Thomas', *ODNB* vol. 51, pp. 976–83.
3. John Ingamells: *The English Episcopal Portrait 1559–1835* (London, 1981) p. 363; followed by Morgan, *loc. cit.*
4. Richard Jeffree: 'Riley, John', *Macmillan Dictionary of Art* ed. Jane Turner, 34 vols (London and New York, 1996) vol. 26, p. 394. Jeffree had earlier said of WAG 2996 that 'it is clearly by Riley – or from his studio, and is, in fact, one of his finest extant works' (*letter*, 13 June 1986, gallery files). When it was acquired by the gallery, WAG 2996 was believed to represent John Tillotson, Archbishop of Canterbury, and it was when it was realised that this identification was incompatible with an attribution to Riley that Closterman was proposed as the artist. Subsequent re-identification of the sitter as Sprat (on the basis of the likeness in Michael Dahl's later portrait of Sprat with his son, engraved by J. Smith) resuscitated the original attribution. However, Ingamells, *loc. cit.*, also proposed that WAG 2996 was the joint work of Riley and Closterman.
5. As is suggested by Jeffree, 'Riley, John', *loc. cit.*
6. This begs the question of whether this painted *VII* is original to the portrait, or a later addition, which it has not been possible to determine.
7. F. O'Donoghue: *Catalogue of Engraved British Portraits Preserved in the Department of Prints and Drawings in the British Museum*, 6 vols (London, 1908–25) vol. 4, p. 168. O'Donoghue does not specify the work on which Loggan's (half-length) print is based but it was identified as WAG 2996 by Dr Christopher Maude Chavasse, Bishop of Rochester, *letter*, 7 July 1959, gallery files.
8. Mrs A. Esdaile, ed.: 'Vertue Notebooks Volume II', *Walpole Society*, vol. 20 1931–32 (1932) p. 89.

George Romney

1734–1802

Portrait of a Lady, Probably Mrs James Collinson

WAG 2602
oil on canvas, 76.5 × 61.5 cm
date: about 1765

This portrait seems always to have been with its companions, WAG 2414–15 (pp. 146-7). A label on the reverse, dated 8 May 1905, identifies the sitter as 'Mrs Collingwood', 'a connection of Lady James Pringle of Richmond, Yorkshire'.[1] The derivation of this identification is unclear, and it appears to have been of very recent origin, for all three paintings had been consigned without name at Christie's in 1903.[2] Since the label was written at the time of a re-lining treatment undertaken by the dealers Shepherd Bros, it probably related to the discovery of an old inscription on the back. The sitters' correct surname was probably Collinson, since portraits of Mrs, Master and Miss Collinson are recorded on a manuscript list of his sitters which Romney drew up shortly after a trip to Lancaster in the mid-1760s.[3] Otherwise unaccounted for, these three portraits seem very likely to be WAG 2602, WAG 2414 and WAG 2415 on grounds of style and other circumstantial evidence.

An inscription on the back of the original canvas was also recorded by Shepherd Bros as *For Mr George Romney / at the Kings Arms / Lancaster.*[4] A plausible interpretation of this is that the canvas was returned to Romney – presumably for alterations – when the artist visited Lancaster in 1767, having originally been painted on his previous trip to the north-west in 1765.[5] Romney's correspondence in the 1760s several times mentions a Mr Collinson, to whom he asks to be remembered,[6] and he appears to have painted this Mr Collinson's portrait at Lancaster also – either in 1760–61, shortly before his first move to London, or else in 1765.[7]

The likeliest candidate for Mr Collinson is James Collinson of Church Street, Lancaster, who was a notary public, became a Freeman of the town in 1755 and died in 1786.[8] Little is known of his wife. She is probably the Jane Collinson who, with James Collinson, witnessed the marriage of Thomas Fryer in Lancaster in 1772; her signature is also recorded on a document dated 1800. She does not appear to have died in Lancaster and her will is untraced.[9] Her two known children were a son James and a daughter Jane, whose baptismal records show that they are of an age to be the children in WAG 2414–15. Mrs Collinson herself was clearly a woman of some pretension: the grey and pink shot silk dress she wears was of a type fashionable in the mid-1760s,[10] and Romney has lavished considerable care on its depiction.

PROVENANCE

…Lady James Pringle;[11] bequeathed to Miss Emily Purvis; Christie 25 April 1903 (56); bt. in; … Shepherd 1905; from whom bt. before 1908[12] by W. Hall Walker (Lord Wavertree); his bequest 1933.

EXHIBITIONS

Spring Exhibition of Selected Pictures by Early British Masters and Modern Painters Shepherd Bros, London 1905 (103); *George Romney* Iveagh Bequest, Kenwood 1961 (13).

NOTES

1. The full text of the label reads: *Mrs Collingwood, painted by George Romney / Mrs Collingwood was a connection of Lady James Pringle of Richmond, / Yorkshire. Behind the original canvas was written 'To Mr George Romney – The King's Arms, Lancaster'. It was relined today. May 8 1905. & the writing / is copied in*

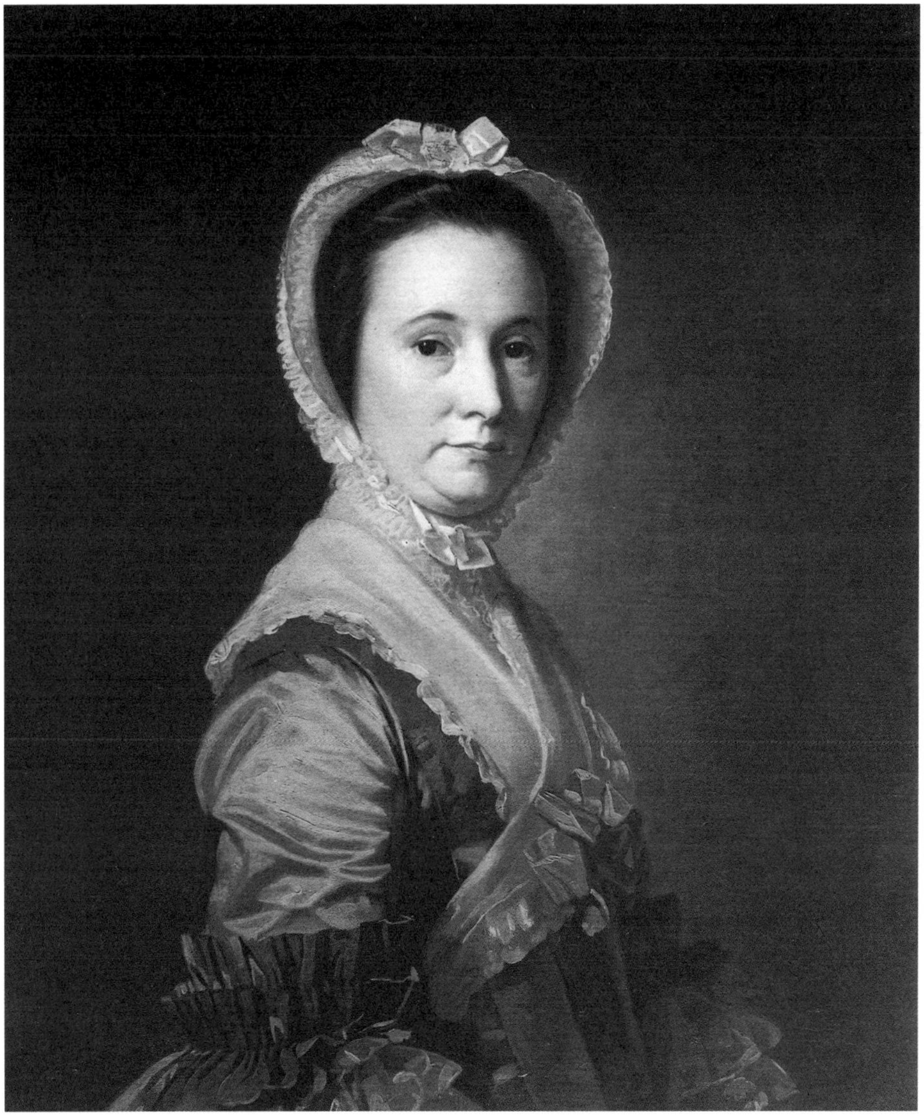

WAG 2602

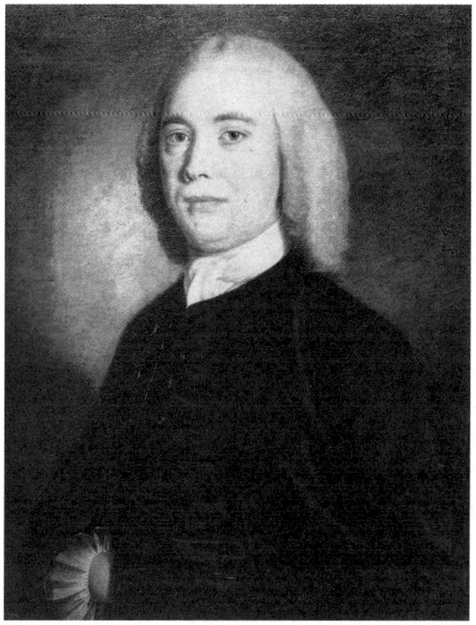

Fig. 61 *James Collinson* by George Romney, oil on canvas. Private collection, UK; photo courtesy the owner.

facsimile.
2. The three paintings were consigned at Christie's in 1903 as the portraits of 'a Lady', 'a Young Boy', and 'a Young Girl'. Another portrait titled *Mrs Collingwood*, the same size as WAG 2602, sold at Christie 28 February 1891 (61); bt. Vokins (£125) appears to have been an unrelated work; this canvas was sold again by E. M. Denny at Christie 31 March 1906 (52); bt. McLean (£84).
3. National Art Library, Victoria & Albert Museum ms L.1957/1455.
4. See n. 1.
5. For these visits see A. Kidson: *George Romney 1734–1802* exh. cat., Walker Art Gallery, National Portrait Gallery, London and Huntington Art Collections, San Marino (2002) pp.16, 59–60, 63–4.
6. See for example Revd John Romney: *Memoirs of the Life and Works of George Romney* [...] (London, 1830) p. 34.
7. The portrait, also consigned by Miss Purvis at Christie's in 25 April 1903 (lot 57, *Portrait of a Gentleman* and also bought in) became separated from the three Walker portraits at the time of the exhibition at Shepherd Bros in 1905. It was returned to Miss Purvis and descended in her family to the present owner. Extensive latterday conservation has made the attribution of this canvas problematic, but a photograph dating from the early twentieth century (fig. 61) does suggest that Romney either painted it *in toto* or else completed a portrait begun by his master Christopher Steele. It has been proposed that WAG 2602 is itself by Steele (Mary E. Burkett: 'Christopher Steele 1733–1767', *Walpole Society* vol. 53 [1987] p. 207) but the evidence of the National Art Library list, if accepted, contradicts this.
8. R. Sharpe France, Lancashire Record Office, *letter*, 15 December 1961, gallery files.
9. Information from Helen Quartermaine, *email*, 3 May 2010, gallery files.
10. Anne Buck, *letter*, 3 January 1962, gallery files.
11. Arthur Chamberlain: *George Romney* (London, 1910) p. 285, stated that Lady Pringle was born Grace Pye and lived in Richmond, North Yorkshire; I am grateful to Helen Quartermaine, *email*, 17 October 2010, for the further information that Grace Pye married James Pringle in Morpeth, Northumberland, in September 1785. Between 1791 and 1810 Morpeth was the home of Admiral Lord Collingwood, and it is conceivable that this was the source of later confusion over the sitter's name.
12. William Roberts, in his own copy, preserved in Christie's archives, of volume 2 of T. H. Ward & W. Roberts: *Romney* 2 vols (London and New York, 1904) noted that he had seen these pictures on a visit to Col. W. Hall Walker's London residence in 1908. He was confused into thinking that the *Mrs Collingwood* was the canvas of that title sold at Christie's in 1906 (see n. 2).

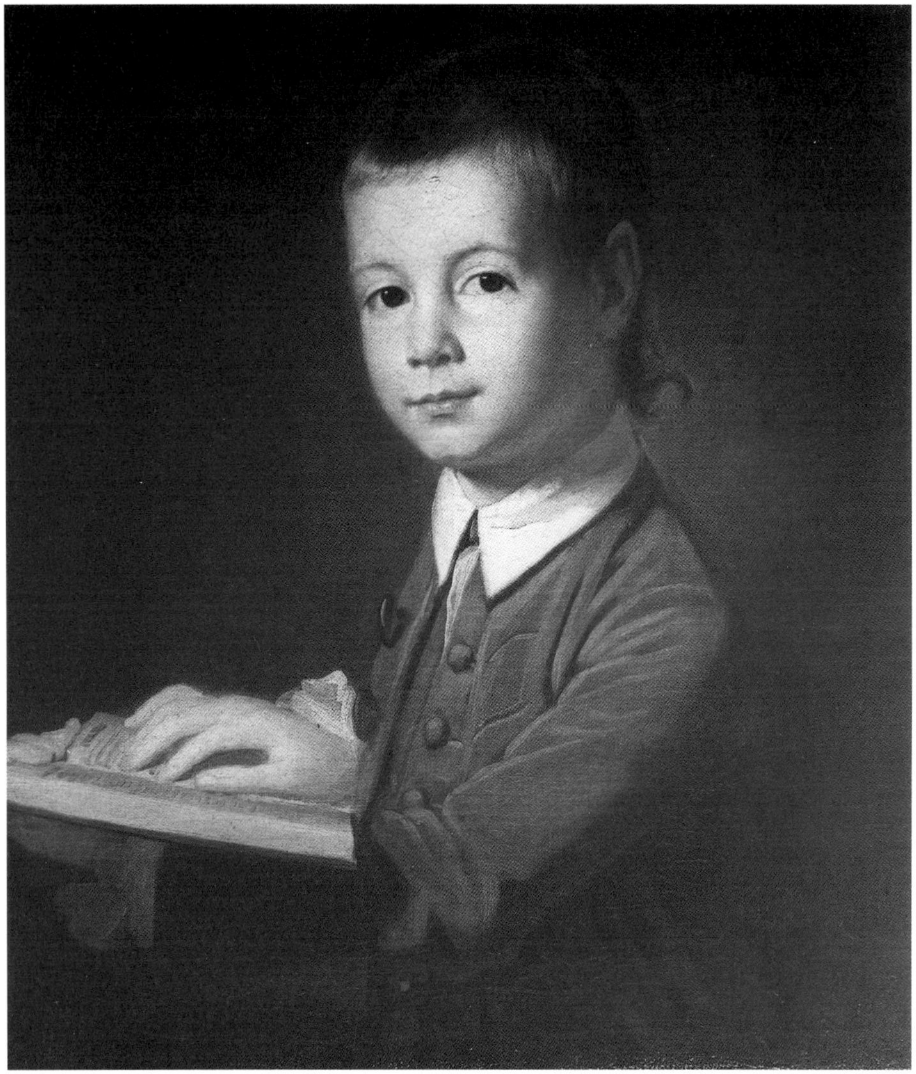

WAG 2414

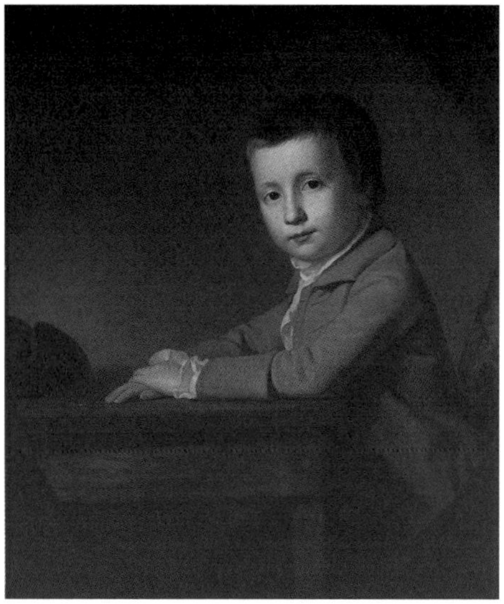

Fig. 62 *Sir John Wells as a Boy* by George Romney, oil on canvas. Private collection, USA; photo courtesy Lowell Libson Ltd.

Portrait of a Boy, Probably James Collinson

WAG 2414
oil on canvas, 51 × 43 cm

Portrait of a Girl, Probably Jane Collinson

WAG 2415
oil on canvas, 51 × 43 cm
date: 1767

A label formerly on the reverse of WAG 2415 reads: *Miss Collingwood, painted by George Romney / Miss Collingwood was a connection of Lady James Pringle of Richmond / Yorkshire. This original canvas was relined today, May 8 1905.*[1] In all probability, however, (see WAG 2602, pp. 144–5) the portrait represents Jane Collinson, daughter of James Collinson of Lancaster, at the age of four. Jane was baptised on 21 August 1763; Romney paid two visits to Lancaster from London in the autumn of 1765 and again in the late summer and autumn of 1767, and on grounds of her apparent age this portrait must have been undertaken on the later visit. Although WAG 2414 has traditionally been titled *Master Collingwood*, he is without doubt Jane Collinson's elder brother James, baptised in Lancaster on 13 January 1762. In 1784 he became a fellow of St. John's College Cambridge.[2]

The style of painting in this pair of works is less sophisticated than in the portrait of the children's mother, but this is more likely to be a deliberate choice on Romney's part than to be an indication of an earlier date of execution. A very similar conception is apparent in Romney's portrait of Sir John Wells as a boy, also dateable to the later 1760s (fig. 62). WAG 2414–15 have been viewed as representative of newly emerging strategies of middle-class portraiture in Britain.[3]

A repaired area of damage to WAG 2414 measuring approximately 2 × 2 cm is visible at lower right, about 6 cm from the right hand edge and the same distance from the bottom of the canvas.

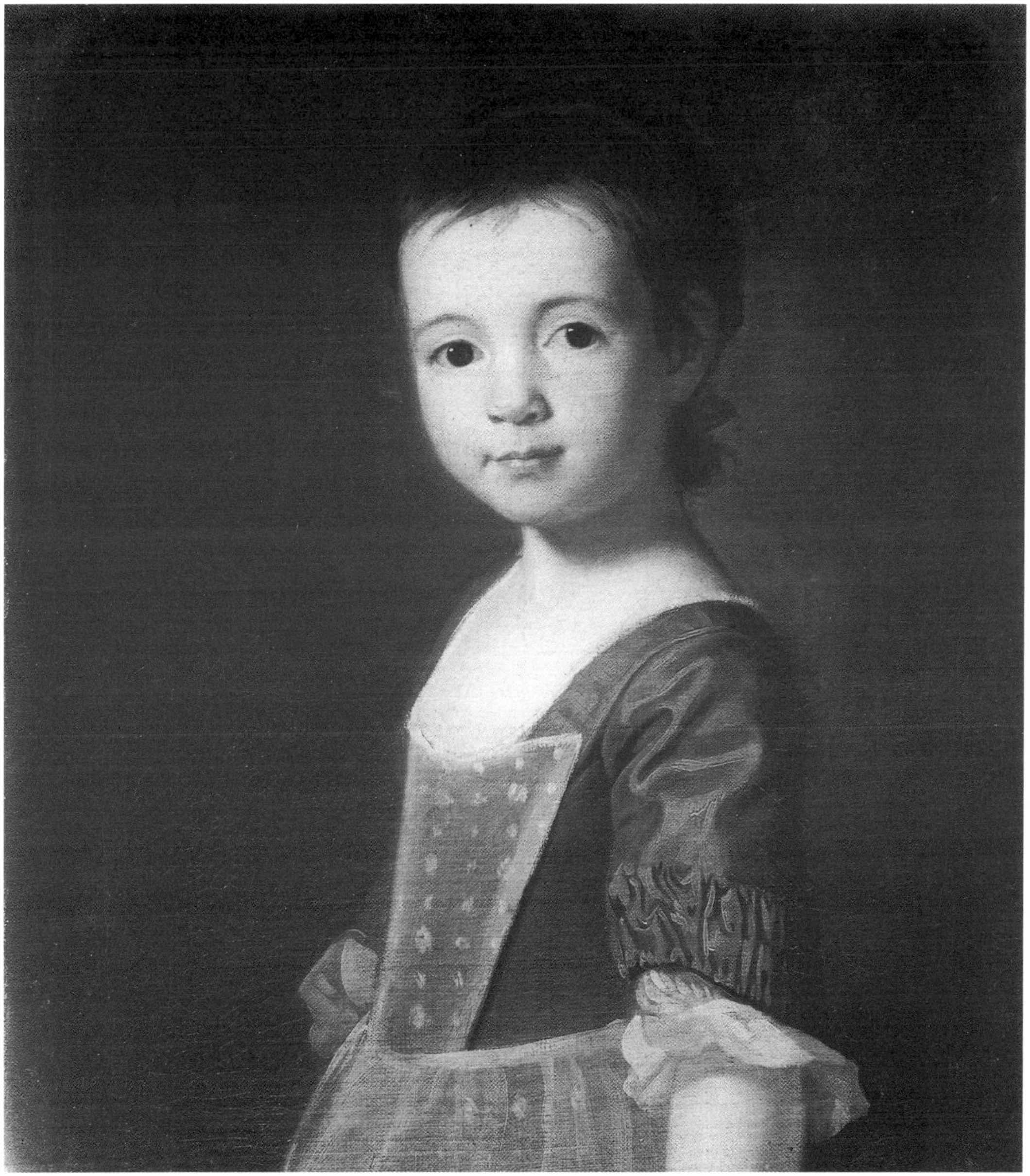

WAG 2415

PROVENANCE

...Lady James Pringle; bequeathed to Miss Emily Purvis; Christie 25 April 1903 (59) [WAG 2414] and (58) [WAG 2415]; bt. in; ...Shepherd 1905; from whom bt. before 1908 by Col. W. Hall Walker (Lord Wavertree);[4] his bequest 1933.

EXHIBITIONS

Spring Exhibition of Selected Pictures by Early British Masters and Modern Painters Shepherd Bros, London 1905 (102) [WAG 2414] and (101) [WAG 2415]; *George Romney* Iveagh Bequest, Kenwood 1961 (15) [WAG 2414] and (14) [WAG 2415]; *Four Kendal Portrait Painters* Abbot Hall Art Gallery, Kendal 1973 (19) [WAG 2414 only]; *George Romney as a Painter of Children* Leger Galleries, London 1984 (2) [WAG 2415] and (3) [WAG 2414].

NOTES

1. The label is preserved in gallery files.
2. R. Sharpe France, Lancashire Record Office, *letter*, 15 December 1961, gallery files. It may not be coincidental that St John's was also the Cambridge college of Romney's son John, and the two may have been friends. No trace has been found of the marriage or death in Lancaster of either James or Jane and it is probable that they moved away from the town (information from Helen Quartermaine, *email*, 3 May 2010, gallery files; and see p. 145, n. 11).
3. G. C. Rump: *George Romney: Zur Bildform der bürgerliche Mitte in der Englischen Neoklassik* 2 vols (Hildesheim, 1974) vol.1, pp. 140–2; vol. 2, pls 82, 84, 87.
4. See p. 145, n. 12.

Charlotte Bettesworth, Mrs John Sargent

WAG 294
oil on canvas, 126.5 × 102 cm
date: 1778

Charlotte Bettesworth was the daughter and heiress of Richard and Charlotte (née Orme) Bettesworth of Lavington Park, near Arundel in Sussex. She was baptised at South Stoke, near Arundel on 5 June 1755[1] and died at Putney 31 March 1841.[2] On 21 December 1778, she married John Sargent, younger son of John Sargent of Halsted Place, Kent;[3] and even though the sittings are undocumented, WAG 294 has every appearance of being a wedding portrait.[4] It was certainly in existence by March 1779 when Romney received total payment for it of £44 14s.10½d.[5]

The commission for the portrait was almost certainly engineered by Romney's friend William Hayley, who lived only a few miles from Lavington Park. In February 1778 Hayley commissioned from Romney a portrait of his friend John Thornton, and later that year Thornton brought his own friend Sargent to Eartham to meet Hayley and his circle, 'and saw him, in consequence of that visit, enamoured of a young Sussex lady whose character and accomplishment afforded him the fairest prospect of matrimonial felicity'.[6] Hayley's letters reveal that he had been amusing himself plotting the match and Romney could conceivably have begun the portrait at Eartham in August or September; although as Hayley chaperoned Miss Bettesworth to London on several occasions during the autumn,[7] the portrait is more likely to have been carried out then. On 23 December Hayley remarked in a letter, 'I presume the Lord of Lavington has recovered his spirits which had totally forsaken him in town, and I should be glad to hear that he was better reconciled to the *Picture*.'[8] Assuming this refers to WAG 294, it suggests that the portrait was finished by the time of the wedding, and may imply that it was carried out for Charlotte's father, rather than bride or groom.

This work is a typical example of Romney's newly fashionable brand of society portraiture, but it is also exceptional for him in the degree of care and contrivance it manifests. The pose is not a standard one but unusual and hard to manage;[9] the sitter's hands are beautifully painted and there is little sense of conventional flattery. In particular, the inclusion in the left background of a relief sculpture version of the antique sardonyx gem *The Marriage of Cupid and Psyche*, then in the collection of the Duke of Marlborough and formerly, as Romney was no doubt aware, in the famous Gem Cabinet of the Earl of Arundel,[10] is unusually loaded. Besides alluding to Charlotte's marriage and her home town, it also underscores the contextual importance of Romney's own friendship with Hayley, friendship which had begun when the two men had projected a new illustrated translation of the tale of Cupid and Psyche, from Apuleius.

A good quality copy of WAG 294, the same size of the original, is in a private collection in Bristol. This is thought to have been made for R. G. Wilberforce at the time he sold the original.[12]

PROVENANCE

By descent to R. G. Wilberforce 1885;[13] …Christie; from whom bt. by Agnew 11 April 1888;[14] bt. by George Holt 11 May 1888 (£1,700);[15] Emma Holt Bequest 1945.

EXHIBITIONS

Old Masters RA 1884 (4); *Loan Exhibition of Pictures… in Aid of the Funds of the Children's Infirmary* Agnew's, Liverpool 1904 (12); *Some Acquisitions of the Walker Art Gallery Liverpool 1935–1945* National Gallery, London 1945 (13); *George Romney 1734–1802* Walker Art Gallery, National Portrait Gallery, London and Huntington Art Collections, San Marino 2002 (93); *Treasures from Sudley: A Liverpool Shipowner's Home* Haworth Art Gallery, Accrington and tour 2005–06 (no cat.).

NOTES

1. P. Gill, West Sussex Record Office, *letter*, 9 January 1984, gallery files.
2. The pedigree of the Sargent family appears in *The Genealogist* NS vol. 33 (1917) p. 191. This source states that Mrs Sargent was 86 at the date of her death.
3. He was author of *The Mine and Other Poems* (1784); MP for Seaford, Queenborough and Bodmin 1790–1806; died 1831 (Roland Thorne: 'Sargent, John', *ODNB* vol. 48, pp. 966–7). A portrait of Sargent attributed to Romney (but not by him) is in the Holburne Museum Bath.
4. T. H. Ward and W. Roberts: *Romney: A Biographical and Critical Essay with a Catalogue Raisonné of His Works* 2 vols (London 1904) vol. 2, pp. 139–40, cite John Romney's 'Rough Lists' of his father's portraits to the effect that it was painted in 1776. This must be a mistake, ascribable to the lack of recorded sittings.
5. *Romney's Account Book, 1777–82*, Huntington Library, HM26343, entry dated 13 March 1779. The cost of the painting itself, 36 guineas, was correctly recorded by John Romney (see n. 4).
6. J. Johnson, ed.: *Memoirs of the Life and Writings of William Hayley, Esq.* 2 vols (London, 1823) vol. 1, p. 175.
7. Johnson, *op. cit.*, pp. 175, 178.
8. *Hayley Mss*, West Sussex Record Office, ms 2816, p. 113.
9. Romney's model may have been Reynolds's *Elizabeth, Lady Harrowby* of 1774–75; see A. Kidson: *George Romney 1734–1802* exh. cat., Walker Art Gallery, National Portrait Gallery, London and Huntington Art Collections, San Marino (2002) p. 161.
10. Diana Scarisbrick: 'The Arundel Gem Chest', *Apollo* vol. 144 (August 1996) pp. 45–8.
11. See Kidson, *op. cit.*, pp. 102–3 for Romney's 1775 painting *[The Wedding of] Cupid and Psyche*, which must have been prominently displayed in Romney's studio on the occasion of Hayley's first visit in 1776.
12. It was sold by Wilberforce's daughters at Christie, 14 July 1939 (25), and bought by their cousin, Mrs G. Franklyn (her letter, 21 February 1945, gallery files); she apparently bequeathed it to her collateral relative Orme Sargent, who already had a number of Sargent and Wilberforce heirlooms (including the portrait of John Sargent mentioned in n. 3); thence it descended to the present owner.
13. Lent by Wilberforce to the 1885 exhibition.
14. Agnew stock books, April 1888. The work was not in a Christie's auction, and had probably been consigned to them for private sale.
15. *George Holt Papers*, gallery archives. Holt paid the Liverpool branch of Agnew £5.15s.6d. for a new frame in July 1888 and a further £4.8s.6d. for repairing and regilding the frame in October 1890.

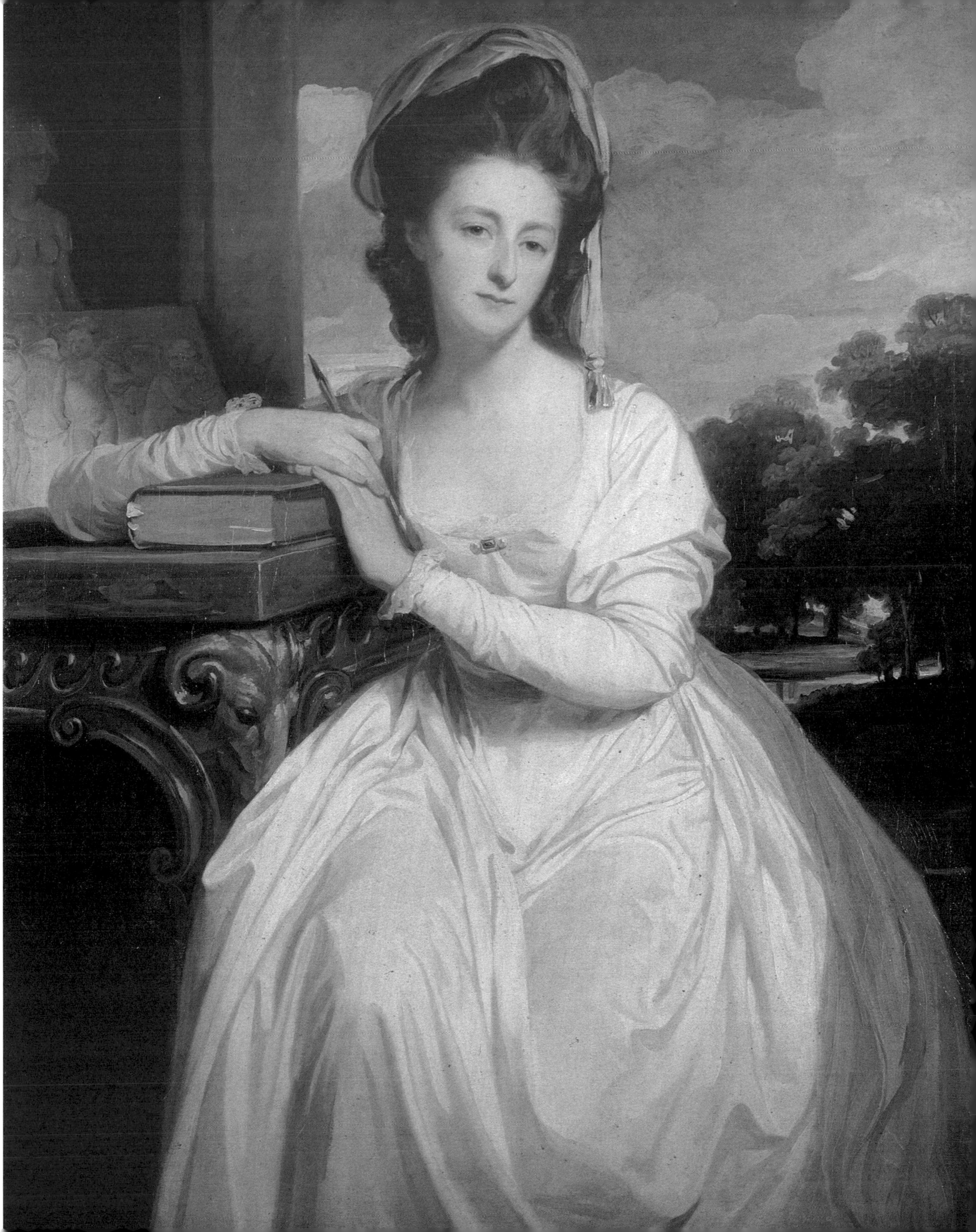

WAG 294

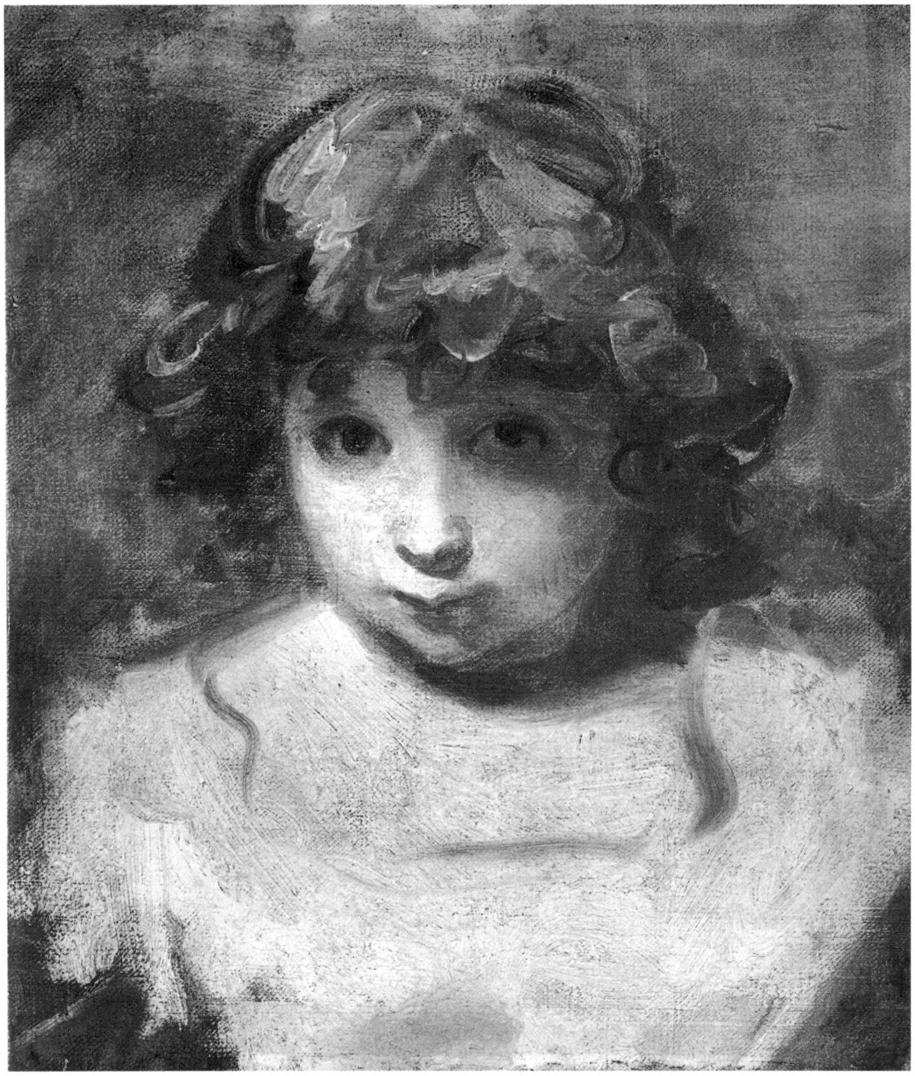

WAG 3104

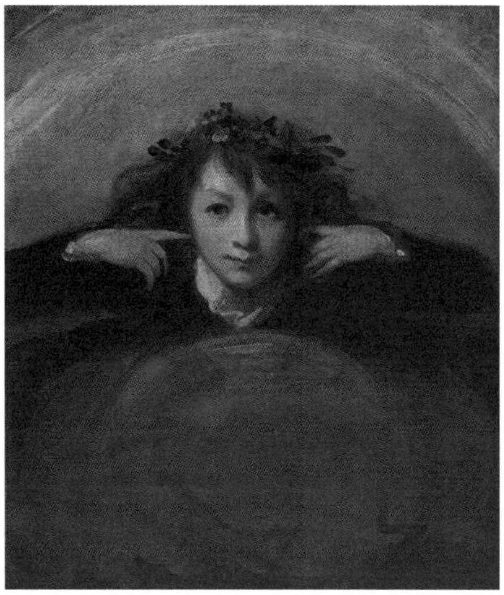

Fig. 63 *Tom Hayley as Robin Goodfellow* by George Romney, oil on canvas. © Tate, London 2011.

Thomas Alphonso Hayley

WAG 3104
oil on canvas, 39 × 33 cm
date: about 1784–85

Thomas Alphonso Hayley was the son of Romney's friend, the poet William Hayley, and one of Hayley's servants, Miss Cockerell. Born in 1780, he was a good-natured, precocious and artistic child, the apple of his father's eye and a great favourite of Romney himself, who painted him on numerous occasions.[1]

Through Romney's intercession Tom was apprenticed in 1795 to the sculptor John Flaxman, but he soon began suffering from a curvature of the spine, from which, after a long and painful decline, he died in 1800.[2]

On the basis of the boy's age, WAG 3104 can be dated to around 1784–85. It has less the character of a proper portrait than a fancy head for which Tom was the model. It must have been painted at William Hayley's villa at Eartham, W. Sussex, where Romney spent some time each summer relaxing, making studies for his works of the imagination and painting portraits of his host's circle. Romney appears to have made this sketch on an already used piece of canvas; the stroke of white paint visible running across the face from upper left to lower right lies underneath the thin paint which establishes Tom's facial features and hair. As the paint continues onto the present tacking margins, the canvas was probably cut down, and it is now on a fairly rough and homespun strainer. An inscription on the reverse of the canvas in ink, *Geo Romney pinx*, is not in the artist's hand.[3]

PROVENANCE

...Liverpool Royal Institution by 1836;[4] deposited at the gallery 1893 and transferred 1948.

EXHIBITIONS

Loan Exhibition of Works of Early British Masters Manchester City Art Gallery 1909 (42); *George Romney 1734–1802* Walker Art Gallery, National Portrait Gallery, London and Huntington Art Collections, San Marino 2002 (112).

NOTES

1. Tom also makes an appearance in Romney's compositions *Tom Hayley as Robin Goodfellow* of 1789 (Tate Britain, London; fig. 63); *Flaxman Modelling the Bust of Hayley* 1795–96 (Yale Center for British Art, New Haven); and *The Four Friends*

1796 (Abbot Hall Art Gallery, Kendal), with related works. He may also be the subject of the sketches sold at Christie 18 June 1971 (5) and Sotheby 9 July 1997 (34). See also T. H. Ward and William Roberts: *Romney: A Biographical and Critical Essay with a Catalogue Raisonné of His Works* 2 vols (London, 1904) vol. 2, pp. 75–6. WAG 3104 was identified as a portrait of Tom in A. Kidson: *George Romney 1734–1802* exh. cat., Walker Art Gallery, National Portrait Gallery, London and Huntington Art Collections, San Marino (2002) p. 190, on the basis of the likeness to the boy in the later, documented Tate painting.
2. For a full survey of Tom's life see J. Johnson, ed.: *Memoirs of the Life and Writings of William Hayley [and] Memoirs of his Son Thomas Alphonso Hayley* 2 vols (London, 1823); especially vol. 2 (section separately paginated).
3. Condition report, National Museums Liverpool Paintings Conservation Department, December 2000.
4. The early history of WAG 3104 is a mystery. It cannot be traced in Romney's studio sale, Christie 27 April 1807, nor Hayley's posthumous sale, Christie 15 February 1821. One hypothesis is that it was presented by Hayley to the artist's son John Romney and given or bequeathed by the latter to the LRI as a companion for Romney's cartoons, donated in 1823.

attributed to

Peter Romney

(1743–77)

Paul Pennington

WAG 10682
oil on canvas, 107 × 92.5 cm
date: 1769

Paul Pennington is listed in Liverpool street directories for 1767, 1769, 1772, 1773 and 1774 as a sailmaker in Atherton Street (later South Castle Street). He is absent from the directories of 1766 and 1777. Portrayed here fashionably dressed in a green suit and making an entry in a ledger, he presents the image of a successful businessman, rather than a worker of sailcloth. The work bears a very indistinct date (inscribed on the ledger) tentatively legible as *September 1769*.[1] On this basis, WAG 10682 may be attributed to Peter Romney, the elusive younger brother and sometime pupil of George Romney. Peter Romney is known to have been working in Liverpool in 1769,[2] and the style of this portrait displays clear affinities to George Romney's work of the second half of the 1760s; it was traditionally attributed to Romney by later owners.[3] Peter Romney's name occurs, together with Paul Pennington's, in a list of 22 founder members of the first Society of Artists in Liverpool, 1769,[4] and although no further information has survived concerning the activities of either man in respect of the society, WAG 10682, from its scale and pretension, may well have been painted with an intended founding exhibition in mind. No other oil painting by Peter Romney is currently known to survive.

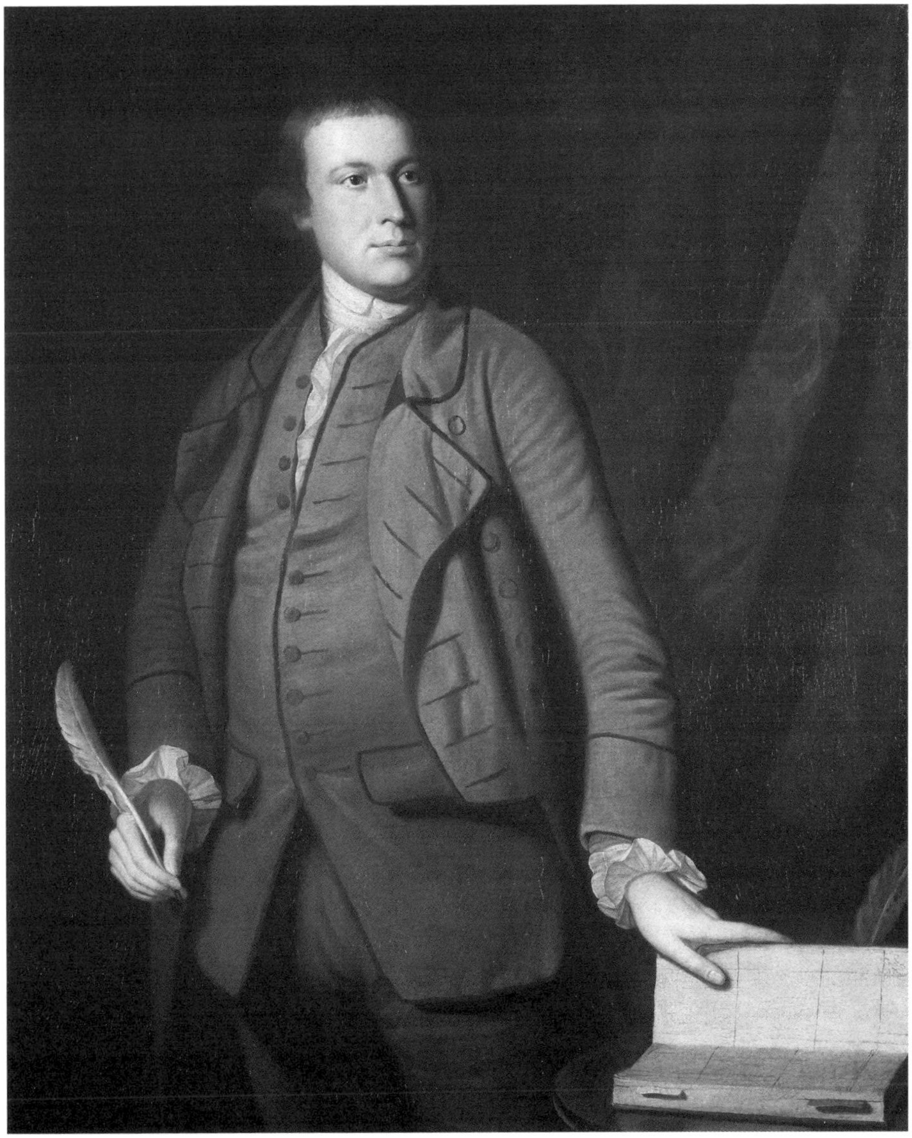

WAG 10682

PROVENANCE

By descent to Mrs H. M. A. Berry, Greetby Hill, Ormskirk, 1935;[5] by descent to Miss M. Berry; from whom bt. 1987.

EXHIBITION

Joseph Wright of Derby in Liverpool Walker Art Gallery and Yale Center for British Art, New Haven 2007–08 (8).[6]

NOTES

1. The date was misread and published as *1767* in CIC, p. 46; the painting itself was attributed to 'British School'.
2. John Romney: *Memoirs of the Life and Works of George Romney, Also Some Particulars of the Life of Peter Romney, His Brother* (London, 1830) p. 300. Peter Romney 'had a dozen pictures in hand' in November 1769 but left Liverpool soon afterwards.
3. Information from Miss Berry, *verbally*, June 1987.
4. Joseph Mayer: *Early Exhibitions of Art in Liverpool, with Some Notes for a Memoir of George Stubbs R.A.* (Liverpool, 1876) p. 4.
5. Christie's stencil 397 *GA* on the reverse; the work was sent to Christie's (presumably for attribution and possible sale as a work by George Romney) in February 1935 but was returned to Mrs Berry without being put into a sale the following month. I am grateful to Marijke Booth for this information.
6. The work was cleaned and restored prior to the exhibition by Larry Keith in the conservation studios of the National Gallery, London.

Francis Sartorius

1734–1804

A Phaeton Drawn by a Pair of Ponies with a Groom

WAG 9815
oil on canvas, 61 × 76 cm
signed and dated: *F Sartorius Pinx 1771* (bottom right)
date: 1771

The subject was described in the *Croxteth 1900s Inventory* as 'Elizabeth, Lady Craven's calache [sic] a pair of greys in the carriage on the panel of which is a cypher EC under a barron's coronet. A groom in Craven livery is standing at the horses heads by the carriage a dalmatian hound'.[1] Elizabeth, daughter of Augustus, 4th Earl of Berkeley married William, 6th Baron Craven in 1767. After his death in 1791, by her second marriage she became Margravine of Anspach; she died in 1818. She was the grandmother of the 3rd Earl of Sefton, her daughter Maria, marrying Lord Molyneux (later 2nd Earl of Sefton) in 1792 (see WAG 10502, pp. 13–5).

The carriage is a pony phaeton, whose construction is carefully depicted by Sartorius. The undercarriage has two cranes with high arches allowing the front wheels to lock underneath. The body with skeleton quarters is suspended by buckle braces from S-springs which are very flat in front and upright behind. Wings are fitted, the offside one appearing to turn up more at the hind end than the nearside one. There is a low platform for the groom. What appears to be a belly strap is visible beneath the nearside pony, to prevent the pole from rising too high. Pony phaetons were described in William Felton's *Treatise on Carriages* (1794) as 'pretty equipages…best adapted for parks only; for, by being so low, the passengers are much annoyed by the dust, if used on the turnpike roads'.[2]

An almost identical phaeton and pair of grey ponies appear, similarly positioned, in Sartorius's portrait of Edward Stratford, 2nd Earl of Aldborough and his second wife Anne, dating from the later 1780s, a work that is the same size as WAG 9815.[3]

PROVENANCE

Presumably given by Lady Craven to her daughter Maria, Countess of Sefton; by descent at Croxteth Hall to Josephine, Countess of Sefton; her bequest 1980.

NOTES

1. *Croxteth 1900s Inventory* Card Room no. 1.
2. This reference, and notes on the carriage, were kindly provided by Chris Nicholson, 1997.
3. Exhibited in *English Sporting Paintings*, Ackermann Ltd, London 1987 (6).

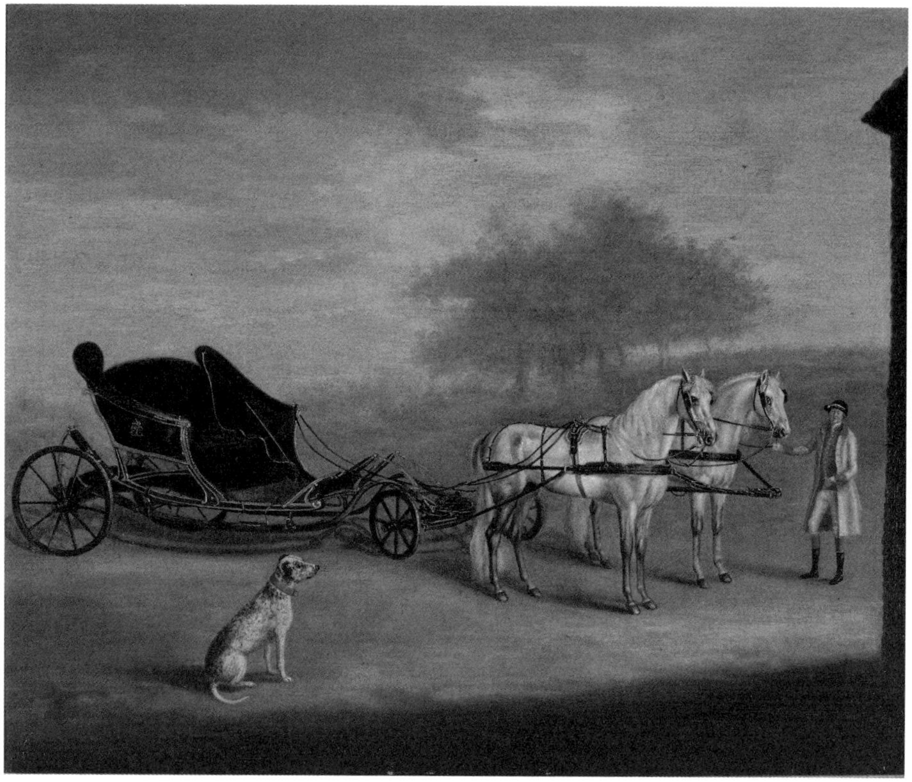

WAG 9815

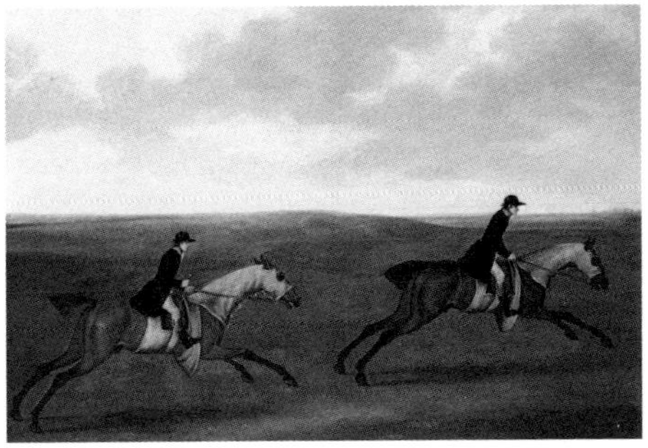

WAG 9814

John Nost Sartorius
1759–1829

Two Racehorses with Liveried Lads up, Exercising on a Heath

WAG 9814
oil on canvas, 57 × 82 cm
date: unknown, perhaps 1795–1800

The painting is unrecorded at Croxteth before 1946, but it could well have been commissioned by the 2nd Earl of Sefton, who was a keen sportsman. The riders, whose features the artist has attempted to portray, wear a livery of navy blue jackets with buff lapels and black caps. In the 1946 inventory the work is attributed to 'School of Sartorius',[1] but John Nost Sartorius's authorship seems plausible. Even though the style is different to that of the works catalogued below, it is likely to be somewhat earlier in date, perhaps from around the 2nd Earl's succession to the title in 1795. The work has been extensively repainted.

PROVENANCE
...Hugh, 7th Earl of Sefton 1946; by descent to Josephine, Countess of Sefton; her bequest 1980.

EXHIBITION
The Noble Horse Metropolitan Teien Art Museum, Tokyo 1998 (23).

REFERENCE
1. *Croxteth 1946 Inventory*, no. 87.

A Huntsman and Fox-hounds Entering a Wood

WAG 2310
oil on canvas, 51 × 61 cm
signed: *J N Sartor*
(bottom right; the *ius* is lacking)
date: unknown, perhaps 1795–1810

Perhaps from a pair or set of hunting scenes, WAG 2310 is of higher quality than the works catalogued below. The horse and the dogs, as well as the rider, are given distinct expressions which, in the case of the dogs, suggest an attempt at humour. The work has been variously dated; it may be from as early as the mid-1790s.[1]

PROVENANCE
...Walter Stone before 1934; Mary Stone Bequest 1944.

EXHIBITIONS
Sporting Pictures from the Walter Stone Collection Bluecoat Gallery, Liverpool 1946 (20); *A Selection of Sporting Pictures from the Walter Stone Collection* Bluecoat Gallery, Liverpool 1953 (16).

REFERENCE
1. The date *1795* is painted on the frame of WAG 2310; the evidence for this date is unknown, but the bottom edge of the canvas is damaged and heavily repainted and it may be that an original signature and date has been lost. However, Walter Stone believed the work to date from around 1820; see *The Walter Stone Collection of Sporting Pictures at Whitton Hall, Westbury, Shropshire* (privately printed, 1938) p. 24 (cat. 32).

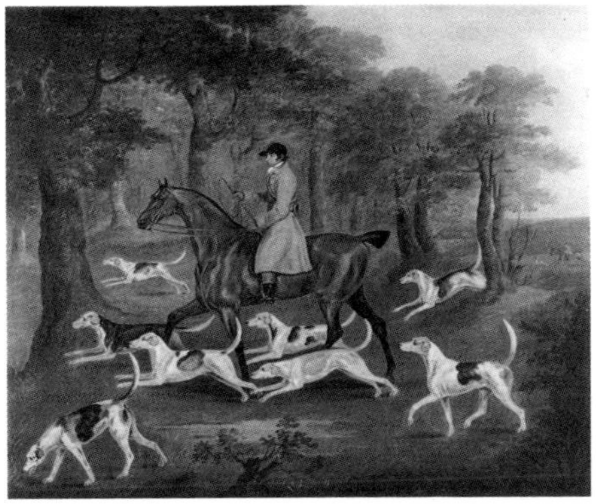

WAG 2310

Setting Out

WAG 36
oil on canvas, 35.5 × 42.5 cm
signed and dated: *J. N. Sartorius 1802*
(bottom right)

Going to Cover

WAG 2334
oil on canvas, 36 × 43 cm
signed and dated: *J. N. Sartorius 1802*
(bottom right)

Full Cry

WAG 2309
oil on canvas, 36 × 43 cm
signed and dated: *J. N. Sartorius 1802*
(bottom right)

Taking a Fence

WAG 2335
oil on canvas, 36 × 43 cm
signed and dated: *J. N. Sartorius 1802*
(bottom right)

The Death

WAG 2336
oil on canvas, 36 × 43 cm
signed and dated: *J. N. Sartorius 1802*
(bottom right)
date: 1802

Sets of fox-hunting scenes such as this formed one of the staples of Sartorius's output. He had established the basic composition of WAG 2334 at least by 1791, the date on a similar-sized but more freshly painted version with the horse differently posed, four hounds and an extensive landscape background (fig. 64).[1] The present set, which is of repetition quality, follows almost identically a set of six signed and dated 1800–01 whose canvases are the same size as the Walker's set, and which was framed as a single piece;[2] another set of six, signed and

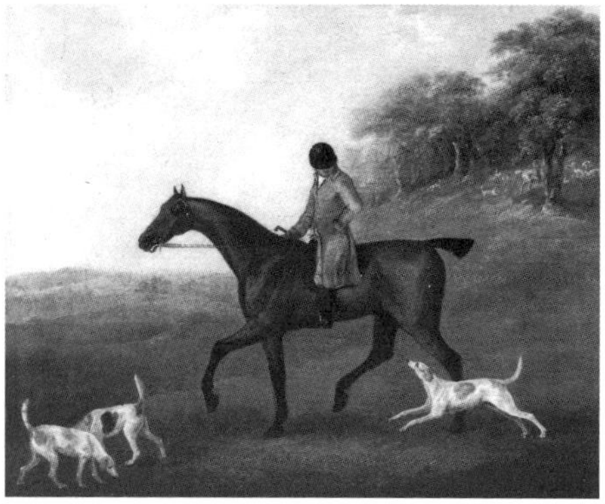

WAG 36

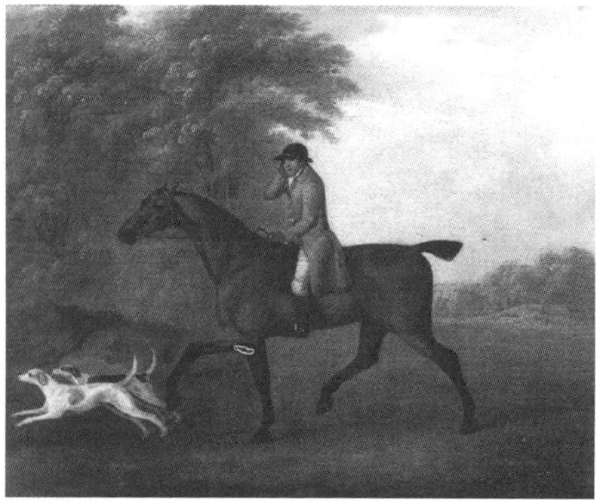

WAG 2334

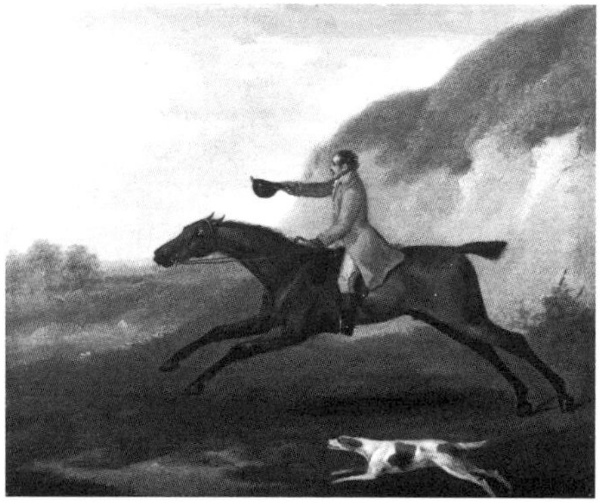

WAG 2309

dated 1809, has the same compositions in reverse with minor variations.[3] The existence of these complete sets confirms that one canvas is missing from the Walker's: the fifth in the sequence, a composition presumably to have been titled *Gone to Earth*, showing the huntsman dismounted and two hounds

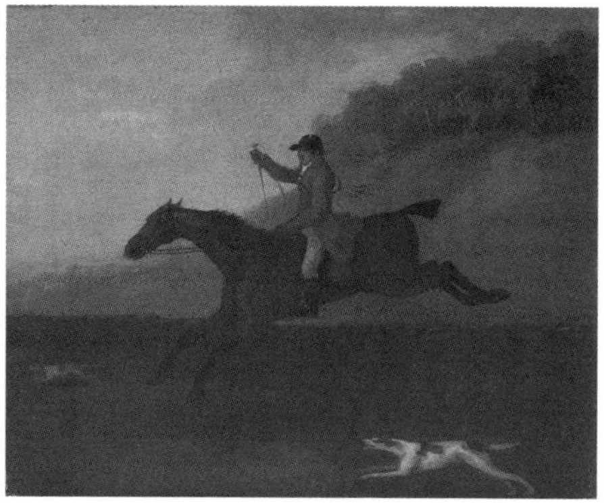

WAG 2335

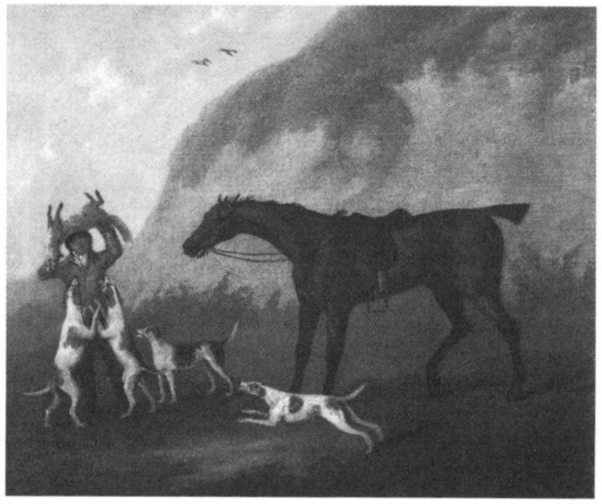

WAG 2336

watching in anticipation as two hunt servants dig the fox out of its bolthole with a pick.[4]

Many other versions of the individual canvases are known,[5] and Sartorius also re-used the poses of the animals in grander commissions. For instance, the first of his series of four paintings *The Earl of Darlington Foxhunting with the Raby Pack* (1804–05; formerly Mellon Collection)[6] incorporates at left in reverse the horse in WAG 36 and WAG 2334, and the running dogs accompanying Lord Darlington are very close to the dogs in WAG 2334.[7]

PROVENANCE

...Walter Stone; Mary Stone Bequest 1944.

EXHIBITIONS

[WAG 36] *Sporting Pictures from the Walter Stone Collection* Bluecoat Gallery, Liverpool 1946 (21);
[WAG 2334] *Sporting Pictures from the Walter Stone Collection* Bluecoat Gallery Liverpool, 1946 (21);
A Selection of Sporting Pictures from the Walter Stone Collection Bluecoat Gallery, Liverpool 1953 (17);
[WAG 2309] *Sporting Pictures from the Walter Stone Collection* Bluecoat Gallery, Liverpool 1946 (23);
[WAG 2335] *Sporting Pictures from the Walter Stone Collection* Bluecoat Gallery, Liverpool 1946 (24);
A Selection of Sporting Pictures from the Walter Stone Collection Bluecoat Gallery, Liverpool 1953 (18);
[WAG 2336] *Sporting Pictures from the Walter Stone Collection* Bluecoat Gallery, Liverpool 1946 (25);
A Selection of Sporting Pictures from the Walter Stone Collection Bluecoat Gallery, Liverpool 1953 (19).

NOTES

1. Christie 22 March 1974 (131); repr. A pendant picture auctioned in the same lot was not related to any of the compositions in the Walker Art Gallery series.
2. Christie New York 28 November 1995 (19); the six works were framed in a sequence running from top right to top left followed by bottom right to bottom left, with *Full Cry* placed third and *Taking a Fence* fourth.
3. Christie 16 July 1982 (10).
4. This subject is titled *The Earth Stopper* in the 1982 sale catalogue (see n. 3).
5. Comparable to WAG 2334 are the horse and rider in a painting 72 × 90 cm formerly with Ackermann & Co.; the horse and rider in a painting 36 × 43 cm, formerly with Knoedler & Co.; and a painting 43 × 34 cm, one of a set of four, with D. H. Farr, Philadelphia, in 1921. Comparable with WAG 2309 are the horse and rider in a painting with Howard Young, New York, 1928 (see the advertisement in *Art News*, 21 February 1928) and horse and rider (reversed) in a painting with Rayner MacConnal, 1935, one of a set of six (repr. *Apollo* (December 1935) p. 132). Comparable with WAG 2336 are: the painting sold at Sotheby 17 July 1974 (166); one of a pair, signed and dated 1806; the painting with Rayner MacConnal (see above, another of his set of six); the painting sold at Parke-Bernet, New York

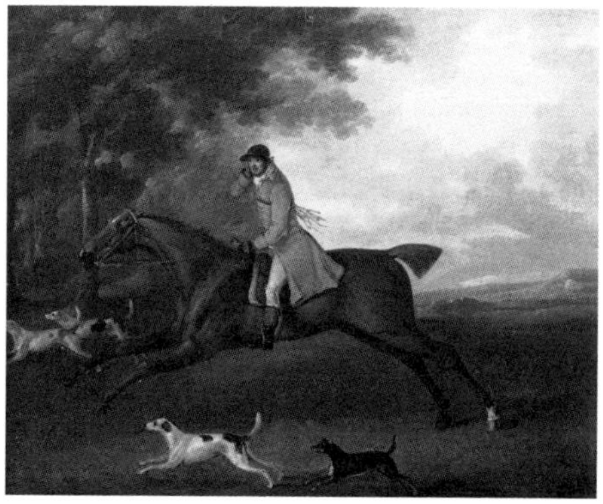

Fig. 64 *Going to Cover* by John Nost Sartorius, oil on canvas. Christie, 22 March 1974 (131, part.); photo A. C. Cooper.

3 December 1974 (31), one of a set of four; and the painting 43 × 34 cm, another of his set of four, with D. H. Farr, Philadelphia, 1921. Photographs of all of these are in the Witt Library.
6. Judy Egerton: *The Paul Mellon Collection: British Sporting and Animal Paintings* (London, 1978) pp. 156–7; repr. pl. 57.
7. I am grateful to Mark Evans for this observation.

A Huntsman Taking a Fence

WAG 2333
oil on canvas, 63 × 76 cm
signed and dated: *J N Sartorius 1807* (bottom right)
date: 1807

This is a work of potboiler quality. The handling is rapid and loose, somewhat in the manner of late George Morland. The size of the fox, barely visible in the lane in front of the thatched cottage, has been miscalculated (it appears to have been painted over the surrounding paint layer and may be a later addition). The horse in the foreground is in a stock pose encountered in numerous other works by or attributed to Sartorius dating from the period 1805–20, in some cases known to be one of a pair.[1] WAG 2333 is likely, too, to be from a pair or set of hunting scenes. It has darkened and the signature is now barely visible.

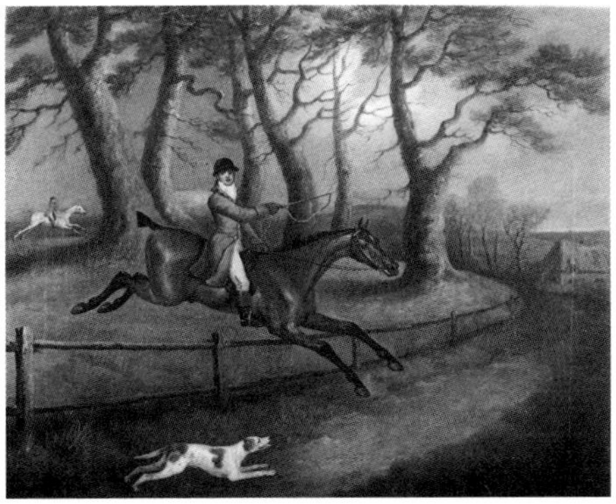

WAG 2333

PROVENANCE
...Walter Stone before 1934;[2] Mary Stone Bequest 1944.

EXHIBITION
A Selection of Sporting Pictures from the Walter Stone Collection Bluecoat Gallery, Liverpool 1953 (15).

NOTES
1. See, for example, Sotheby 17 June 1974 (166), one of a pair dated 1806; Sotheby 18 June 1976 (42), dated 1818; Christie 20 November 1981 (40), dated 1811; photographs of further examples dated 1814 and 1820, each one of a pair, are in Witt Library files.
2. *The Walter Stone Collection of Sporting Pictures at Whitton Hall, Westbury, Shropshire* (privately printed, 1938) p. 23 (cat. 31).

called
Samuel Scott
1702–72

Billingsgate and the Monument

WAG 9823
oil on canvas, 71.5 × 106.5 cm

Fleet Street and Temple Bar

WAG 9824
oil on canvas, 103 × 127 cm

The Thames with Westminster Bridge

WAG 9825
oil on canvas, 76.5 × 127 cm
Inscribed: *WNP*
(on the prow of the boat, left foreground)

St James's Palace and Pall Mall

WAG 9826
oil on canvas, 77 × 128 cm

Old London Bridge

WAG 9827
oil on canvas, 76 × 128 cm

The Thames with the York Buildings Water Tower

WAG 9828
oil on canvas, 76.5 × 127 cm
date: unknown, perhaps 1765–90

Although the name of Samuel Scott was generally applied to works of this type for much of the twentieth century, and was attached to these canvases when they were acquired by the gallery, WAG 9823–28 are certainly not by him. One, WAG 9827, is a copy of a composition by him, and a second, WAG 9828, is based on a view depicted by both Scott and Canaletto at about the same time.[1] Generally, the six works are characteristic examples of the type of tourist view of London which was produced from around 1750 into the nineteenth century, for visitors from the provinces or abroad, presumably in workshops. Canaletto's views were their most obvious prototype.[2] Other artists whose names have been associated with this type of work include Joseph Nickolls (flourished 1726–55), whose known paintings are of much higher quality than WAG 9823–28; William James (active 1754–71), who exhibited at the SA 1761–67, including in 1764 *A View of London Bridge, as Lately Repaired*; Daniel Turner (flourished 1782–1817) and John Paul (1775–1857). It is inconceivable that WAG 9823–28 are autograph works by any of these artists, and although they depict the London of the late 1740s and 1750s, they were probably painted at a slightly later date. All six works remain in their original frames of an egg and dart design characteristic of the third quarter of the eighteenth century, and it is most likely they were framed and sold together as a set, perhaps as decoration for a particular room of a prescribed format. (They may comprise one overdoor [WAG 9823], one overmantel [WAG 9824] and four paintings for side walls [WAG 9825–28].) They are

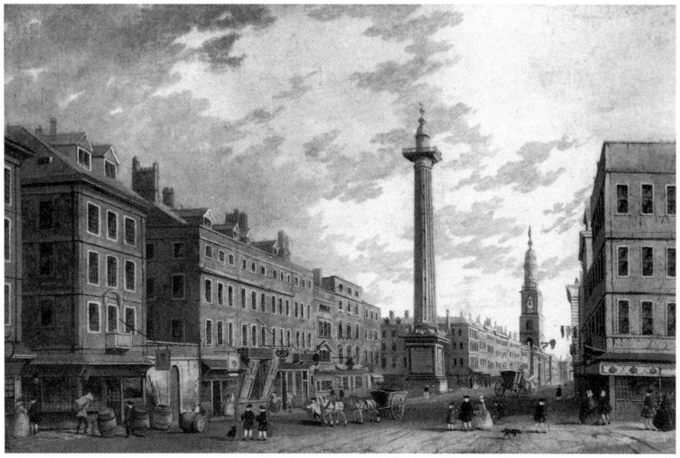

WAG 9823

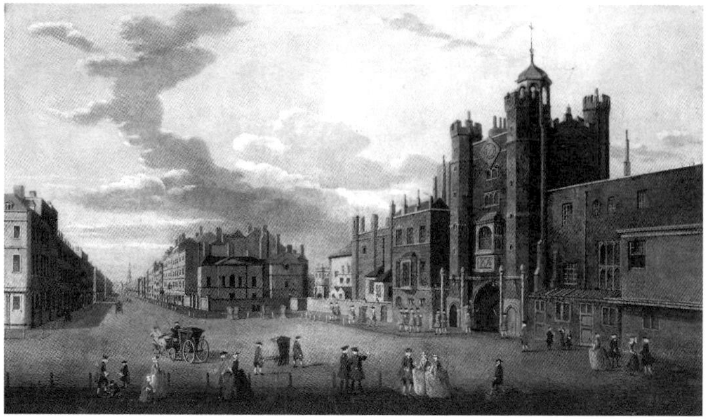

WAG 9826

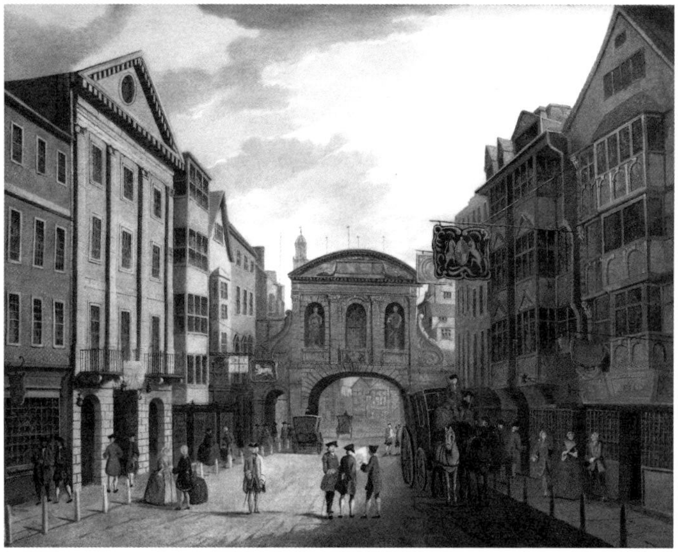

WAG 9824

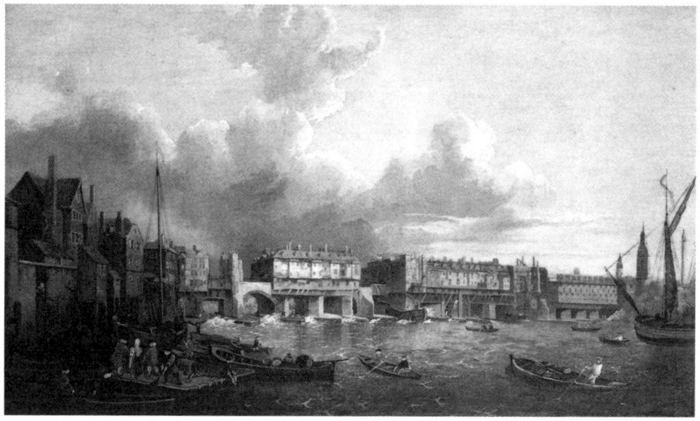

WAG 9827

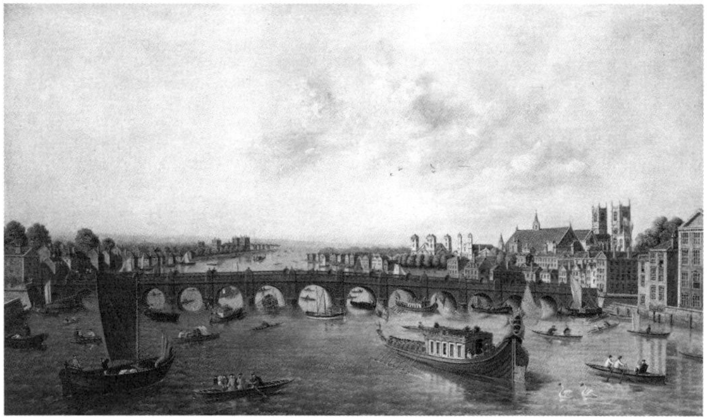

WAG 9825

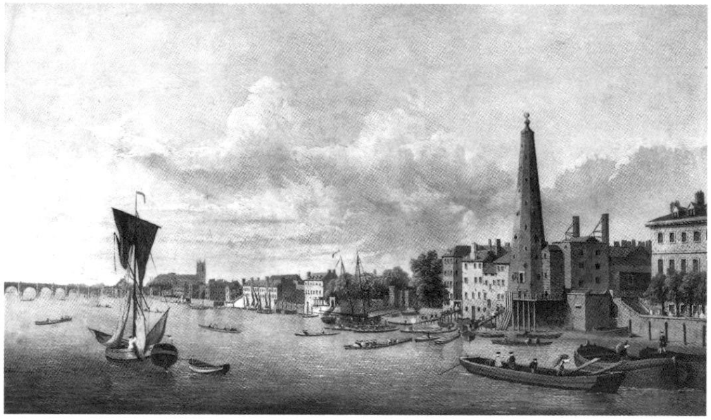

WAG 9828

not all by the same hand. None of them is above workshop quality, but WAG 9824 has claims to be more accomplished than the others. The draughtsmanship of the figures is markedly superior, and it is the only one of the set in which letters on shop fronts are distinguishable. WAG 9825 is by a different, more finicky hand, with a drier touch. The inscription, *WNP*, may be the artist's initials (or the latter may have been WN, with P standing for pinxit); however, no convincing candidate has emerged in support of this notion. WAG 9823 and 9826–28 are cruder in quality. They could well be by the same person.

The focal point of WAG 9823 is Sir Christopher Wren's and Robert Hooke's Monument to the Great Fire of London, built between 1671 and 1677; behind it is Wren's Church of St Magnus (1705). The view is taken at the end of Gracechurch Street, with Great Eastcheap entering in the right foreground, looking south towards London Bridge. The street depicted is not Billingsgate (which was behind St Magnus to the left, running down to the river) but Fish Street Hill; however, 'Billingsgate' seems to have been a term used to refer to the area generally. The two nearest inn signs appear to be those of a Moor's Head and a Copper Kettle; the remainder are indistinguishable.

In WAG 9824, the view is eastwards from the Strand towards Wren's and Hooke's Temple Bar, completed in 1672. Three tourists in the foreground are comparing the original with a print of it. The four buildings in the immediate foreground comprise, to the right, the premises of E. Marlow clock-maker, followed by one prominently displaying the royal coat of arms, and to the left, a stationers', marked by a three compasses shop sign and sporting the word *PARCHMENT* on the fascia, followed by the premises of the Bumpers Society of 1684: the date appears

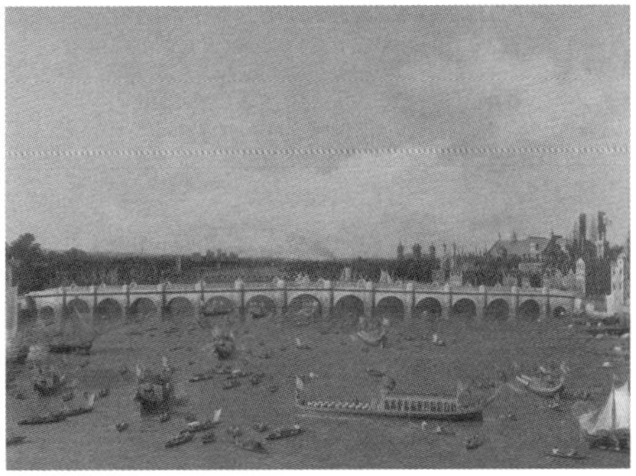

Fig. 65 *Westminster Bridge, with the Lord Mayor's Procession on the Thames* by Antonio Canaletto, oil on canvas. Yale Center for British Art, Paul Mellon Collection.

on the keystone above the entrance.[3] Behind the Temple Bar on the right is the entrance to Middle Temple Lane; on the left is an indication of the church of St Dunstan in the West, just off Fleet Street. The statues on the Bar itself purport to be those of Charles I and Charles II, which were those adorning the western side, but perhaps show different monarchs.[4]

The subject of WAG 9825 is the then new Westminster Bridge, viewed from a vantage point a short distance to the north, as if from the top of a boat's mast. The bridge, designed by the Swiss engineer Charles Labelye, was begun in 1739, took nine years to complete (and even longer to open after one pier subsided and had to be rebuilt) and cost £389,500.[5] In the distance beyond the bridge are Lambeth Palace on the left bank, and on the right, from right to left, Westminster Abbey with Westminster Hall, St Stephen's Chapel (with the twin towers); the building which served as the home of Parliament and was burnt down in 1834, and lastly the church of St John, Smith Square, by Thomas Archer, built between 1713 and 1728. It is depicted here in simplified form, without the distinctive pinnacles to its corner towers.

In the foreground are numerous river craft, including a barge flying the Royal Standard closest to the viewer and five other livery barges behind. Comparable barges were featured in Canaletto's *London, Westminster Bridge from the North on Lord Mayor's Day* of 1746 (Yale Center for British Art, New Haven, fig. 65) – which anticipated the completion of the bridge – and also Samuel Scott's *Building of Westminster Bridge* of 1747 (Metropolitan Museum of Art, New York), which although dating from later than Canaletto's view showed the bridge at an earlier stage of construction. Although Canaletto's work is evidently the prototype for WAG 9825, his treatment of the barges differs significantly, with no prominence being given, as in WAG 9825, to the Royal Standard.[6] WAG 9825 also features two cargo boats with collapsible masts.

Numerous other versions of WAG 9825 are recorded, and the subject seems typically to have been paired with a view of the river in the reverse direction, also generally dependent on Canaletto, of the Thames at Lambeth, with Lambeth Palace in the foreground and the dome of St Paul's on the horizon.[7]

The view in WAG 9826 is eastwards up Pall Mall. At the far end is the church of St Martin-in-the-Fields, rebuilt by James Gibbs between 1722 and 1726. On the right is the main gate of St James's Palace, built for Henry VIII 1532–40: a royal personage is entering in a sedan chair, accompanied by a guard of honour. The building in the centre of the composition is the Fryery.

Many versions of this composition, which appears to be based on a print by Thomas Bowles, are known. One, measuring 59 × 95 cm, with some differences in the figures in the foreground, is in the Lady Lever Art Gallery. This had as its companion a composition titled *Queen Square Bloomsbury*.[8] A version attributed to John Paul measuring 40 × 60 cm, in which the figures are almost identical to those in WAG 9826, was sold in 1990 with two companions, one a version of WAG 9827 and one a Westminster Bridge design (unrelated to WAG 9825).[9]

The scene depicted in WAG 9827 is the eastern side of the medieval London Bridge. At the right, from right to left, are the Monument and the Church of St Magnus, both by Wren (see WAG 9823) and (probably) the tower of All Hallows the Great church in Upper Thames Street. The view is from a position close to St Olave's Stairs on the south bank of the River Thames east of the bridge. WAG 9827 is a copy of Samuel Scott's *Old London Bridge*, one of his most popular compositions, the first version of which is dated 1747.[10] Many copies are known.[11]

In WAG 9828, Westminster Bridge and Westminster Abbey are seen in the background; to the right of the Abbey on the skyline, is the roof of Chapel Royal in Whitehall. Further right are the trees in the garden of Northumberland House. The cone-shaped tower is the York Buildings water works, on the site of the present-day Charing Cross Pier. This was constructed in 1691 to pump river water by means of horse-power to areas such as Whitehall and Piccadilly. The house at the far right is the Office of the Commissioners of the Salt Tax.[12] A painting by Canaletto, *London the Thames, Looking towards Westminster from near York Water Gate*, and one by Scott, *The York Buildings Water Tower*, are the prototypes for WAG 9828, although it is not a copy of either.[13]

PROVENANCE

...Josephine, Countess of Sefton; her bequest 1980.[14]

NOTES

1. R. Kingzett: 'A Catalogue of the Works of Samuel Scott', *Walpole Society*, vol. 48 (1980–82) pp. 42–8 and pp. 54–5; he discusses on p. 54 the possibility that Canaletto worked from a drawing or painting by Scott.
2. For indicative discussions of versions of one London composition by Canaletto, *Northumberland House and Charing Cross* see W. G. Constable and J. G. Links: *Canaletto* 2 vols (2nd edn, reprinted, Oxford, 1989), vol. 2, pp. 411–3, and R. Dorment: *British Paintings in the Philadelphia Museum of Art* (Philadelphia, 1986) p. 438.
3. 'Bumpers' may refer to a jargon trade term for milling stock. For this information, and for work on WAG 9823–28 generally, I am indebted to Susan Lunt, gallery volunteer, June 2005.
4. The artist may have included the 'wrong' statues, from the other side of the Bar, as a way of playing down the Stuart associations of the view from the west; and more generally the prominent inclusion of the Royal coat of arms in WAG 9824 and WAG 9825 suggests that these paintings were designed to appeal to loyal, pro-Hanoverian clients. In the early 1750s, the Young Pretender's rebellion and Culloden were events of the recent past. Viscount Molyneux who may have purchased WAG 9823–28 (see n. 11) converted from Catholicism in the late 1760s and was rewarded with an elevation in the peerage to Earl of Sefton.
5. See, for example, John Summerson: *Georgian London* (1945) pp. 106–9.
6. See n. 4.
7. See, for example, the pair, of the same dimensions as WAG 9825, sold at Christie 12 April 1991 (48), attributed to 'Circle of Joseph Nickolls'.
8. A. Kidson: *Earlier British Paintings in the Lady Lever Art Gallery* (Liverpool, 1999) p. 186.
9. Christie 9 February 1990 (58).
10. Kingzett, *op. cit.*, pp. 42–8, gives further details of the view and lists 11 autograph versions by Scott; the latest dated one is from 1751, but one was probably the work which Scott showed at the SA in 1761 (cat. 99).
11. The version measuring 40 × 60 cm, sold Christie 9 February 1990 (58) (see n. 9), is very close to WAG 9827 in detail, apart from the treatment of the sky.
12. And not, as was supposed when WAG 9828 entered the collection, part of Somerset House.
13. For Canaletto's painting see Constable and Links, *op. cit.*, vol. 2, pp. 417–8 (cat. 427); repr. vol. 1, pl. 78; for Scott's see Kingzett, *op. cit.*, pp. 54–5, listing three versions of the composition, none dated.
14. No trace of WAG 9823–28 appears in known records of works of art owned by the Earls of Sefton at Croxteth Hall or Abbeystead. Possibly they were acquired either by the 1st Earl or by the 2nd Earl as a young man on a visit to London, about 1765–95.

John Thomas Serres

1759–1825

Shipwreck

WAG 6346
oil on canvas, 61 × 77 cm
date: unknown, perhaps 1800–20

When it entered the gallery, WAG 6346 was attributed to Richard Wright of Liverpool (see pp. 295-8) but it was re-ascribed to J. T. Serres soon afterwards.[1] Although storms and shipwreck scenes are not a familiar part of Serres's *oeuvre*, they form a minor strain within his output throughout his career. The distinctive fluffy handling of the wave crests in WAG 6346 is comparable to that in a signed and dated work of 1788, *Shipping off a Rocky Point* (sold Sotheby 23 March 1966 [161]; fig. 66) and even more closely resembles that in a further signed, but undated work, *A Small Fishing Craft, a Frigate and Other Shipping in Rough Seas off Portland, with the Ruins of Weymouth Castle beyond* (sold Christie 14 April 1989 [78]). The conception of this, with a castle overlooking the shipping, is similar to that in WAG 6346, although it is less melodramatic and lurid.

Serres exhibited shipwreck subjects at the Royal Academy between 1788 and 1816 and his painting style seems to have changed little. This makes WAG 6346 very difficult to date. A date of after 1800 has been proposed on the basis of the design of the wrecked frigate.[2] It is possible that the work is one of the shipwrecks that Serres showed at the RA, a number of which remain untraced;[3] but militating against this is the possibility that the castle depicted in WAG 6346 is intended for St Michael's Mount in Cornwall. None of the titles of Serres's exhibits mentions this castle, but it features in works by Serres's exact contemporary, Thomas Luny. The treatment of the clustered and silhouetted

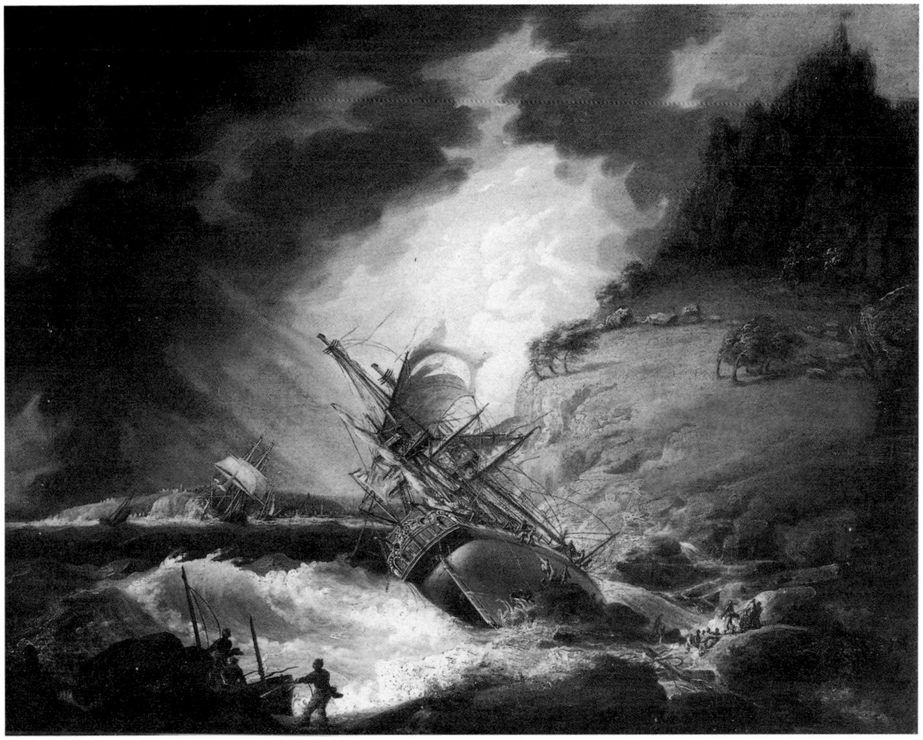

WAG 6346

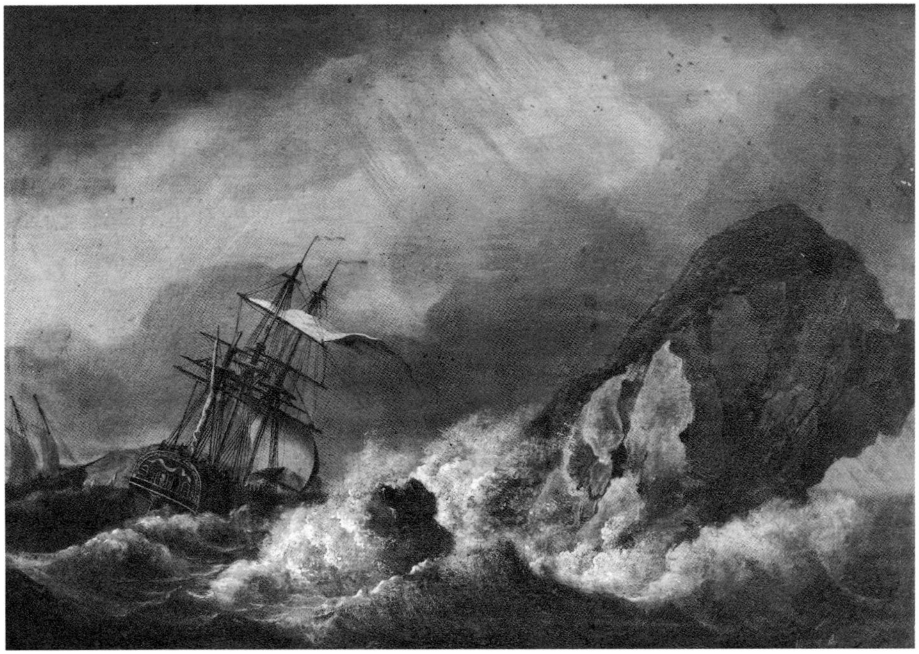

Fig. 66 *Shipping off a Rocky Point* by J. T. Serres, oil on canvas.
Sotheby, 23 March 1966 (161); photo courtesy of Sotheby's Picture Library.

figures in the foreground is also strongly reminiscent of Luny's works and it may be that this is a deliberate exercise in competition or emulation.

PROVENANCE

...Miss Cecilia Dalton; her bequest 1965.

NOTES

1. The attribution was made by Andrew Wilton. It was published in *CIC*, p. 243.
2. H. H. Archibald, National Maritime Museum, *letter*, 17 March 1966, gallery files.
3. The two candidates for exhibits post-1800 are *Mount Orgueil Castle, Jersey, with a Passing Storm* (RA 1802, cat. 193) and *A Squall of Wind, with a Boat on a Lee Shore; North Coast of Devon* (RA 1816, cat. 236). Serres also exhibited storm and shipwreck scenes at the RA in 1788, 1790, 1792 and 1794, although the subjects of these seem less appropriate to the scene depicted in WAG 6346; *GrRA* vol. 7 pp. 78–80.

Martin Archer Shee

1769–1850

William, Duke of Clarence

WAG 7019
oil on canvas, 254 × 174 cm
date: 1799–1800

The sitter was the future King William IV (1765–1837), third son of King George III and Queen Charlotte. He had spent his youth in the navy but upon being promoted Rear-Admiral in 1790 had been retired from active service. He was advanced to the rank of Vice-Admiral in 1794 and Admiral in 1799, and continued to take considerable interest in naval affairs, to the admiration of Nelson, among others. By the late 1790s, however, he was living out of the public limelight as Ranger of Bushey Park, close to his mistress, the actress Mrs Jordan. His liaison with her dominated his public image, together with his propensity for making ill-considered and tactless speeches in the House of Lords, which earned him the nickname 'Silly Billy'.[1]

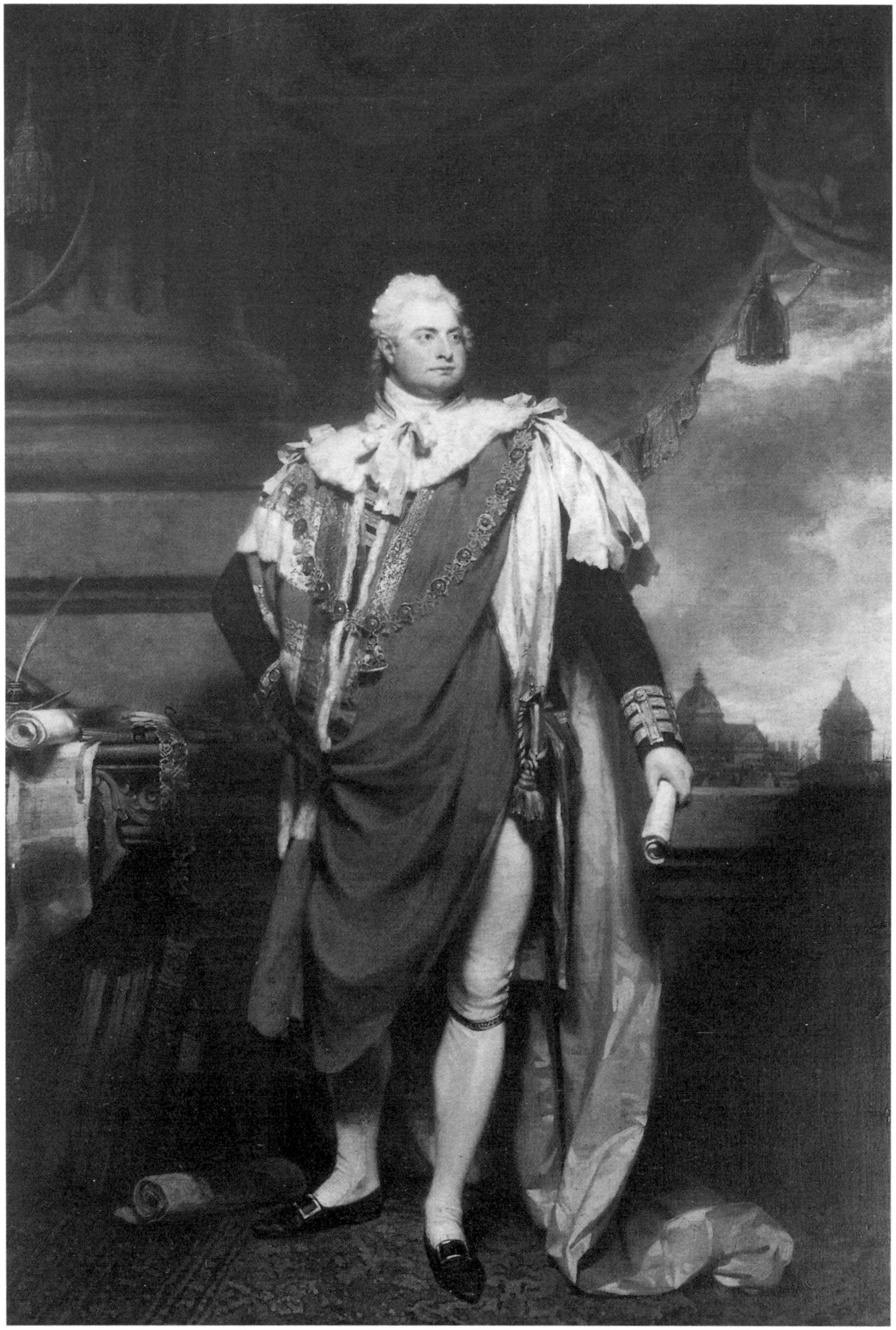

WAG 7019

It was a speech in the Lords that was the direct cause of the present portrait. It was commissioned by the Liverpool Chamber of Commerce, as the artist's son put it, 'as a mark of respect and gratitude to His Royal Highness, – on the occasion of some parliamentary contest in which the commercial interests of that great city had been, as it was thought, effectually served by His Royal Highness's advocacy in the House of Lords'.[2] This is a reference to the Duke's interventions in debates during May 1799 when he confirmed that he would not support the ministry's Slave Limitations Bill and spoke in support of the merchant interest.[3] Joseph Farington, who saw the artist frequently, recorded the fact of the commission in his diary on 13 August 1799.[4] He noted that Shee was proceeding with the portrait following a visit to his studio on 21 September;[5] and the portrait was completed for the Royal Academy exhibition in the spring of the following year.

The Duke is portrayed, as the artist's son pointed out, in the attitude of an orator.[6] He wears Ducal parliamentary robes over his (new) Admiral's uniform, with the collar and chain of the Order of the Garter. To the right, St Paul's Church and the dome of Liverpool Town Hall, together with the windmills of the North Shore and the masts of shipping, are represented with, for a background, unusual specificity (if no concern for topographical accuracy) which may mean that descriptions or engravings were sent down to the artist from Liverpool.

Both the younger Shee and Farington in his *Diary* mention that the artist found the Duke approachable and easy to talk to,[7] and this clearly contributed to the success of the sittings. At the Royal Academy, critics admired the work for its animation and its rich colouring, and observed that it showed the artist to best advantage.[8] After the exhibition was over, it was presumably sent to James Ward whose engraving was published on 2 April 1801. A small version of the portrait on panel, 68 × 54 cm (Brighton Museums; fig.67), has been identified (improbably) as Shee's preliminary sketch (it appears more likely to be a studio or later copy) and WAG 7019 was also used as the basis for a variant full-length of the Duke in Admiral's uniform alone, standing on a rocky seashore by the side of a cannon

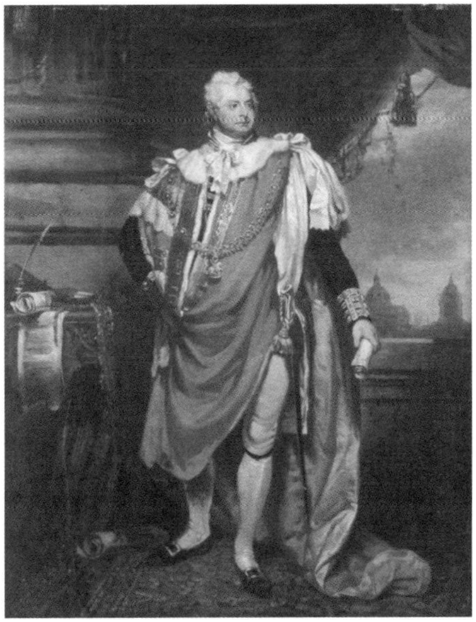

Fig. 67 *William, Duke of Clarence* by Martin Archer Shee, oil on canvas. The Royal Pavilion and Museums, Brighton & Hove.

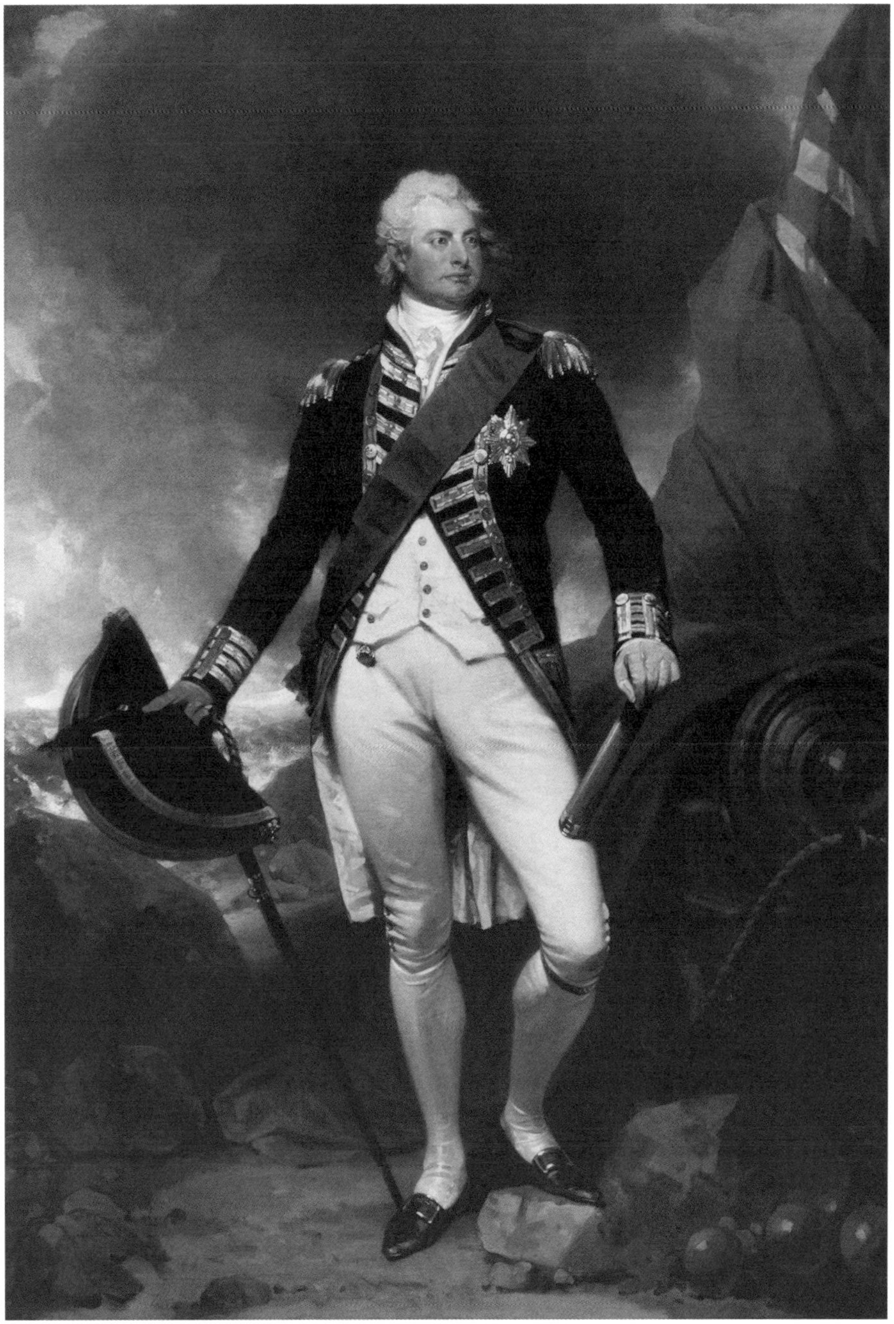

Fig. 68 *William, Duke of Clarence* by Martin Archer Shee, oil on canvas. © National Portrait Gallery, London.

(National Portrait Gallery, no. 2199; fig. 68) in which the pose is varied but the head virtually identical.[9] Shee made further portraits of the Duke in the 1830s when he was King William IV.[10]

PROVENANCE

Commissioned from the artist by Liverpool Chamber of Commerce; transferred from the City Estates Committee 1968.

EXHIBITIONS

RA 1800 (12); Lillymans Hotel, Liverpool 1806; *Kings and Queens of England* Walker Art Gallery 1953 (41).

NOTES

1. *Complete Peerage* vol. 2, pp. 261–2; Michael Brock: 'William IV', ODNB vol. 59, pp. 98–105.
2. M. A. Shee: *The Life of Sir Martin Archer Shee* 2 vols (London, 1860) vol. 1, p. 215. Shee was in error in dating this to the year 1798.
3. See, for example, *The Times* (10 May 1799) p. 2 and (28 May 1799) p. 2.
4. FD, vol. 4, p. 1266 (entry of 13 August 1799).
5. FD, vol. 4, p.1280 (entry of 21 September 1799).
6. Shee, *op. cit.*, p. 216.
7. Shee, *op. cit.*, p. 215; FD, vol. 4, p. 1281 (entry of 22 September 1799).
8. Information from Anne Puetz, Courtauld Institute of Art, *letter*, undated, 2000, gallery files.
9. R. Ormond: *National Portrait Gallery: Early Victorian Portraits* 2 vols (London, 1973) vol. 1, p. 507; dated by Ormond about 1800, who states that it is probably identical with the portrait recorded by George Scharf at Kensington Palace in 1881, as 'apparently by Hoppner'. Shee exhibited another portrait of the Duke at the RA in 1801 (cat. 158); this according to Ormond, *loc. cit.*, was not the NPG canvas, but a further one.
10. These include (i) a whole-length in the Royal Collection, painted 1833, exhibited RA 1834; (ii) a replica of this in the Royal Academy, exhibited RA 1835; and (iii) the portrait exhibited at the RA 1838; Ormond, *op. cit.*, p. 513.

William Roscoe

WAG 3130
oil on canvas, 233 × 166.5 cm
date: 1815–17

William Roscoe (1753–1831) was at the date of this portrait Liverpool's best-known public figure.[1] He enjoyed a European reputation as the author of biographies of Lorenzo de' Medici (1795) and Leo X (1805), and a national one for his stance – controversial in his home town – against slavery. He was also a lawyer, the owner of a (failing) bank, a poet, a collector, a botanist and an agriculturist. He had been MP for Liverpool in 1806–07.[2]

The present work is a friendship portrait. It commemorates the visit which Roscoe paid in late 1814 to T. W. Coke of Holkham Hall, Norfolk (see WAG 2581, pp. 104–5)[3] to study the manuscripts in his library. Coke commissioned Roscoe to catalogue the library, and when he visited Roscoe in Liverpool in October 1815, he asked Roscoe to sit for his portrait, to be placed in the library as a memento of Roscoe's undertaking. Roscoe sat to Shee in London in late November and early December 1815.[4] To Coke he reported at this time that the portrait would be 'so far finished before I leave Town as to prevent any occasion for a journey into Lancashire on so unimportant an occasion'.[5] At this stage, the portrait was a half whole-length measuring 138.5 × 110 cm (55 × 43½ inches) with Roscoe shown standing, his left hand resting against an open book in the right-hand bottom corner of the canvas (as he is shown in WAG 4555; see pp. 164–5).[6] Coke inspected the portrait in Shee's studio and wrote to Roscoe in February 1816 that he highly approved of the likeness, 'but I must have a full length of you sitting in my library, of which I shall be prouder than of any room in the house'.[7] He invited Shee to accompany William Seguier to Holkham in August that year, 'so that no mistake may arise', as Coke put it to Roscoe, 'in the finishing and fixing of your portrait'; and he reported Shee's visit in another letter in October.[8] It was probably at this point that Shee decided to make an oil sketch for the revised composition.[9] His subsequent alterations to the picture, which were evidently calculated with its final hanging position at Holkham in mind, involved adding strips of nearly 11 cm wide to the right and 45 cm to the left, bringing the canvas to its desired (unusual) width of 166.5 cm (65½ inches, some 6–9 inches wider than the standard whole-length); and then, across the top and bottom, strips running the whole new width, 36 cm high at the top and 63.5 cm high at the bottom, which brought the work to roughly the standard whole-length height of 238 cm (91 inches). The new canvas was seen in Shee's studio in February 1817 by William Carey who described it to Roscoe as 'nearly finished and a wonderful likeness'.[10]

Repainting the portrait apparently gave Shee trouble, not only in the management of Roscoe's body, whose torso is markedly disproportionate to the size of his head and legs,[11] but also in the handling of the background, where pentimenti are obvious in the disposition of the curtain and in the shelf of busts above the cornice of the shelving. Shee created an entirely new iconographical framework for the portrait, converting a polite and generic image into one with much more specific allusions to the personal and political ties that had drawn Coke and Roscoe together. With the addition of the shelves of books, the colonnaded architectural setting is now much more recognisably a library. Roscoe is portrayed working amidst its contents and his own credentials as a literary man are emphasised by the inclusion of two volumes of his biography of Leo X standing on the table (three other volumes resting against the leg of the chair are less easy to identify).[12] The two men's shared political beliefs (which were embraced also by Shee himself and may have accounted for his being selected for the commission) are signified by the bust of Charles James Fox (1749–1806), the former leader of the Whig party; identifiable as a version of the second of Joseph Nollekens's two portrait busts of Fox which were shown at the Royal Academy in 1791 and 1802, it was much replicated for Whig patrons for whom ownership of the bust became an ideological statement.[13] On the globe beside the table, the light pointedly falls on West Africa, source of the trade in slaves which Roscoe had made his name opposing. The chair may have been based on Sir Joshua Reynolds's sitters' chair, owned by the RA.[14]

The painting was well received at the RA. *The Literary Gazette* stated that it was 'certainly the finest likeness ever painted of this celebrated man; and altogether, in colouring, disposition and character, does honor [sic] the artist's pencil. We are prevented by our restricted limits only from a detailed notice of this important picture'.[15] One critic praised the perspective of the background as forming 'an original effect in portraiture', adding 'the whole is powerfully impressive'.[16]

The inscriptions at the bottom, *William Roscoe* (on the left) and *Sir M.A. Shee Px / 1822* (on the right), which lie above the final varnish layer, are in the same hand and must have been added after Shee was knighted in 1830. The incorrect date probably derives from the publication of the print, 'drawn and engraved by J. Thomson' in the *European Magazine*, August 1822. The painting was sent to Holkham directly after the finish of the 1817 RA and was recorded as hanging in the ante-room to the Manuscript Library in a guide published in that year.[17]

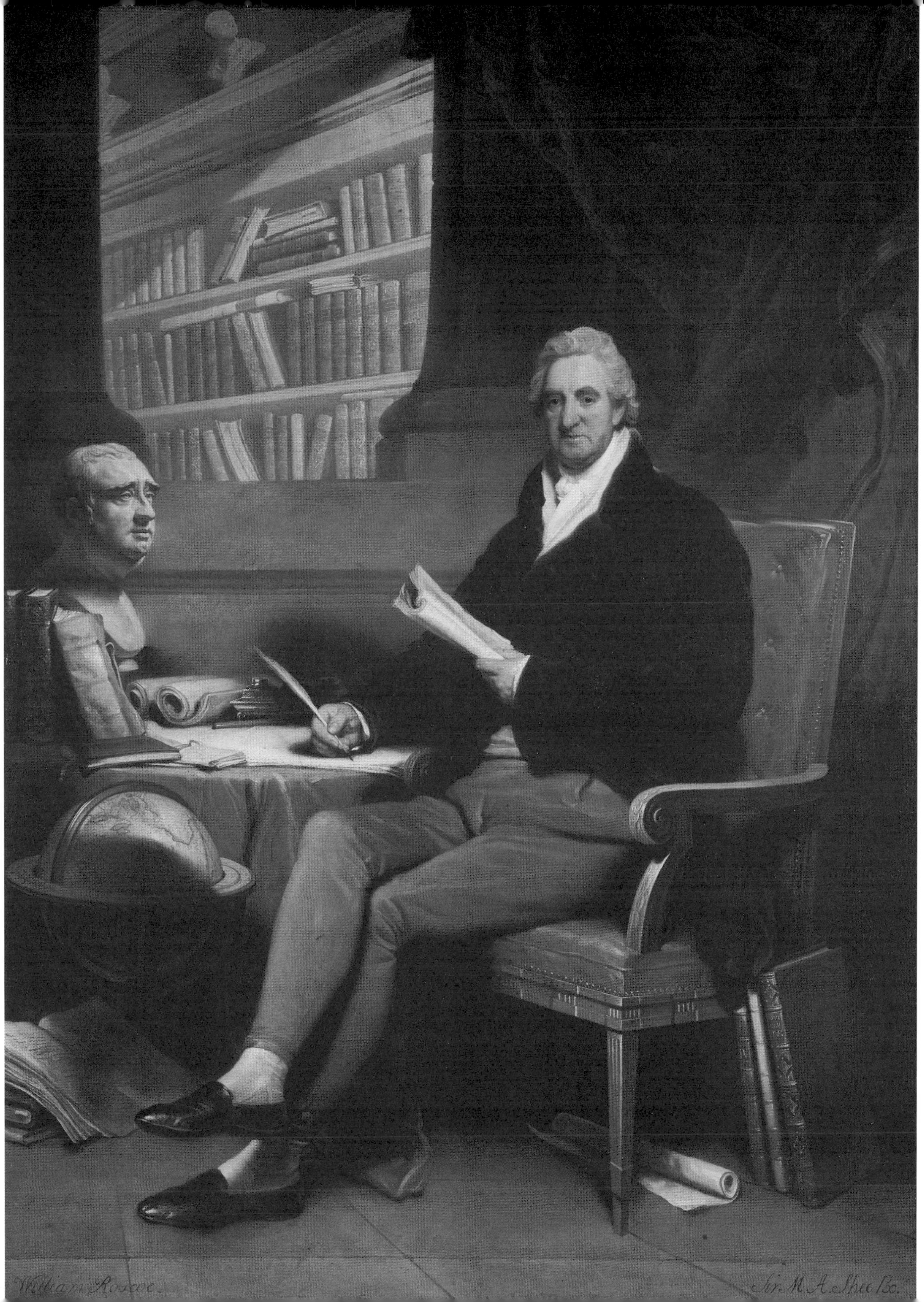

WAG 3130

PROVENANCE

By descent to the 2nd Earl of Leicester; presented by him to Liverpool Corporation 1860 on the occasion of the opening of the William Brown Museum; deposited in the Library and Museum; transferred to the gallery between 1885 and 1903.[18]

EXHIBITIONS

RA 1817 (149); *3rd Special Exhibition of National Portraits* South Kensington 1868 (160); *Cleaned Pictures* Walker Art Gallery 1955 (40).

NOTES

1. The standard biographies of Roscoe are Henry Roscoe: *The Life of William Roscoe* 2 vols (London, 1833); George Chandler: *William Roscoe of Liverpool* (1953); and Arline Wilson: *William Roscoe: Commerce and Culture* (Liverpool, 2008). For his art collecting see especially M. Compton: 'William Roscoe and Early Collectors of Italian Primitives', *Liverpool Bulletin* vol. 9 (1960–61) pp. 27–51, and H. Macandrew: 'Henry Fuseli and William Roscoe', *Liverpool Bulletin* vol. 8 (1959–60) pp. 5–52; also FC, pp. 1–4. The present paragraph is a précis of the biography in *MPPP*, pp. 190–1.

2. R. G. Thorne: *The History of Parliament: The House of Commons 1790–1820* 5 vols (London, 1986) vol. 3, pp. 43–5.

3. Roscoe, *op. cit.*, pp. 84ff.

4. Roscoe to his son W. S. Roscoe, *letters*, 30 November, 4 December and 6 December 1815, *Roscoe Papers*, LRO 920/ROS/4148, 4151 and 4122.

5. Roscoe to Coke, *letter*, 6 December 1815, Holkham Archives, Holkham Hall, F/TWC 5, fol. 33v.

6. NML Conservation Centre condition report and x-radiographs, July–August 2003.

7. Coke to Roscoe, *letter*, 5 February 1816, *Roscoe Papers*, LRO 920/ROS/900.

8. Coke to Roscoe, *letters*, 18 June 1816 and 18 October 1816, *Roscoe Papers*, LRO 920/ROS/905, 925; also Dawson Turner to Roscoe, *letter*, 14 September 1816, *Roscoe Papers*, LRO 920/ROS/4887. Dawson Turner told Roscoe that he had hoped to see Shee's portrait at Holkham on a recent visit but had gathered on that occasion that it might be a further year before the portrait would be delivered.

9. The sketch, which measures approximately 18 × 9 inches, was owned by William Malin Roscoe when it was exhibited in the *Historical Exhibition of Liverpool Antiquities* Walker Art Gallery 1907 (section G, cat. 100a); it is currently untraced.

10. William Carey to William Roscoe, *letter*, 25 February 1817, *Roscoe Papers*, LRO 920/ROS/739.

11. It is possible that this reflects the intended positioning of the portrait and the spectator's viewpoint in the library at Holkham which Shee had been to inspect. W. S. Roscoe commented to his father after a visit to the RA the following year that in Shee's portrait of Lord Albemarle the figure was 'like yours too large' (W. S. Roscoe to Roscoe, *letter*, 6 June 1818, *Roscoe Papers*, LRO 920/ROS/4178).

12. The spine of the left-hand volume is inscribed *IV*; that of the middle volume is uninscribed, and that of the right-hand volume is *JOVI/IN.II/IV:*.

13. Nicholas Penny: 'The Whig Cult of Fox in Early Nineteenth-century Sculpture', *Past and Present* vol. 70 (February 1976), pp. 94–105.

14. D. Shrub, Victoria & Albert Museum, *letter*, 6 June 1966, gallery files. Shee was by this date a member of the inner sanctum of the RA, although he did not become President till 1830. Differences in detail are noted in *MPPP*, p. 191.

15. W. C.: 'Fine Arts: Royal Academy Exhibition Continued', *Literary Gazette* no. 19 (31 May 1817) p. 299.

16. National Art Library, Victoria & Albert Museum, *Press Cuttings Volumes* vol. 4, p. 1110.

17. J. Dawson, *The Stranger's Guide to Holkham, Containing a Description of the Paintings, Statues, etc., of Holkham House, in the County of Norfolk* (Burnham, 1817) p. 80 (cat. 119).

18. The portrait is listed in the 1885 edition of Charles Dyall: *Walker Art Gallery Descriptive Catalogue of the Permanent Collection of Pictures* (Liverpool, 1882) p. 45 (cat. 195) as 'on deposit in the Library and Museum'; it is listed as in the gallery in the 1903 Walker collection catalogue p. 38 (cat. 195).

William Roscoe

WAG 4555

oil on canvas, 141 × 110.5 cm

date: 1816

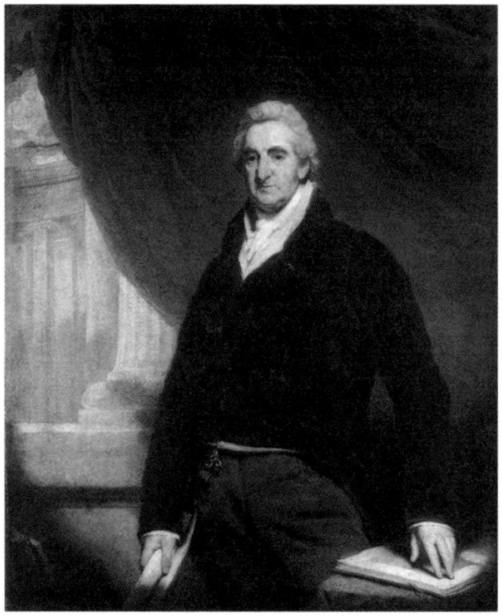

WAG 4555

Shee must have undertaken this canvas in the second half of 1816. In a later letter to Roscoe of April 1819, he wrote that he had made this 'exact duplicate' of WAG 3130 in its original state just before converting that work into a whole-length (see above) and informed Roscoe that he had now decided to submit the duplicate to the forthcoming exhibition at the Royal Academy.[1] Roscoe responded to Shee:

if I were only to consult my own feelings I wou'd rather decline being brought again before the notice of the public, either in the exhibition or in a print, but as I know not that I have any right to interfere with you in your professional labours I must leave you to judge for yourself in this respect, & shall only say that whatever you may decide upon I shall be satisfied with it.[2]

Shee accordingly sent it to the RA where, however, it does not seem to have received much critical attention.

Although WAG 4555 was in Roscoe family ownership by the early twentieth century, there is no evidence that Shee sent it to Roscoe personally. Its ownership by J. Barratt in 1857 has not been accounted for.[3]

Provenance

…J. Barratt, 1857; …Mrs Eliza Roscoe before 1905;[4] F. W. Dunston; …Dr Martin, Salisbury; from whom bt. by Charles Roscoe; by whom presented 1960.[5]

EXHIBITIONS

RA 1819 (174); *Art Treasures* Manchester 1857 (British Portrait Gallery, 320).

NOTES

1. Shee to Roscoe, *letter*, 4 April 1819, *Roscoe Papers*, LRO 920/ROS/4354. Shee wrote:

You are aware that Mr Coke required a portrait of you much larger, & of a character different from that for which you sat, as more appropriate to the situation in which he wished to place it. I took care, however, to make an exact duplicate, the size of the first, & in the standing position for which you may remember to have stood when I had the pleasure of seeing you here. This I have now finished & I am given to understand, with such success, that I am induced to include it in my selection for the forthcoming exhibition.

2. Roscoe to Shee, *letter*, 17 April 1819, sold Sotheby 18 June 1979 (part of lot 12); *draft* in *Roscoe Papers*, LRO

920/ROS/4355.
3. *MPPP*, pp. 192–3 states that WAG 4555 was used by W. C. Edwards in 1824 as the basis of a drawing intended for an engraved frontispiece to Roscoe's catalogue of the Holkham manuscripts (with the apparent implication that at that date the picture was still on Shee's hands). However, the cited letters in the Roscoe papers relating to this, to Roscoe's refusal to have Shee's portrait used for an engraving, and to the suggested employment of a portrait by the Liverpool miniaturist Thomas Hargreaves instead (Coke to Roscoe, *letter*, 8 November 1824; W. C. Edwards to Roscoe, *letter*, undated; Dawson Turner to Roscoe, *letter*, 9 April 1825, *Roscoe Papers*, LRO 920/ROS/963, 1434, 4939), do not explicitly confirm either point. Edwards's letter to Roscoe implies that he had been to Holkham to make the drawing: 'I had great difficulty to see the original in its situation, for it could not be taken down without injury to the house'. WAG 4555 was not included in Shee's studio sale at Christie's on 2 February 1855, but it was lent by Barratt to the 1857 exhibition, where it was recorded by George Scharf; Scharf sketchbooks, National Portrait Gallery Library, vol. 49, p. 20.
4. F. W. Dunston, *Roscoeana* (privately printed, 1905) p. 7, n. 1.
5. Charles Roscoe, *letter*, 28 April 1959, gallery files.

George Stubbs

1724–1806

James Stanley

WAG 8294
oil on canvas, 75 × 62.5 cm
date: 1755

James Stanley was the third surviving son of Thomas Stanley and his wife Catherine, of Cross Hall, near Ormskirk, north of Liverpool. He was baptised at Clitheroe in East Lancashire on 30 May 1722. Thomas, a former High Sheriff of Lancashire who died in 1733, leased Cross Hall from his distant cousin the 10th Earl of Derby, and when the latter died in 1736 he bequeathed the freehold of Cross Hall to James's eldest brother Charles. Charles died in 1754 and Cross Hall was then inherited by the next brother, Thomas. He was the rector of Winwick, some miles away, and it has been conjectured that he permitted his younger brother James, with his wife Ann, to move into Cross Hall in his place, with WAG 8294 perhaps even being commissioned to celebrate his taking up residence.[1] As a younger son, Stanley would have had to carve his own career, and it has also been suggested that this was the James Stanley recorded as living in Ormond Street Liverpool (the same street in which the Stubbs family's currier business had its premises) in 1758.[2]

The back of the lining canvas of WAG 8294 bears the inscription, no doubt copied from the original canvas: *James Stanley / An: AE tat 33. Christ. 1755 / Geo: Stubbs. pinx:.* Evidently completed at Christmas 1755, roughly 15 months after the artist's return to Liverpool from his trip to Rome, it is the only certain portrait among the 'pictures in abundance' that were proposed to him during this Liverpool period, 'which he

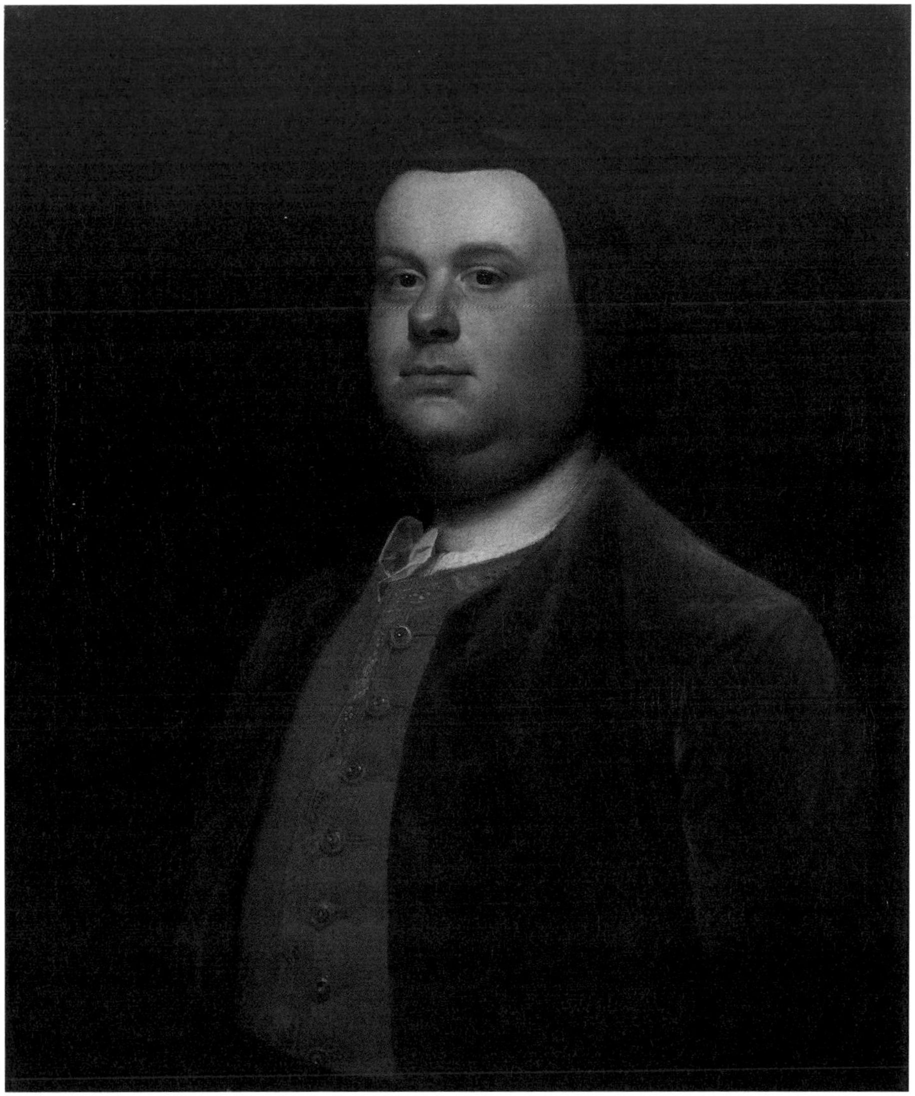

WAG 8294

went on constantly executing', as Ozias Humphry put it in his much later memoir of Stubbs based on his conversations with the artist in the 1790s.[3] The fabric of Stanley's jacket and waistcoat is finely handled but there is an element of caricature in the depiction of the sitter's bluff features which suggests why Stubbs would shortly exchange his career as a portraitist of people for one of animals.

PROVENANCE

By descent to Capt. E. A. V. Stanley, Tixover Grange, near Stamford, Lincs; Knight, Frank & Rutley premises sale 25–26 July 1928 (259); bt. Merrett (31 gns.); ...Mrs Y. N. China; Sotheby 23 June 1971 (91); bt. Spink for the gallery.

EXHIBITIONS

English Paintings, Eighteenth and Nineteenth Centuries Spink & Co., London 1972 (19); *George Stubbs 1724–1806* Tate Gallery, London and Yale Center for British Art, New Haven 1984–85 (26); *George Stubbs: A Celebration* Walker Art Gallery 2006 (no cat. no).

NOTES

1. Robin Blake: *George Stubbs and the Wide Creation* (London, 2005) pp. 106–7; also Judy Egerton: *George Stubbs, Painter. Catalogue Raisonné* (New Haven and London 2007) p. 108 (cat. 4).
2. *MPPP*, p. 196.
3. Ozias Humphry: ms *Life of George Stubbs, Mayer Papers*, LRO 920/MAY/2528A/7, quoted by Blake, *op. cit.*, p. 106.

Molly Long-legs with Her Jockey

WAG 2389
oil on canvas, 101 × 126.8 cm
signed: *Geo: Stubbs/p* (bottom left)
date: 1761–62

The inscription at lower left, *Molly Long-legs*, identifies the subject of WAG 2389: a bay mare bred by Fulke Greville (about 1717–about 1806) of Wilbury House, Wiltshire. She was foaled in 1753: her sire Babram and her dam an unnamed mare sired by Foxhunter. She began life as a brood mare, foaling Young Merlin by Merlin in 1757, before Greville began racing her in 1758, when she was first in a race at Barnet on 12 September and second in a race at Andover on the 27th of the same month. In 1760 at Newmarket she won a match and a rematch both over four miles against Lord March's Rose, and on 18 October beat Lord Gower's Little David in a match for 200 guineas.[1] She was second in a race at Newmarket on 16 April 1761, after which Greville sold her to Frederick St John, 2nd Viscount Bolingbroke (1732–87). For Bolingbroke, a keen sportsman, she won at Oxford in August 1761 and also her last race, in 1762.[2] She then returned to her career as a brood mare at Bolingbroke's estate, Lydiard Tregoze.

Stubbs exhibited WAG 2389 at the Society of Artists in the late spring of 1762 with a companion picture, *A Portrait of a Horse Called Tristram Shandy*. Tristram Shandy was also owned by Viscount Bolingbroke and evidently both works had been commissioned by him from Stubbs some time in the previous few months. Bolingbroke was one of Stubbs's best patrons in the first half of the 1760s, in 1761–62 commissioning him also for portraits of his horses Lustre and Hollyhock as well as at least two pictures of his mares, one of which was the first of his great series of mares and foals; and in 1765–66 for portraits of two of his best-known horses, Gimcrack and Turf.[3] That WAG 2389 was a commission from Bolingbroke has in the past been questioned, partly because (in contrast to some of Stubbs's other paintings) there is no record of its ownership by any member of the Bolingbroke family,[4] but chiefly because the jockey does not wear the racing colours – black jacket, black cap – that Bolingbroke registered at the end of 1762 and which appear in the portraits of Gimcrack and Turf. Instead, his blue jacket and black cap seem to be those associated with the Duke of Grafton.[5] The explanation for this may be that until the Jockey Club regulated the registration of owners' colours in October 1762, horses could be raced at Newmarket under whatever colours the owner chose, and that before that date Bolingbroke may have been competing with Lord Grafton for the use of the sky blue and black outfit.

The jockey in WAG 2389 has not been identified but is almost certainly a portrait. However, the landscape, painted with keen attention to atmospheric effect and as finely composed as the riverscape in the companion picture of Tristram Shandy, must be invented. The suggestion that Molly Long-legs is on a racecourse near the sea can refer neither to Newmarket nor to Lydiard Tregoze, her Wiltshire home.

PROVENANCE

...Sir Walter Gilbey by 1885; Christie 12 March 1910 (150); bt. Vokins (24 gns); [? bt. in for] Tresham Gilbey; Christie 30 May 1947 (82); bt. Bernard (£1942 10s); bt. Walter Hutchinson; Christie 20 July 1951; bt. Agnew (1,000 gns); bt. Messrs Lewis, Liverpool, for presentation to the gallery on its reopening.

EXHIBITIONS

SA 1762 (112); *Loan Collection of Pictures by George Stubbs ARA, and Engravings from His Works* J & W Vokins Gallery, London 1885 (20); *Works of Art illustrative of and Connected with Sport* Grosvenor Gallery, London 1890 (47); *National Gallery of British Sports and Pastimes* Hutchinson House, London 1948 (140); *Selected Acquisitions of the Walker Art Gallery Liverpool 1945–1955* Agnew's, London 1955 (25); *George Stubbs 1724–1806* Whitechapel Art Gallery, London 1957 (17); *Primitives to Picasso* RA 1962 (166); *George Stubbs 1724–1806* Tate Gallery, London 1984 (37); *George Stubbs: A Celebration* Walker Art Gallery, Tate Britain, London and Frick Collection, New York 2006–07 (no cat. no).

NOTES

1. *Racing Calendar* 1758, 1760, communicated by Col. W. N. Gray, Jockey Club, Newmarket, *letter*, 12 December 1961, gallery files.
2. Judy Egerton: *George Stubbs, Painter. Catalogue Raisonné* (New Haven and London, 2007) p. 154 (cat. 25).
3. Egerton, *op. cit.*, pp. 144–9, 154–5 (cats. 17, 19, 20, 26), pp. 226–7 (cat. 70) and pp. 230–1 (cat. 72).
4. Some confusion has been caused by two labels on the back of the frame inscribed *Ashton Court Heirlooms No. 39 and 1885 / No. 59 / March 2nd / Sir Neville Greville Smyth Bt /* [sic] *½ length Portrait of a Lady in White Satin*. In the past these were thought to provide a link with Fulke Greville, but instead

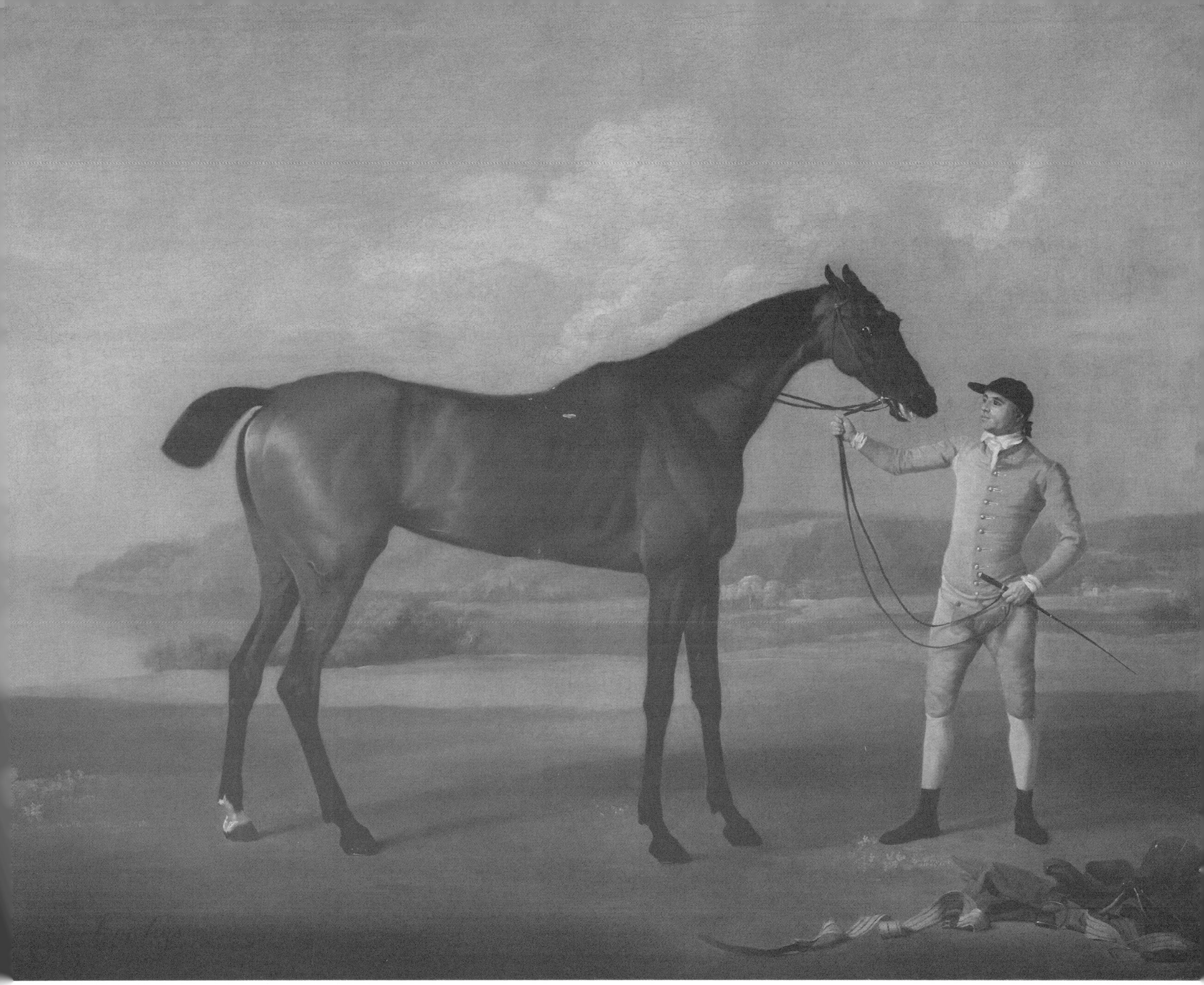

WAG 2389

they indicate that the frame was salvaged from a 50 × 40 inch portrait owned in 1885 by Sir Greville Smyth of Ashton Court, and later included in the Ashton Heirlooms sale of 1947. WAG 2389 was probably disposed of privately by the 5th Viscount Bolingbroke (1820–99), whose lifestyle was unconventional.

5. Stubbs's portrait of the Duke of Grafton's Antinoüs, exhibited in 1764 (Egerton, *op. cit.*, p. 164 [cat. 43]) shows his jockey in the same colours. For a further work including a jockey in the same colours see *The Marquis of Rockingham's Scrub, with John Singleton up* (Egerton, *op. cit.*, pp. 166–7, cat. 32).

Horse Frightened by a Lion

WAG 2387
oil on canvas, 100 × 126 cm
signed and dated: *Geo: Stubbs/pinxit 1770* (bottom right)
date: 1770

This painting and its companion, the *Horse Attacked by a Lion* in Yale University Art Gallery (fig. 69), represent the culmination of Stubbs's engagement with the horse and lion theme which, by 1770, had occupied him for eight years, and which for his contemporaries had become one of his signature subjects. His first painting on the theme had been the very large *Lion Attacking a Horse* carried out for Charles, 2nd Marquis of Rockingham in 1762 (Yale Center for British Art, New Haven; fig. 70).[1] Within a few months of completing this, Stubbs had re-formulated the theme in terms of a pair of works. To offset the depiction of the lion on the back of the horse tearing its flesh, he invented a scene in which the horse is startled into terror by its first glimpse of the lion emerging from cover, the two subjects posing a philosophical question as to whether actual violence or suspense was the true source of terror.[2] In the spring of 1763 Stubbs exhibited at the Society of Artists in London his first pairing of these subjects,[3] of which the *Horse Frightened by a Lion* moved Horace Walpole to pen his poem 'On Seeing the Celebrated Startled Horse, Painted by the Inimitable Mr Stubbs', published in the *Public Advertiser* on 4 November 1763. These paintings were followed by an interim treatment in which the horse, hitherto brown, becomes white (as it is to remain for the remainder of the series).[4] Then, after a gap of about five years, Stubbs painted a pair of small octagonal enamels[5] which, in their close-up concentration on the animals, have the sense of being studies for WAG 2387 and its pendant which are both dated 1770.

As has been widely recognised, Stubbs's chief visual source for the lion attacking the horse was the celebrated Hellenistic sculpture of the subject that had been found in the Tiber in the middle ages and which, heavily restored at the end of the sixteenth century, had been moved to a position in the grounds of the Palazzo dei Conservatori in Rome (where it still is). Stubbs may well have seen this sculpture on his visit to the city in 1754 and stored the memory of it away for future use, but it was in any case available in the shape of reduced replicas and variants, as well as in the form of prints.[6] One variant of the sculpture, in which the head of the horse is bent back towards the lion on its back in the manner of Stubbs's treatment (fig. 71) was acquired at an unknown date by Henry Blundell of Ince, who also owned a version of Stubbs's *Horse Frightened by a Lion*, although it is extremely unlikely that Blundell can have introduced Stubbs to the subject.[7] The story that on his trip to Italy Stubbs had witnessed a fight between a lion and a white Barbary horse in Morocco is no longer credited.[8]

Stubbs's use of a well-known classical source has recently been interpreted as indicative of his wish to be taken seriously by his contemporaries as an academic artist, and not treated merely as a 'horse-painter'.[9] Whilst his decision in 1769–70 to revisit a theme which he had last tackled five years earlier no doubt reflected a wish to improve on his earlier treatments, the form that this 'improvement' took is perhaps surprisingly 'un-academic'. The chief differences between WAG 2387 and its companion on the one hand and the earlier treatments on the other are the much wilder and grander landscape settings and the much more dramatic handling of light and darkness in the later pictures. They are 'sublime' and (as has frequently been stated) 'romantic' in mood,[10] whereas the earlier treatments had a more orderly, staged, and indeed sculpted quality. In WAG 2387 and its companion, Stubbs harnesses all the forms of nature to articulate the unfolding of the drama: in WAG 2387 the tall tree with green foliage appears to shrink back in alarm in sympathy with the horse; the blue sky is just beginning to cloud over. In the pendant work the branches of the tree on the rock in the foreground claw at the horse, trying to deliver it from its assailant, while the brooding black sky conveys that the final tragedy is at hand. But apart from this generic difference, Stubbs has also made more subtle changes to the pose of the horse itself from his 1763 version. The more vertical positioning of the neck and the changes to the legs give a much greater sense of the animal shying back. It was clearly in search of this effect that Stubbs made his own experiments in startling a horse, as was reported by Ozias Humphry in his memoir of the artist:

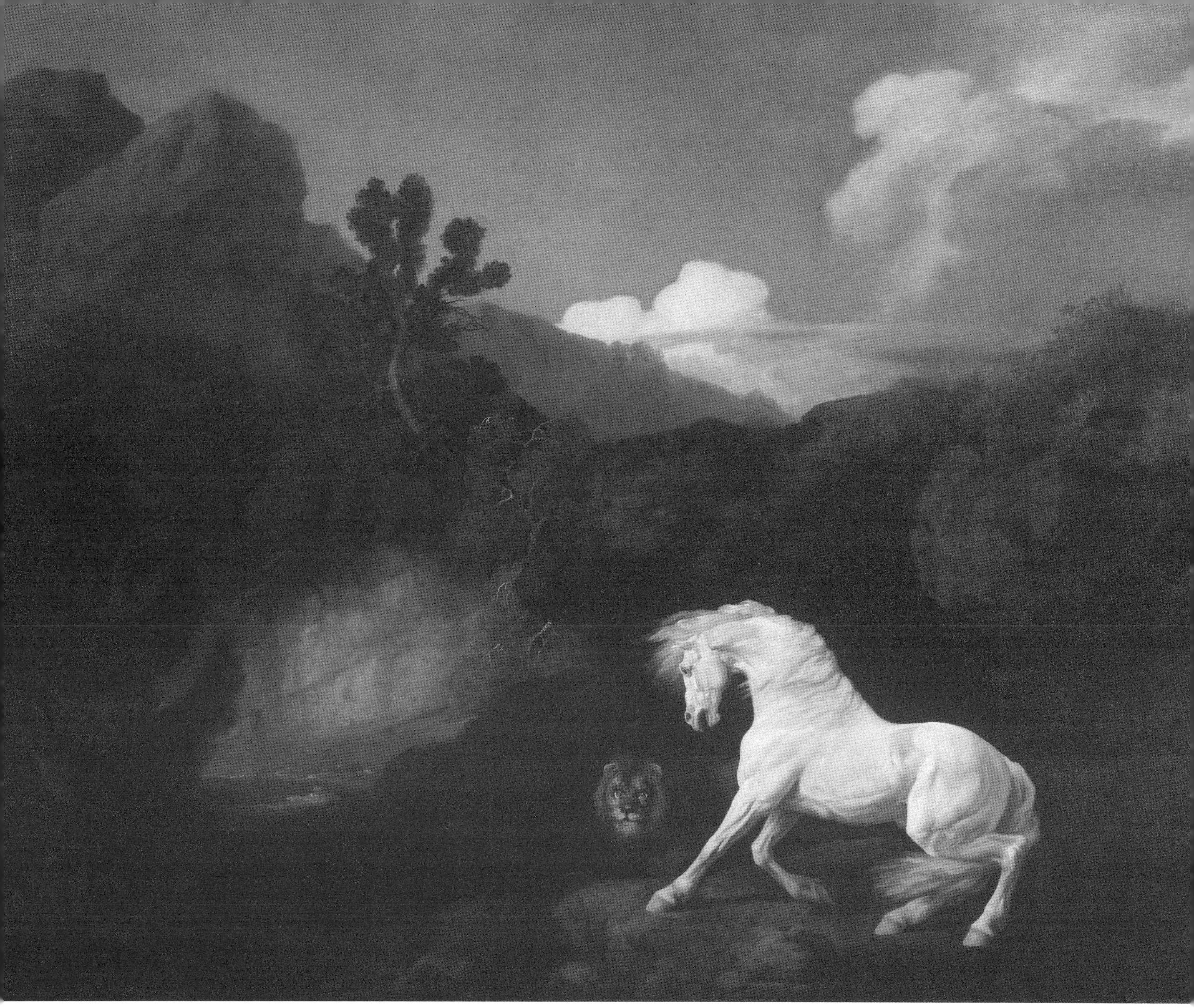

WAG 2387

The white Horse frightened at the Lion was painted from one of the King's Horses in the Mews which Mr Payne the architect [James Paine, Stubbs's close colleague in the SA] procured for him. The expression of Terror was produced repeatedly, from time to time by pushing a brush upon the ground towards him, and this, aided by his anatomical skill, enabled him to give the sentiment of expression & apprehension to the animal which the picture represents.[11]

The chief purpose of the enamel, like WAG 2387 dated 1770 (private collection, USA; fig. 72), may have been to arrive at the definitive treatment of the horse, which is shaped almost identically to the way it is in WAG 2387.

The early history of WAG 2387 and its companion is unknown. That neither was exhibited, and that none of Stubbs's later treatments of the frightened horse theme, namely his 1777 engraving *A Horse Affrighted by a Lion*,[12] his 1780 model for Wedgwood jasperware[13] and his 1788 engraving *A Horse Affrighted at a Lion*[14] were based on WAG 2387, strongly suggests that it and the pendant were sold at once and may even have been commissioned. It seems probable that the two works had been together for virtually the whole of their existence before their separate appearances (WAG 2387 as an exhibition loan and its pendant as a purchase) with the dealer Vokins in 1885 and their subsequent re-union by Sir Walter Gilbey.

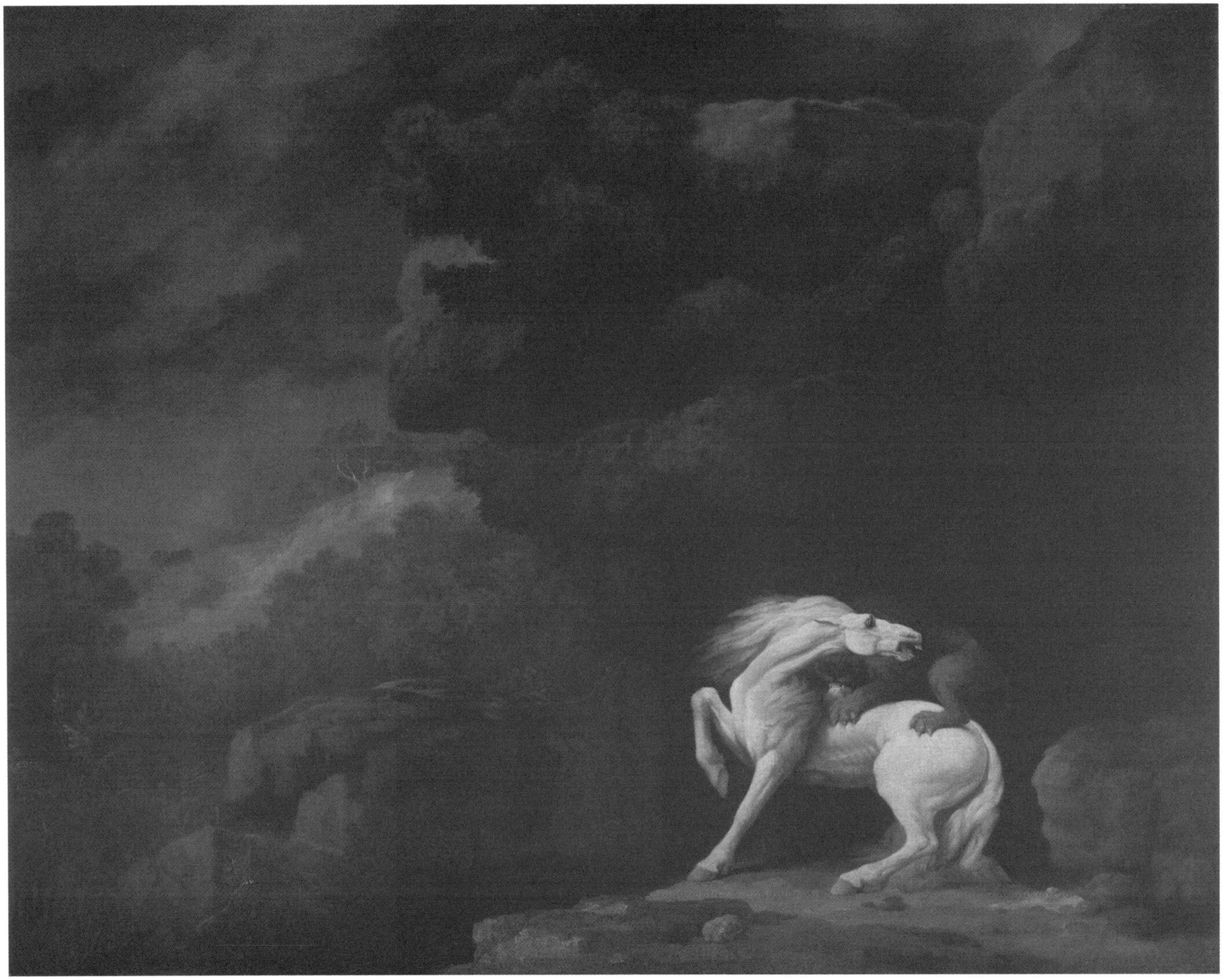

Fig. 69 *Horse Attacked by a Lion* by George Stubbs, oil on canvas.

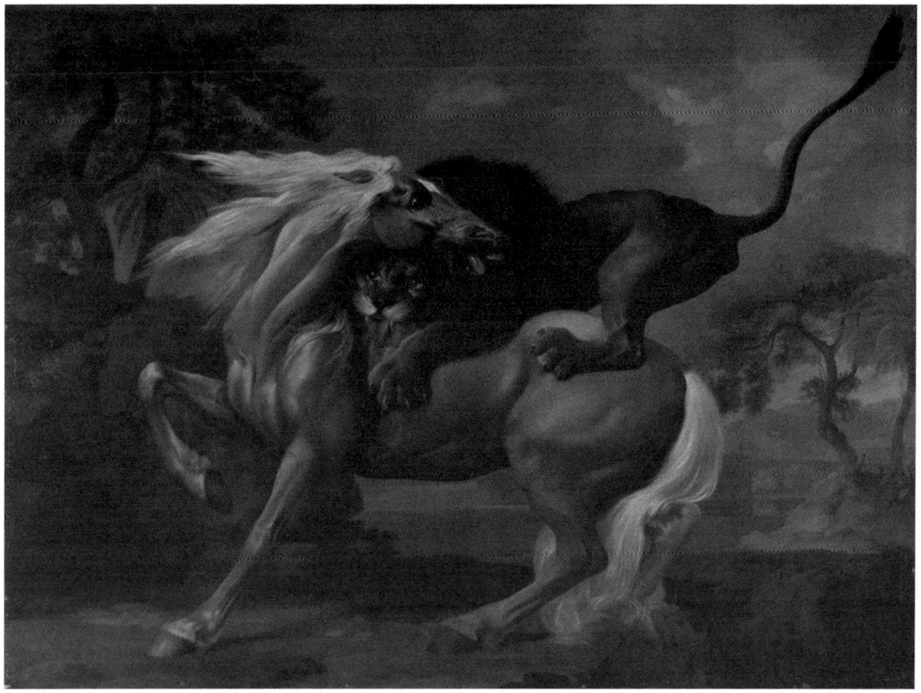

Fig. 70 *A Lion Attacking a Horse* by George Stubbs, oil on canvas. Yale Center for British Art, Paul Mellon Collection.

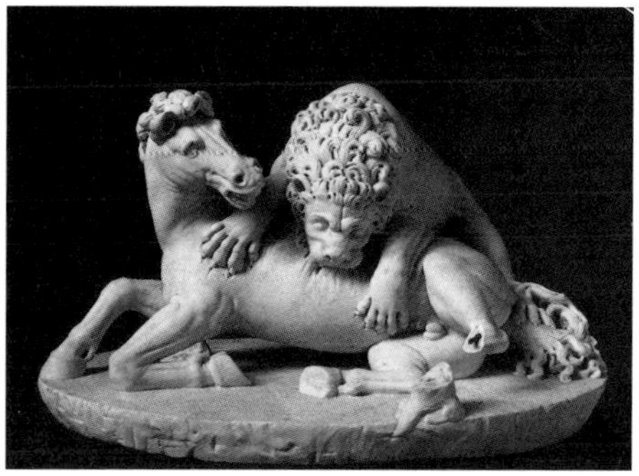

Fig. 71 *Horse Attacked by a Lion* by an unknown artist, marble. Walker Art Gallery

When taken with the fact that the white horse apparently came from the Royal mews, it may not be coincidence that the pendant to WAG 2387 emerged from the collection of Sir William Knighton, son of the doctor of George IV.[15]

PROVENANCE

...Sir Walter Gilbey by 1885; Christie 12 March 1910 (149); bt. Wallis (21 gns.); from whom bt. by the gallery 1910.

EXHIBITIONS

Loan Collection of Pictures by George Stubbs ARA, and Engravings from His Works J & W Vokins Gallery, London 1885 (36); *The Liverpool School of Painters* Harrogate 1924 (26); *Loan Exhibition of Paintings and Drawings from Public Collections* Hanley Museum and Art Gallery, Stoke-on-Trent 1928 (6); *59th Liverpool Autumn Exhibition* Walker Art Gallery 1933 (28); *British Art Exhibition* Manchester City Art Gallery 1934 (25); *British Painting 1730–1850, Hogarth to Turner* Kunsthalle, Hamburg and tour of Scandinavia 1949–50 (90); *George Stubbs* Walker Art Gallery 1951 (11); *English Landscape* Orangerie, Paris 1953 (65); *European Masters of the Eighteenth Century* RA 1954–55 (119); *The Romantic Movement* Tate Gallery, London 1959 (336); *British Painting 1700–1960* Pushkin Museum, Moscow and Hermitage, Leningrad 1960 (25); *George Stubbs 1724–1806* Tate Gallery, London 1984 (66); *Stubbs and the Horse* Kimbell Art Museum, Fort Worth, Walters Art Gallery, Baltimore and National Gallery, London 2004–05 (62); *George Stubbs: A Celebration* Walker Art Gallery, Tate Britain, London and Frick Collection, New York 2006 (no cat. no).

NOTES

1. Judy Egerton: *George Stubbs, Painter. Catalogue Raisonné* (New Haven and London, 2007) pp. 174–5 (cat. 36).
2. The standard discussion of Stubbs's lion and horse subjects, Basil Taylor: 'George Stubbs: "'The Lion and Horse" Theme', *Burlington Magazine* (February 1965) pp. 81–6, obscures this point by describing the various versions in terms of four different episodes, A–D A–B corresponding to the frightening of the horse and C–D to the attack on it.
3. Egerton, *op. cit.*, pp. 178–9 (cats. 38–9); both paintings are now in the collection of Tate Britain, having been separately purchased in 1976 and 1994. In 1765 Stubbs provided Lord Rockingham's picture with an alternative pendant altogether: *Lion Attacking a Stag* (Yale Center for British Art, New Haven; Egerton, *op. cit.*, pp. 292–3 [cat. 111]).
4. National Gallery of Victoria, Melbourne, Felton Bequest; Egerton, *op. cit.*, p. 176 (cat. 37). Egerton argues from the unresolved quality of the background that this is a 'very early' treatment, preceding the 1763 exhibits; yet (plausibly; there seems no other viable candidate) she also identifies it as likely to be the painting *A Lion Seizing a Horse* that Stubbs exhibited at the SA in 1764. It seems very unlikely that Stubbs would have held over for a year a painting that (on Egerton's view) he had already superseded with his 1763 exhibits, and more straightforward to think that Stubbs permanently identified the white colour as an improvement for the horse after painting the brown horses in the 1763 pictures, and that this change was the *raison d'être* of the Melbourne picture (explaining Stubbs's relative lack of interest in the background). Ursula Hoff: *European Paintings in the National Gallery of Victoria* (4th edn, Melbourne, 1995) p. 282, following Taylor, *op. cit.*, p. 81, dates the work to about 1765. On this scenario, a further *Horse Frightened by a Lion* traditionally attributed to Stubbs and showing a brown horse (70.5 × 104 cm; Yale Center for British Art, New Haven, discussed in M. Warner and J. Marciari Alexander: *This Other Eden, Paintings from the Yale Center for British Art*, exh. cat., Art Gallery of New South Wales, Sydney and tour of Australia [1999] pp. 122–3 [cat. 48] as a work dating on stylistic grounds from the 1790s) represents a problem. This work is omitted from Egerton, *op. cit.*, presumably reflecting her conclusion that this painting is not authentic.
5. *Lion Attacking a Horse*, dated 1769 and *Horse Frightened by a Lion* dated 1770 (respectively Egerton, *op. cit.*, pp. 296–7 (cat. 112) and pp. 298–9 (cat. 114). Stubbs painted a replica of the former on panel, probably as a commission from Benjamin West, its first recorded owner (Yale Center for British Art, New Haven; Egerton, *op. cit.*, pp. 296–7 [cat. 113]).
6. For a full discussion, superseding all previous literature, of the background to the antique *Lion and Horse*, and the existing versions, in sculpted and print form, available to Stubbs see Egerton, *op. cit.*, pp. 25–30.
7. Although the exact date of Blundell's acquisition of his *Horse and Lion* sculpture is unknown, it is

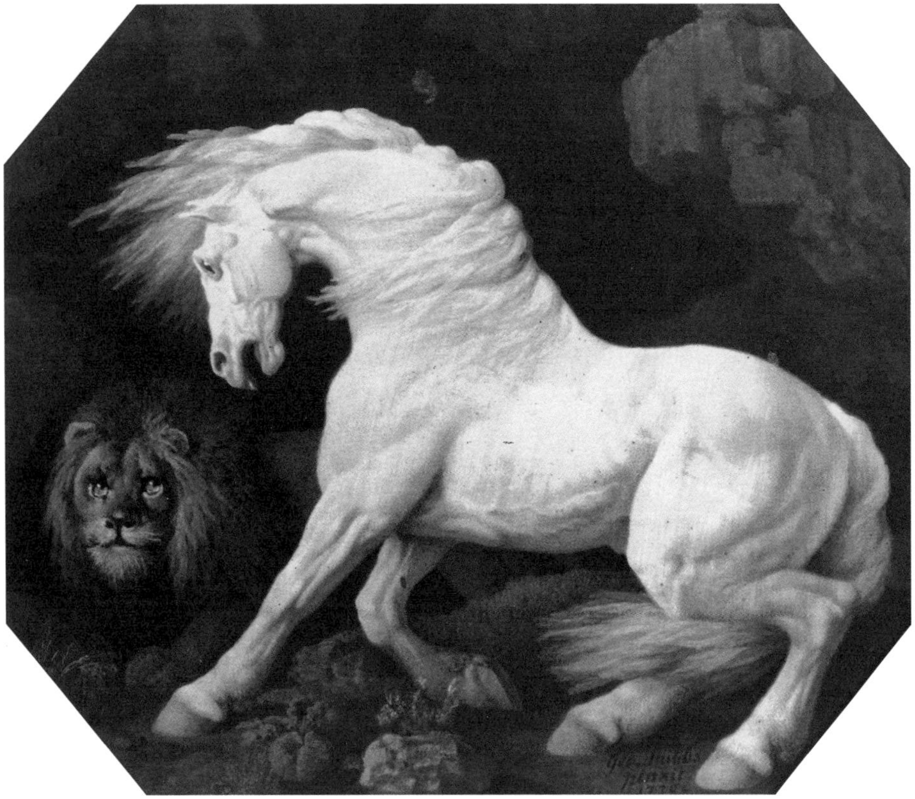

Fig. 72 *Horse Frightened by a Lion* by George Stubbs, enamel on copper. Private collection, USA, photo courtesy Yale Center for British Art.

likely to postdate 1777 when Blundell first visited Italy and began to collect antique sculptures seriously; see J. Ingamells: *A Dictionary of British Travellers in Italy* (New Haven and London, 1997) p. 101 and Gerard Vaughan: 'Henry Blundell's Sculpture Collection at Ince Hall', in Penelope Curtis, ed.: *Patronage and Practice: Sculpture on Merseyside* (Liverpool, 1989) pp. 13–21. The painting *A Horse Attacked by a Lion* owned by Blundell and catalogued by him in his *An Account of the Statues, Busts, Bass-relieves, Cinerary Urns, and Other Ancient Marbles, and Paintings at Ince Collected by H. B.* (Liverpool, 1803) p. 226 (cat. 47; exh: *George Stubbs*, Walker Art Gallery 1951 [15]) was listed by Taylor, *op. cit.*, p. 86, appendix no. 16, as a work by Stubbs but it is by an early imitator and is not catalogued by Egerton, *op. cit.* A similar work to this (and to the Yale picture referred to at n. 4) was sold at Sotheby, 15 July 1992 (89).

8. Sir Walter Gilbey: *Life of George Stubbs R. A.* (London, 1898) pp. 10–2; however, the episode is not mentioned in Ozias Humphry's ms *Life of George Stubbs* (see n. 11).

9. See, for example, Martin Myrone: *George Stubbs* (London, 2002) pp. 39ff.

10. Following the work's inclusion in the Arts Council's 1959 exhibition *The Romantic Movement* (see Exhibitions), WAG 2387 was illustrated in, for example, Pierre Courthion: *Le Romantisme* (Lausanne and Paris, 1961), Marcel Brion: *La Peinture Romantique* (Paris 1966; English version, London 1970), as the front cover for David Wright, ed.: *The Penguin Book of English Romantic Verse* (Harmondsworth, 1968), in Peter Quennell: *Romantic England* (London, 1970) etc.

11. Ozias Humphry: ms *Life of George Stubbs*, *Mayer Papers*, LRO 920/MAY/2528A/7; quoted by Malcolm Warner: *Stubbs and The Horse*, exh. cat, Kimbell Art Museum, Fort Worth, Walters Art Gallery, Baltimore and National Gallery, London (2004–05) p. 197.

12. C. Lennox-Boyd, R. Dixon and T. Clayton: *George Stubbs: the Complete Engraved Works* (Abingdon, 1989) pp. 170–2 (cat. 59); this print adapts the 1763 Tate *Horse Frightened by a Lion*, though the horse is white and the background is different.

13. Egerton, *op. cit.*, pp. 438–9 (cat. 223).

14. Lennox-Boyd, Dixon and Clayton, *op. cit.*, pp. 186–7 (cat. 70); this print adapts the design of the 1770 enamel.

15. The Yale painting was sold from the collection of Sir William W. Knighton, deceased, at Christie 23 May 1885 (448); bought at the sale by Vokins for 21 guineas. It is tempting to wonder if Knighton's executors had been approached by Vokins to sell both works privately, agreed to sell only one (WAG 2387) and insisted on testing the market with the other. However, there is no proof for this speculative suggestion.

A Lion and Tiger

WAG 2393
enamel on Wedgwood ceramic plaque,
43 × 61 cm
signed and dated: *Geo: Stubbs pinxit 1779*
(bottom right)
date: 1779

This is the fourth of Stubbs's surviving works on Wedgwood plaques – his fifth including an initial experiment on a related surface[1] – and it marks the end of the first stage of his experimentation in the medium of enamel on ceramic supports. This itself was a development of his trials with copper supports dating from the end of the 1760s.[2] WAG 2393 is one of two works painted in 1778–79 on rectangular plaques measuring 43 × 61 cm; this seems to have been a trial size of support on the largest durable scale that Wedgwood was initially able to manufacture.[3] Wedgwood's experimentation with his supports for Stubbs continued into the 1780s and in the end yielded larger oval plaques.

All Stubbs's first enamels on ceramic plaques took big cats as their subjects. This was a theme that had preoccupied the artist generally in the previous few years and Stubbs probably chose it because the motifs came easily to him, allowing him to concentrate on the technical aspect of the production. It has been noted that an (otherwise unidentified) Old Master painting of a lion and dead tiger was sold with Stubbs's effects in 1807 and the possibility raised that WAG 2393 was copied from or based on this picture.[4]

Technically, this is one of Stubbs's least successful enamels on Wedgwood plaque paintings. Firing has resulted in the surface buckling in the centre to produce an uneven overall effect and it has also yielded a pitted, blistered effect in the paint layer. The colours themselves are somewhat dull, without the clarity of Stubbs's best works in enamels.[5]

PROVENANCE

Remained with the artist; Coxe 26–27 May 1807 (second day, 82); bt. in (21 gns.); ...J. E. Davis; Christie 16 December 1887 (54); bt. Vokins; ... Sir Walter Gilbey; Christie 12 March 1910 (154); bt. Spencer (5 gns.); ...Edward P. Thompson;[6] by whom presented 1914.

EXHIBITION

Stubbs and Wedgwood Tate Gallery, London 1974 (27).

NOTES

1. The first three were (i) *Lion Seated Overlooking a Rocky Coast*, 1775, 23.5 × 31 cm, private collection Canada, on an unidentified piece of coadestone or similar, perhaps supplied by Wedgwood but not identical to the ceramic plaques he later made for Stubbs; (ii) *Sleeping Leopard*, 1777, 13 × 17 cm, Yale Center for British Art, New Haven, on a fragment of already glazed Wedgwood earthenware, i.e. again not specifically manufactured as a support; and (iii) *Recumbent Panther*, 1778, 19 × 27, Woolavington Collection (Judy Egerton: *George Stubbs, Painter. Catalogue Raisonné* [New Haven and London, 2007] pp. 406–7, 410–1 [cats. 201, 202, 204]). For the fourth work see n. 3.
2. Egerton, *op. cit.*, pp. 296 (cat. 112), 301 (cat. 116) and 402–5 (cats. 197–200) and see also Bruce Tattersall: *Stubbs and Wedgwood*, exh. cat., Tate Gallery London 1974, pp. 7–8, 44–9, 62–5.
3. The other work in this group, dated 1778, is *Lion and Lioness* (private collection UK in 2006; exh. *George Stubbs: A Celebration* Walker Art Gallery, Tate Britain, London and Frick Collection, New York 2006 (no cat. no); see Egerton, *op. cit.*, pp. 408–9 (cat. 203).
4. Second day, lot 41; Hugh Macandrew, draft entry on WAG 2393, about 1962, gallery files.
5. Egerton, *op. cit.*, p. 410, cites the remark by Sir Walter Gilbey: *Life of George Stubbs R. A.* (London, 1898) p. 160: 'as a specimen of enamel painting, this [i.e. WAG 2393] is even superior to the panther picture' and justly adds that this is incomprehensible, unless Gilbey subsequently 'attempted some abortive restoration'.
6. He was the brother of Revd S. A. Thompson Yates, who in 1904 had bequeathed to the gallery numerous items related to and attributed to Stubbs (including WAG 2391, p. 181, and WAG 2392, p. 55).

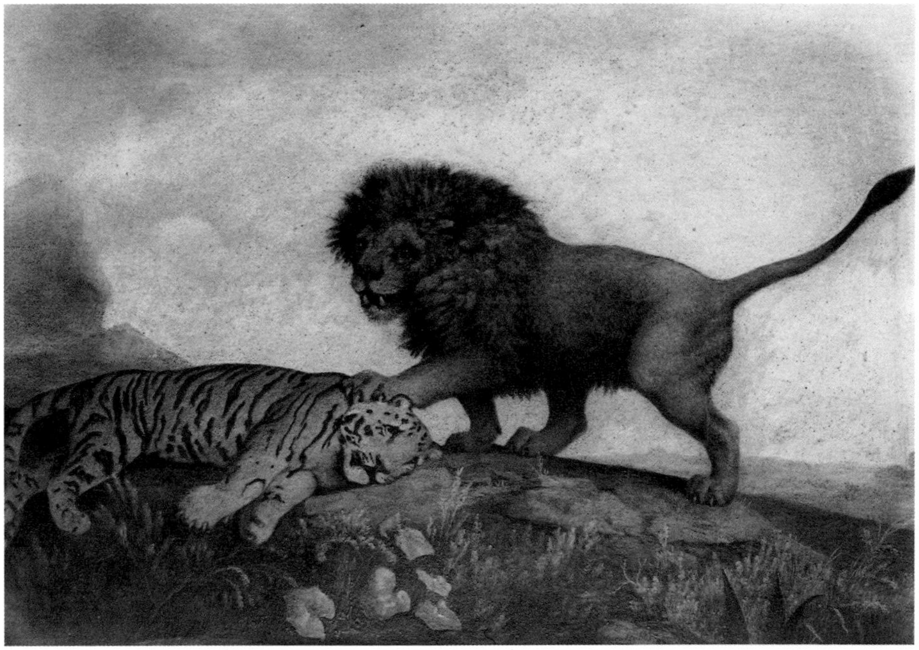

WAG 2393

The Lincolnshire Ox

WAG 2388
oil on panel,[1] 68 × 99 cm
date: 1790

This painting was commissioned from Stubbs in 1790 by John Gibbons, gentleman farmer of Long Sutton in the fens of south-east Lincolnshire, as a portrait of himself with the enormous Herefordshire ox that he had recently won as the prize in a cockfight from a neighbour, John Bough.[2] Bough had bred the ox in November 1782 in the nearby village of Gedney. Gibbons fed the ox up on hay (the ox itself apparently liking to wet the hay in its water trough, a habit to which its great size was imputed)[3] and when he realised that he had a prodigy on his hands, he resolved to take it to London to exhibit it, commission its portrait and organise a subscription for prints, before selling the animal for slaughter.

Gibbons printed advertisements for his enterprise and documented it minutely at every stage.[4] Early in 1790 he set off for London, transporting the ox in a 'machine drawn by eight horses',[5] and showing the animal in public en route. Before departure he had printed a prospectus headed *Long-Sutton Ox / IN A MACHINE / Being on the Road to LONDON, may be seen / This present* [left blank for the insertion of the day by hand] */ Between the hours of 10 & 12 and 2 & 4 o'clock.* The advertisement informed the public that

This Uncommon Animal...is allow'd to be much the LARGEST and FATTEST ever seen in ENGLAND. – His Beef and Tallow are computed to weigh Two Hundred Stone, at 14 lb to the Stone – His Height is near 19 Hands; Girt before the Legs 10 Feet 6 Inches; ditto round the Belly, 11 Feet 3 Inches; across the Hips, 4 feet, and round each Hip, 4 feet. – He never did eat any Oil-Cake.

The Nobility and Gentry are hereby informed,

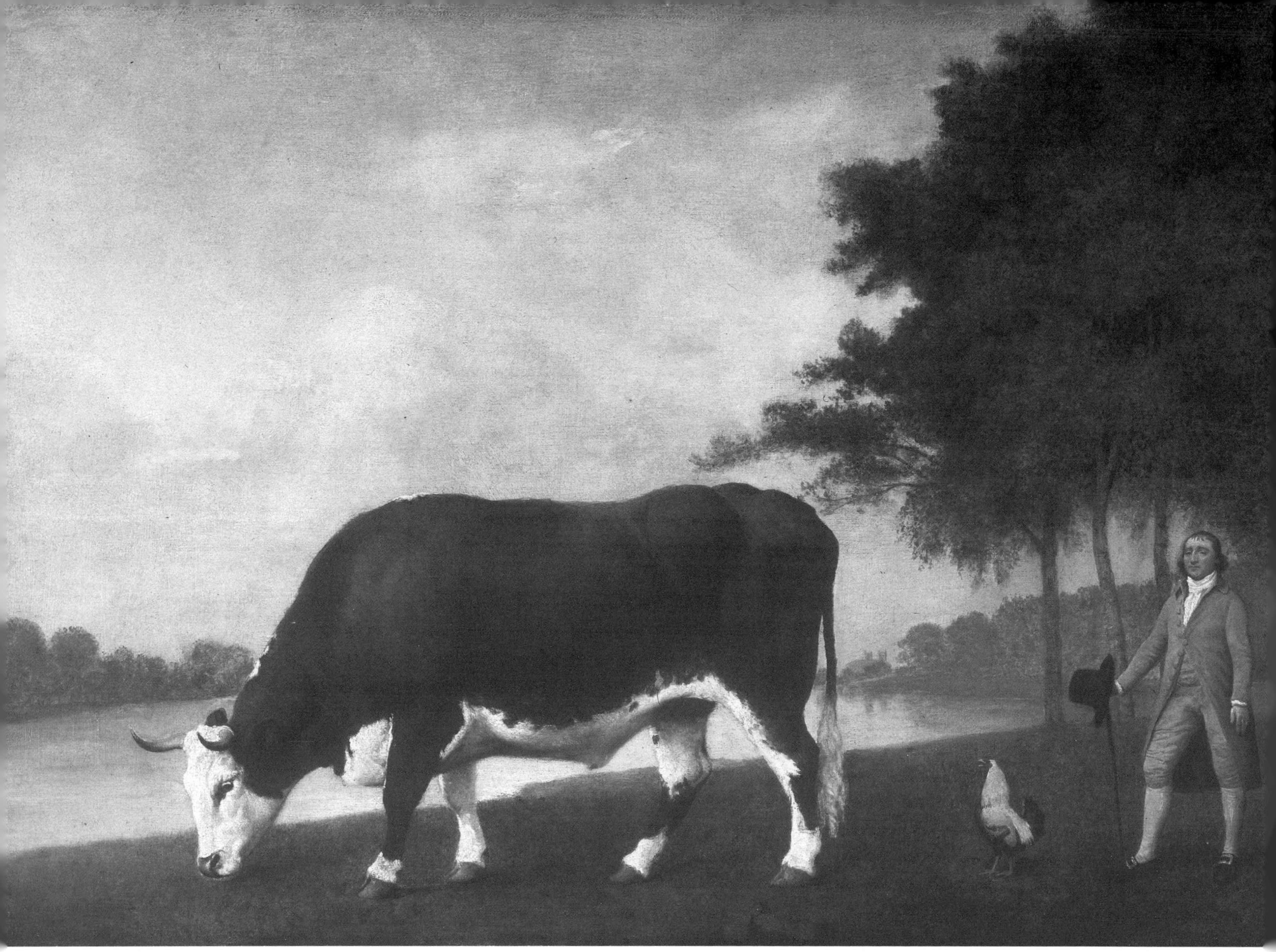

WAG 2388

that a Subscription is begun at Half a Guinea, each Subscriber to have an Engraving of the Ox, which will be engraved by one of the most eminent artists in London, (who will be appointed by Sir Joseph Banks) and a Ticket that will admit each Subscriber to the sight of the Ox, both in London and the Country; which Ticket will be a Security to the Holder for the Delivery of the Print, or the return of the Money, in Case of Failure.

N.B. As the Public may not be aware how much this Ox exceeds any ever seen, it may not be amiss to observe, that before he sets out upon his Journey, he has made nearly 250l. by shewing at 4 Years old, and twice fighting cocks; and that One Hundred and Eighty Five Guineas has been offered for him; – He is so very quiet, as to stand for five or six Ladies to touch him at a time, even when at Liberty in his Pasture.

Admittance 1s, Children 6d

Tickets to be had at the Machine.[6]

Gibbons reached London in early February and had soon engaged Stubbs to paint the ox. Sir Joseph Banks, who himself was from Lincolnshire and evidently acted as Gibbons's intermediary, was familiar with Stubbs's work, having many years previously employed him to make two paintings of a kangaroo and a dingo and three drawings of a mouse lemur.[7] Stubbs had begun work on the picture by the beginning of March (as reported by *The General Advertiser* for 2–4 March)[8] and on the fifth of that month he gave Gibbons a receipt for £20 as part payment for the picture (fig. 73). Stubbs had completed the painting by 9 April when he issued a second receipt to Gibbons for £44 12s 6d 'in full for a Painting of the Lincolnshire Ox' (fig. 74). Later that month he sent the painting to the Royal Academy. It is evident that both he and Gibbons treated the commission as a publicity venture, in which speed and high visibility were of the essence, and in its first notice of the exhibition the *Public Advertiser* duly remarked, 'Stubbs has given the Proprietor of the Lincolnshire Ox a most efficacious advertisement.'[9]

Stubbs's painting shows the ox in Hyde Park,[10] grazing by the Serpentine, with the towers of Westminster Abbey in the distance. The animal was briefly quartered in Hyde Park, at the Duke of Gloucester's riding house, on its first arrival in London, before being moved to public exhibition at the Lyceum in the Strand.[11] Stubbs's treatment of the landscape is perfunctory but his portrayal of the ox leading a lakeside procession consisting of Gibbons's victorious game-cock and Gibbons himself, all strutting in line, is, as has been pointed out, not only slyly humorous but also portentous, anticipating as it does the artist's great project of the 1790s, the *Comparative Anatomy* of the human body, the common fowl, and (in place of an ox) the tiger.[12] The conception is a far cry from earlier, more documentary depictions of large cattle such as George Cuitt's *Blackwell Ox* and Thomas Bewick's *Whitley Large Ox*, two well-known engraved portraits of Teeswater cattle that had appeared during the 1780s and whose example Gibbons was no doubt trying to emulate.[13]

Gibbons closed his subscription for

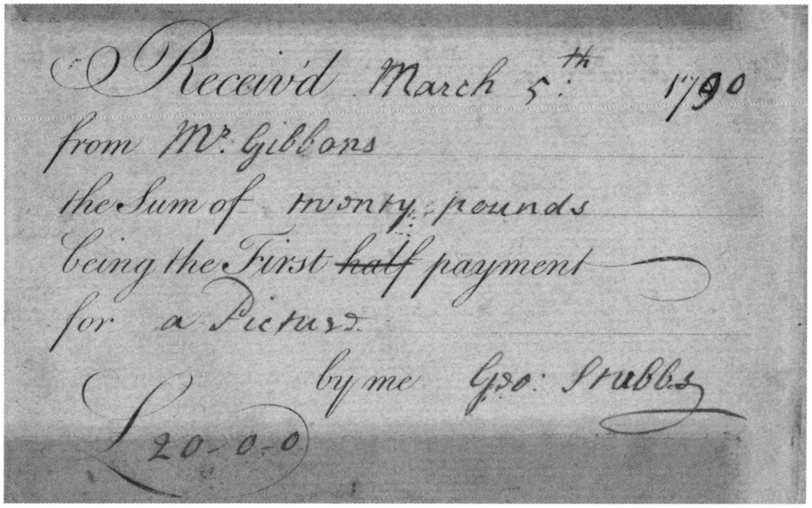
Receiv'd March 5th 1790
from Mr Gibbons
the Sum of twenty pounds
being the First ~~half~~ payment
for a Picture
by me Geo: Stubbs
£20-0-0

Fig. 73 John Gibbons's receipt from George Stubbs for £20 in part payment for *The Lincolnshire Ox*. Walker Art Gallery.

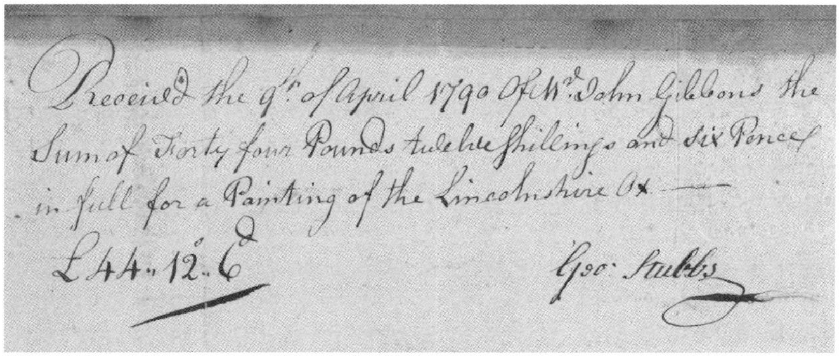
Receiv'd the 9th of April 1790 Of Mr John Gibbons the Sum of Forty four Pounds twelve shillings and six Pence in full for a Painting of the Lincolnshire Ox
£44.12.6
Geo: Stubbs

Fig. 74 John Gibbons's receipt from George Stubbs for £44 12s in full payment for *The Lincolnshire Ox*. Walker Art Gallery.

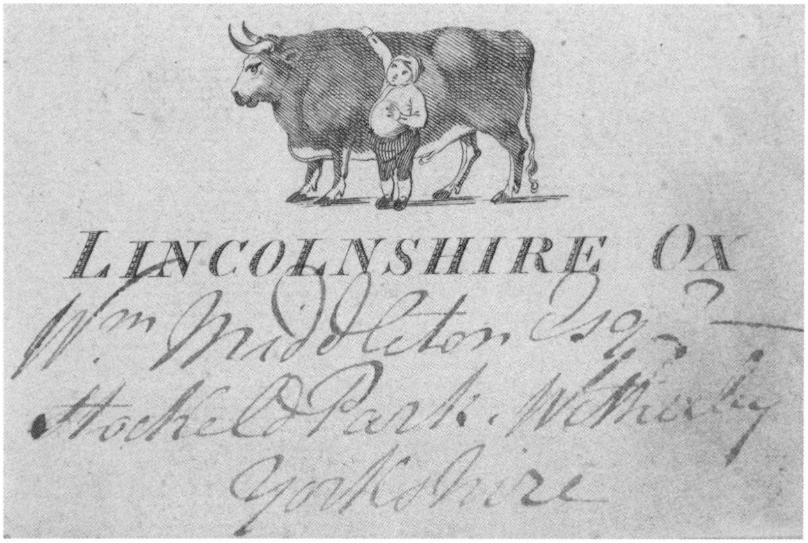

Fig. 75 Admission ticket to see *The Lincolnshire Ox*. Walker Art Gallery.

prints of *The Lincolnshire Ox* in May 1790, when he had over 300 orders for ordinary prints and nearly 100 orders for proofs from subscribers in town and country.[14] At the conclusion of the RA exhibition the painting was sent to George Townly Stubbs in Compton Street, Soho, whose print, an etching with stipple, roulette and rocker work, was published on 20 January 1791. The fact that each subscriber had been given a ticket to see the ox (fig. 75) necessitated keeping it alive, on exhibition, until the prints had been issued, despite the animal's deteriorating health through lack of exercise; but it was finally slaughtered on 20 April 1791. Gibbons retained the beast's horns and hoofs.[15]

Between 2 August 1790 and 3 February 1791 George Townly Stubbs was paid a total of 100 guineas by Gibbons and John Bough, the original owner of the ox (suggesting that the two men had entered into some sort of limited partnership in the print).[16] However, Gibbons seems to have retained proprietorship and the print was dedicated in his name to Sir Joseph Banks. On 6 February 1791 Gibbons paid John Robinson £1 11s 6d for 'Engraving the Writing to the Plate of the Lincolnshire Ox' and four days later he paid Joseph Stewardson 'for paper and printing 500 of the Lincolnshire Ox'.[17] The print was evidently the basis for a copy in silks dated 1794 (fig. 76) by E. Hampton (probably a relation of the Mr Hampton who slaughtered the ox)[18] and perhaps also for a variant in oils discovered in the attic of Great Waldingfield Rectory 1957 (on panel, 38.5 × 56.5 cm; fig. 77), where the central figure of the ox is obviously closely based on the animal depicted by Stubbs.[19] The print was re-issued by Colnaghi, Sala & Co. on 20 January 1798.[20]

PROVENANCE

Painted for John Gibbons; by descent to his great great-grandson Mr George B. Clifton; his bequest 1941.

EXHIBITIONS

RA 1790 (112); *Some Acquisitions of the Walker Art Gallery Liverpool 1935–1945* National Gallery, London 1945 (9); *Pictures of Agricultural and Sporting Interest* Usher Gallery, Lincoln 1947 (4); *Art in the Georgian Home* York City Art Gallery and tour 1949 (22); *George Stubbs* Walker Art Gallery 1951 (25); *First Hundred Years of the Royal Academy 1769–1868* RA 1951–52 (141); *George Stubbs: A Celebration* Walker Art Gallery, Tate Britain, London and Frick Collection, New York 2006–07 (no cat. no).

NOTES

1. Cradled.
2. What is evidently a garbled version of the story of the cockfight for the ox, 'eight gentlemen having subscribed ten guineas each, which is the price of it' was reprinted under the name B. Elliot in *The Parlour Portfolio; or, Post Chaise Companion: Being a Selection of the Most Amusing and Interesting Articles and Anecdotes That Have Appeared in the Magazines, Newspapers and Other Daily and Periodical Journals from the Year 1700 to the Present Time* 2 vols (Glasgow, 1820) vol. 1 p. 102.
3. Bill headed *TO BE SEEN at THE LYCEUM*, gallery files.
4. Gibbons's documentation was preserved with the painting and was also bequeathed to the gallery by George Clifton in 1941.
5. Bill headed *at THE LYCEUM*, gallery files.
6. Bill headed *Long-Sutton Ox*, gallery files.
7. Judy Egerton: *George Stubbs, Painter. Catalogue Raisonné* (New Haven and London, 2007) pp. 336–7 (cats. 143–44) and 340–41 (cat. 146). Stubbs's reputation in Lincolnshire from his long association with the Nelthorpes (who admittedly lived at the other end of the county from Gibbons) may also have weighed with Banks.
8. Egerton, *op. cit.*, p. 510 (cat. 277).
9. *Public Advertiser* (30 April 1790) p. 4. The same notice had appeared the previous day in *The Diary, or Woodfall's Register* (29 April 1790) p. 3. The painting did not attract any more significant reviews.
10. Not St James's Park as is stated by some authors (following Basil Taylor: *Animal Painting in England from Barlow to Landseer* [Harmondsworth, 1955] p. 64).
11. The ox was on exhibition at the Lyceum by April 1790, and Stubbs's painting was titled in the

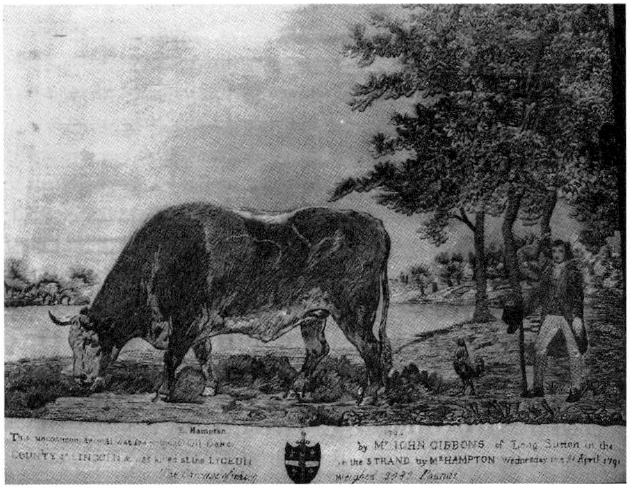

Fig. 76 *The Lincolnshire Ox* after George Stubbs, embroidered silks, by an unknown artist. Private collection; photo courtesy the owner.

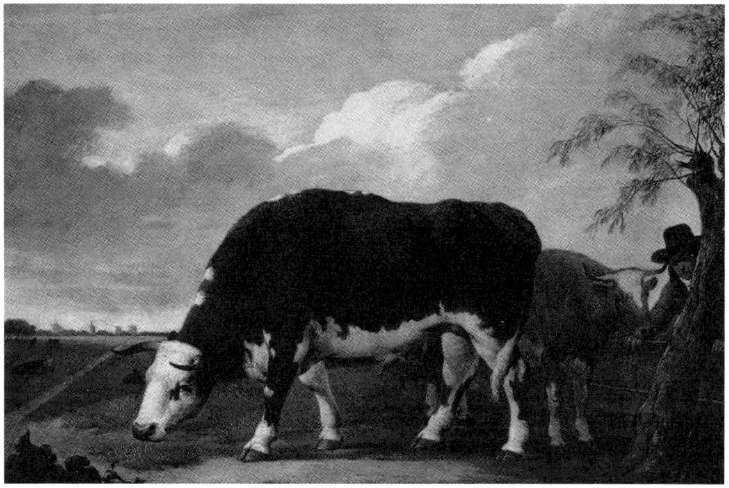

Fig. 77 *Two Oxen* by an unknown artist, oil on panel. Private collection; photo courtesy the owner.

RA catalogue *Portrait of the Lincolnshire Ox, now to be seen at the Lyceum, Strand.*
12. Egerton, *loc. cit.*; and compare A. Kidson: *George Stubbs, A Celebration*, exh. cat., Walker Art Gallery, Tate Britain and Frick Collection New York (2006) p. 8, where the even spacing between the ox, the cock, and Gibbons is contrasted with the uneven spacing employed for similar ends between the figures in Stubbs's 1793 *Soldiers of the 10th Light Dragoons*.
13. Egerton, *loc. cit.*
14. C. Lennox-Boyd, R. Dixon and T. Clayton: *George Stubbs: The Complete Engraved Works* (Abingdon, 1989) p. 225, with an analysis of the social composition of the subscribers. Gibbons had received nearly 100 subscriptions from Lincolnshire farmers and gentry within 16 days of opening the 'country' subscription list on 1 January 1790 (*op. cit.*, p. 223). Gibbons's ms list of *Prints to deliver before I leave town* is in gallery files: among the names on it are the Duke of Clarence, the Duke of Leeds, the Duke of Marlborough, the Marquis of Huntly, Earl Spencer, Sir Peter Burrell and Sir John Sheffield.
15. One of the horns and one of the hoofs was bequeathed to the gallery with the painting.
16. Lennox-Boyd, Dixon and Clayton, *op. cit.*, p. 225.
17. Receipts in gallery files.
18. Communicated by Lt-Col. W. A. Turner, *letter*, 24 July 1973, gallery files.
19. Communicated by Mrs C. S. Darley, *letter*, 15 May 1957, gallery files. Surprisingly, on being shown this picture in London, Basil Taylor was of the opinion it was not a version of Stubbs's ox (note dated June 1957, gallery files).
20. Lennox-Boyd, Dixon and Clayton, *op. cit.*, p. 222.

Gnawpost and Two Other Colts

WAG 2390
oil on canvas, 99.5 × 123 cm
signed and dated: *Geo: Stubbs pinxit 1768* (bottom centre)
date: about 1793

A repetition of a painting that Stubbs had originally made in 1768, WAG 2390 was carried out for *A Review of the Turf*, the huge project that pre-occupied the artist and his son George Townly Stubbs in the first half of the 1790s. The idea of the *Turf Review* was for Stubbs to paint around 150 'original portraits of the most famous racers' to have started 'from the year 1750 to the present time' (as the prospectus of the scheme published in January 1794 put it).[1] These paintings were to be exhibited in London at a dedicated 'Turf Gallery', and engraved by George Townly Stubbs, with the prints being offered in sets to subscribers as well as available for purchase singly.

The scheme was underwritten by an anonymous financial backer who, according to Stubbs, first approached him in 1790. The project was under way by 1793 but, following the backer's withdrawal, had petered out by the end of the following year (although prints continued to be issued at irregular intervals until September 1796). Despite what the prospectus had promised, not all the horses that Stubbs depicted were 'famous', and only four of the 16 pictures that he completed for the project were 'original'; the remainder were copies of earlier horse portraits by him. The source of WAG 2390 was a painting of three yearling colts that had been owned by the breeder Jenison Shafto (now private collection, UK); these were horses of promise rather than achievement and the work may have been done as a publicity venture in anticipation of the horses' success. As a grandson of the Godolphin Arabian, Gnawpost certainly was a horse of high potential not only as a racer but also, as Shafto would have reckoned, as a breeder. However, when Stubbs showed the work at the exhibition of the Society of Artists in 1772 – an indication that it had never passed to Shafto and had remained on the artist's hands – it was simply titled *The Portraits of Three Colts*, a sign not only that Gnawpost was not the prime subject of the picture, over and above the other two horses, but also that the public was unlikely even to recognise his name. In the event, Shafto had died in 1771 and after the horse was sold, his racing career proved to be 'only averagely successful'.[2] By the 1790s his chief claim to fame would have been his colourful habit of 'gnawing at the posts and trees when young at grass'.[3] It must have been this that established his candidacy for inclusion in the *Turf Review*, at which point his name was attached to the composition for the first time.

It is likely that WAG 2390 was one of the last pictures in the series of 16 that Stubbs completed, not only because the horse was one of the least celebrated of the set, but also because it is one of only two of the works that George Townly Stubbs did not get around to engraving.[4] Townly Stubbs did, however, make a watercolour copy of his father's painting, probably to enable him to prepare the print. This drawing (also in the Walker Art Gallery; fig. 78) may have remained with the painting for virtually the entirety of their existence.[5] A similar drawing by Townly Stubbs is known for one other of the *Turf Review* series: Anvil, the print of which was issued in December 1794. Stubbs's Turf Gallery was opened in Conduit Street, off Hanover Square, on 20 January 1794, so it is likely that WAG 2390 was completed in the latter part of 1793.

The absence of the engraving is one of the factors that have helped in the past to disguise the fact that WAG 2390 was a *Turf Review* painting. Another is the fact that the painting bears the date 1768. It was only in the 1960s that it was recognised that Stubbs had inscribed on some of the replicas in the *Turf Review* series the date of the *original* painting rather than the date when he had executed the actual canvas.[6] Eight of the group are inscribed in this way, of which WAG 2390 bears the earliest date of all. To complicate matters further still, when WAG 2390 was acquired by the gallery it bore the title *Three Brood Mares at Grass*, and Gnawpost himself had been repainted to show him eating the grass at the foot of the tree in a pose similar to the horse alongside him (fig. 79). Thus Townly

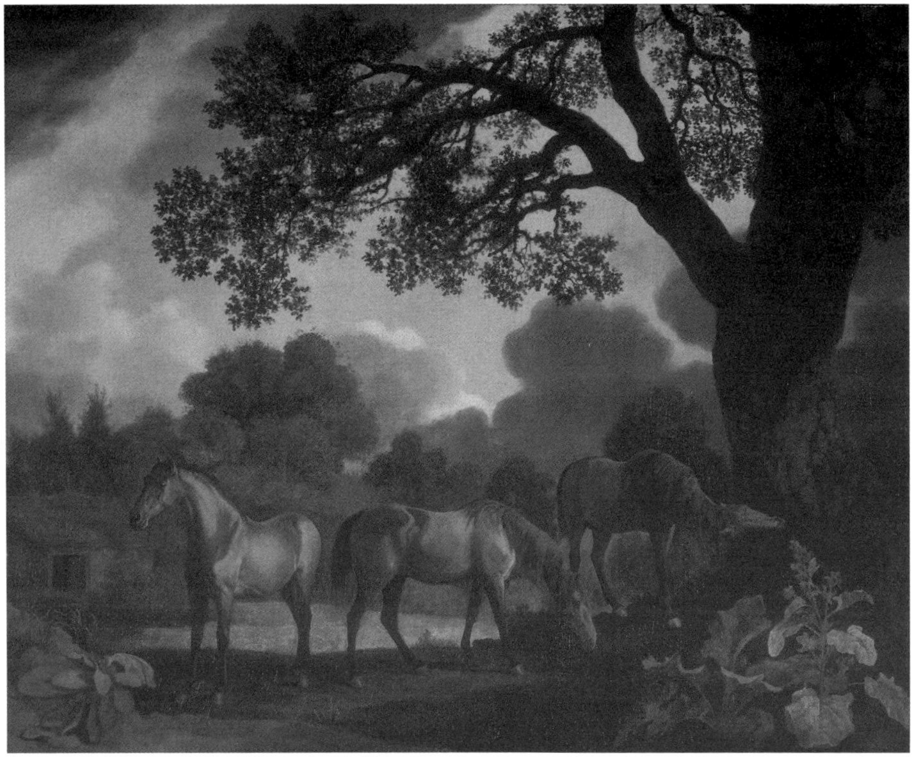

WAG 2390

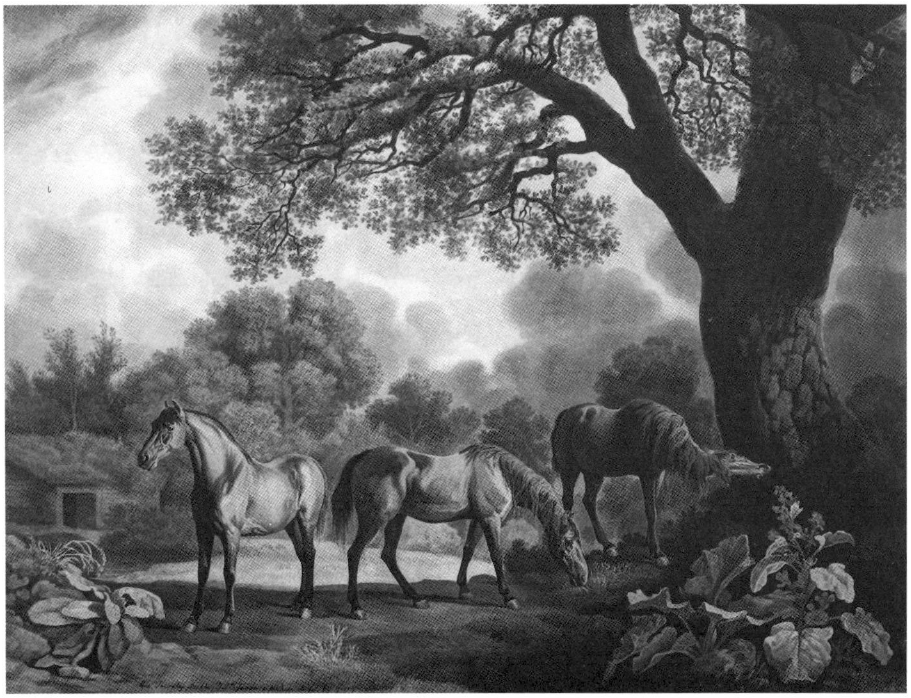

Fig. 78 *Gnawpost and Two Colts*, by G. Townly Stubbs, watercolour on paper. Walker Art Gallery.

Stubbs's watercolour was long assumed to be related to a different version of the picture rather than WAG 2390 itself. It was only following x-radiography in 1997 that the adulteration was discovered and the painting restored to its original design.[7]

PROVENANCE

Remained with the artist; Coxe, 26–27 May 1807 (first day, 93); bt. anon (150 gns.); Colonel Thomas Thornton; Hickman, 11 May 1820 (63);[8] …Walter Hutchinson by about 1947; Christie 20 July 1951 (125); bt. Agnew (1,000 gns.); bt. Messrs Lewis Ltd, Liverpool, for presentation to the gallery on its re-opening.

EXHIBITIONS

Turf Gallery 1794 (XV); *National Gallery of British Sports and Pastimes* Hutchinson House, London 1948 (113); *Selected Acquisitions of the Walker Art Gallery Liverpool 1945–1955* Agnew's, London 1955 (23); *The Noble Horse* Metropolitan Teien Art Museum, Tokyo 1998 (15).

NOTES

1. *Sporting Magazine* (January 1794) p. 214; quoted by Judy Egerton: *George Stubbs, Painter. Catalogue Raisonné* (New Haven and London, 2007) p. 546; and see *ibid.*, pp. 546–9 for a full description of the *Review of the Turf* project.
2. Egerton, *op. cit.*, p. 264.
3. *Ibid.*, citing William Pick: *The Turf Register, and Sportsman and Breeder's Stud-book…* 2 vols (York, 1803–67) vol. 1 pp. 184–5.
4. For the prints see especially C. Lennox-Boyd, R. Dixon and T. Clayton: *George Stubbs: The Complete Engraved Works* (Abingdon, 1989) pp. 235–65 (cats. 99–125). WAG 2390 was no. 15 out of 16 in the numbering of the exhibits in the Turf Gallery but there appears to be no correlation between these numbers and the order in which Townly Stubbs issued, or failed to issue, the engravings.
5. This drawing was also acquired by the Walker from the Walter Hutchinson collection, although not at the same time as WAG 2390. See T. Stevens and E. Morris: *Early English Drawings and Watercolours: Walker Art Gallery* (Liverpool, 1968) pp. 60–1.
6. This was established by Basil Taylor: *Painting in England 1700–1850 from the Collection of Mr and Mrs Paul Mellon*, exh. cat., RA (1964–65) p. 73.
7. WAG 2390 was conserved by Caroline Glover, National Museums and Galleries on Merseyside (later National Museums Liverpool) Conservation Centre, 1997–98, in preparation for its loan to the *Noble Horse* exhibition.
8. Egerton, *op. cit.*, p. 558, argues that WAG 2390 cannot be the painting owned by Thornton which was sold in 1820 under the title *Three Brood Mares* as 'Thornton himself (living at the time of the sale) would certainly have perceived the difference between three colts and three brood mares';

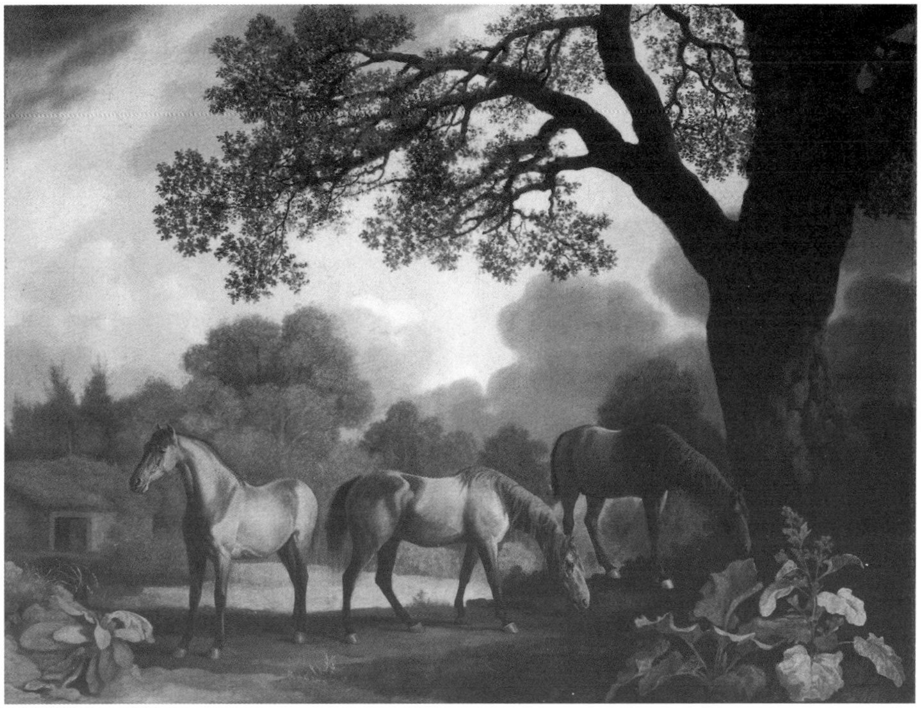

Fig. 79 WAG 2390 as overpainted when it entered the gallery, before conservation in 1998. Walker Art Gallery.

nevertheless, the *Sporting Magazine* in November 1809 reported that 'Colonel Thornton has…a very sweet picture of three horses. The principal of this group is gnawing a tree, for which propensity he was named Gnawpost. He was a famous racer the property of Robert [sic] Shaftoe' (quoted by Sir Walter Gilbey: *Life of George Stubbs R. A.* [London, 1898] p. 230).

A Monkey

WAG 2386
oil on panel, 70 × 56 cm
signed and dated: *Geo: Stubbs/1799* (bottom left)[1]
date: 1799

The monkey depicted in WAG 2386 has been definitively identified as a Malayan long-tailed or crab-eating macaque, also known as Buffon's macaque (*Macaca fascicularis*).[2] From its size, it is probably a juvenile. This monkey was not an unusual or rare species as were some of the exotic animals painted by Stubbs, and it has been pointed out that Stubbs could have seen it in many commercial menageries in London.[3] That the artist seems in this case to have had a more philosophic than scientific intention in painting the subject is suggested by the monkey's directly confrontational, anthropomorphic gaze and by the fact that it is shown holding a peach, which is more likely to have been intended by Stubbs as a symbol than to have been the monkey's actual diet.[4] The significance of the peach has been variously interpreted as an allusion to the Fall of humanity, as a symbol of truth (the fruit and its leaf conjoined denoting the heart and the tongue speaking with one voice) or (in Cesare Ripa's *Iconologia* of 1630) as the fruit sacred to Harpocrates, God of silence.[5] Whichever, it seems that Stubbs is providing his own twist on contemporary scientific debates on the relationship between man and monkeys;[6] and whether he is stressing modern man's distance from, or his closeness to, the monkey, the prominence of the tree reads as a reference to the garden of Eden and to humanity's original state of nature.

That Stubbs renewed his interest in the subject of the monkey and its relationship with the human being in the second half of the 1790s is suggested by the drawing he made of a dissected or desiccated macaque, *Macaca sylvanus*, in connection with his project, *A Comparative Anatomical Exposition of the Human Body with That of a Tiger and a Common Fowl* (1795–1802; Yale Center for British Art).[7] Probably around the same time that he painted WAG 2386, Stubbs also made a replica of his much earlier *A Tigress* (private collection, UK) and these two works, both seemingly painted as an exercise in the course of working on the *Comparative Anatomy*, are the only known instances of the artist making repetitions of his works for his own use, as distinct from commercially.[8] Stubbs showed WAG 2386 at the Royal Academy in 1799. His original version of the subject (private collection, signed and dated 1774)[9] had appeared at the RA in 1775, perhaps significantly, the occasion that had marked his transfer of allegiance from the exhibitions of the Society of Artists. In flirting with (although not strictly breaking) the rule that no artist should show the same work at the RA twice, Stubbs was surely confirming, for his public audience, that the subject held a special personal significance.

PROVENANCE

Remained with the artist; Coxe, 26–27 May 1807 (second day, 70); bt. anon (25 gns.);[10] …T. Humphry Ward by 1907; Christie 17 December 1915 (123); bt. Hood (9 gns.); Christie 31 March 1916 (142); bt. Renton (2 gns.); …Walker's Galleries London 1949; from whom bt. 1950.

EXHIBITIONS

RA 1799 (177); *Animals in Art* Whitechapel Art Gallery, London 1907 (upper gallery, 40); *Historical Exhibition of Liverpool Art* Walker Art Gallery 1908

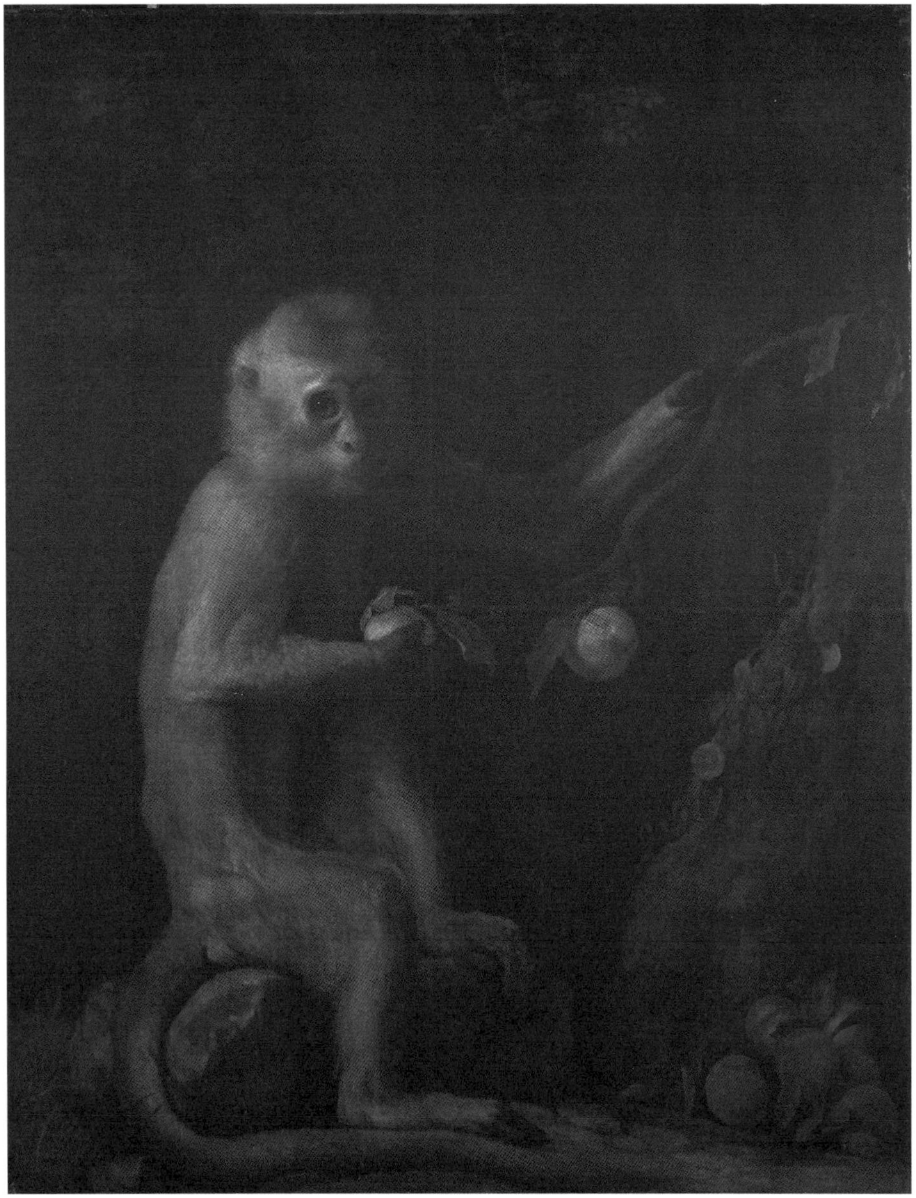

WAG 2386

(119); *George Stubbs* Walker Art Gallery 1951 (66); *First Hundred Years of the Royal Academy 1769–1868* RA 1951–52 (144); *Selected Acquisitions of the Walker Art Gallery Liverpool 1945–1955* Agnew's, London 1955 (14); *Unbekannte Schönheit* Kunsthaus, Zürich 1956 (248); *George Stubbs 1724–1806* Whitechapel Art Gallery, London 1957 (56); *Le Siècle de l'Elégance* Musée des Arts Décoratifs, Paris 1959 (208); *Primitives to Picasso* RA 1962 (171); *George Stubbs: A Celebration* Tate Britain, London and Frick Collection, New York 2006–07 (no cat. no).[11]

NOTES

1. The last digit of the date is difficult to distinguish. Basil Taylor: *Stubbs* (London, 1971) p. 215 published the date as 1798, and this has been followed by Judy Egerton: *George Stubbs 1724–1806* exh. cat, Tate Gallery, London and Yale Center for British Art, New Haven (1984) p. 122; Ian Rolfe and Caroline Grigson: '"Drill and Hamadryas Baboon" in Conjectural Cultural Context', *Archives of Natural History* vol. 33 no. 1 (2006) p. 30; and Egerton: *George Stubbs, Painter. Catalogue Raisonné* (New Haven and London, 2007) p. 364; however, the date was read as 1799 by Hugh Macandrew in 1962 (draft catalogue entry, gallery files), and was thus published in CIC, p. 260.
2. Rolfe and Grigson, *loc. cit.* WAG 2386 was titled *A Green Monkey* when it was acquired by the gallery in 1950 and was exhibited under this title between 1951 and 1962 (see above); it was also given this title in CIC, *loc.cit.* Dr Solly Zuckerman, *letter*, 13 January 1962, identified the monkey as a rhesus; Egerton: *George Stubbs, Anatomist and Animal Painter* exh. cat., Tate Gallery, London (1976) p. 61 (cat. 34) first published the identification as a crab-eating macaque made earlier that year by Prue Napier and Daphne Hills, British Museum. Green monkeys are distinguished by the greenish tinge of their soft outer hair and by their black faces.
3. Egerton, *George Stubbs 1724–1806*, *loc. cit.*
4. *Ibid.*; however, Rolfe and Grigson, *op. cit.*, p. 34, n. 24 point out that fruit at 32 per cent ranks highest in this monkey's dietary proportions and that Buffon in 1766 depicted the species holding a papaya.
5. Rolfe and Grigson, *op. cit.*, p. 30, citing Ronald Paulson: *Emblem and Expression: Meaning in English Art of the Eighteenth Century* (London, 1975) p. 163, n. 22; James Hall: *Dictionary of Subjects and Symbols in Art* (rev. edn, London, 1996) p. 238; and J. Williamson: *The Oak King, the Holly King and the Unicorn: The Myths and Symbolism of the Unicorn Tapestries* (New York, 1986) p. 154.
6. For a discussion of this see Rolfe and Grigson, *op. cit.*, *passim*.
7. The drawing (B.1980.1.126; repr. Egerton, *George Stubbs, Painter*, p. 609) has always been in the portfolios containing Stubbs's drawings for the *Comparative Anatomy*. A sketchbook containing twelve studies of monkeys appeared in Stubbs's studio sale (Peter Coxe, 26–27 May 1807, second day, lot 24; see Rolfe and Grigson, *op. cit.*, p. 35, n. 27).
8. For the original *Tigress* see Egerton, *George Stubbs, Painter*, pp. 240–1 (cat. 77); for the replica, *ibid.*, pp. 610–1 (cat. 328). The replica is dated by Egerton about 1797–98 on the basis that it was made for the engraving published (with a different background) by John Murphy on 27 July 1798.
9. For the 1774 *Monkey* see Egerton (2007) pp. 364–5 (cat. 165); she does not catalogue WAG 2386 although her discussion of it, in the entry on the 1774 painting, suggests that she regards it as autograph.
10. Lot 70 was described in the catalogue as *Portrait of a Monkey Gathering Fruit – An Upright. An exceeding high finished Picture.*
11. Not included in the Walker Art Gallery showing.

091.5 DAU, p. 48 (cat. 67), but is absent from the earlier list of Daulby's paintings preserved with his manuscript *List on the Prices of the Prints* (see WAG 2541, p. 183, n. 2), suggesting that it may have been painted after that list was drawn up.
4. As a grandson of William Roscoe he was a great-nephew of the sitter in WAG 2543; his connection with her presumably explained why WAG 2541–43 were bequeathed to him after the death of Catherine Daulby.

Miss Tate of Toxteth Park

WAG 9281
oil on canvas, 76 × 63.5 cm
date: about 1792–95

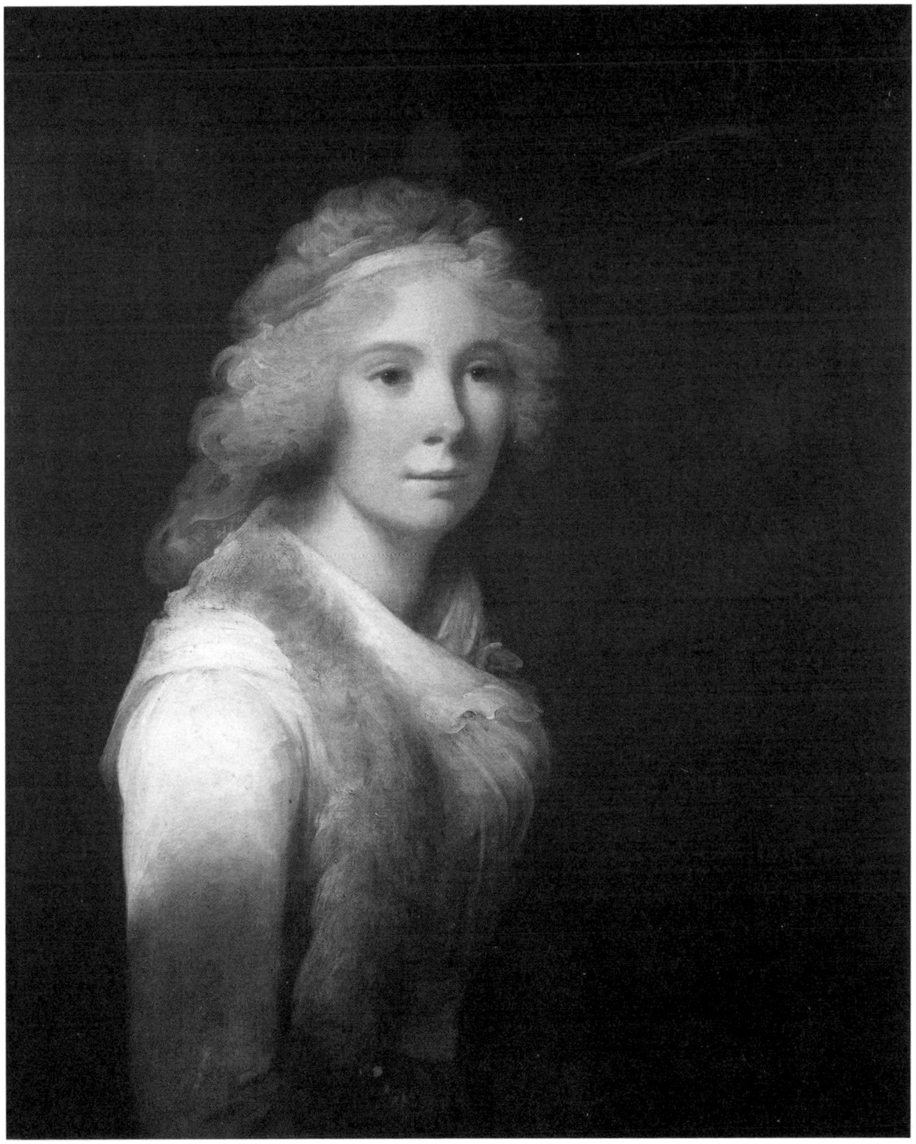

WAG 9281

The sitter is the artist's niece Elizabeth, who was the only daughter of his elder brother Richard Tate.[1] She was baptised at St Thomas's Church, Liverpool, on 26 October 1766[2] and was an amateur artist. She exhibited a landscape drawing at the 1784 exhibition of the Liverpool Society for the Promotion of Painting and Design and two more at the Society's 1787 exhibition.[3] Drawings by her are mentioned in the will of her brother Thomas Moss Tate (for him and other members of the Tate family see WAG 9067, below) and portraits by her of her parents and herself were included in the sale of her husband's effects held by Messrs Trotter & Hodgkins, Liverpool, 7 June 1841.[4] Her husband, whom she married in 1802, was Joseph Williamson, later the celebrated 'Mole of Edge Hill', who constructed miles of tunnelling underneath Liverpool, and who took over the Tate family's tobacco business in Wolstenholme Square in the city.[5] Elizabeth died in 1822 and was buried in St Thomas Church, Liverpool.[6]

On the basis of the sitter's age and costume the portrait can be dated to the early 1790s. William Tate did not exhibit in public exhibitions between 1791 and 1802, and little is known of his career and movements at this juncture. In both 1791 and 1802 he is recorded as living in Manchester but he could easily have painted the work on a visit to his relatives in Liverpool.

PROVENANCE

By descent to Major James Hunter; Bruton, Knowles sale at the Old Rectory, Madresfield, Worcs., 17 February 1976 (303) bt. in;[7] bt. privately from Major Hunter 1977.

NOTES

1. The identification was made in *MPPP*, p. 240.
2. Information from Sonia Addis-Smith, a descendant researching the family, January 2008, gallery files.
3. *LAOE*, p. 586.
4. *Liverpool Mercury* (4 June 1841) p. 185.
5. On Williamson see Charles R. Hand: 'Joseph Williamson, the King of Edge Hill', *Transactions of the Historic Society of Lancashire and Cheshire [for the year 1927]* vol. 79 (1928) pp. 86–111; also *MPPP*, pp. 57–8.
6. Information from Don Higham, *letter*, 15 October 2003 (gallery files).
7. At the 1976 sale the portrait was attributed to Romney.

Mr Tate of Toxteth Park

WAG 9067
oil on canvas, 127 × 100.6 cm
date: about 1800

From the sitter's costume and the general style, WAG 9067 appears to be slightly later in date than the portrait of Miss Tate (portrait of Miss Tate, above). It has been suggested that it could date from around 1800.[1] A portrait by John Boultbee of what were presumably this sitter's horse and the same dog, dated 1801, had the same family provenance as WAG 9067.[2] William Tate was living in Manchester at this date but was no doubt regularly in contact with his Liverpool relations.

The title *Mr Tate of Toxteth Park* could refer to any of the artist's nephews, the sons of Richard Tate, tobacco merchant and amateur artist, established in Liverpool at least by 1766 first in Duke Street and then Wolstenholme Square, who died in 1787. Of these nephews, Richard, Paul and Thomas Moss Tate, Thomas seems much the likeliest candidate for the sitter in WAG 9067. From street directories (which list him from 1790 as a merchant with a tobacco and snuff manufactory), it is evident that he emerged as the head of the family in the period just before 1800; from that year his name alone is listed and in 1803 he is first described as 'gentleman'. Moreover, he is the only brother recorded as living at Toxteth Park (although not before 1821) and it was there that he died on 6 March 1825.[3] In his will of 1816[4] he left small annuities to his brothers, and to Paul he left a reversionary interest in the collection of paintings (including the family portraits) which he bequeathed in the first instance to his wife Emma and their child or children. The wording of the will, in respect of the pictures, emphasises Thomas Moss Tate's friendship with, and esteem for, Joseph Wright of Derby, six paintings by whom, together with a half-length portrait of him ('with Raphael's Bible under one hand'), are specifically mentioned by title.[5] Thomas Moss Tate was an amateur artist who showed a total of seven works at the 1784 and 1787 exhibitions of the Society for the Promotion of Painting and Design in Liverpool. He accompanied Wright on sketching tours of the Lake District in 1793 and 1794[6] and it has been suggested that the present portrait, in which the figure is shown drawing and with its hint of a mountainous lakeland landscape in the background, commemorates these occasions.[7]

Without doubt WAG 9067 must be one of 'the Portraits large and small of or by any of my family' that Thomas Moss Tate left in his will to his wife and then to their daughter Emma. The latter is said to have been a direct ancestor of the last owner.

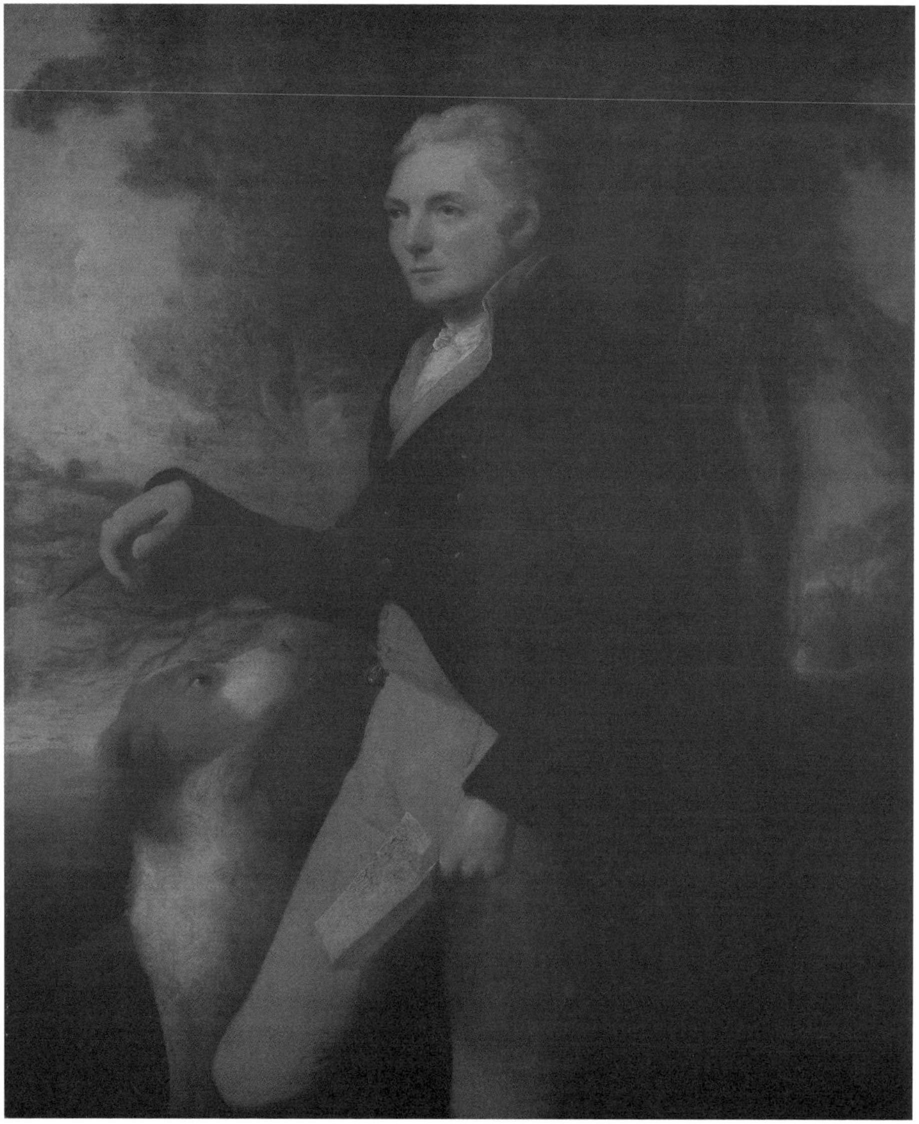

WAG 9067

PROVENANCE

By descent to Major James Hunter; Bruton, Knowles sale at the Old Rectory, Madresfield, Worcs. 17 February 1976 (304);[8] bt. by the gallery.

NOTES

1. MPPP, p. 198.
2. Lot 305 in the 1976 Bruton, Knowles sale.
3. This is the date given by Tate's executors when they proved his will (see n. 4); *Gore's General Advertiser* (10 March 1825) p. 3, gives the date of death as 7 March. Richard Tate, recorded in street directories as merchant at 3 Parr Street in 1796, died on 7 June 1826, aged 56 (*Gore's General Advertiser* [15 June 1826] p. 3). Thomas Moss Tate's date of birth is unknown, but the fact that he exhibited in public in 1784 suggests he was born before 1770. A date of about 1763 has been proposed by Sonia Addis-Smith, January 2008 (note in gallery files).
4. Thomas Moss Tate's will of 8 July 1816, with codicil dated 28 August 1822, Lancashire Record Office, Preston.
5. The titles of the six paintings are *A Philosopher by Lamplight*; *A Landscape View of Langdale Pikes*; *A Moonlight View of Dunkeld* [described as a large picture]; *A Small Moonlight View of Matlock High Tor*; *The Lake of Nemi*; and *Neptune's Grotto*. A seventh painting by Wright, *A Lady in Milton's Comus* (see pp. 290–3) was left by Tate to his wife and then their daughter under the terms of the will's 1822 codicil. The original will directed that Tate's remaining paintings and prints were to be sold after his death. Among the latter (by the date of his death in 1825) were 14 further paintings by Wright, which, together with works by other artists, were auctioned by Winstanley in Liverpool on 13 April 1849, 'the property of a Gentleman recently deceased, and being formerly part of the collection of Thomas Moss Tait Esq., of this town'. No catalogue of this sale is known but the paintings are listed in notices of the sale in the *Liverpool Mercury*, 6 April 1849 p. 4 and 13 April 1849 p. 1.
6. B. Nicolson: *Joseph Wright of Derby, Painter of Light* 2 vols (London 1968) vol. 1, pp. 19, 139.
7. MPPP, *loc. cit.*
8. Attributed at the sale to Wright of Derby.

Charles Towne

1763–1840

Two Gentlemen Setting Out to Hunt

WAG 9818
oil on canvas on board, 41.5 × 48.5 cm
signed: *C Town pinxt* (lower right)

Two Gentlemen Shooting

WAG 9819
oil on canvas on board, 41.5 × 48.5 cm
signed: *C. Town* (centre left)
date: about 1790–95

This pair of ovals depicts two episodes in a day's shooting expedition undertaken by two young gentlemen (who appear in both works) and their attendants (who appear in the first of the pair only). In WAG 9818, the two young men, evidently friends, set out; their attendants, holding their guns, ride a discreet distance behind. In WAG 9819 the huntsman in the red coat and tan breeches, gun cocked, is about to shoot some game, his pointers at the ready. This man is evidently the chief protagonist (his features alone are portrayed in WAG 9818 and he is the dominant figure in WAG 9819) and it may be surmised that he commissioned these paintings from Towne. The style of these works, together with the hats, suggest a date of about 1790–95, and it is tempting to suggest that the man in the red coat is the youthful Viscount Molyneux, who succeeded his father as 2nd Earl of Sefton in 1795.[1]

The scenes are painted as ovals on rectangular pieces of canvas with the cream-coloured ground left bare at the corners. The border of ground at the centre of each edge is approximately 4 cm wide. The canvases appear to have been laid onto board at a later date.

PROVENANCE

...Josephine, Countess of Sefton; her bequest 1980.

NOTES

1. An early dating is supported by the form of Towne's signature, without the final 'e' (which he abandoned in favour of 'Towne' after about 1800). There is, however, no evidence for the existence of these works at Croxteth in such inventories as exist (see, for example, WAG 8635, p. 212, n. 2). Both works are inscribed on the reverse in chalk *BE457*, a code applied to a number of works consigned to Christie's for valuation but not sale after the death of the Countess of Sefton in 1980. It is possible that these were personal acquisitions of the Countess but it may be that they had been taken to the family's second home at Abbeystead in the nineteenth century and were rediscovered by the Countess after she retired there following the death of the 7th Earl of Sefton in 1972.

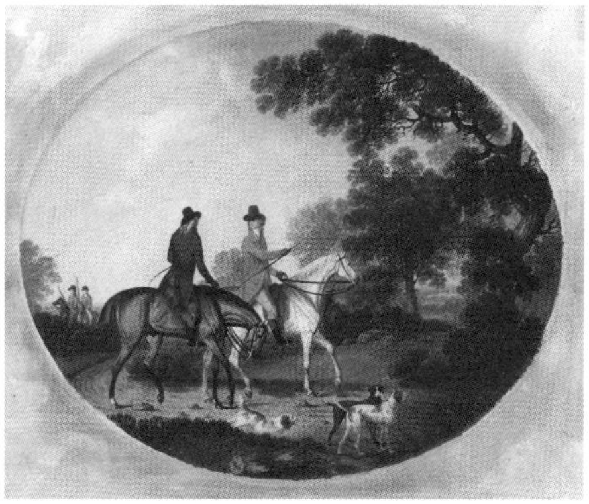

WAG 9818

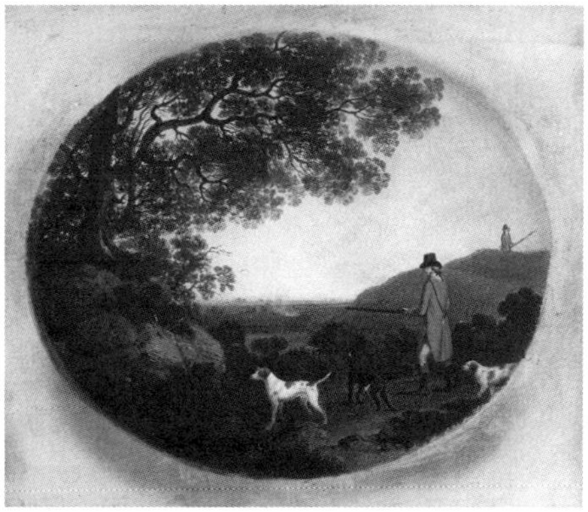

WAG 9819

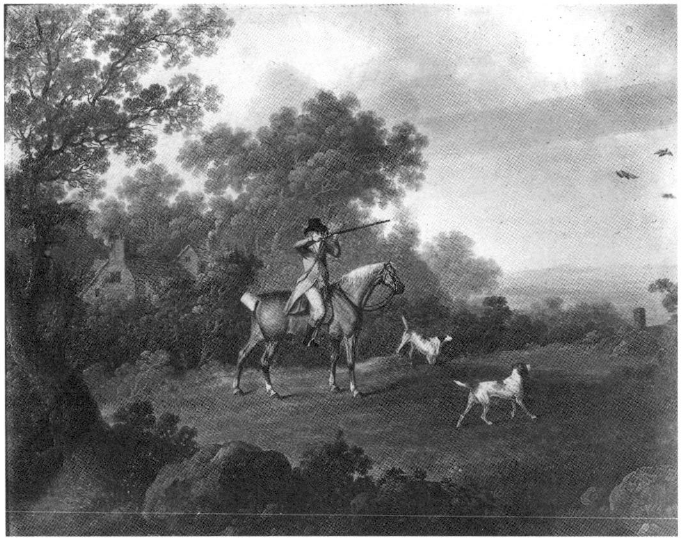

WAG 2340

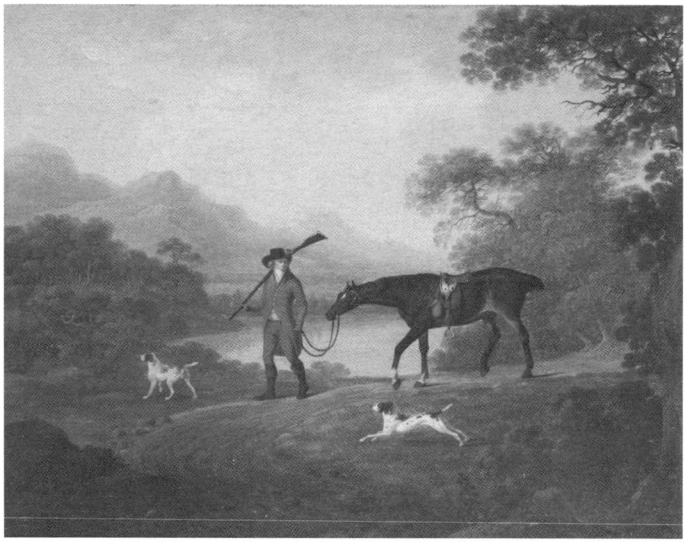

WAG 2341

A Gentleman Shooting Partridges

WAG 2340
oil on panel, 30.5 × 38.5 cm
signed: *Charles Town pinxt* (on rock in left foreground)

A Gentleman Returning from Shooting

WAG 2341
oil on panel, 30.5 × 38.5 cm
signed: *C.T.P.* (bottom centre)
date: about 1790–95

These works, which are very similar in style and in the depiction of costume to WAG 9818–19 (above) may be dated to around 1790–95 (although if de Loutherbourg influenced WAG 2341, as has been argued,[1] they must be from several years later than this). Although they are pendants (being the same size, identically framed and signed in the way Towne appears to have signed pairs generally) they do not function as a pair in the same way that WAG 9818–19 do, as a continuous narrative. Here the two sportsmen are different people: the man in WAG 2340 is in tan breeches and his horse is a chestnut; in 2341 the breeches are grey and the horse is a bay. The landscapes are also strongly contrasted. While that in WAG 2340 lacks a specific northern character, the one in WAG 2341 is evocative of the Lake District,[2] and a 'north versus south' dialogue may have been part of Towne's intention. Nevertheless, the presence of the same two hunting dogs in both pictures establishes an element of continuity, enabling the pictures to function as a narrative in which two sporting friends, each with their horse and dog, enjoy a day's shooting at large. It is possible that the two works were commissioned by two friends in this way.

PROVENANCE

…Walter Stone before 1934; Mary Stone Bequest 1944.

EXHIBITIONS

Some Acquisitions of the Walker Art Gallery Liverpool 1935–1945 National Gallery, London 1945 (84–85); *Sporting Pictures from the Walter Stone Collection* Bluecoat Gallery, Liverpool 1946 (30) [WAG 2341 only]; *Engelse Jachtschilderijen [Merry Old England]* Museum 'het Prinsenhof', Delft 1949–50 (68–69); *English Sporting Pictures* Whitechapel Art Gallery, London 1950 (82–83); *A Selection of Sporting Pictures from the Walter Stone Collection* Bluecoat Gallery, Liverpool 1953 (23) [WAG 2340] and (21) [WAG 2341]; *Charles Towne of Liverpool 1763–1840* Walker Art Gallery 1971 (5–6); *British Sporting Paintings 1650–1850* Hayward Gallery, London and tour 1974–75 (115) [WAG 2341 only].

NOTES

1. Mary Webster and Lionel Lambourne: *British Sporting Paintings 1650–1850*, exh. cat., Hayward Gallery, London and tour (1974) p. 82: the signature *Town* without the final 'e' is characteristic of Towne's eighteenth-century works. Compare *MPPP*, p. 204.
2. It is tempting to suggest that it is a fanciful portrayal of Keswick at the head of Derwentwater, with, from left to right, the three mountains of Skiddaw, Latrigg and Blencathra in approximately correct geographical position behind.

Mare and Foal

WAG 7642
oil on canvas, 33 × 42 cm

The Racehorse

WAG 7643
oil on canvas, 32.5 × 42.5 cm

Fallen in the Shafts of a Huckster's Cart

WAG 7644
oil on canvas, 33 × 42.5 cm

Lying Dead in a Field

WAG 7645
oil on canvas, 33 × 42 cm

Carted Off

WAG 7646
oil on canvas, 32.5 × 42 cm
date: unknown, perhaps 1790–1800

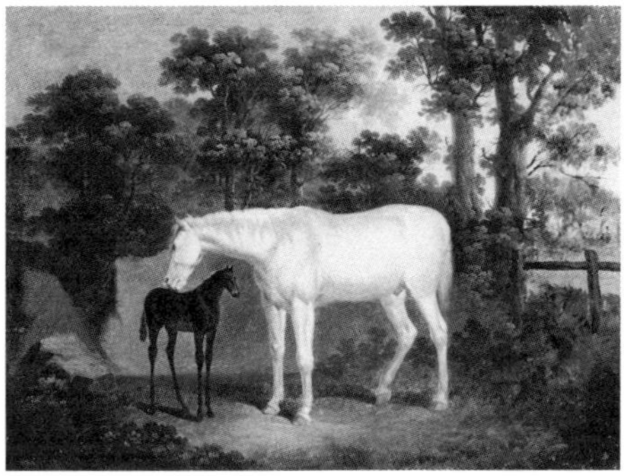

WAG 7642

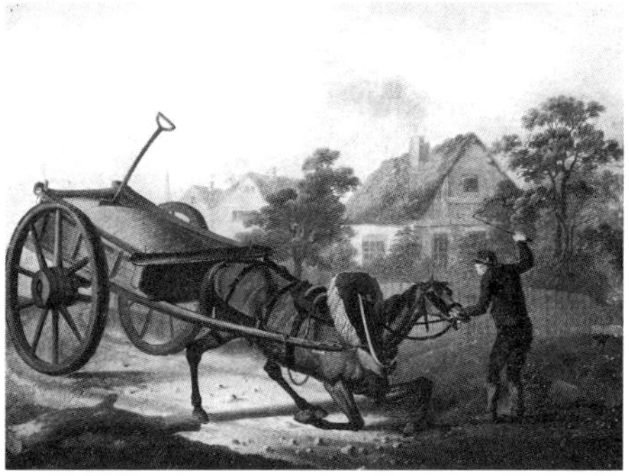

WAG 7644

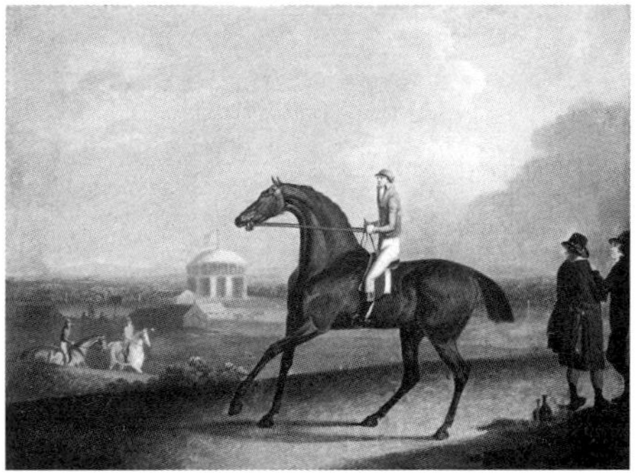

WAG 7643

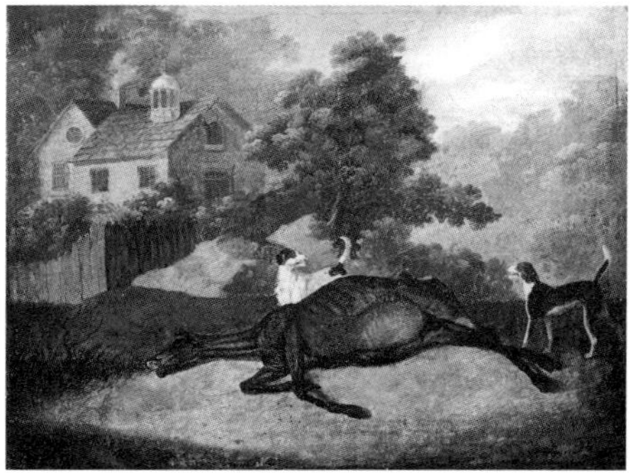

WAG 7645

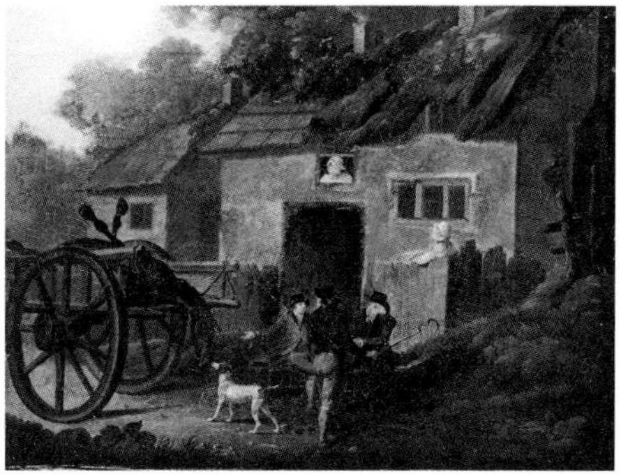

WAG 7646

These are five surviving canvases from an original series of eight on the life of a racehorse.[1] Comparison with a related complete set (Richard Green Gallery London 1972; figs. 81–88)[2] reveals that they are nos 1, 3, 6, 7 and 8 in the sequence; the missing three scenes, nos 2, 4 and 5 being, respectively, *Exercising*; *The Hunter Setting Out*; and *The Carriage Horse* (following the titles given to the Richard Green equivalents, which show a variety of activities, not just racing). WAG 7642–46 display significant variations from the Richard Green canvases and are much inferior in quality; they are also in indifferent condition and appear to have been overpainted, making it hard to judge if they are autograph works by Towne or copies. However, the fact that they are first recorded in the ownership of a Liverpool collector whose life-dates overlap with those of Towne himself suggests that they probably came directly from the artist.

One prototype for Towne's series is a set of six paintings by Thomas Gooch (see p. 56) exhibited at the Royal Academy in 1783.[3] Their theme was popularised with the publication in 1790 of Gooch's aquatint engravings, *The Life and Death of a Racehorse*, whose six plates bore titles virtually identical to those of the paintings shown in 1783;[4] a second set, perhaps from the same pictures, was issued in 1792 'with an Essay tending to excite a benevolent conduct towards the Brute Creation by Dr. Hawksworth'.[5] It is likely that Towne's earliest versions of the subject (which, to judge from their hard, burnished style, included the Richard Green set) date from that decade.[6] His handling of the human figure in these works suggests a close study of the paintings of George Morland, which were especially popular in the 1790s.

It is noticeable how, in extending Gooch's original schema from six works to eight, Towne establishes a very different narrative emphasis. Concentrating on the details of the horse's grisly end, he adds a layer of coarse and mawkish sentiment to the equilibrium of Gooch's set.

PROVENANCE

...Joseph Mayer; bequeathed to the Mayer Trust, Bebington, Cheshire; presented by Bebington Corporation 1971.

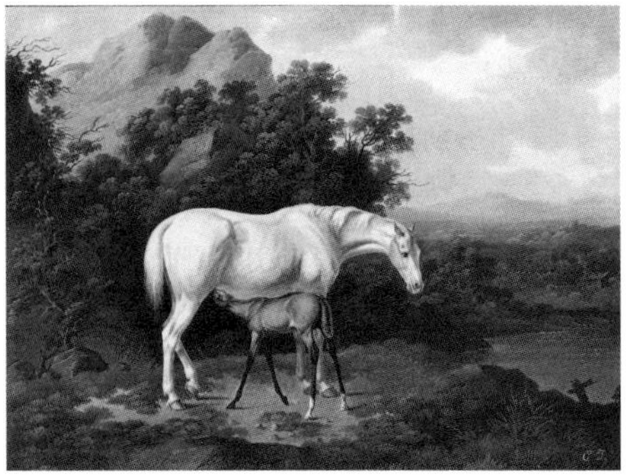
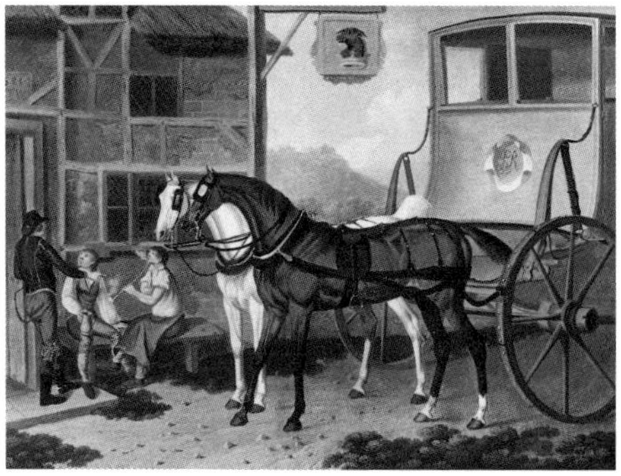
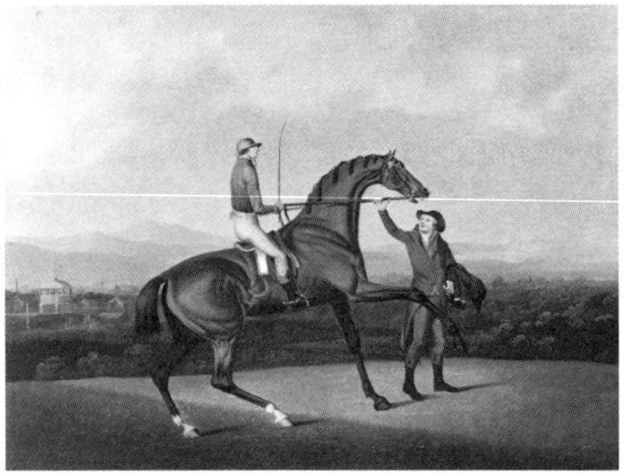
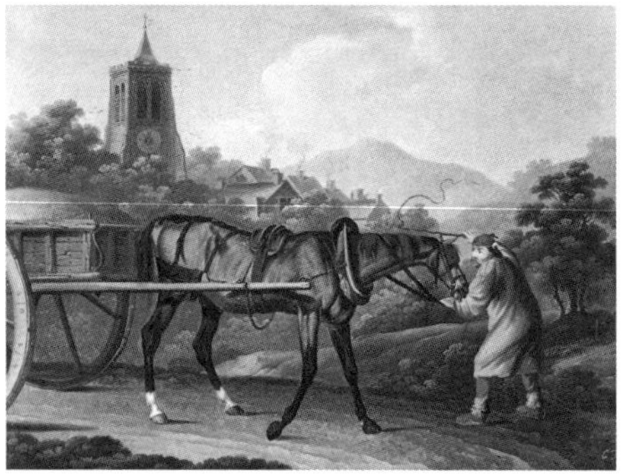
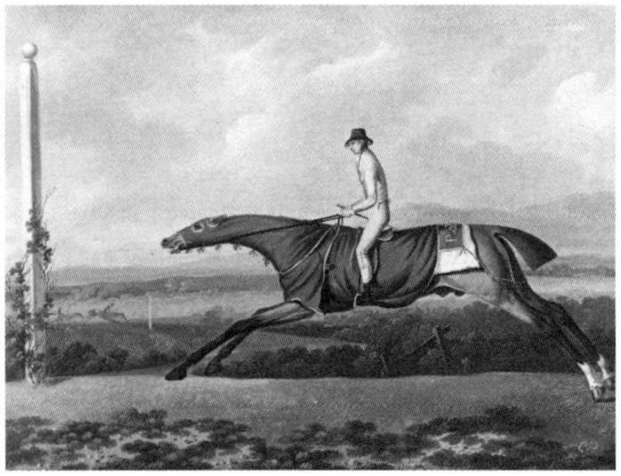
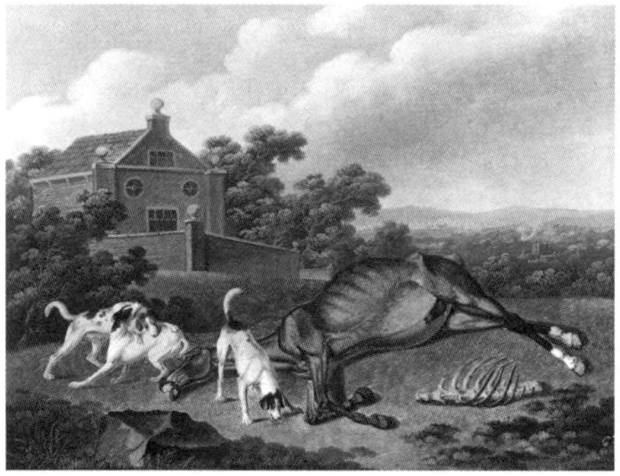
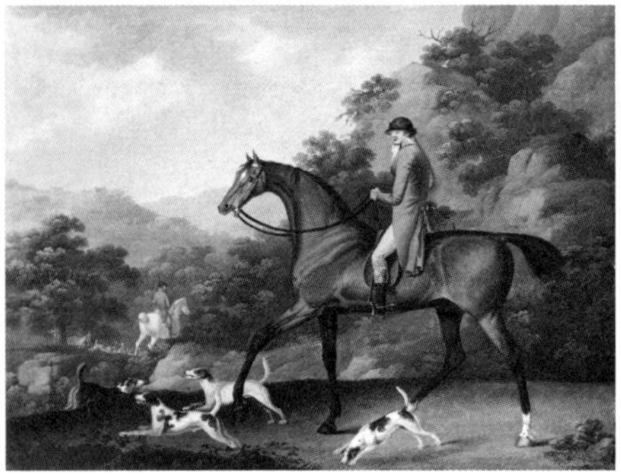
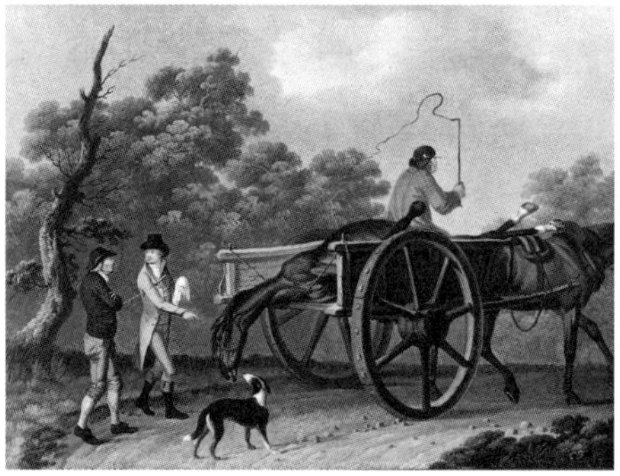

Figs. 81–88 *The Life of A Racehorse* by Charles Towne, eight episodes, oil on canvas. Private collection. Courtesy Richard Green Gallery, London.

EXHIBITION

Charles Towne of Liverpool 1763–1840 Walker Art Gallery 1971 (ex. cat.).

NOTES

1. Apparently all eight were present when the works were in the collection of the Mayer Trust, since they were given the numbers 4–11 in the Trust's *Handlist of Drawings, Prints, Sculpture* [...] (n.d.).
2. Exhibited in his *Annual Exhibition of Sporting Paintings* 1972 (44).
3. GrRA, vol. 3, p. 263; Gooch's titles were: *1st, The Foal, with the Mare, 2nd, The Colt Breaking, 3rd, The Time of Running, 4th, as a hunter, 5th, as a fast horse* and *6th, His Death*.
4. Dudley Snelgrove: *The Paul Mellon Collection: British Sporting and Animal Prints* (London, 1981) p. 81.
5. Judy Egerton: *The Paul Mellon Collection: British Sporting and Animal Paintings* (London, 1978) pp. 146–7.
6. Compare W. Shaw Sparrow: *A Book of Sporting Painters* (London and New York, 1931) fp. 135, 138, where three paintings from a further set (formerly with Spink, London) are illustrated and dated to around 1790.

Drover and Cattle Entering a Valley

WAG 9556
oil on panel, 26.5 × 32 cm
date: unknown, perhaps 1793–96

This small picture is not easy to date,[1] but tentatively it may be identified as an early work, from around 1793–96, when Towne was working around Liverpool and, increasingly, Manchester and before his first visit to London. The tight and rather delicate handling of the figure and the animals recalls that of the artist's first securely dated sporting paintings (see pp. 187–8) while the treatment of the landscape – less contrived and more realistic looking than in Towne's mature work, carries overtones of the work of John Rathbone, whom the artist may well have known in Manchester. The left-hand trees and the mountain profiles also strongly recall the work of Richard Wilson (see pp. 262–273).

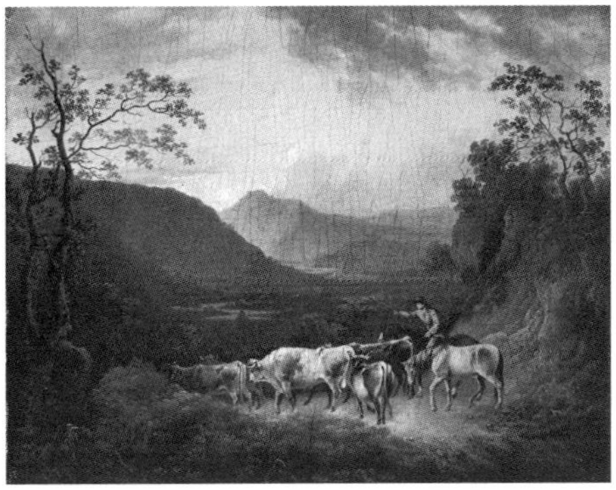

WAG 9556

The panel on which WAG 9556 is painted is slightly bowed at the right and left sides and major abrasions have occurred along all four edges.

PROVENANCE

...Col. J. R. Danson; his bequest 1979.

EXHIBITION

Danson Collection of Paintings by Charles Towne Walker Art Gallery 1977 (35).

REFERENCE

1. The 1977 catalogue, arranged chronologically, placed WAG 9556 between dated works of 1820 and 1822, possibly from the perception that the composition recalls that of *Traveller on a Road in Snowdonia* (1822, second version of 1823; see WAG 9553 and 9552, pp. 215–6); however, the style of the latter works is quite different from that of WAG 9556. CIC proposed a dating of about 1800–10.

Gentleman on a Black Shooting Pony with Beater and Dogs in a Mountain Landscape

WAG 2160
oil on canvas, 61.5 × 77.5 cm
signed: *C. T*
(initials in monogram, bottom centre)
date: about 1796–97

The figures in WAG 2160 both have the appearance of being portraits, and the landscape, too, has the air of a real, studied, location, perhaps in North Wales or the Lake District. It has been dated to the early 1800s,[1] but if the painting is a commission for which Towne travelled to the patron's home, it almost certainly predates the artist's move to London in about 1797–98, after which he seems to have been based in the capital and the Home Counties until 1810. As has been observed, Towne used the present form of monogram at least as early as 1796[2] and the style of WAG 2160 is consonant with a dating in the mid- to later 1790s. The diarist Joseph Farington noted in July 1797 that Towne had 'six months work bespoke' at Manchester;[3] this may have been one of the commissions concerned.

PROVENANCE

...Walter Stone before 1934; Mary Stone Bequest 1944.

EXHIBITIONS

Some Acquisitions of the Walker Art Gallery Liverpool 1935–1945 National Gallery, London 1945 (83); *Sporting Pictures from the Walter Stone Collection* Bluecoat Gallery, Liverpool 1946 (32); *Art in the Georgian Home* York City Art Gallery and tour 1949 (24); *Charles Towne of Liverpool 1763–1840* Walker Art Gallery 1971 (8); *British Sporting Paintings 1650–1850* Hayward Gallery, London and tour 1974–75 (118).

NOTES

1. The 1971 exhibition catalogue, *The Walter Stone Collection of Sporting Pictures at Whitton Hall, Westbury, Shropshire* (privately printed, 1938) p. 27 (cat. 41), suggests 'circa 1800'.
2. *Ibid.*; followed by *MPPP*, p. 204.
3. *FD*, vol. 3, p. 872 (entry of 14 July 1797).

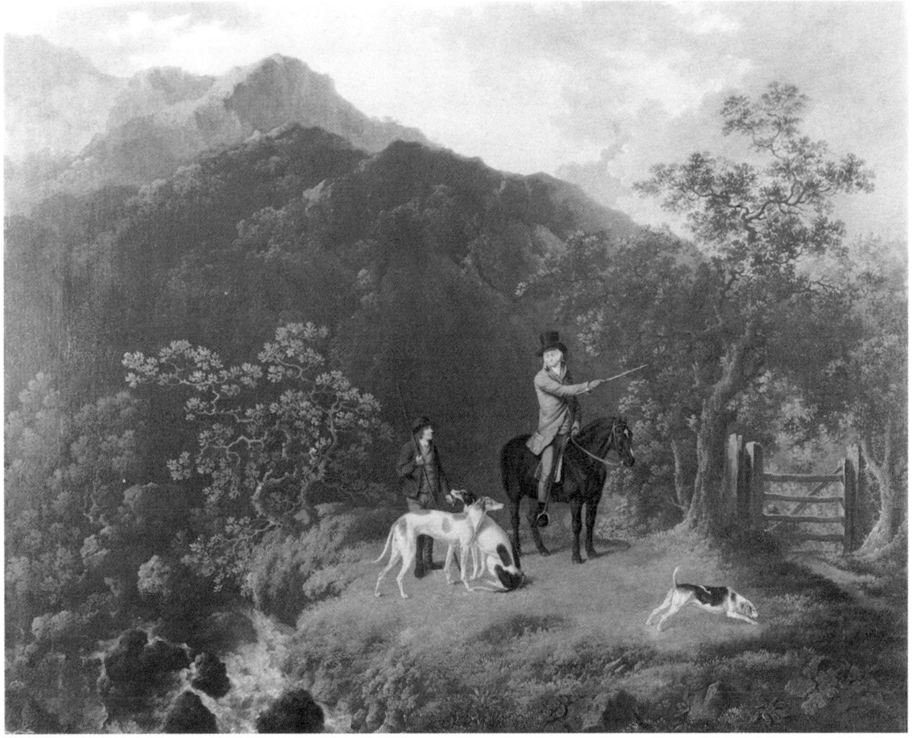

WAG 2160

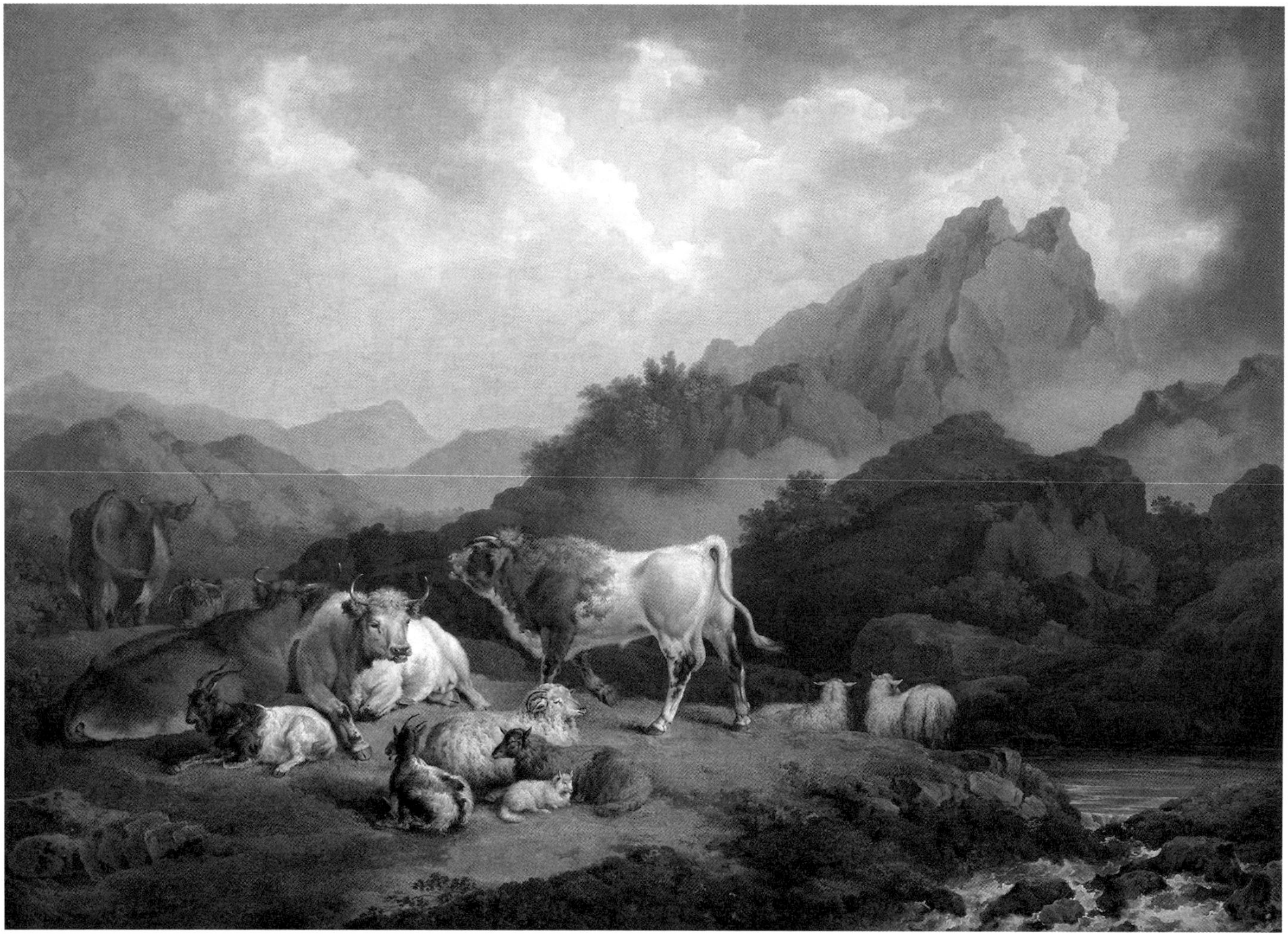

WAG 9567

The Monarch of the Glen[1]

WAG 9567
oil on canvas, 90.5 × 106 cm
signed and dated: *Chas. Towne/1797* (bottom left)
date: 1797

Cool and lucid in manner, WAG 9567 reveals the influence of Philippe de Loutherbourg (1740–1812), whose work made a strong impact on Towne on his first visit to London in 1797.[2] The painting is particularly close to a work of nearly the same dimensions in York City Art Gallery traditionally attributed to de Loutherbourg (fig. 89) in which the same Highland bull in the centre is posed in reverse amidst similar animals and in a closely comparable invented mountain landscape.[3] WAG 9567 is Towne's first securely attributed grand and 'metropolitan' painting and a harbinger of his future specialism in paintings of cattle and sheep.

PROVENANCE

...James Mellor; from whom acquired by Phillips and MacConnal, 40 Bridge Row, Chester, 1940; bt. by Lady Danson;[4] by descent to Col. J. R. Danson; his bequest 1979.

EXHIBITION

Danson Collection of Paintings by Charles Towne Walker Art Gallery 1977 (3).

NOTES

1. This title is traditional but is highly unlikely to be Towne's, or contemporary with the picture. Since Phillips and MacConnal did not refer to it by this title (see n. 4) it is probably Col. Danson's.
2. According to Joseph Farington, writing in July 1797, Towne 'improved much from seeing last Exhibition [i.e. the 1797 Royal Academy], never was in London before – was with Loutherbourgh and saw him paint, surprised at his Exhibition picture...'; *FD*, vol. 3, p. 872 (entry of 14 July 1797). At the 1797 RA, de Loutherbourg's sole exhibit was a painting of banditti attacking travellers in Germany (cat. 37).

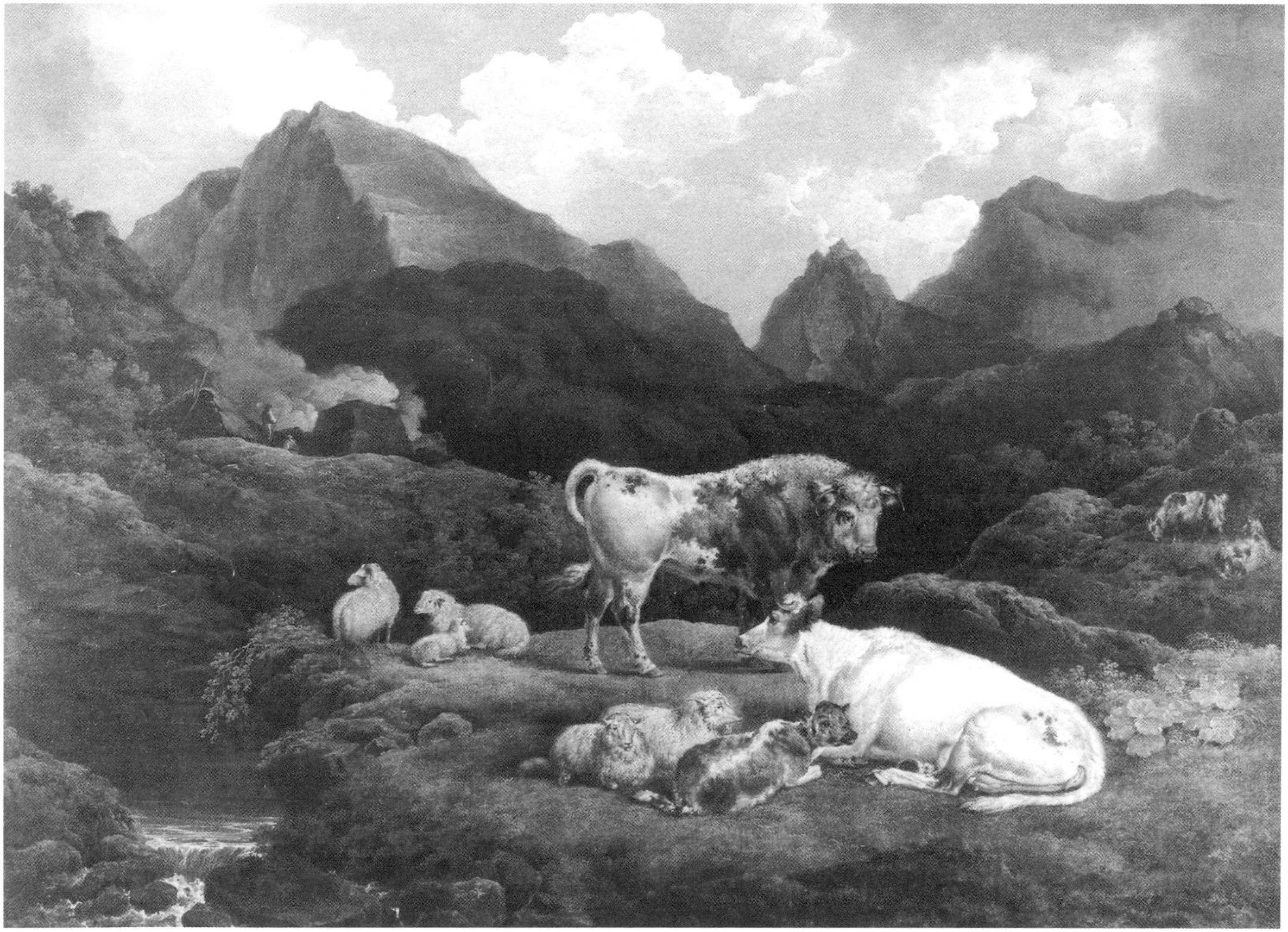

Fig. 89 *Cattle in a Mountain Landscape* by Philippe-Jacques de Loutherbourg, oil on canvas. Courtesy York Museums Trust (York Art Gallery).

3. York City Art Gallery inv. 613, 92 × 116 cm; purchased in 1952 as by James Ward (see p. 235–6) but subsequently attributed to de Loutherbourg; see Hans Hess, ed.: *City of York Art Gallery Catalogue of Paintings* 2 vols (York, 1963) vol. 2, p. 64. This raised the possibility that the cattle were by another hand. After WAG 9567's emergence in the 1977 exhibition, the re-attribution of the York picture to Towne was proposed (Richard Green, *letter*, 5 May 1978, gallery files) but there are distinct stylistic differences between the two works, notably in the treatment of the sky, characteristically Loutherbourg-esque in the York picture and more diffuse in WAG 9567. It seems more likely that Towne either painted his work in direct emulation of de Loutherbourg's or else possibly that de Loutherbourg procured for the younger artist a commission for a pendant for his own picture.

4. Phillips and MacConnal's letter to Mrs [sic] F. C. Danson dated 21 December 1940, offering her two paintings by Towne from Mellor's collection, WAG 9567 for 75 gns., and a smaller *Horsefair* for 85 gns., is in the *Danson Papers*, NML Archives VII.3.7.

Woodmen Carting Timber

WAG 9544
oil on panel, 16 × 21.5 cm
signed: *CT* (monogram) (lower left)

Farmer and His Dog Herding Cattle

WAG 9545
oil on panel, 16 × 21.5 cm
date: unknown, perhaps 1798–1800

These two panel paintings are evidently a pair, being the same size, painted in the

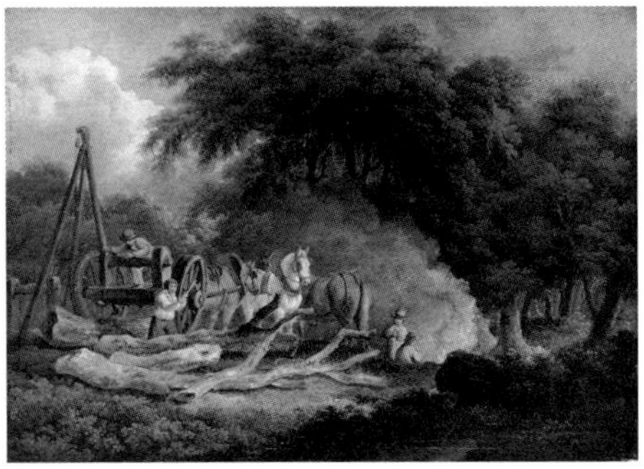

WAG 9544

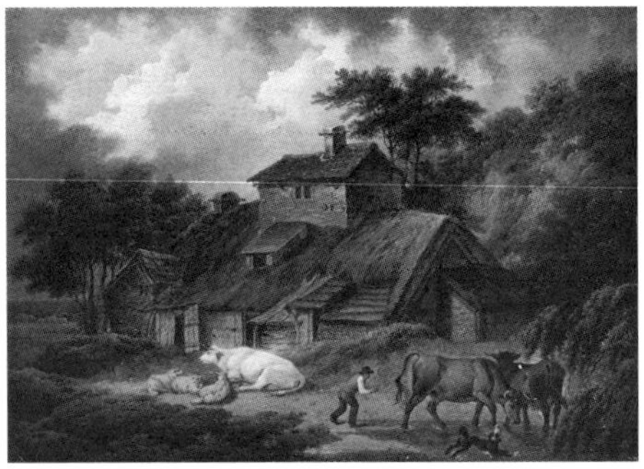

WAG 9545

same extremely fine and delicate manner, and identically framed. The focus in both is a white beast; in WAG 9544 a horse, and in WAG 9545 a cow. This device gives unity to scenes that otherwise form an essay in contrast: WAG 9544 is sober and introverted; WAG 9545 more expansive, with an element of light-heartedness and humour. A date of about 1798–1800 seems likely. The handling of the sky in WAG 9545 suggests the impact on Towne of the work of de Loutherbourg.

PROVENANCE

...[? City Galleries, Liverpool];[1] ...Col. J. R. Danson; his bequest 1979.

EXHIBITION

Danson Collection of Paintings by Charles Towne Walker Art Gallery 1977 (63–64).

REFERENCE

1. The label of Hardy Richards, City Galleries, 1 Tithebarn Street, Liverpool, is on the reverse of both works.

Gentleman on a Grey Mare

WAG 2551
oil on panel, 50.5 × 66 cm
signed and dated: *Chas Towne/1799* (centre right)
date: 1799

This is a mature example of one of Towne's standard types of equestrian portrait in the 1790s: two earlier examples, both signed and dated 1794, depict the horse in a similar trotting pose and the rider comparably dressed in dark hat and dark coat, with an extensive landscape behind.[1] In WAG 2551 the horse is more subtly modelled, and the treatment of the landscape suggests Towne's recent exposure to the work of George Morland. It has been plausibly suggested that WAG 2551 is Towne's exhibit at the 1799 Royal Academy: *Portrait of a Gentleman and Trotting Mare.*[2] The identity of the sitter is unknown. Towne's backwards adjustment of his head and hat is clearly visible.

There is a repaired horizontal split about 5 inches long extending from the left-hand edge of the panel about 5 inches from the top.

PROVENANCE

...Baron Nettelbladt, Glassenbury Park, Cranbrook, Kent; from whom bt. 1934.

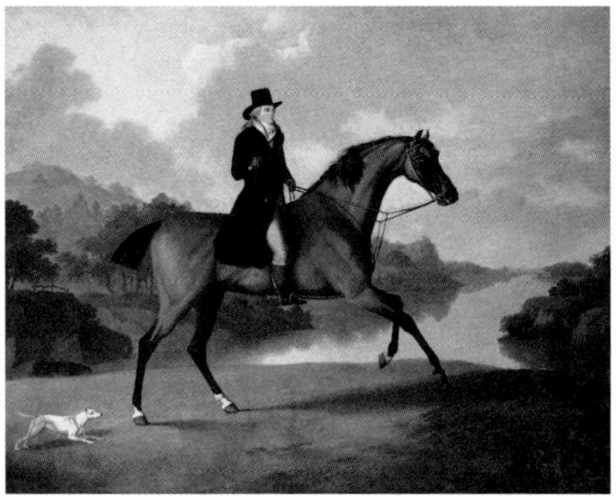

Fig. 90 *John Yates on Ninety-three* by Charles Towne, oil on canvas. Christie, 10 December 1971 (105); photo A. C. Cooper.

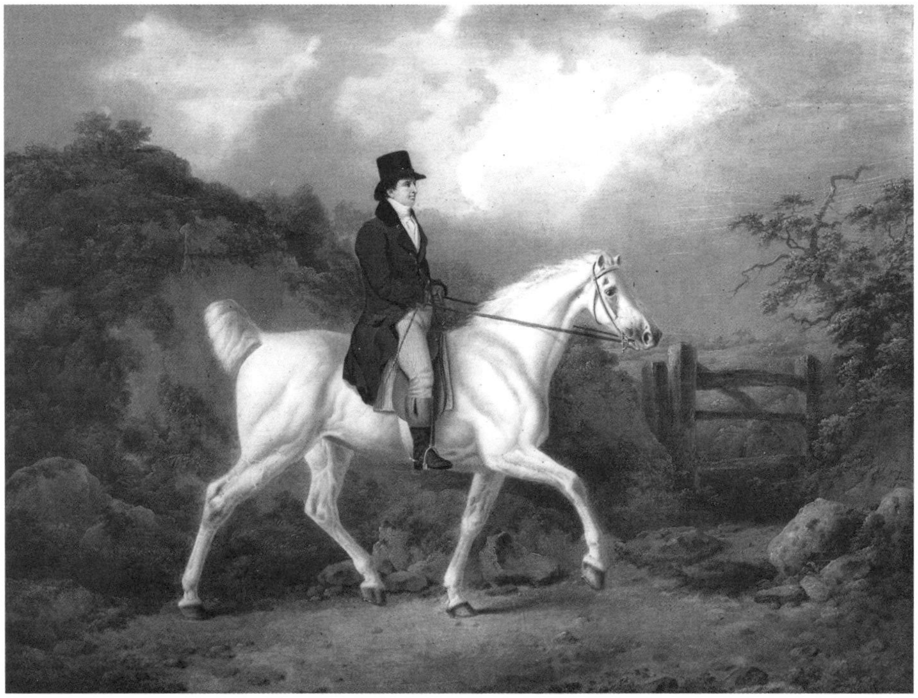

WAG 2551

EXHIBITIONS
(?)RA 1799 (838); *Charles Towne of Liverpool 1763–1840* Walker Art Gallery 1971 (7); *British Sporting Paintings 1650–1850* Hayward Gallery London, and tour 1974–75 (117).

NOTES
1. Compare *John Yates on 'Ninety-three'*, sold Christie 10 December 1971 (105) bt. Roy Miles (fig. 90), and *Portrait of a Gentleman on a Dark Bay Hunter*, Sotheby 21 November 1979 (154).
2. The suggestion was originally made by Charles Carter: 'A Charles Towne for Liverpool', *Connoisseur* vol. 95 (March 1935) p. 151. Carter discerns a debt to George Stubbs in Towne's depiction of the muscles in the mare's off-side back leg.

Evening Landscape with a Herdsman, Cattle and Sheep Crossing a Bridge

WAG 1241
oil on canvas, 72.5 × 91.5 cm
date: about 1800–02

This ambitious painting, with its dramatic shafts of light and gloomy recesses, and its landscape evocative of the atmosphere of the Gothic novel, is dateable on stylistic grounds to the first years of the nineteenth century.[1] It is a possible candidate for the *Evening, Landscape with Cattle* that Towne showed at the Royal Academy in 1801. The gradation of light is convincingly handled; weaker is the crude treatment of the herdsman's left hand clasping the breast of his child. The painting has suffered from endemic flaking along its right-hand and bottom edges.[2]

PROVENANCE
...Prof. R. C. Bosanquet, Liverpool; by whom presented 1920.

EXHIBITIONS
The Liverpool School of Painters Harrogate 1924 (29); *Liverpool Civic Week* Wembley 1924; *The Taste of Yesterday* Walker Art Gallery 1970 (15); *Charles Towne of Liverpool 1763–1840* Walker Art Gallery 1971 (2).

NOTES
1. Both the 1971 exhibition catalogue and MPPP, p. 203 say 'around 1800'.
2. Treated in 1970 by Harriet Owen-Hughes; the problem was recurring in 2008.

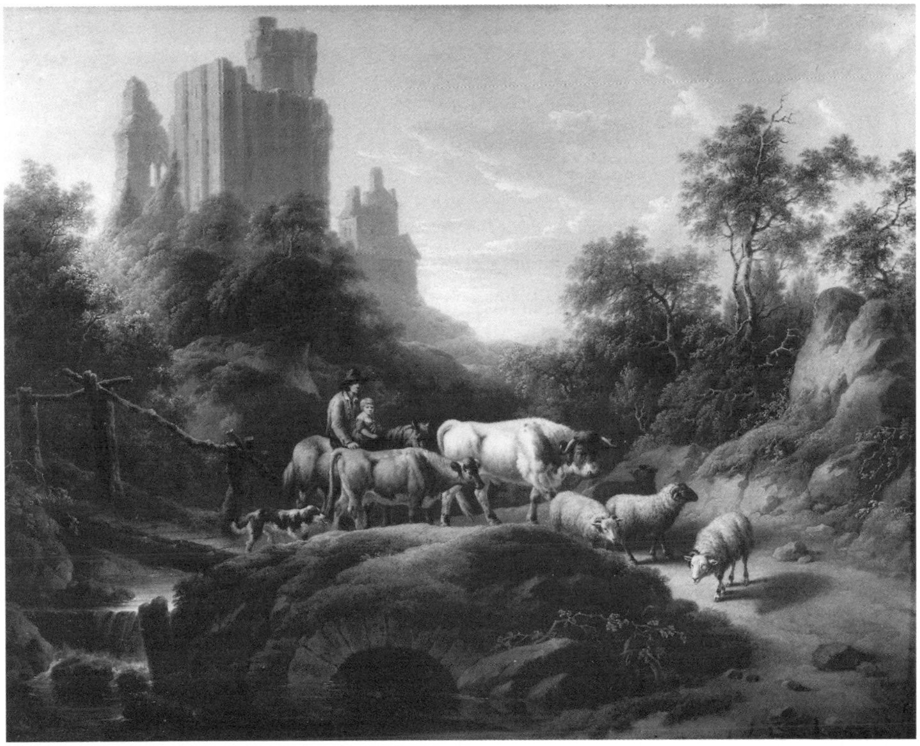

WAG 1241

Two Bull-terriers Attacking a Fox

WAG 2312
oil on panel, 24.5 × 30.5 cm
signed and dated: *C T 1802*
(bottom centre)
date: 1802

The last digit of the date, continuing into a curlicue, is hard to read. It has previously been thought to be a *9*,[1] but the alternative reading of a *2* seems preferable.[2] The work exhibits a degree of finesse that is more in keeping with Towne's early style than with his broad, 'Dutch' phase in the years before 1810. The quality of the handling, however, is not easy to assess since the paint surface has blistered; some pastel green highlights depicting areas of grass are also uncharacteristic. The work was probably executed as a potboiler, rather than on commission.

PROVENANCE
...Walter Stone by 1908; Mary Stone Bequest 1944.

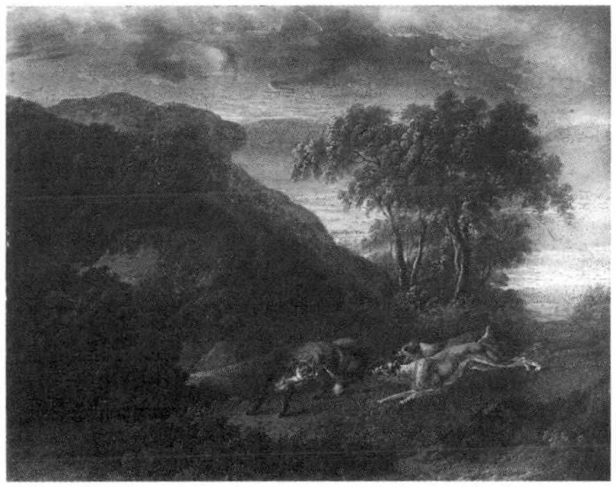

WAG 2312

EXHIBITIONS

Historical Exhibition of Liverpool Art Walker Art Gallery 1908 (201); *Sporting Pictures from the Walter Stone Collection* Bluecoat Gallery, Liverpool 1946 (38); *Charles Towne of Liverpool 1763–1840* Walker Art Gallery 1971 (9).

NOTES

1. *The Walter Stone Collection of Sporting Pictures at Whitton Hall, Westbury, Shropshire* (privately printed, 1938) p. 30 (cat. 51); followed by *MPPP*, p. 205. Sir Walter Gilbey: *Animal Painters of England from the Year 1600* 3 vols (London, 1900–11) vol. 3 (second series) p. 253 (no. 9) listing the work in Stone's collection, erroneously described it as unsigned.
2. As implied by Mary Bennett; ms note on the inventory card, gallery files.

A Wayfarer in a Country Lane

WAG 9575
oil on panel, 17.5 × 19 cm
signed *CT* (monogram, lower left)
date: unknown, perhaps 1802–05

Given the presence of the monogram, the attribution to Towne may be accepted, but neither the paint handling nor the character of the scenery, with its absence of animals and unusually small figures, is wholly characteristic of him. Nor is the work easy to date. A dating of 1809–10 has been proposed,[1] but Towne's characteristic works of this period are much broader than WAG 9575. The Morlandesque quality, taken with the absence of traits found in mature Towne potboilers, argues that it is from the first half of the 1800s.

PROVENANCE

...F. C. Danson before 1911;[2] by descent to Col. J. R. Danson; his bequest 1979.

EXHIBITION

Danson Collection of Paintings by Charles Towne Walker Art Gallery 1977 (11).

NOTES

1. The 1977 exhibition catalogue, which is arranged chronologically, places WAG 9575 with several other undated works between dated pictures of 1809 and 1810.
2. Sir Walter Gilbey: *Animal Painters of England from the Year 1600* 3 vols (London, 1900–11) vol. 3 (second series) p. 251 (no. 4).

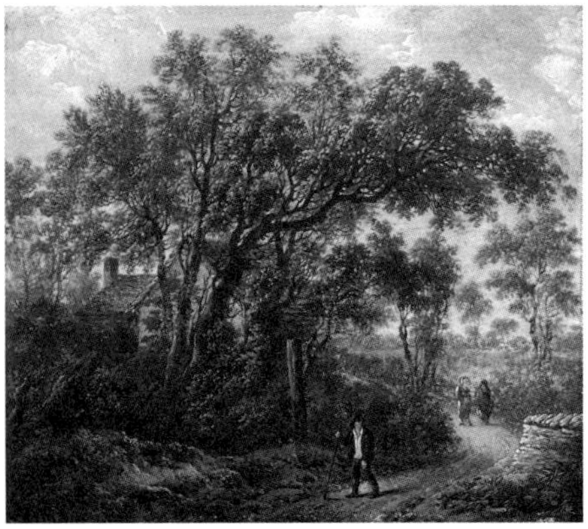

WAG 9575

Shooters Resting

WAG 2342
oil on canvas, 58.5 × 71 cm
date: unknown, perhaps 1803–05

The painting has been dated to both about 1820[1] and more recently implicitly to about 1812,[2] but seems earlier. Despite its relatively small scale, it is a quite ambitious study in the vocabulary of the Picturesque, well observed and carefully painted (especially in the treatment of the dogs at the right) and with strong overtones of George Morland, whose influence on Towne was most pronounced in the first years of the nineteenth century. It was probably painted around 1803–05. There is extensive retouching along the work's right hand edge.

PROVENANCE

...Walter Stone before 1934; Mary Stone Bequest 1944.

EXHIBITIONS

Sporting Pictures from the Walter Stone Collection Bluecoat Gallery, Liverpool 1946 (31); *A Selection of Sporting Pictures from the Walter Stone Collection* Bluecoat Gallery, Liverpool 1953 (27); *Charles Towne of Liverpool 1763–1840* Walker Art Gallery 1971 (11).

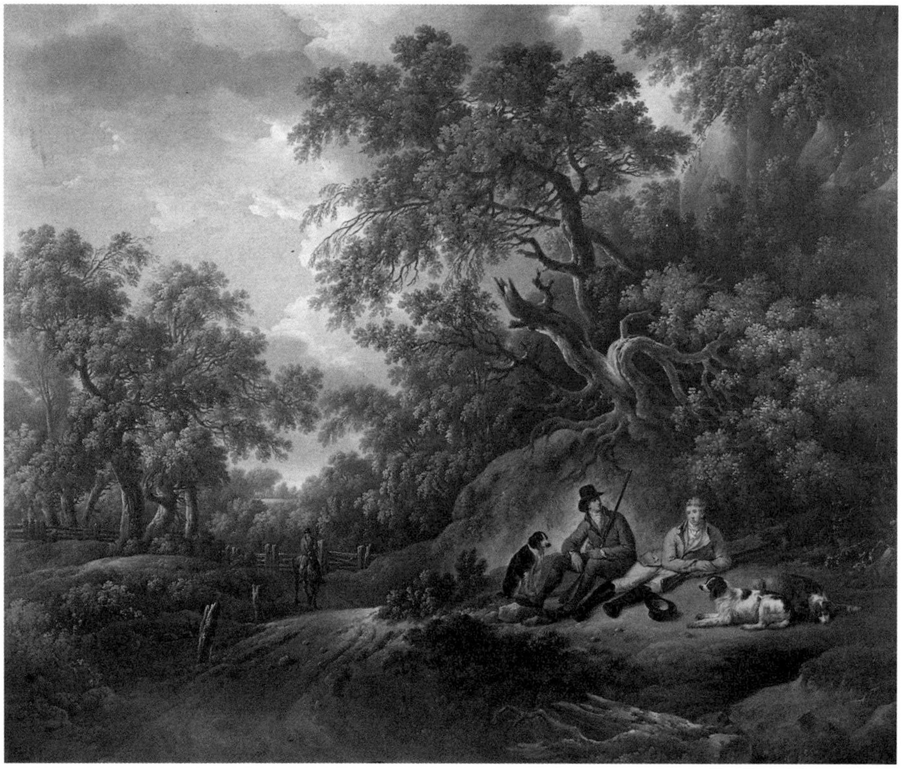

WAG 2342

NOTES

1. *The Walter Stone Collection of Sporting Pictures at Whitton Hall, Westbury, Shropshire* (privately printed, 1938) p. 27 (cat. 40).

2. The 1971 exhibition catalogue, which is ordered chronologically, places WAG 2342 between two dated works of 1812. No date is given in *MPPP*, p. 205, although it adjoins two works of 1812.

Landscape with Cattle by a Stream with Drover

WAG 1240
oil on canvas, 64 × 85 cm
date: unknown, perhaps 1803–07

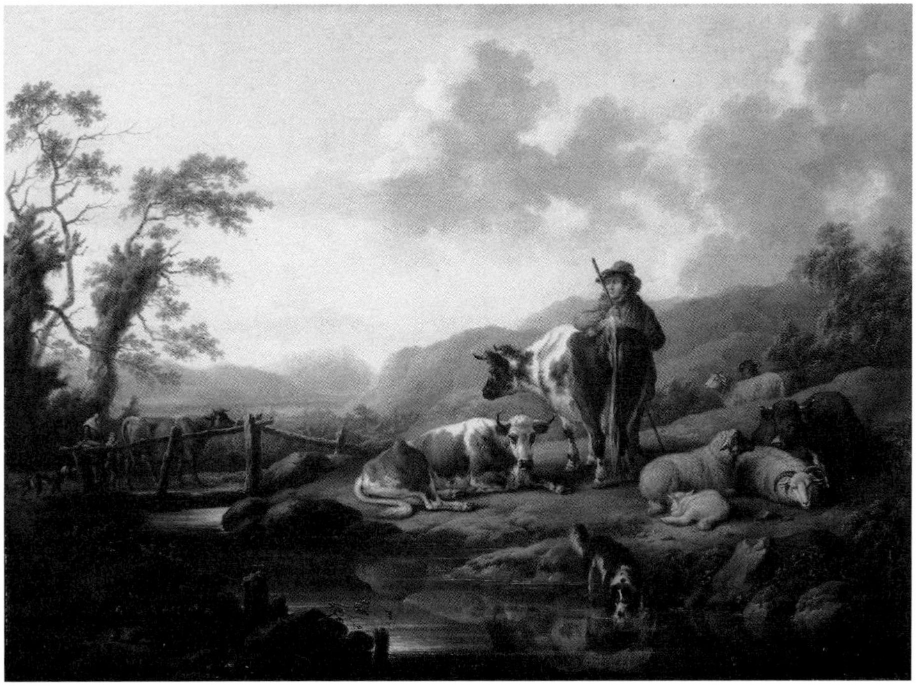

WAG 1240

This ambitious and in some ways uncharacteristic work is not easy to date. Its cool, blue-ish tonality is especially unusual, aligning it most closely, among other works by or ascribed to Towne in the Walker, with WAG 9567 (pp. 192–3) of 1797, with its debt to de Loutherbourg, and the suspect WAG 9568 (see p. 234) whose similarities with WAG 1240, particularly in the treatment of the figure, offer the best argument that that work may be authentic.[1] In the catalogue of the 1971 exhibition, WAG 1240 was dated to the late 1790s, partly on the basis of the costume worn by the woman crossing the bridge in the background. Subsequently, a slightly revised dating of 'around 1800' was proposed,[2] perhaps to factor in the newly recognised possibility that the work was one of Towne's pair of exhibits at the Royal Academy in 1801: *Landscape and Cattle: Morning* (cat. 522) and *Landscape and Cattle: Evening* (cat. 679). This hypothesis is tempting; yet in many respects WAG 1240 has less kinship with the artist's works of the late 1790s made under the influence of de Loutherbourg or Morland than with his characteristic essays in the manner of seventeenth-century Dutch landscape of the later 1800s (for example, WAG 9570 and 9551, pp. 198, 199) and thus a dating of about 1803–07 seems preferable.

Although the composition is invented, a typical *melange* of separate motifs combined to form a pleasing design, the mountainous landscape in the background carries a very general suggestion (without the lake) of Ullswater from the north. On this view, with the light falling from the left, the painting is a morning rather than an evening landscape.

WAG 1240 was the first work by Towne to enter the Walker, and for 35 years the only work by him in the collection.

PROVENANCE

...John King, Liverpool; from whom bt. 1885.

EXHIBITIONS[3]

Historical Exhibition of Liverpool Art Walker Art Gallery 1908 (510); *The Liverpool School of Painters* Harrogate 1924 (30); *Charles Towne of Liverpool 1763–1840* Walker Art Gallery 1971 (1).

NOTES

1. The problematical status of WAG 9568 might justifiably imply that doubt should be cast on the authorship of WAG 1240 also. E. R. Dibdin initially doubted that the latter was a Towne (note in gallery files) before changing his mind and illustrating it as by him in his 'Liverpool Art and Artists in the Eighteenth Century', *Walpole Society* (1917–18) pl. XXVI(a). On balance, despite uncharacteristic aspects of the work (such as the handling of the glittering light on the water in the foreground and the highlighted branch overhanging the stream lower centre) the animals and the foliage in particular seem more characteristic of Towne than their equivalents in WAG 9568.

2. *MPPP*, p. 203.

3. It is likely that WAG 1240 was also exhibited as an interloper in *Sporting Pictures from the Walter Stone Collection* Bluecoat Gallery, Liverpool 1946 (37) as *Landscape with Cows by a Stream*, a work that is not identifiable among the works by Towne in the Stone Bequest.

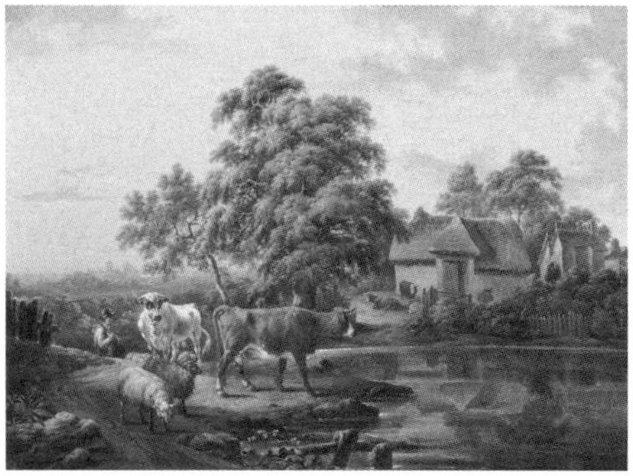

WAG 2313

A Farm Landscape with Cattle and Sheep by a Pond

WAG 2313
oil on canvas, 46 × 61.5 cm
date: unknown, perhaps 1804–08

The work has been variously dated,[1] but seems most likely to be from the earlier part of Towne's Home Counties period, 1804–10. The castle in the background is reminiscent of Windsor – and the work was titled *View of Windsor* when it was shown in Liverpool in 1908 – even though the composition as a whole feels invented. It is perhaps a conscious pastiche of seventeenth-century Dutch landscapes. There are retouched damages in the trees at right and left and in the sheep in the foreground, and there is continuous vertical cracking down the left-hand side about 3 inches from the left edge, probably attributable to pressure from the stretcher.

PROVENANCE

...Walter Stone by 1908;[2] Mary Stone Bequest 1944.

EXHIBITIONS

Historical Exhibition of Liverpool Art Walker Art Gallery 1908 (125); *A Selection of Sporting Pictures from the Walter Stone Collection* Bluecoat Gallery, Liverpool 1953 (32); *Charles Towne of Liverpool 1763–1840* Walker Art Gallery 1971 (4).

NOTES

1. *The Walter Stone Collection of Sporting Paintings at Whitton Hall, Westbury, Shropshire* (privately printed, 1938) p. 29 (cat. 48) dates the work to 'circa 1820'; *MPPP*, p. 204, while conceding that Towne continued to make pastiches of Dutch landscapes into the 1820s, suggested the 1810s; the 1971 exhibition catalogue gave 'possibly around 1800'. Both latter publications noted WAG 2313's close stylistic similarity with WAG 40.
2. Lent by Stone to the 1908 exhibition.

Landscape with Cottage and Herdsman Driving Cattle

WAG 40
oil on canvas, 36 × 44 cm
signed: *C. Towne* (bottom right)
date: unknown, perhaps 1805–10

The painting has been variously dated. When in the Walter Stone collection it was ascribed to about 1800,[1] but more recently it has been suggested that it is from the 1820s.[2] On balance, a date of around 1805–10 seems preferable: Towne's Dutch-manner treatments of bucolic life seem to have been a particular speciality of his Home Counties period before 1810, although they did continue after his return to Liverpool in that year. The style is close to WAG 9551 (p. 199) and WAG 9546 (p. 200–1).

PROVENANCE

...Walter Stone before 1934; Mary Stone Bequest 1944.

EXHIBITION

Charles Towne of Liverpool 1763–1840 Walker Art Gallery 1971 (3).

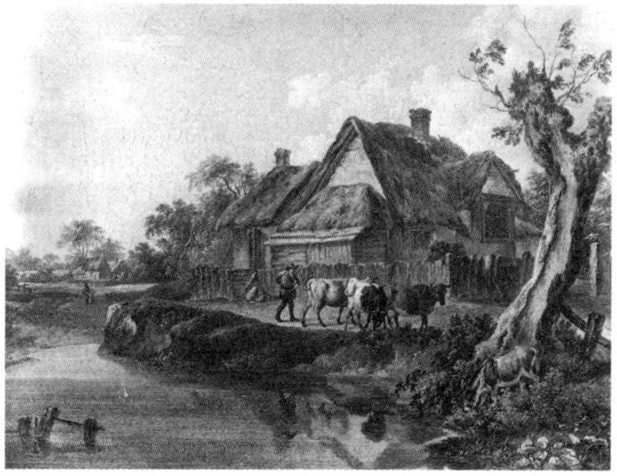

WAG 40

NOTES

1. *The Walter Stone Collection of Sporting Paintings at Whitton Hall, Westbury, Shropshire* (privately printed, 1938), p. 30 (cat. 49): 'A small landscape in the Dutch manner: a herdsman driving cows on the bank of a stream, painted circa. 1800'.
2. *MPPP*, p. 204, with the qualification that it could be from the previous decade.

Farmer on Horseback Carrying a Calf

WAG 9570
oil on canvas, 45 × 54 cm
signed and dated: *CT* [monogram] *1808* (bottom right)
date: 1808

Probably painted for stock rather than as a commission, WAG 9570 is nevertheless carefully composed (around a pair of interlocking diagonals) and is full of gently inflected narrative incident. The somewhat stormy, lurid sky, taken in conjunction with the disrepair to the thatched roof of the cottage at left, and the sick expression of the calf, suggests that Towne intended a threatening, unsettled note to be perceptible beneath the work's ostensibly bucolic character.

PROVENANCE

...Boydell Galleries Liverpool;[1] from whom bt. 8 July 1953[2] by Col. J. R. Danson; his bequest 1979.

EXHIBITION

Danson Collection of Paintings by Charles Towne Walker Art Gallery 1977 (5).

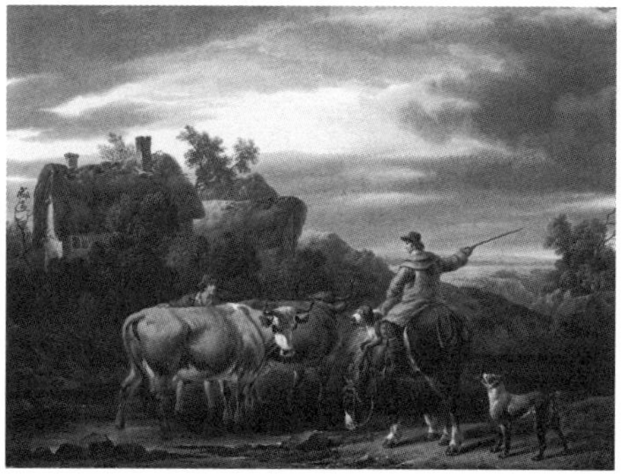

WAG 9570

NOTES

1. A ms note on the reverse of WAG 9570 probably dating from their ownership reads, *CHARLES TOWNE 1808 / signed with initials date / right hand bottom corner / H & F sale 160 D 1850*. The reference to 'H & F sale' presumably denotes a previous owner whose identity, however, remains obscure.

2. Receipt for £72 in *Danson Papers*, NML Archives VII.5.2.

Herdsmen Driving Cattle and Sheep at Sunset

WAG 9551
oil on canvas, 46 × 61 cm
signed: *C T* (monogram, bottom right)
date: unknown, perhaps 1808–10

With its broad handling and warm tonality, together with the 'Home Counties' character of the scenery, WAG 9551 was probably painted about 1808–1810.[1] It is close in style to WAG 9570 (above).

PROVENANCE

...Col. J. R. Danson; his bequest 1979.[2]

EXHIBITION

Danson Collection of Paintings by Charles Towne Walker Art Gallery 1977 (10).

REFERENCE

1. In the 1977 exhibition catalogue, organised chronologically, WAG 9551 was placed between dated pictures of 1809 and 1810.

2. A Boydell Galleries, Liverpool label is pasted to the reverse of the frame.

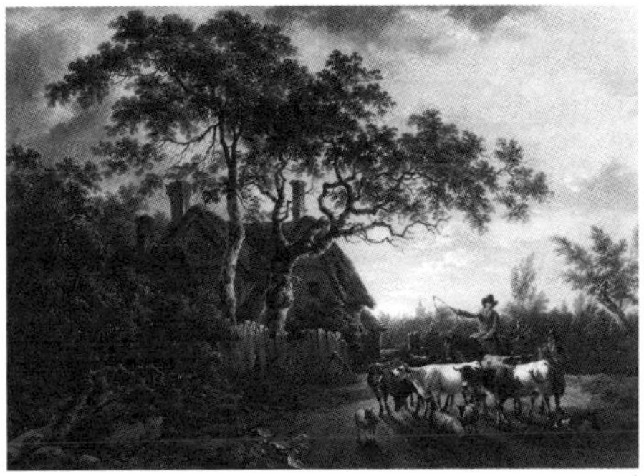

WAG 9551

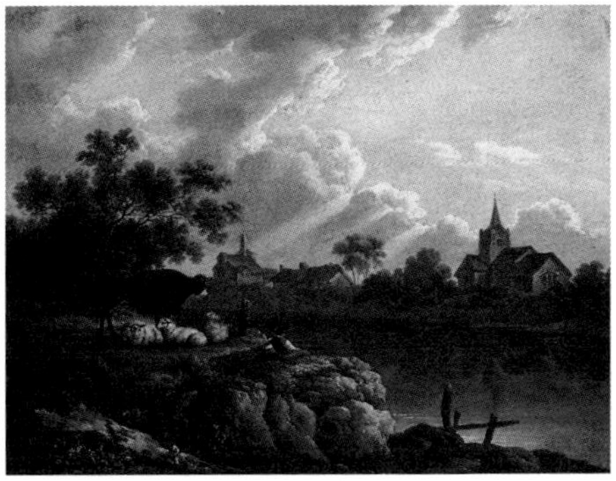

WAG 9554

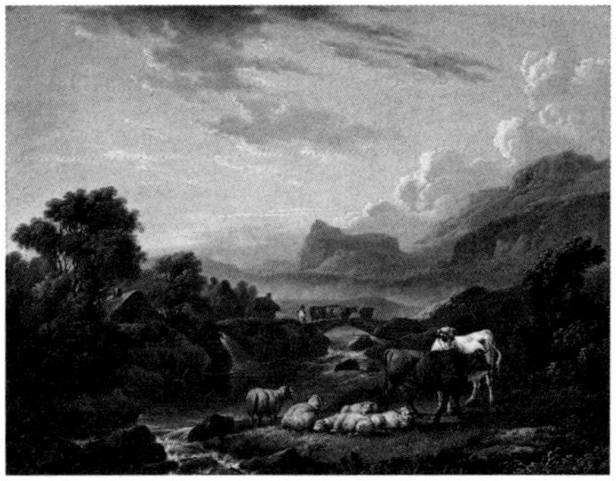

WAG 9555

Boy Resting by a River with Cattle and Sheep

WAG 9554
oil on mahogany panel, 24 × 30.5 cm

Cattle and Sheep by a Mountain Stream

WAG 9555
oil on mahogany panel, 24 × 30.5 cm
signed and dated: *CT1809* (lower left)
date: 1809

Both works are inscribed in chalk on the back: *WESTMORELAND / X / CAIRA*. The landscape in WAG 9555 does bear some resemblance to Lake District scenery,[1] but the presence of the inscription on WAG 9554 (if it does in fact refer to the Lakeland county at all) is more difficult to account for. The two works are studies of sheep and a cow or cows resting in contrasted riverscapes, and that of WAG 9554 has a strong Home Counties feel. As is usual with Towne, only one of the pair is signed and dated. The date on WAG 9555 has been variously read, but 1809 appears correct even though the works diverge stylistically from other paintings of this period.[2] Both are painted in a smooth, waxy manner – WAG 9554 rather more crudely than WAG 9555 – and they have the character of potboilers.

PROVENANCE

...Col. J. R. Danson; his bequest 1979.

EXHIBITION

Danson Collection of Paintings by Charles Towne Walker Art Gallery 1977 (13) [WAG 9554] and (8) [WAG 9555].

NOTES

1. The shape of the mountain in the centre of WAG 9555 bears some resemblance to Blencathra mountain east of Keswick (in Cumberland rather than Westmoreland) viewed from the east, and although the rest of the landscape does not follow the topography of the area accurately, Towne may have been recalling the Derwent valley that runs west to east beneath the mountain.

2. The 1977 exhibition catalogue suggested *1800* as a possible alternative reading for *1809*, but there appears to be a distinct tail on the last digit.

Drovers with Cattle Crossing a Stream

WAG 9573
oil on panel, 15 × 20 cm
date: unknown, perhaps 1809–10

The attribution of WAG 9573 to Towne has been questioned,[1] but on balance the work may be accepted as authentic. The handling of the mounted figure is crude, but the treatment of the cattle, dogs and foliage is characteristic, if of potboiler quality. The work is not easy to date. There is some stylistic similarity with WAG 9555 (above), which is signed and dated 1809, and a similar date for WAG 9573 seems possible.[2]

Paint losses have occurred along the

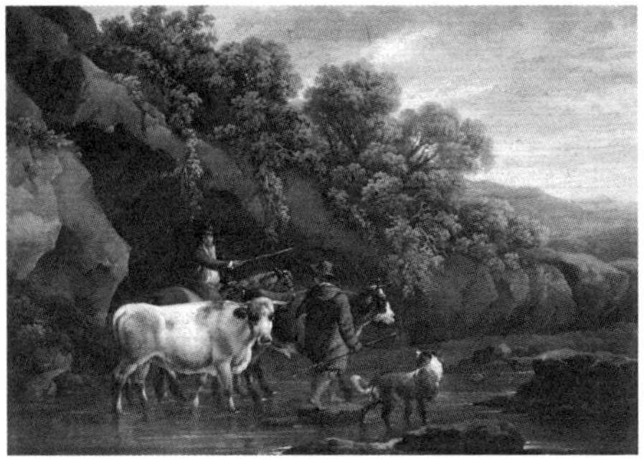

WAG 9573

edges of the work caused by excessive pressure from the inner slip of the frame.

PROVENANCE

...Col. J. R. Danson;[3] his bequest 1979.

EXHIBITION

Danson Collection of Paintings by Charles Towne 1763–1840 Walker Art Gallery 1977 (9).

NOTES

1. The work was listed as 'Manner of Towne' in CIC, p. 282.
2. The 1977 exhibition catalogue, ordered chronologically, placed WAG 9573 immediately after WAG 9555 and before dated works of 1810.
3. The inner flat on the reverse is inscribed in pencil / *Thatcher Esq*. This may refer to a previous owner.

Drover on Horseback with Dog Driving Two Cows and a Calf

WAG 9526
oil on panel, 48 × 60.5 cm
signed: *ct* (on left arm of signpost)

A Farmyard with Horses at a Trough

WAG 9540
oil on panel, 48 × 61 cm
date: 1810

That these two works are the same size, are both on panel, are in frames of identical design, are stylistically from the same period of Towne's career, and were sold together in 1923 all suggests that they were executed as pendants. Formally, the designs are unrelated but together they appear to deliver a single message about farming conditions: the large enclosed farmstead in WAG 9540 is bathed in golden sunlight, an idyll of prosperity; the smallholder in WAG 9526 whose cottage and barn are on open common land has reached the dividing of the ways, and, slumped on his horse, is taking his few remaining animals to market. The two works, although potboilers, are of superior quality. In WAG 9526 the figure of the farmer, the bored expression of his horse and the pose of his dog are well studied; in WAG 9540 the accoutrements of the horses are painted in notable detail.

In WAG 9526 the arms of the signpost are inscribed *ct* on the left and *LONDON* / X[1] on the right. Rather than indicating a spot ten miles from the metropolis this is surely a form of signature: Charles Towne of London painted the work in [18]10. The use of the roman numeral is unusual for Towne,[2] but accords with the ambitious character of the works. In 1810 Towne returned from the south of England to Liverpool, where he was chosen as one of the Vice Presidents of the revived Liverpool Academy, and he may have been signalling his new-found pretensions to colleagues. A dating of 1810 is certainly supported by these works' general style.

The thin wooden panel of WAG 9526 displays a curvature of about 5 mm out

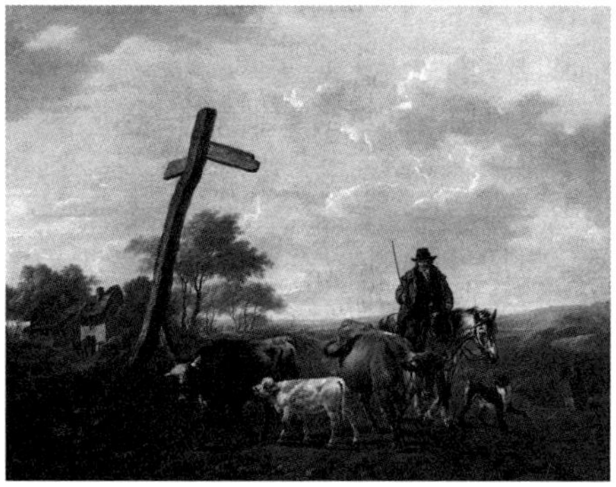

WAG 9526

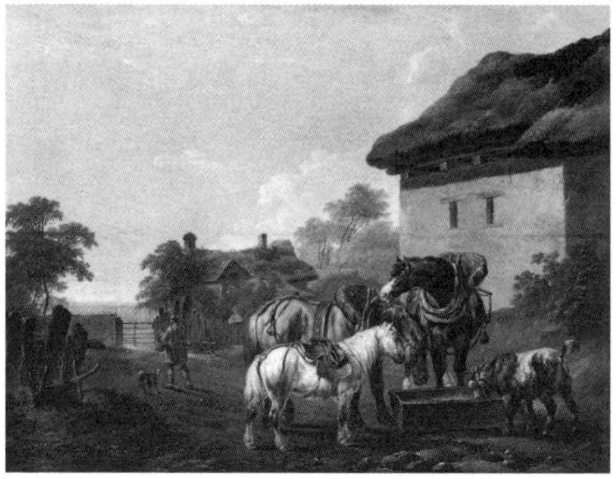

WAG 9540

of true in the vertical plane towards the top. Significant horizontal cracking has occurred at intervals along the left-hand edge which has been filled and retouched. The panel of WAG 9540 is split right across from left to right slightly below centre, and is supported by a cradle.

PROVENANCE

...Miss Oldham, Greystones, Crowborough, Sussex; Christie 17 May 1923 (105) (a pair);[3] bt. Mitchell (£12.1s.6d.); ...Col. J. R. Danson; his bequest 1979.

EXHIBITION

Danson Collection of Paintings by Charles Towne Walker Art Gallery 1977 (6–7).

NOTES

1. The 1977 exhibition catalogue suggests that the X is actually XI but the latter stroke appears to be an old retouching.
2. For another possible case, however, where the Roman numeral may refer to a distance in miles, see WAG 9538, pp. 219–20.
3. At the sale WAG 9526 was titled *Going to Market*.

Old English Homestead

WAG 9546
oil on panel, 35 × 44 cm
signed and dated: *C. TOWN/1810* (bottom right)[1]
date: 1810

The work is a late example of the George Morland-inspired 'cottage-door' type subject that was a staple of Towne's work

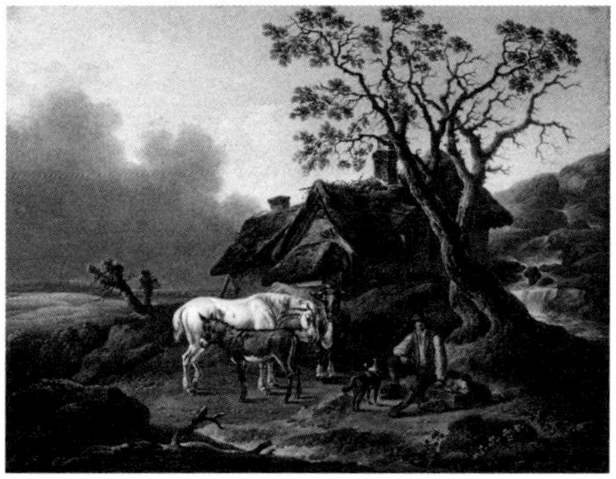

WAG 9546

during his 'Home Counties' period, 1804–1810. The landscape background has a hybrid character: to the left an open plain with distant churches has a pronounced East Anglian feel; the waterfall to the right is more suggestive of the Lake District.

Losses along the top and bottom edges of the panel show that Towne painted over a thin pinky-brown ground. The work has been treated extensively for flaking and for damage to the area around the figures and dog.

PROVENANCE

...Bt. in 1913 by F. C. Danson;[2] by descent to Col. J. R. Danson; his bequest, 1979.

EXHIBITION

Danson Collection of Paintings by Charles Towne Walker Art Gallery 1977 (14).

NOTES

1. This is a rare instance of Towne signing his name without an 'e' after 1800.
2. An ink manuscript label on the back of the frame of WAG 9546 reads *Old English Homestead / by Chas. Towne / Signed and dated 1810. The companion /picture is in Lord Derby's collection* [in a different hand] *Purchased / by FCD / Dec|13 / £ RH*. The supposed companion in the collection of Lord Derby is not recorded in George Scharf: *Catalogue of the Collection of Pictures at Knowsley Hall* (London, 1875) and is not among the pictures by Towne now at Knowsley.

Brown Horse in a Landscape

WAG 9586
oil on panel, 42 × 53.5 cm
signed and dated: *Chas Towne/Pinxit. 1810* (bottom right)
date: 1810

This work epitomises Towne's stock in trade after his return to Liverpool in 1810, when he began to develop a huge clientele among the local landed gentry and middling classes, at first in the north-western counties but gradually over a wider area. Information has seldom survived about the patrons of individual pictures, and the presence of an extensive landscape in the background is no guarantee that a landowner (as distinct from a merchant) commissioned any given work. Occasionally, the name of a horse has come down to us, and Towne sometimes included discreet visual references to the identity, estate or social standing of his client, but WAG 9586 is particularly recalcitrant in these respects, even if the huge thistle in the foreground and the estuary in the distance may be clues. The unusually florid signature, taken with the work's date, perhaps indicates that this is one of the first works Towne painted on his return to Liverpool when he would have been striving to impress a new community of patrons.

PROVENANCE

...Col. J. R. Danson;[1] his bequest 1979.

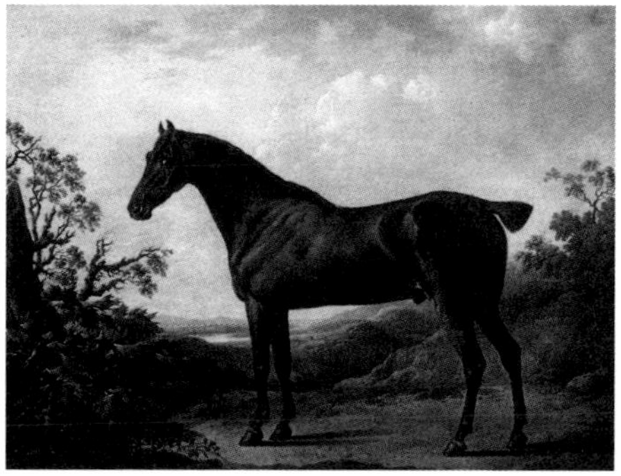

WAG 9586

EXHIBITION

Danson Collection of Paintings by Charles Towne Walker Art Gallery 1977 (15).

REFERENCE

1. Col. Danson may have obtained WAG 9586 from Reginald S. Cross, Fine Art Dealer, 14 Lord Street, Liverpool, whose label is stuck to the reverse of the panel. There is a ms label *4419*, which may be a stock number.

Drovers and Cattle Resting on a Seashore with a Distant Harbour

WAG 9559
oil on canvas, 53.5 × 71 cm
signed: *C Towne/Pinxit* (lower right on rock)
date: unknown, perhaps 1810–15

The painting is a compendium of disparate motifs, possibly intended to provide visitors to Towne's studio with an illustration of his capabilities. It is hard to imagine a patron commissioning such a bizarre image. The work is not easy to date but can perhaps be ascribed to the first half of the 1810s.[1]

There is extensive discoloured repainting in the centre of the sky covering an old damage.

PROVENANCE

...Col. J. R. Danson; his bequest 1979.

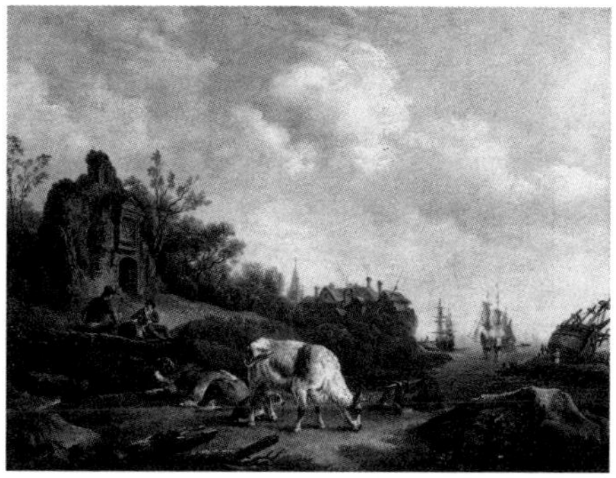

WAG 9559

EXHIBITION

Danson Collection of Paintings by Charles Towne Walker Art Gallery 1977 (34).

REFERENCE

1. In the 1977 exhibition catalogue, which was organised chronologically, WAG 9559 was placed between dated paintings of 1820 and 1822; however, a date of around 1821 seems too late stylistically for this work. For a more thoroughgoing essay in the combination here of Dutch boors and classical ruins see WAG 9562 (dated 1814; p. 207).

Interior of a Stable

WAG 9537
oil on panel, 35 × 44 cm
signed: *C. TOWN* (bottom right)
date: unknown, perhaps 1811–14

That this is a generic stable picture, rather than a view inside the actual stable of a particular patron, is suggested by the artfully contrasted horses' colours and poses, and by the amusing anecdotal detail of the cat and dog facing off at each other. WAG 9537 is neatly and crisply painted for what is essentially a superior potboiler. It is not easy to date but is probably from the first half of the 1810s.[1]

PROVENANCE

...Col. J. R. Danson; his bequest 1979.

EXHIBITION

Danson Collection of Paintings by Charles Towne Walker Art Gallery 1977 (16).

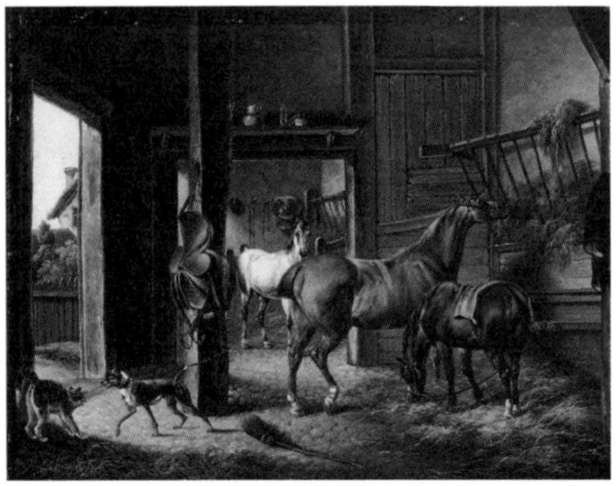

WAG 9537

REFERENCE

1. This view was shared by the 1977 exhibition catalogue, which was organised chronologically, and which placed WAG 9537 between dated paintings of 1810 and 1814. 1810 is perhaps a little early for this work.

Evening Landscape with Cattle and Sheep and a Rider in Conversation with a Herdsman

WAG 2345
oil on canvas, 98 × 132.5 cm
signed and dated: *C Towne 1812*
(bottom right, on rock)
date: 1812

This large and ambitious painting was probably one of Towne's exhibits at the Liverpool Academy in 1812, when, showing for the first time as a Vice President of the institution, he made a special effort to impress. It has previously tentatively been identified as cat. 207, *Landscape with Cattle*,[1] although this seems an inadequate description for the level of incident in the composition, and there are two alternative candidates in the shape of works with literary tags, of which cat. 183, *Landscape – Sunset* appears marginally preferable to cat. 8, *Evening*.[2] The composition is an amalgam of several carefully studied elements: in the foreground, the cattle and sheep are combined in varied, characteristic poses; the chief narrative incident takes place in the centre where a mounted farmer tells his herdsman that it is time to take his animals home, pointing with his stick in the direction of the distant farm at upper right; at the left, another couple herd their cows across a bridge towards their own farm and distant mountains are bathed in a sunset glow. The effect of evening light and long shadows is unusual for Towne and is impressively managed.

The condition of WAG 2345 is now indifferent. Much of the upper left quarter of the painting is disfigured by discoloured retouching of flaking areas and other repairs; there is retouched traction cracking in parts of the foreground and there are very worn areas of the painted surface on the right-hand side of the picture where the off-white ground is exposed in the foliage.

PROVENANCE

... [? James Bremner; Winstanley 21 June 1827 (71); bt. anon. £50 8s.];[3] ...Walter Stone by 1911;[4] Mary Stone Bequest 1944.

EXHIBITIONS

(?) LA 1812 (183); *Sporting Pictures from the Walter Stone Collection* Bluecoat Gallery, Liverpool 1946 (36); *A Selection of Sporting Pictures from the Walter Stone Collection* Bluecoat Gallery, Liverpool 1953 (31); *Liverpool Academy 150th Anniversary* Walker Art Gallery 1960 (22); *Charles Towne of Liverpool 1763–1840* Walker Art Gallery 1971 (12).[5]

NOTES

1. In the catalogue of the 1960 exhibition, p. 15.
2. *Evening* was accompanied in the catalogue by the opening lines of Thomas Gray's *Elegy in a Country Churchyard*, i.e. *The curfew tolls the knell of parting day, / The loving herds wind slowly o'er the lea, / The Ploughman homeward plods his weary way, / And leaves the world to darkness and to me. / Now fades the glimmering landscape on the sight / And all the air a solemn stillness holds. Landscape – Sunset* was accompanied by the lines *On the plain and mountain's sunny side / Large droves of oxen, and the fleecy flock / Feed undisturbed; and fill the echoing air / With music, grateful to the master's ear.* This extract, according to Towne's title, derives from *Loch Leven* (1766) by the Scottish pastoral poet Michael Bruce (1746–67). It has not been traced in editions of the poem consulted, but Bruce's work was appropriated and contested after his early death and Towne may have been quoting from a corrupt source.
3. In the Winstanley sale catalogue lot 71 was titled *A Landscape with Cattle and Figures – Evening* and the measurements given as 4.3 × 3.2 [i.e. 129.5 × 96.5 cm]; it was, however, accompanied (lot 70) by a companion work of the same dimensions titled *A Landscape with Numerous Cattle and Figures – Morning*; conceivably this was cat. 207 in the 1812 exhibition.
4. Sir Walter Gilbey: *Animal Painters of England from the Year 1600* 3 vols (London, 1900–11) vol. 3 (second series) pp. 251–2 (no. 1).
5. Misprinted as WAG 2348 in the catalogue.

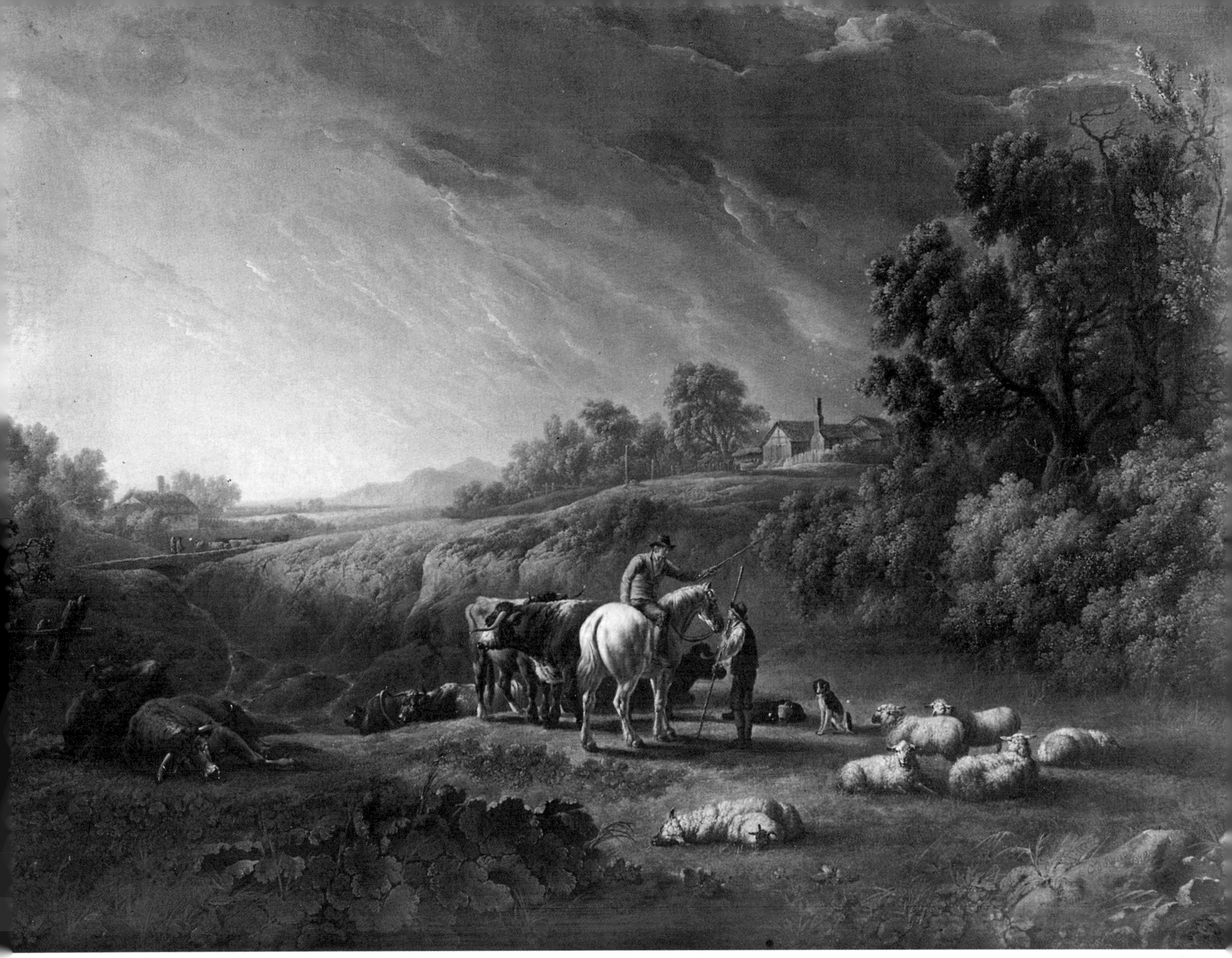

WAG 2345

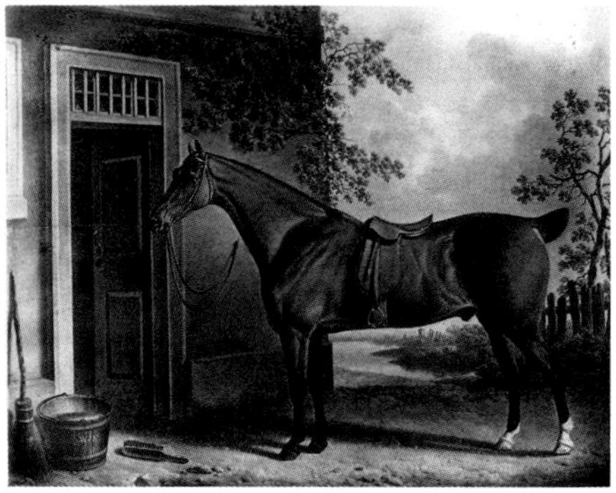

WAG 2348

A Saddled Bay Hunter Tethered outside a Stable

WAG 2348
oil on panel,[1] 48 × 59 cm
signed and dated: *C Towne 1812*
(on the brush)
date: 1812

This is possibly one of the works exhibited by Towne at the Liverpool Academy of 1812. Cat. 32 in that exhibition was his *Portrait of a Well-known Hunter* and cat. 100 was *Portrait of a Hunter.* It must be the *Portrait of a Cob*, 18 × 22 inches, lent by Walter Stone to the 1908 *Historical Exhibition of Liverpool Art.*

What are presumably the original patron's initials, *W.W.*, are inscribed on the pail at the bottom left. He has not been identified.

PROVENANCE
...Walter Stone before 1908; Mary Stone Bequest 1944.

EXHIBITIONS
(?) LA 1812 (32) or (100); *Historical Exhibition of Liverpool Art* Walker Art Gallery 1908 (180); *A Selection of Sporting Pictures from the Walter Stone Collection* Bluecoat Gallery, Liverpool 1953 (25); *Charles Towne of Liverpool 1763–1840* Walker Art Gallery 1971 (13).

NOTES
1. *F.L. CLEMENTS PATENT* is stamped, and 976 incised, in the back of the frame. The frame also bears the label of John King, 83 Renshaw Street Liverpool.

Mischief in a Park

WAG 2346
oil on canvas, 49.5 × 67.3 cm
signed: *CT* (initials in monogram, bottom left)
date: unknown, perhaps 1812

It has been suggested that this is the work exhibited by Towne at the Liverpool Academy in 1812, with the title *Fallow Deer and Dogs: 'But alas, he flies in vain' – Vide Somerville.*[1] The reference is to the long poem *The Chace* (1735) by William Somerville (1675–1742), Book 2, which is largely taken up with a description of the hunting and killing of a hind by a pack of dogs.[2] Towne seldom gave literary tags to his titles, even those of exhibited works, but may have been prompted to in this year because it was the first in which he was showing as a Vice President of the Academy.[3]

It has been pointed out that Towne's idea for the subject may have come from Stubbs's *A Greyhound Attacking a Stag* (about 1762–63; Philadelphia Museum of Art).[4] Although there was no engraving of the original composition and it may not have been seen by Towne, he would almost certainly have been familiar with a variant of it at Ince Blundell, outside Liverpool (the home of the late Henry Blundell, first President of the Liverpool Academy).[5] Stubbs himself had derived his composition from versions of the subject by Frans Snyders, who developed the motif of the staghound springing up on fully extended hind legs.[6]

A related work, titled *The Stag Hunt*, in which the deer is surrounded by four dogs, was sold at Christie, 12 April 1991 (84). This is also a contender for the work exhibited in 1812, although at 42 × 53 cm it is slightly smaller than WAG 2346.

PROVENANCE
...Walter Stone before 1931;[7] Mary Stone Bequest 1944.

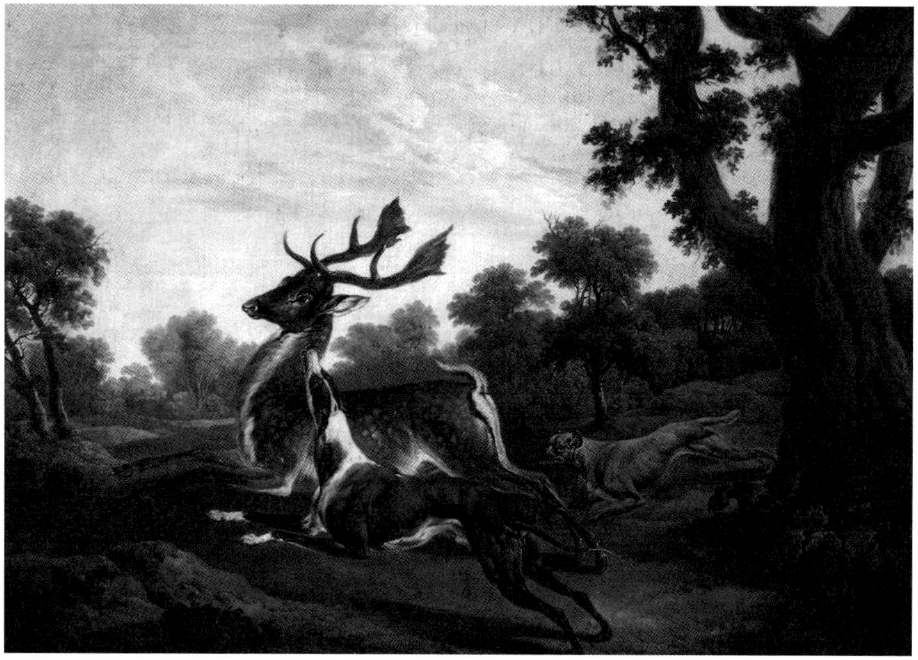

WAG 2346

EXHIBITIONS

[? LA 1812 (48)]; *A Selection of Sporting Pictures from the Walter Stone Collection* Bluecoat Gallery, Liverpool 1953 (33); *Charles Towne of Liverpool 1763–1840* Walker Art Gallery 1971 (10); *British Sporting Paintings 1650–1850* Hayward Gallery, London and tour 1974–75 (120).

NOTES

1. The identification seems to have been first made in the 1971 exhibition catalogue; in the 1953 catalogue the work was still dated 'circa 1800', as it had been in *The Walter Stone Collection of Sporting Pictures at Whitton Hall, Westbury, Shropshire* (privately printed, 1938) p. 30 (cat. 50). A further possibility is that WAG 2346 is *A Scene in Drummond Park, Scotland – Dogs Attacking Deer* which Towne showed at the Royal Manchester Institution in 1830 (cat. 254). The stylistic character of WAG 2346 is not especially distinctive and Towne's treatment of dogs in particular seems relatively consistent throughout his mature career.
2. Somerville's line, which actually occurs just after the death of the hind and describes Orpheus pursued by 'Bacchanals', is 'He flies from Place to Place, but flies in vain'.
3. Towne showed a total of 12 works this year, of which the titles of four were accompanied by literary quotations. See also WAG 2345, p. 202.
4. *MPPP*, p. 205; the general influence of Stubbs on Towne, although not on this work by him, is also suggested by Mary Webster and Lionel Lambourne, *British Sporting Paintings 1650–1850*, exh. cat., Hayward Gallery, London and tour (1974) p. 82. For Stubbs's painting at Philadelphia see Judy Egerton: *George Stubbs, Painter. Catalogue Raisonné* (New Haven and London, 2007) p. 182 (cat. 41).
5. The painting formerly at Ince Blundell was shown in the George Stubbs exhibition at the Walker Art Gallery in 1951 (16) and is now in a private collection.
6. Webster and Lambourne, *loc. cit.*
7. Repr. W. Shaw Sparrow, *A Book of Sporting Painters* (London and New York, 1931) fp. 136.

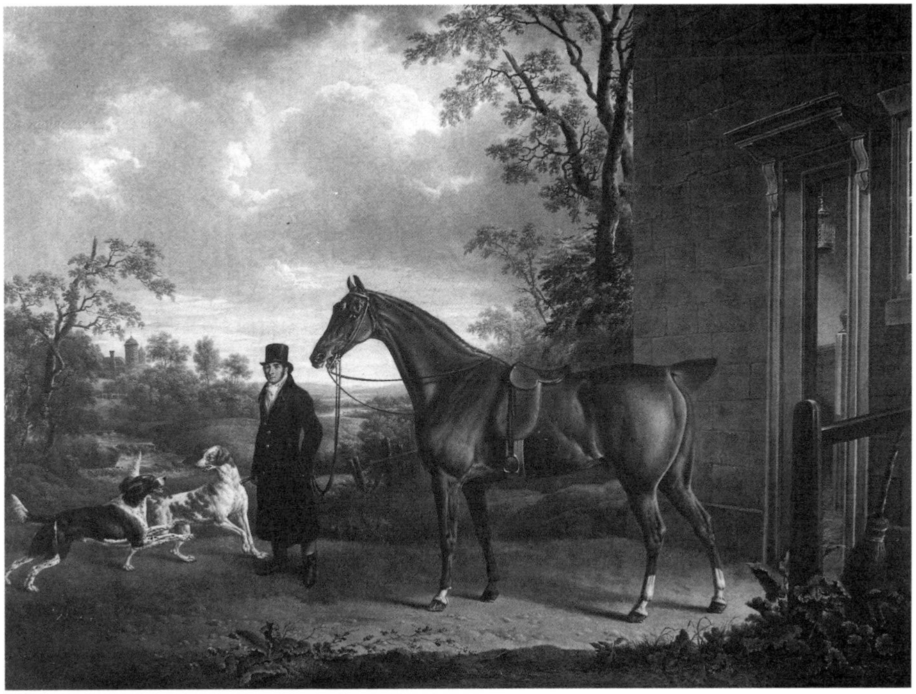

WAG 2319

A Chestnut Hunter with a Groom in a Landscape

WAG 2319
oil on canvas, 81.3 × 107.3 cm
date: unknown, perhaps 1812–15

The inscription *C. Towne/di...it*[1] at the bottom left is uncharacteristic of Towne's signature and appears to be a later addition, but in other respects the work is a classic Towne of the first quality. It is painted with exceptional care and attention to detail. The finely observed animals apart, the late Tudor or Jacobean grange in the left background (presumably the home of Towne's unknown patron) appears much more realistically rendered than is usual with the artist; he has taken care with the interior of the stable glimpsed through the half-open door, with its freshly laid straw and hanging lamp; the cloud pattern is elaborate and beautiful, and above all, the portrait of the groom is of a sensitivity worthy of Towne's mentor, George Stubbs.

When it entered the collection, the work was thought to be from about 1830.[2] However, this date seems impossibly late[3] and one of around 1812–15 much preferable. For stylistic comparison see WAG 2348, dated 1812 (p. 204).

The condition of WAG 2319 is problematic. The original canvas has deteriorated alarmingly around the right, left and bottom edges, where there are extensive retouched damages and where the lining canvas is clearly visible in places.

PROVENANCE

...Walter Stone by 1934; Mary Stone Bequest 1944.

EXHIBITIONS

Sporting Pictures from the Walter Stone Collection Bluecoat Gallery, Liverpool 1946 (35); *A Selection of Sporting Pictures from the Walter Stone Collection* Bluecoat Gallery, Liverpool 1953 (22); *Charles Towne of Liverpool 1763–1840* Walker Art Gallery 1971 (19).

NOTES

1. The word may have been intended as *dipinxit*; damage has obliterated the central letters.
2. *The Walter Stone Collection of Sporting Pictures at Whitton Hall, Westbury, Shropshire* (privately printed, 1938) p. 28 (cat. 45); followed by the 1953 exhibition catalogue.
3. As was recognised in the 1971 exhibition catalogue and in *MPPP*, pp. 206–7.

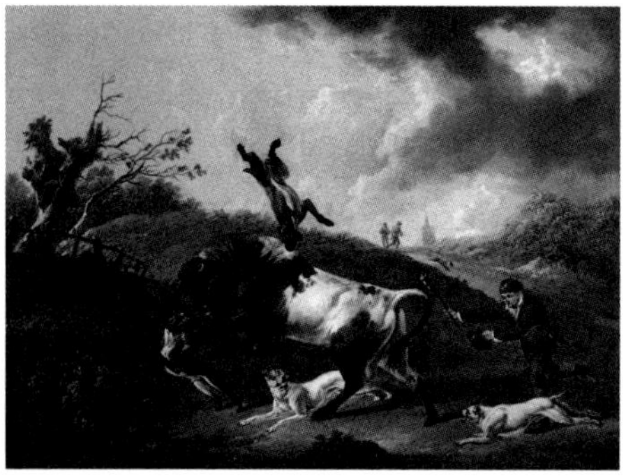

WAG 9572

Bull Terriers Baiting a Bull

WAG 9572
oil on canvas, 29.5 × 39 cm
signed: *CT* (bottom left)
date: unknown, perhaps 1812–15

A humorous and moralistic subject, WAG 9572 is painted in a burnished, meticulous style. Towne may have known Julius Caesar Ibbetson's earlier treatment of the subject (Tabley House, University of Manchester) where a flying dog is also introduced.[1] In Ibbetson's hands the motif is part of a wholly secular scene, but in Towne's the Church presides over affairs. Whether this reflects Towne's philosophy or his patron's is open to question; nothing is known of the work's first owner.

A label on the stretcher, written in ink and of some antiquity, but not contemporary with the artist reads *Charles Towne /1820*.[2] There appears to be no evidence to support this date and stylistically the work looks earlier.

PROVENANCE
…Col. J. R. Danson; his bequest 1979.

EXHIBITION
Danson Collection of Paintings by Charles Towne Walker Art Gallery 1977 (33).

NOTES
1. Repr. James Mitchell: *Julius Caesar Ibbetson (1759–1817) The Berchem of England* (London, 1999) p. 18.
2. Further labels have been removed; the figure 40 is inscribed on both stretcher and frame in blue chalk.

Four Horses in a Landscape

WAG 6107
oil on canvas, 120 × 150.5 cm
signed and dated: *Chas. Towne/ Pinxit/1814* (bottom right)
date: 1814

This large and elaborate composition reflects Towne's long-standing admiration for the work of George Stubbs. The design, with its frieze-like treatment of the foreground horses, clearly recalls Stubbs's *Mares and Foals* subjects. However, in place of the frieze Towne creates a (similarly striking) cruciform motif through his placing of the two dogs in the foreground and the fourth horse in the background carefully framed within the silhouetted muzzles and necks of its companions. The device, leading the viewer's eye back into the distant landscape, is unusually artful for Towne. A label on the reverse states that the horses were the property of Mr Harrison of Urmston, Lancs.[1] William Harrison (1749–1812), a successful cotton merchant of Manchester, had moved with his family to the suburb of Urmston in 1797, and Towne's panoramic background may be intended for the view from that village, five miles south-west of Manchester, eastwards towards the Pennines. Harrison's death led to the removal of his younger son Henry (1795–1871) from Eton in order to join his older cousin Richard, William's nephew, in the Liverpool branch of William's business empire. Although Henry would have been only 19 at the date of WAG 6107's execution, it seems most likely (as the work's provenance implies) that he commissioned it in Liverpool from Towne as a memorial to his father (who was interested in art and owned a supposed Tintoretto).[2] The unusual scale of the work suggests that he gave Towne *carte blanche*. For a later, more modest,

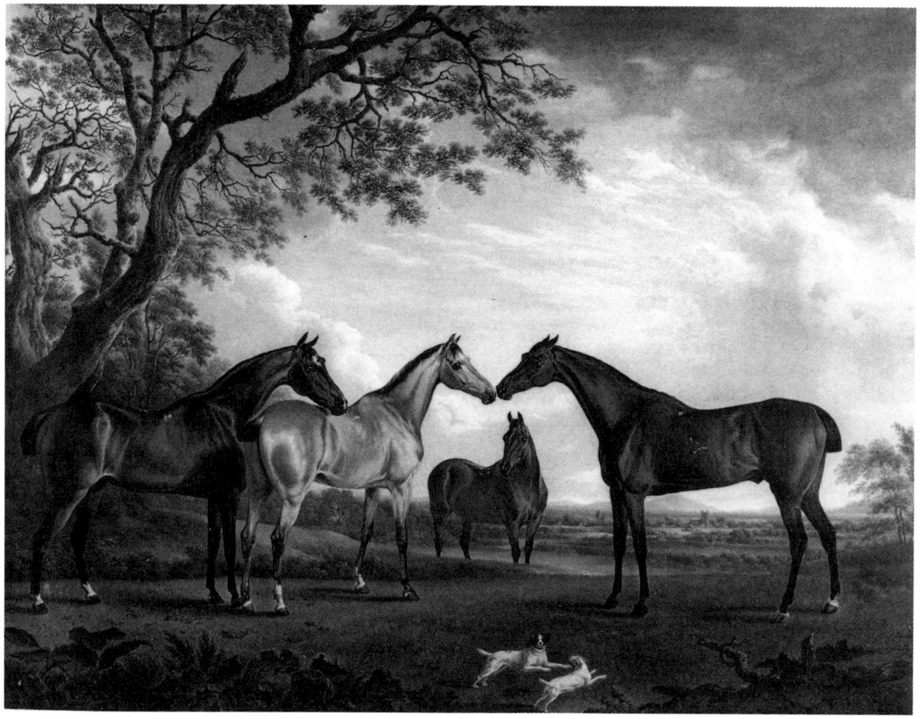

WAG 6107

commission from Towne on Henry Harrison's part see WAG 1164 (p. 225).

PROVENANCE

[? Commissioned by Henry Harrison of Aigburth, Liverpool and by descent to his grandson] Stewart Sandbach Harrison; by descent to Mrs Maxwell-Heron, née Harrison; by whom bequeathed to Mrs H. Bollam, Chirk; by whom presented 1961.

EXHIBITION

Charles Towne of Liverpool 1763–1840 Walker Art Gallery 1971 (14).

NOTES

1. The label reads *This picture of four horses and two dogs which were the property of my grandfather Harrison at Urmston, Cheshire, belongs to my son Stewart Sandbach Harrison* [signed] *William Stewart Harrison.* William Stewart Harrison (1851–1924) was the fourth son of Henry Harrison of Aigburth and his wife Mary Rosina Sandbach.
2. For biographical information on William and Henry Harrison see David Harrison: *The Harrisons of Bankfield* (West Horsley, 2006) especially pp. 74–9, 80 and 90ff.

'Regent', A Favourite Hunter of Sir Thomas Stanley of Hooton, Cheshire

WAG 9531
oil on panel, 57 × 71.5 cm
signed and dated: *Chas. Towne Pinxit/1814*
(bottom right)
date: 1814

The horse and its owner are identified in an early manuscript label on the reverse of WAG 9531, which also gives the (misread) date 1813.

Sir Thomas Massey Stanley, 9th Baronet, of Hooton, was born in 1782. He succeeded his brother to the Baronetcy in 1800, and in 1805 he married Mary, daughter of Sir Carnaby Haggerton of Haggerton, Northumberland, with whom he had four sons and one daughter. He died in 1841.

The Stanleys had been the leading family of Hooton, in the north-east of the Wirral peninsula, since the fourteenth

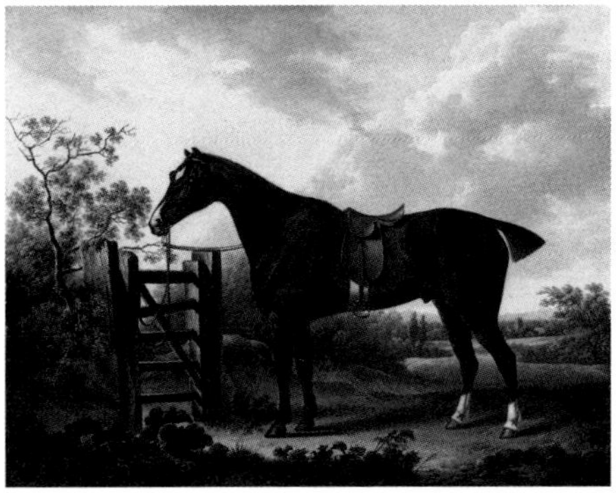

WAG 9531

century. Hooton Hall had been rebuilt for Sir William Stanley, Thomas Stanley's father, in the late 1770s, and the estate was laid out for Sir Thomas himself by Humphrey Repton in 1802. The family were long associated with the Hooton foxhounds, which hunted in the district,[1] and Sir Thomas himself was a keen huntsman. Mrs Fitzherbert, who was Lady Stanley's aunt, wrote from Hooton in 1835, 'Sir Thomas Stanley braves all wind and weather, which he never allows him to stop from hunting and shooting every day.'[2]

PROVENANCE

[? Painted for Sir Thomas Stanley]; ...Col. J. R. Danson; his bequest 1979.

EXHIBITION

Danson Collection of Paintings by Charles Towne, Walker Art Gallery 1977 (19).

NOTES

1. Compare Thomas Weaver's painting of 1833, *William Bolton Aspinall with the Hooton, Cheshire, Foxhounds* (Richard Green Gallery, London, 2006).
2. Quoted by Peter E. Stanley: *The House of Stanley from the Twelfth Century* (Edinburgh, 1998) p. 85.

Classical Ruins with Peasants and Goats

WAG 9562
oil on panel, 59 × 45 cm
signed and dated: *TOWNE 1814*
(bottom right)
date: 1814

An essay in the genre of seventeenth-century Dutch Italianate landscape, WAG 9562 is somewhat coarsely painted. The lines of the forcedly elaborate design converge in somewhat predictable fashion on the group of travellers, whose goats are painted much too large. The work has the appearance of a potboiler and may be a version of an earlier composition. No specific sources in Dutch prints have been identified.

PROVENANCE

...Col. J. R. Danson; his bequest 1979.

EXHIBITION

Danson Collection of Paintings by Charles Towne Walker Art Gallery 1977 (18).

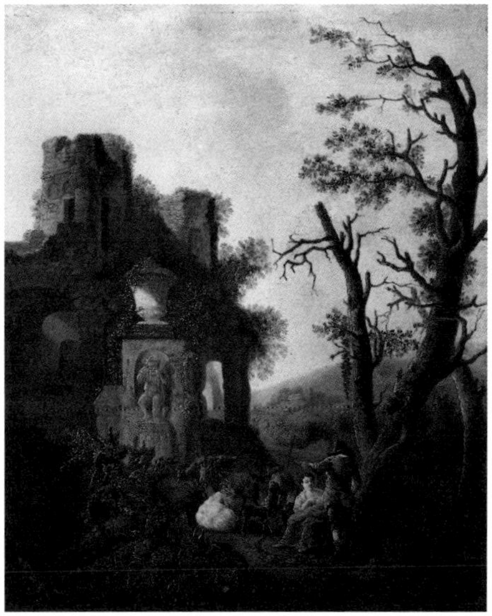

WAG 9562

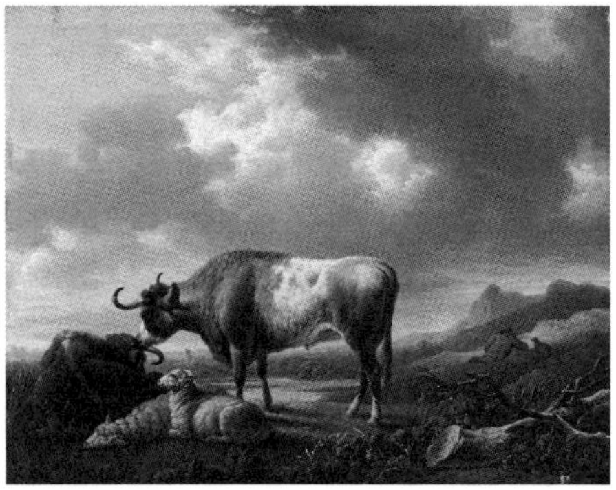

WAG 9569

Cattle and Sheep

WAG 9569
oil on mahogany panel, 24 × 30.5 cm
signed and dated: *C. TOWNE 1814* (bottom right)
date: 1814

Probably painted for stock rather than on commission, WAG 9569 is a study in the grouping and characteristic postures of cattle and sheep of the type developed later in the nineteenth century by Thomas Sidney Cooper (1803–1902). The contrasted poses of the animals are offset by the elaborate play of light and shade across the picture.

PROVENANCE

... Agnew; ...[? City Galleries, Liverpool];[1] ... Col. J. R. Danson; his bequest 1979.

EXHIBITION

Danson Collection of Paintings by Charles Towne Walker Art Gallery 1977 (17).

REFERENCE

1. There are labels on the reverse of Agnew's London gallery, and of Hardy Richards, The City Galleries, 1 Tithebarn Street, Liverpool. This may have been where Col. Danson acquired the painting. A small circular label inscribed in ink *16* also on the back of the frame appears to date from the first half of the twentieth century.

Breaking Cover

WAG 9532
oil on canvas, 84 × 103.5 cm
signed and dated: *Chas. Towne Pinxit 1815* (on bar of fence at right)
date: 1815

Although Towne is often considered a sporting artist, classic fox-hunting scenes are relatively uncommon in his work. That he felt an element of unfamiliarity here in tackling what was presumably, from its size and high finish, a major commissioned work, is suggested by the fact that he adapted its composition from a well-known painting by Philip Reinagle (1749–1833). Reinagle's *Fox Breaking Cover*, commissioned by the famous sportsman Col. Thomas Thornton as a companion to Sawrey Gilpin's *Death of the Fox*, and depicting Thornton as the central figure on the white horse, was well known from the early engraving by John Scott (fig. 91).[1] Close inspection reveals that Towne has discreetly varied each element of the design while preserving a close overall similarity to Reinagle's prototype. For a smaller work of similar character, in which the element of variation is greater, see WAG 2338 (p. 217).

PROVENANCE

[?John Greaves, The Crescent, Salford; Winstanley at The Exchange, Manchester 4–7 May 1836 (141)];[2] ...Alfred Dobell 1886;[3] ...F. C. Danson 1911;[4] by descent to Col. J. R. Danson; his bequest 1979.

EXHIBITIONS

Grand Loan Exhibition of Pictures from Lancashire Collections Walker Art Gallery 1886 (734); *Danson Collection of Paintings by Charles Towne* Walker Art Gallery 1977 (20).

NOTES

1. Judy Egerton: *British Sporting and Animal Paintings 1665–1867: The Paul Mellon Collection* (London, 1978) pp. 143–4. The 1977 exhibition catalogue dates Reinagle's painting to 1811, but this is the date of Scott's engraving, published by James Cunder and John Scott; see *MPPP*, p. 206 and Lionel Lambourne and Mary Webster, eds: *British Sporting Painting*

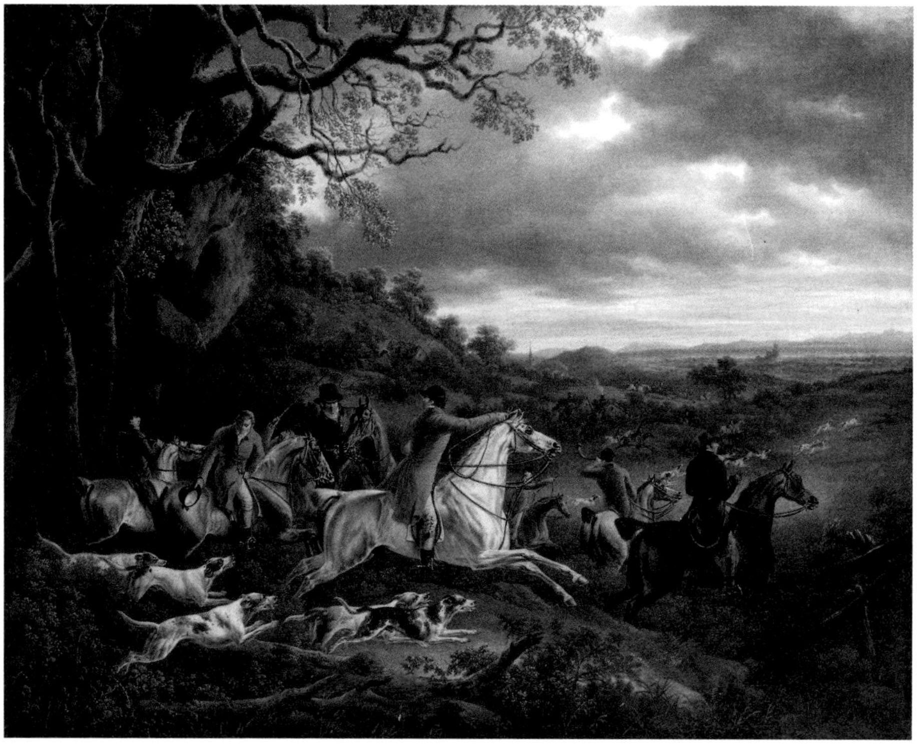

WAG 9532

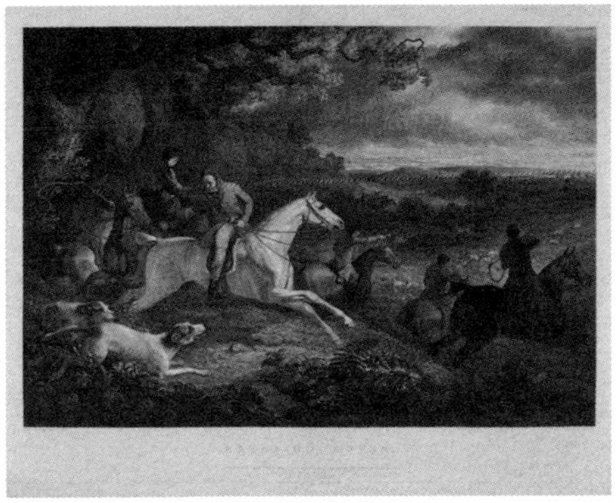

Fig. 91 *Breaking Cover* after Philip Reinagle, engraving by John Scott. © Trustees of the British Museum.

1650–1850, exh. cat., Hayward Gallery London and tour (1974–75) p. 135 (cat. 246).
2. Lot 141 in Greaves's sale, titled *Breaking Cover*, is described in the catalogue as 'A well known Picture' and as measuring 33 × 39 inches, i.e. very nearly the same dimensions as WAG 9532. It is uncertain, however, whether Greaves would have commissioned Towne for this work: he was only 22 in 1815. For other works by Towne owned by Greaves, see WAG 9548, 9553 and 9574 (pp. 214–5, 231).
3. Lent by Dobell to the 1886 exhibition.
4. Sir Walter Gilbey: *Animal Painters of England from the Year 1600* 3 vols (London, 1900–11) vol. 3 (second series) p. 251 (no. 1).

Gentleman on a Bay Horse

WAG 9541
oil on canvas,[1] 33 × 40.5 cm
signed and dated: *Chas Towne 1815* (bottom left)
date: 1815

The identity of the gentleman is unknown. As a clue, the fairground depicted in the background is suggestive, but no connection has been established.

PROVENANCE

…[? City Galleries, Liverpool, about 1950];[2] …Col. J. R. Danson; his bequest 1979.

EXHIBITION

Danson Collection of Paintings by Charles Towne Walker Art Gallery 1977 (21).

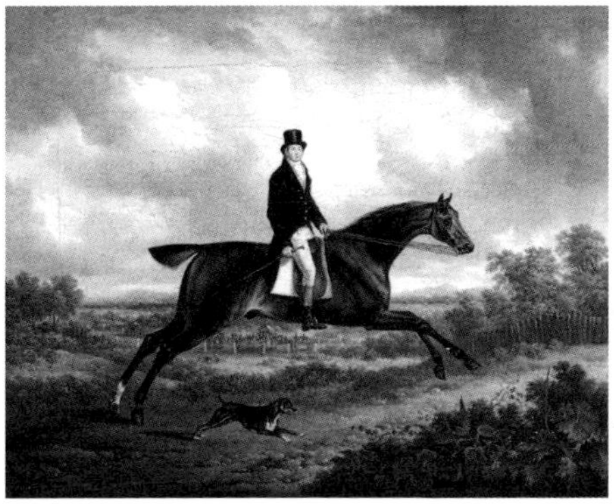

WAG 9541

NOTES

1. The canvas is unlined; it is of a medium tabby weave, degraded and brittle, with a staining pattern present on the reverse corresponding to the cracking pattern in the paint; the ground layer is off-white, perhaps commercially prepared; the paint layer is even, with glazes applied in areas of the horse's body and the foreground (condition report, 12 October 1995, gallery files).
2. Label on the reverse of Hardy Richards, The City Galleries, 1 Tithebarn Street, Liverpool. This may have been where Col. Danson acquired the painting.

Dappled Grey Horse in Landscape

WAG 9533
oil on canvas, 51 × 65 cm
signed and dated: *C. Towne/Pinxit/1816* (bottom left)
date: 1816

Towne's precise portrayal of the very distinctive markings of the horse, as well as of the mountain topography and the unconventional narrative of a group of huntsmen and their pack walking up the path in the background, suggest that he travelled away from Liverpool and stayed with his unidentified patron to receive the commission. The landscape has not been identified, but has some overtones of Ullswater from the Kirkstone Pass in

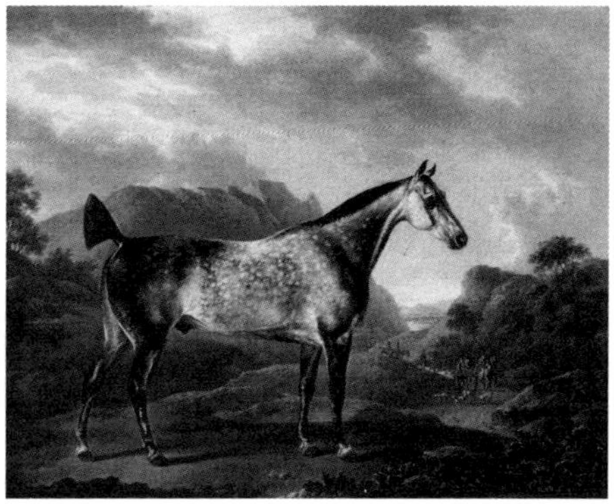

WAG 9533

the Lake District, when the peak in the centre, given artistic licence, could be intended for Helvellyn.

PROVENANCE

…Boydell Galleries Liverpool;[1] from whom bt. by Col. J. R. Danson March 1951;[2] his bequest 1979.

EXHIBITION

Danson Collection of Paintings by Charles Towne Walker Art Gallery 1977 (28).

NOTES

1. Label on stretcher.
2. Receipt for £44, 6 March 1951, *Danson Papers*, NML Archives, VII.5.2.

A Groom Holding an Unsaddled Chestnut Hunter outside a Stable

WAG 2314
oil on canvas, 50.8 × 64.5 cm
signed and dated: *-C Towne- 1817* (bottom right)
date: 1817

Both horse and groom are evidently portraits; however, there is no clue to their identity. It was formerly thought that the church with twin towers in the background was York Minster,[1] implying that Towne's unknown patron came from near the city, but this identification is not correct. A long range of offices

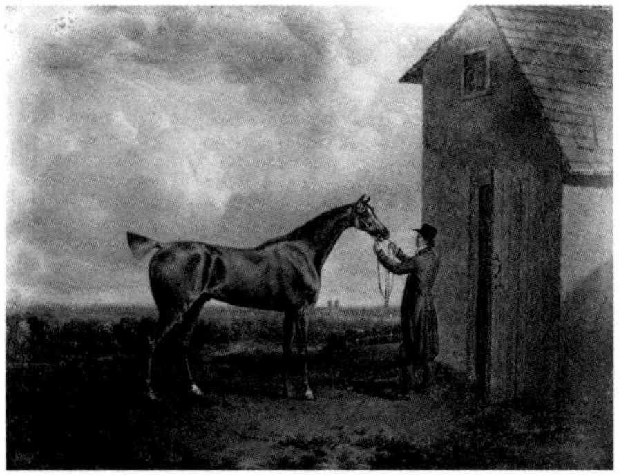

WAG 2314

is visible at right angles to what in a standard church would be the north-west tower, suggesting a monastic foundation; however, the building visibly stands at the centre of a fairly substantial town.

Although carefully painted, the portraits of both horse and man appear miscalculated: the horse's head is very small in proportion to its body, and the figure of the man preternaturally tall and thin. The proportions and perspective of the stable building at the right also seem misjudged and the slates of its roof are much too large. It is tempting to ascribe some of the unsatisfactory visual appearance of WAG 2314 to its physical condition: much of the foreground and right-hand side of the work is damaged and has been extensively repainted. However, the miscalculations appear attributable to Towne himself and seem more likely to reflect a literal-minded patron or a requirement for haste. The signature, although authentic, appears to have been strengthened by a later hand as part of more general restoration.

PROVENANCE

...Walter Stone by 1908;[2] Mary Stone Bequest 1944.

EXHIBITIONS

Historical Exhibition of Liverpool Art Walker Art Gallery 1908 (171); *Sporting Pictures from the Walter Stone Collection* Bluecoat Gallery, Liverpool 1946 (33); *Charles Towne of Liverpool 1763–1840* Walker Art Gallery 1971 (15).

NOTES

1. *MPPP*, p. 206 states that this identification was made by Walter Stone; the work was titled *Portrait of Chestnut Horse – View of York Minster in the Distance* at the 1908 exhibition and York Minster is also referred to in the description by Sir Walter Gilbey: *Animal Painters of England from the Year 1600* 3 vols (London, 1900–11) vol. 3 (second series) p. 252 (no. 5). However, there is no mention of York Minster in the entry in *The Walter Stone Collection of Sporting Pictures at Whitton Hall, Westbury, Shropshire* (privately printed, 1938) p. 29, cat. 46, suggesting that Stone either was not himself responsible for the original identification or else had subsequently recognised the error. For a more accurate depiction of York Minster by Towne see WAG 9549, p. 227.
2. Lent by Stone to the 1908 exhibition.

Saddled Bay Horse and Terrier in a Landscape

WAG 9530
oil on canvas, 77 × 107.5 cm
signed and dated: *Chas. Towne/Pinxit 1817*
(lower left on fence)
date: 1817

There is no clue to the identity of the patron of WAG 9530, but to judge by the extensive and carefully landscaped estate behind the horse, as well as the scale and the careful execution of the painting, he was an important figure.

PROVENANCE

...[? S. Cross, Liverpool]; ...Col. J. R. Danson;[1] his bequest 1979.

EXHIBITION

Danson Collection of Pictures by Charles Towne Walker Art Gallery 1977 (29).

REFERENCE

1. The label of S. Cross Fine Art Dealer, 14 Lord Street, Liverpool, is on the reverse of the stretcher. Danson may have purchased the work from them since he generally employed other firms to conserve his pictures and frames.

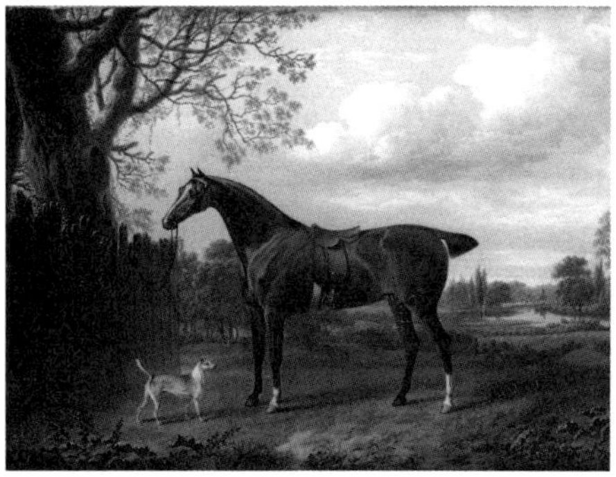

WAG 9530

Cattle in a Wood by a Pond

WAG 9558
oil on canvas, 35 × 45 cm
signed and dated: *C Towne Pinxit 1817*
(bottom centre)
date: 1817

The subject matter of WAG 9558, without human figures or habitation and strongly evocative of a rural mood, is unusual for Towne. The frame is almost certainly the original.[1]

PROVENANCE

...Lady Danson by 1930;[2] by descent to Col. J. R. Danson; his bequest 1979.

EXHIBITION

Danson Collection of Paintings by Charles Towne Walker Art Gallery 1977 (30).

NOTES

1. It bears a period label of Wm. B. Bland, 'carver, gilder and picture frame maker' of 78 Mount Pleasant, Liverpool.
2. Repr. W. Shaw Sparrow: 'Towne-Morland-Bailiffs', *Connoisseur* vol. 86 (July 1930) pl. II, p. 14.

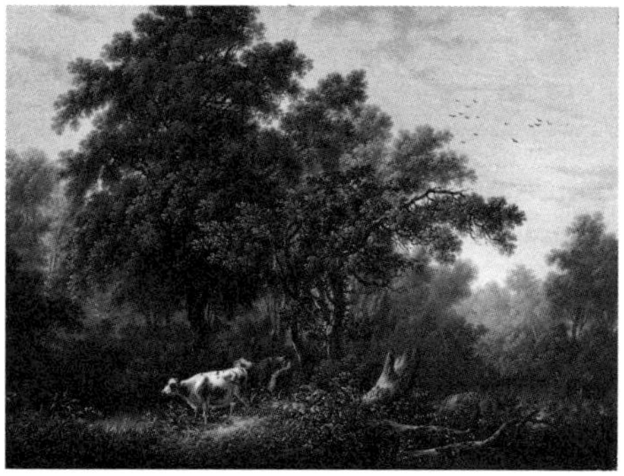

WAG 9558

Landscape with Peasants Fording a Stream

WAG 9563
oil on canvas, 56 × 65 cm
signed and dated: *C. Towne/Pinxit/1818* (bottom right)
date: 1818

An essay in the manner of seventeenth-century Dutch Italianate landscapes, painted in warm tones and a highly finished style.

PROVENANCE
…Agnew, Manchester;[1] …Col. J. R. Danson; his bequest 1979.

EXHIBITION
Danson Collection of Paintings by Charles Towne Walker Art Gallery 1977 (31).

REFERENCE
1. Label on the back of the frame. It suggests that one of the work's early owners may have been one of Towne's Manchester patrons.

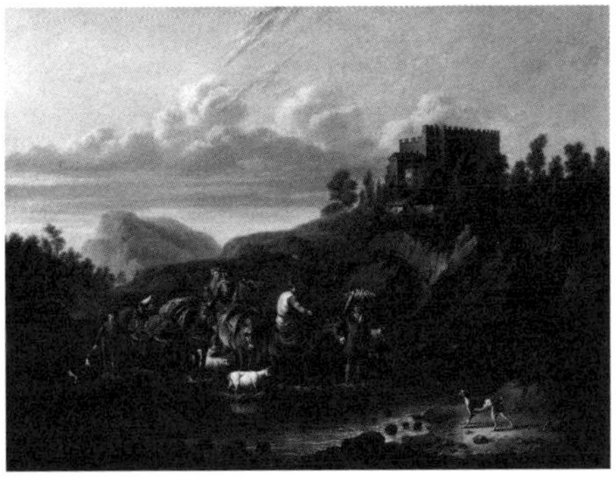

WAG 9563

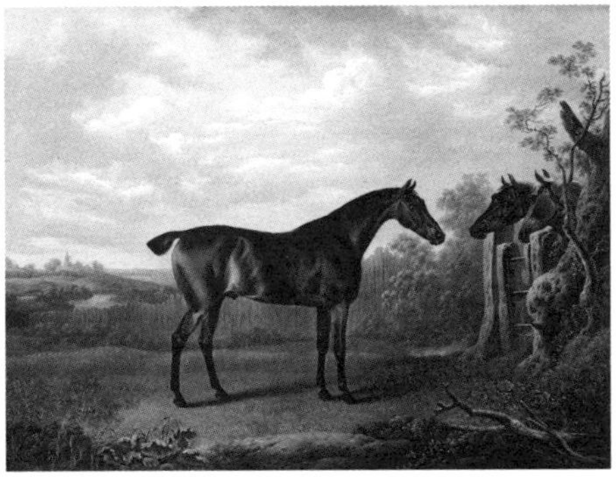

WAG 9816

Bay Hunter in a Field with Two Horses Looking over a Fence

WAG 9816
oil on canvas, 66.5 × 87.5 cm
signed and dated: *C. Towne/1818* (bottom centre)
date: 1818

The horses may well have belonged to the 2nd Earl of Sefton, and WAG 9816 may have been commissioned by him, although there is no positive evidence for this. The earliest record of WAG 9816 at Croxteth is from the first years of the twentieth century.[1]

The castle ruins in the left background of WAG 9816 have not been identified, but the topography as a whole does not appear to be part of the Croxteth estate.

PROVENANCE
…Charles, 5th Earl of Sefton 1900; by descent to Josephine, Countess of Sefton; her bequest 1980.

REFERENCE
1. *Croxteth 1900s Inventory* Billiard Room no.12. None of the works recorded on this inventory is likely to have been a recent acquisition.

A Chestnut Hunter and a Dog in a Park

WAG 9817
oil on canvas, 66 × 87 cm
signed and dated: *CHAS. TOWNE-Pinxit-1819* (top right, on wall)
date: 1819

This work is the same size as WAG 9816 (above), and dates from the following year, which raises the possibility that it was executed as a pendant. The visual language, with the horse posed in the reverse direction to the one in WAG 9816, and again engaged in a slightly humorous narrative of animal curiosity, suggests as much. It is evidently, however, a different animal. The dog, presumably a poodle,

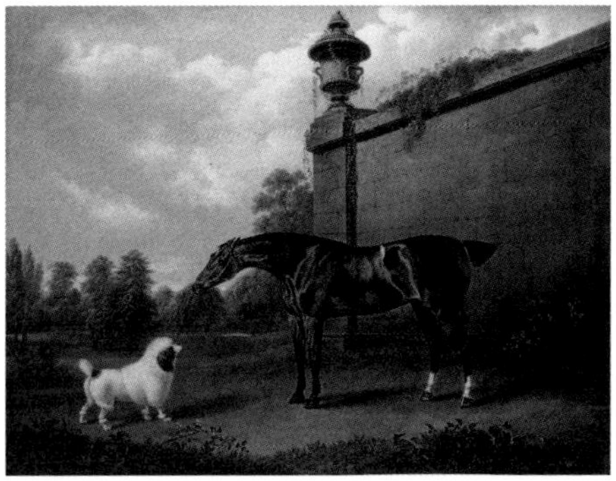

WAG 9817

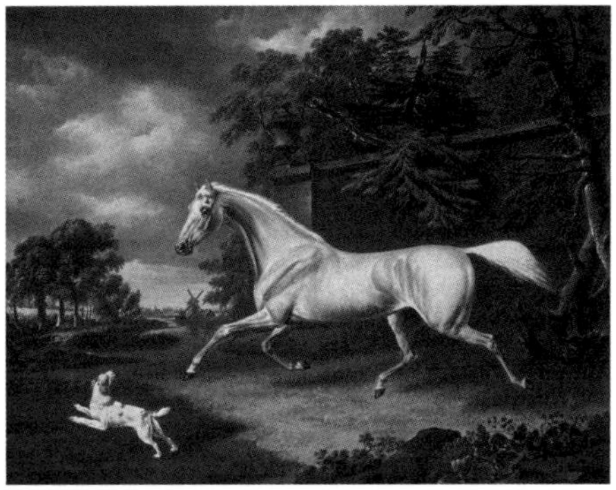

Fig. 92 *Palomino and Spaniel* by Charles Towne, oil on canvas. Private collection/© Partridge Fine Arts, London, UK/The Bridgeman Art Library.

is said to have been Lady Sefton's.[1] The setting may be intended for the Croxteth estate, but the conception perhaps derives from an earlier work, signed and dated 1814, with the traditional title *Palomino Mare and Spaniel* (fig. 92).[2]

PROVENANCE
…Charles, 5th Earl of Sefton 1900; by descent to Josephine, Countess of Sefton; her bequest 1980.

NOTES
1. *Croxteth 1900s Inventory* Billiard Room no. 16, where it is described as *Chestnut Horse with Poodle, Standing by a Garden Wall*; the word *Poodle* has been crossed through and the phrase *Mill. Lady Sefton's Dog* substituted in pencil. None of the works recorded on this inventory is likely to have been a recent acquisition.
2. Formerly in the collection of Col. J. R. Danson; selected from it, under the terms of his will, by Doctor Hardy; subsequently with Partridge Ltd., London (their *Summer Exhibition* 1987 (cat.6); where stated to have descended from Towne's daughter, Elizabeth Forrest Danson); information in gallery files.

A Grey Cob at Croxteth

WAG 8635
oil on canvas,[1] 30.5 × 41 cm
signed and dated: *C.T.P. /1820*
(bottom left)
date: 1820

No doubt commissioned by the 2nd Earl of Sefton (1772–1838), WAG 8635 must portray one of his favourite horses. To judge from the presence of the broom and heavy roller, it was one which worked on the Croxteth estate rather than a hunter or racehorse. WAG 8635 was the latest in date of five paintings by Towne in the collection of the Earls of Sefton, the others being WAG 9816–19 (pp. 187, 211).[2]

The horse faces the main west front of Croxteth Hall, an 11-bay range built for William, 4th Viscount Molyneux in 1702. The flight of steps partially depicted by Towne leads to the main door of the house in the centre of the facade. The two southernmost bays of the house that are visible have been accurately represented. It has been suggested that the spire in the distance may be that of Knowsley Church,[3] but if the topography is accurate, the direction is wrong for Knowsley.[4]

PROVENANCE
Presumably commissioned from the artist by William, 2nd Earl of Sefton; by descent; bt. in 1974 from the executors of Hugh, 7th Earl of Sefton.

NOTES
1. Relined; a *HOGARTH* dealer's label is on the reverse of the stretcher.
2. WAG 8635 is first recorded at Croxteth in the *Croxteth 1900s Inventory*, Billiard Room no. 7. It is *Croxteth 1946 Inventory* no. 26.
3. *MPPP*, p. 206.
4. Julia Carder, Croxteth Hall, *verbally*, 3 February 2005 suggested that it was meant for Prescot Church, which has a spire. Although this too lies in the wrong direction, the degree of error is less than would be the case for Knowsley.

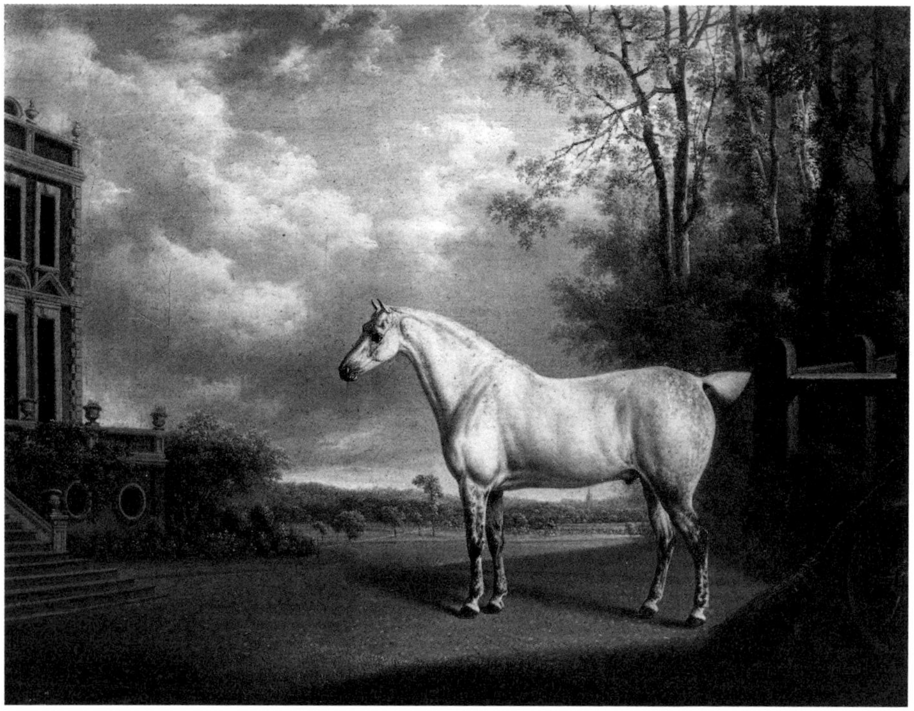

WAG 8635

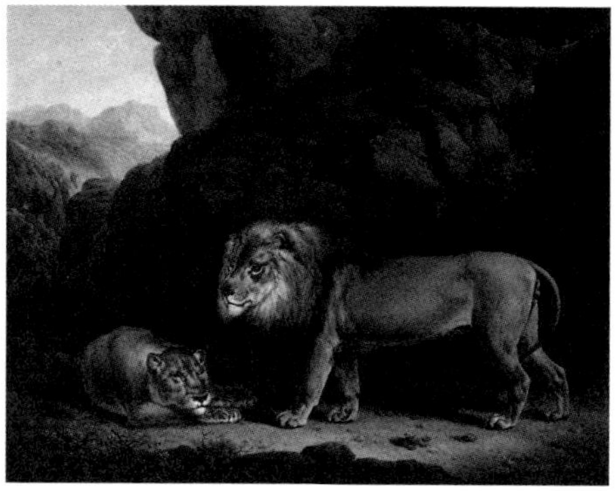

WAG 9589

Lion and Lioness

WAG 9589
oil on canvas, 43.5 × 53.5 cm
signed and dated: *Chas Towne Pinxit 1820*
(lower left on rock by lioness)
date: 1820

The subject matter of WAG 9589 is unusual for Towne. His general inspiration (or that of his patron) was no doubt the *Lion and Lioness* subjects of George Stubbs, two of which were well known in engraved form.[1] Towne's composition is not directly based on either print, nor on any of Stubbs's paintings,[2] which typically place one or other of the animals close to the picture plane and which all evoke a less conventionally domestic male–female relationship between the two animals than the one shown here. Towne had known Stubbs's work since making copies of his *Haymakers* and *Reapers* at the exhibition of the Liverpool Society for Promoting Painting and Design in 1787; for another work generally inspired by Stubbs, see WAG 2346, p. 204.

PROVENANCE
...Col. J. R. Danson;[3] his bequest 1979.

EXHIBITION
Danson Collection of Paintings by Charles Towne
Walker Art Gallery 1977 (32).

NOTES

1. C. Lennox-Boyd, R. Dixon and T. Clayton: *The Complete Engraved Work of George Stubbs* (Abingdon, 1989) pp. 122–3 (cat. 28) and pp. 140–1 (cat. 36).
2. Judy Egerton: *George Stubbs, Painter. Catalogue Raisonné* (New Haven and London, 2007) pp. 301–2, 360–3 (cats. 116–8, 161–4).
3. WAG 9589 bears a label of the Boydell Galleries on the reverse as well as two inscribed *Richard Jones & Chester 218 Samuels* and *Richard Jones & 219 Samuels*. These may relate to a previous owner.

Maghull Racecourse

WAG 2344
oil on canvas, 66.5 × 91.5 cm
signed and dated: *Chas Towne/pinxit/1822* (bottom right)
date: 1822

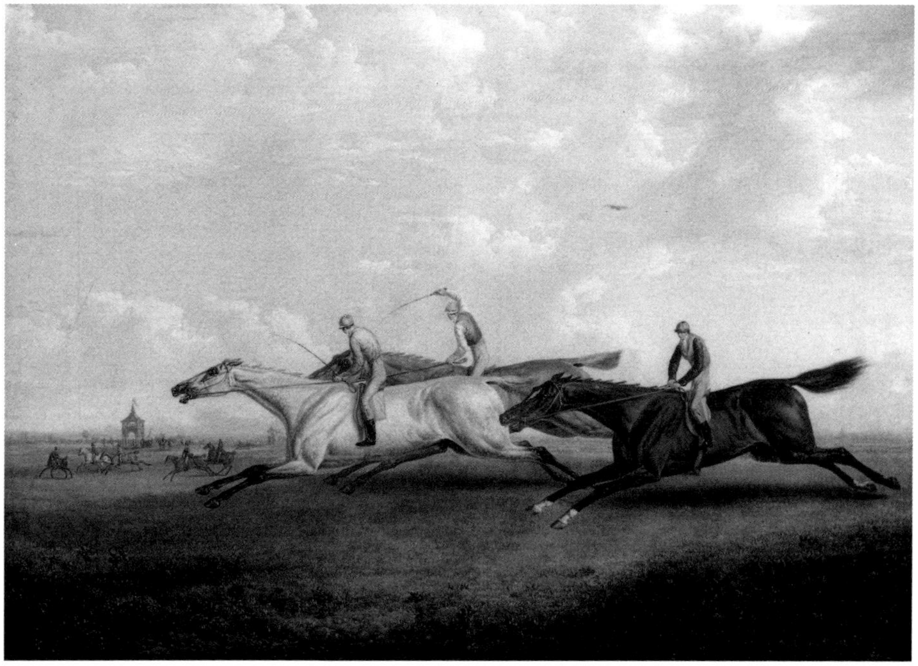

WAG 2344

The title of WAG 2344 is traditional. It was established by 1908, when the work was shown at the Historical Exhibition of Liverpool Art, but the racecourse depicted cannot be Maghull, which was founded only in 1827.[1] It has been suggested that WAG 2344 depicts one of the occasional meetings around Liverpool that provided the impetus for the establishment of the Maghull course,[2] yet no evidence has emerged in local newspapers or from *The Annals of Sporting* that any race or meeting was held in the neighbourhood in 1822. It seems more likely that the idea for setting up the racecourse would have been in the air for some time previously[3] and that Towne made the painting as advance publicity, either for one of the scheme's principal backers, such as John Formby, or else – anticipating future patronage from the owners of the horses that were raced at Maghull; the signature on WAG 2344 is noticeably prominent – on his own initiative. Pictorial interest, rather than historical veracity, is likely to have prompted Towne to show a grey, a chestnut and a bay horse contesting the race, and the colours of the jockeys' silks are also probably invented; it has been pointed out that multi-coloured caps did not feature among the few registered racing colours at this date.[4] It is perhaps significant that rails and finishing post are not depicted, making the view less specific, and that while jockeys are riding the horses in the foreground, gentlemen are mounted on the horses in the ring in the middle ground. Furthermore, for the composition of WAG 2344 Towne has re-used one of his rare earlier racing scenes: *A Match between Sir Joshua and Philo da Puta* (fig. 93). That match took place at Newmarket in 1816 although Towne's painting is dated 1819.[5] For WAG 2344, besides providing an extra horse, Towne replaced the finishing post and buildings at the left in the earlier work with an imaginary judge's Distance Chair[6] and a stand whose position in relation to the course is unresolved. On the right-hand horizon he painted a church tower, possibly a reference to Melling Church about two miles away from John Formby's land at Maghull.

PROVENANCE

...Walter Stone by 1908;[7] Mary Stone Bequest 1944.

EXHIBITIONS

Historical Exhibition of Liverpool Art Walker Art Gallery 1908 (100); *Some Acquisitions of the Walker Art Gallery Liverpool 1935–1945* National Gallery, London 1945 (82); *A Selection of Sporting Pictures from the Walter Stone Collection* Bluecoat Gallery, Liverpool 1953 (29); *150th Anniversary of the Liverpool Academy* Walker Art Gallery 1960 (25); *The Taste of Yesterday* Walker Art Gallery 1970 (25); *Charles Towne of Liverpool 1763–1840* Walker Art Gallery 1971 (16).

NOTES

1. *MPPP*, p. 206; for the course at Maghull, which was the predecessor of Aintree, formed as its rival in 1828, see John Formby: *An Account of the Liverpool Races Established in the Year 1827, with Observations on the Conduct of the Committee Formed in February 1828* (Liverpool, 1828), *passim*. Racing at Maghull continued until 1834.
2. John Rowlands, *verbally*, 4 March 2003. Racing on the marshes at Crosby, the township to the west of Maghull, took place regularly in the eighteenth century but lapsed around 1786; there had also been races at Wallasey on the Wirral opposite Liverpool, and between 1807 and 1816 at Ormskirk, about seven miles north of Maghull (Roger Longrigg:

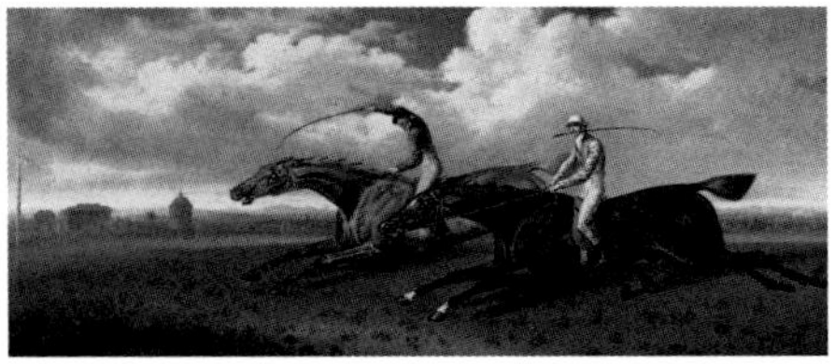

Fig. 93 *A Match between Sir Joshua and Philo di Puta* by Charles Towne. Rutland Gallery, London 1970.

The History of Horse Racing [London, 1972] p. 139). Phil Thompson: *On the Turf: The Origins of Horse Racing in the North-west* (Bebington, 1991) p. 46 states that there was also a racecourse at Melling, but no races there appear to have been officially recorded.

3. See 'Sylvestre': 'Horse-racing at Liverpool – A Hint to Establish Races There', *The Annals of Sporting* vol. 8 (1 October 1825) pp. 239–40 for an article which begins, 'It has long been the regret of the sensible part of the inhabitants of Liverpool that there are no established races within a short distance of this very busy and highly important seaport'. The piece continues with a description of a one-off event that took place at Maghull on 30 August 1825, a race between two horses owned by Mr Thompson and Mr Case, and concludes,

The admirers of the turf in Liverpool and its vicinity are willing to consider this as an earnest of something better, or at least something more extensive; they are willing indeed to regard it as the fore-runner of regularly established races. The ground, with very little trouble, might be converted into a course superior to most in the kingdom, inferior to none…

4. David Oldrey, *letter*, 19 June 2006, gallery files. The colours are as follows: the jockey on the leading grey horse wears a yellow jacket with pink sleeves and a yellow and pink quartered cap; the jockey on the chestnut running second wears a green jacket with white sleeves and a green cap with a white peak; the jockey of the bay horse wears a red jacket with black sleeves and a red cap with a black peak.

5. Exhibited in *This England* Rutland Gallery London 1970 (cat. 45).

6. As suggested by Dr John Pinfold, *copy letter* to Dr John Rowlands, 11 September 1999, gallery files.

7. Lent by Stone to the 1908 exhibition; see also *The Walter Stone Collection of Sporting Paintings at Whitton Hall, Westbury, Shropshire* (privately printed, 1938) p. 27 (cat. 42).

Winter Scene, a Village on the Way from Perth to Birnam Wood

WAG 9548
oil on canvas, 31 × 38.5 cm
signed and dated: *Chas Towne/Pinxit/1822* (bottom right)

Traveller on a Road in Snowdonia

WAG 9553
oil on canvas, 31 × 38.5 cm
signed and dated: *C TOWNE Pinxit 1822* (on rock at left of pond)
date: 1822

Manuscript labels on the reverse of both works, apparently in the artist's own handwriting, record that Towne painted them to order 'for John Greaves Esq. Banker, Manchester' and completed them in December 1822.[1] This, taken with the fact that they are the same size, are similarly framed, and are themed around the contrast between travellers in summer and winter, leaves no doubt that they were painted as a pair. Greaves was a significant collector of Towne's works[2] but the reason behind his specific interest in these locations is unclear. Neither has been precisely identified and it would be highly uncharacteristic for Towne to have depicted them with topographical accuracy; WAG 9553 is especially generic in character. Towne may, however, have visited central Scotland in 1822; it must be significant that he showed a view of the Falls of Tummel at the British Institution in 1823 (after a long absence from London exhibitions).[3] Birnam is a village about 20 miles north of Perth on the main road into the Highlands, familiar chiefly thanks to the prophecy

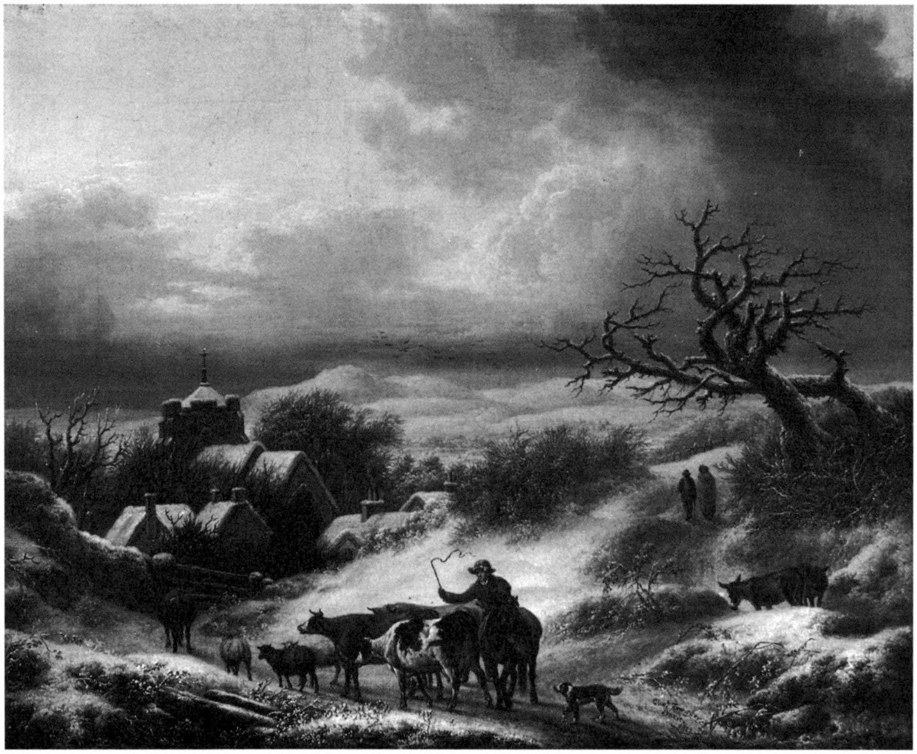

WAG 9548

in Shakespeare's *Macbeth* that the troubled king will remain safe until 'Great Birnam wood to high Dunsinane hill shall come against him'.[4] There are numerous small settlements between there and Perth but whether Towne's view is of one of these is uncertain.[5]

Towne made a repetition with variations of WAG 9553 the following year (WAG 9552; below).

PROVENANCE

Painted for John Greaves; …Lt. Col. R. Cross, Ballymoyer House, Co. Armagh; Christie 6 April 1925 (133) (a pair);[6] bt. Mitchell (16 gns.); …Lady Danson by 1930;[7] by descent to Col. J. R. Danson; his bequest 1979.

EXHIBITION

Danson Collection of Paintings by Charles Towne Walker Art Gallery 1977 (36–37).

NOTES

1. The label on WAG 9548 reads: *This view is from a village on the way from / Pearth to Burnham Woods – / Painted to order for John Greaves Esq. / Banker Manchester Finished Decr. 19 1822 / Charles Towne*; that on WAG 9553 reads *This view is from the neighbourhood of / Snowdon in Wales and painted to the order of / John Greaves Esq. Banker Manchester / Finished Decr. 9th* [or perhaps 19th, as suggested in the 1977 exhibition catalogue, though there is no reason that Towne should have completed them on the same day] *1822 / Charles Towne*.
2. John Greaves (1793–1847) was the eldest son of John and Mary Greaves of Irlam Hall, between Manchester and Warrington; the elder John was one of Manchester's wealthiest men and a partner of Robert Peel in the banking house of Peel, Greaves & Co. The younger John lived in Salford until the later 1830s; his residence is recorded as The Crescent, Salford in Burke's *Genealogical and Heraldic History of the Commoners of Great Britain* (London, 1838) p.106, though his 'seat' is given as Irlam Hall; however he held a clearance sale of his art collection in Manchester in 1836 (Thomas Winstanley at the Exchange, 4–7 May). The catalogue, which states that the sale was occasioned by an impending change of residence, lists seven works by Towne, one of which is almost certainly WAG 9574 (p. 231), and another probably WAG 9532 (pp. 208–9). WAG 9548 and WAG 9553 are not among the seven Townes in the sale, implying that they were (as the catalogue put it) among the 'small selection of such Pictures as, for various reasons, he [Greaves] wishes to retain'; however, it is not entirely certain that Greaves ever took delivery of the works from Towne and this may indeed be the implication of the presence of the labels on the reverse. Possibly WAG 9548 and WAG 9553 are the works titled *Summer* and *Winter* lent by R. Hornby to the *Third Exhibition Illustrative of Objects Illustrative of the Fine Arts* […] at the Liverpool Mechanics Institution 1844 (cats. 72 and 104).
3. Algernon Graves: *The British Institution 1806–1867. A Complete Dictionary of Contributors and their Work from the Foundation of the Institution* (London, 1908) p. 541 (Tummel misprinted as Jumel).
4. William Shakespeare: *Macbeth*, Act 4, Scene 1.
5. Possible candidates for the village depicted by Towne between Perth and Birnam are Bankfoot and Stanley but the churches in these places do not resemble the one in WAG 9548. I am grateful to Maria Devaney, Perth Museum and Art Gallery, for this information.
6. Christie's stencil *187 EA* on the reverse of both works.
7. W. Shaw Sparrow: 'Chas. Towne The Last Phase', *Connoisseur* vol. 86 (August 1930) pp. 93, 96; Sir Francis Danson (d. 1926), Lady Danson's husband, probably purchased both works and may have bought them directly from Mitchell.

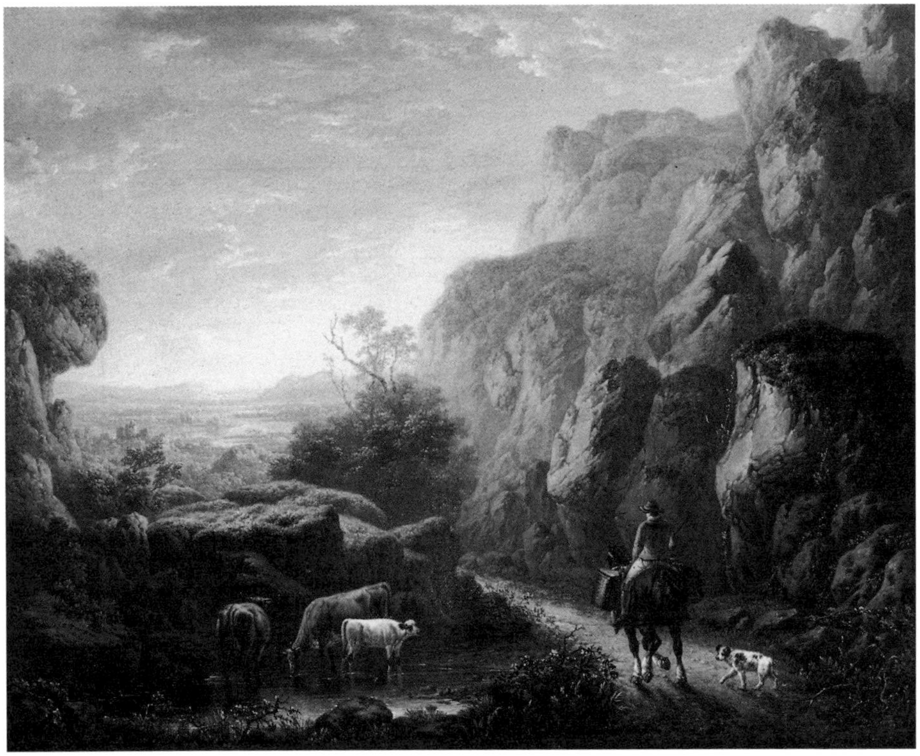

WAG 9553

Traveller on a Road in Snowdonia

WAG 9552
oil on canvas, 31 × 38 cm
signed and dated: *C Towne/Pinxit/1823* (at edge of pond)
date: 1823

This is a second version of WAG 9553 (above). Its quality is scarcely inferior

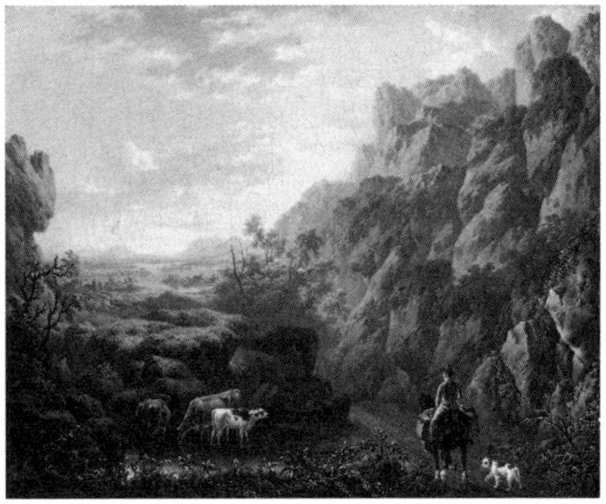

WAG 9552

and it has the character of a variant rather than a replica or copy. There are minor differences all across the canvas but the two most significant are the more subdued effect of light overall, and the more consciously picturesque and patterned handling of the natural forms, particularly the rock forms at both left and right as well as the clouds. WAG 9552 lacks the three huge boulders at the right of the path and Towne has painted the foliage covering the rocks at the right in a much more consciously decorative way. With the same decorative effect in view, the man on horseback is less prominent and smaller in scale, and the right-hand cow has a patterned back rather than a plain one.

There is considerable craquelure in the sky of WAG 9552 and an old repaired damage in the sky above the left-hand hill in the distance, about 8.5 cm from the left edge.

PROVENANCE
...Col. J. R. Danson; his bequest 1979.

EXHIBITION
Danson Collection of Paintings by Charles Towne Walker Art Gallery 1977 (38).

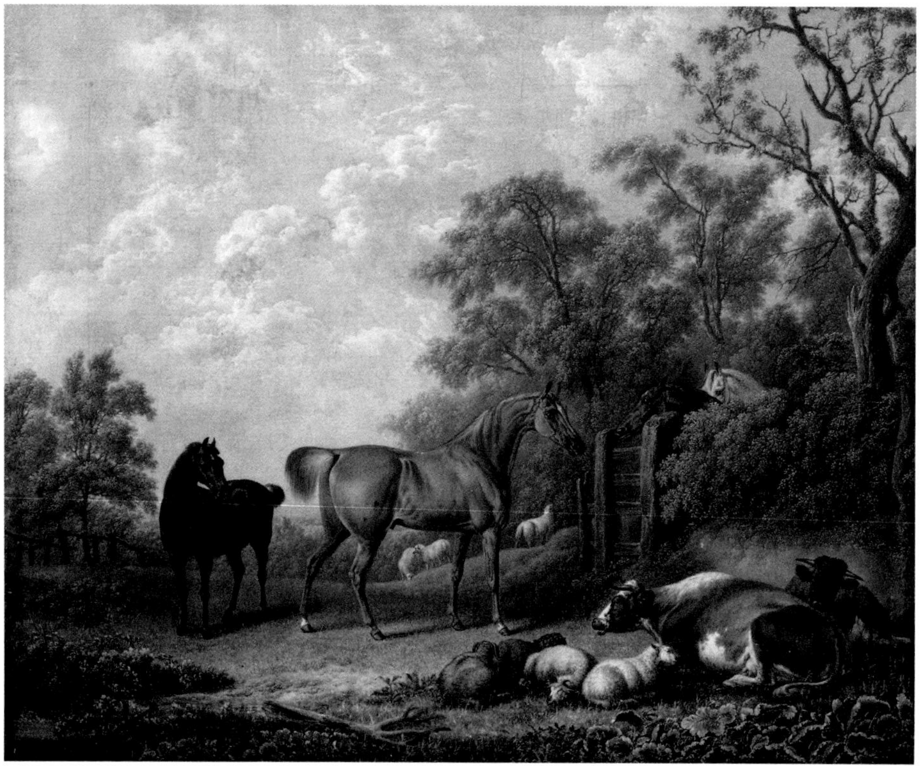

WAG 9539

Chestnut and Black Racehorses with Cattle in a Field

WAG 9539
oil on canvas, 70.5 × 86.3 cm
signed and dated: *C TOWNE/Pinxit/1823* (bottom right)
date: 1823

The unidentified patron of WAG 9539 was evidently a gentleman of consequence. His house (in the background between the two horses) appears to be castellated; he farms both sheep and cattle, while his horses are clearly racehorses, rather than farm horses or even hunters. The motif of the horse greeting his fellows over a stile is a favourite one of Towne's (compare WAG 9816, p. 211).

Damage from an old re-lining remains visible especially towards the right-hand side of the canvas. The early history of WAG 9539 is unknown.

PROVENANCE
...Col. J. R. Danson; his bequest 1979.

EXHIBITION
Danson Collection of Paintings by Charles Towne Walker Art Gallery 1977 (39).

Spaniel Putting up a Woodcock

WAG 9577
oil on mahogany panel, 25.5 × 30.5 cm
signed and dated: *C. Towne 1824* (bottom right)
date: 1824

This is an early example of Towne's last manner, characterised by the highly detailed treatment of foliage and the elaborate pattern made by clouds and the trunks and branches of trees. The prominence given to the memorial and church is suggestive of a recent bereavement. A slightly larger variant

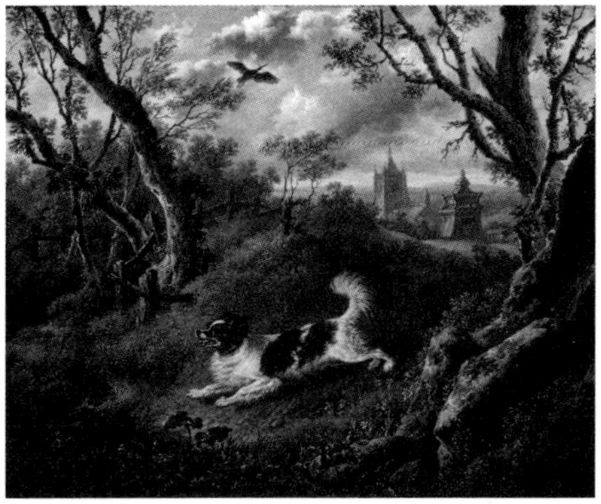

WAG 9577

work, *Spaniel Barking at a Stoat*, is signed and dated 1826.[1]

PROVENANCE

John Bentley;[2] Christie 15 May 1886 (47) [*a spaniel in a landscape*]; bt. Vokins (£12 15s 6d); ...Charles Burt, Hillside House, Richmond, Surrey; Christie 8 December 1913 (26);[3] bt. Pawsey & Payne (7 gns.); ...Joseph R. Bell Liverpool, June 1914;[4] ...Col. J. R. Danson; his bequest 1979.

EXHIBITION

Danson Collection of Paintings by Charles Towne Walker Art Gallery 1977 (41).

NOTES

1. On panel, 30.5 × 35.5 cm; sold Sotheby 31 October 1973 (40).
2. Label on the verso bearing the motto *Benigno Numene* and inscribed *Bentley Birch House*. Birch House near Bury was the chief residence of the Lancashire magistrate John Bentley (b. 1797). He also had a town house in the Crescent, Salford, and would very likely have been familiar with the collection of John Greaves (see WAG 9532, pp. 208–9). See John Burke: *A Genealogical and Heraldic History of the Commoners of Great Britain and Ireland* 4 vols (London, 1834–38) vol. 4, p. 683. Bentley appears to have been buying paintings in the later 1820s (see WAG 2139, p. 294).
3. Titled in the catalogue *A Spaniel and a Woodcock in a Landscape* and described as a panel measuring 9¾ × 11¾ ins.
4. Ms label on the reverse: *Joseph R. Bell / Fine Art Dealer / 14 Cook Street / Liverpool / 4 / 6 / 14.*

Fox-hunting: Full Cry

WAG 2338
oil on canvas, 51 × 68.5 cm
signed and dated: *C. TOWNE 1825*
(on the fence, lower left)
date: 1825

As with WAG 9532 (pp. 208–9), the conception and basic composition of this work derive from Philip Reinagle's *Fox Breaking Cover*, as engraved by John Scott.[1] The element of variation is greater than in the earlier work, but both canvases contain a sportsman on a galloping grey horse in the middle of the picture, dogs in the foreground, a large tree framing the design at the left, and a gradually unfolding background landscape in which rolling contours give onto distant hills on the horizon. There is no sense in WAG 2338, as there is in WAG 9532, that some of the figures are portraits, and the degree to which Towne has miscalculated the relative size of the distant dogs at the right and the fallen huntsman in the middle ground, suggests that he undertook the work for stock rather than as a commissioned piece.

The paint surface of WAG 2338 is worn following relining and there are visible losses and damages at edges of the canvas at the top right and at the horizon far right.

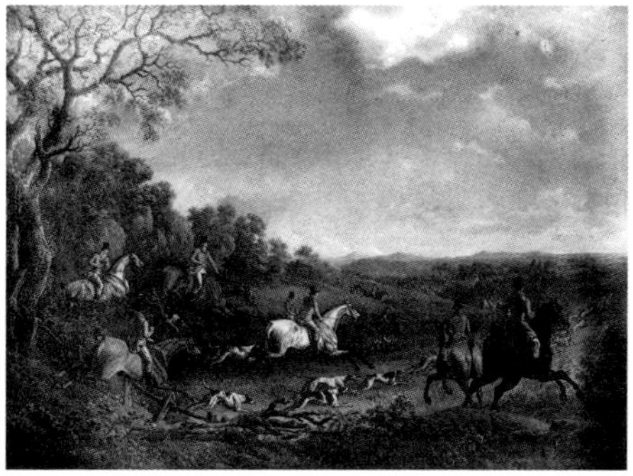

WAG 2338

PROVENANCE

...Agnew; Christie 28 March 1913 (53); bt. King (£63); ...Walter Stone by 1931;[2] Mary Stone Bequest 1944.

EXHIBITIONS

Sporting Pictures from the Walter Stone Collection Bluecoat Gallery, Liverpool 1946 (28); *A Selection of Sporting Pictures from the Walter Stone Collection* Bluecoat Gallery, Liverpool 1953 (26); *Charles Towne of Liverpool 1763–1840* Walker Art Gallery 1971 (17).

NOTES

1. MPPP, p. 206.
2. Repr. W. Shaw Sparrow: *A Book of Sporting Painters* (London and New York, 1931) fp. 144; *The Walter Stone Collection of Sporting Pictures at Whitton Hall, Westbury, Shropshire* (privately printed, 1938) p. 25 (cat. 37).

Saddled Bay Horse Tied to a Cottage Gate

WAG 9534
oil on board, 40 × 50.5 cm
signed and dated: *C. TOWN 1825*
(over cottage door)
date: 1825

This is perhaps a commission from one of Towne's more modest clients. The family home has only one chimney and there is no sign of a stable. The landscape in the background is also dotted with domestic-scale buildings, cottages and a small church, rather than a castle or estate. The form of the signature, without the final 'e', which is unusual in the artist's

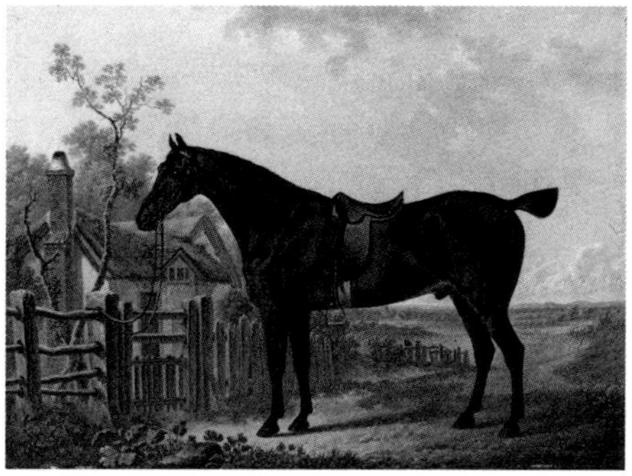

WAG 9534

work after about 1800, may also reflect an instinctual solidarity with a no-nonsense, man-of-the-people type patron.[1]

PROVENANCE

...Dr Glynn Morris, Basil Grange, Sandfield Park, Liverpool; ...Boydell Galleries, Liverpool; from whom bt. 1 September 1950 (£60) by Col. J. R. Danson;[2] his bequest 1979.

EXHIBITION

Danson Collection of Paintings by Charles Towne Walker Art Gallery 1977 (42).

NOTES

1. The 'N' of *TOWN* is adjacent to the bridle; no 'E' is visible.
2. Danson's receipt from Boydell's recording the earlier provenance is preserved in the *Danson Papers*, NML Archives, VII.5.2.

Grey Horse in a Landscape

WAG 9528
oil on canvas, 69.5 × 87.5 cm
date: unknown, perhaps 1825–30

On balance, WAG 9528 may be accepted as an authentic work by Towne despite certain problematic features. One is the lack of a signature, somewhat unexpected in a work of this size and pretension. Another is the stiff treatment of the horse (reminiscent of the horse in WAG 9525; see p. 234), although this may reflect a conscious effort on Towne's part to convey that the horse is old. The general composition and the handling of the sky, foliage and landscape background are all characteristic of the artist. There are several areas of very prominent retouching both on the horse and in the sky and a miscalculated restoration treatment may be to blame for the work's unsympathetic quality.

Not easy to date, WAG 9528 can perhaps be placed around 1825–30 rather than around 1815 as has hitherto been supposed.[1]

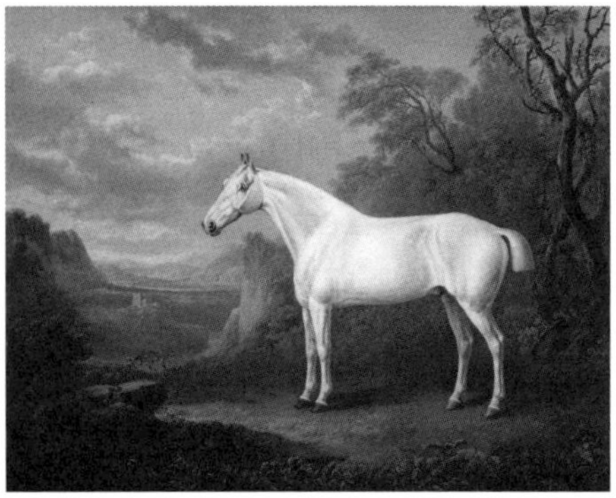

WAG 9528

PROVENANCE

...[? Boydell Galleries, Liverpool; from whom bt. by] Col. J. R. Danson;[2] his bequest 1979.

EXHIBITION

Danson Collection of Paintings by Charles Towne Walker Art Gallery 1977 (27).

NOTES

1. The 1977 catalogue, organised chronologically, placed WAG 9528 between dated works of 1815 and 1816. The detailed, fussy handling of the foliage and distant landscape indicates that the work belongs, if not firmly to, then at least on the cusp of, Towne's later manner. It is a possible candidate for Towne's 1830 exhibit at the Royal Manchester Institution (cat. 305), *A Portrait of a Grey Horse, the Property of a Gentleman in Manchester.*
2. A label of the Boydell Galleries is on the reverse of the frame.

Cattle and Sheep with a Goat in a Mountain Landscape with a Castle

WAG 9565
oil on panel, 25 × 35 cm
date: unknown, perhaps 1825–30

The inscription *Chas Towne Pinxt* at the bottom right of WAG 9565 does not resemble Towne's normal signatures, but despite the likelihood that this is inauthentic, the picture itself seems acceptable as his work.[1] The handling of the foliage suggests a date of about 1825 or later. Towne may have reworked the upper left hand corner where the towers of the castle appear to be added over the rock forms and the sky, and the dabs of creamy white paint for the cloud forms are inconsistent with the treatment of the clouds in the right-hand side of the picture. The landscape is unidentified but has a distinct character and taken in conjunction with the castle it suggests that a specific location is intended.[2]

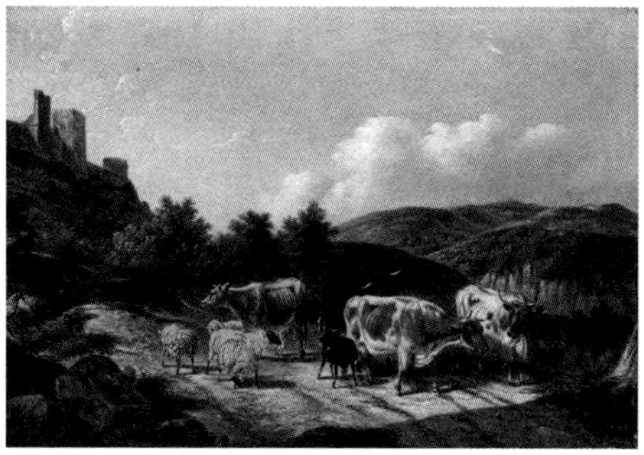

WAG 9565

PROVENANCE

...Col. J. R. Danson; his bequest 1979.

EXHIBITION

Danson Collection of Paintings by Charles Towne Walker Art Gallery 1977 (62).

NOTES

1. On account of the signature WAG 9565 was rejected as an autograph Towne in *CIC*, p. 282.
2. It is tempting to suggest that the landscape is the Forest of Bowland, east of Lancaster, and that the castle is meant as a representation of Abbeystead, then the property of the Earls of Sefton. There is, however, no evidence of any Sefton connection with WAG 9565.

Bay Horse in a Mountain Landscape

WAG 9536
oil on canvas, 50.6 × 65 cm
signed and dated: *C. Towne/1826* (bottom right)
date: 1826

An inscription on the reverse states that WAG 9536 was owned by S. B. Mercer of Liverpool 'whose father was a friend of C. Towne'.[1] The best candidate for this

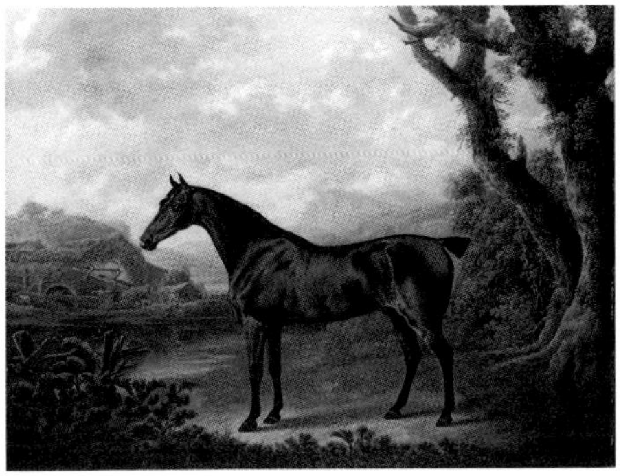

WAG 9536

man appears to be the Samuel Mercer, land agent, recorded in Liverpool street directories at 2 Irvine Street, Edge Hill in 1835 in succession to the William Mercer, 'gentleman' listed at that address in 1829 and 1832.[2] William Mercer himself (presumably Samuel's father) is recorded as living at 2 Kensington in 1825 and 1827, which would have placed him in fairly close proximity to Towne, if not quite as a neighbour. The label does not explicitly state, however, that WAG 9536 was commissioned by either Samuel or William, and it is somewhat tempting to suspect from the inclusion of the mill that the artist's original patron was a miller who failed to take delivery of his picture.

Although relined, WAG 9536 has remained in fresh condition and is a fine example of Towne's staple product.

PROVENANCE

...S. B. Mercer, Liverpool; ...Col. J. R. Danson; his bequest 1979.

EXHIBITION

Danson Collection of Paintings by Charles Towne Walker Art Gallery 1977 (43).

NOTES

1. The ms label reads in full, *Portrait of a horse, size of canvas / 25in × 19½ dated 1826. Formerly / the property of S.B. Mercer of / L'pool, whose father was a / friend of C. Towne.* Mercer is also stated to have owned WAG 9538 (below), which dates from the same year as the present work.

2. Samuel Mercer is not recorded in Liverpool street directories after 1835. However, Sir Walter Gilbey: *Animal Painters of England from the year 1600* 3 vols (London, 1900–11) vol. 3 (second series) p. 254 in his list of owners of works by Towne wrote, 'Mr S.B. Mercer of Liverpool, whose father was a friend of Towne, has [sic] four works'. These are given as WAG 9536, WAG 9538 (below), a *Portrait of a Horse* on mahogany panel, 15 × 10¼ ins., dated 1825, and a *Portrait of a Dog*, 11 × 9 inches, dated 1828. If S. B. Mercer was alive in 1911, it seems extremely unlikely he was Samuel the land agent, although it is possible he was his son, and that the land agent was Towne's friend. However, it seems more likely that Gilbey had simply been informed of the labels recording Mercer's ownership of the works and erroneously jumped to the conclusion that Mercer was still alive.

Chestnut Driven in a Gig

WAG 9538
oil on canvas, 25.5 × 33.6 cm
signed and dated: *C. Towne/1826* (bottom right)
date: 1826

As with WAG 9536 (above), WAG 9538 bears a label on the reverse stating that it was formerly owned by S. B. Mercer of Liverpool, 'whose father was a friend of Charles Towne'.[1] Mercer is recorded as a land agent living in Edge Hill outside Liverpool in the mid-1830s but although both horse and man are clearly portraits, and carried out with considerable affection and attention to detail, it seems doubtful that the man is Mercer himself. The milepost to the left of the horse is inscribed (apparently) *V / TO / WHELANS*. The meaning of this is unclear but may indicate that the family name of Towne's patron was Whelan, and that the gig with its driver is supposed to be five miles from Whelan's house.[2] In the left background, the three figures walking along the road that wends into the distance may form another element in such a narrative.

It has been observed that Towne's depiction of the gig is unusual and interesting. With its long floor line and shallow seat, the body does not appear to conform precisely to the known contemporary styles. The metal rail

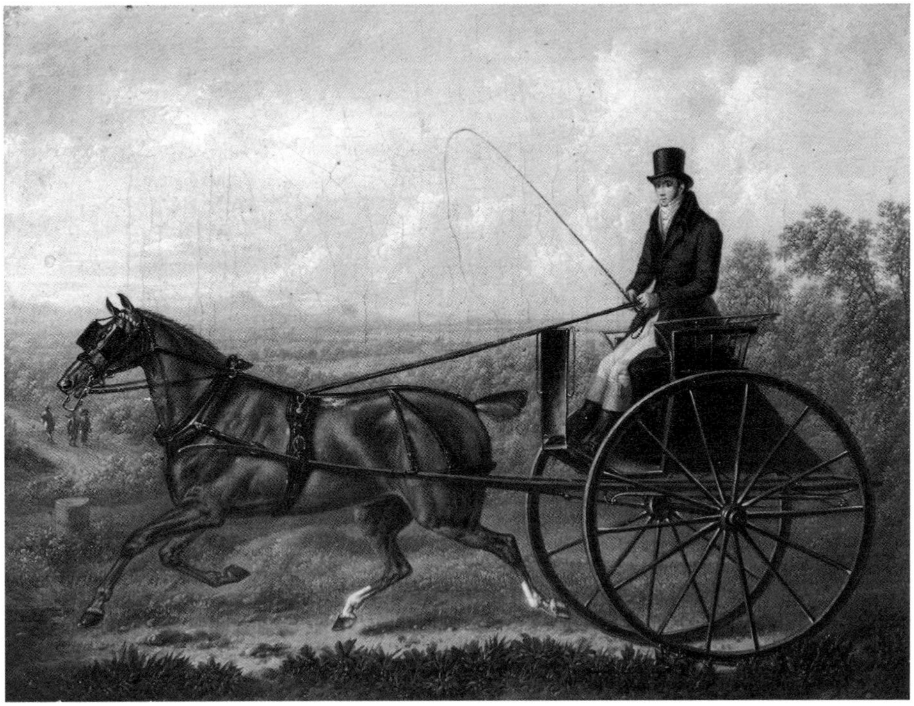

WAG 9538

fitted around the seat-back is a special addition, perhaps to create a handrail used to mount the gig, for it appears to have no steps, without which the occupant would have to mount by climbing on the wheel spokes.[3]

PROVENANCE
...S. B. Mercer, Liverpool; ...Col. J. R. Danson; his bequest 1979.

EXHIBITION
Danson Collection of Paintings by Charles Towne Walker Art Gallery 1977 (44).

NOTES
1. The inscription on the label reads, in full, *Horse and Gig with driver 13" × 10 dated 1826 formerly belonged to S.B. Mercer of Liverpool whose father was a friend of Towne*. A label of Middleton & Co. Liners is also present on the reverse.
2. Towne's use of the Roman numeral is unusual but for another instance see WAG 9526 (p. 200).
3. Notes forwarded by Chris Nicholson in 1997, gallery files; he points out that the gig is none of the Stanhope, Tilbury or Denner types recorded in W. B. Adams: *English Pleasure Carriages* (London, 1837). Nicholson suggests that the omission of the steps was simply an error on Towne's part.

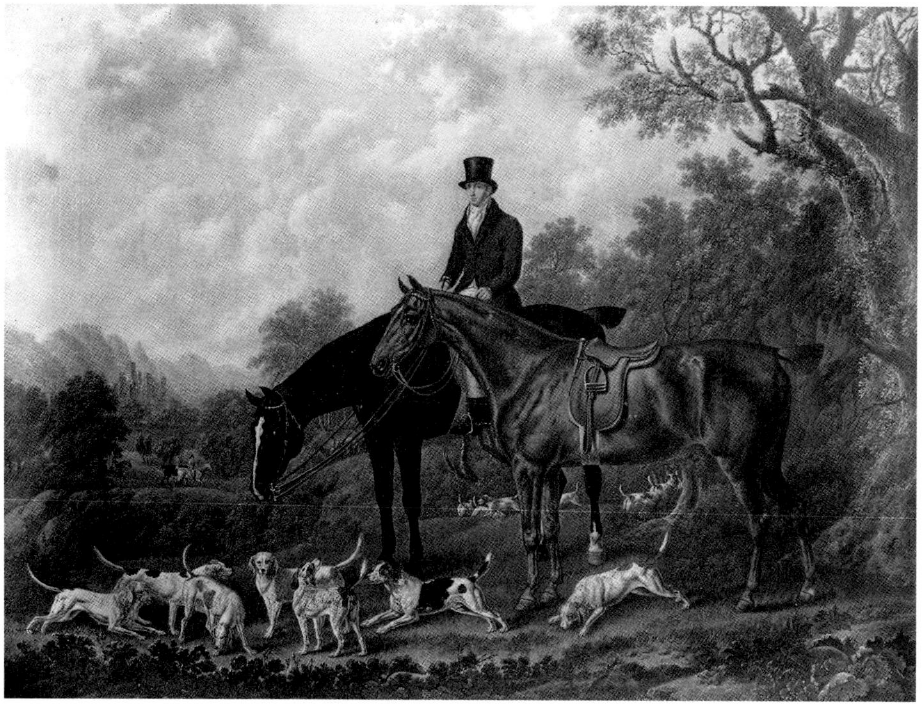

WAG 2339

The Second Horse

WAG 2339
oil on canvas, 51 × 65.2 cm
signed and dated: *C Towne/1828* (bottom left)
date: 1828

The precise subject of WAG 2339 is uncertain. The central figure, ostensibly a groom or hunt servant leading his master's spare horse during a hunt, is well studied, suggesting that he is in fact Towne's patron. His black formal attire contrasts with the red hunting coats worn by the huntsmen visible in the background, and it is tempting to wonder whether the work commemorates the death of the absent master in a hunting accident. The dogs, painted with unusual sophistication, have been described alternatively as lap beagles and harriers.[1] They have been identified as a northern pack because they are lighter than southern dogs, and the mountainous background suggests that the setting is the Lake District[2] or possibly North Wales.

There is substantial retouching of old damage along the work's bottom edge.

PROVENANCE
...Walter Stone by 1930;[3] Mary Stone Bequest 1944.

EXHIBITIONS
Sporting Pictures from the Walter Stone Collection Bluecoat Gallery, Liverpool 1946 (29); *A Selection of Sporting Pictures from the Walter Stone Collection* Bluecoat Gallery, Liverpool 1953 (24); *Charles Towne of Liverpool 1763–1840* Walker Art Gallery 1971 (18).

NOTES
1. Respectively by W. Shaw Sparrow: 'Charles Towne: The Last Phase', *Connoisseur*, vol. 86 (August 1930) p. 90 and pl. II; and by members of the British Sporting Art Trust, *verbally*, on a visit to the gallery, 6 June 2006.
2. Conjecturally, the scene is intended for the Blencathra hunt with the triple-peaked mountain, Blencathra, east of Keswick, depicted very fancifully in the background. If the view were looking east, Sharp Edge, the celebrated spur of Blencathra (although in real life it is more behind the mountain) would be at the far end of the massif, as here.
3. Shaw Sparrow, *loc. cit.*; this painting is not among those listed as in Stone's collection in Sir Walter Gilbey: *Animal Painters of England from the Year 1600* 3 vols (London, 1900–11) vol. 3 (second series) pp. 251–3, suggesting that Stone acquired it between 1911 and 1930.

A Chestnut Horse in a Landscape

WAG 2347
oil on canvas, 39.5 × 47.5 cm
signed and dated: *C. Towne 1828* (lower left)
date: 1828

Nothing is known about Towne's patron but the landscape background suggests he may have come from the Lake District. WAG 2347 is in unusualy fresh condition apart from an area of visibly restored impact damage in the landscape immediately beneath the horse's stomach.

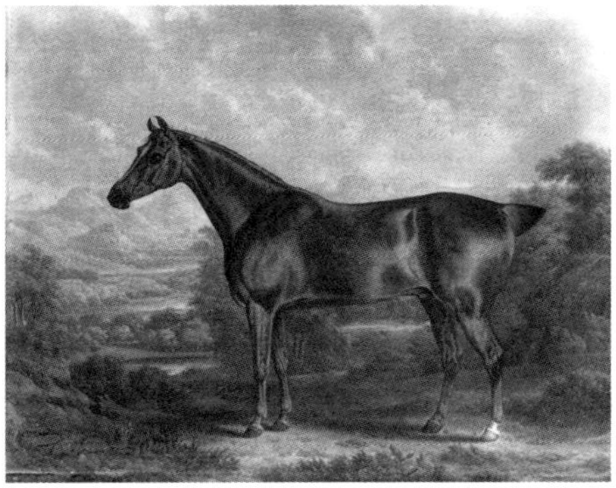

WAG 2347

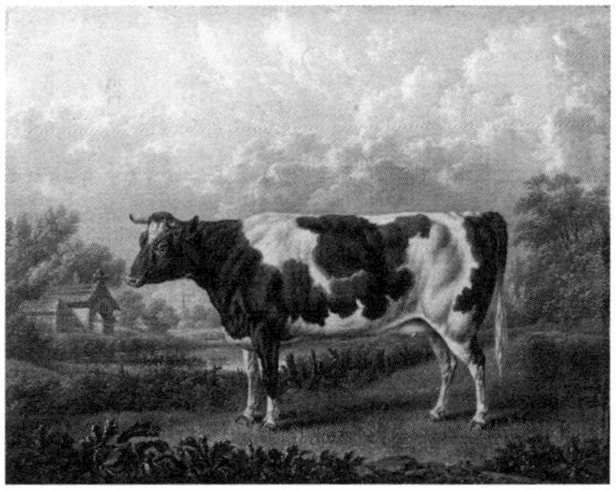

WAG 9571

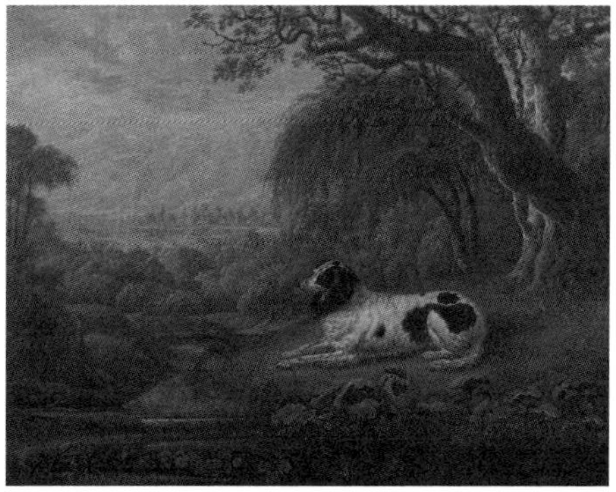

WAG 9576

PROVENANCE

...Walter Stone by 1934;[1] Mary Stone Bequest 1944.

EXHIBITIONS

Sporting Pictures from the Walter Stone Collection Bluecoat Gallery, Liverpool 1946 (39); *A Selection of Sporting Pictures from the Walter Stone Collection* Bluecoat Gallery, Liverpool 1953 (28); *The Taste of Yesterday* Walker Art Gallery 1970 (17); *Charles Towne of Liverpool 1763–1840* Walker Art Gallery 1971 (20).

REFERENCE

1. *The Walter Stone Collection of Sporting Pictures at Whitton Hall, Westbury, Shropshire* (privately printed, 1938) p. 31 (cat. 52). An inscription *GARSON* in graphite along one of the inner stretcher members may be the name of a previous owner. An illegible nineteenth-century London frame-maker's label is also present on the reverse of the frame.

Prize Cow in a Landscape

WAG 9571
oil on canvas, 23 × 28.5 cm
signed and dated: *C. Towne/1828*
(bottom right)
date: 1828

Judging by WAG 9571's small size and by the nature of the buildings in the background – a cottage, a chapel and a church, rather than a country house – Towne's patron was a man of relatively modest social standing, perhaps the farmer that bred the animal. The cow is probably a young Ayrshire.[1] The paint surface of WAG 9571 has been flattened in re-lining; the weave pattern of the canvas is prominent and there are numerous tiny losses of paint in the sky which reveal the brown ground beneath.

PROVENANCE

...F. C. Danson; by descent to Col. J. R. Danson;[2] his bequest 1979.

EXHIBITION

Danson Collection of Paintings by Charles Towne Walker Art Gallery 1977 (47).

NOTES

1. Ayrshires are typically mottled red and white and their markings often have jagged edges, as in WAG 9571 (www.moocow.com/info/breeds [of cows], accessed 30 June 2008).
2. The remains of a ms label on the reverse of WAG 9571 read *See Animal Painters / Gilbey / Vol. III p. 251, No. 5*, a reference to Sir Walter Gilbey: *Animal Painters of England from the Year 1600* 3 vols (London, 1900–11) vol. 3 (second series) p. 251, no. 5 on the list of works in the possession of F. C. Danson, where, however, it is dated to 1815.

Black and White Spaniel in a Landscape

WAG 9576
oil on canvas, 31 × 41.5 cm
signed and dated: *C. Towne /1828*
(bottom left)
date: 1828

Towne's last style, characterised by its fussy depiction of foliage and landscape detail, is epitomised in this work. The identity of the patron is unknown, but from the background, he or she may have been from the Lake District.[1]

PROVENANCE

...Col. J. R. Danson; his bequest 1979.

EXHIBITION

Danson Collection of Paintings by Charles Towne Walker Art Gallery 1977 (46).

REFERENCE

1. The character of the landscape is reminiscent, without being an accurate representation of, the area around Friar's Crag at the head of Derwentwater.

Parson's Jack Russell Terrier[1]

WAG 9578
oil on canvas, 23 × 28 cm
signed and dated: *C Towne/1828*
(bottom left centre)
date: 1828

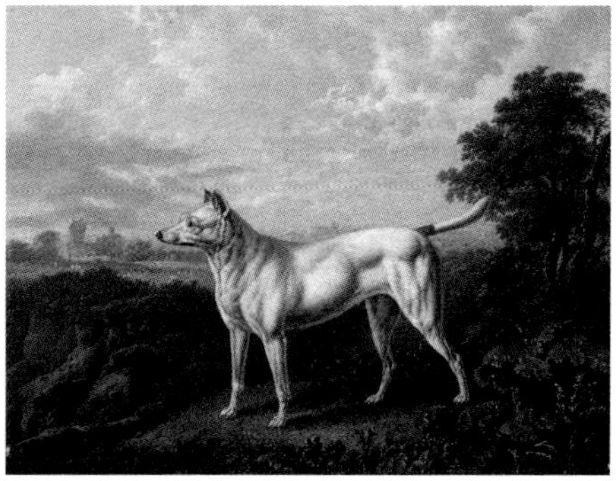

WAG 9578

In contrast to WAG 9579–83 (below), this appears to be a commissioned work: a view of the patron's seat is included in the background. Neither patron nor animal is identified.

PROVENANCE
...Col. J. R. Danson; his bequest 1979.

EXHIBITION
Danson Collection of Paintings by Charles Towne Walker Art Gallery 1977 (48).

REFERENCE
1. The breed was identified by Jenny Sneddon, Liverpool John Moores University, *verbally*, June 2005.

Jack Russell Terrier[1]

WAG 9579
oil on mahogany panel, 13.5 × 18 cm
date: unknown, perhaps 1828–30

The work is inscribed at bottom left *Charles Towne / 1815* in an uncharacteristic and suspect style.[2] However, the painting itself appears authentic.[3] It is unclear whether it forms part of the same group as WAG 9580–83 (below). The panel on which it is painted is larger than those works and is also about 1 cm thicker, yet it is not out of the question that the work was designed to form a decorative scheme with them, whether a generic one or for a specific location in a particular patron's house. Equally possibly, it may have been part of a different, larger set of dogs, although if so, it has been separated from its companions.

On the view that the inscribed date *1815* is a later addition and invented, it may be proposed on grounds of style that WAG 9579 is a late work, dating from the later 1820s or early 1830s.

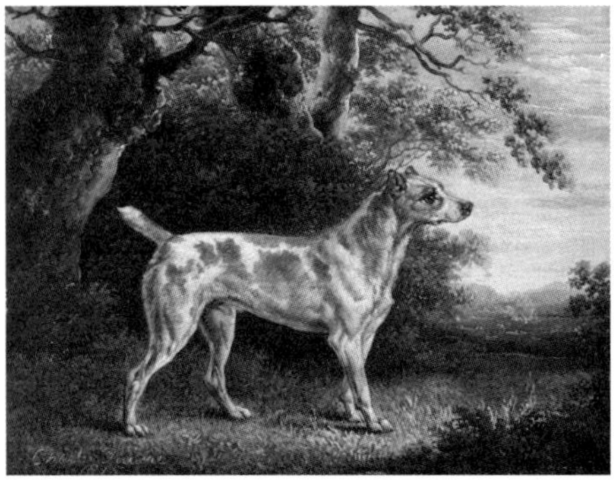

WAG 9579

PROVENANCE
...Col. J. R. Danson; his bequest 1979.

EXHIBITION
Danson Collection of Paintings by Charles Towne Walker Art Gallery 1977 (22).

NOTES
1. The breed was identified by Jenny Sneddon, Liverpool John Moores University, *verbally*, June 2005.
2. The inscription has apparently been made by the tip of the brush handle being drawn through the paint surface to reveal the lighter ground beneath.
3. Because of doubts over the signature WAG 9579 was attributed to 'manner of Charles Towne' in *CIC*, p. 283.

Bull Terrier

WAG 9580
oil on mahogany panel, 8 × 10.5 cm
signed: *C.T.* (lower left)

Greyhound

WAG 9581
oil on mahogany panel, 8 × 10 cm
signed: *C.T.* (lower right)

Cocker Spaniel

WAG 9582
oil on mahogany panel, 8.5 × 10.5 cm
signed: *C.T.* [twice] (bottom right)

Wire-haired Terrier

WAG 9583
oil on mahogany panel, 8.5 × 10 cm
signed *C.T. / P.* (lower right)
date: unknown, perhaps 1828–30

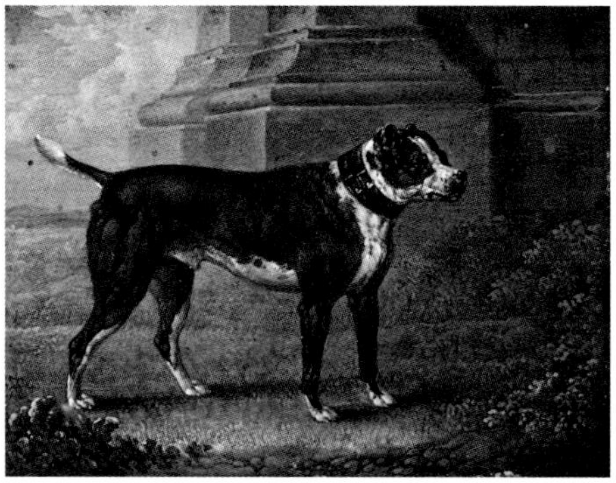

WAG 9580

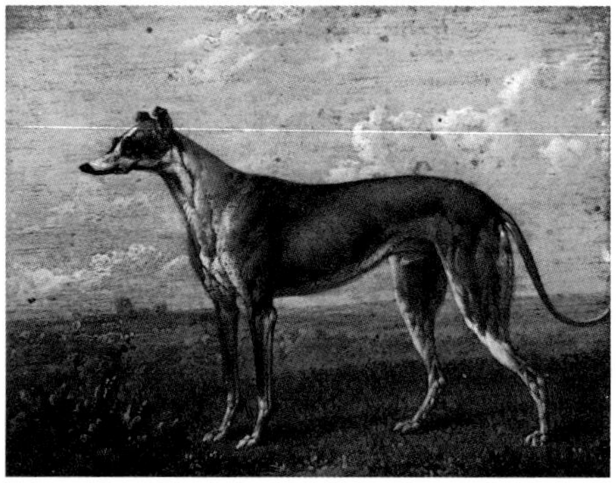

WAG 9581

These four works appear to have been painted as a set. They are (effectively) the same size, and are painted on the same type of support, a rough mahogany panel approximately 7.5 mm thick, but occasionally tapering to a lesser thickness. Each work is signed, and they are in matching frames. Their delicacy and detail suggests they are late works: perhaps, to judge from stylistic comparison with WAG 9578, from around 1828–30.[1]

There is no evidence to show that these paintings were commissioned by a single owner as portraits of individual dogs, and the conception of the set indicates otherwise: that they are typological portraits aimed for sale to generic dog lovers. Each dog is portrayed in a setting appropriate to his character: the bull terrier guards an imposing edifice; the greyhound is placed in a flat, open expanse ideal for running in; the spaniel

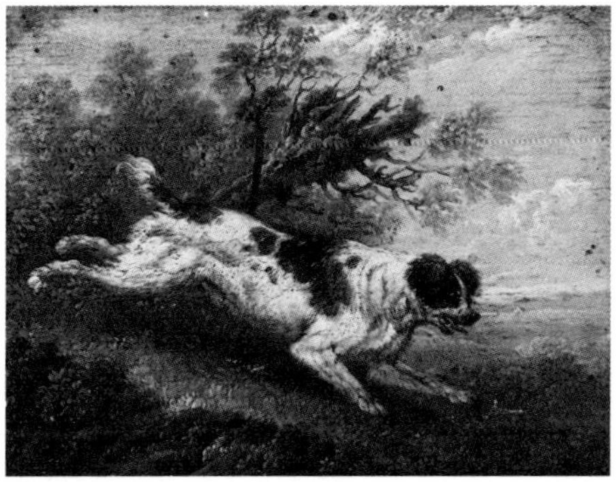

WAG 9582

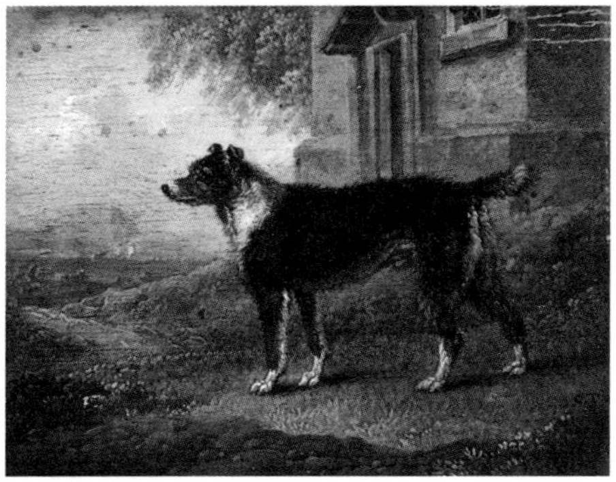

WAG 9583

is in hunting terrain; the wire-haired terrier stands outside a cottage door. They may have been undertaken as stock in trade, to show prospective clients in the studio.

PROVENANCE

...Col. J. R. Danson;[2] his bequest 1979.

EXHIBITION

Danson Collection of Paintings by Charles Towne Walker Art Gallery 1977 (23–26).

NOTES

1. Following the view taken that the stylistically related WAG 9579, WAG 9580–83 were attributed to 'manner of Charles Towne' in *CIC*, p. 283.
2. Inscriptions on the reverse of the frames, which to judge from their apparent age were made by or for Danson, are as follows: (WAG 9580) label (ink) *22*; chalk mss *18* and *16*; (WAG 9581) label (ink) 34; chalk ms [illegible]; pencil ms *No 12 right on* [? *of*] *Entrance*; (WAG 9582) label (ink) *32*; chalk ms *15*; (WAG 9583) label (ink) *18*; chalk ms *13*; pencil ms *26*.

Colonel Bolton Reviewing Volunteers

WAG 9547
oil on canvas, 87.5 × 118 cm
date: unknown, perhaps 1828–30

In 1797 the Liverpool merchant John Bolton (for whom see WAG 3059, pp. 4–5) contributed £500 to the government scheme to defend Britain against French invasion and in 1803 he raised and equipped 800 men – 'Bolton's Invincibles' – for the First Battalion of Liverpool Volunteers, a regiment which he commanded until 1806, when it was disbanded. James Aspinall later described them

as fine and well-disciplined a body of men as ever mounted guard in St. James's or Buckingham Palace. In what awe we used to stand of the tall, upright and somewhat prim and starched old Colonel as mounted on his favourite white charger he marched, band playing, colours flying, at the head of his men, round and round Mosslake fields looking, both he and they, defiance at the world in general and Napoleon and Ney and Soult and Lannes and Davouse and Murat and all the rest of the frog eaters in particular...[1]

In 1808 Bolton retired to live in the Lake District, where he became a pillar of local society and a friend of Wordsworth. In the foreground of WAG 9547 Col. Bolton is shown mounted on a grey horse in the uniform of commanding officer of his 'Invincibles', but he also appears as a tiny figure in the background actually reviewing his battalion. This counter-realistic device, together with the mountainous scenery, indicates that WAG 9547 does not date, as has been supposed, from the years 1803–06,[2] but must have been commissioned from Towne many years afterwards, when Bolton was living on his memories. Stylistically WAG 9547 belongs to Towne's last phase, distinguished by his highly detailed depiction of foliage and other natural forms, and by his abandonment of warm 'Old Master' tonalities for fresher colours. It can perhaps be dated to around 1828–30.[3] The lifelike portrayals of Bolton himself and his groom are unusual for Towne. Whether they were done from the life or, as seems more likely, from earlier portraits or miniatures, they testify to the special effort the artist has put into the work.

The background of WAG 9547 has been extensively retouched, and there are many areas of discolouration in the landscape and the sky.

PROVENANCE

Presumably commissioned by the sitter; passed to relations of his wife and by descent to T. Alfred Fletcher of Allerton Hall, Liverpool; Christie 23 June 1922 (156);[4] bt. Gooden & Fox (£33.12s.0d.);[5] ...Col. J. R. Danson; his bequest 1979.

EXHIBITION

Danson Collection of Paintings by Charles Towne Walker Art Gallery 1977 (4).

NOTES

1. *Liverpool a Few Years Since* by an Old Stager, quoted by G. W. Mathews: 'John Bolton, a Liverpool Merchant 1756–1837', *Transactions of the Historic Society of Lancashire and Cheshire [for the Year 1941]* vol. 93 (1942), p. 100.
2. When exhibited in 1977 WAG 9547 was catalogued as no. 4 in a chronological treatment of the works, between paintings of 1797 and 1808.
3. 1828 would have been the 25th anniversary of the formation of 'Bolton's Invincibles'.
4. Christie's stencil 469 *DN* on the stretcher.
5. An unsourced note in gallery files suggests that the work passed from a collection in Oxton, Birkenhead, to the Boydell Galleries, Liverpool in about 1957, and was acquired from them by Col. Danson.

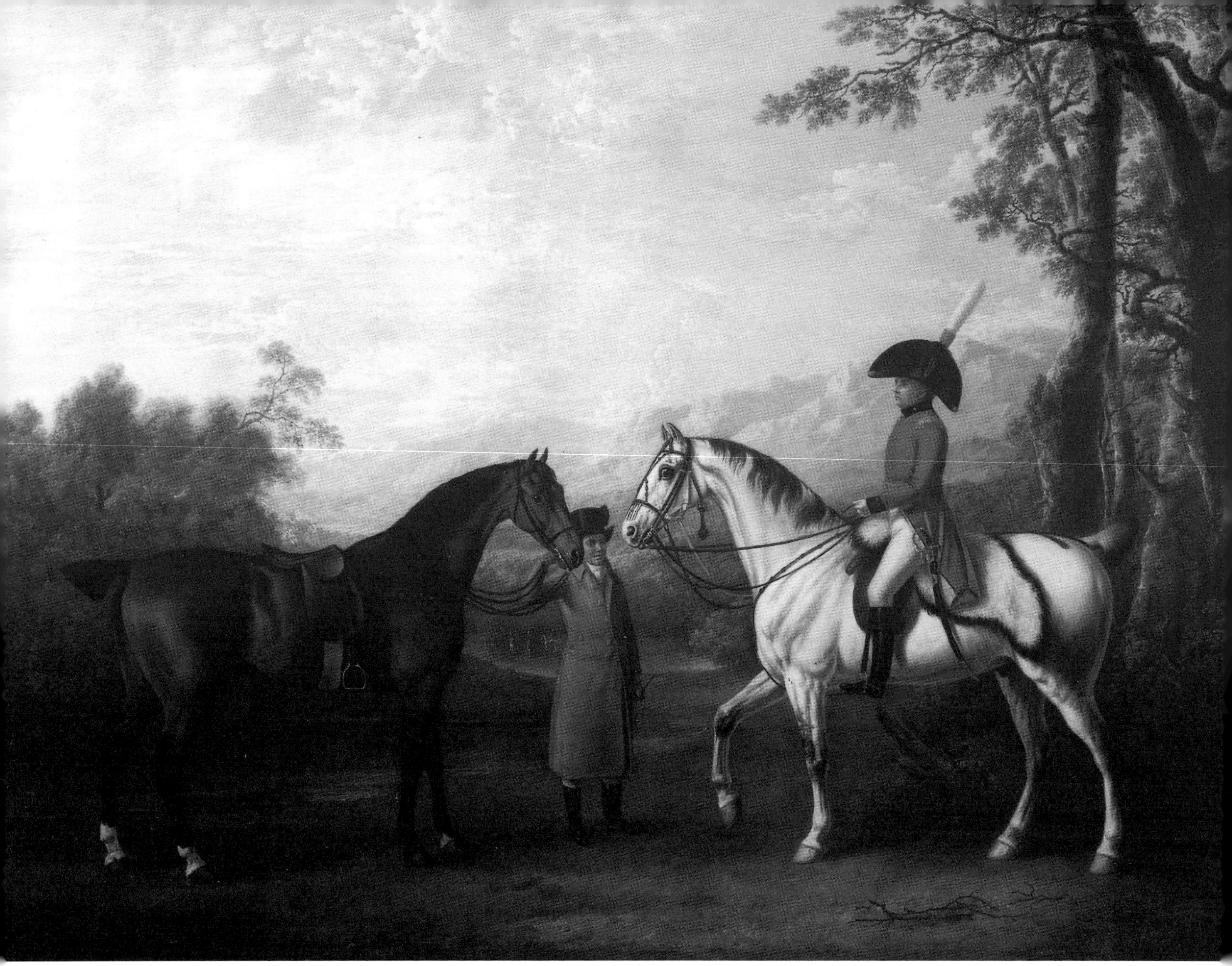

WAG 9547

The Intruder

WAG 1164
oil on canvas, 61 × 71.5 cm
signed and dated: *C. Towne 1829*
(bottom right)
date: 1829

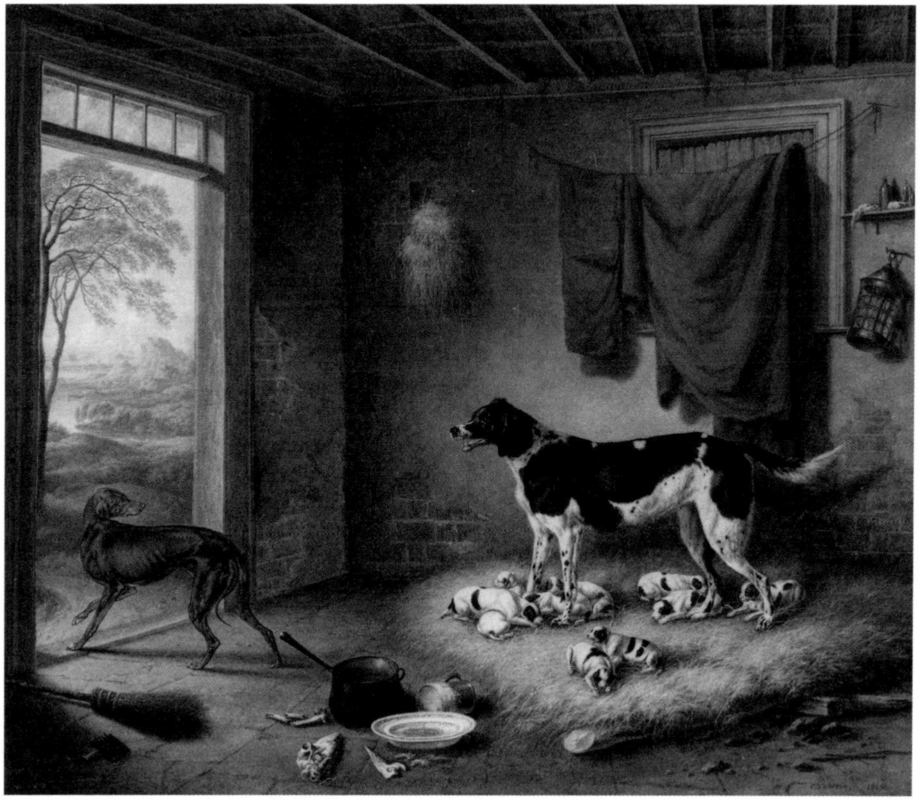

WAG 1164

According to a label on the back of the stretcher, WAG 1164 was painted for Henry Harrison of 'Mostyn', Aigburth.[1] The son of William Harrison, cotton merchant of Manchester, Henry (1795–1871) came to Liverpool to join his older cousin Richard in 1812 as partner in the business of Harrison, Arnold and Latham (later Harrisons and Latham), 3 George's Dock Gates, and from 1851 at Bank Chambers, 3 Cook Street, Liverpool. He is is recorded in Liverpool street directories as 'merchant, Aigburth' between 1825 and 1860, in succession to Richard who is similarly listed in 1816 and 1821. After a period working in Brazil (whence his cousins Richard and Arnold had long imported orchids to Liverpool) he returned to England and married Mary Rosina Sandbach, 20 years younger than himself, in 1835. The couple moved to the grand house of 'Holmefield' in Aigburth, where they brought up 11 children. Business reverses from the mid-1850s forced Henry Harrison to sell 'Holmefield' and move to a smaller home, 'Mostyn', where street directories record him from 1865 until the year of his death.[2]

It seems very likely that the dogs portrayed in WAG 1164 were Harrison's own. According to family tradition he was very fond of dogs[3] and called this painting *Sal and Her Puppies*.[4] Harrison had known Towne's work for some years, having almost certainly commissioned from him a large painting – one of Towne's masterpieces – of his father's horses in 1814 (see WAG 6107, pp. 206–7). The unusual subject of a confrontation between two bitches, one guarding her ten puppies, is depicted with a literalism that suggests Towne was commissioned to record a recent happening, and the riverside setting visible outside the stable door, though fanciful in the extreme as a depiction of the bank of the Mersey at Aigburth, is generally appropriate to the location of Harrison's home (at that time, when he was still a bachelor, Aigburth Hall). In 1957 WAG 1164 was noted as being in poor condition with substantial flaking to the lower centre; it was relined and restored the following year.[5]

PROVENANCE

Henry Harrison; his son, Sandbach Percy Harrison (1847–1910); his bequest, following a life interest to his youngest sister, 1929.[6]

EXHIBITIONS

Charles Towne of Liverpool 1763–1840 Walker Art Gallery 1971 (21); *British Sporting Paintings 1650–1850* Hayward Gallery, London and tour 1974–75 (123).

NOTES

1. The label reads, in full, *The picture was painted for Mr Henry Harrison of Mostyn, Aigburth and left to his son, Mr S. Percy Harrison. The latter directed that on the death of his last surviving sister the picture should be offered to the Walker Art Gallery.* It must date from the 1860s (see main text).
2. MPPP, p. 207; and see especially David Harrison: *The Harrisons of Bankfield 1500–2006* (West Horsley, 2006) pp. 104ff.
3. Harrison, *op. cit.*, p. 119.
4. Harrison, *op. cit.*, p. 106; also his *email*, 31 December 2002, gallery files.
5. Condition note in gallery files.
6. Sandbach Percy Harrison's youngest sister Evelyn Sara (b. 1857) died in 1920; from her the painting evidently passed to their sister Jessie (b. 1842) who died in 1929.

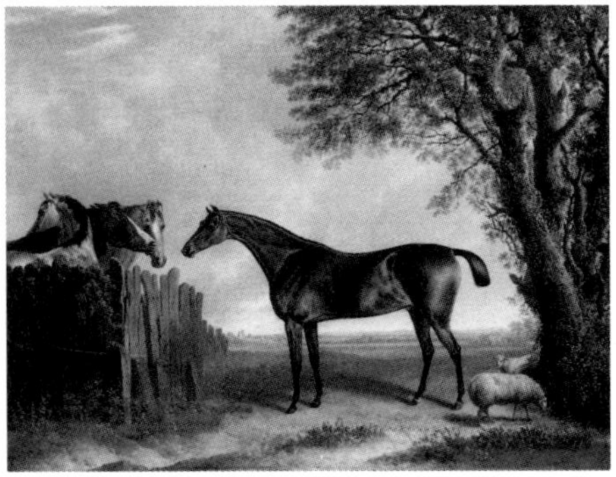

WAG 9542

Mr Jackson's 'Hazard'

WAG 9542
oil on canvas, 71 × 91.5 cm
signed and dated: *C. Towne/1830*
(on cross bar of fence at left)
date: 1830

The racehorse Hazard won five victories in 1829: at the Liverpool spring meeting, the Maiden Plate at Chester in May, and three sweepstakes, at Derby and Stourbridge in August and Walsall in September.[1] His owner has not been identified. The motif of the portrayed horse leaning over a fence to commune with others was a favourite with Towne; see also WAG 9816, dated 1818 (p. 211).

PROVENANCE

...Col. J. R. Danson; his bequest 1979.

EXHIBITION

Danson Collection of Paintings by Charles Towne Walker Art Gallery 1977 (50).

REFERENCE

1. This information is given on a typescript label on the reverse.

The Home Park Windsor with Grey Mare in the Foreground

WAG 9527
oil on canvas, 56 × 72.5 cm
signed and dated: *C. Towne/1830*
(left of horse)
date: 1830

From the care with which it is executed, WAG 9527 appears to be an important commission, possibly from a member of the Royal Household based at Windsor Castle.[1] The mare portrayed in the foreground is almost certainly the same animal as appears in the left middle ground drawing a carriage in which a well-dressed couple, the woman holding a parasol, are taking a drive. These are presumably Towne's patrons. The lodge visible through the trees behind them, which has not been identified, may well be their house and they are accompanied on their excursion by their dog (painted somewhat out of proportion). The depiction of the distant north terrace of Windsor Castle, seen from the Home Park, is relatively accurate. Whether or not Towne travelled to Windsor and the work was based on studies from the life, WAG 9527 is a measure of Towne's reputation as a sporting artist by the end of the 1820s.

PROVENANCE

...F. C. Danson 1911;[2] by descent to Col. J. R. Danson; his bequest 1979.

EXHIBITION

Danson Collection of Paintings by Charles Towne Walker Art Gallery 1977 (51).[3]

NOTES

1. The frame of WAG 9527, which must be the original, is decorated at the centre of the inside bar on all four sides with a small design of Prince of Wales's feathers. In 1830 there was no Prince of Wales but it is not out of the question that Towne's patron had been a member of George IV's household while he was Prince of Wales before ascending the throne in 1820.
2. Listed as in Danson's ownership by Sir Walter

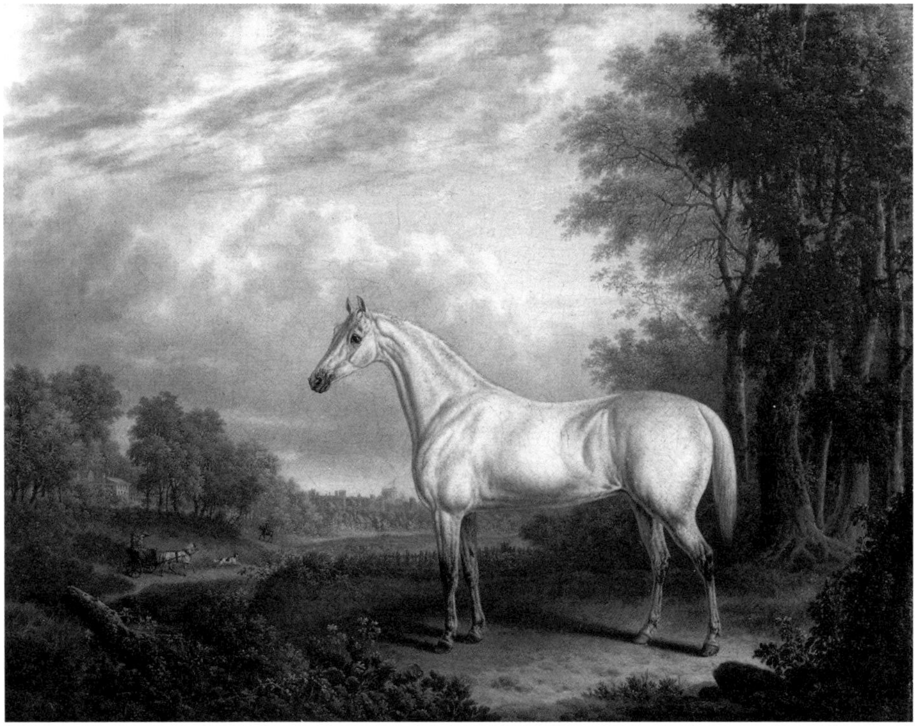

WAG 9527

Gilbey: *Animal Painters of England from the Year 1600* 3 vols (London, 1900–11) vol. 3 (second series) p. 251 (no. 6). A label on the reverse of the stretcher inscribed *72 The Home Park Windsor with Portrait of a Horse in the Foreground. A most admirable and carefully studied composition in this artist's well-known style* appears to reproduce an entry in an unidentified earlier sale or exhibition catalogue.
3. The illustration of WAG 9527 in the exhibition catalogue has lopped off about a quarter of the composition at the left.

Bay Horse in a Landscape with Farm Buildings

WAG 9585
oil on canvas,[1] 43.5 × 51 cm
signed and dated: *C. Towne 1830*
(bottom right)
date: 1830

The mountainous landscape background suggests Towne's patron was from North Wales or the Lake District, while the presence of farm cottages rather than a castle or substantial country house may imply that he was a man of fairly modest means.

PROVENANCE

...Grindley & Palmer Liverpool;[2] from whom bt. by Col. J. R. Danson 30 June 1934;[3] his bequest 1979.

EXHIBITION

Danson Collection of Paintings by Charles Towne Walker Art Gallery 1977 (49).

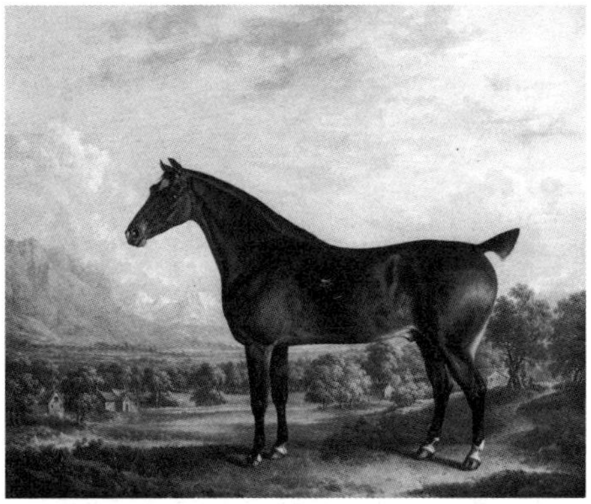

WAG 9585

NOTES

1. Canvas stamp of Rowney & Co. Rathbone Place.
2. Ms framing instructions in pencil while the work was with Grindley & Palmer are on the reverse of the frame.
3. Receipt in *Danson Papers*, NML Archives, VII.5.2.

Landscape with York Minster

WAG 9549
oil on canvas, 33.5 × 46 cm

Landscape with Bolton Abbey

WAG 9550
oil on canvas, 33.5 × 46 cm
signed and dated: *C. Towne 1831*
(on rocks at left)
date: 1831

These pictures form a pair. The depictions of both buildings are inexact and their surroundings are wholly fictitious. The traditional title of WAG 9550 has been retained, although another version of the work is titled *Melrose Abbey.*[1] Both works were clearly intended as decorative and Towne may well have vested at least as much importance in the contrasted treatments of cow herding in the pictures' foregrounds.

Discoloured overpaint is visible in the skies of both works but is particularly evident in WAG 9549.

PROVENANCE

...Lady Danson by 1930;[2] by descent to Col. J. R. Danson;[3] his bequest 1979.

EXHIBITION

Danson Collection of Paintings by Charles Towne Walker Art Gallery 1977 (53) [WAG 9549] and (52) [WAG 9550].

NOTES

1. Variants of WAG 9550 include the *Landscape with a Ruined Abbey*, 32.5 × 46 cm, sold at Christie 2 February 1962 (95); what seems to be the same picture, recorded as signed and dated 1824, was at Christie 20 June 1975 (15) and apparently again, cut down to 16 × 46 cm, at Sotheby 12 March 1986 (104); also *A Dark Bay Hunter with Melrose Abbey beyond*, sold Christie 21 November 1986 (33).

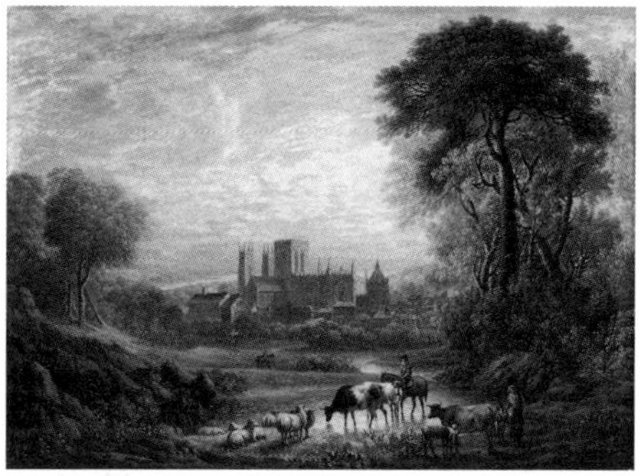

WAG 9549

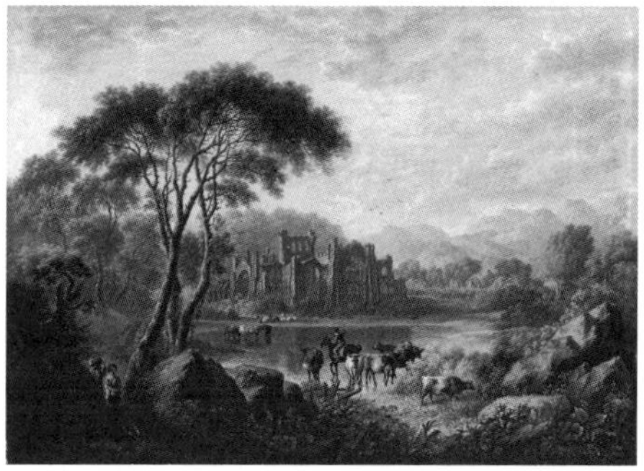

WAG 9550

2. See W. Shaw Sparrow: 'Charles Towne: The Last Phase', *Connoisseur*, vol. 86 (August 1930), p. 97 (pl. IV) for WAG 9550's presence in Lady Danson's collection by that date. Presumably WAG 9549 and WAG 9550 have always been together.
3. WAG 9549 bears the label of A. and J. Polak; both WAG 9549 and WAG 9550 bear the labels of the Boydell Galleries, Liverpool.

The Monarch of Pasture Land

WAG 9566
oil on canvas, 91.5 × 112 cm
signed and dated: *Chas. Towne/ Pinxit/1831*
(lower right on grass, near cattle)
date: 1831

The date on WAG 9566 has been variously read as 1821,[1] 1824[2] and 1831.[3] On stylistic grounds the last of these has claims to preference: the work exhibits numerous features of the artist's late manner, with its lighter tonality and highly detailed

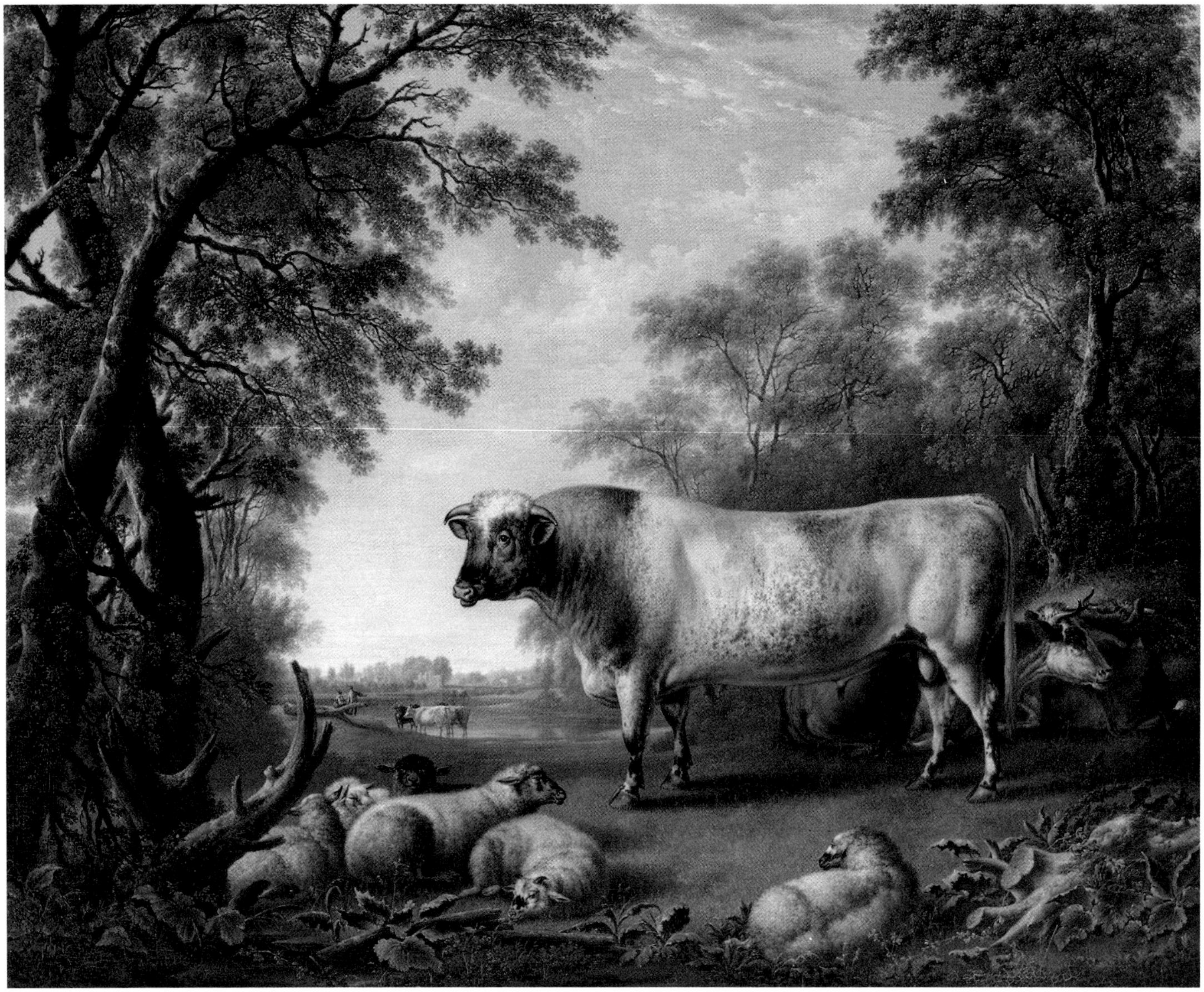

WAG 9566

depiction of foliage. It also seems significant that Towne's three exhibits at the 1831 Royal Manchester Institution were all titled *Landscape and Cattle*.[4]

The work stands in the tradition of commissioned portraits of huge cattle that were triumphs of the breeder's skill and of agricultural progress. Towne's mentor, George Stubbs, had made a memorable contribution to the genre with his *Lincolnshire Ox* – see pp. 173–7 – which was well known from the print by George Townly Stubbs. The present beast has been identified as a brindled shorthorn bull[5] and its owner, Towne's presumed patron, is likely to be the right-hand of the two gentlemen in the background who is pointing out to his companion further cattle in his herd. No information about his identity has emerged.

PROVENANCE

...Mr Phillips of Liverpool 1911;[6] by descent to his widow; from whom bt. before 1926 by F. C. Danson;[7] by descent to Col. J. R. Danson; his bequest 1979.

EXHIBITION

Danson Collection of Paintings by Charles Towne Walker Art Gallery 1977 (40).

NOTES

1. 1821 is given on the inventory card, gallery files; and in CIC, p. 277.
2. *1824* is inscribed on the frame of WAG 9566. This date was given by W. Shaw Sparrow, 'Charles

Towne of Liverpool: His Youth', *Connoisseur* vol. 85 (May 1930) p. 291, and was followed in the catalogue of the 1977 exhibition.
3. As read by the present compiler.
4. Cats. 146, 152 and 300; Towne exhibited a further *Landscape with Cattle* at the Royal Manchester Institution in 1832 (cat. 399).
5. Shaw Sparrow, *loc. cit.*
6. Sir Walter Gilbey: *Animal Painters of England from the Year 1600* 3 vols (London, 1900–11) vol. 3 (second series) p. 253 (no. 1).
7. Ms label on the reverse of WAG 9566 inscribed *Purchased by F.C.D. from Mrs. Phillips.* Danson died in 1926 and Shaw Sparrow, *loc. cit.*, recorded the work in Lady Danson's possession.

Billy – A Favourite Horse of James Dearden Esq.

WAG 9529
oil on canvas, 56.5 × 69.5 cm
signed and dated: *C. Towne 1832*
(left edge below fence)
date: 1832

Labels on the reverse of WAG 9529 identify the horse as Billy, a grey owned by James Dearden[1] and give details of the horse's ancestry.[2] This horse is not to be confused with Old Billy, the celebrated barge-horse who worked on the Manchester and Irwell Navigation and lived to the age of 63, whom Towne painted several times.[3] James Dearden was a member of a Rochdale family. His father, enriched by a seam of coal on land whose ownership was disputed with Lord Byron, in 1823 bought the manor of Rochdale from the Byron family. James himself was a barrister, moving to Dearden Castle outside Caernarvon where he induged his interest in archaeology and became a fellow of the Society of Antiquaries. A portrait of his daughters by John Simpson was exhibited at the Royal Academy in 1839. He died in 1862.[4] In the background Towne appropriately includes a view of Caernarvon Castle and behind it a mountain no doubt meant to represent Snowdon. The work is carefully observed – even down to Billy's flea-bites – and is highly finished.

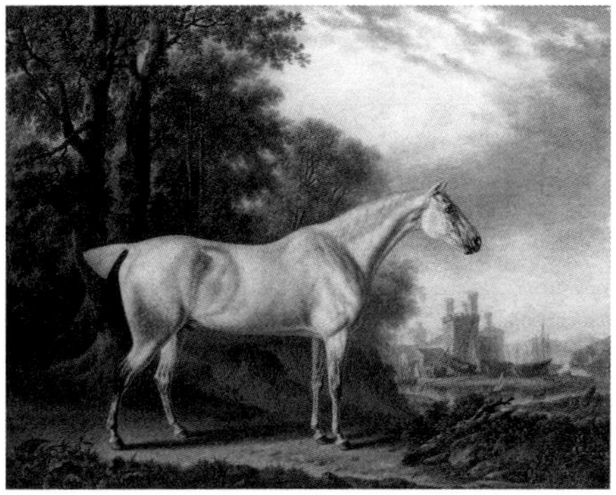

WAG 9529

PROVENANCE
James Dearden; by descent to his grandson J. Griffith Dearden of Walcot Park Stamford and the Manor House, Rochdale; Christie 27 February 1914 (116); bt. Permain (14 gns.); ...Lady Danson by 1930;[5] by descent to Col. J. R. Danson; his bequest 1979.

EXHIBITION
Danson Collection of Paintings by Charles Towne Walker Art Gallery 1977 (54).

NOTES
1. Ms label: *1832 November this picture of my / James Dearden / old grey Horse Billy was painted by Towne of Liverpool J.D.*
2. Ms label: *Billy's sire was Sir Percy [?] / Dimsdale dam by Adonis / Grandam by Enchanter / Greatgrandam by Royal Slave.*
3. One, described as Towne's first portrait of him and as dating from 1822, the year of Old Billy's death, was reproduced in *Country Life* (8 December 1955) p. 1385. Another small portrait, in which Billy is identically posed but against a different canal background, and dated 1823, is now in the Yale Center for British Art, New Haven; see Judy Egerton: *British Sporting and Animal Paintings 1665–1867: The Paul Mellon Collection* (London, 1978) p. 175.
4. See W. Farrer and J. Brownbill, eds: *Victoria County History: A History of the County of Lancaster Volume* 5 (London, 1911) p. 191 and nn. 45–46; Edward Parry: *Cambrian Mirror, or a New Tourist Companion through North Wales* (2nd edn, London, 1846, p. 205); for Simpson's portrait see *GrRA*, vol. 7, p. 131.
5. Reproduced as in Lady Danson's collection by W. Shaw Sparrow: 'Charles Towne: the Last Phase', *Connoisseur* vol. 86 (August 1930) p. 95.

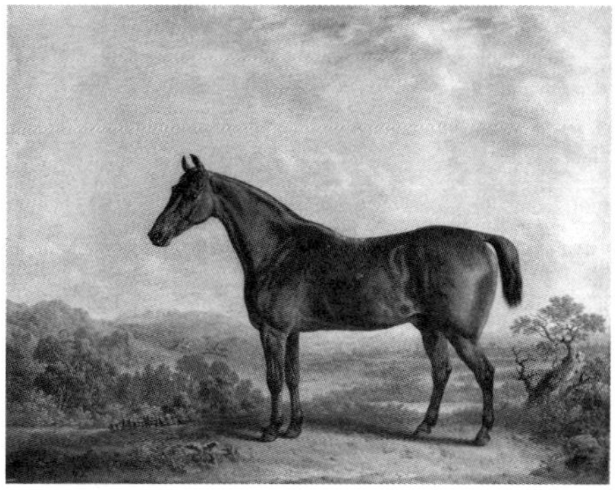

WAG 9535

Chestnut Horse in a Landscape with a Fox Hunt

WAG 9535
oil on canvas, 51 × 64 cm
signed and dated: *C. Towne, 1833*
(bottom left)
date: 1833

The work doubles as a portrait of the unidentified patron's favourite horse and a record of his involvement with a local hunt. Towne has miscalculated the scale of the distant figures of the huntsmen, which loom over the trees in front of them.

PROVENANCE
...C. B. Morgan, Blakemore, Sandiway, Cheshire; Christie 7 December 1934 (148);[1] bt. in; ...Col. J. R. Danson; his bequest 1979.

EXHIBITION
Danson Collection of Paintings by Charles Towne Walker Art Gallery 1977 (55).

REFERENCE
1. Christie's stencil 75 *FY* on the stretcher.

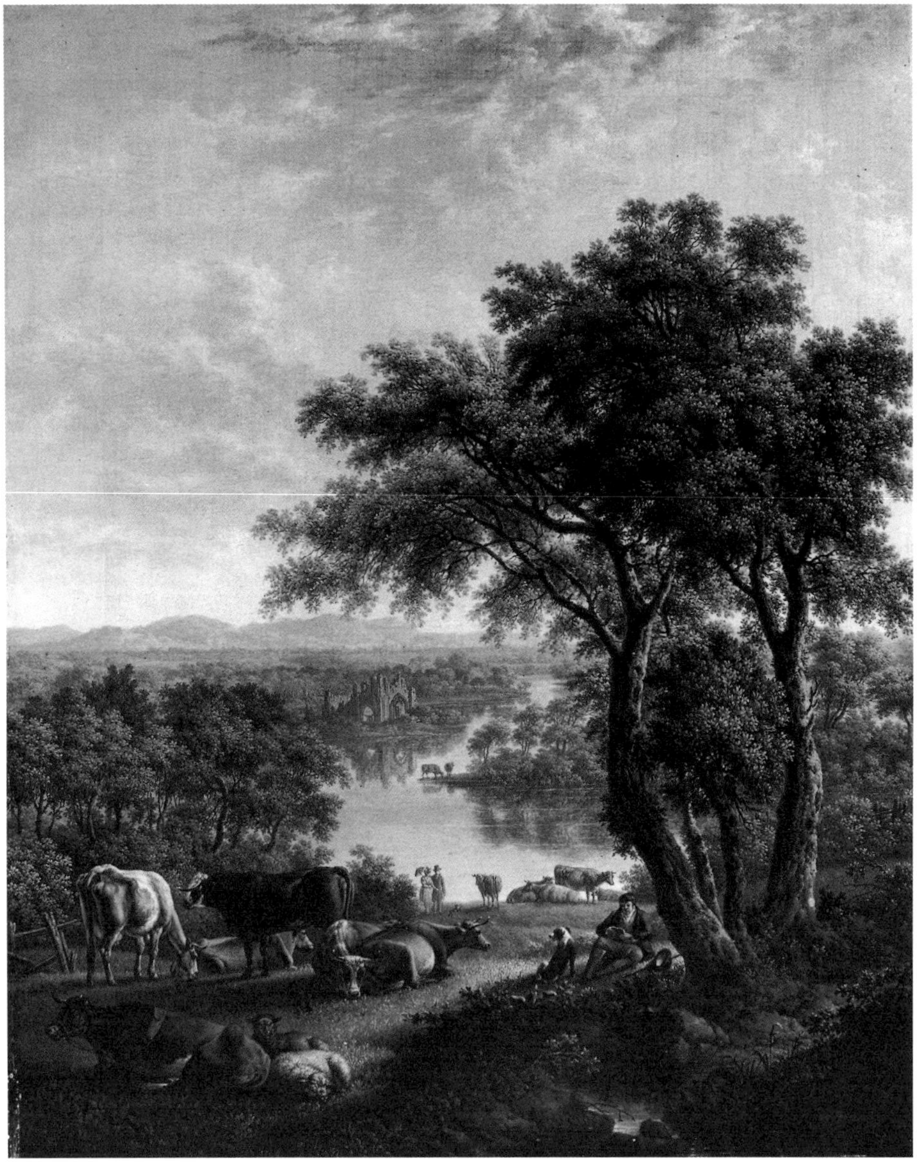

WAG 9564

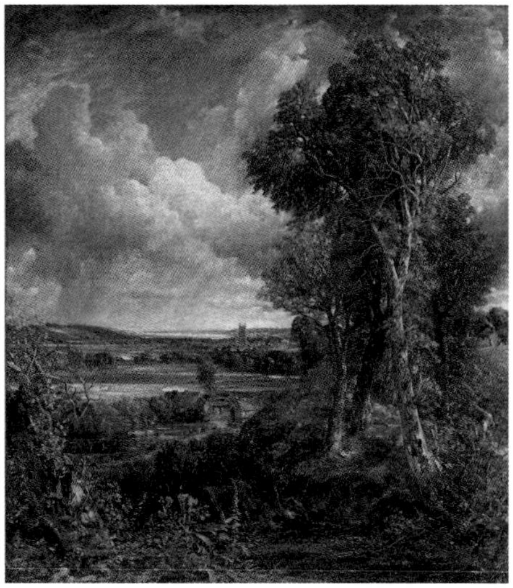

Fig. 94 *Dedham Vale* by John Constable, oil on canvas. © National Galleries of Scotland.

Man Reading under a Tree in a Landscape

WAG 9564
oil on canvas, 65 × 51 cm
signed and dated: *C TOWNE 1833* (bottom left)
date: 1833

Although moderate in scale, WAG 9564 is an ambitious imitation of landscapes by Claude Lorrain. It evokes a poetic and Arcadian mood designed to amplify the central image of the man reading a book in the shade of a tree. This figure has been described as a 'gentleman',[1] but his closeness to his sheepdog and to the other farm animals suggests that he is more probably the factor or estate manager of the more elderly couple who are seen strolling, with their own little dog, in the middle ground. Towne's perhaps deliberate mismanagement of the foreshortening in this area has the effect of making the pasture appear to overhang the riverscape, rather than abut it, increasing the panoramic and epic feel of the work. The landscape appears idealised (the abbey ruins are not identifiable as a real place) and the composition bears sufficient resemblance to Claude Lorrain's *Hagar and the Angel* and its modern offspring, Constable's *Dedham Vale* (National Gallery of Scotland; fig. 94) as to warrant the suggestion that Towne may have recently seen and have been paying homage to one or other of them. Constable's painting had been shown at the Royal Academy in 1828 and the Claude had been on view at the National Gallery in London since 1824.

PROVENANCE

...Agnew about 1850;[2] ...Col. J. R. Danson; his bequest 1979.

EXHIBITION

Danson Collection of Paintings by Charles Towne Walker Art Gallery 1977 (56).

REFERENCE

1. WAG 9564 was titled *Cattle on a Hillside with Gentleman Reading under a Tree; a Ruined Abbey on a River in Distant Valley* at the 1977 exhibition.
2. A label on the reverse of the frame, only partly legible, reads *THOMAS AGNEW / LATE AGNEW & ZANETTI / Carver, Gilder*; the wording and style indicate a date of the mid-nineteenth century.

Mastiff and Terrier in the Drive of a House

WAG 9584
oil on canvas, 51.5 × 64 cm
signed and dated: *Cha.s Towne /1834*
(bottom left)
date: 1834

The unusually large and florid signature, taken in conjunction with the careful depiction of the two dogs, suggests that this is a commission with which Towne took particular trouble. There is no clue to the identity of his patron, but the artist has made a special effort to capture the individual, contrasted personalities of both animals, and there is a strong suggestion that not only are the portraits accurate, but also, unusually, that they were taken on the spot. The background is entirely lacking in the kind of conventional clue that Towne habitually introduced into his animal portraits to convey the social standing and even the locality inhabited by his patron. Here, the view is an anonymous and literal view of the gates and drive of an estate. The smaller dog has been identified as an Airedale terrier.[1]

PROVENANCE

...Col. J. R. Danson;[2] his bequest 1979.

EXHIBITION

Danson Collection of Paintings by Charles Towne Walker Art Gallery 1977 (57).

NOTES

1. Note in gallery files.
2. A Boydell Galleries Liverpool label is on the reverse.

Italian Seaport with Ruined Castle at Sunset, with Cattle and Donkey

WAG 9574
oil on canvas, 17.5 × 46 cm
signed and dated: *C Towne 1835*
(on rock at left)
date: 1835

The conception of this late picture, which pays homage to Claude Lorrain, Carle Vernet and perhaps Richard Wright of Liverpool, is unusual in Towne's *oeuvre*. Another version of the composition is known, the same size but with variations especially in the foreground.[1]

The retouching of a horizontal crack in the sky about 4 cm from the top edge – probably caused by pressure from the upper stretcher member – has discoloured.

PROVENANCE

[? Acquired from the artist by] John Greaves of Salford; Winstanley 4–7 May 1836 (71);[2] ...Boydell Galleries Liverpool; from whom bt. in 1954 by Col. J. R. Danson;[3] his bequest 1979.

EXHIBITION

Danson Collection of Paintings by Charles Towne Walker Art Gallery 1977 (59).

NOTES

1. Sold Christie 17 May 1946 (97); the date on this version was read as *1825*.
2. The work in the Greaves sale was titled *Italian Sea Port with Cattle and Figures in Foreground and Vessels in Distance* and measured 6 × 18 inches; it was sold with a companion the same size: *Landscape with Waterfall and River in the Distance*. Assuming WAG 9574 is the work owned by Greaves, it has become separated from the companion. For other works by Towne in Greaves's collection, see WAG 9532, 9548 and 9553 (pp. 208–9, 214–5).
3. Boydell Galleries' receipt dated 23 May 1954, *Danson Papers*, NML Archives VII.5.2; Boydell's label is on the reverse of the frame.

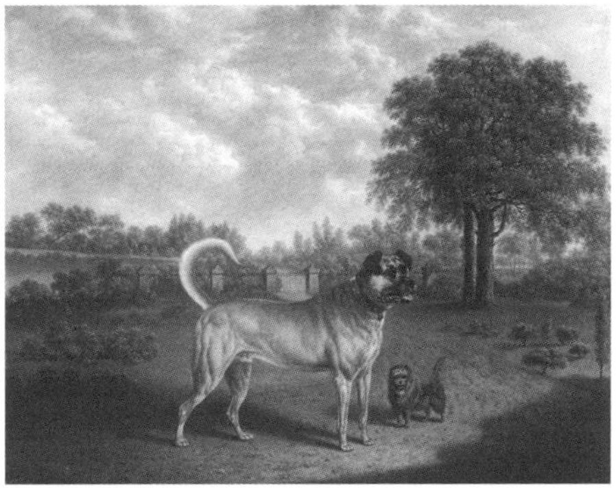

WAG 9584

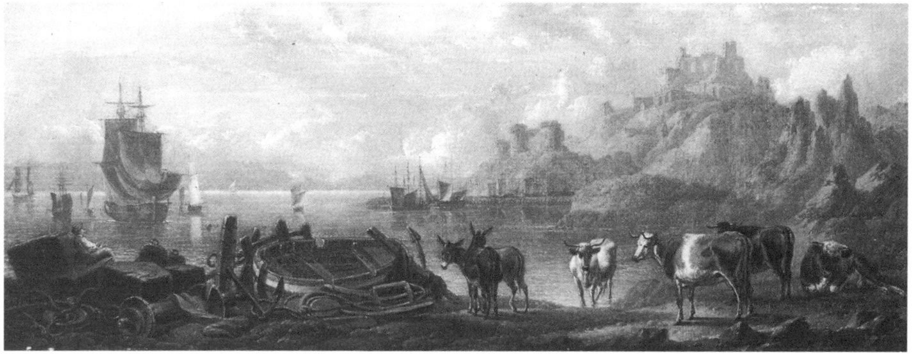

WAG 9574

Bull and Cattle and Herdsman Resting in Valley Pasture

WAG 9561
oil on canvas, 51.5 × 64 cm
signed and dated: *C Towne /1836*
(bottom left)
date: 1836

To judge by the costume of the herdsman reclining on the bank, Towne may have envisaged this as an essay in the manner of Cuyp, although the mountainous background and the walled town in the distance have a German rather than Netherlandish feel. The inscribed date has been variously read as *1835* and *1836*.[1]

PROVENANCE

...F. C. Danson by 1911;[2] by descent to Col. J. R. Danson; his bequest 1979.

EXHIBITION

Danson Collection of Paintings by Charles Towne Walker Art Gallery 1977 (58).

NOTES

1. *1835* is inscribed on the frame; followed by Sir Walter Gilbey: *Animal Painters of England from the Year 1600* 3 vols (London, 1900–11) vol. 3 (second series) p. 251 (no. 2). 1836 is given in the 1977 catalogue; close visual inspection suggests that the last digit is a 6.
2. Gilbey, *loc. cit.*

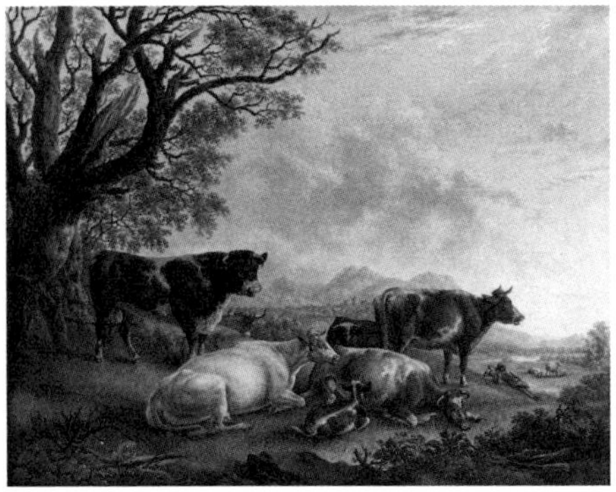

WAG 9561

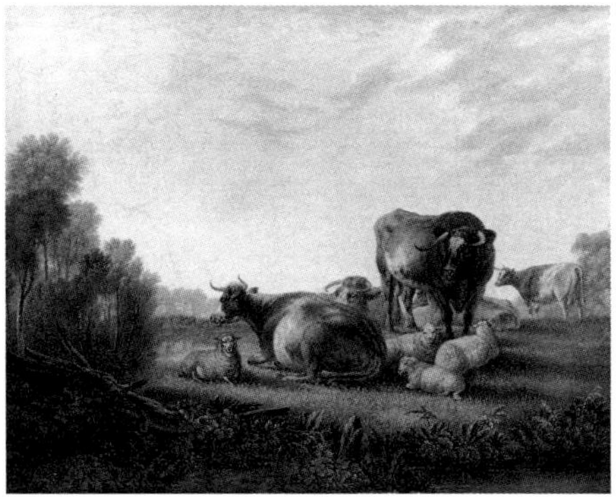

WAG 9560

Cattle and Sheep in a Pasture

WAG 9560
oil on canvas, 39.5 × 48 cm[1]
signed and dated: *C Towne 1837*
(lower left)
date: 1837

One of Towne's last works, WAG 9560 is painted in his typically detailed late style, with an extraordinary close focus on the individual shrubs in the foreground. The open composition and strong warm light suggests Towne's awareness of the growing reputation of Thomas Sidney Cooper. The patron is unknown but the palatial house in the background suggests he was a person of consequence.

PROVENANCE

...Col. J. R. Danson; his bequest 1979.

EXHIBITION

Danson Collection of Paintings by Charles Towne Walker Art Gallery 1977 (60).

NOTES

1. Framer's label of Grindley & Palmer, Liverpool, on the stretcher bar.

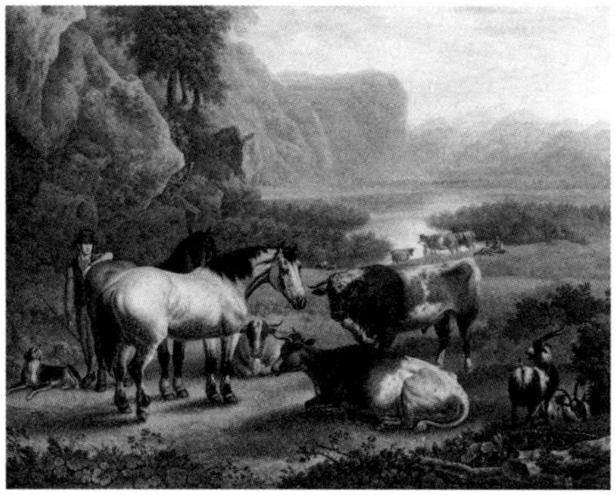

WAG 9543

Mountain Landscape with Horses, Cattle and Goats

WAG 9543
oil on canvas, 72 × 86.5 cm
signed and dated: *C. TOWNE/1838*
(bottom left)
date: 1838

This is the latest-dated painting by the artist in the collection. It shows no serious falling-off in quality despite the fact that by 1838, Towne was suffering seriously from the dropsy that killed him two years later. The background may be intended as a view of Derwentwater from Keswick, to judge from the landscape forms.

PROVENANCE

...Boydell Galleries Liverpool; from whom bt. (£45) by Col. J. R. Danson 8 July 1953;[1] his bequest 1979.

EXHIBITION

Danson Collection of Paintings by Charles Towne Walker Art Gallery 1977 (61).

REFERENCE

1. Receipt in the *Danson papers*, VII.5.2., NML archives.

called

Charles Towne

A Grey Racehorse and Brown Foal Standing outside a Stable

WAG 2315
oil on canvas, 51.5 × 67.5 cm
date: unknown, perhaps 1820–25

The nineteenth-century frame on WAG 2315 bears a plaque inscribed *Chanticleer.* When carrying out research on this picture and WAG 2343 (below) which appears to depict the same horse, Walter Stone established that the Chanticleer concerned was foaled only in 1843 and proposed an alternative identification, Mr Garforth's Pyramus.[1] A grey colt of this name, by Black Charles out of Vesta, was foaled in 1816; he was owned by W. Garforth and raced on the flat (with limited success) in 1819–20, chiefly in Yorkshire.[2] This identification not only conformed much better with the work's style in general, it also permitted the traditional attribution to Towne to stand. However, even making allowances for WAG 2315's poor condition – it has been flattened in lining and has pronounced weave distortion – it is not possible to accept that the painting is by Towne. The horses themselves somewhat resemble his work but other elements of the picture, especially the landscape background

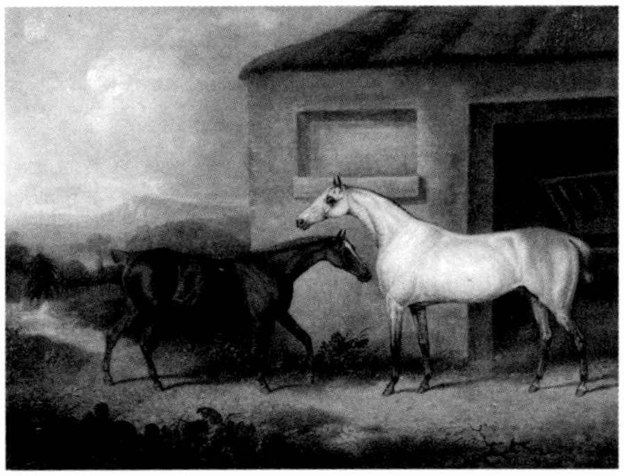

WAG 2315

and the cool, silvery tonality overall, are much less characteristic. Daniel Clowes (1790–1849) has been suggested as an alternative candidate for the artist, but this remains tentative.[3]

PROVENANCE

...Walter Stone by 1911;[4] Mary Stone Bequest 1944.

EXHIBITION

Charles Towne of Liverpool 1763–1840 Walker Art Gallery 1971 (22).

NOTES

1. *The Walter Stone Collection of Sporting Pictures at Whitton Hall, Westbury, Shropshire* (privately printed, 1938) p. 28 (cat. 44). The source of his information is unknown. In 1911, when the painting was already in Stone's collection, the horse was still identified as Chanticleer; see Sir Walter Gilbey: *Animal Painters of England from the Year 1600* 3 vols (London, 1900–11) vol. 3 (second series) p. 252 (no. 4).
2. *MPPP*, p. 207.
3. Mary Bennett, note in gallery files. Compare, for example, Clowes's *A Gentleman Holding a Grey Racehorse; a View of a Racecourse beyond*, 55.5 × 75 cm; Sotheby 19 November 1986 (123); the style is also close to a signed horse portrait by Clowes in a private collection in North Yorkshire.
4. Gilbey, *loc. cit.*; but if Stone acquired WAG 2315 with WAG 2343, it would have been in his possession before 1908; see WAG 2343, n. 5 (below).

A Grey Racehorse with Jockey up on a Racecourse

WAG 2343
oil on canvas, 58.5 × 77 cm
date: unknown, perhaps 1820–25

As with WAG 2315 (above), the horse in WAG 2343 was identified as Chanticleer in the early years of the twentieth century,[1] and was re-identified by Walter Stone as Pyramus, owned by W. Garforth.[2] It has been suggested that the racecourse depicted is Doncaster.[3] WAG 2343 appears to be by the same hand as WAG 2315 and is even less characteristic of Towne (strengthening the argument that WAG 2315 is not by him); it also has been tentatively ascribed to Daniel Clowes (1790–1849).[4] Stone presumably acquired

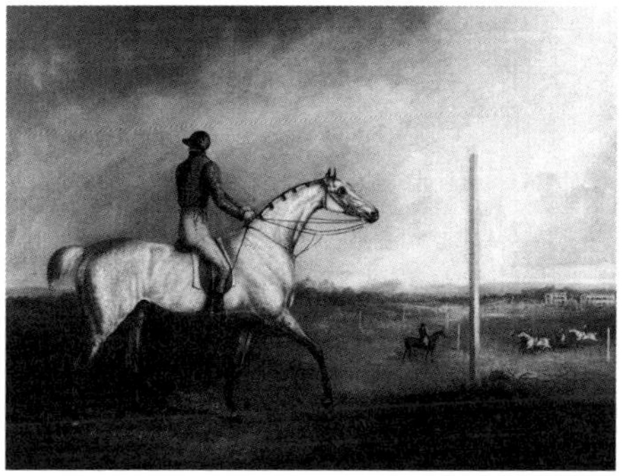

WAG 2343

both works from the same source at the same time.

PROVENANCE

...Walter Stone probably by 1908;[5] Mary Stone Bequest 1944.

EXHIBITIONS

[? *Historical Exhibition of Liverpool Art* Walker Art Gallery 1908 (250)]; *Some Acquisitions of the Walker Art Gallery Liverpool 1935–1945* National Gallery, London 1945 (86); *Sporting Pictures from the Walter Stone Collection* Bluecoat Gallery, Liverpool 1946 (34); *A Selection of Sporting Pictures from the Walter Stone Collection* Bluecoat Gallery, Liverpool 1953 (30); *Charles Towne of Liverpool 1763–1840* Walker Art Gallery 1971 (23).

NOTES

1. A label inscribed *Chanticleer* is stuck to the stretcher on the reverse.
2. *The Walter Stone Collection of Sporting Pictures at Whitton Hall, Westbury, Shropshire* (privately printed, 1938) p. 28 (cat. 43).
3. Sir Walter Gilbey: *Animal Painters of England from the Year 1600* 3 vols (London, 1900–11) vol. 3 (second series) p. 252 (no. 3). Gilbey describes the subject as '"Chanticleer", grey horse (Mr Merry's), jockey wearing blue or green jacket and black cap on a racecourse (Doncaster?), going to the post'.
4. Mary Bennett, ms note in gallery files.
5. This, rather than WAG 2315, is probably the *Chanticleer* lent by Stone to the 1908 exhibition, whose dimensions are given in the catalogue as 21 × 28 inches. WAG 2343 measures 22½ × 30½ inches, WAG 2315 20 × 25½.

Dappled Grey Horse Saddled in a Stable

WAG 9525
oil on canvas, 60.5 × 79.5 cm
date: unknown, perhaps 1820–45

Although a characteristic Towne subject, WAG 9525 cannot be accepted as his work. The inscription *C Town pinxt.* at the bottom right is inauthentic, and probably represents a fraudulent attempt to market the picture as by Towne (perhaps with Col. Danson, a noted enthusiast, in view). The horse itself is painted in a stiff, angular manner at odds with Towne's usual style (the treatment of the head and neck is especially mannered) and the overall tonality of the picture is cooler than that of most Townes. When WAG 9525 was exhibited at the Walker in 1977 it was identified as an immature early canvas,[1] but this seems wrong. For one thing, the earliest certain examples of Towne's work (such as WAG 9818–19, p. 187) do not at all resemble WAG 9525 in their handling. For another, there are passages within WAG 9525 which suggest it is the work of an accomplished professional artist in his own right: the treatment of the saddle, the riding accoutrements and the landscape through the door is distinctive. A further factor to take into account is that the work is extensively restored; there is an old mend on the back of the stall, and there are many discoloured retouchings throughout the background, as well as a wide area of pentiment above the outline of the horse's neck. Thus the present appearance of WAG 9525 may differ significantly from its original one. The scenario that a painting by an artist conversant with Towne's work has been reworked at a later date – and then 'signed' – seems the most probable.

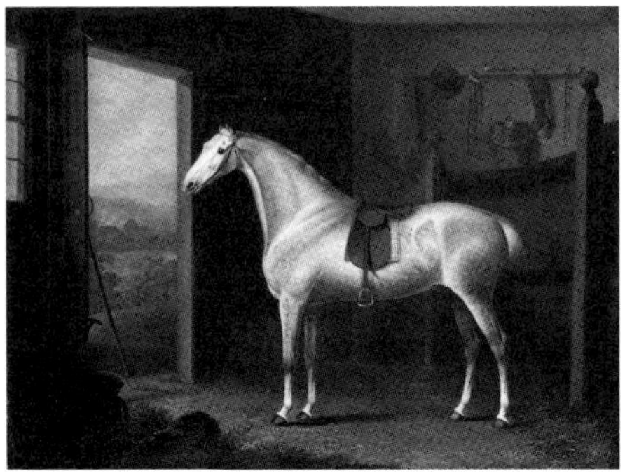

WAG 9525

PROVENANCE
…Col. J. R. Danson; his bequest 1979.

EXHIBITION
Danson Collection of Paintings by Charles Towne Walker Art Gallery 1977 (2).

REFERENCE
1. The 1977 exhibits were catalogued chronologically, and WAG 9525 was placed before every other work in the exhibition apart from the portrait of the artist as a young man, then believed to be a self-portrait (see WAG 9587, p. 235). The spelling of the artist's name in the signature is that found on Towne's early works, before about 1800.

Italianate Landscape with a Peasant Woman Spinning

WAG 9568
oil on canvas, 85 × 112 cm
date: unknown, perhaps 1820–40

The inscription *C. TOWNE. 1827* on WAG 9568 at the lower right is uncharacteristic and must be a later addition. There are numerous other problematical aspects of the painting that raise doubts over Towne's authorship. These include the untypical subdued light and the cool aerial perspective, the uncharacteristic treatment of the foliage throughout, and even the handling of the animals, notably the two sheep closest to the girl and the goat sprawled on the rock in the left foreground. Although Towne did occasionally paint Italianate subjects (and it may be significant that he exhibited a now unidentified *Landscape with Cattle in the Style of Berghem* at the Liverpool Academy in 1825) they are relatively uncommon and are also more readily associated with earlier phases of his career (see, for example, WAG 9562, from 1814, p. 207). This raises the suspicion that the date of 1827 has been plucked at random simply to re-inforce the impression of a mature production. Keeping an open mind on WAG 9568, it is perhaps just possible that it is an ambitious and experimental one-off, but on balance it seems more likely that it is the work of another animal painter contemporary with Towne sharing certain similarities with the latter's style. The clichéd phrase 'too good to be by Towne' comes to mind.

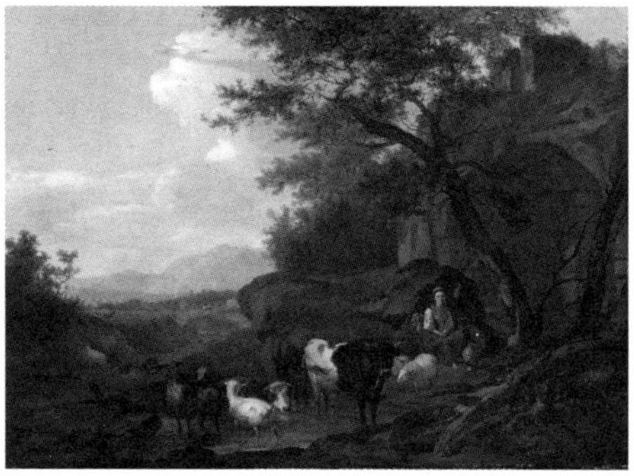

WAG 9568

PROVENANCE
…Col. J. R. Danson;[1] his bequest 1979.

EXHIBITION
Danson Collection of Paintings by Charles Towne Walker Art Gallery 1977 (45).

REFERENCE
1. A note on the accession card, gallery files, presumably recording verbal information from Col. Danson, states that the painting was bought from a collection in Oxton, Birkenhead, before the Second World War.

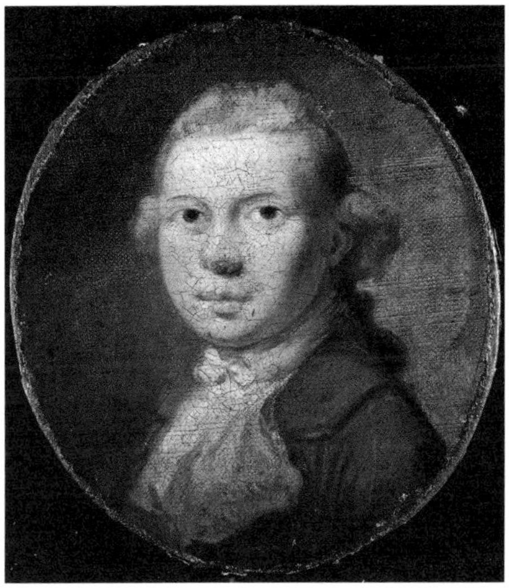

WAG 9587

Self-portrait as a Young Man

WAG 9587
oil on canvas, 21.5 × 19.5 cm (oval)
date: unknown, perhaps 1782–84

Comparison between WAG 9587 and the much later self-portrait by Towne in watercolour (Walker Art Gallery; fig. 95),[1] an engraving of which was published by H. Fisher in 1824,[2] reveals considerable facial resemblance: in both cases the sitter has a short, straight, fleshy nose, thickish lips, a round, jowly chin, and short hair sweeping back off the forehead. On this basis, WAG 9587 can be accepted as a portrait of Towne aged about 20 and carried out in the early 1780s, a dating supported by general considerations of style. There are strong grounds, however, for doubting that at that date Towne could have executed the work in this manner himself. No work by the artist is documented before the copies after Stubbs's *Haymakers* and *Reapers* that he executed in Liverpool in 1787, and the loose technique of WAG 9587 is about as far removed from the finicky manner of Towne's earliest sporting pictures (see pp. 187–8) as it would be possible to get. WAG 9587 had been identified as a self-portrait by 1911,[3] at which date it was already in Danson family ownership, but it seems probable that this was a case of wishful thinking and that the work is by a friend or professional colleague of Towne's which passed to him and was perhaps among his effects at his death.

The portrait, on an oval stretcher, is in poor condition with flattened paint and weave distortion following relining.

PROVENANCE
...F. C. Danson by 1911;[4] by descent to Col. J. R. Danson; his bequest 1979.

EXHIBITION
Danson Collection of Paintings by Charles Towne Walker Art Gallery 1977 (1).

NOTES
1. The watercolour, measuring 16.5 × 12 cm, was purchased at Sotheby 23 October 1986 (325).
2. Repr. W. Shaw Sparrow, 'Charles Towne of Liverpool, Early Bitterness', *Connoisseur* vol. 85 (June 1930) p. 376.
3. Sir Walter Gilbey: *Animal Painters of England from the Year 1600* 3 vols (London, 1900–11) vol. 3 (second series) p. 251 (no. 8); this source is given on a ms ink label on the reverse of WAG 9587.
4. Gilbey, *op. cit.*, p. 251; and repr. as in Lady Danson's ownership by W. Shaw Sparrow, 'Charles Towne of Liverpool: His Youth', *Connoisseur* vol. 85 (May 1930) p. 287.

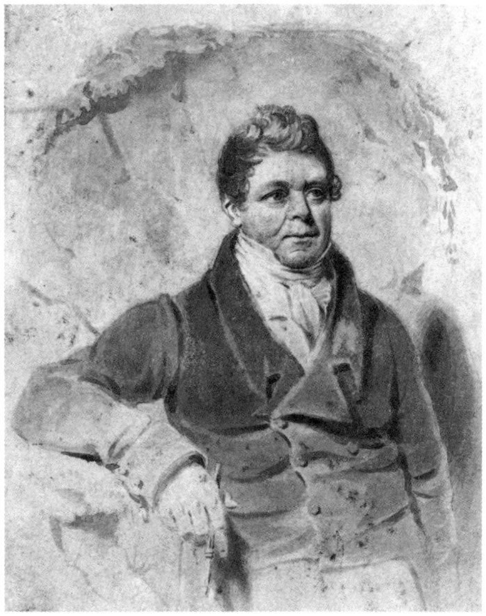

Fig. 95 *Self-portrait* by Charles Towne, watercolour on paper. Walker Art Gallery.

James Ward

1769–1859

Huntsmen Drawing Covert

WAG 2385
oil on canvas, 89 × 128.5 cm
signed: *J. Ward* (bottom left)
date: about 1795–97

The style of WAG 2385 suggests a date in the mid- to late 1790s, when Ward's work was at its closest to George Morland.[1] The treatment of the nearest rider is slovenly in Morland's manner whereas his horse (rather small in proportion) is depicted in fine detail. The scenery looks as if it is based on an actual landscape. The locale has not been identified, but a tall church spire and old tower are visible in close proximity in the left background, and just below the right horizon Ward has casually indicated what appears to be a navigable river with two sailing ships, suggesting that the setting is close to the coast. If the setting is specific it seems likely that the work was a commission. There is no evidence that the picture was exhibited by Ward and no reference to it can be traced in his surviving papers.

PROVENANCE
...Mrs MacDonald Close; Christie 31 May 1946 (159);[2] bt. Ellis and Smith; Walter Hutchinson; Christie 20 July 1951 (139); bt. Agnew for the gallery.

EXHIBITIONS
Selected Acquisitions of the Walker Art Gallery Liverpool 1945–1955 Agnew's, London 1955 (21); *James Ward* Tate Gallery, London 1960 (25).

NOTES
1. Ed Nygren, *verbally*, 22 October 1970.
2. The vendor sold a second Ward, *A Gypsy Encampment* (a title with Morland associations) as the following lot but there is no evidence that the two works were pendants.

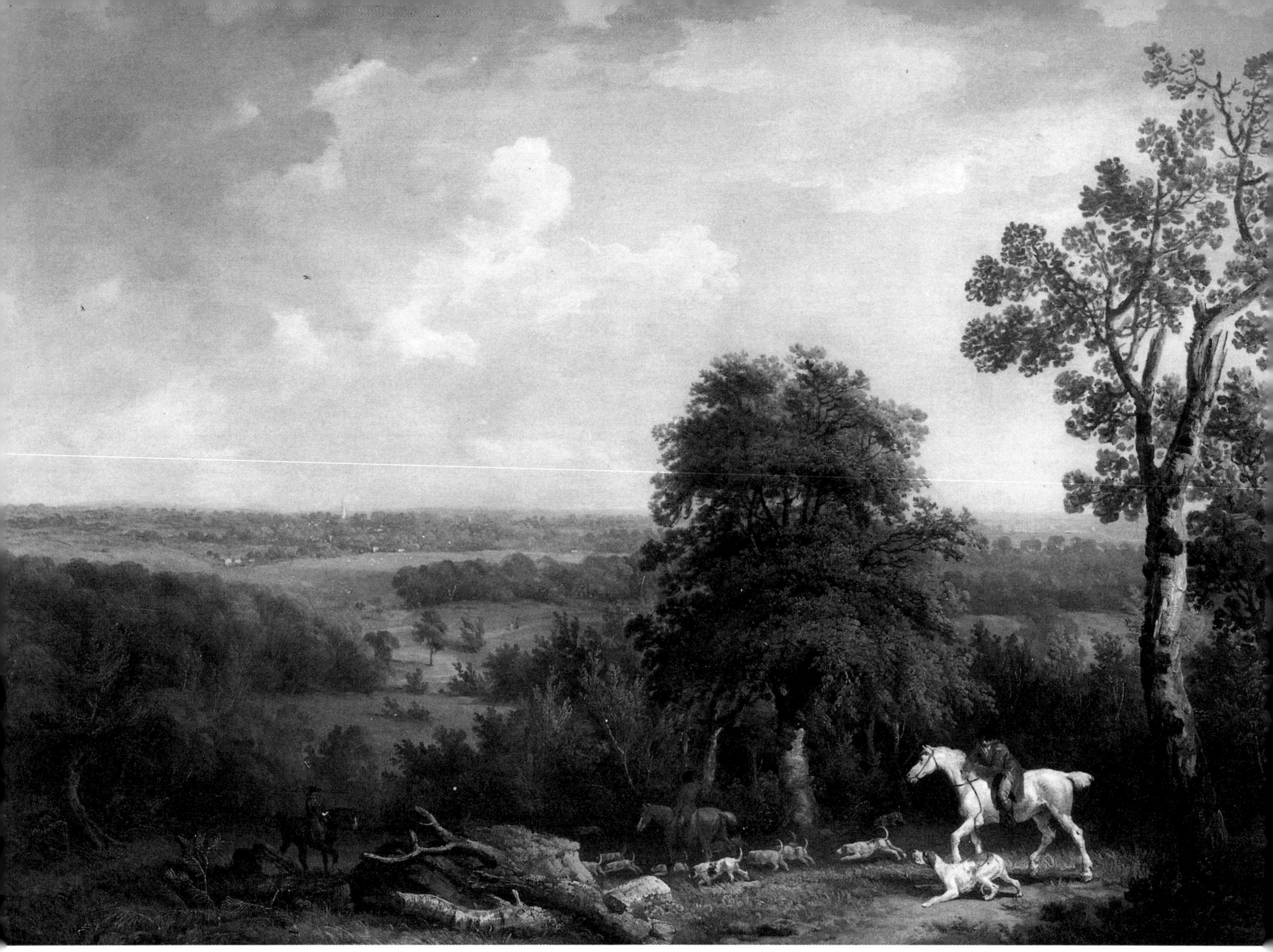

WAG 2385

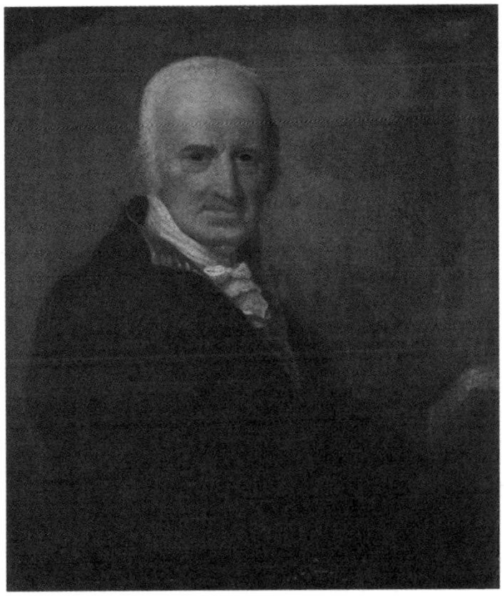

WAG 6941

after
George Watson
1767–1837

Benjamin West

WAG 6941
oil on canvas,[1] 77 × 63 cm
date: unknown, perhaps 1824–45

Watson's original, now in the National Gallery of Scotland (fig. 96) was painted during the artist's stay in London around 1815 and exhibited at the Royal Academy in 1816 (cat.350). It was presented by Watson's son, W. S. Watson, to the Royal Scottish Academy in 1859.[2] WAG 6941, which is in poor condition, extensively abraded and holed in three places, is an indifferent although early copy. A manuscript inscription on the reverse of the canvas reads: *copy from Watson's portrait presented to the Academy of Fine Arts, 1823–1824* [signed] *L.J.S. Cogd...* It has been suggested that the Academy concerned was the Academy of Fine Arts in Charleston, South Carolina, founded in 1821, to which Watson is stated to have been elected an honorary member, and to which he is known to have presented an autograph copy of his portrait of West.[3] The inscription implies that WAG 6941 is not Watson's autograph replica but a further copy, presumably made in Charleston.

The American painter Benjamin West (1738–1820) is shown in Watson's original at the age of 77. Born in Pennsylvania, West came to Europe at the age of 21 to study and remained there for the rest of his life. He emerged as the leading historical painter in Britain in the late 1760s (for three varied but characteristic works by him, see below). He enjoyed extensive patronage from King George III, and in 1792 he succeeded Sir Joshua Reynolds as President of the Royal Academy. West's posthumous reputation in America was at its height during the 1820s and the painting in the background of Watson's portrait is his 1815 version of *Christ Healing the Sick*, commissioned for the Pennsylvania Hospital, Philadelphia, exhibited in London in 1815 and 1816.[4] The artist of WAG 6941 has considerably departed from Watson's relatively faithful rendition of the figures in West's painting.

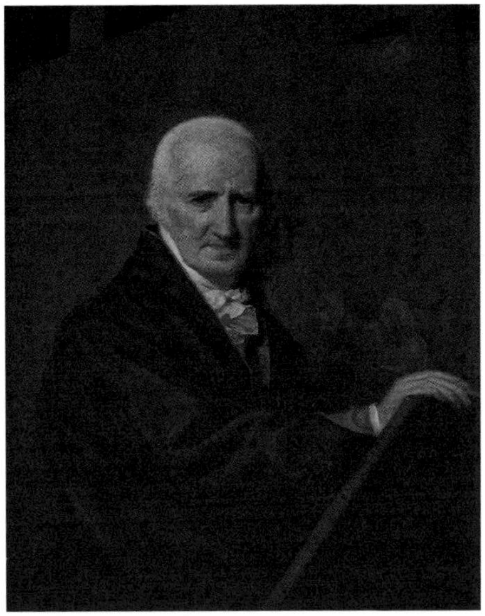

Fig. 96 *Portrait of Benjamin West* by George Watson, oil on canvas. © National Galleries of Scotland.

PROVENANCE
...Liverpool Royal Institution;[5] by whom presented 1969.

NOTES
1. Label of John H. Paris, frame-maker.
2. Julia Lloyd Williams, ed.: *The National Gallery of Scotland, Concise Catalogue of Paintings* (Edinburgh, 1997) p. 368.
3. Helen Smailes, National Gallery of Scotland, *letter*, 16 March 2006, gallery files, citing information in Robert Brydall: *Art in Scotland, Its Origin and Progress* (Edinburgh and London, 1889), p. 229.
4. See H. von Erffa and A. Staley: *The Paintings of Benjamin West* (New Haven and London, 1986) pp. 349–50; also, for Watson's picture, p. 348.
5. WAG 6941 is not traceable in LRI catalogues. However, it may be the 'Framed oil painting' *Portrait of a Gentleman* by an unknown artist listed as in the basement of the Institution in Lumb & Matthison's [typed] *Inventory of the Furniture, Fixtures, Fittings and Pictures on the Premises of the Royal Institution, Colquitt Street, Liverpool Made the Third Day of May 1946*; copy in gallery archives.

Benjamin West
1738–1820

Family Group (Called 'The Sheridan Family')

WAG 3127
oil on canvas, 228 × 160.5 cm
date: about 1776

This imposing portrait entered the collection as *The Sheridan Family* by Nathaniel Dance. The attribution to Dance was always doubted and was eventually corrected,[1] but the traditional identification of the sitters has proved more tenacious. The aspiring Irish-born playwright Richard Brinsley Sheridan (1751–1816) eloped with and married the singer Elizabeth Linley (1754–92) daughter of Thomas Linley of Bath in 1773; their son Thomas was born on 17 March 1775. It seems extraordinary that such a grand portrait of celebrities could remain totally undocumented both in Sheridan's circle and in

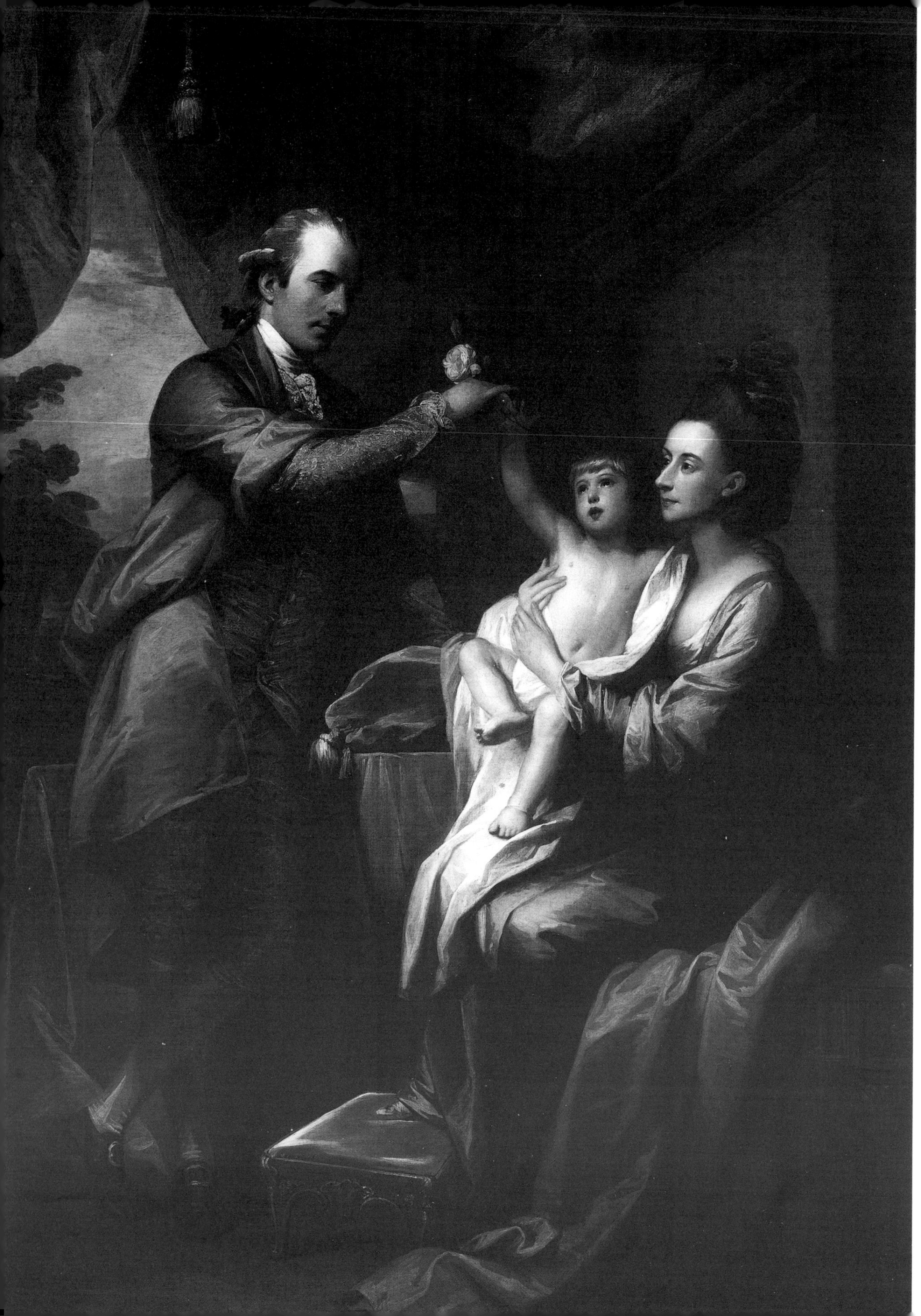

WAG 3127

West's,[2] yet the style of the work, the sitters' apparent ages and their costumes and hairstyles all accord with the notion that they sat for this picture in the latter part of 1775 or early in 1776. The adult likenesses, moreover, if somewhat generalised, do seem comparable to other portraits of Sheridan (for example, by Romney, of about 1785; Burrell Collection, Glasgow) and his wife (for example, by Gainsborough, in *The Linley Sisters*, 1772; Dulwich Picture Gallery).[3] The period 1775–76 was a heady one for Sheridan: apart from the birth of his first child, it witnessed his first successes as a playwright with *The Rivals* and *The Duenna* (both 1775) and the start of his managerial career at Drury Lane Theatre in succession to David Garrick (1776).

If the portrait is of the Sheridans, explanation of its descent into complete anonymity must reside in its having been regarded as a total failure (its formal language of decorous politeness does indeed seem completely alien to the raffish, bohemian *persona* of the youthful Sheridan).[4] It has been proposed that the work is identifiable with the *Portrait of a Gentleman, His Wife and Child* by West sold by the artist's sons at Robins's Rooms, 20–22 June 1829 (171), a work for which no other candidate is known in West's *oeuvre*.[5] If this work was a portrait of the Sheridans, and either the identity of the sitters had already been lost or else was being deliberately concealed, this might well suggest that the work had been rejected by Sheridan in such forcible terms as to encourage West to keep it under wraps for the rest of his life. In the same sale, lot 141 was a supposed portrait of Mrs Sheridan, circumstantial evidence for the existence of a tradition that she had sat to West; this has remained untraced and no image of it is known.[6] But if WAG 3127 is the work sold in 1829, the question then becomes how the identity of the Sheridan family was resurrected at the end of the nineteenth century, particularly if by then it was being mis-attributed to Dance. So far no information has emerged to shed light on any of these mysterious aspects of the work's history.

PROVENANCE

[? Sold by the artist's sons at Robins, 20–22 June 1829 (171); …Turner & Horsley 1897];[7] …bt. from an unknown source by Sophie, Lady Wavertree;[8] acquired by the gallery in 1933 under the terms of the bequest of her husband, Lord Wavertree.[9]

EXHIBITIONS

[? *Exhibition of Dramatic and Musical Art* Grafton Galleries London 1897 (157)]; *American Artists in Europe 1800–1900* Walker Art Gallery 1976 (70).

NOTES

1. John Kerslake, *letter*, 19 June 1968, and Helmut von Erffa, *letter*, 15 April 1976, gallery files, endorsed the re-attribution from Dance to West.
2. Such considerations led to the identification being doubted in the 1976 exhibition catalogue.
3. Helmut von Erffa and Allen Staley: *The Paintings of Benjamin West* (New Haven and London, 1986) p. 552 (cat. 696).
4. If the portrait is of Sheridan, it is much the earliest significant depiction of him, and the idea that it left a bad taste might explain why he seems to have avoided sitting for his portrait for some years afterwards; see Richard Walker: *National Portrait Gallery: Regency Portraits* 2 vols (London, 1985) vol. 1, pp. 451–2.
5. Von Erffa and Staley, *loc. cit.*
6. Von Erffa and Staley, *loc. cit.* (cat. 697).
7. Lent by Turner & Horsley to the 1897 exhibition. That WAG 3127 is the portrait exhibited in 1897, when it was attributed to Dance, is very likely, but wholly certain.
8. Lady Wavertree, *letter*, 27 October 1933, gallery files, stated that she bought the work 'many years ago'. She was born Sophie Sheridan, daughter of Algernon Thomas Brinsley Sheridan, and was the great-great-grand-daughter of Richard Brinsley Sheridan.
9. A dispute over the work's bequest arose when it was discovered that it should not have been available for selection by the gallery from the estate of Lord Wavertree, being the personal property of Lady Wavertree. By the time the error was discovered, the legal position was held by the gallery's lawyers to be irreversible; correspondence October–December 1933, gallery files.

The Presentation of the Crown to William I

WAG 6946
oil on canvas, 198 × 152 cm
date: about 1792–97

In the centre of the composition Edgar Atheling, chosen as the successor to King Harold after the latter's death at the Battle of Hastings on 14 October 1066, kneels as he resigns the crown to the victor of the battle, William of Normandy, who steps forward on the left. On the right, the Archbishop of Canterbury, Stigand, accompanied by another bishop, makes a gesture of benediction but with a sullen and even hostile expression on his face. The bystanders – Norman soldiers on the left, Saxon nobles and citizens of London on the right – are shown in a variety of awestruck poses.[1] West's design, a simple X-shape with the crown at its centre, is stagy, but effectively conveys his understanding of the event as a historical crossroads, a critical moment in the development of British ethnic diversity. He sets the scene outside an invented Westminster Abbey, where William would shortly be crowned King William I. The anachronistic Gothic features of the abbey would later cause the subject of the picture to be mis-identified as the presentation of the crown to Lord Bolingbroke.[2]

The painting was made for the miniature painter turned print publisher Robert Bowyer (1758–1834). In about 1791, under the impact of the recently opened Boydell Shakespeare Gallery, Bowyer conceived the idea of a new edition of David Hume's popular *History of England*[3] lavishly illustrated by prints made from specially commissioned paintings of scenes from British history. The paintings themselves would be displayed in a special 'Historic Gallery' in Bowyer's new house in Pall Mall.

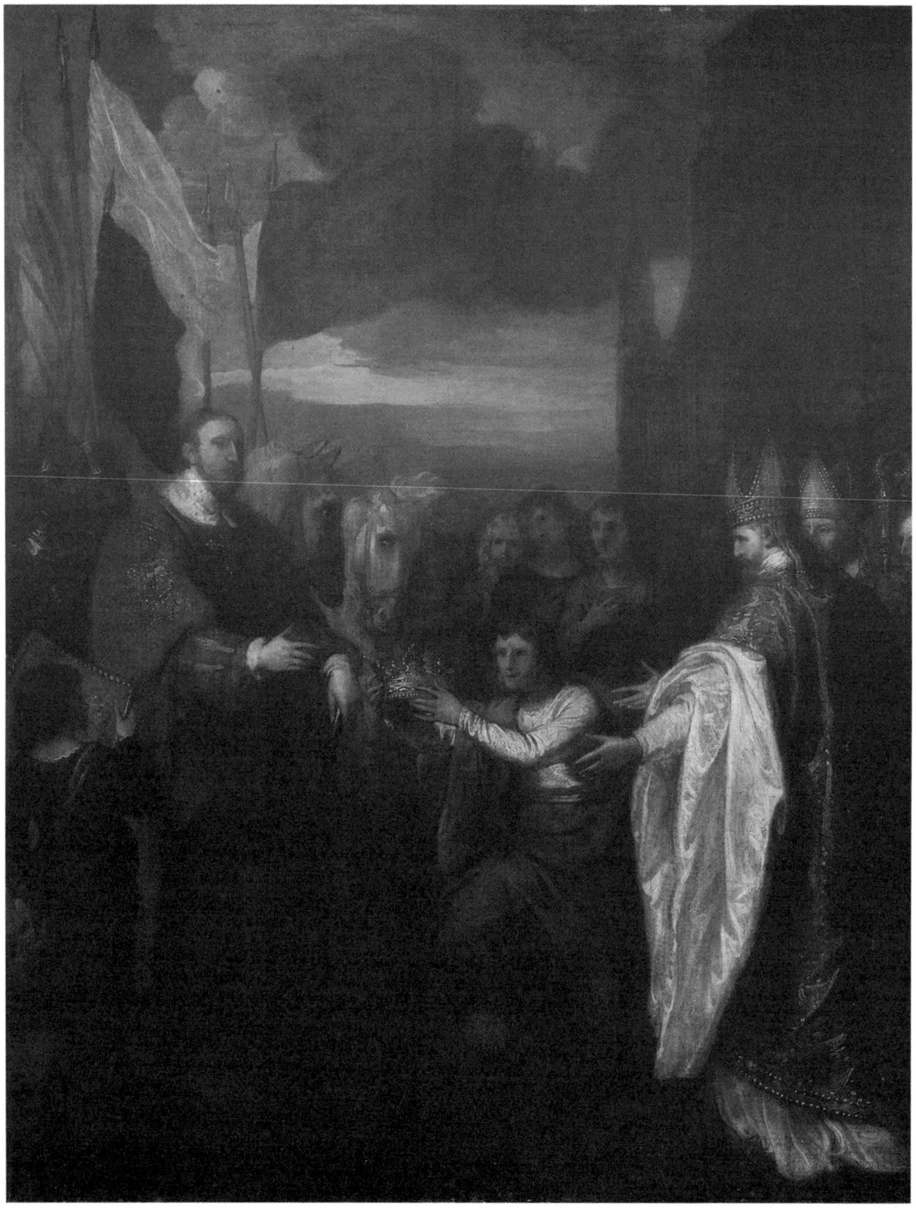

WAG 6946

Between 1793 and 1806, despite the adverse economic conditions caused by the French Revolutionary wars, Bowyer succeeded in issuing five volumes of Hume's history, but the effort crippled him and the project was abandoned. In 1807 the paintings which formed the 'Historic Gallery' were sold at auction.[4]

One of two works that West painted for the project, WAG 6946 dates from between January 1792, when an unidentified newspaper reported that West was one of the artists involved in Bowyer's scheme,[5] and 1797; George Noble's engraving for the book (fig. 97) was published on 1 December that year. West also made a preliminary oil sketch for the work (untraced) which he eventually exhibited at the Royal Academy in 1808.[6]

WAG 6946 is in poor condition. The paint surface has darkened and is very worn and damaged,[7] to the point where much of the detail in the engraving is invisible. Its size notwithstanding, West may have painted the work specifically for the purpose of the engraving, and not have concerned himself with the high finish and detail that he would have applied to an intended exhibition picture.

PROVENANCE

Painted for Robert Bowyer; Coxe, 29–30 May 1807 (56); ...acquired between 1893 and 1946 by the Liverpool Royal Institution;[8] by whom presented 1969.

EXHIBITIONS

Bowyer's Historic Gallery Pall Mall until 1807; *Mythen der Nationen: Ein Europäisches Panorama* Deutsches Historisches Museum, Berlin 1998 (GB 6).

NOTES

1. The figures were identified in Helmut von Erffa and Allen Staley: *The Paintings of Benjamin West* (New Haven and London, 1986) p. 188 (cat. 50).
2. WAG 6946 entered the gallery under the latter title, which refers to Henry IV's usurpation of the crown from Richard II in 1399; the subject had, however, previously been correctly identified by David Irwin: *English Neo-classical Art* (London, 1966) pp. 96–7. It was Irwin who pointed out the anachronism of West's treatment of Westminster Abbey.
3. Hume's *History* was written and published in four volumes between 1754 and 1762; it was noted, and after initial criticism, quickly admired, for its free-thinking, anti-Whig viewpoint.
4. For Bowyer's project see Deborah Graham-Vernon: 'Bowyer, Robert', *ODNB* vol. 6, pp. 995–7, and T. Boase: 'Macklin and Bowyer', *Journal of the Courtauld and Warburg Institutes* (1963) pp. 148–77, especially pp. 169–76. Boase discusses Bowyer's scheme within the context of earlier similar illustrated histories of Britain, and lists currently identified works painted for Bowyer (not including WAG 6946).
5. National Art Library, Victoria & Albert Museum, *Press Cuttings Volumes* vol. 3, p. 617 (article titled 'Complete History of England superbly Ornamented', dated 2 January 1792). West's other painting for Bowyer was *The Intercession of the Queen Mother with Richard I to Pardon His Brother John* (Washington University, St Louis); von Erffa and Staley, *op. cit.*, p. 189 (cat. 52).
6. Von Erffa and Staley, *op. cit.*, p. 189 (cat. 51).
7. WAG 6946 was described as 'stained' on its arrival

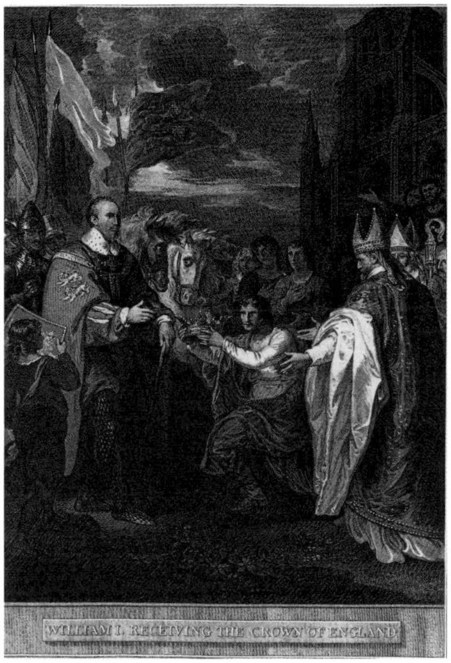

Fig. 97 *William I Receiving the Crown of England* after Benjamin West, engraving by George Noble. Private collection.

at the gallery (note in gallery files).
8. The work is not included in the *List of Paintings, &c, on the Institution Premises* in the *Liverpool Royal Institution Annual Report* (1893) pp. 53–4; it is, however, present on Lumb & Matthison's [typed] *Inventory of the Furniture, Fixtures, Fittings and Pictures on the Premises of the Royal Institution, Colquitt Street, Liverpool Made the Third Day of May 1946* ('framed oil painting, 'Group Offering a Crown', 'Artist unknown'); copy in gallery archives. WAG 6946 had been on long-term loan from the LRI to the University of Liverpool prior to its presentation to the gallery in 1969.

The Death of Nelson

WAG 3132
oil on canvas and panel, 182 × 247.5 cm
signed and dated: *B West 1806*
(bottom centre)
date: 1806

The artist began work on WAG 3132 within days of the arrival in London, on 6 November 1805, of the news of Lord Nelson's death at the Battle of Trafalgar. Joseph Farington, West's friend and fellow academician, wrote in his diary on 29 November that West

told me that [James] Heath, the Engraver, called upon him sometime since and proposed to him to paint a picture of Lord Nelson's Victory & Death, and that he would engrave a Plate from it, and that they should make it a partnership concern. The picture to be considered as a companion to that of the death of General Wolfe. – Terms had been settled between them and he had begun the design.[1]

This was before HMS Victory, with Nelson's body preserved in a barrel of spirits, had even reached England, but at some point soon afterwards West may have gone on board the ship. A drawing of the deck survives (Yale Center for British Art, New Haven) to which West is thought to have added the figures of the dying Nelson and three companions.[2] In January 1806, in a response to a request from West to the Admiralty, master's mate Thomas Goble, who had been promoted to Admiral's secretary during the action, visited the artist in order to give him detailed information about the battle. Goble returned to West's house in Newman Street on an almost daily basis until the middle of March.[3] During this period, West introduced Goble's portrait into the picture, as well as the likenesses of many other sailors who had been present at Trafalgar, in a quest for documentary accuracy. Several of them were paid a guinea by West for their expenses in travelling to London from Chatham.[4] It was presumably at this period that West made two chalk studies for the figures of master's mate Thomas Robins and second lieutenant of marines Lewis Reeves, who had been badly wounded in the battle (Walker Art Gallery; figs. 98–99).[5]

On 16 March Farington visited West and saw the picture, noting that it was 'all painted in & would employ him a month more to harmonise and give effect to it'.[6] A long description and explanation of the picture appeared in the May issue of *La Belle Assemblée* and on 10 May West called on Farington to invite him to come and see the finished picture, which he did the following day.[7] Soon after this West, in a calculated snub to the Royal Academy, who had forced him to resign the Presidency the previous year,[8] put the painting on public exhibition in his house, accompanied by autograph copies of the artist's *Death of General Wolfe* and *Battle of La Hogue*. Crowds flocked to see the picture; West himself estimated 30,000 people by the beginning of July, and told Farington that he had issued 6,500 cards for admittance, some of them for parties of eight to ten people. Other friends (including Farington himself) wrote notes of introduction for visitors and there had been a special private viewing for King George III.[9] According to a later article in the *Monthly Magazine* people 'thronged the painting room, passages, doorways, the very street in which [West's] house was situated in order to obtain a view of so interesting a public work. The crowds of visitants continued for many weeks'.[10]

The work's popularity gave West an immediate and visible precedence over the other artists who had also responded at once to the news of Trafalgar, including Arthur William Devis, Samuel Drummond (see pp. 36–9), J. M. W. Turner and even John Constable,[11] but it soon became apparent that popularity did not equate to critical approval. Farington, who was pointedly silent about his own opinion of the picture although West was a friend, recorded the response of fellow artist Thomas Hearne to the effect that it was a remarkable performance for a man of West's age, and Sir Nathaniel Dance-Holland that the picture was 'far inferior' to *The Death of Wolfe*.[12] He also recorded

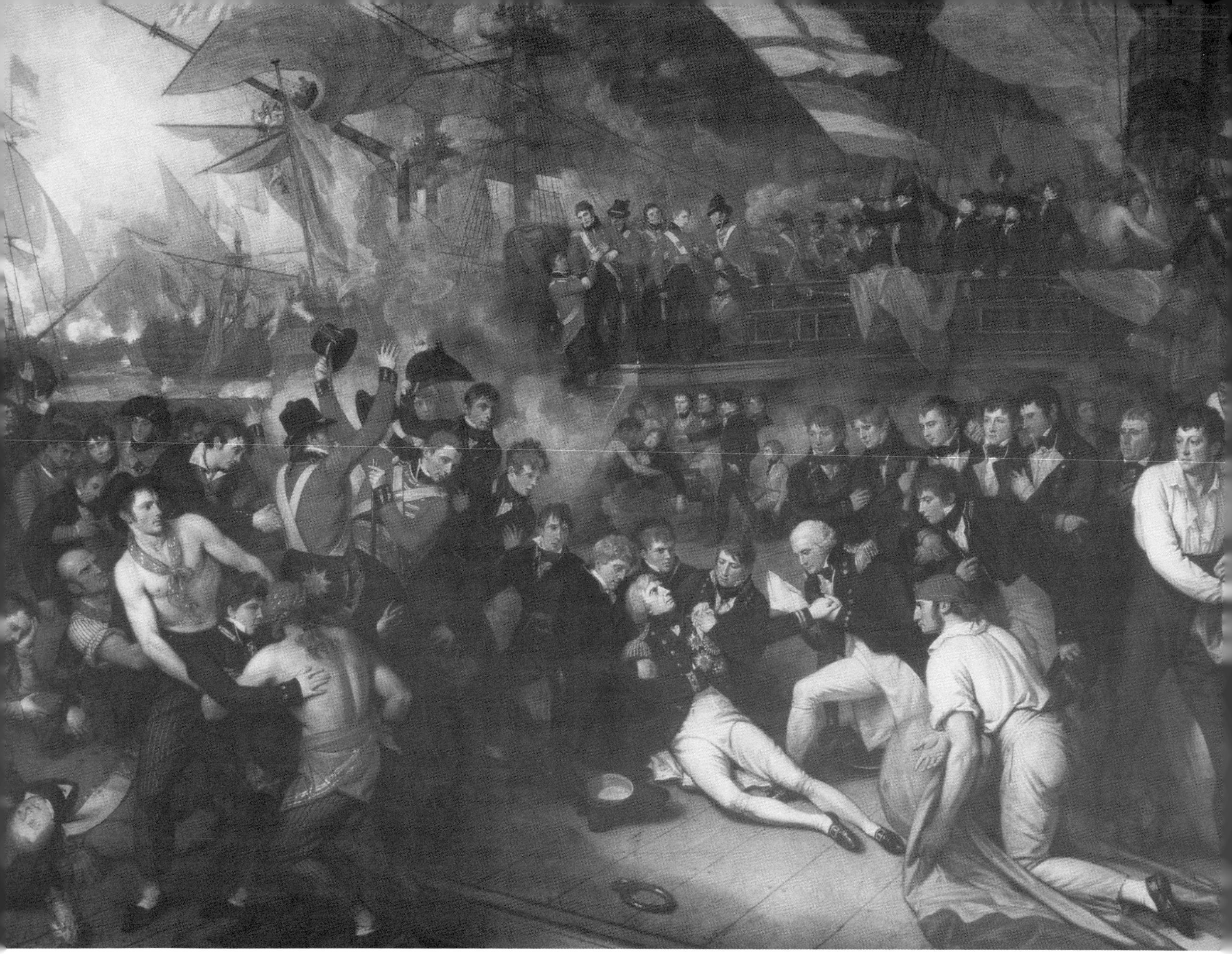

WAG 3132

meeting Able Seaman William Saunders, the figure in the painting kneeling in front of Nelson, at West's house on 8 July. Saunders told him that in point of fact he had never seen Lord Nelson after he had been wounded, as he had been carried below immediately, and that West had painted 'a picture of what might have been, not the circumstances as they had happened'.[13] This seems to have been the burden of reaction to the painting, as is apparent from West's own defensive remarks to Farington following his visit in June 1807 to see the rival, and very contrasted treatment of Nelson's death by Devis (now National Maritime Museum, Greenwich). It had

more convinced Him that there was no other way of representing the death of a Hero but by an Epic representation of it. It must exhibit the event in a way to excite awe & veneration & that which may be required to give superior interest to the representation must be introduced, all that can show the importance of the Hero. Wolfe must not die like a common soldier under a bush, nor should Nelson be represented dying in the gloomy hold of a ship, like a sick man in a Prison Hole… No boy, sd. West, wd. be animated by a representation of Nelson dying like an ordinary man, His feelings must be roused & His mind inflamed by a scene great & extraordinary. A mere matter of fact will never produce this effect.[14]

As against this, when Josiah Boydell issued Bromley's print of Devis's *Death of Nelson* in 1812, the accompanying text concluded: 'Mr Devis has adopted the plan of making TRUTH alone the object of his delineation, and has consequently depicted this awful scene with respect to time, place, and persons present, exactly as it occurred,'[15] pointedly a reference to the consensual view of West's treatment.

West evidently regarded *The Death of Nelson* as a belated sequel to his much earlier *Death of Wolfe*, and he seems to have viewed their intellectual underpinning as identical.[16] He failed to discern the fundamental differences between the two historical events and the demands of their respective audiences. In the first place, *The Death of Nelson* dealt with an event much closer to home and of far greater public emotive impact than the earlier picture did. This meant that the historical anomalies in the picture would inevitably be much more visible and contested than those in *The Death of Wolfe*. Apart from showing Nelson dying above decks, West, for instance, also included in the picture at the left the figure of Admiral's secretary John Scott (the man whose role was taken by Thomas Goble), whose dead body had in fact been thrown overboard some time before Nelson himself was felled. On the far right he inserted a Mr Wynn holding captured French colours, who it has been shown was not present on the Victory at all.[17] Such inaccuracies undoubtedly registered with contemporaries eager to participate vicariously in a moment of national triumph. Second, West failed to calculate at the outset the extent to which the intended commercial use of the painting as the basis for an engraving would colour his approach. He was constrained towards a decorous and even-handed treatment of the event, with results that are a kind of visual equivalent of a court circular in *The Times*. Tacitly, West seems soon to have accepted the limitations of his conception in WAG 3132, for he explored a much more Devis-like realistic treatment and a much more idealistic and allegorical one in two further paintings of the death of Nelson painted in 1807–08.[18] These were commissioned for engravings for Clarke and M'Arthur's *Life of Nelson* (published 1809); the second also featured in West's related *Sketch for a Monument to Lord Nelson* (Yale Center for British Art, New Haven), his response to the king's appeal to the Royal Academy in December 1805 for proposals to commemorate Nelson in monument form.[19]

James Heath's engraving of WAG 3132 soon ran into difficulties. According to Farington, Heath told West when he first saw the finished picture in the summer of 1806, 'he must have 600 guineas more for the engraving than He had first proposed. The price of the print was then advanced to *Proofs* 6 guineas, Common Impressions 3 *guineas*; before the Proofs were charged 4 guineas & the Common impressions 2 guineas.'[20] This price hike resulted in a large number of cancellations from subscribers. Heath had completed a preliminary etching of West's picture by June 1807, and in December that year calculated it would take him another two years to finish the engraving, but he was worried that because of the number of heads West had included in the painting, which he had not anticipated, 'something of a spotty effect' was produced, which would 'be difficult to regulate'.[21] In the event it was the spring of 1811 before Heath finished the engraving. He showed a proof at that year's RA exhibition[22] and West agreed to show the painting itself in the same exhibition.[23]

Although West seems at some point to have presented the work to his wife for her to bequeath, and at her death she willed the picture to Maria, daughter of Raphael West,[24] the painting was still on his hands in 1815 when he was visited by the Bostonian George Ticknor. West told Ticknor, according to the latter's memoirs, that

Just before [Nelson] went to sea for the last time, West sat next to him at a large entertainment given to him here, and in the course of the dinner Nelson expressed to Sir William Hamilton his regret, that in his youth he had not acquired some taste for art and some power of discrimination. 'But', said he, turning to West, 'there is one picture whose power I do feel. I never pass a printshop where your

"Death of Wolfe" is in the window, without being stopped by it'. West of course made his acknowledgements, and Nelson went on to ask why he had painted no more like it. 'Because, my Lord, there are no more subjects.' 'D-n it,' said the sailor, 'I didn't think of that,' and asked him to take a glass of champagne. 'But my lord, I fear your intrepidity will yet furnish me such another scene; and if it should, I shall certainly avail myself of it.' 'Will you?', said Nelson, pouring out bumpers, and touching his glass violently against West's, – 'will you, Mr West? Then I hope I shall die in the next battle.' He sailed a few days after, and the result was on the canvas before us.[25]

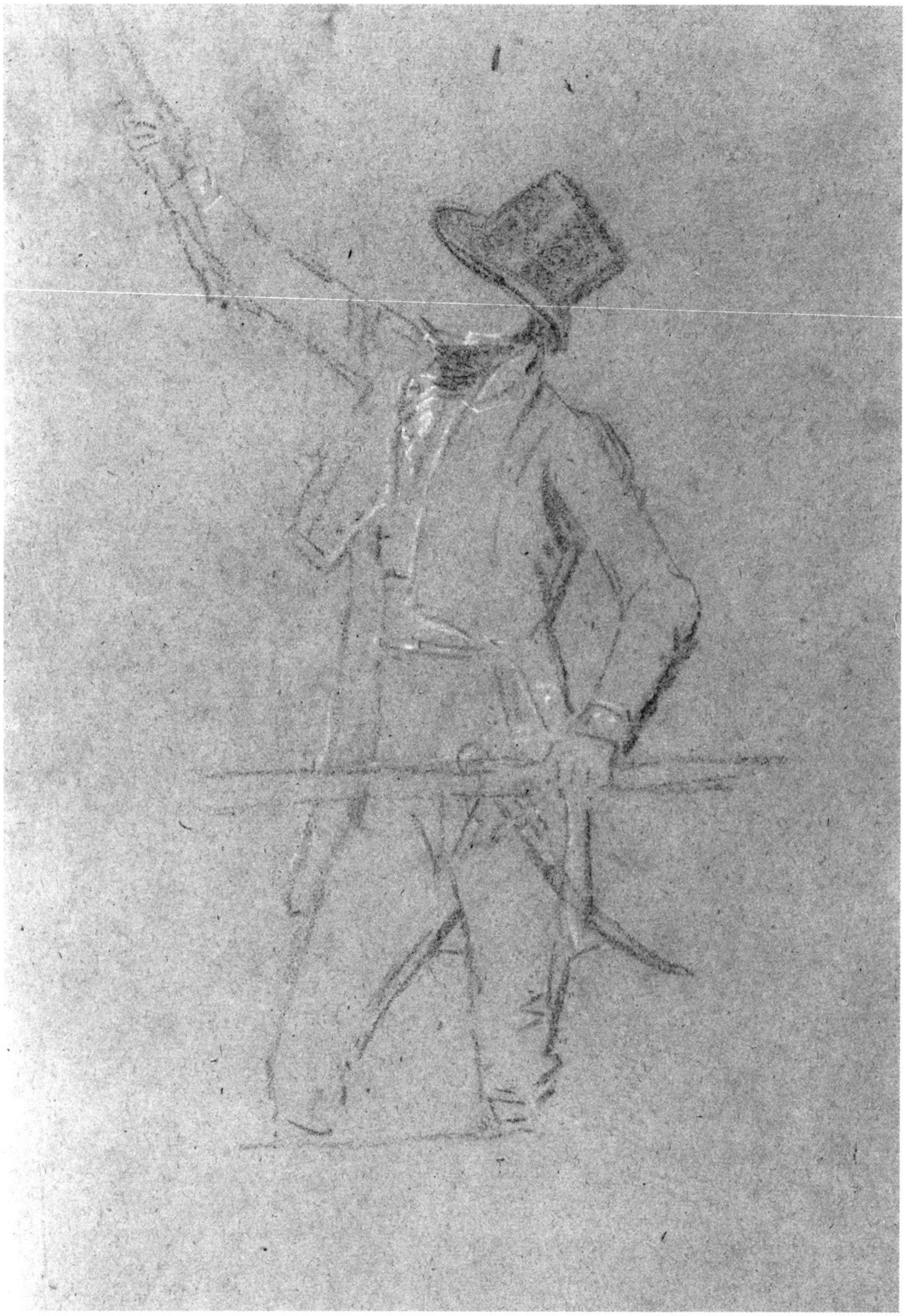

Fig. 98 *Study for the Figure of Lieut. Lewis Reeves in 'The Death of Nelson'* by Benjamin West, black and white chalks on paper. Walker Art Gallery.

Though obviously fictive (it has been pointed out that Sir William Hamilton died two years before Nelson)[26] this story may nevertheless contain some grains of truth. West had met Nelson and Sir William Hamilton at a dinner at Fonthill in December 1800[27] and as the two men were lionised together in society for a period there could have been other opportunities for West to have encountered them together. West had made a drawing on the subject of the triumph of Nelson as long before as 1798 (Courtauld Institute Gallery, London)[28] and Heath may have been aware that he held views on the potential of Nelson's death as a subject before he approached him in November 1805.

West initially priced WAG 3132 at £2,000, but found no takers, a situation 'almost passing belief' according to the *Monthly Magazine* in 1809.[29] By 1820, when Raphael West asked Farington to assist his daughter Maria in an (ultimately vain) attempt to sell the painting to Greenwich Hospital, the family were asking £1,000 to £1,500, 'with £1,200 as a medium price'.[30] The work was eventually sold at auction in 1829 for 850 guineas.

PROVENANCE

By descent to West's grand-daughter Maria; sold on her behalf by her father Raphael West, Robins 22–25 May 1829 (91); bt. H. Sandby (£892 10s.); ... bt. by Bristow H. Hughes;[31] presented in 1866 to the Corporation of Liverpool;[32] transferred to the gallery before 1882.[33]

EXHIBITIONS

West's house 1806; RA 1811 (116); West's Gallery 1822–28 (131); *Royal Naval Exhibition* Chelsea 1891 (585); *American Artists in Europe 1800–1900* Walker Art Gallery 1976 (73) *Mythen der Nationen: Ein Europäisches Panorama* Deutsches Historisches Museum, Berlin 1998 (GB 24).

NOTES

1. FD, vol. 7, p. 2652 (entry of 29 November 1805); for West's *Death of General Wolfe* see n. 16.
2. Helmut von Erffa and Allen Staley: *The Paintings of Benjamin West* (New Haven and London 1986) p. 222 (cat. 108); West later re-used the verso as part of a larger drawing on several sheets for a monument to Nelson (see main text). A further study for the figure of Nelson with three companions was with the Bernard Black Gallery in 1968 (von Erffa and Staley, *loc. cit.*).
3. Brenda Paton, *letter*, 19 July 1972, and Mike Windle, *letter*, 12 August 2001, gallery files. Mrs Paton was Thomas Goble's grand-daughter; Mr Windle was researching a book on the life and times of Goble, who went on to enjoy a colourful career in the navy as an Admiral's secretary before being court martialled for 'improper use of his office' in August 1825.
4. Von Erffa and Staley, *loc. cit.*, citing a letter from West to Watkins Trench of 17 February 1806 (Historical Society of Pennsylvania).
5. Black chalk heightened with white on grey paper, 38.5 x 26 cm; bought Sotheby 22 March 1979 (1); formerly in the collection of Mrs F. Howard.
6. FD, vol. 7, p. 2694 (entry of 16 March 1806).
7. FD, vol. 7, pp. 2756–7 (entries of 10 and 11 May 1806).
8. FD, vol. 7, p. 2757 (entry of 11 May 1806): 'When I was left alone with West He spoke of the Academy. He said it had been a great motive to induce him to paint that picture "The Death of Lord Nelson", to shew the Academy what they had done in causing the Author of it to withdraw himself.' The 1806 RA exhibition was the only one between 1769 and West's death at which he showed nothing.
9. FD, vol. 8, pp. 2802–3 (entry of 2 July 1806).
10. *Monthly Magazine* vol. 27 (1809) p. 325, quoted by Arthur S. Marks: 'The Impact of Admiral Horatio Nelson's Death on English Art', MA report, Columbia University, 1965, pp. 31–2.
11. Constable exhibited at the RA in 1806 (no. 787) his only treatment of a naval subject, the watercolour *His Majesty's Ship Victory, Capt. T. Hardy, in the Memorable Battle of Trafalgar, between Two Ships of the Line* (Victoria & Albert Museum, London). The work has been persistently mis-titled, with the captain's name being given as *E. Harvey*, presumably as a result of a misprint in the exhibition catalogue. For a full discussion of the wide-ranging responses by artists to Trafalgar, and their wider cultural context, see Marks, *op. cit.*, *passim*.
12. FD, vol. 7, p. 2782 (entry of 12 June 1806) and vol. 8, p. 3029 (entry of 21 April 1807).
13. FD, vol. 8, p. 2806 (entry of 8 July 1806).
14. FD, vol. 8, p. 3064 (entry of 10 June 1807).
15. Marks, *op. cit.*, pp. 21–2.
16. For a discussion of this, and especially of the influence on West's retrospective thinking of the writer Robert Bromley, see Charles Mitchell: 'Benjamin West's *Death of Nelson*', in Douglas Fraser, Howard Hibbard and Milton J. Lewine, eds: *Essays in the History of Art Presented to Rudolf Wittkower* (Oxford, 1967) pp. 265–73. West seems to have been encouraged in his views by James Heath.
17. His identity remains unknown; Lt-Commander C. P. Addis MBE, *letter*, 25 March 1990, gallery files. See Addis's *The Men Who Fought with Nelson in H.M.S. Victory at Trafalgar* (Nelson Society, 1988) for biographical summaries of many of the figures in WAG 3132.
18. Von Erffa and Staley, *op. cit.*, pp. 222–3 (cat. 109) and pp. 224–5 (cat. 111). Both are in the National

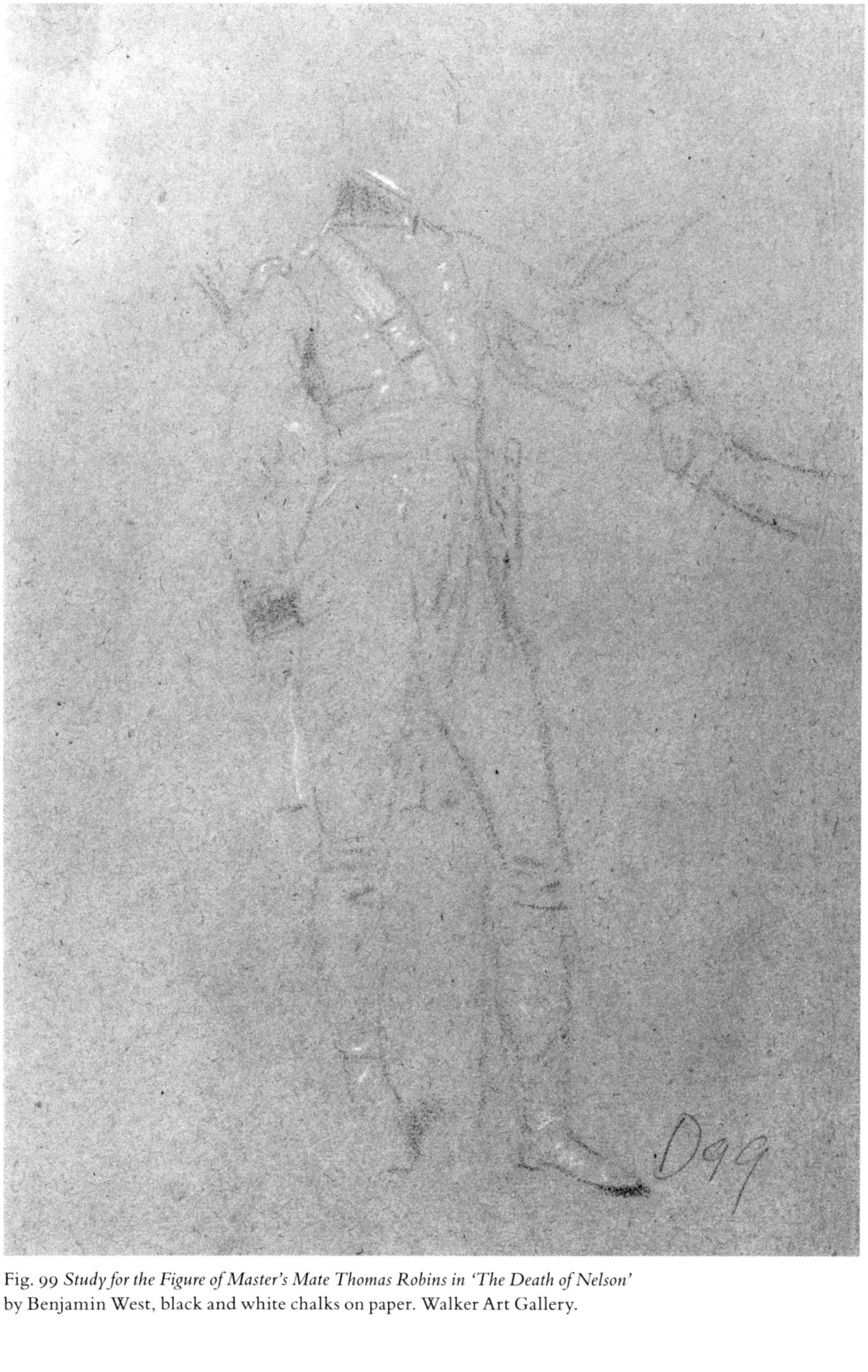

Fig. 99 *Study for the Figure of Master's Mate Thomas Robins in 'The Death of Nelson'* by Benjamin West, black and white chalks on paper. Walker Art Gallery.

Maritime Museum, Greenwich.
19. Von Erffa and Staley, *op. cit.*, pp. 223–4 (cat. 110).
20. FD, vol. 8, p. 2806 (entry of 8 July 1806).
21. FD, vol. 8, pp. 3064, 3162 (entries of 10 June and 12 December 1807)
22. In the catalogue the title was followed by an explanation written by West:
23. To coincide with the publication of Heath's print a key-plate was issued identifying the figures portrayed; this carried a version of West's 'explanation' cited above (n. 22).

The Death of Lord Nelson, or the Naval Victory off Trafalgar; being one of the most distinguished that ever occurred in the annals of Great Britain, for heroism and national importance. Mr West, conceiving that such an event demanded a composition every way appropriate to its dignity and high importance, formed it into an Epic Composition. This enabled him to give it that character and interest which the subject demanded. Availing himself of that character in composition, he laid the heroic Nelson wounded on the quarter-deck of his ship, the Victory, with his Captain (now Sir Thomas Hardy) holding the Dying Hero by the hand, and from a paper in the other, announcing to him the number of ships taken from the enemy's Combined Fleet. The surrounding groups of gallant officers and men are sympathizing with each other in the suffering of their wounded Friend and expiring Commander: and the dead and wounded in the several groups are introduced as episodes, to commemorate these with honour, who fell on board the Hero's ship in that distinguished action. The ships in the distance display the flags and signals of the other triumphant British Admirals, which are marked with all the wrack of battle, and that defeat which took place on the 21st of October, 1805.

24. FD, vol. 16, p. 5534 (entry of 6 July 1820).
25. George S. Hillard, ed.: *Life, Letters and Journals of George Ticknor* 2 vols (London, 1876) vol. 1, p. 63.
26. Mitchell, *op. cit.*, p. 365.
27. Von Erffa and Staley, *op. cit.*, p. 222.
28. Marks, *op. cit.*, pp. 68–9. The drawing is inscribed *made this sketch on the fifth of October 1798 when at the Castle Inn in Windsor.*
29. Marks, *op. cit.*, p. 32.
30. FD, *loc. cit.*
31. According to Thomas B. Hughes, *letter*, 18 September 2001, gallery files, his grandfather purchased the work (supposedly for £72) at an unidentified auction on his return from Australia, aged 37; Hughes's dates are unknown.
32. Liverpool Corporation's receipt, dated 22 June 1866 (gallery files) was presented by Thomas B. Hughes in 1967.
33. Charles Dyall; *Walker Art Gallery Descriptive Catalogue of the Collection of Pictures* (Liverpool, 1882) p. 15 (cat. 37).

Richard Westall

1766–1836

The Last Request

WAG 2839
oil on canvas, 205.5 × 175 cm
date: about 1807

The subject of WAG 2839 is taken from the poem *Monody to the Memory of a Young Lady Who Died in Childbed by an Afflicted Husband* (1768) by Cuthbert Shaw (1739–71).[1] In the poem, the dying wife Emma requests her husband, when he re-marries, to keep their child separated from its stepmother, so that it will not transfer its affection to her or know her dislike, and will enjoy its father's love in isolation: 'Wilt thou – / I know thou will…and silence speaks assent / And in that pleasing hope thy Emma dies content.' The poem was Shaw's most popular, and went through four editions in the 11 years after its publication.

Ostensibly Westall's painting was in

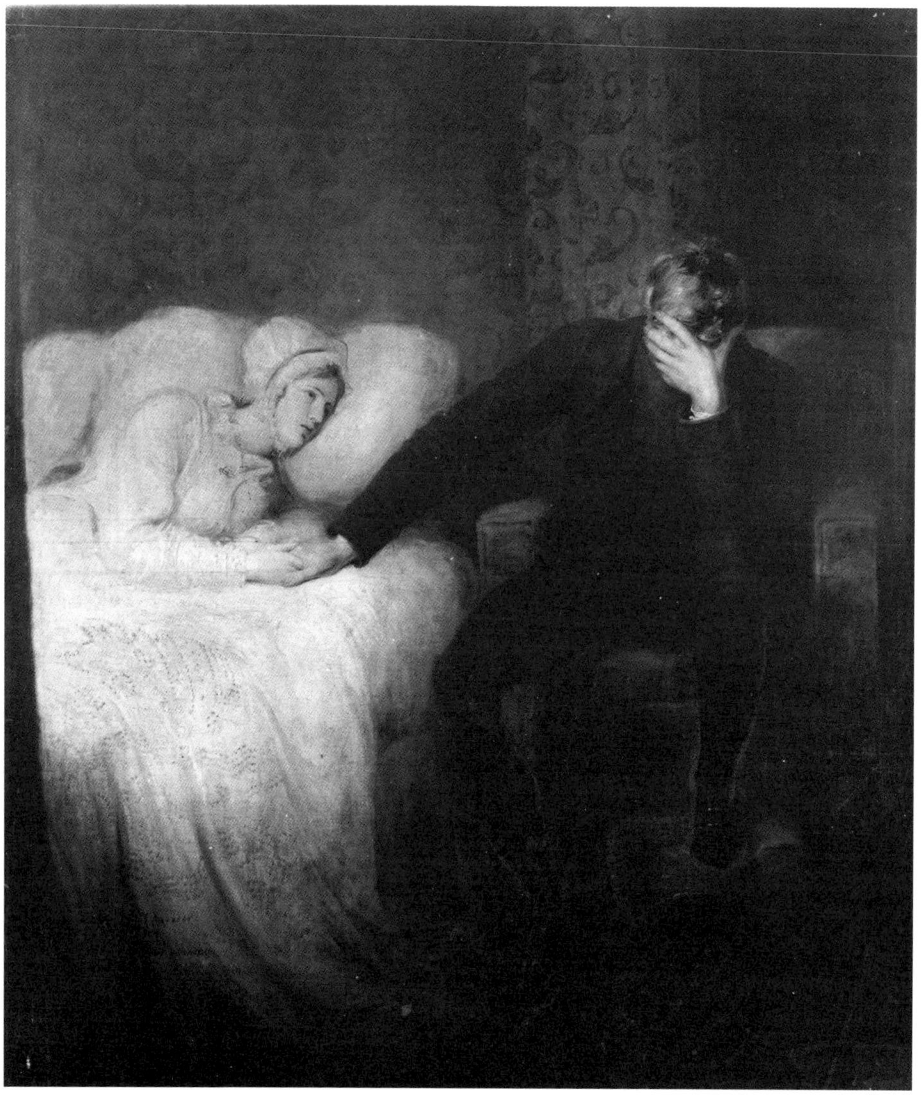

WAG 2839

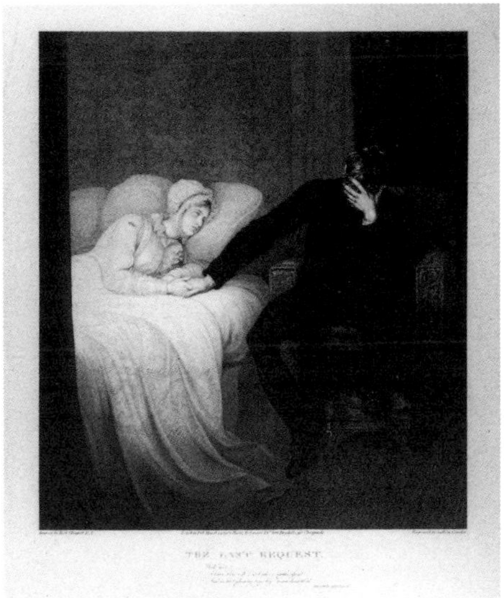

Fig. 100 *The Last Request* after Richard Westall, engraving by Anthony Cardon.
© Trustees of the British Museum.

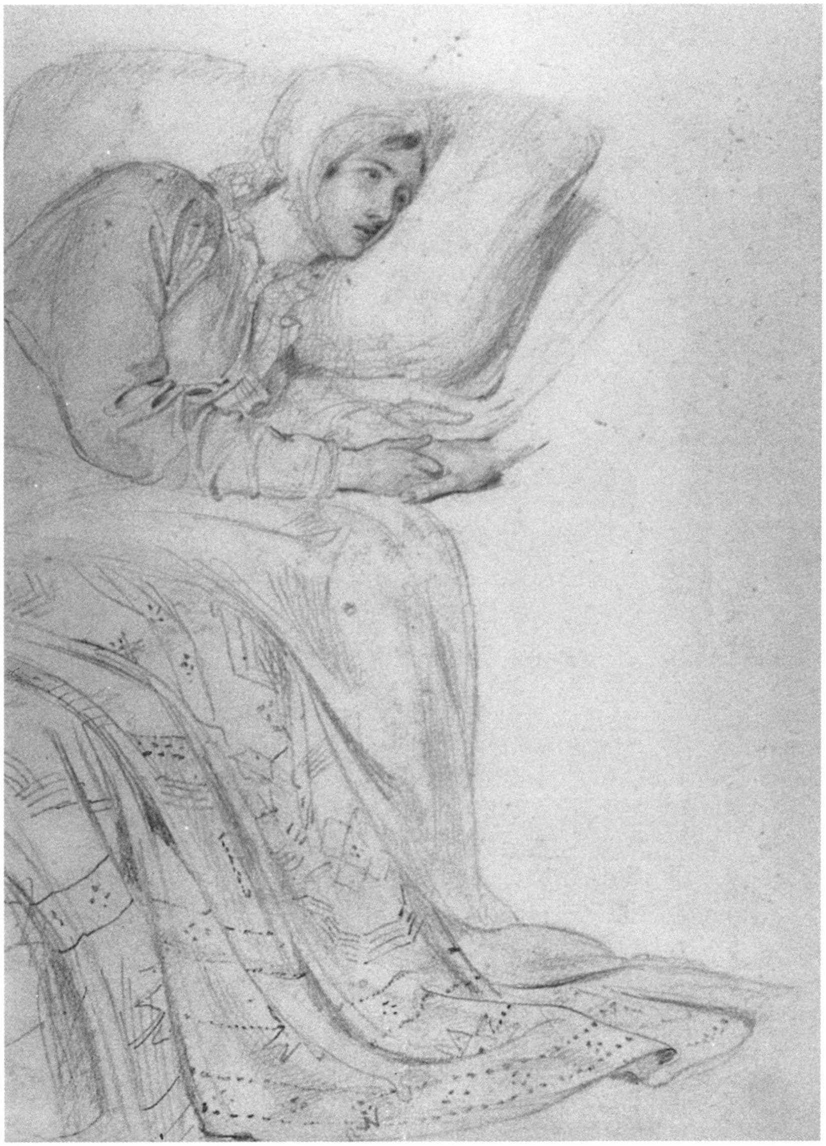

Fig. 101 *The Last Request* by Richard Westall, graphite on paper. Walker Art Gallery.

existence by 1807, since a large etching of it by Anthony Cardon (1772–1813) was published on 1 February that year by John Sharp. Cardon's print was re-worked and re-issued, in colour which generally follows WAG 2839, by Hurst, Robinson & Co. in 1819 (fig. 100). The letters of this version state that the subject was 'drawn' (rather than painted) by Richard Westall, and given that the painting itself was not exhibited and has a slightly unfinished air, it is tempting to wonder whether Westall's treatment enjoyed a more complex gestation than would at first sight appear.[2]

A signed but undated pencil study for the figure of Emma holding her husband's hand is also in the Walker Art Gallery (fig. 101).[3]

PROVENANCE

…S. J. Arnold; by whom presented to Liverpool Corporation in 1862;[4] transferred to the gallery before 1882.[5]

EXHIBITION

The Taste of Yesterday Walker Art Gallery 1970 (7).

NOTES

1. Shaw was a teacher (and acted as tutor to Philip Stanhope, 5th Earl of Chesterfield), actor, journalist and purveyor of quack medicines, as well as a poet; see James Sambrook: 'Shaw, Cuthbert', ODNB, vol. 50, pp. 77–8.

2. The contrast between WAG 2839 and Westall's 13 × 10 cm pencil drawing of a similar subject, *A Woman Ministering to Another, with Three Weeping Children (Young's 'Night Thoughts')*, one of seven drawings for an edition of the English Poets (Tate Britain, London T08656), is striking. The latter is far more characteristic of Westall's work as a literary illustrator. WAG 2839 has the appearance o a contemporary rather than eighteenth-century deathbed scene, belatedly put at the service of an engraving after Shaw's poem.

3. 36 × 23.5 cm; purchased from Abbott & Holder 1995.

4. Charles Dyall: *First Decade of the Walker Art Gallery: A Report of Its Operations from 1877–1887* (Liverpool, 1888) p. 7.

5. Charles Dyall: *Walker Art Gallery Descriptive Catalogue of the Permanent Collection of Pictures* (Liverpool, 1882) p. 27 (cat. 102).

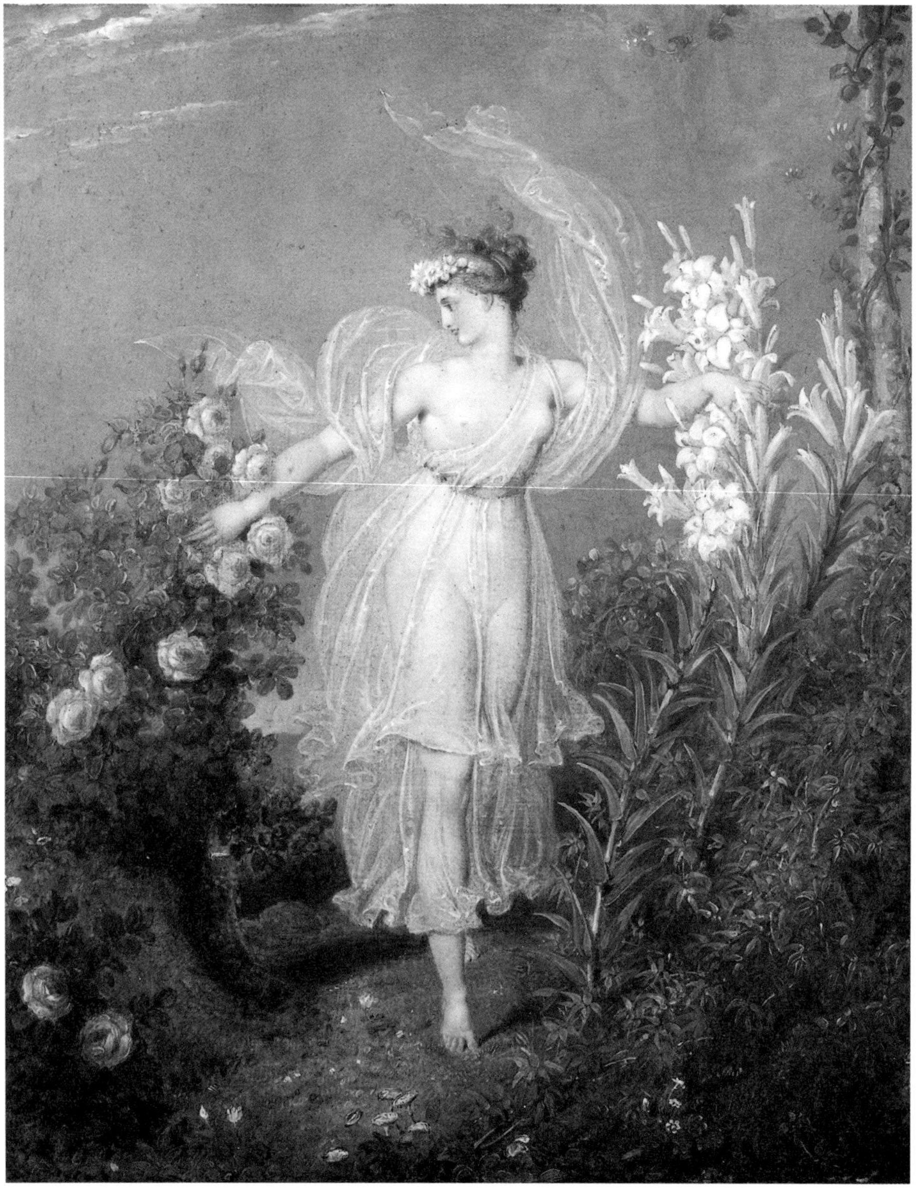

WAG 8468

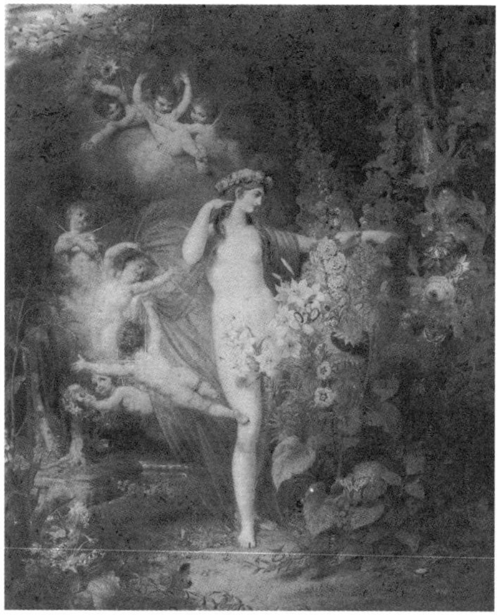

Fig. 102 *Flora Unveiled* by the Zephyrs, oil on canvas. Formerly Downton Castle. Photograph: Photographic Survey, Courtauld Institute of Art.

Flora

WAG 8468
oil on panel,[1] 45.5 × 38 cm
date: about 1825–30

On the reverse of WAG 8468 is a label inscribed *90 Flora in the late Mr Farrer's sale 15 June 1866 at Messrs. Christie Manson and Woods this beautiful little picture painted for Sir Thomas Lawrence sold for 9½ guineas* and in a different hand *BY RICHD. WESTALL R.A.*[2] (A second, printed label, repeats this information and gives the dimensions as 18 × 14½ inches.) The work is a simplified, cabinet-sized variant, concentrating on the figure of Flora alone, of the *Flora Unveiled by Zephyrs* that Westall had exhibited at the Royal Academy in 1807 and which had been acquired by his great patron and admirer Richard Payne Knight (formerly Downton Castle; sold at Hall's, Shrewsbury 28 June 2006 [297]; fig. 102).[3] Flora, the Roman goddess of flowers and gardens, and associated with fertility rites, had been frequently depicted in Western art since the Renaissance (particularly in continental Europe; less so in Britain). She is often in the company of her consort Zephyr, the West wind.[4] On stylistic grounds, WAG 8468 may be dated to the second half of the 1820s; the treatment of the female figure is comparable to that of Comedy in Westall's *Shakespeare between Tragedy and Comedy* signed and dated 1825 (exhibited in *The Painted Word, British History Painting 1750–1830*, Heim Gallery London 1991, cat. 141) and of Lilith in his *Faust and Lilith* (RA 1831, cat. 33; private collection, London).[5] The supplier of the panel, R. Davy of Wardour Street, was a company that was patronised by Lawrence himself in the 1820s.[6]

PROVENANCE
Painted for Sir Thomas Lawrence; Christie 15 May 1830 (82); ...Henry Farrer; Christie 15 June 1866 (90); ...[? private collection, France];[7] ...private collection London; Mr A. A. Ballard, Kingswear, Devon about 1970;[8] Bearne and Waycott, Torquay 6 March 1973 (454); bt. by the gallery.

NOTES
1. Stamp of R. Davy, 16 Wardour Street.
2. The label is printed *GOYARD/ emballeur / rue St. Honoré / 233 Paris* (a firm of packers founded at this address in 1853).
3. For Westall's patronage from Payne Knight see especially Andrew Ballantyne: 'The Most Interesting and Affecting Pictures: Richard Westall and Richard Payne Knight', *Sheffield Arts Review* (1995) pp. 5–17, and Richard J. Westall: 'The Westall Brothers', *Turner Studies* vol. 4 no. 1 (1984) pp. 23–38, especially pp. 24–5. Neither article refers to WAG 8468.
4. See Jane Davidson Reid: *The Oxford Guide to Classical Mythology in the Arts* 2 vols (New York and Oxford, 1993) vol. 1, pp. 434–42.
5. Photographs in the Witt Library, Courtauld Institute of Art.
6. The firm stated on their labels of the late 1820s that they supplied Sir Thomas Lawrence, President of the Royal Academy.
7. See n. 2.
8. Alexander Ballard, *letter*, 11 April 1973, gallery files.

Francis Wheatley

1747–1801

The Careless Servant

WAG 1625
oil on canvas, 78 × 64 cm
signed: *F. W.* (on the barrel, lower left)
date: unknown, perhaps about 1791–95

Although apparently an autograph work by Wheatley, WAG 1625 is rather perfunctorily painted. It was probably done expressly for an engraver.[1] C. G. Playter's stipple print titled as above, which reverses the design, is undated, but was presumably executed shortly after the picture's completion.[2]

Genre subjects of this type proliferate in Wheatley's *oeuvre* from the mid-1780s until the mid-1790s. Tentatively, it might be proposed that WAG 1625, with its element of rustic humour, aimed to exploit the popularity of George Morland's pig subjects, which seem to have emerged around 1790,[3] while at the same time extending Wheatley's own well-established repertoire of courtship themes.[4] WAG 1625 (which bore the title *Courtship* when it was acquired by the gallery) is thus perhaps most plausibly to be dated about 1791–95.

What appears from a photograph to be a copy of WAG 1625, rather than WAG 1625 itself, was in the collection of Charles Bechmann in 1910.[5]

PROVENANCE
...A. L. R. Rathbone; his bequest 1923.

NOTES
1. No work of this title appears among Wheatley's exhibited subjects, and no preparatory drawings are known. See Mary Webster: *Francis Wheatley* (London, 1970), appendices. Webster does not catalogue WAG 1625, but lists Playter's engraving (see above and n. 2) as E189, among 'undated

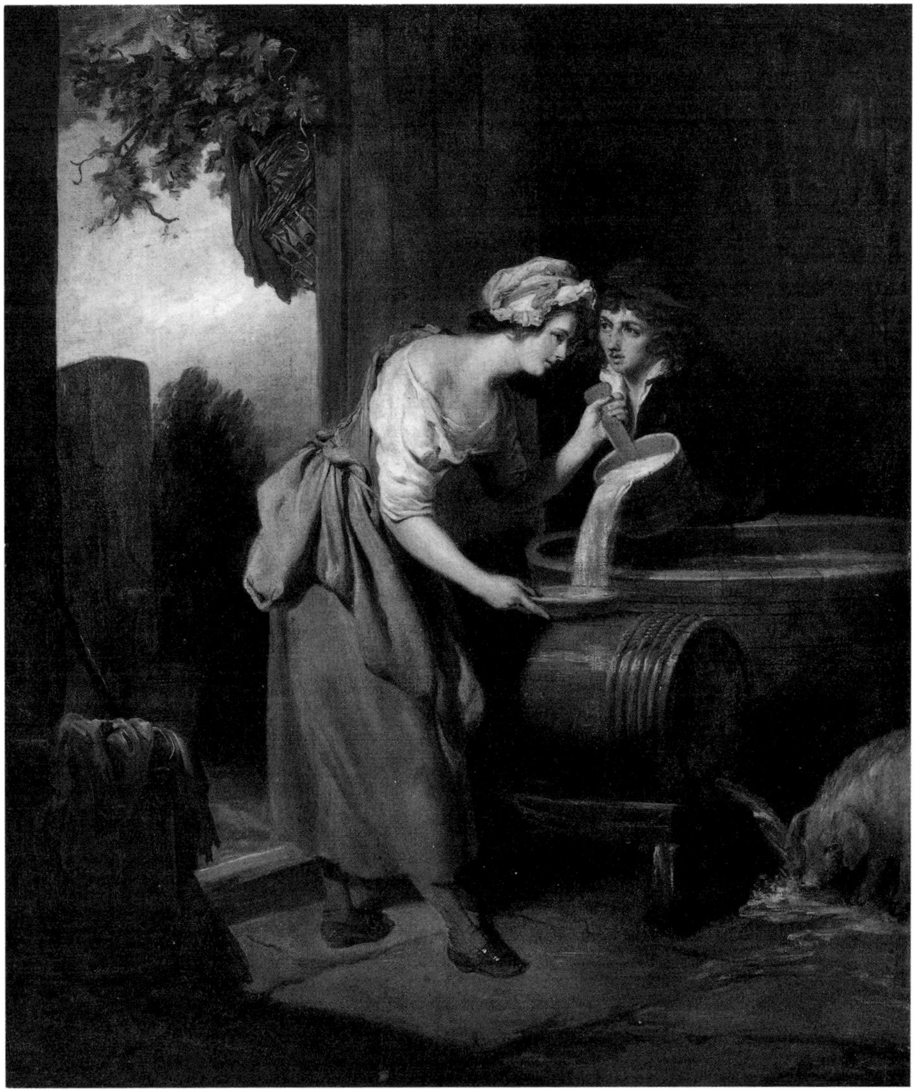

WAG 1625

engravings after Wheatley'.
2. Playter is stated (Department of Prints and Drawings, British Museum files) to have died in 1809, and to have been active between 1786 and 1803. He executed a handful of prints for the Boydells' Shakespeare Gallery, 1793–1800.
3. D. Winter: 'George Morland', PhD thesis, Stanford University, 1977, *passim*.
4. See, for example, *The Recruiting Officer* (RA 1787 [212]; Webster, *op. cit.*, pp. 74, 165, 205); the drawings *Love in a Mill*, dated 1786 (Webster, *op. cit.*, p. 73) and *A Country Girl Offering Refreshment to a Harvester* dated 1791 (Sotheby 10 July 1988 [53]); and particularly the painting *Courtship, Scene in a Dairy* (Sotheby 25 April 1934 [145, part]).
5. W. Roberts: *F. Wheatley, R.A. His Life and Works, with a Catalogue of His Engraved Pictures* (London, 1910), pl. xxxi. Small differences in detail are apparent, notably in the faces of the two figures.

John Williamson

1751–1818

William Roscoe

WAG 6136
oil on canvas, 43 × 36 cm
date: 1783–84

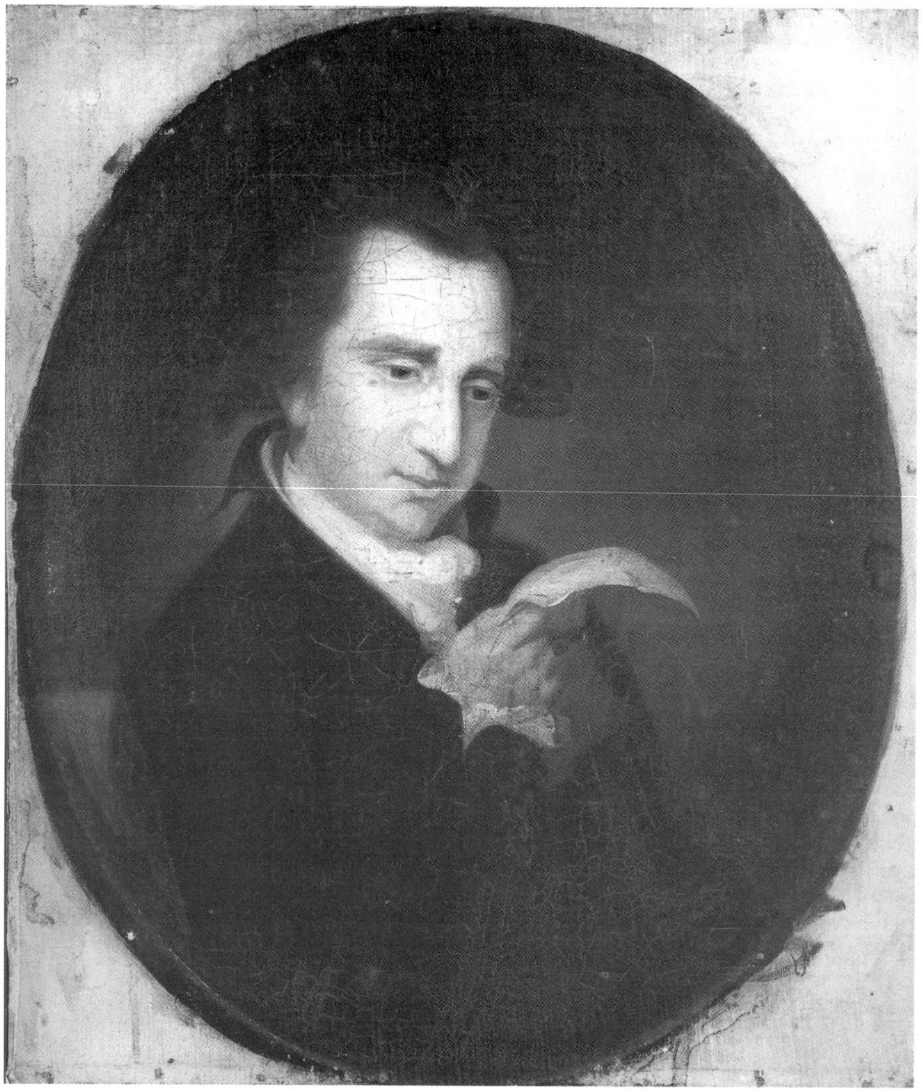

WAG 6136

The work's former owner Joseph Mayer described WAG 6136 as 'the first portrait [Roscoe] ever sat for', and he also believed it to be the *Portrait of a Gentleman* exhibited by Williamson at the Society for the Promotion of Painting and Design in Liverpool, 1784 (109)[1] (one of several works by the artist in the exhibition). The small-scale and delicate handling of WAG 6136 supports a dating to 1783–84, as does Roscoe's apparent age.

A watercolour sketch of Roscoe's head as it appears in WAG 6136 was also owned by Joseph Mayer, who believed it to be a preparatory study for WAG 6136;[2] however, the attribution of this to Williamson seems doubtful and it was probably copied from the oil.[3] Another version, in oils, on a standard 30 × 25 inch canvas, descended in Roscoe's family to his grandson Sir Henry Enfield Roscoe and was presented by him to the National Portrait Gallery in 1894. This differs from WAG 6136 in showing Roscoe reading a printed pamphlet, rather than a letter (fig. 103). It has been identified as Williamson's original[4] but with its somewhat waxy quality it seems likely to be a later variant of WAG 6136.

Possibly WAG 6136 is to be identified as the 'capital original Portrait of Roscoe' advertised as 'to be disposed of by private sale' in the *Literary Gazette* in August 1831 (a month after Roscoe's death), 'representing him in the middle period of life and finely executed by the elder Williamson, of Liverpool. It has never been engraved.'[5]

PROVENANCE

...Joseph Mayer; his bequest to Bebington Borough Council; presented to the gallery 1962.

EXHIBITION

[? Society for the Promotion of Painting and Design in Liverpool 1784 (109)].

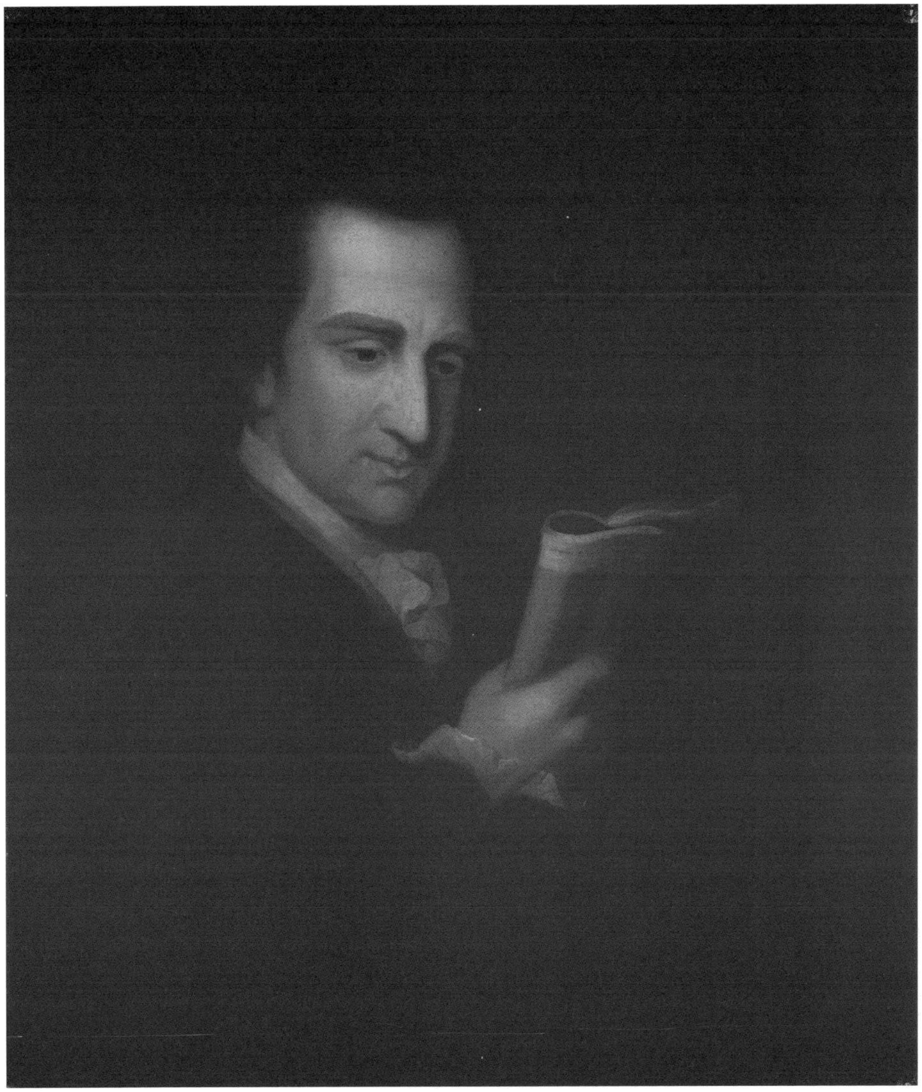

Fig. 103 *William Roscoe* after John Williamson, oil on canvas. © National Portrait Gallery, London.

William Roscoe

WAG 2547
oil on canvas, 38.5 × 30 cm

Mrs Jane Roscoe and Her Son William Stanley Roscoe

WAG 2267
oil on canvas, 38.5 × 30 cm
date: 1784–85

Of identical dimensions and provenance, WAG 2547 and WAG 2267 are painted in a similar style and have every appearance of being pendants.[1] Roscoe's son Henry, in his biography of his father of 1833, wrote of WAG 2547, 'painted about the year 1791 by Williamson, an artist of considerable ability at Liverpool'.[2] He had the portrait engraved by W. C. Edwards for the frontispiece of the biography and the engraving accordingly is inscribed *aetat* 38. But Henry (who was born only in 1799) was surely in error over the date. Roscoe (born 1753; see WAG 3130, pp. 162–4 for biography) looks younger than 38 and not much older than how he appears in WAG 6136, which is probably to be related to the portrait – presumably painted in 1783 or early 1784 – that was exhibited at the Society for the Promotion of Painting and Design in Liverpool in the latter year. Furthermore, the relatively small-scale and tight handling stands in marked contrast to Williamson's more expansive later manner (as witnessed in WAG 2589 and WAG 3167, pp. 255–6), and even with the portrait of Fuseli of 1789 (WAG 1542, pp. 254–5). It seems preferable to describe WAG 2547 as the work of a young, careful artist and to date it to within a couple of years of WAG 6136, that is, to about 1784–85. This fits well with the traditional identification of the sitters in the pendant picture, WAG 2267, as Mrs Jane Roscoe (b. 1757; see WAG 2589, pp. 255–6) with her eldest son, William Stanley, who was born in 1782 and who

NOTES

1. Joseph Mayer: *Early Exhibitions of Art in Liverpool, with Some Notes for a Memoir of George Stubbs R.A.* (Liverpool, 1876) p. 61; cf. Mayer's ms *List of Oil Paintings in the Lecture Theatre, Bebington, September 1873* (copy in gallery archives) no. 31: 'the first painted portrait of him'.
2. The sketch is in the *Roscoe Memorials*, part 1, *Mayer Papers*, LRO 920/MAY/11, p. 2 and is inscribed in pencil *John Williamson // the first sketch Roscoe ever sat to.*
3. As suggested in *MPPP*, p. 225.
4. Implicitly, by being selected (rather than WAG 6136, which was then in the possession of Bebington Borough Council) for the exhibition *150 Years of the Liverpool Academy* Walker Art Gallery 1960 (2). On its arrival at the Walker WAG 6136 was regarded by Hugh Macandrew as a copy of the National Portrait Gallery picture (draft catalogue entry, gallery files); and *MPPP* describes it as 'after John Williamson' although qualifies this by saying it is 'possibly autograph'. Richard Walker: *Regency Portraits* 2 vols (London, 1985) vol. 1, pp. 424–5, offers no qualitative judgements concerning the National Portrait Gallery painting's relationship to WAG 6136.
5. *The Literary Gazette and Journal of the Belles Lettres* (6 August 1831) p. 511. Another candidate for this is the unattributed portrait illustrated in H. Stansfield: 'William Roscoe, Botanist', *Liverpool Bulletin* vol. 5 (1955) fp. 19, but this appears to show him in later life.

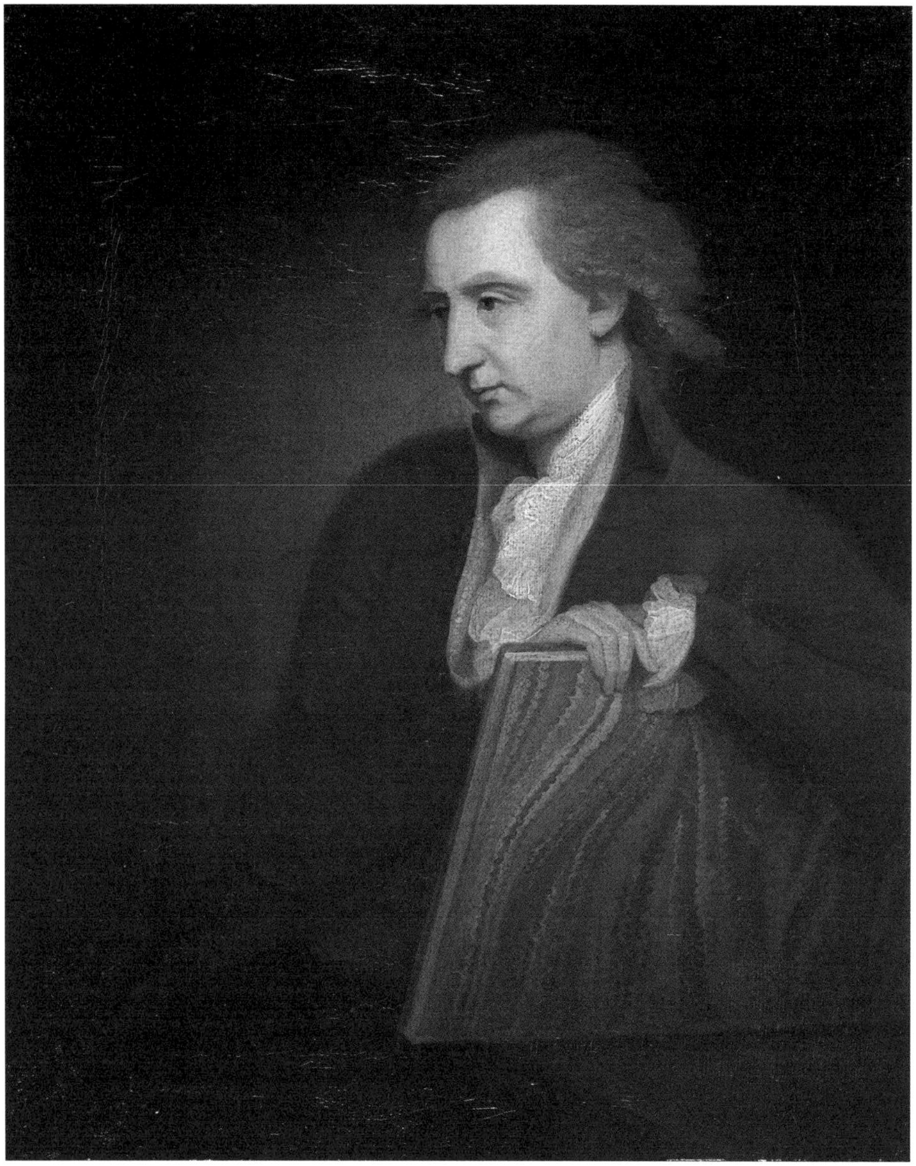

WAG 2547

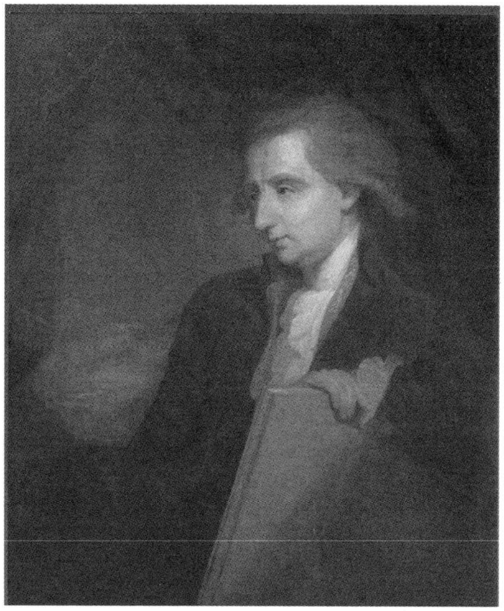

Fig. 104 *William Roscoe* after John Williamson, oil on canvas. Private collection, UK; photo Mills Media, Liverpool.

appears about two or three years old in the picture.[3] The couple's second son, Edward, was born in 1785 and his absence from the portrait tends to suggest that it pre-dates his birth; there is even perhaps a visual hint that Mrs Roscoe was pregnant when she sat for the portrait. The traditional identification of both sitters in WAG 2267 was subsequently overturned on the grounds that 'the costume makes a date in the 1800s certain',[4] yet if the style of the dress is to be ascribed to the 1800s,[5] a possible explanation is that Mrs Roscoe later had the work 'updated'. Comparison with Williamson's portrait of Mrs Roscoe dateable to the early 1790s (WAG 2589) confirms the likeness and suggests that she is between five and ten years younger here.

Two other versions of WAG 2547 are recorded: one, of good quality, in which Roscoe holds a red leather-bound folio rather than a marbled one and is posed against a curtain opening out on a stormy sea (fig. 104), was successively in Rathbone and Cotton family ownership; the other, measuring 15 × 12 inches and of replica quality, descended in the family of Roscoe's second son, Edward.[6]

PROVENANCE

By descent to William Malin Roscoe, great-grandson of William Roscoe; his widow Mrs A. M. Roscoe; her bequest 1950.

EXHIBITION

Historical Exhibition of Liverpool Antiquities Walker Art Gallery 1907 (section G, 97) [WAG 2547] and (section G, 93) [WAG 2267].

NOTES

1. This point was not made in *MPPP*, in which a divergent view of these two works was offered.
2. Henry Roscoe: *The Life of William Roscoe* 2 vols (London, 1833) vol. 2, p. 474.
3. F. W. Dunston: *Roscoeana* (privately printed, 1905) p. 7, n. 3; William Roscoe of Birchamp, Glos., to George H. Parry, City Librarian, *letter*, 2 May 1932, *Roscoe Memorials* part 2, *Mayer Papers* LRO 920/MAY/11, p. 131.
4. *MPPP*, p. 224.
5. A dating for the dress to the early nineteenth

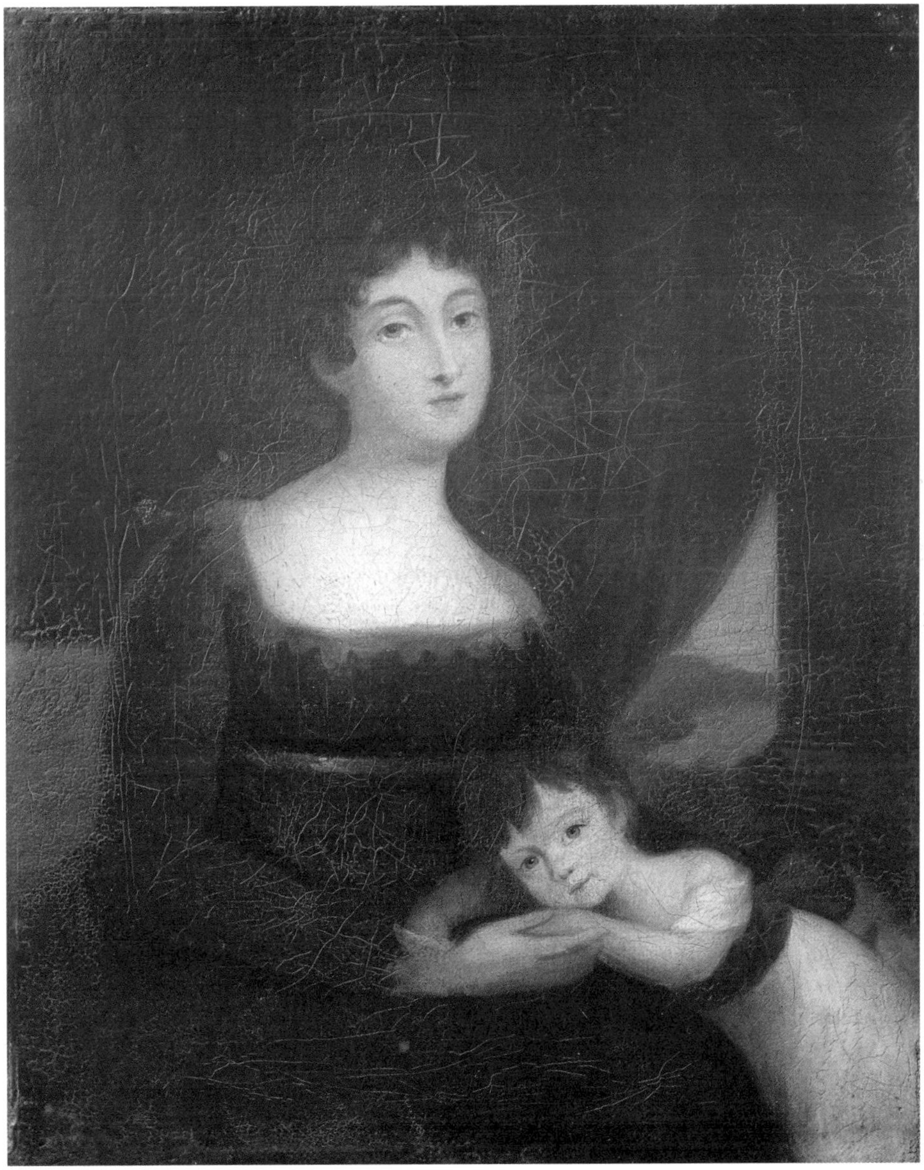

WAG 2267

century was confirmed by Pauline Rushton, Curator of Decorative Art, National Museums Liverpool, *verbally*, 1 August 2007. She pointed out that the ruffle round the neckline could be the cotton muslin or fine linen edge of the shift worn beneath the dress.
6. See *MPPP*, p. 223.

William Roscoe

WAG 2266
oil on canvas, 33 × 28 cm
date: about 1787

A manuscript label on the reverse of WAG 2266, contemporary in date with the picture, reads, *Portrait of William Roscoe / by Williamson*. It has been generally agreed that Roscoe appears to be a

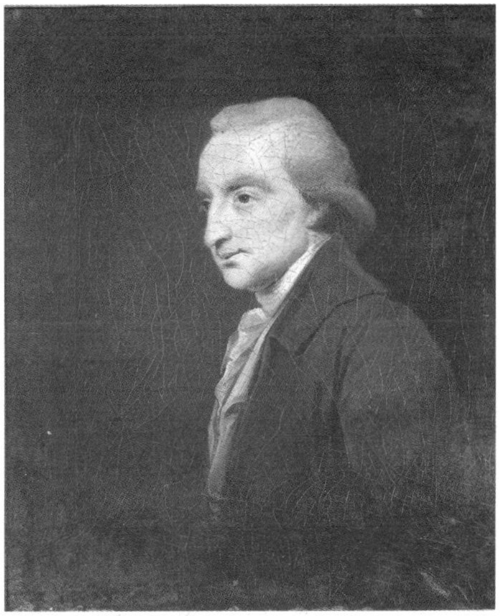

WAG 2266

few years older here than in WAG 2547 (above).[1] The style is a little looser than in that work, yet it still seems delicate by the side of the more confident and broadly handled portrait of Fuseli of 1789 (see below), arguing that it is earlier in date. If so, it was perhaps painted about 1787, when Roscoe would have been 34 years old.[2]

PROVENANCE
By descent to William Malin Roscoe; his widow Mrs A. M. Roscoe; her bequest 1950.

EXHIBITION
Historical Exhibition of Liverpool Antiquities Walker Art Gallery 1907 (section G, 96).

NOTES
1. *MPPP*, p. 223; on the view that WAG 2547 dated from 1791, a dating of the mid-1790s for WAG 2266 was proposed. Hugh Macandrew, in a draft entry dating from about 1960 (gallery files) also suggested that WAG 2266 dated from the 1790s.
2. In default of any other known candidate, WAG 2266 might have been the *Portrait of a Gentleman* exhibited by Williamson at the 1787 Liverpool Society for the Promotion of Painting and Design (122); Roscoe was Williamson's chief patron and closely involved with the Society. The suggestion, however, is speculative.

Henry Fuseli

WAG 1542
oil on canvas, 61.5 × 52 cm
date: 1789

Henry Fuseli, the Swiss-born artist domiciled in London (see pp. 40–7) became friendly with William Roscoe of Liverpool about 1779,[1] and WAG 1542 is a friendship portrait for which Fuseli sat, to Roscoe's favourite local artist, on a visit to Liverpool in the later part of 1789. The date was established by Fuseli's first biographer, John Knowles,[2] who at the end of 1825, the year of Fuseli's death, wrote to Roscoe's son: 'Did you not tell me that he sat for his Portrait in Liverpool, do you know in what year, and who the artist was?'[3] The following year he wrote again: 'Did you not say that a Mr Williamson painted a portrait of Fuseli now in your possession, if so in what ye[ar]?'[4] William Stanley Roscoe's replies do not survive but evidently Knowles used the information that he supplied in his published biography. There is no reason to question the date since independent evidence exists to show that Fuseli did visit Roscoe in Liverpool in the autumn of 1789.[5]

Whether the portrait is a good likeness of Fuseli is open to question.[6] Informal in conception and loosely brushed, it must be the product of few sittings; perhaps only one. A later inventory of Roscoe's possessions taken in 1820 describes it as 'a present',[7] and it seems likely that Fuseli sat for WAG 1542 at Roscoe's request and gave it to him at the time it was painted.

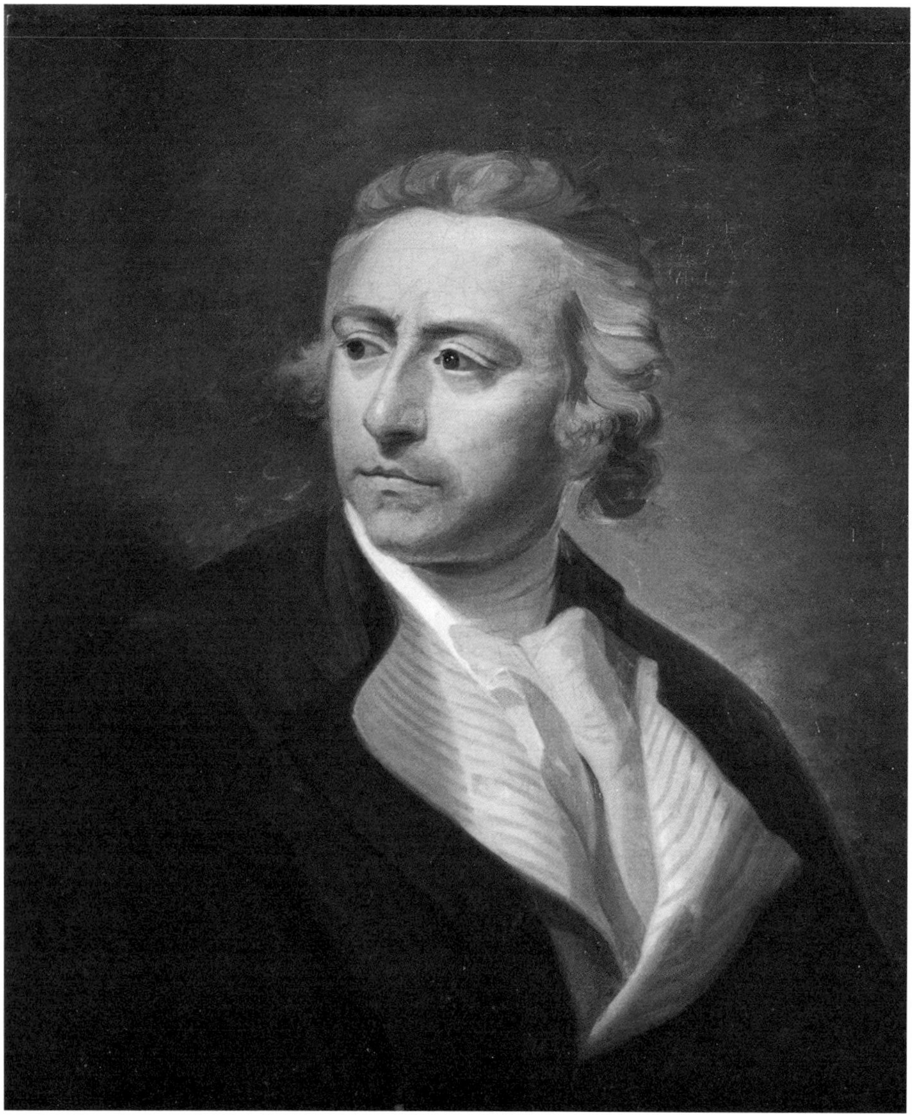

WAG 1542

PROVENANCE

...William Roscoe by 1820; by descent to Mrs A. M. Roscoe; her bequest 1950.

NOTES

1. For the relationship between Roscoe and Fuseli see especially Hugh Macandrew: 'Henry Fuseli and William Roscoe', *Liverpool Bulletin*, vol. 8 (1959–60), pp. 5–52; also Macandrew: 'Selected Letters from the Correspondence of Henry Fuseli and William Roscoe of Liverpool', *Gazette des Beaux-Arts*, vol. 62 (1963) pp. 205–28. Fuseli had first visited Liverpool in 1767 with his friend Joseph Johnson, who was a Liverpudlian, and on that occasion (according to his biographer John Knowles: *The Life and Writings of Henry Fuseli*, 3 vols [London, 1831] vol. 1, p. 44) 'became acquainted with men who, in after life, were the greatest patrons of his pencil'; however, these cannot have included Roscoe, who in 1767 was only 14 years old. That Fuseli's friendship with Roscoe dated from 1779 was stated by Knowles, *op. cit.*, vol. 1, pp. 66–7.
2. Knowles, *op. cit.*, vol. 1, p. 352.
3. Knowles to W. S. Roscoe, *letter*, 29 December 1825; *Roscoe Papers*, LRO 920/ROS/2280.
4. Knowles to W. S. Roscoe, *letter*, 27 November 1826; *Roscoe Papers*, LRO 920/ROS/2281.
5. A letter from Fuseli to Roscoe dated November 1789 describes his journey home from Liverpool by coach; *Roscoe Papers*, LRO 920/ROS/1599.
6. The obituary of Williamson in the *Liverpool Mercury* (5 June 1818) included WAG 1542 among the works by him that 'will ever hold a highly respectable rank in the Arts, standing second only to a Reynolds or a Lawrence, and in the estimation of some, equal to them'; cited in *MPPP*, p. 222. *MPPP* states that WAG 1542 shows Fuseli with the white hair that resulted from his catching a fever in Rome in 1774; however, the white is much less prominent than it is in Opie's portrait of Fuseli of 1794 (National Portrait Gallery) and is more like

the 'salt and pepper' effect visible in Northcote's portrait (also National Portrait Gallery) of 1778. Both the latter works are more characterful and less deferential than WAG 1542.
7. *Inventory of Household Furniture etc. Belonging to William Roscoe*, 9 February 1820, *Roscoe Papers*, LRO 920/ROS/3906, p. 6.

The Five Elder Sons of William Roscoe

WAG 3167
oil on canvas, 74.5 × 91.5 cm
date: 1792

The sitters are William Stanley (1782–1843), Edward (1785–1840), James (1787–1829), Robert (1789–1884) and Thomas (1791–1871), the elder sons of William Roscoe and his wife Jane.[1] William and Jane had ten children in all: one girl, Elizabeth, was born and died in 1783 and four more children, two boys and two girls, were born between 1793 and 1799.[2] On the basis of the children's age, WAG 3167 may be dated to 1792: the youngest boy, Thomas, appears no older than one and William Stanley, at left, could well be ten. He rests his hand on a sheet of unrolled paper; a portfolio is visible resting against the table around which the boys are crowded.

The five boys would have comprised all Mr and Mrs Roscoe's living children at the date of the portrait. If the work was intended as a complete record of the next generation of the family, Mrs Roscoe's discovery that she was again pregnant in late 1792 may well have caused the work to be abandoned, and this in turn could explain its very broadly laid-in and incomplete treatment. The very perfunctory appearance of WAG 3167 has led to the suggestion that it is not an autograph work by Williamson;[3] however, the one other known version of the composition, the same size,[4] is said to have been of no higher quality.

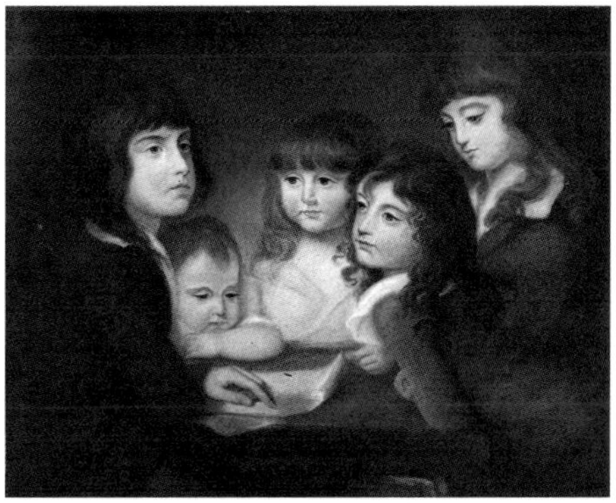

WAG 3167

Assessment of the work's status is complicated by its indifferent condition. An earlier relining has flattened the paint surface and may have resulted in a substantial loss of detail. The tacking edge of the original canvas is visible at the top, while at the right-hand side the presence of a continuous seam about two inches from the edge suggests that the canvas has been extended. An old repaired tear extends about 25 cm diagonally into the painting from just below the top right-hand corner.[5] On balance the original attribution to Williamson appears acceptable.

PROVENANCE
By descent to William Roscoe's eldest daughter Mary Ann Roscoe; by descent to Miss H. Winefrid Jevons; by whom presented 1950.

NOTES
1. For further biographical information about the five boys see F. W. Dunston: *Roscoeana* (privately printed, 1905) pp. 8–30. William Stanley married Hannah Eliza Caldwell in 1818 and was a banker; Edward married his second cousin Margaret Lace in 1810 and was a merchant. Little is known about James beyond the fact of his marriage to Jane Douglas in 1817; Robert married Martha Walker in 1819 and was a solicitor in London. Thomas married his wife Elizabeth about 1816 and had five children born between about 1817 and 1834 (ms addition to the copy of *Roscoeana* inscribed *No. 1*, LRO, p. 28) and was a writer; William and Robert also published volumes of poetry. Between them the five boys had 31 children.
2. The four youngest children were Richard (1793–1864), Mary Ann (1795–1845), into whose possession WAG 3167 came, Elizabeth (1797–1853) and Henry (1799–1836); Dunston, *loc. cit.*
3. *MPPP*, p. 223, describes WAG 3167 as 'of poor quality and possibly a copy of a lost original'; *CIC* catalogued it as 'after John Williamson'.
4. The other version, bearing a traditional attribution to Hoppner, was owned in 1972 by E. J. T. Roscoe (a descendant of Edward Roscoe); note in gallery files. Its dimensions are the same as WAG 3167 and it is described as 'an exact replica'.
5. Miss Winefrid Jevons had the picture cleaned 'several years ago…by a firm undertaking that work for the National Gallery', *letter*, 6 October 1950, gallery files.

Mrs Jane Roscoe

WAG 2589
oil on canvas, 61 × 51 cm
date: 1792–93

The identity of the sitter in WAG 2589 was traditional in the Roscoe family. Jane Griffies, born in 1757, was the second daughter of William Griffies, a draper in Castle Street, Liverpool and his wife Anne, née Lace. She married William Roscoe on 22 February 1781 at St Anne's Chapel and with him had ten children, seven sons and three daughters, who were born between 1782 and 1800. Their happy

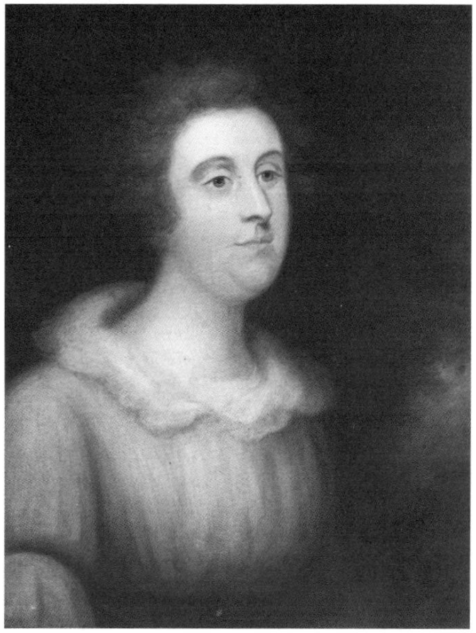

WAG 2589

marriage ended only with her death in 1824.

The portrait was presented to the gallery without attribution and in 1978 the ascription to Williamson was described as 'recent'.[1] WAG 2589 was clearly intended as an informal portrait that was not intended to flatter: the handling of the facial features is literal and almost wooden and of the rest of the work is very loose and skimpy. A date of about 1792–93 seems the most likely on the basis of the sitter's apparent age and her dress, as well as from its stylistic similarity to WAG 3167 (above). It was perhaps left unfinished when Mrs Roscoe became pregnant with her seventh child, born in 1793.

PROVENANCE

By descent to Charlotte Alicia Roscoe, the sitter's grand-daughter-in-law, 1905;[2] by descent to Mrs Philip Roscoe; by whom presented 1931.

EXHIBITION

Roscoe Centenary Liverpool City Library 1931 (4).

NOTES

1. *MPPP*, p. 223; the attribution, which must be correct although the work is one of the erratic artist's less endearing productions, was made by Hugh Macandrew in a draft entry of about 1960, gallery files. Macandrew suggested the work dated from about 1783, shortly after Williamson's arrival in Liverpool, perhaps on the view that the undoubted coarseness of the paint handling might reflect a relatively immature artist. *MPPP* did not suggest a date.
2. F. W. Dunston, *Roscoeana* (privately printed, 1905) p. 7, n. 3.

Peter Litherland

WAG 2265
oil on canvas, 76 × 62 cm
date: about 1796–1800

The watchmaker Peter Litherland was born in Warrington in 1756 and worked there, at an address in Wilderspool Causeway, until 1790. He moved to Latchford, outside Warrington and while there in 1791 took out his first patent for the rack-lever escapement. The following year he moved to Liverpool and took out a second patent.[1] He is recorded as living at 21 Mount Pleasant in 1796 and at 12 Commutation Row in 1800. From 1800 the business of Litherland, Whiteside & Co., patent lever watchmakers, is also recorded in Ranelagh Street; this subsequently became the firm Litherland, Davies & Co., of Church Street and Bold Street which remained in business until 1876. Peter Litherland died in December 1804, leaving a wife, Lydia, with whom he had had at least one son, Peter, and four daughters.[2]

Unattributed when presented to the Corporation, WAG 2265 was identified as by Williamson in 1926 by a descendant of the sitter.[3] The attribution is unarguable on stylistic grounds but is also supported by circumstantial evidence: Williamson's artist son Daniel acted as a bondsman to Litherland's estate when he died intestate, and is believed to have been married to one of Litherland's daughters;[4] if so, it would have been natural for Litherland to have given preference to his in-law when selecting an artist to sit to. Furthermore, the obituary of the artist published on 5 June 1818 by the *Liverpool Mercury* referred to Williamson's portrait of 'the late Mr Litherland' as one of his works 'that will ever hold a highly respectable rank in the arts'.[5] WAG 2265 was no doubt painted during the 12 years that Litherland lived in Liverpool; a date of about 1796–1800 may tentatively be proposed on the basis of style, costume, and the sitter's age. Litherland is shown holding an open watch which exhibits one of his own mechanisms; a second watch and its opened glass-fronted case is on the table in front of him. The canvas has suffered from bituminous cracking and flaking paint, and the paint surface is considerably worn following relining.[6]

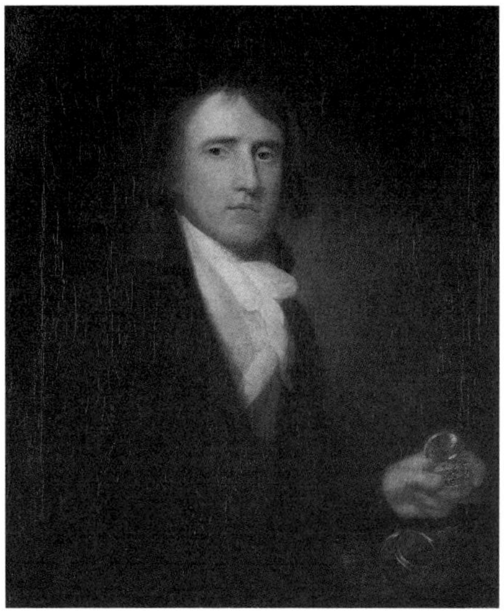

WAG 2265

PROVENANCE

Presented to Liverpool Corporation before 1873;[7] deposited in the Library & Museum; transferred to the gallery between 1908 and 1927.[8]

EXHIBITIONS

Historical Exhibition of Liverpool Antiquities Walker Art Gallery 1907 (section F, 14[a]); *Historical Exhibition of Liverpool Art* Walker Art Gallery 1908 (153).

NOTES

1. The first patent (no. 1830) describes a straight-line rack lever escapement with a 4-wheel train and a 15-tooth escape wheel with radial teeth; a similar movement with right angle escapement, and a method of using a rack to wind a watch. The second patent (no.1889) describes a rack lever escapement with a 3-wheel train and a 30-tooth escape with inclined teeth; a similar escapement with an extra wheel between the rack and balance which provided a watch with balance beating once a second; a compensation curb; and a method of winding watches by means of a slide. See G. H. Baillie et al., eds: *Britten's Old Clocks and Watches and Their Makers*

(7th edn, New York, 1956) p. 426, and R. Vaudrey Mercer, 'Peter Litherland & Co.', *Antiquarian Horology* vol. 3, no.11 (June 1962) pp. 316–23.
2. Vaudrey Mercer, *op. cit.*, pp. 316–7; *MPPP*, pp. 223–4. Peter junior and Lydia are referred to in the Administration Bonds of Litherland's estate, Lancashire Record Office; communicated by R. Sharpe France, *letter*, 21 July 1961, gallery files; Litherland's four daughters are referred to in notes by Robert Williamson dating from about 1900–10, stated by *MPPP*, p. 224, to be in gallery files (untraced).
3. *MPPP*, *loc. cit.*
4. See n. 2.
5. Cited in *MPPP*, p. 222.
6. Condition notes by J. Coburn Witherop, September 1958, gallery files; Witherop conserved WAG 2265 in 1970.
7. Charles Dyall: *First Decade of the Walker Art Gallery: A Report of Its Operations from 1877–1887* (Liverpool, 1888) p. 7.
8. The portrait, which is listed in Charles Dyall: *Walker Art Gallery Descriptive Catalogue of the Permanent Collection of Pictures* (Liverpool, 1882) p. 45 (cat. 190) as 'on deposit in the Library and Museum', was lent by the Libraries Sub-committee to the 1908 exhibition; it was included in the 1927 Walker Art Gallery collection catalogue, p. 216.

John Shepherd

WAG 2585
oil on canvas, 76 × 65.5 cm
date: unknown, perhaps 1802–14

John Shepherd (1764–1836), naturalist, was the first curator of the Liverpool Botanic Garden. He was appointed in 1802, when the Garden opened, on being recommended to William Roscoe by J. L. Philips of Manchester (where Shepherd then lived). Shepherd's catalogue of the Garden's plants was published in 1808. With his friend John Bostock he contributed to the fifth edition of Withering's *Arrangement of British Plants*, in 1818 he gave his name of the genus *Shepherdia*, and he collaborated with Roscoe on his *Monandrian Plants* (1828). His obituary in the *Liverpool Mercury*, 30 September 1836, observed that 'indefatigable in his exertions, he succeeded in raising the establishment over which he was placed, to a state of competition with the first gardens of Europe.'[1]

The attribution of WAG 2585 to Williamson seems correct not only on stylistic grounds but also circumstantial ones.[2] He was a favoured artist of Roscoe's and the latter may well have commissioned this portrait for presentation to the Garden. Furthermore, Williamson exhibited a portrait of Shepherd at the Liverpool Academy in 1814, which seems very likely to have been the present work, commissioned to mark the sitter's 50th birthday. Although, as has been pointed out, Shepherd seems too young to be aged 50 here,[3] the question of his likely age is impossible to resolve owing to the work's very degraded condition. Suffering from extreme bituminous cracking across its entire surface (see fig. 105) it was in effect completely repainted in 1971[4] to make it exhibitable in the context of museum displays on botanical themes. A further possibility, although this would be contrary to early nineteenth-century exhibiting practice, is that the portrait was actually painted earlier – perhaps around the time of the opening of the Garden – and simply borrowed to include in the 1814 exhibition as a mark of respect.

PROVENANCE
...Liverpool Corporation Parks and Gardens Department; transferred to the gallery at an unknown date.[5]

EXHIBITION
[? LA 1814 (42)].

NOTES
1. Summarising the biography in *MPPP*, pp. 224–5, where earlier biographical sources are cited.
2. The painting entered the gallery without attribution and seems to have been first ascribed to Williamson by Mary Bennett in *MPPP*.
3. *MPPP*, p. 224.
4. *MPPP*, p. 225. The circumstances of this are not recorded.
5. The Corporation took over the administration of the Botanic Garden in 1836 after it had been removed from its original site in Mosslake Fields, off Myrtle Street, to a site adjoining Edge Lane. In the twentieth century the Garden was moved again to Calderstones Park. I am grateful to Jyll Bradley for the suggestion, *verbally*, March 2008, that WAG 2585 was transferred in 1908 when the Edge Lane herbarium and library were transferred to the Liverpool Museum and Liverpool City Libraries respectively.

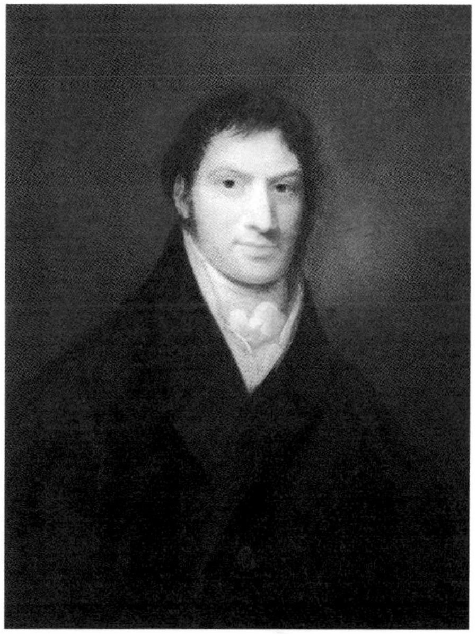

WAG 2585

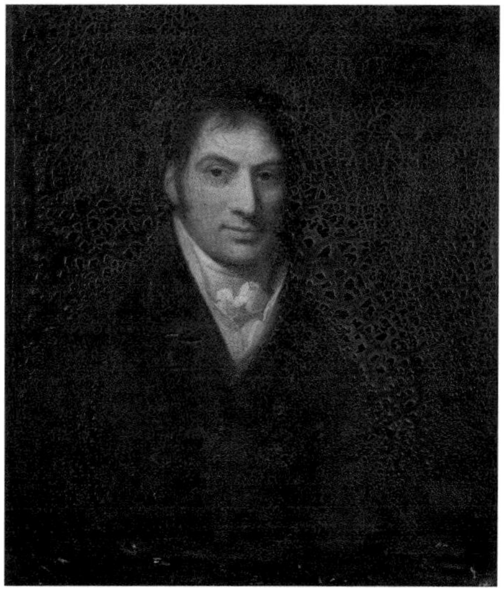

Fig. 105 WAG 2585 prior to being repainted. Walker Art Gallery.

William Durning

WAG 8706
oil on canvas, 76 × 64.5 cm

John Durning

WAG 8707
oil on canvas, 87.5 × 71.5 cm

Anne Durning

WAG 8708
oil on canvas, 72.5 × 61 cm
date: about 1803

William Durning (about 1714–1803), a yeoman of Edge Hill, outside Liverpool, was the son of William Durning (1667–1727) and Sarah (d. 1748), niece and co-heiress of Richard Wainwright, also of Edge Hill. The family, Presbyterians and later Unitarians, were said to have been of Dutch origin. They had owned their small estate on Edge Lane, the road leading eastwards from Liverpool towards the township of West Derby, since at least the mid-seventeenth century. William married Anne Hill (d. 1776) of Denton's Green and the couple had three children (see below). William made a living farming, creating what was originally called Rake Lane (later re-named Durning Road) as a path to move his cattle from one pasture to another. He was fabled among later generations of the Durning family for refusing to add to his estate a large area of adjoining common land, which he was offered on the condition that he enclosed it and kept it up, supposedly saying that it was not worth his trouble. He was buried in the Nonconformist Park Road Chapel, Toxteth.[1]

John Durning appears to have been William's second son, born about 1752. (A first son, William, is said to have died young in 1751.) John was a land agent for the Watt family of Speke and celebrated for the minute accuracy of his book-keeping. He remained unmarried and died suddenly of heart disease, aged about 49, in 1802.[2]

Anne Durning (1754–1831), known as Nancy, daughter and heiress of William, married after his death a younger man, Robert Nuttall, who changed his name to Durning in pursuance of a promise Anne had made to her father never to change her name. Shortly before her death she was forced to sell part of her estate to the newly founded Liverpool and Manchester Railway Company, whose Liverpool terminus was at Edge Hill. The remainder, after descending to her husband for his life's interest, eventually passed to her first cousins once removed, Emma Holt and her sister Jemima.[3]

Although WAG 8706–08 are each a different size and not pendants, they are stylistically homogenous, and may be assumed to have been painted in a single campaign. The portrait of John Durning, but not that of William, who died the year after his son, is said to have been executed posthumously,[4] which may mean that the three works were executed in the year 1803. On this view, the paintings seem likely to have been commissioned by Anne Durning, an impression reinforced by the much greater freshness and vivacity of WAG 8708 compared with the portraits of the two men. The flat and mechanical effect of WAG 8706 may be partly explained by wear to the paint surface (there are numerous visible retouchings in the background) but it can never have been more than a plain, slightly caricatured likeness.[5] The portrait of John, which is larger than the others, was perhaps intended for a place of honour in Anne's house and its outdoor setting may allude to his profession as a land agent. The depiction of his features is wooden but the ruddy glow of his cheeks may have been a deliberate allusion to his heart disease. The portrait of Anne has subsequently been altered in conjunction with its reframing as an oval; black paint has been applied over part of the sitter's bust and arms although the original surface remains visible at the corners of the canvas.

PROVENANCE

Painted for, or passed to, Anne Durning; by descent to her first cousin once removed, Emma Durning

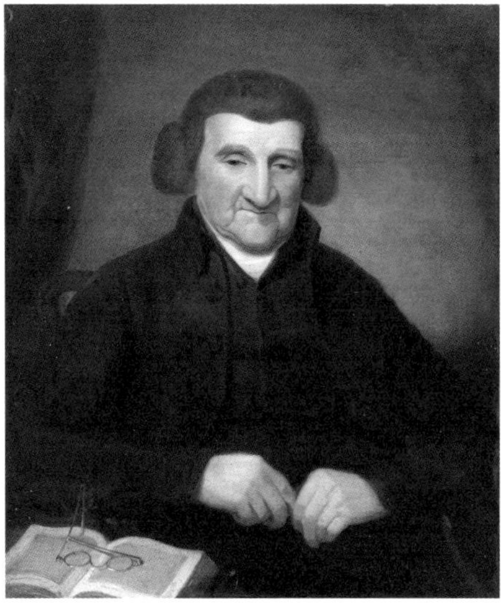

WAG 8706

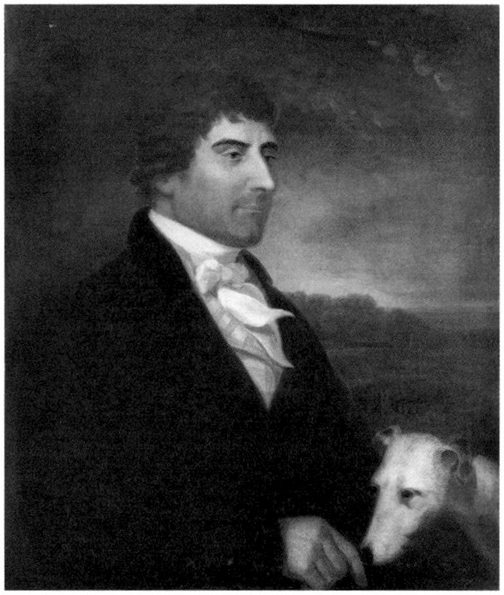

WAG 8707

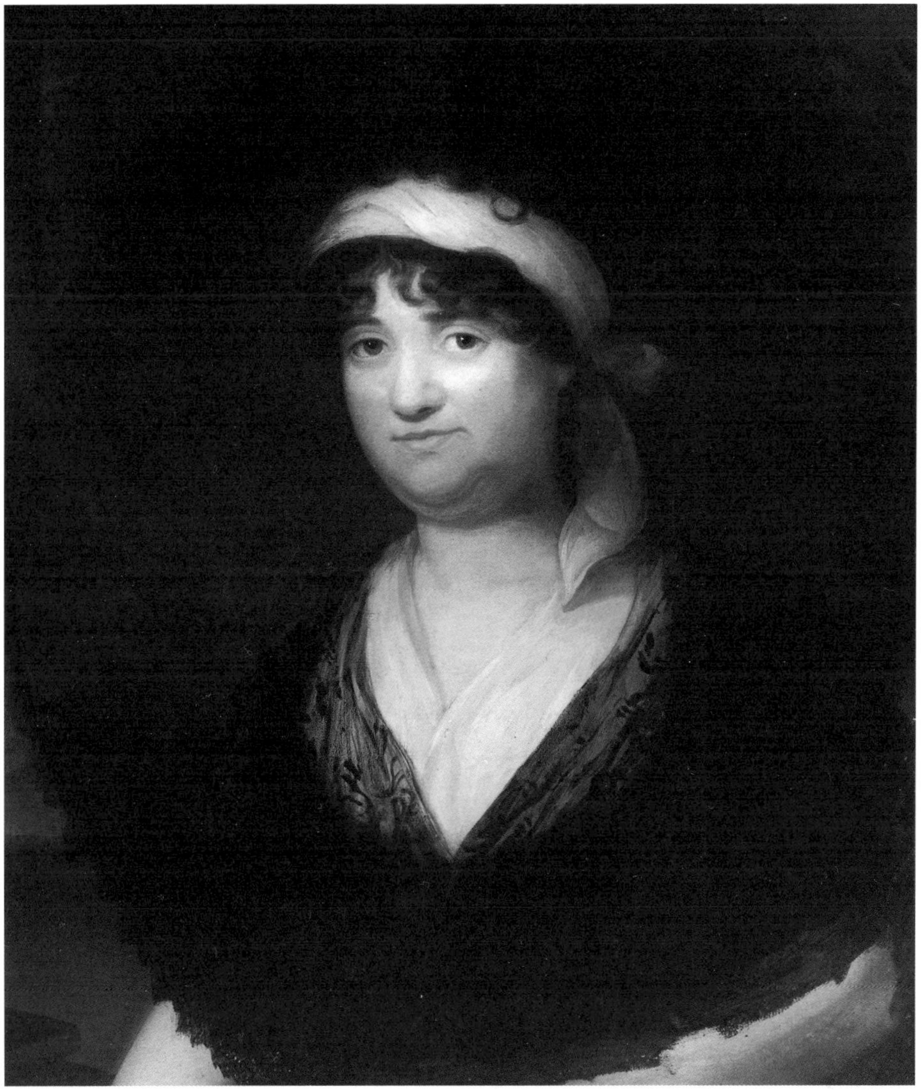

WAG 8708

Holt; her daughter Anne by 1871;[6] presumably passed to her younger brother Robert Durning Holt; by descent to his grand-daughter Anne Holt; by whom presented 1974.

NOTES

1. Anne Holt: ms *Emma Durning and the Durning Family* (1871), *Durning Holt Papers*, LRO 920/DUR/4/31/1; typescript copy in gallery files, pp. 2–4.
2. Anne Holt, *op. cit.*, p. 4, erroneously stating that John died aged 'about forty'; *MPPP*, p. 224.
3. *MPPP*, p. 224. The account given by Anne Holt, *op. cit.*, pp. 5–6, is unclear about the descent of the estate and implies that all or part of it passed to the Nuttall family.
4. Anne Holt, *op. cit.*, p. 3.
5. However, in the view of Anne Holt, *ibid.*, WAG 8706 is the best of the three portraits.
6. Anne Holt, *ibid.*

attributed to

John Williamson

Mary Wollstonecraft

WAG 1541
oil on canvas, 76 × 63 cm
date: 1791–92

A letter from Mary Wollstonecraft to William Roscoe of October 1791[1] implies that she was then sitting for a portrait which Roscoe had commissioned some time previously. Since WAG 1541 descended in Roscoe's family together with Williamson's portraits of Roscoe himself, his wife and children and Henry Fuseli (see pp. 251–5), it is virtually certain that this is that work, and it seems very plausible, even though the identity of the artist subsequently became lost, that Williamson painted it. In support of this notion is Mary Wollstonecraft's own remark to Roscoe that 'I do not imagine that it will be a very striking likeness',[2] which is much more likely to have applied to the provincial Williamson than, say, to John Opie, whose first portrait of her (National Portrait Gallery, fig. 106) dates from the same period. Williamson is known to have been living in Liverpool in 1790 and to have been in London in May 1792,[3] but no further information about his movements has emerged. The style of the work is not similar to that of Williamson's earlier portrait of Fuseli, yet Williamson was an inconsistent artist whose stylistic development is hard to plot. The rather stiff quality of the handling in WAG 1541 recurs elsewhere in his work, and is present in some of the Roscoe portraits. These could in certain cases be replicas of Williamson's originals, and WAG 1541 may also be a copy.[4]

The circumstances in which Roscoe commissioned the portrait are unknown. He first met Mary Wollstonecraft early in 1791, probably through Fuseli, at

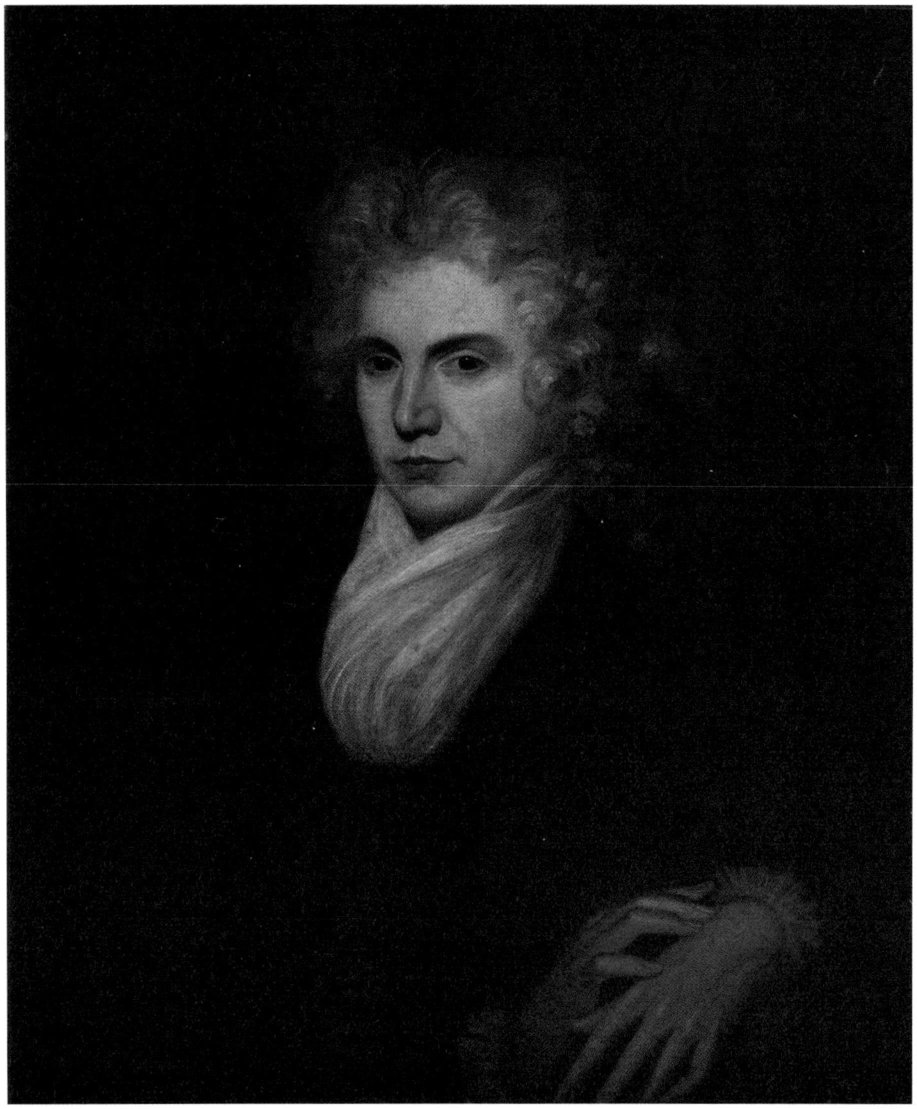

WAG 1541

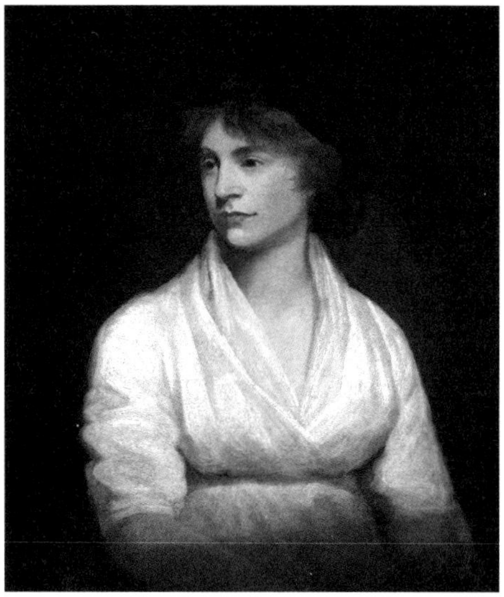

Fig. 106 *Mary Wollstonecraft* by John Opie, oil on canvas. © National Portrait Gallery, London.

the London house of Joseph Johnson, the Radical publisher who had issued Wollstonecraft's *Thoughts on the Education of Daughters* in 1787.[5] Roscoe shared her views on equality and freedom for women and WAG 1541 may be viewed as an important icon of the network of Radical friendships which flourished in England at the time of the French Revolution.

PROVENANCE

Painted for William Roscoe; by descent to Mrs A. M. Roscoe; her bequest 1950.

EXHIBITION

EUROPA 1789: Aufklärung Verklärung Verfall Kunsthalle, Hamburg 1989 (68).

NOTES

1. Mary Wollstonecraft to William Roscoe, *letter*, 6 October 1791, *Roscoe Papers*, LRO 920/ROS/5328: 'Be it known to you, my dear Sir, that I am actually sitting for the picture and that it will be very shortly forthcoming'.
2. *Loc. cit.* Wollstonecraft's own letters do not mention the artist (see Ralph M. Wardle, ed: *The Collected Letters of Mary Wollstonecraft* [New York and London, 1979] pp. 207ff.).
3. *MPPP*, p. 221.
4. No other version of WAG 1541 is known. Hugh Macandrew, in letters to Eleanor Nicholes, Harvard College Library, 1961 (gallery files) stated that he had attributed WAG 1541 to Williamson on stylistic grounds and had then changed his mind: 'some of my colleagues do not agree with me that it is related in style with the other Williamsons in the collection'. Nevertheless, Macandrew's instincts seem sound.
5. A contemporary portrait of Johnson, now lost, but known from an unattributed engraving in the British Museum, may also be by Williamson.

Robert Williamson

WAG 3019
oil on canvas, 124.5 × 101.5 cm
date: unknown, perhaps 1803–06

Although Robert Williamson was a significant figure in the development of literary culture in Liverpool in the mid-eighteenth century, biographical information about him is elusive. It is not known when or where he was born and died. From the 1750s he was

Liverpool's leading printer, publisher and bookseller, with an address in Castle Street in the heart of the town, and he was also a stationer, editor, broker, auctioneer, house agent and agent for the lottery. His first listed publication was the *Liverpool Memorandum Book* for 1753 (issued 1752), a cross between a diary and a tourist guide for visitors, which reveals an already considerable familiarity with the Liverpool scene. On 28 May 1756 he published the first number of *Williamson's Weekly Advertiser* which ran (with a gap in 1764) until 31 March 1769.[1] In 1767 he printed *A Catalogue of Paintings Perform'd by Nathaniel Tucker to Be Seen (at the Exhibition at the Golden Lion Dale Street) as Likewise the Rules of Painting.*[2] WAG 3019 has hitherto been identified as a work of the late 1760s, and although Tucker's work remains unfamiliar, he is known to have been resident in Liverpool in 1766–67,[3] and his authorship has been very tentatively suggested.[4]

On stylistic grounds, however, WAG 3019 cannot be a work of the 1760s. Its language is characteristic of substantially later portraiture, and its similarity to mature works by John Williamson is striking. It is particularly close to Williamson's portrait of William Durning (WAG 8706, p. 258), notably in the treatment of the hands. That work is traditionally dated to 1802–03 and WAG 3019 may be ascribed to about the same time. From the presence on the frame of a plaque bearing an inscription referring to the foundation date of *Williamson's Weekly Advertiser*, 1756, it is tempting to wonder if WAG 3019 was commissioned to mark the newspaper's 50th anniversary in 1806.[5] On this scenario, whether or not Robert Williamson was still alive at this period, which seems extremely doubtful,[6] it is evident from the sitter's age that the artist would have been working from an earlier likeness. That supposition would help explain the somewhat wooden and generalised treatment; yet the work's large scale and strong contrasts of light and shade do suggest that it was intended as a presentation portrait and for a public setting. It is tempting, although perhaps pressing conjecture too far, to suspect that John Williamson could have been selected for the commission because he was in some way related to Robert, and may have had a good recollection of the latter's features.[7]

PROVENANCE

Presented to Liverpool Corporation before 1873;[8] deposited in the Library and Museum; transferred to the gallery between 1903 and 1927.[9]

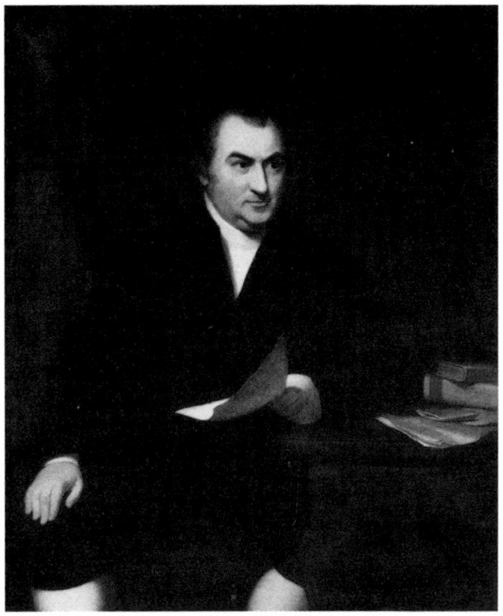

WAG 3019

NOTES

1. MPPP, p. 51; citing also Sir J. A. Picton, *Memorials of Liverpool* 2 vols (1873) vol. 2, p. 21, and A. H. Arkle, 'Some Notes on Robert Williamson, Printer and Stationer', *Transactions of the Historic Society of Lancashire and Cheshire [for the Year 1928]* vol. 80 (1929) pp. 147–9.
2. A. J. Hawkes, *Lancashire Printed Books: A Bibliography* (Wigan, 1925) p. 41; the copy of the 1767 catalogue in Liverpool City Libraries was destroyed in the Second World War.
3. Gore's street directory for 1767; see H. I. A.: 'Tucker and Caddick, Portrait Painters at Liverpool, 1767', *Notes and Queries* vol. 165 (5 August 1933) p. 81; also A. Kidson, 'The Liverpool Art Scene 1745–1770', in E. Barker and A. Kidson, *Joseph Wright of Derby in Liverpool*, exh. cat., Walker Art Gallery and Yale Center for British Art, New Haven (2007) pp. 28–9 and p. 38, n. 29.
4. MPPP, loc. cit.
5. *Williamson's Liverpool Advertiser and Mercantile Register* was first published on 28 May 1756. In 1758 it changed its name to *Williamson's Liverpool Advertiser and Mercantile Chronicle*, under which name it ran until August 1769. After a gap of three years it resumed publication (under the proprietorship of Alice Williamson, believed to be Robert's sister, although she was described as Mrs Alice Williamson in street directories). From December 1772 until 1781 its title was unchanged; then it was simply *Williamson's Liverpool Advertiser* until 1789, then until 30 December 1793 it was *Williamson's Liverpool Advertiser and Marine Intelligencer*. From the issue of 6 January 1794 it became *Billinge's Liverpool Advertiser and Marine Intelligencer*. Robert Williamson is last recorded in Liverpool street directories in 1769 and Alice Williamson in 1787; in 1790 the business is listed as 'Williamson and Billinge, Publishers of the Liverpool Advertiser'. Thomas Billinge was listed as sole proprietor in the directory of 1796.
6. See n. 5; after 1769 Robert is thought to have left Liverpool for Madras; Arkle, *loc. cit.*
7. John Williamson was born at Ripon in Yorkshire and worked as a japanner in Birmingham before moving to Liverpool in or shortly before 1783. His decision to settle in the town may mean that he had relations there.
8. Picton, *loc. cit.*
9. Listed as in the Library and Museum in Charles Dyall: *Walker Art Gallery Descriptive Catalogue of the Permanent Collection of Pictures* (Liverpool, 1882) p. 45 (cat. 196); and as still there in the 1903 Walker collection catalogue, p. 33. It was included in the 1927 Walker Art Gallery collection catalogue, p. 197.

Richard Wilson

1713–82

Landscape with Phaeton's Petition to Apollo

WAG 1999.58
oil on canvas, 229 × 224 cm
date: about 1763–67

The subject of WAG 1999.58 is taken from Book 2 of Ovid's *Metamorphoses*. The sun-god, Apollo, is visited at dawn at his palace by his mortal son, the impetuous Phaeton. In order to prove his love for Phaeton, Apollo swears to grant any request his son makes of him, but Phaeton makes the one wish that Apollo dreads: that he be allowed to drive the chariot of the sun for a day. Despite Apollo's attempts to dissuade him (and to the consternation of Phaeton's sisters, who as a result of his folly will be turned into trees) he gets his way; but he will soon lose control of the chariot and burn up huge swathes of the earth's surface before Jupiter destroys him with a thunderbolt (for another treatment of the subject see WAG 6221, pp. 325–7). Wilson depicts the outset of the story, partly in order to illustrate the moment of portentous suspense rather than the inevitable denouement, and partly no doubt as an excuse to paint one of his trademark pearly dawn skies. Wilson's patron Henry Blundell (1724–1810), in his catalogue of the pictures and statues at Ince Blundell written in 1803, misunderstood what time of day it was, describing the picture as finely expressing the warm glow of evening. Indeed by that date the painting had been given the title *A Summer's Evening*.[1]

Wilson's painting is one of a set of four commissioned by Blundell for the saloon at Ince Blundell Hall, north of Liverpool. According to Joseph Farington, who was a pupil of Wilson at the time of the commission, Wilson was recommended to Blundell by Edward Penny (see pp. 118–9).[2] Wilson travelled to Ince to inspect the room the paintings were destined for before embarking on the commission, which he entrusted mainly to assistants to carry out. In Farington's words, the paintings 'were prepared and far advanced towards finishing by his pupils, but Wilson went over and regulated them'.[3] Again according to Farington, Wilson asked £50 per picture, but Blundell voluntarily paid him £70.[4] The exact date of the commission is unknown but Farington was Wilson's student between June 1763 and at the latest 1767,[5] so the paintings must date from between those years.

All four of the Ince Blundell paintings were repetitions, or more accurately variants, on a larger scale and to a square or nearly square format, of subjects that Wilson had already painted.[6] WAG 1999.58 was based on a work that Wilson had showed at the Society of Artists' exhibition in London in the spring of 1763 (cat. 133): *A Large Landskip with Phaeton's Petition to Apollo*, which had been purchased by Francis, 3rd Duke of Bridgewater. William Woollett's engraving of this, reversing the design, was published by John Boydell in 1763, and it is tempting to suppose that Wilson reversed the design of the Ince Blundell canvas, too, in order to enable his pupils to make direct use of the engraving, no other repetition of the *Phaeton* then being in existence.[7]

The painting and its companions were seen at Ince Blundell on a visit to England in 1816 by S. H. Spiker, librarian to the King of Prussia, who wrote in his travel memoir : 'the room in which we took our wine after dinner was ornamented with five [sic] beautiful landscapes, of the celebrated English landscape painter, Wilson'. Spiker believed that Wilson had painted them in Italy.[8] Not long after this, WAG 1999.58 and one of its companions, the *Landscape with Diana and Callisto* (now Bristol Museum and Art Gallery) were given by Charles Blundell to John Gladstone, father of the Prime Minister William Ewart Gladstone; the latter was the recorded lender of WAG 1999.58 to an exhibition at the British Institution in 1856. Sometime before 1893, the *Phaeton*, but not the *Diana and Callisto*, was bought back from the Gladstones by the (as they now were) Weld-Blundells.[9]

PROVENANCE

Painted for Henry Blundell of Ince Blundell; by descent to his son Charles Blundell; by whom given to John Gladstone; by descent to William Ewart Gladstone 1857;[10] bt. back by [?] Charles Weld-Blundell; by descent to Sir Joseph Weld; offered by his executors to HM Government in lieu of inheritance tax; by whom allocated to the gallery in 1999.

EXHIBITION

BI 1856 (123).

NOTES

1. [Henry Blundell]: *An Account of the Statues, Busts, Bass-relieves, Cinerary Urns, and Other Ancient Marbles, and Paintings at Ince Collected by H. B.* (Liverpool, 1803) p. 225.
2. FD, vol. 3, p. 683 (entry of 28 October 1796). David Solkin, *Richard Wilson* exh. cat., Tate Gallery, London and tour (1982) pp. 216–7, has pointed out that Wilson had a distant family connection with Blundell, whose wife Elizabeth Mostyn of the Flintshire Mostyns was a relation of Wilson's mother.
3. FD, vol. 7, p. 2797 (entry of 26 June 1806).
4. *Ibid.*
5. W. G. Constable: *Wilson* (London, 1953) p. 164.
6. The three other paintings in the set were *Diana and Callisto* (Constable, *op. cit.*, p. 164, cat. 23b), *Tivoli, with the Temple of the Sibyl and a View of the Campagna* (Constable, *op. cit.*, p. 222, cat. 115b), and *The Villa of Maecenas at Tivoli* (Constable, *op. cit.*, pp. 225–6, cat. 119a). These three paintings were the same height as WAG 1999.58, but narrower, at 183 cm (72 inches) rather than 224 cm (88 inches). This suggests that the *Phaeton* enjoyed pre-eminence within the decorative scheme. Constable's captions misprint the sizes of the *Phaeton* (given as 96 × 96 inches; it is 90 × 88), and the *Diana and Callisto* (given as 84 × 96 inches).
7. Apart from the Bridgewater painting and WAG 1999.58, three further versions of the painting are discussed by Constable, *op. cit.*, pp. 163–4: (i) a painting measuring 124.5 × 176.5 cm which was sold by Walsh Porter at Christie, 22 March 1803,

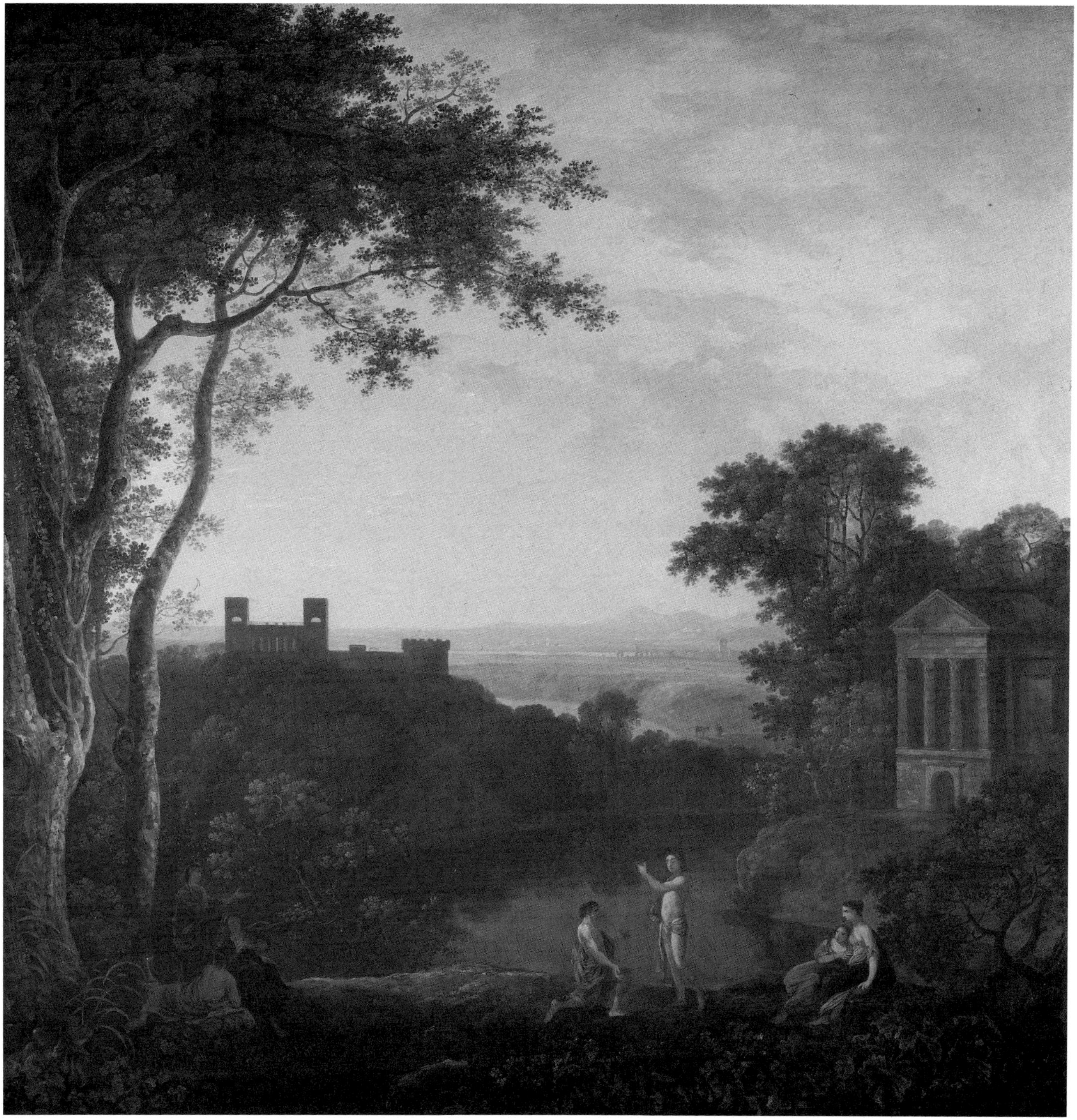

WAG 1999.58

bought by Lord Cowper (this was sold at Christie 12 November 1999 [41]); (ii) a large painting with Angerstein provenance which was sold at Christie 24 February 1883 (265): *Phaeton; A Grand Landscape, with Buildings and Figures by P. Battoni. Engraved by Woollett*; bought in, and (iii) a canvas measuring 70 × 91.5 cm which was in a private collection in Kent in 1953. The Bridgewater painting, which was sold privately by the 3rd Duke in 1801, was considered likely by Constable to be (i) above, but when this re-appeared at Christie's in 1999 it seemed on visual grounds a poor candidate to be Wilson's prime version and much more likely to be a copy, leaving the Bridgewater picture most likely to be identifiable with (ii).

8. S. H. Spiker: *Travels through England, Wales and Scotland in the Year 1816* 2 vols (London, 1820), vol. 1, p. 314.

9. Charles Weld-Blundell wrote on 9 May 1893 to the National Gallery offering it 'a very large Rd Wilson (*Summer Evening* somewhat similar to the one ordered at the same time at Rome [*sic*] by the Duke of Bridgewater)' for £2000.

10. The *Phaeton* has been identified by Constable, *op. cit.*, p. 164, as probably the work at the house of William Gladstone, MP described by Gustav Waagen in his *Galleries and Cabinets of Art in Great Britain* (London, 1857; the supplement to his three-volume *Treasures of Art in Great Britain* of 1854) p. 153 as 'A landscape which for size, beauty of composition, powerful effect and careful rendering, may be considered one of [Wilson's] chief works.'

Snowdon from Llyn Nantlle

WAG 2429
oil on canvas, 101 × 127 cm
date: 1765–66

Wilson's view is from the north-west. Y Wyddfa, the summit of Snowdon, dominates the centre of the composition; in the middle ground to the left are the slopes of Mynydd Mawr, with, just in view at the left-hand edge of the picture, the crest of the precipice Craig y Bere; below the summit of Snowdon is the little knoll of Clogwyn y Gareg, and to the right the ridge named Trum y Ddysgl. In the foreground is the small lake Llyn Nantlle (or Llyn Nantlle Uchaf). Today it is one single expanse of water, but in the eighteenth century there were two lakes divided by a spit of land.[1] Issuing from the near end of the western lake, in the right foreground, is the stream Afon Llynfnwy. Comparison with a photograph of the scene (fig. 107) shows that Wilson has dramatised the view by making the right-hand ridge steeper (his change to the outline is clearly visible as a pentiment, as well as the pentiment to its reflection in the lake) and by bringing the central massif closer to the viewer. Nevertheless, the topography is surprisingly accurate by the standards of eighteenth-century landscape painting.

Of numerous known versions of the composition,[2] WAG 2429 has been held to be Wilson's first,[3] and on this basis it is identifiable as the canvas titled *North-west View of Snowdon and Its Environs* exhibited at the Society of Artists in 1766 (189). Presumably, therefore, Wilson painted it in 1765 or the first months of 1766. Although the presence of the pentimenti reinforces the notion that this canvas is Wilson's original, doubts have been voiced that this is the case. WAG 2429 appears to have been the version of *Snowdon* seen by Farington in 1800 with whose quality he was disappointed;[4] and furthermore, there are significant differences between the painting and the engraving issued by William Woollett in 1775, in which the composition is extended on both sides. A preliminary pencil study for the subject by Wilson (Huntington Art Collections, San Marino, 63.52.296; fig. 108) is of similar proportions to the engraving. It has extensions to the view at either side, and is inscribed in the artist's hand *rain/bow* on the lower left slopes of the Snowdon massif, a feature which is missing in WAG 2429. On the other hand, no rainbow is present in any other known oil version either, and moreover WAG 2429 is on a standard size of prepared canvas in continuous use throughout the eighteenth century. Given that Woollett's engraving was issued as much as ten years after the first version of the subject was made, the differences between them may be explicable in terms of there being no version in oil available for him to work from, and Wilson having to produce a new one. A candidate for this is known, uniquely of the same proportion as the engraving and probably autograph, but considerably smaller than WAG 2429 and of copyish quality (with Tooth & Sons, London 1956, 58.5 × 89 cm; fig. 109). In such circumstances, Wilson could well have reverted more directly to the original drawing from which, in making his first painted versions, he had made some significant deviations.[5]

WAG 2429 was apparently one of three paintings by Wilson purchased by William Vaughan of Corsygedol, a wealthy landowner in North Wales who was a distant kinsman of the artist and a man in the forefront of the movement to revive native Welsh culture.[6] In this context it seems significant that Wilson has chosen a viewpoint on the opposite side of the mountain to the approach from England (through the Llanberis pass) but one familiar to the indigenous population of the remote north-west of Wales centred on Caernarvon, only a few miles from Llyn Nantlle. Equally, it has been held that *Snowdon* marks a turning point in Wilson's conception of landscape painting, where the explicitly classicising bent of his art, honed in Italy in the 1750s, gave way to a more 'native' and literal approach; perhaps one geared to the growth of tourism.[7] Thomas Pennant, in his 1783 *Tour of Wales*, wrote of the 'two fine lakes called *Llynnieu Nantlle* which form two handsome expanses, with a very small distance between each. From here is a noble view of the *Wyddfa* which terminates the view through the visto of *Drws y Coed*. It is from this spot Mr Wilson has favoured us with a view, as magnificent as it is faithful.'[8] If Wilson

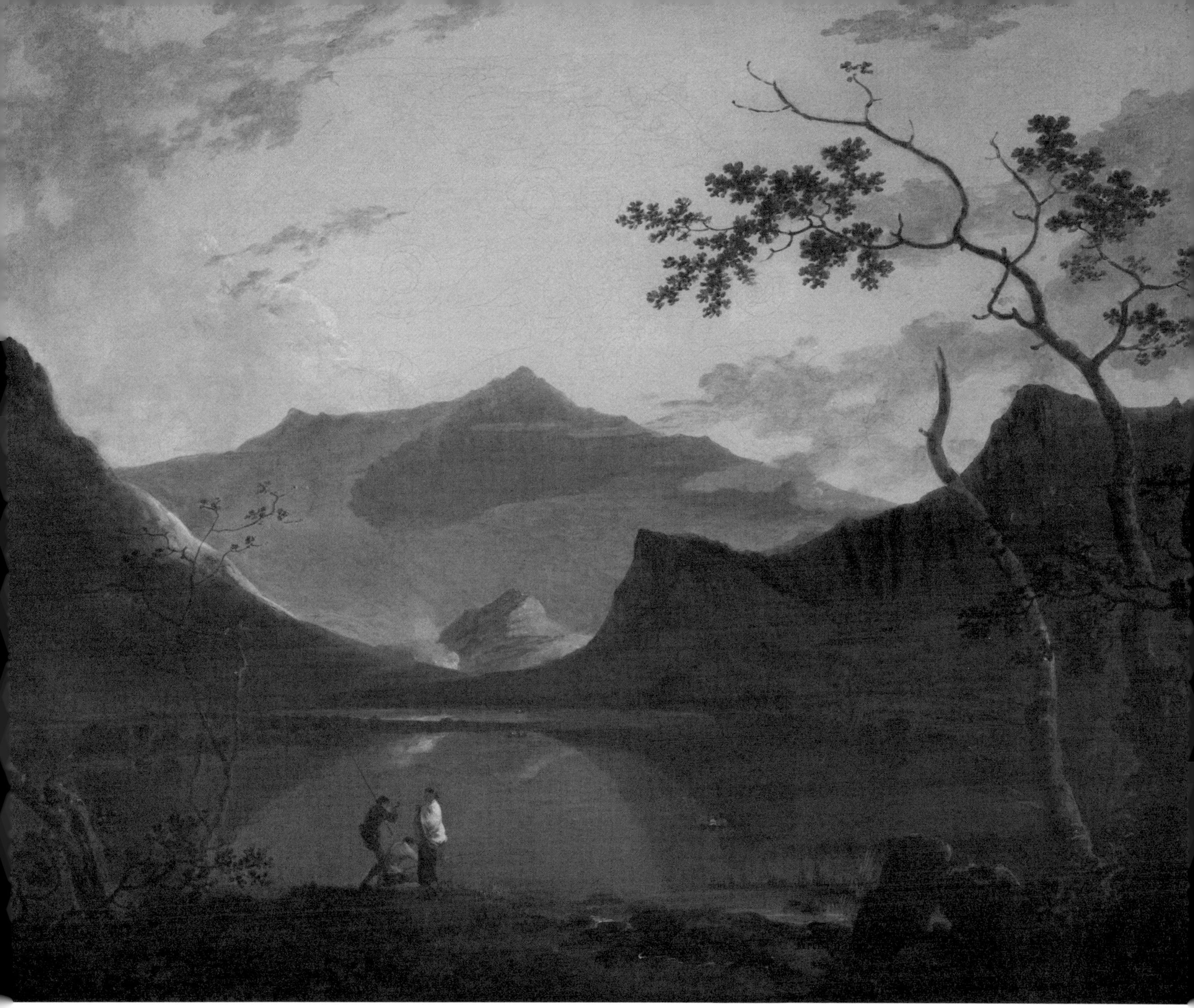

WAG 2429

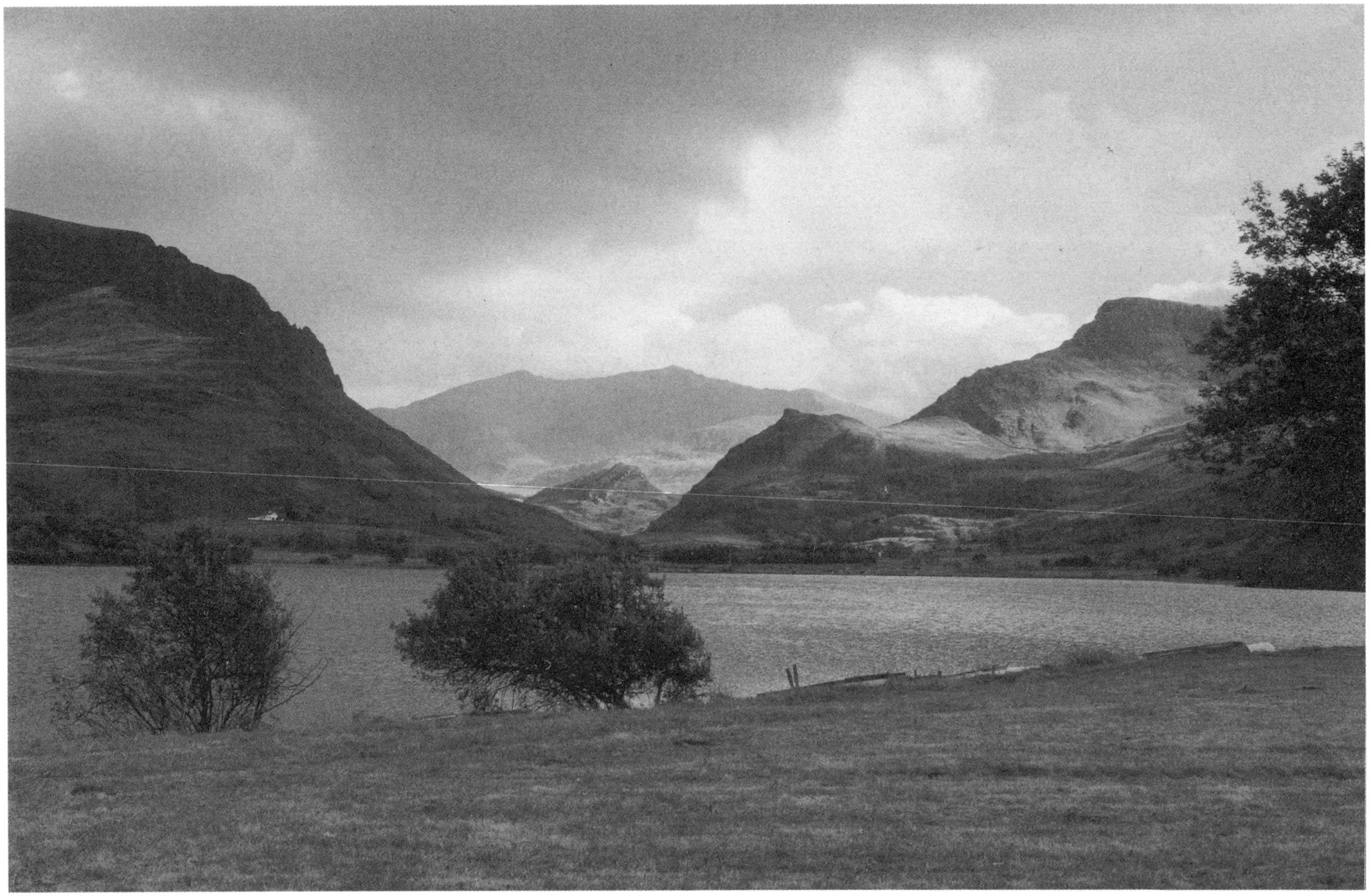

Fig. 107 Snowdon from the north-west. Photograph by Frank Milner.

continued to echo Gaspard Dughet's and Claude Lorrain's feeling for the structure of the landscape, their sense of balance and order, and their attraction to soft and beautiful effects of light, in *Snowdon* he has fused with these precepts a marvellous sense of place and truth to locality; a concern with the particular in nature which would become one of the mainsprings of Romanticism.

A further, little-observed factor in the gestation of *Snowdon* is the emerging competition for Wilson from the Irish painter George Barret, who arrived in London in 1763 (see pp. 9–11). The following year Barret won the Free Society of Artists' prize for landscape painting with *A Large Landscape with Figures*, a work which letters written in 1765 by Barret's compatriot James Barry suggest was a North Welsh subject.[9] In travelling from Ireland to London Barret must have passed through Snowdonia, and experienced at first hand its potential for an essay in the Burkean landscape sublime. As has been recognised, this success marked Barret as 'in the forefront of the discovery of the Welsh picturesque'.[10] The painting concerned was probably Barret's large *Llyn Nantlle* (Royal Albert Memorial Museum, Exeter; fig. 110). Its grandeur notwithstanding, the rustic and anecdotal character of this work might well have prompted Wilson to attempt a more distilled version of the same scene for exhibition at the rival London exhibiting society. Undoubtedly, Barret's later North Welsh subjects, such as the *Dolbadarn Castle* at Nottingham, and the related *Llyn Peris with Dolbadarn Castle* (Christie 7 May 2009 [46]) betray strong evidence of the influence of Wilson's aesthetic of order and calm as encapsulated in WAG 2429.

PROVENANCE

Bt. from the artist by William Vaughan; by descent to General J. V. Vaughan; Christie 20 June 1930 (114); bt. Agnew; from whom bt. 1935.

EXHIBITIONS

SA 1766 (189); BI 1849 (115); *Works by Richard Wilson R.A.* Ferens Art Gallery, Hull 1936 (53); *Some Acquisitions of the Walker Art Gallery Liverpool 1935–1945* National Gallery, London 1945 (5); *Richard Wilson and His Circle* Birmingham Museum and

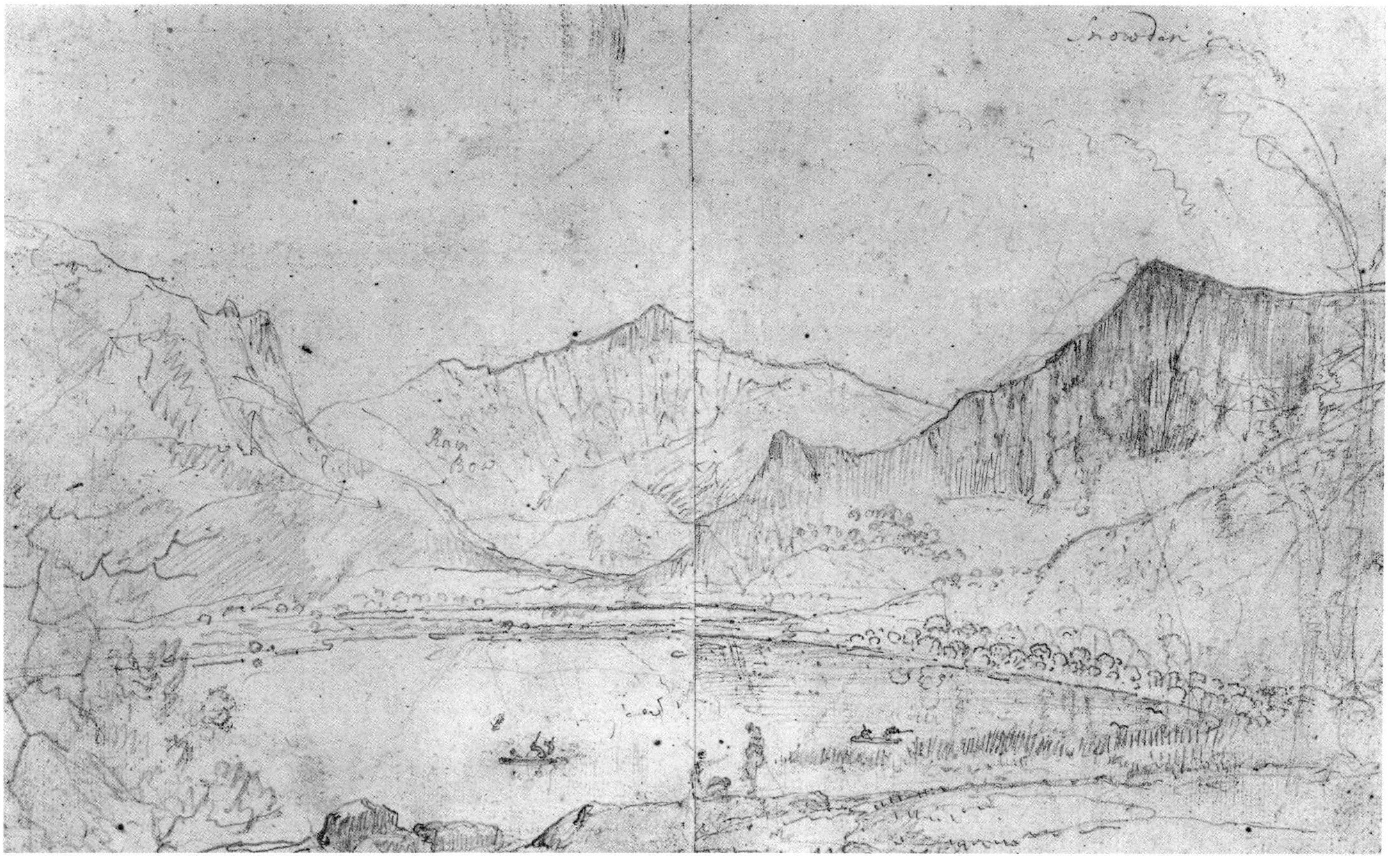

Fig. 108 *Snowdon from Llyn Nantlle* by Richard Wilson, graphite on paper. Courtesy of the Huntington Art Collections, San Marino, California.

Art Gallery 1948–49 (35) and Tate Gallery, London (34); *British Painting 1730–1850, Hogarth to Turner* Kunsthalle, Hamburg and tour of Scandinavia 1949–50 (118); *Le Paysage Anglais de Gainsborough à Turner* Orangerie, Paris 1953 (96); *Unknown Masterpieces* Kunsthaus, Zürich 1956 (278); *Age of Rococo* Residenz, Munich 1958 (226); *Art in Wales: A Survey of* 4,000 *years to* A.D. *1850* Glynn Vivian Art Gallery, Swansea 1964 (114); *Richard Wilson* Tate Gallery, London 1982 (117a).[11]

NOTES

1. There were still two lakes in 1931, but one was 'almost filled in by debris from slate heaps and silted mud'; Frank Ward: *The Lakes of Wales* (London, 1931) p. 177.

2. W. G. Constable: *Wilson* (London, 1953) p. 186, pl. 55, lists the following other versions: (i) 101 × 127 cm, Castle Museum, Nottingham (regarded by Constable as autograph; this was described by David Solkin, *letter*, 1 August 1984, gallery files, as a 'rather slick repetition'; in it, the left-hand ridge is substantially taller and steeper than it is in WAG 2429, destroying the balance of the composition); (ii) possibly the same work as the above, the version lent to the *Old Masters* exhibition at the RA in 1872 by the sculptor Thomas Woolner; the size given (evidently in error) as 48 × 48½ inches; (iii) the version lent to the *Old Masters* exhibition at the RA in 1892 by H. W. Worsley-Taylor and (evidently the same work) lent to the Guildhall in 1899 by F. Worsley-Taylor (this in 1977 was owned by Miss Dorothea Worsley-Taylor, Surrey [Solkin, *loc. cit.*] and seems to be the canvas measuring 101.5 × 127 cm, with Henry Strachey in 1989; from photographs apparently the same picture by 1993 was in the Shizuoka Prefectural Museum, Japan; according to *A Catalogue of Paintings and Watercolours Presented by Sven Bruntjen, Henry Strachey [and] Michael and Steven Rich, Ltd* [London, 1989], cat. 10, this picture bore a label inscribed *Sir James Worsley-Taylor.* Its earlier provenance was given as …Theobold Smith, 23 Jermyn St, London W1; his sale at Christie, 8 December 1889 [23]; bt. in [and sold to] Major Corbett Winder of Vainol Park, Montgomeryshire; Christie 25 May 1890 [106]; bt. G. Bartrop). (iv) a *View of Snowdon*, dimensions unknown, recorded by Benjamin Booth in the late eighteenth century in the possession of Sir Watkin Williams Wynn at Wynnstay; this is likely to be the same as (iii) (see p. 271, n. 4) although Booth's reliability is doubted by Solkin, *loc. cit.*; and (v) a copy, dimensions unknown, not by Wilson, in a private collection in Stockholm. To these should be added the small version with Tooth in 1956 (see main text; this may be the same as a version mentioned by Solkin, *loc. cit.*, in a private collection in Johannesburg).

3. WAG 2429 is listed first by Constable, *loc. cit.*, and was described as 'Wilson's prime original' by Solkin, *loc.cit.*

4. FD, vol. 4, p. 1441 (entry of 13 October 1800). Farington, visiting Col. Salesbury with Sir George and Lady Beaumont, saw 'Wilson's pictures of Snowdon, Pembroke Castle & Kilgarren Castle. We were disappointed in finding the two former pictures colder in colour & inferior in all respects to what we expected.' W. G. Constable: 'Richard Wilson: Some Pentimenti', *Burlington Magazine*

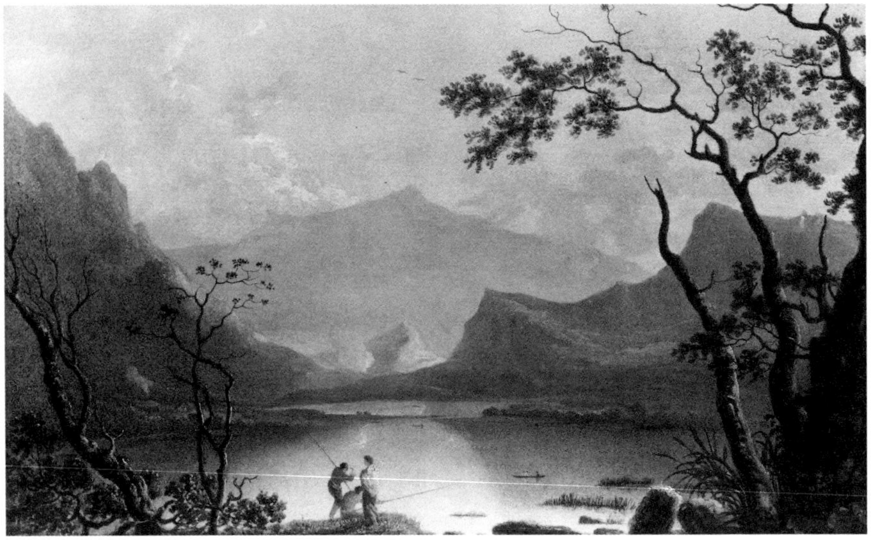

Fig. 109 *Snowdon from Llyn Nantlle* by Richard Wilson, oil on canvas.
Photo courtesy Arthur Tooth & Sons.

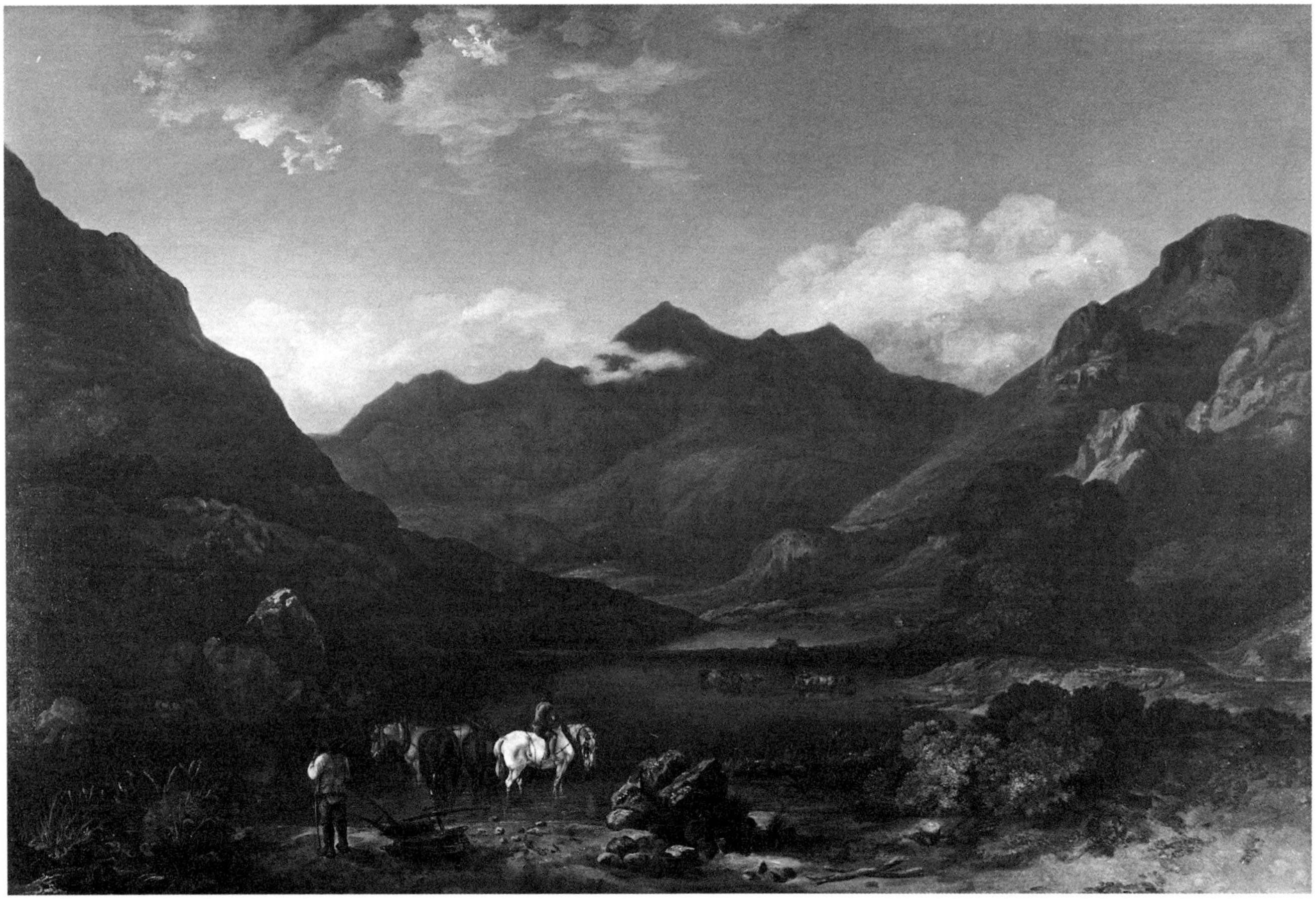

Fig. 110 *Llyn Nantlle, North Wales* by George Barret, oil on canvas.
Courtesy Royal Albert Memorial Museum & Art Gallery, Exeter.

(May 1954) p. 143, established that the subjects of the three paintings seen by Farington were identical with three pictures later owned by R. W. Vaughan (who lent WAG 2429 to the BI in 1849). In 1800 the paintings were at 'Reig' (i.e. Rûg, a property of the Vaughan family; Col. Salesbury had changed his name from Vaughan and after his death his estate passed to a younger brother, Griffith Howel Vaughan).
5. The differences include the relative positioning of the fishermen on the shore of the lake and the boat on the lake, and the treatment of the framing trees. Also in the drawing the artist is positioned on the opposite bank of the Afon Llynfnwy. One noticeable similarity is that in the drawing as well as in WAG 2429, Wilson has had difficulty in establishing the right-hand ridge to his liking. This suggests that the drawing was produced in advance of WAG 2429 and was not executed as preparation for the engraving.
6. David Solkin, *Richard Wilson*, exh. cat., Tate Gallery, London and tour (1982) pp. 101, 225–6.
7. However, Solkin, who argues this in respect of Wilson's later landscapes generally, views *Snowdon* as an image of order, designed to provide reassurance to an audience of conservative Welsh landowners who felt destabilised by the politics of popular discontent in London in the mid-1760s; *Richard Wilson*, pp. 96–103.
8. Thomas Pennant: *A Tour in Wales* 2 vols (London, 1778–81) vol. 2, p. 183.
9. Christie's sale catalogue 7 May 2009 (lot 46).
10. Anne Crookshank and the Knight of Glin: *Ireland's Painters* (New Haven and London, 2002) p. 135.
11. Illustrated as cat. 117b.

The Valley of the Mawddach and Cader Idris Mountain

WAG 2428
oil on canvas, 92 × 110 cm
date: 1773–74

Wilson's view is taken from high ground overlooking the Mawddach valley about seven miles north-east of Cader Idris mountain and about two and a half miles north-east of the small town of Dolgellau (which is hidden by the bank on the right of the picture, but indicated by the rising smoke). Cader Idris is the right hand of the two peaks, the centre one being the slightly lower Mynydd Moel. In the right foreground is the house of Gelligemlyn. Immediately behind the spectator is the peak of Bryn-prydydd, around whose slopes there winds a small country lane high above the valley. The spot at which Wilson has taken the view remains to this day a classic (if defiantly inaccessible) tourist 'viewing point' on this road.[1]

The composition has generally been recognised as one of Wilson's last major works, dateable on stylistic grounds to the early 1770s.[2] More recently it has been identified as the *View of Caderidris Mountain* that Wilson exhibited at the Royal Academy in 1774.[3] Several versions of the work are known but WAG 2428 has traditionally been regarded as the prime one.[4]

Within the sequence of Wilson's Welsh landscapes, WAG 2428 has been taken to mark a move away from an interest in didactic, 'sublime' scenery (represented most notably by *Snowdon from Llyn Nantlle* [WAG 2429] and *Cader Idris, Llyn-y-cau* [Tate Britain, London]) in favour of more pleasing, Picturesque views. This in turn has been linked with the opening up of the remoter parts of Wales to tourists in the 1770s.[5] It has also been suggested that Wilson was attracted to Cader Idris as a subject because it was a focus of Welsh legend: supposedly the site of one of King Arthur's castles and also the home of a monstrous giant. Thus it was a repository of myth equivalent to the classical sites that he had earlier depicted in Italy.[6]

PROVENANCE

...P. H.;[7] Christie 14 June 1879 (397); bt. Agnew (£105); bt. Robert Rankin; Christie 14 May 1898 (86); bt. Agnew (£84; ? bt. in); John Rankin; by descent to Sir Robert and James Rankin; by whom presented 1937.

EXHIBITIONS

[? RA 1774 (316)];[8] Liverpool Art Club 1881 (130); *Some Acquisitions of the Walker Art Gallery Liverpool 1935–1945* National Gallery, London 1945 (6); *Richard Wilson* Birmingham Museum and Art Gallery 1948–49 (34) and Tate Gallery, London 1949 (33); *The Influence of Wales on Painting* Brighton Museum and Art Gallery 1957 (39); *Richard Wilson* Tate Gallery, London 1982 (136a); *British Vision: Observation and Inspiration in British Art 1750–1950* Museum voor Schone Kunsten, Ghent 2007–08 (114).

NOTES

1. The viewpoint in WAG 2428 was correctly identified, from information provided by the National Museum of Wales, by W. G. Constable: *Wilson* (London, 1953) p. 180 (cat. 45). The painting had entered the gallery as a view on the Mawddach between Barmouth and Dolgellau, i.e. from the west of Cader Idris. A belief that Cader Idris was the peak in the centre of the composition may have been to blame for this error. The same assumption may have caused David Solkin: *Richard Wilson*, exh. cat., Tate Gallery, London and tour (1982) p. 241 (cat. 136a–b) to state that the viewpoint was from 'several miles to the south-east', despite the fact that no view from the south-east could incorporate the valley of the Mawddach.
2. Constable, *op. cit.*, p. 93; he linked the work stylistically with three other compositions, *On Hounslow Heath*, one version of which was exhibited in 1770, *Between Dolgellau and Barmouth*, and *Cader Idris: Llyn-y-cau* (which was, however, later shown by Solkin, *op. cit.*, pp. 223–4 [cat. 116] to have been painted no later than 1767).
3. Solkin, *op. cit.*, p. 241.
4. Constable, *op. cit.*, p. 181, lists (i) the canvas measuring 91.5 × 106.5 cm at Manchester Art Gallery (fig. 111); this version is very worn but according to Constable is autograph (although the treatment of the summit of Mynydd Moel and its relative height to Cader Idris beyond might rather suggest a copyist) ; (ii) the canvas measuring 59.5 × 75.5 cm in the National Museum and Gallery, Cardiff (described by David Solkin, *letter*, 1 August 1984, gallery files, as a small sketch version); and (iii) a version 90 × 101.5 cm, formerly in the collection

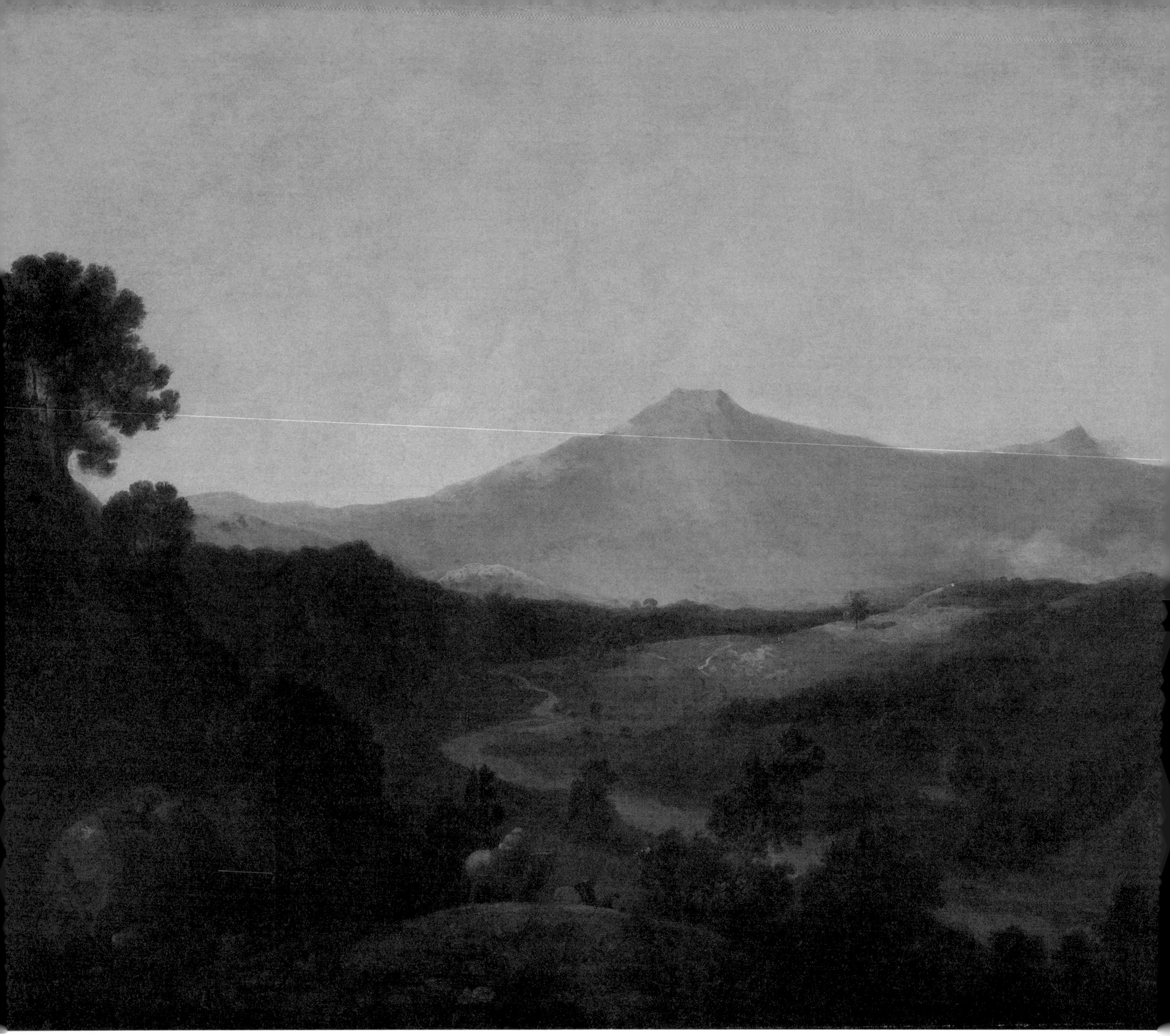

WAG 2428

of H. W. Worsley-Taylor, described by Constable as untraced (bought at Sotheby in 1978 by a UK private collector). This, given that Worsley-Taylor also owned a version of *Snowdon*, is likely to be the *View of Cader Ydris* recorded by Benjamin Booth with a *Snowdon* in the collection of Sir Watkin Williams-Wynn at Wynnstay in the late eighteenth century. To these should be added the important version, not listed by Constable, with Leggatt 1982 (exh. in the Cardiff and New Haven showings of *Richard Wilson*, cat. 136b; the exhibition catalogue transposes the illustration with that of WAG 2428) and now in the Cleveland Museum of Art (fig. 112). The depiction of the river in particular in the Cleveland canvas seems superior to that in WAG 2428; but at 89.5 × 105.5 cm it is appreciably smaller, leaving open the question of which is the original version.
5. Solkin, *op. cit.*, p. 242.
6. Martin Postle, entry in *British Vision: Observation and Inspiration in British Art 1750–1950*, exh. cat, Museum voor Schone Kunsten, Ghent (2007) p. 196 (cat. 114).
7. These initials of the previous owner are given in Constable, *op. cit.*, p. 180; at Christie's the work was consigned by the 'Trustees of the Manor of Sidmouth'.
8. One version of the present composition; not certainly WAG 2428. The work was noticed, with its three companion exhibits, by the *Public Advertiser* (3 May 1774) p. 2, as 'delightful Views of Nature, painted with Freedom and Taste, but slight, and somewhat too green in the Colouring'; and by the *Morning Chronicle* (4 May 1774) p. 2, whose critic wrote: 'there is an unconfined simplicity in these views, which, without that high finish of colouring, or laboured precision which belong to other landscape painters more immediately in fashion, cannot fail of being pleasing to all those who prefer the unadulterated traces of nature to the pedantry of profession.'

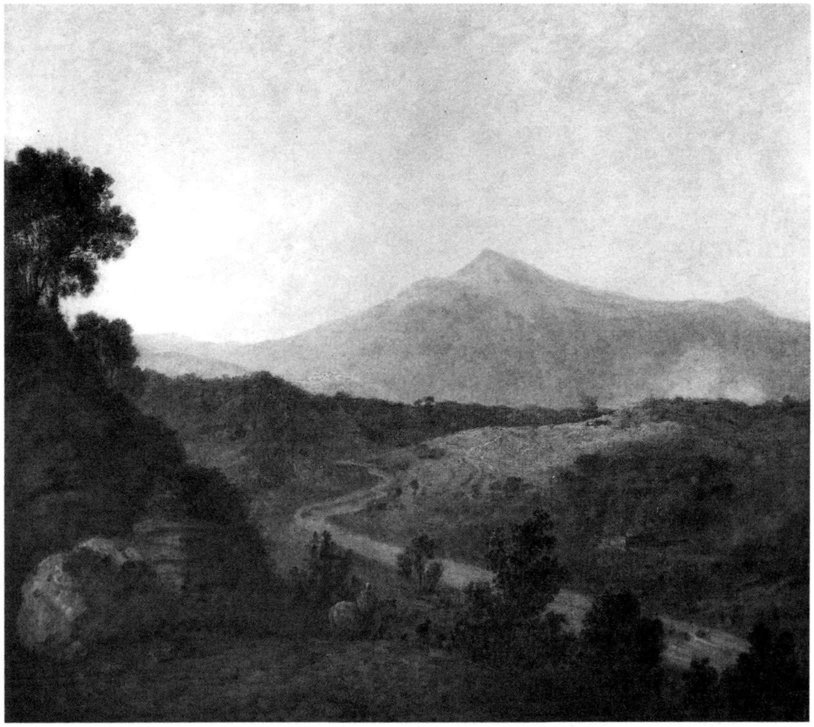

Fig. 111 *The Valley of the Mawddach* by Richard Wilson, oil on canvas. © Manchester Art Gallery.

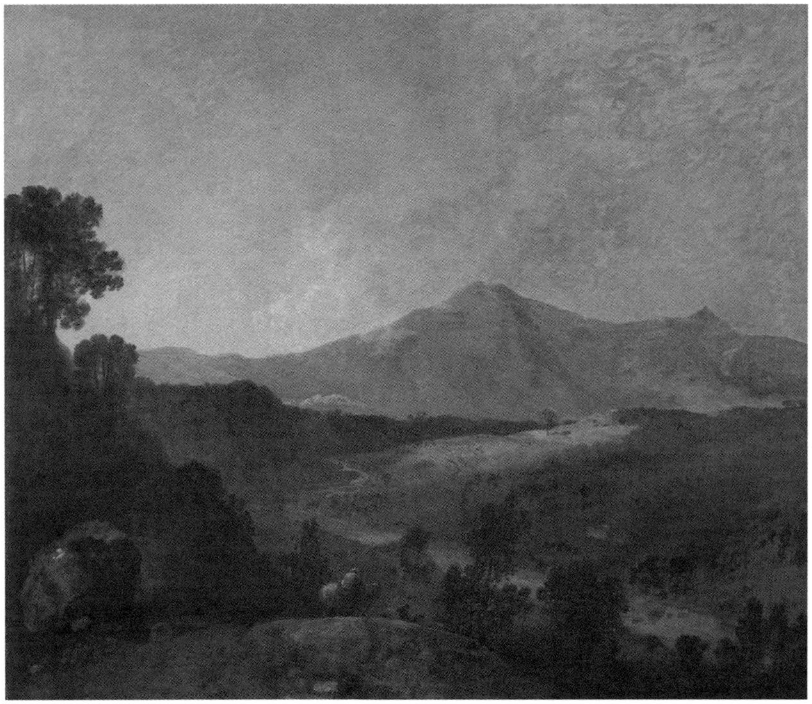

Fig. 112 *Cader Idris, with the Mawddach River* by Richard Wilson. Oil on canvas. © The Cleveland Museum of Art, Leonard C Hanna Jr Fund.

after

Richard Wilson

Landscape with Lake Avernus

WAG 317
oil on canvas, 40.5 × 51 cm
date: unknown, perhaps 1765–75

Lake Avernus (in Italian Lago d'Averno) is a small lake formed in a deep volcanic crater three miles north-west of Pozzuoli, a short distance north of Naples. It is one of a cluster of such lakes which also include the Lago Lucrino, Lago d'Agnano and the Lake of Baiae. For the Grand Tourist, Lake Avernus possessed the special significance that in Roman mythology it was one of the entrances to the underworld; most notably, in Book VI of Virgil's *Aeneid* it is where Aeneas meets the Cumaean sibyl, who informs him that he can only enter the depths in search of the shade of his father if he carries a golden bough in order to placate Persephone. Wilson's composition is a familiar meditation on the spiritual distance between ancient Italy, represented by the ruined temple on the lakeshore and the opened sarcophagus, and the modern landscape in which the local inhabitants are unconcernedly fishing the lake for their daily catch. Breaching the space between the two worlds is a figure in dark robes and carrying a cross: a learned monk cautioning the fishermen about the lake's infernal reputation.

During the five years that Wilson spent in Rome, 1752–57, he is thought to have made at least three visits to the region around Naples, where he was particularly drawn to the countryside north of the city.[1] The view in WAG 317 is not strictly topographically accurate: the classical buildings in the centre-left of the composition, which Wilson must have intended to allude to the ancient temple of Apollo (or, in other accounts, Pluto or Mercury)[2] and to the remains of Roman bathhouses on the lakeside, were in reality situated on its eastern shore. But the broader topography appears to show the view from approximately the north-eastern corner of the lake looking south-west or south.[3] Initially, Wilson appears to have used a version of the Lake Avernus design, while in Rome, as the basis for a heavily idealised composition in the vein of Gaspar Dughet,[4] only later evolving it into its present, more familiar form after his return to England. It became one of his staples; one that he and his students repeated and varied endlessly. The only two versions that Wilson appears to have signed and dated bear the date 1764 and

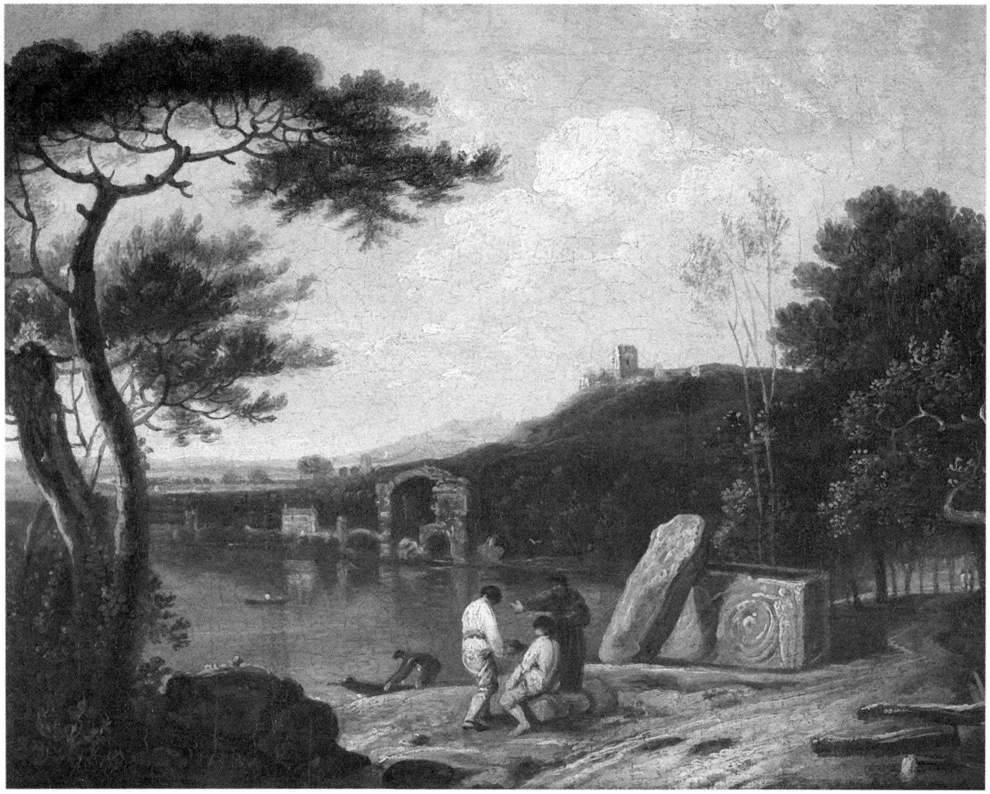

WAG 317

James Roberts's engraving of this picture, reversed, and titled *View in Italy*, appeared in 1765.

Of the five variants of the subject that have been identified, WAG 317 belongs with the most numerous, which has traditionally been given the title *Lake Avernus I*.[5] The largest known *Lake Avernus I* (Philadelphia Museum of Art) uniquely measures 70.5 × 89.5 cm and may thus be the original;[6] nearly all the others in the group have the same measurements as WAG 317.[7] In comparison with some of these other canvases, WAG 317, although a little coarse, is of fair quality (and noticeably close in detail to Roberts's engraving) and it is not unreasonable to suggest that even if it is largely the work of pupils working in his studio, Wilson himself may have touched on it. WAG 317 is notable for revealing more clearly than any of the other versions that the robed figure in the centre is a monk, and that he carries a cross – this figure has elsewhere been identified as a sibyl or as a local woman who has come to buy fish.[8]

PROVENANCE

...F. W. Crossley; bt. Agnew; from whom bt. by George Holt December 1895; Emma Holt Bequest 1945.

NOTES

1. W. G. Constable: *Wilson* (London, 1953) p. 37.
2. Richard Dorment: *British Paintings in the Philadelphia Museum of Art* (Philadelphia, 1986) p. 423.
3. This is also suggested by St John Gore, in his entry in [multiple authors:] *European Paintings in the Worcester Art Museum* (Worcester, 1974) p. 71.
4. Dorment, *loc. cit.* and p. 424, n. 3; Constable, *op. cit.*, p. 195; this is Constable's *Lake Avernus III* (see n. 5).
5. Dorment, *op. cit.*, p. 423; the five variants were described by Constable, *op. cit.*, pp. 194–5, as follows: (i) the present design, with three figures in the foreground, and closely approximating to Roberts's engraving, reversed. Constable identified the prime version, bearing Wilson's RW monogram and the date 1764, as the canvas, 42 × 52 cm, owned by F. S. Clarke by 1925; formerly in the collection of Louis Huth, by whom it was lent to the *Old Masters* exhibition at the Royal Academy in 1884; (ii) a version in which the centre background is occupied by an arched bridge of four spans, and which lacks the church on the hilltop but has a tall turret further over to the left; the most familiar version of this, in Tate Britain, London (originally bequeathed to the National Gallery by Richard and Catherine Jones Garnons in 1854), however, measures only 23 × 29 cm and is of indifferent quality; a larger version of this type, measuring 44 × 55 cm, not listed by Constable or Dorment, was consigned at Phillips 13 December 1994 (40); (iii) a version with only two figures in the foreground, with taller and more silhouetted trees (characteristic of Wilson's Roman period), with a tall hill in the centre background, and lacking the temple and bathhouse by the lakeside, of which the best known canvas, 62 × 83.5 cm, was in 1953 in the collection of the Duke of Buccleugh at Boughton House (see n. 4); (iv) a composition that reverses the prototype and follows Roberts's engraving of 1765. Constable is sensitive to differences from the print but essentially makes no case that any of the versions of this type are anything other than later variants based upon the print; (v) a variant displaying considerable differences in the centre background, where a tall rocky outcrop surmounted by a turret replaces the lower ridge in type (i); and also at right where the pattern of the trees varies from the original design; the version 61.5 × 76.5 cm in the Worcester Art Museum, designated as type (i) by both Constable and Dorment, seems rightly to belong to this group; for other versions of each type see Constable, *loc. cit.*, and Dorment, *loc. cit.*
6. Constable, *op. cit.*, p. 194, described this painting as 'doubtfully by Wilson'; Dorment, perhaps unwilling to challenge Constable's opinion openly, hinted at the possibility that it was autograph; the painting shows some signs of having been repainted but intrinsically it appears to be of hitherto unacknowledged quality.
7. The versions of *Lake Avernus I* listed by Constable, *loc. cit.*, and Dorment, *loc. cit.*, do not include WAG 317, which eluded their detection. Apart from (i) the version formerly in the collection of F. S. Clarke (see n. 5), Dorment recorded (ii) the version formerly owned by Capt. E. G. Spencer-Churchill, Northwick Park; most recently traced at Christie, 25 June 1965 (78); (iii) the version at Worcester (but see n. 5); (iv) the version in the Museum of Fine Arts, Boston; (v) a version formerly in the collection of R. B. Beckett, sold Christie 17 November 1967 (98); (vi) a version in the collection of Hugh Brocklebank, 1953; (vii) a version formerly owned by Sir Robert Dick-Conyngham, Prestonfield House; and (viii) the version in York City Art Gallery, like version (i) signed in monogram and dated 1764, which according to an inscription on the reverse was owned by John White in 1820; of these eight paintings, all but (iii) – certainly – and (vii) – possibly – measure approximately the same as WAG 317. To the above may be added two more versions measuring about 41 × 52 cm that have emerged since 1986 (and which may be identical with one or other of the above): (ix) with Galerie Hans, Hamburg 1996, of good quality; and (not the same as this) (x) Sotheby 26 March 2004 (59); in which the 'monk' figure seems much more like a female.
8. Constable, *op. cit.*, p. 194.

called

Richard Wilson

Classical Landscape

WAG 2963
oil on canvas, 127 × 102 cm
date: unknown, perhaps 1850–80

In the Holt family diary, which he was then keeping, Robert Durning Holt recorded on 23 January 1887: 'when in London I purchased of Mr White of King St a somewhat important picture by Richard Wilson R.A. intended to hang over the dining room fireplace – the picture arrived yesterday – and have since been studying the hanging'.[1] There is evidence that the attribution was doubted even before WAG 2963 was presented to

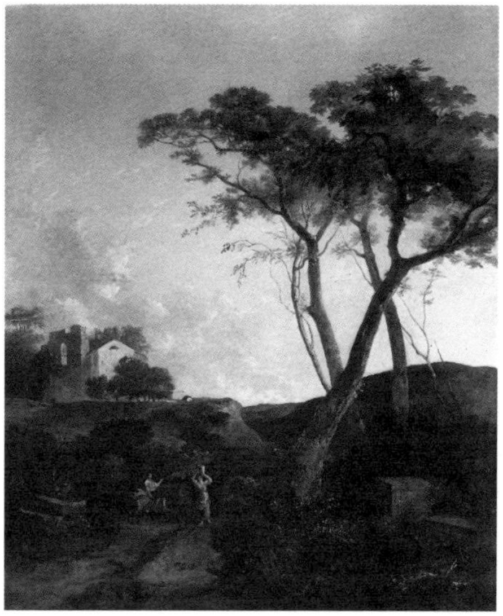

WAG 2963

the gallery in 1946,[2] but it was definitively overturned in 1953.[3] To judge by the handling of the foliage of the trees especially, the work is a later pastiche. It has been queried whether the artist is even British.[4]

PROVENANCE

...Edward F. White; from whom bt. by Robert Durning Holt, 18 January 1887; by descent to his daughter-in-law, Eliza, Lady Holt; by whom presented in memory of her husband 1946.

NOTES

1. Ms *Holt Family Diary* (vol. 6, 1885–93), *Durning Holt Papers*, LRO 920/DUR/1/6.
2. According to an undated letter from Anne Holt, gallery files, her father (Richard Durning Holt, 1st Bt, eldest son of Robert Durning Holt) some years previously had showed the picture 'to some representative of Agnew's who told him it was almost too good for Wilson'.
3. W. G. Constable: *Wilson* (London, 1953) p. 105.
4. Elizabeth Einberg, *letter*, 1 December 1983, gallery files.

Hamlet Winstanley

1694–1756

Self-portrait

WAG 10396
oil on canvas, 125.5 × 100.5 cm
date: about 1720

The artist was the second son of William Winstanley, a tradesman of Warrington, and his wife Ellen. He showed talent in drawing at school and after attracting the notice of Revd John Finch, Rector of Winwick and the brother of the Earl of Nottingham, he travelled to London in 1718 where he worked at the Academy in Great Queen Street (often referred to as Kneller's Academy; Kneller is said to have been Winstanley's 'particular friend' and 'great master'). He returned to Warrington in 1721 to paint the portrait of Sir Edward Stanley of Bickerstaffe (the future 11th Earl of Derby), and was soon being patronised by Stanley's kinsman, James, 10th Earl of Derby, who assisted him to travel to Rome and Venice between 1723 and 1725. While in Italy Winstanley copied and purchased pictures for Lord Derby's collection and on his return spent three years engraving some of these, and other works in the collection at Knowsley, which he published as *The Knowsley Gallery* (1729). He remained active at least into the 1740s in the Warrington area, carrying out further commissions at Knowsley, including a large family picture, a type of work for which he seems to have become particularly noted. According to George Vertue, he was responsible for 'a method quite new and extraordinary' of painting portraits, namely sending heads on small canvases to London to be inset into large canvases and completed by drapery painters. Winstanley has a further claim to fame as the first master of George Stubbs, who worked with him at Knowsley in 1740; however, their association seems to have been brief and possibly acrimonious. In later years, Winstanley built Stanley Street in Warrington and he died in the town on 16 May 1756, aged 61.[1]

The present self-portrait was in existence by 1731, when John Faber's engraving of it (fig. 113) was published.[2] It seems natural to assume from the Knowsley provenance and from the wording of the title on Faber's engraving that the picture was executed in conjunction with the publication of *The Knowsley Gallery* at the end of the 1720s. But it is not out of the question that it was painted some years earlier. One tenuous piece of evidence may lie with Alexander Bannerman's engraving of the portrait (in reverse) for the 1762/63 edition of Walpole's *Anecdotes of Painters* (fig. 114) which shows Winstanley working on a portrait inscribed *Dorigny*.[3] This must refer to the French engraver Nicolas Dorigny (1658–1746), who was in London when Winstanley first arrived there, engaged on the high-profile project of engraving the Raphael Cartoons in the Royal Collection (for which he was knighted by King George I in 1720). There is no visual evidence on WAG 10396 that the portrait Winstanley is painting can ever have resembled the one in Bannerman's print – and indeed the white outlines of a female face in profile which are faintly visible on the painting are present, much more clearly delineated, in Faber's engraving[4] – but there may have been a verbal tradition that linked the gestation of the self-portrait to Dorigny. It does not seem unlikely, for example, that Dorigny gave Winstanley tuition in engraving. If there is some at present concealed link with the Frenchman, then it is likely that the self-portrait dates from around 1720. Such a dating would perhaps be borne out by the artist's apparent youth in the picture (by 1730 he would have been in his 36th year), as well as by the Knelleresque spareness and angularity of the painting style, which contrasts with Winstanley's later coarser, more Hogarthian manner.[5]

A further small piece of circumstantial evidence is that WAG 10396 is first recorded in the collection at Knowsley only in the inventory taken in 1850.[6] If the work was in fact painted for the 10th Earl of Derby around the time of the publication of *The Knowsley Gallery*, it is surprising that its existence at Knowsley was not acknowledged from the outset, in eighteenth-century inventories. On the view that the work genuinely only came to Knowsley in the mid-nineteenth century, it would make sense that it was painted before Winstanley became intimately connected with the Stanley family.

PROVENANCE

...Earls of Derby, Knowsley Hall by 1850; by descent to Edward, 18th Earl of Derby; Christie 8 October 1954 (139); bt. Appleby (£21); ...Leger; Phillips 6 December 1983 (38); bt. by the gallery.

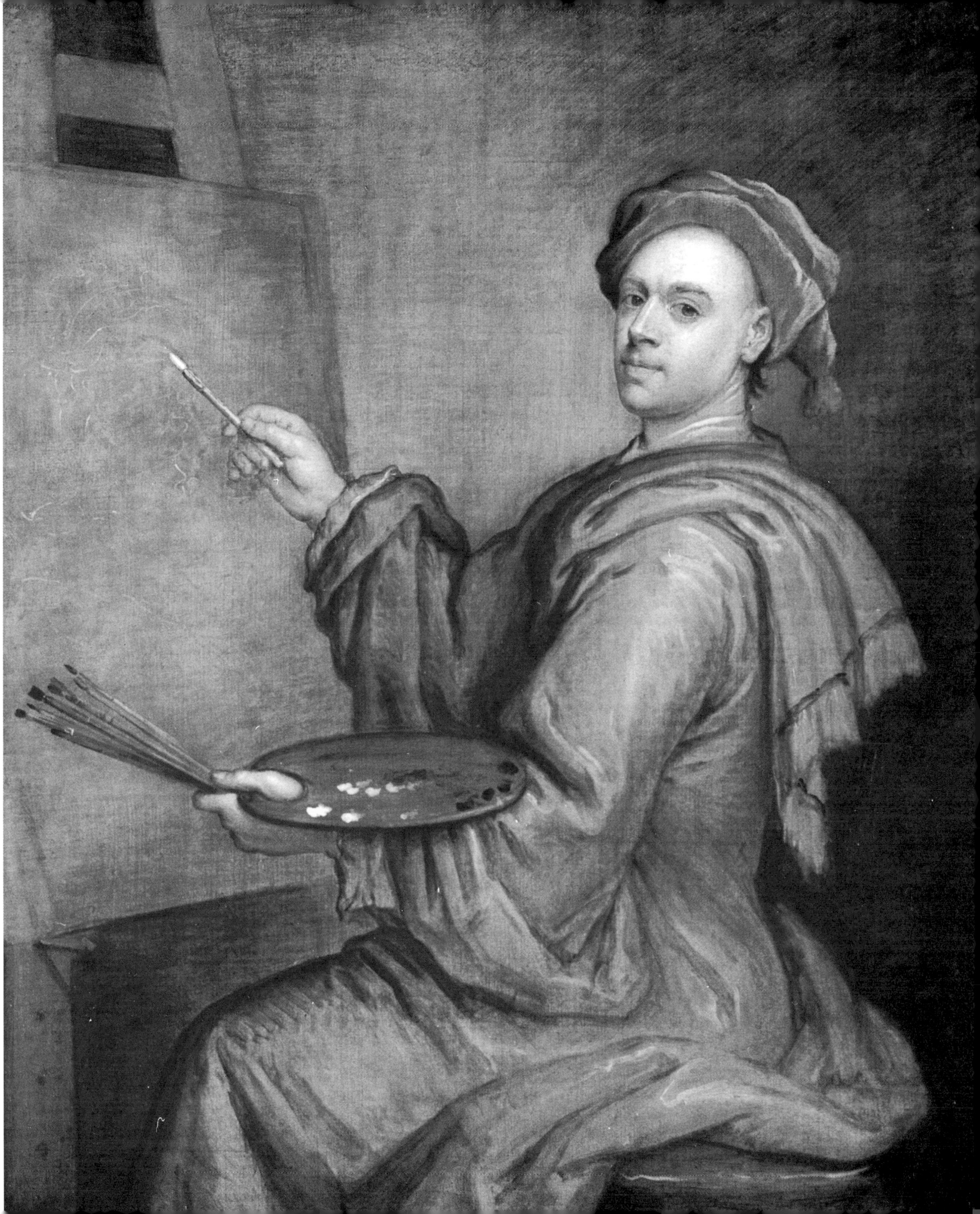

WAG 10396

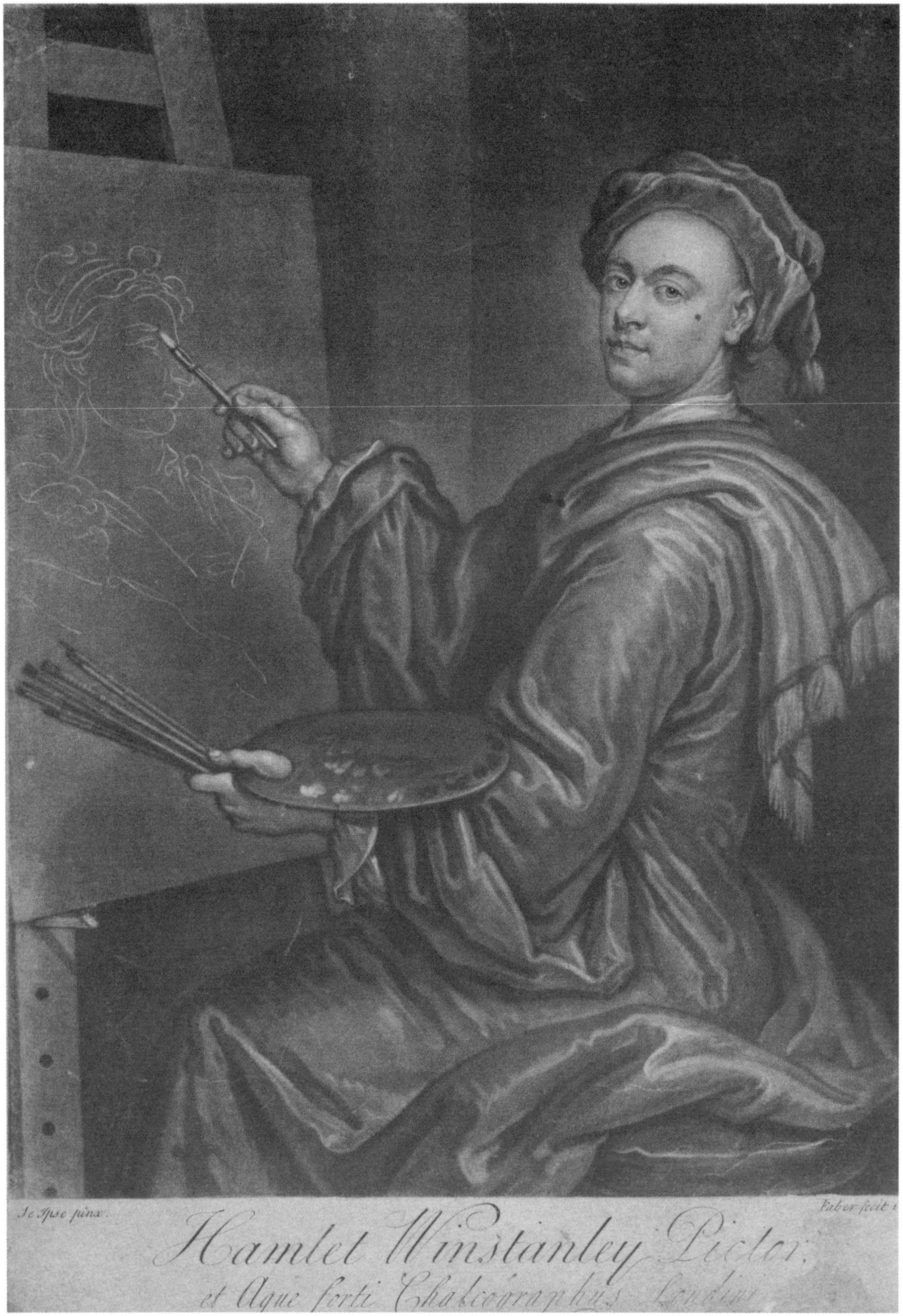

Fig. 113 *Self-portrait* after Hamlet Winstanley, engraving by John Faber.
Yale Center for British Art, Paul Mellon Collection.

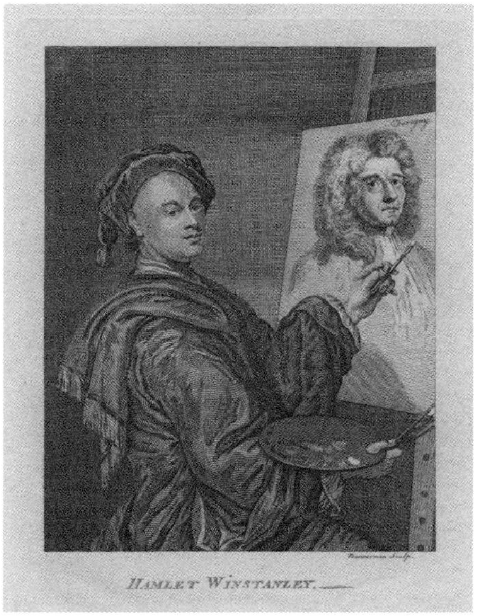

Fig. 114 *Self-portrait* after Hamlet Winstanley, engraving by Alexander Bannerman. Yale Center for British Art, Paul Mellon Collection.

EXHIBITIONS

2nd Special Exhibition of Portraits South Kensington 1867 (248); *Face to Face: Three Centuries of Artists' Self-portraiture* Walker Art Gallery 1994 (36).

NOTES

1. This account summarises the longer one in *MPPP*, p. 233, and see Judy Egerton: 'Winstanley, Hamlet', *ODNB* vol. 59, pp. 770–1.
2. The caption to the illustration of WAG 10396 in Egerton, *op. cit.*, dates the painting to 'c. 1730', revising the statement by Thomas Seccombe: 'Winstanley, Hamlet' in Leslie Stephen et al., *The Dictionary of National Biography* 63 vols (London, 1885–1900) vol. 62, p. 208, that the painting is actually dated 1730. There is no date on the work itself and nor is it dated by George Scharf: *Catalogue of the Collection of Pictures at Knowsley Hall* (London, 1875) pp. 182–3 (cat. 353).
3. WAG 10396 was re-engraved by J. Thomson for Ralph Wornum's 1849 edition of Walpole's *Anecdotes*, vol. 3, fp. 955, and this engraving was re-used in subsequent editions.
4. Xanthe Brooke: *Face to Face: Three Centuries of Artists' Self-portraiture* exh. cat., Walker Art Gallery (1994) p. 89, suggests that the portrait on Winstanley's easel is that of the artist's wife Catherine, known from an engraving by Faber which was issued as a pair to his print of the self-portrait itself.
5. WAG 10396 is unrelated to the painting in Tate Britain, London formerly identified as a (youthful) self-portrait by Winstanley (N10176).
6. Scharf, *loc. cit.*

Elizabeth, Countess of Derby and Her Son, Hon. Edward Stanley

WAG 139
oil on canvas, 127 × 101.5 cm
date: 1740

The sitters are identified by an inscription in the bottom right hand corner of the canvas: *Elizh. Countess of Derby / Wife to Edward Earl of / Derby & Edward their / Son 1740 – / Hal. Winstanly pinxt.* Elizabeth (1694–1776) was the daughter and heiress of Robert Hesketh of Rufford Hall, near Ormskirk (died about 1697) and his wife Elizabeth, daughter of Hon. William Spencer of Ashton, Lancs. In 1714 she married Sir Edward Stanley of Bickerstaffe, Bt. (1689–1776), who in 1735 succeeded his sixth cousin as 11th Earl of Derby. Years before, Sir Edward had effectively launched Winstanley's career by commissioning a portrait of himself and then introducing him to his kinsman the 10th Earl. Once Earl of Derby himself, he commissioned further works, including WAG 139 but most notably a *Family Piece* containing depictions of himself, his wife and their eight children. Edward (about 1732–45), the boy in WAG 139, was their youngest son.

WAG 139 may have been carried out in conjunction with, and possibly even as a preparatory exercise for, the *Family Piece*, although as the latter remains untraced it is impossible to confirm this. A head-and-shoulders variant of the portrait of the Countess in WAG 139, in which she wears a pink fur-lined cloak, remains at Knowsley but appears inferior to the present portrait;[1] also at Knowsley is Winstanley's earlier half-length of her seated front-on in a white dress. This shows her a good deal younger, and may date from her husband's first patronage of the artist in 1721.[2] It must be this work, rather than WAG 139, which is listed in the 1772 manuscript inventory of paintings at Knowsley, without attribution, as *Elizabeth Countess of Derby Half Length.* WAG 139 is not present on this list and is apparently unrecorded in any of the Knowsley inventories, which argues that it may always have been regarded in an inferior light and perhaps even withdrawn to one of the family's smaller properties.

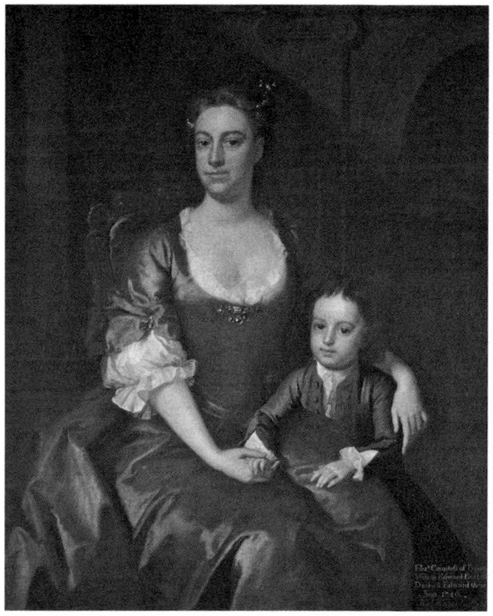

WAG 139

PROVENANCE

Commissioned by Edward, 11th Earl of Derby; by descent to the 18th Earl of Derby; Christie 8 October 1954 (140); bt. Agnew for the gallery.

NOTES

1. Diana Kay: [unpublished typescript] *Catalogue of the Knowsley Collection of Pictures* (1985) cat. 295; copy in gallery archives.
2. Kay, *op. cit.*, cat. 294. This painting was recorded by George Scharf: *Catalogue of the Collection of Pictures at Knowsley Hall* (London, 1875), p. 98 (cat. 173). Several half-length portraits of her husband exist as candidates for pendants of this work and WAG 139: (i) Kay, *op. cit.*, cat. 292 (Scharf, *op. cit.*, p. 98; cat. 172), half-length in a blue suit, first recorded at Knowsley in 1736; (ii) Kay, *op. cit.*, cat. 293, where said to measure 44 × 36 inches and bear a date in the 1740s; in a pink coat; not recorded by Scharf, *op. cit.*; (iii) *Edward Earl of Derby and One of His Daughters*, listed in the 1772 manuscript inventory of paintings at Knowsley without attribution but in a group of family portraits listed immediately after the *Family Piece*; not listed in Scharf, *op. cit.*, but presumably the portrait sold at Christie 8 October 1954 (107).

Dean Wolstenholme

1757–1837

A Huntsman and Hounds Coming out of Cover

WAG 2351
oil on canvas, 51 × 61.5 cm
date: unknown, perhaps 1795–1805

The identity of the huntsman – presumably Wolstenholme's patron – is unknown. The scale of the figure is unusual for the artist's hunting scenes, which traditionally feature a more panoramic viewpoint and smaller figures. However, the traditional attribution seems warranted; the treatment of the dogs and the handling of the foliage interrupting the branch formation of the tree is characteristic.[1] WAG 2351 has been dated to about 1800.[2]

PROVENANCE

...Walter Stone before 1934; Mary Stone Bequest 1944.

EXHIBITIONS

Sporting Pictures from the Walter Stone Collection Bluecoat Gallery, Liverpool 1946 (44); *A Selection of Sporting Pictures from the Walter Stone Collection* Bluecoat Gallery, Liverpool 1953 (36).

NOTES

1. See, for example, the signed small version of Wolstenholme's *Epping Forest Hunt* (1811); Christie 16 November 1999 (96).
2. *The Walter Stone Collection of Sporting Pictures at Whitton Hall, Westbury, Shropshire* (privately printed, 1938) p. 33, cat. 59.

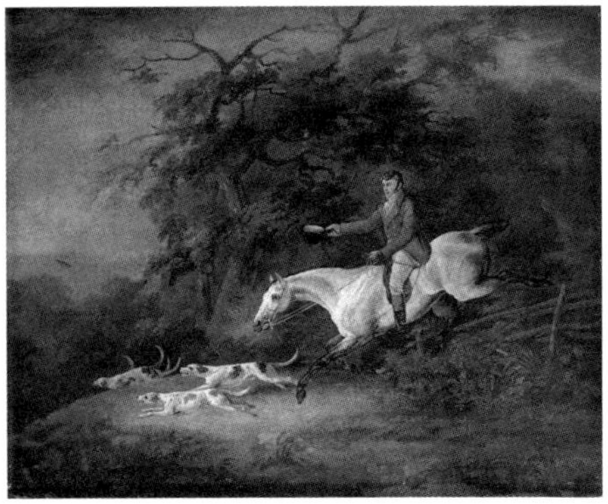

WAG 2351

Joseph Wright (of Derby)

1734–97

Richard Gildart

WAG 10637
oil on canvas, 125 × 100 cm
signed and dated: *J. Wright pinxt 1768* (lower left)
date: 1768

Richard Gildart was the son of James Geldart of Middleham, Yorkshire and his wife Elizabeth, née Sweeting. If the inscription in the bottom left-hand corner of WAG 10637, *AET* 95, is accurate, he was born in 1673, and this is substantiated by the report in the *Liverpool General Advertiser*, 2 February 1770, of his death a week previously, which states that Gildart was aged 96; other sources, however, claim that he died at the age of 99.[1] He came to Liverpool as a young man and was sworn a freeman of the town on 2 November 1698. In 1707 he married Ann Johnson, daughter of Thomas Johnson, MP for Liverpool 1701–23, with whose fortunes his early business career was closely linked. The Gildarts had 13 children, seven sons and six daughters, of whom James (1711–90) was Mayor of Liverpool 1750, Francis (about 1718–80) was Town Clerk from the year 1742 to his death and Ann (1721–1800) married Spencer Steers, son of Thomas Steers, the engineer of Liverpool's first dock.[2] Gildart became a Common Councillor on 4 August 1708; he was Bailiff in 1712 and Mayor three times, in 1714–15, 1731–32 and 1736–37. From 1734 to 1754 he was MP for Liverpool, being described in an electoral survey drawn up by Lord Egmont in about 1750 as 'always under the lash of the Customs', a reference to a history of unpaid customs dues that had plagued both himself and his father-in-law for decades past.[3] His varied commercial interests included tobacco, rock salt and principally sugar, but also slaves.[4] He traded chiefly with Virginia and his son James, who carried on the family firm, incurred huge losses during the American War of Independence.[5]

Wright arrived in Liverpool towards the end of 1768, having been persuaded to try his fortune in the town by his friend the map-maker Peter Perez Burdett. WAG 10637 is the only known portrait by Wright of a Liverpool sitter to bear that year's date, and it has been suggested that the portrait was a publicity stunt organised on the artist's behalf to enable him to introduce himself to potential patrons (it seems highly unlikely that Liverpool's senior citizen, whose features would no doubt have been familiar to every prospective patron in Liverpool, would have felt the need to commission such a work privately at the age of 95).[6] The work may have been painted at one sitting and in a public or semi-public setting.[7] Wright is thought to have rented a studio and public exhibition space in Liverpool,[8] and conceivably WAG 10637 was the first work that he displayed there. The half-length format of the painting (127 × 101 cm; 50 × 40 inches) was the one that would dominate Wright's Liverpool output, and the work's concentration on establishing a likeness and on demonstrating a skill in rendering the textures of fabric and polished wood appears deliberately tailored to the perceived tastes of the artist's new fellow-citizens. Gildart's coat, with its wide cuffs, is of a fashion of about ten years before.

The line painted down the right side of the background has been interpreted as a demonstration on Wright's part that he was capable of painting a straight line freehand, a further piece of showmanship.[9]

Two copies of WAG 10637 are known, one of which is WAG 2506 (see p. 295).[10]

PROVENANCE

By descent to the sitter's youngest son, Thomas Gildart (1731–1816); his daughter, Mrs Elizabeth

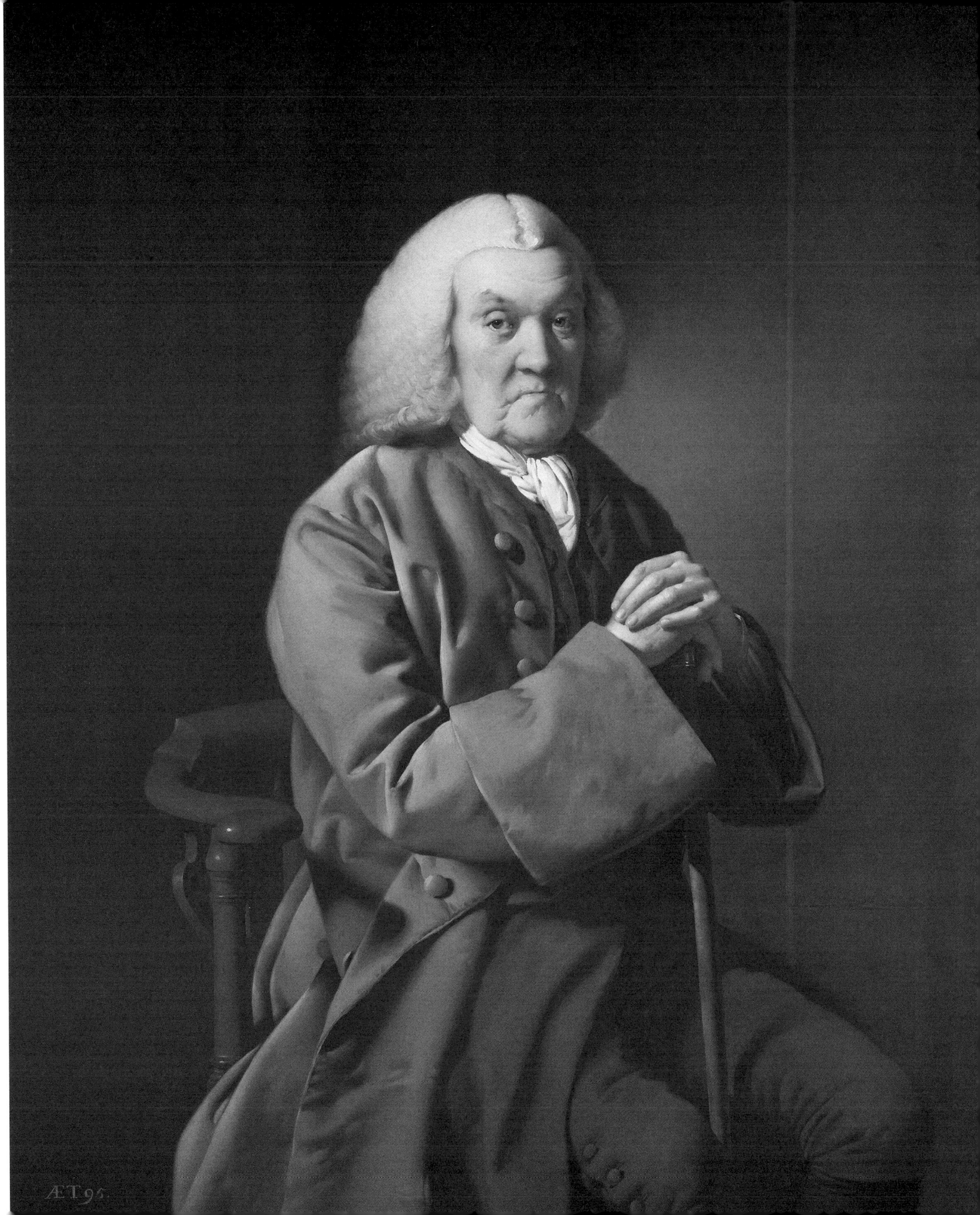

WAG 10637

Worsley; by descent to Mr J. R. Worsley; from whom bt. through Agnew 1987.

EXHIBITION

Joseph Wright of Derby in Liverpool Walker Art Gallery and Yale Center for British Art, New Haven 2007–08 (12).

NOTES

1. H. Peet: 'Thomas Steers, the Engineer of Liverpool's First Dock', *Transactions of the Historic Society of Lancashire and Cheshire [for the Year 1930]* vol. 82 (1932) pp. 221–3 [appendix D: 'The Gildarts']; followed by R. Sedgwick: *The History of Parliament: The House of Commons* 2 vols (London, 1970) vol. 2, p. 63; also J. R. Worsley, typescript notes on the Gildart family, 1987, gallery files.
2. Worsley, *loc. cit.*
3. Sedgwick, *loc. cit.*
4. His ship the Walpole, built in Liverpool in 1718, is recorded as docking on the Upper James river, Richmond, Virginia with 180 slaves on 3 July 1738; information from K. Calos, *Richmond Times-dispatch, email*, 27 February 2008, gallery files.
5. Worsley, *loc. cit.*
6. Alex Kidson: 'The Liverpool Art Scene 1745–1770', talk in the *Wright of Derby in Liverpool* symposium, Merseyside Maritime Museum, 15 November 2007.
7. *Ibid.*
8. E. Barker: 'Swallowing Up All the Business: Joseph Wright of Derby in Liverpool', in E. Barker and A. Kidson: *Joseph Wright of Derby in Liverpool*, exh. cat., Walker Art Gallery and Yale Center for British Art, New Haven (2007) p. 47; the evidence relates to Wright's possible rental of a public space in 1772 but it seems likely that he would have shown his work in public as soon as he arrived in Liverpool.
9. Kidson, *loc. cit.*
10. The second, presumably a copy after Wright and described as measuring 60 × 40 inches (but perhaps a misprint for 50 × 40 inches), was offered to the gallery in 1933 by J. Geldart Riadore and declined; *MPPP*, p. 51.

Fleetwood Hesketh

WAG 10846
oil on canvas, 127 × 102 cm

Mrs Frances Hesketh

WAG 10847
oil on canvas, 127 × 101.5 cm
date: 1769

Fleetwood Hesketh (1738–69) was the son of Roger Hesketh (1711–91) of North Meols Hall, Lancashire (on the outskirts of present-day Southport) and his wife Margaret, daughter and heiress of Edward Fleetwood of Rossall (north of present-day Blackpool). In 1759 he married Frances Bold, one of the six daughters of Peter and Anna Maria Bold of Bold Hall, near Prescot, about ten miles east of Liverpool, with whom he had two sons, Bold and Robert. The two marriages had expanded the horizons of the Hesketh family and by the 1760s

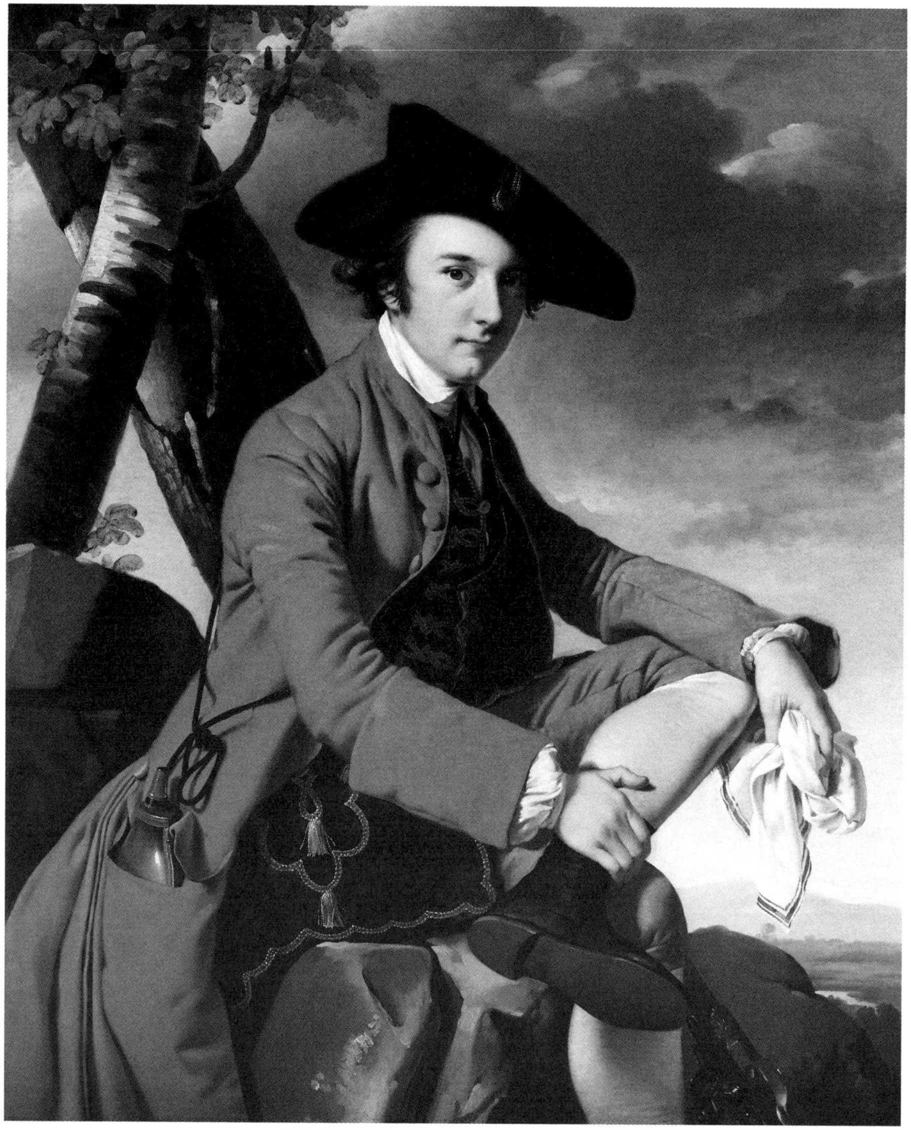

WAG 10846

they had developed considerable shipping interests in Liverpool.[1] Fleetwood Hesketh probably became aware of Wright on a visit to Liverpool early in 1769 (he was to die later that same year). Even though – unusually among Wright's male Liverpool sitters – he chose to be portrayed not as a businessman but in his *alter ego* of country gentleman, participating in a hunt, the portrait, together with the pendant of his wife, was almost certainly carried out in Liverpool, rather than Wright travelling to Meols for the purpose.

Wright recorded the portraits in his account book (National Portrait Gallery archives) under the heading *Sitters at Liverpool 1769*, 'Mr & Mrs Hisketh – 21 0 0'.[2] The price of each canvas, 10 guineas, is Wright's standard one for a portrait at that date (he charged the same for smaller portraits; see *Thomas Parke* and *Mrs Thomas Parke*, pp. 283–4) but he clearly regarded the commission as a significant one, for he took the unusual step of studying Fleetwood Hesketh's cross-legged seated pose in a preparatory drawing (Derby Museums and Art Gallery; fig. 115). The conception of this unusually relaxed and casual figure – even down to the black tricorne that he wears on his head – is closely comparable to that of Peter Perez Burdett in Wright's imposing earlier double portrait *Peter Perez and Hannah Burdett* of 1765 (Narodnì Galerie, Prague; fig. 116), and since the latter work must have accompanied the Burdetts to Liverpool when they came to live there in 1768, there is good reason to think that Hesketh had the opportunity to see it, and asked Wright for something similar. Despite Wright having made the drawing, the pose looks miscalculated: in both drawing and painting, Hesketh's left leg appears to emerge from his abdomen rather than its proper anatomical position. Nevertheless, the intricate grid of limbs and tree-trunks that underpins the design is notably arresting and ambitious.

The portrait of the fashionably attired Mrs Hesketh, as has been observed, is more conventional.[3] Wright had recently posed a figure against an almost identical balustrade, this time in the male half of a pair of half-length portraits, *Robert Vernon Atherton Gwillym* of 1766 (St Louis Art Museum).[4] Although Mrs Hesketh is not dressed in mourning, it is tempting to wonder whether the portrait was completed after her husband's death in view of the size of the huge urn behind her, which threatens to de-stabilise the composition. Partly in order to offset this, but partly in order to provide a formal link with the portrait of her husband, Wright introduced the very broad slanting tree trunk whose diagonal emphasis in conjunction with the balustrade creates a much more severe geometrical rigour than is present in the portrait of Fleetwood Hesketh.

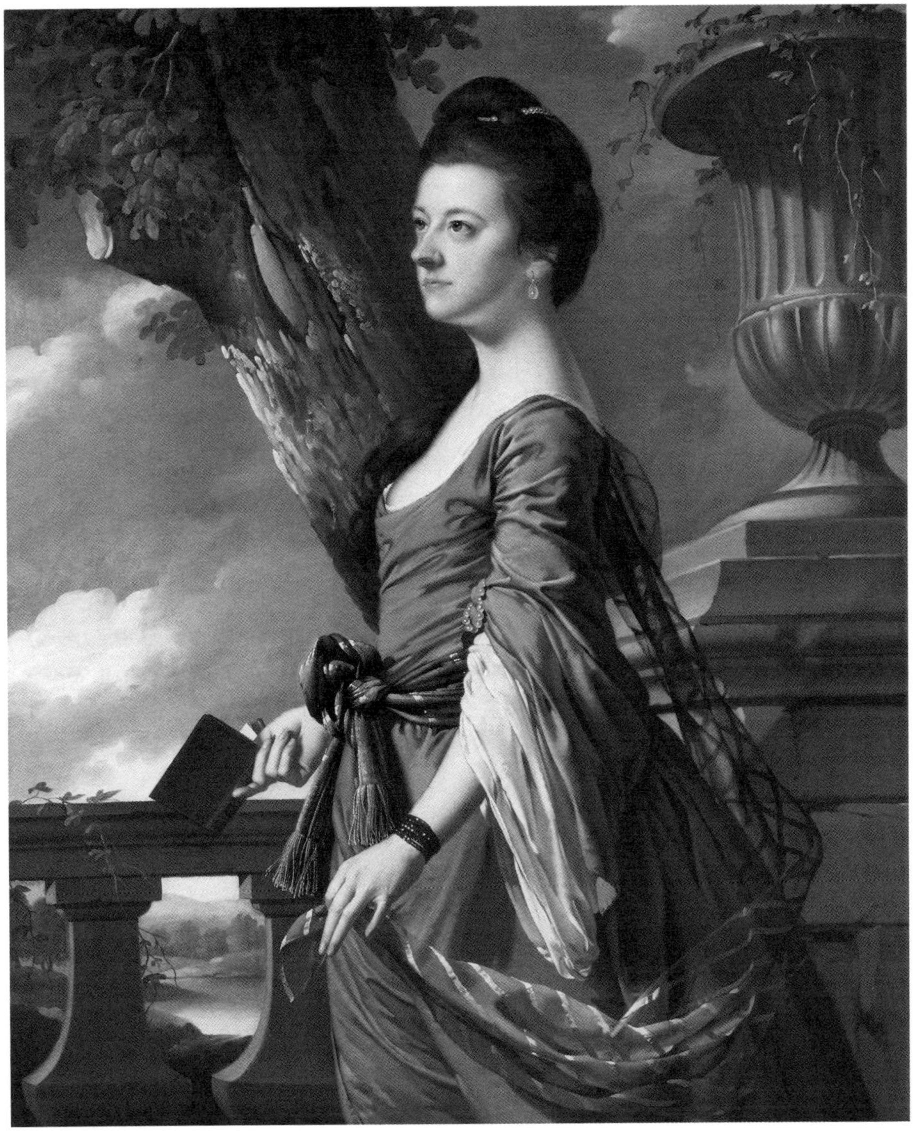

WAG 10847

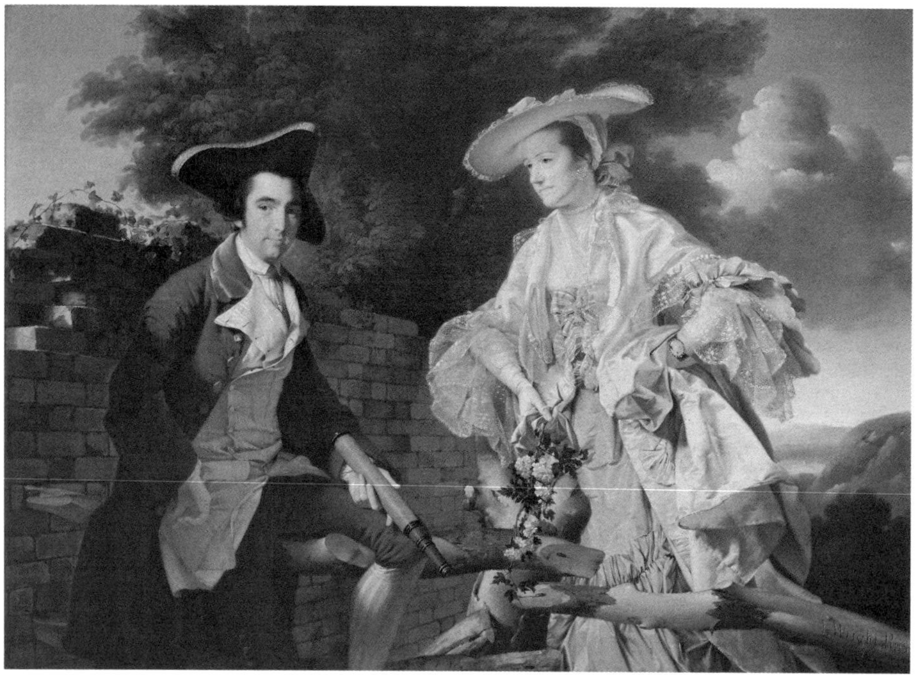

Fig. 115 *Peter Perez Burdett and Hannah Burdett* by Joseph Wright of Derby, oil on canvas. Narodnì Galerie, Prague.

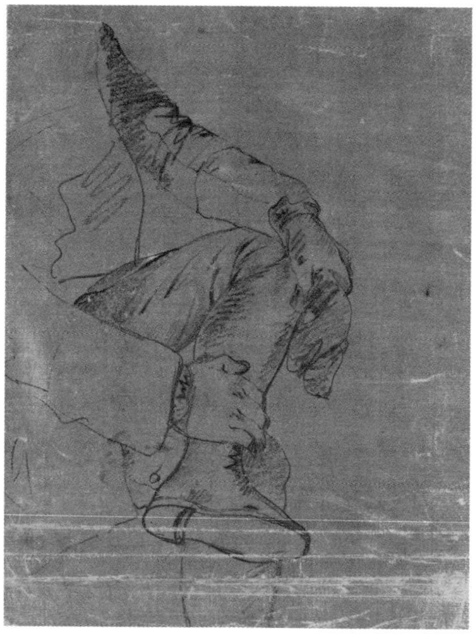

Fig. 116 *Study for the Portrait of Fleetwood Hesketh* by Joseph Wright of Derby, black and brown chalks on grey paper. © 2011 Derby Museums and Art Gallery.

Again Wright's ambition has led to visual solecism; the lost-profile pose of the face is not managed with complete conviction, as a result of which Mrs Hesketh's expression lacks definition (let alone the engaging quality of her husband's). Yet the effect must have been approved, for Wright was commissioned to paint the portrait of Mrs Hesketh's sister Mary Hunt soon afterwards.[5]

Both paintings were cleaned for the 2007–08 exhibition. It had previously been noted that Wright had used a cream-coloured ground.[6]

PROVENANCE

[Both works] By descent to the sitters' second son, Robert Hesketh; [WAG 10846] his son Peter Hesketh; his second wife Virginia Maria; by whom bequeathed in 1894 to her great-nephew, Thomas Knowlys Parr; [WAG 10847] his daughter Anna Maria, Mrs Thomas Knowlys; by descent to her grandson, Thomas Knowlys Parr 1893;[7] [both works] bequeathed by Thomas Knowlys Parr in 1938 to his collateral relations, the Fleetwood-Hesketh family of North Meols Hall; bt. by the gallery in 1990 from the Trustees of the Roger Hesketh 1987 Settlement, with the assistance of the National Heritage Memorial Fund, the Art Fund, the Hope Fund, the Friends of National Museums and Galleries on Merseyside and other sources.

EXHIBITIONS

Festival Exhibition of Local Art Treasures Atkinson Art Gallery, Southport 1951 (153) [WAG 10846] and (149) [WAG 10847]; *Works of Art from Private Collections in the North West and North Wales* Manchester City Art Gallery 1960 (141) [WAG 10846] and (143) [WAG 10847]; *Treasure Houses of Britain* National Gallery of Art, Washington DC 1985 (447) [WAG 10846 only];[8] *Joseph Wright of Derby in Liverpool* Walker Art Gallery and Yale Center for British Art, New Haven 2007–08 (18–19).

NOTES

1. B. Nicolson: *Joseph Wright of Derby, Painter of Light* 2 vols (London 1968) vol. 1, p. 99.
2. Elizabeth E. Barker: 'Documents Relating to Joseph Wright "of Derby"', *Walpole Society* vol. 71 (2009) p. 14.
3. For example, by Francis Russell in *Treasure Houses of Britain*, exh. cat., National Gallery of Art, Washington DC (1985) p. 508.
4. Repr. Judy Egerton: *Wright of Derby* exh. cat., Tate Gallery, London, Musée du Louvre, Paris and Metropolitan Museum of Art, New York (1990) p. 80 (cat. 35).
5. Lanhydrock House (The Robartes Collection) The National Trust; repr. E. Barker and A. Kidson: *Joseph Wright of Derby in Liverpool* exh. cat., Walker Art Gallery and Yale Center for British Art, New Haven (2007) p. 153 (cat. 26). The attribution of this portrait to Wright was first published by Alastair Laing in Michael Trinick et al.: *Lanhydrock* (London, 1995) p. 24.
6. Jacqueline Ridge and Katherine Stainer-Hutchins, condition reports dated July 1991, gallery files.
7. That the two paintings were separated at the death of Robert Hesketh, the male portrait going to his elder son and the female portrait to his daughter, and were reunited in Thomas Knowlys Parr's possession in 1894 is confirmed by long ms memoranda written by him which survive on the backs of the two paintings. They read as follows: [on the reverse of WAG 10846]:

This Fleetwood Hesketh Esquire of Rossall Hall & North Meols Co. Lancaster son of Roger Hesketh by Margaret Fleetwood married Frances Bold of Bold and had issue Robert Hesketh Esquire of Rossall he married Maria Rawlinson and had issue Peter of Rossall, Charles of North Meols and a daughter Anna Maria Martha of Heysham they were born at Wennington Hall which Mrs Hesketh hired for many years and were all baptised at Melling Church. she married Thomas John Knowlys Esquire of Hollybrook with Blighmount Co. Hants and inherited the Heysham land from Mr Hesketh they had with other issue a daughter Louisa Debonnaire who married on 1st January 1862 Thomas Parr Esquire son of Robert Henning Parr of Parkston Co. Dorset descended from the Parr's of Ormskirk and Kendal (see histories of Lancashire and Westmorland) & they had issue a son Thomas Knowlys Parr the present owner of this picture AD *1894 when it came to him through his great-aunt Virginia Maria Fleetwood-Hesketh widow (and 2nd wife) of the above mentioned Peter Hesketh brother of Mrs Knowlys of Heysham Tower.*

[on the reverse of WAG 10847]: (written in ink on a sheet of vellum sealed in four places to the stretcher, and superseding a first attempt written on the canvas itself, and broken off):

The Bolds of Bold Hall in the Co. Lancaster. This is the portrait of Frances Bold Mrs Hesketh of Rossall Painted by Wright of Derby Bold Hall the principal house in the township of Bold was the house of this lady before her marriage. It is the primary residence of her ancient family which was seated here before the conquest. John de Bold in the VII *and* VIII *of Henry* IV *obtained a grant of free Warren in Bold & Prescott within the forest of Symond –es-Mode in the wapentake of West Derby. It was the singular good fortune of this family to retain their possession uninterrupted in the male line down to the death of Mrs Hesketh's father Peter Bold Esquire* MP *for Lancaster who died* AD *1761 leaving several daughters but no son. Anna Maria Bold his eldest daughter succeeded her father in his estate and died in her 82nd year November 1813 his daughter Frances Bold married* A.D. *1759 Fleetwood Hesketh Esquire, of Rossall Hall Co. Lancaster and of North Meols they had issue Bold Fleetwood Hesketh Esquire who died unmarried in 1819 when Rossall was inherited by their second son Robert Hesketh Sqre who married 11th Sept 1790 Maria eldest daughter of Henry Rawlinson* M.P. *for Liverpool they had issue two sons and one daughter. Peter Hesketh the elder died without issue Charles Hesketh Rector of North Meols see histories of Lancashire and their daughter Anna Maria Martha married Thomas John Knollys Esqr of Heysham Tower in the Co. Lancaster and had with other issue a daughter Louisa Debonnaire Knowlys who married on 1st Jan 1862 at Clifton Parish Church Thomas Parr Esqr and they had issue a son Thomas Knowlys Parr the present owner of this picture* AD *1893.*

8. WAG 10846 was requested for loan from the Hesketh Family Trustees to the 1990 Tate Gallery Wright exhibition, and was included as no. 37 in the catalogue (see n. 4), but could not be shown because of legal technicalities.

Thomas Parke

WAG 10768
oil on canvas, 76 × 63.5 cm

Mrs Thomas Parke

WAG 10769
oil on canvas, 77 × 64 cm
date: 1769

Thomas Parke (1729–1819) was the son of a Liverpool ironmonger and anchorsmith of the same name.[1] He is recorded in the first (1766) Liverpool street directory as a linen draper living in Covent Garden. By 1769 he had moved to Old Church Yard, and by 1784 he had a house in the fashionable Duke Street. About 1781 he also purchased Highfield House, a mansion in the countryside a few miles east of Liverpool (in what became the suburb of Old Swan) that had been built in 1763 by the sugar merchant Thomas Wakefield and had subsequently been owned by the Dowager Duchess of Atholl and her son.[2] By 1785 he was senior partner in the Liverpool bank Parke & Heywood, and by 1790 he was a partner in a new bank, Gregson, Parke and Morland. He amassed great wealth and added purchases of land to the Highfield estate, which by the late 1820s comprised 120 acres. His wife Anne (1740–1827) was the daughter of William Preston. The couple had 13 children, four daughters and nine sons, of whom the youngest, James (1782–1868) became the noted Victorian judge Lord Wensleydale. WAG 10768–69 descended to him and his heirs.[3]

Wright's account book records, among his *Sitters at Liverpool 1769*, 'Mr & Mrs Park – 21 0 0'.[4] WAG 10768–69 have been identified as the portraits corresponding to this entry. At this date, although Wright occasionally charged more in special cases, 10 guineas seems to have been his standard fee for a portrait, whether of a 'three-quarters' (i.e. 76 × 63 cm) or 'half-length' (127 × 101 cm) format; that he charged the normal amount here confirms that the commission was an ordinary one. Nevertheless, the characteristic close-focused and intense qualities of many of Wright's Liverpool portraits (including those of Richard Gildart and the Hesketh; see above) are scarcely in evidence and it seems possible that Wright may have had some assistance in completing the works (WAG 10768 in particular; WAG 10769 seems more typical).[5] The asymmetry of the framing devices, with Mrs Parke's portrait set within an oval cartouche, is a standard device of the period. No other versions of these works are known.

PROVENANCE

By family descent; Christie 15 July 1988 (88–89); bt. Agnew for the gallery.

NOTES

1. John Hughes: *Liverpool Banks and Bankers 1760–1837* (Liverpool, 1906) p. 111. It was this Thomas Parke, and not the sitter in WAG 10768, who had interests in the privateer *King of Prussia*; Gomer Williams: *The Liverpool Privateers* (Liverpool, 1897), pp. 110–2; Hughes *op. cit.*, p. 112. Both authors note that he was declared bankrupt in 1758. For further biographical details of Thomas Parke the younger, the subject of WAG 10768, see Elizabeth E. Barker: 'Documents Relating to Joseph Wright "of Derby"', *Walpole Society* vol. 71 (2009) p. 200.
2. Hughes, *op. cit.*, pp. 112–3; and see also *Liverpool Post and Mercury* (9 May 1932) p. 5 and 'A Picturesque Line', *Liverpool Post* (6 April 1945) p. 2. The latter dates Parke's purchase of Highfield to 1791, but according to Gareth H. Jones: 'Parke, James', ODNB vol. 42 p. 648, James Parke was born at Highfield in 1782.
3. The paintings passed to Lord Wensleydale's youngest daughter, Mrs Lowther, and thence to her son, Lord Ullswater.
4. The account book is in the archives of the National Portrait Gallery. See Barker, *op. cit.*, p. 14.
5. Barker, *op. cit.*, p. 52 (n. 172) observes that 'presumably' WAG 10768–69 are identifiable as Wright's portraits. In 1919 James Lowther completed a National Portrait Gallery questionnaire to the effect that the portraits were by Cotes, indicating that no firm tradition of Wright's authorship survived in the family (notes on collections, National Portrait Gallery archives).

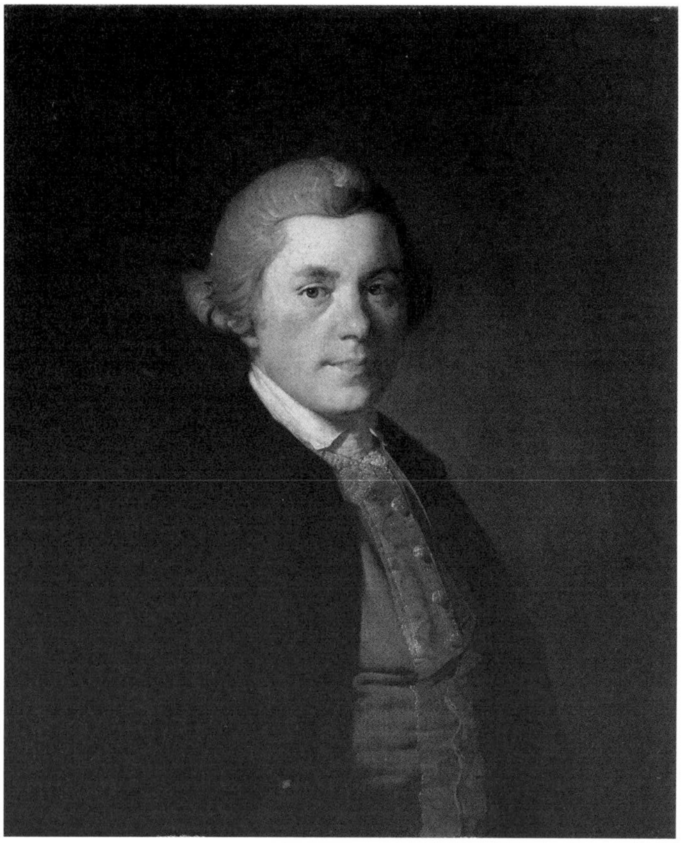

WAG 10768

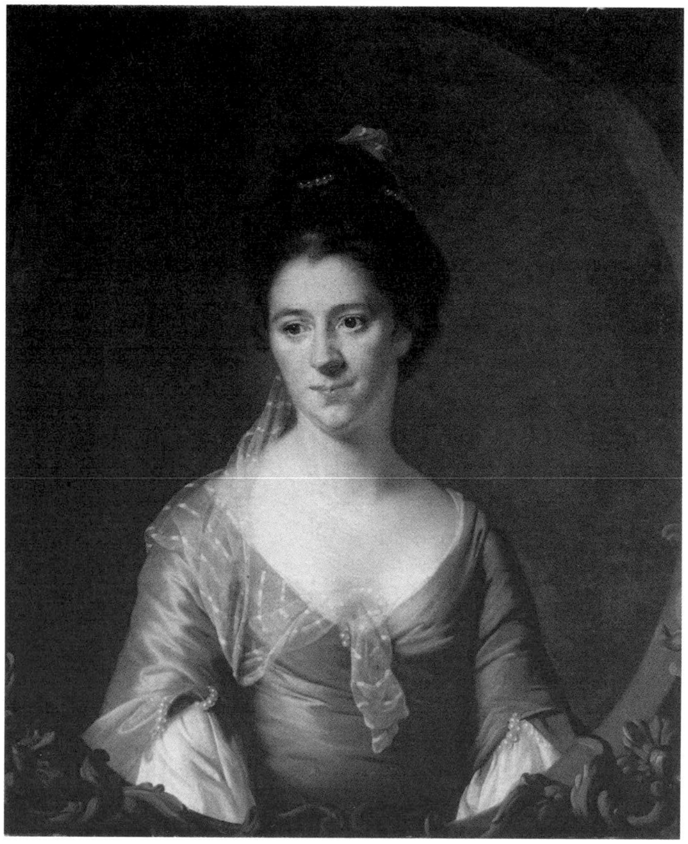

WAG 10769

The Old Man and Death

WAG 6123
oil on canvas, 63.5 × 77 cm
date: about 1775

This is a version of the lower left-hand part of Wright's exhibit at the Society of Artists in London in 1774 (Wadsworth Atheneum, Hartford; fig. 117).[1] The works are to the same scale, WAG 6123 merely eliminating the sky and the river landscape at the top and right-hand side of the larger version. Both are on standard-size canvases (WAG 6123 on a conventional 'three-quarters', the large picture on a 'half-length', 101 × 127 cm). WAG 6123 does not have the character of a preliminary study and the absence of variation and the slightly coarser finish argue that it is a replica. Wright failed to sell the large picture at the 1774 exhibition, which took place during his absence in Italy, and on his return to England in 1775 may well have taken it with him, hoping to find a buyer for it, when he went to live in Bath. It seems likely (see Provenance) that he was commissioned for this smaller version there. There is no evidence that WAG 6123 was once itself on a half-length canvas and has been cut down. The attribution to Wright himself has never seriously been questioned.[2]

The chief visible difference between WAG 6123 and the same area of the large version, apart from the slight but perceptible loss of intensity throughout, is that in WAG 6123 the tip of Death's spear projecting above the right shoulder is missing. The whole upper part of the figure of Death has suffered from damage in the past and has been repainted;[3] the restorer, however, omitting to replace the top of the spear, with the curious effect that Death appears to be impaling himself rather than simply 'reversing arms'. The elimination of the sky and the landscape

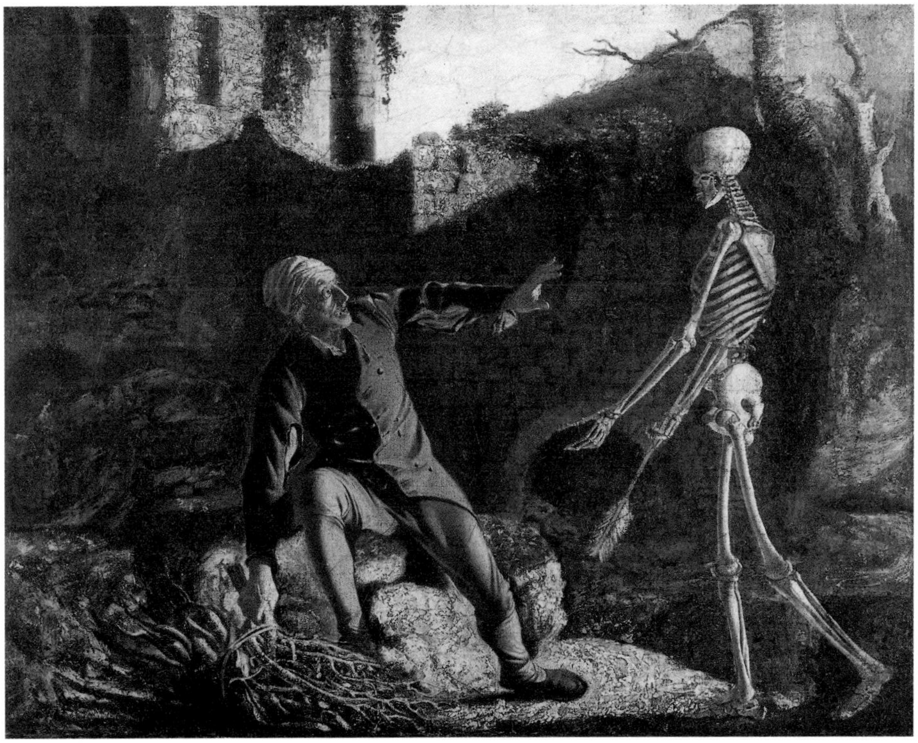

WAG 6123

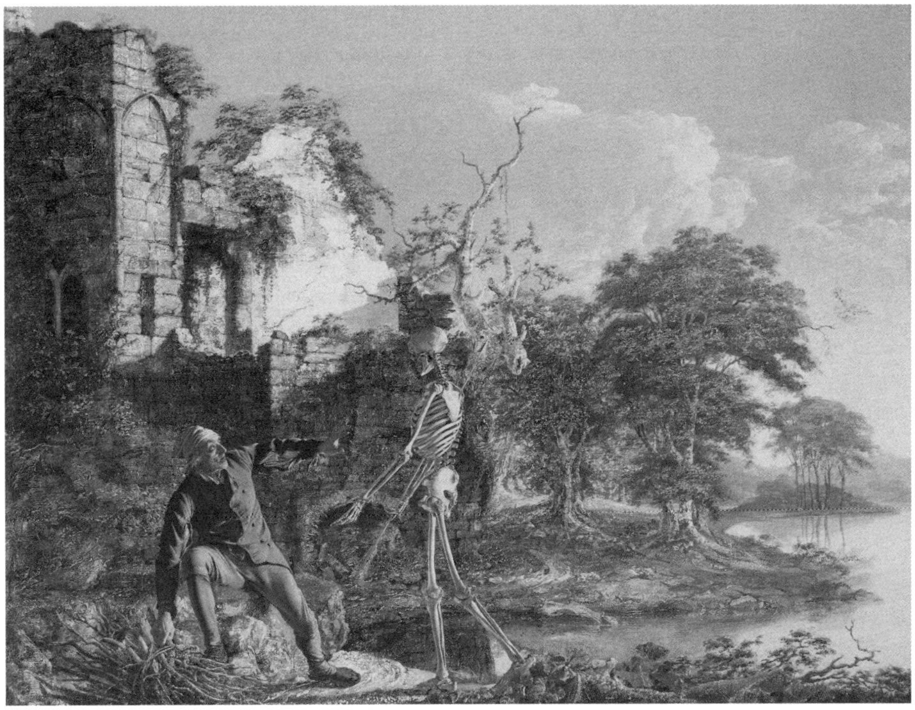

Fig. 117 *The Old Man and Death* by Joseph Wright of Derby, oil on canvas. Wadsworth Atheneum Hartford; photo E. Irving Blomstrann.

setting profoundly alters the character of the painting, increasing a sense of claustrophobia but paradoxically reducing the surreal and visionary element of Death appearing out of the blue on an English riverside.[4]

The source of Wright's subject is one of Aesop's fables (Wright may have seen an edition, *Select Fables of Esop and Other Fabulists*, published in Birmingham in 1761 which includes a small circular printed illustration of his chosen episode).[5] The fable relates how a poor old man sets down his heavy load of faggots and calls on Death to put him out of his misery, but when Death unexpectedly appears, the old man thinks better of it and tells Death he was merely asking him to carry his faggots. The moral is that any suffering is preferable to Death, and it has been suggested that the way Death carries the spear, not actually pointing it at the old man, emphasises that he is to be spared.[6] For the skeleton Wright adapted the third table of Bernhard Siegfried Albinus's *Tables of the Skeleton and Muscles of the Human Body* (1749), a copy of which was owned by Wright's friend John Hamilton Mortimer.[7] However, Wright altered the arms and the right foot of the Albinus skeleton, creating a more conciliatory, less coercive image of Death.

PROVENANCE

[? Bt. from Wright by William Gilbert Podd, 'picture dealer of Bell Savage Yard, Ludgate Hill and late from Bath, a Bankrupt'; his sale, Richards, Haymarket London 17 February 1798 (47); … Towne and Wigley, Princes Street, Leicester Square, London 27 May 1807 (23); bt. anon (£2 4s); …Robins 11 March 1811 (29) ('the property of a gentleman, deceased, and removed from Gloucestershire'); …Dr Solomon, Gilead House; Winstanley & Crole Liverpool 3–4 December 1818 (lot number unknown);[8] ? bt. by] Revd John Yates (1758–1826); his daughter, Helen Yates of Fairfield House, Liverpool 1860; Revd Samuel Yates; by descent to his nephew (or great-nephew) Allan Heywood Bright; Mrs Bright 1934; by descent to their daughter Mrs E. M. Lloyd; by whom presented 1962.

EXHIBITIONS

Exhibition of Ancient and Modern Paintings, Engravings and Photographs Liverpool Society of Fine Arts, Queen's Hall, Bold St Liverpool 1860 (127);[9] Wright of Derby Bi-centenary Exhibition Derby Museum and Art Gallery 1934 (86); The Profane and Symbolic in the Art of the Symbolists Galleria d'Arte Moderna, Turin 1969 (1).

NOTES

1. Not the central portion, as stated by Benedict Nicolson *Joseph Wright of Derby, Painter of Light* 2 vols (London, 1968), vol. 1, p. 243 (cat. 221), and followed by Judy Egerton: *Wright of Derby*, exh. cat., Tate Gallery, London, Musée du Louvre, Paris and Metropolitan Museum of Art, New York (1990) p. 84 (cat. 38).
2. Nicolson, *loc. cit.*, wrote, referring to Yates's ownership, that 'the highly impressive provenance dispels whatever doubts one might have had about the authenticity'.
3. J. Coburn Witherop, condition report dated 8 April 1969, gallery files.
4. Wright may originally have conceived the subject as a pendant for his 1773 Society of Artists exhibit *The Earth-stopper on the Banks of the Derwent*; the two pictures are (virtually) the same size and both feature a river bank setting in which death is foretold, one by day and one by night. If so, this adds weight to the argument that the landscape is a key element of *The Old Man and Death* and thus that WAG 6123 cannot be a preliminary study for the work.
5. Robert Rosenblum: 'Sources of Two Paintings by Joseph Wright of Derby', *Journal of the Warburg and Courtauld Institutes* vol. 25 nos 1–2 (1962) pp. 135–6; this, Nicolson, *op. cit.*, pp. 55–6 and p. 243 (cat. 220) and Egerton, *op. cit.* pp. 83–4, comprise the standard literature for the large version and add further bibliographical references.
6. Frederick Cummings: *Romantic Art in Britain: Paintings and Drawings 1760–1860* exh. cat., Detroit Institute of Arts and Philadelphia Museum of Art (1968) pp. 28–9 (cat. 29).
7. Nicolson, *op. cit.*, p. 56, where Albinus's illustration is reproduced.
8. Martin Hopkinson, who discovered these references, pointed out that the known provenance of Wright's large painting excluded the possibility that this was the work sold in these sales, and also that no other version of the painting is known, leaving WAG 6123 as the sole candidate (note in gallery files). The painting's impending appearance in the Winstanley and Crole sale of 1818 is reported in the *Liverpool Mercury* (27 November 1818) p. 172; no copy of the catalogue is known.
9. As *Death and the Woodman*, lent by the Misses Yates. This exhibition is not to be confused with the Liverpool Society of Fine Arts's exhibition of contemporary art which took place in the same premises in 1860 (and annually between the years 1858 and 1862).

The Annual Girandola at the Castel Sant'Angelo, Rome

WAG 1428
oil on canvas, 138 × 173 cm
date: 1775–76

The *girandola* was the spectacular firework display staged every Easter Monday from the roof of the Castel Sant'Angelo in Rome; *girandole* were also held on the feast day of Saints Peter and Paul (29 June) and on the inauguration of a new Pope.[1] The word literally means the revolving wheel from which the rockets were fired. While in Rome, Wright could have witnessed several *girandole* (including the one which inaugurated the papacy of Pius VI in February 1775), but the inscription *Rome June 4th 1774* on a drawing which he seems to have used as the basis for the composition of WAG 1428 (Derby Museums and Art Gallery; fig. 118) offers evidence that it was the *girandola* of Easter Monday 1774 that provided the inspiration for his later paintings of the subject. The drawing is carefully studied, itself evidently the product of a two-month incubation period.

In WAG 1428, as in all Wright's versions of the *Girandola*, the topography of Rome is not presented accurately; at the left, Trajan's column stands cheek by jowl with the Pantheon, while in the centre, St Peter's towers implausibly over the much closer Castel Sant' Angelo.[2] The work is a traditional (and even old-fashioned) *capriccio* of familiar Roman tourist sights, including the two colossal Italian stone pines, given novelty by the spectacular effect of light – Wright's trademark, in the eyes of his contemporaries.

Wright was working on his first major version of the *Girandola* (he may previously have made a small version of the subject in oil)[3] by the end of 1775. Writing to his brother Richard

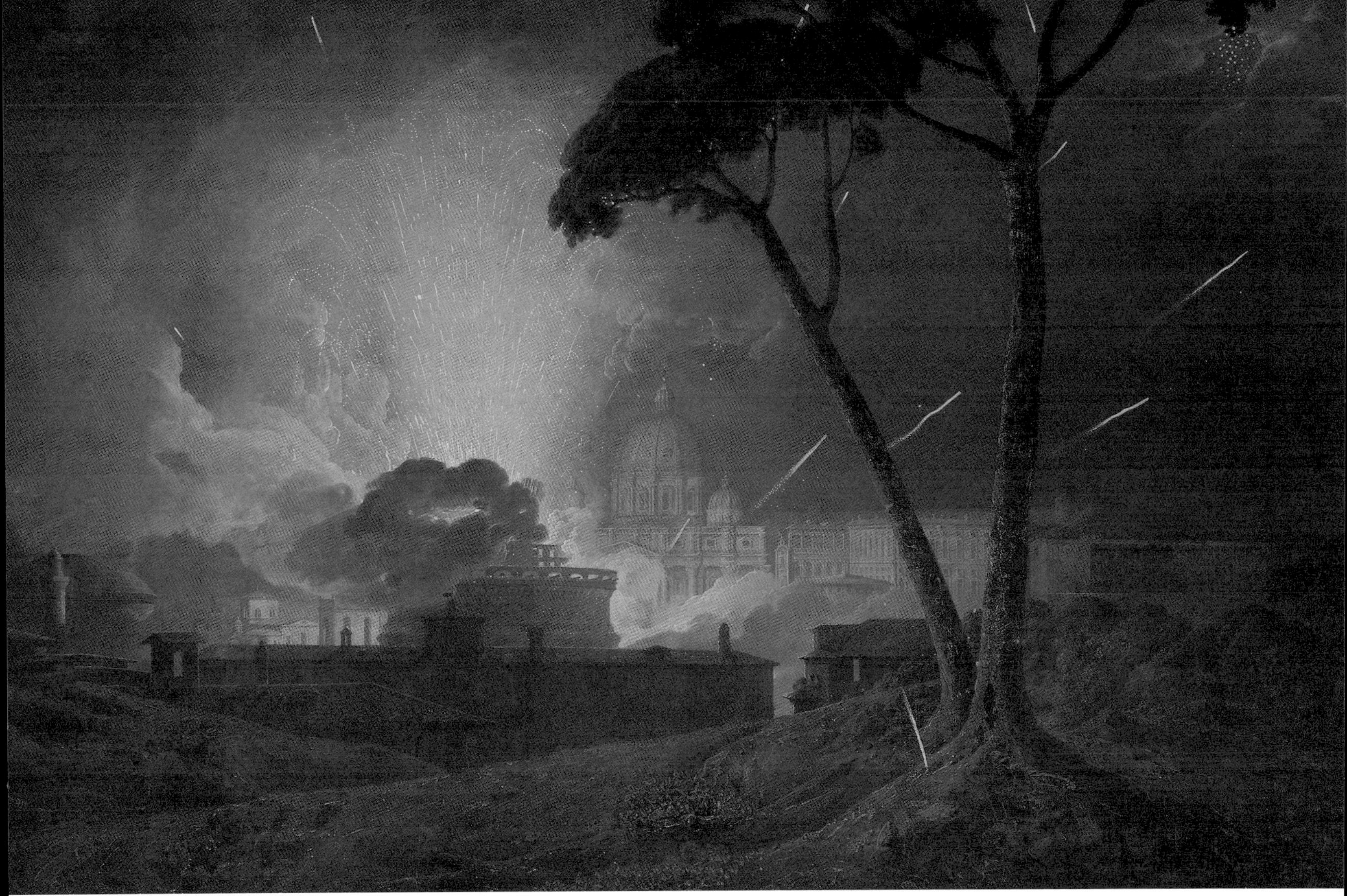

WAG 1428

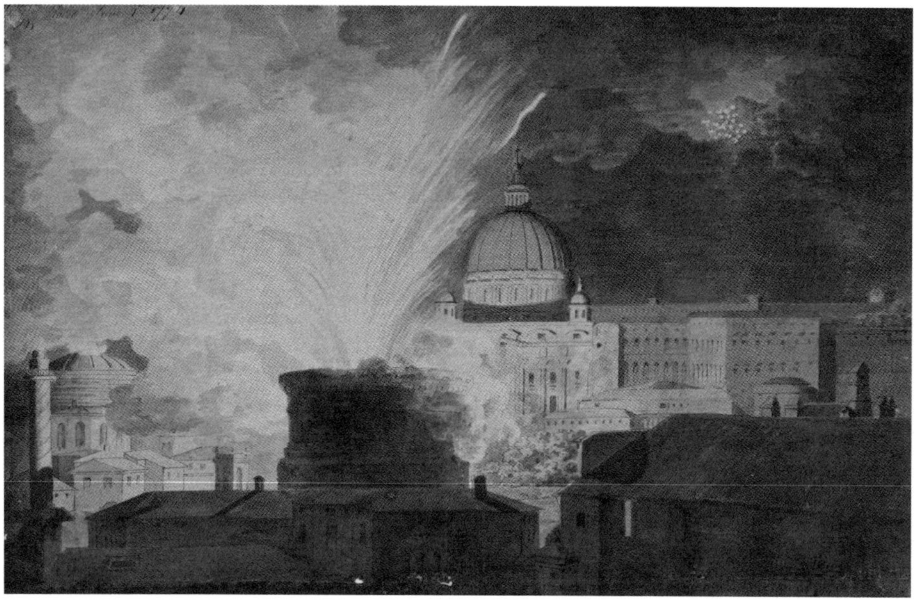

Fig. 118 *Girandola at the Castel Sant' Angelo* by Joseph Wright of Derby, sepia wash with brown ink on paper. © 2011 Derby Museums and Art Gallery.

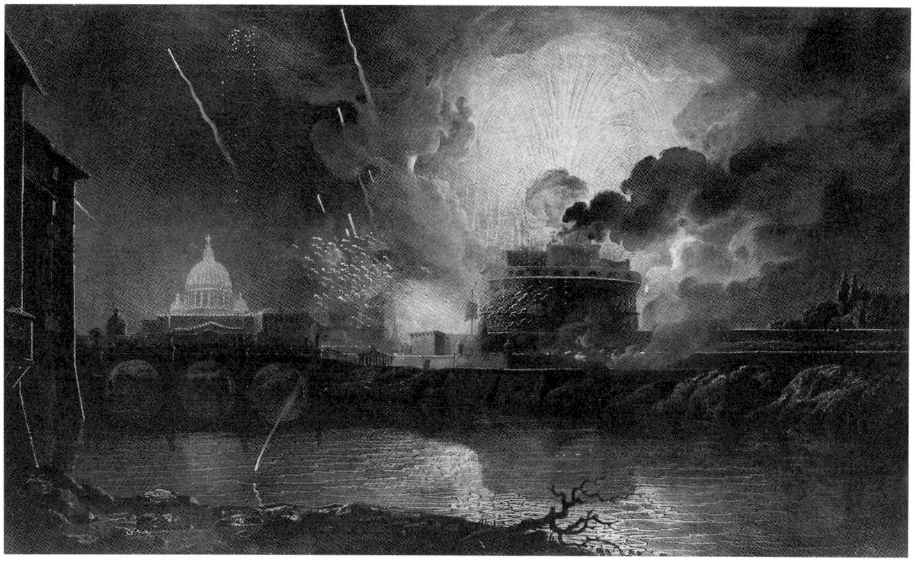

Fig. 119 *Girandola at the Castel Sant' Angelo* by Joseph Wright of Derby, oil on canvas. Birmingham Museums and Art Gallery.

from Bath on 15 January 1776 about the *éclat* being enjoyed in the town by his previously painted *The Eruption of Mount Vesuvius*,[4] he reported, 'I have just now finished a Companion to it. The Exhibition of a great Fire work from the Castle of St Angelo in Rome, the one the greatest Effect of Nature the other of Art that I suppose can be. This last picture I have painted to keep me from Idleness –' (continuing that he had had no commissions for portraits at all since he had been in the town).[5] He exhibited both works as pendants at the Society of Artists in the spring of 1776, where they were purchased by John Milnes of Wakefield. Wright was working on a portrait of Milnes in Bath at the time he must have been negotiating the despatch of the pictures from his studio to London[6] and although in a later letter he stated that Milnes bought the paintings on seeing them at the exhibition,[7] it seems very probable that Milnes was already familiar with them from sitting to Wright in Bath. Although the fate of Milnes's collection of pictures remains unknown, WAG 1428 has convincingly been identified as the version of the *Girandola* which he owned:[8] its scale and degree of finish is certainly that of an exhibition picture. Its companion of *Vesuvius*, which may have been, but was not certainly, the same size, remains untraced.[9]

Despite the fact that WAG 1428 was one of the first masterpieces of eighteenth-century English painting to be acquired by the fledgling Walker Art Gallery (see pp. XVI–XVIII), its history between its acquisition by Milnes and its presentation to Liverpool in 1880 by the local farmer and JP Robert Neilson has remained surprisingly obscure. It is unknown whether Neilson – himself an elusive figure[10] – purchased or inherited the work. In the past it has been assumed, erroneously, that WAG 1428 must be the *Girandola* purchased from Wright by the Liverpool collector Daniel Daulby in 1780,[11] which was the version that Wright had exhibited at the RA in 1778 and which Daulby himself lent to the Liverpool Society for Promoting Painting and Design in 1784 and 1787. Currently untraced, this canvas passed after Daulby's death in 1798 into the collection of Thomas Norris of Manchester and thence to John Moss, who lent it to the 1823 exhibition at the Royal Institution in Liverpool, but it is known from Daulby's sale catalogue to have measured only 38 × 48 inches.[12] There is a strong possibility, however, that WAG 1428 is the *Girandola* that was among 14 paintings by Wright sold by Thomas Winstanley in Liverpool, 13 April 1849, 'being formerly part of the Collection of the late Thomas Moss Tait, Esq., of this town' (i.e. Wright's friend T. Moss Tate; for whom see pp. 186–7). Nothing more is known of this picture.[13]

PROVENANCE

Bt. from Wright by John Milnes;[14] [...? Thomas Moss Tate; ...Winstanley, Liverpool 13 April 1849 (lot no. unknown)]; ...Robert Neilson; by whom presented to Liverpool Corporation for the gallery 1880.

EXHIBITIONS

SA 1776 (148); *Paintings by Joseph Wright* [...] Corporation Art Gallery Derby 1883 (49); *Joseph Wright of Derby* Tate Gallery, London and Walker Art Gallery 1958 (15); *Il Settecento a Roma* Rome 1959 (690); *Italian Art and Britain* RA 1960 (213); *R.A. Bi-centenary* RA 1968–69 (31); *Joseph Wright of Derby* Derby Museums and Art Gallery 1979 (21); *Wright of Derby* Tate Gallery, London, Musée du Louvre, Paris and Metropolitan Museum of Art, New York 1990 (104).

NOTES

1. The standard discussion of Wright's *Girandola* pictures is Judy Egerton: *Wright of Derby*, exh. cat., Tate Gallery, London, Musée du Louvre, Paris and Metropolitan Museum of Art, New York (1990) p. 172 (cat. 104). This supersedes Benedict Nicolson: *Joseph Wright of Derby, Painter of Light* 2 vols (London, 1968), vol. 1, pp. 279–84, Appendix B: 'Paintings of "Vesuvius" and the "Girandola"' (although the latter remains valuable for its full listing of (the much more numerous) versions of the *Vesuvius*). The present entry is indebted to Egerton's account. For a recent summary of the literature on WAG 1428 see also A. J. Fox: '"A World of Trouble": Joseph Wright of Derby in Bath', MA report, University of Maryland, 2009, especially pp. 48ff.
2. The church or churches between the Pantheon and the Castel Sant'Angelo have not been conclusively identified. Jane Martineau, *email*, 7 September 2010, gallery files, has suggested the church with the octagonal crossing tower is intended for S. Maria di Loreto.
3. The small version of the *Girandola* now at Birmingham Museum and Art Gallery (fig. 119) was identified by Nicolson, *loc. cit.*, as likely to be Wright's first treatment of the theme, on the basis of its close similarity to a drawing that Wright sent to an unknown correspondent from Rome in 1774; he considered this oil likely to be a preparatory study for the painting exhibited at the SA in 1776. Fox, *loc. cit.*, also considers the 1776 exhibit to be Wright's second treatment, and the Birmingham picture the first. Egerton, recognising that the relationship between the Birmingham picture and the earlier drawing is scarcely closer than that of WAG 1428 to the Rome drawing inscribed *June 4th 1774*, describes the role assigned by Nicolson to the Birmingham canvas as 'entirely hypothetical'. The Birmingham work is not identifiable as an exhibited picture and it might convincingly be argued that it has the character of a potboiler, rather than a preliminary study.
4. The *Vesuvius* had been painted in Italy, under the immediate impression of a trip to Naples in October–November 1774, and was finished by January 1775 when it was mentioned by Father Thorpe in a letter to Lord Arundell of Wardour; Egerton, *op. cit.*, p. 166 (cat. 101). It had been the subject of abortive interest from Empress Catherine of Russia, who later purchased versions of both the *Vesuvius* and the *Girandola* (the very large paintings exhibited by Wright at the RA in 1778 and 1779 respectively; Egerton, *op. cit.*, pp. 174–6; cats. 105–106).
5. Elizabeth E. Barker: 'Documents Relating to Joseph Wright "of Derby"', *Walpole Society* vol. 71 (2009) p. 88 (Letter 23).
6. Egerton, *op. cit.*, pp. 68–9 (cat. 27).
7. Barker, *op. cit.*, p. 96 (letter 35).
8. Egerton, *op. cit.*, p. 172 (cat. 104).
9. Egerton, *op. cit.*, p. 166 (cat. 101) implicitly (although not explicitly) casts the version of the *Vesuvius* in the collection of the University of Wales, Aberystwyth, as this work; it is likely to have been the *Vesuvius* sold by John Leigh Philips in 1814, but that leaves room for it to have been owned previously by Milnes. Its size is not identical to WAG 1428, being only 101.5 × 127 cm; however, it appears that Wright did not necessarily exhibit the subjects as identically sized pendants. In 1778 he exhibited at the RA a *Vesuvius* that measured 162 × 213.5 cm (the Empress Catherine's) together with a *Girandola* that measured 99 × 124 cm (Daulby's). On the other hand, it is tempting to think that the Aberystwyth canvas, which is the same size as Daulby's *Girandola*, may originally have been planned by Wright as its pendant, in the same way that the 1779 *Girandola* was clearly planned as the companion of the 1778 *Vesuvius*.
10. Neilson appears to have begun life as a Liverpool merchant (Samuel Sidney: *Rides on Railways* [London, 1851] p. 158, describes him as 'a mercantile notability'). However, already by 1848 he was leasing the 300-acre Halewood Farm south-east of Liverpool from Lord Stanley and was gaining a reputation as a progressive farmer. By the last quarter of the nineteenth century he was 'possibly the best-known farmer in Lancashire, having used steam for ploughing since 1867 and making his own gas to power a threshing mill and bone mill. He was a JP and on the committee of the Liverpool Farmers Club' (A. Mutch: 'The Mechanization of the Harvest in South-west Lancashire 1850–1914', *Agricultural History Review* vol. 29, part 2 [1981] p. 130); and see also S. Lewis: *A Topographical Dictionary of England* (London, 1848) p. 375. He presented no other works of art to Liverpool and, indeed, is not known to have owned any others.
11. This assumption was made, for example, by S. C. Kaines Smith and H. Cheney Bemrose: *Wright of Derby* (London, 1922) pp. 28–9. For Wright's letters to Daulby regarding the purchase see Barker, *op. cit.*, pp. 96–7 (letters 34–6).
12. Nicolson, *op. cit.*, vol. 1, p. 280; Egerton, *op. cit.*, p. 172 (cat. 104). The work was lot 81 in Daulby's sale, Thomas Vernon, Liverpool 27 August 1798; bt. Norris £87 3s.
13. Notices of the sale listing the works were published in the *Liverpool Mercury* 6 April 1849 p. 4 and 13 April 1849 p. 1. However, no catalogue for the sale survives and the dimensions of the work are unknown. Neither Nicolson, *op. cit.*, nor Egerton, *op. cit.*, makes reference to this appearance of a *Girandola* subject.
14. Milnes certainly owned WAG 1428 and its companion in 1787; Nicolson, *op. cit.*, vol. 1, p. 279. They may have been included in one of his sales: of 1806 (Nicolson, *op. cit.*, vol. 1, p. 250) or 1808 (Egerton, *op. cit.*, p. 69 [cat. 27]). No catalogue for either sale survives and it is thus impossible to state whether Tate bought Milnes's picture at one or other of them. No *Vesuvius* was among the paintings sold by Winstanley in 1849 but the painting listed after the *Girandola* was titled *An Illumination*, which could conceivably be Milnes's *Vesuvius*.

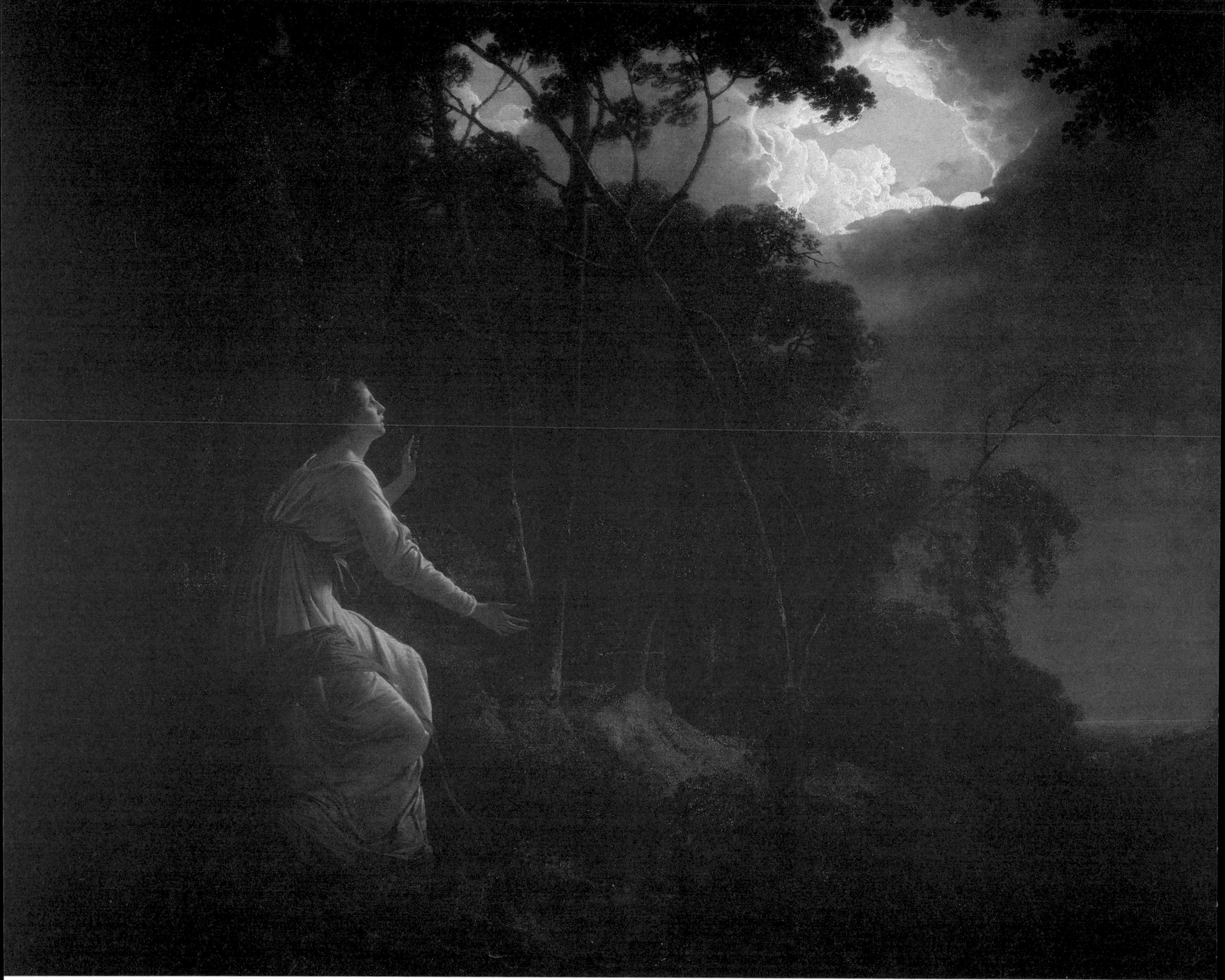

WAG 2500

The Lady in Milton's 'Comus'

WAG 2500
oil on canvas, 101 × 127 cm
date: 1783–84

Wright's painting depicts one of the climactic moments in John Milton's masque *Comus*, first performed at Ludlow Castle on Michaelmas night, 1634. Comus, a pagan god invented by Milton as the offspring of Bacchus and Circe, is the leader of a rabble who waylay travellers by night and transform them into monsters; he has a particular preference for virgins. The Lady, having gone for a walk in the woods with her two brothers, has become separated from them. Left alone, she has heard distant sinister calls and noises and has become prey to fear, but when she voices the conviction that God will 'send a glist'ring Guardian if need were / To keep my life and honour unassail'd', the moon breaks through the clouds, and gives her the emotional strength she needs to keep her virtue intact from Comus's menaces. In the catalogue of Wright's one-man exhibition at Robins's Rooms, London in 1785, at which the work was first shown, the five lines spoken by the Lady at the appearance of the moon were quoted:

Was I deceived, or did a sable cloud
Turn forth her silver lining on the night?
I did not err, there does a sable cloud
Turn forth her silver lining on the night
And cast a gleam over this tufted grove.

Wright conceived WAG 2500 as a pendant to *The Indian Widow* (Derby Museums and Art Gallery, fig. 120). The subject of *The Indian Widow* had been suggested to him in 1783 by his friend the poet William Hayley, and it appears to have been Hayley's friend in Derby, Mrs Beridge, no doubt aware that he was casting around for another noble woman at an emotionally charged moment and seated under a spectacularly lit sky, who directed Wright's attention to Milton's lines.[1] Wright began *The Lady in Milton's 'Comus'* some time after *The Indian Widow*, but the two are clearly designed as a pair, with the compositions mirroring each other. By April 1784, having been held up on the first picture, Wright was writing to Hayley that he had 'nearly finished' its companion. He added that 'I have never painted a picture so universally liked',[2] indicating that he had shown the picture to friends in Derby and was unusually confident of its success. The work's blend of sentiment, its appeal to national cultural pride (in the selection of a passage from a great English poet), its refined classicism (in the handling of the drapery, one of the finest instances of Wright's skill with female robes), its sublimity (in its exploitation of fear and darkness) and its incipient Romanticism (in its depiction of a particular effect in nature) seem, indeed, to have touched a deep chord with contemporaries,[3] and this in spite of the fact (or perhaps because of it) that the subject was completely unfamiliar to viewers, being unique in British art to that date.[4] The picture was bought immediately, before the 1785 exhibition, by Josiah Wedgwood, and when it was shown in London it drew considerable critical attention. *The General Evening Post* enthused,

this, we presume to say, is one of the most beautiful performances that ever came from the hand of this excellent artist. The fine disposition of the light, thrown on the face, hands, and neck of this amiable virgin, is inimitably pencilled... Indeed too much cannot be said in commendation of the picture, which in drawing, composition and effect, shows the hand of a great and original genius. – The happy choice of the subject, the delicate manner in which it is treated, and the brilliancy of the colouring, proclaims it one of the best productions that has ever been exhibited by the greatest ancient or modern professors.[5]

In similar vein, *The Morning Post and Daily Advertiser* wrote that 'this, among the minor pictures [Wright's exhibits included several larger paintings, including the colossal *View of Gibraltar during the Destruction of the Floating Batteries*] is perhaps the most perfect in the room. It is difficult to say whether it most excels in drawing, composition or effect'.[6]

John Raphael Smith's mezzotint engravings of *The Indian Widow* and WAG 2500 were issued in January and February 1789 respectively.[7] A 25 × 30 inch copy of WAG 2500 was sold at Sotheby 11 March 1987 (117) where it was stated to be by Wright himself.[8] No second version by him is documented, but he is known to have made a replica of *The Indian Widow*[9] and is also known to have made 'three-quarters' versions of pictures he had originally painted on 'half-length' (101 × 127 cm) canvases (including *The Old Man and Death*, pp. 285–6).

PROVENANCE

Bt. from the artist by Josiah Wedgwood; by descent; consigned by a member of the Wedgwood family to the European Museum, King Street London after May 1813 and before May 1814, whence sold between April 1817 and March 1818;[10] ...Thomas Moss Tate of Liverpool by 1822;[11] ...William Rathbone, Liverpool 1881;[12] presented to the gallery by Mrs William Rathbone in memory of her husband 1902.

EXHIBITIONS

Pictures Painted by J. Wright, of Derby [...] Robins's Room, Covent Garden 1785 (1); European Gallery 1814 (433); Liverpool Art Club 1881 (24); *Wright of Derby Bi-centenary Exhibition* Derby Museum and Art Gallery 1934 (139); *The Romantic Movement* Tate Gallery, London 1959 (381); *Primitives to Picasso* RA 1962 (299); *Joseph Wright of Derby* Derby Museums and Art Gallery 1979 (21); *Wright of Derby* Tate Gallery, London, Musée du Louvre, Paris and Metropolitan Museum of Art, New York 1990 (66).

NOTES

1. Judy Egerton: *Wright of Derby*, exh. cat., Tate Gallery, London, Musée du Louvre, Paris and Metropolitan Museum of Art, New York (1990) pp. 127–8 (cat. 66) – to which this entry is much indebted – suggests that Wright had already identified his subject in Milton's work and that

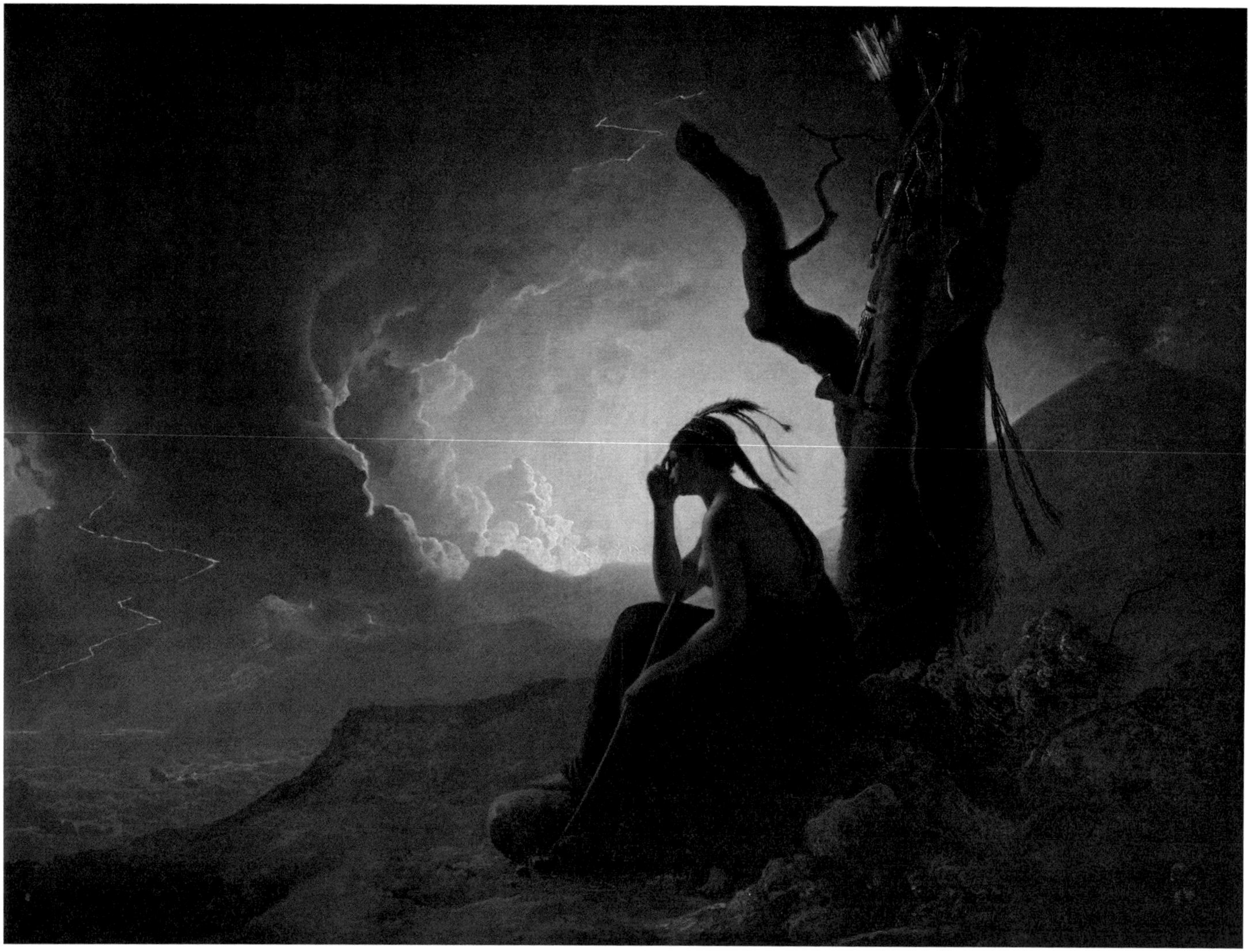

Fig. 120 *The Indian Widow* by Joseph Wright of Derby, oil on canvas.

Mrs Beridge merely directed him to the specific lines; but it seems more likely that Wright informed Mrs Beridge that he needed another subject with a female protagonist and a strong effect of light and that she gave him the idea of the Lady in *Comus*. For Wright's reliance on literary advisers generally see Suzanne E. May: 'Attempts towards Fame and Fortune: Joseph Wright of Derby and Late Renaissance Humanism', *British Art Journal* vol. 11 no. 1 (2010) pp. 41–52.
2. Elizabeth E. Barker: 'Documents Relating to Joseph Wright "of Derby"', *Walpole Society* vol. 71 (2009) p. 111 (Letter 57).
3. For discussions of the work's place in late eighteenth-century art and culture see, for example, Michael Kitson: 'Romantic and "Romantic"', *The Studio* vol. 158, no. 797 (August–September 1959) pp. 33–40, esp. pp. 36–7; Benedict Nicolson: 'Two Companion Pieces by Wright of Derby', *Burlington Magazine* vol. 155 (March 1962) pp. 113–7; Benedict Nicolson: *Joseph Wright of Derby, Painter of Light* 2 vols (London, 1968), vol. 1, esp. p. 65; also pp. 16–7, 148, 153, and 245 (cat. 234); Marcia Pointon: *Milton and English Art* (Manchester, 1970) pp. 70–3, and Eric Adams: *Francis Danby: Varieties of Poetic Landscape* (New Haven and London, 1973) pp. 13, 26.
4. Pointon, *loc. cit.*
5. *General Evening Post* (14–16 April 1785) p. 4. The writer may have been Hayley.
6. *Morning Post and Daily Advertiser* (20 April 1785) p. 2.
7. Tim Clayton: 'Catalogue of the Engraved Works of Joseph Wright of Derby', in Egerton, *op. cit.*, pp. 250–1 (cats. P30–1); both originally priced by Smith at 10s 6d.
8. The attribution had been confirmed by David Fraser of Derby Museums and Art Gallery.
9. Nicolson (1968) vol. 1 p. 247 (cat. 244); dimensions unknown.
10. Burton B. Fredericksen, *letter*, 27 August, gallery files.
11. In the codicil, dated 28 August 1822, of his will of 1816 (Lancashire Record Office, Preston) Thomas Moss Tate bequeathed *The Lady in*

Milton's 'Comus' to his wife and then to their daughter Emma.

12. Lent by Rathbone to the 1881 exhibition. When the Rathbone family acquired the work is not known; however, the picture was not among the 14 works by Wright formerly owned by Thomas Moss Tate auctioned by Winstanley in Liverpool, 13 April 1849 (for this sale see p. 187, n. 5).

The Convent of San Cosimato

WAG 2139
oil on canvas, 50.5 × 63.5 cm
signed: *J. W. Pt.* (on rock, bottom right)
date: about 1787–88

Wright's view depicts the convent of San Cosimato, situated on the Roman Via Valeria outside the town of Vicovaro slightly over 30 miles east-south-east of Rome. The convent overlooks the gorge of the river Aniene, which seven miles downstream will pass through the more popular tourist site of Tivoli. In the foreground of the view is part of the Claudian Aqueduct (completed by the Emperor Claudius in 52 CE). The medieval convent was built on the site of a sixth-century oratory dedicated to Saints Cosma and Damian which itself had been erected upon the remains of a Roman villa, and a complex system of tunnels links it with the riverbank below. The area is traditionally said to have been frequented by hermits.[1]

An inscription on the stretcher of WAG 2139 reads as follows: *Convent of Cosimato / Bought by Wm Claxton of South Hill Grove, Liverpool / in April 1849 / having formerly belonged to his friend / Thos Moss Tate Esq. / by Wright of Derby Pt. 1774 a gift to Thos. Moss Tate Esq.* In two respects this text is misleading.[2] First, the date of 1774 may refer to Wright's visit to Italy but cannot be the date of the painting itself. It has been suggested that Wright may in fact have visited the area in the summer of 1775 when he travelled from Rome to Florence 'by the way of Narni, Terni, Perugio &c'[3] and that he based this and other later Italian landscapes on sketches made on the spot;[4] but the actual work dates from the later 1780s. Second, the painting was given not to Thomas Moss Tate but to his uncle, Wright's Liverpool friend and pupil William Tate, as an entry in Wright's account book makes clear: *A small picture of Cosmato given to my friend W: Tate – .*[5] On his death in 1806, William Tate bequeathed it to his nephew, who himself had enjoyed a close association with Wright in the four or five years before the artist's death.

Wright's account book records four other *San Cosimato* pictures apart from WAG 2139. The earliest chronologically is the *com[panion] of Cosmato* which accompanied a *View in Dovedale* sold to Mr [Revd Thomas] Gisborne for 50 guineas the pair; of these (at Kedleston until sold in 2007) the *Dovedale* is signed and dated 1786.[6] Although Wright played skilfully on the visual parallels between the gorges of the Dove and the Aniene in these paintings, he appears to have regarded the pairing as unsatisfactory, for he thereafter twinned Dovedale by day with Dovedale by moonlight subjects, freeing up *The Convent of Cosimato* to stand by itself. Chronologically, the next version recorded in Wright's account book must be WAG 2139, which from the surrounding entries on the page appears to have been presented to Tate in about 1787–88; then comes *A View at Cosimato on panel sold to Honble A Thompson pd. £42.0*, which is identifiable as the panel measuring 61 × 81.5 cm, dated 1789, formerly in the Blundell-Turner collection, whence it was on long loan to Derby Museums and Art Gallery (fig. 121).[7] Compositionally, this work is very close to WAG 2139, but both

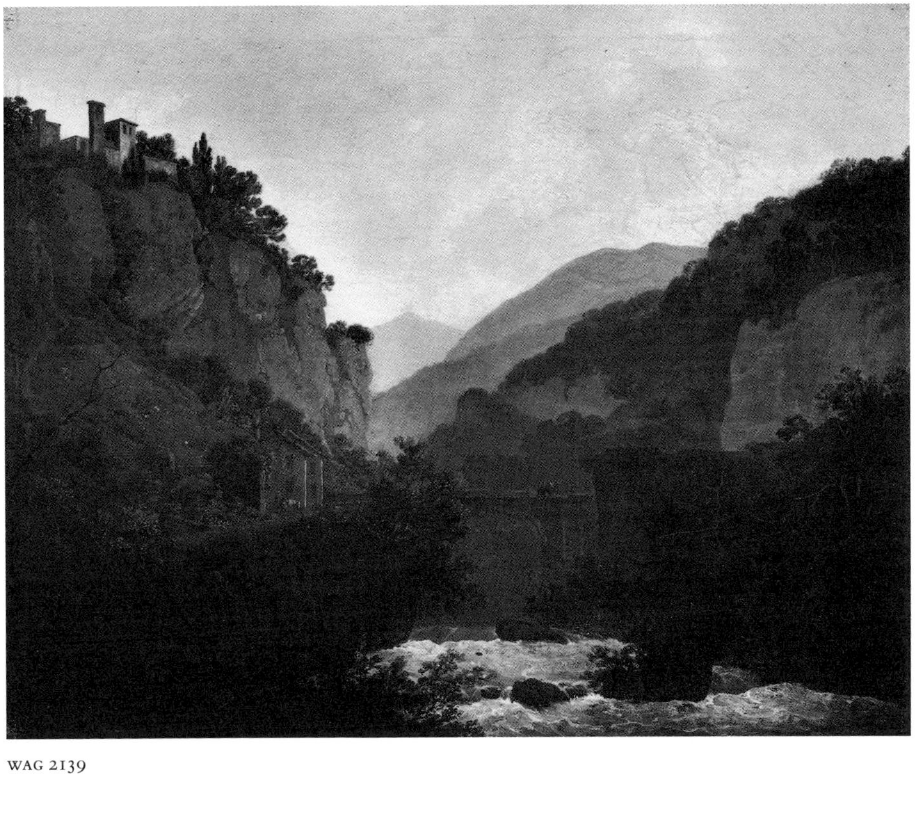

WAG 2139

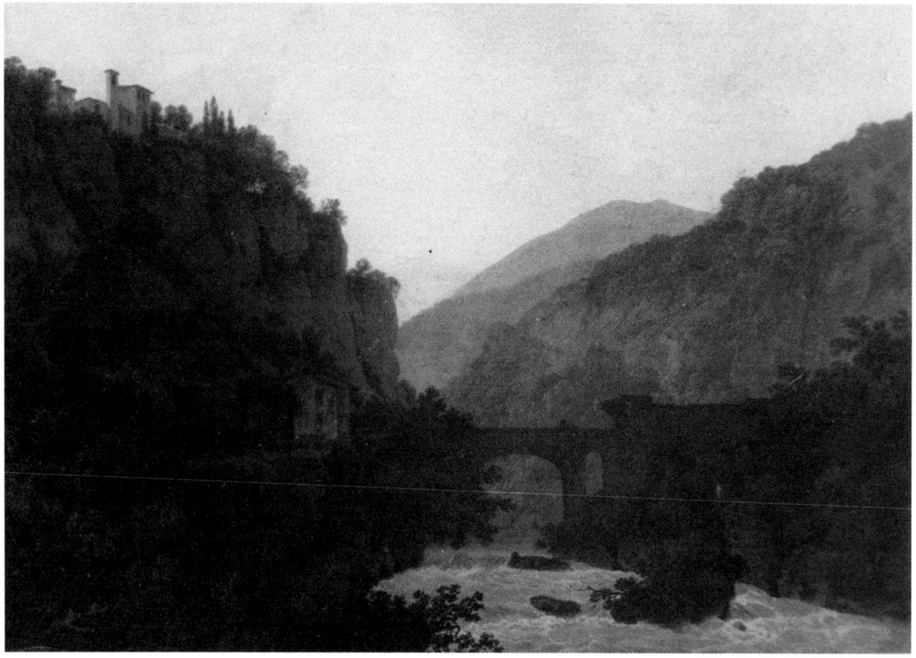

Fig. 121 *The Convent of San Cosimato* by Joseph Wright of Derby, oil on canvas. Private collection; image courtesy of Derby Museums and Art Gallery.

exhibit some significant variations from the Kedleston version. In the latter the viewpoint is from the right-hand bank of the Aniene, but in WAG 2139 and the Blundell-Turner picture, Wright has switched to the left bank, compressing the rock face below the convent and opening out the view of the mountains to the right and giving the arches of the aqueduct a more central position. Two further versions of the subject are listed in the account book among pictures of the 1790s: *The Convent of St Cosimato 26 5/ D° for Mrs Hayley – Mem – Not Paid.*[8] These remain untraced. A version said to be by Tate was sold from the collection of John Pooley by Winstanley, Manchester, 30 March 1827 (17), and this may be the *Italian Scene – Convent of St. Cosimata* lent by J. Bentley (as by Wright) to the Royal Manchester Institution's *Old Masters* exhibition of 1831 (cat. 145).

Wright himself showed one version of the subject at the Royal Academy in 1788, under the title *The Convent of St Cosimato, near Vicobaro,* [sic] *and Remains of the Claudian Aqueduct, on the River Arno* [sic]. On balance, WAG 2139 is the best candidate for this picture.[9] Of his exhibits generally the *Gazetteer and New Daily Advertiser* remarked,

The modest and unobtruding Wright, who hides the brightest talents among the hills of Derbyshire, has greatly contributed this year to the splendor of the exhibition. He has some most exquisite landscapes, in which his comparative excellence, both in fire and water, is fully ascertained.[10]

The critic of the *St James's Chronicle* commented of the *Convent of Cosimato*, 'The Artist has here placed the principal Light in the Sky, which has a beautiful Effect; though not often seen in Painting. The Objects are distinct, clear, well-coloured, and highly finished.'[11]

PROVENANCE

Given by the artist to William Tate; bequeathed to his nephew, Thomas Moss Tate; ...Winstanley, Liverpool 13 April 1849 (cat. no. unknown);[12] bt. William Claxton; by descent to Dr Ecroyde I. Claxton; his bequest through his widow Mrs G. Claxton 1958.

EXHIBITION

[? RA 1788 (98)].

NOTES

1. Judy Egerton: *Wright of Derby*, exh. cat., Tate Gallery, London, Musée du Louvre, Paris and Metropolitan Museum of Art, New York (1990) p. 192 (cat. 121); also www.tibursburn.it/escursioni/sancosimato/SanCosimato.htm, accessed 3 October 2009.
2. Benedict Nicolson: *Joseph Wright of Derby: Painter of Light* 2 vols (London, 1968) vol. 1 p. 253 (cat. 264) compounded the confusion by mis-transcribing *1774* as *1794* and *Thos Moss Tate* as *Jno Moss Tate.*
3. Wright's 'Italian Journal', in Elizabeth E. Barker: 'Documents Relating to Joseph Wright "of Derby"', *Walpole Society* vol. 71 (2009) p. 65.
4. John Jacob, draft catalogue entry, gallery files.
5. Wright's Account Book (National Portrait Gallery Archives) p. 63^r; Barker, *op. cit.*, p. 40.
6. Wright's Account Book (National Portrait Gallery Archives) p. 65^v; Barker, *op. cit.*, p. 41; and see Egerton, *op. cit.*, pp. 191–2 where both works are reproduced in colour. They were sold at Christie 5 July 2007 (41).
7. Wright's Account Book (National Portrait Gallery Archives) p. 61^v; Barker, *op. cit.*, p. 40; and see Nicolson, *op. cit.*, vol. 1, p. 252 (cat. 263); this painting was sold at Sotheby in 1973 and bought by Colnaghi; exh. *An Exhibition of English Drawings, Watercolours and Paintings* Colnaghi, London 1973 (95).
8. Wright's Account Book (National Portrait Gallery Archives) p. 51^v; Barker, *op. cit.*, p. 33.
9. Nicolson, *op. cit.*, vol. 1, p. 263, observes that the only two candidates for the exhibited picture are WAG 2139 and Gisborne's. But it would seem unlikely that Wright would have requested to borrow an old painting that had already been sold, or that he would have wanted to show only one painting of a designated pair.
10. *The Gazetteer and New Daily Advertiser* (29 April 1788) p. 2.
11. *St James's Chronicle* (3–6 May 1788) p. 4
12. No catalogue for this sale survives, but 14 works by Wright 'being formerly part of the Collection of the late Thomas Moss Tait [sic], Esq., of this town' [for whom see pp. 186–7] were auctioned by Winstanley on 13 April 1849 and are listed in notices of the sale printed in the *Liverpool Mercury* (6 April 1849) p. 4 and (13 April 1849) p. 1. *The Convent of Cosimato* is among them. The intervening owner may have been Tate's cousin and executor Robert Benson.

after

Joseph Wright (of Derby)

1734–97

Richard Gildart

WAG 2506
oil on canvas, 81 × 61 cm
date: unknown, perhaps 1800–25

Of very mediocre quality, WAG 2506 is a copy of the upper part of Wright's portrait also in the collection (see WAG 10637, pp. 278–80). It may derive from an intervening copy for there are a number of differences: the proper right hand is positioned more horizontally, the cuff and the number of buttons on the coat are altered, and the head and wig are shaped differently. Little or no effort has been made to imitate Wright's painting style. It is not certain that WAG 2506 is the work of a single artist: the depiction of the hands is in a markedly different technique from that of the head and neckcloth. The inscription *Richard Gildart M.P./aet 95* in the lower left corner is fuller than that on the original and is in a much more cursive hand, suggestive of the nineteenth century. Folds across the canvas about 6 cm and 3 cm from the bottom suggest that WAG 2506 was previously a larger canvas whose bottom edge was at one point folded round the bottom edge of the stretcher, and which was subsequently trimmed at the top (Gildart's head is closer to the top of the picture space than in the original). Nothing is known of the history of the work. It is thought to have entered the gallery about 1920[1] but there is nothing to confirm that it was executed in Liverpool.

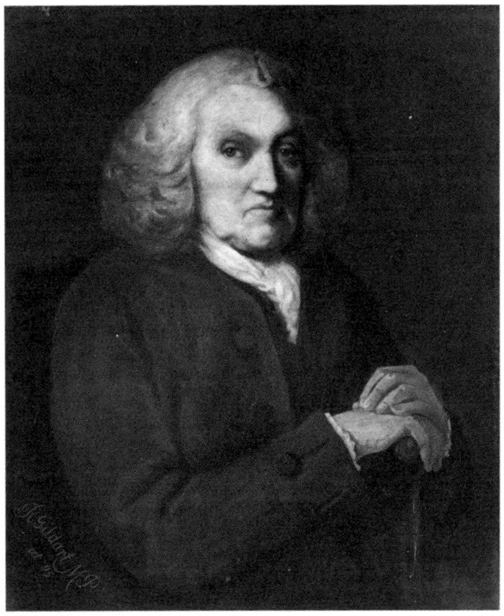

WAG 2506

PROVENANCE

Found in the gallery; transferred to the permanent collection at an unknown date.

REFERENCE

1. *MPPP*, p. 51. It may be identifiable with the copy of Wright's portrait of Gildart that was offered to Liverpool Corporation for purchase by Miss Mary R. Gildart of Dunain Lodge, York Road, Harrogate in 1920, and was declined (Minutes of the Arts and Exhibitions Sub-committee dated 9 July 1920, in the volume covering meetings 7 January 1916–23 July 1920, p. 199 (gallery archives). I am grateful to Edward Morris for this reference. The work is not included in the 1927 Walker Art Gallery catalogue (under Wright, British School or Unknown).

Richard Wright

about 1723 – about 1775

Man of War in a Harbour

WAG 2006.21
oil on canvas, 106.5 × 167.5 cm
date: about 1765–70

The ship in WAG 2006.21 remains unidentified, although clues to its identity are provided by the flag of an admiral of the white flying at the mainmast and the white ensign at the stern, and by the distinctive figurehead at her bows of a man wearing (apparently) a tricorne and a tartan jacket with matching knee-breeches (he is bare-legged below the knees). The vessel is leaving harbour at the rear of a small squadron of warships sailing in line ahead in the distance, and is still towing her longboat in which two seamen are visible. She has already hoisted her spritsail whose drainage holes Wright has carefully depicted.[1] That she appears to have fewer guns than the standard 74-gun ship of the line casts doubt on a recent identification of the work as Wright's 1767 Society of Artists exhibit, *A Man of War of 74 Guns, with Some Shipping at a Distance, Taken in a Squall of Rain.*[2] All the same, WAG 2006.21 is a significant work of Wright's London period (after 1760), and is on a scale that suggests it was intended for public exhibition. The elements of caprice within the composition, such as the still-life of varied marine life in the foreground,[3] and the dramatic invented harbourscape, reinforce this impression.

Although the work may have been commissioned by the captain of the ship portrayed, Wright seems to have sold it instead to Jervoise Clarke (later Clarke-Jervoise, 1733–1808), MP for Yarmouth, Isle of Wight, 1768–69 and 1774–79, and later for Hampshire.[4] He is not known to have had any direct connection with the Royal Navy but the fact that he

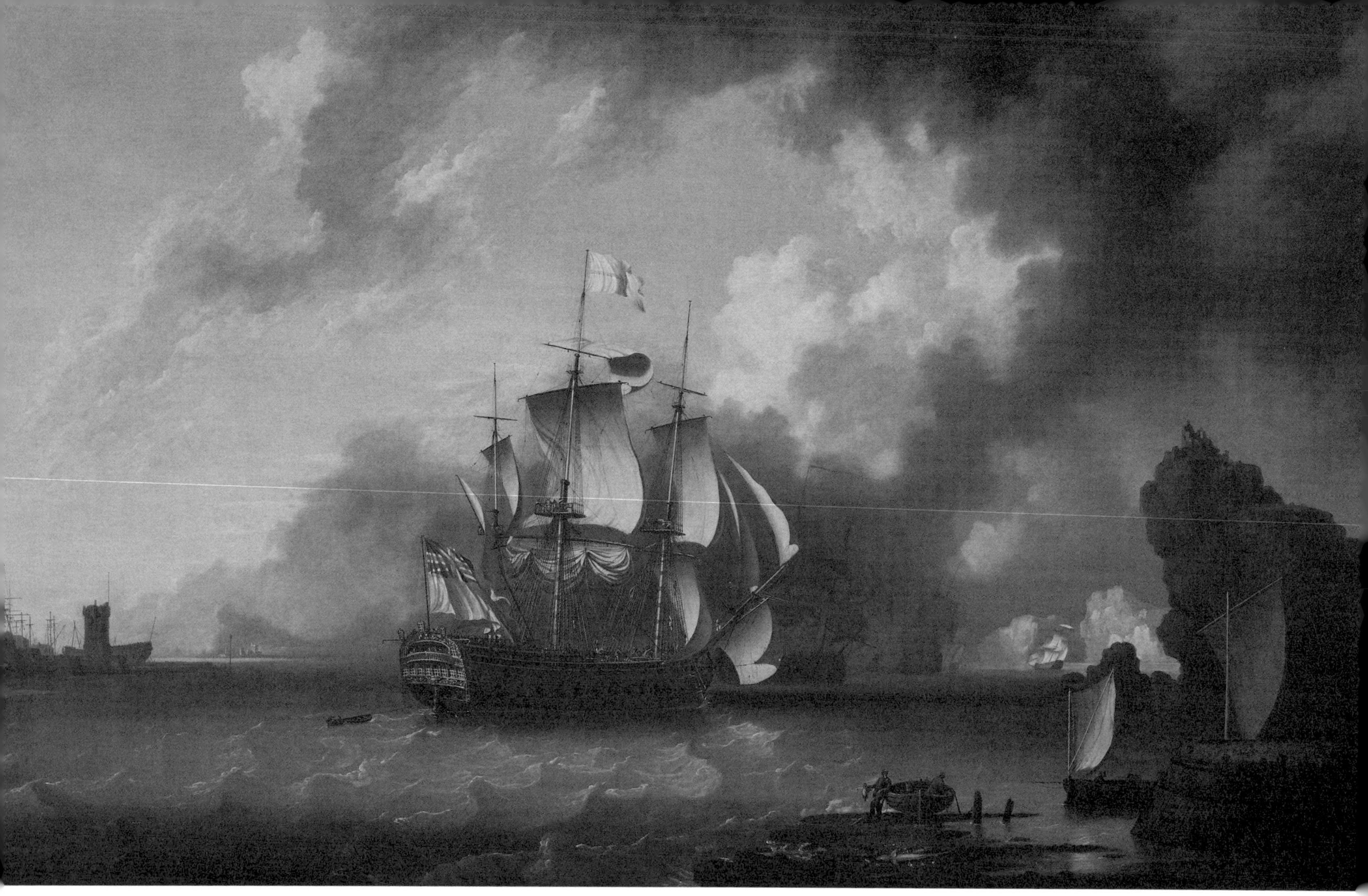

WAG 2006.21

represented an Isle of Wight constituency in Parliament may be significant in accounting for the subject's appeal to him.

The painting, which is not on its original stretcher, has been lined twice, and the edges of the original canvas have been trimmed and overpainted, but the paint layer itself is in good condition.[5]

PROVENANCE

Bt. from the artist for £63 plus 16 gns. for the frame by Jervoise Clarke;[6] by descent to Major A. F. Clarke-Jervoise; Christie 21 March 1975 (135); bt. Simon Carter Gallery; bt. Mrs Vivien Cole; from whom bt. 2006 with assistance from the Friends of National Museums Liverpool.

EXHIBITION

Joseph Wright of Derby in Liverpool Walker Art Gallery and Yale Center for British Art, New Haven 2007–08 (5).

NOTES

1. Notes made by Sam Davidson, gallery files.
2. This was the suggestion of Mrs Cole, *verbally*, to the compiler, 1995. It was not made in the 1975 sale catalogue.
3. The fish have been identified as John Dory, smooth hound, red mullet, squid and whelks (information from Rachel Porter, World Museum Liverpool, gallery files).
4. L. Namier and J. Brooke, eds: *The History of Parliament: The House of Commons 1754–1790* 3 vols (London, 1964) vol. 2, p. 216.
5. Conservation and treatment report dated 2007, gallery files.
6. A manuscript list of his art purchases, apparently written by Clarke himself, survived with WAG 2006.21 until the 1975 sale. The work is in its original frame.

after

Richard Wright

about 1723 – about 1775

The Fishery

WAG 2164
oil on canvas, 51 × 69 cm
date: unknown, perhaps 1764–68

This is a small version of Wright's best-known composition, which was exhibited at the Free Society of Artists in 1764 as *A Sea Piece, with a Squall of Rain*. Its traditional (later) title, *The Fishery*, alludes to the activity in the foreground of the scene, where Wright depicts his imagined realisation of a scheme for transporting fresh fish inland by means of refrigerated wagon that had recently been promoted by the Society for the Encouragement of Arts, Manufacturers and Commerce. Wright's passing allusion to this project – in a work teeming with incident – was probably what earned the painting the Society's £30 prize for the best marine painting of the year. According to the Society's minutes, Wright's original (which is currently not certainly traced)[1] measured 3 ft by 4 ft 6 inches.[2] Its celebrity, which may have been partly fuelled by a controversy over the value of the prize given to the artist,[3] led to the publication on 30 June 1768 of an engraving by William Woollett (fig. 122); this was given the title *The Fishery* and it was dedicated to Sir John Hort (from 1767 British consul-general in Lisbon).[4] WAG 2164, which has frequently been assumed to be Wright's original,[5] is one of many known copies.[6] It is of fair quality and captures much of the detail of the composition but it is much too small to have any claim to be the first version. Whether Wright made autograph replicas of his works is unknown, but on balance it seems probable that WAG 2164 was carried out by a studio assistant or

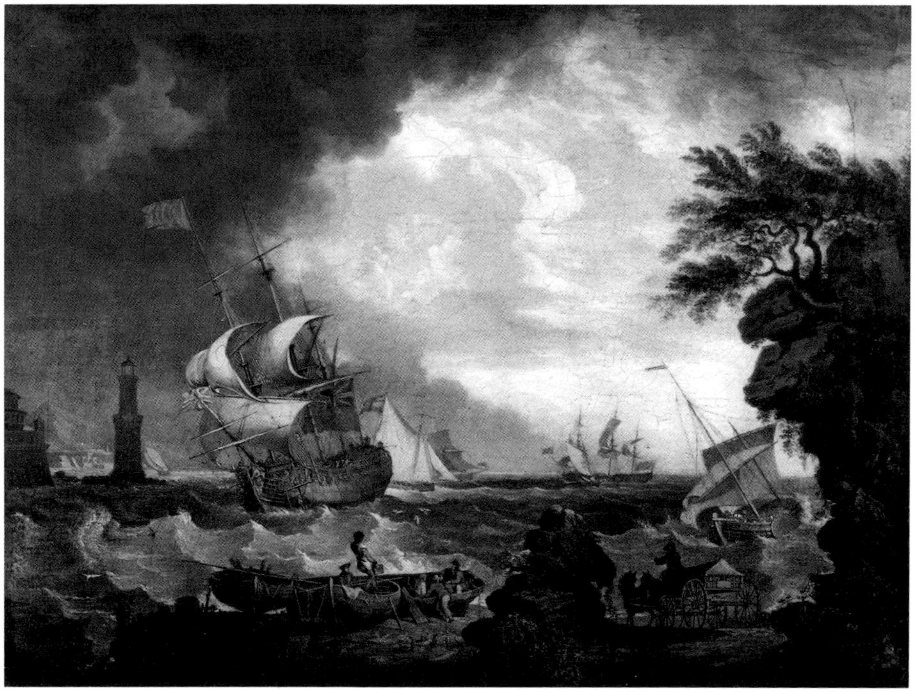

WAG 2164

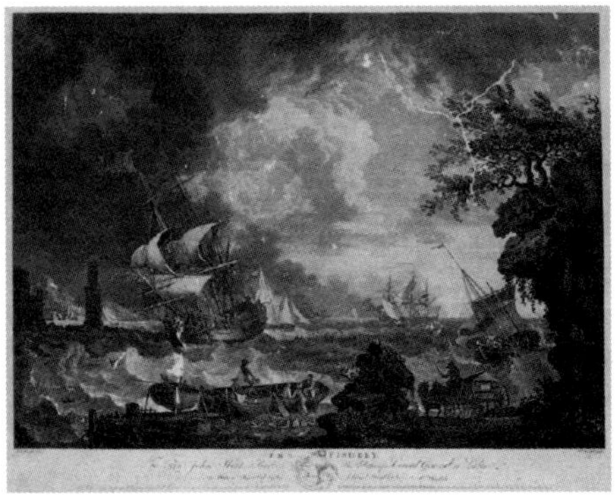

Fig. 122 *The Fishery* after Richard Wright, engraving by William Woollett.
© Walker Art Gallery.

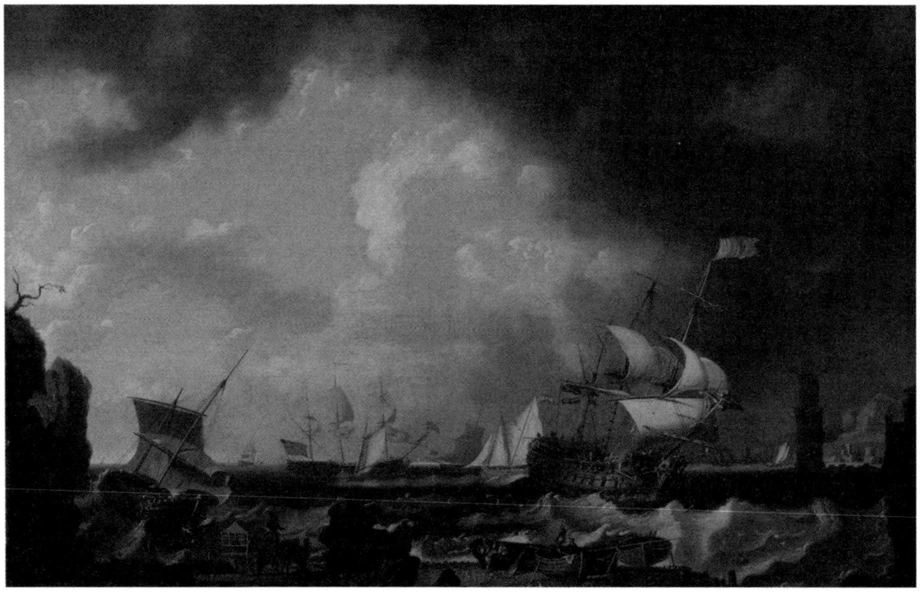

Fig. 123 *The Fishery* attributed to Richard Wright, oil on canvas.
Yale Center for British Art, Paul Mellon Collection.

pupil.[7] The ship in the left foreground has been identified as HMS Neptune from its figurehead.[8]

PROVENANCE

...Colonel Fox, London Salvage Corps; from whom bt. November 1914.

EXHIBITION

The Liverpool School of Painters Harrogate 1924 (36).

NOTES

1. Arguably the best candidate for the original at present is the canvas in the Yale Center for British Art, New Haven (inventory B-1981.25.723[a]; sold at Sotheby's 23 November 1966; bt. Colnaghi for Paul Mellon; fig. 123). At 35½ × 54 inches, it is the closest known to the presumed dimensions of Wright's original. It is of fair quality, and it is the only one of all the versions which is in reverse to Woollett's engraving, prompting the speculation that Woollett may simply have engraved Wright's picture 'straight' without using a mirror. However, pirated French engravings after Woollett (one inscribed *Vernet pinxit / La Peege / J.J. A[vril] Sculp / A Paris Crepy rue St Jacques près la rue de la Parcheminerie*, for which see Col. M. H. Grant: *A Chronological History of the Old English Landscape Painters in Oil from the XVIth Century to the XIXth Century, etc.*, 8 vols [rev. edn, Leigh-on-Sea, 1957–61] vol. 3, p. 212) were in reverse to Woollett's, and conceivably one of these could have formed the basis for the Yale picture. Moreover, there are substantial differences between the Yale picture and Woollett's engraving, including the cliff on the right-hand side (of the engraving) which simply does not exist in the painting, the treatment of the sky, and the size of rock in the centre of the foreground; in the painting there is extra shipping in the middle background and the gun ports on the large vessel are open. Sarah Monks, *letter*, 13 July 2001, Yale Center for British Art files, discussing the YCBA picture, notes 'additions [in Woollett's print] which are clearly to be seen in Woollett's preparatory sketches' as evidence that the variations were invented by Woollett; however, see also n. 7 below for a further argument that the Yale picture cannot be Wright's original.
2. James Taylor, National Maritime Museum Greenwich, *verbally*, 18 February 1994; and Monks, *loc. cit.*
3. According to Taylor, *ibid.*, the minutes state that Wright was originally going to receive a £50 premium but this was reduced to £30, presumably on the grounds that Wright's canvas as originally sized was only eligible for the prize allocated to smaller pictures. Realising this, Wright appears to have extended his canvas in order to make it eligible for the larger award.
4. John Hort was elected a member of the Royal Society of Arts in November 1761 and remained a member until his departure for Lisbon in 1767. He does not appear to have played any part in the award of the RSA's 1764 prize for marine painting to Wright (Rebecca Short, Royal Society of Arts, *emails*, 5 and 14 October 2010, gallery files).
5. WAG 2164 was first published as Wright's original by E. Rimbault Dibdin: 'Liverpool Art and Artists in the Eighteenth Century', *Walpole Society* vol. 6 (1917–18) pp. 60–1, repr. pl. XXIV(b). A. S. Davidson was still referring to it as Wright's original in his *Marine Art and Liverpool* (Wolverhampton, 1986) p. 16. In *MPPP*, p. 236, WAG 2164 was more cautiously referred to as 'a likely candidate for the original picture'; this assessment was based on its relatively superior quality.
6. Fourteen documented versions (not including the Yale picture; see n. 1) are listed in *MPPP*, p. 237. Since the publication of *MPPP*, the version cited there as no.12 was re-sold at Christie 15 July 1987 (8); a copy by Henry Ninham (1793–1874) (illustrating the popularity of Wright's subject well into the nineteenth century) was sold at Christie 13 October 1989 (58); a large version measuring 83 × 114.5 cm was sold at Christie 12 July 1990 (64); a version was with the Norsk Institutt for Kulturminneforskning, Oslo, 1993; a small copy on panel, 43.5 × 57 cm, was sold at Bearne's, Torquay 25–27 October 1994 (669), and a version measuring about 90 × 120 cm was sold at Bearne's, Exeter 2 November 2005 (370).
7. However, the sign inscribed *FISH MACHINE* fixed to the back of the cart that is visible in the engraving (and in many of the other copies) is not present in WAG 2164: this has led to the supposition (*MPPP*, p. 236) that WAG 2164 represents Wright's original conception and the introduction of the 'Fishery' theme into the picture was an afterthought on the artist's part. But as Edward Edwards implied in his *Anecdotes of Painters* (London, 1808) p. 48, Wright's 'compliment' to the Society of Arts must have been intended from the outset; and it seems most probable that the Fish Machine sign was added by Woollett to make Wright's otherwise highly topical and arcane reference more legible. Accordingly, versions of the composition lacking the inscribed words *FISH MACHINE*, such as WAG 2164, presumably derive from Wright's original canvas, not the print; this in turn might suggest that they were executed between 1764 and the publication of the print in 1768.
8. Davidson, *loc. cit.*

Johan Zoffany

1733–1810

The Family of Sir William Young

WAG 2395
oil on canvas, 114.5 × 167.5 cm
date: about 1767–69

The sitters in WAG 2395 are Sir William Young, 1st Baronet (1725–88), his second wife Elizabeth (1729–1801), their nine children and their slave named John Brook. The children are as follows: the eldest daughter, Sarah, is in the centre of the composition holding open an album of music, evidently about to join her mother and father, who are playing the theorbo and cello respectively, in a musical party. The eldest son, William (born at Charlton, Kent, 1749; died in Tobago 1815, who had recently completed his education at Eton and would succeed his father as 2nd Baronet)[1] is at far right with his favourite sister Mary (later Mrs Sewel), who leans her elbow affectionately on her brother's shoulder. At the left are the three younger sons: on the horse, Brook (died unmarried at Marseilles before 1788), Henry (died of wounds in the American war of Independence) who is being greeted by the family dog while reaching up to his younger brother John (baptised in Antigua 10 September 1761, married Jane Blizard of Antigua between 1784 and 1788, and lived in later life at Bath where he wrote a life of his father and his Young ancestors, died 1834).[2] The three youngest daughters are ranged to the right of their mother: behind her are Portia (died unmarried in 1832) and next to her, holding garlands of flowers, Elizabeth (married firstly before 1788 James Hartley and secondly a Mr Summers, died at her home in Margaret Street, Cavendish Square 1823); in the foreground is the youngest child, Olivia (died unmarried).[3]

Sir William himself was the son of a doctor, William Young of Leny, Perthshire, an estate which had been granted to his forebears in the reign of Mary Queen of Scots. William Young of Leny had been implicated in the Old Pretender's rebellion in 1715 and emigrated to the West Indies, where he married Margaret Nauton, daughter of a wealthy plantation owner. The plantations which their son inherited formed the basis of his wealth and enabled him to adopt a cultivated lifestyle. Shortly after he arrived in Europe, he married (probably in 1746) Sarah Fagg of Mystole, Chartham, Kent, who died after only seven months of wedlock, aged 18, in 1747. Young expressed his grief at her loss by commissioning an imposing funerary monument for her from Michael Rysbrack, which he adorned with lines written by himself,[4] but very soon afterwards he married his second wife, who was the only child of Brook Taylor of Bifrons, Kent, secretary to the Royal Society and leading authority on perspective and optics. In 1749 Young was elected a member of the Society of Antiquities and he bought an estate in Wiltshire, Standlynch in the parish of Downton.[5] By 1758 he and his wife, who performed amateur theatricals and were passionately fond of the theatre – witnessed in WAG 2395 by their choice to sit in 'masquerade' or 'Van Dyck' costume – had also became friendly with David Garrick.[6] It was probably Garrick who in due course provided the Youngs with an introduction to Zoffany, for he was the German-born artist's leading patron and supporter during the 1760s, Zoffany's first decade in London.[7]

Young divided his time between England and the West Indies. In 1764 he was appointed Commissioner and Receiver for sale of lands in the islands of Dominica, St Vincent and Tobago, and responded by publishing two pamphlets: *Some Observations Which May Contribute to Afford a Just Idea of the Nature and Importance, and Settlement of Our New West-India Colonies* and *Considerations Which May Tend to Promote the Settlement of Our New West India Colonies.*[8] He was in England in 1767, when he commissioned portraits of his eldest son William and of himself and his wife with their youngest child, from Benjamin West[9] (whose *Venus Lamenting the Death of Adonis* he purchased shortly afterwards). In the same year, Sir William purchased the Elizabethan manor house and estate of Delaford, near Iver, Bucks, where he gave land to the parish to enable improvements to the local highways.[10] In March 1768 he was appointed Lieutenant-Governor of Dominica. In 1769 he was created a Baronet, and in October 1770 he was appointed Lieutenant-Governor of Tobago. On this trip he seems to have remained in England for several years, at least until the summer of 1770, the date of his eldest daughter Sarah's marriage to Richard Ottley.[11] The central positioning of Sarah, with the huge tree flourishing behind her as an augury of abundant progeny, may perhaps offer a clue to the date of WAG 2395, which has been contested. Traditionally the work has been dated to around 1770,[12] but more recently the suggestion has been made that it may have been commissioned as early as 1764.[13] The argument turns on the apparent age of John, who is recorded as having been baptised in Antigua on 10 September 1761.[14] Since John appears older than just three, a dating of 1764 seems improbable. More persuasive is the view that the work was carried out about 1766, on the basis that John can be no older than five, and that William, at the far right, looks younger here than he does in his Eton leaving portrait of 1767.[15] Both points are perhaps arguable; certainly, Sir William and his wife themselves

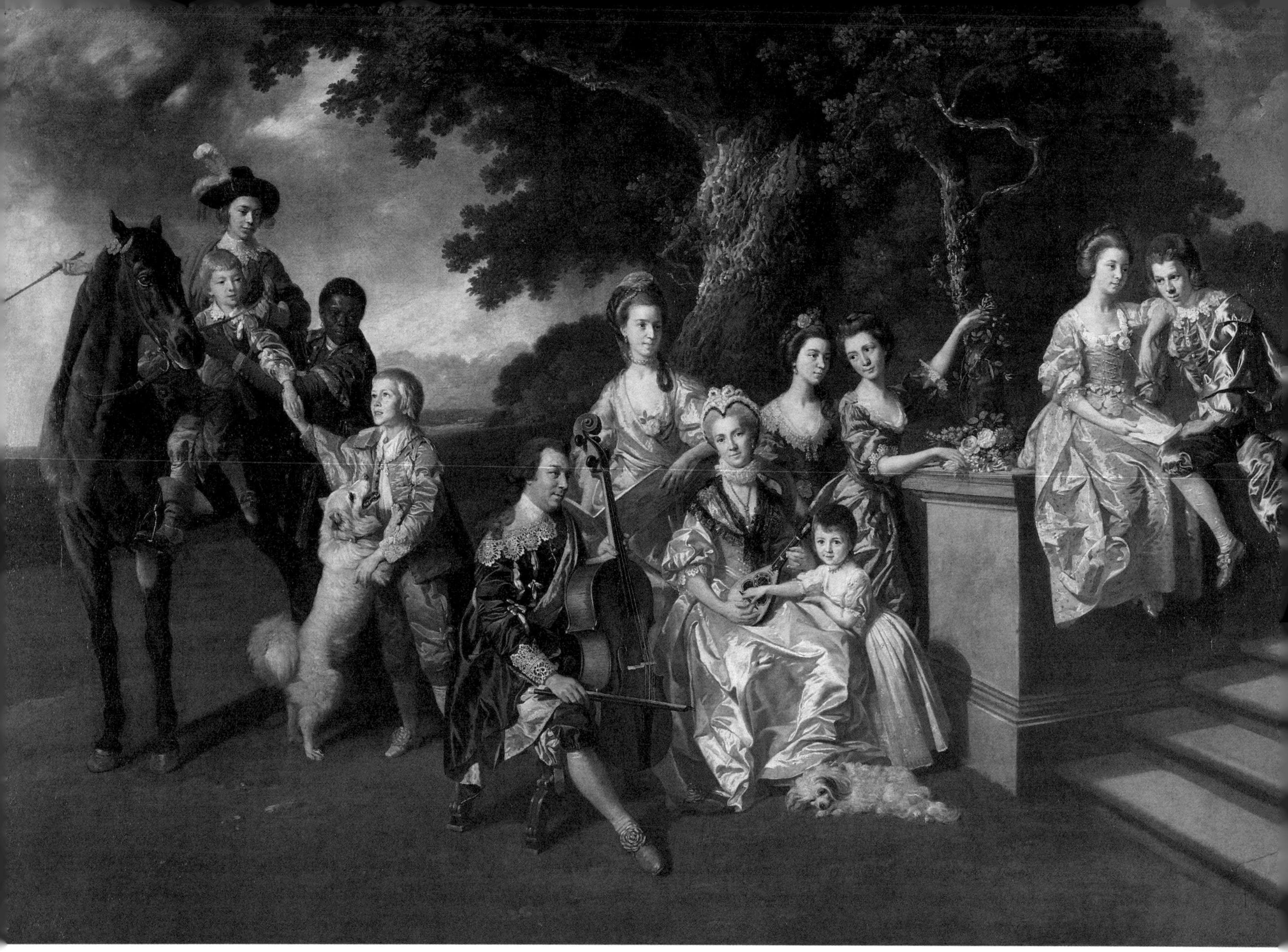

WAG 2395

both appear distinctly older in Zoffany's painting than they do under the hands of West, although this may reflect the American artist's greater propensity for flattery as against Zoffany's instinctive literalism. On balance, a date of 1768, with the work intended to serve as a generic reminder of life at Delaford[16] in the context of Sir William's recent appointment as Governor of Dominica and likely imminent return to the West Indies, and with John shown as a rather youthful six or seven, seems preferable.

However, the question of the work's date is further complicated by the existence of two small oil variants of the left- and right-hand sections of the work (private collection; figs. 124–25). The former of these is inscribed, in a later hand *Brook, John and Harry Young / Zoffany and Stubbs pinx. 1770.* If this inscription is correct, it raises the issue of the precise relationship of these small canvases to WAG 2395. They are far too finished to be described as studies in a normal sense and they bear no stylistic resemblance to the few known preparatory oil sketches by Zoffany; but nor are they straightforward copies, for they both exhibit differences to the finished painting, most noticeably in the pose of John and the dress worn by Mary. These changes register as improvements in WAG 2395 rather than in the smaller pictures, suggesting that the latter came first. The attribution of the horse in the

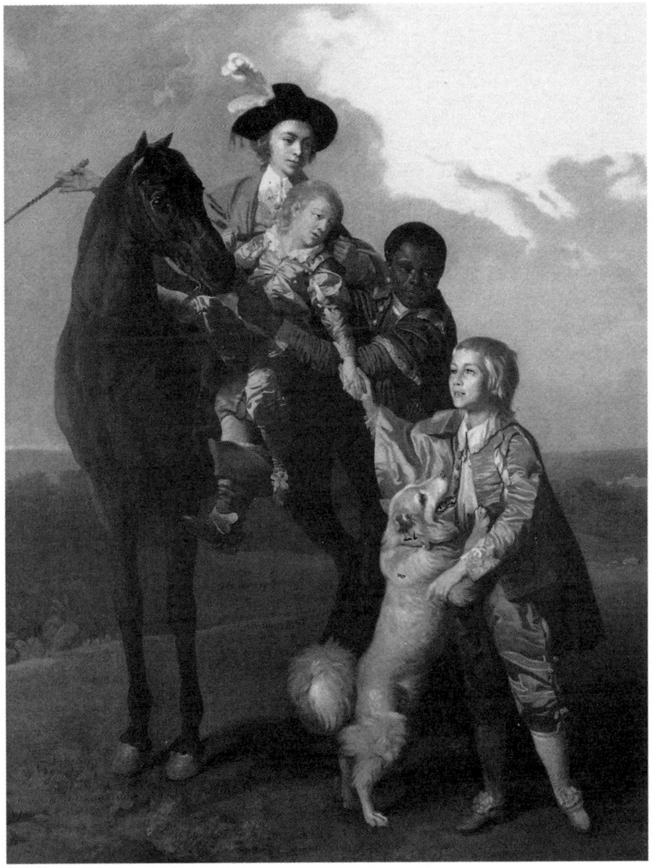

Fig. 124 *Brook, Henry and John Young, with John Brook* by or after Johan Zoffany, oil on canvas. Private collection, UK; photo courtesy National Portrait Gallery, London.

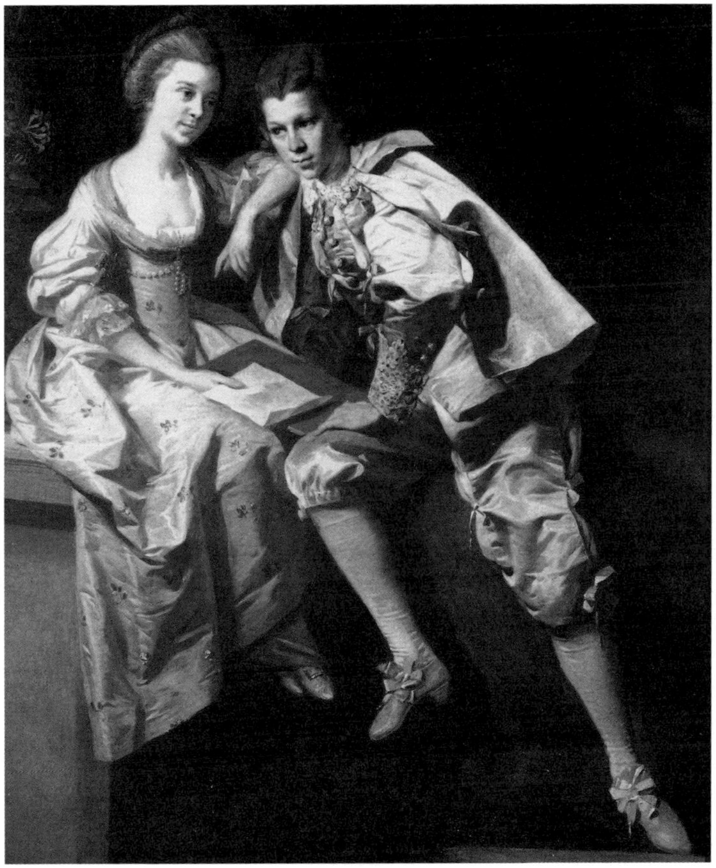

Fig. 125 *William and Mary Young* by or after Johan Zoffany, oil on canvas. Private collection, UK; photo courtesy National Portrait Gallery, London.

sketch to Stubbs – which has never been stated with respect to WAG 2395 – suggests that the information in the inscription is suspect and that the date of 1770 should be disregarded, unless the contrary view is to be taken that the sketches postdate the large canvas after all. Given that the number of figures in WAG 2395 makes it the most populous of all Zoffany's known conversation pieces of the 1760s, it may be that he felt the challenge of combining all the figures and, uniquely, decided to make finished studies for the outer parts of the composition before integrating them into the work's very schematic tri-partite structure.[17] In this connection, it may be significant that the upper paint layers of WAG 2395 have been described as lying over an already textured surface, as though a different composition had been started underneath.[18]

In other respects, however, WAG 2395 is the epitome of Zoffany's conversation pieces in which the ostensibly polite grouping of the figures in fact articulates the artist's careful personal observation of the dynamics within the family.[19] Thus the eldest son William is grouped slightly apart with his favourite sister, Sarah's quickening desire to be married and have children is understood and articulated, while the slave John Brook, smartly dressed as a page and shown on terms of affection with his white owners, is neatly grouped with John and Brook Young. Much recent discussion of WAG 2395 has centred on the depiction of John Brook.[20] It seems fair to suggest that Zoffany's image seems designed as an embodiment of Sir William and his son's deeply held belief, expressed in their writings, in the possibility of integrating improved conditions of slavery within a more cultivated, sociable and civilised style of life in the West Indies.

The second codicil of Sir William's will in which 'my family picture at the old Road' is bequeathed directly to his grandson Billy (the future 3rd Baronet) has been assumed to refer to WAG 2395[21] – a clear indication of his dynastic view of the painting.

PROVENANCE

By descent;[22] Christie 14 December 1928 (96); bt. Knoedler (7,000 gns.); Sir Philip Sassoon; Christie 2 July 1937 (34); bt. in and sold privately to the gallery.

EXHIBITIONS

English Conversation Pieces 25 Park Lane, London 1930 (7); *Twee Eeuwen Engelsche Kunst* [*Two Centuries of English Art*] Stedelijk Museum, Amsterdam 1936 (183); *Some Acquisitions of the Walker Art Gallery Liverpool 1935–1945* National Gallery, London 1945 (12); *English Conversation Pieces of the Eighteenth Century* Arts Council Gallery, London 1946 (22); *One Hundred Years of British Painting 1730–1830* Museu de Arte Antiga, Lisbon and Prado, Madrid 1949 (55); *British Painting 1730–1850, Hogarth to Turner* Kunsthalle Hamburg, and tour of Scandinavia 1949–50 (120); *Johan Zoffany 1733–1810* National Portrait Gallery, London 1977 (41); *Masquerade* Museum of London 1983 (no cat. no.).

Notes

1. For him see E. I. Carlyle: 'Young, Sir William, Second Baronet', rev. Richard B. Sheridan, ODNB vol. 60, pp. 950–1.
2. This *Life* is referred to by Jennifer Leigh Marais, a descendant of Sir William Young, *letter*, 2 November 1992, gallery files.
3. Biographical information about Sir William's younger children is sparse; some details may be gleaned from Sir William Young's will (Public Record Office, PROB/11/1168 20320; copy in gallery files); further information was provided by Charles Robson (see n. 22) *copy letter*, 14 August 1937, gallery files.
4. For a discussion of Rysbrack's monument and Young's sentiments expressed by it see Matthew Craske: *The Silent Rhetoric of the Body* (New Haven and London, 2007) pp. 329–33; Craske describes Young as 'a Nabob of feeling'.
5. See David M. Little and George M. Kahrl, eds: *Letters of David Garrick*, 3 vols (London, 1963) vol. 1 p. 205. Kay Dian Kriz: *Slavery, Sugar and the Culture of Refinement: Picturing the British West Indies 1700–1840* (New Haven and London, 2008) p. 40 says only that it was at Downton.
6. Mary Webster: *Johan Zoffany 1733–1810*, exh. cat., National Portrait Gallery, London (1977) p. 42 (cat. 41).
7. Penny Treadwell: *Johan Zoffany, Artist and Adventurer* (London, 2009) p. 155.
8. Kriz, *op. cit.*, pp. 41, 211.
9. Helmut von Erffa and Allen Staley: *The Paintings of Benjamin West* (New Haven and London, 1986) cats. 725 and 723, pp. 569–70. A version of the portrait of the younger William was presented to Eton College as a leaving portrait (cat. 724, p. 470).
10. W. H. Ward and K. S. Block: *A History of Iver* (London, 1933) p. 198.
11. FC, p. 232 points out that letters from Garrick to Young dated 1772 imply that he remained in England until then, but it is possible that he had been in the West Indies in the interim.
12. Kriz, *op. cit.*, p. 211 argues that it seems 'likely that the painting would have been commissioned no later than the end of 1764, when Young left for the West Indies, although it may have been completed and delivered after his departure'.
13. The 1928 and 1937 Christie's sale catalogues; Craske, *op. cit.*, p. 331, says 'around 1769'; Beth Fowkes Tobin: *Picturing Imperial Power: Colonial Subjects in Eighteenth-century British Painting* (Durham, NC and London, 1999) p. 40, says 1770.
14. Webster, *loc. cit.*
15. *Ibid.*
16. Craske, *loc. cit.* states that WAG 2395 is set in the gardens at Delaford. FC, *loc. cit.*, quotes the suggestion by A. Atkinson: 'William Young Ottley, Artist and Collector', *Notes and Queries* (2 April 1936) p. 236 and (12 November 1938) p. 346 that the setting is Dunston House, Thatcham, Berks (called by Atkinson 'St Dunstan's Park'), home of Sarah's husband Richard Ottley. The treatment of the terrace and the gardens in WAG 2395 seems generic rather than particular.
17. Webster, *op. cit.*, p. 42, cats. 39–40, says that they are probably studies for WAG 2395. According to G. C. Williamson: *English Conversation Pieces* (London, 1931) pp. 3, 19 (quoted by FC, *loc. cit.*), they were commissioned as autograph replicas by the godparents of the respective groups of children. The source of this story is unknown. Clare, Lady Young, *letter*, 14 March 1958, gallery files, mentioned a third work, depicting the central group, as having been sold at an unknown date in the past but it is unclear whether she knew of this work or was merely assuming its existence. Conceivably it is, or is related to, the otherwise unknown 75 × 62 cm. *Portrait of Sir William Young, Bart. of Delaford, Full-length, Standing by a Table*, the property of W. Ottley Esq (and thus descended from Sir William's eldest daughter) sold at Sotheby 13 May 1931 (19) as by Zoffany; bt. Lewis (£36).
18. Condition report of 1991, National Museums Liverpool conservation files. Recent X-radiographs have shown, however, that the heavily brushed surface does not lie over a significantly different composition beneath. All that they reveal are minor alterations to the position of the hose's legs, the legs of Sir William's chair, and the garden wall. The 1991 report notes that WAG 2395 is relined, and that its original tacking edges have been cut off.
19. Treadwell, *op. cit.*, pp. 99–100.
20. Tobin, *op. cit.*, pp. 21, 39–43, 45–6, 55; she argues that the figure of the slave 'reminds us of Sir William's West Indian legacy but immediately transforms that brutal colonial power into an elegant, graceful and refined celebration of English art, music and domestic life' (p. 46); Kriz, *op. cit.*, p. 40, observes that the slave is the emblem of Young's involvement with the West Indies whose 'apparently happy and harmonious insertion into the family is suggested by the way that his body and gestures smoothly interlink with those of Young's sons. The wealth generated from West Indian sugar helped to finance innumerable cultural performances and artefacts such as this elaborately staged conversation piece.' Sarah Parsons: '"A Conversation of Girls": Wright and the British Visual Culture of Slavery', in Elizabeth E. Barker and A. Kidson: *Joseph Wright of Derby in Liverpool*, exh. cat., Walker Art Gallery and Yale Center for British Art, New Haven (2007) p. 110, points out that the Moorish character of the slave's costume, while of a piece with the uniform elegance, sets him apart from the family in their Van Dyck dress; also that while many of the figures physically interact, he is the only one actually performing a service for another figure.
21. Webster, *loc. cit.*, quoting a version of Sir William's will published by Vere L. Oliver: *The History of the Island of Antigua*, 3 vols, (London, 1899) vol. 3, p. 281; this codicil is not present in the copy of the will in the Public Record Office (see main text). The meaning of the expression 'at the old road' is almost certainly 'the old mansion of my ancestors' on Antigua referred to by William Young, 2nd Baronet, in his *Tour through Several Islands* of 1801 (quoted by Tobin, *op. cit.*, p. 42).
22. WAG 2395 passed initially into the possession of John Young, the fourth son of the 1st Baronet; at his wife Jane's death without direct heirs in 1838 it went to his nephew George Young, fourth son of the 2nd Baronet, and thence after his wife Mary's death in 1882 to their only son Julian Young. Although willed by him to Charles Robson, a descendant of the 2nd Baronet's daughter Caroline, the portrait was consigned at Christie's in 1928 by Julian Young's widow with Robson agreeing to take half the proceeds from the sale; information from family letters kindly supplied by Sir William Young, *email*, 12 February 2010, gallery files.

after

Johan Zoffany

1733–1810

George Nassau Clavering Cowper, 3rd Earl Cowper

WAG 1513
oil on canvas, 115.5 × 85 cm
date: unknown, perhaps 1800–30

This is a reduced and simplified version of Zoffany's portrait of Lord Cowper painted in Florence probably in 1773 (142 × 111 cm; private collection, Sussex; fig. 126).[1] Set within a painted oval with a plain sky background instead of an elaborate landscape and truncating the figure to just below the waist instead of at the calf, it lacks the detail and the play of light and shade of the original; the gold braid on the waistcoat and the lace at the cuffs are treated more schematically, while Lord Cowper's firm-jawed, confident expression is watered down into a more complaisant look. The figure is the same size as in the original, the reduction having been achieved simply by cropping the design. Although WAG 1513 has been attributed to Zoffany himself,[2] the stylistic differences suggest that it is the work of a later copyist.[3]

Lord Cowper (1738–89) was one of the most celebrated British residents in Florence. By 1772, the date of Zoffany's arrival in Florence to undertake his *Tribuna of the Uffizi* for King George III and Queen Charlotte, he had established a reputation as a serious art collector and as the confidant of Prince Pietro Leopoldo of Tuscany. He acted as a hub for English tourists and travellers and gave celebrated parties at his Villa Palmieri at Fiesole outside the city.[4] He had been instrumental in procuring permission for Zoffany to work in the Tribuna and he figured prominently as one of the connoisseurs portrayed in that work. Besides sitting to Zoffany for his own portrait, Lord Cowper also commissioned from him portraits of his fiancée and of her family.[5]

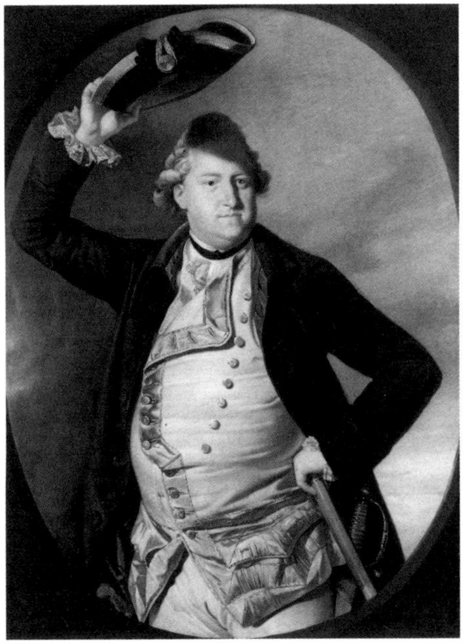

WAG 1513

PROVENANCE

By descent to Auberon, 9th Baron Lucas of Crudwell, Wrest Park (d. 1916); Christie 6 November 1917 (129); …Tooth; …H. Buttery; bt. in 1926 by Leggatt; bt. by Lord Brocket; Sotheby 16 July 1952 (102); bt. by the gallery.

EXHIBITIONS

Selected Acquisitions of the Walker Art Gallery Liverpool 1945–1955 Agnew's, London 1955 (18); *Eighteenth Century Italy and the Grand Tour* Norwich Castle Museum 1958 (102).

NOTES

1. See Mary Webster: *Johan Zoffany 1733–1810*, exh. cat., National Portrait Gallery, London (1977) pp. 60–1 (cat. 77).
2. FC, p. 230.
3. WAG 1513 emerged in the collection of Auberon, 9th Baron Lucas (1876–1916), son of Hon. Florence Amabel Herbert who was the daughter of the 6th Earl Cowper. Zoffany's original entered the possession of another of the 6th Earl's daughters, Adine (about 1840–68). It is tempting to think that the original was a wedding gift to Adine from her brother, the 7th Earl, and that WAG 1513 was later painted as a wedding gift for Florence Amabel, but this is conjectural. It is also possible that WAG 1513 was regarded as a Lucas heirloom and descended directly from the 7th Earl Cowper (who was also 8th Baron Lucas) to his grandson, the 9th Baron. The known provenance of a further copy, 51 × 41 cm, sold most recently at Sotheby 5 June 2008 (45), also begins in the later nineteenth century; it was owned by Sir Edmund Charles Nugent, 3rd Bt. (1839–1928).
4. For a biographical summary see Hugh Belsey: 'Cowper, George Nassau Clavering, Third Earl Cowper', ODNB vol. 13, pp. 805–6; Lord Cowper features regularly in the correspondence of Horace Walpole.
5. See Webster, *op. cit.*, pp. 61–3 (cats. 78–9); the portrait of Miss Gore as a Savoyarde is in the same collection as Zoffany's portrait of Lord Cowper, and the portrait of the Gore family is now in the Yale Center for British Art, New Haven.

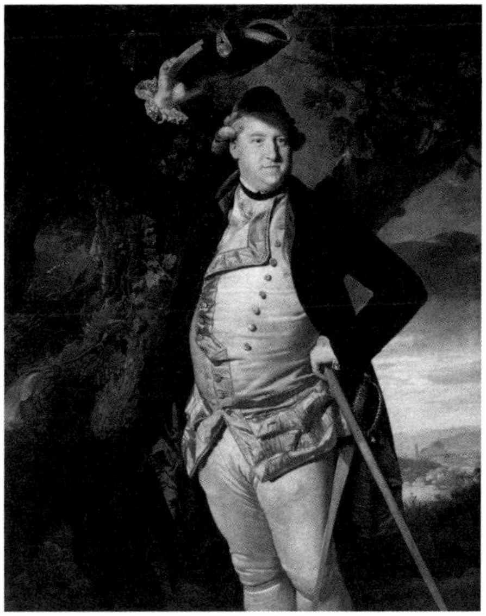

Fig. 126 *George, 3rd Earl Cowper* by Johan Zoffany, oil on canvas. Private collection/ The Bridgeman Art Library.

British School

Child with Dog

WAG 217
oil on canvas, 126.5 × 101 cm
date: unknown, perhaps 1770–75

The portrait entered the collection of George Holt, presumably between 1885 and 1896 when he acquired virtually all his eighteenth-century paintings, as by 'Miss Reynolds'.[1] Frances Reynolds (1729–1807), the sister of Sir Joshua Reynolds, is known to have copied her brother's works and independently to have made a number of portraits, chiefly miniatures.[2] Her known work lacks the imposing, professional character of WAG 217 and the attribution cannot be accepted.

Some connection with Reynolds's studio is nevertheless suggested by the handling of certain areas of the work, notably the trees at the left, the middle ground, the background and the sky, together with the fabric and the ribbon of the little girl's skirt. On the other hand, the painting of the girl's face, her bonnet and her upper torso, together with the dog, is carried out in a tighter, more meticulous fashion.[3] It is tempting, therefore, to speculate that WAG 217 is the work of two artists, the second completing a commission left unfinished by the first.

The sitter is unknown and clues to her identity are completely lacking. She appears around five years old, and her costume indicates a date for the work in the early 1770s.[4]

PROVENANCE

...Agnew; from whom bt. at an unknown date by George Holt; Emma Holt Bequest 1945.

NOTES

1. *George Holt's Ms Picture Catalogue*, n.d., gallery archives.
2. Sir Ellis Waterhouse: *Dictionary of British Eighteenth Century Painters* (Woodbridge, 1981) p. 300.
3. The girl's eyes appear to have been enlarged by a later artist.
4. One possible candidate for the (?first) artist is George James (fl. 1755–80, d. 1795), for whom see Waterhouse, *op. cit.*, p. 193, illustrating James's *The Three Misses Walpole*, 1768. Compare also James's *Emily and Georgiana Mason*, sold Sotheby 3 April 1996 (64).

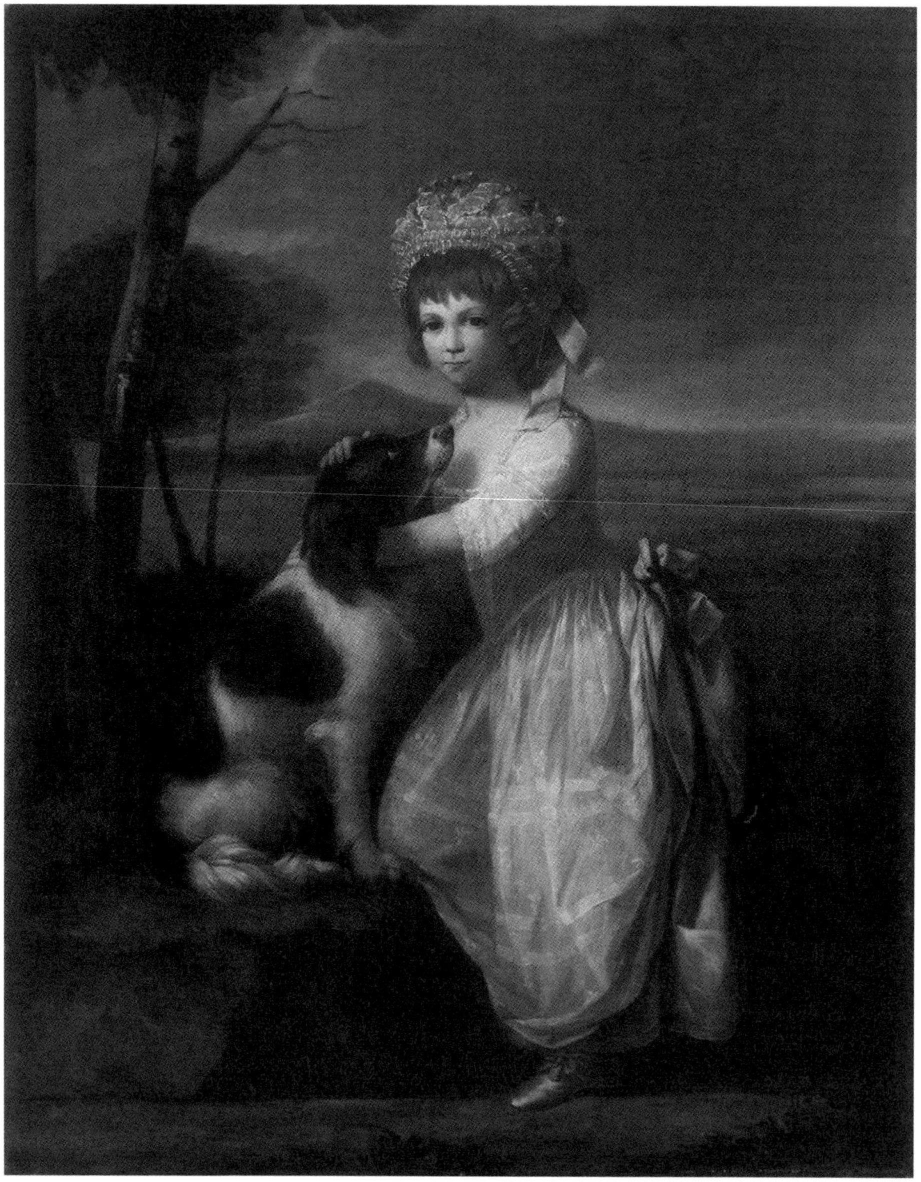

WAG 217

Portrait of a Lady

WAG 253
oil on canvas, 76 × 63.5 cm
date: unknown, perhaps 1825–35

George Holt acquired WAG 253 as a portrait of Mrs Morant by Thomas Lawrence. This attribution cannot be accepted,[1] although no convincing alternative candidate for the artist has emerged. The style of the hair and the general treatment suggest a date of about 1825. The painting of the sitter's head recalls the work of Lawrence and may be by a pupil, but the rest of the canvas is executed in a more old-fashioned idiom (the background especially is suggestive of Beechey)[2] and it is tempting to wonder if the work is by more than one artist. Furthermore, the painting has undergone significant structural alteration and may well have been extensively repainted in connection with this.[3]

No patron of artists of the name Morant in the 1820s has been traced, and the title may well have been invented at the time of the work's sale to Agnew's by the firm Morant & Co.[4]

PROVENANCE

...Morant & Co.; from whom bt. by Agnew October 1890; bt. by George Holt April 1891 (£525); Emma Holt Bequest 1945.

EXHIBITIONS

Loan Exhibition of Pictures... in Aid of the Funds of the Children's Infirmary Agnew's, Liverpool 1904 (7); *Pictures by Artists Contemporary with Those Represented in the Wrigley Collection* Bury Art Gallery 1913 (40).

NOTES

1. The attribution to Lawrence was rejected before 1971; Mary Bennett and Edward Morris: *Sudley* (Liverpool, 1971) p. 14. WAG 253 was not included in Kenneth Garlick: *Lawrence* (London, 1954) nor in his 'A Catalogue of the Paintings, Drawings and Pastels of Sir Thomas Lawrence', *Walpole Society* vol. 39 (1964).
2. No portrait of Mrs Morant is recorded in Beechey's account book, printed in W. Roberts: *Sir William Beechey* (London, 1907) (copy in the National Portrait Gallery Library corrected by Jacob Simon against the ms original in the Royal Academy Library).
3. WAG 253 has an added strip of canvas approximately 2 inches high at the top, the original top edge of the canvas having been folded over before being sewn to the extension. Although the new strip of canvas is of similar weave and weight to the original, which may suggest that this is the artist's own work, a chalk inscription on the reverse of the top stretcher member *[?to] be lowered 1½ times the Top* implies that this was an instruction to a conservator. The stretcher itself is of standard 'head and shoulders' dimensions, which suggests that the canvas has been trimmed or repositioned at the bottom. The handling of the sitter's brown cloak in the lower part of the picture, which is in a coarser style than the rest of the work, also supports the view that a second artist altered or completed WAG 253.
4. There are no other portraits of a Mrs Morant of this period in the Heinz Archive, National Portrait Gallery. Two potential candidates for her, however, are (i) Lady Caroline Hay, daughter of the 17th Earl of Erroll, who married John Morant of Brockenhurst Park, Hants in 1823. She would presumably have been referred to as Lady Caroline Morant after her marriage but this nicety may have become obscured by 1890; (ii) (if different) the currently unidentified mother of Sir Robert Morant (d. 1873) 'designer of high-class furniture and silk fabrics' of Hampstead (who may provide a direct connection with 'Morant & Co.'); for him see Geoffrey K. Fry: 'Morant, Sir Robert Laurie', ODNB vol. 39, p. 5.

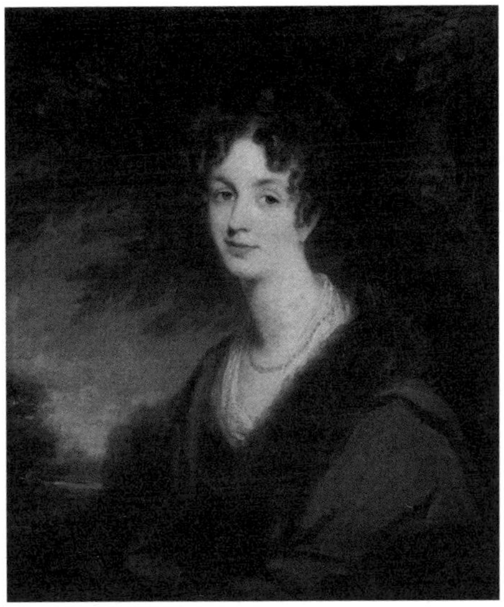

WAG 253

A Lady in Tudor Dress

WAG 828
oil on canvas, 48.5 × 43 cm
date: unknown, perhaps 1850–75

It is unclear whether WAG 828 is a copy of an authentic portrait or whether it is a pastiche (perhaps done in good faith, for example as an educational tool). It purports to depict a lady of the early Tudor period, but it has not been possible

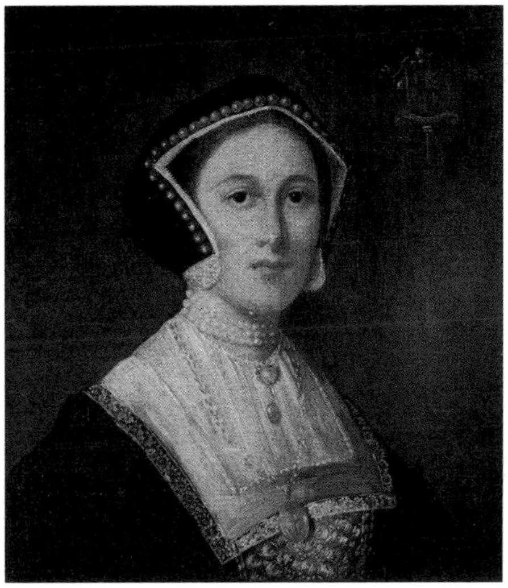

WAG 828

to identify any specific prototype. There are certain generic similarities with known portraits of Katherine of Aragon and Anne Boleyn.[1] The sitter wears an English, or gable, hood characteristic of the 1520s or 1530s.[2] The coat of arms is indistinctly painted in a manner antithetical to their traditionally highly specific rendering in dynastic portraiture.[3] From the painting style WAG 828 can date from no earlier than the mid-nineteenth century and may well be later.

PROVENANCE

...William Hall Walker, Lord Wavertree; his bequest 1933.

NOTES

1. See, for example, in the National Portrait Gallery, NPG 163, *Katherine of Aragon*, by an unknown artist, and NPG 668, *Anne Boleyn* by an unknown artist (repr. Roy Strong: *National Portrait Gallery: Tudor and Jacobean Portraits* 2 vols [London, 1969] vol. 2, pls 73 and 8).
2. I am grateful to Pauline Rushton, Curator of Decorative Art, for discussing the costume with me, 22 August 2008.
3. The coat of arms quarters a pale cross on a dark ground and three descending [?] martlets on a light ground. The colours are muted and unspecific.

The Child of Hale

WAG 1608
oil on canvas, 310 × 155 cm
date: unknown, perhaps 1700–30

John Middleton (1578–1623) was born and died in the village of Hale, eight miles south-east of Liverpool. He grew to a gigantic height, nine feet three inches according to the later inscription on his gravestone in Hale churchyard,[1] and was known as the Child of Hale on account of his simplicity. Matthew Gregson, in his *Portfolio of Fragments Relating to Lancashire*, relates that

Sir Gilbert Ireland Knt about 1617 took him up to the court of James I where he wrestled with the King's wrestler and put out his thumb, by which awkwardness he disobliged the courtiers and was sent back, the King giving him, as it is said, £20. He returned by Brazenose College Oxford, which was full of Lancashire students, and where his picture was taken and now exists. A likeness of this English giant is also preserved at High Leigh [sic] and one at Hale.[2]

Gregson's mention of the portrait at High Legh in 1817 is the earliest documentary reference to WAG 1608. In the High Legh picture catalogue of 1884 it was attributed to Marcus Gheeraerdts.[3] According to family tradition, it was originally owned by Thomas Legh, brother-in-law of the Child's patron, Sir Gilbert Ireland; Ireland himself was presumably the original owner of the portrait described by Gregson as 'at Hale'. This portrait remained with Ireland's descendants at Hale Hall until it was presented to Brasenose College in 1924 (fig. 127).[4] The two portraits are evidently closely related; they are very similar in size and in both the Child wears the same costume, which has been identified as the one he wore on his presentation at Court,[5] and which embodies, in the fleur-de-lys pattern on the breeches, a reference to the Ireland arms. The Brasenose picture, however, is the cruder of the two, and a difficulty exists in explaining how the Child's patron should have had this while a superior version belonged to his brother-in-law. To account for the respective works' provenances, it has been suggested that WAG 1608 is a somewhat later painting, implicitly by a technically more advanced artist, than the 'contemporary' Ireland prototype. Visual inspection does indeed suggest that the painting technique employed in WAG 1608 is of the eighteenth century, and not of the early seventeenth century at all. [6]

It is possible to interpret Gregson's reference to the portrait at Brasenose in 1817 as to a putative prototype, itself full-length, for both the Ireland portrait and WAG 1608. That such a portrait did once hang in Brasenose College Library appears to be confirmed by a statement made in 1686 by Robert Plot, a former Keeper of the Ashmolean Museum. He wrote a description of the Child of Hale: 'his whole height 9 foot 3 inches, wanting but six inches of the height of Goliah, if that [portrait] in Brasen-Nose College Library (drawn at length, as 'tis said, in his just proportion) be a true piece of him.'[7] However, no such portrait has subsequently been recorded[8] or traced and more recently it has been argued (somewhat implausibly)[9] that Plot's remark really refers to the celebrated impression of the Child's hand preserved for many years in one of the Brasenose cellars (it was seen there by Samuel Pepys in 1668);[10] and in turn that Gregson's own reference is either to this or to one of the smaller portraits of the Child or his hand now in the College's possession, at least some of which pre-date the early nineteenth century.[11]

By the eighteenth century, a number of other full-length portraits of the Child were in existence in the North-west. These included a portrait in a Liverpool inn (identified by Gregson as the Folly) which was seen by a visitor, Joseph Taylor, in 1705; this must have been of considerable size as it had to be nailed to the ceiling. A copy was at the Red Lion inn, Warrington.[12] Another portrait is listed in the MS catalogue of paintings at Knowsley, 1772,[13] where it was seen on one of his northern tours (posthumously published in 1801) by Thomas Pennant, and described as a 'Gigantic figure'.[14] Pennant himself mentioned another version of the portrait 'in the Museum at Oxford' and this may represent evidence for the existence at a later date of the portrait described by Plot.[15] Given the uncertain early history of WAG 1608, it may well be identical with one of the paintings in the inns, the 'gigantic' canvas at Knowsley – or conceivably even the portrait described by Plot.

PROVENANCE

...At High Legh House near Warrington by 1817; by descent to C. L. S. Cornwall-Legh; by whom presented 1955.

NOTES

1. *Here lyeth the body of John Middleton the Childe Nine Feet Three Borne 1578 Dyede 1623*. The inscription is spaced around a crack in the stone which is thought to have occurred when the body was disinterred in the late eighteenth century, but it probably reproduced an earlier inscription.
2. Matthew Gregson: *Portfolio of Fragments relative to the History and Antiquities of the County Palatine and Duchy of Lancaster* (Liverpool, 1817) p. 212, cited in R. Stewart-Brown: 'The Childe of Hale' (John Middleton); some Portraits' *Transactions of the Historic Society of Lancashire and Cheshire [for the Year 1934]* vol. 86 (1935) pp. 73–83.
3. Stewart-Brown, *op. cit.*, p. 79.
4. Stewart-Brown, *op. cit.*, p. 76.
5. Stewart-Brown, *op. cit.*, p. 79, citing G. Ormerod: *History of the County Palatine and City of Chester* [...] *2nd Edn, Revised and Enlarged by T. Helsby* 3 vols (London, 1882). It seems likely, however, that the portraits provided the source for the descriptions, rather than independent confirmation.
6. *MPPP*, p. 47. The most recent condition report on WAG 1608, made in 1990 by Brian Cardy (gallery files) does not offer any direct dating evidence. It observes that the original support is a linen canvas of conventional weave, that the original edges have been cut on all sides during relining and that the

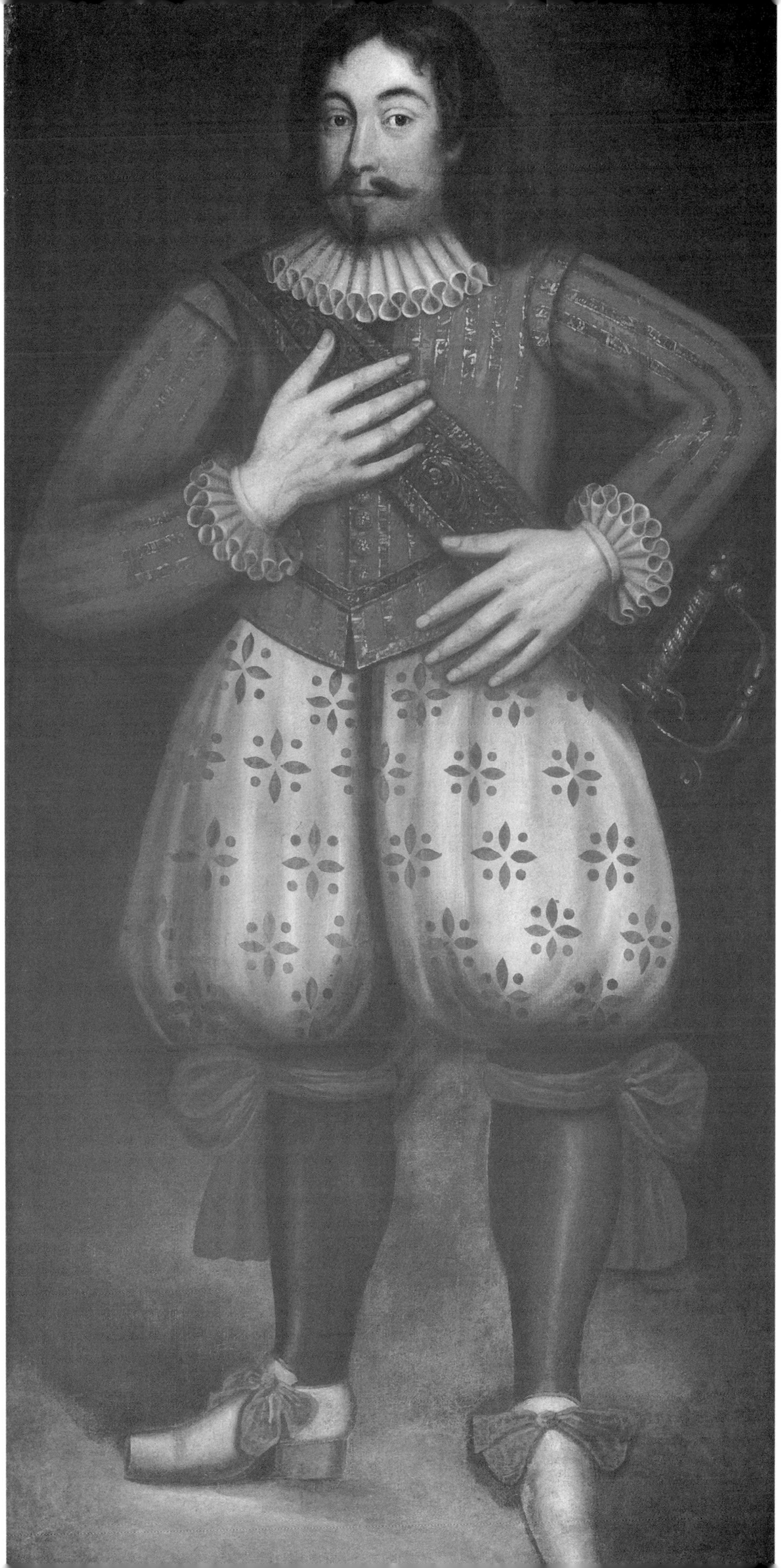

WAG 1608

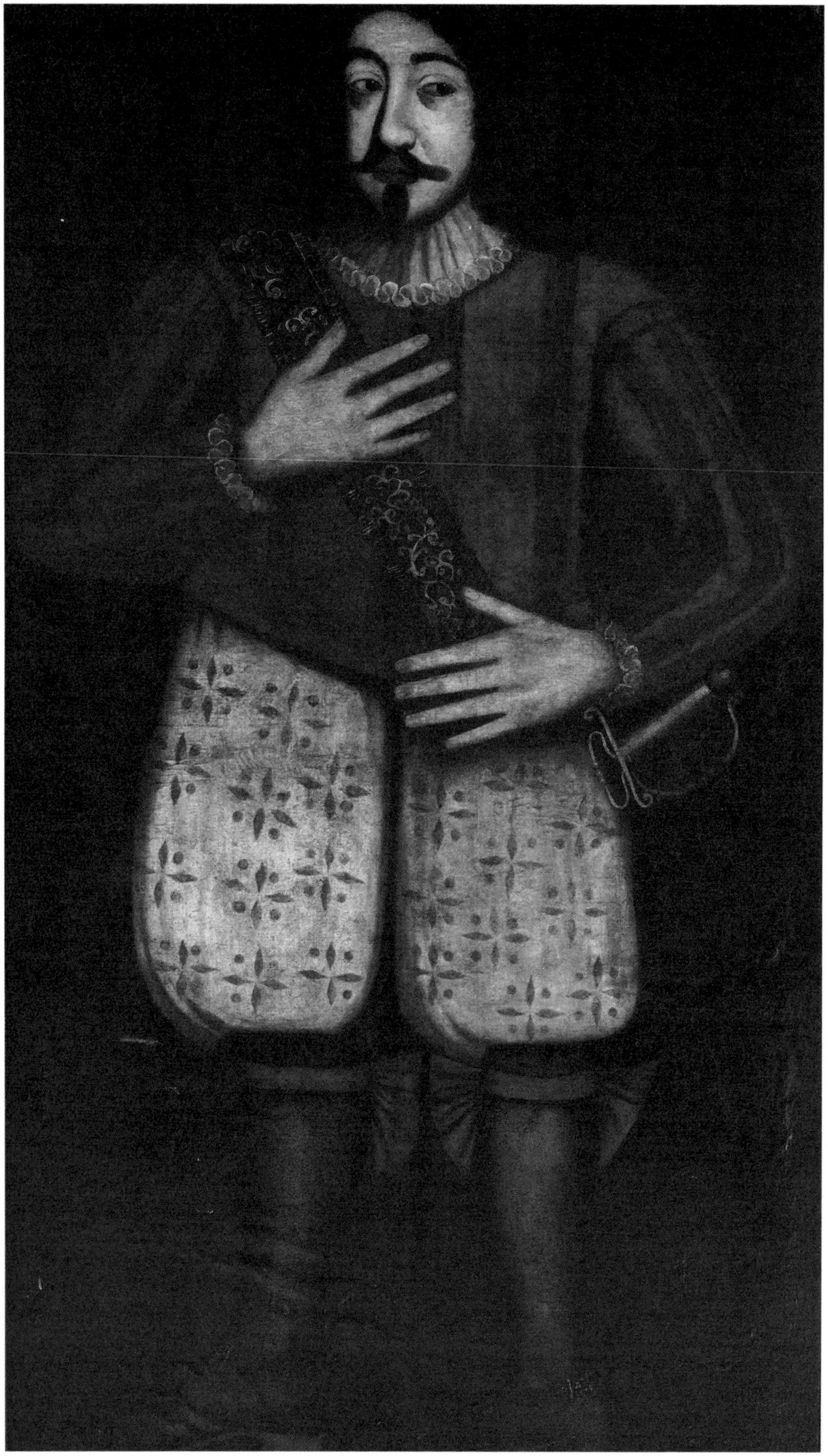

Fig. 127 *The Childe of Hale* by an unknown artist, oil on wood. Brasenose College Oxford.

surface is covered with areas of retouching and overpainting, especially in the background. WAG 1608 is painted on two pieces of canvas joined horizontally about four-sevenths up from the bottom edge.

7. R. Plot: *Natural History of Staffordshire* (Oxford, 1686) p. 295; cited by Stewart-Brown, *op. cit.*, p. 76.

8. Stewart-Brown, *op. cit.*, p. 81, mentions an anonymous mid-eighteenth century note which alludes to the existence of this portrait in the college library, but the writer of this note may not have seen the portrait.

9. Stewart-Brown, *op. cit.*, p. 76.

10. R. Latham and W. Matthews, eds: *The Diary of Samuel Pepys* 11 vols (London, 1970–83) vol. 9 p. 226 (entry of 9 June 1668).

11. The smaller works at Brasenose College are: (i) a small copy of the Ireland (Hale Hall) portrait made by T. B. Banner in 1842; (ii) a small watercolour portrait of the Child, differently costumed but with his hands in a similar pose, which has been dated to the eighteenth century but which may well be a copy of an earlier work; (iii) and (iv), two portraits of the Child's hand, the earlier of which is stated to record, actual size, the impression left in the buttery cellar. The impression itself no longer survives. All four works are reproduced in Stewart-Brown, *op. cit.* Frank Hird: *Lancashire Stories* 2 vols (London and Edinburgh, 1912) vol. 1 p. 40, reproduces a sketch taken from a picture of the Child standing next to the King's wrestler; the source of this is unknown.

12. Matthew Gregson: ms addition to an interleaved copy of the *Portfolio* [...] owned by John Foster of Liverpool, now in the John Rylands Library, University of Manchester; cited by Stewart-Brown, *op. cit.*, p. 75.

13. Knowsley archives, cited in *MPPP*, p. 47.

14. Thomas Pennant: *A Tour from Downing to Alston-Moor* (London, 1801) p. 41, cited in *MPPP*, p. 47.

15. *Ibid.*

The Burning of the Liverpool Exchange

WAG 1740
oil on canvas, 92 × 122.5 cm
date: 1795

Liverpool's new Exchange, built by John Wood of Bath between 1749 and 1754, was the most prominent architectural symbol of the town's commercial and cultural expansion in the mid-eighteenth century. It acted as the meeting place for the leaders of the town's society, who met fortnightly in its assembly rooms,[1] and it boasted fine interior decoration. On 18 January 1795, fire broke out in the small hours of the morning in an upstairs room of the building, owing to a fault in a chimney.[2] Despite the gathering of a large crowd and the arrival of a number of private water-carts, it proved impossible to control the blaze because of an inadequate supply of water, and eventually much of the interior of the building was gutted, among the works of art lost being an admired series of allegorical paintings by Daniel Stringer of Knutsford.[3] The building (now Liverpool's Town Hall) was reconstructed over the next twelve years by James Wyatt, who created a deeper, more imposing portico, and rebuilt the dome on a higher base.

Attrributed to Wright of Derby when it entered the possession of Liverpool Corporation in 1865, WAG 1740 cannot be by him, but it might well be by a local artist who had made some study of Wright's firelight paintings.[4] The effect of the firelight itself, as well as the reflected light cast on the neighbouring buildings, is well handled, without any effect of garishness. It is tempting to think that the artist witnessed and sketched the event on the spot, for the work shows the fire at an early stage, when it was still confined to the room on the left of the façade on the first floor, rather than the more spectacular blaze it must have presented later on when the whole building had caught alight. The depiction of the scene in the foreground, with the crowds watching in orderly fashion and with water-carts and pumping engine drawn up and attempting to control the fire, accords with the description given by the mayor of Liverpool, printed in *Gore's Liverpool Advertiser*, of 'the very great Order which [Major Clarkson and the officers of the Southern Fencibles] were the means of

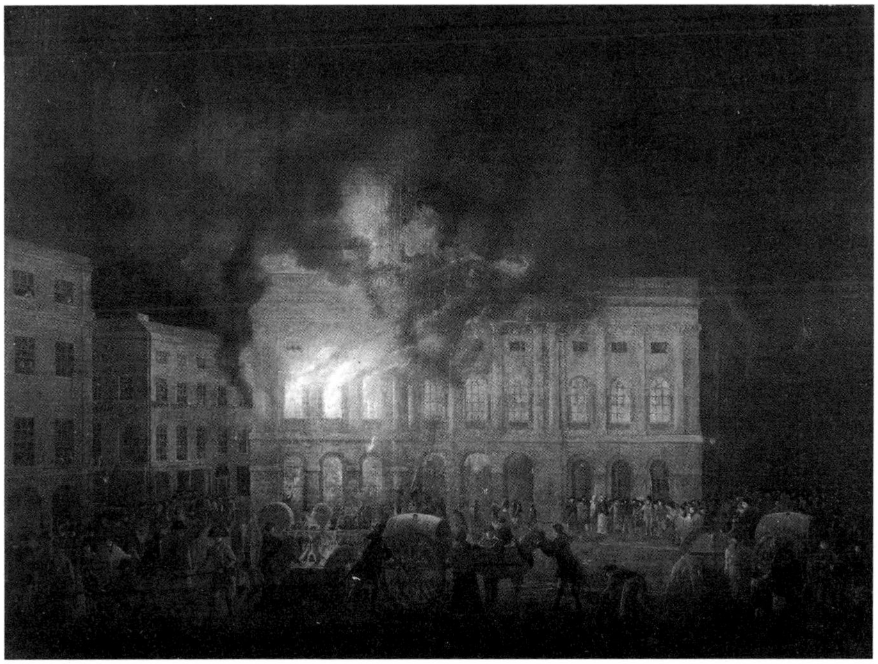

WAG 1740

preserving at the unfortunate FIRE which took place this day in the Exchange'.[5] It seems possible that WAG 1740 was commissioned by the Corporation as a propaganda exercise to demonstrate that the response to the fire had been as effective as possible, for the Corporation's insurers initially declined to pay out on the damage.[6] Two sketches of the event by John Foster, the town's own surveyor, depict a much more confused scene than that shown in WAG 1740.[7]

PROVENANCE

...E. S. Samuell; by whom presented to Liverpool Corporation 1865;[8] deposited in the Library and Museum; transferred to the gallery between 1903 and 1927.[9]

NOTES

1. Samuel Derrick: *Letters Written from Leverpoole, Chester, Corke, the Lake of Killarney [etc...]* 2 vols (London, 1767), vol. 1, p. 20.
2. For a fuller description see *MPPP*, pp. 54–5.
3. E. Barker and A. Kidson: *Wright of Derby in Liverpool*, exh. cat, Walker Art Gallery and Yale Center for British Art, New Haven (2007) p. 195.
4. One candidate is Thomas Chubbard (see p. 28), who, although not known for this type of picture, was very familiar with Wright's work and was the most eclectic of Liverpool's artists; he was still active in the mid-1790s although no oils by him of this period are recorded. But perhaps the likeliest candidate for the artist is William Jackson of 21 Gibraltar Street Liverpool, uniquely described as 'Perspective Painter' in the 1796 edition of *Gore's Liverpool Street Directory*. He had exhibited a view of Liverpool in the 1784 exhibition of the Society for Promoting Painting and Design, and seems to have been in the city ever since, being recorded in Bailey's Liverpool Directory in 1787 (p. 47) as a 'Portrait and Sea-Piece Painter' living in Williamson St; in Gore's 1790 Directory (p. 87) as a 'Prospect Painter' living at 35 Sir Thomas's Buildings, and in the Universal Directory of 1794 (section on Liverpool, p. 705) as a 'Limner' living in Gibraltar Row.
5. *Gore's Liverpool Advertiser* 22 January 1795, p. 3 (written on 18 January); quoted by *MPPP*, p. 54.
6. *MPPP*, *loc. cit.*
7. The drawings were reproduced as lithographs by H. Greenwood in W. G. Herdman: *Pictorial Relics of Ancient Liverpool* (Liverpool, 1856) pls 22 and 23, between pp. 68 and 69.
8. Charles Dyall: *First Decade of the Walker Art Gallery: A Report of Its Operations from 1877–1887* (Liverpool, 1888) p. 7.
9. Charles Dyall: *Walker Art Gallery Descriptive Catalogue of the Permanent Collection of Pictures* (Liverpool, 1882) p. 44 (cat. 187) as 'on deposit in the Library and Museum'; it was listed as still there in the 1903 edition, p. 33; it was included in the 1927 Walker Art Gallery collection catalogue, p. 221, still attributed to Wright of Derby.

Portrait of a Gentleman

WAG 2383
oil on canvas, 73.5 × 61 cm
date: about 1765–70

On the basis of an ink inscription on a small rectangle of canvas glued to the top stretcher bar, WAG 2383 was purchased as a portrait of the Duke of Grafton by Henry Walton (1745–1813). The inscription, which is undoubtedly of considerable age, reads *Duke of Grafton / A* [sic] *Walton 1787* and its two lines appear to have been written by different hands. The origins of this piece of canvas are unclear: it appears too deep to have formed part of the turnover of the original support, but it may have come from a former lining canvas, since the present one appears of relatively recent origin.

Although the work is executed in a style generally reminiscent of Walton's small whole-lengths, with their closely observed and intimate quality,[1] the attribution does not bear close scrutiny. The sitter's jacket, with its turned back cuffs, and the style of his wig have been dated to no later than the mid-1760s[2], a date which must rule Walton's authorship out, since he did not begin to train as an artist until the end of that decade. Recent conservation of WAG 2383 has revealed a work of previously unsuspected quality; the colour is well harmonised and the modelling of the gentleman's face, with its reflected lights and subtle changes of hue, is of exceptional skill and sophistication.[3]

The sitter cannot be either the 3rd or the 4th Duke of Grafton. His costume suggests a country squire or a yeoman farmer rather than a member of the aristocracy. From other portraits, for example by Reynolds (Sotheby, 20 November 1985 [40]) and Jeremiah Meyer (Euston Hall, Duke of Grafton), the 3rd Duke (1735–1811) seems to have looked nothing like this man, but to have had a prominent Roman nose and thick, flat eyebrows. The 4th Duke (1760–1844) was painted by Walton in the mid-1780s as part of his group portrait *The Holme Park Hunt* (untraced);[4] (and the inscription on the reverse may turn out to have some connection with that commission) but the evidence of the costume appears to rule him out completely as the sitter.

PROVENANCE

...Sir H. Hughes-Stanton;[5] from whom bt. (£175) through Dunthorne 1935.

EXHIBITIONS

English Eighteenth Century Conversations and Small Portraits Rembrandt Gallery, London 1935 (catalogue number unknown);[6] *Some Acquisitions of the Walker Art Gallery Liverpool 1935–1945* National Gallery, London 1945 (14).

NOTES

1. For a summary of Walton's work and a representative sample of illustrations see Evelyne Bell: 'The Life and Work of Henry Walton', *Gainsborough's House Review* (1998/99) pp. 40ff.
2. Pauline Rushton, Curator of Decorative Art, National Museums Liverpool, *verbally*, February 2004; confirming the view of John Steegmann, *letter*, 2 March 1937, gallery files. However, Anne Buck, *letter*, 7 January 1978, gallery files, believed it could possibly date from as late as 1770.
3. The painting was conserved by Jevon Thistlewood, NML Paintings Conservation Department, in 2003. One fanciful hypothesis is that the face and perhaps part of the rest of the figure is by Zoffany; and that as an unfinished or aborted commission perhaps dating from some

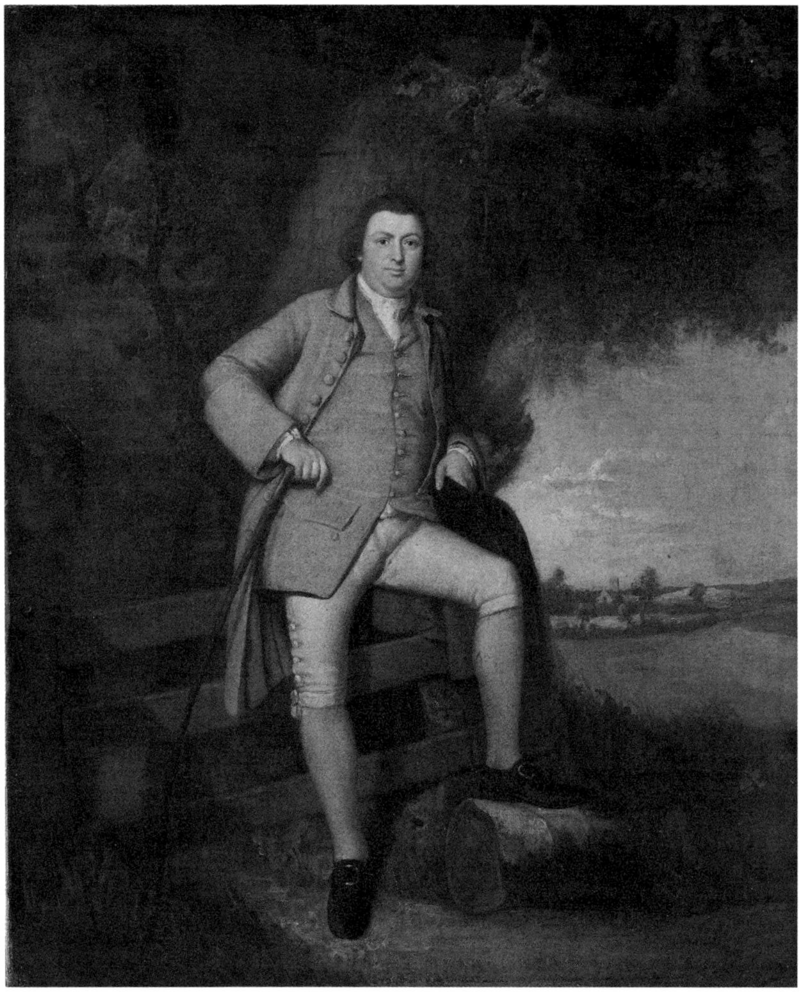

WAG 2383

years earlier, the canvas was given by Zoffany to Walton as a completion exercise when Walton was his pupil at the end of the 1760s. Walton could in theory have taken the canvas away with him and completed it later. A further very speculative idea is that it is the work of Oldfield Bowles, based on stylistic comparison with the latter's self-portrait at Clevedon.
4. Bell, *op. cit.*, pp. 67–8, repr. fig. 18.
5. In a letter to Frank Lambert, Director of the Walker Art Gallery, dated 14 December 1936 (copy in gallery files) Hughes-Stanton wrote that he had bought it many years previously from a dealer and that he believed it had previously been through one of the London sale rooms. Neither dealer nor sale has been traced.
6. It has not been possible to trace a copy of the catalogue. '"The Second Duke of Grafton", by Henry Walton is an excellent full length in landscape' (*The Times*, review of the Rembrandt Gallery exhibition [11 June 1935] p. 14).

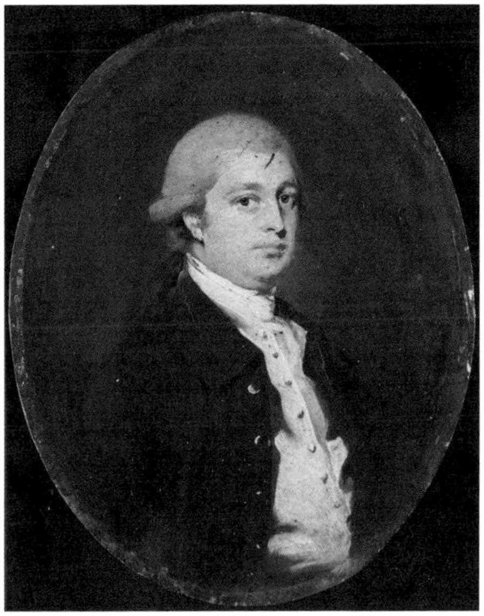
WAG 2397

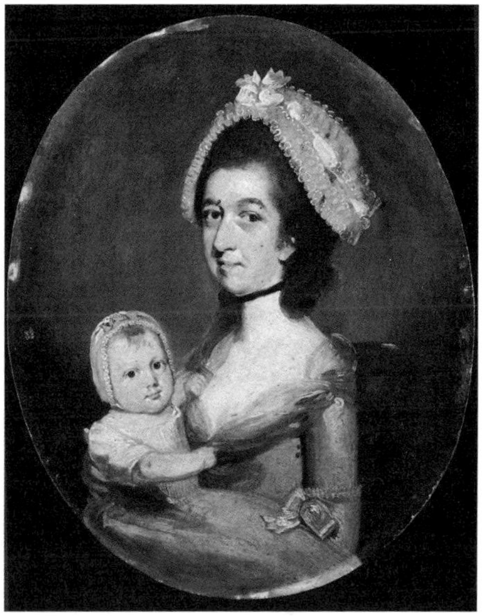
WAG 2398

Portrait of a Man

WAG 2397
oil on copper, 17.5 × 14 cm

Portrait of a Lady and Child

WAG 2398
oil on copper, 17.5 × 14.5 cm
date: about 1775–80

The provenance of WAG 2397–98 suggests that these works originated in Liverpool. However, the identity of both the artist and the sitters is unknown. The costumes suggest they were executed in the second half of the 1770s. The lively, rather loose handling suggests a portrait painter working 'in small' rather than a professional miniaturist.[1]

PROVENANCE
...Mrs A. M. Roscoe; her bequest 1950.

REFERENCE
1. WAG 2397 and 2398 are not immediately identifiable on a schedule of Mrs Roscoe's collection dated 1946 (gallery files) but may be part of item 44: *Four Miniatures*. These included two of Thomas Roscoe (brother of William Roscoe) and his wife. The collection as a whole is said to have consisted entirely of the personal property of William Roscoe (1753–1831). Candidates for the artist include Thomas Chubbard (1737/38–1809), William Jackson and 'Mr Sharples', probably James Sharples, of Duke Street, Liverpool, each of whom showed miniatures at the 1774 exhibition of the Society of Artists in Liverpool; the last two showed paired portraits of a lady and gentleman. Patrick McMorland (active 1784–91), whose miniature of Roscoe's brother-in-law Daniel Daulby is recorded in Daulby's collection may be a further possibility although he is not known to have been in Liverpool as early as the 1770s. Also recorded in Daulby's collection is a pair of miniatures of himself and his first wife Eliza by William Woodworth (1749–87). The presence of the child makes it unlikely that WAG 2398 depicts Eliza as she died when her only child was only six weeks old; however, it is not absolutely ruled out, and comparison with the portraits of the couple by Tate (see WAG 2541 and 2542, pp. 182–4) leaves the possibility open.

John Bridge Aspinall, Mayor of Liverpool

WAG 2587
oil on canvas,[1] 72.5 × 49 cm
date: 1803–04

For the sitter, see WAG 7041 under Mather Brown (p. 19). WAG 2587 is a reduction of Aspinall's full-length portrait as Lord Mayor (WAG 7026, p. 328), and was presumably carried out by the same artist in conjunction with that work in 1803 or shortly after.[2] Its domestic scale, together with the fact that trees, rather than Liverpool Town Hall, occupy the right background, suggest that it was intended

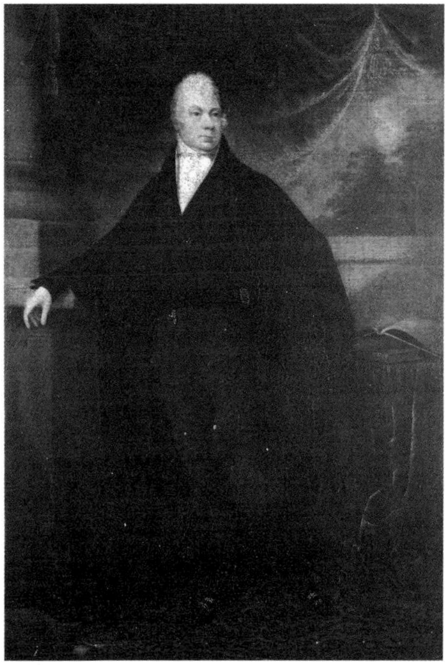
WAG 2587

for Aspinall's own house. The artist is unknown, but for a discussion of possible candidates see WAG 7026.

PROVENANCE

By descent to the sitter's son, R. A. Aspinall; by whom presented through Sir J. A. Picton in 1858 to the Library and Museum Committee of Liverpool Corporation; transferred to the gallery before 1885.[3]

NOTES

1. Relined.
2. It has, however, been suggested (*MPPP*, p. 55) that WAG 2587 is 'a first design on which WAG 7026 was based rather than a reduced version'.
3. WAG 2587 is recorded as being displayed in the Library and Museum in the 1885 and 1903 gallery catalogues.

Portrait of a Lady

WAG 2588
oil on canvas, 91 × 71 cm
date: unknown, perhaps 1890–1925

The portrait purports to date from the very early years of the nineteenth century, and seems to have been acquired by the gallery as something of a gamble that it might turn out to be a Raeburn.[1]

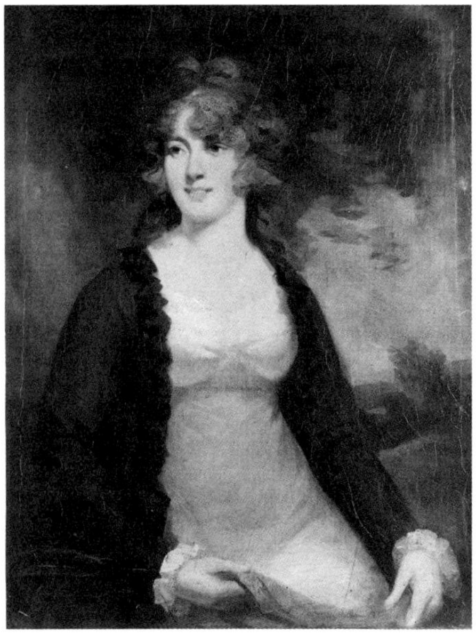

WAG 2588

It has subsequently been attributed to John James Masquerier (1778–1825),[2] but despite some superficial stylistic similarities to his work this cannot be accepted. WAG 2588 has all the appearances of a pastiche and may well have been executed only shortly before it was offered to the gallery.

PROVENANCE

...Boydell & Co., Liverpool; from whom bt. (300 gns.) 1925.

NOTES

1. See p. XXI, n. 6.
2. *Curatorial note*, gallery files.

Lady and Child

WAG 2985
oil on canvas, 127 × 101.5 cm
date: about 1710–25

The portrait – the gallery's first purchase of an early British painting – was initially ascribed to Sir Godfrey Kneller (1646–1723) but this attribution had been abandoned at least by the 1950s.[1] The work may, however, be by an artist trained in the Great Queen Street ('Kneller's') Academy. Conservation in 2003–04 which removed a thick varnish layer revealed a painting of hitherto unsuspected quality: the faces are modelled with considerable sensitivity and the expressions have individuality. The use of blue to create reflected lights in the faces has been seen as a sign of possible Dutch training.[2] Also of a vaguely Dutch character is the turreted building in the background. The handling of the drapery is more schematic and may be by the hand of an assistant.

The identity of the sitters is unknown and no clue is provided by the work's provenance. Tentatively the work may be dated around 1710–25.

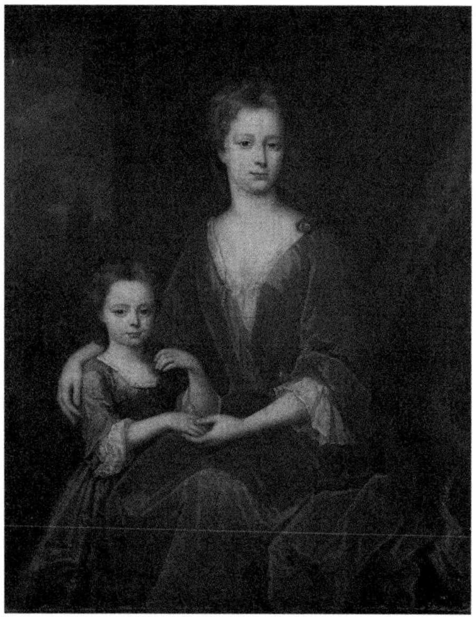

WAG 2985

PROVENANCE

...P. H. Scott of James Street Liverpool; from whom bt. for £35 August 1879.

EXHIBITION

Loan Exhibition of Works of Early British Masters Manchester City Art Gallery 1909 (60).

NOTES

1. Gallery accession files compiled in the 1950s; the work was still attributed to Kneller in the gallery's 1927 catalogue.
2. Jevon Thistlewood, NML Paintings Conservation Department, *verbally*, December 2003; he, however, suggested WAG 2985 might be by Charles Jervas (about 1675–1739), a view tentatively also expressed by Tabitha Barber, Tate Britain. Sir Oliver Millar, *letter*, 14 December 2003, suggested an attribution to Thomas Gibson (about 1680–1751). The distinctive outlines around the eyelids observable in Gibson's portraits are certainly present in WAG 2985.

King George III

WAG 2998
oil on canvas, 244 × 158.8 cm
date: about 1783–90

This depiction of George III is a conflation, with variations, of two portrait types: the whole-length by Thomas Gainsborough exhibited at the Royal Academy in 1781 (Royal Collection; fig. 128) and the earlier coronation portrait of 1760 by Allan Ramsay (Royal Collection; fig. 129). The treatment of the column springing from the plinth at shoulder height and the prominence of the coronation robes, by establishing an immediate visual relationship with Ramsay's 'official' portrait, suggests that WAG 2998, too, was commissioned for an official purpose. However, WAG 2998 is much more closely based in detail on Gainsborough's type: in the face, which copies Gainsborough's likeness; in the pose of the torso and the legs (the left one with the Garter prominent) and in the treatment of the landscape background at the right-hand side. The pose of the arms has, however, been re-invented.

The artist of WAG 2998 has not been identified and the work's origins remain obscure. A very similar work (differing chiefly in the replacement of the landscape background by a further column) is in the Guildhall at Worcester (fig. 130).[1] The circumstances of the commissioning of this work are also unknown. It does not appear to be by the same hand as WAG 2998 and the figure is thinner and less directly derived from Gainsborough's prototype, suggesting that it is a little later in date. The exhibition of Gainsborough's portrait in 1781 provides a *terminus a quo* for the production of both works and they cannot be from much more than a decade later when other likenesses of the King (for

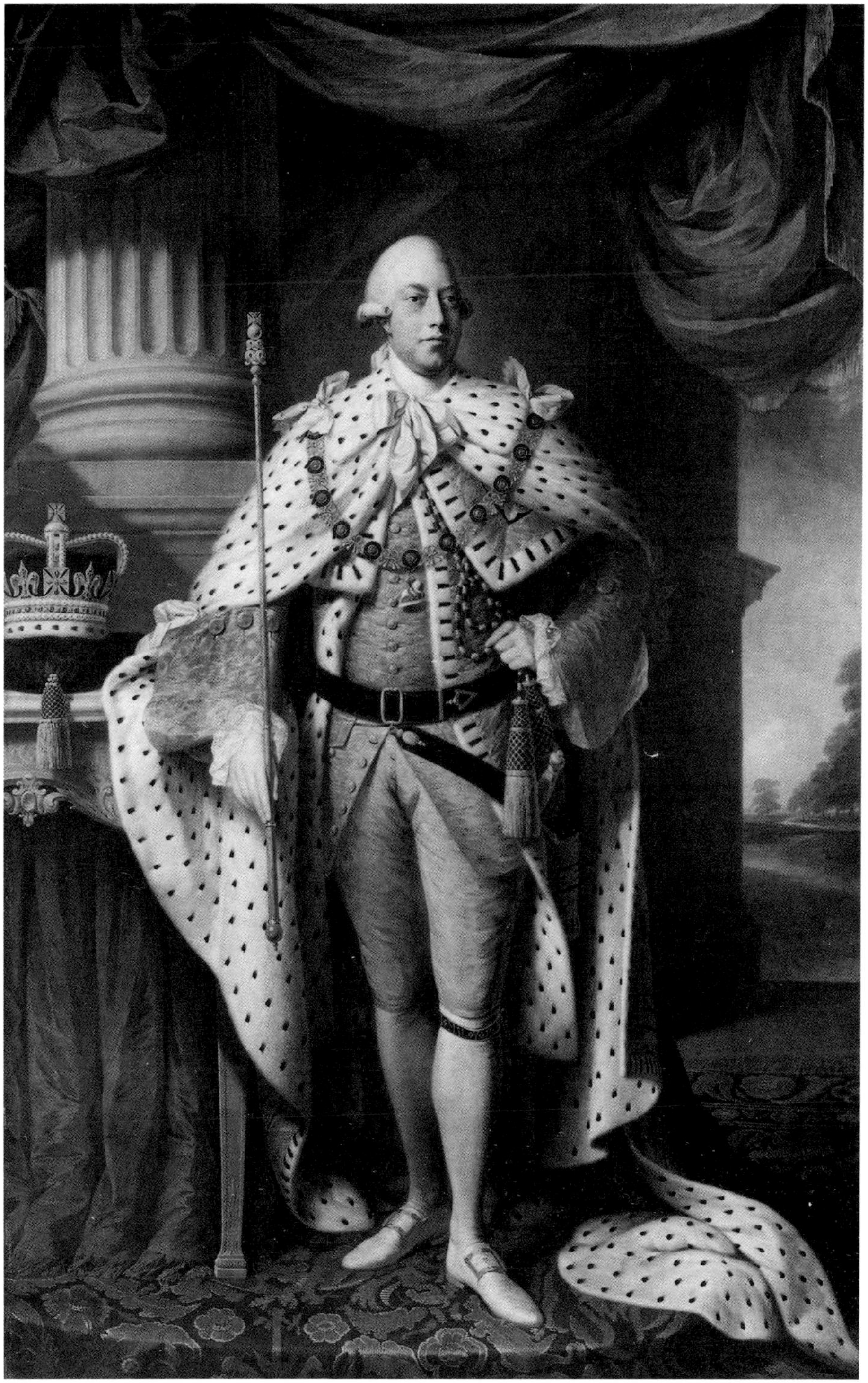

WAG 2998

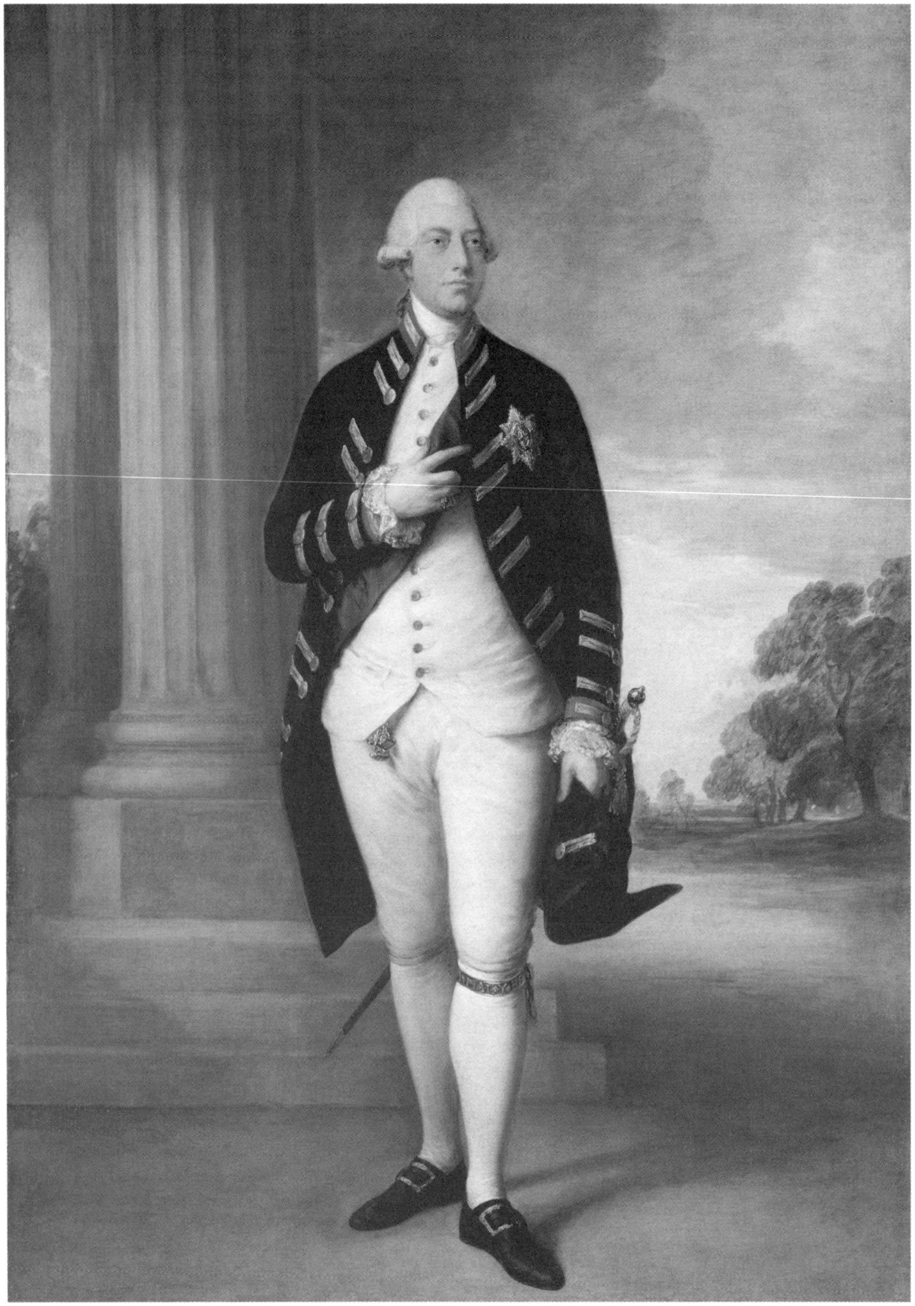

Fig. 128 *King George III* by Thomas Gainsborough, oil on canvas. The Royal Collection © 2011 Her Majesty Queen Elizabeth II.

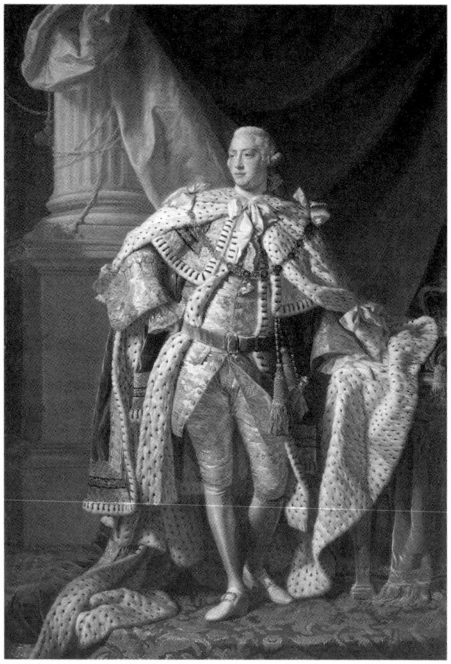

Fig. 129 *King George III* by Allan Ramsay, oil on canvas. The Royal Collection © 2011 Her Majesty Queen Elizabeth II.

example by Lawrence; see WAG 7021, pp. 101–3) became current. Neither can WAG 2998 be by Gainsborough's only known assistant, his nephew Gainsborough Dupont, whose characteristic loose manner is totally at variance with the hard, wooden paint handling of WAG 2998. The former suggestion that it is the work of Richard Broughton must be discounted;[2] another idea is that Philip Reinagle (1749–1833), Ramsay's pupil, who was employed to make copies of his master's coronation portrait, later updated it by grafting onto it the basic features of Gainsborough's work.[3]

PROVENANCE

...Sir Ernest Royden; by whom presented 1953.

NOTES

1. Oliver Millar: *Later Georgian Pictures in the Collection of Her Majesty the Queen* 2 vols (London, 1969) vol. 1, pp. 35–6. The Worcester picture is now attributed to the 'circle of Christopher William Hunnemann' on the basis that in 1788, George III presented Worcester with further full-lengths of himself and Queen Charlotte copied by Hunnemann from Gainsborough's original; these are also in Worcester Guildhall (Philippa Tinsley, *email*, 21 September 2010, gallery files).
2. John Woodward: 'Four Royal Portraits at the Walker Art Gallery' *Liverpool Bulletin* vol. 4, nos 1–2 (October 1954) p. 14; however, Broughton had left England for Russia – where he died in 1783 – before the completion of Gainsborough's painting.
3. Hugh Belsey, to whom I am grateful for discussing the work, tentatively made this suggestion, *verbally*, 24 October 2008.

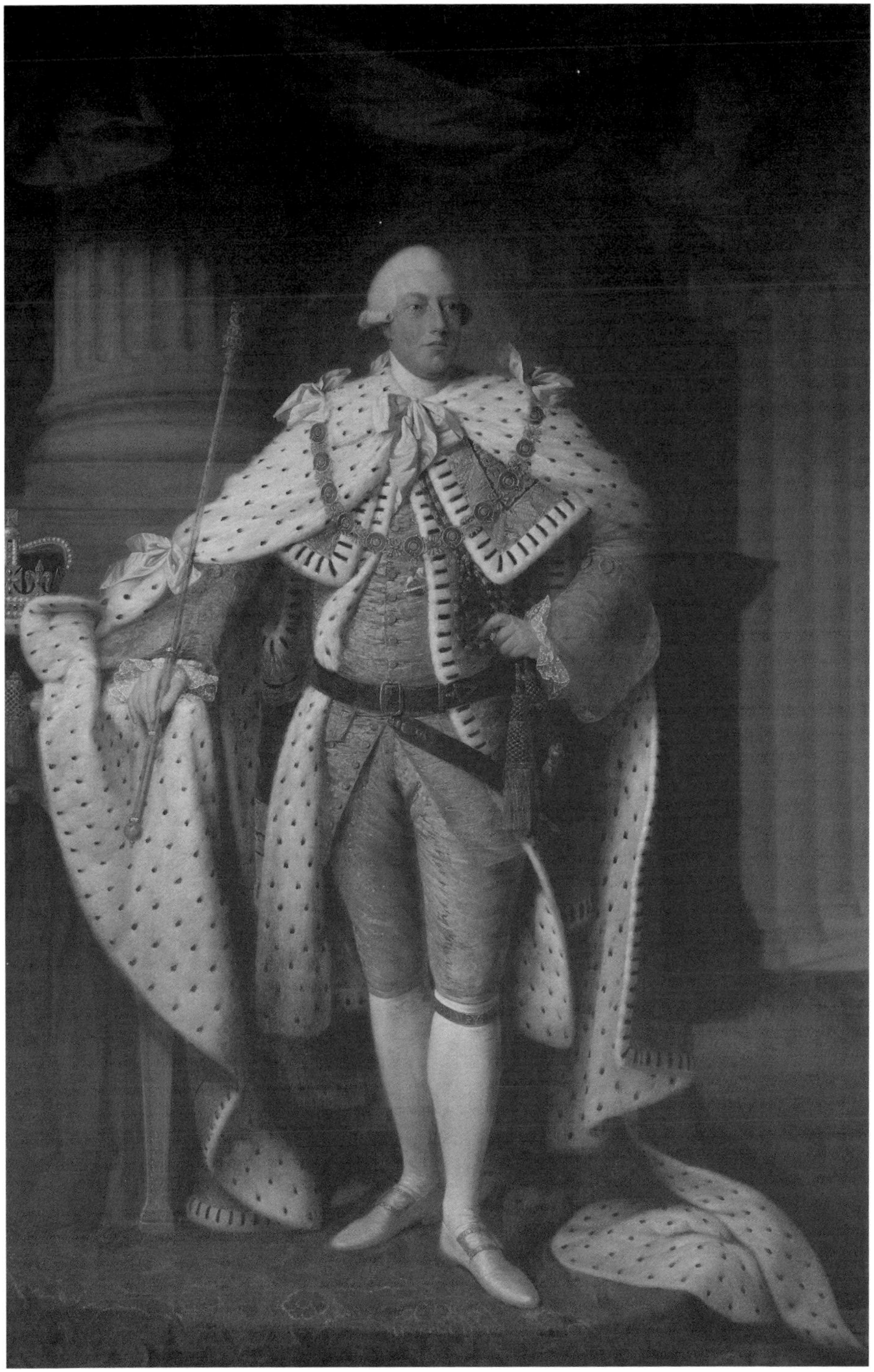

Fig. 130 *George III* after Thomas Gainsborough, oil on canvas. Collection of the City of Worcester.

A Mediterranean Port with British Ships

WAG 3087
oil on canvas, 115.5 × 183.5 cm
date: unknown, perhaps 1735–60

To the left and right are four British ships, including, second from the left, an 88-gun warship flying the union jack from the main mast and with a carved royal standard roundel below the gallery. All four ships are flying red ensigns. Between them is a felucca or galley characteristic of the Mediterranean. This is flying at its mainmast an unidentifiable flag comprising a red design on a white field.[1] This ship and the two smaller vessels making their way towards the British warships are also flying identical red flags with a red and white quartering. At the extreme left is the turreted end of a harbour wall and in the right distance a fortress whose white walls and single tower are catching the sun.

This large and problematical painting is not easy to date and its precise subject remains unidentified. From the costumes worn by the figures in the left foreground, it would appear to date from the late seventeenth century, but the warships themselves and the design of the union flag (as well as the general style of the picture) are of the mid-eighteenth century; this suggests that the artist was less concerned with historical accuracy than in reproducing conventions of earlier maritime painting in the manner of a capriccio. It is unclear where the scene is set and whether a specific historical event is depicted, even if loosely.[2] Ostensibly, the scene is a diplomatic one in which British vessels visit a friendly foreign port and are formally welcomed.

When it was acquired by the gallery, WAG 3087 was believed to be by the Dutch artist Johannes Lingelbach (1622–74); this attribution was soon rejected, but no satisfactory candidate for the artist has

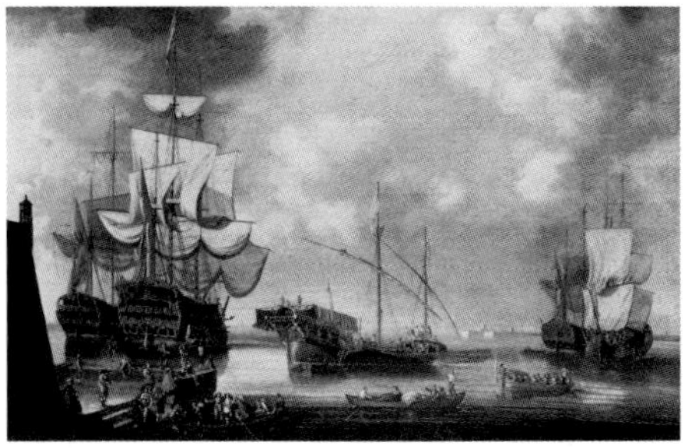

WAG 3087

emerged.[3] The depiction of the warships is skilled, in a style suggestive of the circle of Peter Monamy; but the handling of the foreground detail is relatively wooden. On the basis of the artistic quality it has been suggested that WAG 3087 is a replica, rather than a unique work.[4]

PROVENANCE

...Maritime Insurance Company;[5] by whom presented 1951.

NOTES

1. See n. 2.
2. It has been suggested that the setting is Venice, looking from the Lido towards the Forte San Andrea in the background (James Byam-Shaw, *letter*, 22 August 1959, gallery files) and that the craft in the centre is distinctively Venetian. However, there is no sign of the city of Venice which in this scenario ought to be visible in the left background. It has also been suggested (by Roger Quarm, National Maritime Museum, Greenwich, *verbally*, 10 March 2010) that the port is Valletta, and the white and red flag flown by the barge in the centre could be the eighteenth-century red Maltese Cross on a white ground; or else Naples, with the flag being the Papal ensign.
3. One possibility may be Thomas Allin or Allen, works by whom at Goodwood House bear some stylistic resemblance to WAG 3087. Allen's dates are unknown but the Goodwood paintings have been dated to the late 1730s (Rosemary Baird, *email*, 17 March 2010, gallery files). It is unclear, but seems likely, that this is the same Thomas Allen who exhibited 14 works at the Free Society of Artists between 1767 and 1772 (*GrSA*, p. 2).
4. Ellie Hughes, Yale Center for British Art, New Haven, *verbally*, February 2008.
5. Christie's stencil *136 CZ* on the back of the work. Christie's used this stencil for a single (unidentified) painting consigned by Messrs Philpotts and Shepland, London, 2 October 1919, which was forwarded to the auction house Foster's for onward sale. I am grateful to Marijke Booth for this information.

George Delves and a Female Companion

WAG 3089
oil on oak panel, 218.5 × 133.5 cm[1]
date: 1577

The painted inscriptions on WAG 3089 are as follows:

(upper left)

ALTRO NON MI VAGLIA CHE AMOR E FAMA[2]

(upper right)

THE COVRE WHOES OUTWARD SHOES
SETS FORTH A WORLD OF IOYES
HATH FLATTRED ME TO LONG
THAT WANDRED IN HER TOYES
WHEAR SHULD HE THIRSTI DRINK
BUT WHEAR THE FOUNTAIN RON
THE HOEP OF SVCH RELEEF
HATH ALMOST ME VNDON

(bottom centre)

THE WARS HAVTH WAST ME WEALTH
AND TIME CONSUEM BY STEALTH
AS TROETH CAN WEL DECLAER
WHEALIN I SOCHT FOR FAEM
OR AT THE LEAST SOM GAYN
IN FINE MY HOEL REWARD
WAS NOGHT BUT WOE AND PA(IN)

(lower left)

ANNO DOMINI	*Aetatis suae*
1577	*40*

There is no reason to doubt the date of the painting as given by the last of these inscriptions,[3] and this evidence, in conjunction with the coat of arms and the Delves family motto *Defy Fortune* on the pennant above the discarded suit of armour, has led to the sitter being identified as George Delves (d. 1604), a younger son[4] of Sir Henry Delves of Doddington, Cheshire (d. 1560) and his wife Cicely (d. 1563),[5] daughter of Sir Richard Broke, a baron of the exchequer in London. The date of George's birth is not known, but if the inscription on WAG 3089 is right, it was in 1536–37. George Delves is known to have been an officer in Queen Elizabeth I's army in Ireland by 1560 and to have been a captain of a troop by 1561, by which date he had been appointed a Gentleman Pensioner. He was granted an estate in Ireland, Shian Castle, near present-day Portlaoise, in 1563 and spent the next six years there working and fighting (not always successfully) for the English cause before selling up and returning to England in 1569.[6] The fact that these biographical details coincide both with the iconography of the discarded armour in the portrait and also with the tone of the inscribed verses, which express a weariness of court life and disillusionment that war has brought neither fame nor wealth, strongly support the notion that George Delves is the sitter.[7]

After his return to England, Delves marked time for several years. In 1572 he was elected MP for East Retford through the influence of the Duke of Rutland, who had family estates in Cheshire of which Delves's father had been the steward; and in 1573 he was appointed a Justice of the Peace for Cheshire, suggesting that around this time he resided in the county when he was not at court.[8] Even though he is not known to have lived at Doddington itself, the character of the painting encourages the belief that it was made for the family (at a time when it seems that he was its senior male member); and he may have commissioned it to present to his young nephew at Doddington, Henry Delves (1555–1606). It may be significant that Henry reached his majority the year before the picture was completed.[9]

The female figure in WAG 3089 may be meant to represent George Delves's first wife Christian, the daughter of

painting, the priming and underpainting (especially of the costume) and the order in which the image was built up.

16. Roy Strong: *The Artist and the Garden* (New Haven and London, 2000) p. 93, writes, 'the painter is certainly not English but Netherlandish'. Katherine Stainer-Hutchins (note in gallery files) proposed an attribution to Quentin Matsys the younger (1534–89) on the basis of a perceived similarity to his 1583 portrait of Queen Elizabeth I (Siena); he is listed as a visitor to the Dutch church in London in 1581, but it is not known that he was in England before this date.

17. This paragraph and the next are largely based on ms notes on the costumes by Janet Arnold, April 1995, gallery files.

18. Illustrated by Aileen Ribeiro and Valerie Cumming: *The Visual History of Costume* (London, 1989) p. 86 (cat. 45).

19. Bird et al., *op. cit.*, p. 169. Arnold, *loc. cit.*, conjectures that the cord attaching the ring to Delves's wrist may be of plaited hair, rather than ribbon or plaited silk.

20. A. V. B. Norman, *letter*, 17 September 1995, gallery files.

21. Hearn, *op. cit.*, p. 106.

22. Stainer-Hutchins, *loc. cit.*

23. Bird et. al., *op. cit.*, pp. 175–82, provide a detailed description and analysis of the garden, whose size they calculate 'conservatively covering around 2.7 acres' (p. 178); and see also Strong, *loc. cit.*, who describes this as 'the most comprehensive representation of a large garden from the period'.

24. Bird et al., *op. cit.*, p. 181.

25. Bird et al., *op. cit.*, p. 179; Strong, *op. cit.*, pp. 93–4.

26. The relationship between the house at Doddington and the house as painted in WAG 3089 is fully discussed by Bird et al., *op. cit.*, pp. 173–5.

27. Dr Victor Morgan, *letter*, 27 January 1996, gallery files.

28. I am grateful to Dr Hester Lees-Jeffries for discussing WAG 3089 in the context of her work on fountain imagery in Elizabethan literature, and for pointing out the development of a corruptive strain in the notion of the fountain of love, particularly in Ben Jonson's *The Fountain of Self-love* of 1584.

Liverpool from Tranmere

WAG 3115
oil on canvas, 67 × 102.5 cm
date: about 1770–75

The view is from the Cheshire side of the Mersey, looking almost due east. Tranmere Pool is in the foreground, with a longboat carrying travellers across the river depicted approaching the shore. Behind the pool is the site of the present-day Woodside and Hamilton Square areas of Birkenhead.

The painting must date from between 1769 and 1784; St Paul's Church, which was consecrated in Liverpool in the former year, is visible as the left-hand of the two domed buildings; but there is no sign of St John's Church, finished in 1784, at the then north-eastern edge of the town. A dating of WAG 3115 close to the beginning of this period seems preferable, partly on the basis of the relatively old-fashioned style of the painting itself and partly from the dress of the couple promenading in the foreground (which seems outmoded even for the 1760s).

The other prominent buildings in WAG 3115 are, from left to right: St Nicholas's Parish Church, with its short spire, on the dock front a little to the right of St Paul's; the second Exchange (or Town Hall) designed by John Wood of Bath 1754–55 and badly damaged by fire in 1795 (see pp. 308–9), with its dome, smaller than St Paul's; St George's Church, the corporation church consecrated in 1734, marked by the left-hand of the two spires; and the even newer St Thomas's of 1750 with the taller spire. Much of the space between the two latter churches was occupied by the Old Dock, not visible in this view. On the right, the buildings on Duke Street may be seen straggling up to the site of the Bowling Green and beyond.

WAG 3115 was called *Liverpool in 1769* by an unknown artist when presented to the Corporation in 1873 and also when it was catalogued in 1885;[1] but by 1917 it had been given the title *Tranmere Pool in 1810* and attributed to Charles Eyes junior (1786–1833).[2] Although he cannot have painted the work, it is not out of the question that WAG 3115 has something to do with the surveying activities of his better-known great-uncle John Eyes (d. 1773); or more likely, Eyes's rivals as surveyors in Liverpool in the late 1760s and early 1770s, George Perry (d. 1771) and Peter Perez Burdett. When Perry completed his large map of Liverpool in 1769, his intention was to issue it to subscribers with views of Liverpool – ultimately carried out in the form of prints by Edward Rooker from watercolours by his son, Michael 'Angelo' Rooker (figs. 132–33). It is tempting to wonder whether WAG 3115 represents an earlier effort on Perry's part to procure a panoramic view of the town. The possibility that it is by Burdett, who was an accomplished draughtsman, is tantalising, even if nothing is known of his talents as a painter.

Two further suggestions have been made concerning WAG 3115.[3] One is that it could be the *View from the River Mersey on the Cheshire Side with a Distant Prospect of Liverpool* shown by the local landscape and marine painter William Jackson at the 1787 exhibition of the Society for Promoting Painting and Design in Liverpool (cat. 50). But unless WAG 3115 was an old painting by Jackson dusted off for the purpose, this seems wrong. Jackson had submitted other works to the Liverpool exhibitions of 1774 and 1784, and presumably would have sent this picture to one or other of those had it been available. The second suggestion is that WAG 3115 is the *View on the River Mersey* shown at the 1771 exhibition of the Free Society of Artists in London

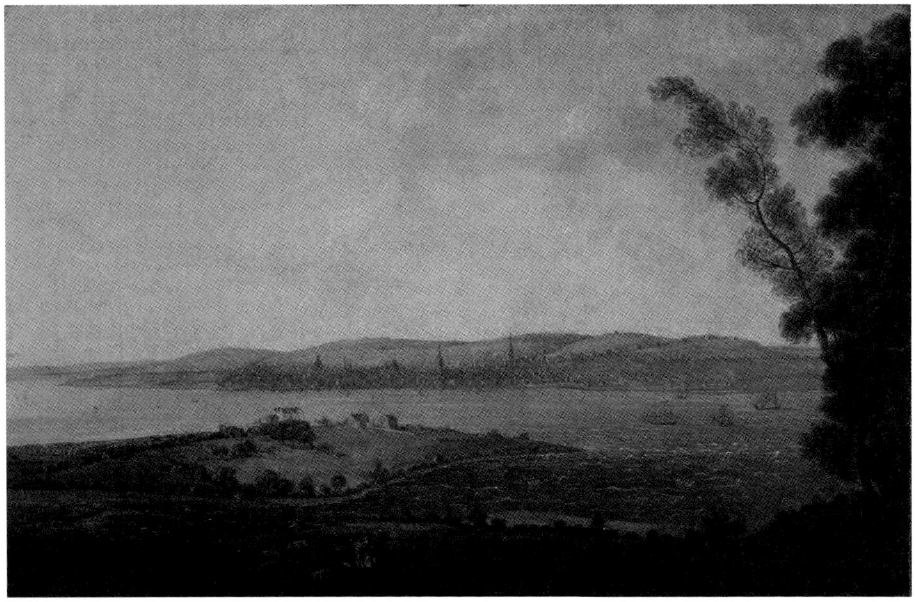

WAG 3115

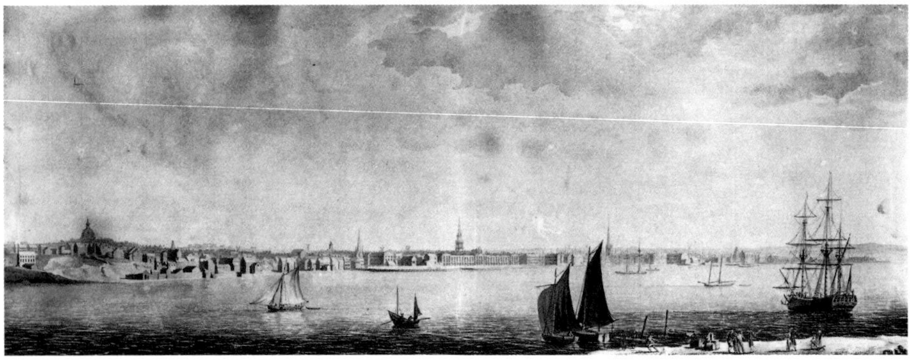

Fig. 132 *Liverpool from Seacombe* by Michael Angelo Rooker, watercolour on paper. Walker Art Gallery.

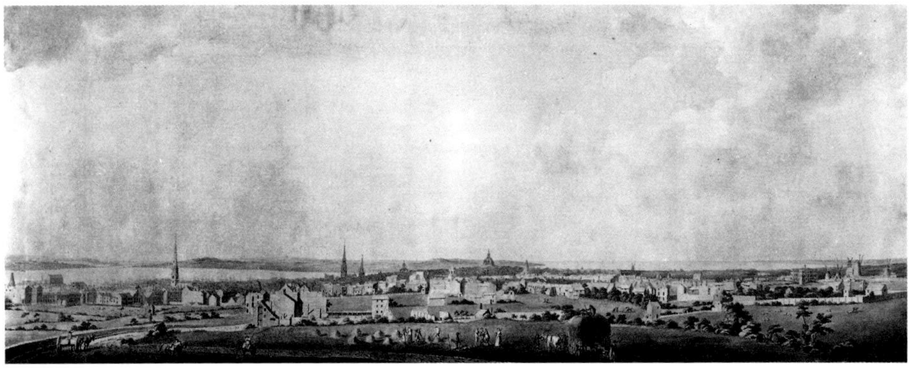

Fig. 133 *Liverpool from the Bowling Green* by Michael Angelo Rooker, watercolour on paper. Walker Art Gallery.

(cat. 46) by Thomas Chubbard. In terms of the dating, this seems much more plausible, and although little of Chubbard's work in landscape is known, comparison between the elaborately decorative tree-forms in WAG 3115 and those in the smaller, and later, landscapes in the collection (WAG 8653–54, p. 28) does suggest the artist could be the same.

PROVENANCE

...Presented to the Corporation by Sir J. A. Picton 1873; deposited in the Library and Museum; transferred to the gallery between 1903 and 1917.[4]

EXHIBITIONS

Liverpool Civic Week Wembley 1924; *Jubilee Celebration* Birkenhead 1927; *Pictures of Old Liverpool* Bluecoat Gallery, Liverpool 1945 (1); *The Taste of Yesterday* Walker Art Gallery 1970 (5).

NOTES

1. Charles Dyall: *Walker Art Gallery Descriptive Catalogue of the Permanent Collection of Pictures* (Liverpool, 1882) p. 44 (cat. 186); the work was listed as on deposit in the Library and Museum.
2. E. R. Dibdin: 'Liverpool Art and Artists in the Eighteenth Century', *Walpole Society*, vol. 6 (1917–18) p. 72. Dibdin described it as 'the work of an efficient painter' but noted that it was in poor condition; an old repair in the sky is now clearly visible.
3. *MPPP*, p. 50.
4. It was still listed as in the Library in the 1903 Walker collection catalogue, p. 33 (cat. 186) but was in the Walker when published by Dibdin, *loc. cit*.

Erasmus Earle

WAG 3164
oil on canvas, 126 × 102 cm
date: about 1690–95

The sitter (1666–1721)[1] was the second, but eldest surviving son of John Earle of Heydon Hall, Norfolk and his wife Sarah, née Hare; and the grandson of the more noted Erasmus Earle (1590–1667) who was Oliver Cromwell's serjeant-at-law and who established the Earles at Heydon.[2] The younger Erasmus married Eleanor, daughter and heir of Augustine Castell of Raveningham. In 1690 he was appointed High Sheriff of Norfolk, an event that, judging by his apparent age, this portrait may have been intended to commemorate.[3] WAG 3164 may be related to the portrait recorded at Heydon in the early years of the twentieth century which was sold with most of the contents of the house in 1950.[4] No convincing candidate for the artist has been put forward,[5] and the quality of the picture is very hard to determine owing to the darkened varnish covering most of its surface.

PROVENANCE

...J. Davey and Sons, Liverpool; from whom bt. 1951.[6]

NOTES

1. Prince F. Duleep Singh: *Portraits in Norfolk Houses* ed. E. Farrer 2 vols (Norwich, 1927) vol. 1, p. 234, with the note that Earle was buried at Heydon.
2. WAG 3164 has hitherto been thought to represent this Erasmus Earle within the gallery; hence the proposed dating 'about 1625 / about 1660' in *CIC*, p. 37.
3. Duleep Singh, *loc. cit.*, gives 'about 1688' for the portrait at Heydon (see main text and n. 4).
4. *Ibid.* It is tempting to suspect, from the absence of any earlier provenance for WAG 3164 than 1951, the year after the contents of Heydon were dispersed, that it actually is the Heydon picture, even though that work, as described by Duleep Singh, differs in some details, notably the presence of a 'dove-coloured curtain on the sinister side' (i.e. the viewer's right). This could have been altered to the present landscape after the sale to disguise the work's provenance; it is noticeably more modern-looking than any other passage of the painting.
5. The copy of Duleep Singh in the National Portrait Gallery Library is annotated *Riley tradition / ? Closterman*.
6. According to a note in gallery files, WAG 3164 was purchased for the frame. It may have been acquired by the Liverpool dealers Davey's in the mistaken belief that the sitter was a member of the well-known Liverpool family of Earles (for whom see WAG 9283, p. 337).

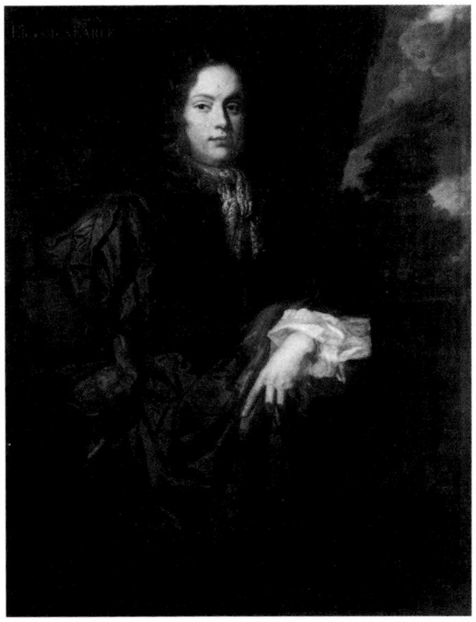

WAG 3164

George, Lord Anson

WAG 4540
oil on canvas, 101.5 × 79 cm
date: unknown, perhaps 1750–53

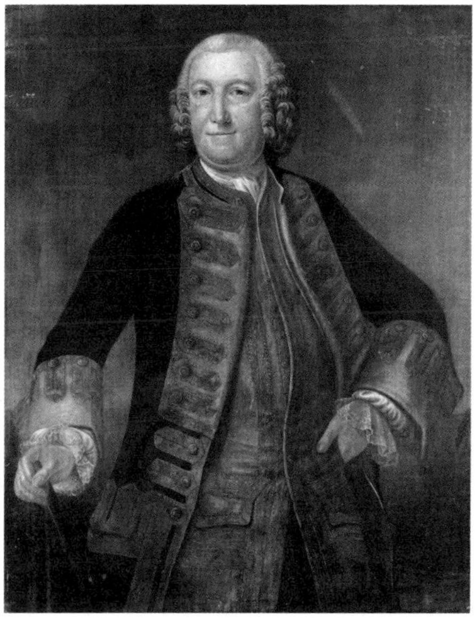

WAG 4540

Anson (1697–1762) achieved celebrity in 1744 when he returned to London following a five-year circumnavigation of the world. In 1739, as a naval captain with considerable experience in protecting British merchant shipping sailing to and from the American Colonies, he had been given command of a small squadron despatched to harass Spanish settlements in South America. The expedition had many adventures and suffered numerous setbacks, but Anson emerged from it with great credit, and is said to have re-entered London with booty worth ten million pounds. Following this exploit he was made in quick succession a Rear-Admiral of the Blue, a Lord of the Admiralty, a Rear-Admiral of the White (April 1745) and Vice-Admiral of the Blue (July 1746). After his defeat of the French Admiral La Jonquière off Finistère in 1747 he was created Baron Soberton; he was First Lord of the Admiralty 1751–56 and again from 1757 to his death; and he commanded the squadron which brought Queen Charlotte, consort of George III, to England in 1761.[1]

Anson was one of the most portrayed persons in Britain in the period 1745–60. Without being a simple copy, WAG 4540 appears to relate closely to a type by the Dutch artist Jan Wandelaar (1690–1759), a version of which is at Goodwood House. The exact date of WAG 4540 is unknown, but Anson is shown in flag officer's undress uniform of the period 1748–67,[2] and he appears plausibly three to six years younger than in his best-known portrait, by Reynolds, which dates from 1754 (Shugborough; copy at the National Portrait Gallery, London). Wandelaar's portrait was certainly engraved in 1751 by his Dutch colleague Jacobus Houbraken,[3] whose print was used as the basis of the engraving by Thomas Rothwell published in the *Biographical Magazine* in 1795 (fig. 134).[4] J. Jenkins's similar engraving, published by Thomas Kelly, Paternoster Row, in 1828, acknowledges Wandelaar's original authorship, whereas Rothwell's does not. A further closely comparable engraving by the Tuscan-based Giovanni Lapi, active in the 1740s and 1750s, must date from the period 1747–51 since the

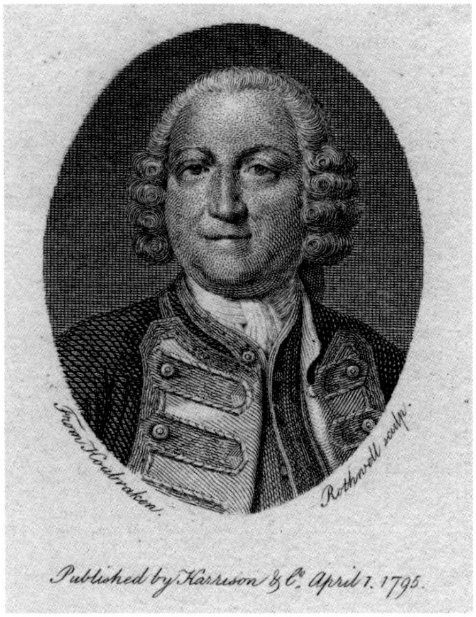

Fig. 134 *Admiral Lord Anson* after Houbraken, engraving published by Harrison & Co. © National Portrait Gallery, London.

letters describe Anson as Baron Soberton without calling him First Lord of the Admiralty. This derives either directly from Wandelaar or possibly from Houbraken.[5] Although no other painted version of WAG 4540 is currently known, its quality seems much too stiff for it to be Wandelaar's original, and it, too, may derive from one of the printed sources.[6]

PROVENANCE

...Revd Augustus Campbell;[7] by whom presented to Sir J. A. Picton for the City of Liverpool 1865; passed to the Corporation in 1873; deposited in the Library and Museum; transferred to the gallery between 1917 and 1927.[8]

NOTES

1. *The Biographical Magazine, Containing Portraits and Characters of Eminent and Ingenious Persons of Every Age and Nation* (London, 1794) p. 3; N. A. M. Rodger: 'Anson, George, Baron Anson', ODNB vol. 2 pp. 260–6.
2. Roger Quarm, *email*, 1 October 2010, gallery files. Quarm points out that Anson appears to be wearing the undress uniform of a Rear-Admiral of the Blue even though he had been promoted to the rank of Vice-Admiral of the Blue in 1746. This may mean that the portrait was made for someone whose intimacy with Anson dated from before his promotion (see n. 7).
3. See *Catalogue* 3, The Print Room, London (1989) p. 27, no. 52; listed as a copper engraving, 40 × 25 cm.
4. *Biographical Magazine*, *loc. cit.*, described as 'From Houbraken'.
5. E. H. H. Archibald, National Maritime Museum, Greenwich, *letter*, 22 December 1977, gallery files, suggested that WAG 4540 was based directly on Lapi's print.
6. WAG 4540 has some similarity, although it exhibits differences in detail, with a portrait of Anson in the collection of the Dukes of Richmond at Goodwood House (as noted by Archibald, *loc. cit.*).
7. According to Campbell, who was Vicar of Childwall in the suburbs of Liverpool, the portrait came to him from his uncle, 'who was an admiral and sailed around the world with [Anson]' (*copy letter*, Revd A. Campbell to Sir J. A. Picton, 27 May 1865, gallery files).
8. Charles Dyall: *First Decade of the Walker Art Gallery: A Report of Its Operations from 1877–1887* (Liverpool, 1888) p. 7, states that the work was given to the Corporation in 1873. Dyall: *Walker Art Gallery Descriptive Catalogue of the Permanent Collection of Pictures* (1882) p. 44 (cat. 189) lists the work as on deposit in the Library and Museum, and according to a ms curatorial note, gallery files, it was still in the Library in October 1917. It was included in the 1927 Walker Art Gallery collection catalogue, p. 194.

View of Conway

WAG 5601
oil on canvas, 101.5 × 127 cm
date: about 1775–80

The view is from the east, with the estuary of the River Conwy in the foreground. The sun is in the west, indicating that the time is afternoon, and the tide is out. On the riverbank, figures await the arrival of an open-ended ferry being punted across the calm water. The bulk of the castle, one of the chain of Edward I's Welsh fortresses, and begun in 1283, is at the left, underneath the 610-metre high mountain Tal-y-fan. In the early seventeenth century the castle had become the property of the Earls of Conway; after the English Civil War the third Earl had stripped it out and during the eighteenth century it had been allowed to fall into decay.

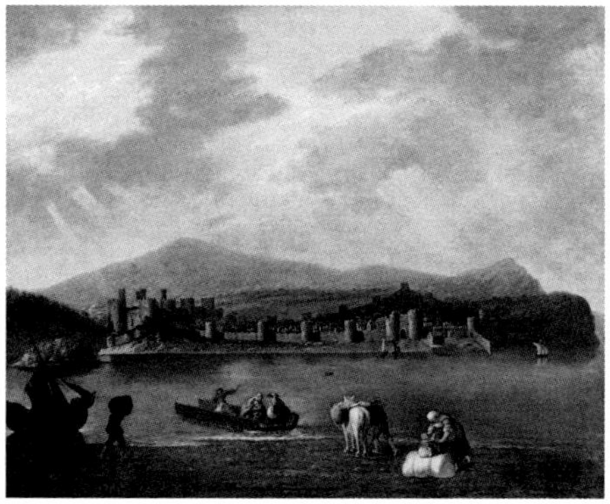

WAG 5601

It is not known who painted WAG 5601. On grounds of style, it can be dated to around 1775–80. There is a distinct similarity with the handling of WAG 3115 (pp. 308–9), and it is not out of the question that they are by the same artist, though perhaps painted some years apart.[1] Although the scale of the distant boats is mismanaged, the painting is impressive in its handling of the fall of light and its panoramic sweep and is clearly by a provincial figure of some significance.

PROVENANCE

Found in the gallery; transferred to the permanent collection in 1961.

REFERENCE

1. The hypothesis that WAG 3115 is the work of Thomas Chubbard (see p. 28) might equally apply, by extension, to WAG 5601. No view of Conway by Chubbard or any other artist is recorded among the exhibits at the 1774, 1784 or 1787 exhibitions of the Liverpool Society of Artists; nor is any work of this title recorded in Daniel Daulby's ms catalogues of his paintings (LRO); these do, however, list other Welsh subjects by Chubbard, including a *Caernarvon Castle*.

Index

The Story of Diana and Actaeon

WAG 6220
oil on wood, 115.5 × 129.5 cm

The Story of Phaeton

WAG 6221
oil on wood, 104 × 223.5 cm
date: about 1605

When they were acquired by the gallery, WAG 6220–21 were stated to have come from Grafton Hall, Malpas, and they were believed to have formed part of the decoration of one of the rooms there since the early seventeenth century.[1] The Hall was built by Sir Peter Warburton (d. 1621) in the decade after his acquisition of the land at Grafton from the Massey family in 1602,[2] and the style of the paintings and of the costumes worn by the figures in them is consonant with a date of about 1605. Decorative schemes making use of episodes from Ovid's *Metamorphoses*, which are the source of the subjects of WAG 6220–21, were commonplace throughout Europe during the Renaissance. Other examples from the period in Britain include a grisaille plaster frieze at Stodmarsh Court near Canterbury, which includes representations of the planets and *Diana and Actaeon* (now in the Victoria & Albert Museum, London), and three embroidered cushion-covers at Hardwick Hall with representations of *Diana and Actaeon*, *The Fall of Phaeton* and *The Rape of Europa*.[3] The fact that the two panels are not the same size suggests that they were not pendants and are likely to have been part of a larger cycle of Ovidian subjects.

Both paintings, adopting the conventions of contemporary embroideries and tapestries, combine several episodes from the respective stories. In WAG 6220, Actaeon, whilst hunting, encounters the goddess Diana and her nymphs bathing in a pool; Diana transforms him into a stag by splashing water in his face. In the centre background he is pursued across a field by his own hounds and companions, and in the left middle ground he is brought down and killed.[4] The castle on the hill to the right may be intended to depict Actaeon's royal palace. When WAG 6220 was acquired by the gallery, the nude figures were covered by an overpainted curtain extending from just beneath their faces down to the leading edge of the bath. This was removed in subsequent cleaning.

In WAG 6221, the action moves from left to right: at bottom left, Clymene informs her son Phaeton that his father is the sun god. Above this Phaeton pleads with his father to be allowed to drive the chariot of the sun for a day (for Richard Wilson's depiction of this moment see WAG 1999.58, pp. 262–4). Phaeton sets off in his father's chariot, driving past the signs of the zodiac but getting too close to the earth and causing fires, and further to the right people hide in caves and sea animals die from the heat. Further over still, Zeus strikes Phaeton with a thunderbolt, bringing him crashing down into the river Eridanus, and he is buried by naiads.[5] Ovid's narrative is followed closely in both pictures, although the foreground of WAG 6221, depicting a castle and its estates with promenading figures and others driving in a carriage, is more fanciful. It is tempting to suspect that the figures under the sunshade are portraits of the artist's patron and his family; the costumes worn by them have been identified as the only ones in the two

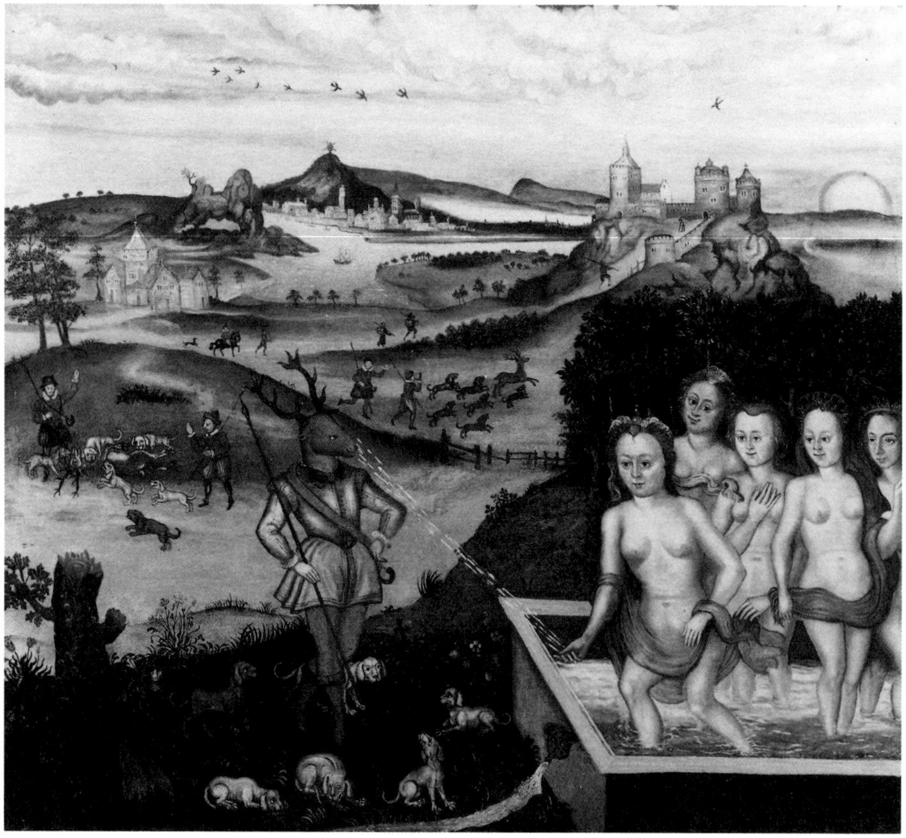

WAG 6220

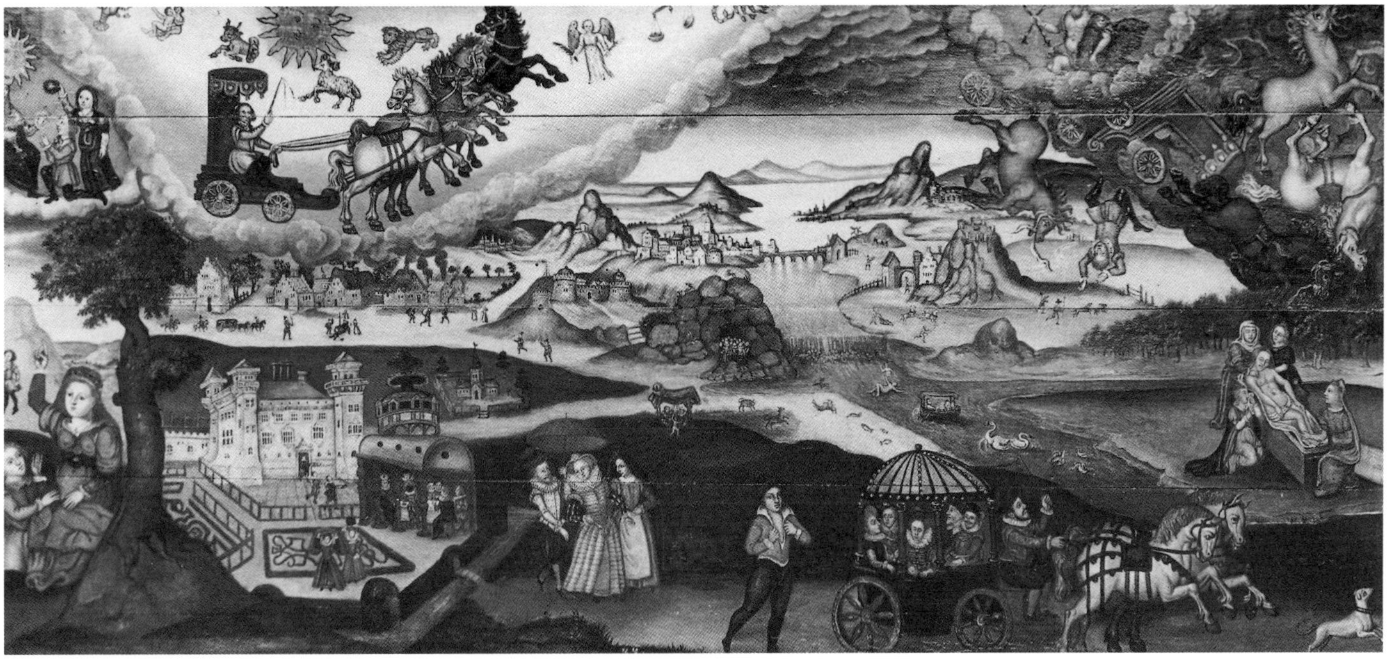

WAG 6221

works that are distinctively contemporary and English.[6]

The iconography of both works probably derives from prints, although only one specific borrowing has so far been identified. This is the castle in WAG 6221 which has been shown to be based on a building in the print *Wealth Brings forth Pride* from *The Cycle of the Vicissitudes of Human Affairs* (*Circulus Vicissitudinis rerum humanorum*) designed by Maarten de Vos and engraved by Karel van Mallery.[7] It has also been suggested that the treatment of the chariot in the sky, separated by a formalised band of cloud from a panoramic landscape peopled with small figures, may derive from two series of engravings of *The Planets* by Virgil Solis.[8] With regard to WAG 6220 the treatment of the foreground scene of Actaeon being turned into a stag is very similar to the more sophisticated depiction of the subject in a painting of 1561 by Bernaert De Rijckere (Prague Castle; fig. 135) and presumably both derive from the same printed source. It has been noted that the cistern-like bath with its lion's head spout may be found in prints published by Gerard de Jode as part of his *Thesaurus Sacrarum*[9] and also in a woodcut by Bernard Salomon published in Lyon in 1557.[10] A panoramic background with a view of a castle on a hill appears in a woodcut of *Diana and Actaeon* by George Pencz of 1530.[11]

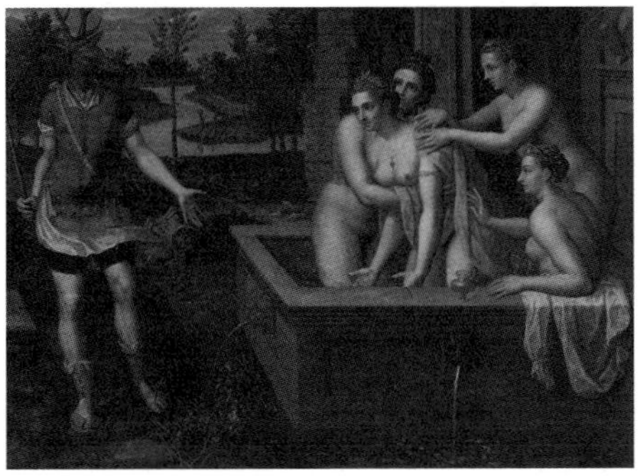

Fig. 135 *Diana and Actaeon* by Bernaert De Rijckere, oil on panel; © Prague Castle Administration; photo Prokop Paul.

Both WAG 6220 and WAG 6221 are painted on panels comprising four horizontal planks of roughly the same height (approximately 29 cm in the case of WAG 6220, 25 cm in the case of WAG 6221). It appears that both are by the same hand. The quality of the paintings is no more than provincial and no candidate for the artist has emerged.

PROVENANCE

...[? Sir Peter Warburton of Grafton Hall, Malpas]; by descent at Grafton Hall to Sir Peter Egerton-Warburton; from whom bt. on the demolition of the house in 1963 by Mrs C. Needham; from whom bt. (£850) 1964.

NOTES

1. Mrs C. Needham, *letter*, 18 November 1963, gallery files. Mrs Needham believed that the paintings were made for Sir Hugh Massey, who sold the Grafton estate to Sir Peter Warburton.
2. Peter Egerton-Warburton, *letter*, 5 May 1974, gallery files; he noted that Grafton Hall was largely rebuilt in the 1880s by the Stanley family, raising the possibility that the panels were introduced as period decoration at this point from another source.
3. G. Wingfield Digby: *Elizabethan Embroidery* (London, 1963) p. 112.
4. Ovid: *Metamorphoses* Book 3, lines 138–252.
5. Ovid: *Metamorphoses* Book 2, lines 1–366.
6. Stella Mary Newton, *letter*, 7 December 1973,

gallery files; she adds, however, that the mantle worn by the woman on the right of the group is 'of a kind...only found in Netherlandish works of art'.
7. Anthony Wells-Cole: *Art and Decoration in Elizabethan and Jacobean England: The Influence of Continental Prints* (New Haven and London, 1997) p. 209. Wells-Cole observes that WAG 6221 provides 'the only evidence to date that this important moralistic print series was known in England'.
8. Mark Evans, draft entry on WAG 6220–21, gallery files, citing Ilse O'Dell-Franke: *Kupferstiche und Radierungen aus der Werkstatt des Virgil Solis* (Wiesbaden, 1977), pp. 102–5 and pls 39–41. The present entry is greatly indebted to Mark Evans's work on these pictures.
9. Xanthe Brooke (to Anthony Wells-Cole), *copy letter*, 6 December 1993, gallery files.
10. Reproduced by E. Panofsky: *Problems in Titian, Mostly Iconographic* (London, 1969) fig. 168.
11. D. Landau: *Catalogo Completo dell'opera grafica di Georg Pencz* (Milan, 1978) p. 151.

The Leicester Family

WAG 6252
oil on canvas, 100.5 × 121.5 cm
date: about 1790–92

In the centre is Mrs Ellen Leicester (1767–1830)[1] and her child, probably (on the view that the portrait was commissioned as a dynastic statement) her first-born and a boy who will continue the family name into the next generation. The identities of the remaining figures are uncertain, but they read as Mrs Leicester's own father, at the left, reaching forward to pet his grandchild, and at the right Mrs Leicester's husband, Peter Leicester, merchant of Liverpool,[2] with, next to him, his own father.[3]

The work may be dated from the costumes to the early 1790s. No convincing attribution has emerged but the artist may well have been based in Liverpool. In its general ambience WAG 6252 is not unlike Richard Caddick's *Caddick Family* (WAG 3108, pp. 22–3) but the handling of proportion and perspective is weak in comparison.[4]

PROVENANCE
By descent in the Leicester family to Miss Mary Leicester (grand-daughter of the woman in the picture); by whom bequeathed to John Lindsay; his sister, Miss Mary G. Lindsay; her bequest 1964.

NOTES
1. A memorial to her in Woolton Church, Liverpool, placed there by her son Robert, who was first vicar of Much Woolton from 1826 until his death in 1875, describes her as 'a beloved mother' and states that she died on 13 January 1830 aged 62; R. Stewart-Brown: 'Leicester Family of Hale Lowe and Pickmere', *Cheshire Sheaf* (n.d.) [1920]; copy in gallery files.
2. Peter Leicester is first recorded in Liverpool street directories in 1790 as a cheese and porter merchant at 18 King Street. He is thereafter listed as a merchant, with from 1800 his private residence in Rodney Street and his 'provision warehouse' in King Street or Seel Street. From the same year he is recorded in partnership with John Gouthwaite, whose house was also in Rodney Street. He last appears in 1807 and in the 1810 directory Thomas Leicester (who may be a candidate for the child in WAG 6252) is given as the proprietor of the provision warehouse (by now in Dale Street) and Ellen Leicester herself as the owner of the house in Rodney Street. Between 1811 and 1813 Thomas was succeeded as the proprietor of the Dale Street warehouse by John Leicester.
3. The same interpretation was put forward by *MPPP*, p. 54. WAG 6252 descended to Mary, the daughter of Revd Robert Leicester, but it seems unlikely that Robert is the child in the painting. He was probably born about 1800–01 (he left Shrewsbury School in 1818; Stewart-Brown, *loc. cit.*) and stylistically WAG 6252 seems earlier in date than this. The last owner of WAG 6252, Miss Lindsay, presumably recording family tradition, stated that the child was a brother of Robert Leicester; note dated 13 January 1954, gallery files.
4. The best candidates for the artist, going by painters listed specifically as 'portrait painters' in mid-1790s Liverpool street directories are the following: Thomas Chubbard (see p. 28), whose late portraiture remains an unknown quantity, Peter Holland (who is better known as a landscapist), John McCree and Samuel Moore. Nothing is known of the last two. Thomas Hazlehurst (chiefly but not wholly a miniature painter), Richard Caddick (see pp. 20–5) and John Williamson (see pp. 250–61) were also in Liverpool in the mid-1790s but stylistic considerations are against WAG 6252 being by them.

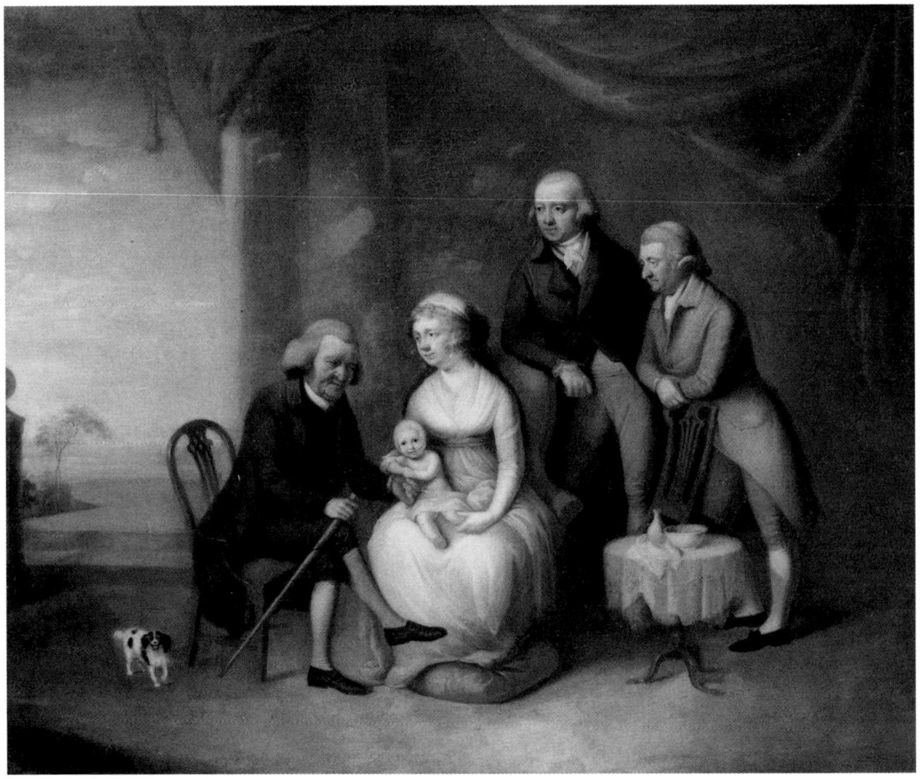

WAG 6252

Portrait of a Boy in Classical Dress with a Bow and Arrow

WAG 6659
oil on canvas, 105 × 77.5 cm
date: unknown, perhaps 1850–75

The portrait purports to be a work of around 1690–1700,[1] of a well-known classicising type associated with such names as John Michael Wright (1617–94), Henri Gascars (1635–1701) and others. However, the technique is from no earlier than the middle of the nineteenth century, and perhaps considerably later. It is unclear that the work is a deliberate forgery; it was part of a collection of portraits ostensibly from different periods that were originally presented to Liverpool Museum, not the Art Gallery, and which may always have had an educative purpose.

PROVENANCE

...Miss Porter, Liverpool; by whom presented to Liverpool Museum 1953; transferred to the gallery in 1968.

REFERENCE

1. I am grateful to Catharine MacLeod for confirming this dating.

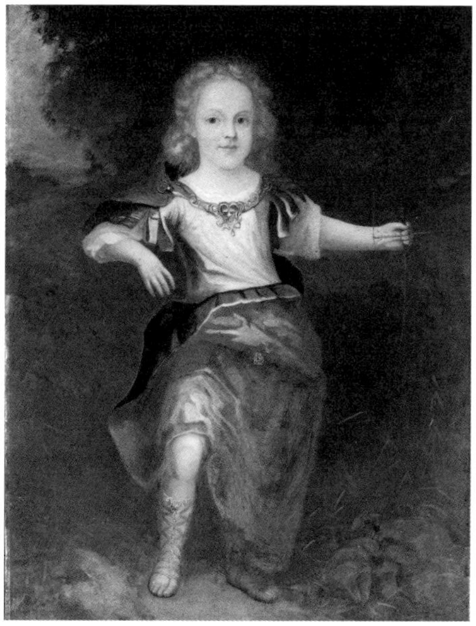

WAG 6659

John Bridge Aspinall

WAG 7026
oil on canvas,[1] 237 × 148 cm
date: 1803–04

For the sitter, see WAG 7041 under Mather Brown (p. 19). Aspinall is portrayed in mayoral robes, and presumably commissioned WAG 7026 as a presentation portrait for the Town Hall (which is shown in the background with, apparently, St Paul's Church behind it). Since Aspinall was Mayor in 1803, the work can presumably be dated to late 1803 or 1804. In the event, the work was not presented to the Corporation until 1851, which may argue that at the time it was not considered a success. The artist has not been identified.[2] For a smaller version of the portrait see WAG 2587 (pp. 311–2).

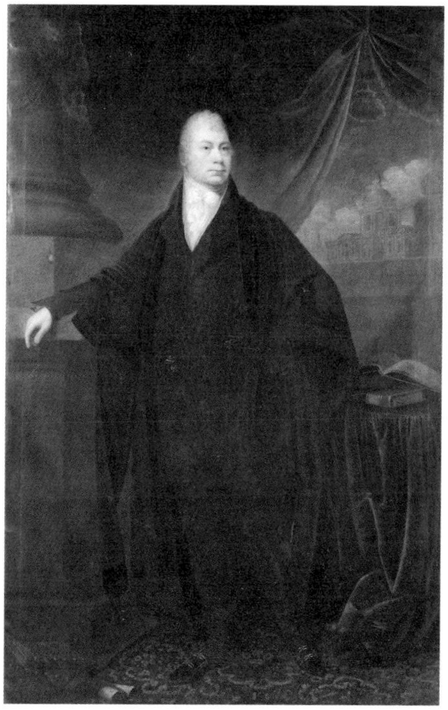

WAG 7026

PROVENANCE

By descent to the sitter's grandson, Clarke Aspinall; by whom presented to Liverpool Corporation 1851;[3] transferred from the City Estates Committee 1968.

NOTES

1. Relined, and with an unidentified wax seal on the back.
2. It is very likely that WAG 7026 is by a local artist, and the 1803 Liverpool street directory lists five 'portrait painters' (as distinct from miniaturists etc.) as follows: (i) Thomas Chubbard (1737–1809), landscapes by whom are catalogued on p. 28. Almost nothing is known of his portraiture, and by this date Chubbard was living in Soho, an unfashionable district of Liverpool, so that it seems unlikely he would have been selected for his portrait by the mayor; (ii) Thomas Hargreaves (1774–1847), for whose works in the collection see *MPPP*, vol. 1, p. 109 and vol. 2 p. 62; these are disparate in date and style but none is close to WAG 7026; (iii) William Higgins, who is listed in the 1800 and 1803 street directories at 107 Park Lane, the street in which the Aspinalls had their plumbing and glazing workshop, but is absent from the 1804 directory. He is possibly to be identified with the William Higgin[s] born 1759 who entered the RA Schools in 1784 and exhibited *Portrait of a Lady* at the RA in 1786 (see Sir Ellis Waterhouse: *The Dictionary of British Eighteenth Century Painters* [Woodbridge, 1981] p.169). His portrait of Charles Robert Blundell of 1803, which was in the Weld-Blundell family in the late twentieth century, is in a hand style unlike WAG 7026; (iv) Frederick Plowman, no work by whom is currently identified. He is listed in 1803 at 66 Dale Street, an address very close to Liverpool Town Hall, and in 1804 at 123 Duke Street, only a few doors from John Bridge Aspinall's private address; (v) John Williams (sic), listed at 35 Brownlow Hill; this is John Williamson (1751–1818), for whom see pp. 250–61. Uneven in ability but arguably Liverpool's leading resident portraitist at this time, Williamson does not seem to have specialised in mayoral portraits, but stylistically WAG 7026 does somewhat resemble other works by him.
3. According to Charles Dyall: *First Decade of the Walker Art Gallery: A Report of Its Operations from 1877–1887* (Liverpool, 1888) p. 7, the gift dates from 1858.

A Scholar

WAG 7478
oil on canvas, 75 × 64 cm
date: about 1650–65

The sitter is unidentified. He appears to be a Fellow-Commoner of the University of Cambridge, as the gown he wears is close to one illustrated in Loggan's *Cantabrigia Illustrata* of 1690.[1] WAG 7478 has been dated to around 1650–65.[2] A similar portrait of a Cambridge student is in the Fitzwilliam Museum.[3]

PROVENANCE
...Lieut-Col. Vere Cotton; his bequest 1970.

NOTES
1. David Loggan: *Cantabrigia Illustrata* (Cambridge, 1690) pl. VII, no. 4.
2. J. W. Goodison, *letter*, 18 June 1971 (gallery files) proposed 1660–65. David Moore-Gwyn, *verbally*, 22 July 2010 proposed a date in the 1650s.
3. J. W. Goodison: *Fitzwilliam Museum Cambridge Catalogue of Paintings, Vol. III, British School* (Cambridge, 1977) pp. 28–9.

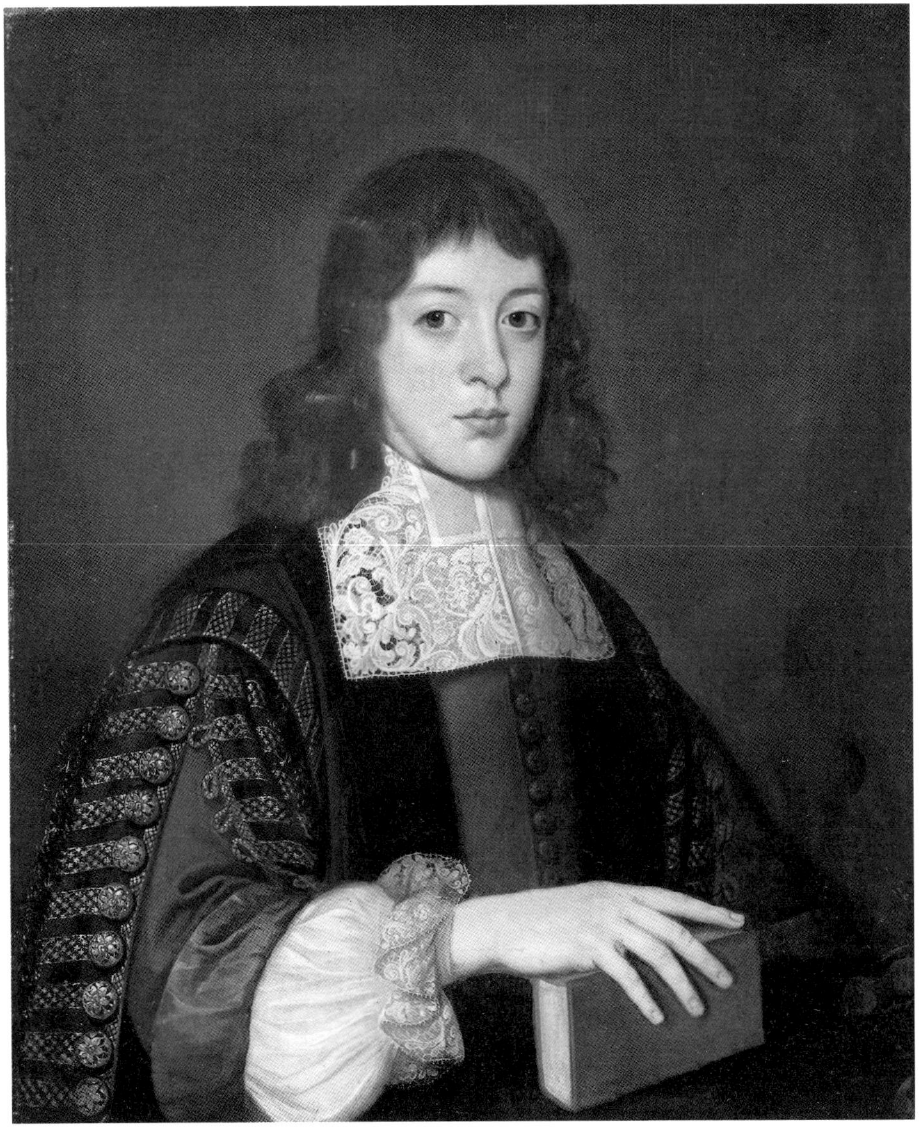

WAG 7478

Hon. Richard Molyneux

WAG 8627
oil on canvas, 128 × 102 cm
date: unknown, perhaps 1695–1720

This is one of a group of eight late seventeenth- and early eighteenth-century Molyneux family portraits which were formerly part of the historic collection at Croxteth Hall outside Liverpool, the main residence of the family from the eighteenth century. The others are WAG 8628, 8631, 8638 and 8641 (catalogued under British School, pp. 331–2, 344–5), WAG 8629–30 (catalogued under Garret Morphy, pp. 114–5) and WAG 8640 (catalogued under Jacob Huysmans, p. 79). (One further portrait, WAG 8637, pp. 332–3, stands outside the group as being later in date, although its provenance is identical.) None of these works is certainly documented at Croxteth before 1946 and the precise circumstances in which they came into the collection are unknown. Although the identifications of the sitters are traditional, and in some cases contested, it is clear they spread over at least two (and perhaps three or even four) generations. Nevertheless, the fact that the works are all or nearly all copies argues that they may have been made as part of a single campaign, within a fairly narrow timespan, perhaps in connection with the decoration of the new wing built at Croxteth between 1702 and 1714 by William, 4th Viscount Molyneux. It is noticeable that William is the core figure of those family members depicted, for putatively at least, the portraits represent himself, his elder brother, whose premature death opened the way to his own succession to the Viscountcy (this is WAG 8627), his elder sister (WAG 8640), his eldest son and heir and the latter's wife (WAG 8629–30), the latter's eldest surviving child, a daughter (WAG

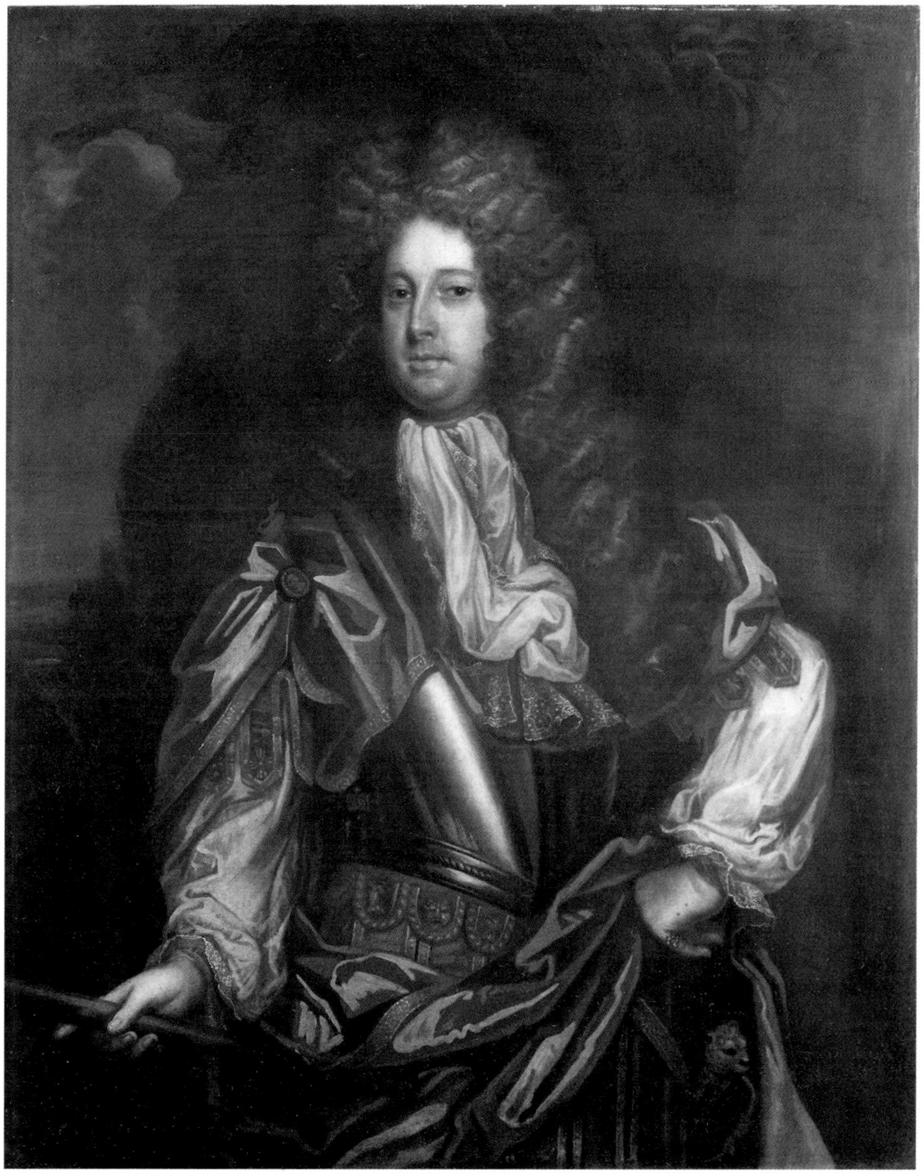

WAG 8627

8638), and the heir to their title, the 4th Viscount's second son (WAG 8641). Not represented is the 4th Viscount's first wife, Bridget Lucy, which may argue that all these works were commissioned after her death in 1713, and before the Viscount's own death in 1718. However, it is not out of the question that the group, or part of it, emerged under the auspices of his successor, the 5th Viscount, even if the poor quality of his portrait (WAG 8629) and the presence of two putative portraits of the 4th Viscount militate against this scenario. The actual canvases are by more than one hand, but this may simply reflect the disparateness of the works sourced.

The present work, perhaps the most imposing of the group, traditionally depicts Hon. Richard Molyneux, the eldest son of Caryll, 3rd Viscount Molyneux and his wife Mary, née Barlow.[1] Born about 1652, he was, like his father, a confirmed Jacobite, and it has been suggested that the portrait was produced to celebrate the succession of James II in 1685.[2] The precise date of Richard's death is unrecorded but he pre-deceased his father (who died in 1700). WAG 8627, which shows him in half armour and carrying a baton, is the same size as, and similarly framed to, WAG 8640, and may have been executed by the same hand. No convincing attribution has emerged.

PROVENANCE

By descent at Croxteth Hall; bt. in 1974 from the executors of Hugh, 7th Earl of Sefton.

NOTES

1. *Croxteth 1946 Inventory*, no. 3.
2. *MPPP*, p. 48; however, a date in the 1690s was suggested by Catharine MacLeod, *verbally*, 9 December 2008.

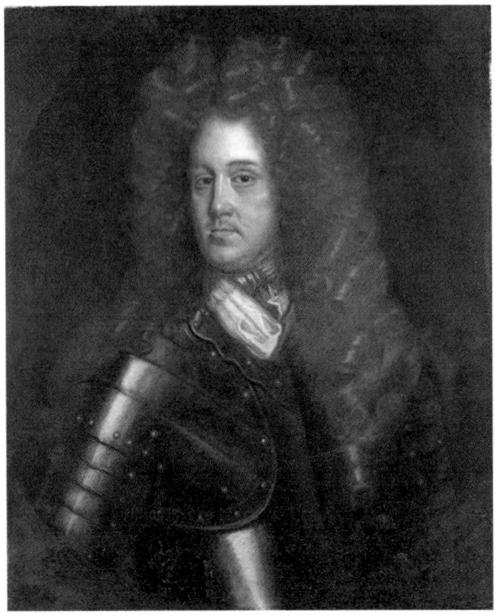

WAG 8628

A Man of the Molyneux Family, Perhaps William, 4th Viscount Molyneux

WAG 8628
oil on canvas,[1] 77 × 63 cm
date: unknown, perhaps 1695–1720

The head in WAG 8628 is the same type as in WAG 8631 (below) and was either copied from it or both were copied from the same source (the same artist was probably responsible for both works). The suit of armour is also the same but the neckcloth is treated differently and the body is turned in the opposite direction. The portrait is within a painted oval. No convincing attribution has emerged. For a discussion of the likely identity of the sitter see WAG 8631.[2]

PROVENANCE

By descent at Croxteth Hall; bt. in 1974 from the executors of Hugh, 7th Earl of Sefton.

NOTES

1. Re-lined.
2. WAG 8628 has been identified as *Croxteth 1946 Inventory* no. 70: 'Caryll, 3rd Viscount Molyneux, in Armour', 30 × 25 inches, by 'School of Kneller'; *MPPP*, p. 48.

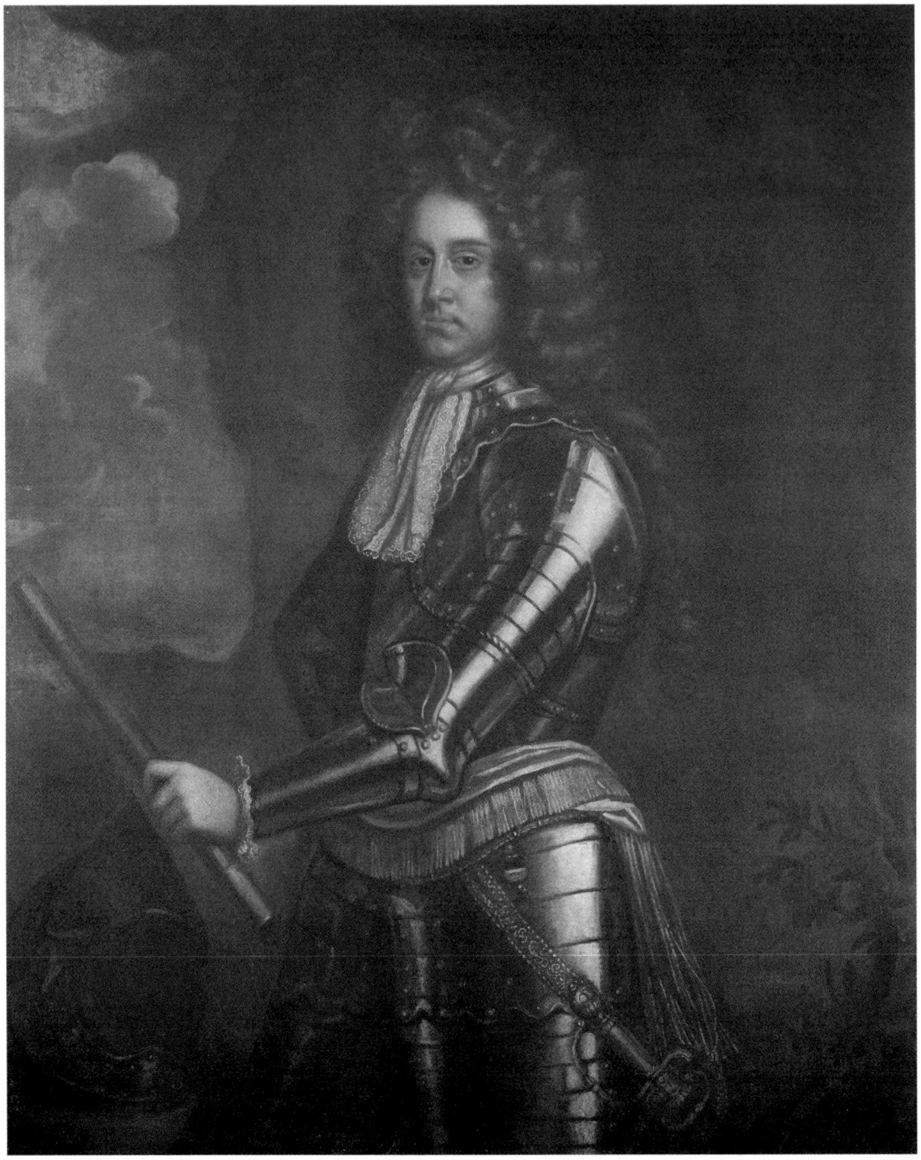

WAG 8631

A Man of the Molyneux Family, Perhaps William, 4th Viscount Molyneux

WAG 8631
oil on canvas, 128 × 102.5 cm
date: unknown, perhaps 1695–1720

WAG 8631 is one of two portraits of the same sitter among the late seventeenth- and early eighteenth-century Molyneux family portraits from Croxteth Hall outside Liverpool (for the other see WAG 8628, above). Curiously, they were traditionally identified at Croxteth as of different men: WAG 8628 as of Caryll, 3rd Viscount (1622–1700), but WAG 8631 as of his third son William (1655–1718), who succeeded him as 4th Viscount in 1700.[1] The latter identification seems more likely to be correct given the sitter's apparent age. On stylistic grounds, these

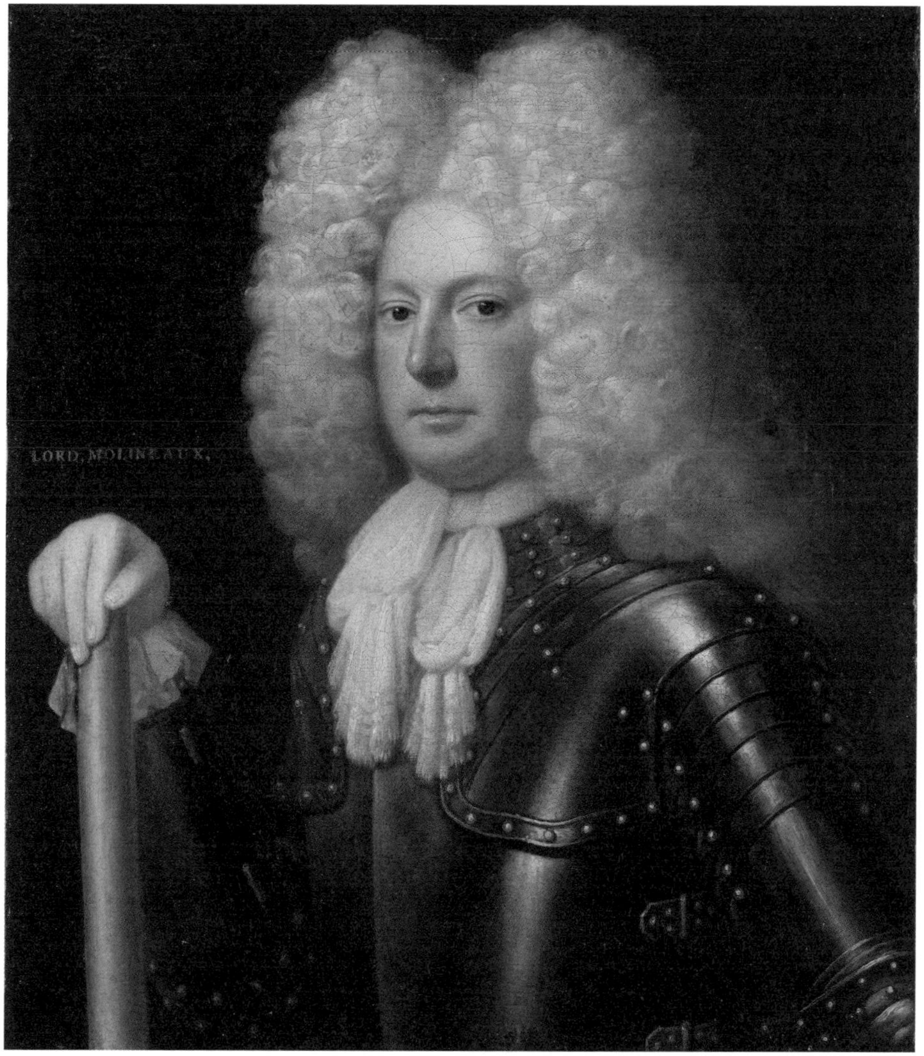

Fig. 136 Portrait of Viscount Molyneux by Garret Morphy, oil on canvas. National Gallery of Ireland, Dublin; photo © National Gallery of Ireland.

portraits, or the putative portrait of which they are copies, must date from around 1688–95,[2] and it is hard to accept that this man can be around 70. The armour might perhaps refer to the Colonel's commission which the younger William received from King James II, an offence with which he was charged in the reign of William III.[3] Later, as 4th Viscount, William was responsible for making Croxteth Hall the main home of the Molyneux family and he built the new Queen Anne-style wing there between 1702 and 1714. He was twice married, first to Bridget Lucy, second in 1716 to Mary, daughter of Lieutenant-General Bevil Skelton.

Complicating the question of the sitter's identity is WAG 8631's relationship to a portrait by Garret Morphy now in the National Gallery of Ireland (fig. 136) which itself has successively been thought to show both the 3rd and 4th Viscounts Molyneux.[4] Although the similarities between the two depictions are considerable, it is far from clear that the two portraits are of the same man.[5] Both men wear what appears to be the same suit of armour, but this could simply allude to the hereditary position claimed by successive Viscounts Molyneux of Constable of Liverpool Castle (which, according to family tradition, is the building in the background of WAG 8631).[6] If the view is taken that the two men are not the same, the fact that the portrait by Morphy is now held to depict the 4th Viscount around 1700 might suggest that WAG 8631 does not show him but his father instead.

As with WAG 8628, WAG 8631 is rather woodenly painted and is of copyish or at best provincial quality. No convincing attribution has emerged.

PROVENANCE

By descent at Croxteth Hall; bt. in 1974 from the executors of Hugh, 7th Earl of Sefton.

NOTES

1. WAG 8631 is identified as *Croxteth 1946 Inventory* no. 5; *MPPP*, p. 48.
2. This dating was confirmed by Catharine MacLeod, *verbally*, 9 December 2008.
3. *MPPP*, *loc. cit.*
4. Nicola Figgis and Brendan Rooney: *Irish Paintings in the National Gallery of Ireland, Vol. 1* (Dublin, 2001), pp. 367–8. The re-identification of Morphy's sitter from 3rd to 4th Viscount was first proposed by Jane Fenlon: 'Garret Morphy and His Circle', *Irish Arts Review Yearbook* (*1991–2*), p. 142, partly on grounds of style and of the sitter's apparent age, but partly from the assumption that Morphy's portrait depicted the same man as WAG 8631; Fenlon's article was written after a visit to Liverpool to see the Molyneux portraits.
5. *MPPP*, *loc. cit.* (under WAG 8628, n. 3), states categorically that the two men do not resemble each other. Ironically, at that point, Morphy's portrait was held to represent the 3rd Viscount, which strengthened the argument advanced in *MPPP* that WAG 8628 and 8631 showed the 4th Viscount. However, it appears less than self-evident that the two men are different and it is perhaps not out of the question that WAG 8631 and WAG 8628 were freely adapted from Morphy's type rather in the way that Morphy's portraits of the 5th Viscount Molyneux and his wife were somewhat loosely copied for Croxteth (see pp. 114–5).
6. *MPPP*, *loc. cit.*

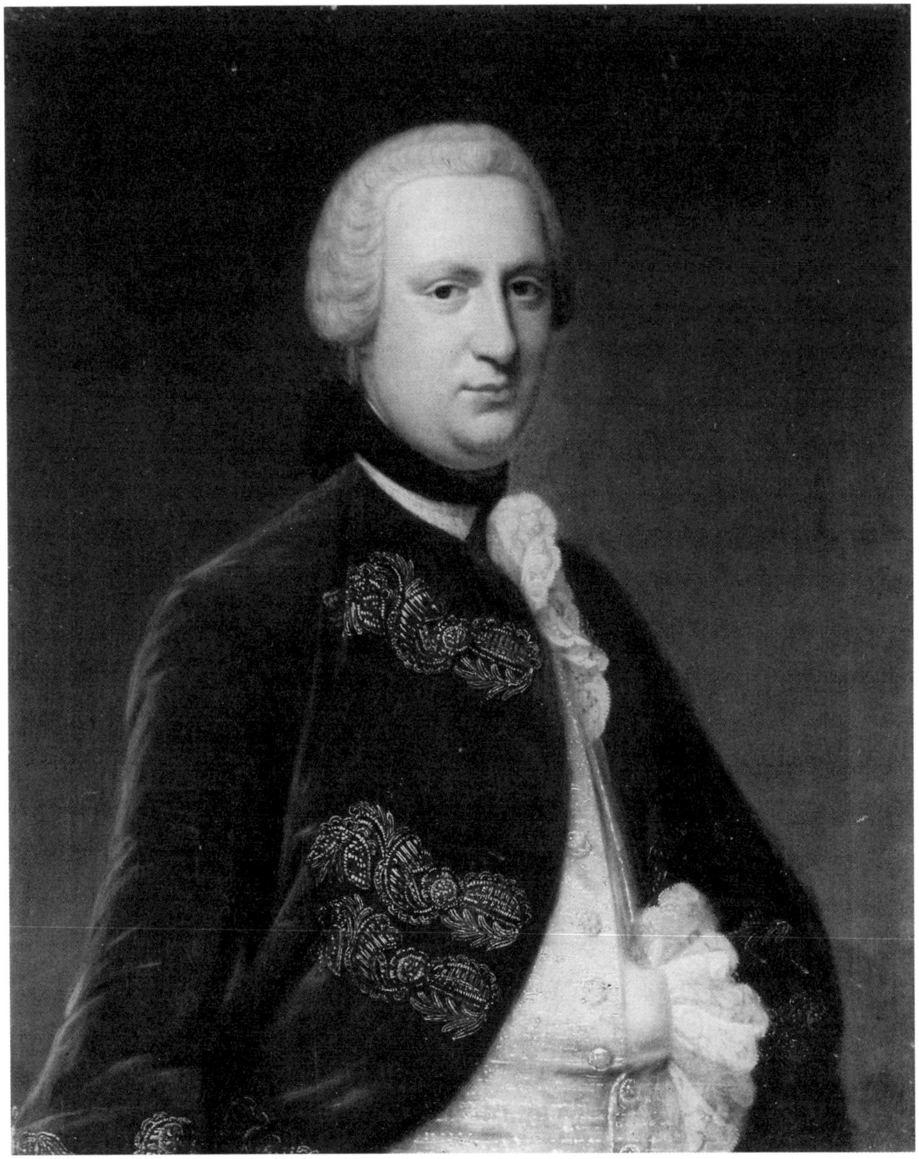

WAG 8637

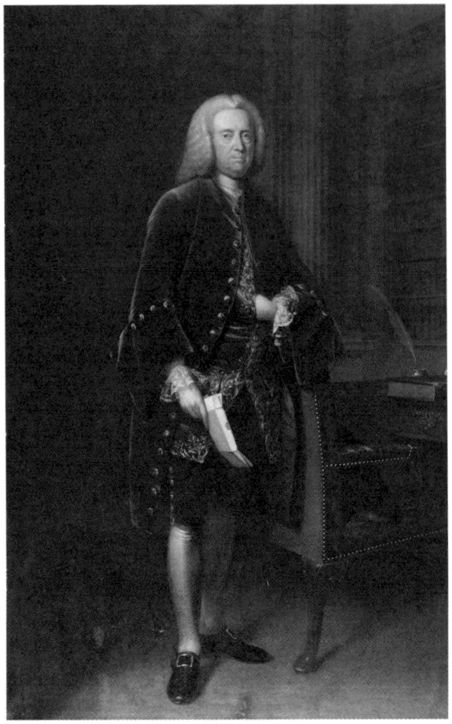

Fig. 137 *Nicholas Fazackerley* by Arthur Devis, oil on canvas. Harris Museum and Art Gallery, Preston/The Bridgeman Art Library.

Portrait of a Man

WAG 8637
oil on canvas, 75.5 × 62.5 cm
date: about 1748–53

This is one of the series of portraits from the late seventeenth through to the mid-eighteenth centuries which formed part of the historic collection at Croxteth Hall (for a general discussion of which see British School WAG 8627, pp. 329–30). This one, however, stands apart in the set as being of somewhat later date than the others. It has traditionally been identified as a portrait of Charles William Molyneux, 8th Viscount Molyneux, later 1st Earl of Sefton (1748–95),[1] but cannot depict him. The sitter in WAG 8637 must be at least in his mid-twenties, whereas the style and costume indicate this is a work of the very late 1740s or early 1750s.[2]

There is no candidate for the sitter among members of the Molyneux family and his identity must be sought elsewhere. A visual similarity has been noticed between WAG 8637 and Arthur Devis's 1763 portrait of Nicholas Fazackerley of Preston (fig. 137);[3] and although there is no question of WAG 8637 being by Devis, the possible identification is of interest given Fazackerley's high Tory politics and reputation as a covert Jacobite,[4] sentiments which were undoubtedly shared by the Molyneux family. But in this connection an even more tempting possibility is that this is Charles Edward Stuart, Bonnie Prince Charlie (1720–88), himself. His political profile in Britain as a figurehead for Catholic families was at its height in the late 1740s following his doomed but surprisingly effective

invasion attempt in 1745. Comparison with other likenesses of the Prince of around 1750 (including some made for Catholic houses in the north)[5] reveals considerable facial similarity, although no other version of this precise portrait is known. It may turn out that WAG 8637 is by a continental, rather than British artist,[6] especially given that the Viscount Molyneux of the day, William, 7th Viscount Molyneux, was a Jesuit priest and thus well placed to commission a copy of a foreign likeness.

PROVENANCE

By descent at Croxteth Hall; bt. 1974 from the executors of Hugh, 7th Earl of Sefton.

NOTES

1. A partially surviving ms inscription in ink on a label on the reverse reads [...] *Portrait of / [...] William Earl of Sefton / perh Thomas Gainsborough*. The usage 'Earl of Sefton', with the implied suggestion that the work is related to Gainsborough's portrait of Viscountess Molyneux, Countess of Sefton (pp. 49–51), is an indication that the inscription must considerably postdate the period.

2. Sir Ellis Waterhouse, *letters*, 10 September and 17 September 1977, gallery files, dated WAG 8637 from the costume to between 1747 and 1756. Anne Buck, *letter*, 23 October 1977, gallery files, dated the coat to the 1740s but the wig to the 1750s. *MPPP*, p. 50, titled the work *Charles William 1st Earl of Sefton* without qualification but noted the possibility of a misidentification; *CIC*, p. 44, titled the work *A Member of the Molyneux Family* with the dating 1745–60. Hugh Belsey also dated the work to about 1750, *verbally*, 30 April 2009.

3. Mary Bennett, note in gallery files.

4. For Fazackerley see Stephen Sartin: *Polite Society by Arthur Devis*, exh. cat., Harris Museum and Art Gallery, Preston and National Portrait Gallery, London (1983) p. 65.

5. See Edward Corp: *The King over the Water* (Edinburgh, 2001), especially pp. 98 and 111, and Robin Nicholson: *Bonnie Prince Charlie and the Making of a Myth: A Study in Portraiture 1720–1892* (Lewisburg and London, 2002) for example pp. 72, 86 for portraits by (and after) Cosmo Alexander, Louis Tocque and Robert Strange.

6. The French character of WAG 8637 was noted both by Waterhouse, *letter*, 17 September 1977 and by Buck, *loc. cit.*

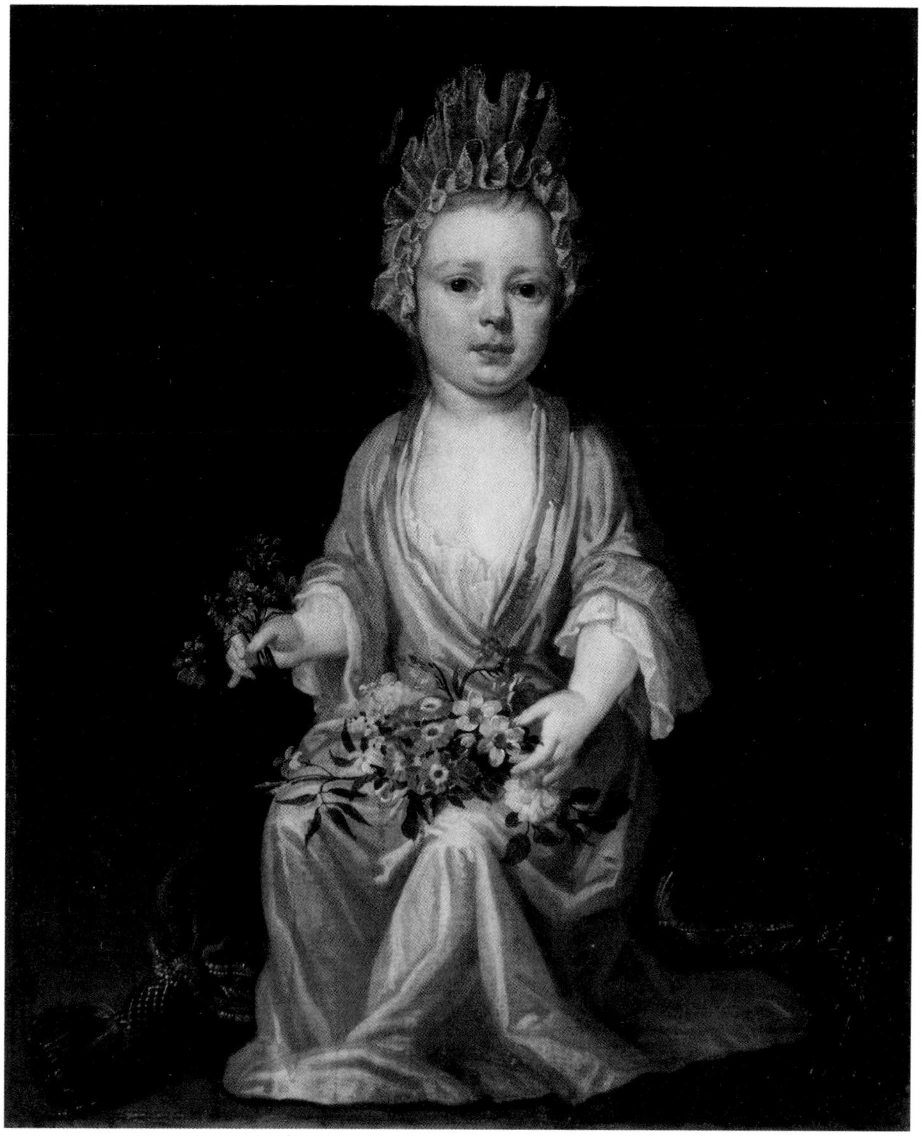

WAG 8638

A Young Girl Holding a Bouquet of Flowers

WAG 8638
oil on canvas,[1] 75.5 × 63 cm
date: about 1712–15

This is one of the group of late seventeenth- and early eighteenth-century Molyneux family portraits which formed part of the historic collection at Croxteth Hall (for a general discussion of the group see British School WAG 8627, pp. 329–30). It is much less obviously a copy than other pictures in the group and is a work of fair quality. It was attributed to Caspar Netscher (1639–84) when acquired by the gallery but it must date from after his death: the distinctive 'fontange' head-dress worn by the sitter became fashionable in the 1690s and continued to be worn

into the 1700s.[2] The girl is wearing a pink robe with a pale blue silk lining and a white undershirt. Her face is white, suggesting that despite her young age she may be wearing powder. Her identity is unknown, and there is no certainty that she is a Molyneux, for within the family the only viable candidates are one or other of the daughters of Richard, 5th Viscount Molyneux and his wife Mary née Brudenell (see WAG 8629–30, after Garret Morphy) which would date the portrait to no earlier than about 1710. The two girls concerned (whose exact birthdates, probably around 1707–08, are unknown) were Mary, later Mrs Thomas Clifton (and later still Mrs William Anderton) and Dorothy, later Mrs John Caryll (see p. 96).

An area of crude overpainting covers old damage at the upper left about 6 inches from the top and left-hand sides.

PROVENANCE
By descent at Croxteth Hall; bt. 1974 from the executors of Hugh, 7th Earl of Sefton.

NOTES
1. Re-lined.
2. I am grateful to Catharine MacLeod for discussing the dating of the work with me.

A Man of the Molyneux Family

WAG 8641
oil on canvas, 75 × 62 cm
date: unknown, perhaps 1710–30

The work is one of the late seventeenth- and early eighteenth-century family portraits from Croxteth Hall (for further discussion of which see British School WAG 8627, pp. 329–30). A plaque on the frame identifies the sitter as William, 4th Viscount Molyneux, and the artist as Kneller,[1] but neither name is correct. The sitter here can scarcely be older than 30, an age that the future 4th Viscount attained in 1685, but on stylistic grounds WAG 8641 dates from around 1710 or even later. It has been proposed that the sitter is Richard, 5th Viscount on the basis of comparison with the likeness in WAG 8629 (after Garret Morphy) and even more closely, the likeness in Morphy's original (National Gallery of Ireland, Dublin; see fig. 49, p. 114).[2] This cannot be ruled out, although the sitter in WAG 8641 has a squarer, fleshier head and less full lips than Morphy gives Richard. A better candidate, however, is Richard's younger brother Caryll, later 6th Viscount (1683–1745).[3] Arthur Devis's portrait of him with his great-niece, although taken later in his life (fig. 138) shows him with a pudgy nose, thin lips and jowly face that recall the likeness here.

No convincing alternative has emerged to the attribution to Kneller, but the quality of WAG 8641 is that of a provincial artist or copyist.

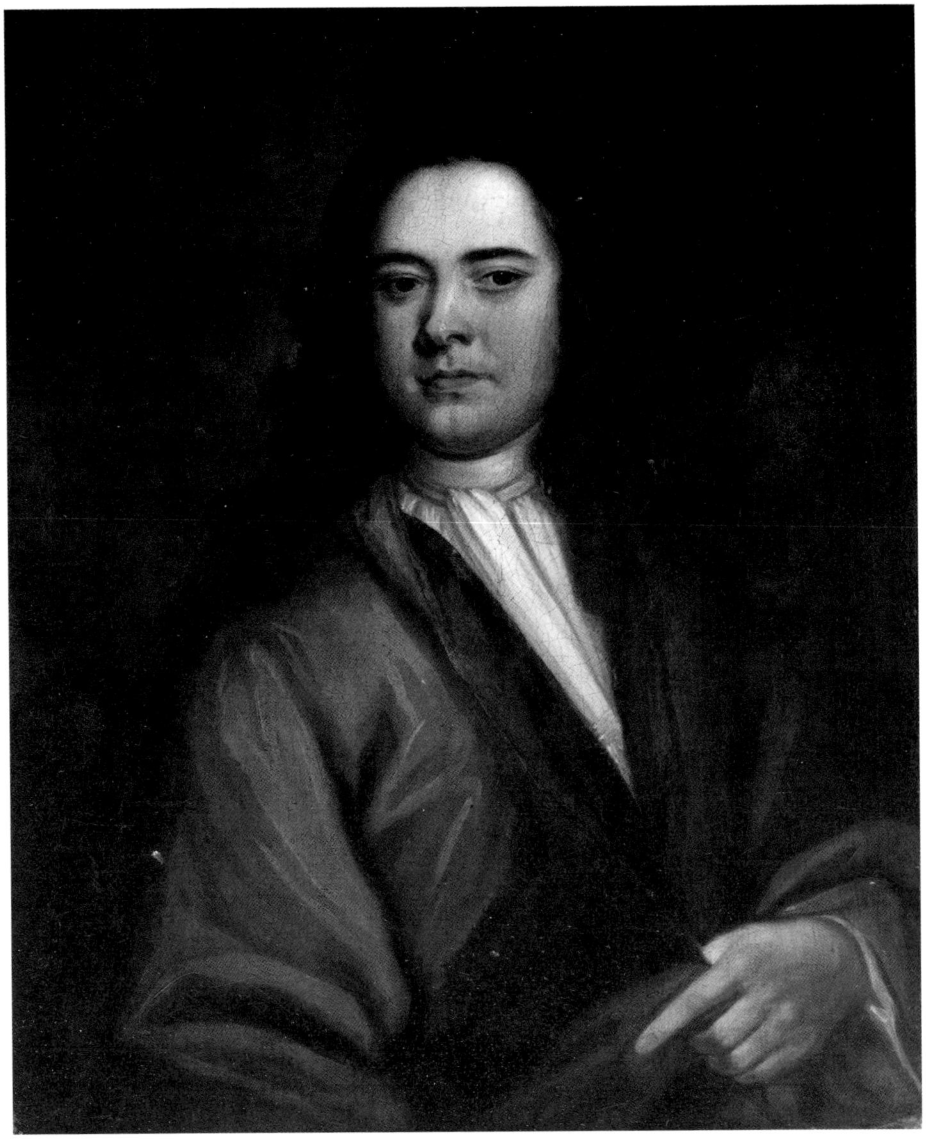

WAG 8641

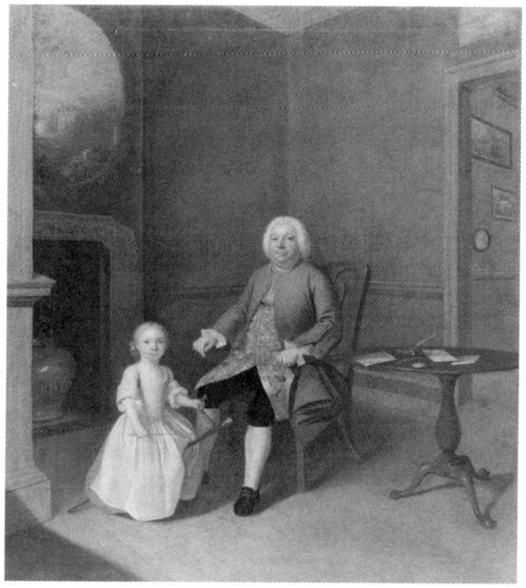

Fig. 138 *Caryll, 6th Viscount Molyneux and His Great-niece* by Arthur Devis, oil on canvas. Sotheby, 16 November 1969 (79). © Sotheby's/photo National Portrait Gallery, London.

PROVENANCE

By descent at Croxteth Hall; bt. 1974 from the executors of Hugh, 7th Earl of Sefton.

NOTES

1. WAG 8641 may be the unattributed portrait of the 4th Viscount listed in *Croxteth 1946 Inventory* no. 96.
2. *MPPP*, p. 49.
3. The *Croxteth 1746 Inventory* p. 1 lists in the Large Dining Room a *Lord Caryl Half Length* valued at 1 guinea. No other candidate for this work (assuming *Lord Caryl* refers to the 6th Viscount rather than the 3rd) is known. (The Inventory lists a total of 29 paintings at Croxteth and at 'Mrs Anderton's house in Preston', but none of these is securely identifiable with any other of the early to mid-eighteenth-century paintings of Molyneux provenance now in the gallery; the latter may already have been regarded as family heirlooms and not as Lord Molyneux's disposable property.)

Landscape with River and Castle[1]

WAG 8983
oil on canvas, 158.5 × 114.5 cm
date: unknown, perhaps 1710–20

This work has been identified as an overmantel from one of the suite of rooms built at Croxteth Hall by William, 4th Viscount Molyneux between 1702 and 1714.[2] Its seriously deteriorated condition indicates that it was in one of the rooms consumed in the fire at Croxteth in 1952. It appears to have been considered not worth restoring, and, having been abandoned, entered the collection by main force when Merseyside County Council began to look after the house in 1974.

The clue to the meaning of the picture is the pennant being flown by the barge in the river, which shows the arms of the Molyneux family.[3] The painting is evidently an allegorical view of a preternaturally calm river Mersey. Liverpool Castle, of which successive Viscounts Molyneux were hereditary Constables, is in the centre, and descending from the castle to enter the barge are a couple who may be identifiable as the 4th Viscount and his first wife, Bridget Lucy. In the background, in what may be an attempt to imitate works by Claude Lorrain, is a building on a rocky outcrop which is probably intended for Croxteth Hall itself (the relationship between its two blocks seems to be that of the old and new wings at Croxteth as they would have appeared in 1714). The building strategically placed beneath it may be intended to represent Knowsley, home of the Molyneux' rivals, the Stanleys.

The picture must date from the second decade of the eighteenth century. No clue exists as to the identity of the artist but the work must always have been of mediocre

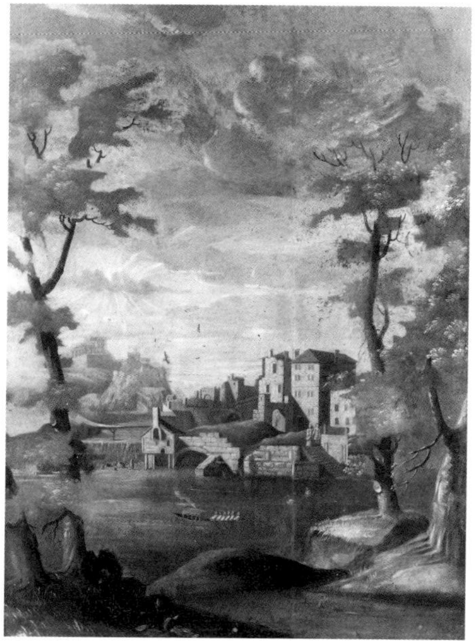

WAG 8983

quality and is perhaps by a local favourite of Viscount Molyneux.

PROVENANCE

By descent at Croxteth Hall; transferred to the gallery 1974.

NOTES

1. Titled *Landscape with Water-mill* in *CIC*, p. 44.
2. Draft catalogue entry by Mary Bennett, gallery files. The painting was omitted from *MPPP*.
3. *Ibid*.

Lord Sefton's Black Breasted Reds after a Fight

WAG 9023
oil on canvas, 101 × 127.5 cm
date: unknown, perhaps 1800–10

The title given above does not seem to be traditional and was given to the work only at Bonham's sale in 1975. Nevertheless, WAG 9023 and a companion work (fig. 139) appear in a list of works of art at Croxteth taken for probate in 1930,[1] and it seems likely that they had been in the Molyneux family for much

longer.[2] Two paintings of cocks valued at £1 10s are listed in the *Croxteth 1746 Inventory*, but if the present title of WAG 9023, indicating that the cocks were owned by Lord Sefton, is the original one, then the work must date from after 1771, when the Sefton peerage was granted. This impression is re-inforced by stylistic considerations, although it is not out of the question that a later artist was commissioned to make new versions of two old family heirlooms. The most likely Lord Sefton to have placed such a commission was William, 2nd Earl of Sefton (1772–1837), a keen sportsman. He succeeded to the title in 1795, and a dating of about 1800–10 seems acceptable for the two pictures.[3]

No convincing attribution has been put forward. When they were sold at the Croxteth premises sale in 1973, WAG 9023 and its companion were attributed to 'Alken'. It is unclear which member of the Alken family of sporting artists was meant, but the attribution may have derived from the cockfighting pictures of Henry Alken (1785–1851) and their related prints. Between 1973 and 1975 the attribution was changed to Francis Sartorius (see p. 152).[4] Both the scale and the conception of WAG 9023 and its companion, with their grisly documentary accuracy underpinned

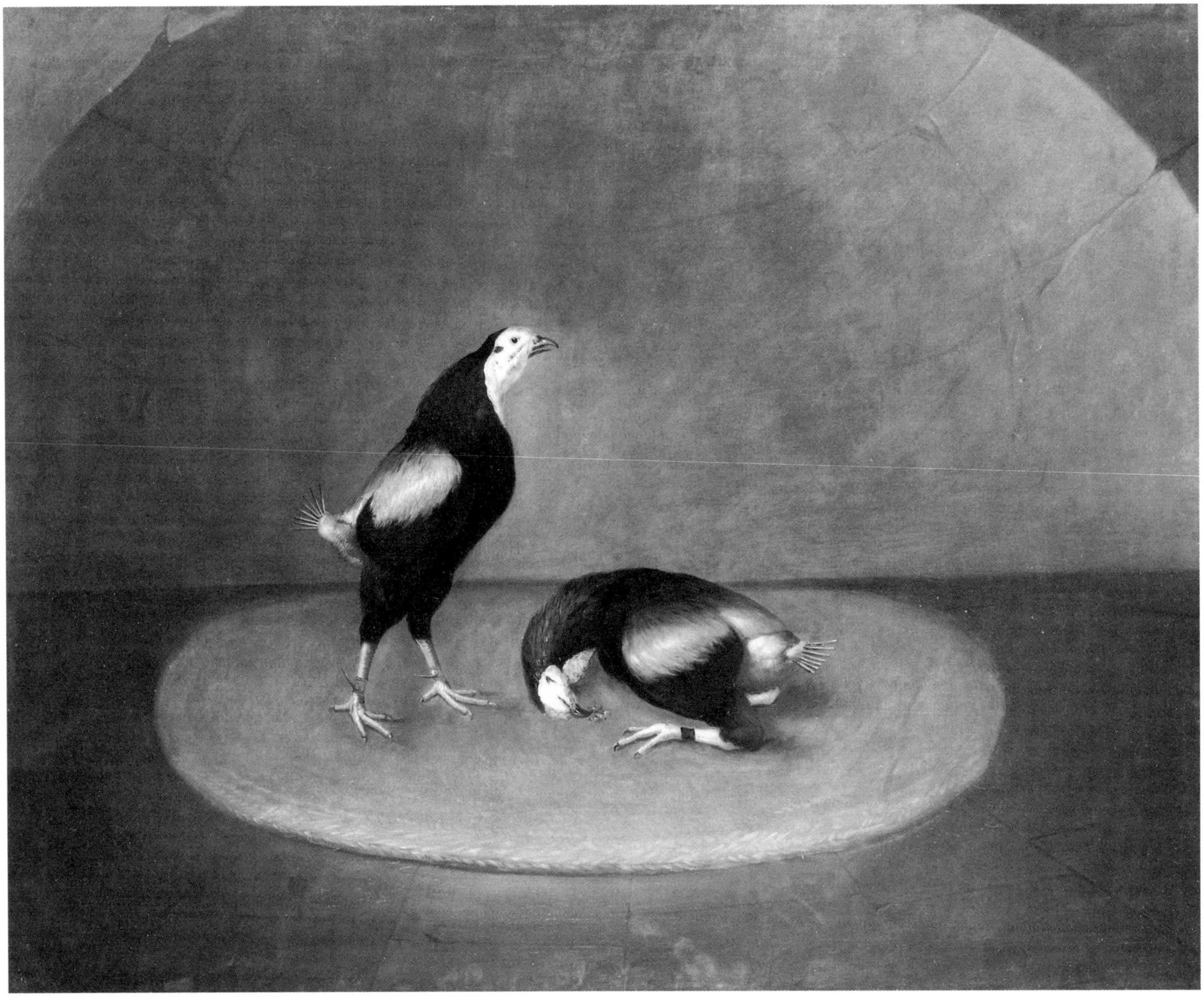

WAG 9023

by a strong sense of emptiness at the death of the losing cock, indicates an unusual artistic sensibility rather than a purveyor of conventional sporting scenes.

Discoloured retouchings on WAG 9023 are visible along all four edges, which have been trimmed at the time of an earlier relining; at upper centre (where there is some indication that a small handbill or publicity advertisement on the upper wall of the cockpit has been painted out) and at lower left below the rush matting.

PROVENANCE

...[? By descent to] Hugh, 7th Earl of Sefton; Christie premises sale at Croxteth Hall 17–20 September 1973 (1022, part); bt. Miles; Bonham 6 November 1975 (220); bt. John Baskett for the gallery.

NOTES

1. They are nos 165–66 on the 1930 probate list, which is cross-referenced in the *Croxteth 1946 Inventory*. On the latter the two works are nos 71–72, *Two Cockfighting Scenes* attributed to 'English School, Early nineteenth century'.

2. The gallery's inventory card records four separate ms inscriptions on the reverse of the frame, as well as an Agnew's printed label indicating that they had regilded the frame for the Seftons. None of these are present on the back of the work's present frame. It appears that the inscriptions were recorded either when the work was still at Croxteth or at a point before the work finally entered the gallery's possession (both pictures were loaned to the gallery for a short period in 1975), and that the frame was replaced or switched with that of the companion work before the Bonham's sale.

3. See n. 1.

4. The attribution to Francis Sartorius was made by Roy Miles Fine Paintings, and WAG 9023 was sold under this attribution at Bonham's in 1975. This may have come about through a simple misreading of the Christie's catalogue of 1973, in which the next lot to the two cockfighting scenes was a set of four works by Francis Sartorius.

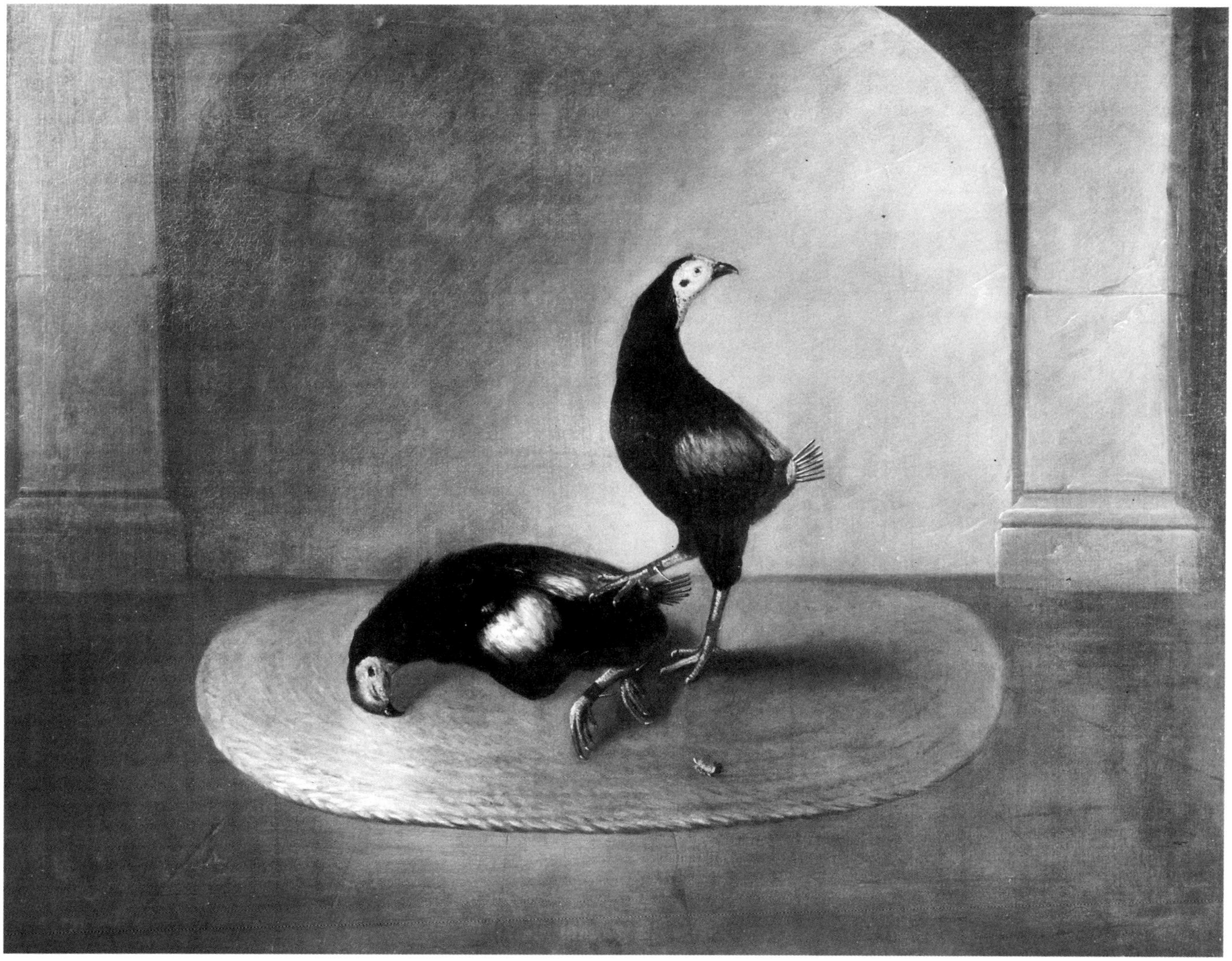

Fig. 139 *Two Fighting Cocks* by an unknown artist, oil on canvas. Roy Miles Fine Art 1975; photo Rodney Wright-Watson.

John Earle

WAG 9283
oil on canvas, 76 × 63.5 cm
date: unknown, perhaps 1710–20

The inscription in the lower left corner of the canvas reads *John Earle Mayor of / Liverpool 1703* [sic] *married Mary / only Daughter and Heiress of Ralph Finch Esquire / & Elizabeth De Anyers Coheiress with her Sister Ellen / Willis of Colonel Willm. de Anyers.* The inscription's emphasis on Earle's in-laws suggests that WAG 9283 was executed for that branch of the family;[1] although of much better than average copy quality, the work appears to have been based on a portrait that exhibits variations in facial feature and shows him as a younger man, but wearing the same costume.[2] Here, he looks as though he is in his mid- to late thirties.

John Earle (1674–1749) was the founder of one of the great eighteenth-century Liverpool merchant dynasties. The son of a Warrington brewer of the same name, he came to Liverpool in 1688 to work for the merchant and shipowner William Clayton, later MP for Liverpool and a Tory, whose politics he followed. Earle set up on his own in 1700, trading primarily in wine but also in iron, tobacco, sugar and slaves. In that year he married Eleanor Tyrer (who died in 1702) with whom he had one son, who died an infant. He was co-opted onto the town council in 1703 and became Bailiff in 1705 and Mayor in 1709. In that year he married Mary Finch, with whom he had seven children. His sons, Ralph (1715–90), Thomas (1719–81) and William (1721–88) were later all prominent as merchants and by the 1780s they were the tenth largest British slave trading concern. Ralph followed his father as Mayor of Liverpool in 1769.[3]

The present canvas has been relined and fixed to a new stretcher.

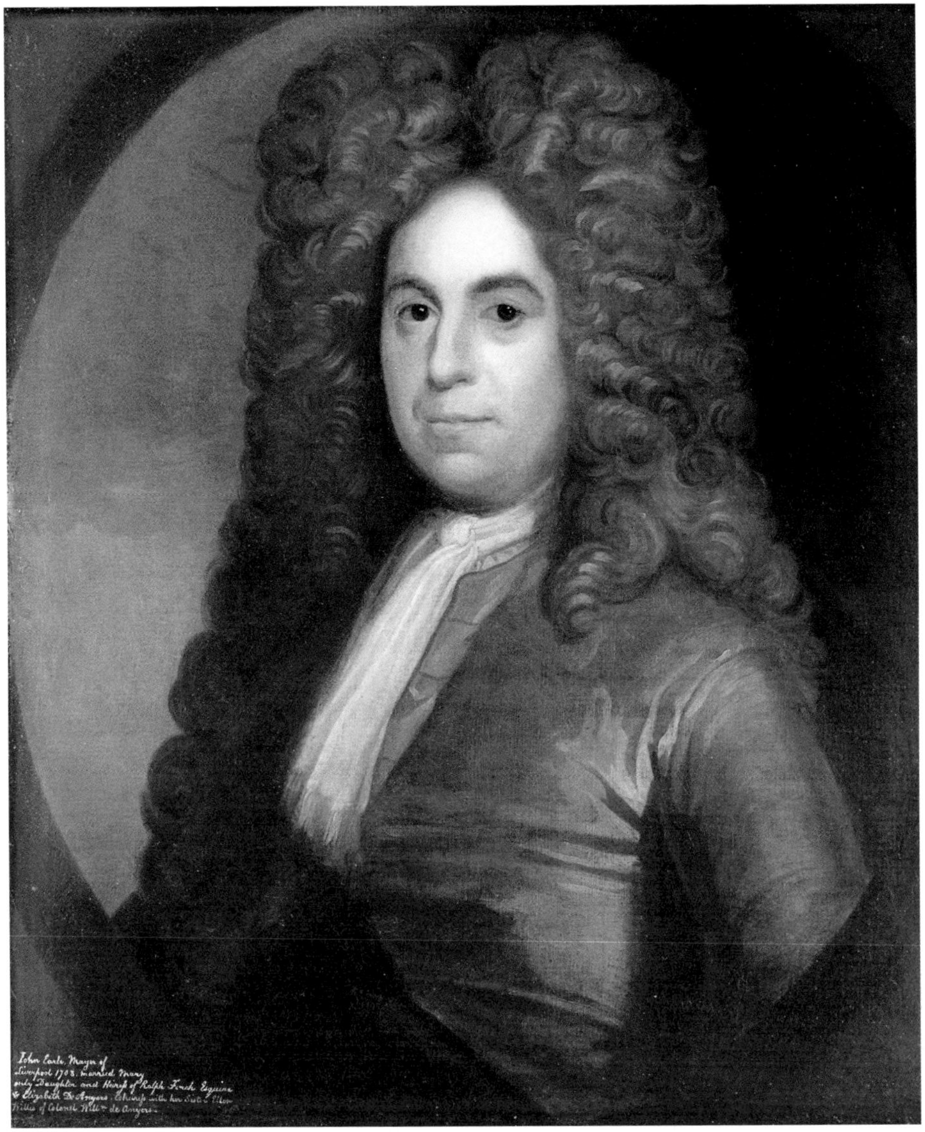

WAG 9283

PROVENANCE
...Bonham 9 March 1978 (186); bt. Agnew for the gallery.

NOTES
1. *MPPP*, p. 238 suggests that the inscription may have been added after 1788 (when Ralph Earle, John Earle's son succeeded to the Willis estates); however, the succession should seemingly have made the need for such an inscription superfluous.
2. Reproduced by T. Algernon Earle: 'Earle of Allerton Tower', *Transactions of the Historic Society of Lancashire and Cheshire [for the Year 1890]* vol. 42 (1892) p. 31. *MPPP*, *loc. cit.*, describes this original portrait as 'an elaborate drawing' but this is not apparent from the reproduction. WAG 9283 was sold in 1978 as by Kneller but this attribution cannot be accepted. Kneller's pupil Hamlet Winstanley (see pp. 274–7) would have been too young to have painted the original if it marked Earle's mayoralty, 1709–10, but it is not out of the question that he painted this version if it is a later copy.
3. *MPPP*, *loc. cit.*; Earle, *op. cit.*, pp. 15–76; Dawn Littler: 'The Earle Collection: Records of a Liverpool Family of Merchants and Shipowners', *Transactions of the Historic Society of Lancashire and Cheshire [for the Year 1996]* vol. 146 (1997) pp. 93–106.

Index of names and places

Authors and publications cited in the references have been omitted. British and Irish counties and American states have not been indexed separately from places therein. Names asterisked are those of collectors, and purchasers and vendors at sales, whose full names have not been cited and are in most cases unknown. **Names in bold** refer to artists included in the catalogue; **numbers in bold** refer to pages on which an illustration of the artist's work, or the subject, appears.